THE
MACMILLAN
WRITER

Rhetoric, Reader, Handbook

THE MACMILLAN WRITER

Rhetoric, Reader, Handbook

FOURTH EDITION

JUDITH NADELL

LINDA McMENIMAN
Rowan University

JOHN LANGAN
Atlantic Community College

ALLYN AND BACON

Boston   London   Toronto   Sydney   Tokyo   Singapore

VICE PRESIDENT: Eben Ludlow
EDITORIAL ASSISTANT: Grace Trudo
EXECUTIVE MARKETING MANAGER: Lisa Kimball
EDITORIAL-PRODUCTION ADMINISTRATOR: Annette Joseph
EDITORIAL-PRODUCTION SERVICE/ELECTRONIC COMPOSITION: Omegatype Typography, Inc.
COMPOSITION BUYER: Linda Cox
MANUFACTURING BUYER: Suzanne Lareau
COVER ADMINISTRATOR: Linda Knowles

Library of Congress Cataloging-in-Publication Data

Nadell, Judith.
    The Macmillan writer : rhetoric, reader, handbook / Judith Nadell,
Linda McMeniman, John Langan. — 4th ed.
      p. cm.
    Includes index.
    ISBN 0-205-29854-0 (alk. paper)
    1. English language—Rhetoric. 2. English language—Grammar
Handbooks, manuals, etc. 3. College readers. 4. Report writing.
I. McMeniman, Linda. II. Langan, John. III. Title.
PE1408.N19 2000
808'.0427—dc21   99-22375
                                                   CIP

Printed in the United States of America

10 9 8 7 6 5 4 3 2 1   04 03 02 01 00 99

Permission acknowledgments begin on page 699, which constitutes a continuation of the
copyright page.

BRIEF CONTENTS

(A Detailed Contents follows this Brief Contents.)

DETAILED CONTENTS

PREFACE

IN our more than sixty years of combined experience teaching composition, the three of us have gathered ideas from colleagues, journals, books, and conferences. Mindful of shifting trends in composition theory and practice, we've experimented with a variety of instructional methods. We've also risked the deflation of our egos as we've tested numerous hunches of our own. And so, when we started thinking about writing the first edition of this book, we looked as objectively as we could at our classroom experiences. Which approaches, we asked ourselves, had truly helped students become more confident, more skilled, more insightful writers?

Like the first three editions, the fourth edition of *The Macmillan Writer: Rhetoric, Reader, Handbook* represents a distillation of what we've learned about writing these many years. We continue to adopt an eclectic approach in the book, bringing together the best from often conflicting schools of thought, blending in class-tested strategies of our own. The mix we've come up with works for our students; we think it will for yours, too.

In the book, as in our classes, we try to strike a balance between product and process. Stressing the connection between reading and writing, we describe possible sequences and structures. At the same time, we emphasize that these steps and formats shouldn't be viewed as rigid prescriptions but as strategies for helping students discover what works best for them. This flexibility means that the book can fit a wide range of teaching philosophies and learning styles.

The Macmillan Writer includes everything that instructors and students need in a one- or two-semester first-year college composition course: (1) a comprehensive *rhetoric,* including chapters on each stage of the writing process, discussions of the exam essay and the literary paper, and an in-depth treatment of the research paper; (2) a *reader* with thirty-five *professional selections* and thirteen *student essays* integrated into the rhetoric; plus (3) a concise, easy-to-use *Handbook.* Throughout the text, we aim for a supportive, conversational tone that inspires students' confidence without being patronizing. Numerous *activities* and *writing assignments—over three hundred in all—*develop awareness of rhetorical choices and encourage students to explore a range of composing strategies.

THE BOOK'S PLAN

Gratified by the first three editions' warm, enthusiastic reception, we have—once again—decided not to tinker with the book's essential structure. The book's format remains as follows:

Part I, "The Reading Process," provides guided practice in a three-step process for reading with close attention and interpretive skill. An activity at the end of Chapter 1, "Becoming a Strong Reader," gives students a chance to put the sequence to use. First, they read Ellen Goodman's essay "Family Counterculture." The essay has been annotated both to show the reading process in action and to illustrate how close critical reading can suggest promising writing topics.

Students then respond to sample questions and writing assignments, all similar to those that accompany the professional selections in Part III. Part I thus does more than just tell students how to sharpen their reading abilities; it guides them through a clearly sequenced plan for developing critical reading skills.

Part II, "The Writing Process," takes students, step by step, through a multistage composing sequence. To make the writing process easier for students to understand, we provide a separate chapter for each of the following stages:

- Chapter 2, "Getting Started Through Prewriting"
- Chapter 3, "Identifying a Thesis"
- Chapter 4, "Supporting the Thesis with Evidence"
- Chapter 5, "Organizing the Evidence"
- Chapter 6, "Writing the Paragraphs in the First Draft"
- Chapter 7, "Revising Overall Meaning, Structure, and Paragraph Development"
- Chapter 8, "Revising Sentences and Words"
- Chapter 9, "Editing and Proofreading"

In Chapter 2, we introduce students to a range of prewriting techniques, including brainstorming, mapping, and journal writing. Stressing the need for students to analyze their purpose and audience, we explain how to limit a broad topic and how to generate raw, preliminary material about the topic. Chapter 2, like the other chapters in Part II, ends with an array of practical activities.

At this point, students are ready for our discussion of thesis statements in Chapter 3. Numerous examples illustrate how to frame an effective thesis, how to position it in an essay, and what pitfalls to avoid. The chapter also encourages students to view their first thesis as tentative; they learn that as writing continues, new ideas emerge that may force them to reformulate their initial thesis.

Chapter 4 starts with a description of strategies for gathering evidence to support a thesis. Then we discuss techniques for evaluating the relevance, specificity, accuracy, and persuasiveness of supporting material. Numerous suggestions for organizing evidence are presented in Chapter 5. Besides describing chronological, spatial, emphatic, and simple-to-complex methods for sequencing material, the chapter illustrates various approaches for preparing effective outlines.

In Chapter 6, students learn how to move from an outline to a first draft. Urging students to view the first draft as work in progress, we describe ways to avoid getting bogged down. Plentiful "before" and "after" examples show how to write unified, specific, and coherent paragraphs and essays. The chapter concludes with techniques for writing strong introductions, conclusions, and titles.

Emphasizing how helpful peer feedback can be, Chapters 7 and 8 introduce students to a multistage revising process. In Chapter 7, students learn how to respond to instructor feedback and how to evaluate an essay's overall content and structure. Once they know how to rework an essay at this level, they are ready to move ahead to Chapter 8. This chapter begins with abundant "before" and "after" examples that illustrate strategies for making sentences clear, concise, and emphatic. The chapter then describes approaches for refining word choice, with extensive examples showing how to make language natural, vigorous, and specific. Rounding out the chapter is a section on nonsexist language. Throughout Chapters 7 and 8, handy checklists make revision more manageable by focusing students on one rewriting stage at a time. And a series of structured activities helps them apply the checklists when they revise their own and other students' papers. Chapter 9 offers hints for editing and proofreading.

We continually point out in Part II that the stages in the writing process are fluid. Indeed, the case history of an evolving student paper dramatically illustrates just how recursive and individualized the writing process can be. Similarly, we stress that there's no single correct way to write. Focusing on the excitement and sheer fun of exploring ideas on paper, we explain that everyone must tailor the writing process to fit his or her own needs.

Throughout Part II, three instructional devices are used to strengthen students' understanding of the writing process. *Checklists* summarize key concepts and keep students focused on the essentials. Extensive *end-of-chapter activities* also reinforce pivotal skills. Designed to highlight the way invention and revision come into play throughout the writing process, the activities involve students in making rhetorical decisions about such matters as purpose, audience, tone, point of view, organization, paragraph development, and sentence structure. And numerous *guided exercises* involve students in writing—right from the start—showing them how to take their papers through successive stages in the composing process.

Finally, to illustrate the link between reading and writing, the chapters in Part II present—from prewriting through revision—the progressive stages of a student essay written in response to Ellen Goodman's "Family Counterculture" (the professional selection in Part I). In short, *by the end of Part II, the entire reading-writing process has been illustrated,* from reading a selection to writing about it.

Part III, "The Patterns of Development," opens with Chapter 10, which provides a concise overview that reinforces two key points: that the patterns come into play throughout the writing process and that most writers combine patterns in their work. The rest of Part III consists of nine chapters, each covering a different pattern: description, narration, illustration, division-classification, process analysis, comparison-contrast, cause-effect, definition, and argumentation-persuasion. The first few chapters address the more personal and expressive patterns of development, while later chapters move to the more public and analytic patterns. However, because they are self-contained, the chapters can be covered in any order. Part III's thirty-one professional essays are grouped according to the nine patterns of development.

We recognize that some instructors are reluctant to teach the patterns of development as discrete forms; they fear that doing so implies that writers set out to prepare an essay using a specific pattern and that an essay contains only one pattern. Of course, writing usually doesn't work that way at all. So throughout Parts II and III, we provide numerous examples and activities to illustrate that writers select a pattern because it helps them generate material and organize their ideas—that is, it helps serve their rhetorical purposes. We also show that most writing combines two or more patterns, with one pattern usually providing the organizational framework for a piece.

The nine pattern-of-development chapters also illustrate that the multi-stage composing sequence described in Part II has relevance no matter which pattern or combination of patterns is used in an essay. Each chapter in Part II thus follows the same format:

- *A detailed explanation of the pattern* begins the chapter. The explanation includes these sections: (1) a definition of the pattern, (2) a description of the way the pattern helps writers accommodate their purpose and audience, (3) a Prewriting Checklist to spark creativity and help students get started, (4) step-by-step guidelines for using the pattern, and (5) a Revision Checklist to focus students' efforts when they rework their papers.

  The argumentation-persuasion chapter is even more extensive. Besides the sections described above, it includes a clearly explained section on Toulmin logic, a chart on refutation strategies, and a full discussion of induction, deduction, and logical fallacies.

- Following the explanation of each pattern of development is an *annotated student essay, from prewriting through revision.* Written in response to one of the professional selections in the chapter, each essay clearly illustrates the pattern under discussion. By comparing successive stages of the essay, students come to appreciate the way material is progressively reshaped and refined.

- *Commentary* after the student essay points out the blend of patterns in the paper, identifies the paper's strengths, and pinpoints areas needing improvement. "First draft" and "revised" versions of one section of the essay reveal how the student writer went about revising, thus illustrating the relationship between the final draft and the steps taken to produce it.

- Next come *extensive prewriting and revising activities*. Together, these two sets of activities help students appreciate the distinctive features of the pattern being studied. The first prewriting activity asks students to generate raw material for an essay and helps them see that the essay may include more than one pattern of development. The last revising activity gives students a chance to rework a paragraph that needs strengthening. Other activities encourage students, working alone or in groups, to examine rhetorical options, to anticipate the consequences of such choices, and to experiment with a variety of composing techniques.

- The *professional selections* follow the activities. Representing a variety of subjects, tones, and points of view, the selections include tried and true classics like George Orwell's "Shooting an Elephant" and E. B. White's "Once More to the Lake." Other selections have rarely, if ever, been included in a composition text. Among these are Meg Greenfield's "Why Nothing Is 'Wrong' Anymore," John Leo's "Absolutophobia," and Ann McClintock's "Propaganda Techniques in Today's Advertising." Of course, each selection clearly illustrates a specific pattern of development or combination of patterns.

  Extensive instructional apparatus accompanies each professional selection:

  1. *A biographical note* gives background on the author and provides a context for the selection.

  2. *Questions for Close Reading* help students dig into and interpret the selection. The first question asks them to identify the selection's thesis; the last provides work on vocabulary development.

  3. *Questions About the Writer's Craft* deal with such matters as purpose, audience, tone, point of view, organization, sentence structure, diction, and figurative language. The first question (labeled "The Pattern") focuses on the distinctive features of the pattern(s) used in the selection. And often there's another question (labeled "Other Patterns") that asks students to analyze the writer's use of additional patterns in the piece.

  4. Next come *four writing assignments,* all prompted by the selection and packed with suggestions on how to proceed. The first two assignments ask students to write an essay using the same pattern(s) as the selection; the last two invite students to discover for themselves which pattern(s) would be most appropriate for an essay. Frequently, the writing assignments are preceded by a special symbol (∞), indicating a cross-reference to another professional selection in the book. By encouraging students to make connections between selections, these assignments broaden students' perspective and give them additional material to draw upon when they write. Such paired assignments will be especially welcome to instructors stressing recurring ideas and themes.

- At the end of each pattern-of-development chapter are two sets of Additional Writing Topics: *General Assignments* and *Assignments with a Specific Purpose, Audience, and Point of View.* The first set provides open-ended topics that prompt students to discover for themselves the best way to use a specific pattern. The second set, problem-solving in nature, develops students' sensitivity to rhetorical context by asking them to apply the pattern in a real-world setting.

Part IV consists of two chapters on **"The Research Paper."** In this practical, comprehensive guide, we demonstrate how to tailor the multi-stage composing process described in Part II to the demands of writing a research paper. This section is filled with hints on all of the following: using the library, drawing upon the Internet, taking notes, introducing quoted material, interpreting statistics, evaluating conflicting sources, documenting material, and avoiding plagiarism. A fully annotated research paper illustrates MLA documentation, while a separate section provides guidelines for using the APA system. Activities at the end of both chapters help ensure mastery of key research skills.

Part V includes two chapters, **"Writing About Literature"** and **"Writing Exam Essays."** Besides showing students how to adapt the composing process to fit the requirements of these highly specific writing situations, each chapter includes a student essay and commentary, as well as helpful end-of-chapter activities.

The book concludes with **Part VI, "A Concise Handbook."** * Detailed and user-friendly, the Handbook offers easy-to-grasp explanations of those areas that most often give students trouble. Boxed *"Cautions"* help students focus on the essentials. When appropriate, alternative correction strategies are presented so that students come to see that there may be more than one way to remedy a problem. Plentiful *practice activities* encourage mastery of important skills.

WHAT'S NEW IN THE FOURTH EDITION

Before beginning work on the fourth edition of *The Macmillan Writer,* we looked closely at the scores of questionnaires completed by instructors using the long version. The instructors' comments, always discerning and constructive, helped us identify additional material the book might include. Here, then, are the most important new features of *The Macmillan Writer, Fourth Edition*:

- *Roughly one-third of the selections are new.* Many of these new readings were suggested by instructors across the country; others were chosen after a lengthy search of magazines, nonfiction collections, newspapers, autobiographies, and the like. Whether written by a well-known figure like Maya Angelou ("Sister Flowers") or a relative newcomer like Susan Douglas ("Managing Mixed Messages"), the new selections are bound to stimulate strong writing on a variety of

*Note: Part VI is *not* included in *The Macmillan Writer, Fourth Edition/Brief Edition.* The *Brief Edition* is appropriate in those classes where students are likely to have purchased a separate English handbook.

topics—ethics, prejudice, gender identity, family life, and ethnicity, to name just a few. When selecting new readings, we took special care to include several *longer, more sustained pieces*, written from the *third person point of view*.

- A provocative *new essay* in the reading-process chapter *clearly paves the way* for the *student paper* presented in the writing-process chapters. Seeing such a direct connection between the essay and the writing it inspires helps students appreciate the interdependence of the reading and writing process.

- New illustrative material highlights the *techniques that writers use to craft a tone consistent with their purpose.*

- The discussion of *strategies for revising sentences* and *words* has been *streamlined*, making it easier for students to grasp key revising concepts.

- *The value of collaborative learning is underscored more than ever.* Many assignments encourage students to investigate various sides of an issue by brainstorming with classmates, questioning friends, speaking with family members, or interviewing "experts." Such assignments help students formulate sound, well-reasoned opinions and steer them away from reflexive, off-the-cuff positions.

- *A greater number of linked assignments* (indicated by ∞) help students make connections between selections, thus broadening their perspectives and giving them additional material to draw upon when they write.

- A concise *new explanation of the purposes underlying comparison-contrast* helps students see that this all-important pattern is at the heart of much college writing.

- *The argumentation-persuasion chapter, already more comprehensive than any comparable text's, expands the discussion of refutation strategies* by presenting a new *pair of professional essays, with one essay having been written in rebuttal to the other.*

- *Additional information* is provided on *computerized card catalogs* and on *computerized indexes, abstracts, and bibliographies.*

- *A helpful, completely up-to-date section on the Internet* offers hints for accessing the Net, discusses the advantages and pitfalls of conducting research online, shows how to use online time efficiently, and provides guidelines for evaluating materials retrieved electronically.

- The *critical link between taking effective notes and writing a strong research paper is underscored* by presenting a series of notecards based on an article about homelessness—the same subject that the research paper explores.

- *The research paper and the sample MLA and APA bibliographic entries have been updated to reflect the most recent guidelines regarding the citation of electronic sources.*

TEACHING ANCILLARIES

An Instructor's Edition of *The Macmillan Writer, Fourth Edition*, includes a comprehensive Instructor's Manual. The manual includes the following: a thematic table of contents; lists of the book's paired writing assignments and collaborative and/or problem-solving exercises; pointers about using the book; suggested activities; a detailed syllabus; answers to the Handbook exercises; and in-depth responses to the end-of-chapter activities, Questions for Close Reading, and Questions About the Writer's Craft.

ACKNOWLEDGMENTS

Throughout our teaching and certainly in writing this book, we've drawn upon the expertise and wisdom of many composition scholars and practitioners. Although we cannot list all those who have influenced us, we owe a special debt to James Britton, Kenneth Bruffee, Frances Christensen, Edward P. J. Corbett, Peter Elbow, Janet Emig, Linda Flower, Donald Hall, Ken Macrorie, James Moffett, Donald Murray, Frank O'Hare, Mina Shaughnessy, Nancy Sommers, and W. Ross Winterowd.

Over the years, many writing instructors have reviewed *The Macmillan Writer*. These colleagues' hard-hitting, practical comments guided our work every step of the way. To the following reviewers we are indeed grateful: Thomas G. Beverage, Coastal Carolina Community College; Barry Brunetti, Gulf Coast Community College; Tony C. Clark, Scottsdale Community College; Bruce Coad, Mountain View College; Beatrice I. Curry, Columbia State Community College; Juanita Davis, Columbia State Community College; William Dyer, Mankato State University; Jo Nell Farrar, San Jacinto College Central; Adam Fischer, Coastal Carolina Community College; Andrea Glebe, University of Nevada, Las Vegas; Linda Hasley, Redlands Community College; M. Jean Jones, Columbia State Community College; Rowena R. Jones, Northern Michigan University; Leela Kapai, University of the District of Columbia; Anne M. Kuhta, Northern Virginia Community College; William B. Lalicker, West Chester University of Pennsylvania; Joe Law, Wright State University; Carol Owen Lewis, Trident Technical College; James L. Madachy, Gallaudet University; Rita M. Mignacca, State University of New York at Brockport; Margaret Kissam Morris, Mercy College; Betty P. Nelson, Volunteer State Community College; Douglas L. Okey, Spoon River College; Doris Osborn, Northern Oklahoma College; Mack A. Perry, Jackson State Community College; John S. Ramsey, State University of New York at Fredonia; Clay Randolph, Oklahoma City Community College; Gladys C. Rosser, Fayetteville Technical Community College; Peggy Ruff, DeVry Institute of Technology; Elizabeth Sarcone, Delta State University; Laura A. Scibona, State University of New York at Brockport; Marilyn Segal,

California State University at Northridge; Rodger Slater, Scottsdale Community College; Richard Stoner, Broome Community College; Martha Coultas Strode, Spoon River College; Carole F. Taylor, University of Dayton; Delores Waters, Delgado Community College; Wendy F. Weiner, Northern Virginia Community College; Carol Wershoven, Palm Beach Community College; Stephen Wilhoit, University of Dayton; and Gene Young, Morehead State University.

For help in preparing the fourth edition, we owe thanks to the perceptive comments of these reviewers: John C. Baker, Concord College; Joyce L. Cherry, Albany State University; M. Jean Jones, Columbia State Community College; Joe Law, Wright State University; Jeffrey Maxson, Rowan University; Nancy McGee, Detroit College of Business; and Richard C. Zath, DeVry Institute of Technology.

At Allyn and Bacon, our thanks go to Eben Ludlow, who has played a key role in helping to shape the book from the very start. We're also indebted to Bonny Graham for skillfully handling the complex details of the production process.

Several individuals from our in-home office deserve special thanks. Karen Beardslee, Eliza Comodromos, Beth Johnson, and Frank Smigiel—four talented composition instructors—helped us with instructional apparatus and the research chapters. Janet Goldstein, upon whose peerless proofreading abilities we always rely, provided valuable assistance as we finetuned the Instructor's Manual. And Greg Giuffrida eased the demands of the project by supplying strong word-processing skills.

Of course, much appreciation goes to our families. To both sides of Judy Nadell and John Langan's family go affectionate thanks for being so supportive of our work. To Linda McMeniman's husband, Larry Schwab, and their children, Laurel, Emily, and Jeremy, much love and thanks for their charm, playfulness, patience, and support.

Finally, we're grateful to our students. Their candid reactions to various drafts of the text sharpened our thinking and kept us honest. We're especially indebted to the thirteen students whose work is included in the book. Their essays illustrate dramatically the potential and the power of student writing.

Judith Nadell
Linda McMeniman
John Langan

ABOUT THE AUTHORS

Judith Nadell was until several years ago Associate Professor of Communications at Rowan University (New Jersey). During her eighteen years at Rowan, she coordinated the introductory course in the Freshman Writing Sequence and served as Director of the Writing Lab. In the past several years, she has developed a special interest in grassroots literacy. Besides designing the instructional sequence for an adult-literacy project, a children's reading-enrichment program, and a family-literacy initiative, she has worked as a volunteer tutor and a tutor trainer in the programs. A Phi Beta Kappa graduate of Tufts University, she received a doctorate from Columbia University. She is the founder of the consulting firm Communication Training Associates and coauthor of *Doing Well in College* (McGraw-Hill), *Vocabulary Basics* (Townsend Press), and *The Macmillan Reader*. The recipient of a New Jersey award for excellence in the teaching of writing, Judith Nadell lives with her coauthor husband, John Langan, near Philadelphia.

Linda McMeniman has taught in the College Writing Department in the College of Communication at Rowan University for over twenty years. At Rowan, she teaches courses in composition, research, business writing, advanced writing, and semantics. A Phi Beta Kappa graduate of New York University, she holds a Ph.D. from the University of Pennsylvania. She has been a free-lance writer and editorial consultant. Coauthor of *The Macmillan Reader*, she is author of the Macmillan textbook *From Inquiry to Argument*. Linda McMeniman lives in Pennsylvania with her husband and family.

John Langan has taught reading and writing courses at Atlantic Community College near the New Jersey shore for the past twenty-three years. He earned an advanced degree in reading at Glassboro State College and another in writing at Rutgers University. Active in a mentoring program, he recently sponsored a reading-enrichment program for inner-city high school students. Coauthor of *The Macmillan Reader* and author of a series of college textbooks on both reading and writing, he has published widely with McGraw-Hill Book Company, Townsend Press, and Allyn and Bacon. His books include *English Skills, Reading and Study Skills,* and *College Writing Skills.*

THE MACMILLAN WRITER

Rhetoric, Reader, Handbook

PART I

THE
READING
PROCESS

1
BECOMING A STRONG READER

MORE than two hundred years ago, essayist Joseph Addison commented, "Of all the diversions of life, there is none so proper to fill up its empty spaces as the reading of useful and entertaining authors." Addison might have added that reading also challenges our beliefs, deepens our awareness, and stimulates our imagination.

Why, then, don't more people delight in reading? After all, most children feel great pleasure and pride when they first learn to read. As children grow older, though, the initially magical world of books is increasingly associated with homework, tests, and grades. Reading turns into an anxiety-producing chore. Also, as demands on a person's time accumulate throughout adolescence and adulthood, reading often gets pushed aside in favor of something that takes less effort. It's easier simply to switch on the television and passively view the ready-made images that flash across the screen. In contrast, it's almost impossible to remain passive while reading. Even a slick best-seller requires that the reader decode, visualize, and interpret what's on the page. The more challenging the materials, the more actively involved the reader must be.

The essays we selected for Part III of this book call for active reading. Representing a broad mix of styles and subjects, the essays range from the classic to the contemporary. They contain language that will move you, images that will enlarge your understanding of other people, ideas that will transform your views on complex issues.

The selections in Part III serve other purposes as well. For one thing, they'll help you develop a repertoire of reading skills—abilities that will benefit you throughout life. Second, as you become a better reader, your own writing style will become more insightful and polished. Increasingly, you'll be able to draw on the ideas presented in the selections and employ the techniques that professional writers use to express such ideas. As novelist Saul Bellow has observed, "A writer is a reader moved to emulation."

In the pages ahead, we outline a three-stage approach for getting the most out of this book's selections. Our suggestions will enhance your understanding of the book's essays, as well as help you read other material with greater ease and assurance.

STAGE 1: GET AN OVERVIEW OF THE SELECTION

Ideally, you should get settled in a quiet place that encourages concentration. If you can focus your attention while sprawled on a bed or curled up in a chair, that's fine. But if you find that being very comfortable is more conducive to daydreaming and dozing off than it is to studying, avoid getting too relaxed.

Once you're settled, it's time to read the selection. To ensure a good first reading, try the following hints:

- Get an overview of the essay and its author. Start by reading the biographical note that precedes the selection. By providing background information about the author, the note helps you evaluate the writer's credibility as well as his or her slant on the subject. For example, if you know that Deborah Tannen is a widely published linguistics professor at Georgetown University, you can better assess whether she is a credible source for the analysis she presents in her essay "But What Do You Mean?" (reprinted in Chapter 14).

- Consider the selection's title. A good title often expresses the essay's main idea, giving you insight into the selection even before you read it. For example, the title of Ann McClintock's essay, "Propaganda Techniques in Today's Advertising" (Chapter 14) suggests that the piece will examine the dark side of the advertising world. A title may also hint at a selection's tone. The title of Robert Barry's piece, "Becoming a Videoholic" (the student essay in Chapter 15), points to an essay that's light in spirit, whereas George Orwell's "Shooting an Elephant" (Chapter 12) suggests a piece with a serious mood.

- Read the selection straight through purely for pleasure. Allow yourself to be drawn into the world the author has created. Just as you first see a painting from the doorway of a room and form an overall impression without perceiving the details, you can have a preliminary, subjective feeling about a reading selection. Moreover, because you bring your own experiences and viewpoints to the piece, your reading will be unique. As Emerson said, "Take the book, my friend, and read your eyes out; you will never find there what I find."

- After this initial reading of the selection, focus your first impressions by asking yourself whether you like the selection. In your own words, briefly describe the piece and your reaction to it.

STAGE 2: DEEPEN YOUR SENSE OF THE SELECTION

At this point, you're ready to move further into the selection. A second reading will help you identify the specific features that triggered your initial reaction. Here are some suggestions on how to proceed:

- Mark off the selection's main idea, or thesis, often found near the beginning or end. If the thesis isn't stated explicitly, write down your own version of the selection's main idea.
- Locate the main supporting evidence used to develop the thesis. You may even want to number in the margin each key supporting point.
- Take a minute to write "Yes" or "No" beside points with which you strongly agree or disagree. Your reaction to these points often explains your feelings about the aptness of the selection's ideas.
- Return to any unclear passages you encountered during the first reading. The feeling you now have for the piece as a whole will probably help you make sense of initially confusing spots. However, this second reading may also reveal that, in places, the writer's thinking isn't as clear as it could be.
- Use your dictionary to check the meanings of any unfamiliar words.
- Ask yourself if your initial impression of the selection has changed in any way as a result of this second reading. If your feelings *have* changed, try to determine why you reacted differently on this reading.

STAGE 3: EVALUATE THE SELECTION

Now that you have a good grasp of the selection, you may want to read it a third time, especially if the piece is long or complex. This time, your goal is to make judgments about the essay's effectiveness. Keep in mind, though, that you shouldn't evaluate the selection until after you have a strong hold on it. A negative, even a positive reaction is valid only if it's based on an accurate reading.

At first, you may feel uncomfortable about evaluating the work of a professional writer. But remember: Written material set in type only *seems* perfect; all writing can be finetuned. By identifying what does and doesn't work in others' writing, you're taking an important first step toward developing your own power as a writer. You might find it helpful at this point to get together with other students to discuss the selection. Comparing viewpoints often opens up a piece, enabling you to gain a clearer perspective on the selection and the author's approach.

To evaluate the essay, ask yourself the following questions:

Questions for Evaluating a Selection

1. *Where does support for the selection's thesis seem logical and sufficient? Where does support seem weak?* Which of the author's supporting facts, arguments, and examples seem pertinent and convincing? Which don't?

2. *Is the selection unified? If not, why not?* Where does something in the selection not seem relevant? Where are there any unnecessary digressions or detours?

3. *How does the writing make the selection move smoothly from beginning to end?* How does the writer create an easy flow between ideas? Are any parts of the essay abrupt and jarring? Which ones?

4. *Which stylistic devices are used to good effect in the selection?* Which pattern of development or combination of patterns does the writer use to develop the piece? Why do you think those patterns were selected? How do paragraph development, sentence structure, and word choice (diction) contribute to the piece's overall effect? What tone does the writer adopt? Where does the writer use figures of speech effectively? (The terms *patterns of development, sentence structure, diction,* and the like are explained in Chapter 2.)

5. *How does the selection encourage further thought?* What new perspective on an issue does the writer provide? What ideas has the selection prompted you to explore in an essay of your own?

It takes some work to follow the three-stage approach just described, but the selections in Part III make it worth the effort. Bear in mind that none of the selections you'll read in Part III sprang full-blown from the pen of its author. Rather, each essay is the result of hours of work—hours of thinking, writing, rethinking, and revising. As a reader, you should show the same willingness to work with the selections, to read them carefully and thoughtfully. Henry David Thoreau, an avid reader and prolific writer, emphasized the importance of this kind of attentive reading when he advised that "books must be read as deliberately and unreservedly as they were written."

To illustrate the multistage reading process, we've annotated the professional essay that follows: Ellen Goodman's "Family Counterculture." Note that annotations are provided in the margin of the essay as well as at the end of the essay. As you read Goodman's essay, try applying the three-stage sequence. You can measure your ability to dig into the selection by making your own annotations on Goodman's essay and then comparing them to ours. You can also see how well you evaluated the piece by answering the preceding five questions and then comparing your responses to ours on pages 9–10.

ELLEN GOODMAN

The recipient of a Pulitzer Prize, Ellen Goodman (1941–) worked for *Newsweek* and the *Detroit Free Press* before joining the staff of the *Boston Globe* in the mid-1970s. A resident of the Boston area, Goodman writes a popular syndicated column. Her pieces have appeared in a number of national publications, including *The Village Voice* and *McCalls.* Collections of her columns have been published in *Close to Home* (1979), *Turning Points* (1979), *At Large* (1981), *Keeping in Touch* (1985), *Making Sense* (1989), and *Value Judgments* (1993). The following selection is from *Value Judgments.*

FAMILY COUNTERCULTURE

1   Sooner or later, most Americans become card-carrying members of the counterculture. This is not an underground holdout of hippies. No beads are required. All you need to join is a child.

2   At some point between Lamaze and the PTA, it becomes clear that one of your main jobs as a parent is to counter the culture. What the media delivers to children by the masses, you are expected to rebut one at a time.

3   The latest evidence of this frustrating piece of the parenting job description came from pediatricians. This summer, the American Academy of Pediatrics called for a ban on television food ads. Their plea was hard on the heels of a study showing that one Saturday morning of TV cartoons contained 202 junk-food ads.

4   The kids see, want, and nag. That is, after all, the theory behind advertising to children, since few six-year-olds have their own trust funds. The end result, said the pediatricians, is obesity and high cholesterol.

5   Their call for a ban was predictably attacked by the grocers' association. But it was also attacked by people assembled under the umbrella marked "parental responsibility." We don't need bans, said these "PR" people, we need parents who know how to say "no."

6   Well, I bow to no one in my capacity for naysaying. I agree that it's a well-honed skill of child raising. By the time my daughter was seven, she qualified as a media critic.

7   But it occurs to me now that the call for "parental responsibility" is increasing in direct proportion to the irresponsibility of the marketplace. Parents are expected to protect their children from an increasingly hostile environment.

8   Are the kids being sold junk food? Just say no. Is TV bad? Turn it off. Are there messages about sex, drugs, violence all around? Counter the culture.

9   Mothers and fathers are expected to screen virtually every aspect of their children's lives. To check the ratings on the movies, to read the labels on the CDs, to find out if there's MTV in the house next door. All the while keeping in touch with school and, in their free time, earning a living.

10   In real life, most parents do a great deal of this monitoring and just-say-no-ing. Any trip to the supermarket produces at least one scene of a child

Annotations in margin:
- Interesting take on the term "counterculture"
- Time frame established
- Light humor. Easy, casual tone
- Time frame picked up
- Thesis, developed overall by cause-effect pattern
- First research-based example to support thesis
- Relevant paragraph? Identifies Goodman as a parent, but interrupts flow
- Transition doesn't work but would if ¶6 cut.
- Series of questions and brief answers consistent with overall casual tone.
- Brief real-life examples support thesis.
- Fragments
- More examples

grabbing for something only to have it returned to the shelf by a frazzled parent. An extraordinary number of the family arguments are over the goodies—sneakers, clothes, games—that the young know only because of ads.

Another weak transition—no contrast → But at times it seems that the media have become the mainstream cul- 11 ture in children's lives. Parents have become the alternative.

Restatement of thesis

Second research-based example to support thesis → Barbara Dafoe Whitehead, a research associate at the Institute for Amer- 12 ican Values, found this out in interviews with middle-class parents. "A common complaint I heard from parents was their sense of being over-

Citing an expert reinforces thesis. whelmed by the culture. They felt their voice was a lot weaker. And they felt relatively more helpless than their parents.

Restatement of thesis → "Parents," she notes, "see themselves in a struggle for the hearts and 13 minds of their own children." It isn't that they can't say no. It's that there's so much more to say no to.

Comparison-contrast pattern—signaled by "Today," "Once," and "Now" Without wallowing in false nostalgia, there has been a fundamental 14 shift. Americans once expected parents to raise their children in accor- dance with the dominant cultural messages. Today they are expected to raise their children in opposition.

Once the chorus of cultural values was full of ministers, teachers, neigh- 15 bors, leaders. They demanded more conformity, but offered more support. Now the messengers are Ninja Turtles, Madonna, rap groups, and celebri- ties pushing sneakers. Parents are considered "responsible" only if they are successful in their resistance.

It's what makes child raising harder. It's why parents feel more isolated. 16

Restatement of thesis → It's not just that American families have less time with their kids. It's that we have to spend more of this time doing battle with our own culture.

Conveys the challeng- es that parents face It's rather like trying to get your kids to eat their green beans after 17 they've been told all day about the wonders of Milky Way. Come to think of it, it's exactly like that.

Thesis: First stated in paragraph 2 ("…it becomes clear that one of your main jobs as a parent is to counter the culture. What the media delivers to children by the mass- es, you are expected to rebut one at a time.") and then restated in paragraphs 11 ("the media have become the mainstream culture in children's lives. Parents have become the alternative."); 13 (Parents are frustrated, not because "…they can't say no. It's that there's so much more to say no to.") and 16 ("It's not just that American families have less time with their kids; it's that we have to spend more of this time doing bat- tle with our own culture.").

First Reading: A quick take on a serious subject. Informal tone and to-the-point style gets to the heart of the media vs. parenting problem. Easy to relate to.

Second and Third Readings:

1. Uses the findings of the American Academy of Pediatrics, a statement made by Barbara Dafoe Whitehead, and a number of brief examples to illustrate the relentless work parents must do to counter the culture.
2. Uses cause-effect overall to support thesis and comparison/contrast to show how parenting nowadays is more difficult than it used to be.
3. Not everything works (reference to her daughter as a media critic, repetitive and often inappropriate use of "but" as a transition), but overall the essay succeeds.
4. At first, the ending seems weak. But it feels just right after an additional reading. Shows how parents' attempts to counter the culture are as commonplace as their attempts to get kids to eat vegetables. It's an ongoing and constant battle that makes parenting more difficult than it has to be and less enjoyable than it should be.
5. Possible essay topics: A humorous paper about the strategies kids use to get around their parents' saying "no" or a serious paper on the negative effects on kids of another aspect of television culture (cable television, MTV, tabloid-style talk shows, and so on).

The following answers to the questions on pages 5–6 will help crystalize your reaction to Goodman's essay.

1. *Where does support for the selection's thesis seem logical and sufficient? Where does support seem weak?* Goodman begins to provide evidence for her thesis when she cites the American Academy of Pediatrics' call for a "ban on television food ads" (paragraphs 3–5). The ban followed a study showing that kids are exposed to 202 junk-food ads during a single Saturday morning of television cartoons. Goodman further buoys her thesis with a list of brief "countering the culture" examples (8–10) and a slightly more detailed example (10) describing the parent-child conflicts that occur on a typical trip to the supermarket. By citing Barbara Dafoe Whitehead's findings (12–13) later on, Goodman further reinforces her point that the need for constant rebuttal makes parenting especially frustrating: Because parents have to say no to virtually everything, more and more family time ends up being spent "doing battle" with the culture (16).

2. *Is the selection unified? If not, why not?* In the first two paragraphs, Goodman identifies the problem and then provides solid evidence of its existence (3–4, 8–10). But Goodman's comments in paragraph 6 about her daughter's skill as a media critic seem distracting. Even so, paragraph 6 serves a purpose because it establishes Goodman's credibility by showing that she, too, is a parent and has been compelled to be a constant naysayer with her child. From paragraph 7 on, the piece stays on course by focusing on the way parents have to compete with the media for control of their children. The concluding paragraphs (16–17) reinforce Goodman's thesis by suggesting that parents' struggle to counteract the media is as common—and as exasperating—as trying to get children to eat their vegetables when all the kids want is to gorge on candy.

3. *How does the writer make the selection move smoothly from beginning to end?* The first two paragraphs of Goodman's essay are clearly connected: The phrase "sooner or later" at the beginning of the first paragraph establishes a time frame that is then picked up at the beginning of of the second paragraph with the phrase "at some point between Lamaze and the PTA." And Goodman's use in paragraph 3 of the word *this* ("The latest evidence of *this* frustrating piece of the parenting job description...") provides a link to the preceding paragraph. Other connecting strategies can be found in the piece. For example, the words *Today, Once,* and *Now* in paragraphs 14–15 provide an easy-to-follow contrast between parenting in earlier times and parenting in this era. However, because paragraph 6 contains a distracting aside, the contrast implied by the word *But* at the beginning of paragraph 7 doesn't work. Nor does Goodman's use of the word *But* at the beginning of paragraph 11 work; the point there emphasizes rather than contrasts with the one made in paragraph 10. From this point on, though, the essay is tightly written and moves smoothly along to its conclusion.

4. *Which stylistic devices are used to good effect in the selection?* Goodman uses several patterns of development in her essay. The selection as a whole shows the *effect* of the mass media on kids and their parents. In paragraphs 3 and 12, Goodman provides *examples in the form of research data* to support her thesis, while paragraphs 8–10 provide a series of *brief real-life examples.* Paragraphs 12–15 use a *contrast,* and paragraph 17 makes a *comparison* to punctuate Goodman's concluding point. Throughout, Goodman's *informal, conversational tone* draws readers in, and her *no-holds-barred style* drives her point home forcefully. In paragraph 8, she uses a *question and answer format* ("Are the kids being sold junk food? Just say no.") and *short sentences* ("Turn it off" and "Counter the culture") to illustrate how pervasive the situation is. And in paragraph 9, she uses *fragments* ("To check the ratings..." and "All the while keeping in touch with school...") to focus attention on the problem. These varied stylistic devices help make the essay a quick, enjoyable read. Finally, although Goodman is concerned about the corrosive effects of the media, she leavens her essay with dashes of *humor.* For example, the image of parents as card-carrying hippies (1) and the comments about green beans and Milky Ways (17) probably elicit smiles or gentle laughter from most readers.

5. *How does the selection encourage further thought?* Goodman's essay touches on a problem most parents face at some time or another—having to counter the culture in order to protect their children. Her main concern is how difficult it is for parents to say "no" to virtually every aspect of the culture. Although Goodman offers no immediate solutions, her presentation of the issue urges us to decide for ourselves which aspects of the culture should be countered and which should not.

　　If, for each essay you read in this book, you consider the preceding questions, you'll be able to respond thoughtfully to the *Questions for Close Reading* and *Questions About the Writer's Craft* presented after each selection. Your responses will, in turn, prepare you for the writing assignments that follow the questions. Interesting and varied, the assignments invite you to examine issues raised by the selections and encourage you to experiment with various writing styles and organizational patterns.

Following are some sample questions and writing assignments based on the Goodman essay; all are similar to the sort that appear later in this book. Note that the final writing assignment paves the way for the successive stages of a student essay presented in Part II, "The Writing Process." (The final version of the essay appears on pages 137–139.)

QUESTIONS FOR CLOSE READING

1. According to Goodman, what does it mean to "counter the culture"? Why is it harder now than ever before?

2. Which two groups, according to Goodman, protested the American Academy of Pediatrics' ban on television food ads? Which of these two groups does she take more seriously? Why?

QUESTIONS ABOUT THE WRITER'S CRAFT

1. What audience do you think Goodman had in mind when she wrote this piece? How do you know? Where does she address this audience directly?

2. What word appears four times in paragraph 16? Why do you think Goodman repeats this word so often? What is the effect of this repetition?

WRITING ASSIGNMENTS

1. Goodman believes that parents are forced to say "no" to almost everything the media offer. Write an essay supporting the idea that not everything the media present is bad for children.

2. Goodman implies that, in some ways, today's world is hostile to children. Do you agree? Write an essay supporting or rejecting this viewpoint.

The benefits of active reading are many. Books in general and the selections in Part III in particular will bring you face to face with issues that concern all of us. If you study the selections and the questions that follow them, you'll be on your way to discovering ideas for your own papers. Part II offers practical suggestions for turning those ideas into well-organized, thoughtful essays.

PART II

THE WRITING PROCESS

2
GETTING STARTED THROUGH PREWRITING

OBSERVATIONS ABOUT THE WRITING PROCESS

NOT many people retire at age thirty-eight. But Michel Montaigne, a sixteenth-century French attorney, did exactly that. Montaigne retired at a young age because he wanted to read, think, and write about all the subjects that interested him. After spending years getting his ideas down on paper, Montaigne finally published his short prose pieces. He called them *"essais"*—French for "trials" or "attempts."

In fact, all writing is an attempt to transform ideas into words, thus giving order and meaning to life. By using the term *essais,* Montaigne acknowledged that a written piece is never really finished. Of course, writers have to stop at some point, especially if they have deadlines to meet. But, as all experienced writers know, even after they dot the final *i,* cross the final *t,* and say "That's it," there's always something that could have been explored further or expressed a little better.

When we read a piece of writing, we see only the finished product. Not being privy to the writer's effort to convey meaning, we may hold a romanticized notion of what it means to be a writer. We may imagine the writer transported by flashes of creativity, polished prose appearing—as if by magic—on the page. In practice, though, most writers do anything but pour out well-formed thoughts. Rather, they stare into space, dash off a few pages, crumple them up, and start all over. Even E. B. White, the American essayist celebrated for his eloquent, seemingly effortless prose, confessed, "Writing . . . is a hell of a chore for me, closely related to acid indigestion."

If White, who made his living as a writer, admitted such anxiety, you shouldn't be surprised if you feel some apprehension when it's time to write a paper. Your uneasiness may stem in part from your belief that some people are born writers, others are not—and that you're one of the latter. Some people *do* seem to be born with a gift for language, just as some people seem to be born with a gift for athletics or music. But with practice, just about anyone can learn to play a solid game of tennis or to sing on key. And that's what most of us are aiming for—not to be the Martina Navratilovas, the Pavarottis, or the E. B. Whites of the world, but to perform skillfully and confidently.

As with singing or playing tennis, learning to write well is a challenge. Shaky starts and changes in direction aren't uncommon. Although there's no way to eliminate the work needed to write effectively, certain approaches can make the process more manageable and rewarding. In Chapters 2–9, we describe a sequence of steps for writing essays. Familiarity with a specific sequence develops your awareness of strategies and choices, making you feel more confident when it comes time to write. You're less likely to look at a blank piece of paper and think, "Help! Now what do I do?" During the sequence, you do the following:

- Prewrite
- Identify your thesis
- Support the thesis with evidence
- Organize the evidence
- Write the paragraphs of the first draft
- Revise meaning, structure, and paragraph development
- Revise sentences and words
- Edit and proofread

Even though we present the sequence as a series of steps, it's not a rigid formula that you must follow step by unchanging step. Somewhere in school we were taught that a straight line is the shortest distance between two points. But writing isn't as simple or tidy as that. Most people develop personalized approaches to the writing process. Some writers mull over a topic in their heads, then move quickly into a promising first draft; others outline their essays in detail before beginning to write. Between these two extremes are any number of effective approaches.

Most of us tend to be creatures of habit; we feel secure and comfortable doing things the way we always have. You've probably approached writing in much the same way for many years. At first, you may be reluctant to try the techniques we describe here and in the following chapters. That's understandable. But we urge you to experiment with the strategies we present. Try them, use what works, discard what doesn't. And always feel free to streamline or alter the steps in the sequence to suit your individual needs and the requirements of specific writing assignments.

USE PREWRITING TO GET STARTED

Prewriting refers to strategies you can use to generate ideas *before* starting the first draft of a paper. Prewriting techniques are like the warm-ups you do before going out to jog—they loosen you up, get you moving, and help you to develop a sense of well-being and confidence. Since prewriting techniques encourage imaginative exploration, they also help you discover what interests you most about your subject. Having such a focus early in the writing process keeps you from plunging into your initial draft without first giving some thought to what you want to say. Prewriting thus saves you time in the long run by keeping you on course.

Prewriting can help in other ways, too. When we write, we often sabotage our ability to generate material because we continually critique what we put down on paper. "This makes no sense," "This is stupid," "I can't say that," and other critical thoughts pop into our minds. Such negative, self-critical comments stop the flow of our thoughts and reinforce the fear that we have nothing to say and aren't very good at writing. During prewriting, you deliberately ignore your internal critic. Your purpose is simply to get ideas down on paper *without evaluating* their effectiveness. Writing without immediately judging what you produce can be liberating. Once you feel less pressure, you'll probably find that you can generate a good deal of material. And that can make your confidence soar.

One final advantage of prewriting: The random associations typical of prewriting tap the mind's ability to make unusual connections. When you prewrite, you're like an archaeologist going on a dig. On the one hand, you may not unearth anything; on the other hand, you may stumble upon one interesting find after another. Prewriting helps you appreciate—right from the start—this element of surprise in the writing process.

Keep a Journal

Of all the prewriting techniques, keeping a **journal** (daily or almost daily) is the one most likely to make writing a part of your life. If you prefer keeping a handwritten journal, consider using a small notebook that you can carry with you for on-the-spot writing. If you feel more comfortable working at a typewriter or word processor, keep your typed pages or printouts in a loose-leaf notebook. No matter how you proceed, be sure to date all entries.

Some journal entries focus on a single theme; others wander from topic to topic. Your starting point may be a dream, a snippet of overheard conversation, a video on MTV, a political cartoon, an issue raised in class or in your reading—anything that surprises, interests, angers, depresses, confuses, or amuses you. You may also use a journal to experiment with your writing style—say, to vary your sentence structure if you tend to use predictable patterns.

Here is a fairly focused excerpt from a student's journal:

> Today I had to show Paul around school. He and Mom got here
> by 9. I didn't let on that this was the earliest I've gotten up
> all semester! He got out of the car looking kind of nervous.
> Maybe he thought his big brother would be different after a cou-
> ple of months of college. I walked him around part of the campus
> and then he went with me to Am. Civ. and then to lunch. He met
> Greg and some other guys. Everyone seemed to like him. He's got a
> nice, quiet sense of humor. When I went to Bio., I told him that
> he could walk around on his own since he wasn't crazy about sit-
> ting in on a science class. But he said "I'd rather stick with
> you." Was he flattering me or was he just scared? Anyway it made
> me feel good. Later when he was leaving, he told me he's defi-
> nitely going to apply. I guess that'd be kind of nice, having him
> here. Mom thinks it's great and she's pushing it. I don't know. I
> feel kind of like it would invade my privacy. I found this school
> and have made a life for myself here. Let him find his own
> school! But it could be great having my kid brother here. I guess
> this is a classic case of what my psych teacher calls ambiva-
> lence. Part of me wants him to come, and part of me doesn't.
> (November 10)

The journal is a place for you to get in touch with the writer inside you. Although some instructors collect students' journals, you needn't be overly concerned with spelling, grammar, sentence structure, or organization. While journal writing is typically more structured than freewriting (see page 27), you don't have to strive for entries that read like mini-essays. You may leave loose ends, drift to new topics, and evoke the personal and private without fully explaining or describing. The most important thing is to let your journal writing prompt reflection and insights.

Writing openly and fluently doesn't happen overnight; you need to keep at it. Try to complete a page-long journal entry three to five times a week. It's also a good idea to reread each week's entries to identify recurring themes and concerns. Keep a list of these issues at the back of your journal, under a heading like "Possible Essay Subjects." Here, for instance, are a few topics suggested by the preceding journal entry: deciding which college to attend, leaving home, sibling rivalry. Each of these topics could be developed in a full-length essay.

Using the journal to identify potential essay subjects helps you see that everyday life can be the source of meaningful writing. Most of us have become so accustomed to the routines of our lives that we cannot see the interesting in the ordinary. In *Walden*, a collection of journal entries, Henry David Thoreau wrote

that our lives would be enriched immeasurably if we "employ[ed] a certain portion of each day looking back upon the time which has passed and in writing
down...[our] thoughts and feelings." Keeping a journal does indeed foster an
awareness of our own lives. It prevents us from thinking of ourselves as dull,
dreary people to whom nothing happens. And it provides a wealth of material to
draw on in our writing.

Journal writing stimulates thinking in a loose, unstructured way. But when you
have a specific piece to write, you should approach prewriting in a purposeful,
focused manner. You need to:

- Understand the boundaries of the assignment
- Determine your purpose, audience, tone, and point of view
- Discover your essay's limited subject
- Generate raw material about your limited subject
- Organize the raw material

We'll discuss each of these steps in turn. But first, here's a practical tip: If you don't
use a word processor during the prewriting stage, try using a pencil and scrap
paper. They're less intimidating than pen, typewriter, and "official" paper; they
also reinforce the notion that prewriting is tentative and exploratory.

Understand the Boundaries of the Assignment

Most likely, you'll find considerable variety in your college writing assignments. Sometimes a professor will indicate that you can write on a topic of your
own choosing; other times you may be given a highly specific assignment. Most
assignments, though, will fit somewhere in between. In any case, you shouldn't
start writing a paper until you know what's expected. First, clarify the *kind of paper*
the instructor has in mind. Assume the instructor asks you to discuss the key ideas
in an assigned reading. What exactly does the instructor want you to do? Should
you include a brief summary of the selection? Should you compare the author's
ideas with your own view of the subject? Should you determine if the author's
view is supported by valid evidence? If you're not sure about an assignment, ask
your instructor—not the student next to you, who may be as confused as you—to
make the requirements clear. Most instructors are more than willing to provide an
explanation. They would rather take a few minutes of class time to explain the
assignment than spend hours reading dozens of student essays that miss the
mark.

Second, find out *how long* the paper is expected to be. Many instructors will
indicate the approximate length of the papers they assign. If no length requirements are provided, discuss with the instructor what you plan to cover and indicate how long you think your paper will be. The instructor will either give you the
go-ahead or help you refine the direction and scope of your work.

Determine Your Purpose, Audience, Tone, and Point of View

Once you understand the requirements for a writing assignment, you're ready to begin thinking about the essay. What is its *purpose*? For what *audience* will it be written? What *tone* and *point of view* will you use? Later on, you may modify your decisions about these issues. That's fine. But you need to understand the way these considerations influence your work in the early phases of the writing process.

Purpose

Start by clarifying to yourself the essay's broad **purpose.** What do you want the essay to accomplish? The papers you write in college are usually meant to *inform* or *explain*, to *convince* or *persuade,* and sometimes to *entertain.*

In practice, writing often combines purposes. You might, for example, write an essay trying to *convince* people to support a new trash recycling program in your community. But before you win readers over, you most likely would have to *explain* something about current waste-disposal technology.

When purposes blend in this way, the predominant one influences the essay's content, organization, pattern of development, emphasis, and language. Assume you're writing about a political campaign. If your primary goal is to *entertain*, to take a gentle poke at two candidates, you might use the comparison-contrast pattern to organize your essay. You might, for example, start with several accounts of one candidate's "foot-in-mouth disease" and then describe the attempts of the other candidate, a multimillionaire, to portray himself as an average Joe. Your language, full of exaggeration, would reflect your objective. But if your primary purpose is to *persuade* readers that the candidates are incompetent and shouldn't be elected, you might adopt a serious, straightforward style. Selecting the argumentation-persuasion pattern to structure the essay, you might use one candidate's gaffes and the other's posturings to build a case that neither is worthy of public office.

Audience

Writing is a social act and thus implies a reader or an **audience.** To write effectively, you need to identify who your readers are and to take their expectations and needs into account. An essay about the artificial preservatives in the food served by the campus cafeteria would take one form if submitted to your chemistry professor and a very different form if written for the college newspaper. The chemistry paper would probably be formal and technical, complete with chemical formulations and scientific data: "Distillation revealed sodium benzoate particles suspended in a gelatinous medium." But such technical material would be inappropriate in a newspaper column intended for general readers. In this case, you might provide specific examples of cafeteria foods containing additives—"Those deliciously smoky cold cuts are loaded with nitrates and nitrites, both known to cause cancer in laboratory animals"—and suggest ways to eat more healthfully—"Pass by the deli counter and fill up instead on vegetarian pizza and fruit juices."

If you forget your readers, your essay can run into problems. Consider what happened when one student, Roger Salucci, submitted a draft of his essay to his instructor for feedback. The assignment was to write about an experience that demonstrated the value of education. Here's the opening paragraph from Roger's first draft:

> When I received my first page as an EMT, I realized pretty quickly that all the weeks of KED and CPR training paid off. At first, when the call came in, it was nerve city for this guy, I can tell you. When the heat is on, my mind tends to go as blank as a TV screen at 2:00 a.m. in the morning. But I beat it to the van right away. After a couple of false turns, my partner and I finally got the right house and found a woman fibrillating and suffering severe myocardial arrhythmia. Despite our anxiety, our heads were on straight; we knew exactly what to do.

Roger's instructor found his essay unclear because she knew nothing about being an EMT (Emergency Medical Technician). When writing the essay, Roger neglected to consider his audience; specifically, he forgot that college instructors are no more knowledgeable than anyone else about subjects outside their specialty. Roger's instructor also commented that she was thrown off guard by the paper's casual, slangy approach ("It was nerve city for this guy, I can tell you"; "I beat it to the van right away"). Roger used a breezy, colloquial style—almost as though he were chatting about the experience with friends—but the instructor had expected a more formal approach.

The more you know about your readers, the more you can adapt your writing to fit their needs and expectations. The accompanying checklist will help you analyze your audience.

✔ ANALYZING YOUR AUDIENCE: A CHECKLIST

- ☐ What are my readers' age, sex, and educational levels? How do these factors affect what I need to tell and don't need to tell my readers?
- ☐ What are my readers' political, religious, and other beliefs? How do these beliefs influence their attitudes and actions?
- ☐ What interests and needs motivate my audience?
- ☐ How much do my readers already know about my subject? Do they have any misconceptions?
- ☐ What biases do they have about me, my subject, and my opinion?
- ☐ How do my readers expect me to relate to them?
- ☐ What values do I share with my readers that will help me communicate with them?

Tone

Just as your voice may project a range of feelings, your writing can convey one or more **tones,** or emotional states: enthusiasm, anger, resignation, and so on. Tone isn't a decorative adornment tacked on as an afterthought. Rather, tone is integral to meaning. It permeates writing and reflects your attitude toward yourself, your purpose, your subject, and your readers.

In everyday conversation, vocal inflections, facial expressions, and body gestures help convey tone. In writing, how do you project tone without these aids? You pay close attention to *sentence structure* and *word choice.* In Chapter 8, we present detailed strategies for finetuning sentences and words during the revision stage. Here we simply want to help you see that determining your tone should come early in the writing process because the tone you select influences the sentences and words you use later.

Sentence structure refers to the way sentences are shaped. Although the two paragraphs that follow deal with exactly the same subject, note how differences in sentence structure create sharply dissimilar tones:

> During the 1960s, many inner-city minorities considered the police an occupying force and an oppressive agent of control. As a result, violence grew against police in poorer neighborhoods, as did the number of residents killed by police.

> An occupying force. An agent of control. An oppressor. That's how many inner-city minorities in the '60s viewed the police. Violence against police soared. Police killings of residents mounted.

Informative in its approach, the first paragraph projects a neutral, almost dispassionate tone. The sentences are fairly long, and clear transitions ("During the 1960s"; "As a result") mark the progression of thought. But the second paragraph, with its dramatic, almost alarmist tone, seems intended to elicit a strong emotional response; its short sentences, fragments, and abrupt transitions reflect the turbulence of earlier times.

Word choice also plays a role in establishing the tone of an essay. Words have **denotations,** neutral dictionary meanings, as well as **connotations,** emotional associations that go beyond the literal meaning. The word *beach,* for instance, is defined in the dictionary as "a nearly level stretch of pebbles and sand beside a body of water." This definition, however, doesn't capture individual responses to the word. For some, *beach* suggests warmth and relaxation; for others, it calls up images of hospital waste and sewage washed up on a once-clean stretch of shoreline.

Since tone and meaning are tightly bound, you must be sensitive to the emotional nuances of words. Think about some of the terms denoting *adult human female: woman, fox, broad, member of the fair sex.* While all of these words denote the same thing, their connotations—the pictures they call up—are sharply different. Similarly, in a respectful essay about police officers, you wouldn't refer to *cops, narcs,* or *flatfoots;* such terms convey a contempt inconsistent with the tone intended. Your words must also convey tone clearly; otherwise, meaning is lost.

Suppose you're writing a satirical piece criticizing a local beauty pageant. Dubbing the participants "livestock on view" leaves no question about your tone. But if you simply referred to the participants as "attractive young women," readers might be unsure of your attitude. Remember, readers can't read your mind, only your paper.

Point of View

When you write, you speak to your audience as a unique individual. **Point of view** reveals the person you decide to be as you write. Like tone, point of view is closely tied to your purpose, audience, and subject. Imagine you want to convey to students in your composition class the way your grandfather's death—on your eighth birthday—impressed you with life's fragility. To capture that day's impact on you, you might tell what happened from the point of view of a child: "Today is my birthday. I'm eight. Grandpa died an hour before I was supposed to have my party." Or you might choose instead to recount the event speaking as the adult you are today: "My grandfather died an hour before my eighth birthday party." Your point of view will obviously affect the essay's content and organization.

The most strongly individualized point of view is the **first person** (*I, me, mine, we, us, our*). Because it focuses on the writer, the first-person point of view is appropriate in narrative and descriptive essays based on personal experience. It also suits other types of essays (for example, causal analyses and process analyses) when the bulk of evidence presented consists of personal observation. In such essays, avoiding the first person often leads to stilted sentences like "There was strong parental opposition to the decision" or "Although Organic Chemistry had been dreaded, it became a passion." In contrast, the sentences sound much more natural when the first person is used: "*Our* parents strongly opposed the decision" and "Although *I* had dreaded Organic Chemistry, it became *my* passion."

Like many students, you may feel that a lightning bolt will strike you if you use the first person when writing. Indeed, in high school, you may have been warned away from (even forbidden to use) the first person. And it does have its dangers. For one thing, in essays voicing an opinion, most first-person expressions ("I believe that ..." and "In my opinion ...") are unnecessary; the point of view stated is assumed to be the writer's unless another source is indicated. Second, in a paper intended to be an objective presentation of an issue, the first person distracts from the issue by drawing unwarranted attention to the writer: "I think it's important to realize that most violent crime in this country is directly related to substance abuse." By way of contrast, note how the matter under discussion is clearly highlighted when the first person is omitted: "Most violent crime in this country is directly related to substance abuse."

In some situations, writers use the **second person** (*you, your, yours*), alone or in combination with the first person. In fact, we frequently use forms of *you* in this book. For instance, we write, "If *you're* the kind of person who doodles while thinking, *you* may want to try mapping ..." rather than "If a *writer* is the kind of person who doodles while thinking, *he or she* may want to try mapping. ..." As you can see, the second person simplifies style and involves the reader in a more personal way. You'll also find that the *imperative* form of the verb ("*Send* letters of protest to the television networks") engages readers in much the same way. The implied *you* speaks to the audience directly and lends immediacy to the directions. Despite these advantages, the second-person point of view often isn't appropriate in many college courses where more formal, less conversational writing is called for.

The **third-person** point of view is by far the most common in academic writing. The third person gets its name from the stance it conveys—that of an outsider or "third person" observing and reporting on matters of primarily public rather than private importance: "The international team of negotiators failed to resolve the border dispute between the two nations." In discussions of historical events, scientific phenomena, works of art, and the like, the third-person point of view conveys a feeling of distance and objectivity. When you write in the third person, though, don't adopt such a detached stance that you end up using a stiff, artificial style: "On this campus, approximately two-thirds of the student body is dependent on bicycles as the primary mode of transportation to class." Aim instead for a more natural and personable quality: "Two-thirds of the students on campus ride their bikes to class." (For a more detailed discussion of levels of formality, see pages 119–120 in Chapter 8.)

Discover Your Essay's Limited Subject

Once you have a firm grasp of the assignment's boundaries and have determined your purpose, audience, tone, and point of view, you're ready to focus on a **limited subject** of the general assignment. Because too broad a subject can result in a diffuse, rambling essay, be sure to restrict your general subject before starting to write.

The following examples show the difference between general subjects that are too broad for an essay and limited subjects that are appropriate and workable. The examples, of course, represent only a few among many possibilities.

General Subject	Less General	Limited Subject
Education	Computers in education	Computers in elementary school arithmetic classes
	High school education	High school electives
Transportation	Low-cost travel	Hitchhiking
	Getting around a metropolitan area	The transit system in a nearby city
Work	Planning for a career	College internships
	Women in the work force	Women's success as managers

How do you move from a general to a narrow subject? Imagine that you're asked to prepare a straightforward, informative essay for your writing class. The assignment, prompted by Ellen Goodman's essay "Family Counterculture" (page 6), is as follows:

Assignment
> Goodman implies that, in some ways, today's world is hostile to children. Do you
> agree? Write an essay supporting or rejecting this viewpoint.

You might feel unsure about how to proceed. But two techniques can help you
limit such a general assignment. Keeping your purpose, audience, tone, and point
of view in mind, you may **question** or **brainstorm** the general subject. These two
techniques have a paradoxical effect. Although they encourage you to roam freely
over a subject, they also help restrict the discussion by revealing which aspects of
the subject interest you most.

Question the General Subject

One way to narrow a subject is to ask a series of *who, how, why, where, when,* and
what questions. The following example shows how one student, Harriet Davids,
used this technique to limit the Goodman assignment. A thirty-eight-year-old college student and mother of two teenagers, Harriet was understandably intrigued
by the assignment. Generally in agreement with Goodman, she started by asking
a number of pointed questions about the general topic. As she proceeded, she was
aware that the same questions could have led to different limited subjects—just as
other questions would have.

> Student
> essay in
> progress

General Assignment: We live in a world that is difficult, even hostile toward
children.

Question	Limited Subject
<u>Who</u> is to blame for the diffi-cult conditions under which children grow up?	Parents' casual attitude toward childrearing
<u>How</u> have schools contributed to the problems children face?	Not enough counseling programs for kids in distress
<u>Why</u> do children feel fright-ened?	Divorce
<u>Where</u> do kids go to escape?	Television, which makes the world seem even more dangerous
<u>When</u> are children most vulner-able?	The special problems of adolescents
<u>What</u> dangers or fears should parents discuss with their children?	AIDS, drugs, alcohol, war, terrorism

Brainstorm the General Subject

Another way to focus on a limited subject is to list quickly everything about the
general topic that pops into your mind. Working vertically down the page, jot
down brief words, phrases, and abbreviations to capture your free-floating
thoughts. Writing in complete sentences will slow you down. Don't try to organize

or censor your ideas. Even the most fleeting, random, or seemingly outrageous thoughts can be productive.

Here's an example of the brainstorming that Harriet Davids decided to do in an effort to gather even more material for the Goodman assignment:

General Subject: We live in a world that is difficult, even hostile for children.

```
Too many divorces
Parents squabbling over material goods in settlements
Money too important
Kids feel unimportant
Child abuse growing
Families move a lot
I moved in fourth grade--hated it
Rootless feeling
Nobody graduates from high school in same district they went to
kindergarten in
Drug abuse all over, in little kids' schools
Pop music glorifies drugs
Kids not innocent--know too much
TV shows--corrupt politicians, sex, pollution, violence
Kids babysat by TV
Not enough guidance from parents
Kids raise selves
Single-parent homes
Day-care problems
Abuse of little children in day care
TV coverage of abuse--frightens kids
Unrealistic, perfect families on TV make kids feel inadequate
```

As you can see, questioning and brainstorming suggest many possible limited subjects. To identify especially promising ones, reread your material with pen or pencil in hand. What arouses your interest, anger, or curiosity? What themes seem to dominate and cut to the heart of the matter? Star or circle ideas with potential. Be sure to pay close attention to material generated at the end of your questioning and brainstorming. Often your mind takes a few minutes to warm up, with the best ideas popping out last.

After marking the material, write several phrases or sentences summarizing the most promising limited subjects. These, for example, are just a few that emerged from Harriet Davids's questioning and brainstorming the Goodman assignment:

```
TV partly to blame for children having such a hard time
Relocation stressful to children
```

```
Schools also at fault
The special problems that parents face raising children today
```

Harriet decided to write on the last of these limited subjects. This topic, in turn, is the focus of our discussion on the pages ahead.

Generate Raw Material About Your Limited Subject

When a limited subject strikes you as having possibilities, your next step is to begin generating material about that topic. If you do this now, in the prewriting stage, you'll find it easier to write the paper later on. Since you'll already have amassed much of the material for your essay, you'll be able to concentrate on other matters—say, finding just the right words to convey your ideas. Taking the time to sound out your limited subject during the prewriting stage also means you won't find yourself halfway through the first draft without much to say.

To generate raw material, you may use *freewriting, brainstorming, mapping,* and other techniques.

Freewrite on Your Limited Subject

Although freewriting can help you narrow a general subject, it's more valuable once you have limited your topic. **Freewriting** means jotting down in rough sentences or phrases everything that comes to mind. Although freewriting looks like regular prose because it is recorded horizontally, from margin to margin, it's much more fragmented. As you freewrite, you get swept along and go wherever your thoughts take you. You may skip back and forth between ideas, taking off in a more focused manner when you stumble across something interesting.

To capture this continuous stream of thought, write nonstop for ten minutes or more. Don't censor anything; put down whatever pops into your head. Don't reread, edit, or pay attention to organization, spelling, or grammar. If your mind goes blank, repeat words until another thought emerges.

Consider part of the freewriting that Harriet Davids generated about her limited subject, "The special problems that parents face raising children today":

> Student essay in progress

```
    Parents today have tough problems to face. Lots of dangers.
Drugs and alcohol for one thing. Also crimes of violence against
kids. Parents also have to keep up with cost of living, everything
costs more, kids want and expect more. Television? Another thing
is Playboy, Penthouse. Sexy ads on TV, movies deal with sex. Kids
grow up too fast, too fast. Drugs. Little kids can't handle know-
ing too much at an early age. Both parents at work much of the day.
Finding good day care a real problem. Lots of latchkey kids.
Another problem is getting kids to do homework, lots of other
things to do. Especially like going to the mall! When I was young,
we did homework after dinner, no excuses accepted by my parents.
```

Brainstorm Your Limited Subject

Let your mind wander freely, as you did when narrowing your general subject. This time, though, list every idea, fact, and example that occurs to you about your limited subject. Use brief words and phrases, so you don't get bogged down writing full sentences. For now, don't worry whether ideas fit together or whether the points listed make sense.

Student essay in progress

To gather additional material on her limited subject for the Theroux assignment ("The special problems that parents face raising children today"), Harriet brainstormed the following list:

```
Trying to raise kids when both parents work
Prices of everything outrageous, even when both parents work
Commercials make everyone want more of everything
Clothes so important
Day care not always the answer--cases of abuse
Day care very expensive
Sex everywhere--TV, movies, magazines
Sexy clothes on little kids. Absurd!
Sexual abuse of kids
Violence against kids
Violence against kids when parents abuse drugs
Cocaine, crack, AIDS
Schools have to teach kids about these things
Schools doing too much--not as good as they used to be
Not enough homework assigned--kids unprepared
Distractions from homework--malls, TV, phones, stereos, MTV
```

Use Group Brainstorming

Brainstorming can also be conducted as a group activity. Thrashing out ideas with other people stretches the imagination, revealing possibilities you may not have considered on your own. Group brainstorming doesn't have to be conducted in a formal classroom situation. You can bounce ideas around with friends and family anywhere—over lunch, at the student center, and so on.

Map Out the Limited Subject

If you're the kind of person who doodles while thinking, you may want to try **mapping,** sometimes called **diagraming** or **clustering.** Like other prewriting techniques, mapping proceeds rapidly and encourages the free flow of ideas.

Begin by expressing your limited subject in a crisp phrase and placing it in the center of a blank sheet of paper. As ideas come to you, put them along lines or in boxes or circles around the limited subject. Draw arrows and lines to show the relationships among ideas. Don't stop there, however. Focus on each idea; as subpoints and details come to you, connect them to their source idea, again using boxes, lines, circles, or arrows to clarify how everything relates.

Here's an example of the kind of map that Harriet Davids could have drawn to generate material for her limited subject based on the Theroux assignment.

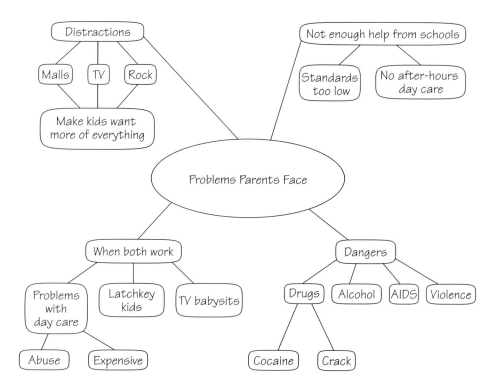

There's no right or wrong way to do mapping. Sometimes you'll move from the limited subject to a key related idea and all the details it prompts before moving to the next key idea; other times you'll map all the major divisions of a limited subject before mapping the details of any one idea.

Use the Patterns of Development

Throughout this book, we show how writers use various **patterns of development,** singly or in combination, to develop and organize their ideas. Because each pattern has its own distinctive logic, the patterns encourage you to think about a limited subject in surprising new ways.

The various patterns of development are discussed in detail in Chapters 10–19 of Part III. At this point, though, you should find the chart on page 30 helpful. It not only summarizes the broad purpose of each pattern but also shows the way each pattern could generate different raw material for the limited subject of Harriet Davids's essay.

Limited Subject: The special problems that parents face raising children today.

Pattern of Development	Purpose	Raw Material
Description	To detail what a person, place, or object is like	Detail the sights and sounds of a glitzy mall that attracts lots of kids
Narration	To relate an event	Recount what happened when neighbors tried to forbid their kids to go to a rock concert
Illustration	To provide specific instances or examples	Offer examples of family arguments nowadays: Can a friend known to use drugs visit? Will permission be given to go to a party where alcohol will be served? Can parents outlaw MTV?
Division-classification	To divide something into parts or to group related things into categories	Identify the components of a TV commercial that distorts kids' values / Classify the kinds of commercials that make it difficult to teach kids values
Process analysis	To explain how something happens or how something is done	Explain step by step how family life can disintegrate when parents have to work all the time to make ends meet
Comparison-contrast	To point out similarities and/or dissimilarities	Contrast families today with those of a generation ago
Cause-effect	To analyze reasons and consequences	Explain why parents are not around to be with their kids: industry's failure to provide day care and its inflexibility about granting time off for parents with sick kids / Explain the consequences of absentee parents: Kids feel unloved; they turn to TV for role models; they're undisciplined; they take on adult responsibility too early
Definition	To explain the meaning of a term or concept	What is meant by "tough love"
Argumentation-persuasion	To win people over to a point of view	Convince parents that they must work with the schools to develop programs that make kids feel safer and more secure

(For more on ways to use the patterns of development in different phases of the writing process, see pages 38, 45–46, 53–54, 67–68, and Chapter 10.)

Conduct Research

Some limited subjects (for example, "Industry's day-care policies") can be developed only if you do some research. You may conduct **primary research,** in which you interview experts, conduct your own studies, compile your own statistics, and the like. Or you may conduct **secondary research,** in which you visit the library and look for books and articles about your limited subject in the card catalog, the *Readers' Guide to Periodical Literature,* or a computerized reference system. (See pages 505–507 Part IV on how to conduct research.) At this point, you don't need to read closely the material you find. Just skim and perhaps take a few brief notes on ideas and points that could be useful.

If researching the Goodman assignment, for instance, Harriet Davids could look under the following headings and subheadings:

Day care
Drug abuse
Family
Parent-child relationship
   Child abuse
   Children of divorced parents
   Children of working mothers
School and home

Student
essay in
progress

Organize the Raw Material

Some students prefer to wait until after they have formulated a thesis to shape their prewriting material. (For information on thesis statements, see Chapter 3.) But if you find that imposing a preliminary order on your prewriting provides the focus needed to devise an effective thesis, you'll probably want to prepare a **scratch list** or **outline** at this point. In Chapter 5, we talk about the more formal outline you may need later on in the writing process (pages 56–59). Here we show how a rough outline or scratch list can help shape the tentative ideas generated during prewriting.

As you reread your exploratory thoughts about the limited subject, keep the following questions in mind: What *purpose* have you decided on? What are the characteristics of your *audience*? What *tone* will be effective in achieving your purpose with your audience? What *point of view* will you adopt? Record your responses to these questions at the top of your prewriting material.

Now go to work on the raw material itself. Cross out anything not appropriate for your purpose, audience, tone, and point of view; add points that didn't originally occur to you. Star or circle compelling items that warrant further development. Then draw arrows between related items, your goal being to group such material under a common heading. Finally, determine what seems to be the best order for the headings.

By giving you a sense of the way your free-form material might fit together, a scratch outline makes the writing process more manageable. You're less likely to feel overwhelmed once you actually start writing because you'll already have some idea about how to shape your material into a meaningful statement. Remember, though, the scratch outline can, and most likely will, be modified along the way.

Harriet Davids's handwritten annotations on her brainstormed list (page 28) illustrate the way Harriet began shaping her raw prewriting material. Note how she started by recording at the top her limited subject as well as her decisions about purpose, audience, tone, and point of view:

Purpose: To inform

Audience: Instructor as well as class members, most of whom are 18-20 years old

Tone: Serious and straightforward

Point of view: Third person (mother of two teenage girls)

Limited subject: The special problems that parents face raising children today

① Day Care

Trying to raise kids when both parents work

Prices of everything outrageous, even when both parents work

Commercials make everyone want more of everything

Clothes so important

Day care not always the answer--cases of abuse   *problems—before and after school*

Day care very expensive

③ Sexual material everywhere

Sex everywhere--TV, movies, magazines

Sexy clothes on little kids. Absurd!

Sexual abuse of kids

④ Dangers

Violence against kids

Violence against kids when parents abuse drugs

Cocaine, crack, AIDS *—also drinking*

Schools have to teach kids about these things

Schools doing too much--not as good as they used to be

Not enough homework assigned--kids unprepared

② Homework distractions

Distractions from homework--malls, TV, phones, stereos, MTV, *video arcades, rock concerts*

The scratch outline that starts below and continues on the next page shows how Harriet translated the annotations on her prewriting into a more organized format. (If you'd like to see Harriet's more formal outline and her first draft, turn to pages 58–59 and 83–84.)

Purpose: To inform

Audience: Instructor as well as class members, most of whom are 18-20 years old

Tone: Serious and straightforward

Point of view: Third person (mother of two teenage girls)

Limited subject: The special problems that parents face raising children today

1. Day care for two-career families
   - Expensive
   - Before-school problems
   - After-school problems
2. Distractions from homework
   - Stereos, televisions in room at home
   - Places to go--malls, video arcades, fast-food restaurants, rock concerts
3. Sexually explicit materials
   - Magazines and books
   - Television shows
   - MTV
   - Movies
   - Rock posters
4. Life-threatening dangers
   - AIDS
   - Drugs
   - Drinking
   - Violence against children (by sitters, in day care, etc.)

Continues on page 37

The prewriting strategies described in this chapter provide a solid foundation for the next stages of your work. But invention and imaginative exploration don't end when prewriting is completed. As you'll see, remaining open to new ideas is crucial during all phases of the writing process.

ACTIVITIES: GETTING STARTED THROUGH PREWRITING

1. Number the items in each set from 1 (*broadest subject*) to 5 (*most limited subject*):

Set A	Set B
Abortion	Business majors
Controversial social issue	Students' majors
Cutting state abortion funds	College students
Federal funding of abortions	Kinds of students on campus
Social issues	Why students major in business

2. Which of the following topics are too broad for an essay of two to five typewritten pages: soap operas' appeal to college students; day care; trying to "kick" junk food; male and female relationships; international terrorism?

3. Assume you're writing essays on two of the topics below. For each one, explain how you might adapt your purpose, tone, and point of view to the audiences indicated in parentheses. (You may find it helpful to work with others on this activity.)

  a. Overcoming shyness (ten-year-olds; teachers of ten-year-olds; young singles living in large apartment buildings)
  b. Telephone solicitations (people training for a job in this field; homeowners; readers of a humorous magazine)
  c. Smoking (people who have quit; smokers; elementary school children)

4. Choose one of the following general topics for a roughly five-hundred-word essay. Then use the prewriting technique indicated in parentheses to identify several limited topics. Next, with the help of one or more patterns of development, generate raw material on the limited subject you consider most interesting.

  a. Friendship (*journal writing*)
  b. Malls (*mapping*)
  c. Leisure (*freewriting*)
  d. Television (*brainstorming*)
  e. Required courses (*group brainstorming*)
  f. Manners (*questioning*)

5. For each set of limited subjects and purposes that follows, determine which pattern(s) of development would be most useful. (Save this material so you can work with it further after reading the next chapter.)

  a. The failure of recycling efforts on campus

     Purpose: to explain why students and faculty tend to disregard recycling guidelines

  b. The worst personality trait that a teacher, parent, boss, or friend can have

     Purpose: to poke fun at this personality trait

  c. The importance of being knowledgeable about national affairs

     Purpose: to convince students to stay informed about current events

6. Select *one* of the following limited subjects. Then, given the purpose and audience indicated, draft a paragraph using the first-, second-, or third-person point of view. Next, rewrite the paragraph two more times, each time using a different point of view. What differences do you see in the three versions? Which version do you prefer? Why?

  a. American action movies like *The Terminator* and *Lethal Weapon*

     Purpose: to defend the enjoyment of such films

     Audience: those who like foreign "art" films

    b. Senioritis

      Purpose: to explain why high school seniors lose interest in school

      Audience: parents and teachers

    c. Television commercials aimed at teens and young adults

      Purpose: to make fun of the commercials' persuasive appeals

      Audience: advertising executives

7. Select *one* of the following general subjects. Keeping in mind the indicated purpose, audience, tone, and point of view, use a prewriting technique to limit the subject. Next, by means of another prewriting strategy, generate relevant information about the restricted topic. Finally, shape your raw material into a scratch outline—crossing out, combining, and adding ideas as needed. (Save your scratch outline so you can work with it further after reading the next chapter.)

    a. Rock music

      Purpose: to explain its attraction

      Audience: classical music fans

      Tone: playful

      Writer's point of view: a rock fan

    b. Becoming a volunteer

      Purpose: to recruit

      Audience: ambitious young professionals

      Tone: straightforward

      Writer's point of view: head of a volunteer organization

    c. Sexist attitudes in music videos

      Purpose: to inform

      Audience: teenagers of both sexes

      Tone: objective but with some emotion

      Writer's point of view: a teenage male

    d. Major problems in high school education

      Purpose: to create awareness of the problems

      Audience: teachers

      Tone: serious and concerned

      Writer's point of view: a former high school student

3
IDENTIFYING A THESIS

THE process of prewriting—discovering a limited subject and generating ideas about it—prepares you for the next stage in writing an essay: identifying the paper's *thesis*, or controlling idea.

WHAT IS A THESIS?

Presenting your position on a subject, the **thesis** should focus on an interesting and significant issue, one that engages your energies and merits your consideration. You may think of the thesis as the essay's hub—the central point around which all the other material revolves. Your thesis determines what does and does not belong in the essay. The thesis, especially when it occurs early in an essay, also helps focus the reader on the piece's central point and thus helps you achieve your writing purpose.

FINDING A THESIS

Sometimes the thesis emerges early in the prewriting stage, particularly if a special angle on your limited topic sparks your interest or becomes readily apparent. Often, though, you'll need to do some work to determine your thesis. For some topics, you may need to do some library research. For other subjects, the best way to identify a promising thesis is to look through your prewriting and ask yourself questions like these: "What statement does all this prewriting support? What aspect of the limited subject is covered in most detail? What is the focus of the most provocative material?"

For a look at the process of finding the thesis within prewriting material, glance back in Chapter 2 at the annotated brainstorming (page 32) and the resulting scratch outline (pages 32–33) that Harriet Davids prepared for her limited subject, "The special problems that parents face raising children today." Harriet eventually devised the following thesis to capture the focus of her prewriting: "Being a parent today is much more difficult than it was a generation ago." (For more on how Harriet arrived at her thesis, see pages 40–41.)

Student essay in progress

Sometimes the thesis won't be easy to pinpoint. Indeed, you may find that you need to refocus your thesis as you move through the stages of the writing process. To see how this progressive clarification might work, imagine you're writing a paper about adjusting to the academic demands of college life. After looking over your prewriting, you might identify this preliminary thesis: "Many college students flounder during the first semester because they have trouble adjusting to the amount of work required by their professors." However, once you start writing the essay, you might realize that students' increased personal freedom, not their increased workload, is the primary problem. You would revise your thesis accordingly: "Many college students flounder the first semester because they become so distracted by new freedoms in their personal lives that they don't give enough attention to academics."

WRITING AN EFFECTIVE THESIS

What makes a thesis effective? Generally expressed in one or two sentences, a thesis statement often has two parts. One part presents your paper's *limited subject*; the other presents your *point of view,* or *attitude,* about that subject. Here are some examples of the way you might move from general subject to limited subject to thesis statement. In each thesis statement, the limited subject is underlined once and the attitude twice.

General Subject	Limited Subject	Thesis Statement
Education	Computers in elementary school arithmetic classes	Computer programs in arithmetic can individualize instruction more effectively than the average elementary school teacher can.
Transportation	A metropolitan transit system	Although the city's transit system still has problems, it has become safer and more efficient in the last two years.
Work	College internships	The college internship program has had positive consequences for students.
Drugs	Driving while intoxicated	Individuals found guilty of drunk driving should have their licenses revoked for five years.

Tone and Point of View

An effective thesis establishes a tone and point of view suitable for a given purpose and audience. If you're writing an essay arguing that multi-media equipment can never replace a live teacher in the classroom, you need to frame a thesis that matches your and your readers' concerns about the subject. Instead of breezily writing, "Parents, schoolboards, principals: ditch the boob tube and the cutesy interactive computer and put the bucks where it counts—in teachers," you would aim for a more thoughtful and serious tone: "Education won't be improved by purchasing more electronic teaching tools but by allocating more money to hire and develop good teachers."

Implied Pattern of Development

On page 20, we show how an essay's purpose may suggest a pattern of development. In the same way, an effective thesis may point the way to a pattern of development that would be appropriate for developing the essay. Consider the thesis statements in the preceding list. The first thesis might use *comparison-contrast*; the second *illustration*; the third *cause-effect*; and the fourth *argumentation-persuasion*. (For more information about the relationship between an essay's purpose and its pattern of development, see the chart on page 30.)

Including a Plan of Development

Sometimes a thesis will include a **plan of development**: a concise *overview of the essay's main points in the exact order* in which those points will be discussed. To incorporate a plan of development into your thesis, use single words or brief phrases that convey—in a nutshell—your essay's key points; then add those summarized points to the end of the thesis, being sure to present them in the order they will appear in the essay. Note, for example, the way a plan of development (in italics) is included in the following thesis: "Baseball's inflated salaries hurt *the fans, the sport, and most of all, the athletes.*"

A thesis with a plan of development is an effective strategy for keeping readers focused on an essay's main points. If you decide to prepare such a thesis, be careful not to overload it with too much information. Rather than writing "An after-school job can promote a sense of responsibility in young people, teach important human-relations skills, and create awareness of career options," tighten the plan of development so it reads more crisply: "An after-school job develops responsibility, human-relations skills, and an awareness of career options."

If the essay's key points resist your efforts to reduce them to crisp phrases, you can place the plan of development in a separate sentence, directly *after* the thesis. Consider the plan of development (in italics) that comes after the following thesis: "Many parents have unrealistic expectations for their children. These parents want their children to *accept their values, follow their paths, and succeed where they have failed.*" Note that the points in a plan of development are expressed in grammatically parallel terms: The plan of development for the paper on baseball salaries contains nouns in series ("the fans," "the sport," "the athletes"), while the plan of development for the paper on parental expectations contains verb phrases ("accept their values," "follow their paths," "succeed where they have failed").

Because preparing an effective thesis is such a critical step in writing a sharply focused essay, you need to avoid the following four common problems.

1. Don't Write a Highly Opinionated Statement

Although your thesis should express your attitude toward your subject, don't go overboard and write a dogmatic, overstated thesis: "With characteristic clumsiness, campus officials bumbled their way through the recent budget crisis." A more moderate thesis can make the same point, *without alienating readers:* "Campus officials had trouble managing the recent budget crisis effectively."

2. Don't Make an Announcement

Some writers use the thesis statement merely to announce the limited subject of their paper and forget to indicate their attitude toward the subject. Such statements are announcements of intent, not thesis statements.

Compare the following three announcements with the thesis statements beside them:

Announcement	Thesis Statement
My essay will discuss whether a student pub should exist on campus.	This college should not allow a student pub on campus.
Handgun legislation will be the subject of my paper.	Banning handguns is the first step toward controlling crime in America.
I want to discuss cable television.	Cable television has not delivered on its promise to provide an alternative to network programming.

3. Don't Make a Factual Statement

Your thesis and thus your essay should focus on an issue capable of being developed. If a fact is used as a thesis, you have no place to go; a fact generally doesn't invite much discussion.

Notice the difference between the following factual statements and thesis statements:

Factual Statement	Thesis Statement
Many businesses pollute the environment.	Tax penalties should be levied against businesses that pollute the environment.

Movies nowadays are often violent.

Movie violence provides a healthy outlet for aggression.

America's population is growing older.

The aging of the American population will eventually create a crisis in the delivery of health-care services.

4. Don't Make a Broad Statement

Avoid stating your thesis in vague, general, or sweeping terms. Broad statements make it difficult for readers to grasp your essay's point. Moreover, if you start with a broad thesis, you're saddled with the impossible task of trying to develop a book-length idea with an essay that runs only several pages.

The following examples contrast thesis statements that are too broad with effectively focused statements:

Broad Statement	Thesis Statement
Nowadays, high school education is often meaningless.	High school diplomas have been devalued by grade inflation.
Newspapers cater to the taste of the American public.	The success of *USA Today* indicates that people want newspapers that are easy to read and entertaining.
The computer revolution is not all that we have been led to believe it is.	Home computers are still an impractical purchase for many people.

ARRIVING AT AN EFFECTIVE THESIS

Student essay in progress

On pages 36–37, we discussed the basic process for finding a thesis; we also pointed out how Harriet Davids—after reviewing her prewriting—identified her paper's thesis: "Being a parent today is much more difficult than it was a generation ago." But Harriet didn't discover her thesis immediately; she went through several stages before she came up with the final wording. The following paragraph describes the steps Harriet took when formulating her essay's central point. In all likelihood, you too will need to experiment a bit before arriving at an effective thesis.

Starting with her limited subject ("The special problems that parents face raising children today"), Harriet at first worded her thesis to read "My essay will show that raising children today is a horror show compared to how it was when my parents raised me." As soon as she read what she had written, Harriet saw that she had prepared an *announcement* rather than a thesis. Rephrasing the statement to do away with the announcement, she next wrote "Raising children today is a horror show compared to how it was when my parents raised me." When Harriet read this version out loud, she was pleased to hear that the rewording eliminated the announcement—but she was surprised to discover that the rephrasing highlighted two problems she hadn't detected earlier. For one thing, her statement was *highly opinionated* and *slangy* ("horror show"). Second, the statement *misrepresented* what she intended to do by suggesting—incorrectly—that she was going to (1) discuss the child-rearing process and (2) contrast her parents' and her own child-raising experiences. She planned to do neither. Instead, she intended to (1) emphasize parenthood's challenges and (2) address—in a general way—the difference between parenting today and parenting years ago. So, recasting her statement one more time to eliminate these problems, Harriet arrived at the final wording of her thesis: "Being a parent today is much more difficult than it was a generation ago."

Continues on page 47

PLACING THE THESIS IN AN ESSAY

The thesis is often located in the middle or at the end of the introduction. But considerations about audience, purpose, and tone should always guide your decision about its placement. You may, for example, choose to delay the thesis if you feel that background information needs to be provided before readers can fully understand your key point—especially if the concept is complex and best taken in slowly. Similarly, if you sense your audience is resistant to your thesis, you may wish to lead readers to it gradually. Conversely, if you feel that readers would appreciate a direct, forthright approach, you might place the thesis early in the essay—perhaps even at the very beginning of the introduction.

Sometimes the thesis is reiterated—using fresh words—in the essay's conclusion or elsewhere. If done well, this repetition keeps readers focused on the essay's key point. You may even leave the thesis implied, relying on strong support, tone, and style to convey the essay's central idea.

One final point: Once you start writing your first draft, some feelings, thoughts, and examples may emerge that modify, even contradict your initial thesis. Don't resist these new ideas. Keep them in mind as you revise the thesis and—in the process—move toward a more valid and richer view of your subject.

ACTIVITIES: IDENTIFYING A THESIS

1. For each of the following limited subjects, four possible thesis statements are given. Indicate whether each thesis is an announcement (A), a factual statement (FS), too broad a statement (TB), or an acceptable thesis (OK). Revise the flawed statements. Then, for each effective thesis statement, identify a possible purpose, audience, tone, and point of view.

a. *Limited subject:* The ethics of treating severely disabled infants

- Some babies born with severe disabilities have been allowed to die.
- There are many serious issues involved in the treatment of newborns with disabilities.
- The government should pass legislation requiring medical treatment for newborns with disabilities.
- This essay will analyze the controversy surrounding the treatment of severely disabled babies who would die without medical care.

b. *Limited subject:* Privacy and computerized records

- Computers raise some significant questions for all of us.
- Computerized records keep track of consumer spending habits, credit records, travel patterns, and other personal information.
- Computerized records have turned our private lives into public property.
- In this paper, the relationship between computerized records and the right to privacy will be discussed.

2. Turn back to activity 5 on page 34. For each set of limited subjects listed there, develop an effective thesis. Select *one* of the thesis statements. Then, keeping in mind the purpose indicated and the pattern of development you identified earlier, draft a paragraph developing the point expressed in the thesis. (Save the paragraph so you can work with it further after reading the next chapter.)

3. Following are four pairs of general and limited subjects. Generate an appropriate thesis for each pair. Select one of the thesis statements, and determine which pattern of development would support the thesis most effectively. Use that pattern to draft a paragraph developing the thesis. (Save the paragraph so you can work with it further after reading the next chapter.)

General Subject	Limited Subject
Psychology	The power struggles in a classroom
Health	Doctors' attitudes toward patients
The elderly	Television's depiction of the elderly
Work	Minimum-wage jobs for young people

4. Each set that follows lists the key points for an essay. Based on the information provided, prepare a possible thesis for each essay. Then propose a possible purpose, audience, tone, and point of view.

Set A

- One evidence of this growing conservatism is the re-emerging popularity of fraternities and sororities.
- Beauty contests, ROTC training, and corporate recruiting—once rejected by students on many campuses—are again popular.

- Most important, many students no longer choose possibly risky careers that enable them to contribute to society but instead select safe fields with money-making potential.

Set B

- We do not know how engineering new forms of life might affect the earth's delicate ecological balance.
- Another danger of genetic research is its potential for unleashing new forms of disease.
- Even beneficial attempts to eliminate genetic defects could contribute to the dangerous idea that only perfect individuals are entitled to live.

5. Keep a journal for several weeks. Then reread a number of entries, identifying two or three recurring themes or subjects. Narrow the subjects and, for each one, generate possible thesis statements. Finally, using an appropriate pattern of development, draft a paragraph for one of the thesis statements. (Save the paragraph so you can work with it further after reading the next chapter.)

6. Select a broad topic—either your own or one of the following: animals, popularity, the homeless, money, fashion trends, race relations, parties. Working with a partner, use a prewriting technique to narrow the topic so that it's suitable for an essay of two to five typed pages. Using another prewriting strategy, generate details on the limited topic. Next, examine the material and identify at least two possible thesis statements. Then, for each thesis, reshape your prewriting, determining which items are appropriate, which are not, and where more material is needed.

7. Return to the scratch outline you prepared in response to activity 7 on page 35. After examining the outline, identify a thesis that conveys the central idea behind most of the raw material. Then, ask others to evaluate your thesis in light of the material in your scratch outline. Finally, keeping the thesis—as well as your purpose, audience, and tone—in mind, refine the scratch outline by deleting inappropriate items, adding relevant ones, and indicating where more material is needed. (Save your refined scratch outline and thesis so you can work with them further after reading the next chapter.)

4
SUPPORTING THE THESIS WITH EVIDENCE

AFTER identifying a preliminary thesis, you should develop the evidence needed to support that central idea. This supporting material grounds your essay, showing readers you have good reason for feeling as you do about your subject. Your evidence also adds interest and color to your writing.

In college essays of 500 to 1,500 words, you usually need at least three major points of evidence to develop your thesis. These major points—each focusing on related but separate aspects of the thesis—eventually become the supporting paragraphs (see pages 65–75) in the body of the essay.

WHAT IS EVIDENCE?

By **evidence,** we mean a number of different kinds of support. *Reasons* are just one option. To develop your thesis, you might also include *examples, facts, details statistics, personal observation* or *experience, anecdotes,* and *expert opinions* and *quotations* (gathered from books, articles, interviews, documentaries, and the like). Imagine you're writing an essay with the thesis, "People normally unconcerned about the environment can be galvanized to constructive action if they feel personally affected by an environmental problem." You could support this thesis with any combination of the following types of evidence:

- *Reasons* why people become involved in the environmental movement: they believe the situation endangers the health of their families; they fear the value of their homes will plummet; they feel deceived by officials' assurances that there's nothing to worry about.
- *Examples* of neighborhood recycling efforts succeeding in communities once plagued by trash-disposal problems.
- *Facts* about residents' efforts to preserve the quality of well water in a community undergoing widespread industrial development.
- *Details* about the specific steps the average person can take to get involved in environmental issues.
- *Statistics* showing the growing number of Americans concerned about the environment.
- A *personal experience* telling about the way you became involved in an effort to stop a local business from dumping waste in a neighborhood stream.
- An *anecdote* about an ordinarily apathetic friend who protested the commercial development of a wooded area where he jogs.
- A *quotation* from a well-known scientist about the considerable impact that well-organized, well-informed citizens can have on environmental legislation.

HOW DO YOU FIND EVIDENCE?

Where do you find the examples, anecdotes, details, and other types of evidence needed to support your thesis? As you saw when you followed Harriet Davids's strategies for gathering material for an essay (pages 25–33), a good deal of information is generated during the prewriting stage. In this phase of the writing process, you tap into your personal experiences, draw upon other people's observations, perhaps interview a person with special knowledge about your subject. The library, with its abundant material, is another rich source of supporting evidence. (For information on using the library, see Chapter 20.) In addition, the various patterns of development are a valuable source of evidence.

How the Patterns of Development Help Generate Evidence

In Chapter 2, we discussed how the patterns of development could help generate material about Harriet Davids's limited subject (pages 29–30). The same patterns also help develop support for a thesis. The following chart shows how they generate evidence for this thesis: "To those who haven't done it, babysitting looks easy. In practice, though, babysitting can be difficult, frightening, even dangerous."

Pattern of Development	Evidence Generated
Description	Details about a child who, while being babysat, was badly hurt playing on a backyard swing.
Narration	Story about the time a friend babysat a child who became seriously ill and whose condition was worsened by the babysitter's remedies.
Illustration	Examples of potential babysitting problems: an infant who rolls off a changing table; a toddler who sticks objects in an electric outlet; a school-age child who is bitten by a neighborhood dog.
Division-classification	A typical babysitting evening divided into stages: playing with the kids; putting them to bed; dealing with their nighttime fears once they're in bed. Classify kids' nighttime fears: of monsters under their beds; of bad dreams, of being abandoned by their parents.
Process analysis	Step-by-step account of what a babysitter should do if a child becomes ill or injured.
Comparison-contrast	Contrast between two babysitters: one well-prepared, the other unprepared.
Cause-effect	Why children have temper tantrums; the effect of such tantrums on an unskilled babysitter.
Definition	What is meant by a *skilled* babysitter?
Argumentation-persuasion	A proposal for a babysitting training program to be offered by the local community center.

(For further discussion of ways to use the patterns of development in different phases of the writing process, see pages 29–30, 38, 53–54, 67–68, and Chapter 10.)

CHARACTERISTICS OF EVIDENCE

No matter how it is generated, all types of supporting evidence share the characteristics described in the following sections. You should keep these characteristics in mind as you review your thesis and scratch list. That way, you can make the changes needed to strengthen the evidence gathered earlier. As you'll see shortly, Harriet Davids focused on many of these issues as she worked with the evidence she collected during the prewriting phase.

The Evidence Is Relevant and Unified

All the evidence in an essay must clearly support the thesis. It makes no difference how riveting material might be; if it doesn't *relate directly* to the essay's central point, the evidence should be eliminated. Irrelevant material can weaken your position by implying that no relevant support exists. It also distracts readers from your controlling idea, thus disrupting the paper's overall unity.

Suppose you want to write an essay with the thesis "Fairly fought arguments can strengthen relationships." To support your thesis, you could adapt prewriting material about an argument you had with a friend: how the disagreement started, how you and your friend worked out your differences, how your friendship deepened because of what you learned about each other. Also to the point would be statements from your sister who found, after reading a book on conflict management, that her relationship with her co-workers improved significantly. Similarly relevant would be an account of a conflict-ridden family whose tensions eased once a counselor taught them how to air their differences. It would *not* serve your thesis, however, to include details about the way negotiating strategies can backfire. This material wouldn't be appropriate because it contradicts the point you want to make.

Early in the writing process, Harriet Davids was aware of the importance of relevant evidence. Take a moment to review Harriet's annotated prewriting (page 32). Even though Harriet hadn't yet identified her thesis, she realized she should delete a number of items on the reshaped version of her brainstormed list—for example, "prices of everything outrageous..." and "Not enough homework assigned—kids unprepared." Harriet eliminated these points because they weren't consistent with the focus of her limited subject.

> Student essay in progress

The Evidence Is Specific

When evidence is vague and general, readers lose interest in what you're saying, become skeptical of your ideas' validity, and feel puzzled about your meaning. In contrast, *specific, concrete evidence* provides sharp *word pictures* that engage your readers, persuade them that your thinking is sound, and clarify meaning.

Consider a paper with this thesis: "College students should not automatically dismiss working in fast-food restaurants; such jobs can provide valuable learning experiences." Here's how you might go wrong trying to support the thesis: Suppose you begin with the broad claim that these admittedly lackluster jobs can teach students a good deal about themselves. In a similarly abstract fashion, you go on to say that such jobs can affect students' self-concepts in positive ways. You end by declaring that such changes in self-perception lead to greater maturity.

To prevent readers from thinking "Who cares?" or "Who says?" you need to replace these vague generalities with specific, concrete evidence. For example, focusing on your own experience working at a fast-food restaurant, you might start by describing how you learned to control your sarcasm; such an attitude, you discovered, alienated co-workers and almost caused your boss to fire you. You could also recount the time you administered the Heimlich maneuver to a choking customer; your quick thinking and failure to panic increased your self-esteem. Finally, you could explain that the job encouraged you to question some of your values; you became close friends with a bookish, introspective co-worker—the kind of person you used to spurn. This specific, particularized evidence would support your thesis and help readers "see" the point you're making. (Pages 69–71 describe strategies for making evidence specific.)

Student
essay in
progress

At this point, it will be helpful to look once again at the annotations that Harriet Davids entered on her prewriting material (page 32). Note the way she jotted down new details to make her prewriting more specific. For instance, to the item "Distractions from homework," she added the examples "video arcades" and "rock concerts." And once Harriet arrived at her thesis ("Being a parent today is much more difficult than it was a generation ago"), she realized that she needed to provide even more specifics. With her thesis firmly in mind, she expanded her prewriting material—for instance, the point about sexuality on television. To develop that item, she specified three kinds of TV programming that depict sexuality offensively: soap operas, R-rated comedians, R-rated cable movies. And, as you'll soon discover, Harriet added many more specific details when she prepared her final outline (pages 58–59) and her first and final drafts (pages 83–84 and 137–139).

The Evidence Is Adequate

Readers won't automatically accept your thesis; you need to provide *enough specific evidence* to support your viewpoint. On occasion, a single extended example will suffice. Generally, though, you'll need a variety of evidence: facts, examples, reasons, personal observations, expert opinion, and so on.

Assume you want to write an essay arguing that "college students living on campus should register and vote where they attend school." Hoping the essay will be published in the campus newspaper, you write it in the form of an open letter to the student body. One reason in support of your thesis strikes you immediately: that eighteen-year-olds should act as the adults they are and become involved in the electoral process. You also present as evidence a description of how good you felt during the last election when you walked into the voting booth set up in the student center. If this is all the support you provide, students probably won't be convinced; you haven't offered *sufficient* evidence. You need to present additional material—statistics on the shockingly low number of students registered to vote at your school; an account of a voter-registration drive at a nearby university that got students involved in the community and thus reduced traditional "town-gown" tensions; quotations from several students who voted against an anti-student housing ordinance and saw the ordinance defeated; an explanation of how easy it is to register.

Student
essay in
progress

Now take a final look at Harriet's annotations on her prewriting (page 32). As you can see, Harriet realized she needed more than one block of supporting material to develop her limited subject; that's why she identified four separate blocks of evidence (day care, homework distractions, sexual material, and dangers). As soon as Harriet formulated her thesis, she re-examined her prewriting to see if it provided sufficient support for her essay's central point. Luckily, Harriet recognized that these four blocks of evidence needed to be developed further. She thus decided to enlarge the "Distractions from homework" block by drawing upon her daughters' love affair with MTV and the "Life-threatening dangers" block by including details about the way peer pressure to experiment with drugs and alcohol endangers young people. Harriet's final outline (pages 58–59) reflects these decisions. When you look at the outline, you'll also note that Harriet ended up eliminating one of the four blocks of evidence ("Day care") she had identified earlier. But she added so many specific and dramatic details when writing her first and final drafts (pages 83–84 and 137–139) that her evidence was more than sufficient.

Continues on page 58

The Evidence Is Dramatic

The most effective evidence enlarges the reader's experience by *dramatizing reality.* Say you plan to write an essay with the thesis "People who affirm the value of life refuse to wear fur coats." If, as support, you state only that most animals killed for their fur are caught in leg-hold traps, your readers will have little sense of the suffering involved. But if you write that steel-jaw, leg-hold traps snap shut on an animal's limb, crushing tissue and bone and leaving the animal to die, in severe pain, from exposure or starvation, your readers can better envision the animal's plight.

The Evidence Is Accurate

Make your evidence as dramatic as you can, but be sure it is *accurate.* When you have a strong belief and want readers to see things your way, you may be tempted to overstate or downplay facts, disregard information, misquote, or make up details. Suppose you plan to write an essay making the point that dormitory security is lax. You begin supporting your thesis by narrating the time you were nearly mugged in your dorm hallway. Realizing the essay would be more persuasive if you also mentioned other episodes, you decide to invent some material. Perhaps you describe several supposed burglaries on your dorm floor or exaggerate the amount of time it took campus security to respond to an emergency call from a residence hall. Yes, you've supported your point—but at the expense of truth.

The Evidence Is Representative

Using *representative* evidence means that you rely on the *typical,* the *usual,* to show that your point is valid. Contrary to the maxim, exceptions don't prove the rule. Perhaps you plan to write an essay contending that the value of seat belts has been exaggerated. To support your position, you mention a friend who survived a head-on collision without wearing a seat belt. Such an example isn't representative because the facts and figures on accidents suggest your friend's survival was a fluke.

Borrowed Evidence Is Documented

If you include evidence from outside sources (books, articles, interviews), you need to *acknowledge* where that information comes from. If you don't, readers may consider your evidence nothing more than your point of view, or they may regard as dishonest your failure to cite your indebtedness to others for ideas that obviously aren't your own.

The rules for crediting sources in informal writing are less established than they are for formal research. Follow any guidelines your instructor provides, and try to keep your notations, like those that follow, as simple as possible.

<u>Business Life</u> (March 16, 1999) reports that corporate wrongdoing has led to a rash of consumer protests.

Science writer Natalie Angier believes that private zoos may be the only hope for some endangered species.

In formal research, you need to provide much more detailed documentation of sources. For information on formal documentation, see Chapter 21.

Strong supporting evidence is at the heart of effective writing. Without it, essays lack energy and fail to project the writer's voice and perspective. Such lifeless writing is also more apt to put readers to sleep than to engage their interest and convince them that the points being made are valid. Taking the time to accumulate solid supporting material is, then, a critical step in the writing process. (If you'd like to read more about the characteristics of strong evidence, see pages 69–75. If you'd like suggestions for organizing an essay's evidence, see the diagram on page 82.)

ACTIVITIES: SUPPORTING THE THESIS WITH EVIDENCE

1. Imagine you're writing an essay with the following thesis in mind. Which of the statements in the list support the thesis? Label each statement acceptable (OK), irrelevant (IR), inaccurate (IA), or too general (TG).

Thesis: Colleges should put less emphasis on sports.

a. High-powered athletic programs can encourage grade fixing.
b. Too much value is attached to college sports.
c. Athletics have no educational value.
d. Competitive athletics can lead to extensive and expensive injuries.
e. Athletes can spend too much time on the field and not enough on their studies.
f. Good athletic programs create a strong following among former under-graduates.

2. For each of the following thesis statements, list at least three supporting points that convey vivid word pictures.

a. Rude behavior in movie theaters seems to be on the rise.
b. Recent television commercials portray men as incompetent creatures.
c. The local library fails to meet the public's needs.
d. People often abuse public parks.

3. Turn back to the paragraphs you prepared in response to activity 2, activity 3, or activity 5 in Chapter 3 (pages 42–43). Select one paragraph and strengthen its evidence, using the guidelines presented in this chapter.

4. Choose one of the following thesis statements. Then identify an appropriate purpose, audience, tone, and point of view for an essay with this thesis. Using freewriting, mapping, or the questioning technique, generate at least three supporting points for the thesis. Last, write a paragraph about one of the points, making sure your evidence reflects the characteristics discussed in this chapter. Alternatively, you may go ahead and prepare the first draft of an essay having the selected thesis. (If you choose the second option, you may want to turn to page 82 to see a diagram showing how to organize a first draft.) Save whatever you prepare so you can work with it further after reading the next chapter.

a. Winning the lottery may not always be a blessing.
b. All of us can take steps to reduce the country's trash crisis.
c. Drug education programs in public schools are (or are not) effective.

5. Select one of the following thesis statements. Then determine your purpose, audience, tone, and point of view for an essay with this thesis. Next, use the patterns of development to generate at least three supporting points for the thesis. Finally, write a paragraph about one of the points, making sure that your evidence demonstrates the characteristics discussed in this chapter. Alternatively, you may go ahead and prepare a first draft of an essay having the thesis selected. (If you choose the latter option, you may want to turn to page 82 to see a diagram showing how to organize a first draft.) Save whatever you prepare so you can work with it further after reading the next chapter.

a. Teenagers should (or should not) be able to obtain birth-control devices without their parents' permission.

    b. The college's system for awarding student loans needs to be overhauled.

    c. VCRs have changed for the worse (or the better) the way Americans entertain themselves.

6. Look at the thesis and refined scratch outline you prepared in response to activity 7 in Chapter 3 (page 43). Where do you see gaps in the support for your thesis? By brainstorming with others, generate material to fill these gaps. If some of the new points generated suggest that you should modify your thesis, make the appropriate changes now. (Save this material so you can work with it further after reading the next chapter.)

(For more activities on generating evidence, see pages 86–89 in Chapter 6 as well as pages 132–133 in Chapter 8.)

5
ORGANIZING THE EVIDENCE

Once you've generated supporting evidence, you're ready to *organize* that material. Even highly compelling evidence won't illustrate the validity of your thesis or achieve your purpose if it isn't organized properly. Some writers can move quickly from generating support to writing a clearly structured first draft. (They usually say they have sequenced their ideas in their heads.) Most, however, need to spend some time sorting out their thoughts on paper before starting the first draft; otherwise, they tend to lose their way in a tangle of ideas.

When moving to the organizing stage, you should have in front of you your scratch list (see pages 32–33) and thesis, plus any supporting material you've accumulated since you did your prewriting. To find a logical framework for all this material, you'll need to (1) determine which pattern of development is implied in your evidence, (2) select one of four basic approaches for organizing your evidence, and (3) outline your evidence. These issues are discussed in the following sections.

USE THE PATTERNS OF DEVELOPMENT

As you saw on pages 30 and 45–46, the patterns of development (definition, narration, process analysis, and others) can help you develop prewriting material and generate evidence for a thesis. In the organizing stage, the patterns provide frameworks for presenting the evidence in an orderly, accessible way. Here's how.

Each pattern of development has its own internal logic that makes it appropriate for some writing purposes but not for others. (You may find it helpful at this point to turn to pages 29–30 so you can review the broad purpose of each pattern.) Imagine that you want to write an essay *explaining why* some students drop out of college during the first semester. If your essay consisted only of a lengthy narrative of two friends floundering through the first month of college, you wouldn't achieve your purpose. A condensed version of the narrative might be appropriate at some point in the essay, but—to meet your objective—most of the paper would have to focus on *causes* and *effects.*

Once you see which pattern (or combination of patterns) is implied by your purpose, you can block out your paper's general structure. For instance, in the preceding example, you might organize the essay around a three-part discussion of the key reasons that students have difficulty adjusting to college: (1) they miss friends and family, (2) they take inappropriate courses, and (3) they experience conflicts with roommates. As you can see, your choice of pattern of development significantly influences your essay's content and organization.

Some essays follow a single pattern, but most blend them, with a predominant pattern providing the piece's organizational framework. In our example essay, you might include a brief *description* of an overwhelmed first-year college student; you might *define* the psychological term *separation anxiety;* you might end the paper by briefly explaining a *process* for making students' adjustment to college easier. Still, the essay's overall organizational pattern would be *cause-effect* because the paper's primary purpose is to explain why students drop out of college. (See pages 67–68 and Chapter 10 for more information on the way patterns often mix.)

Although writers often combine the patterns of development, your composition instructor may ask you to write an essay organized according to a single pattern. Such an assignment helps you understand a particular pattern's unique demands. Keep in mind, though, that most writing begins not with a specific pattern but with a specific *purpose.* The pattern or combination of patterns used to develop and organize an essay evolves out of that purpose.

SELECT AN ORGANIZATIONAL APPROACH

No matter which pattern(s) of development you select, you need to know four general approaches for organizing the supporting evidence in an essay: chronological, spatial, emphatic, and simple-to-complex.

Chronological Approach

When an essay is organized **chronologically,** supporting material is arranged in a clear time sequence, usually starting with what happened first and ending with what happened last. Occasionally, chronological arrangements can be resequenced to create flashback or flashforward effects, two techniques discussed in Chapter 12 on narration.

Essays using narration (for example, an experience with prejudice) or process analysis (for instance, how to deliver an effective speech) are most likely to be organized chronologically. The paper on public speaking might use a time sequence to present its points: how to prepare a few days before the presentation is due; what to do right before the speech; what to concentrate on during the speech itself. (For examples of chronologically arranged student essays, turn to pages 198–199 in Chapter 12 and pages 306–309 in Chapter 15.)

Spatial Approach

When you arrange supporting evidence **spatially,** you discuss details as they occur in space, or from certain locations. This strategy is particularly appropriate for description. Imagine that you plan to write an essay describing the joyous times you spent as a child playing by a towering old oak tree in the neighborhood park. Using spatial organization, you start by describing the rich animal life (the plump earthworms, swarming anthills, and numerous animal tracks) you observed while hunkered down *at the base* of the tree. Next, you re-create the contented feeling you experienced sitting on a branch *in the middle* of the tree. Finally, you describe the glorious view of the world you had *from the top* of the tree.

Although spatial arrangement is flexible (you could, for instance, start with a description from the top of the tree), you should always proceed systematically. And once you select a particular spatial order, you should usually maintain that sequence throughout the essay; otherwise, readers may get lost along the way. (A spatially arranged student essay appears in Chapter 11 on pages 162–164.)

Emphatic Approach

In **emphatic** order, the most compelling evidence is saved for last. This arrangement is based on the psychological principle that people remember best what they experience most recently. Emphatic order has built-in momentum because it starts with the least important point and builds to the most significant. This method is especially effective in argumentation-persuasion essays, in papers developed through examples, and in pieces involving comparison-contrast, division-classification, or causal analysis.

Consider an essay analyzing the negative effect that workaholic parents can have on their children. The paper might start with a brief discussion of relatively minor effects, such as the family's eating mostly frozen or take-out foods. Paragraphs on more serious effects might follow: children get no parental help with homework; they try to resolve personal problems without parental advice. Finally, the essay might close with a detailed discussion of the most significant effect— children's lack of self-esteem because they feel unimportant in their parents' lives. (The student essays on pages 233–235 in Chapter 13, pages 344–346 in Chapter 16, and pages 412–414 in Chapter 18 all use an emphatic arrangement.)

Simple-to-Complex Approach

A final way to organize an essay is to proceed with relatively **simple** concepts to more **complex** ones. By starting with easy-to-grasp, generally accepted evidence, you establish rapport with your readers and assure them that the essay is firmly grounded in shared experience. In contrast, if you open with difficult or highly technical material, you risk confusing and alienating your audience.

Assume you plan to write a paper arguing that your college has endangered students' health by not making an all-out effort to remove asbestos from dormitories and classroom buildings. It probably wouldn't be a good idea to begin with a medically sophisticated explanation of precisely how asbestos damages lung tissue. Instead, you might start with an observation that is likely to be familiar to your readers—one that is part of their everyday experience. You could, for example, open with a description of asbestos—as readers might see it—wrapped around air ducts and furnaces or used as electrical insulation and fireproofing material. Having provided a basic, easy-to-visualize description, you could then go on to explain the complicated process by which asbestos can cause chronic lung inflammation. (See pages 380–382 in Chapter 17 for an example of a student essay using the simple-to-complex arrangement.)

Depending on your purpose, any one of these four organizational approaches might be appropriate. For example, assume you planned to write an essay developing Harriet Davids's thesis: "Being a parent today is much more difficult than it was a generation ago." To emphasize that the various stages in children's lives present parents with different difficulties, you'd probably select a *chronological* sequence. To show that the challenges parents face vary depending on whether children are at home, at school, or in the world at large, you'd probably choose a *spatial* sequence. To stress the range of problems that parents face (from less to more serious), you'd probably use an *emphatic* sequence. Finally, to illustrate today's confusing array of theories for raising children, you might take a *simple-to-complex* approach, moving from the basic to the most sophisticated theory.

PREPARE AN OUTLINE

Do you, like many students, react with fear and loathing to the dreaded word *outline*? Do you, if asked to submit an outline, prepare it *after* you've written the essay? If you do, we hope to convince you that having an outline—a skeletal version of your paper—*before* you begin the first draft makes the writing process much more manageable. The outline helps you organize your thoughts beforehand, and it guides your writing as you work on the draft. Even though ideas continue to evolve during the draft, an outline clarifies how ideas fit together, which points are major, which should come first, and so on. An outline may also reveal places where evidence is weak, prompting you to eliminate the material altogether, retain it in an unemphatic position, or do more prewriting to generate additional support.

Like previous stages in the writing process, outlining is individualized. Some people prepare highly structured, detailed outlines; others make only a few informal jottings. Sometimes outlining will go quickly, with points falling easily into place; at other times you'll have to work hard to figure out how points are related. If that happens, be glad you caught the problem while outlining, rather than while writing or revising.

To prepare an effective outline, you should reread and evaluate your scratch list and thesis as well as any other evidence you've generated since the prewriting stage. Then decide which pattern of development (description, cause-effect, and so on) seems to be suggested by your evidence. Also determine whether your evidence lends itself to a chronological, a spatial, an emphatic, or a simple-to-complex order. Having done all that, you're ready to identify and sequence your main and supporting points.

The amount of detail in an outline will vary according to the paper's length and the instructor's requirements. A scratch outline consisting of words or phrases (such as the one on pages 32–33 in Chapter 2) is often sufficient, but for longer papers, you'll probably need a more detailed and formal outline. In such cases, the suggestions in the accompanying checklist will help you develop a sound plan. Feel free to modify these guidelines to suit your needs.

✔ GUIDELINES FOR OUTLINING: A CHECKLIST

☐ Write your purpose, audience, tone, point of view, and thesis at the top of the outlining page.

☐ Below the thesis, enter the pattern of development that seems to be implied by the evidence you've accumulated.

☐ Also record which of the four organizational approaches would be most effective in sequencing your evidence.

☐ Reevaluate your supporting material. Delete anything that doesn't develop the thesis or that isn't appropriate for your purpose, audience, tone, and point of view.

☐ Add any new points or material.

☐ Group related items together. Give each group a heading that represents a main topic in support of your thesis.

☐ Label these main topics with roman numerals (I, II, III, and so on). Let the order of numerals indicate the best sequence.

☐ Identify subtopics and group them under the appropriate main topics. Indent and label these subtopics with capital letters (A, B, C, and so on). Let the order of the letters indicate the best sequence.

☐ Identify supporting points (often reasons and examples) and group them under the appropriate subtopics. Indent and label these supporting points with arabic numbers (1, 2, 3, and so on). Let the numbers indicate the best sequence.

> ☐ Identify specific details (secondary examples, facts, statistics, expert opinions, quotations) and group them under the appropriate supporting points. Indent and label these specific details with lowercase letters (a, b, c, and so on). Let the letters indicate the best sequence.
> ☐ Examine your outline, looking for places where evidence is weak. Where appropriate, add new evidence.
> ☐ Doublecheck that all main topics, subtopics, supporting points, and specific details develop some aspect of the thesis. Also confirm that all items are arranged in the most logical order.

<table>
<tr><td>Student essay in progress</td></tr>
</table>

The sample outline that starts below and continues on the next page develops the thesis "Being a parent today is much more difficult than it was a generation ago." You may remember that this is the thesis that Harriet Davids devised for the essay she planned to write in response to the assignment on page 25. Harriet's scratch list, based on her brainstorming, appears on pages 32–33. (You may want to review pages 47–49 to see how Harriet later reconsidered material on the scratch list in light of her thesis.) When you compare Harriet's scratch list and outline, you'll find some differences. On the one hand, the outline tends to contain more specifics (for instance, the details about sexually explicit materials—in magazines and books, in movies, and on television). On the other hand, the outline doesn't include all the material in the scratch list. For example, after reconsidering her purpose, audience, tone, point of view, and thesis, Harriet decided to omit from her outline the section on day care and the points about AIDS and rock posters.

Harriet's outline is called a **topic outline** because it uses phrases, or topics, for each entry. (See pages 305–306, 343–344, and 458–459 for other examples of topic outlines.) For a more complex paper, a **sentence outline** might be more appropriate (see pages 232–233 and 584–586). You can also mix phrases and sentences (see pages 379–380), as long as you are consistent about where you use each.

In Harriet's outline, note that indentations signal the relationships among the essay's points and that the same grammatical form is used to begin each entry on a particular level. For instance, since a noun phrase ("Distractions from homework") follows roman numeral *I*, noun phrases also follow subsequent roman numerals. Such consistency helps writers see if items at a particular level are comparable.

```
Purpose: To inform
Audience: Instructor as well as class members, most of whom are
18-20 years old
Tone: Serious and straightforward
```

Point of view: Third person (mother of two teenage girls)

Thesis: Being a parent today is much more difficult than it was a generation ago.

Pattern of development: Illustration

Organizational approach: Emphatic order

I. Distractions from homework

   A. At home

      1. Stereos, radios, tapes

      2. Television--MTV and my kids

   B. Outside home

      1. Malls

      2. Video arcades

      3. Fast-food restaurants

II. Sexually explicit materials

   A. In print

      1. Sex magazines

         a. Playboy

         b. Penthouse

      2. Pornographic books

   B. In movies

      1. Seduction scenes

      2. Casual sex

   C. On television

      1. Soap operas

      2. R-rated comedians

      3. R-rated movies on cable

III. Increased dangers

   A. Drugs--peer pressure

   B. Alcohol--peer pressure

   C. Violent crimes against children

Continues on page 66

Hints for moving from an outline to a first draft appear on pages 63–65. For additional suggestions on organizing a first draft, see the diagram on page 82.

Before starting to write your first draft, show your outline to several people (your instructor, friends, classmates). Their reactions will indicate whether your proposed organization is appropriate for your thesis, purpose, audience, tone, and point of view. Their comments can also highlight areas needing additional work. After making whatever changes are needed, you're in a good position to go ahead and write the first draft of your essay.

ACTIVITIES: ORGANIZING THE EVIDENCE

1. The following thesis statement is accompanied by a scrambled list of supporting points. Prepare a topic outline for a potential essay, being sure to distinguish between major and secondary points.

Thesis: Our schools, now in crisis, could be improved in several ways.

Certificate requirements for teachers
Schedules
Teachers
Longer school year
Merit pay for outstanding teachers
Curriculum
Better textbooks
Longer school days
More challenging course content

2. For each of the following thesis statements, there are two purposes given. Determine whether each purpose suggests an emphatic, chronological, spatial, or simple-to-complex approach. Note the way the approach varies as the purpose changes.

a. *Thesis:* Traveling in a large city can be an unexpected education.

   Purpose 1: To explain, in a humorous way, the stages in learning to cope with the city's cab system

   Purpose 2: To describe, in a serious manner, the vastly different sections of the city as viewed from a cab

b. *Thesis:* The student government seems determined to improve its relations with the college administration.

   Purpose 1: To inform readers by describing efforts that student leaders took, month by month, to win administrative support

   Purpose 2: To convince readers by explaining straightforward as well as intricate pro-administration resolutions that student leaders passed

c. *Thesis:* Supermarkets use sophisticated marketing techniques to prod consumers into buying more than they need.

Purpose 1: To inform readers that positioning products in certain locations encourages impulse buying

Purpose 2: To persuade readers not to patronize those chains using especially objectionable sales strategies

3. Return to the paragraph or first draft you prepared in response to activity 4 or activity 5 in Chapter 4. Applying the principles discussed in Chapter 5, strengthen the organization of the evidence you generated. (If you rework a first draft, save the draft so you can refine it further after reading the next chapter.)

4. Each of the following brief essay outlines consists of a thesis and several points of support. Which pattern of development would you probably use to develop the overall organizational framework for each essay? Which pattern(s) would you use to develop each point of support? Why?

a. *Thesis:* Friends of the opposite sex fall into one of several categories: the pal, the confidante, or the pest.

Points of Support

- Frequently, an opposite-sex friend is simply a "pal."
- Sometimes, though, a pal turns, step by step, into a confidante.
- If a confidante begins to have romantic thoughts, he or she may become a pest, thus disrupting the friendship.

b. *Thesis:* What happens when a child gets sick in a two-income household? Numerous problems occur.

Points of Support

- Parents often encounter difficulties as they take steps to locate a babysitter or make other child-care arrangements.
- If no child-care helper can be found, a couple must decide which parent will stay at home—a decision that may create conflict between husband and wife.
- No matter what they do, parents inevitably will incur at least one of several kinds of expenses.

5. For one of the thesis statements given in activity 4, identify a possible purpose, audience, tone, and point of view. Then, use one or more patterns to generate material to develop the points of support listed. Get together with someone else to review the generated material, deleting, adding, combining, and arranging ideas in logical order. Finally, make an outline for the body of the essay. (Save your outline. After reading the next chapter, you can use it to write the essay's first draft.)

6. Look again at the thesis and scratch outline you refined and elaborated in response to activity 6 in Chapter 4. Reevaluate this material by deleting, adding, combining, and rearranging ideas as needed. Then, in preparation for writing an essay, outline your ideas. Consider whether an emphatic, chronological, spatial, or simple-to-complex approach will be most appropriate. Finally, ask at least one other person to evaluate your organizational plan. (Save your outline. After reading the next chapter, you can use it to write the essay's first draft.)

6
WRITING THE PARAGRAPHS IN THE FIRST DRAFT

AFTER prewriting, deciding on a thesis, and developing and organizing evidence, you're ready to write a first draft—a rough, provisional version of your essay. Some people work slowly as they prepare their drafts, while others quickly dash off their drafts. No matter how you proceed, you should concentrate on providing paragraphs that support your thesis. Also try to include all relevant examples, facts, and opinions, sequencing this material as effectively as you can.

Because of your work in the preceding stages, the first draft may flow quite smoothly. But don't be discouraged if it doesn't. You may find that your thesis has to be reshaped, that a point no longer fits, that you need to return to a prewriting activity to generate additional material. Such stopping and starting is to be expected. Writing the first draft is a process of discovery, involving the continual clarification and refining of ideas.

HOW TO MOVE FROM OUTLINE TO FIRST DRAFT

There's no single right way to prepare a first draft. With experience, you'll undoubtedly find your own basic approach, adapting it to suit each paper's length, the time available, and the instructor's requirements. Some writers rely heavily on their scratch lists or outlines; others glance at them only occasionally.

Some people write the first draft in longhand; others use a typewriter or computer.

However you choose to proceed, consider the following general suggestions when moving from an outline or scratch list to a first draft:

- Make the outline's *main topics* (I, II, III) the *topic sentences* of the essay's supporting paragraphs. (Topic sentences are discussed later in this chapter.)
- Make the outline's *subtopics* (A, B, C) the *subpoints* in each paragraph.
- Make the outline's *supporting points* (1, 2, 3) the *key examples* and *reasons* in each paragraph.
- Make the outline's *specific details* (a, b, c) the *secondary examples,* facts, statistics, expert opinion, and quotations in each paragraph.

(To see how one student, Harriet Davids, moved from outline to first draft, turn to pages 83–84.)

GENERAL SUGGESTIONS ON HOW TO PROCEED

Although outlines and lists are valuable for guiding your work, don't be so dependent on them that you shy away from new ideas that surface during your writing of the first draft. It's during this time that promising new thoughts often pop up; as they do, jot them down. Then, at the appropriate point, go back and evaluate them: Do they support your thesis? Are they appropriate for your essay's purpose, audience, tone, and point of view? If so, go ahead and include the material in your draft.

It's easy to get stuck while preparing the first draft if you try to edit as you write. Remember: A draft isn't intended to be perfect. For the time being, adopt a relaxed, noncritical attitude. Working as quickly as you can, don't stop to check spelling, correct grammar, or refine sentence structure. Save these tasks for later. One good way to help remind you that the first draft is tentative is to prepare it in longhand, using scrap paper and pencil. Writing on alternate lines also underscores your intention to revise later on, when the extra space will make it easier to add and delete material. Similarly, writing on only one side of the paper can prove helpful if, during revision, you decide to move a section to another part of the paper.

IF YOU GET BOGGED DOWN

All writers get bogged down now and then. The best thing to do is accept that sooner or later it will happen to you. When it does, keep calm and try to write something—no matter how awkward or imprecise it may seem. Just jot a reminder to yourself in the margin ("Fix this," "Redo," or "Ugh!") to finetune the section later. Or leave a blank space to hold a spot for the right words when they finally break loose. It may also help to reread—out loud is best—what you've already written. Regaining a sense of the larger context is often enough to get you moving again. You might also try talking your way through a troublesome section. Like most people, you probably speak more easily than you write; by speaking aloud, you tap this oral fluency and put it to work in your writing.

If a section of the essay strikes you as particularly difficult, don't spend time struggling with it. Move on to an easier section, write that, and then return to the challenging part. If you're still getting nowhere, take a break. Watch television, listen to music, talk with friends. While you're relaxing, your thoughts may loosen up and untangle the knotty section. If, on the other hand, an obligation such as a class or an appointment forces you to stop writing when the draft is going well, jot down a few notes in the margin to remind yourself of your train of thought. The notes will keep you from getting stuck when you pick up the draft later.

A SUGGESTED SEQUENCE FOR WRITING THE FIRST DRAFT

Because you read essays from beginning to end, you may assume that writers work the same way, starting with the introduction and going straight through to the conclusion. Often, however, this isn't the case. In fact, since an introduction depends so heavily on everything that follows, it's usually best to write the introduction *after* the essay's body.

When preparing your first draft, you may find it helpful to follow this sequence:

1. Write the essay's supporting paragraphs.
2. Write the other paragraphs in the essay's body.
3. Write the introduction.
4. Write the conclusion.

Write the Supporting Paragraphs

Before starting to write the essay's **supporting paragraphs,** enter your thesis at the top of the page. You might even underline key words in the thesis to keep yourself focused on the central ideas you plan to develop. Also, now that you've planned the essay's overall organization, you may want to add to your thesis a **plan of development:** a brief *overview* of the essay's *major points in the exact order* in which you will discuss those points. (For more on plans of development, see pages 38–39.)

Not every essay needs a plan of development. In a brief paper, readers can often keep track of ideas without this extra help. But in a longer, more complex essay, a plan of development helps readers follow the progression of main points in the supporting paragraphs. Whether or not you include a plan of development, always keep in mind that writing the draft often leads to new ideas; you may have to revise your thesis, plan of development, and supporting paragraphs as the draft unfolds.

Drawn from the main sections in your outline or scratch list, each supporting paragraph should develop an aspect of your essay's thesis or plan of development. Although there are no hard-and-fast rules, strong supporting paragraphs are (1) often focused by topic sentences, (2) organized around one or more patterns of development, (3) unified, (4) specific, (5) adequately supported, and (6) coherent. Aim for as many of these qualities as you can in the first draft. The material on the following pages will help keep you focused on your goal. But don't expect the draft paragraphs to be perfect; you'll have the chance to revise them later on.

Use Topic Sentences

Frequently, each supporting paragraph in an essay is focused by a **topic sentence.** This sentence usually states a main point in support of the thesis. In a formal outline, such a point customarily appears, often in abbreviated form, as a *main topic* marked with a roman numeral (I, II, III).

The transformation of an outline's main topic to a paragraph's topic sentence is often a matter of stating your attitude toward the outline topic. When changing from main outline topic to topic sentence, you may also add details that make the topic sentence more specific and concrete. Compare, for example, Harriet Davids's outline on pages 58–59 with her first draft on pages 83–84. You'll see that the outline entry "I. Distractions from homework" turned into the topic sentence "Parents have to control all the new distractions/temptations that turn kids away from schoolwork" (paragraph 2). The difference between the outline topic and the topic sentence is thus twofold: The topic sentence has an *element of opinion* ("have to control"), and it is focused by *added details* (in this case, the people involved— parents and children).

The topic sentence functions as a kind of mini-thesis for the paragraph. Generally one or two sentences in length, the topic sentence usually appears at or near the beginning of the paragraph. However, it may also appear at the end, in the middle, or—with varied wording—several times within the paragraph. In still other cases, a single topic sentence may state an idea developed in more than one paragraph. When a paragraph is intended primarily to clarify or inform, you may want to place its topic sentence at the beginning; that way, readers are prepared to view everything that follows in light of that main idea. If, though, you intend a paragraph to heighten suspense or to convey a feeling of discovery, you may prefer to delay the topic sentence until the end.

Regardless of its length or location, the topic sentence states the paragraph's main idea. The other sentences in the paragraph provide support for this central point in the form of examples, facts, expert opinion, and so on. Like a thesis statement, the topic sentence *signals the paragraph's subject* and frequently *indicates the writer's attitude* toward that subject. In the topic sentences that follow, the subject of the paragraph is underlined once and the attitude toward that subject is underlined twice:

> **Student essay in progress**

Topic Sentences

Some students select a particular field of study for the wrong reasons.

The ocean dumping of radioactive waste is a ticking time bomb.

Several contemporary rock groups show unexpected sensitivity to social issues.

Political candidates are sold like slickly packaged products.

As you work on the first draft, you may find yourself writing paragraphs without paying too much attention to topic sentences. That's fine, as long as you remember to evaluate the paragraphs later on. When revising, you can provide a topic sentence for a paragraph that needs a sharper focus, recast a topic sentence for a paragraph that ended up taking an unexpected turn, even eliminate a topic sentence altogether if a paragraph's content is sufficiently unified to imply its point.

With experience, you'll develop an instinct for writing focused paragraphs without having to pay such close attention to topic sentences. A good way to develop such an instinct is to note how the writers in this book use topic sentences to shape paragraphs and clarify meaning. (If you'd like some practice in identifying topic sentences, see pages 85–86.)

Use the Patterns of Development

As you saw on pages 53–54, an entire essay can be organized around one or more patterns of development. These patterns can also provide the organizational framework for an essay's supporting paragraphs. Assume you're writing an article for your town newspaper with the thesis "Year-round residents of an ocean community must take an active role in safeguarding the seashore environment." As the following examples indicate, your supporting paragraphs could develop this thesis through a variety of patterns, with each paragraph's topic sentence suggesting a specific pattern or combination of patterns.

Topic Sentence	Possible Pattern of Development
In a nearby ocean community, signs of environmental damage are everywhere.	*Description* of a seaside town with polluted waters, blighted trees, and diseased marine life
Typically, residents blame industry or tourists for such damage.	*Narration* of a conversation among seaside residents
Residents' careless behavior is also to blame, however.	*Illustrations* of residents' littering the beach, injuring marine life while motor boating, walking over fragile sand dunes
Even environmentally concerned residents may contribute to the problem.	*Cause-effect* explanation of the way styrofoam packaging and plastic food wrap, even when properly disposed of in a trash can, can harm scavenging seagulls
Fortunately, not all seaside towns are plagued by such environmental problems.	*Comparison-contrast* of one troubled shore community with another more ecologically sound one

Topic Sentence	Possible Pattern of Development
It's clear that shore residents must become "environmental activists."	*Definition* of an *environmental activist*
Residents can get involved in a variety of pro-environmental activities.	*Division-classification* of activities at the neighborhood, town, and municipal levels
Moreover, getting involved is an easy matter.	*Process analysis* of the steps for getting involved at the various levels
Such activism yields significant rewards.	A final *argumentation-persuasion* pitch showing residents the benefits of responsible action

Of course, each supporting paragraph in an essay doesn't have to be organized according to a different pattern of development; several paragraphs may use the same pattern. Nor is it necessary for any one paragraph to be restricted to a single pattern; supporting paragraphs often combine patterns. For example, the topic sentence "Fortunately, not all seaside towns are plagued by such environmental problems" might be developed primarily through *comparison-contrast,* but the paragraph would need a fair amount of *description* to clarify the differences between towns. (For more on the way the patterns of development come into play throughout the writing process, see pages 29–30, 38, 45–46, 53–54, and Chapter 10.)

Make the Paragraphs Unified

Just as overall evidence must support an essay's thesis (pages 46–47), the facts, opinions, and examples in each supporting paragraph must have *direct bearing* on the paragraph's topic sentence. If the paragraph has no topic sentence, the supporting material must be *consistent* with the paragraph's *implied focus.* A paragraph is **unified** when it meets these requirements.

Consider the following sample paragraph, taken from an essay illustrating recent changes in Americans' television-viewing habits. The paragraph focuses on people's reasons for switching from network to cable television. As you'll see, though, the paragraph lacks unity because it contains points (underlined) unrelated to its main idea. Specifically, the criticism of cable's foul language contradicts the paragraph's topic sentence—"Many people consider cable TV an improvement over network television." To present a balanced view of cable versus network television, the writer should discuss these points, but in *another paragraph.*

Nonunified Support

Many people consider cable TV an improvement over network television. For one thing, viewers usually prefer the movies on cable. Unlike network films, cable movies are often only months old, they have not been edited by censors, and they are not interrupted by commercials. Growing numbers of people also feel that cable specials are superior to the ones the networks grind out. Cable viewers may enjoy such pop stars as Billy Joel, Mariah Carey, or Chris Rock in concert, whereas the networks continue to broadcast tired Bill Cosby variety shows and boring awards ceremonies. <u>There is, however, one problem with cable comedians. The foul language many of them use makes it hard to watch these cable specials with children. The networks, in contrast, generally present "clean" shows that parents and children can watch together</u>. Then, too, cable TV offers viewers more flexibility since it schedules shows at various times over the month. People working night shifts or attending evening classes can see movies in the afternoon, and viewers missing the first twenty minutes of a show can always catch them later. It's not surprising that cable viewership is growing while network ratings have taken a plunge.

Make the Paragraphs Specific

If your supporting paragraphs are vague, readers will lose interest, remain unconvinced of your thesis, even have trouble deciphering your meaning. In contrast, paragraphs filled with **concrete, specific details** engage readers, lend force to ideas, and clarify meaning.

Following are two versions of a paragraph from an essay about trends in the business community. Although both paragraphs focus on one such trend—flexible working hours—note how the first version's vague generalities leave meaning unclear. *What,* for example, is meant by "flex-time scheduling"? *Which* companies have tried it? *Where,* specifically, are these companies located? *How,* exactly, does flex-time increase productivity, lessen conflict, and reduce accidents? The second paragraph answers these questions with specifics and, as a result, is more informative and interesting.

Nonspecific Support

More and more companies have begun to realize that flex-time scheduling offers advantages. Several companies outside Boston have tried flex-time scheduling and are pleased with the way the system reduces the difficulties their employees face getting to work. Studies show that flex-time scheduling also increases productivity, reduces on-the-job conflict, and minimizes work-related accidents.

Specific Support

More and more companies have begun to realize that flex-time scheduling offers advantages over a rigid 9-to-5 routine. Along suburban Boston's Route 128, such companies as Compugraphics and Consolidated Paper now permit employees to schedule their arrival any

time between 6 a.m. and 11 a.m. The corporations report that the
number of rush-hour jams and accidents has fallen dramatically.
As a result, employees no longer arrive at work weighed down by
tension induced by choking clouds of exhaust fumes and the blaring
horns of gridlocked drivers. Studies sponsored by the journal
Business Quarterly show that this more mellow state of mind benefits
corporations. Traffic-stressed employees begin their workday
anxious and exasperated, still grinding their teeth at their fellow
commuters, their frustration often spilling over into their performance at work. By contrast, stress-free employees work more
productively and take fewer days off. They are more tolerant
of co-workers and customers, and less likely to balloon minor
irritations into major confrontations. Perhaps most important,
employees arriving at work relatively free of stress can focus
their attention on working safely. They rack up significantly
fewer on-the-job accidents, such as falls and injuries resulting from careless handling of dangerous equipment. Flex-time
improves employee well-being, and as well-being rises, so do
company profits.

Five Strategies for Making Paragraphs Specific.   How can you make the evidence in your paragraphs specific? The following techniques should help.

1. Provide examples that answer *who, which, what,* and similar questions. In
contrast to the vague generalities in the first paragraph on flex-time scheduling,
the second paragraph provides examples that answer a series of basic questions.
For instance, the general comment "Several companies outside of Boston" (*which*
companies?) is replaced by "Compugraphics and Consolidated Paper." The vague
phrase "difficulties their employees face getting to work" (*what* difficulties?) is
dramatized with the examples "rush-hour jams and accidents." Similarly, "work-
related accidents" (*which* accidents?) is illustrated with "injuries resulting from a
fall or improper handling of dangerous equipment."

2. Replace general nouns and adjectives with precise ones. In the following sentences, note how much sharper images become when exact nouns and adjectives
replace imprecise ones:

General	**More Specific**	**Most Specific**
A *man* had trouble lifting the *box* out of the *old* car.	A *young man, out of shape,* struggled to lift the *heavy crate* out of the *beat-up sports car.*	*Joe, only twenty years old but more than fifty pounds over- weight,* struggled to lift the *heavy wooden crate* out of the *rusty* and *dented Corvette.*

3. Replace abstract words with concrete ones. Notice the way the example on the right, firmly grounded in the physical, clarifies the intangible concepts in the example on the left:

Abstract	Concrete
The fall day had great *beauty*, despite its *dreariness*.	*Red, yellow,* and *orange* leaves *gleamed wetly* through the *gray mist*.

(For more on making abstract language concrete, see pages 121–122 in Chapter 8.)

4. Use words that appeal to the five senses (sight, touch, taste, smell, sound). The sentence on the left lacks impact because it fails to convey any sensory impressions; the sentence on the right, though, gains power through the use of sensory details:

Without Sensory Images	With Sensory Images
The computer room is eerie.	In the computer room, keys *click* and printers *grate* while row after row of students stare into screens that *glow without shedding any light*. (sound and sight)

(For more on sensory language, see pages 158–159 in Chapter 11.)

5. Use vigorous verbs. Linking verbs (such as *seem* and *appear*) and *to be* verbs (such as *is* and *were*) paint no pictures. Strong verbs, however, create sharp visual images. Compare the following examples:

Weak Verbs	Strong Verbs
The spectators *seemed* pleased and *were* enthusiastic when the wheelchair marathoners *went* by.	The spectators *cheered* and *whistled* when the wheelchair marathoners *whizzed* by.

(For more on strong verbs, see pages 122–123 in Chapter 8.)

Provide Adequate Support

Each supporting paragraph should also have **adequate support** so that your readers can see clearly the validity of the topic sentence. At times, a single extended example is sufficient; generally, however, an assortment of examples, facts, personal observations, and so forth is more effective.

Following are two versions of a paragraph from a paper showing how difficult it is to get personal, attentive service nowadays at gas stations, supermarkets, and department stores. Both paragraphs focus on the problem at gas stations, but one paragraph is much more effective. As you'll see, the first paragraph starts with good specific support, yet fails to provide enough of it. The second paragraph offers additional examples, descriptive details, and dialog—all of which make the writing stronger and more convincing.

Inadequate Support

Gas stations are a good example of this impersonal attitude. At many stations, attendants have even stopped pumping gas. Motorists pull up to a combination convenience store and gas island where an attendant is enclosed in a glass booth with a tray for taking money. The driver must get out of the car, pump the gas, and walk over to the booth to pay. That's a real inconvenience, especially when compared with the way service stations used to be run.

Adequate Support

Gas stations are a good example of this impersonal attitude. At many stations, attendants have even stopped pumping gas. Motorists pull up to a combination convenience store and gas island where an attendant is enclosed in a glass booth with a tray for taking money. The driver must get out of the car, pump the gas, and walk over to the booth to pay. Even at stations that still have "pump jockeys," employees seldom ask, "Check your oil?" or wash windshields, although they may grudgingly point out the location of the bucket and squeegee. And customers with a balky engine or a nonfunctioning heater are usually out of luck. Why? Many gas stations have eliminated on-duty mechanics. The skillful mechanic who could replace a belt or fix a tire in a few minutes has been replaced by a teenager in a jumpsuit who doesn't know a carburetor from a charge card and couldn't care less.

Make the Paragraphs Coherent

A jigsaw puzzle with all the pieces heaped on a table remains a baffling jumble unless it's clear how the pieces fit together. Similarly, paragraphs can be unified, specific, and adequately supported, yet—if internally disjointed or inadequately connected to each other—leave readers feeling confused. Readers need to be able to follow with ease the progression of thought within and between paragraphs. One idea must flow smoothly and logically into the next; that is, your writing must be **coherent.**

The following paragraph lacks coherence for two main reasons. First, it sequences ideas improperly. (The idea about toll attendants' being cut off from co-workers is introduced, dropped, then picked up again. References to motorists are similarly scattered throughout the paragraph.) Second, it doesn't indicate how individual ideas are related. (What, for example, is the connection between drivers who pass by without saying anything and attendants who have to work at night?)

Incoherent Support

Collecting tolls on the turnpike must be one of the loneliest jobs in the world. Each toll attendant sits in his or her booth, cut off from other attendants. Many drivers pass by each booth. None stays long enough for a brief "hello." Most don't acknowledge the attendant at all. Many toll attendants work at night, pushing them "out of synch" with the rest of the world. The attendants have to deal with rude drivers who treat them like non-people, swearing at them for the long lines at the tollgate. Attendants dislike how cut off they feel from their co-workers. Except for infrequent breaks, they have little chance to chat with each other and swap horror stories--small pleasures that would make their otherwise routine jobs bearable.

Coherent Support

Collecting tolls on the turnpike must be one of the loneliest jobs in the world. First of all, although many drivers pass by the attendants, none stays long enough for more than a brief "hello." Most drivers, in fact, don't acknowledge the toll collectors at all, with the exception of those rude drivers who treat the attendants like non-people, swearing at them for the long lines at the toll-gate. Then, too, many toll attendants work at night, pushing them further "out of synch" with the rest of the world. Worst of all, attendants say, is how isolated they feel from their co-workers. Each attendant sits in his or her booth, cut off from other atten-dants. Except for infrequent breaks, they have little chance to chat with each other and swap horror stories--small pleasures that would make their otherwise routine jobs bearable.

To avoid the kinds of problems found in the incoherent paragraph, use—as the revised version does—two key strategies: (1) a clearly *chronological, spatial,* or *emphatic order* ("*Worst of all,* the attendants say…") and (2) *signal devices* ("*First of all,* although many drivers pass by…") to show how ideas are connected. The following sections discuss these two strategies.

Chronological, Spatial, and Emphatic Order.   As you learned in Chapter 5, an entire essay can be organized using chronological, spatial, or emphatic order (pages 54–55). These strategies can also be used to make a paragraph coherent.
   Imagine you plan to write an essay showing the difficulties many immigrants face when they first come to this country. Let's consider how you might structure

the essay's supporting paragraphs, particularly the way each paragraph's organizational approach can help you arrange ideas in a logical, easy-to-follow sequence.

One paragraph, focused by the topic sentence "The everyday life of a typical immigrant family is arduous," might be developed through a **chronological** account of the family's daily routine: purchasing, before dawn, fruits and vegetables for their produce stand; setting up the stand early in the morning; working there for ten hours; attending English class at night. Another paragraph might develop its topic sentence—"Many immigrant families get along without the technology that others take for granted"—through **spatial** order, taking readers on a brief tour of an immigrant family's rented home: the kitchen lacks a dishwasher or microwave; the living room has no stereo or VCR, only a small black-and-white TV; the basement has just a washtub and clothesline instead of a washer and dryer. Finally, a third paragraph with the topic sentence "A number of worries typically beset immigrant families" might use an **emphatic** sequence, moving from less significant concerns (having to wear old, unfashionable clothes) to more critical issues (having to deal with isolation and discrimination).

Signal Devices. Once you determine a logical sequence for your points, you need to make sure that readers can follow the progression of those points within and between paragraphs. **Signal devices** provide readers with cues, reminding them where they have been and indicating where they are going.

Try to include some signals—however awkward or temporary—in your first draft. If you find you *can't,* that's probably a warning that your ideas may not be arranged logically—in which case, it's better to find that out now rather than later on.

Useful signal devices include *transitions, bridging sentences, repeated words, synonyms,* and *pronouns.* Keep in mind, though, that a light touch should be your goal with such signals. Too many call attention to themselves, making the essay mechanical and plodding.

1. Transitions. Words and phrases that ease readers from one idea to another are called **transitions.** Among such signals are the following:

Time	Space	Addition	Examples
first	above	moreover	for instance
next	below	also	for example
during	next to	furthermore	to illustrate
finally	behind	in addition	specifically

Contrast	Comparison	Summary
but	similarly	therefore
however	also	thus
in contrast	likewise	in short
on the one/ other hand	too	in conclusion

Note how the underlined transitions in the following paragraph provide clear cues to readers, showing how ideas fit together:

> Although the effect of air pollution on the human body is distressing, its effect on global ecology is even more troubling. In the Bavarian, French, and Italian Alps, <u>for example</u>, once magnificent forests are slowly being destroyed by air pollution. Trees dying from pollution lose their leaves or needles, allowing sunlight to reach the forest floor. <u>During</u> this process, grass prospers in the increased light and pushes out the native plants and moss that help hold rainwater. The soil <u>thus</u> loses absorbency and becomes hard, causing rain and snow to slide over the ground instead of sinking into it. This, <u>in turn</u>, leads to erosion of the soil. <u>After</u> a heavy rain, the eroded land <u>finally</u> falls away in giant rockslides and avalanches, destroying entire villages and causing life-threatening floods.

2. Bridging sentences. Although **bridging sentences** may be used within a paragraph, they are more often used to move readers from one paragraph to the next. Look again at the first sentence in the preceding paragraph on pollution. Note that the sentence consists of two parts: The first part reminds readers that the previous discussion focused on pollution's effect on the body; the second part tells readers that the focus will now be pollution's effect on ecology.

3. Repeated words, synonyms, and pronouns. The **repetition** of important words maintains continuity, reassures readers that they are on the right track, and highlights key ideas. **Synonyms**—words similar in meaning to key words or phrases—also provide coherence, while making it possible to avoid unimaginative and tedious repetitions. Finally, **pronouns** (*he, she, it, they, this, that*) enhance coherence by causing readers to think back to the original word (antecedent) the pronoun replaces. When using pronouns, however, be sure there is no ambiguity about antecedents. (See pages 660–661 in the Handbook.)

The following paragraph uses repeated words (underlined once), synonyms (underlined twice), and pronouns (underlined three times) to integrate ideas:

> <u>Studies</u> have shown that color is also an important part of the way <u>people</u> experience <u>food</u>. In one <u>study</u>, <u>individuals</u> fed a rich red tomato sauce didn't notice <u>it</u> had no flavor until <u>they</u> were nearly finished eating. Similarly, in another <u>experiment</u>, <u>people</u> were offered strangely colored <u>foods</u>: gray pork chops, lavender mashed potatoes, dark blue peas, dessert topped with yellow whipped cream. Not one of the <u>subjects</u> would eat the strange-looking <u>food</u>, even though <u>it</u> smelled and tasted normal.

Write Other Paragraphs in the Essay's Body

Paragraphs supporting the thesis are not necessarily the only kind in the body of an essay. You may also include paragraphs that give background information or provide transitions.

Background Paragraphs

Usually found near the essay's beginning, **background paragraphs** provide information that doesn't directly support the thesis but that helps the reader understand or accept the discussion that follows. Such paragraphs may consist of a definition, brief historical overview, or short description. For example, in the student essay "Salt Marsh" on pages 162–164, the paragraph following the introduction defines a salt marsh and summarizes some of its features. This background information serves as a lead-in to the detailed description that makes up the rest of the essay.

Because you don't want to distract readers from your essay's main point, background paragraphs should be kept as brief as possible. In a paper outlining a program that you believe your college should adopt to beautify its grounds, you would probably need a background paragraph describing typical campus eyesores. Too lengthy a description, though, would detract from the presentation of your step-by-step program.

Transitional Paragraphs

Another kind of paragraph, generally one to three sentences long, may appear between supporting paragraphs to help readers keep track of your discussion. Like the bridging sentences discussed earlier in the chapter, **transitional paragraphs** usually sum up what has been discussed so far and then indicate the direction the essay will take next.

Although too many transitional paragraphs make writing stiff and mechanical, they can be effective when used sparingly, especially in essays with sharp turns in direction. For example, in a paper showing how to purchase a car, you might start by explaining the research a potential buyer should do beforehand: Consult publications like *Consumer Reports*; check performance records published by the automotive industry; call several dealerships for price information. Then, as a transition to the next section—how to negotiate at the dealership—you might provide the following paragraph:

```
Once you have armed yourself with the necessary information,
you are ready to meet with a salesperson at the showroom. Your expe-
rience at the dealership should not be intimidating as long as you
follow the guidelines below.
```

Write the Introduction

Many writers don't prepare an **introduction** until they have started to revise; others feel more comfortable if their first draft includes in basic form all parts of the final essay. If that's how you feel, you'll probably write the introduction as you

complete your first draft. No matter when you prepare it, keep in mind how crucial the introduction is to your essay's success. First impressions count heavily.
More specifically, the introduction serves three distinct functions: It arouses readers' interest, introduces your subject, and presents your thesis.

Introductions are difficult to write—so difficult, in fact, that you may be
tempted to take the easy way out and use a stale beginning like "According to
Webster...." Equally yawn-inducing are sweeping generalizations that sound
grand but say little: "Throughout human history, people have waged war" or
"Affection is important in all our lives." Don't, however, go too far in the other
direction and come up with a gimmicky opening: "I don't know about you, but in
my life, love is the next best thing to being there. Where? Heaven, that's where!"
Contrived and coy, such introductions are bound to be inconsistent with your
essay's purpose, tone, and point of view. Remember, the introduction's style and
content should flow into the rest of the essay.

The length of your introduction will vary according to your paper's scope and
purpose. Most essays you write, however, will be served best by a one- or two-
paragraph beginning. To write an effective introduction, use any of the following
methods, singly or in combination. The thesis statement in each sample introduction is underlined. Note, too, that the first thesis includes a plan of development,
whereas the last thesis is followed by a plan of development (see pages 38–39).

Broad Statement Narrowing to a Limited Subject

For generations, morality has been molded primarily by parents,
religion, and schools. Children traditionally acquired their ideas
about what is right and wrong, which goals are important in life,
and how others should be treated from these three sources collec-
tively. But in the past few decades, a single force--television--has
undermined the beneficial influence that parents, religion, and
school have on children's moral development. Indeed, television
often implants in children negative values about sex, work, and family life.

Brief Anecdote

At a local high school recently, students in a psychology course
were given a hint of what it is like to be the parents of a newborn.
Each "parent" had to carry a raw egg around at all times to
symbolize the responsibilities of parenthood. The egg could not be
left alone; it limited the "parents'" activities; it placed a
full-time emotional burden on "Mom" and "Dad." This class exercise
illustrates a common problem facing the majority of new mothers
and fathers. Most people receive little preparation for the job of
being parents.

Starting with an Idea That Is the Opposite of the One Actually Developed

We hear a great deal about divorce's disastrous impact on children. We are deluged with advice on ways to make divorce as painless as possible for youngsters; we listen to heartbreaking stories about the confused, grieving children of divorced parents. Little attention has been paid, however, to a different kind of effect that divorce may have on children. <u>Children from divorced families may become skilled manipulators, playing off one parent against the other, worsening an already painful situation.</u>

Series of Short Questions

What happens if a child is caught vandalizing school property? What happens if a child goes for a joyride in a stolen car and accidentally hits a pedestrian? Should parents be liable for their children's mistakes? Should parents have to pay what might be hundreds of thousands of dollars in damages? Adults have begun to think seriously about such questions because the laws concerning the limits of parental responsibility are changing rapidly. <u>With unfortunate frequency, courts have begun to hold parents legally and financially responsible for their children's misbehavior.</u>

Quotation

Educator Neil Postman believes that television has blurred the line between childhood and adulthood. According to Postman, "All the secrets that a print culture kept from children . . . are revealed all at once by media that do not, and cannot, exclude any audience." <u>This media barrage of information, once intended only for adults, has changed childhood for the worse.</u>

Brief Background on the Topic

For a long time, adults believed that "children should be seen, not heard." On special occasions, youngsters were dressed up and told to sit quietly while adults socialized. Even when they were alone with their parents, children were not supposed to bother adults with their concerns. However, beginning with psychologist Arnold Gesell in the 1940s, childraising experts began to question the wisdom of an approach that blocked communication. In 1965, Haim

Ginott's ground-breaking book *Between Parent and Child* stressed the importance of conversing with children. More recently, two of Ginott's disciples, Adele Sager and Elaine Mazlich, wrote a book on this subject: *How to Talk So Children Will Listen and Listen So Children Will Talk.* <u>These days, experts agree, successful parents are those who encourage their children to share their thoughts and concerns</u>.

Refutation of a Common Belief

Adolescents care only about material things; their lives revolve around brand-name sneakers, designer jeans, the latest fad in stereo equipment. They resist education, don't read, barely know who is president, mainline rock 'n' roll, experiment with drugs, and exist on a steady diet of Ring-Dings, nachos, and beer. This is what many adults, including parents, seem to believe about the young. <u>The reality is, however, that young people today show more maturity and common sense than most adults give them credit for</u>.

Dramatic Fact or Statistic

Seventy percent of the respondents in a poll conducted by columnist Ann Landers stated that, if they could live their lives over, they would choose not to have children. This startling statistic makes one wonder what these people believed parenthood would be like. <u>Many parents have unrealistic expectations for their children</u>. Parents want their children to accept their values, follow their paths, and succeed where they failed.

Write the Conclusion

You may have come across essays that ended with jarring abruptness because they had no conclusions at all. Other papers may have had conclusions, but they sputtered to a weak close, a sure sign that the writers had run out of steam and wanted to finish as quickly as possible. Just as satisfying closes are an important part of everyday life (we feel cheated if dinner doesn't end with dessert or if a friend leaves without saying goodbye), a strong **conclusion** is an important part of an effective essay.

However important conclusions may be, they're often difficult to write. When it comes time to write one, you may feel you've said all there is to say. To prevent such an impasse, you can try saving a compelling statistic, quotation, or detail for the end. Just make sure that this interesting item fits in the conclusion and that the essay's body contains sufficient support without it.

Occasionally, an essay doesn't need a separate conclusion. This is often the case with narration or description. For instance, in a narrative showing how a crisis can strengthen a faltering friendship, your point will probably be made with sufficient force without a final "this is what the narrative is all about" paragraph.

Usually, though, a conclusion is necessary. Generally one or two paragraphs in length, the conclusion should give the reader a feeling of completeness and finality. One way to achieve this sense of "rounding off" is to return to an image, idea, or anecdote from the introduction.

Because people tend to remember most clearly the points they read last, the conclusion is also a good place to remind readers of your thesis, phrasing this central idea somewhat differently than you did earlier in the essay. You may also use the conclusion to make a final point about your subject. This way, you leave your readers with something to mull over. Be careful, though, not to open an entirely new line of thought at the essay's close. If you do, readers may feel puzzled and frustrated, wishing you had provided evidence for your final point. And, of course, always be sure that concluding material fits your thesis and is consistent with your purpose, tone, and point of view.

In your conclusion, it's best to steer away from stock phrases like "In sum," "In conclusion," and "This paper has shown that. . . ." Also avoid lengthy conclusions. As in everyday life, prolonged farewells are tedious.

Following are examples of some of the techniques you can use to write effective conclusions. These strategies may be used singly or in combination. The first strategy, the *summary conclusion*, can be especially helpful in long, complex essays since readers may appreciate a review of your points. Tacked onto a short essay, though, a summary conclusion often seems boring and mechanical.

Summary

Contrary to what many adults think, most adolescents are not only aware of the important issues of the times but also deeply concerned about them. They are sensitive to the plight of the homeless, the destruction of the environment, and the pitfalls of rampant materialism. Indeed, today's young people are not less mature and sensible than their parents were. If anything, they are more so.

Prediction

The growing tendency on the part of the judicial system to hold parents responsible for the actions of their delinquent children can have a disturbing impact on all of us. Parents will feel bitter toward their own children and cynical about a system that holds them accountable for the actions of minors. Children, continuing to escape the consequences of their actions, will become even more law-less and destructive. Society cannot afford two such possibilities.

Quotation

The comic W. C. Fields is reputed to have said, "Anyone who hates children and dogs can't be all bad." Most people do not share Fields's cynicism. Viewing childhood as a time of purity, they are alarmed at the way television exposes children to the seamy side of life, stripping youngsters of their innocence and giving them a glib sophistication that is a poor substitute for wisdom.

Statistic

Granted, divorce may, in some cases, be the best thing for fam-ilies torn apart by parents battling one another. However, in lon-gitudinal studies of children from divorced families, psychologist Judith Wallerstein found that only 10 percent of the youngsters felt relief at their parents' divorce; the remaining 90 percent felt dev-astated. Such statistics surely call into question parents' claims that they are divorcing for their children's sake.

Recommendation or Call for Action

It is a mistake to leave parenting to instinct. Instead, we should make parenting skills a required course in schools. In addi-tion, a nationwide hotline should be established to help parents deal with crises. Such training and continuing support would help adults deal more effectively with many of the problems they face as parents.

Write the Title

Some writers say that they often begin a piece with only a title in mind. But for most, writing the **title** is the finishing touch. Although creating a title is usually one of the last steps in writing an essay, it shouldn't be done haphazardly. It may take time to write an effective title—one that hints at the essay's thesis and snares the reader's interest.

Good titles may make use of the following techniques: *repetition of sounds* ("The Plot Against People"), *humor* ("Neat People versus Sloppy People"), and *questions* ("Am I Blue?"). More often, though, titles are straightforward phrases derived from the essay's subject or thesis: "Shooting an Elephant" and "Our Drug Prob-lem," for example.

PULLING IT ALL TOGETHER

Now that you know how to prepare a first draft, you might find it helpful to examine the illustration below to see how the different parts of a draft can fit together. Keep in mind that not every essay you write will take this shape. As your purpose, audience, tone, and point of view change, so will your essay's structure. An introduction or conclusion, for instance, may be developed in more than one paragraph; the thesis statement may be implied or delayed until the essay's middle or end; not all paragraphs may have topic sentences; and several supporting paragraphs may be needed to develop a single topic sentence. Even so, the basic format presented here offers a strategy for organizing a variety of writing assignments—from term papers to lab reports. Once you feel comfortable with the structure, you have a foundation on which to base your variations. (This book's student and professional essays illustrate some possibilities.) Even when using a specific format, you always have room to give your spirit and imagination free play. The language you use, the details you select, the perspective you offer are uniquely yours. They are what make your essay different from anyone else's.

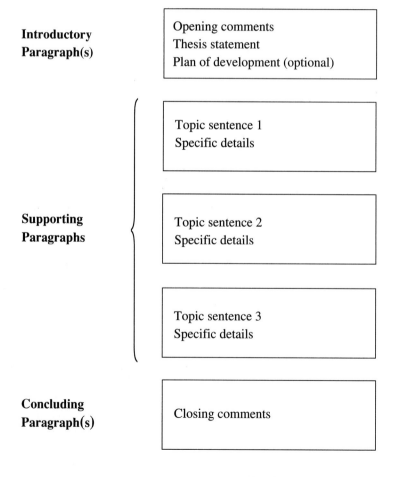

Introductory Paragraph(s)

Opening comments
Thesis statement
Plan of development (optional)

Supporting Paragraphs

Topic sentence 1
Specific details

Topic sentence 2
Specific details

Topic sentence 3
Specific details

Concluding Paragraph(s)

Closing comments

SAMPLE FIRST DRAFT

Here is the first draft of Harriet Davids's essay. (You saw Harriet's prewriting scratch list on pages 32–33, her thesis on page 32, and so on). Harriet wrote the draft in one sitting. Working at a computer, she started by typing her thesis at the top of the first page. Then, following the guidelines on pages 63–64, she moved the material in her outline (pages 58–59) to her draft. (See page 66 for an explanation of the differences between her outline and draft.) Harriet worked rapidly; she started with the first body paragraph and wrote straight through to the last supporting paragraph.

By moving quickly, Harriet got down her essay's basic text rather easily. Once she felt she had captured in rough form what she wanted to say, she reread her draft to get a sense of how she might open and close the essay. Then she drafted her introduction and conclusion; both appear here, together with the body of the essay. (The commentary following the draft will give you an even clearer sense of how Harriet proceeded.)

Challenges for Today's Parents

by Harriet Davids

Thesis: Being a parent today is much more difficult than it was a generation ago.

Raising children used to be much simpler in the 50s and 60s. I remember TV images from that era showing that parenting involved simply teaching kids to clean their rooms, do their homework, and _____ . But being a parent today is much more difficult because nowadays parents have to shield/protect kids from lots of things, like distractions from schoolwork, from sexual material, and from dangerous situations.

Add specifics

Parents have to control all the new distractions/temptations that turn kids away from schoolwork. These days many kids have stereos and televisions in their rooms. Certainly, my girls can't resist the urge to listen to MTV, especially if it's time to do homework. Unfortunately, though, kids aren't assigned much homework and what is assigned too often is busywork. And there are even more distractions outside the home. Teens no longer hang out/congregate on the corner where Dad and Mom can yell to them to come home and do homework. Instead they hang out at the mall, in video arcades, and at fast-food restaurants. Obviously, parents and school can't compete with all this.

Weak transition   (Also,) parents have to help kids develop responsible sexual
values even though sex is everywhere. Kids see sex magazines
and dirty paperbacks in the corner store where they used to get
candy and comic books. And instead of the artsy nude shots of
the past, kids see ronchey (sp?), explicit shots in <u>Playboy</u> and
<u>Hustler</u>. And movies have sexy stuff in them today. Teachers
seduce students and people treat sex casually/as a sport. Not
exactly traditional values. Even worse is what's on TV. Kids
see soap-opera characters in bed and cable shows full of nudity
by just flipping the dial. (FIX) The situation has gotten so
out of hand that maybe the government should establish
guidelines on what's permissible.

   Worst of all are the life-threatening dangers that parents
must help children fend off over the years. With older kids,
drugs fall into place as a main concern (Awk). Peer pressure to
try drugs is bigger (wrong word) to kids than their parents'
warnings. Other kinds of warnings are common when children are
small. Then parents fear violence since news shows constantly
report stories of little children being abused (add specifics).
And when kids aren't much older, they have to resist the
pressure to drink.(Alcohol has always attracted kids, but
nowadays they are drinking more and this can be deadly,   *Redo*
especially when drinking is combined with driving.)

   Most adults love their children and want to be good
parents. But it's difficult because the world seems stacked
against young people. Even Holden Caufield (sp?) had trouble
dealing with society's confusing pressures. Parents must give
their children some freedom but not so much that the kids lose
sight of what's important.

<table>
<tr><td>Student
essay in
progress</td></tr>
</table>

Commentary

   As you can see, Harriet's draft is rough. Because she knew she would revise
later on (pages 101 and 129), she "zapped out" the draft in an informal, colloquial
style. For example, she occasionally expressed her thoughts in fragments ("Not
exactly traditional values"), relied heavily on "and" as a transition, and used
slangy expressions such as "kids," "dirty paperbacks," and "lots of things." Similarly, rather than finetuning, Harriet simply made marginal or parenthetical notes
to herself: "redo" or "fix" to signal awkward sentences; "add specifics" to mark
overly general statements; "wrong word" after an imprecise word; "sp" to remind
herself to check spelling in the dictionary; "weak transition" to indicate where a

stronger signaling device was needed. Note, too, that she used slashes between alternative word choices and left a blank space when wording just wouldn't come. (Harriet's final draft appears on pages 137–139.)

Contin-
ues on
page 101

Writing a first draft may seem like quite a challenge, but the tips offered in this chapter should help you proceed with confidence. Indeed, as you work on the draft, you may be surprised by how much you enjoy writing. After all, this is your chance to get down on paper something you want to say.

ACTIVITIES: WRITING THE PARAGRAPHS IN THE FIRST DRAFT

1. For each paragraph that follows, determine whether the topic sentence is stated or implied. If the topic sentence is explicit, indicate its location in the paragraph (beginning, end, middle, or both beginning and end). If the topic sentence is implied, state it in your own words.

a.   In 1902, a well-known mathematician wrote an article "prov-
    ing" that no airplane could ever fly. Just a year later, the
    Wright brothers made their first flight. In the 1950s, a famed
    British astronomer said in an interview that the idea of space
    travel was "utter bilge." Similarly, noted scholars in this
    country and abroad claimed that automobiles would never replace
    the trolley car and that the electric light was an impractical
    gimmick. Clearly, being an expert doesn't guarantee a clear
    vision of the future.

b.   Motorists in Caracas, Venezuela, must follow an odd/even
    license-number system for driving their cars on any given day.
    Cars with license plates ending in even numbers can drive down-
    town only on even-numbered days. Similarly, in Los Angeles sev-
    eral summers ago, an experimental program required businesses
    with more than one hundred employees to form "Don't drive to
    work" programs. Such programs established ride-sharing sched-
    ules and offered employees incentives for using mass transpor-
    tation. Even more extreme is Singapore's method for limiting

downtown traffic--most private vehicles are completely banned
from central sections of the city.

c.   A small town in Massachusetts that badly needed extra space
for grade school classes found it in an unlikely spot. Most of
the town's available buildings were too far from the main
school or too small. One building, however, was nearby and spacious; it even offered excellent lunchroom and recreation
facilities. Despite some objections, the building was chosen--
a former saloon, complete with bar, bar stools, cocktail
lounge, and pool hall.

d.   The physical complaints of neurotics--people who are
exceptionally anxious, pessimistic, hostile, or tense--were
once largely ignored by physicians. Many doctors believed that
neurotics' frequent health complaints simply reflected their
emotional distress. New research, though, shows that neurotics
are indeed likely to have physical problems. Specifically,
researchers have found that neurotics stand a greater chance
of suffering from arthritis, asthma, ulcers, headaches, and
heart disease. In addition, there is growing evidence that
people who were chronically anxious or depressed in their
teens and twenties are more likely to become ill, even die,
in their forties.

e.   Many American companies have learned the hard way that they
need to know the language of their foreign customers. When
Chevrolet began selling its Nova cars in Latin America, hardly
anyone would buy them. The company finally realized that Spanish speakers read the car's name as the Spanish phrase "no va,"
meaning "doesn't go." When Pepsi-Cola ran its "Pepsi gives you
life" ads in China, consumers either laughed or were offended.
The company hadn't translated its slogan quite right. In Chinese, the slogan came out "Pepsi brings your ancestors back
from the dead."

2. Using the strategies described on pages 70–71, strengthen the following vague
paragraphs. Elaborate each one with striking specifics that clarify meaning and
add interest. As you provide specifics, you may need to break each paragraph into
several.

a.   Other students can make studying in the college library
difficult. For one thing, they take up so much space that they

leave little room for anyone else. By being inconsiderate in other ways, they make it hard to concentrate on the task at hand. Worst of all, they do things that make it almost impossible to find needed books and magazines.

b.   Some people have dangerous driving habits. They act as though there's no one else on the road. They also seem unsure of where they're going. Changing their minds from second to second, they leave it up to others to figure out what they're going to do. Finally, too many people drive at speeds that are either too slow or too fast, creating dangerous situations for both drivers and pedestrians.

c.   Things people used to think were safe are now considered dangerous. This goes for certain foods that are now considered unhealthy. Similarly, some habits people thought were harmless have been found to be risky. Even things in the home, in the workplace, and in the air have been found to cause harm. So much has been discovered in recent years about what is harmful that it makes you wonder: What additional dangers lurk in the environment?

d.   Society encourages young people to drink. For one thing, youngsters learn early that alcohol plays a prominent role in family and business celebrations. Children also see that liquor is an important part of adults' celebration of national holidays. But the place where youngsters see alcohol depicted most enticingly is on TV. Prime-time shows and beer commercials imply that alcohol is an essential part of a good life.

3. Using the designations indicated in parentheses, identify the flaw(s) in the development of each of the following paragraphs. The paragraphs may lack one or more of the following: unity (U), specific and sufficient support (S), coherence (C). The paragraphs may also needlessly repeat a point (R). Revise the paragraphs, deleting, combining, and rearranging material. Also, add supporting evidence and signal devices where needed.

a.   Studies reveal that individuals' first names can influence other people's perceptions. Some names reflect favorably on individuals. For example, a survey conducted by Opinion Masters, Inc., showed that male business executives thought the names <u>Dorothy</u> and <u>Katherine</u> conveyed competence and professionalism. And participants in a British study reported that names like <u>Richard</u> and <u>Charles</u> commanded respect and sounded "classy." Of course, participants' observations also reflect the fairly rigid stratification of British society. Other names, however, can have a negative impact. In one study, for instance, teachers gave lower grades to essays supposedly written by boys named <u>Hubert</u> and <u>Elmer</u> than to the very same essays when credited to boys with more popular names. Another study found that girls with unpopular names (like <u>Gertrude</u> or <u>Gladys</u>) did worse on tests than girls with more appealing names. Such findings underscore the arbitrary nature of the grading process.

b.   This "me first" attitude is also behind the cheating that seems prevalent nowadays. School is perhaps the first place where widespread cheating occurs, with students devising shrewd strategies to do well--often at the expense of others. And since schools are reluctant to teach morality, children grow up with distorted values. The same exaggerated self-interest often causes people, once they reach adulthood, to cheat their companies and co-workers. It's no wonder American business is in such trouble.

c.   Despite widespread belief to the contrary, brain size within a species has little to do with how intelligent a particular individual is. A human brain can range from 900 cubic centimeters to as much as 2,500 cubic centimeters, but a large brain does not indicate an equally large degree of intelligence. If humans could see the size of other people's brains, they would probably judge each other accordingly, even though brain size has no real significance.

d.   For the 50 percent of adult Americans with high cholesterol, heart disease is a constant threat. Americans can reduce their cholesterol significantly by taking a number of easy steps. Since only foods derived from animals contain cholesterol, eating a strict vegetarian diet is the best way to beat the cholesterol problem. Also, losing weight is known to reduce cholesterol levels--even in those who were as little as ten pounds overweight. Physicians warn, though, that quick weight loss almost always leads to an equally rapid regaining of the lost pounds. For those unwilling to try a vegetarian diet, poultry, fish, and low-fat dairy products can substitute for such high-cholesterol foods as red meat, eggs, cream, and butter. Adding oat bran to the diet has been shown to lower cholesterol. The bran absorbs excess cholesterol in the blood and removes it from the body through waste matter.

4. Strengthen the coherence of the following paragraphs by providing a clear organizational structure and by adding appropriate signal devices. To improve the flow of ideas, you may also need to combine and resequence sentences.

I was a camp counselor this past summer. I learned that leading young children is different from leading people your own age. I was president of my high school Ecology Club. I ran it democratically. We wanted to bring a speaker to the school. We decided to do a fund-raiser. I solicited ideas from everybody. We got together to figure out which was best. It became obvious which was the most profitable and workable fund-raiser. Everybody got behind the effort. The discussion showed that the idea of a raffle with prizes donated by local merchants was the most profitable.

I learned that little kids operate differently. I had to be more of a boss rather than a democratic leader. I took suggestions from the group on the main activity of the day. Everyone voted for the best suggestion. Some kids got especially upset. There was a problem with kids whose ideas were voted down. I learned to make the suggestions myself. The children could vote on my suggestions. No one was overly attached to any of the suggestions. They felt that the outcome of the voting was fair. Basically, I got to be in charge.

5. For an essay with the thesis shown here, indicate the implied pattern(s) of development for each topic sentence that follows.

Thesis: The college should make community service a requirement for graduation.

Topic Sentences

a. "Mandatory community service" is a fairly new and often misunderstood concept.
b. Certainly, the conditions in many communities signal serious need.
c. Here's the story of one student's community involvement.
d. There are, though, many other kinds of programs in which students can become involved.
e. Indeed, a single program offers students numerous opportunities.

    f. Such involvement can have a real impact on students' lives.

    g. This is the way mandatory community service might work on this campus.

    h. However, the college could adopt two very different approaches—one developed by a university, the other by a community college.

    i. In any case, the college should begin exploring the possibility of making community service a graduation requirement.

6. Select one of the topic sentences listed in activity 5. Use individual or group brainstorming to generate support for it. After reviewing your raw material, delete, add, and combine points as needed. Finally, with the thesis in mind, write a rough draft of the paragraph.

7. Imagine you plan to write a serious essay on one of the following thesis statements. The paper will be read by students in your composition class. After determining your point of view, use any prewriting techniques you want to identify the essay's major and supporting points. Arrange the points in order and determine where background and/or transitional paragraphs might be helpful.

    a. Society needs stricter laws against noise pollution.

    b. The traditional lecture format used in many large colleges and universities discourages independent thinking.

    c. Public buildings in this town should be redesigned to accommodate the disabled.

    d. Long-standing discrimination against women in college athletics must stop.

8. Use any of the techniques described on pages 76–81 to revise the opening and closing paragraphs of two of your own papers. When rewriting, don't forget to keep your purpose, audience, tone, and point of view in mind.

9. Reread Harriet Davids's first draft on pages 83–84. Overall, does it support Harriet's thesis? Which topic sentences focus paragraphs effectively? Where is evidence specific, unified, and coherent? Where does Harriet run into some problems? Make a list of the draft's strengths and weaknesses. Save your list for later review. (In the next chapter, you'll be asked to revise Harriet's draft.)

10. Freewrite or write in your journal about a subject that's been on your mind lately. Reread your raw material to see what thesis seems to emerge. What might your purpose, audience, tone, and point of view be if you wrote an essay with this thesis? What primary and secondary points would you cover? Prepare an outline of your ideas. Then draft the essay's body, providing background and transitional paragraphs if appropriate. Finally, write a rough version of the essay's introduction, conclusion, and title. (Save your draft so you can revise it after reading the next chapter.)

11. If you prepared a first draft in response to activity 3 in Chapter 5 (page 61), work with at least one other person to strengthen that early draft by applying the ideas presented in this chapter. (Save this stronger version of your draft so you can refine it further after reading the next chapter.)

12. Referring to the outline you prepared in response to activity 5 or activity 6 in Chapter 5 (pages 61–62), draft the body of an essay. After reviewing the draft, prepare background and transitional paragraphs as needed. Then draft a rough introduction, conclusion, and title. Ask several people to react to what you've prepared, and save your draft so you can work with it further after reading the next chapter.

7
REVISING OVERALL MEANING, STRUCTURE, AND PARAGRAPH DEVELOPMENT

BY now, you've probably abandoned any preconceptions you might have had about good writers sitting down and creating a finished product in one easy step. Alexander Pope's comment that "true ease in writing comes from art, not chance" is as true today as it was more than two hundred years ago. Writing that seems effortlessly clear is often the result of sustained work, not of good luck or even inborn talent. And much of this work takes place during the final stage of the writing process, when ideas, paragraphs, sentences, and words are refined and reshaped.

You've most likely seen cartoons picturing writers plugging away at their typewriters, filling their wastebaskets with sheet after sheet of crumpled paper. It's true. Professional writers—novelists, journalists, textbook authors—seldom submit a piece of writing that hasn't been revised. They recognize that rough, unpolished work doesn't do them justice. What's more, they often look forward to revising. Columnist Ellen Goodman puts it this way: "What makes me happy is rewriting. ... It's like cleaning house, getting rid of all the junk, getting things in the right order, tightening up."

In a sense, revision occurs throughout the writing process: At some earlier stage, you may have dropped an idea, overhauled your thesis, or shifted paragraph order. What, then, is different about the rewriting that occurs in the revision stage? The answer has to do with the literal meaning of the word *revision*—reseeing, or seeing again. Genuine revision involves casting clear eyes on your work, viewing it as though you're a reader rather than the writer. Revision is not, as some believe, simply touch-up work—changing a sentence here, a word there, eliminating spelling errors, typing a neat final copy. Revision means that you go through your paper looking for trouble, ready to pick a fight with your own writing. And then you must be willing to sit down and make the changes needed for your writing to be as effective as possible.

Throughout this book, we emphasize that everyone approaches early stages in the writing process differently. The same is true for the revision stage. Some people dash off a draft, knowing they'll spend hours reworking it later. Others find that writing the first draft slowly yields such good results that wholesale revision isn't necessary. Some writers revise neatly, while others fill their drafts with messily scribbled changes. Then there are those who find that the more they revise, the more they overcomplicate their writing and rob it of spontaneity. So, for each writer and for each piece of writing, the amount and kind of revision will vary.

Because revision is hard work, you may resist it. After putting the final period in your first draft, you may feel done and have trouble accepting that more work remains. Or, as you read the draft, you may see so many weak spots that you view revision as punishment for not getting things right the first time. And, if you feel shaky about how to proceed, you may be tempted to skip revising altogether.

If all this sounds as though we're talking about you, don't give up. Here are seven strategies to help you get going if you balk at or feel overwhelmed by revising.

STRATEGIES TO MAKE REVISION EASIER

Keep in mind that the revision strategies discussed here should be adapted to each writing situation. Revising an answer on an essay exam is quite different from revising a paper you've spent several weeks preparing. Other considerations include your professor's requirements and expectations, the time available, and the paper's bearing on your grade. In any case, the following strategies will help you approach revision more confidently.

Set Your First Draft Aside for a While

When you pick up your draft after having set it aside for a time, you'll approach it with a fresh, more objective point of view. How much of an interval to leave depends on the time available to you. In general, though, the more time between finishing the draft and starting to revise, the better.

Work from Typed or Printed Text

Working with an essay in impersonal typewritten form, instead of in your own familiar handwriting, helps you see the paper impartially, as if someone else had written it. Each time you make major changes, try to retype your essay so that you can see it anew. Using a word processor makes it easy to prepare successive copies. If, however, you work from handwritten drafts, don't boldly strike out or erase as you revise. Instead, lightly cross out material, in case you want to retrieve it later on.

Read the Draft Aloud

Hearing how your writing sounds helps you pick up problems that might otherwise go undetected: places where sentences are awkward, meaning is ambiguous, words are imprecise. Even better, have another person read your draft aloud to you. The thought of this probably makes you shudder, but it's worth the risk. Someone else doesn't have—as you do—a vested interest in making your writing sound good. If a reader slows to a crawl over a murky paragraph or trips over a convoluted sentence, you know where you have to do some rewriting.

React to Your Instructor's Comments

Your instructor may use several methods to give feedback on your writing. You may submit a first draft and then meet with the instructor to go over it in conference. At the conference, you may see your instructor's comments recorded on the draft, or the draft may be unmarked because your instructor—thinking you may be distracted by comments—has made notes on a separate piece of paper. Alternatively, your instructor may return your draft accompanied by typed, written, or taped feedback to you to consider before you resubmit the paper for a grade. And, of course, there's the traditional kind of instructor feedback: comments entered in the margin and at the end of the paper, including a grade.

Like many students, you may be tempted to look only briefly at your instructor's comments. Perhaps you've "had it" with the essay and don't want to think about preparing a revised version that reflects the instructor's remarks. And if there's a grade on the essay, you may think that's the only thing that counts. But remember: Although grades are important, comments are even more so. They can help you *improve* your writing—if not in this paper, then in the next one. So, if you're reading or listening to your instructor's feedback, pay close attention and take notes. Then use a modified version of the feedback chart or a system of marginal annotations (see pages 96–97) to help you evaluate and react to the instructor's comments. If you don't understand or don't agree with the instructor's observations, don't hesitate to request a conference. Be sure to go to the conference prepared. You might, for example, put a check next to the instructor's comments you want to discuss. Your instructor will appreciate your thoughtful planning; getting together gives both you and the instructor a chance to clarify your respective points of view.

Participate in Peer Feedback Sessions

Writing is social and interactive; it promotes dialog. For this reason, many instructors include peer feedback sessions as a regular part of a composition course. Or, if you like, you can set up feedback sessions on your own, adapting the suggestions in this and the following section to fit your needs.

Perhaps the idea of receiving (and giving) peer feedback seems strange to you. After all, what can "mere" students learn from each other? But collaborative feedback can be invaluable. For one thing, it increases your writing options by showing you how other students handle the same assignment. Peer feedback also reinforces the importance of audience analysis by reminding you that your instructor isn't your only reader. Finally, collaborative feedback encourages you to take a conscientious approach to your writing. Your classmates' comments can help you strengthen your writing before it undergoes your instructor's scrutiny. This fact alone will motivate you to put forth your best, most serious effort.

If you do set up your own peer feedback sessions, *select readers* who are *critical* (not a love-struck admirer or a doting grandparent) and who are *skilled* enough to provide useful commentary: other students taking similar courses, friends or family members who write on the job, staff in your college writing lab. To ensure that you leave feedback sessions with specific observations about what does and doesn't work in your writing, give your readers a clear sense of what you want from them. If you simply ask, "How's this?" you'll probably receive vague comments like "It's good" or "It's not very effective." What you want are *concrete observations and suggestions:* "I'm confused because what you say in the fifth sentence contradicts what you say in the second" or "You make the same point in the second and fourth paragraphs. Shouldn't the paragraphs be combined?"

To promote such specific responses, ask your readers *targeted questions:* "My introduction seems bland. What ideas do you have for perking it up?" or "I'm having trouble moving from my second to my third point. How can I make the transition smoother?" Questions like these require more than "yes" or "no" responses; they encourage readers to dig into your writing where you sense it needs work. You may develop your own questions or adapt the revision checklists in this and the following chapter.

If you're most concerned about your draft's overall meaning (pages 98–99), your readers don't necessarily need a copy of your essay. The draft can be read aloud so everyone can hear it. However, if you want feedback on individual paragraphs (pages 99–101) or on specific sentences and words (see Chapter 8), you must supply readers with copies of your draft.

Evaluate and Act on Peer Feedback

Accepting criticism isn't easy (even if you asked for it), and not all readers will be tactful. Even so, try to listen to others with an open mind and take notes on their observations. When everyone is finished commenting, reread your notes. Which remarks seem valid? Which recommendations are workable? Which are not? In addition, try using a feedback chart or a system of marginal annotations to help you evaluate and remedy any perceived weaknesses in your draft.

Here's how to use a three-column **feedback chart.** In the first column, list the major problems you and your readers see in the draft. Next, rank the problems, designating the most critical as 1. Then, in the second column, jot down possible solutions—your own as well as your readers'. Finally, in the third column, briefly describe what action you'll take to correct each problem. Here is a sample chart:

	Problems	Suggestions	Decisions
④	Informal expressions in paragraph 3 seem out of keeping with the rest of the essay.	Lighten language elsewhere. Make the language in paragraph 3 less slangy.	Make language in paragraph 3 a bit more formal. Also make overall language less stiff, especially in paragraphs 2 and 5.
①	Thesis in introduction contradicted by paragraph 2.	Delete paragraph 2. Qualify the thesis so that there's no contradiction.	Qualify thesis.
②	Chronological order used until paragraph 4. That background paragraph breaks the flow.	Delete background paragraph. Move paragraph to beginning. Add transition so paragraph fits more easily.	Delete background paragraph--not needed, except for definition, which can be added to introduction.
③	Too many long sentences	Eliminate some prepositional phrases. Break up long sentences into shorter ones.	Take out some prepositional phrases.

If you don't use a feedback chart, be sure to enter **marginal annotations** on your draft before revising it. In the margins, jot down any major problems, numbered in order of importance, along with possible remedies. Marking your draft this way, much as an instructor might, helps you view your paper as though it were written by someone else. Then, keeping the draft's problems in mind, start revising. You may make changes directly above the appropriate line, or, when necessary, rework sections on a separate sheet of paper. To see how such marginal annotations work, turn to page 101 or look at the sample first drafts of student essays in Chapters 11–19.

View Revision as a Series of Steps

The six revision techniques described so far will help you approach revision with more confidence. We've saved for last, though, the strategy we consider most critical: dividing revision into steps.

You can overcome a bad case of revision jitters simply by viewing revision as a process. Instead of trying to tackle all of a draft's problems at once, proceed step by step. (The feedback chart and annotation system will help you do just that.) If time allows, read your essay several times. Move from a broad overview (the *macro* level) to an up-close look at mechanics (the *micro* level). With each reading, focus on different issues and ask different questions about the draft.

Here is a recommended series of revision steps:

First step: Revise overall meaning and structure.

Second step: Revise paragraph development.

Third step: Revise sentences and words.

At first, the prospect of reading and rewriting a paper several times may seem to make revision more, not less, overwhelming. Eventually, though, you'll become accustomed to revision as a process, and you'll appreciate the way such an approach improves your writing.

Ernest Hemingway once told an interviewer that he had revised the last page of one of his novels thirty-nine times. When the interviewer asked, "What was it that had you stumped?" Hemingway answered, "Getting the words right." We don't expect you to revise your paper thirty-nine times. Whenever possible, though, you should aim for three readings. Resist the impulse to tinker with, say, an unclear sentence until you're sure the essay as a whole makes its point clearly. After all, it can be difficult to rephrase a muddy sentence until you have the essay's overall meaning well in hand.

Remember, though: There are no hard-and-fast rules about the revision steps. For one thing, there are bound to be occasions when you have time for, at best, only one quick pass over a draft. Moreover, as you gain experience revising, you'll probably streamline the process or shift the steps around. Assume, for example, that you get bogged down trying to recast the thesis so it more accurately reflects the draft's overall meaning (the first step). You might take a break by fastforwarding to the final stage and using the dictionary to check the spelling of several words. Or, while reorganizing a paragraph (the second step), you might realize you need to rephrase some sentences (the third step).

The remainder of this chapter discusses the first and second steps in the revision process—revising overall meaning and structure and paragraph development. Chapter 8 focuses on the third step—revising sentences and words.

REVISING OVERALL MEANING AND STRUCTURE

During this first step in the revision process, you (and any readers you may have) should read the draft quickly to assess its *general effect* and *clarity.* Does the draft accomplish what you set out to do? Does it develop a central point clearly and logically? Does it merit and hold the reader's attention?

It's not uncommon when revising at this stage to find that the draft doesn't fully convey what you had in mind. Perhaps your intended thesis ends up being overshadowed by another idea. (If that happens, you have two options: (1) you may pursue the new line of thought as your revised thesis, or (2) you may bring the paper back into line with your original thesis by deleting extraneous material.) Another problem might be that readers miss a key point. Perhaps you initially believed the point could be implied, but you now realize it needs to be stated explicitly.

Preparing a *brief outline* of a draft can help evaluate the essay's overall structure. Either you or another reader can prepare the outline. In either case, your thesis, reflecting any changes made during the first draft, should be written at the top of the outline page. Then you or your readers jot down in brief outline form the paper's basic structure. With the draft pared down to its essentials, you can see more easily how parts contribute to the whole and how points do or do not fit together. This bare-bones rendering often reveals the changes needed to remedy any fuzziness or illogic in the development of the draft's central idea and key supporting points.

The following checklist is designed to help you and your readers evaluate a draft's overall meaning and structure. As with other checklists in the book, you may either use all the checklist questions or focus only on those especially relevant to a particular essay. (Activities at the end of the chapter will refer you to this checklist when you revise several essays.) To see how one student used the checklist when revising, turn to page 101.

☑ REVISING OVERALL MEANING AND STRUCTURE:
A CHECKLIST

☐ What is your initial reaction to the draft? What do you like and dislike?

☐ What audience does the essay address? How suited to this audience are the essay's purpose, tone, and point of view?

☐ What is the essay's thesis? Is it explicitly stated or implied? If the perceived thesis isn't what was intended, what changes need to be made?

☐ What are the essay's main points? If any stray from or contradict the thesis, what changes need to be made?

☐ According to what organizing principle(s)—spatial, chronological, emphatic, simple to complex—are the main points arranged? How does this organizational scheme reinforce the thesis?

☐ Which patterns of development (narration, description, comparison-contrast, and so on) help shape the draft? How do these patterns reinforce the thesis?

☐ Where would background information, definition of terms, or additional material clarify meaning?

You are now ready to focus on the second step in the revising process.

REVISING PARAGRAPH DEVELOPMENT

After you use feedback to refine the paper's fundamental meaning and structure, it's time to look closely at the essay's paragraphs. At this point, you and those giving you feedback should read the draft more slowly. How can the essay's paragraphs be made more unified (see pages 68–69) and more specific (pages 69–71)? Which paragraphs seem to lack sufficient support (pages 71–72)? Which would profit from more attention to coherence (pages 72–75)?

At this stage, you may find that a paragraph needs more examples to make its point or that a paragraph should be deleted because it doesn't develop the thesis. Or perhaps you realize that a paragraph should be placed earlier in the essay because it defines a term that readers need to understand from the outset.

Here's a strategy to help assess your paragraphs' effectiveness. In the margin next to each paragraph, make a brief notation that answers these two questions: (1) What is the paragraph's *purpose*? and (2) What is its *content*? Then skim the marginal notes to see if each paragraph does what you intended.

During this stage, you should also examine the *length of your paragraphs.* Here's why.

You know how boring it can be to travel long stretches of unvarying highway. Without interesting twists and turns, sweeping views, and occasional rest stops, you struggle to stay awake. The same is true in writing. Paragraphs all the same length dull your readers' response, while variations encourage them to sit up and take notice. (We imagine, for example, that the two-sentence paragraph above got your attention.)

If your paragraphs tend to run long, try breaking some of them into shorter, crisper chunks. Be sure, however, not to break paragraphs just anywhere. To preserve the paragraphs' logic, you may need to reshape and add material, always keeping in mind that each paragraph should have a clear and distinctive focus.

However, don't go overboard and break up all your paragraphs. Too many short paragraphs become as predictable as too many long ones. An abundance of brief paragraphs also makes it difficult for readers to see how points are related. (In such cases, you might combine short paragraphs containing similar ideas.) Furthermore, overreliance on short paragraphs may mean that you haven't provided sufficient evidence for your ideas. Finally, a succession of short paragraphs (as in a newspaper article) encourages readers to skim when, of course, you want them to consider carefully what you have to say. So use short paragraphs, but save them for places in the essay where you want to introduce variation or achieve emphasis.

The following checklist is designed to help you and your readers evaluate a draft's paragraph development. (Activities at the end of the chapter will refer you to the checklist when you revise several essays.) To see how a student used the checklist when revising, turn to page 101.

✔ REVISING PARAGRAPH DEVELOPMENT: A CHECKLIST

☐ In what way does each supporting paragraph develop the essay's thesis? Which paragraphs fail to develop the thesis? Should they be deleted or revised?

☐ What is each paragraph's central idea? If this idea is expressed in a topic sentence, where is this sentence located? Where does something stray from or contradict the paragraph's main idea? How could the paragraph's focus be sharpened?

☐ Where in each paragraph does support seem irrelevant, vague, insufficient, inaccurate, nonrepresentative, or disorganized? What could be done to remedy these problems? Where would additional sensory details, examples, facts, statistics, expert authority, and personal observations be appropriate?

☐ By what organizational principle (spatial, chronological, or emphatic) are each paragraph's ideas arranged? Why is this the most effective order?

☐ How could paragraph coherence be strengthened? What signal devices are used to relate ideas within and between paragraphs? Where are there too few signals? Too many?

☐ Where do too many paragraphs of the same length dull interest? Where would a short paragraph be more effective? A long one?

☐ How could the introduction be strengthened? What striking anecdote, fact, or statistic elsewhere in the essay might be moved to the introduction? How does the introduction establish the essay's purpose, audience, tone, and point of view? What strategy links the introduction to the essay's body?

> ☐ How could the conclusion be strengthened? What striking anecdote, fact, or statistic elsewhere in the essay might be moved to the conclusion? Would echoing something from the introduction help round off the essay more effectively? How has the conclusion been made an integral part of the essay?

SAMPLE STUDENT REVISION OF OVERALL MEANING, STRUCTURE, AND PARAGRAPH DEVELOPMENT

The introduction to Harriet Davids's first draft that we saw in Chapter 6 (pages 83–84) is reprinted here with Harriet's revisions. In the margin, numbered in order of importance, are the problems with the introduction's meaning, structure, and paragraph development—as noted by Harriet's editing group. (The group used the checklists on pages 98–99 and 100–101 to focus their critique.) The above-line changes show Harriet's first efforts to eliminate these problems through revision.

> Student essay in progress

In the 50s and 60s, parents had it easy. TV comedies of that period show the ~~Raising children used to be much simpler in the 50s and 60s. I~~

Cleavers scolding Beaver about his dirty hands, the Andersons telling Bud to do his ~~remember TV images from that era showing that parenting involved~~ homework, and the Nelsons telling Ricky to clean his room. ~~simply teaching kids to clean their rooms, do their homework,~~

> ② Take out personal reference

> ③ Give specific TV shows

and _____. ~~But~~ (B) being a parent today is much more difficult.

~~because~~ N~~owadays~~ parents ~~have to shield~~/ must protect ~~kids~~ their children from ~~lots of~~ many

—from a growing number of

things ~~like~~ distractions ~~from schoolwork,~~ from sexual material, and ly explicit

from dangerous situations.

> ① Thesis too long. Make plan of development separate sentence.

> Continues on page 128

(If you'd like to see Harriet's final draft, turn to page 137.)

There's no doubt about it: As Harriet's reworked introduction shows, revision is challenging. But once you learn how to approach it step by step, you'll have the pleasure of seeing a draft become sharper and more focused. The rather global work you do early in the revision process puts you in a good position to concentrate on sentences and words—our focus in the following chapter.

ACTIVITIES: REVISING OVERALL MEANING, STRUCTURE, AND PARAGRAPH DEVELOPMENT

An important note: When revising essay drafts in activities 1–3, don't worry too much about sentence structure and word choice. However, do save your revisions so you can focus on these matters after you read the next chapter.

1. On page 101, you saw the marginal notes and above-line changes that Harriet Davids added to her first draft introduction. Now look at the draft's other paragraphs on pages 83–84 and identify problems in overall meaning, structure, and paragraph development. Working alone or in a group, start by asking questions like these: "Where does the essay stray from the thesis?" and "Where does a paragraph fail to present points in the most logical and compelling order?" (The critique you prepared for activity 9 in Chapter 6 should help.) For further guidance, refer to the checklists on pages 98–99 and 100–101. Summarize and rank the perceived problems in marginal annotations or on a feedback chart. Then type your changes (into a word processor, if you use one), or enter them between the lines of the draft (work on a newly typed copy, a photocopy, or the textbook pages themselves). Don't forget to save your revision.

2. Retrieve the draft you prepared in response to activity 12 in Chapter 6 (page 91). Outline the draft. Does your outline reveal any problems in the draft's overall meaning and structure? If it does, make whatever changes are needed. The checklists on pages 98–99 and 100–101 will help focus your revising efforts. (Save your revised draft so you can work with it further after reading the next chapter.)

3. On the next page is the first draft of an essay advocating a longer elementary school day. Read it closely. Are tone and point of view consistent throughout? Is the thesis clear? Is the support in each body paragraph relevant, specific, and adequate? Are ideas arranged in the most effective order? Working alone or in a group, use the checklists on pages 98–99 and 100–101 to identify problems with the draft's overall meaning, structure, and paragraph development. Summarize and rank the perceived problems on a feedback chart or in marginal annotations. Then revise the draft by typing a new version or by entering your changes by hand (on a photocopy of the draft, a typed copy, or the textbook pages themselves). Don't forget to save your revision.

The Extended School Day

Imagine a seven-year-old whose parents work until five each night. When she arrives home after school, she is on her own. She's a good girl, but still a lot of things could happen. She could get into trouble just by being curious. Or something could happen through no fault of her own. All over the country, there are many "latchkey" children like this little girl. Some way must be found to deal with the problem. One suggestion is to keep elementary schools open longer than they now are. There are many advantages to this idea.

Parents wouldn't have to be in a state of uneasiness about whether their child is safe and happy at home. They wouldn't get uptight about whether their child's needs are being met. They also wouldn't have to feel guilty because they are not able to help a child with homework. The longer day would make it possible for the teacher to provide such help. Extended school hours would also relieve families of the financial burden of hiring a home sitter. As my family learned, having a sitter can wipe out the budget. And having a sitter doesn't necessarily eliminate all problems. Parents still have the hassle of worrying whether the person will show up and be reliable.

It's a fact of life that many children dislike school, which is a sad commentary on the state of education in this country. Even so, the longer school day would benefit children as well. Obviously, the dangers of their being home alone after school would disappear because by the time the bus dropped them off after the longer school day, at least one parent would be home. The unnameable horrors feared by parents would not have a chance to happen. Instead, the children would be in school, under trained supervision. There, they would have a chance to work on subjects that give them trouble. In contrast, when my younger brother had difficulty with subtraction in second grade, he had to struggle along because there wasn't enough time to give him the help he needed. The longer day would also give children a chance to participate in extracurricular activities. They could join a science club, play on a softball team, sing in a school chorus, take an art class. Because school districts are try-ing to save money, they often cut back on such extracurricular activities. They don't realize how important such experiences are.

Finally, the longer school day would also benefit teachers. Having more hours in each day would relieve them of a lot of pressure. This longer workday would obviously require schools to increase teachers' pay. The added salary would be an incentive for teachers to stay in the profession.

Implementing an extended school day would be expensive, but I feel that many communities would willingly finance its costs because it provides benefits to parents, children, and even teachers. Young children, home alone, wondering whether to watch another TV show or to wander outside to see what's happening, need this longer school day now.

4. Look closely at your instructor's comments on an ungraded draft of one of your essays. Using a feedback chart, summarize and evaluate your instructor's comments. That done, rework the essay. Type your new version, or make your changes by hand. In either case, save the revision so you can work with it further after reading the next chapter.

5. Return to the draft you wrote in response to activity 10 or activity 11 in Chapter 6 (page 90). To identify any problems, meet with several people and request that one of them read the draft aloud. Then ask your listeners focused questions about the areas you sense need work. Alternatively, you may use the checklist on pages 98–99 to focus the group's feedback. In either case, summarize and rank the comments on a feedback chart or in marginal annotations. Then, using the comments as a guide, revise the draft. Either type a new version or do your revising by hand. (Save your revision so you can work with it further after reading the next chapter.)

8
REVISING SENTENCES AND WORDS

REVISING SENTENCES

HAVING refined your essay's overall meaning, structure, and paragraph development, you can concentrate on sharpening individual sentences. Although polishing sentences inevitably involves decisions about individual words, for now focus on each sentence *as a whole;* you can evaluate individual words later. At this point, work to make your sentences

- consistent with your intended tone,
- economical,
- varied in type,
- varied in length, and
- emphatic.

Make Sentences Consistent with Your Tone

In Chapter 2, we saw how integral **tone** is to meaning (pages 22–23). As you revise, be sure each sentence's **content** (its images and ideas) and **style** (its structure and length) reinforce your intended tone: Both *what* you say and *how* you say it should support the essay's overall mood.

Consider the following excerpt from a piece by *Philadelphia Inquirer* columnist Melissa Dribben. Responding to the ongoing debate over gun control, Dribben

supports legislation sought by the mayor of Philadelphia to limit handgun purchases to one per person per month. She writes:

> There are people who buy a new toothbrush every month. A new vacuum-cleaner
> bag. A fresh box of baking soda. A pair of $5 sunglasses. This you understand. You
> can never have too many.
> But when you reach the point where you have a stash of .38-caliber pistols bigger
> than your supply of clean underwear, you have a problem. And it isn't a shopping
> addiction.

Dribben's tone here is biting and sarcastic; her attitude exasperated and mocking. She establishes this tone partly through sentence content (what she says). For
example, to her it is outrageous that people would want to buy guns more frequently than they purchase basic household and personal necessities. Dribben's
style (how she says it) also contributes to her overall tone. The three fragments in
the first paragraph convey an attitude of angry disbelief. These fragments, followed by two brief but complete sentences, build to the longer, climactic sentence
at the beginning of the second paragraph. That sentence, especially when combined with the crisp last sentence, delivers a final, quick jab to those opposed to
the proposed legislation. In short, content and style help express Dribben's impassioned attitude toward her subject.

Make Sentences Economical

Besides reinforcing your tone, your sentences should be **economical** rather
than wordy. Use as few, not as many, words as possible. Students sometimes pad
their writing because they think the longer a paper is, the higher grade it will
receive. Most instructors, though, are skilled at spotting wordiness intended only
to fill pages. Your sentences won't be wordy if you (1) eliminate redundancy,
(2) delete weak phrases, and (3) remove unnecessary *who, which,* and *that* clauses.

Eliminate Redundancy

Redundancy means unnecessary repetition. Sometimes words are repeated
exactly; sometimes they are repeated by way of *synonyms,* other words or phrases
that mean the same thing. When writing is redundant, words can be trimmed
away without sacrificing meaning or effect. Why, for example, write "In the expert
opinion of one expert" and needlessly repeat the word *expert*? Similarly, "They
found it difficult to get consensus or agreement about the proposal" contains an
unnecessary synonym (*agreement*) for *consensus.*
Redundancy isn't the same as repetition for dramatic emphasis. Consider the
following excerpt from an address to the United Nations by John F. Kennedy:

> Unconditional war can no longer lead to unconditional victory. It can no longer
> serve to settle disputes. It can no longer be of concern to great powers alone....

Here the repetition of *unconditional* and *can no longer* drives home the urgency of
Kennedy's message. Repetition used, in this way, to underscore the relationship

among sentences or ideas is called *parallelism*. (For more on parallelism, see pages 115–116.)

When not used as a stylistic device, however, repetition weakens prose. Take a look at the sentence pairs below. Note how the revised versions are clearer and stronger because the redundancy in the original sentences (italicized) has been eliminated:

Original   While under the *influence* of alcohol, many people insist they are not under the *influence* and *swear* they are sober.

Revised   While under the influence of alcohol, many people insist they are sober.

Original   *They designed a computer program* that increased sales by 50 percent. The *computer program they designed* showed how the TRS-80 can be *used* and *implemented* in small *businesses* and *firms*.

Revised   Their program, which showed how the TRS-80 computer can be used in small businesses, increased sales by 50 percent.

Delete Weak Phrases

In addition to eliminating redundancy, you can make sentences more economical by **deleting the three types of weak phrases** described here.

1. *Empty Phrases.* In speaking, we frequently use empty phrases that give us time to think but don't add to our message—expressions such as "Okay?" and "You know what I mean?" In writing, though, we have the chance to eliminate such deadwood. Here are some common culprits—expressions that are needlessly awkward and wordy—along with their one-word alternatives:

Wordy Expressions	Revised
due to the fact that	because
in light of the fact that	since
regardless of the fact that	although
in the event that	if
in many cases	often
in that period	then
at the present time	now
at this point in time	now
in the not-too-distant future	soon
for the purpose of	to
has the ability to	can
be aware of the fact that	know
is necessary that	must

Notice the improvement in the following sentences when wordy, often awkward phrases are replaced with one-word substitutes:

Original *It is necessary that* the government outlaw the production of carcinogenic pesticides.
Revised The government *must* outlaw the production of carcinogenic pesticides.

Original Student leaders were upset by *the fact that* no one in the administration consulted them.
Revised Student leaders were upset *because* no one in the administration consulted them.

Some phrases don't even call for concise substitutes. Because they add nothing at all to a sentence's meaning, they can simply be deleted. Here are some examples: "shy *type of* child," "*kind of* person," "*field of* communications," "small *in size.*" The revised sentence that follows has exactly the same meaning as the original, but the meaning is expressed without the empty phrase *in color:*

Original The hybrid azaleas were light blue *in color.*
Revised The hybrid azaleas were light blue.

Other times, to avoid an empty phrase, you may need to recast a sentence slightly:

Original The midterm assessment is *for the purpose of letting* students know if they are failing a course.
Revised The midterm assessment *lets* students know if they are failing a course.

2. *Roundabout Openings with* **There, It, and Question Words like How and What.** At the beginning of a sentence, you're formulating a new thought, so you may grope around a bit before pinning down what you want to say. For this rea-
son, the openings of sentences are especially vulnerable to unnecessary phrases. Common culprits include phrases beginning with *There* and *It* (when *It* does not refer to a specific noun), and words like *How* and *What* (when they don't actually ask a question). In the following examples, note that trimming away excess words highlights the subject and verb, thus clarifying meaning:

Original It was their belief that the problem had been solved.
Revised They believed the problem had been solved.

Original There are now computer courses offered by many high schools.
Revised Many high schools now offer computer courses.

Original What should be done in this crisis is to transport food to the victims' homes.
Revised Food must be transported to the victims' homes.

Original How to simplify the college's registration process should be a priority.
Revised Simplifying the college's registration process should be a priority.

Of course, feel free to open with *There* or *It* when some other construction would be less clear or effective. For example, don't write "Many reasons can be cited why students avoid art courses" when you can say "There are many reasons why students avoid art courses."

3. *Excessive Prepositional Phrases.* Strings of prepositional phrases (word groups beginning with *at, on,* and the like) tend to make writing choppy; they weigh sentences down and hide main ideas. Note how much smoother and clearer sentences become when prepositional phrases (italicized in the following examples) are eliminated:

Original   Growth *in the greenhouse effect* may result *in increases in the intensity of hurricanes.*
Revised   The growing greenhouse effect may intensify hurricanes.

Original   The reassurance *of a neighbor* who was the owner *of a pit bull* that his dog was incapable *of harm* would not be sufficient to prevent most parents *from calling* the authorities if the dog ran loose.
Revised   Despite a neighbor's reassurance that his pit bull was harmless, most parents would call the authorities if the dog ran loose.

These examples show that prepositional phrases can sometimes be eliminated by substituting one strong verb (*intensify*) or by using the possessive form (*neighbor's reassurance, his pit bull*) rather than an *of* phrase.

Remove Unnecessary *Who, Which,* and *That* Clauses

Often *who, which,* or *that* clauses can be removed with no loss of meaning. Consider the tightening possible in these sentences:

Original   The townsfolk misunderstood the main point *that the developer made.*
Revised   The townsfolk misunderstood *the developer's main point.*

Original   The employees *who protested* the restrictions went on strike, *which was a real surprise to management.*
Revised   The employees *protesting* the restrictions *surprised management* by going on strike.

Vary Sentence Type

Another way to invigorate writing is to **vary sentence type.** Since the predictable soon becomes dull, try to offer a mixture of simple, compound, complex, and compound-complex sentences.

Simple Sentences

A **clause** is a group of words with both a subject and a verb. Clauses can be **independent** (able to stand alone) or **dependent** (unable to stand alone). A **simple**

sentence consists of a single independent clause (whose subject and verb are italicized here):

> The *president serves* four years.
>
> *Marie Curie investigated* radioactivity and *died* from its effects.
>
> Unlike most mammals, *birds* and *fish see* color.

Notice that a simple sentence can have more than one verb (sentence 2) or more than one subject (sentence 3). In addition, any number of modifying phrases (such as *Unlike most mammals*) can extend the sentence's length and add information. What distinguishes a simple sentence is its single *subject-verb combination*.

Simple sentences can convey dramatic urgency:

> Suddenly we heard the screech of brakes. Across the street, a small boy lay sprawled in front of a car. We started to run toward the child. Seeing us, the driver sped away.

Simple sentences are also excellent for singling out a climactic point: "They found the solution." In a series, however, they soon lose their impact and become boring. Also, because simple sentences highlight one idea at a time, they don't clarify the relationships among ideas. Consider these two versions of a passage:

Original

> Many first-year college students are apprehensive. They won't admit it to themselves. They hesitate to confide in their friends. They never find out that everyone else is anxious, too. They are nervous about being disliked and feeling lonely. They fear not "knowing the ropes."

Revised

> Many first-year college students are apprehensive, but they won't admit it to themselves. Because they hesitate to confide in their friends, they never find out that everyone else is anxious, too. Being disliked, feeling lonely, not "knowing the ropes"—these are what beginning college students fear.

In addition to sounding repetitive and childish, the simple sentences in the original version fragment the passage into a series of disconnected ideas. In contrast, the revised version includes a variety of sentence types and patterns, all of which are discussed on the pages ahead. This variety clarifies the relationships among ideas, so that the passage reads more easily.

Compound Sentences

Compound sentences consist of two or more independent clauses. There are four types of compound sentences. The most basic type consists of two simple sentences joined by a *coordinating conjunction* (*and, but, for, nor, or, so,* or *yet*). Here's an example:

Chimpanzees and gorillas can learn sign language, *and* they have been seen teaching this language to others.

Another type of compound sentence has a semicolon (;), rather than a comma and coordinating conjunction, between the two simple sentences:

Yesterday, editorials attacked the plan; a week ago, they praised it.

A third type of compound sentence links two simple sentences with a semicolon plus a *conjunctive adverb* such as *however, moreover, nevertheless, therefore,* and *thus:*

Every year billions of U.S. dollars go to researching AIDS; *however,* recent studies show that a large percentage of the money has been mismanaged.

A final type of compound sentence consists of two simple sentences connected by a *correlative conjunction,* a word pair such as *either...or, neither...nor,* or *not only...but also:*

Either the litigants will win the lawsuit, *or* they will end up in debt from court costs.

Compound sentences help clarify the relationship between ideas. Similarities are signaled by such words as *and* and *moreover,* contrasts by *but* and *however,* cause-effect by *so* and *therefore.* When only a semicolon separates the two parts of a compound sentence, the relationship between those two parts is often a contrast. ("Yesterday, editorials attacked the plan; a week ago, they praised it.")

Complex Sentences

In a **complex sentence,** a dependent (subordinate) clause is joined to an independent clause. Sometimes the dependent clause (italicized in the following examples) is introduced by a subordinating conjunction such as *although, because, if, since,* or *when:*

Since they have relatively small circulations, specialty magazines tend to be expensive.

We knew there had been a power failure *because all the clocks in the building were two hours slow.*

Other dependent clauses are introduced by a relative pronoun such as *that, which,* or *who:*

Several celebrities revealed *that they have been stalked by delusional fans.*

Fame and wealth from his writings had little effect on author J. R. R. Tolkien, *who continued to teach until reaching retirement age.*

As you can see, the order of the dependent and independent clause isn't fixed. The dependent clause may come first, last, or even in the middle of the independent clause, as in this example:

Nurses' uniforms, *although they are no longer the norm,* are still required by some hospitals.

Whether to use a comma between a dependent and an independent clause depends on a number of factors, including the location of the dependent clause and whether it's *restrictive* (essential for identifying the thing it modifies) or *nonrestrictive*. (For more information on punctuating clauses, see page 642 in the Handbook.)

Because a dependent clause is subordinate to an independent one, complex sentences can clarify the relationships among ideas. Consider the two paragraphs that follow. The first merely strings together a series of simple and compound sentences, all of them carrying roughly the same weight. In contrast, the complex sentences in the revised version use subordination to connect ideas and signal their relative importance.

Original

Are you the "average American"? Then take heed. Here are the results of a time-management survey. You might want to budget your time differently. According to the survey, you spend six years of your life eating. Also, you're likely to spend two years trying to reach people by telephone, so you should convince your friends to get answering machines. Finally, you may be married and expect long conversations with your spouse to occur spontaneously, but you'll have to make a special effort. Ordinarily, your discussions will average only four minutes a day.

Revised

If you're the "average American," take heed. After you hear the results of a time-management survey, you might want to budget your time differently. According to the survey, you spend six years of your life eating. Also, unless you convince your friends to get an answering machine, you're likely to spend two years trying to reach them by telephone. Finally, if you're married, you shouldn't expect long conversations with your spouse to occur spontaneously. Unless you make a special effort, your discussions will average only four minutes a day.

If you find that the original paragraph resembles your writing more than the revised, don't despair. With experience, you'll develop a strong sense of how to connect and rank ideas through subordination. For now, just remember the following: Expressed as a dependent clause, an idea is relegated to a position of secondary importance; expressed as an independent clause, it's emphasized. So reserve for the independent clause the point you want to highlight.

The following sentences illustrate how meaning shifts depending on what is put in the main clause and what is subordinated:

Although most fraternities and sororities no longer have hazing, pledging is still a big event on many campuses.

Although pledging is still a big event on many campuses, most fraternities and sororities no longer have hazing.

In the first sentence, the focus is on *pledging;* in the second, it is on the *discontinuation of hazing.*

Compound-Complex Sentences

A **compound-complex sentence** connects one or more dependent clauses to two or more independent clauses. In the following example, the two independent clauses are underscored once and the two dependent clauses twice:

> The Procrastinators' Club, which is based in Philadelphia, issues a small magazine, but it appears infrequently, only when members get around to writing it.

Go easy on the number of compound-complex sentences you use. Because they tend to be long, a string of them is likely to overwhelm the reader and cloud meaning.

Vary Sentence Length

You've probably noticed that simple sentences tend to be short, compound and complex sentences tend to be of medium length, and compound-complex sentences tend to be long. Generally, by varying sentence type, a writer automatically **varies sentence length** as well. However, sentence type doesn't always determine length. In this example, the simple sentence is longer than the complex one:

Simple Sentence

> Hot and thirsty, exhausted from the effort of carrying so many groceries, I desired nothing more than an ice-cold glass of lemonade.

Complex Sentence

> Because I was hot and thirsty, I craved lemonade.

The difference lies in the number of **modifiers**—words or groups of words used to describe another word or group of words. So, besides considering sentence type, check on sentence length when revising.

Short Sentences

Too many short sentences, like too many simple ones, can sound childish and create a choppy effect that muddies the relationship among ideas. Used wisely, though, a series of short sentences gives writing a staccato rhythm that carries more punch and conveys a faster pace than the same number of words gathered into longer sentences. As you read the two passages that follow, note how the first version's clipped rhythms are more effective for conveying a rush of terrifying events:

> Witches bring their faces close. Goblins glare with fiery eyes. Fiendish devils stealthily approach to claw a beloved stuffed bear. The toy recoils in horror. These are among the terrifying happenings in the world of children's nightmares.

> Witches bring their faces close as goblins glare, their eyes fiery. Approaching stealthily, fiendish devils come to claw a beloved stuffed bear that recoils in horror. These are among the terrifying happenings in the world of children's nightmares.

Brevity also highlights a sentence, especially when surrounding sentences are longer. Consider the dramatic effect of the final sentence in this paragraph:

> Starting in June, millions of Americans pour onto the highways, eager to begin vacation. At the same time, city, state, and federal agencies deploy hundreds, even thousands of workers to repair roads that have, until now, managed to escape bureaucratic attention. Chaos results.

The short sentence "Chaos results" stands out because it's so much shorter than the preceding sentences. The emphasis is appropriate because, in the writer's view, chaos is the dramatic consequence of prolonged bureaucratic inertia.

Long Sentences

Long sentences often convey a leisurely pace and establish a calm tone:

> As I look across the lake, I see the steady light of a campfire at the water's edge, the flames tinting to copper an aluminum rowboat tied to the dock, the boat glimmering in the darkness.

However, as with short sentences, don't overdo it. Too many long sentences can be hard to follow. And remember: A sentence stands out most when it differs in length from surrounding sentences. Glance back at the first paragraph on children's nightmares (page 113). The final long sentence stands in contrast to the preceding short ones. The resulting emphasis works because the final sentence is also the paragraph's topic sentence.

Make Sentences Emphatic

The previous section shows how sentence length affects meaning by highlighting some sentences in a paragraph but not others. Within a single sentence, you can use a number of techniques to make parts of the sentence stand out from the rest. To achieve such **emphasis**, you can: (1) place key ideas at the beginning or end, (2) set them in parallel constructions, (3) express them as fragments, or (4) express them in inverted word order.

Place Key Points at the Beginning or End

A sentence's start and close are its most prominent positions. So, keeping your overall meaning in mind, use those two spots to highlight key ideas.

Let's look first at the **beginning** position. Here are two versions of a sentence; the meanings differ because the openers differ.

> The potentially life-saving drug, developed by junior researchers at the medical school, will be available next month.

> Developed by junior researchers at the medical school, the potentially life-saving drug will be available next month.

In the first version, the emphasis is on the life-saving potential of a drug. Reordering the sentence shifts attention to those responsible for discovering the drug.

An even more emphatic position than a sentence's beginning is its **end.** Put at the close of a sentence whatever you want to emphasize:

Kindergarten is wasted on the young—especially the co-ed naptime.

Now look at two versions of another sentence, each with a slightly different meaning because of what's at the end:

Increasingly, overt racism is showing up in—of all places—popular song lyrics.

Popular song lyrics are showing—of all things—increasingly overt racism.

In the first version, the emphasis is on lyrics; in the second, it's on racism.

Be sure, though, that whatever you place in the climactic position merits the emphasis. The following sentence is so anticlimactic that it's unintentionally humorous:

The family, waiting anxiously for the results of the medical tests, sat.

Similarly, don't build toward a strong climax only to defuse it with some less important material:

On the narrow parts of the trail, where jagged cliffs drop steeply from the path, keep your eyes straight ahead and don't look down, toward the town of Belmont in the east.

In the preceding sentence, "toward the town of Belmont in the east" should be deleted. The important point surely isn't Belmont's location but how to avoid an accident.

Use Parallelism

Parallelism occurs when ideas of comparable weight are expressed in the same grammatical form, thus underscoring their equality. Parallel elements may be words, phrases, clauses, or full sentences. Here are some examples:

Parallel Nouns

We bought *pretzels, nachos,* and *candy bars* to feed our pre-exam jitters.

Parallel Adverbs

Smoothly, steadily, quietly, the sails tipped toward the sun.

Parallel Verbs

The guest lecturer *spoke* to the group, *showed* her slides, and then *invited* questions.

Parallel Adjective Phrases

Playful as a kitten but *wise as a street Tom,* the old cat played with the string while keeping a watchful eye on his surroundings.

Parallel Prepositional Phrases

Gloomy predictions came *from political analysts, from the candidate's staff,* and, surprisingly, *from the candidate herself.*

Parallel Dependent Clauses

Since our rivals were in top form, since their top player would soon come up to bat, we knew that all was lost.

As you can see, the repetition of grammatical forms creates a pleasing symmetry that emphasizes the sequenced ideas. Parallel structure also conveys meaning economically. Look at the way the following sentences can be tightened using parallelism:

Nonparallel

Studies show that most women today are different from those in the past. They want to have their own careers. They want to be successful. They also want to enjoy financial independence.

Parallel

Studies show that most women today are different from those in the past. They want to have careers, be successful, and enjoy financial independence.

Parallel constructions are often signaled by word pairs (correlative conjunctions) such as *either...or, neither...nor,* and *not only...but also.* To maintain parallelism, the same grammatical form must follow each half of the word pair.

Either professors are too rigorous, *or* they are too lax.

The company is interested in *neither* financing the project *nor* helping locate other funding sources.

When my roommate argues, she tends to be *not only* totally stubborn *but also* totally wrong.

Parallelism can create elegant and dramatic writing. Too much, though, seems artificial, so use it sparingly. Save it for your most important points.

Use Fragments

A **fragment** is part of a sentence punctuated as if it were a whole sentence—that is, with a period at the end. A sentence fragment consists of words, phrases, and/or dependent clauses, *without an independent clause.* Here are some examples:

Resting quietly.

Except for the trees.

Because they admired her.

A demanding boss who accepted no excuses.

Ordinarily, we advise students to stay clear of fragments. However, like most rules, this one may at times be broken—*if* you do so intentionally and skillfully. To be on the safe side, ask your composition instructor whether an occasional frag-ment—used as a stylistic device—will be considered acceptable. Here's an exam-ple showing the way fragments (underlined) can be used effectively for emphasis:

> One of my aunt's eccentricities is her belief that only person-ally made gifts show the proper amount of love. Her gifts are often strange. <u>Hand-drawn calendars</u>. <u>Home-brewed cologne that smells like jam</u>. <u>Crocheted washcloths</u>. Frankly, I'd rather receive a gift cer-tificate from a department store.

Notice how the three fragments focus attention on the aunt's charmingly off-beat gifts. Remember, though: When overused, fragments lose their effect, so draw on them sparingly. (See pages 638–643 in the Handbook.)

Use Inverted Word Order

In most English sentences, the subject comes before the verb. When you use **inverted word order,** however, at least part of the verb comes before the subject. The resulting sentence is so atypical that it automatically stands out.

Inverted statements, like those that follow, are used to emphasize an idea:

Normal   My Uncle Bill is a strange man.
Inverted   A strange man is my Uncle Bill.

Normal   Their lies about the test scores were especially brazen.
Inverted   Especially brazen were their lies about the test scores.

Normal   The age-old tree would never again bear fruit.
Inverted   Never again would the age-old tree bear fruit.

A note of caution: Inverted statements should be used infrequently and with special care. Bizarre can they easily sound.

Another form of inversion, the question, also acts as emphasis. A question may be a genuine inquiry, one that focuses attention on the issue at hand, as in the fol-lowing example:

> Since the 1960s, only about half of this country's eligible voters have gone to the polls during national elections. *Why are Americans so apathetic*? Let's look at some of the reasons.

Or a question may be *rhetorical;* that is, one that implies its own answer and encourages the reader to share the writer's view:

> Yesterday, there was yet another accident at the intersection of Fairview and Springdale. Given the disproportionately high number of collisions at that crossing, *can anyone question the need for a traffic light*?

The following checklist is designed to help you and your readers evaluate the sentences in a first draft. (Activities at the end of the chapter will refer you to this checklist when you revise several essays.) To see how one student, Harriet Davids, used the checklist when revising, turn to page 129.

✔ REVISING SENTENCES: A CHECKLIST

☐ Which sentences are inconsistent with the essay's intended tone? How could the problem be corrected?

☐ Which sentences could be more economical? Where could unnecessary repetition, empty phrases, and weak openings be eliminated? Which prepositional phrases could be deleted? Where are there unnecessary *who, which,* and *that* clauses?

☐ Where should sentence type be more varied? Where would subordination clarify the connections among ideas? Where would simpler sentences make the writing less inflated and easier to understand?

☐ Where does sentence length become monotonous? Which short sentences should be connected to enhance flow and convey a more leisurely pace? Which long sentences would be more effective if broken into crisp, short ones?

☐ Where would a different sentence pattern add variety? Better highlight key sentence elements? Seem more natural?

☐ Which sentences could be more emphatic? Which strategy would be most effective—expressing the main point at the beginning or end, using parallelism, or rewriting the sentence as a fragment, question, or inverted-word-order statement?

REVISING WORDS

After refining the sentences in your first draft, you're in a good position to look closely at individual words. During this stage, you should aim for

- words consistent with your intended tone,
- an appropriate level of diction,
- words that neither overstate nor understate,
- words with appropriate connotations,
- specific rather than general words,
- strong verbs,
- no unnecessary adverbs,
- original figures of speech, and
- nonsexist language.

Make Words Consistent with Your Tone

Like full sentences, individual words and phrases should also reinforce your intended tone. Reread the Melissa Dribben excerpt on gun control (see page 106). Earlier we discussed how sentence structure and length contribute to the excerpt's biting tone. Word choice also plays an important role. The word *stash* mocks the impulse to hoard guns as if they were essential but depletable goods—like clean underwear. And the specific phrase *.38-caliber pistols* evokes the image of a weapon with frightening lethal power. Such word choices reinforce the overall tone Dribben wants to convey.

Use an Appropriate Level of Diction

Diction refers to the words a writer selects. Those words should be appropriate for the writer's purpose, audience, point of view, and tone. If, for example, you are writing a straightforward, serious piece about on-the-job incompetence, you would be better off saying people "don't concentrate on their work" and they "make frequent errors," rather than saying they "screw up" or "goof off."

There are three broad levels of diction: *formal, popular,* and *informal.* To describe feelings of pervasive sadness, clinical psychologists might use the highly formal term *dysthymia,* while the popular term for such emotions is *depression.* At the other end of the continuum, someone might use the informal phrase *down in the dumps.* Within each level of diction, there are degrees of formality and informality: *Down in the dumps* and *bummed out* are both informal, but *bummed out* is the slangier expression.

Formal Diction

Impersonal and distant in tone, **formal diction** is the type of language found in scholarly journals. Contractions are rare; long, specialized, technical words are common. Unfortunately, many people mistakenly equate word length with education: The longer the words, they think, the more impressed readers will be. So rather than using the familiar and natural words *improve* and *think,* they thumb through a thesaurus (literally or figuratively) for such fancy-sounding alternatives as *ameliorate* and *conceptualize.* They write "That is the optimum consequence we have the expectation of attaining" rather than "That is the best result we can expect." Remember: It's a word's ability to convey meaning clearly that counts, not its number of syllables.

Similarly, when writing for a general audience, don't show off specialized knowledge by throwing in **jargon,** insiders' terms from a particular area of expertise (say, a term like *authorial omniscience* from literary theory). Such "shop-talk" should be used only when less specialized words would lack the necessary precision. If readers are apt to be unfamiliar with a term, provide a definition.

Some degree of formality is appropriate—when, for example, you write up survey results for a sociology class. In such a case, your instructor may expect you to avoid the pronoun *I* (see page 23). Other instructors may think it's pretentious for a student to refer to himself or herself in the third person ("The writer observed that...."). These instructors may be equally put off by the artificiality of the passive voice (pages 123–124): "It was observed that...." To be safe, find out what your instructors expect. If possible, use *I* when you mean "I." Your writing will be no less objective—unless using *I* tempts you to highly personal remarks and opinions. Even in more formal situations, resist the temptation to dazzle readers by piling up multi-syllable words. (For more on avoiding pretentious language, see below.)

Popular Diction

Popular, or **mainstream,** diction is found in most magazines, newspapers, books, and texts (including this one). In such prose, the writer may use the first person and address the reader as "you." Contractions appear frequently; specialized vocabulary is kept to a minimum.

You should aim for popular diction in most of the writing you do—in and out of college. Also keep in mind that an abrupt downshift to slang (*freaked out* instead of *lost control*) or a sudden turn to highly formal language (*myocardial infarction* instead of *heart attack*) will disconcert readers and undermine your credibility.

Informal Diction

Informal diction, which conveys a sense of everyday speech, is friendly and casual. First-person and second-person pronouns are common, as are contractions and fragments. Colloquial expressions (*rub the wrong way*) and slang (*You wimp*) are used freely. Informal diction isn't appropriate for academic papers, except where it is used to indicate *someone else's* speech.

Avoid Words That Overstate or Understate

When revising, be on the lookout for **doublespeak,** language that deliberately overstates or understates reality. Here's an example of each.

In their correspondence, Public Works Departments often refer to "ground-mounted confirmatory route markers"—a grandiose way of saying "road signs." Other organizations go to the other extreme and use **euphemisms,** words that minimize something's genuine gravity or importance. Hospital officials, for instance, sometimes call deaths resulting from staff negligence "unanticipated therapeutic misadventures." When revising, check that you haven't used words that exaggerate or downplay something's significance.

Select Words with Appropriate Connotations

Mark Twain once said, "The difference between the right word and the almost right word is the difference between lightning and the lightning bug." Even two words listed as synonyms in a dictionary or thesaurus can differ in meaning in important ways.

The dictionary meaning of a word is its **denotation.** The word *motorcycle,* for example, is defined as "a two- or three-wheeled vehicle propelled by an internal-combustion engine that resembles a bicycle, but is usually larger and heavier, and often has two saddles." Yet how many of us think of a motorcycle in these terms?

Certainly, there is more to a word than its denotation. A word also comes surrounded by **connotations**—associated sensations, emotions, images, and ideas. For some, the word *motorcycle* probably calls to mind danger and noise. For motorcyclists themselves, the word most likely summons pleasant memories of high-speed movement through the open air.

Given the wide range of responses that any one word can elicit, you need to be sensitive to each word's shades of meaning, so you can judge when to use it rather than some other word. Examine the following word series to get a better feel for the subtle but often critical differences between similar words:

contribution, donation, handout

quiet, reserved, closemouthed

everyday, common, trite

follower, disciple, groupie

Notice the extent to which words' connotations create different impressions in these two examples:

The young woman emerged from the interview, her face *aglow*. Moving *briskly* to the coatrack, she *tossed* her raincoat over one arm. After a *carefree* "Thank you" to the receptionist, she *glided* from the room.

The young woman emerged from the interview, her face *aflame*. Moving *hurriedly* to the coatrack, she *flung* her raincoat over one arm. After a *perfunctory* "Thank you" to the receptionist, she *bolted* from the room.

In the first paragraph, the words *aglow, carefree,* and *glided* have positive connotations, so the reader surmises that the interview was a success. In contrast, the second paragraph contains words loaded with negative connotations: *aflame, perfunctory,* and *bolted.* Reading this paragraph, the reader assumes something went awry.

A thesaurus can help you select words with the right connotations. Just look up any word with which you aren't satisfied, and you'll find a list of synonyms. To be safe, stay away from unfamiliar words. Otherwise, you stand a good chance of using a word incorrectly and creating a howler. Several years ago, one of our students wrote in an essay, "I wanted to *bequeath* the party by midnight." What he meant was that he wanted to "*leave* the party by midnight." He had, though, already used the word *leave* several times, so, looking for a synonym, he turned to the thesaurus, where he came across the word *bequeath*. But writing "I wanted to *bequeath* the party by midnight" doesn't work because *bequeath* means to leave property or goods by means of a will. Our advice? Choose only those words whose nuances you understand.

Use Specific Rather Than General Words

Besides carrying the right connotations, words should be **specific** rather than general. That is, they must avoid vagueness and ambiguity by referring to *particular* people, animals, events, objects, and phenomena. If they don't, readers may misinterpret what you mean.

Assume you're writing an essay about the demise of neighborhood movie houses. If, at one point, you refer to the "theaters' poor facilities," readers may imagine you're referring to faulty sound quality and projection. If you mean the theaters' messy physical surroundings, you need specific language to send the right message: wads of gum stuck under the seats, crushed popcorn tubs everywhere, a sticky film coating the floor. Precise words like these eliminate confusion.

Besides clarifying meaning, specific words enliven writing and make it more convincing. Compare these two paragraphs:

Original

Sponsored by a charitable organization, a group of children from a nearby town visited a theme park. The kids had a great time. They went on several rides and ate a variety of foods. Reporters and a TV crew shared in the fun.

Revised

Sponsored by the United Glendale Charities, twenty-five underprivileged Glendale grade-schoolers visited the Universe of Fun Themepark. The kids had a great time. They roller-coastered through a meteor shower on the Space Probe, encountered a giant squid on the Submarine Voyage, and screamed their way past coffins and ghosts in the House of Horrors. At the International Cuisine arcade, they sampled foods ranging from Hawaiian poi to German strudel. Reporters from the *Texas Herald* and a camera crew from WGLD, the Glendale cable station, shared in the fun.

You may have noticed that the specific words in the second paragraph provide answers to "which," "how," and similar questions. In contrast, when reading the first paragraph, you probably wondered, "*Which* charitable organization? *Which* theme park? *Which* rides?" Similarly, you may have asked, "*How* large a group? *How* young were the kids?" Specific language also answers "In what way?" The revised paragraph details *in what way* the children "had a great time." They didn't just eat "a variety of foods." Rather, they "sampled foods ranging from Hawaiian poi to German strudel." So, when you revise, check to make sure that your wording doesn't leave unanswered questions like "How?" "Why?" and "In what way?" (For more on making writing specific, see pages 47–48 and 69–70.)

Use Strong Verbs

Because a verb is the source of action in a sentence, it carries more weight than any other element. Replacing weak verbs and nouns with **strong verbs** is, then, another way to tighten and energize language. Consider the following strategies.

Replace *To Be* and Linking Verbs with Action Verbs

Overreliance on *to be* verbs (*is, were, has been,* and so on) tends to stretch sentences, making them flat and wordy. The same is true of motionless **linking verbs** such as *appear, become, sound, feel, look,* and *seem.* Since these verbs don't communicate any action, more words are required to complete their meaning and explain what is happening. Even *to be* verb forms combined with present participles (*is laughing, were running*) are weaker than bare **action verbs** (*laughs, ran*). Similarly, linking verbs combined with adjectives (*becomes shiny, seemed offensive*) aren't as vigorous as the action verb alone (*shines, offended*). Look how much more effective a paragraph becomes when weak verbs are replaced with dynamic ones:

Original

The waves *were* so high that the boat *was* nearly *tipping* on end. The wind *felt* rough against our faces, and the salt spray *became* so strong that we *felt* our breath *would be* cut off. Suddenly, in the air *was* the sound I had dreaded most—the snap of the rigging. I *felt* panicky.

Revised

The waves *towered* until the boat nearly *tipped* on end. The wind *lashed* our faces, while the salt spray *clogged* our throats and *cut* off our breath. Suddenly, the sound I had dreaded most *splintered* the air—the snap of the rigging. Panic *gripped* me.

The second paragraph is not only less wordy; it's also more vivid.

When you revise, look closely at your verbs. If you find too many *to be* and linking verb forms, ask yourself, "What's happening in the sentence?" Your response will help you substitute stronger verbs that will make your writing more compelling.

Change Passive Verbs to Active Ones

To be verb forms (*is, has been,* and so on) may also be combined with a past participle (*cooked, stung*), resulting in a **passive verb.** A passive verb creates a sentence structure in which the subject is *acted on* and, therefore, is placed in a secondary or passive position. In contrast, the subject of an **active verb** *performs* the action. Consider the following active and passive forms:

Passive	Active
A suggestion was made by the instructor that the project plan be revised by the students.	The instructor suggested that the students revise the project plan.
The employees' grievances will be considered by the union-management team when contract terms are being negotiated.	The union-management team will consider employees' grievances when negotiating contract terms.

Although they're not grammatically incorrect, passive verbs generally weaken writing, making it wordy and stiffly formal. Sometimes, though, it makes sense to use the passive voice. Perhaps you don't know who performed an action. ("When I returned to my car, I noticed the door had been dented.") Or you may want to emphasize an event, not the agent responsible for the event. For example, in an article about academic dishonesty on your campus, you might deliberately use the passive voice: "Every semester, research papers are plagiarized and lab reports falsified."

Unfortunately, corporations, government agencies, and other institutions often use the passive voice to avoid taking responsibility for controversial actions. Notice how easily the passive conceals the agent: "The rabbits were injected with a cancer-causing chemical."

Because the passive voice *is* associated with "official" writing, you may think it sounds scholarly and impressive. It doesn't. Unless you have good reason for de-emphasizing the agent, change passive verbs to active ones.

Replace Weak Verb-Noun Combinations

Just as *to be,* linking, and passive verbs tend to lengthen sentences needlessly, so do weak verb-noun combinations. Whenever possible, replace such combinations with their strong verb counterparts. Change "made an estimate" to "estimated," "gave approval" to "approved." Notice how revision tightens these sentences, making them livelier and less pretentious:

Original   They *were* of the *belief* that the report was due next week.
Revised   They *believed* the report was due next week.

Original   The technical adviser *effected* a *replacement* of the system.
Revised   The technical advisor *replaced* the system.

Delete Unnecessary Adverbs

Strong verbs can further tighten your writing by ridding it of unnecessary adverbs. "She *strolled* down the path" conveys the same message as "She *walked slowly* and *leisurely* down the path"—but more economically. Similarly, why write "The crime was *extremely difficult* for the police to solve" when you can simply write "The crime *mystified* the police"?

Adverbs such *as extremely, really,* and *very* usually weaken writing. Although they are called "intensifiers," they make writing less, not more, intense. Notice that the following sentence reads more emphatically *without* the intensifier:

Original   Although the professor's lectures are controversial, no one denies that they are *really* brilliant.
Revised   Although the professor's lectures are controversial, no one denies that they are brilliant.

"Qualifiers" such as *quite, rather,* and *somewhat* also tend to weaken writing. When you spot one, try to delete it:

Original   When planning a summer trip to the mountains, remember to pack warm clothes; it turns *quite* cool at night.
Revised   When planning a summer trip to the mountains, remember to pack warm clothes; it turns cool at night.

Use Original Figures of Speech

Another strategy for adding vitality to your writing is to create imaginative, nonliteral comparisons, called **figures of speech.** For example, you might describe midsummer humidity this way: "Going from an air-conditioned building to the street is like being hit in the face with peanut butter." Or you might describe someone's raw, sunburned face by saying it is "as red as a skinned tomato." Notice that in both cases the comparisons yoke essentially dissimilar things (humidity and peanut butter, a face and a tomato). Such unexpected connections surprise readers and help keep their interest.

Figures of speech also tighten writing. Since they create sharp images in the reader's mind, you don't need many words to convey as much information. If someone writes "My teenage years were like perpetual root canal," the reader immediately knows how painful and never-ending the author found adolescence.

Similes, Metaphors, Personification

Figures of speech come in several varieties. A **simile** is a direct comparison of two unlike things using the word *like* or *as:* "The moon brightened the yard *like* a floodlight." In a **metaphor,** the comparison is implied rather than directly stated: "The girl's *barbed-wire hair* set off *electric shocks* in her parents." In **personification,** an inanimate object is given human characteristics: "The couple robbed the store without noticing a silent, hidden eyewitness who later would tell all—a video camera." (For more on figures of speech, see page 159.)

Avoid Clichés

Trite and overused, some figures of speech signal a lack of imagination: *a tough nut to crack, cool as a cucumber, green with envy.* Such expressions, called **clichés,** are so predictable that you can hear the first few words (*Life is a bowl of...*) and fill in the rest (*cherries*). Clichés lull writer and reader alike into passivity since they encourage rote, habitual thinking.

When revising, either eliminate tired figures of speech or give them an unexpected twist. For example, seeking a humorous effect, you might write "Beneath his rough exterior beat a heart of lead" (instead of "gold"); rather than "Last but not least," you might write "Last but also least."

Two Other Cautions

First, if you include figures of speech, *don't pile one on top of the other,* as in the following sentence:

> Whenever the dorm residents prepared for the first party of the season, hairdryers howled like a windstorm, hairspray rained down in torrents, stereos vibrated like an earthquake, and shouts of excitement shook the walls like an avalanche.

Second, guard against *illogical* or *mixed* figures of speech. In the following example, note the ludicrous and contradictory comparisons:

> They rode the roller coaster of high finance, dodging bullets and avoiding ambushes from those trying to lasso their streak of good luck.

To detect outlandish comparisons, visualize each figure of speech. If it calls up some unintentionally humorous or impossible image, revise or eliminate it.

Avoid Sexist Language

Sexist language gives the impression that one sex is more important, powerful, or valuable than the other. You may have noticed such language in certain reading selections in this book—for example, selections that refer to the average person as *he*. Some of these essays were written before people became alert to sexist overtones; others reveal the tenacity of long-standing habits and attitudes. Fortunately, a growing number of writers—female and male—are replacing sexist language with **gender-neutral** or **nonsexist** terms that convey no sexual prejudice. You, too, can avoid sexist language. But to do so, you need to be aware of the situations in which it is apt to occur.

Sexist Vocabulary

Using nonsexist vocabulary means staying away from terms that demean or exclude one of the sexes. Such slang words as *stud, jock, chick,* and *fox* portray people as one-dimensional. Just as adult males should be called *men,* adult females should be referred to as *women,* not *girls.* Similarly, men shouldn't be empowered with professional and honorary titles while professional women are assigned only personal titles. Why, for example, years ago should Ronald Reagan have been referred to as *President* Reagan while the Prime Minister of England, Margaret Thatcher, was called *Mrs.* Thatcher? In addition, consider replacing *Mrs.* and *Miss* with *Ms.;* like *Mr., Ms.* doesn't indicate marital status.

Be alert as well to the fact that words not inherently sexist can become so in certain contexts. Asking "What does the *man* in the street think of the teachers' strike?" excludes the possibility of asking women for their reactions.

Because language in our culture tends to exclude women rather than men, we list here a number of common words that exclude women. When you write (or speak), make an effort to use the more inclusive alternatives given.

Sexist	Nonsexist
the average guy	the average person
chairman	chairperson, chair
congressman	congressional representative
fireman	fire fighter
foreman	supervisor
layman	layperson
mailman	mail carrier, letter carrier
mankind, man	people, humans, human beings
policeman	police officer
salesman	salesperson
statesman	diplomat
spokesman	spokesperson
workmen	workers

Also, be on the lookout for phrases that suggest a given profession or talent is unusual for someone of a particular sex: *woman judge, woman doctor, male secretary, male nurse.*

Sexist Pronoun Use

Indefinite singular nouns—those representing a general group of people consisting of both genders—can lead to **sexist pronoun use:** "On *his* first day of school, a young child often experiences separation anxiety," or "Each professor should be responsible for monitoring *his* own students' progress." These sentences exclude female children and female professors from consideration, although the situations being described apply equally to them. But writing "On *her* first day of school, a young child often experiences separation anxiety" or "Each professor should be responsible for monitoring *her* own students' progress" is similarly sexist because the language excludes males.

Indefinite *pronouns* such as *anyone, each,* and *everybody* may also pave the way to sexist language. Although such pronouns often refer to a number of individuals, they are considered singular. So, wanting to be grammatically correct, you may write a sentence like the following: "Everybody wants *his* favorite candidate to win." The sentence, however, is sexist because *everybody* is certainly not restricted to men. But writing "Everybody wants *her* candidate to win" is equally sexist because now males aren't included.

Here's one way to avoid these kinds of sexist constructions: Use *both* male and female pronouns, instead of just one or the other. For example, you could write "On *his or her* first day of school, a young child often experiences separation anxiety" or "Everybody wants *his or her* favorite candidate to win." If you use both pronouns, you might try to vary their order; that is, alternate *he/she* with *she/he, his or her* with *her or his,* and so on. Another approach is to use *s/he* in place of *he* or *she* alone. A third possibility is to use the gender-neutral pronouns *they, their,* or *themselves:* "Everybody wants *their* favorite candidate to win." Be warned, though. Some people object to using these plural pronouns with singular indefinite pronouns, even though the practice is common in everyday speech. To be on the safe side, ask your instructors if they object to any of the approaches described here. If not, feel free to choose whichever nonsexist construction seems most graceful and least obtrusive.

If you're still unhappy with the result, two alternative strategies enable you to eliminate the need for *any* gender-marked singular pronouns. First, you can change singular general nouns or indefinite pronouns to their plural equivalents and then use nonsexist plural pronouns:

Original   A *workaholic* feels anxious when *he* isn't involved in a task-related project.
Revised   *Workaholics* feel anxious when *they*'re not involved in task-related projects.

Original   *Everyone* in the room expressed *his* opinion freely.
Revised   *Those* in the room expressed *their* opinions freely.

Second, you can recast the sentence to omit the singular pronoun:

Original   A *manager* usually spends part of each day settling squabbles among *his* staff.
Revised   A manager usually spends part of each day settling *staff squabbles.*

Original No *one* wants *his* taxes raised.
Revised   No one wants *to pay more taxes.*

The following checklist is designed to help you and your readers evaluate the words in a draft. (Activities at the end of the chapter will refer you to this checklist when you revise several essays.) To see how one student, Harriet Davids, used the checklist when revising, turn to page 129.

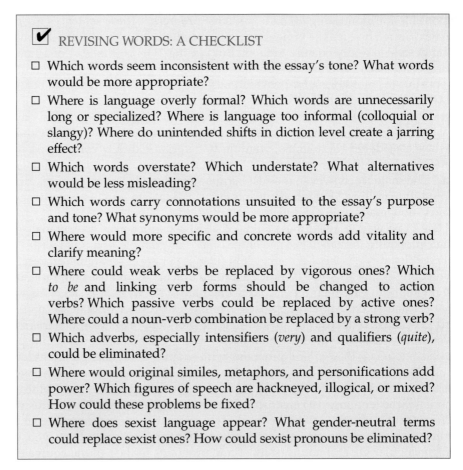

✔ REVISING WORDS: A CHECKLIST

☐ Which words seem inconsistent with the essay's tone? What words would be more appropriate?

☐ Where is language overly formal? Which words are unnecessarily long or specialized? Where is language too informal (colloquial or slangy)? Where do unintended shifts in diction level create a jarring effect?

☐ Which words overstate? Which understate? What alternatives would be less misleading?

☐ Which words carry connotations unsuited to the essay's purpose and tone? What synonyms would be more appropriate?

☐ Where would more specific and concrete words add vitality and clarify meaning?

☐ Where could weak verbs be replaced by vigorous ones? Which *to be* and linking verb forms should be changed to action verbs? Which passive verbs could be replaced by active ones? Where could a noun-verb combination be replaced by a strong verb?

☐ Which adverbs, especially intensifiers (*very*) and qualifiers (*quite*), could be eliminated?

☐ Where would original similes, metaphors, and personifications add power? Which figures of speech are hackneyed, illogical, or mixed? How could these problems be fixed?

☐ Where does sexist language appear? What gender-neutral terms could replace sexist ones? How could sexist pronouns be eliminated?

SAMPLE STUDENT REVISION OF SENTENCES AND WORDS

Student essay in progress

Reprinted here is the introduction to Harriet Davids's first draft—as it looked after she entered on a word processor the changes she made in overall meaning, structure, and paragraph development (see page 101). To help identify problems with words and sentences, Harriet asked someone in her editing group to read the revised version aloud. Then she asked the group to comment on her paper, using the checklists on pages 118 and 128. The marginal notes indicate her ranking of the group's comments in order of importance. The above-line changes show how Harriet revised in response to these suggestions for improving the paragraph's sentences and words.

                                                                    Reruns of   from the
        ~~In the 50s and 60s, parents had it easy~~, TV comedies ~~of that~~

    50s and 60s dramatize the kinds of problems that parents used to have.
    ~~period show~~/the Cleavers scolding Beaver about his dirty hands~~,~~

                    ground   for not   *ing*
        the Andersons ~~telling~~ Bud to do his homework ~~and~~ the Nelsons

        dock   *'s allowance because he forgets*
    ~~telling~~ Ricky to clean his room. Being a parent today is much

                    than it was a generation ago.
    more difficult. Nowadays parents must protect their children from

    many things--from a growing number of distractions, from sexually

                        life-threatening
    explicit material, and from ~~dangerous~~ situations.

① Combine into one
   sentence idea of
   50s/60s parents
   and TV shows

② Make each
   family's problems
   a separate
   sentence

③ Use stronger
   verbs (not
   "telling")

④ Make "dangerous
   situations" more
   specific

Once you, like Harriet, have carefully revised sentences and words, your essay needs only to be edited (for errors in grammar, punctuation, and spelling) and proofread. In the next chapter, you'll read about these final steps. You'll also see a student essay that has gone through all phases of the writing process.

Continues on page 137

ACTIVITIES: REVISING SENTENCES AND WORDS

1. Revise the following wordy, muddy sentences, making them economical and clear.

   a. What a person should do before subletting a rental apartment is make sure to have the sublet agreement written up in a formal contract.

   b. In high school, it often happens that young people deny liking poetry because of the fact that they fear running the risk of having people mock or make fun of them because they actually enjoy poetry.

c. In light of the fact that college students are rare in my home neighborhood, being a college student gives me immediate and instant status.

d. There were a number of people who have made the observation that the new wing of the library looks similar in appearance to several nearby buildings with considerable historical significance.

e. It was, in my opinion, an apt comment when the professor noted that most of the students who complain about how demanding the requirements of a course are tend to work at part-time or even full-time jobs.

2. Using only simple or simple and compound sentences, write a paragraph based on one of the following topic sentences. Then rewrite the paragraph, making some of the sentences complex and others compound-complex. Examine your two versions of the paragraph. What differences do you see in meaning and emphasis?

a. The campus parking lot is dangerous at night.

b. Some students have trouble getting along with their roommates.

c. Silent body language speaks loudly.

d. Getting on a teacher's good side is an easily mastered skill.

3. The following sentences could be more emphatic. Examine each one to determine its focus; then revise the sentence, using one of the following strategies: placing the most important item first or last, parallelism, inverted word order, a fragment. Try to use a different strategy in each sentence.

a. The old stallion's mane was tangled, and he had chipped hooves, and his coat was scraggly.

b. Most of us find rude salespeople difficult to deal with.

c. The politician promises, "I'll solve all your problems."

d. We meet female stereotypes such as the gold digger, the dangerous vixen, and the "girl next door" in the movies.

e. It's a wise teacher who encourages discussion of controversial issues in the classroom.

4. The following paragraph is pretentious and murky. Revise to make it crisp and clear.

Since its founding, the student senate on this campus has maintained essentially one goal: to upgrade the quality of its student-related services. Two years ago, the senate, supported by the opinions of three consultants provided by the National Council of Student Governing Boards, was confident it was operating from a base of quality but felt that, if given additional monetary support from the administration, a significant improvement in student services would be facilitated. This was a valid prediction, for that is exactly

what transpired in the past fifteen months once additional monetary
resources were, in fact, allocated by the administration to the senate and its activities.

5. Write a sentence for each word in the series that follows, making sure your details reinforce each word's connotations:

   a. chubby, voluptuous, portly

   b. stroll, trudge, loiter

   c. turmoil, anarchy, hubbub

6. Write three versions of a brief letter voicing a complaint to a store, a person, or an organization. One version should be charged with negative connotations; another should "soft pedal" the problem. The final version should present your complaint using neutral, objective words. Which letter do you prefer? Why?

7. Describe each of the following in one or two sentences, using a creative figure of speech to convey each item's distinctive quality:

   a. a baby's hand

   b. a pile of dead leaves

   c. a sophisticated personal computer

   d. an empty room

   e. an old car

8. Enliven the following dull, vague sentences. Use your knowledge of sentence structure to dramatize key elements. Also, replace weak verbs with vigorous ones and make language more specific.

   a. I got sick on the holiday.

   b. He stopped the car at the crowded intersection.

   c. A bird appeared in the corner of the yard.

   d. The class grew restless.

   e. The TV broadcaster put on a concerned air as she announced the tragedy.

9. The following paragraph contains too many linking verbs, passives, adverbs, and prepositions. In addition, noun forms are sometimes used where their verb counterparts would be more effective. Revise the paragraph by eliminating unnecessary prepositions and providing more vigorous verbs. Then add specific, concrete words that dramatize what is being described.

The farmers in the area conducted a meeting during which they
formulated a discussion of the vandalism problem in the county in
which they live. They made the estimate that, on the average, each
of them had at least an acre of crops destroyed the past few weekends by gangs of motorcyclists who have been driving maliciously

```
over their land. The increase in such vandalism has been caused by
the encroachment of the suburbs on rural areas.
```

10. Revise the following sentences to eliminate sexist language.

    a. The manager of a convenience store has to guard his cash register carefully.

    b. When I broke my arm in a car accident, a male nurse, aided by a physician's assistant, treated my injury.

    c. All of us should contact our congressman if we're not satisfied with his performance.

    d. The chemistry professors agree that nobody should have to buy her own Bunsen burner.

An important note: When revising essay drafts in activities 11 and 12, don't worry too much about grammar, punctuation, and spelling. However, do save your revisions, so you can focus on these matters after reading the next chapter.

11. In response to activity 1 in Chapter 7 (page 102), you revised the overall meaning, structure, and paragraph development of Harriet Davids's first draft. Find that revision so that you can now focus on its sentences and words. Get together with at least one other person and ask yourselves questions like these: "Where should sentence type, length, or pattern be more varied?" and "Where would more specific and concrete words add vitality and clarify meaning?" For further guidance, refer to the checklists on pages 118 and 128. Summarize and rank any perceived problems in marginal annotations or a feedback chart. Then type your changes into a word processor or enter them between the lines of the draft. (Save your revision so you can edit and proofread it after reading the next chapter.)

12. Return to the draft you prepared in response to activity 2, activity 3, activity 4, or activity 5 in Chapter 7 (pages 102–104). Get together with several people and request that one of them read the draft aloud. Then, using the checklists on pages 118 and 128, ask the group members focused questions about any sentences and words that you feel need sharpening. After evaluating the feedback, revise the draft. Either key your changes into a word processor or do your revising by hand. (Save your revision so you can edit and proofread it after reading the next chapter.)

9
EDITING AND PROOFREADING

IT happens all too often. A student works hard to revise an essay—reading it over, making changes (some of them extensive), refining sentences and words— all to arrive at the best version possible. Then the student types the paper and hands it in without even a glance.

Wanting to get a piece of writing off your desk is a normal human response to so much work. But if you don't edit and proofread—that is, closely check your writing for grammar, spelling, and typographical errors—you run the risk of sabotaging your previous efforts. Readers may assume that a piece of writing isn't worth their time if they're jolted by surface flaws that make it difficult to read. So, to make sure that your good ideas get a fair hearing, you should do the following:

- Edit,
- Use the appropriate manuscript format, and
- Proofread.

EDIT CAREFULLY

When revising the paper, you probably spotted some errors in grammar, punctuation, or spelling, perhaps flagging them for later correction. Now—after you're satisfied with the essay's organization, development, and style—it's time to fix these errors. It's also time to search for and correct errors that have slipped by you so far.

If you're working with pen and paper or on a typewritten or word-processed draft with handwritten annotations, use a different color ink, so your new corrections will stand out. Because most writers find it easier to locate errors on a clean copy of their text, consider retyping your draft before editing it. If you use a word processor, search for errors both on the screen and on a printout. If your software includes a spelling check, your search for misspellings will be greatly simplified. Be aware, however, that such programs may not find errors in the spelling of proper nouns, and that they won't flag errors that constitute legitimate words (for example, *he* when you meant *the* or *their* when you meant *there*).

To be a successful editor of your own work, you need two standard tools: a grammar handbook (like the one on pages 633–697) and a good dictionary. One way to keep track of the errors you're prone to make is to record them on a simple chart. Divide the chart into three columns: (1) *Error,* (2) *Rules for Correcting Error,* and (3) *Error Corrected.* When your instructor returns an essay, copy representative mistakes you've made into the first column. Look up in a handbook the rules that apply and enter them in the second column. Then, in the last column, rewrite the phrase or sentence from your paper with the error corrected. As the semester goes on, you'll develop a *personalized inventory* of writing errors to use in checking your own work.

If you're weak in spelling, make a similar inventory of spelling errors and corrections. Use four columns for this list: (1) *Word Misspelled,* (2) *Part of Word Misspelled,* (3) *Spelling Rule,* and (4) *Word Corrected.* (For more on spelling, see pages 694–696 in the Handbook.)

USE THE APPROPRIATE MANUSCRIPT FORMAT

After correcting all grammar and spelling problems, you're ready to produce the final copy. In doing so, you should follow accepted academic practice, adapted to your instructor's requirements. Most instructors will require that you type your papers. Even if this isn't the case, typed or computer-printed papers look neater, are easier to grade, and show that you have made the transition to college-level format.

The following checklist on manuscript format describes the basic rules for college essays as well as special rules for typed, computer-generated, and handwritten papers.

✔ APPROPRIATE MANUSCRIPT FORMAT: A CHECKLIST

Computer-Generated Papers

☐ Use good-quality white paper.

☐ Never hand in a written piece on spread-sheet paper. Tear off sheet edges at the perforations, separate the pages, and arrange them in correct order. Don't rip the paper from the printer, rush to class, and hand in the accordion-folded sheets!

□ Double-space throughout the paper, and make sure your printer uses legible, easy-to-read characters. An ink-jet, daisy wheel, or laser printer is best, but a dot-matrix printer that approximates "letter quality" is also acceptable.

Typed Papers

□ Use standard-size (8-½ by 11 inches), good-quality white typing paper. Don't use "erasable" paper or onion skin. The result is often a smudged look, and the instructor may have a difficult time getting the paper to accept inked-in comments.

□ Use a typewriter with a standard type style. Avoid script or other hard-to-read typefaces.

□ Make sure the typewriter prints in dark black ink. Keep the type clean and change the ribbon as needed.

□ Double-space throughout the paper, and type on only one side of the page.

Handwritten Papers

□ Use white, lined paper with a margin rule on the left side. The paper may have holes for insertion in a notebook, but don't rip pages out of a spiral notebook unless there are perforations that permit you to do so neatly.

□ Use only standard-size paper: 8-½ by 10 or 11 inches.

□ Write on only one side of the page, using dark blue or black ink, never pencil.

□ Don't skip lines, except between paragraphs.

□ Write legibly and carefully, in a moderate size. Eliminate exaggerated mannerisms from your handwriting, such as curlicues and extreme slants.

All Papers

□ Leave adequate margins: one inch at the top and bottom and right and left of each page should be sufficient.

□ If you include a title page, place the title about one-third of the way down the page. Enter the title, and double-space between lines of the title and your name. Course and section, instructor's name, and date, on separate lines, are double-spaced and centered.

□ If you don't include a title page, use a standard heading, as specified by your instructor, at the top of the first page. One standard format for the heading consists of your name, the instructor's name, the course title and number, and the date on double-spaced lines in the upper-left corner, an inch from the top.

☐ Center the title of your paper one double space below the heading. Capitalize only the first letters of all main words. Don't use all caps, underlining, or quotation marks. Double-space a title having more than one line.

☐ Double-space between the title and the first paragraph of your essay.

☐ With the exception of the title page, number each page, including the first, by putting an arabic numeral in the upper-right corner one-half inch below the top of the page. Avoid putting *p.* or *page* with the page number. Include your last name before each page number, in case pages become separated.

☐ Indent the first line of each paragraph five spaces.

☐ Paper clip or staple your essay's pages, placing the outline wherever your instructor requests. Don't use the corner "rip and fold" method; it doesn't hold, and it spoils the look of a carefully typed paper.

☐ Don't use a report cover unless your instructor requests it.

(For examples of correct manuscript format, see pages 137 and 582–583.)

PROOFREAD CLOSELY

Proofreading means checking your final copy carefully for "typos" or other mistakes. One trick is to read your material backwards: If you read from the end of each paragraph to the beginning, you can focus on each word individually to make sure no letters have been left out or transposed. This technique prevents you from getting caught up in the flow of ideas and missing small defects, which is easy to do when you've read your own words many times.

What should you do when you find a typo? Simply use a pen with dark ink to make an above-line correction. The following standard proofreader's marks will help you indicate some common types of corrections:

Proofreader's Mark	Meaning	Example
∧	insert missing letter or word	televᵢsion
ℓ	delete	reports the ~~the~~ findings
∾	reverse order	the gang's here all
⁋	start new paragraph	to dry. Next, put
#	add space	thegirls
◡	close up space	boy cott

If you make so many corrections on a page that it begins to look like a draft, retype the page. If you're using a computer, make the corrections on the disk and reprint the page.

STUDENT ESSAY: FROM PREWRITING THROUGH PROOFREADING

In the last several chapters, we've taken you through the various stages in the writing process—from prewriting to proofreading. You've seen how Harriet Davids used prewriting (pages 25–32) and outlining (pages 32–33) to arrive at her thesis (pages 37 and 40–41) and her first draft (pages 83–84). You also saw how Harriet revised, first, her draft's overall meaning and paragraph development (page 101) and, second, its sentences and words (pages 128–129). In this chapter, you'll look at Harriet's final draft—the paper she submitted to her instructor after completing all the stages of the writing process.

> Student essay in progress

Harriet, a thirty-eight-year-old college student and mother of two teenagers, wanted to write an informative paper with a straightforward, serious tone. While preparing her essay, she kept in mind that her audience would include her course instructor as well as her classmates, most of them considerably younger than she. This is the assignment that prompted Harriet's essay:

> Because the world these days is a difficult, even dangerous place, parents understandably worry about their children. Write an essay supporting the idea that today's world is, in many ways, hostile—particularly to children.

Harriet's essay is annotated so you can see how it illustrates the essay format described in Chapter 6 (page 82). As you read the essay, try to determine how well it reflects the principles of effective writing. The commentary following the paper will help you look at the essay more closely and give you some sense of the way Harriet went about revising her first draft.

```
Harriet Davids
Professor Kinne
College Composition, Section 203
October 4, 19__
```

Challenges for Today's Parents

1   Reruns of situation comedies from the 1950s and early 1960s   Introduction
dramatize the kinds of problems that parents used to have with
their children. The Cleavers scold Beaver for not washing his
hands before dinner; the Andersons ground Bud for not doing his
homework; the Nelsons dock little Ricky's allowance because
he keeps forgetting to clean his room. But times have changed   Thesis
dramatically. Being a parent today is much more difficult than
it was a generation ago. Parents nowadays must protect their   Plan of
                                                                 development

children from a growing number of distractions, from sexually
explicit material, and from life-threatening situations.

First supporting
paragraph

Topic sentence ———

Today's parents must try, first of all, to control all the
new distractions that tempt children away from schoolwork. At
home, a child may have a room furnished with a stereo and television. Not many young people can resist the urge to listen to
a CD or watch MTV--especially if it is time to do schoolwork.
Outside the home, the distractions are even more alluring.
Children no longer "hang out" on a neighborhood corner within
earshot of Mom or Dad's reminder to come in and do homework.
Instead, they congregate in vast shopping malls, buzzing video
arcades, and gleaming fast-food restaurants. Parents and school
assignments have obvious difficulty competing with such enticing alternatives.

Second
supporting
paragraph

Topic sentence
with link to
previous
paragraph

3

Besides dealing with these distractions, parents have to
shield their children from a flood of sexually explicit materials. Today, children can find sex magazines and pornographic
paperbacks in the same corner store that once offered only comics and candy. Children will not see the fuzzily photographed
nudes that a previous generation did but will encounter the
hard-core raunchiness of <u>Playboy</u> or <u>Penthouse</u>. Moreover, the
movies young people rent from the neighborhood video store or
see at the local theater often focus on highly sexual situations. It is difficult to teach children traditional values when
films show teachers seducing students and young people treating
sex as a casual sport. An even more difficult matter for parents
is the heavily sexual content of programs on television. With
just a flick of the dial, children can see soap-opera stars
cavorting in bed or watch cable programs where nudity is common.

Third supporting
paragraph

Topic sentence
with emphasis
signal

Most disturbing to parents today, however, is the increase
in life-threatening dangers that face young people, When children are small, parents fear that their youngsters may be victims of violence. Every news program seems to carry a report
about a mass murderer who preys on young girls, a deviant who
has buried six boys in his backyard, or an organized child pornography ring that molests preschoolers. When children are
older, parents begin to worry about their kids' use of drugs.
Peer pressure to experiment with drugs is often stronger than
parents' warnings. This pressure to experiment can be fatal.

Finally, even if young people escape the hazards associated with drugs, they must still resist the pressure to drink. Although alcohol has always held an attraction for teenagers, reports indicate that they are drinking more than ever before. As many parents know, the consequences of this attraction can be deadly--especially when drinking is combined with driving.

5   Within one generation, the world as a place to raise children has changed dramatically. One wonders how yesterday's parents would have dealt with today's problems. Could the Andersons have kept Bud away from MTV? Could the Nelsons have shielded little Ricky from sexually explicit material? Could the Cleavers have protected Beaver from drugs and alcohol? Parents must be aware of all these distractions and dangers yet be willing to give their children the freedom they need to become responsible adults. It is not an easy task.

> Conclusion
>
> References to TV shows recall introduction

Commentary

> Student essay in progress

Introduction and Thesis

The opening paragraph attracts readers' interest by recalling several vintage television shows that have almost become part of our cultural heritage. Harriet begins with these examples from the past because they offer such a sharp contrast to the present, thus underscoring the idea expressed in her *thesis:* "Being a parent today is much more difficult than it was a generation ago." Opening in this way, with material that serves as a striking contrast to what follows, is a common and effective strategy. Note, too, that Harriet's thesis states the paper's subject (being a parent) as well as her attitude toward the subject (the job is more demanding than it was years ago).

Plan of Development

Harriet follows her thesis with a *plan of development* that anticipates the three major points to be covered in the essay's supporting paragraphs. Unfortunately, this particular plan of development is somewhat mechanical, with the major points being trotted past the reader in one long, awkward sentence. To deal with the problem, Harriet could have rewritten the sentence or eliminated the plan of development altogether, ending the introduction with her thesis.

Patterns of Development

Although Harriet develops her thesis primarily through *examples,* she also draws on two other patterns of development. The whole paper implies a *contrast* between the way life and parenting are now and the way they used to be. The essay also contains an element of *causal analysis* since all the factors that Harriet cites affect children and the way they are raised.

Purpose, Audience, Tone, and Point of View

Given the essay's *purpose* and *audience*, Harriet adopts a serious *tone*, providing no-nonsense evidence to support her thesis. Note, too, that she uses the *third-person point of view*. Although she writes from the perspective of a mother of two teenage daughters, she doesn't write in the first person or refer specifically to her own experiences and those of her daughters. She adopts this objective stance because she wants to keep the focus on the issue rather than on her family.

What if Harriet had been asked by her daughters' school newspaper to write a humorous column about the trials and tribulations that parents face raising children? Aiming for a different tone, purpose, and audience, Harriet probably would have taken another approach. Drawing upon her personal experience, she might have confessed how she survives MTV's flash and dazzle, as well as the din of stereos blasting rock music at all hours: she stuffs her ears with cotton, hides her daughters' tapes, and cuts off the electricity. This material—with its first-person perspective, exaggeration, and light tone—would be appropriate.

Organization

Structuring the essay around a series of *relevant* and *specific examples*, Harriet uses *emphatic order* to sequence the paper's three main points: that a growing number of distractions, sexually explicit materials, and life-threatening situations make parenting difficult nowadays. The third supporting paragraph begins with the words "Most disturbing to parents today...," signaling that Harriet feels particular concern about the physical dangers children face. Moreover, she uses basic organizational strategies to sequence the supporting examples within each paragraph. The details in the first supporting paragraph are organized *spatially*, starting with distractions at home and moving to those outside the home. The second supporting paragraph arranges examples *emphatically*. Harriet starts with sexually explicit publications and ends with the "even more difficult matter" of sexuality on television. The third and final supporting paragraph is organized *chronologically*; it begins by discussing dangers to small children and concludes by talking about teenagers.

The essay also displays Harriet's familiarity with other kinds of organizational strategies. Each supporting paragraph opens with a *topic sentence*. Further, *signal devices* are used throughout the paper to show the relationship among ideas: *transitions* ("*Instead,* they congregate in vast shopping malls"; "*Moreover,* the movies young people attend often focus on highly sexual situations"); *repetition* ("*sexual* situations" and "*sexual* content"); *synonyms* ("distractions ... enticing alternatives" and "life-threatening ... fatal"); *pronouns* ("young people ... *they*"); and *bridging sentences* ("Besides dealing with these distractions, parents have to shield their children from a flood of sexually explicit materials").

A Minor Problem

Harriet's efforts to write a well-organized essay result in a somewhat predictable structure. It might have been better had she rewritten one of the paragraphs, perhaps embedding the topic sentence in the middle of the paragraph or saving it for the end. Similarly, Harriet's signal devices are a little heavy-handed. Even so, an essay with a sharp focus and clear signals is preferable to one with a confusing or inaccessible structure. As she gains more experience, Harriet can work on making the structure of her essays more subtle.

Conclusion

Harriet brings the essay to a satisfying *close* by reminding readers of the paper's central idea and three main points. The final paragraph also extends the essay's scope by introducing a new but related issue: that parents have to strike a balance between their need to provide limitations and their children's need for freedom.

Revising the First Draft

As you saw on pages 101 and 128–129, Harriet reworked her essay a number of times. For a clearer sense of her revision process, compare the final version of her conclusion (on page 139) with the original version reprinted here. Harriet wisely waited to rework her conclusion until after she had finetuned the rest of the essay. The marginal annotations, ranked in order of importance, indicate the problems that Harriet and her editing group detected in the conclusion:

Student essay in progress

Original Conclusion

Most adults love their children and want to be good parents. But it's difficult because the world seems stacked against young people. Even Holden Caulfield had trouble dealing with society's pressures. Parents must give their children some freedom but not so much that kids lose sight of what's important.

(1) Paragraph seems tacked on

(3) Boring sentence— too vague

(2) Inappropriate reference to Holden

As soon as Harriet heard her paper read aloud during a group session, she realized her conclusion didn't work at all. Rather than bringing the essay to a pleasing finish, the final paragraph seemed like a tired afterthought. A classmate also pointed out that her allusion to *The Catcher in the Rye* misrepresented the essay's focus since Harriet discusses children of all ages, not just teens.

Keeping these points in mind, Harriet decided to scrap her original conclusion. Working at a word processor, she prepared a new, much stronger concluding paragraph. Besides eliminating the distracting reference to Holden Caulfield, she replaced the shopworn opening sentence ("Most adults love their children....") with three interesting and rhythmical questions ("Could the Andersons...Could the Nelsons...Could the Cleavers...?"). Because these questions recall the essay's main points and echo the introduction's reference to vintage television shows, they help unify Harriet's paper and bring it to a satisfying close.

These are just a few of the changes Harriet made when reworking her essay. Realizing that writing is a process, she left herself enough time to revise. She was gratified by her classmates' responses to what she had written and pleased by the lively discussion her essay provoked. Early in her composition course, Harriet learned that attention to the various stages in the writing process yields satisfying results, for writer and reader alike.

ACTIVITIES: EDITING AND PROOFREADING

1. Applying for a job, a student wrote the following letter. Edit and proofread it carefully, as if it were your own. If you have trouble spotting many grammar, spelling, and typing errors, that's a sign you need to review the appropriate sections of the Handbook (page 636).

Dear Mr. Eno:

I am a sophomore at Harper College who will be returning home to Brooktown this June, hopefully, to fine a job for the the summer. One that would give me further experience in the retail field. I have heard from my freind, Sarah Snyder, that your hiring college studnets as assistant mangers, I would be greatly intrested in such a postion.

I have quite a bit of experience in retail sales. Having worked after school in a "Dress Place" shop at Mason Mall, Pennsylvania. I started their as a sales clerk, by my second year I was serving as assistant manger.

I am reliable and responsible, and truely enjoy sales work. Mary Carver, the owner of the "Dress Place," can verify my qualifications, she was my supervisor for two years.

I will be visiting Brooktown from April 25 to 30. I hope to have an oppurtunity to speak to you about possible summer jobs at that time, and will be available for interview at your convience. Thank-you for you're consideration.

Sincerley,

Joan Ackerman

Joan Ackerman

2. Retrieve the revised essay you prepared in response to either activity 11 or activity 12 in Chapter 8 (page 132). Following the guidelines described on the preceding pages, edit and proofread your revision. After making the needed changes, prepare your final draft of the essay, using the appropriate manuscript format. Before submitting your paper to your instructor, ask someone to check it for grammar, spelling, and typographical errors that may have slipped by you undetected.

THE PATTERNS OF DEVELOPMENT

10
AN OVERVIEW OF THE PATTERNS OF DEVELOPMENT

Throughout Part II, you saw how the patterns of development—narration, process analysis, definition, and so on—are used as strategies for generating, developing, and organizing ideas for essays. You also learned that, in practice, most types of writing combine two or more patterns. This chapter, the first in Part III, provides additional information about these important points. Once you have a clear understanding of the patterns in general, you'll be ready to move on to the remaining chapters in Part III. There you'll learn more about the unique characteristics of each pattern.

THE PATTERNS IN ACTION: DURING THE WRITING PROCESS

As you know, the patterns of development come into play throughout the composing process. In the prewriting stage, awareness of the patterns encourages you to think about your subject in fresh, new ways. Assume, for example, that you've been asked to write an essay about the way children are disciplined in school. However, you draw a blank as soon as you try to limit this general subject. To break the logjam, you could apply one or more patterns of development to your subject. *Comparison-contrast* might prompt you to write an essay investigating the differences between your parents' and your own feelings about school discipline.

Division-classification might lead you to another paper—one that categorizes the kinds of discipline used in school. And *cause-effect* might point to still another essay—one that explores the way students react to being suspended.

Further along in the writing process—after you've identified your limited subject and your thesis—the patterns of development can help you generate your paper's evidence. Imagine that your thesis is "Teachers shouldn't discipline students publicly just to make an example of them." You're not sure, though, how to develop this thesis. Calling on the patterns might spark some promising possibilities. *Narration* might encourage you to recount the disastrous time you were singled out and punished for the misdeeds of an entire class. Using *definition,* you might explain what is meant by an *autocratic* disciplinary style. *Argumentation-persuasion* might prompt you to advocate a new plan for disciplining students fairly and effectively.

The patterns of development also help you organize your ideas by pointing the way to an appropriate framework for a paper. Suppose you plan to write an essay for the campus newspaper about the disturbingly high incidence of shoplifting among college students; your purpose is to *persuade* young people not to get involved in this tempting, supposedly victimless crime. You believe that many readers will be deterred from shoplifting if you tell them about the harrowing *process* set in motion once a shoplifter is detected. With this step-by-step explanation in mind, you can now map out the essay's content: what happens when a shoplifter is detained by a salesperson, questioned by store security personnel, led to a police car, booked at the police station, and tried in a courtroom.

THE PATTERNS IN ACTION: IN AN ESSAY

Although Part III devotes a separate chapter to each of the nine patterns of development, all chapters emphasize the same important point: Most writing consists of several patterns, with the dominant pattern providing the piece's organizational framework. To reinforce this point, each chapter contains a section, "How [the Pattern] Fits Your Purpose and Audience," that shows how a writer's purpose often leads to a blending of patterns. You'll also notice that one of the "Questions About the Writer's Craft" following each professional selection often asks you to analyze the piece's combination of patterns. Further, the "Writing Assignments Using Other Patterns of Development" encourage you to discover for yourself which mix of patterns would work best in a given piece of writing. In short, all through *The Macmillan Writer,* we emphasize that the patterns of development are far from being mechanical formulas. On the contrary: They are practical strategies that open up options in every stage of the composing process.

Before studying how the writers in Part III combine patterns of development, you'll probably find it helpful to glance back at pages 29–30 so you can review the broad purpose of each pattern. That done, you'll be ready to analyze the selections in this part of the book. The following checklist will help you look more closely at the selections.

☑ ANALYZING HOW A WRITER COMBINES PATTERNS:
   A CHECKLIST

☐ What are the writer's purpose and thesis?

☐ Which pattern of development dominates this essay? How does this pattern help the writer support the essay's thesis and fulfill the essay's purpose?

☐ What other patterns appear in the essay? How do these secondary patterns help the writer support the essay's thesis and fulfill the essay's purpose?

Your responses to these three questions will reward you with a richer understanding of the way skilled prose stylists use the patterns of development in their work. To give you an even clearer sense of how writers mix patterns, we have annotated the essay "The Death of the Moth" by Virginia Woolf, using the preceding three questions as a guide. By making your own annotations on Woolf's essay and then comparing them to ours, you can measure your ability to analyze Woolf's use of the patterns. You can further evaluate your analysis of the piece by answering the three questions on your own and then comparing your responses to ours on pages 150–152.

VIRGINIA WOOLF

Virginia Woolf (1882–1941) is considered one of the most innovative writers of the twentieth century. Born in London, Woolf became a key member of the Bloomsbury Group, a circle of writers and artists committed to the highest standards in art and literature. Woolf's works include the novels *Mrs. Dalloway* (1923) and *To the Lighthouse* (1927), as well as the collection of essays *A Room of One's Own* (1920). Although her work met with critical acclaim, Woolf was troubled all her life by severe depression and committed suicide in 1941. The following selection first appeared in the volume *The Death of the Moth and Other Essays* (1948).

THE DEATH OF THE MOTH

1   Moths that fly by day are not properly to be called moths; they do not excite that pleasant sense of dark autumn nights and ivy-blossom which the commonest yellow-underwing asleep in the shadow of the curtain never fails to rouse in us. They are hybrid creatures, neither gay like butterflies nor sombre like their own species. Nevertheless the present specimen, with his narrow hay-coloured wings, fringed with a tassel of the same colour, seemed to be content with life. It was a pleasant morning, mid-September,

Description of the moth

Definition (by negation): How this moth differs from the usual kind mild, benignant, yet with a keener breath than that of the summer months. The plough was already scoring the field opposite the window, and where the share had been, the earth was pressed flat and gleamed with moisture.

Part of implied
purpose/thesis:
Nature's energy

Description of nature's
energy here *contrasts*
with *description* of
nature in ¶5 (part
of purpose/thesis).

Such vigour came rolling in from the fields and the down beyond that it was difficult to keep the eyes strictly turned upon the book. The rooks too were keeping one of their annual festivities; soaring round the tree tops until it looked as if a vast net with thousands of black knots in it had been cast up into the air; which, after a few moments, sank slowly down upon the trees until every twig seemed to have a knot at the end of it. Then, suddenly, the net would be thrown into the air again in a wider circle this time, with the utmost clamour and vociferation, as though to be thrown into the air and settle slowly down upon the tree tops were a tremendously exciting experience.

Comparison between
nature's energy and
the moth's strong
life force (part of
purpose/thesis)

Start of *narrative* (main
pattern) about the
moth's plight

Start of *narrative* about
Woolf's reaction to the
moth's plight

Description of moth's
strong life force—
despite his small size
(these two contrasting
qualities are part of
purpose/thesis)

The same energy which inspired the rooks, the ploughmen, the   2
horses, and even, it seemed, the lean bare-backed downs, sent the moth fluttering from side to side of his square of the windowpane. One could not help watching him. One was, indeed, conscious of a queer feeling of pity for him. The possibilities of pleasure seemed that morning so enormous and so various that to have only a moth's part in life, and a day moth's at that, appeared a hard fate, and his zest in enjoying his meagre opportunities to the full, pathetic. He flew vigorously to one corner of his compartment, and, after waiting there a second, flew across to the other. What remained for him but to fly to a third corner and then to a fourth? That was all he could do, in spite of the size of the downs, the width of the sky, the far-off smoke of houses, and the romantic voice, now and then, of a steamer out at sea. What he could do he did. Watching him, it seemed as if a fibre, very thin but pure, of the enormous energy of the world had been thrust into his frail and diminutive body. As often as he crossed the pane, I could fancy that a thread of vital light became visible. He was little or nothing but life.

Part of purpose/
thesis: The moth
represents life.

Narrative about
Woolf's reaction
continues.

Restatement of part
of purpose/thesis:
The moth's two
contrasting qualities

Yet, because he was so small, and so simple a form of the energy that   3
was rolling in at the open window and driving its way through so many narrow and intricate corridors in my own brain and in those of other human beings, there was something marvellous as well as pathetic about him. It

was as if someone had taken a tiny bead of pure life and decking it as lightly as possible with down and feathers, had set it dancing and zigzagging to show us the true nature of life. Thus displayed one could not get over the strangeness of it. One is apt to forget all about life, seeing it humped and bossed and garnished and cumbered so that it has to move with the greatest circumspection and dignity. Again, the thought of all that life might have been had he been born in any other shape caused one to view his simple activities with a kind of pity.

Restatement of part of purpose/thesis: The moth represents life.

4   After a time, tired by his dancing apparently, he settled on the window ledge in the sun, and, the queer spectacle being at an end, I forgot about him. Then, looking up, my eye was caught by him. He was trying to resume his dancing, but seemed either so stiff or so awkward that he could only flutter to the bottom of the window-pane; and when he tried to fly across it he failed. Being intent on other matters I watched these futile attempts for a time without thinking, unconsciously waiting for him to resume his flight, as one waits for a machine, that has stopped momentarily, to start again without considering the reason of its failure. After perhaps a seventh attempt he slipped from the wooden ledge and fell, fluttering his wings, on to his back on the window sill. The helplessness of his attitude roused me. It flashed upon me that he was in difficulties; he could no longer raise himself; his legs struggled vainly. But, as I stretched out a pencil, meaning to help him to right himself, it came over me that the failure and awkwardness were the approach of death. I laid the pencil down again.

Narrative about the moth's plight continues; tension builds.

Narrative about Woolf's reaction continues.

Hint of the resolution of the narrative about the moth

5   The legs agitated themselves once more. I looked as if for the enemy against which he struggled. I looked out of doors. What had happened there? Presumably it was midday, and work in the fields had stopped. Stillness and quiet had replaced the previous animation. The birds had taken themselves off to feed in the brooks. The horses stood still. Yet the power was there all the same, massed outside, indifferent, impersonal, not attending to anything in particular. Somehow it was opposed to the little hay-coloured moth. It was useless to try to do anything. One could only watch the extraordinary efforts made by those tiny legs against an oncoming doom which could, had it chosen, have submerged an entire city, not merely a city, but masses of human beings; nothing, I knew, had any chance

Narrative about Woolf's reaction continues.

Description of nature's indifference here contrasts with description of nature in ¶1 (part of purpose/thesis).

Restatement of part of purpose/thesis: The strength of the moth's life force—despite small size

Part of purpose/thesis: Death's inevitability

Narrative about moth continues. against death. Nevertheless after a pause of exhaustion the legs fluttered again. It was superb, this last protest, and so frantic that he succeeded at last in righting himself. One's sympathies, of course, were all on the side of

Narrative about Woolf's reaction continues. life. Also, when there was nobody to care or to know, this gigantic effort on the part of an insignificant little moth, against a power of such magnitude, to retain what no one else valued or desired to keep, moved one strangely.

Restatement of part of purpose/thesis: The strength of the moth's life force— despite his size Again, somehow, one saw life, a pure bead. I lifted the pencil again, useless though I knew it to be. But even as I did so, the unmistakable tokens of death showed themselves. The body relaxed, and instantly grew stiff. The

Resolution of the *narrative* about the moth struggle was over. The insignificant little creature now knew death. As I looked at the dead moth, this minute wayside triumph of so great a force over so mean an antagonist filled me with wonder. Just as life had been strange a few minutes before, so death was now as strange. The moth having righted himself now lay most decently, and uncomplainingly composed.

Restatement of part of purpose/thesis: Death's inevitability O yes, he seemed to say, death is stronger than I am.

The following answers to the questions on page 147 will help you analyze Virginia Woolf's use of the patterns of development in the essay "The Death of the Moth."

1. *What is the writer's purpose and thesis?* *Woolf's purpose* is to show that the tiny moth's courageous but ultimately futile battle to cling to life embodies the struggle at the very heart of all existence. Woolf achieves her purpose by relating the story of the moth's efforts to resist death. Her *thesis* might be expressed this way: Although living creatures may make "extraordinary efforts" (paragraph 5) to hold on to life, these attempts aren't strong enough to defy death. Nothing, Woolf writes, has "any chance against death" (5).

Woolf's purpose and thesis first become apparent at the end of paragraph 2. There she shows that the moth, with his "frail and diminutive body," represents "nothing but life." Although "small...and simple" (3), the moth is suffused with the same extraordinary energy that is evident in the natural world beyond Woolf's window. This energy, combined with the moth's tiny size, makes the creature both "marvellous" and "pathetic" (3)—two qualities that are particularly apparent during the moth's final struggles. During those moments, the moth makes a final "superb" (5) protest against death, but ultimately the "insignificant" (5) creature— like all forms of life—must cease his valiant struggle and die.

2. *What pattern of development dominates the essay? How does this pattern help the writer support the essay's thesis and fulfill the essay's purpose?* Although the essay's first paragraph is largely descriptive, it becomes clear by paragraph 2 that the description is in service of a larger *narrative* about the moth's struggles. It's this narrative that dominates the essay.

At the beginning, the moth is imbued with vitality, as he flies "vigorously" (paragraph 2) and with "zest" (2) from one side of the window to the other. But narrative tension begins to build in paragraph 4. There Woolf writes that the moth tries once again to cross the windowpane, fails repeatedly, and slips "onto his back," seemingly defeated. However, even then, the moth doesn't abandon his hold on life, for—as Woolf relates in paragraph 5—he tries, despite exhaustion, to right himself. Against all odds, he finally succeeds, but his frantic struggle to hold on to life takes its toll, and the tiny creature soon dies. This detailed story of the moth's futile battle against death is presented as an emblem of the fate of all life. Through this narrative, Woolf achieves her purpose and thesis: to convey the power of nature and the inability of living creatures—despite heroic efforts—to defy this power.

Paralleling the tale of the moth's struggle is another *narrative*: the story of Woolf's changing understanding of the event that unfolds before her. When the moth is "dancing" (3), energetic, and vital, Woolf "can't help watching him" (2) and feels a kind of wonderment at this "tiny bead of pure life" (3). Then in paragraph 4, Woolf writes that she forgets about the moth for a while until she happens to look up and see his "futile attempts" to "resume dancing." For a few moments, she watches the moth's "stiff" and "awkward" efforts to fly, expecting him to demonstrate the same vitality as before. Suddenly, she understands that the moth is "in difficulties" and can no longer lift himself up. She tries to help but abandons her efforts when she realizes that the moth's labored efforts signify the "approach of death." Paragraph 5 presents the final stage of Woolf's interior narrative. She looks outside her window for an explanation of the moth's plight. But now she finds that the forces of nature—earlier so exuberant and vibrant—are, if anything, "opposed to the little hay-colored moth." With that, her attention is once again drawn to the moth and the fluttering of his legs. Although drained, the tiny creature makes one last effort to resist death—and, improbably enough, picks himself up one more time. Struck by the sheer power of the moth's life force, Woolf is prompted, as before, to help the creature, even though she recognizes the futility. But then the "unmistakable" tokens of death appear, and the moth gives up his struggle, succumbing—as all forms of life must—to the forces of nature. With the moth lying "uncomplainingly composed," Woolf comes to accept the fact that "death is stronger than life."

3. *What other patterns appear in the essay? How do these secondary patterns help the writer support the essay's thesis and fulfill the essay's purpose?* Although the essay is predominantly a narrative, it also contains other patterns. The *descriptive* passage at the beginning of the essay includes a brief *definition by negation* in which Woolf explains how the creature she is observing differs from the usual, more colorful night moth. The rest of paragraph 1 draws upon description to evoke the sense of early autumn and nature's extraordinary energy. This description of the natural world's vibrancy and abundance, exemplified by the rooks and plowed earth, *contrasts* with Woolf's later characterization of the natural world in paragraph 5. There she writes, "Stillness and quiet...replaced the previous animation," and she senses not that nature fosters vitality, but that it is "indifferent, impersonal, not attending to anything in particular."

Shifting her focus in paragraph 2 from the natural world to the moth, Woolf exercises her *descriptive* powers to convey the moth's extraordinary zest as he flies across the windowpane. In this paragraph, Woolf also draws upon *comparison-contrast* to show that despite *differences* in their sizes, the tiny moth and the vast natural world embody the *same* primal energy. Woolf's consideration of this elemental similarity leads her to the basic *contrast* at the heart of the essay: While the moth's tiny size makes him "pathetic," his formidable life spirit makes him "marvellous." He may be small and lightweight, but he is abuzz with vitality. When contrasted to the enormous power of nature, the moth—like all forms of life—may be puny, but his impulse to defy such power inspires awe and reverence.

11
DESCRIPTION

WHAT IS DESCRIPTION?

ALL of us respond in a strong way to sensory stimulation. The sweet perfume of a candy shop takes us back to childhood; the blank white walls of the campus infirmary remind us of long vigils at a hospital where a grandmother lay dying; the screech of a subway car sets our nerves on edge.

Without any sensory stimulation, we sink into a less-than-human state. Neglected babies, left alone with no human touch, no colors, no lullabies, become withdrawn and unresponsive. And prisoners dread solitary confinement, knowing that the sensory deprivation can be unbearable, even to the point of madness.

Because sensory impressions are so potent, descriptive writing has a unique power and appeal. **Description** can be defined as the expression, in vivid language, of what the five senses experience. A richly rendered description freezes a subject in time, evoking sights, smells, sounds, textures, and tastes in such a way that readers become one with the writer's world.

HOW DESCRIPTION FITS YOUR PURPOSE AND AUDIENCE

Description can be a supportive technique that develops part of an essay, or it can be the dominant technique used throughout an essay. Here are some examples of the way description can help you meet the objective of an essay developed chiefly through another pattern of development:

• In a *causal analysis* showing the *consequences* of pet overpopulation, you might describe the desperate appearance of a pack of starving stray dogs.

- In an *argumentation-persuasion essay* urging more rigorous handgun control, you might start with a description of a violent family confrontation that ended in murder.
- In a *process analysis* explaining the pleasure of making ice cream at home, you might describe the beauty of an old-fashioned, hand-cranked ice cream maker.
- In a *narrative essay* recounting a day in the life of a street musician, you might describe the musician's energy and the joyous appreciation of passersby.

In each case, the essay's overall purpose would affect the amount of description needed.

Your readers also influence how much description to include. As you write, ask yourself, "What do my particular readers need to know to understand and experience keenly what I'm describing? What descriptive details will they enjoy most?" Your answers to these and similar questions will help you tailor your description to specific readers. Consider an article intended for professional horticulturists; its purpose is to explain a new technique for controlling spider mites. Because of readers' expertise, there would be little need for a lengthy description of the insects. Written for a college newspaper, however, the article would probably provide a detailed description of the mites so student gardeners could spot them with ease.

While your purpose and audience define *how much* to describe, you have great freedom deciding *what* to describe. Description is especially suited to objects (your car or desk, for example), but you can also describe a person, an animal, a place, a time, and a phenomenon or concept. You might write an effective description about a friend who runs marathons (person), a pair of ducks that returns each year to a neighbor's pond (animals), the kitchen of a fast-food restaurant (place), a period when you were unemployed (time), the "fight or flight" response to danger (phenomenon or concept).

Description can be divided into two types: objective and subjective. In an **objective description,** you describe the subject in a straightforward and literal way, without revealing your attitude or feelings. Reporters, as well as technical and scientific writers, specialize in objective description; their jobs depend on their ability to detail experiences without emotional bias. For example, a reporter may write an unemotional account of a township meeting that ended in a fistfight. Or a marine biologist may write a factual report describing the way sea mammals are killed by the plastic refuse (sandwich wrappings, straws, fishing lines) that humans throw into the ocean.

In contrast, when writing a **subjective description,** you convey a highly personal view of your subject and seek to elicit a strong emotional response from your readers. Such subjective descriptions often take the form of reflective pieces or character studies. For example, in an essay describing the rich plant life in an inner-city garden, you might reflect on people's longing to connect with the soil and express admiration for the gardeners' hard work—an admiration you'd like readers to share. Or, in a character study of your grandfather, you might describe his stern appearance and gentle behavior, hoping that the contradiction will move readers as much as it moves you.

The *tone* of a subjective description is determined by your purpose, your attitude toward the subject, and the reader response you wish to evoke. Consider an essay about a dynamic woman who runs a center for disturbed children. If your goal is to make readers admire the woman, your tone will be serious and appreciative. But if you want to criticize the woman's high-pressure tactics and create distaste for her management style, your tone will be disapproving and severe.

The language of a descriptive piece also depends, to a great extent, on whether your purpose is primarily objective or subjective. If the description is objective, the language is straightforward, precise, and factual. Such *denotative* language consists of neutral dictionary meanings. If you want to describe as dispassionately as possible fans' violent behavior at a football game, you might write about the "large crowd" and its "mass movement onto the field." But if you are shocked by the fans' behavior and want to write a subjective piece that inspires similar outrage in readers, then you might write about the "swelling mob" and its "rowdy stampede onto the field." In the latter case, the language used would be *connotative* and emotionally charged so that readers would share your feelings. (For more on denotation and connotation, see pages 22–23 and pages 120–121.)

Subjective and objective descriptions often overlap. Sometimes a single sentence contains both objective and subjective elements: "Although his hands were large and misshapen by arthritis, they were gentle to the touch, inspiring confidence and trust." Other times, part of an essay may provide a factual description (the physical appearance of a summer cabin your family rented), while another part of the essay may be highly subjective (how you felt in the cabin, sitting in front of a fire on a rainy day).

PREWRITING STRATEGIES

The following checklist shows how you can apply to description some of the prewriting strategies discussed in Chapter 2.

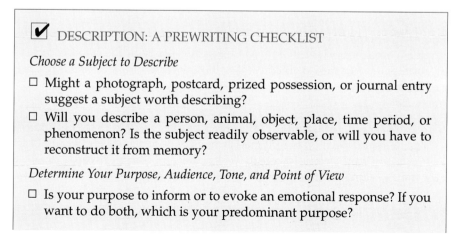

✔ DESCRIPTION: A PREWRITING CHECKLIST

Choose a Subject to Describe

☐ Might a photograph, postcard, prized possession, or journal entry suggest a subject worth describing?

☐ Will you describe a person, animal, object, place, time period, or phenomenon? Is the subject readily observable, or will you have to reconstruct it from memory?

Determine Your Purpose, Audience, Tone, and Point of View

☐ Is your purpose to inform or to evoke an emotional response? If you want to do both, which is your predominant purpose?

☐ What audience are you writing for? How much does the audience already know about the subject you plan to describe?

☐ What tone and point of view will best serve your purpose and make readers receptive to your description?

Use Prewriting to Generate Details About the Subject

☐ How could freewriting, journal entries, or brainstorming help you gather sensory specifics about your subject?

☐ What relevant details about your subject come to mind when you apply the questioning technique to each of the five senses? What sounds (pitch, volume, and quality) predominate? What can you touch and how does it feel (temperature, weight, texture)? What do you see (color, pattern, shape, size)? What smells (pleasant, unpleasant) can't you forget? What tastes (agreeable, disagreeable) remain memorable?

STRATEGIES FOR USING DESCRIPTION IN AN ESSAY

After prewriting, you're ready to draft your essay. The following suggestions will be helpful whether you use description as a dominant or supportive pattern of development.

1. Focus a descriptive essay around a dominant impression.   Like other kinds of writing, a descriptive essay must have a thesis, or main point. In a descriptive essay with a subjective slant, the thesis usually centers on the **dominant impression** you have about your subject. Suppose you decide to write an essay on your ninth-grade history teacher, Ms. Hazzard. You want the paper to convey how unconventional and flamboyant she was. The essay could, of course, focus on a different dominant impression—how insensitive she could be to students, for example. What's important is that you establish—early in the paper—the dominant impression you intend to convey. Although descriptive essays often imply, rather than explicitly state, the dominant impression, that impression should be unmistakable.

2. Select the details to include.   The prewriting techniques discussed on pages 25–31 can help you develop heightened powers of observation and recall. Practice in noting significant details can lead you to become—in the words of novelist Henry James—"one of those people on whom nothing is lost." The power of description hinges on your ability to select from all possible details *only those that support the dominant impression*. All others—no matter how vivid or interesting—

must be left out. If you were describing how flamboyant Ms. Hazzard could be, the details in the following paragraph would be appropriate:

> A large-boned woman, Ms. Hazzard wore her bright red hair piled on top of her head, where it perched precariously. By the end of class, wayward strands of hair tumbled down and fell into eyes fringed by spiky false eyelashes. Ms. Hazzard's nails, filed into crisp points, were painted either bloody burgundy or neon pink. Plastic bangle bracelets, also either burgundy or pink, clattered up and down her ample arms as she scrawled on the board the historical dates that had, she claimed, "changed the world."

Such details—the heavy eye makeup, stiletto nails, gaudy bracelets—contribute to the impression of a flamboyant, unusual person. Even if you remembered times that Ms. Hazzard seemed perfectly conventional and understated, most likely you wouldn't describe those times because they would contradict the dominant impression.

You must also be selective in the *number of details* you include. Having a dominant impression helps you eliminate many details gathered during prewriting, but there still will be choices to make. For example, it would be inappropriate to describe in exhaustive detail everything in a messy room:

> The brown desk, made of a grained plastic laminate, is directly under a small window covered by a torn yellow-and-gold plaid curtain. In the left corner of the desk are four crumbled balls of blue-lined yellow paper, three red markers (all without caps), two fine-point blue pens, a crumbling pink eraser, and four letters, two bearing special wildlife stamps. A green down-filled vest and an out-of-shape red cable-knit sweater are thrown over the back of the bright blue metal bridge chair pushed under the desk. Under the chair is an oval braided rug, its once brilliant blues and greens spotted by soda and coffee stains.

Readers will be reluctant to wade through such undifferentiated specifics. Even more important, such excessive detailing dilutes the essay's focus. You end up with a seemingly endless list of specifics, rather than with a carefully crafted word picture. In this regard, sculptors and writers are similar—what they take away is as important as what they leave in.

3. Organize the descriptive details.   It's important to select the organizational pattern (or combination of patterns) that best supports your dominant impression. The paragraphs in a descriptive essay are usually sequenced *spatially* (from top to bottom, interior to exterior, near to far) or *chronologically* (as the subject is experienced in time). But the paragraphs can also be ordered *emphatically* (ending with your subject's most striking elements) or by *sensory impression* (first smell, then taste, then touch, and so on).

You might, for instance, use a *spatial* pattern to organize a description of a large city as you viewed it from the air, a taxi, or a subway car. A description of your first day on a new job might move *chronologically*, starting with how you felt the first hour on the job and proceeding through the rest of the day. In a paper describing a bout with the flu, you might arrange details *emphatically*, beginning with a description of your low-level aches and pains and concluding with an account of your raging fever. An essay about a neighborhood garbage dump could be organized by *sensory impressions:* the sights of the dump, its smells, its sounds. Regardless of the organizational pattern you use, provide enough *signal devices* (for example, *about, next, worst of all*) so that readers can follow the description easily.

Finally, although descriptive essays don't always have conventional topic sentences, each descriptive paragraph should have a clear focus. Often this focus is indicated by a sentence early in the paragraph that names the scene, object, or individual to be described. Such a sentence functions as a kind of *informal topic sentence;* the paragraph's descriptive details then develop that topic sentence.

4. Use vivid sensory language and varied sentence structure.   The connotative language typical of subjective description should be richly evocative. The words you select must etch in readers' minds the same picture that you have in yours. For this reason, rather than relying on vague generalities, you must use language that involves readers' senses. Consider the difference between the following paired descriptions:

Vague	Vivid
The food was unappetizing.	The stew congealed into an oval pool of muddy-brown fat.
The toothpaste was refreshing.	The toothpaste, minty sweet, tingled against my bare teeth, finally free from braces.
Filled with passengers and baggage, the car moved slowly down the road.	Burdened with its load of clamoring children and bulging suitcases, the car labored down the interstate on bald tires and worn shocks, emitting puffs of blue exhaust and an occasional backfire.

Unlike the *concrete, sensory-packed* sentences on the right, the sentences on the left fail to create vivid word pictures that engage readers. While all good writing blends abstract and concrete language, descriptive writing demands an abundance of specific sensory language. (For more on specific language, see pages 121–122 in Chapter 8.)

Although you should aim for rich, sensory images, avoid overloading your sentences with *too many adjectives:* "A stark, smooth, blinding glass cylinder, the fifty-story skyscraper dominated the crowded city street." Delete unnecessary words, retaining only the most powerful: "A blinding glass cylinder, the skyscraper dominated the street."

Remember, too, that *verbs pack more of a wallop* than adverbs. The following sentence has to rely on adverbs (italicized) because its verbs are so weak: "She walked *casually* into the room and *deliberately* tried not to pay attention to their stares." Rewritten, so that verbs (italicized), not adverbs, do the bulk of the work, the sentence becomes more powerful: "She *strolled* into the room and *ignored* their stares." *Onomatopoetic* verbs, like *buzz, sizzle,* and *zoom,* can be especially effective because their sounds convey their meaning. (For more on vigorous verbs, see pages 122–124 in Chapter 8).

Figures of speech—nonliteral, imaginative comparisons between two basically dissimilar things—are another way to enliven descriptive writing. *Similes* use the word *like* or *as* when comparing; *metaphors* state or imply that the two things being compared are alike; and *personification* attributes human characteristics to inanimate things. (For further discussion of figures of speech, refer to pages 125–126 in Chapter 8.)

The examples that follow show how effective figurative language can be in descriptive writing:

Simile

Moving as jerkily as a marionette on strings, the old man picked himself up off the sidewalk and staggered down the street.

Metaphor

Stalking their prey, the hall monitors remained hidden in the corridors, motionless and ready to spring on any unsuspecting student who tried to sneak into class late.

Personification

The scoop of vanilla ice cream, plain and unadorned, cried out for hot fudge sauce and a sprinkling of sliced pecans.

(For suggestions on avoiding clichéd figures of speech, see page 125 in Chapter 8.)

Finally, when writing descriptive passages, you need to *vary sentence structure.* Don't use the same subject-verb pattern in all sentences. The second example above, for instance, could have been written as follows: "The hall monitors stalked their prey. They hid in the corridors. They remained motionless and ready to spring on any unsuspecting student who tried to sneak into class late." But the sentence is richer and more interesting when the descriptive elements are embedded, eliminating what would otherwise have been a clipped and predictable subject-verb pattern. (For more on sentence variety, see pages 109–114 in Chapter 8.)

REVISION STRATEGIES

Once you have a draft of the essay, you're ready to revise. The following checklist will help you and those giving you feedback apply to description some of the revision techniques discussed in Chapters 7 and 8.

☑ DESCRIPTION: A REVISION CHECKLIST

Revise Overall Meaning and Structure

☐ What dominant impression does the essay convey? Is the dominant impression stated or implied? Where? Should it be made more obvious or more subtle? Why?

☐ Is the essay primarily objective or subjective? Should the essay be more personal and emotionally charged or less so?

☐ Which descriptive details don't support the dominant impression? Should they be deleted, or should the dominant impression be adjusted to encompass the details?

Revise Paragraph Development

☐ How are the essay's descriptive paragraphs (or passages) organized—spatially, chronologically, emphatically, or by sensory impressions? Would another organizational pattern be more effective? Which one(s)? Why?

☐ Which paragraphs lack a distinctive focus?

☐ Which descriptive paragraphs (or passages) deteriorate into a mere list of sensory impressions?

☐ Which descriptive paragraphs (or passages) are too abstract or general? Which fail to engage the reader's senses? How could they be made more concrete and specific?

Revise Sentences and Words

☐ What signal devices (such as *above, next, worst of all*) guide readers through the description? Are there enough signals? Too many?

☐ Where should sentence structure be varied so that it is less predictable and monotonous?

☐ Which sentences lack sensory images? How could they be made more evocative?

☐ Where should flat verbs and adverbs be replaced with vigorous verbs? Where would onomatopoeia enliven a sentence?

☐ Where are there too many adjectives? Which could be deleted?

☐ What figures of speech appear in the essay? Which seem contrived or trite?

STUDENT ESSAY: FROM PREWRITING THROUGH REVISION

The student essay that follows was written by Marie Martinez in response to this assignment:

> The essay "Once More to the Lake" is an evocative piece about a spot that had special meaning in E. B. White's life. Write an essay about a place that holds rich significance for you, centering the description on a dominant impression.

After deciding to write about the salt marsh near her grandparents' home, Marie used the prewriting technique of *questioning* to gather sensory details about this special place. To enhance her power of recall, she focused, one at a time, on each of the five senses. Then, typing as quickly as she could, she listed the sensory specifics that came to mind.

When Marie later reviewed the details listed under each sensory heading, she concluded that her essay's dominant impression should be the marsh's peaceful beauty. With that dominant impression in mind, she added some details to her prewriting and deleted others. Below and on the next page is Marie's original prewriting; the handwritten insertions indicate her later efforts to develop the material:

Questioning Technique

See: What do I see at the marsh?

- line of tall, waving reeds *bordering the creek*
- path--flattened grass
- spring--bright green (brilliant green)
- autumn--gold (tawny)
- winter--gray
- soil--spongy
- dark soil
- blue crabs
- creek--narrow, sinuous, can't see beginning or end *less than 15' wide*

- birds--little, brown
- low tide--steep bank of creek
- ~~an occasional beer can or potato chip bag~~
- grass under the water--green waves, shimmers
- fish--tiny, with silvery (minnows) sides, dart through water and vegetation *and underwater tangles*
- center of creek--everything water and sky

Hear: How does it sound there?

- chirping of birds ("tweep, tweep")
- splash of turtle or otter
- mainly silent

Feel: How does it feel?

- soil--spongy
- water--warmer than ocean; rub my face and neck; mucky and oily
- mud--slimy (through toes)

- crabs brush my legs
- feel buoyant, weightless

Smell: Why can't I forget its smell?

- salt
- soil

When Marie reviewed her annotated prewriting, she decided that, in the essay, she would order her brainstormed impressions by location rather than by sensory type. Using a spatial method of organization, she would present details as she moved from place to place—from her grandparents' home to the creek. The arrangement of details was now so clear to Marie that she felt comfortable moving to a first draft without further shaping her prewriting or preparing an outline. As she wrote, though, she frequently referred to her prewriting to retrieve sensory details about each location.

Now read Marie's paper, "Salt Marsh," noting the similarities and differences between her prewriting and final essay. You'll see that the essay's introduction and conclusion weren't drawn from the prewriting material, whereas most of the sensory details were. Notice, too, that when she wrote the essay, Marie expanded these details by adding more specifics and providing several powerful similes. Finally, consider how well the essay applies the principles of description discussed in this chapter. (The commentary that follows the paper will help you look at the essay more closely and will give you some sense of how Marie went about revising her first draft.)

Salt Marsh

by Marie Martinez

Introduction

In one of his journals, Thoreau told of the difficulty he   1
had escaping the obligations and cares of society: "It sometimes happens that I cannot easily shake off the village. The
thought of some work will run in my head and I am not where my
body is--I am out of my senses. In my walks I . . . return to my
senses." All of us feel out of our senses at times. Overwhelmed

by problems or everyday annoyances, we lose touch with sensory pleasures as we spend our days in noisy cities and stuffy classrooms. Just as Thoreau walked in the woods to return to his senses, I have a special place where I return to mine: the salt marsh behind my grandparents' house.   — Dominant impression (thesis)

2   My grandparents live on the East Coast, a mile or so inland from the sea. Between the ocean and the mainland is a wide fringe of salt marsh. A salt marsh is not a swamp, but an expanse of dark, spongy soil threaded with saltwater creeks and clothed in a kind of grass called salt meadow hay. All the water in the marsh rises and falls daily with the ocean tides, an endless cycle that changes the look of the marsh--partly flooded or mostly dry--as the day progresses.   — Informal topic sentence: Definition paragraph

3   Heading out to the marsh from my grandparents' house, I follow a short path through the woods. As I walk along, a sharp smell of salt mixed with the rich aroma of peaty soil fills my nostrils. I am always amazed by the way the path changes with the seasons. Sometimes I walk in the brilliant green of spring, sometimes in the tawny gold of autumn, sometimes in the grayish-tan of winter. No matter the season, the grass flanking the trail is often flattened into swirls, like thick Van Gogh brush strokes that curve and recurve in circular patterns. No people come here. The peacefulness heals me like a soothing drug.   — Informal topic sentence: First paragraph in a four-part spatial sequence
— Simile

4   After a few minutes, the trail suddenly opens up to a view that calms me no matter how upset or discouraged I might be: a line of tall waving reeds bordering and nearly hiding the salt marsh creek. To get to the creek, I part the reeds.   ← Informal topic sentence: Second paragraph in the spatial sequence

5   The creek is a narrow body of water no more than fifteen feet wide, and it ebbs and flows as the ocean currents sweep toward the land or rush back toward the sea. The creek winds in a sinuous pattern so that I cannot see its beginning or end, the places where it trickles into the marsh or spills into the open ocean. Little brown birds dip in and out of the reeds on the far shore of the creek, making a special "tweep-tweep" sound peculiar to the marsh. When I stand at low tide on the shore of the creek, I am on a miniature cliff, for the bank of the creek falls abruptly and steeply into the water. Below me, green grasses wave and shimmer under the water while tiny minnows   ← Informal topic sentence: Third paragraph in the spatial sequence

flash their silvery sides as they dart through the underwater tangles.

Informal topic sentence: Last paragraph in the spatial sequence →

The creek water is often much warmer than the ocean, so I   6
can swim there in three seasons. Sitting on the edge of the
creek, I scoop some water into my hand, rub my face and neck,
then ease into the water. Where the creek is shallow, my feet
sink into a foot of muck that feels like mashed potatoes mixed

Simile ————

with motor oil. But once I become accustomed to it, I enjoy
squishing the slimy mud through my toes. Sometimes I feel
brushing past my legs the blue crabs that live in the creek.
Other times, I hear the splash of a turtle or an otter as it
slips from the shore into the water. Otherwise, it is silent.
The salty water is buoyant and lifts my spirits as I stroke
through it to reach the middle of the creek. There in the center, I float weightlessly, surrounded by tall reeds that reduce
the world to water and sky. I am at peace.

Conclusion

The salt marsh is not the kind of dramatic landscape found   7
on picture postcards. There are no soaring mountains, sandy
beaches, or lush valleys. The marsh is a flat world that some
consider dull and uninviting. I am glad most people do not
respond to the marsh's subtle beauty because that means I can
be alone there. Just as the rising tide sweeps over the marsh,
floating debris out to the ocean, the marsh washes away my con-

Echo of idea in introduction →

cerns and restores me to my senses.

Commentary

The Dominant Impression

Marie responded to the assignment by writing a moving tribute to a place having special meaning for her—the salt marsh near her grandparents' home. Like
most descriptive pieces, Marie's essay is organized around a *dominant impression*:
the marsh's peaceful solitude and gentle, natural beauty. The essay's introduction
provides a context for the dominant impression by comparing the pleasure Marie
experiences in the marsh to the happiness Thoreau felt in his walks around
Walden Pond.

Other Patterns of Development

Before developing the essay's dominant impression, Marie uses the second
paragraph to *define* a salt marsh. An *objective description*, the definition clarifies that
a salt marsh—with its spongy soil, haylike grass, and ebbing tides—is not to be

confused with a swamp. Because Marie offers such a factual definition, readers have the background needed to enjoy the personalized view that follows.

Besides the definition paragraph and the comparison in the opening paragraph, the essay contains a strong element of *causal analysis:* Throughout, Marie describes the marsh's effect on her.

Sensory Language

At times, Marie develops the essay's dominant impression explicitly, as when she writes "No people come here" (paragraph 3) and "I am at peace" (6). But Marie generally uses the more subtle techniques characteristic of *subjective description* to convey the dominant impression. First of all, she fills the essay with strong *connotative language*, rich with *sensory images.* The third paragraph describes what she smells (the "sharp smell of salt mixed with the rich aroma of peaty soil") and what she sees ("brilliant green," "tawny gold," and "grayish-tan"). In the fifth paragraph, she uses *onomatopoeia* ("tweep tweep") to convey the birds' chirping sound. And the sixth paragraph includes vigorous descriptions of how the marsh feels to Marie's touch. She splashes water on her face and neck; she digs her toes into the mud at the bottom of the creek; she delights in the delicate brushing of crabs against her legs.

Figurative Language, Vigorous Verbs, and Varied Sentence Structure

You might also have noted that *figurative language, energetic verbs,* and *varied sentence patterns* contribute to the essay's descriptive power. Marie develops a simile in the third paragraph when she compares the flattened swirls of swamp grass to the brush strokes in a painting by Van Gogh. Later she uses another simile when she writes that the creek's thick mud feels "like mashed potatoes mixed with motor oil." Moreover, throughout the essay, she uses lively verbs ("shimmer," "flash") to capture the marsh's magical quality. Similarly, Marie enhances descriptive passages by varying the length of her sentences. Long, fairly elaborate sentences are interspersed with short, dramatic statements. In the third paragraph, for example, the long sentence describing the circular swirls of swamp grass is followed by the brief statement "No people come here." And the sixth paragraph uses two short sentences ("Otherwise, it is silent" and "I am at peace") to punctuate the paragraph's longer sentences.

Organization

We can follow Marie's journey through the marsh because she uses an easy-to-follow combination of *spatial, chronological,* and *emphatic* patterns to sequence her experience. The essay relies primarily on a spatial arrangement since the four body paragraphs focus on the different spots that Marie reaches: first, the path behind her grandparents' house (paragraph 3); then the area bordering the creek (4); next, her view of the creek (5); last, the creek itself (6). Each stage of her walk is signaled by an *informal topic sentence* near the start of each paragraph. Furthermore, *signal devices* (marked by italics here) indicate not only her location but also the chronological passage of time: "*As* I walk along, a sharp smell…fills my nostrils" (3); "*After* a few minutes, the trail suddenly opens up…" (4); "*Below* me, green grasses wave…" (5). And to call attention to the creek's serene beauty, Marie saves for last the description of the peace she feels while floating in the creek.

An Inappropriate Figure of Speech

Although the four body paragraphs focus on the distinctive qualities of each location, Marie runs into a minor problem in the third paragraph. Take a moment to reread that paragraph's last sentence. Comparing the peace of the marsh to the effect of a "soothing drug" is jarring. The effectiveness of Marie's essay hinges on her ability to create a picture of a pure, natural world. A reference to drugs is inappropriate. Now, reread the paragraph aloud, stopping after "No people come here." Note how much more in keeping with the essay's dominant impression the paragraph is when the reference to drugs is omitted.

Conclusion

The concluding paragraph brings the essay to a graceful close. The powerful *simile* found in the last sentence contains an implied reference to Thoreau and to Marie's earlier statement about the joy to be found in special places having restorative powers. Such an allusion echoes, with good effect, the paper's opening comments.

Revising the First Draft

When Marie met with some classmates during a group feedback session, the students agreed that Marie's first draft was strong and moving. But they also said that they had difficulty following her route through the marsh; they found her third paragraph especially confusing. Marie kept track of her classmates' comments on a separate piece of paper and then entered them, numbered in order of importance, in the margin of her first draft. Reprinted here is the original version of Marie's third paragraph, along with her annotations:

Original Version of Third Paragraph

① Chronology is
confusing

As I head out to the marsh from the house, I follow a short trail through the woods. A smell of salt and soil fills my nostrils. The end of the trail suddenly opens up to a view that calms me no matter how upset or discouraged I might be: a line of tall, waving reeds bordering the salt marsh creek. Civilization seems far away as I walk the path of flattened grass and finally reach my goal, the salt marsh creek hidden behind the tall, waving reeds. The path changes with the seasons; sometimes I walk in the brilliant green of spring, sometimes in the tawny

gold of autumn, sometimes in the <u>gray of winter.</u> In some areas,   ③ Make more
the grass is flattened into swirls that make the <u>marsh resemble</u>   specific
<u>one of those paintings by Van Gogh.</u> No people come here. The   ② Develop more
peacefulness heals me like a soothing drug. The path stops at   fully—maybe
the line of tall, waving reeds standing upright at the border of   use a simile
the creek. I part the reeds to get to the creek.

When Marie looked more carefully at the paragraph, she agreed it was confusing. For one thing, the paragraph's third and fourth sentences indicated that she had come to the path's end and had reached the reeds bordering the creek. In the following sentences, however, she was on the path again. Then, at the end, she was back at the creek, as if she had just arrived there. Marie resolved this confusion by breaking the single paragraph into two separate ones—the first describing the walk along the path, the second describing her arrival at the creek. This restructuring, especially when combined with clearer transitions, eliminated the confusion.

While revising her essay, Marie also intensified the sensory images in her original paragraph. She changed the "smell of salt and soil" to the "sharp smell of salt mixed with the rich aroma of peaty soil." And when she added the phrase "thick Van Gogh brush strokes that curve and recurve in circular patterns," she made the comparison between the marsh grass and a Van Gogh painting more vivid.

These are just some of the changes Marie made while rewriting the paper. Her skillful revisions provided the polish needed to make an already strong essay even more evocative.

ACTIVITIES: DESCRIPTION

Prewriting Activities

1. Imagine you're writing two essays: One explains how students get "burned out"; the other contends that being a spendthrift is better (or worse) than being frugal. Jot down ways you might use description in each essay.

2. Go to a place on campus where students congregate. In preparation for an *objective* description of this place, make notes of various sights, sounds, smells, and textures, as well as the overall "feel" of the place. Then, in preparation for a *subjective* description, observe and take notes on another sheet of paper. Compare the two sets of material. What differences do you see in word choice and selection of details?

3. Prepare to interview an interesting person by outlining several questions ahead of time. When you visit that person's home or workplace, bring a notebook in which to record his or her responses. During the interview, observe the person's surroundings, voice, body language, dress, and so on. As soon as the interview is over, make notes on these matters. Then review your notes and identify your dominant impression of the person. With that impression in mind, which details would you omit if you were writing an essay? Which would you elaborate? Which organizational pattern (spatial, emphatic, chronological, or sensory) would you select to organize your description? Why?

Revising Activities

4. Revise each of the following sentence sets twice. The first time, create an unmistakable mood; the second time, create a sharply contrasting mood. To convey atmosphere, vary sentence structure, use vigorous verbs, provide rich sensory details, and pay special attention to words' connotations.

   a. The card players sat around the table. The table was old. The players were, too.
   b. A long line formed outside the movie theater. People didn't want to miss the show. The movie had received a lot of attention recently.
   c. A girl walked down the street in her first pair of high heels. This was a new experience for her.

5. The following sentences contain clichés. Rewrite each sentence, supplying a fresh and imaginative figure of speech. Add whatever descriptive details are needed to provide a context for the figure of speech.

   a. They were as quiet as mice.
   b. My brother used to get green with envy if I had a date and he didn't.
   c. The little girl is proud as a peacock of her Girl Scout uniform.
   d. The professor is as dull as dishwater.

6. The following descriptive paragraph is from the first draft of an essay showing that personal growth may result when romanticized notions and reality collide. How effective is the paragraph in illustrating the essay's thesis? Which details are powerful? Which could be more concrete? Which should be deleted? Where should sentence structure be more varied? How could the description be made more coherent? Revise the paragraph, correcting any problems you discover and adding whatever sensory details are needed to enliven the description. Feel free to break the paragraph into two or more separate ones.

        As a child, I was intrigued by stories about the farm in Harrison County, Maine, where my father spent his teens. Being raised on a farm seemed more interesting than growing up in the suburbs. So about a year ago, I decided to see for myself what the farm was like. I got there by driving on Route 334, a surprisingly easy-to-drive, four-lane highway that had recently been built with matching state and federal funds. I turned into the dirt road leading to the farm and got out of my car. It had been washed and waxed for the occasion. Then I headed for a dirt-colored barn. Its roof was full of huge, rotted holes. As I rounded the bushes, I saw the house. It too was dirt-colored. Its paint must have worn off decades ago. A couple of dead-looking old cars were sprawled in front of the barn. They were dented and windowless. Also by the barn was an ancient refrigerator, crushed like a discarded accordion. The porch steps to the house were slanted and wobbly. Through the open windows came a stale small and the sound of television. Looking in the front door screen, I could see two chickens jumping around inside. Everything looked dirty both inside and out. Secretly grateful that no one answered my knock, I bolted down the stairs, got into my clean, shiny car, and drove away.

PROFESSIONAL
SELECTIONS:
DESCRIPTION

E. B. WHITE

Recipient of the Presidential Medal of Freedom and the National Medal for Literature, Elwyn Brooks White (1899–1985) is considered one of America's foremost essayists. Known for his graceful prose, White wrote *The New Yorker's* "Talk of the Town" column for many years. He also authored, with William Strunk, Jr., the renowned guide for writers *The Elements of Style.* White's books for children include the beloved classic *Charlotte's Web* (1952). This selection is taken from *The Essays of E. B. White* (1977).

ONCE MORE TO THE LAKE

1   One summer, along about 1904, my father rented a camp on a lake in Maine and took us all there for the month of August. We all got ringworm from some kittens and had to rub Pond's Extract on our arms and legs night and morning, and my father rolled over in a canoe with all his clothes on; but outside of that the vacation was a success

and from then on none of us ever thought there was any place in the world like that lake in Maine. We returned summer after summer—always on August 1 for one month. I have since become a salt-water man, but sometimes in summer there are days when the restlessness of the tides and the fearful cold of the sea water and the incessant wind that blows across the afternoon and into the evening make me wish for the placidity of a lake in the woods. A few weeks ago this feeling got so strong I bought myself a couple of bass hooks and a spinner and returned to the lake where we used to go, for a week's fishing and to revisit old haunts.

I took along my son, who had never had any fresh water up his nose and who had seen lily pads only from train windows. On the journey over to the lake I began to wonder what it would be like. I wondered how time would have marred this unique, this holy spot—the coves and streams, the hills that the sun set behind, the camps and the paths behind the camps. I was sure that the tarred road would have found it out, and I wondered in what other ways it would be desolated. It is strange how much you can remember about places like that once you allow your mind to return into the grooves that lead back. You remember one thing, and that suddenly reminds you of another thing. I guess I remembered clearest of all the early mornings, when the lake was cool and motionless, remembered how the bedroom smelled of the lumber it was made of and of the wet woods whose scent entered through the screen. The partitions in the camp were thin and did not extend clear to the top of the rooms, and as I was always the first up I would dress softly so as not to wake the others, and sneak out into the sweet outdoors and start out in the canoe, keeping close along the shore in the long shadows of the pines. I remembered being very careful never to rub my paddle against the gunwale for fear of disturbing the stillness of the cathedral.

The lake had never been what you would call a wild lake. There were cottages sprinkled around the shores, and it was in farming country although the shores of the lake were quite heavily wooded. Some of the cottages were owned by nearby farmers, and you would live at the shore and eat your meals at the farmhouse. That's what our family did. But although it wasn't wild, it was a fairly large and undisturbed lake and there were places in it that, to a child at least, seemed infinitely remote and primeval.

I was right about the tar: it led to within half a mile of the shore. But when I got back there, with my boy, and we settled into a camp near a farmhouse and into the kind of summertime I had known, I could tell that it was going to be pretty much the same as it had been before—I knew it, lying in bed the first morning, smelling the bedroom and hearing the boy sneak quietly out and go off along the shore in a boat. I began to sustain the illusion that he was I, and therefore, by simple transposition, that I was my father. This sensation persisted, kept cropping up all the time we were there. It was not an entirely new feeling, but in this setting it grew much stronger. I seemed to be living a dual existence. I would be in the middle of some simple act, I would be picking up a bait box or laying down a table fork, or I would be saying something, and suddenly it would be not I but my father who was saying the words or making the gesture. It gave me a creepy sensation.

We went fishing the first morning. I felt the same damp moss covering the worms in the bait can, and saw the dragonfly alight on the tip of my rod as it hovered a few inches from the surface of the water. It was the arrival of this fly that convinced me beyond any doubt that everything was as it always had been, that the years were a mirage and that there had been no years. The small waves were the same, chucking the rowboat under the chin as we fished at anchor, and the boat was the same boat, the same color green and the ribs broken in the same places, and under the floorboards the same fresh-water leavings and débris—the dead helgramite, the wisps of moss, the rusty discarded fishhook, the dried blood from yesterday's catch. We stared silently at the tips of our rods, at the dragonflies that came and went. I lowered the tip of mine into the water, tentatively, pensively dislodging the fly, which darted two feet away, poised, darted two feet back, and came to rest again a little farther up the rod. There had been no years between the ducking of this dragonfly and the other one—the one that was part of memory. I looked at the boy, who was silently watching his fly, and it was my hands that held his rod, my eyes watching. I felt dizzy and didn't know which rod I was at the end of.

6   We caught two bass, hauling them in briskly as though they were mackerel, pulling them over the side of the boat in a businesslike manner without any landing net, and stunning them with a blow on the back of the head. When we got back for a swim before lunch, the lake was exactly where we had left it, the same number of inches from the dock, and there was only the merest suggestion of a breeze. This seemed an utterly enchanted sea, this lake you could leave to its own devices for a few hours and come back to, and find that it had not stirred, this constant and trustworthy body of water. In the shallows, the dark, water-soaked sticks and twigs, smooth and old, were undulating in clusters on the bottom against the clean ribbed sand, and the track of the mussel was plain. A school of minnows swam by, each minnow with its small individual shadow, doubling the attendance, so clear and sharp in the sunlight. Some of the other campers were in swimming, along the shore, one of them with a cake of soap, and the water felt thin and clear and unsubstantial. Over the years there had been this person with the cake of soap, this cultist, and here he was. There had been no years.

7   Up to the farmhouse to dinner through the teeming, dusty field, the road under our sneakers was only a two-track road. The middle track was missing, the one with the marks of the hooves and the splotches of dried, flaky manure. There had always been three tracks to choose from in choosing which track to walk in; now the choice was narrowed down to two. For a moment I missed terribly the middle alternative. But the way led past the tennis court, and something about the way it lay there in the sun reassured me; the tape had loosened along the backline, the alleys were green with plantains and other weeds, and the net (installed in June and removed in September) sagged in the dry noon, and the whole place steamed with midday heat and hunger and emptiness. There was a choice of pie for dessert, and one was blueberry and one was apple, and the waitresses were the same country girls, there having been no passage of time, only the illusion of it as in a dropped curtain—the waitresses were still fifteen; their hair had been washed, that was the only difference—they had been to the movies and seen the pretty girls with the clean hair.

8   Summertime, oh, summertime, pattern of life indelible, the fade-proof lake, the woods unshatterable, the pasture with the sweetfern and the juniper forever and ever, summer without end; this was the background, and the life along the shore was the design, the cottagers with their innocent and tranquil design, their tiny docks with the flagpole and the American flag floating against the white clouds in the blue sky, the little paths over the roots of the trees leading from camp to camp and the paths leading back to the outhouses and the can of lime for sprinkling, and at the souvenir counters at the store the miniature birch-bark canoes and the postcards that showed things looking a little better than they looked. This was the American family at play, escaping the city heat, wondering whether the newcomers in the camp at the head of the cove were

"common" or "nice," wondering whether it was true that the people who drove up for Sunday dinner at the farmhouse were turned away because there wasn't enough chicken.

It seemed to me, as I kept remembering all this, that those times and those summers   9 had been infinitely precious and worth saving. There had been jollity and peace and goodness. The arriving (at the beginning of August) had been so big a business in itself, at the railway station the farm wagon drawn up, the first smell of the pine-laden air, the first glimpse of the smiling farmer, and the great importance of the trunks and your father's enormous authority in such matters, and the feel of the wagon under you for the long ten-mile haul, and at the top of the last long hill catching the first view of the lake after eleven months of not seeing this cherished body of water. The shouts and cries of the other campers when they saw you, and the trunks to be unpacked, to give up their rich burden. (Arriving was less exciting nowadays, when you sneaked up in your car and parked it under a tree near the camp and took out the bags and in five minutes it was all over, no fuss, no loud wonderful fuss about trunks.)

Peace and goodness and jollity. The only thing that was wrong now, really, was the 10 sound of the place, an unfamiliar nervous sound of the outboard motors. This was the note that jarred, the one thing that would sometimes break the illusion and set the years moving. In those other summertimes all motors were inboard; and when they were at a little distance, the noise they made was a sedative, an ingredient of summer sleep. They were one-cylinder and two-cylinder engines, and some were make-and-break and some were jump-spark, but they all made a sleepy sound across the lake. The one-lungers throbbed and fluttered, and the twin-cylinder ones purred and purred, and that was a quiet sound, too. But now the campers all had outboards. In the daytime, in the hot mornings, these motors made a petulant, irritable sound; at night, in the still evening when the afterglow lit the water, they whined about one's ears like mosquitoes. My boy loved our rented outboard, and his great desire was to achieve single-handed mastery over it, and authority, and he soon learned the trick of choking it a little (but not too much), and the adjustment of the needle valve. Watching him I would remember the things you could do with the old one-cylinder engine with the heavy flywheel, how you could have it eating out of your hand if you got really close to it spiritually. Motorboats in those days didn't have clutches, and you would make a landing by shutting off the motor at the proper time and coasting in with a dead rudder. But there was a way of reversing them, if you learned the trick, by cutting the switch and putting it on again exactly on the final dying revolution of the flywheel, so that it would kick back against compression and begin reversing. Approaching a dock in a strong following breeze, it was difficult to slow up sufficiently by the ordinary coasting method, and if a boy felt he had complete mastery over his motor, he was tempted to keep it running beyond its time and then reverse it a few feet from the dock. It took a cool nerve, because if you threw the switch a twentieth of a second too soon you would catch the flywheel when it still had speed enough to go up past center, and the boat would leap ahead, charging bull-fashion at the dock.

We had a good week at the camp. The bass were biting well and the sun shone end- 11 lessly, day after day. We would be tired at night and lie down in the accumulated heat of the little bedrooms after the long hot day and the breeze would stir almost imperceptibly outside and the smell of the swamp drift in through the rusty screens. Sleep would come easily and in the morning the red squirrel would be on the roof, tapping out his gay routine. I kept remembering everything, lying in bed in the mornings—the small steamboat that had a long rounded stern like the lip of a Ubangi, and how quietly she ran on the moonlight sails, when the older boys played their mandolins and the girls sang and we ate doughnuts dipped in sugar, and how sweet the music was on the water in the shining night, and what it had felt like to think about girls then. After breakfast we would go up to the store and the things were in the same place—the minnows in a bottle, the plugs and spinners disarranged and pawed over by the youngsters from the boys' camp, the Fig Newtons and the Beeman's gum. Outside, the road was tarred and cars stood in front of the store. Inside, all was just as it had always been, except there was more Coca-Cola and not so much Moxie and root beer and birch beer and sarsaparilla. We would walk out with the bottle of pop apiece and sometimes the pop would backfire up our noses and hurt. We explored the streams, quietly, where the turtles slid off the sunny logs and dug their way into the soft bottom; and we lay on the town wharf and fed worms to the tame bass. Everywhere we went I had trouble making out which was I, the one walking at my side, the one walking in my pants.

12   One afternoon while we were there at the lake a thunderstorm came up. It was like the revival of an old melodrama that I had seen long ago with childish awe. The second-act climax of the drama of the electrical disturbance over a lake in America had not changed in any important respect. This was the big scene, still the big scene. The whole thing was so familiar, the first feeling of oppression and heat and a general air around camp of not wanting to go very far away. In midafternoon (it was all the same) a curious darkening of the sky, and a lull in everything that had made life tick; and then the way the boats suddenly swung the other way at their moorings with the coming of a breeze out of the new quarter, and the premonitory rumble. Then the kettle drum, then the snare, then the bass drum and cymbals, then crackling light against the dark, and the gods grinning and licking their chops in the hills. Afterward the calm, the rain steadily rustling in the calm lake, the return of light and hope and spirits, and the campers running out in joy and relief to go swimming in the rain, their bright cries perpetuating the deathless joke about how they were getting simply drenched, and the children screaming with delight at the new sensation of bathing in the rain, and the joke about getting drenched linking the generations in a strong indestructible chain. And the comedian who waded in carrying an umbrella.

13   When the others went swimming, my son said he was going in, too. He pulled his dripping trunks from the line where they had hung all through the shower and wrung them out. Languidly, and with no thought of going in, I watched him, his hard little body, skinny and bare, saw him wince slightly as he pulled up around his vitals the small, soggy, icy garment. As he buckled the swollen belt, suddenly my groin felt the chill of death.

Questions for Close Reading

1. What is the selection's thesis (or dominant impression)? Locate the sentence(s) in which White states his main idea. If he doesn't state the thesis explicitly, express it in your own words.

2. Why does White return to the lake in Maine he had visited as a child? Why do you think he has waited to revisit it until he has a young son to bring along?

3. Several times in the essay, White notes that he felt as if he were his own father—and that his son became his childhood self. What event first prompts this sensation? What actions and thoughts cause it to recur?

4. How is the latest visit to the lake similar to White's childhood summers? What differences does White notice? What effects do the differences have on him?

5. Refer to your dictionary as needed to define the following words used in the selection: *incessant* (paragraph 1), *placidity* (1), *primeval* (3), *transposition* (4), *undulating* (6), *indelible* (8), *petulant* (10), and *languidly* (13).

Questions About the Writer's Craft

1. The pattern. Through vivid language, descriptive writing evokes sensory experiences. In "Once More to the Lake," White overlays two sets of sensory details: those of the present-day lake and those of the lake as it was in his boyhood. Which set of details is more objective? Which seems sharper and more powerful? Why?

2. To describe the lake, White chooses many words and phrases with religious connotations. Give some examples. What might have been his purpose in using such language?

3. Other patterns. In paragraph 12, White uses a metaphor to describe a thunderstorm. To what does he compare a thunderstorm? Why does he make this comparison?

4. White refers to "the chill of death" in the final paragraph. What brings on this feeling? Why does he feel it "in his groin"? Where has this idea been hinted at previously in the essay?

Writing Assignments Using Description as a Pattern of Development

1. Write a descriptive essay about a special place in your life. The place need not be a natural setting like White's lake; it could be a city or building that has meant a great deal to you. Use sensory details and figurative language, as White does, to enliven your description and convey the place's significance for you.

∞ **2.** White was fortunate that his lake had remained virtually unchanged. But many other special spots have been destroyed or are threatened with destruction. Write a descriptive essay about a place (a park, a school, an old-fashioned ice cream parlor) that is "infinitely precious and worth saving." For your dominant theme, show which aspects of your subject make it worthy of being preserved for future generations. Joseph H. Suina's "And Then I Went to School" (page 361) may spark some helpful ideas since it details the special qualities of a place threatened with extinction.

Writing Assignments Using Other Patterns of Development

∞ **3.** Sometimes, we, like White, are suddenly reminded of the nearness of death: a crushed animal lies in the road, a politician is assassinated, a classmate is killed in a car crash. Write an essay about a time you were forced to think about mortality. Explain what happened and describe your thoughts and feelings afterwards. Before writing your essay, be sure to read Natalie Angier's "A Granddaughter's Fear" (page 388), a powerful account of the author's reaction to impending death.

∞ **4.** Have your older relatives attempted to share with you some special experiences of their younger years? Have you done the same thing with your own children, nephews, or nieces? You may have taken loved ones to a special place, as White did, or listened to stories or looked at photographs. Write an essay recounting such an experience. Explain the motivations of the older generation and the effects on the younger one. Before planning your paper, you may want to read Toni Morrison's "A Slow Walk of Trees" (page 351); it depicts two generations' views of the past as well as the effect of those views on the present.

MAYA ANGELOU

Born Marguerite Johnson in 1928, Maya Angelou rose from a difficult childhood in Stamps, Arkansas, to become a multitalented performer and writer. A professor at Wake Forest University since 1991, she has danced professionally; starred in an off-Broadway play; acted on television; and become a prolific, highly regarded writer. Her work includes poetry, *Oh Pray My Wings Are Gonna Fit Me Well* (1975), *Now Sheba Sings the Song* (1988), and *A Brave and Startling Truth* (1995), as well as a series of autobiographical books, beginning with *I Know Why the Caged Bird Sings* (1969), from which the following selection is taken. Raped at the age of eight in St. Louis, Angelou responded by speaking to no one but her brother Bailey. She and Bailey were soon sent to Stamps to live with their grandmother (Momma), at which point this excerpt begins.

SISTER FLOWERS

1   For nearly a year [after the rape], I sopped around the house, the Store, the school and the church, like an old biscuit, dirty and inedible. Then I met, or rather got to know, the lady who threw me my first life line.

2   Mrs. Bertha Flowers was the aristocrat of Black Stamps. She had the grace of control to appear warm in the coldest weather, and on the Arkansas summer days it seemed she had a private breeze which swirled around, cooling her. She was thin without the taut look of wiry people, and her printed voile dresses and flowered hats were as right for her as denim overalls for a farmer. She was our side's answer to the richest white woman in town.

3   Her skin was a rich black that would have peeled like a plum if snagged, but then no one would have thought of getting close enough to Mrs. Flowers to ruffle her dress, let alone snag her skin. She didn't encourage familiarity. She wore gloves too.

I don't think I ever saw Mrs. Flowers laugh, but she smiled often. A slow widening   4
of her thin black lips to show even, small white teeth, then the slow effortless closing.
When she chose to smile on me, I always wanted to thank her. The action was so
graceful and inclusively benign.

She was one of the few gentlewomen I have ever known, and has remained   5
throughout my life the measure of what a human being can be.

Momma had a strange relationship with her. Most often when she passed on the   6
road in front of the Store, she spoke to Momma in that soft yet carrying voice, "Good
day, Mrs. Henderson." Momma responded with "How you, Sister Flowers?"

Mrs. Flowers didn't belong to our church, nor was she Momma's familiar. Why on   7
earth did she insist on calling her Sister Flowers? Shame made me want to hide my
face. Mrs. Flowers deserved better than to be called Sister. Then, Momma left out the
verb. Why not ask, "How *are* you, *Mrs.* Flowers?" With the unbalanced passion of the
young, I hated her for showing her ignorance to Mrs. Flowers. It didn't occur to me for
many years that they were as alike as sisters, separated only by formal education.

Although I was upset, neither of the women was in the least shaken by what I   8
thought an unceremonious greeting. Mrs. Flowers would continue her easy gait up the
hill to her little bungalow, and Momma kept on shelling peas or doing whatever had
brought her to the front porch.

Occasionally, though, Mrs. Flowers would drift off the road and down to the Store   9
and Momma would say to me, "Sister, you go on and play." As she left I would hear the
beginning of an intimate conversation. Momma persistently using the wrong verb, or
none at all.

"Brother and Sister Wilcox is sho'ly the meanest—" "Is," Momma? "Is"? Oh,   10
please, not "is," Momma, for two or more. But they talked, and from the side of the
building where I waited for the ground to open up and swallow me, I heard the soft-
voiced Mrs. Flowers and the textured voice of my grandmother merging and melting.
They were interrupted from time to time by giggles that must have come from Mrs.
Flowers (Momma never giggled in her life). Then she was gone.

She appealed to me because she was like people I had never met personally. Like   11
women in English novels who walked the moors (whatever they were) with their loyal
dogs racing at a respectful distance. Like the women who sat in front of roaring fireplaces, drinking tea incessantly from silver trays full of scones and crumpets. Women
who walked over the "heath" and read morocco-bound books and had two last names
divided by a hyphen. It would be safe to say that she made me proud to be Negro, just
by being herself.

She acted just as refined as whitefolks in the movies and books and she was more   12
beautiful, for none of them could have come near that warm color without looking gray
by comparison.

It was fortunate that I never saw her in the company of powhitefolks. For since they   13
tend to think of their whiteness as an evenizer, I'm certain that I would have had to
hear her spoken to commonly as Bertha, and my image of her would have been shattered like the unmendable Humpty-Dumpty.

One summer afternoon, sweet-milk fresh in my memory, she stopped at the Store to   14
buy provisions. Another Negro woman of her health and age would have been
expected to carry the paper sacks home in one hand, but Momma said, "Sister Flowers,
I'll send Bailey up to your house with these things."

15   She smiled that slow dragging smile, "Thank you, Mrs. Henderson. I'd prefer Marguerite, though." My name was beautiful when she said it. "I've been meaning to talk to her, anyway." They gave each other age-group looks.

16   Momma said, "Well, that's all right then. Sister, go and change your dress. You going to Sister Flowers's."

17   The chifforobe was a maze. What on earth did one put on to go to Mrs. Flowers's house? I knew I shouldn't put on a Sunday dress. It might be sacrilegious. Certainly not a house dress, since I was already wearing a fresh one. I chose a school dress, naturally. It was formal without suggesting that going to Mrs. Flowers's house was equivalent to attending church.

18   I trusted myself back into the Store.

19   "Now, don't you look nice." I had chosen the right thing, for once....

20   There was a little path beside the rocky road, and Mrs. Flowers walked in front swinging her arms and picking her way over the stones.

21   She said, without turning her head, to me, "I hear you're doing very good school work, Marguerite, but that it's all written. The teachers report that they have trouble getting you to talk in class." We passed the triangular farm on our left and the path widened to allow us to walk together. I hung back in the separate unasked and unanswerable questions.

22   "Come and walk along with me, Marguerite." I couldn't have refused even if I wanted to. She pronounced my name so nicely. Or more correctly, she spoke each word with such clarity that I was certain a foreigner who didn't understand English could have understood her.

23   "Now no one is going to make you talk—possibly no one can. But bear in mind, language is man's way of communicating with his fellow man and it is language alone which separates him from the lower animals." That was a totally new idea to me, and I would need time to think about it.

24   "Your grandmother says you read a lot. Every chance you get. That's good, but not good enough. Words mean more than what is set down on paper. It takes the human voice to infuse them with the shades of deeper meaning."

25   I memorized the part about the human voice infusing words. It seemed so valid and poetic.

26   She said she was going to give me some books and that I not only must read them, I must read them aloud. She suggested that I try to make a sentence sound in as many different ways as possible.

27   "I'll accept no excuse if you return a book to me that has been badly handled." My imagination boggled at the punishment I would deserve if in fact I did abuse a book of Mrs. Flowers's. Death would be too kind and brief.

28   The odors in the house surprised me. Somehow I had never connected Mrs. Flowers with food or eating or any other common experience of common people. There must have been an outhouse, too, but my mind never recorded it.

29   The sweet scent of vanilla had met us as she opened the door.

30   "I made tea cookies this morning. You see, I had planned to invite you for cookies and lemonade so we could have this little chat. The lemonade is in the icebox."

31   It followed that Mrs. Flowers would have ice on an ordinary day, when most families in our town bought ice late on Saturdays only a few times during the summer to be used in the wooden ice-cream freezers.

She took the bags from me and disappeared through the kitchen door. I looked 32
around the room that I had never in my wildest fantasies imagined I would see.
Browned photographs leered or threatened from the walls and the white, freshly done
curtains pushed against themselves and against the wind. I wanted to gobble up the
room entire and take it to Bailey, who would help me analyze and enjoy it.

"Have a seat, Marguerite. Over there by the table." She carried a platter covered with 33
a tea towel. Although she warned that she hadn't tried her hand at baking sweets for
some time, I was certain that like everything else about her the cookies would be perfect.

They were flat round wafers, slightly browned on the edges and butter-yellow in the 34
center. With the cold lemonade they were sufficient for childhood's lifelong diet.
Remembering my manners, I took nice little lady-like bites off the edges. She said she
had made them expressly for me and that she had a few in the kitchen that I could take
home to my brother. So I jammed one whole cake in my mouth and the rough crumbs
scratched the insides of my jaws, and if I hadn't had to swallow, it would have been a
dream come true.

As I ate she began the first of what we later called "my lessons in living." She said that 35
I must always be intolerant of ignorance but understanding of illiteracy. That some people, unable to go to school, were more educated and even more intelligent than college
professors. She encouraged me to listen carefully to what country people called mother
wit. That in those homely sayings was couched the collective wisdom of generations.

When I finished the cookies she brushed off the table and brought a thick, small 36
book from the bookcase. I had read *A Tale of Two Cities* and found it up to my standards as a romantic novel. She opened the first page and I heard poetry for the first
time in my life.

"It was the best of times and the worst of times..." Her voice slid in and curved 37
down through and over the words. She was nearly singing. I wanted to look at the
pages. Were they the same that I had read? Or were there notes, music, lined on the
pages, as in a hymn book? Her sounds began cascading gently. I knew from listening to
a thousand preachers that she was nearing the end of her reading, and I hadn't really
heard, heard to understand, a single word.

"How do you like that?"   38

It occurred to me that she expected a response. The sweet vanilla flavor was still on 39
my tongue and her reading was a wonder in my ears. I had to speak.

I said, "Yes, ma'am." It was the least I could do, but it was the most also.   40

"There's one more thing. Take this book of poems and memorize one for me. Next 41
time you pay me a visit, I want you to recite."

I have tried often to search behind the sophistication of years for the enchantment I 42
so easily found in those gifts. The essence escapes but its aura remains. To be allowed,
no, invited, into the private lives of strangers, and to share their joys and fears, was a
chance to exchange the Southern bitter wormwood for a cup of mead with Beowulf* or
a hot cup of tea and milk with Oliver Twist.† When I said aloud, "It is a far, far better
thing that I do, than I have ever done..."‡ tears of love filled my eyes at my selflessness.

---

*The hero of an Old English epic poem dating from the eighth century (editors' note).

†The main character in Charles Dickens's novel *Oliver Twist* (1837) (editors' note).

‡The last words of Sydney Carton, the selfless hero of Charles Dickens's novel *A Tale of Two Cities*
(1859) (editors' note).

43   On that first day, I ran down the hill and into the road (few cars ever came along it) and had the good sense to stop running before I reached the Store.

44   I was liked, and what a difference it made. I was respected not as Mrs. Henderson's grandchild or Bailey's sister but for just being Marguerite Johnson.

45   Childhood's logic never asks to be proved (all conclusions are absolute). I didn't question why Mrs. Flowers had singled me out for attention, nor did it occur to me that Momma might have asked her to give me a little talking to. All I cared about was that she had made tea cookies for *me* and read to *me* from her favorite book. It was enough to prove that she liked me.

Questions for Close Reading

1. What is the selection's thesis (or dominant impression)? Locate the sentence(s) in which Angelou states her main idea. If she doesn't state the thesis explicitly, express it in your own words.

2. Angelou states that Mrs. Flowers "has remained throughout my life the measure of what a human being can be" (5). What does Angelou admire about Mrs. Flowers?

3. Why is young Angelou so ashamed of Momma when Mrs. Flowers is around? How do Momma and Mrs. Flowers behave with each other?

4. What are the "lessons in living" that Angelou receives from Mrs. Flowers during their first visit? How do you think these lessons might have subsequently influenced Angelou?

5. Refer to your dictionary as needed to define the following words used in the selection: *taut* (paragraph 2), *voile* (2), *benign* (4), *unceremonious* (8), *gait* (8), *moors* (11), *incessantly* (11), *scones* (11), *crumpets* (11), *heath* (11), *chifforobe* (17), *sacrilegious* (17), *infuse* (24), *couched* (35), and *aura* (42).

Questions About the Writer's Craft

1. The pattern. Reread the essay, focusing on the descriptive passages first of Mrs. Flowers and then of Angelou's visit to Mrs. Flowers's house. To what senses does Angelou appeal in these passages? What method of organization (see pages 157–158) does she use to order these sensory details?

2. To enrich the description of her eventful encounter with Mrs. Flowers, Angelou draws upon figures of speech (see pages 125–126). Consider, for example, the similes in paragraphs 1 and 11. How do these figures of speech contribute to the essay's dominant impression?

3. Other patterns. Because Angelou's description has a strong narrative component, it isn't surprising that there's a considerable amount of dialogue in the selection. For example, in paragraphs 7 and 10, Angelou quotes Momma's incorrect grammar. She then provides an imagined conversation in which the young

Angelou scolds Momma and corrects her speech. What do these imagined scoldings of Momma reveal about young Angelou? How do they relate to Mrs. Flowers's subsequent "lessons in life"?

4. Although it's not the focus of this selection, the issue of race remains in the background of Angelou's portrait of Mrs. Flowers. Where in the selection does Angelou imply that race was a fact of life in her town? How does this specter of racism help Angelou underscore the significance of her encounter with Mrs. Flowers?

Writing Assignments Using Description as a Pattern of Development

1. At one time or another, just about all of us have met someone who taught us to see ourselves more clearly and helped us understand what we wanted from life. Write an essay describing such a person. Focus on the individual's personal qualities, as a way of depicting the role he or she played in your life. Be sure not to limit yourself to an objective description. Subjective description, filled with lively language and figures of speech, will serve you well as you provide a portrait of this special person.

2. Thrilled by the spectacle of Mrs. Flowers's interesting home, Angelou says she wanted to "gobble up the room entire" and share it with her brother. Write an essay describing in detail a place that vividly survives in your memory. You may describe a setting that you visited only once or a familiar setting that holds a special place in your heart. Before you write, list the qualities and sensory impressions you associate with this special place; then refine the list so that all details support your dominant impression. You may want to read E. B. White's "Once More to the Lake" (page 169), John Ciardi's "Dawn Watch" (page 181), and Joseph A. Suina's "And Then I Went to School" (page 361) to see how three very different writers evoke the qualities of special places in their lives.

Writing Assignments Using Other Patterns of Development

3. When the young Angelou discovers, thanks to Mrs. Flowers, the thrill of acceptance, she experiences a kind of *epiphany*—a moment of enlightenment. Write an essay about an event in your life that represented a kind of epiphany. You might write about a positive discovery, such as when you realized you had a special talent for something, or about a negative discovery, such as when you realized that a beloved family member had a serious flaw. To make the point that the moment was a turning point in your life, start by describing what kind of person you were before the discovery. Then narrate the actual incident, using vivid details and dialogue to make the event come alive. End by discussing the importance of this epiphany in your life.

4. Think of an activity that engages you completely, one that provides—as reading does for Angelou—an opportunity for growth and expansion. Possibilities include reading, writing, playing an instrument, doing crafts, dancing, hiking, playing a sport, cooking, or traveling. Write an essay in which you argue the merits of your chosen pastime. Assume that some of your readers are highly skeptical. To win them over, you'll need to provide convincing examples that demonstrate the pleasure and benefits you have discovered in the activity.

JOHN CIARDI

John Ciardi (1916–86) was born in Boston and is known primarily for his richly textured yet accessible poetry. He taught at Rutgers University in the 1950s and for almost twenty years served as the poetry editor of the magazine *Saturday Review.* In addition to translating the medieval epic poem *The Divine Comedy,* Ciardi wrote several children's books and a college-level text on poetry, *How Does a Poem Mean?* (1959). His own poetry is available in the collections *As If: New and Selected Poems* (1955) and *For Instance* (1979). The following essay is from *Manner of Speaking* (1982).

DAWN WATCH

1   Unless a man is up for the dawn and for the half hour or so of first light, he has missed the best of the day.

2   The traffic has just started, not yet a roar and a stink. One car at a time goes by, the tires humming almost like the sound of a brook a half mile down in the crease of a mountain I know—a sound that carries not because it is loud but because everything else is still.

3   It isn't exactly a mist that hangs in the thickets but more nearly the ghost of a mist— a phenomenon like side vision. Look hard and it isn't there, but glance without focusing and something registers, an exhalation that will be gone three minutes after the sun comes over the treetops.

4   The lawns shine with a dew not exactly dew. There is a rabbit bobbing about on the lawn and then freezing. If it were truly a dew, his tracks would shine black on the grass, and he leaves no visible track. Yet, there is something on the grass that makes it glow a depth of green it will not show again all day. Or is that something in the dawn air?

5   Our cardinals know what time it is. They drop pure tones from the hemlock tops. The gang of grackles that makes a slum of the pin oak also knows the time but can only grate at it. They sound like a convention of broken universal joints grating uphill. The grackles creak and squeak, and the cardinals form tones that only occasionally sound through the noise. I scatter sunflower seeds by the birdbath for the cardinals and hope the grackles won't find them.

6   My neighbor's tomcat comes across the lawn, probably on his way home from passion, or only acting as if he had had a big night. I suspect him of being one of those poolroom braggarts who can't get next to a girl but who likes to let on that he is a hot stud. This one is too can-fed and too lazy to hunt for anything. Here he comes now, ignoring the rabbit. And there he goes.

As soon as he has hopped the fence, I let my dog out. The dog charges the rabbit, 7
watches it jump the fence, shakes himself in a self-satisfied way, then trots dutifully
into the thicket for his morning service, stopping to sniff everything on the way back.

There is an old mountain laurel on the island of the driveway turnaround. From 8
somewhere on the wind a white morning-glory rooted next to it and has climbed it.
Now the laurel is woven full of white bells tinged pink by the first rays through the not
quite mist. Only in earliest morning can they be seen. Come out two hours from now
and there will be no morning-glories.

Dawn, too, is the hour of a weed I know only as day flower—a bright blue button 9
that closes in full sunlight. I have weeded bales of it out of my flower beds, its one daytime virtue being the shallowness of its root system that allows it to be pulled out
effortlessly in great handfuls. Yet, now it shines. Had it a few more hours of such shining in its cycle, I would cultivate it as a ground cover, but dawn is its one hour, and a
garden is for whole days.

There is another blue morning weed whose name I do not know. This one grows 10
from a bulb to pulpy stems and a bedraggled daytime sprawl. Only a shovel will dig it
out. Try weeding it by hand and the stems will break off to be replaced by new ones and
to sprawl over the chosen plants in the flower bed. Yet, now and for another hour it out-
shines its betters, its flowers about the size of a quarter and paler than those of the day
flower but somehow more brilliant, perhaps because of the contrast of its paler foliage.

And now the sun is slanting in full. It is bright enough to make the leaves of the Jap- 11
anese red maple seem a transparent red bronze when the tree is between me and the
light. There must be others, but this is the only tree I know whose leaves let the sun
through in this way—except, that is, when the fall colors start. Aspen leaves, when
they first yellow and before they dry, are transparent in this way. I tell myself it must
have something to do with the red-yellow range of the spectrum. Green takes sunlight
and holds it, but red and yellow let it through.

The damned crabgrass is wrestling with the zinnias, and I stop to weed it out. The 12
stuff weaves too close to the zinnias to make the iron claw usable. And it won't do to
pull at the stalks. Crabgrass (at least in a mulched bed) can be weeded only with dirty
fingers. Thumb and forefinger have to pincer into the dirt and grab the root-center.
Weeding, of course, is an illusion of hope. Pulling out the root only stirs the soil and
brings new crabgrass seeds into germinating position. Take a walk around the block
and a new clump will have sprouted by the time you get back. But I am not ready to
walk around the block. I fill a small basket with the plucked clumps, and for the instant
I look at them, the zinnias are weedless.

Don't look back. I dump the weeds in the thicket where they will be smothered by 13
the grass clippings I will pile on at the next cutting. On the way back I see the cardinals
come down for the sunflower seeds, and the jays join them, and then the grackles
start ganging in, gatecrashing the buffet and clattering all over it. The dog stops chewing
his rawhide and makes a dash into the puddle of birds, which splashes away from him.

I hear a brake-squeak I have been waiting for and know the paper has arrived. As 14
usual, the news turns out to be another disaster count. The function of the wire services is to bring us tragedies faster than we can pity. In the end we shall all be inured,
numb, and ready for emotionless programming. I sit on the patio and read until the sun
grows too bright on the page. The cardinals have stopped singing, and the grackles
have flown off. It's the end of birdsong again.

15   Then suddenly—better than song for its instant—a hummingbird the color of green crushed velvet hovers in the throat of my favorite lily, a lovely high-bloomer I got the bulbs for but not the name. The lily is a crest of white horns with red dots and red velvet tongues along the insides of the petals and with an odor that drowns the patio. The hummingbird darts in and out of each horn in turn, then hovers an instant, and disappears.

16   Even without the sun, I have had enough of the paper. I'll take that hummingbird as my news for this dawn. It is over now. I smoke one more cigarette too many and decide that, if I go to bed now, no one in the family need know I have stayed up for it again. Why do they insist on shaking their heads when they find me still up for breakfast, after having scribbled through the dark hours? They always do. They seem compelled to express pity for an old loony who can't find his own way to bed. Why won't they understand that this is the one hour of any day that must not be missed, as it is the one hour I couldn't imagine getting up for, though I can still get to it by staying up? It makes sense to me. There comes a time when the windows lighten and the twittering starts. I look up and know it's time to leave the papers in their mess. I could slip quietly into bed and avoid the family's headshakes, but this stroll-around first hour is too good to miss. Even my dog, still sniffing and circling, knows what hour this is.

17   Come on, boy. It's time to go in. The rabbit won't come back till tomorrow, and the birds have work to do. The dawn's over. It's time to call it a day.

Questions for Close Reading

1. What is the selection's thesis (or dominant impression)? Locate the sentence(s) in which Ciardi states his main idea. If he doesn't state the thesis explicitly, express it in your own words.

2. What might Ciardi mean by saying that dawn is the "best" part of the day?

3. What details indicate that the scene Ciardi observes is one with which he is thoroughly familiar and one in which he himself plays a role?

4. What do you think Ciardi means by saying he has had "enough of the paper" and will "take that hummingbird as my news for this dawn" (paragraph 16)? What can you infer from these statements about Ciardi's view of the everyday world?

5. Refer to your dictionary as needed to define the following words used in the selection: *exhalation* (paragraph 3), *grackles* (5 and 13), *aspen* (11), *spectrum* (11), *germinating* (12), and *inured* (14).

Questions About the Writer's Craft

1. The pattern. What sensory impressions does Ciardi draw upon when describing the dawn? What method of organization does he use to structure these impressions?

2. Ciardi uses several striking metaphors to convey the dawn's sensory richness. Locate some of these metaphors. How do they reinforce the essay's dominant impression?

3. Other patterns. In detailing the scenes and events of the dawn, Ciardi describes several processes. Locate some of these in his essay and explain what they reveal about Ciardi's attitude toward the dawn.

4. Examine Ciardi's concluding paragraph. To whom is Ciardi talking? What is the effect of this sudden shift away from speaking to the reader? Why does the sentence "It's time to call it a day" make an especially apt closing line?

Writing Assignments Using Description as a Pattern of Development

1. Like Ciardi, most people have fond feelings about a specific place at a specific time of day. Brainstorm the sensory details that make a particular place and time especially attractive to you. Then write a description of your subject. Include both conventionally beautiful and nonpoetic elements so that your description, like Ciardi's, is down-to-earth rather than romanticized or sentimentalized.

∞ **2.** Solitude is a major component of Ciardi's dawn watch. Write an essay about a place whose essential nature emerges in the absence of people. Possible subjects include a vacant city lot, a neighborhood garden, a section of ocean boardwalk. Rather than stating your thesis explicitly, choose sensory details that convey what it is about your subject that makes it worth describing. To see how three skilled prose stylists write about places having a magic of their own, you might want to read E. B. White's "Once More to the Lake" (page 169) and Anne Morrow Lindbergh's "Channelled Whelk" (page 241).

Writing Assignments Using Other Patterns of Development

3. Choose a block of time that you feel too few people appreciate. Then write an essay that refutes the reasons people might have for overlooking the value of this span of time. You might, for example, argue the importance of time spent commuting in a car, waiting for class to begin, or standing in line at the supermarket. Your essay may be serious or light in tone.

4. In his essay, Ciardi defines the "best" of the day. In an essay of your own, define the "best" of some important aspect of your life. For instance, you could define your "best" learning experience, your "best" decision, your "best" accomplishment. Use evocative sensory images and strong narrative details to support your definition of the "best."

ADDITIONAL WRITING TOPICS: DESCRIPTION

General Assignments

Write an essay using description to develop one of the following topics.

1. A favorite item of clothing

2. A school as a young child sees it

3. A hospital room you have visited or stayed in

4. An individualist's appearance

5. A coffee shop, bus shelter, newsstand, or some other small place

6. A parade or victory celebration

7. A banana, squash, or other fruit or vegetable

8. A particular drawer

9. A houseplant

10. A "media event"

11. A dorm room

12. An elderly person

13. An attractive man or woman

14. A prosthetic device or wheelchair

15. A TV, film, or music celebrity

16. A student lounge

17. A once-in-a-lifetime event

18. The inside of something, such as a cave, boat, car, shed, or machine

19. A friend, roommate, or other person you know well

20. An essential gadget or a useless gadget

Assignments with a Specific Purpose, Audience, and Point of View

1. For an audience of incoming first-year students, prepare a speech describing registration day at your college. Use specific details to help prepare students for the actual event. Choose an adjective that represents your dominant impression of the experience, and keep that word in mind as you write.

2. As a subscriber to a dating service, you've been asked to submit a description of the kind of person you'd like to meet. Describe your ideal date. Focus on specifics about physical appearance, personal habits, character traits, and interests.

3. Your college has decided to replace an old campus structure (for example, a dorm or dining hall) with a new version. Write a letter of protest to the administration, describing the place so vividly and appealingly that its value and need for preservation are unquestionable.

4. As a staff member of the campus newspaper, you have been asked to write a weekly column of social news and gossip. For your first column, you plan to describe a recent campus event—a dance, party, concert, or other social activity. With a straightforward or tongue-in-cheek tone, describe where the event was held, the appearance of the people who attended, and so on.

5. You are part of a student–faculty group responsible for revising the college catalog at your school. Write a full and accurate description of a course with which you're familiar. Tell exactly what the course is about, who teaches it, and how it is run.

6. As a resident of a particular town, you're angered by the appearance of a certain spot and by the activities that take place there. Write a letter to the town council, describing in detail the undesirable nature of this place (a video arcade, an adult bookstore, a bar, a bus station, a neglected park or beach). End with some suggestions about ways to improve the situation.

12
NARRATION

WHAT IS NARRATION?

HUMAN beings are instinctively storytellers. In prehistoric times, our ancestors huddled around campfires to hear tales of hunting and magic. In ancient times, warriors gathered in halls to listen to bards praise in song the exploits of epic heroes. Things are no different today. Boisterous children invariably settle down to listen when their parents read to them; millions of people tune in day after day to the ongoing drama of their favorite soap operas; vacationers sit motionless on the beach, caught up in the latest best-sellers; and all of us enjoy saying, "Just listen to what happened to me today." Our hunger for storytelling is basic.

Narration means telling a single story or several related stories. The story can be a means to an end, a way to support a main idea or thesis. To demonstrate that television has become the constant companion of many children, you might narrate a typical child's day in front of the television—starting with cartoons in the morning and ending with situation comedies at night. Or to support the point that the college registration process should be reformed, you could tell the tale of a chaotic morning spent trying to enroll in classes.

Narration is powerful. Every public speaker, from politician to classroom teacher, knows that stories capture the attention of listeners as nothing else can. We want to know what happened to others, not simply because we're curious, but also because their experiences shed light on our own lives. Narration lends force to opinion, triggers the flow of memory, and evokes places, times, and people in ways that are compelling and affecting.

HOW NARRATION FITS YOUR PURPOSE AND AUDIENCE

Since narratives tell a story, you may think they're found only in novels or short stories. But narration can also appear in essays, sometimes as a supplemental pattern of development. For example, if your purpose in a paper is to *persuade* apathetic readers that airport security regulations must be followed strictly, you might lead off with a brief account of an armed terrorist who easily boarded a plane. In a paper *defining* good teaching, you might keep readers engaged by including satirical anecdotes about one hapless instructor, the antithesis of an effective teacher. An essay on the *effects* of an overburdened judicial system might provide—in an attempt to involve readers—a dramatic account of the way one clearly guilty murderer plea-bargained his way to freedom.

In addition to providing effective support in one section of your paper, narration can also serve as an essay's dominant pattern of development. In fact, most of this chapter shows you how to use a single narrative to convey a central point and share with readers your view of what happened. You might choose to narrate the events of an afternoon spent with your three-year-old nephew as a way of revealing how you rediscovered the importance of family life. Or you might relate the story of your roommate's mugging, evoking the powerlessness and terror of being a victim.

Although some narratives relate unusual experiences, most tread familiar ground, telling tales of joy, love, loss, frustration, fear—all common emotions experienced during life. Narratives can take the ordinary and transmute it into something significant, even extraordinary. As Willa Cather, the American novelist, wrote: "There are only two or three human stories and they go on repeating themselves as fiercely as if they had never happened before." The challenge lies in applying your own vision to a tale, thereby making it unique.

PREWRITING STRATEGIES

The following checklist shows how you can apply to narration some of the prewriting strategies discussed in Chapter 2.

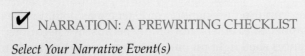 NARRATION: A PREWRITING CHECKLIST

Select Your Narrative Event(s)

☐ What event evokes strong emotion in you and is likely to have a powerful effect on your readers?

☐ Does your journal suggest any promising subjects—for example, an entry about a bully's surprisingly respectful behavior toward a disabled student or a painful encounter with racial prejudice?

☐ Does a scrapbook souvenir, snapshot, old letter, or prized object (an athletic trophy, a political button) point to an event worth writing about?

☐ Will you focus on a personal experience (your high school graduation ceremony), an incident in someone else's life (a friend's battle with chronic illness), or a public event (a community effort to save a beached whale)?

☐ Can you recount your story effectively, given the length of a typical college essay? If not, will relating one key incident from the fuller, more complete event enable you to convey the point and feeling of the entire experience?

☐ If you write about an event in someone else's life, will you have time to interview the person? ("Why did you cross the picket line?" "What did you do when your boss told you to lie?")

Focus on the Conflict in the Event

☐ What is the source of tension in the event: one person's internal dilemma, a conflict between characters, or a struggle between a character and a social institution or natural phenomenon?

☐ Will the conflict create enough tension to "hook" readers and keep them interested?

☐ What point does the conflict and its resolution convey to readers?

☐ What tone is appropriate for recounting the conflict?

Use Prewriting to Generate Specifics About the Conflict

☐ Would the questioning technique ("Why did the argument occur?"), brainstorming, freewriting, mapping, or interviewing help you generate details about the conflict? Does your journal suggest ways to explore aspects of the conflict? ("When my friends participated in the violence at the rock concert, why didn't I try to stop them?")

STRATEGIES FOR USING NARRATION IN AN ESSAY

After prewriting, you're ready to draft your essay. The following suggestions will be helpful whether you use narration as a dominant or supportive pattern of development.

1. Identify the point of the narrative conflict. As you know, most narratives center around a conflict (see the preceding checklist). When you relate a story, it's up to you to convey the *significance* or *meaning* of the event's conflict. In *The Adventures* *of Huckleberry Finn,* Mark Twain warned: "Persons attempting to find a motive in this narrative will be prosecuted; persons attempting to find a moral in it will be banished...." Twain was, of course, being ironic; his novel's richness lies in its "motives" and "morals." Similarly, when recounting your narrative, be sure to begin with a clear sense of your *narrative point,* or *thesis.* Then either state that point directly or select details and a tone that imply the point you want readers to take away from your story.

For example, suppose you decide to write about the time you got locked in a mall late at night. Your narrative might focus on the way the mall looked after hours and the way you struggled with mounting terror. But you would also use the narrative to make a point. Perhaps you want to emphasize that fear can be instructive. Or your point might be that malls have a disturbing, surreal underside. You could state this thesis explicitly. ("After hours, the mall shed its cheerful daytime demeanor and took on a more sinister quality.") Or you could refrain from stating the thesis directly, relying on your details and language to convey the point of the narrative: "The mannequins stared at me with glazed eyes and frozen smiles" and "The steel grates pulled over each store entrance glinted in the cold light, making each shop look like a prison cell."

2. Develop only those details that advance the narrative point. Nothing is more boring than a storyteller who gets sidetracked and drags out a story with nonessential details. When telling a story, you maintain an effective narrative pace by focusing on your point and eliminating any details that don't support it. A good narrative depends not only on what is included, but also on what has been left out.

How do you determine which specifics to omit, which to treat briefly, and which to emphasize? Having a clear sense of your narrative point and knowing your audience are crucial. Assume you're writing a narrative about a disastrous get-acquainted dance sponsored by your college the first week of the academic year. In addition to telling what happened, you also want to make a point; perhaps you want to emphasize that, despite the college's good intentions, such "official" events actually make it difficult to meet people. With this purpose in mind, you might write about how stiff and unnatural students seemed, all dressed up in their best clothes; you might narrate snatches of strained conversation you overheard; you might describe the way males gathered on one side of the room, females on the other—reverting to behaviors supposedly abandoned in fifth grade. All these details would support your narrative point.

Because you don't want to lead away from that point, you would leave out details about the top-notch band and the appetizing refreshments at the dance. The music and food may have been surprisingly good, but since these details don't advance the point you want to make, they should not be included in your narrative.

You also need to keep your audience in mind when selecting narrative details. If the audience consists of your instructor and other students—all of them familiar with the new student center where the dance was held—specific details about the center probably wouldn't have to be provided. But imagine that the essay is going to appear in the quarterly magazine published by the college's community relations office. Many of the magazine's readers are former graduates who haven't been on campus for several years. They may need additional specifics about the student center: its location, how many people it holds, how it is furnished.

As you write, keep asking yourself, "Is this detail or character or snippet of conversation essential? Does my audience need this detail to understand the conflict in the situation? Does this detail advance or intensify the narrative action?" Summarize details that have some importance but do not deserve lengthy treatment ("Two hours went by..."). And try to limit *narrative commentary*—statements that tell rather than show what happened—since such remarks interrupt the narrative flow. Focus instead on the specifics that propel action forward in a vigorous way.

Sometimes, especially if the narrative re-creates an event from the past, you won't be able to remember what happened detail for detail. In such a case, you should take advantage of what is called **dramatic license.** Using your current perspective as a guide, feel free to add or reshape details to suit your narrative point.

3. Organize the narrative sequence. All of us know the traditional beginning of fairy tales: "Once upon a time...." Every narrative begins somewhere, presents a span of time, and ends at a certain point. Frequently, you will want to use a straightforward time order, following the event *chronologically* from beginning to end: first this happened, next this happened, finally this happened.

But sometimes a strict chronological recounting may not be effective—especially if the high point of the narrative gets lost somewhere in the middle of the time sequence. To avoid that possibility, you may want to disrupt chronology, plunge the reader into the middle of the story, and then return in a **flashback** to the tale's beginning. You are probably familiar with the way flashback is used on television and in film. You see someone appealing to the main characters for financial help, then return in a flashback to an earlier time when both were students in the same class. Narratives can also use **flashforward**—you give readers a glimpse of the future (the main character being jailed) before the story continues in the present (the events leading to the arrest). These techniques shift the story onto several planes and keep it from becoming a step-by-step, predictable account. Reserve flashforwards and flashbacks, however, for crucial incidents only, since breaking out of chronological order acts as emphasis. Here are examples of how flashback and flashforward can be used in narrative writing:

Flashback

Standing behind the wooden counter, Greg wielded his knife expertly as he shucked clams--one every ten seconds--with practiced ease. The scene contrasted sharply with his first day on the job, when his hands broke out in blisters and when splitting each shell was like prying open a safe.

Flashforward

> Rushing to move my car from the no-parking zone, I waved a quick goodbye to Karen as she climbed the steps to the bus. I didn't know then that by the time I picked her up at the bus station later that day, she had made a decision that would affect both our lives.

Whether or not you choose to include flashbacks or flashforwards in an essay, remember to limit the time span covered by the narrative. Otherwise, you'll have trouble generating the details needed to give the story depth and meaning. Also, regardless of the time sequence you select, organize the tale so it drives toward a strong finish. Be careful that your story doesn't trail off into minor, anticlimactic details.

4. Make the narrative easy to follow. Describing each distinct action in a separate paragraph helps readers grasp the flow of events. Although narrative essays don't always have conventional topic sentences, each narrative paragraph should have a clear focus. Often this focus is indicated by a sentence early in the paragraph that directs attention to the action taking place. Such a sentence functions as a kind of *informal topic sentence;* the rest of the paragraph then develops that topic sentence. You should also be sure to use time signals when narrating a story. Words like *now, then, next, after,* and *later* ensure that your reader won't get lost as the story progresses.

5. Make the narrative vigorous and immediate. A compelling narrative provides an abundance of specific details, making readers feel as if they're experiencing the story being told. Readers must be able to see, hear, touch, smell, and taste the event you're narrating. *Vivid sensory description* is, therefore, an essential part of an effective narrative. (See page 71 in Chapter 6 and pages 121–122 in Chapter 8 for more on concrete, sensory language.) Not only do specific sensory details make writing a pleasure to read—we all enjoy learning the particulars about people, places, and things—but they also give the narrative the stamp of reality. The specifics convince the reader that the event being described actually did, or could, occur.

Compare the following excerpts from a narrative essay. The first version is lifeless and dull; the revised version, packed with sensory images, grabs readers with its sense of foreboding:

Original Version

> That eventful day started out like every other summer day. My sister Tricia and I made several elaborate mud pies which we decorated with care. A little later on, as we were spraying each other with the garden hose, we heard my father walk up the path.

Revised

That sad summer day started out uneventfully enough. My sister Tricia and I spent a few hours mixing and decorating mud pies. Our hands caked with dry mud, we sprinkled each lopsided pie with alternating rows of dandelion and clover petals. Later, when the sun got hotter, we tossed our white T-shirts over the red picket fence--forgetting my grandmother's frequent warnings to be more ladylike. Our sweaty backs bared to the sun, we doused each other with icy sprays from the garden hose. Caught up in the primitive pleasure of it all, we barely heard my father as he walked up the garden path, the gravel crunching under his heavy work boots.

A caution: Sensory language enlivens narration, but it also slows the pace. Be sure that the slower pace suits your purpose. For example, a lengthy description fits an account of a leisurely summer vacation but is inappropriate in a tale about a frantic search for a misplaced wallet.

Another way to create an aura of narrative immediacy is to use **dialog** while telling a story. Our sense of other people comes, in part, from what they say and the way they sound. Conversational exchanges allow the reader to experience characters directly. Compare the following fragments of a narrative, one with dialog and one without, noting how much more energetic the second version is.

Original

As soon as I found my way back to the campsite, the trail guide commented on my disheveled appearance. I explained that I had heard some gunshots and had run back to camp as soon as I could.

Revised

As soon as I found my way back to the campsite, the trail guide took one look at me and drawled, "What on earth happened to you, Daniel Boone? You look as though you've been dragged through a haystack backwards."

"I'd look a lot worse if I hadn't run back here. When a bullet whizzes by me, I don't stick around to see who's doing the shooting."

Note that, when using dialog, you generally begin a new paragraph to indicate a shift from one person's speech to another's (as in the second example above). Dialog can also be used to convey a person's inner thoughts. Like conversation between people, such interior dialog is enclosed in quotation marks.

The challenge in writing dialog, both exterior and interior, is to make each character's speech distinctive and convincing. Reading the dialog aloud—even asking friends or family members to speak the lines—will help you develop an ear for authentic speech. What sounds most natural is often a compressed and reshaped version of what was actually said. As with other narrative details, include only those portions of dialog that serve your purpose, fit the mood you want to create, and reveal character. (For guidelines on punctuating dialog, see pages 676–678 of the Handbook.)

Another way to enliven narratives is to use *varied sentence structure*. Sentences that plod along with the same predictable pattern put readers to sleep. Experiment with your sentences by varying their length and type; mix long and short sentences, simple and complex. (For more on sentence structure, see pages 109–114 in Chapter 8.) Compare the following original and revised versions to get an idea of how effective varied sentence structure can be in narrative writing:

Original

```
    The store manager went to the walk-in refrigerator every day.
The heavy metal door clanged shut behind her. I had visions of her
freezing to death among the hanging carcasses. The shiny door
finally swung open. She waddled out.
```

Revised

```
    Each time the store manager went to the walk-in refrigerator,
the heavy metal door clanged shut behind her. Visions of her freez-
ing to death among the hanging carcasses crept into my mind until,
finally, the shiny door swung open and out she waddled.
```

Original

```
    The yellow-and-blue striped fish struggled on the line. Its
scales shimmered in the sunlight. Its tail waved frantically. I saw
its desire to live. I decided to let it go.
```

Revised

```
    Scales shimmering in the sunlight, tail waving frantically, the
yellow-and-blue striped fish struggled on the line. Seeing its
desire to live, I let it go.
```

Finally, *vigorous verbs* lend energy to narratives. Use active verb forms ("The boss *yelled at* him") rather than passive ones ("He *was yelled at* by the boss"), and try to replace anemic *to be* verbs ("She *was* a good basketball player") with more dynamic constructions ("She *played* basketball well"). (For more on strong verbs, see pages 122–124 in Chapter 8.)

6. Keep your point of view and verb tense consistent. All stories have a *narrator,* the person who tells the story. If you, as narrator, tell a story as you experienced it, the story is written in the *first-person point of view* ("I saw the dog pull loose"). But if you observed the event (or heard about it from others) and want to tell how someone else experienced the incident, you would use the *third-person point of view* ("Anne saw the dog pull loose"). Each point of view has advantages and limitations. First person allows you to express ordinarily private thoughts and to recreate an event as you actually experienced it. This point of view is limited, though, in its ability to depict the inner thoughts of other people involved in the event. By way of contrast, third person makes it easier to provide insight into the thoughts of all the participants. However, its objective, broad perspective may undercut some of the subjective immediacy typical of the "I was there" point of view. No matter which point of view you select, stay with that vantage point throughout the entire narrative. (For more on point of view, see pages 23–24 in Chapter 2.)

Knowing whether to use the *past* or *present tense* ("I *strolled* into the room" as opposed to "I *stroll* into the room") is important. In most narrations, the past tense predominates, enabling the writer to span a considerable period of time. Although more rarely used, the present tense can be powerful for events of short durations—a wrestling match or a medical emergency, for instance. A narrative in the present tense prolongs each moment, intensifying the reader's sense of participation. Be careful, though; unless the event is intense and fast-paced, the present tense can seem contrived. Whichever tense you choose, avoid shifting midstream—starting, let's say, in the past tense ("she skated") and switching to the present tense ("she runs").

REVISION STRATEGIES

Once you have a draft of the essay, you're ready to revise. The following checklist will help you and those giving you feedback apply to narration some of the revision techniques discussed in Chapters 7 and 8.

 NARRATION: A REVISION CHECKLIST

Revise Overall Meaning and Structure

☐ What is the essay's narrative point? Is it stated explicitly? If so, where? If not, where is it implied? Could the point be conveyed more clearly? How?

☐ What is the narrative's conflict? Is it stated explicitly? If so, where? If not, where is it implied? Could the conflict be made more dramatic? How?

☐ From what point of view is the narrative told? Is that the most effective point of view for this essay? Why or why not?

Revise Paragraph Development

☐ Which paragraphs (or passages) fail to advance the action, reveal character, or contribute to the story's mood? Should these sections be condensed or eliminated?

☐ Where do commentary and description slow the narrative pace? Is such an effect intended? If not, should the sections be tightened or eliminated?

☐ Where is it difficult to follow the chronology of events? Where should paragraph order be changed? Why? Where would chronology be clearer if there were separate paragraphs for distinct time periods? Where would additional time signals help?

☐ How could flashback or flashforward paragraphs (or passages) be used to highlight key events?

☐ What can be done to make the essay's opening paragraph more compelling? Would a dramatic bit of dialog or a mood-setting descriptive passage help?

☐ What could be done to make the essay's closing paragraph more effective? If the final paragraph seems anticlimactic, would it help to end earlier? If the ending doesn't round off the essay in a satisfying way, what could be added that would echo an idea or image in the opening?

Revise Sentences and Words

☐ Where is sentence structure monotonous? How would combining sentences, mixing sentence type, and alternating sentence length help?

☐ Where should the narrative pace be slowed down with long sentences or quickened with short ones?

☐ Where could dialog effectively convey character and propel the story forward? Where could dialog replace commentary?

☐ Which sentences and words are inconsistent with the essay's tone?

☐ Which sentences would benefit from sensory details that heighten the narrative mood?

☐ Where do vigorous verbs convey action? Where could active verbs ("Many of us *made* the same error") replace passive ones ("The same error *was made* by many of us")? Where could dull *to be* verbs ("The room *was* dark") be converted to more dynamic forms ("The room *darkened*")?

☐ Where are there inappropriate shifts in point of view or verb tense?

STUDENT ESSAY: FROM PREWRITING THROUGH REVISION

The student essay that follows was written by Paul Monahan in response to this assignment:

> In "Shooting an Elephant," George Orwell tells about an incident that forced him to act in a manner contrary to his better instincts. Write a narrative about a time you faced a disturbing conflict and ended up doing something you later regretted.

After deciding to write about an encounter he had with an elderly woman in the store where he worked, Paul did some *freewriting* on a word processor to gather material on his subject. When he later reviewed this freewriting, he crossed out unnecessary commentary, wrote notes signaling where dialog and descriptive details were needed, and indicated where paragraph breaks might occur. After annotating his freewriting in this manner, Paul felt comfortable launching into his first draft, without further shaping his freewriting or preparing an outline. As he wrote, though, he frequently referred to his warm-up material to organize his narrative and retrieve details. Paul's original freewriting is shown here; the handwritten marks indicate Paul's later efforts to shape and develop this material:

Freewriting

An (old woman) entered the (store). She pushed the door, hob-   *Set up contrast*
bled in, coughed, and seemed to be in pain. She wore a faded   *Give details about her*
dress and a sweater that was much too small for her. The night   *appearance*
was cold, but she didn't wear any stockings. You could see her
veins. She strolled around the store, sneezing and hacking. She
picked up a can of corn and stared at it. She made me nervous.
I walked over to see what was going on. Asked if she needed   *Add dialog*
help.

I was the one to do this because I was on duty. Had worked   *Background*
at 7-11 for two years. Felt confident. Always tried to be   *information—move to*
friendly and polite. Hadn't had any trouble. But the old woman   *first paragraph*
worried me.

"I need food," she said. I told her how much the corn cost   *Add dialog*
and also that the bologna was on sale (what a stupid, insensitive thing to do!). She said she couldn't pay. I almost told her
to take the can of corn, but all the rules stopped me. Be
polite, stay in control. I told her I couldn't give anything
away. Her face looked even more saggy. She kind of shook and put
the can back. She left, I rushed out after her. Too late. Felt   *More specifics*

Good title?   ashamed about acting like a robot. Mad at myself. (If only I'd
                acted differently.)

Now read Paul's paper, "If Only," noting the similarities and differences between his prewriting and final essay. You'll notice, for example, that Paul decided to move background information to the essay's opening, and that he ended up using as his title a shortened version of the final sentence in his prewriting. Finally, consider how well the essay applies the principles of narration discussed in this chapter. (The commentary that follows the paper will help you look at Paul's essay more closely and will give you some sense of how he went about revising his first draft.)

If Only

by Paul Monahan

Introduction   Having worked at a 7-Eleven store for two years, I   1
                       thought I had become successful at what our manager calls
                       "customer relations." I firmly believed that a friendly smile
                       and an automatic "sir," "ma'am," and "thank you" would see me
                       through any situation that might arise, from soothing impa-
                       tient or unpleasant people to apologizing for giving out the
Narrative point ────── wrong change. But the other night an old woman shattered my
(thesis)   belief that a glib response could smooth over the rough spots
                       of dealing with other human beings.
Informal topic ──────→ The moment she entered, the woman presented a sharp con-   2
sentence   trast to our shiny store with its bright lighting and neatly
                       arranged shelves. Walking as if each step were painful, she
                       slowly pushed open the glass door and hobbled down the near-
Sensory details ────── est aisle. She coughed dryly, wheezing with each breath. On a
                       forty-degree night, she was wearing only a faded print dress,
                       a thin, light-beige sweater too small to button, and black
                       vinyl slippers with the backs cut out to expose calloused
                       heels. There no stockings or socks on her splotchy,
                       blue-veined legs.
                           After strolling around the store for several minutes, the   3
                       old woman stopped in front of the rows of canned vegetables.
                       She picked up some corn niblets and stared with a strange
                       intensity at the label. At that point, I decided to be a
Informal topic ────── good, courteous employee and asked her if she needed help. As
sentence   I stood close to her, my smile became harder to maintain; her

red-rimmed eyes were partially closed by yellowish crusts; her hands were covered with layer upon layer of grime, and the stale smell of sweat rose in a thick vaporous cloud from her clothes. — Sensory details

4   "I need some food," she muttered in reply to my bright "Can I help you?" — Start of dialog

5   "Are you looking for corn, ma'am?"

6   "I need some food," she repeated. "Any kind."

7   "Well, the corn is ninety-five cents," I said in my most helpful voice. "Or, if you like, we have a special on bologna today."

8   "I can't pay," she said.

9   For a second, I was tempted to say, "Take the corn." But ← Conflict established the employee rules flooded into my mind: Remain polite, but do not let customers get the best of you. Let them know that you are in control. For a moment, I even entertained the idea that this was some sort of test, and that this woman was someone from the head office, testing my loyalty. I responded dutifully, "I'm sorry, ma'am, but I can't give away anything for free."

10   The old woman's face collapsed a bit more, if that were possible, and her hands trembled as she put the can back on the shelf. She shuffled past me toward the door, her torn and dirty clothing barely covering her bent back. — Informal topic sentence

11   Moments after she left, I rushed out the door with the can of corn, but she was nowhere in sight. For the rest of my shift, the image of the woman haunted me. I had been young, healthy, and smug. She had been old, sick, and desperate. Wishing with all my heart that I had acted like a human being rather than a robot, I was saddened to realize how fragile a hold we have on our better instincts. — Conclusion / Echoing of narrative point in the introduction

Commentary

Point of View, Tense, and Conflict

Paul chose to write "If Only" from the *first-person point of view,* a logical choice because he appears as a main character in his own story. Using the *past tense,* Paul recounts an incident filled with *conflict*—between him and the woman and between his fear of breaking the rules and his human instinct to help someone in need.

Narrative Point

It isn't always necessary to state the *narrative point* of an essay; it can be implied. But Paul decided to express the controlling idea of his narrative in two places—in the introduction ("But the other night an old woman shattered my belief that a glib response could smooth over the rough spots of dealing with other human beings") and again in the conclusion, where he expands his idea about rote responses overriding impulses of independent judgment and compassion. All of the essay's *narrative details* contribute to the point of the piece; Paul does not include any extraneous information that would detract from the central idea he wants to convey.

Organization and Other Patterns of Development

The narrative is *organized chronologically,* from the moment the woman enters the store to Paul's reaction after she leaves. Paul limits the narrative's time span. The entire incident probably occurs in under ten minutes, yet the introduction serves as a kind of *flashback* by providing some necessary background about Paul's past experiences. To help the reader follow the course of the narrative, Paul uses *time signals: "The moment* she entered, the woman presented a sharp contrast" (paragraph 2); "*At that point,* I decided to be a good, courteous employee" (3); "*For the rest of my shift,* the image of the woman haunted me" (11).

The paragraphs (except for those consisting solely of dialog) also contain *informal topic sentences* that direct attention to the specific stage of action being narrated. Indeed, each paragraph focuses on a distinct event: the elderly woman's actions when she first enters the store, the encounter between Paul and the woman, Paul's resulting inner conflict, the woman's subsequent response, and Paul's delayed reaction.

This chain of events, with one action leading to another, illustrates that the *cause-effect* pattern underlies the essay's basic structure. And another pattern— *description*—gives dramatic immediacy to the events being recounted. Throughout, rich sensory details engage the reader's interest. For instance, the sentence "her red-rimmed eyes were partially closed by yellowish crusts" (3) vividly recreates the woman's appearance while also suggesting Paul's inner reaction to the woman.

Dialog and Sentence Structure

Paul uses other techniques to add energy and interest to his narrative. For one thing, he dramatizes his conflict with the woman through *dialog* that crackles with tension. And he achieves a vigorous narrative pace by *varying the length and structure of his sentences.* In the second paragraph, a short sentence ("There were no stockings or socks on her splotchy, blue-veined legs") alternates with a longer one ("On a forty-degree night, she was wearing only a faded print dress, a thin, light-beige sweater too small to button, and black vinyl slippers with the backs cut out to expose calloused heels"). Some sentences in the essay open with a subject and verb ("She coughed dryly"), while others start with dependent clauses or participial phrases ("As I stood close to her, my smile became harder to maintain"; "Walking as if each step were painful, she slowly pushed open the glass door") or with a prepositional phrase ("For a second, I was tempted").

Revising the First Draft

To get a sense of how Paul went about revising his essay, take a moment to look at the original version of his third paragraph shown here. The handwritten annotations, numbered in order of importance, represent Paul's ideas for revision. Compare this preliminary version with the final version in the full essay:

Original Version of Third Paragraph

    After sneezing and hacking her way around the store, the
old woman stopped in front of the vegetable shelves. She picked
up a can of corn and stared at the label. She stayed like this
for several minutes. Then I walked over to her and asked if I
could be of help.

③ Inappropriate words—sound humorous

① Boring—not enough details

② Choppy sentences

As you can see, Paul realized the paragraph lacked power, so he decided to add compelling descriptive details about the woman ("the stale smell of sweat," for example). When revising, he also worked to reduce the paragraph's choppiness. By expanding and combining sentences, he gave the paragraph an easier, more graceful rhythm. Much of the time, revision involves paring down excess material. In this case, though, Paul made the right decision to elaborate his sentences. Furthermore, he added the following comment to the third paragraph: "I decided to be a good, courteous employee." These few words introduce an appropriate note of irony and serve to echo the essay's controlling idea.

Finally, Paul decided to omit the words "sneezing and hacking" because he realized they were too comic or light for his subject. Still, the first sentence in the revised paragraph is somewhat jarring. The word *strolling* isn't quite appropriate since it implies a leisurely grace inconsistent with the impression he wants to convey. Replacing *strolling* with, say, *shuffling* would bring the image more into line with the essay's overall mood.

Despite this slight problem, Paul's revisions are right on the mark. The changes he made strengthened his essay, turning it into a more evocative, more polished piece of narrative writing.

ACTIVITIES: NARRATION

Prewriting Activities

1. Imagine you're writing two essays: One analyzes the effect of insensitive teachers on young children; the other argues the importance of family traditions. With the help of your journal or freewriting, identify different narratives you could use to open each essay.

2. Use brainstorming or any other prewriting technique to generate narrative details about *one* of the following events. After examining your raw material, identify two or three narrative points (thesis statements) that might focus an essay. Then edit the prewriting material for each narrative point, noting which items would be appropriate, which would be inappropriate, which would have to be developed more fully.

   a. An injury you received
   b. The loss of an important object
   c. An event that made you wish you had a certain skill

3. For each of the following situations, identify two different conflicts that would make a story worth relating:

   a. Going to the supermarket with a friend
   b. Telling your parents which college you've decided to attend
   c. Participating in a demonstration
   d. Preparing for an exam in a difficult course

4. Prepare six to ten lines of vivid and natural-sounding dialog to convey the conflict in *two* of the following situations:

   a. One member of a couple trying to break up with the other
   b. A ten-year-old brother and a teenage sister shopping for a parent's birthday present
   c. A teacher talking to a student who plagiarized a paper
   d. A young person talking to his or her parents about dropping out of college for a semester

Revising Activities

5. Revise each of the following narrative sentence groups twice: once with words that carry negative connotations, and again with words that carry positive connotations. Use varied sentence structure, sensory details, and vigorous verbs to convey mood.

a. The bell rang. It rang loudly. Students knew the last day of class was over.
b. Last weekend, our neighbors burned leaves in their yard. We went over to speak with them.
c. The sun shone in through my bedroom window. It made me sit up in bed. Daylight was finally here, I told myself.

6. The following paragraph is the introduction from the first draft of an essay proposing harsher penalties for drunk drivers. Revise this narrative paragraph to make it more effective. How can you make sentence structure less predictable? Which details should you delete? As you revise, provide language that conveys the event's sights, smells, and sounds. Also, clarify the chronological sequence.

```
As I drove down the street in my bright blue sports car, I saw
a car coming rapidly around the curve. The car didn't slow down as
it headed toward the traffic light. The light turned yellow and then
red. A young couple, dressed like models, started crossing the
street. When the woman saw the car, she called out to her husband.
He jumped onto the shoulder. The man wasn't hurt but, seconds later,
it was clear the woman was. I ran to a nearby emergency phone and
called the police. The ambulance arrived, but the woman was already
dead. The driver, who looked terrible, failed the sobriety test, and
the police found out that he had two previous offenses. It's appar-
ent that better ways have to be found for getting drunk drivers off
the road.
```

PROFESSIONAL
SELECTIONS:
NARRATION

GEORGE ORWELL

Born Eric Blair in the British colony of India, George Orwell (1903–50) is best known for his two novels *Animal Farm* (1946) and *1984* (1949)—both searing depictions of totalitarian societies. A fierce critic of political and economic injustice, Orwell also wrote a number of essays about the desperate lives of English factory workers and miners. Orwell's position with the Indian Imperial Police provided the basis for the following essay, which is taken from the collection *"Shooting an Elephant" and Other Essays* (1950).

SHOOTING AN ELEPHANT

In Moulmein, in Lower Burma, I was hated by large numbers of people—the only 1
time in my life that I have been important enough for this to happen to me. I was sub-
divisional police officer of the town, and in an aimless, petty kind of way anti-European
feeling was very bitter. No one had the guts to raise a riot, but if a European woman
went through the bazaars alone somebody would probably spit betel juice over her
dress. As a police officer I was an obvious target and was baited whenever it seemed
safe to do so. When a nimble Burman tripped me up on the football field and the ref-
eree (another Burman) looked the other way, the crowd yelled with hideous laughter.
This happened more than once. In the end the sneering yellow faces of young men that
met me everywhere, the insults hooted after me when I was at a safe distance, got
badly on my nerves. The young Buddhist priests were the worst of all. There were several thousand of them in the town and none of them seemed to have anything to do
except stand on street corners and jeer at Europeans.

All this was perplexing and upsetting. For at that time I had already made up my 2
mind that imperialism was an evil thing and the sooner I chucked up my job and got
out of it the better. Theoretically—and secretly, of course—I was all for the Burmese
and all against their oppressors, the British. As for the job I was doing, I hated it more
bitterly than I can perhaps make clear. In a job like that you see the dirty work of
Empire at close quarters. The wretched prisoners huddling in the stinking cages of the
lock-ups, the grey, cowed faces of the long-term convicts, the scarred buttocks of the
men who had been flogged with bamboos—all these oppressed me with an intolerable
sense of guilt. But I could get nothing into perspective. I was young and ill-educated
and I had to think out my problems in the utter silence that is imposed on every
Englishman in the East. I did not even know that the British Empire is dying, still less
did I know that it is a great deal better than the younger empires that are going to supplant it. All I knew was that I was stuck between my hatred of the empire I served and
my rage against the evil-spirited little beasts who tried to make my job impossible.
With one part of my mind I thought of the British Raj as an unbreakable tyranny, as
something clamped down, *in saecula saeculorum,** upon the will of prostrate peoples;
with another part I thought that the greatest joy in the world would be to drive a bayo-
net into a Buddhist priest's guts. Feelings like these are the normal by-products of
imperialism; ask any Anglo-Indian official, if you can catch him off duty.

One day something happened which in a roundabout way was enlightening. It was 3
a tiny incident in itself, but it gave me a better glimpse than I had had before of the real
nature of imperialism—the real motives for which despotic governments act. Early one
morning the sub-inspector at a police station the other end of the town rang me up on
the 'phone and said that an elephant was ravaging the bazaar. Would I please come and
do something about it? I did not know what I could do, but I wanted to see what was
happening and I got onto a pony and started out. I took my rifle, an old .44 Winchester
and much too small to kill an elephant, but I thought the noise might be useful *in ter-
rorem.*† Various Burmans stopped me on the way and told me about the elephant's
doings. It was not, of course, a wild elephant, but a tame one which had gone "must."

---

*For ever and ever (editors' note).
†As a warning (editors' note).

It had been chained up, as tame elephants always are when their attack of "must" is due, but on the previous night it had broken its chain and escaped. Its mahout, the only person who could manage it when it was in that state, had set out in pursuit, but had taken the wrong direction and was now twelve hours' journey away, and in the morning the elephant had suddenly reappeared in the town. The Burmese population had no weapons and were quite helpless against it. It had already destroyed some-body's bamboo hut, killed a cow and raided some fruit-stalls and devoured the stock; also it had met the municipal rubbish van and, when the driver jumped out and took to his heels, had turned the van over and inflicted violences upon it.

4   The Burmese sub-inspector and some Indian constables were waiting for me in the quarter where the elephant had been seen. It was a very poor quarter, a labyrinth of squalid bamboo huts, thatched with palm-leaf, winding all over a steep hillside. I remember that it was a cloudy, stuffy morning at the beginning of the rains. We began questioning the people as to where the elephant had gone and, as usual, failed to get any definite information. That is invariably the case in the East; a story always sounds clear enough at a distance, but the nearer you get to the scene of events the vaguer it becomes. Some of the people said that the elephant had gone in one direction, some said that he had gone in another, some professed not even to have heard of any ele-phant. I had almost made up my mind that the whole story was a pack of lies, when we heard yells a little distance away. There was a loud, scandalized cry of 'Go away, child! Go away this instant!' and an old woman with a switch in her hand came round the corner of a hut, violently shooing away a crowd of naked children. Some more women followed, clicking their tongues and exclaiming; evidently there was something that the children ought not to have seen. I rounded the hut and saw a man's dead body sprawling in the mud. He was an Indian, a black Dravidian coolie, almost naked, and he could not have been dead many minutes. The people said that the elephant had come suddenly upon him round the corner of the hut, caught him with its trunk, put its foot on his back and ground him into the earth. This was the rainy season and the ground was soft, and his face had scored a trench a foot deep and a couple of yards long. He was lying on his belly with arms crucified and head sharply twisted to one side. His face was coated with mud, the eyes wide open, the teeth bared and grinning with an expression of unendurable agony. (Never tell me, by the way, that the dead look peaceful. Most of the corpses I have seen looked devilish.) The friction of the great beast's foot had stripped the skin from his back as neatly as one skins a rabbit. As soon as I saw the dead man I sent an orderly to a friend's house nearby to borrow an ele-phant rifle. I had already sent back the pony, not wanting it to go mad with fright and throw me if it smelt the elephant.

5   The orderly came back in a few minutes with a rifle and five cartridges, and mean-while some Burmans had arrived and told us that the elephant was in the paddy fields below, only a few hundred yards away. As I started forward practically the whole pop-ulation of the quarter flocked out of the houses and followed me. They had seen the rifle and were all shouting excitedly that I was going to shoot the elephant. They had not shown much interest in the elephant when he was merely ravaging their homes, but it was different now that he was going to be shot. It was a bit of fun to them, as it would be to an English crowd; besides they wanted the meat. It made me vaguely uneasy. I had no intention of shooting the elephant—I had merely sent for the rifle to defend myself if necessary—and it is always unnerving to have a crowd following you. I marched down the hill looking and feeling a fool, with the rifle over my shoulder and

an ever-growing army of people jostling at my heels. At the bottom, when you got away from the huts, there was a metalled road and beyond that a miry waste of paddy fields a thousand yards across, not yet ploughed but soggy from the first rains and dotted with coarse grass. The elephant was standing eight yards from the road, his left side towards us. He took not the slightest notice of the crowd's approach. He was tearing up bunches of grass, beating them against his knees to clean them and stuffing them into his mouth.

I had halted on the road. As soon as I saw the elephant I knew with perfect certainty   6
that I ought not to shoot him. It is a serious matter to shoot a working elephant—it is comparable to destroying a huge and costly piece of machinery—and obviously one ought not to do it if it can possibly be avoided. And at that distance, peacefully eating, the elephant looked no more dangerous than a cow. I thought then and I think now that his attack of "must" was already passing off; in which case he would merely wander harmlessly about until the mahout came back and caught him. Moreover, I did not in the least want to shoot him. I decided that I would watch him for a little while to make sure that he did not turn savage again, and then go home.

But at that moment I glanced round at the crowd that had followed me. It was an   7
immense crowd, two thousand at the least and growing every minute. It blocked the road for a long distance on either side. I looked at the sea of yellow faces above the garish clothes—faces all happy and excited over this bit of fun, all certain that the elephant was going to be shot. They were watching me as they would watch a conjurer about to perform a trick. They did not like me, but with the magical rifle in my hands I was momentarily worth watching. And suddenly I realized that I should have to shoot the elephant after all. The people expected it of me and I had got to do it; I could feel their two thousand wills pressing me forward, irresistibly. And it was at this moment, as I stood there with the rifle in my hands, that I first grasped the hollowness, the futility of the white man's dominion in the East. Here was I, the white man with his gun, standing in front of the unarmed native crowd—seemingly the leading actor of the piece; but in reality I was only an absurd puppet pushed to and fro by the will of those yellow faces behind. I perceived in this moment that when the white man turns tyrant it is his own freedom that he destroys. He becomes a sort of hollow, posing dummy, the conventionalized figure of a sahib. For it is the condition of his rule that he shall spend his life in trying to impress the "natives," and so in every crisis he has got to do what the "natives" expect of him. He wears a mask, and his face grows to fit it. I had got to shoot the elephant. I had committed myself to doing it when I sent for the rifle. A sahib has got to act like a sahib; he has got to appear resolute, to know his own mind and do definite things. To come all that way, rifle in hand, with two thousand people marching at my heels, and then to trail feebly away, having done nothing—no, that was impossible. The crowd would laugh at me. And my whole life, every white man's life in the East, was one long struggle not to be laughed at.

But I did not want to shoot the elephant. I watched him beating his bunch of grass   8
against his knees, with that preoccupied grandmotherly air that elephants have. It seemed to me that it would be murder to shoot him. At that age I was not squeamish about killing animals, but I had never shot an elephant and never wanted to. (Somehow it always seems worse to kill a *large* animal.) Besides, there was the beast's owner to be considered. Alive, the elephant was worth at least a hundred pounds; dead, he would only be worth the value of his tusks, five pounds, possibly. But I had got to act quickly. I turned to some experienced-looking Burmans who had been there when we arrived, and asked them how the elephant had been behaving. They all said the same

thing: he took no notice of you if you left him alone, but he might charge if you went too close to him.

9   It was perfectly clear to me what I ought to do. I ought to walk up to within, say, twenty-five yards of the elephant and test his behavior. If he charged, I could shoot; if he took notice of me, it would be safe to leave him until the mahout came back. But also I knew that I was going to do no such thing. I was a poor shot with a rifle and the ground was soft mud into which one would sink at every step. If the elephant charged and I missed him, I should have about as much chance as a toad under a steam-roller. But even then I was not thinking particularly of my own skin, only of the watchful yellow faces behind. For at that moment, with the crowd watching me, I was not afraid in the ordinary sense, as I would have been if I had been alone. A white man mustn't be frightened in front of "natives"; and so, in general he isn't frightened. The sole thought in my mind was that if anything went wrong those two thousand Burmans would see me pursued, caught, trampled on and reduced to a grinning corpse like that Indian up the hill. And if that happened it was quite probable that some of them would laugh. That would never do. There was only one alternative. I shoved the cartridges into the magazine and lay down on the road to get a better aim.

10   The crowd grew very still, and a deep, low, happy sigh, as of people who see the theatre curtain go up at last, breathed from innumerable throats. They were going to have their bit of fun after all. The rifle was a beautiful German thing with cross-hair sights. I did not then know that in shooting an elephant one would shoot to cut an imaginary bar running from ear-hole to ear-hole. I ought, therefore, as the elephant was sideway on, to have aimed straight at his ear-hole; actually I aimed several inches in front of this, thinking the brain would be further forward.

11   When I pulled the trigger I did not hear the bang or feel the kick—one never does when a shot goes home—but I heard the devilish roar of glee that went up from the crowd. In that instant, in too short a time, one would have thought, even for the bullet to get there, a mysterious, terrible change had come over the elephant. He neither stirred nor fell, but every line of his body had altered. He looked suddenly stricken, shrunken, immensely old, as though the frightful impact of the bullet had paralyzed him without knocking him down. At last, after what seemed a long time—it might have been five seconds, I dare say—he sagged flabbily to his knees. His mouth slobbered. An enormous senility seemed to have settled upon him. One could have imagined him thousands of years old. I fired again into the same spot. At the second shot he did not collapse but climbed with desperate slowness to his feet and stood weakly upright, with legs sagging and head drooping. I fired a third time. That was the shot that did for him. You could see the agony of it jolt his whole body and knock the last remnant of strength from his legs. But in falling he seemed for a moment to rise, for as his hind legs collapsed beneath him he seemed to tower upward like a huge rock toppling, his trunk reaching skywards like a tree. He trumpeted, for the first and only time. And then down he came, his belly towards me, with a crash that seemed to shake the ground even where I lay.

12   I got up. The Burmans were already racing past me across the mud. It was obvious that the elephant would never rise again, but he was not dead. He was breathing very rhythmically with long rattling gasps, his great mound of a side painfully rising and falling. His mouth was wide open—I could see far down into caverns of pale pink throat. I waited a long time for him to die, but his breathing did not weaken. Finally I fired my two remaining shots into the spot where I thought his heart must be. The thick blood welled out of him like red velvet, but still he did not die. His body did not even jerk

when the shots hit him, the tortured breathing continued without a pause. He was dying, very slowly and in great agony, but in some world remote from me where not even a bullet could damage him further. I felt that I had got to put an end to that dreadful noise. It seemed dreadful to see the great beast lying there, powerless to move and yet powerless to die, and not even to be able to finish him. I sent back for my small rifle and poured shot after shot into his heart and down his throat. They seemed to make no impression. The tortured gasps continued as steadily as the ticking of a clock.

In the end I could not stand it any longer and went away. I heard later that it took 13 him half an hour to die. Burmans were bringing dahs and baskets even before I left, and I was told they had stripped the body almost to the bones by the afternoon.

Afterwards, of course, there were endless discussions about the shooting of the ele- 14 phant. The owner was furious, but he was only an Indian and could do nothing. Besides, legally I had done the right thing, for a mad elephant has to be killed, like a mad dog, if its owner fails to control it. Among the Europeans opinion was divided. The older men said I was right, the younger men said it was a damn shame to shoot an elephant for killing a coolie, because an elephant was worth more than any damn Coringhee coolie. And afterwards I was very glad that the coolie had been killed; it put me legally in the right and it gave me a sufficient pretext for shooting the elephant. I often wondered whether any of the others grasped that I had done it solely to avoid looking a fool.

Questions for Close Reading

1. What is the selection's thesis (or narrative point)? Locate the sentence(s) in which Orwell states his main idea. If he doesn't state the thesis explicitly, express it in your own words.

2. How does Orwell feel about the Burmans? What words does he use to describe them?

3. What reasons does Orwell give for shooting the elephant?

4. In paragraph 3, Orwell says that the elephant incident gave him a better understanding of "the real motives for which despotic governments act." What do you think he means? Before you answer, reread paragraph 7 carefully.

5. Refer to your dictionary as needed to define the following words used in the selection: *imperialism* (paragraph 2), *prostrate* (2), *despotic* (3), *mahout* (3), *miry* (5), *conjurer* (7), *futility* (7), and *sahib* (7).

Questions About the Writer's Craft

1. The pattern. Most effective narratives encompass a restricted time span. How much time elapses from the moment Orwell gets his gun to the death of the elephant? What time signals does Orwell provide to help the reader follow the sequence of events in this limited time span?

2. Orwell doesn't actually begin his narrative until the third paragraph. What purposes do the first two paragraphs serve?

3. In paragraph 6, Orwell says that shooting a working elephant "is comparable to destroying a huge and costly piece of machinery." This kind of comparison is called an *analogy*—describing something unfamiliar, often abstract, in terms of something more familiar and concrete. Find at least three additional analogies in Orwell's essay. What effect do they have?

4. Other patterns. Much of the power of Orwell's narrative comes from his ability to convey sensory impressions—what he saw, heard, smelled. Orwell's description becomes most vivid when he writes about the elephant's death in paragraphs 11 and 12. Find some evocative words and phrases that give the description its power.

Writing Assignments Using Narration as a Pattern of Development

∞ **1.** Orwell recounts a time he acted under great pressure. Write a narrative about an action you once took simply because you felt pressured. Perhaps you were attempting to avoid ridicule or to fulfill someone else's expectations. Like Orwell, use vivid details to bring the incident to life and to convey its effect on you. Reading Malcolm X's "My First Conk" (page 321) will help you appreciate the power of the need to conform.

∞ **2.** Write a narrative essay about an experience that gave you, like Orwell, a deeper insight into your own nature. You may have discovered, for instance, that you can be surprisingly naive, compassionate, petty, brave, rebellious, or good at something. Your essay may be serious or light in tone. Before writing, you might want to read two very different pieces: Russell Baker's "Selling the Post" (page 214), a humorous essay that recounts Baker's encounter with his own regrettable "lack of gumption," and Natalie Angier's "A Granddaughter's Fear" (page 388), a harrowing essay that describes Angier's confrontation with her dark side.

Writing Assignments Using Other Patterns of Development

3. Was Orwell justified in shooting the elephant? Write an essay arguing either that Orwell was justified *or* that he was not. To develop your thesis, cite several specific reasons, each supported by details drawn from the essay. Here are some points you might consider: the legality of Orwell's act, the elephant's temperament, the crowd's presence, the aftermath of the elephant's death, the death itself.

4. Orwell's essay concerns, in part, the tendency to conceal indecision and confusion behind a facade of authority. Focusing on one or two groups of people (parents, teachers, doctors, politicians, and so on), write an essay about the way people in authority sometimes *pretend* to know what they are doing so that subordinates won't suspect their insecurity or incompetence. Part of your essay should focus on the consequences of such behaviors.

AUDRE LORDE

Named poet laureate of the state of New York in 1991, Audre Lorde (1934–92) was a New Yorker born of African-Caribbean parents. Lorde taught at Hunter College for many years and published numerous poems and nonfiction pieces in a variety of magazines and literary journals. Her books include *The Black Unicorn: Poems* (1995), *A Burst of Light* (1988), and *Sister Outsider: Essays and Speeches* (1984). "The Fourth of July" is an excerpt from her autobiography, *Zami: A New Spelling of My Name* (1982).

THE FOURTH OF JULY

The first time I went to Washington, D.C., was on the edge of the summer when I 1 was supposed to stop being a child. At least that's what they said to us all at graduation from the eighth grade. My sister Phyllis graduated at the same time from high school. I don't know what she was supposed to stop being. But as graduation presents for us both, the whole family took a Fourth of July trip to Washington, D.C., the fabled and famous capital of our country.

It was the first time I'd ever been on a railroad train during the day. When I was lit- 2 tle, and we used to go to the Connecticut shore, we always went at night on the milk train, because it was cheaper.

Preparations were in the air around our house before school was even over. We 3 packed for a week. There were two very large suitcases that my father carried, and a box filled with food. In fact, my first trip to Washington was a mobile feast; I started eating as soon as we were comfortably ensconced in our seats, and did not stop until somewhere after Philadelphia. I remember it was Philadelphia because I was disappointed not to have passed by the Liberty Bell.

My mother had roasted two chickens and cut them up into dainty bite-size pieces. 4 She packed slices of brown bread and butter and green pepper and carrot sticks. There were little violently yellow iced cakes with scalloped edges called "marigolds," that came from Cushman's Bakery. There was a spice bun and rock-cakes from Newton's, the West Indian bakery across Lenox Avenue from St. Mark's School, and iced tea in a wrapped mayonnaise jar. There were sweet pickles for us and dill pickles for my father, and peaches with the fuzz still on them, individually wrapped to keep them from bruising. And, for neatness, there were piles of napkins and a little tin box with a washcloth dampened with rosewater and glycerine for wiping sticky mouths.

I wanted to eat in the dining car because I had read all about them, but my mother 5 reminded me for the umpteenth time that dining car food always cost too much money and besides, you never could tell whose hands had been playing all over that food, nor where those same hands had been just before. My mother never mentioned that Black people were not allowed into railroad dining cars headed south in 1947. As usual, whatever my mother did not like and could not change, she ignored. Perhaps it would go away, deprived of her attention.

I learned later that Phyllis's high school senior class trip had been to Washington, 6 but the nuns had given her back her deposit in private, explaining to her that the class, all of whom were white, except Phyllis, would be staying in a hotel where Phyllis "would not be happy," meaning, Daddy explained to her, also in private, that they did not rent rooms to Negroes. "We will take you to Washington, ourselves," my father had avowed, "and not just for an overnight in some measly fleabag hotel."

7   American racism was a new and crushing reality that my parents had to deal with every day of their lives once they came to this country. They handled it as a private woe. My mother and father believed that they could best protect their children from the realities of race in america and the fact of american racism by never giving them name, much less discussing their nature. We were told we must never trust white people, but *why* was never explained, nor the nature of their ill will. Like so many other vital pieces of information in my childhood, I was supposed to know without being told. It always seemed like a very strange injunction coming from my mother, who looked so much like one of those people we were never supposed to trust. But something always warned me not to ask my mother why she wasn't white, and why Auntie Lillah and Auntie Etta weren't, even though they were all that same problematic color so different from my father and me, even from my sisters, who were somewhere in-between.

8   In Washington, D.C., we had one large room with two double beds and an extra cot for me. It was a back-street hotel that belonged to a friend of my father's who was in real estate, and I spent the whole next day after Mass squinting up at the Lincoln Memorial where Marian Anderson had sung after the D.A.R. refused to allow her to sing in their auditorium because she was Black. Or because she was "Colored," my father said as he told us the story. Except that what he probably said was "Negro," because for his time, my father was quite progressive.

9   I was squinting because I was in that silent agony that characterized all of my childhood summers, from the time school let out in June to the end of July, brought about by my dilated and vulnerable eyes exposed to the summer brightness.

10   I viewed Julys through an agonizing corolla of dazzling whiteness and I always hated the Fourth of July, even before I came to realize the travesty such a celebration was for Black people in this country.

11   My parents did not approve of sunglasses, nor of their expense.

12   I spent the afternoon squinting up at monuments to freedom and past presidencies and democracy, and wondering why the light and heat were both so much stronger in Washington, D.C., than back home in New York City. Even the pavement on the streets was a shade lighter in color than back home.

13   Late that Washington afternoon my family and I walked back down Pennsylvania Avenue. We were a proper caravan, mother bright and father brown, the three of us girls step-standards in-between. Moved by our historical surroundings and the heat of the early evening, my father decreed yet another treat. He had a great sense of history, a flair for the quietly dramatic and the sense of specialness of an occasion and a trip.

14   "Shall we stop and have a little something to cool off, Lin?"

15   Two blocks away from our hotel, the family stopped for a dish of vanilla ice cream at a Breyer's ice cream and soda fountain. Indoors, the soda fountain was dim and fan-cooled, deliciously relieving to my scorched eyes.

16   Corded and crisp and pinafored, the five of us seated ourselves one by one at the counter. There was I between my mother and father, and my two sisters on the other side of my mother. We settled ourselves along the white mottled marble counter, and when the waitress spoke at first no one understood what she was saying, and so the five of us just sat there.

The waitress moved along the line of us closer to my father and spoke again. "I said 17 I kin give you to take out, but you can't eat here. Sorry." Then she dropped her eyes looking very embarrassed, and suddenly we heard what it was she was saying all at the same time, loud and clear.

Straight-backed and indignant, one by one, my family and I got down from the 18 counter stools and turned around and marched out of the store, quiet and outraged, as if we had never been Black before. No one would answer my emphatic questions with anything other than a guilty silence. "But we hadn't done anything!" This wasn't right or fair! Hadn't I written poems about Bataan and freedom and democracy for all?

My parents wouldn't speak of this injustice, not because they had contributed to it, 19 but because they felt they should have anticipated it and avoided it. This made me even angrier. My fury was not going to be acknowledged by a like fury. Even my two sisters copied my parents' pretense that nothing unusual and anti-american had occurred. I was left to write my angry letter to the president of the united states all by myself, although my father did promise I could type it out on the office typewriter next week, after I showed it to him in my copybook diary.

The waitress was white, and the counter was white, and the ice cream I never ate 20 in Washington, D.C., that summer I left childhood was white, and the white heat and the white pavement and the white stone monuments of my first Washington summer made me sick to my stomach for the whole rest of that trip and it wasn't much of a graduation present after all.

Questions for Close Reading

1. What is the selection's thesis (or narrative point)? Locate the sentence(s) in which Lorde states her main idea. If she doesn't state the thesis explicitly, express it in your own words.

2. In paragraph 4, Lorde describes the elaborate picnic her mother prepared for the trip to Washington, D.C. Why did Lorde's mother make such elaborate preparations? What do these preparations tell us about Lorde's mother?

3. Why does Lorde have trouble understanding her parents' dictate that she "never trust white people" (paragraph 7)?

4. In general, how do Lorde's parents handle racism? How does the family as a whole deal with the racism they encounter in the ice cream parlor? How does the family's reaction to the ice cream parlor incident make Lorde feel?

5. Refer to your dictionary as needed to define the following words used in the selection: *fabled* (paragraph 1), *injunction* (7), *progressive* (8), *dilated* (9), *vulnerable* (9), *travesty* (10), *decreed* (13), *pretense* (19).

Questions About the Writer's Craft

1. The pattern. What techniques does Lorde use to help readers follow the unfolding of the story as it occurs in both time and space?

2. When telling a story, skilled writers limit narrative commentary—statements that tell rather than show what happened—because such commentary tends to interrupt the narrative flow. Lorde, however, provides narrative commentary in several spots. Find these instances. How is the information she provides in these places essential to her narrative?

3. In paragraphs 7 and 19, Lorde uses all lowercase letters when referring to America/American and to the President of the United States. Why do you suppose she doesn't follow the rules of capitalization? In what ways does her rejection of these rules reinforce what she is trying to convey through the essay's title?

4. What key word does Lorde repeat in paragraph 20? What effect do you think she hopes the repetition will have on readers?

Writing Assignments Using Narration as a Pattern of Development

∞ **1.** Lorde recounts an incident during which she was treated unfairly. Write a narrative about a time when either you were treated unjustly or you treated someone else in an unfair manner. Like Lorde, use vivid details to make the incident come alive and to convey how it affected you. George Orwell's "Shooting an Elephant" (page 203), Natalie Angier's "A Granddaughter's Fear" (page 388), and Brent Staples's "Black Men and Public Space" (page 398) will prompt some ideas worth exploring.

∞ **2.** Write a narrative about an experience that dramatically changed your view of the world. The experience might have been jarring and painful, or it may have been positive and uplifting. In either case, recount the incident with compelling narrative details. To illustrate the shift in your perspective, begin with a brief statement of the way you viewed the world before the experience. The following essays provide insight into the way a single experience can alter one's understanding of the world: Maya Angelou's "Sister Flowers" (page 175), Diane Cole's "Don't Just Stand There" (page 315), Richard Rhodes's "Watching the Animals" (page 324), and Joseph Suina's "And Then I Went to School" (page 361).

Writing Assignments Using Other Patterns of Development

3. Lorde suggests that her parents use the coping mechanism of denial to deal with life's harsh realities. For example, she writes that whatever her mother "did not like and could not change, she ignored." Refer to a psychology textbook to learn more about denial as a coping mechanism. When is it productive? When is it counterproductive? Drawing upon your own experiences as well as those of friends, family, and classmates, write an essay contrasting effective and ineffective uses of denial. Near the end of the paper, present brief guidelines that will help readers identify when denial may be detrimental.

∞ **4.** In her essay, Lorde decries and by implication takes a strong stance against racial discrimination. Brainstorm with friends, family members, and classmates to identify other injustices in American society. To prompt discussion, you might begin by considering attitudes toward the elderly, the overweight, the physically disabled; the funding of schools in poor and affluent neighborhoods; the portrayal of a specific ethnic group on television; and so on. Focusing on *one* such injustice, write an essay arguing that such an injustice indeed exists. To document the nature and extent of the injustice, use library research as well as your own and other people's experiences. Acknowledge and, when you can, dismantle the views of those who think there isn't a problem. The following essays will alert you to several issues you may want to explore: Susan Douglas's "Managing Mixed Messages" (page 247), Richard Rhodes's "Watching the Animals" (page 324), Brent Staples's "Black Men and Public Space" (page 398), and Nancy Gibbs's "When Is It Rape?" (423).

RUSSELL BAKER

A Pulitzer Prize-winning journalist and wry social commentator, Russell Baker (1925–) is the author of two highly acclaimed autobiographies, *Growing Up* (1982) and *The Good Times* (1989). Baker began his career as a writer for the *Baltimore Sun* and later joined the *New York Times,* for whom he writes a popular column, "The Observer." Baker's columns have been collected in several books, including *So This Is Depravity* (1980) and *There's a Country in My Cellar* (1990). Editor of *The Norton Book of Light Verse* (1986), Baker is also the host of the popular PBS series *Masterpiece Theatre.* The selection reprinted here is taken from *Growing Up.*

SELLING THE POST

I began working in journalism when I was eight years old. It was my mother's idea. 1
She wanted me to "make something" of myself and, after a levelheaded appraisal of my strengths, decided I had better start young if I was to have any chance of keeping up with the competition.

The flaw in my character which she had already spotted was lack of "gumption." My 2
idea of a perfect afternoon was lying in front of the radio rereading my favorite Big Little Book, *Dick Tracy Meets Stooge Viller.* My mother despised inactivity. Seeing me having a good time in repose, she was powerless to hide her disgust. "You've got no more gumption than a bump on a log," she said. "Get out in the kitchen and help Doris do those dirty dishes."

My sister Doris, though two years younger than I, had enough gumption for a dozen 3
people. She positively enjoyed washing dishes, making beds, and cleaning the house. When she was only seven she could carry a piece of short-weighted cheese back to the A&P, threaten the manager with legal action, and come back triumphantly with the full quarter-pound we'd paid for and a few ounces extra thrown in for forgiveness. Doris could have made something of herself if she hadn't been a girl. Because of this defect,

however, the best she could hope for was a career as a nurse or schoolteacher, the only work that capable females were considered up to in those days.

4   This must have saddened my mother, this twist of fate that had allocated all the gumption to the daughter and left her with a son who was content with Dick Tracy and Stooge Viller. If disappointed, though, she wasted no energy on self-pity. She would make me make something of myself whether I wanted to or not. "The Lord helps those who help themselves," she said. That was the way her mind worked.

5   She was realistic about the difficulty. Having sized up the material the Lord had given her to mold, she didn't overestimate what she could do with it. She didn't insist that I grow up to be President of the United States.

6   Fifty years ago parents still asked boys if they wanted to grow up to be President, and asked it not jokingly but seriously. Many parents who were hardly more than paupers still believed their sons could do it. Abraham Lincoln had done it. We were only sixty-five years from Lincoln. Many a grandfather who walked among us could remember Lincoln's time. Men of grandfatherly age were the worst for asking if you wanted to grow up to be President. A surprising number of little boys said yes and meant it.

7   I was asked many times myself. No, I would say, I didn't want to grow up to be President. My mother was present during one of these interrogations. An elderly uncle, having posed the usual question and exposed my lack of interest in the Presidency, asked, "Well, what *do* you want to be when you grow up?"

8   I loved to pick through trash piles and collect empty bottles, tin cans with pretty labels, and discarded magazines. The most desirable job on earth sprang instantly to mind. "I want to be a garbage man," I said.

9   My uncle smiled, but my mother had seen the first distressing evidence of a bump budding on a log. "Have a little gumption, Russell," she said. Her calling me Russell was a signal of unhappiness. When she approved of me I was always "Buddy."

10   When I turned eight years old she decided that the job of starting me on the road toward making something of myself could no longer be safely delayed. "Buddy," she said one day, "I want you to come home right after school this afternoon. Somebody's coming and I want you to meet him."

11   When I burst in that afternoon she was in conference in the parlor with an executive of the Curtis Publishing Company. She introduced me. He bent low from the waist and shook my hand. Was it true as my mother had told him, he asked, that I longed for the opportunity to conquer the world of business?

12   My mother replied that I was blessed with a rare determination to make something of myself.

13   "That's right," I whispered.

14   "But have you got the grit, the character, the never-say-quit spirit it takes to succeed in business?"

15   My mother said I certainly did.

16   "That's right," I said.

17   He eyed me silently for a long pause, as though weighing whether I could be trusted to keep his confidence, then spoke man-to-man. Before taking a crucial step, he said, he wanted to advise me that working for the Curtis Publishing Company placed enormous responsibility on a young man. It was one of the great companies of America. Perhaps the greatest publishing house in the world. I had heard, no doubt, of the *Saturday Evening Post*?

Heard of it? My mother said that everyone in our house had heard of the *Saturday* 18
Evening Post and that I, in fact, read it with religious devotion.

Then doubtless, he said, we were also familiar with those two monthly pillars of the 19
magazine world, the *Ladies Home Journal* and the *Country Gentleman*.

Indeed we were familiar with them, said my mother.   20

Representing the *Saturday Evening Post* was one of the weightiest honors that could 21
be bestowed in the world of business, he said. He was personally proud of being a part
of that great corporation.

My mother said he had every right to be.   22

Again he studied me as though debating whether I was worthy of a knighthood. 23
Finally: "Are you trustworthy?"

My mother said I was the soul of honesty.   24

"That's right," I said.   25

The caller smiled for the first time. He told me I was a lucky young man. He admired 26
my spunk. Too many young men thought life was all play. Those young men would not
go far in this world. Only a young man willing to work and save and keep his face
washed and his hair neatly combed could hope to come out on top in a world such as
ours. Did I truly and sincerely believe that I was such a young man?

"He certainly does," said my mother.   27

"That's right," I said.   28

He said he had been so impressed by what he had seen of me that he was going to 29
make me a representative of the Curtis Publishing Company. On the following Tuesday,
he said, thirty freshly printed copies of the *Saturday Evening Post* would be delivered
at our door. I would place these magazines, still damp with the ink of the presses, in a
handsome canvas bag, sling it over my shoulder, and set forth through the streets to
bring the best in journalism, fiction, and cartoons to the American public.

He had brought the canvas bag with him. He presented it with reverence fit for a 30
chasuble. He showed me how to drape the sling over my left shoulder and across the
chest so that the pouch lay easily accessible to my right hand, allowing the best in journalism, fiction, and cartoons to be swiftly extracted and sold to a citizenry whose happiness and security depended upon us soldiers of the free press.

The following Tuesday I raced home from school, put the canvas bag over my shoul- 31
der, dumped the magazines in, and, tilting to the left to balance their weight on my
right hip, embarked on the highway of journalism.

We lived in Belleville, New Jersey, a commuter town at the northern fringe of New- 32
ark. It was 1932, the bleakest year of the Depression. My father had died two years
before, leaving us with a few pieces of Sears, Roebuck furniture and not much else, and
my mother had taken Doris and me to live with one of her younger brothers. This was
my Uncle Allen. Uncle Allen had made something of himself by 1932. As salesman for
a soft-drink bottler in Newark, he had an income of $30 a week; wore pearl-gray spats,
detachable collars, and a three-piece suit; was happily married; and took in threadbare
relatives.

With my load of magazines I headed toward Belleville Avenue. That's where the 33
people were. There were two filling stations at the intersection with Union Avenue, as
well as an A&P, a fruit stand, a bakery, a barber shop, Zuccarelli's drugstore, and a diner
shaped like a railroad car. For several hours I made myself highly visible, shifting position now and then from corner to corner, from shop window to shop window, to make
sure everyone could see the heavy black lettering on the canvas bag that said the

Saturday Evening Post. When the angle of the light indicated it was suppertime, I walked back to the house.

34   "How many did you sell, Buddy?" my mother asked.

35   "None."

36   "Where did you go?"

37   "The corner of Belleville and Union Avenues."

38   "What did you do?"

39   "Stood on the corner waiting for somebody to buy a *Saturday Evening Post.*"

40   "You just stood there?"

41   "Didn't sell a single one."

42   "For God's sake, Russell!"

43   Uncle Allen intervened. "I've been thinking about it for some time," he said, "and I've about decided to take the *Post* regularly. Put me down as a regular customer." I handed him a magazine and he paid me a nickel. It was the first nickel I earned.

44   Afterwards my mother instructed me in salesmanship. I would have to ring door-bells, address adults with charming self-confidence, and break down resistance with a sales talk pointing out that no one, no matter how poor, could afford to be without the *Saturday Evening Post* in the home.

45   I told my mother I'd changed my mind about wanting to succeed in the magazine business.

46   "If you think I'm going to raise a good-for-nothing," she replied, "you've got another think coming." She told me to hit the streets with the canvas bag and start ringing doorbells the instant school was out next day. When I objected that I didn't feel any aptitude for salesmanship, she asked how I'd like to lend her my leather belt so she could whack some sense into me. I bowed to superior will and entered journalism with a heavy heart.

47   My mother and I had fought this battle almost as long as I could remember. It prob-ably started even before memory began, when I was a country child in northern Vir-ginia and my mother, dissatisfied with my father's plain workman's life, determined that I would not grow up like him and his people, with calluses on their hands, overalls on their backs, and fourth-grade educations in their heads. She had fancier ideas of life's possibilities. Introducing me to the *Saturday Evening Post,* she was trying to wean me as early as possible from my father's world where men left with their lunch pails at sunup, worked with their hands until the grime ate into the pores, and died with a few sticks of mail-order furniture as their legacy. In my mother's vision of the better life there were desks and white collars, well-pressed suits, evenings of reading and lively talk, and perhaps—if a man were very, very lucky and hit the jackpot, really made something important of himself—perhaps there might be a fantastic salary of $5,000 a year to support a big house and a Buick with a rumble seat and a vacation in Atlantic City.

48   And so I set forth with my sack of magazines. I was afraid of the dogs that snarled behind the doors of potential buyers. I was timid about ringing the doorbells of strang-ers, relieved when no one came to the door, and scared when someone did. Despite my mother's instructions, I could not deliver an engaging sales pitch. When a door opened I simply asked, "Want to buy a *Saturday Evening Post*?" In Belleville few per-sons did. It was a town of 30,000 people, and most weeks I rang a fair majority of its doorbells. But I rarely sold my thirty copies. Some weeks I canvassed the entire town for six days and still had four or five unsold magazines on Monday evening; then I

dreaded the coming of Tuesday morning, when a batch of thirty fresh *Saturday Evening Posts* was due at the front door.

"Better get out there and sell the rest of those magazines tonight," my mother 49 would say.

I usually posted myself then at a busy intersection where a traffic light controlled 50 commuter flow from Newark. When the light turned red I stood on the curb and shouted my sales pitch at the motorists.

"Want to buy a *Saturday Evening Post*?"   51

One rainy night when car windows were sealed against me I came back soaked and 52 with not a single sale to report. My mother beckoned to Doris.

"Go back down there with Buddy and show him how to sell these magazines," she 53 said.

Brimming with zest, Doris, who was then seven years old, returned with me to the 54 corner. She took a magazine from the bag, and when the light turned red she strode to the nearest car and banged her small fist against the closed window. The driver, probably startled at what he took to be a midget assaulting his car, lowered the window to stare, and Doris thrust a *Saturday Evening Post* at him.

"You need this magazine," she piped, "and it only costs a nickel."   55

Her salesmanship was irresistible. Before the light changed half a dozen times she 56 disposed of the entire batch. I didn't feel humiliated. To the contrary. I was so happy I decided to give her a treat. Leading her to the vegetable store on Belleville Avenue, I bought three apples, which cost a nickel, and gave her one.

"You shouldn't waste money," she said.   57

"Eat your apple." I bit into mine.   58

"You shouldn't eat before supper," she said. "It'll spoil your appetite."   59

Back at the house that evening, she dutifully reported me for wasting a nickel. 60 Instead of a scolding, I was rewarded with a pat on the back for having the good sense to buy fruit instead of candy. My mother reached into her bottomless supply of maxims and told Doris, "An apple a day keeps the doctor away."

By the time I was ten I had learned all my mother's maxims by heart. Asking to stay 61 up past normal bedtime, I knew that a refusal would be explained with "Early to bed and early to rise, makes a man healthy, wealthy, and wise." If I whimpered about having to get up early in the morning, I could depend on her to say, "The early bird gets the worm."

The one I most despised was, "If at first you don't succeed, try, try again." This was 62 the battle cry with which she constantly sent me back into the hopeless struggle whenever I moaned that I had rung every doorbell in town and knew there wasn't a single potential buyer left in Belleville that week. After listening to my explanation, she handed me the canvas bag and said, "If at first you don't succeed..."

Three years in that job, which I would gladly have quit after the first day except for 63 her insistence, produced at least one valuable result. My mother finally concluded that I would never make something of myself by pursuing a life in business and started considering careers that demanded less competitive zeal.

One evening when I was eleven I brought home a short "composition" on my summer 64 vacation which the teacher had graded with an A. Reading it with her own schoolteacher's eye, my mother agreed that it was top-drawer seventh grade prose and complimented me. Nothing more was said about it immediately, but a new idea had taken life in her mind. Halfway through supper she suddenly interrupted the conversation.

65   "Buddy," she said, "maybe you could be a writer."

66   I clasped the idea to my heart. I had never met a writer, had shown no previous urge to write, and hadn't a notion how to become a writer, but I loved stories and thought that making up stories must surely be almost as much fun as reading them. Best of all, though, and what really gladdened my heart, was the ease of the writer's life. Writers did not have to trudge through the town peddling from canvas bags, defending themselves against angry dogs, being rejected by surly strangers. Writers did not have to ring doorbells. So far as I could make out, what writers did couldn't even be classified as work.

67   I was enchanted. Writers didn't have to have any gumption at all. I did not dare tell anybody for fear of being laughed at in the schoolyard, but secretly I decided that what I'd like to be when I grew up was a writer.

Questions for Close Reading

1. What is the selection's thesis (or narrative point)? Locate the sentence(s) in which Baker states his main idea. If he doesn't state the thesis explicitly, express it in your own words.

2. What was Baker like as an eight-year-old? How was he different from his sister Doris?

3. Why is Baker's mother so intent on developing her son's ability to succeed in the working world?

4. How did Mrs. Baker influence Baker's decision to become a writer?

5. Refer to your dictionary as needed to define the following words used in the selection: *gumption* (paragraph 2), *repose* (2), *interrogations* (7), *grit* (14), *spunk* (26), *chasuble* (30), *extracted* (30), *intervened* (43), *aptitude* (46), *wean* (47), *canvassed* (48), *zeal* (63), and *prose* (64).

Questions About the Writer's Craft

1. The pattern. Why might Baker have chosen to include so much dialog in his narrative? What purpose does the dialog serve?

2. Other patterns. Baker's narrative hinges on the contrast between his temperament and his mother's. What other set of contrasting personalities does Baker present in his narrative? What does this secondary set of contrasts add to the essay?

3. Baker's narrative spans three years. Identify some of the techniques Baker uses to help readers follow the progression of events during this time.

4. Even though Baker doesn't use much sensory language, he clearly conveys to readers the setting of his tale. What details does he use to establish the story's time and place? What do these details add to the narrative?

Writing Assignments Using Narration as a Pattern of Development

∞ 1. With humor and gentle self-mockery, Baker recounts his youthful lack of gumption. Write an essay in which you use narration to poke gentle fun at some character trait of your own—for example, your tendency to procrastinate, to be a compulsive collector, to indulge a passion for practical jokes. Like Baker, use dialog and humor to enliven the narrative and to illustrate the trait in question. To see how skilled writers use humor to make their points, read—if you haven't already done so—two student essays, Gail Oremland's "The Truth About College Teachers" (page 269) and Robert Barry's "Becoming a Videoholic" (page 306).

2. In a delightfully roundabout way, Baker tells us how he chose his career. In a narrative essay of your own, recount one or two events that helped you realize what you want to do as your life's work. If you haven't yet decided, focus on one or two events that suggest to you a strong possibility for a career choice. Include only those narrative details that help explain the reasons for your decision.

Writing Assignments Using Other Patterns of Development

3. Baker points out that opportunities for girls, when he was growing up, were sorely limited. Speak with members of earlier generations to find out what opportunities or expectations there were for girls and women in their day. Be sure to cover a broad range of areas—for example, employment choices, home life, academic pursuits, participation in sports, career advancement. Then decide whether you think women's and girls' possibilities have improved over time. Focusing on two or three areas of life, write an essay in which you support your conclusion by comparing and contrasting females' possibilities today with those in the past.

4. Baker started working when he was only eight. Many psychologists and educators argue that such employment can have serious disadvantages for young people—even for high school students. Working, these experts argue, limits the time students can spend on academics, encourages them to think like employees rather than like kids, and fosters an excessive attachment to money. Write an essay arguing that teenagers should *or* should not hold jobs during the academic year. At some point, acknowledge or even refute opposing views. To gain a wider perspective on the issue, interview teenagers and older adults with varying viewpoints before you begin writing.

ADDITIONAL WRITING TOPICS: NARRATION

General Assignments

Write an essay using description to develop one of the following topics.

1. An emergency that brought out the best or worst in you

2. The hazards of taking children out to eat

3. An incident that made you believe in fate

4. Your best or worst day at school or work

5. A major decision

6. An encounter with a machine

7. An important learning experience

8. A narrow escape

9. Your first date, first day on the job, or first anything

10. A memorable childhood experience

11. A fairy tale the way you would like to hear it told

12. A painful moment

13. An incredible but true story

14. A significant family event

15. An experience in which a certain emotion (pride, anger, regret, or some other) was dominant

Assignments with a Specific Purpose, Audience, and Point of View

1. As fund-raiser for a particular organization (for example, Red Cross, SPCA, Big Brothers/Big Sisters), you're sending a newsletter to contributors. Support your

cause by telling the story of a time when your organization made all the differ-ence—the blood donation that saved a life, the animal that was rescued from abuse, and so on.

2. A friend of yours has seen someone cheat on a test, shoplift, or violate an employer's trust. In a letter, convince this friend to inform the instructor, store owner, or employer, by narrating an incident in which a witness did (or did not) speak up in such a situation. Tell what happened as a result.

3. You have had a disturbing encounter with one of the people who seems to have "fallen through the cracks" of society—a street person, an unwanted child, or any-one else who is alone and abandoned. Write a letter to the local newspaper describing this encounter. Your purpose is to arouse people's indignation and compassion and to get help for such unfortunates.

4. Write an article for your old high school newspaper. The article will be read pri-marily by seniors who are planning to go away to college next year. In the article, narrate a story that points to some truth about the "breaking away" stage of life.

5. A close friend has written a letter to you telling about a bad experience that he or she had with a teacher, employer, doctor, repairperson, or some other profes-sional. On the basis of that single experience, your friend now negatively stereo-types the entire profession. Write a letter to your friend balancing his or her cynical picture by narrating a story that shows the "flip side" of this profession—someone who made every effort to help.

6. Your younger brother, sister, relative, or neighborhood friend can't wait to be your age. By narrating an appropriate story, show the young person that your age isn't as wonderful as he or she thinks. Be sure to select a story that the person can understand and appreciate.

13
ILLUSTRATION

WHAT IS ILLUSTRATION?

IF someone asked you, "Have you been to any good restaurants lately?" you probably wouldn't answer "Yes" and then immediately change the subject. Most likely, you would go on to **illustrate** with examples. Perhaps you'd give the names of restaurants you've enjoyed and talk briefly about the specific things you liked: the attractive prices, the tasty main courses, the pleasant service, the tempting desserts. Such examples and details are needed to convince others that your opinion—in this or any matter—is valid. Similarly, when you talk about larger and more important issues, people won't pay much attention to your opinion if all you do is string together vague generalizations: "We have to do something about acid rain. It's had disastrous consequences for the environment. Its negative effects increase every year. Action must be taken to control the problem." To be taken seriously and convince others that your point is well-founded, you must provide specific supporting examples: "The forests in the Adirondacks are dying"; "yesterday's rainfall was fifty times more acidic than normal"; "Pine Lake, in the northern part of the state, was once a great fishing spot but now has no fish population."

Examples are equally important when you write an essay. It's not vague generalities and highfaluting abstractions that make writing impressive. Just the opposite is true. Facts, details, anecdotes, statistics, expert opinion, and personal observations are at the heart of effective writing, giving your work substance and solidity.

HOW ILLUSTRATION FITS YOUR PURPOSE AND AUDIENCE

The wording of assignments and essay exam questions may signal the need for illustration:

> Soap operas, whether shown during the day or in the evening, are among the most popular television programs. Why do you think this is so? Provide specific examples to support your position.

> Some observers claim that college students are less interested in learning than in getting ahead in their careers. Cite evidence to support or refute this claim.

> A growing number of people feel that parents should not allow young children to participate in highly competitive team sports. Basing your conclusion on your own experiences and observations, indicate whether you think this point of view is reasonable.

Such phrases as "Provide specific examples," "Cite evidence," and "Basing your conclusion on your own experiences and observations" signal that each essay would be developed through illustration.

Usually, though, you won't be told so explicitly to provide examples. Instead, as you think about the best way to achieve your essay's purpose, you'll see the need for illustrative details—no matter which patterns of development you use. For instance, to *persuade* skeptical readers that the country needs a national health system, you might mention specific cases to dramatize the inadequacy of our current health-care system: a family bankrupted by medical bills; an uninsured accident victim turned away by a hospital; a chronically ill person rapidly deteriorating because he didn't have enough money to visit a doctor. Or imagine a lightly satiric piece that pokes fun at cat lovers. Insisting that "cat people" are pretty strange creatures, you might make your point—and make readers chuckle—with a series of examples *contrasting* cat lovers and dog lovers: the qualities admired by each group (loyalty in dogs versus independence in cats) and the different expectations each group has for its pets (dog lovers want Fido to be obedient and lovable, whereas cat lovers are satisfied with Felix's occasional spurts of docility and affection). Similarly, you would supply examples in a *causal analysis* speculating on the likely impact of a proposed tuition hike at your college. To convince the college administration of the probable negative effects of such a hike, you might cite the following examples: articles reporting a nationwide upswing in student transfers to less expensive schools; statistics indicating a significant drop in grades among already employed students forced to work more hours to pay increased tuition costs; interviews with students too financially strapped to continue their college education.

Whether you use illustration as a primary or supplemental method of development, it serves a number of important purposes. For one thing, illustrations make writing *interesting*. Assume you're writing an essay showing that television commercials are biased against women. Your essay would be lifeless and boring if all it did was repeat, in a general way, that commercials present stereotyped views of women:

Illustration 225

Original

    `An anti-female bias is rampant in television commercials. It is`
`very much alive, yet most viewers seem to take it all in stride. Few`
`people protest the obviously sexist characters and statements on`
`such commercials. Surely, these commercials misrepresent the way`
`most of us live.`

Without interesting particulars, readers may respond, "Who cares?" But if you provide specific examples, you'll attract your readers' attention:

Revised

    `An anti-female bias is rampant in television commercials.`
`Although millions of women hold responsible jobs outside the`
`home, commercials continue to portray women as simple creatures`
`who spend much of their time thinking about wax buildup, cottony-`
`soft bathroom tissue, and static-free clothes. Men, apparently,`
`have better things to do than fret over such mundane household`
`matters. How many commercials can you recall that depict men pro-`
`claiming the virtues of squeaky-clean dishes or sparkling bath-`
`rooms? Not many.`

    Illustrations also make writing *persuasive.* Most writing conveys a point, but many readers are reluctant to accept someone else's point of view unless evidence demonstrates its validity. Imagine you're writing an essay showing that latchkey children are more self-sufficient and emotionally secure than children who return from school to a home where a parent awaits them. Your thesis is obviously controversial. Without specific examples—from your own experience, personal observations, or research studies—your readers would undoubtedly question your position's validity.

    Further, illustrations help *explain* difficult, abstract, or unusual ideas. Suppose you're assigned an essay on a complex subject such as inflation, zero population growth, or radiation exposure. As a writer, you have a responsibility to your readers to make these difficult concepts concrete and understandable. If writing an essay on radiation exposure in everyday life, you might start by providing specific examples of home appliances that emit radiation—color televisions, computers, and microwave ovens—and tell exactly how much radiation we absorb in a typical day from such equipment. To illustrate further the extent of our radiation exposure, you could also provide specifics about unavoidable sources of natural radiation (the sun, for instance) and details about the widespread use of radiation in medicine (X-rays, radiation therapy). These examples would ground your discussion, making it immediate and concrete, preventing it from flying off into the vague and theoretical.

Finally, examples help *prevent unintended ambiguity.* All of us have experienced the frustration of having someone misinterpret what we say. In face-to-face communication, we can provide on-the-spot clarification. In writing, however, instantaneous feedback isn't available, so it's crucial that meaning be as unambiguous as possible. Illustrations will help. Assume you're writing an essay asserting that ineffective teaching is on the rise in today's high schools. To clarify what you mean by "ineffective," you provide illustrations: the instructor who spends so much time disciplining unruly students that he never gets around to teaching; the moonlighting teacher who is so tired in class that she regularly takes naps during tests; the teacher who accepts obviously plagiarized reports because he's grateful that students hand in something. Without such concrete examples, your readers will supply their own ideas—and these may not be what you had in mind. Readers might imagine "ineffective" to mean harsh and punitive, whereas concrete examples would show that you intend it to mean out of control and irresponsible.

PREWRITING STRATEGIES

The following checklist shows how you can apply to illustration some of the prewriting techniques discussed in Chapter 2.

☑ ILLUSTRATION: A PREWRITING CHECKLIST

Choose a Subject to Illustrate

☐ What general situation or phenomenon (for example, campus apathy, organic farming) can you depict through illustration?

☐ What difficult or misunderstood concept (nuclear winter, passive aggression) would examples help to explain and make concrete?

Determine Your Purpose, Audience, Tone, and Point of View

☐ What is your purpose in writing?

☐ What audience do you have in mind?

☐ What tone and point of view will best serve your purpose and lead readers to adopt the desired attitude toward the subject being illustrated?

Use Prewriting to Generate Examples

☐ How can brainstorming, freewriting, journal entries, or mapping help you generate relevant examples (events, facts, anecdotes, quotations) from your own or others' experiences?

☐ How could library research help you gather pertinent examples (expert opinion, case studies, statistics)?

Illustration   227

STRATEGIES FOR USING ILLUSTRATION IN AN ESSAY

After prewriting, you're ready to draft your essay. The following suggestions will be helpful whether you use illustration as a dominant or supportive pattern of development.

1. Select the examples to include.   Examples can take several forms, including specific names (of people, places, products, and so on), anecdotes, personal observations, expert opinion, as well as facts, statistics, and case studies gathered through research. Once you've used prewriting to generate as many examples as possible, you're ready to limit your examples to the strongest. Keeping your thesis, audience, tone, and point of view in mind, ask yourself several key questions: "Which examples support my thesis? Which do not? Which are most convincing? Which are most likely to interest readers and clarify meaning?"

You may include several brief examples within a single sentence:

> The French people's fascination with some American literary figures, such as Poe and Hawthorne, is understandable, but their great respect for "artists" like comedian Jerry Lewis is a mystery.

Or you may develop a paragraph with a number of "for instances":

> A uniquely American style of movie-acting reached its peak in the 1950s. Certain charismatic actors completely abandoned the stage techniques and tradition that had been the foundation of acting up to that time. Instead of articulating their lines clearly, the actors mumbled; instead of making firm eye contact with their colleagues, they hung their heads, shifted their eyes, even talked with their eyes closed. Marlon Brando, Montgomery Clift, and then James Dean were three actors who exemplified this new trend.

As the preceding paragraph shows, *several examples* are usually needed to achieve your purpose. An essay with the thesis "Rock videos are dangerously violent" wouldn't be convincing if you gave only one example of a violent rock video. Several strong examples would be needed for readers to feel you had illustrated your point sufficiently.

As a general rule, you should strive for variety in the kinds of examples you include. For instance, you might choose a *personal-experience example* drawn from your own life or from the life of someone you know. Such examples pack the wallop of personal authority and lend drama to writing. Or you might include a *typical-case example,* an actual event or situation that did occur—but not to you or to anyone you know. (Perhaps you learned about the event through a magazine article, newspaper account, or television report.) The objective nature of such cases makes them especially convincing. You might also include a speculative or *hypothetical example* ("Imagine how difficult it must be for an elderly person to carry bags of groceries from the market to a bus stop several blocks away"). You'll find that hypothetical cases are effective for clarifying and dramatizing key points, but be sure to acknowledge that the example is indeed invented (*"Suppose* that..." or "Let's for a moment *assume* that..."). Make certain, too, that the invented situation is easily imagined and could conceivably happen. Finally, you might create a *generalized example*—one that is a composite of the typical or usual. Such generalized examples are often signaled by words that involve the reader (*"All of us,* at one time or another, have been driven to distraction by a trivial annoyance like the buzzing of a fly or the sting of a papercut"), or they may refer to humanity in general ("When *most people* get a compliment, they perk up, preen, and think the praise-giver is blessed with astute powers of observation").

Occasionally, *one extended example,* fully developed with many details, can support an essay. It might be possible, for instance, to support the thesis "Federal legislation should raise the legal drinking age to twenty-one" with a single compelling, highly detailed example of the effects of one teenager's drunken-driving spree.

The examples you choose must also be *relevant;* that is, they must have direct bearing on the point you want to make. You would have a hard time convincing readers that Americans have callous attitudes toward the elderly if you described the wide range of new programs, all staffed by volunteers, at a well-financed center for senior citizens. Because these examples *contradict,* rather than support, your thesis, readers are apt to dismiss what you have to say.

In addition, try to select *dramatic* examples. Say you're writing an essay to show that society needs to take more steps to protect children from abuse. Simply stating that many parents hit their children isn't likely to form a strong impression in the reader's mind. However, graphic examples (children with stab wounds, welts, and burn marks) are apt to create a sense of urgency in the reader.

Make certain, too, that your examples are *accurate.* Exercise special caution when using statistics. An old saying warns that there are lies, damned lies, and statistics—meaning that statistics can be misleading. A commercial may claim, "In a taste test, eighty percent of those questioned indicated that they preferred Fizzy Cola." Impressed? Don't be—at least, not until you find out how the test was conducted. Perhaps the participants had to choose between Fizzy Cola and battery acid, or perhaps there were only five participants, all Fizzy Cola vice presidents.

Finally, select *representative* examples. Picking the oddball, one-in-a-million example to support a point—and passing it off as typical—is dishonest. Consider an essay with the thesis "Part-time jobs contribute to academic success." Citing only one example of a student who works at a job twenty-five hours a week while earning straight *A's* isn't playing fair. Why not? You've made a *hasty generalization* based on only one case. To be convincing, you need to show how holding down a job affects *most* students' academic performance. (For more on hasty generalizations, see pages 448–450.)

2. Develop your examples sufficiently. To ensure that you get your ideas across, your examples must be *specific.* An essay on the types of heroes in American movies wouldn't succeed if you simply strung together a series of undeveloped examples in paragraphs like this one:

Illustration   229

Original

    Heroes in American movies usually fall into types. One kind of hero is the tight-lipped loner, men like Clint Eastwood and Humphrey Bogart. Another movie hero is the quiet, shy, or fumbling type who has appeared in movies since the beginning. The main characteristic of this hero is lovableness, as seen in actors like Jimmy Stewart. Perhaps the most one-dimensional and predictable hero is the super-man who battles tough odds. This kind of hero is best illustrated by Sylvester Stallone as Rocky and Rambo.

If you developed the essay in this way—moving from one undeveloped example to another—you would be doing little more than making a list. To be effective, key examples must be expanded in sufficient detail. The examples in the preceding paragraph could be developed in paragraphs of their own. You could, for instance, develop the first example this way:

Revised

    Heroes can be tight-lipped loners who appear out of nowhere, form no permanent attachments, and walk, drive, or ride off into the sunset. In most of his Westerns, from the low-budget "spaghetti Westerns" of the 1960s to Unforgiven in 1992, Clint Eastwood person-ifies this kind of hero. He is remote, mysterious, and untalkative. Yet he guns down an evil sheriff, runs other villains out of town, and helps a handicapped girl--acts that cement his heroic status. The loner might also be Sam Spade as played by Humphrey Bogart. Spade solves the crime and sends the guilty off to jail, yet he holds his emotions in check and has no permanent ties beyond his faithful secretary and shabby office. One gets the feeling that he could walk away from these, too, if necessary. Even in The Right Stuff, an account of America's early astronauts, the scriptwriters mold Chuck Yeager, the man who broke the sound barrier, into a clas-sic loner. Yeager, portrayed by the aloof Sam Shepherd, has a wife, but he is nevertheless insular. Taking mute pride in his ability to distance himself from politicians, bureaucrats, even colleagues, he soars into space, dignified and detached.

(For hints on making evidence specific, see pages 69–72 in Chapter 6.)

3. Organize the examples. If, as is usually the case, several examples support your point, be sure to present the examples in an *organized* manner. Often you'll find that other *patterns of development* (cause-effect, comparison-contrast, definition, and so on) suggest ways to sequence examples. Let's say you're writing an essay showing that stay-at-home vacations offer numerous opportunities to relax. You might begin the essay with examples that *contrast* stay-at-home and get-away vacations. Then you might move to a *process analysis* that illustrates different techniques for unwinding at home. The essay might end with examples showing the *effect* of such leisurely at-home breaks.

Finally, you need to select an *organizational approach consistent* with your *purpose* and *thesis.* Imagine you're writing an essay about students' adjustment during the first months of college. The supporting examples could be arranged *chronologically.* You might start by illustrating the ambivalence many students feel the first day of college when their parents leave for home; you might then offer an anecdote or two about students' frequent calls to Mom and Dad during the opening weeks of the semester; the essay might close with an account of students' reluctance to leave campus at the midyear break.

Similarly, an essay demonstrating that a room often reflects the character of its occupant might be organized *spatially:* from the empty soda cans on the floor to the spitballs on the ceiling. In an essay illustrating the kinds of skills taught in a composition course, you might move from *simple* to *complex* examples: starting with relatively matter-of-fact skills like spelling and punctuation and ending with more conceptually difficult skills like formulating a thesis and organizing an essay. Last, the *emphatic sequence*—in which you lead from your first example to your final, most significant one—is another effective way to organize an essay with many examples. A paper about Americans' characteristic impatience might progress from minor examples (dependence on fast food, obsession with ever-faster mail delivery) to more disturbing manifestations of impatience (using drugs as quick solutions to problems, advocating simple answers to complex international problems: "Bomb them!").

4. Choose a point of view. Many essays developed by illustration place the subject in the foreground and the writer in the background. Such an approach calls for the *third-person point of view.* For example, even if you draw examples from your own personal experience, you can present them without using the *first-person* "I." You might convert such personal material into generalized examples (see page 228), or you might describe the personal experience as if it happened to someone else. Of course, you may use the first person if the use of "I" will make the example more believable and dramatic. But remember: Just because an event happened to you personally doesn't mean you have to use the first-person point of view.

REVISION STRATEGIES

Once you have a draft of the essay, you're ready to revise. The following checklist will help you and those giving you feedback apply to illustration some of the revision techniques discussed in Chapters 7 and 8.

Illustration   231

✔ ILLUSTRATION: A REVISION CHECKLIST

Revise Overall Meaning and Structure

☐ What thesis is being advanced? Which examples don't support the thesis? Should these examples be deleted, or should the thesis be reshaped to fit the examples? Why?

☐ Which patterns of development and methods of organization (chronological, spatial, simple-to-complex, emphatic) provide the essay's framework? Would other ordering principles be more effective? If so, which ones?

Revise Paragraph Development

☐ Which paragraphs contain too many or too few examples? Which contain examples that are too brief or too extended? Which include insufficiently or overly detailed examples?

☐ Which paragraphs rely on predictable examples? How could the examples be made more compelling?

☐ Which paragraphs include examples that are atypical or inaccurate?

Revise Sentences and Words

☐ What signal devices (*for example, for instance, in particular, such as*) introduce examples and clarify the line of thought? Where are there too many or too few of these devices?

☐ Where would more varied sentence structure heighten the effect of the essay's illustrations?

☐ Where would more concrete and specific words make the examples more effective?

STUDENT ESSAY: FROM PREWRITING THROUGH REVISION

The student essay that follows was written by Michael Pagano in response to this assignment:

Anne Morrow Lindbergh states in "Channelled Whelk" that Americans impose unnecessary complications on their lives. Observe closely the way you and others conduct your daily lives. Use your observations to generate evidence for an essay that supports or refutes Lindbergh's point of view.

After deciding to write an essay on the way possessions complicate life, Michael sat down at his word processor and did some *freewriting* to generate material on the topic. His original freewriting follows; the handwritten comments indicate Michael's later efforts to develop and shape this material. Note that Michael deleted some points, added others, and made several items more specific; he also labeled and sequenced key ideas. These annotations paved the way for a sentence outline, which is presented after the freewriting.

Freewriting

①Buying

④Discarding items

⑤Running into debt

②Running out of room

③Having maintenance problems

> I shop too much. So do my parents--practically every week-end and ~~nearly every holiday except Christmas and Easter. All those Washington's Birthday sales~~. Then they yell at us kids for watching so much TV, although they're not around to do much with us. In fact, Mom and Dad were the ones who thought our old *19-inch* TV wasn't good enough anymore so they replaced it with a *35-inch* huge color set. I remember all those annoying phone calls when they put the ad in the paper to sell *classified section* the old set. People coming and going. Then Mom and Dad only got $25 for it anyway. It wasn't worth paying for ~~the ad. They never seem to come~~ out ahead. No wonder Mom works part-time at the library and Dad stays so late *2nd job* at the office *overtime*. I'm getting into the same situation. Already up to my ears in debt, paying off the car. I spend hours washing *time payments* it and waxing it, and it doesn't even fit into the garage, which *③ vacuuming car—maintenance* is loaded with discarded junk. The whole house is cluttered. Maybe that's why people move so much--to escape the clutter. There was hardly room for my new word processor in my room. I also have to shove my new clothes into the closets and drawers. My snazzy new jeans get all wrinkled. They shrank when I washed them. Now they're too tight. I should have sent them to the dry cleaners. But I'd already paid enough for them. ~~Well, everything's shoddy nowadays~~. *My computer's giving me trouble.* Possessions don't hold up. So what lasts? Basic values--love, family, friends. *conclusion?*

Outline

Thesis: We clutter our lives with material goods.
  I. We waste a lot of time deciding what to buy.
    A. We window-shop for good-looking footwear.
    B. We look through magazines for stereos and exercise equipment.
    C. Family life suffers when everyone is out shopping.
 II. Once we take our new purchases home, we find we don't have enough room for them.

Illustration   233

       A. We stack things in crowded closets, garages, and basements.

       B. When things get too cluttered, we simply move.

   III. Our possessions require continual maintenance.

       A. Cars have to be washed and waxed.

       B. New jeans have to go to the cleaners.

       C. Word processors and other items break down and have to be replaced.

   IV. Before we replace broken items, we try to get rid of them by placing ads in the classified section.

       A. We have to deal with annoying phone calls.

       B. We have to deal with people coming to the house to see the items.

   V. Our mania for possessions puts us in debt.

       A. We accumulate enormous credit-card balances.

       B. We take second jobs or work overtime to make time payments.

Now read Michael's paper, "Pursuit of Possessions," noting the similarities and differences among his freewriting, outline, and final essay. You'll see, for example, that Michael changed the "I" of his freewriting to the more general "We" in the outline and essay. He made this change because he wanted readers to see themselves in the situations being illustrated. In addition, Michael's outline, while more detailed than his freewriting, doesn't include highly concrete examples, but the essay does. In the outline, for instance, he simply states, "Word processors and other items break down...." In the essay, though, he spins out this point with vivid details: "The home computer starts to lose data, the microwave has to have its temperature controls adjusted, and the videotape recorder has to be serviced when a cassette becomes jammed."

As you read Michael's essay, also consider how well it applies the principles of illustration. (The commentary that follows the paper will help you look at the essay more closely and will give you some sense of how Michael went about revising his first draft.)

Pursuit of Possessions

by Michael Pagano

1   In the essay "Channelled Whelk," Anne Morrow Lindbergh   *Introduction*
states that Americans "who could choose simplicity, choose
complication." Lindbergh herself is a prime example of the
phenomenon she discusses. A wife and a mother, as well as a
writer, Lindbergh has many obligations that make for a complicated life. Even so, Lindbergh attempts to simplify her life by

escaping to a beach cottage that is bare except for driftwood
and shells for decoration; there she is happy. But very few
of us would be willing to simplify our lives as Lindbergh does.

Thesis ──────────→ Instead, we choose to clutter our lives with a stream of
material possessions. And what is the result of this mania for

Plan of ─────────── possessions? Much of our time goes into buying new things,
development   dealing with the complications they create, and working madly
to buy more things or pay for the things we already have.

Topic sentence ──────→ We devote a great deal of our lives to acquiring the   2
material goods we imagine are essential to our well-being.
Hours are spent planning and thinking about our future
purchases. We window-shop for designer jogging shoes; we
leaf through magazines looking at ads for elaborate stereo

The first of   equipment; we research back issues of Consumer Reports to find
three paragraphs   out about recent developments in exercise equipment. Moreover,
in a chronological   once we find what we are looking for, more time is taken up when
sequence   we decide to actually buy the items. How do we find this time?
That's easy. We turn evenings, weekends, and holidays--times
that used to be set aside for family and friends--into shopping
expeditions. No wonder family life is deteriorating and children spend so much time in front of television sets. Their
parents are seldom around.

Topic sentence ──────→ As soon as we take our new purchases home, they begin to   3
complicate our lives. A sleek new sports car has to be washed,
The second   waxed, and vacuumed. A fashionable pair of skintight jeans
paragraph in   can't be thrown in the washing machine but has to be taken to
the chronological   the dry cleaner. New stereo equipment has to be connected with
sequence   a tangled network of cables to the TV, radio, and cassette
deck. Eventually, of course, the inevitable happens. Our
indispensable possessions break down and need to be repaired.

A paragraph with   The home computer starts to lose data, the microwave has to
many specific   have its temperature controls adjusted, and the videotape
examples   recorder has to be serviced when a cassette becomes jammed in
the machine.

Topic sentence ─────→ After more time has gone by, we sometimes discover that our   4
purchases don't suit us anymore, and so we decide to replace
The third paragraph   them. Before making our replacement purchases, though, we have
in the chronological   to find ways to get rid of the old items. If we want to replace
sequence   our 19-inch television set with a 35-inch color set, we have to

Illustration   235

find time to put an ad in the classified section of the paper. Then we have to handle phone calls and set up times people can come to look at the old TV. We could store the set in the base-ment--if we are lucky enough to find a spot that isn't already filled with other discarded purchases.

5   Worst of all, this mania for possessions often influences our approach to work. It is not unusual for people to take a second or even a third job to pay off the debt they fall into because they have overbought. After paying for food, clothing, and shelter, many people see the rest of their pay-check go to Visa, MasterCard, department store charge accounts, and time payments. Panic sets in when they realize there simply is not enough money to cover all their expenses. Just to stay afloat, people may have to work overtime or take on additional jobs.

Topic sentence with emphasis signal

6   It is clear that many of us have allowed the pursuit of possessions to dominate our lives. We are so busy buying, maintaining, and paying for our worldly goods that we do not have much time to think about what is really important. We should try to step back from our compulsive need for more of everything and get in touch with the basic values that are the real point of our lives.

Conclusion

Commentary

Thesis, Other Patterns of Development, and Plan of Development

In "Pursuit of Possessions," Michael analyzes the American mania for acquir-ing material goods. He begins with a quotation from Anne Morrow Lindbergh's "Channelled Whelk" and briefly explains Lindbergh's strategy for simplifying her life. The reference to Lindbergh gives Michael a chance to *contrast* the way she tries to lead her life with the acquisitive and frenzied way many Americans lead theirs. This contrast leads logically to the essay's *thesis:* "We choose to clutter our lives with a stream of material possessions."

Besides introducing the basic contrast at the heart of the essay, Michael's open-ing paragraph helps readers see that the essay contains an element of *causal analy-sis.* Michael asks, "What is the result of this mania for possessions?" and then answers that question in the next sequence. This sentence also serves as the essay's *plan of development* and reveals that Michael feels the pursuit of possessions negatively affects our lives in three key ways.

Essays of this length often don't need a plan of development. But since Michael's paper is filled with many *examples*, the plan of development helps readers see how all the details relate to the essay's central point.

Evidence

Support for the thesis consists of numerous examples presented in the *first-person plural point of view* ("*We* choose to clutter our lives...," "*We* devote a great deal of our lives...," and so on). Many of these examples seem drawn from Michael's, his friends', or his family's experiences; however, to emphasize the events' universality, Michael converts these essentially personal examples into generalized ones that "we" all experience.

These examples, in turn, are organized around the three major points signaled by the plan of development. Michael uses one paragraph to develop his first and third points and two paragraphs to develop his second point. Each of the four supporting paragraphs is focused by a *topic sentence* that appears at the beginning of the paragraph. The transitional phrase "Worst of all" (paragraph 5) signals that Michael has sequenced his major points *emphatically,* saving for last the issue he considers most significant: how the "mania for possessions...influences our approach to work."

Organizational Strategies

Emphatic order isn't Michael's only organizational technique. When reading the paper, you probably felt that there was an easy flow from one supporting paragraph to the next. How does Michael achieve such *coherence between paragraphs*? For one thing, he sequences paragraphs 2–4 *chronologically:* what happens before a purchase is made; what happens afterward. Secondly, topic sentences in paragraphs 3 and 4 include *signal devices* that indicate this passage of time. The topic sentences also strengthen coherence by *linking back* to the preceding paragraph: "*As soon as we take our new purchases home,* they...complicate our lives" and "*After more time has gone by,* we...discover that our purchases don't suit us anymore."

The same organizing strategies are used *within paragraphs* to make the essay coherent. Details in paragraphs 2–4 are sequenced *chronologically,* and to help readers follow the chronology, Michael uses *signal devices*: "*Moreover, once* we find what we are looking for, more time is taken up..." (2); "*Eventually,* of course, the inevitable happens" (3); "*Then* we have to handle phone calls..." (4).

Problems with Paragraph Development

You probably recall that an essay developed primarily through illustration must include examples that are *relevant, interesting, convincing, representative, accurate,* and *specific.* On the whole, Michael's examples meet these requirements. The third and fourth paragraphs, especially, include vigorous details that show how our mania for buying things can govern our lives. We may even laugh with self-recognition when reading about "skintight jeans that can't be thrown in the washing machine" or a basement "filled...with discarded purchases."

The fifth paragraph, however, is underdeveloped. We know that this paragraph presents what Michael considers his most significant point, but the paragraph's

Illustration   237

examples are rather *flat* and *unconvincing.* To make this final section more compelling, Michael could mention specific people who overspend, revealing how much they are in debt and how much they have to work to become solvent again. Or he could cite a television documentary or magazine article dealing with the issue of consumer debt. Such specifics would give the paragraph the solidity it now lacks.

Shift in Tone

The fifth paragraph has a second, more subtle problem: a *shift in tone.* Although Michael has, up to this point, been critical of our possession-mad culture, he has poked fun at our obsession and kept his tone conversational and gently satiric. In this paragraph, though, he adopts a serious tone, and, in the next paragraph, his tone becomes even weightier, almost preachy. It is, of course, legitimate to have a serious message in a lightly satiric piece. In fact, most satiric writing has such an additional layer of meaning. But because Michael has trouble blending these two moods, there's a jarring shift in the essay.

Shift in Focus

The second paragraph shows another kind of shift—in *focus.* The paragraph's controlling idea is that too much time is spent acquiring possessions. However, starting with "No wonder family life is deteriorating," Michael includes two sentences that introduce a complex issue beyond the scope of the essay. Since the sentences disrupt the paragraph's unity, they should be deleted.

Revising the First Draft

Although the final version of the essay needs work in spots, it's much stronger than Michael's first draft. To see how Michael went about revising the draft, compare his paper's second and third supporting paragraphs with his draft version reprinted here. The annotations, numbered in order of importance, show the ideas Michael hit upon when he returned to his first draft and reworked this section.

Original Version of the Second Paragraph

Our lives are spent not only buying things but in dealing with the inevitable complications that are created by our newly acquired possessions. First, we have to find places to put all the objects we bring home. More clothes demand more closets; a second car demands more garage space; a home-entertainment center requires elaborate shelving. We shouldn't be surprised that the average American family moves once every three years. A good many families move simply because they need more space to store all the things they buy. In addition, our possessions demand maintenance time. A person who gets a new car will spend hours washing it, waxing it, and vacuuming it. A new

② Awkward first sentence

① Paragraph goes in too many directions. Cut idea about moving since not enough space.

③ Make problem
with jeans
more specific

④ Develop
more fully

pair of jeans has to go to the dry cleaners. New stereo
systems have to be connected to already existing equipment.
Eventually, of course, the inevitable happens. Our new
items need to be repaired. Or we get sick of them and
decide to replace them. Before making our replacement purchases, though, we have to get rid of the old items. That
can be a real inconvenience.

Referring to the revision checklist on page 231 helped Michael see that the paragraph rambled and lacked energy. He started to revise by tightening the first sentence, making it more focused and less awkward. Certainly, the revised sentence
("As soon as we take our new purchases home, they begin to complicate our
lives") is crisper than the original. Next, he decided to omit the discussion about
finding places to put new possessions; these sentences about inadequate closet,
garage, and shelf space were so exaggerated that they undercut the valid point he
wanted to make. He also chose to eliminate the sentences about the mobility of
American families. This was, he felt, an interesting point, but it introduced an
issue too complex to be included in the paragraph.

Michael strengthened the rest of the paragraph by making his examples more
specific. A "new car" became a "sleek new sports car," and a "pair of jeans"
became a "fashionable pair of skintight jeans." Michael also realized he had to do
more than merely write, "Eventually,... our new items need to be repaired." This
point had to be dramatized by sharp, convincing details. Therefore, Michael
added lively examples to describe how high-tech possessions—microwaves,
home computers, VCRs—break down. Similarly, Michael realized it wasn't
enough simply to say, as he had in the original, that we run into problems when
we try to replace out-of-favor purchases. Vigorous details were again needed to
illustrate the point. Michael thus used a typical "replaceable" (an old TV) as his
key example and showed the annoyance involved in handling phone calls and setting up appointments so that people could see the TV.

After adding these specifics, Michael realized that he had enough material to
devote a separate paragraph to the problems associated with replacing old purchases. By dividing his original paragraph, Michael ended up with two well-
focused paragraphs, rather than a single rambling one.

In short, Michael strengthened his essay through substantial revision. Another
round of rewriting would have made the essay stronger still. Even without this
additional work, Michael's essay provides an interesting perspective on an American preoccupation.

Illustration   239

ACTIVITIES: ILLUSTRATION

Prewriting Activities

1. Imagine you're writing two essays: One is a serious paper analyzing why large numbers of public school teachers leave the profession each year; the other is a light essay defining *preppie, head banger,* or some other slang term used to describe a kind of person. Jot down ways you might use examples in each essay

2. Use mapping or another prewriting technique to gather examples illustrating the truth of *one* of the following familiar sayings. Then, using the same or a different prewriting technique, accumulate examples that counter the saying. Weigh both sets of examples to determine the saying's validity. After developing an appropriate thesis, decide which examples you would elaborate in an essay.

   a. Haste makes waste.
   b. There's no use crying over spilled milk.
   c. A bird in the hand is worth two in the bush.

3. Turn back to activity 4 and activity 5 in Chapter 4, and select *one* thesis statement for which you didn't develop supporting evidence earlier. Identify a purpose, audience, tone, and point of view for an essay with this thesis. Then meet with at least one other person to generate as many examples as possible to support the thesis. Next, evaluate the material to determine which examples should be eliminated. Finally, from the remaining examples, take the strongest one and develop it as fully as you can.

4. Freewrite or use your journal to generate examples illustrating how widespread a recent fad or trend has become. After reviewing your prewriting to determine a possible thesis, narrow the examples to those you would retain for an essay. How might the patterns of development or a chronological, emphatic, spatial, or simple-to-complex approach help you sequence the examples?

Revising Activities

5. The following paragraph is from the first draft of an essay about the decline of small-town shopping districts. The paragraph is meant to show what small towns can do to revitalize business. Revise the paragraph, strengthening it with specific and convincing examples.

A small town can compete with a large new mall for shoppers.
But merchants must work together, modernizing the stores and making
the town's main street pleasant, even fun to walk. They should also
copy the malls' example by including attention-getting events as
often as possible.

6. The paragraph that follows is from the first draft of an essay showing how
knowledge of psychology can help us understand behavior that might otherwise
seem baffling. The paragraph is intended to illustrate the meaning of the psychological term *superego.* Revise the paragraph, replacing its vague, unconvincing
examples with one extended example that conveys the meaning of *superego* clearly
and dramatically.

The superego is the part of us that makes us feel guilty when
we do something that we know is wrong. When we act foolishly or
wildly, we usually feel qualms about our actions later on. If we
imagine ourselves getting revenge, we most likely discover that the
thoughts make us feel bad. All of these are examples of the superego
at work.

7. Reprinted here is a paragraph from the first draft of a light-spirited essay showing that Americans' pursuit of change for change's sake has drawbacks. The paragraph is meant to illustrate that infatuation with newness costs consumers money
yet leads to no improvement in product quality. How effective is the paragraph?
Which examples are specific and convincing? Which are not? Do any seem nonrepresentative, offensive, or sexist? How could the paragraph's organization be
improved? Consider these questions as you rewrite the paragraph. Add specific
examples where needed. Depending on the way you revise, you may want to
break this one paragraph into several.

We end up paying for our passion for the new and improved.
Trendy clothing styles convince us that last year's outfits are outdated, even though our old clothes are fine. Women are especially
vulnerable in this regard. What, though, about items that have to be
replaced periodically, like shampoo? Even slight changes lead to new
formulations requiring retooling of the production process. That
means increased manufacturing costs per item--all of which get
passed on to us, the consumer. Then there are those items that tout
new, trend-setting features that make earlier versions supposedly
obsolete. Some manufacturers, for example, boast that their stereo
or CD systems transmit an expanded-frequency range. The problem
is that humans can't even hear such frequencies, But the high-tech
feature dazzles men who are too naive to realize they're being
hoodwinked.

Illustration   241

ANNE MORROW LINDBERGH

Anne Morrow Lindbergh (1906–) is a distinguished novelist, diarist, essayist, and poet. Her books include the novels *Dearly Beloved* (1962), *Earth Shine* (1969), and *War Within and War Without* (1995), as well as the essay collection *Gift from the Sea* (1955), where the following selection first appeared.

CHANNELLED WHELK

1   The shell in my hand is deserted. It once housed a whelk, a snail-like creature, and then temporarily, after the death of the first occupant, a little hermit crab, who has run away, leaving his tracks behind him like a delicate vine on the sand. He ran away, and left me his shell. It was once a protection to him. I turn the shell in my hand, gazing into the wide open door from which he made his exit. Had it become an encumbrance? Why did he run away? Did he hope to find a better home, a better mode of living? I too have run away, I realize, I have shed the shell of my life, for these few weeks of vacation.

2   But his shell—it is simple; it is bare, it is beautiful. Small, only the size of my thumb, its architecture is perfect, down to the finest detail. Its shape, swelling like a pear in the center, winds in a gentle spiral to the pointed apex. Its color, dull gold, is whitened by a wash of salt from the sea. Each whorl, each faint knob, each criss-cross vein in its egg-shell texture, is as clearly defined as on the day of creation. My eye follows with delight the outer circumference of that diminutive winding staircase up which this tenant used to travel.

3   My shell is not like this, I think. How untidy it has become! Blurred with moss, knobby with barnacles, its shape is hardly recognizable any more. Surely, it had a shape once. It has a shape still in my mind. What is the shape of my life?

4   The shape of my life today starts with a family. I have a husband, five children and a home just beyond the suburbs of New York. I have also a craft, writing, and therefore work I want to pursue. The shape of my life is, of course, determined by many other things; my background and childhood, my mind and its education, my conscience and its pressures, my heart and its desires. I want to give and take from my children and husband, to share with friends and community, to carry out my obligations to man and to the world as a woman, as an artist, as a citizen.

5   But I want first of all—in fact, as an end to these other desires—to be at peace with myself. I want a singleness of eye, a purity of intention, a central core to my life that will enable me to carry out these obligations and activities as well as I can. I want, in fact—

to borrow from the language of the saints—to live "in grace" as much of the time as possible. I am not using this term in a strictly theological sense. By grace I mean an inner harmony, essentially spiritual, which can be translated into outward harmony. I am seeking perhaps what Socrates asked for in the prayer from the *Phaedrus* when he said, "May the outward and inward man be at one." I would like to achieve a state of inner spiritual grace from which I could function and give as I was meant to in the eye of God.

Vague as this definition may be, I believe most people are aware of periods in their 6 lives when they seem to be "in grace" and other periods when they feel "out of grace," even though they may use different words to describe these states. In the first happy condition, one seems to carry all one's tasks before one lightly, as if borne along on a great tide; and in the opposite state one can hardly tie a shoe-string. It is true that a large part of life consists in learning a technique of tying the shoe-string, whether one is in grace or not. But there are techniques of living too; there are even techniques in the search for grace. And techniques can be cultivated. I have learned by some experience, by many examples, and by the writings of countless others before me, also occupied in the search, that certain environments, certain modes of life, certain rules of conduct are more conducive to inner and outer harmony than others. There are, in fact, certain roads that one may follow. Simplification of life is one of them.

I mean to lead a simple life, to choose a simple shell I can carry easily—like a hermit 7 crab. But I do not. I find that my frame of life does not foster simplicity. My husband and five children must make their way in the world. The life I have chosen as wife and mother entrains a whole caravan of complications. It involves a house in the suburbs and either household drudgery or household help which wavers between scarcity and non-existence for most of us. It involves food and shelter; meals, planning, marketing, bills, and making the ends meet in a thousand ways. It involves not only the butcher, the baker, the candlestick maker but countless other experts to keep my modern house with its modern "simplifications" (electricity, plumbing, refrigerator, gas-stove, oil-burner, dish-washer, radios, car, and numerous other labor-saving devices) functioning properly. It involves health; doctors, dentists, appointments, medicine, cod-liver oil, vitamins, trips to the drugstore. It involves education, spiritual, intellectual, physical; schools, school conferences, carpools, extra trips for basket-ball or orchestra practice; tutoring; camps, camp equipment and transportation. It involves clothes, shopping, laundry, cleaning, mending, letting skirts down and sewing buttons on, or finding someone else to do it. It involves friends, my husband's, my children's, my own, and endless arrangements to get together; letters, invitations, telephone calls and transportation hither and yon.

For life today in America is based on the premise of ever-widening circles of contact 8 and communication. It involves not only family demands, but community demands, national demands, international demands on the good citizen, through social and cultural pressures, through newspapers, magazines, radio programs, political drives, charitable appeals, and so on. My mind reels with it. What a circus act we women perform every day of our lives. It puts the trapeze artist to shame. Look at us. We run a tight-rope daily, balancing a pile of books on the head. Baby-carriage, parasol, kitchen chair, still under control. Steady now!

This is not the life of simplicity but the life of multiplicity that the wise men warn us 9 of. It leads not to unification but to fragmentation. It does not bring grace; it destroys the soul. And this is not only true of my life, I am forced to conclude; it is the life of

Illustration   243

millions of women in America. I stress America, because today, the American woman more than any other has the privilege of choosing such a life. Woman in large parts of the civilized world has been forced back by war, by poverty, by collapse, by the sheer struggle to survive, into a smaller circle of immediate time and space, immediate family life, immediate problems of existence. The American woman is still relatively free to choose the wider life. How long she will hold this enviable and precarious position no one knows. But her particular situation has a significance far above its apparent economic, national or even sex limitations.

10   For the problem of the multiplicity of life not only confronts the American woman, but also the American man. And it is not merely the concern of the American as such, but of our whole modern civilization, since life in America today is held up as the ideal of a large part of the rest of the world. And finally, it is not limited to our present civilization, though we are faced with it now in an exaggerated form. It has always been one of the pitfalls of mankind. Plotinus was preaching the dangers of multiplicity of the world back in the third century. Yet, the problem is particularly and essentially woman's. Distraction is, always has been, and probably always will be, inherent in woman's life.

11   For to be a woman is to have interests and duties, raying out in all directions from the central mother-core, like spokes from the hub of a wheel. The pattern of our lives is essentially circular. We must be open to all points of the compass; husband, children, friends, home, community; stretched out, exposed, sensitive like a spider's web to each breeze that blows, to each call that comes. How difficult for us, then, to achieve a balance in the midst of these contradictory tensions, and yet how necessary for the proper functioning of our lives. How much we need, and how arduous of attainment is that steadiness preached in all rules for holy living. How desirable and distant is the ideal of the contemplative, artist, or saint—the inner inviolable core, the single eye.

12   With a new awareness, both painful and humorous, I begin to understand why the saints were rarely married women. I am convinced it has nothing inherently to do, as I once supposed, with chastity or children. It has to do primarily with distractions. The bearing, rearing, feeding and educating of children; the running of a house with its thousand details; human relationships with their myriad pulls—woman's normal occupations in general run counter to creative life, or contemplative life, or saintly life. The problem is not merely one of *Woman and Career, Woman and the Home, Woman and Independence.* It is more basically: how to remain whole in the midst of the distractions of life; how to remain balanced, no matter what centrifugal forces tend to pull one off center; how to remain strong, no matter what shocks come in at the periphery and tend to crack the hub of the wheel.

13   What is the answer? There is no easy answer, no complete answer. I have only clues, shells from the sea. The bare beauty of the channelled whelk tells me that one answer, and perhaps a first step, is in simplification of life, in cutting out some of the distractions. But how? Total retirement is not possible. I cannot shed my responsibilities. I cannot permanently inhabit a desert island. I cannot be a nun in the midst of family life. I would not want to be. The solution for me, surely, is neither in total renunciation of the world, nor in total acceptance of it. I must find a balance somewhere, or an alternating rhythm between these two extremes; a swinging of the pendulum between solitude and communion, between retreat and return. In my periods of retreat, perhaps I can learn something to carry back into my worldly life. I can at least

practice for these two weeks the simplification of outward life, as a beginning. I can follow this superficial clue, and see where it leads. Here, in beach living, I can try.

One learns first of all in beach living the art of shedding; how little one can get along 14 with, not how much. Physical shedding to begin with, which then mysteriously spreads into other fields. Clothes, first. Of course, one needs less in the sun. But one needs less anyway, one finds suddenly. One does not need a closet-full, only a small suitcase-full. And what a relief it is! Less taking up and down of hems, less mending, and—best of all—less worry about what to wear. One finds one is shedding not only clothes—but vanity.

Next, shelter. One does not need the airtight shelter one has in winter in the North. 15 Here I live in a bare sea-shell of a cottage. No heat, no telephone, no plumbing to speak of, no hot water, a two-burner oil stove, no gadgets to go wrong. No rugs. There were some, but I rolled them up the first day; it is easier to sweep the sand off a bare floor. But I find I don't bustle about with unnecessary sweeping and cleaning here. I am no longer aware of the dust. I have shed my Puritan conscience about absolute tidiness and cleanliness. Is it possible that, too, is a material burden? No curtains. I do not need them for privacy; the pines around my house are enough protection. I want the windows open all the time, and I don't want to worry about rain. I begin to shed my Martha-like anxiety about many things. Washable slipcovers, faded and old—I hardly see them; I don't worry about the impression they make on other people. I am shedding pride. As little furniture as possible; I shall not need much. I shall ask into my shell only those friends with whom I can be completely honest. I find I am shedding hypocrisy in human relationships. What a rest that will be! The most exhausting thing in life, I have discovered, is being insincere. That is why so much of social life is exhausting; one is wearing a mask. I have shed my mask.

I find I live quite happily without those things I think necessary in winter in the 16 North. And as I write these words, I remember, with some shock at the disparity in our lives, a similar statement made by a friend of mine in France who spent three years in a German prison camp. Of course, he said, qualifying his remark, they did not get enough to eat, they were sometimes atrociously treated, they had little physical freedom. And yet, prison life taught him how little one can get along with, and what extraordinary spiritual freedom and peace such simplification can bring. I remember again, ironically, that today more of us in America than anywhere else in the world have the luxury of choice between simplicity and complication of life. And for the most part, we, who could choose simplicity, choose complication. War, prison, survival periods, enforce a form of simplicity on man. The monk and the nun choose it of their own free will. But if one accidentally finds it, as I have for a few days, one finds also the serenity it brings.

Is it not rather ugly, one may ask? One collects material possessions not only for 17 security, comfort or vanity, but for beauty as well. Is your sea-shell house not ugly and bare? No, it is beautiful, my house. It is bare, of course, but the wind, the sun, the smell of the pines blow through its bareness. The unfinished beams in the roof are veiled by cobwebs. They are lovely, I think, gazing up at them with new eyes; they soften the hard lines of the rafters as grey hairs soften the lines on a middle-aged face. I no longer pull out grey hairs or sweep down cobwebs. As for the walls, it is true they looked forbidding at first. I felt cramped and enclosed by their blank faces. I wanted to

Illustration   245

knock holes in them, to give them another dimension with pictures or windows. So I dragged home from the beach grey arms of driftwood, worn satin-smooth by wind and sand. I gathered trailing green vines with floppy red-tipped leaves. I picked up the whitened skeletons of conchshells, their curious hollowed-out shapes faintly reminiscent of abstract sculpture. With these tacked to walls and propped up in corners, I am satisfied. I have a periscope out to the world. I have a window, a view, a point of flight from my sedentary base.

18   I am content. I sit down at my desk, a bare kitchen table with a blotter, a bottle of ink, a sand dollar to weight down one corner, a clam shell for a pen tray, the broken tip of a conch, pink-tinged, to finger, and a row of shells to set my thoughts spinning.

19   I love my sea-shell of a house. I wish I could live in it always. I wish I could transport it home. But I cannot. It will not hold a husband, five children and the necessities and trappings of daily life. I can only carry back my little channelled whelk. It will sit on my desk in Connecticut, to remind me of the ideal of a simplified life, to encourage me in the game I played on the beach. To ask how little, not how much, can I get along with. To say—is it necessary?—when I am tempted to add one more accumulation to my life, when I am pulled toward one more centrifugal activity.

20   Simplification of outward life is not enough. It is merely the outside. But I am starting with the outside. I am looking at the outside of a shell, the outside of my life—the shell. The complete answer is not to be found on the outside, in an outward mode of living. This is only a technique, a road to grace. The final answer, I know, is always inside. But the outside can give a clue, can help one to find the inside answer. One is free, like the hermit crab, to change one's shell.

21   Channelled whelk, I put you down again, but you have set my mind on a journey, up an inwardly winding spiral staircase of thought.

Questions for Close Reading

1. What is the selection's thesis? Locate the sentence(s) in which Lindbergh states her main idea. If she doesn't state the thesis explicitly, express it in your own words.

2. What does Lindbergh find appealing about the shell of the channelled whelk?

3. Why, according to Lindbergh, are distraction and "multiplicity" so much a problem for women? Why are they less of a problem for men?

4. Since Lindbergh prefers the life at the beach house, why doesn't she remain there? Why does she take the shell away with her?

5. Refer to your dictionary as needed to define the following words used in the selection: *apex* (paragraph 2), *conducive* (6), *myriad* (12), *periphery* (12), and *sedentary* (17).

Questions About the Writer's Craft

1. The pattern. Illustrative essays often develop key points through extended examples. In what paragraphs does Lindbergh use extended illustrations to clarify what she means by "simplification"? What's the effect of these extended illustrations?

2. Other patterns. Why do you suppose Lindbergh begins her essay with a few paragraphs describing a whelk shell? Where does she return to the shell? What does the shell come to represent?

3. In paragraph 6, the author uses the image of "tying a shoe-string." To what aspects of life is she referring? At what point do you recognize that "tying a shoe-string" serves as a metaphor for a larger part of life?

4. Why do you think Lindbergh ends the essay with a short "speech" or address to the whelk shell? How does this last paragraph extend an idea suggested in the preceding paragraph?

Writing Assignments Using Illustration as a Pattern of Development

1. Write an essay about the excess of possessions in people's lives today. Give examples of people you know or have heard about who are obsessed with possessions. Part of your essay should discuss the effect these possessions have on people's lives.

2. Lindbergh writes that she often feels fragmented into a series of selves because of the numerous demands—family, community, and political—made on her. Analyze your own life to identify the different roles you play. Write an essay detailing the "balancing act" you perform in your life. When describing each of your roles, be sure to provide specific examples of the demands claiming your attention. In the conclusion, point briefly to some things you could do to make your life less fragmented and more harmonious.

Writing Assignments Using Other Patterns of Development

3. Imagine simplifying your own life to achieve greater inner harmony. How would you go about it? Write an essay describing such a process. For each step, include specific examples of activities, objects, relationships, and the like that you would eliminate.

∞ **4.** Focus on *one* aspect of American mass culture (for example, TV situation comedies, pop music, movies, MTV, magazines, ads and commercials), and write an essay showing how that particular medium helps create a society obsessed with possessions. Support your point with a number of vivid and persuasive examples. Joyce Garity's "Is Sex All That Matters?" (page 252), Ann McClintock's "Propa-

Illustration 247

ganda Techniques in Today's Advertising" (page 277), and Pete Hamill's "Crack and the Box" (page 356) will deepen your understanding of mass culture's powerful effect.

SUSAN DOUGLAS

Susan J. Douglas (1950–), professor of communication studies at the University of Michigan, is the media critic for *The Progressive*. She has written for the *Village Voice* and the *Nation* and is the author of three books: *Inventing American Broadcasting: 1899–1922* (1987), *Where the Girls Are: Growing Up Female With the Mass Media* (1994), and *Listening In: Radio and the American Imagination* (1999). "Managing Mixed Messages" is an excerpt from *Where the Girls Are.*

MANAGING MIXED MESSAGES

1   "Mommy, Mommy, hurry, come quickly, *now*!" implores my daughter at 8:16 a.m. on Saturday. This is the one time of the week she's allowed to watch commercial television, and the price is heavy. I drag my hungover and inadequately caffeinated butt over to the TV set. Her eyes shine like moonstones as I see what's on the screen. "Can I get that, Mommy, can I, puleeze? Please, Mommy." I see before me some hideous plastic doll, or pony, or troll, being pitched by a combination of elated little girls, flashing lights, and rap music. Everything seems to be colored hot pink or lilac. Sometimes it's one of these dolls you can put fake jewels all over, other times it's a troll doll in a wedding dress, or it's something really bad, like Kitty Surprise or Cheerleader Skipper. It is always something specifically targeted to little girls. She is four years old, and she understands, completely, the semiotics of gender differentiation. She never calls me when they're selling Killer Commando Unit, G.I. Joe, and all the other Pentagon-inspired stuff obviously for boys. She knows better. She knows she's a girl, and she knows what's for her. Twenty years of feminist politics and here I am, with a daughter who wants nothing more in the whole wide world than to buy Rollerblade Barbie.

2   Having grown up with the mass media myself, and considering what that has done for me and to me, I bring all that to bear as I raise my own little girl, who will, in her own way, and with her own generation, have her hopes and fears shaped by the mass media too. Ever since she was old enough to understand books, kids' movies, and *Sesame Street,* I have looked, in vain, for strong and appealing female characters for her to identify with. With a few exceptions, like *The Paperbag Princess,* shrewd, daring girls who outsmart monsters and value their freedom and self-esteem more than marrying some prince are hard to find. There's Maria, who knows how to fix toasters and stereos, on *Sesame Street.* But little kids are, at first, most drawn to the Muppets, and until recently, not one of the main stars—Big Bird, Kermit, the Count, Elmo, Snuffy, or Oscar—was female. Children's books are not much better. Even if they feature animals as the main protagonists, stories for kids too readily assume, automatically, that the main actor is male. Television cartoons, from Winnie the Pooh (no females except Kanga, and she's always doing laundry or cooking), to Garfield to Doug, not to mention

the more obnoxious superhero action ones, still treat females either as nonexistent or as ancillary afterthoughts. We have the cartoon *James Bond, Jr.,* but no *Emma Peel, Jr.* And it goes without saying that nearly all the little girls she sees on TV and elsewhere are white.

And then there are the movies. When mothers cling to *The Little Mermaid* as one of the few positive representations of girls, we see how far we have not come. Ariel, the little mermaid in question, is indeed brave, curious, feisty, and defiant. She stands up to her father, saves Prince Eric from drowning, and stares down great white sharks as she hunts for sunken treasure. But her waist is the diameter of a chive, and her salvation comes through her marriage—at the age of sixteen, no less—to Eric. And the sadistic, consummately evil demon in the movie is, you guessed it, an older, overweight woman with too much purple eyeshadow and eyeliner, a female octopus who craves too much power and whose nether regions evoke the dreaded vagina dentate.

Belle, in *Beauty and the Beast,* dreams of escaping from the narrow confines of her small town, of having great adventures, and has nothing but contempt for the local cleft-chinned lout and macho beefcake Gaston. Her dreams of a more interesting, exciting life, however, are also fulfilled through marriage alone. The most important quality of these characters remains their beauty, followed closely by their selflessness and the ability to sing. There are gestures to feminism—Ariel's physical courage, Belle's love of books, and, in *Aladdin,* Jasmine's defiance of an arbitrary law that dictates when and whom she must marry. These are welcome flourishes, and many of us milk them for all they're worth—"See how *strong* she is, honey?"—but they are still only flourishes, overwhelmed by the age-old narrative that selfless, beautiful girls are rewarded by the love of a prince they barely know. Nonanimated movies for kids are no better. Hollywood simply takes it for granted that little heroes, like big ones, are always boys. So little girls get *Home Alone* and who knows how many sequels, *Cop and a Half, The Karate Kid, Rookie of the Year, Free Willy,* and *Dennis the Menace,* all with little boy leads, little boy adventures, and little boy heroism, while gutsy, smart, enterprising, and sassy little girls remain, after all this time, absent, invisible, denied. Even my daughter, at the age of four, volunteered one day, "Mommy, there should be more movies with girls."

The one movie that I was happy to have my daughter embrace was made over fifty years ago, and judging from anecdotal evidence, it's been enjoying an enormous resurgence among the preschool set. No narrative has gripped my daughter's imagination more than *The Wizard of Oz.* And why not? Finally, here's a *girl* who has an adventure and doesn't get married at the end. She runs away from home, flies to Oz in a cyclone, kills one wicked witch and then another—although never on purpose—and helps Scarecrow get a brain, Tin Man get a heart, and Lion get some courage, all of which Dorothy already has in spades. Throughout the movie, Dorothy is caring, thoughtful, nurturing, and empathetic, but she's also adventuresome, determined, and courageous. She tells off Miss Gulch, slaps the lion while her male friends cower in the bushes, refuses to give the witch her slippers, and chastises the Wizard himself when she feels he is bullying her friends. Of course, when she's older, my daughter will learn the truth about Dorothy: that Judy Garland had to have her breasts strapped down for the part and was fed bucketfuls of amphetamines so she'd remain as slim as the studio wanted. This, too, I think, will speak to my daughter.

Illustration   249

6   Shortly after seeing a few of the Disney fairy tales, both old and new, my daughter announced, at age three and a half, that she would no longer wear the unisex sweat suits and overalls I'd been dressing her in. It was dresses or nothing. Her favorite pretend games became "wedding" and "family," with her as either the bride or the mom. She loved playing Wizard of Oz—she was always Dorothy, of course—but she also loved playing Snow White, dropping like a sack of onions to the kitchen floor after she'd bitten into the pretend apple. The blocks, the Tinkertoys, and the trucks I had gotten her lay neglected, while the Barbie population began to multiply like fruit flies.

7   One of the things that feminist moms, and dads, for that matter, confront is the force of genetics. In the 1970s, I was convinced that most of the differences between men and women were the results of socialization. In the nature-nurture debate, I gave nature very little due. But now, as a parent, I have seen my daughter, long before she ever watched television, prefer dolls to trucks, use blocks to build enclosures instead of towers, and focus on interpersonal relationships in her play rather than on hurling projectiles into things. But at the same time, I have seen children's television (which, if anything, is even more retrograde than it was in the 1970s) reinforce and exaggerate these gender differences with a vengeance as if there were no overlap of traits at all between boys and girls...

8   In fact, kids' TV is worse than ever, and certainly more crass, more sexist...than much of the programming pitched to adults. In addition to all the war toys that train little boys to be cannon fodder and/or gun collectors, and the makeup kits and dolls that train little girls to be sex objects and/or moms, the overall message is about regarding yourself and everyone else you know as a commodity to be bought and sold. Ads geared to each gender encourage kids to dehumanize themselves and one another, to regard people as objects to be acquired or discarded. "Get the right boyfriend! Get the right friends!" commands an ad for a game for girls, Spring Valley High School (or maybe it was called Shop 'Til You Drop). To be a desirable commodity, a little girl must herself consume the right goods so she can make herself pretty and ornament herself properly. Being able to sing and smile admiringly at boys is highly desirable. Being smart, brave, or assertive isn't. On Saturday morning, boys are "cool"; girls are their mirrors, flat, shiny surfaces whose function is to reflect all this coolness back to them and on them. Girls watch boys be "awesome" and do "awesome" things. Girls aren't awesome; they're only spectators.

9   Already I see my little girl, at the age of four, managing the mixed messages around her. I see her process them, try to control them, and allow them into her sense of her place in the world. She wants to be at the center of the action, and she dictates the precise direction of her pretend games with the authority of a field marshal. In the books she has about rabbits, cats, alligators, and the like, she insists that I change all the pronouns from *he* to *she* so the story will be about a girl, not a boy. Already, she is resisting, without yet knowing it, certain sexist presumptions of the media. But she succumbs to them too. For it is also important to her that she be pretty, desired, and the one who beats out the ugly stepsisters for the prince's attention. She wants control and she wants love, and she is growing up in a culture as confused about how much of each a woman can have as it was in the 1950s and '60s. So she will be surrounded by media imagery that holds out promises of female achievement with one hand and slaps her down with the other.

One recourse we…have is to teach our daughters how to talk back to and make fun 10
of the mass media. This is especially satisfying since, thanks to Nickelodeon, we sometimes see them watching the same stuff we grew up with. In an episode of *Lassie* my
daughter and I watched one morning, a ranger comes to the house to warn the mom
that there are some mountain lions in the area. As he tries to show her, on a map,
where they'd been spotted, she demurs, confessing that she can't read maps and they
just confuse her. Then, on her way to meet Dad and Timmy at a Grange dinner, she
gets a flat—which, of course, she hasn't a clue how to change—and then gets caught in
one of the traps set for the mountain lions. Lassie—a dog—has more brains than she
does and has to save her. Such scenes provide the feminist mom with an opportunity to
impart a few words of wisdom about how silly and unrealistic TV can be when it comes
to women.

But…I don't want to monitor my daughter's TV viewing on Saturday morning, I 11
want to go back to bed. How many mothers have the time or the energy for such interventions? Why should such interventions be so constantly necessary? And even the
most conscientious and unharried mom can't compensate for the absences, the era-
sures, of what their daughters don't see, may never see, about women and bravery,
intelligence, and courage…. Of one thing I am certain. Like us, our daughters will
make their own meanings out of much that they see, reading between the lines,
absorbing exhortations to be feisty side by side with exhortations to be passive. Like
us, they will have to work hard to fend off what cripples them and amplify what
empowers them. But why, after all these years, should they still have to work so hard
and to resist so much?

Questions for Close Reading

1. What is the selection's thesis? Locate the sentence(s) in which Douglas states
her main idea. If she doesn't state the thesis explicitly, express it in your own
words.

2. What, according to Douglas, is good about animated movies like *The Little Mermaid* and *Beauty and the Beast?* What is bad about both these animated movies and
nonanimated movies like *Home Alone* and *Free Willy?*

3. Why is Douglas happy to have her daughter "embrace" (5) *The Wizard of Oz?*
What makes this movie different from the others she mentioned earlier? What, if
anything, does she find problematic about it?

4. How does Douglas's daughter react to the media presentation of gender roles?
How does the girl's reaction reinforce Douglas's thesis?

5. Refer to your dictionary as needed to define the following words used in the
selection: *implores* (paragraph 1), *semiotics* (1), *consummately* (3), *nether* (3), *arbitrary*
(4), *flourishes* (4), *resurgence* (5), *retrograde* (7), *succumbs* (9), *demurs* (10), *impart* (10),
unharried (11), *exhortations* (11).

Illustration 251

Questions About the Writer's Craft

1. The pattern. In the course of her essay, Douglas cites television commercials, books, television shows, and movies to support her thesis. How does she signal movement from one medium to the other?

2. How would you characterize Douglas's tone in the first paragraph of the essay? What words and phrases reveal this tone? How does this tone help Douglas reinforce her thesis?

3. Other patterns. The brief personal narrative that opens the essay lets us hear the voice of Douglas's daughter. Where in the essay do we hear Douglas herself speaking? What do these two instances of dialogue contribute to the essay?

4. Why do you think Douglas ends her essay with a question? What effect do you think she wanted the question to have on her readers?

Writing Assignments Using Illustration as a Pattern of Development

∞ 1. Douglas provides numerous examples to show how media messages shape her daughter's understanding of what it means to be female. Write an essay in which you cite the experiences and sources of information that shaped your understanding of your gender. Before writing your paper, you may want to read the following essays, all of which provide insight into gender expectations: Maya Angelou's "Sister Flowers" (page 175), Deborah Tannen's "But What Do You Mean?" (page 283), and Nancy Gibbs's "When Is It Rape?" (page 423).

∞ 2. Douglas claims that the media glorify males at the expense of females. Are there other aspects of our culture that value the behavior and attitudes of males more than those of females? With friends, classmates, and relatives, discuss other areas, such as dating, marriage, academics, athletics, and friendships. Then, focusing on *one* area, write an essay illustrating that a particular aspect of contemporary society values one sex more than the other. To support your point of view, draw upon others' experiences as well as your own. If appropriate, include points made in any of the following essays: Deborah Tannen's "But What Do You Mean?" (page 283) and Nancy Gibbs's "When Is It Rape?" (page 423).

Writing Assignments Using Other Patterns of Development

∞ 3. In paragraph 7, Douglas alludes to the "nature-nurture" debate—in this case, whether the gender differences are a result of primarily genetics or socialization.

To gain insight into the complexities of the nature-nurture debate, brainstorm with others and conduct some library research. Then write an essay arguing your position about the controversy: Is it biology or the environment that plays the predominant role in determining sex-role attitudes and behavior? Remember to defend your viewpoint with plentiful examples based on research as well as your own and other people's experiences. Acknowledge the opposing viewpoint, dismantling as much of it as you can. The following essays will provide insights to draw upon in your paper: Deborah Tannen's "But What Do You Mean?" (page 283) and Nancy Gibbs's "When Is It Rape?" (page 423).

4. In paragraph 9, Douglas says that her daughter wants love and control but is growing up in a culture "as confused about how much of each a woman can have as…in the 1950s and '60s." Interview several people who grew up in that period to gather information on gender expectations a generation ago. Using their experiences and observations as well as your own, write an essay comparing and contrasting gender expectations now and in the past. Focus your discussions on *one* sex, and reach some conclusions about how much or how little has changed since that earlier time.

JOYCE GARITY

Social worker Joyce Garity (1955–) has served as the supervisor of county foster-child services in two Midwestern states. Garity derived her essay "Is Sex All That Matters?" from a highly regarded presentation she made several years ago at a social workers' conference on teenage parenthood.

IS SEX ALL THAT MATTERS?

A few years ago, a young girl lived with me, my husband, and our children for several months. The circumstances of Elaine's coming to us don't matter here; suffice it to say that she was troubled and nearly alone in the world. She was also pregnant—hugely, clumsily pregnant with her second child. Elaine was seventeen. Her pregnancy, she said, was an accident; she also said she wasn't sure who had fathered her child. There had been several sex partners and no contraception. Yet, she repeated blandly, gazing at me with clear blue eyes, the pregnancy was an accident, and one she would certainly never repeat. 1

Eventually I asked Elaine, after we had grown to know each other well enough for such conversations, why neither she nor her lovers had used birth control. She blushed—this porcelain-skinned girl with one child in foster care and another swelling the bib of her fashionably faded overalls—she stammered, she blushed some more. Birth control, she finally got out, was "embarrassing." It wasn't "romantic." You couldn't be really passionate, she explained, and worry about birth control at the same time. 2

I haven't seen Elaine for quite a long time. I think about her often, though. I think of her as I page through teen fashion magazines in the salon where I have my hair cut. 3

Illustration   253

Although intended to be mainstream and wholesome, these magazines trumpet sexuality page after leering page. On the inside front cover, an advertisement for Guess jeans features junior fashion models in snug denim dresses, their legs bared to just below the crotch. An advertisement for Liz Claiborne fragrances shows a barely clad young couple sprawled on a bed, him painting her toenails. An advertisement for Obsession cologne displays a waif-thin girl draped stomach-down across a couch, naked, her startled expression suggesting helplessness against an unseen yet approaching threat.

4   I think of Elaine because I know she would love these ads. "They're so beautiful," she would croon, and of course they are. The faces and bodies they show are lovely. The lighting is superb. The hair and makeup are faultless. In the Claiborne ad, the laughing girl whose toenails are being painted by her handsome lover is obviously having the time of her life. She stretches luxuriously on a bed heaped with clean white linen and fluffy pillows. Beyond the sheer blowing curtains of her room, we can glimpse a graceful wrought-iron balcony. Looking at the ad, Elaine could only want to be her. Any girl would want to be her. Heck, *I* want to be her.

5   But my momentary desire to move into the Claiborne picture, to trade lives with the exquisite young creature pictured there, is just that—momentary. I've lived long enough to know that what I see is a marketing invention. I know that a moment after the photo shoot was over, the beautiful room was dismantled, the models moved on to their next job, and the technicians took over the task of doctoring the photograph until it reached full-blown fantasy proportions. I know all that.

6   Not so Elaine. After months of living together and countless hours of watching her yearn after magazine images, soap-opera heroines, and rock goddesses, I have a pretty good idea of why she likes ads such as Claiborne's. She sees the way life—her life—is *supposed* to be. She sees a world characterized by sexual spontaneity, playfulness, and abandon. She sees people who don't worry about such unsexy details as birth control. Nor, apparently, do they spend much time thinking about such pedestrian topics as commitment or whether they should act on their sexual impulses. Their clean sunlit rooms are never invaded by the fear of AIDS, of unwanted pregnancy, of shattered lives. For all her apparent lack of defense, the girl on the couch in the Obsession ad will surely never experience the brutality of rape.

7   Years of exposure to this media-invented, sex-saturated universe have done their work on Elaine. She is, I'm sure, completely unaware of the irony in her situation: She melts over images from a sexual Shangri-la, never realizing that her attempts to mirror those images left her pregnant, abandoned, living in the spare bedroom of a stranger's house, relying on charity for rides to the welfare office and supervised visits with her toddler daughter.

8   Of course, Elaine is not the first to be suckered by the cynical practice of using sex to sell underwear, rock groups, or sneakers. Using sex as a sales tool is hardly new. At the beginning of this century, British actress Lily Langtry shocked her contemporaries by posing, clothed somewhat scantily, with a bar of Pear's soap. Advertisers have always known that the masses are susceptible to the notion that a particular product will make them more sexually attractive. In the past, though, ads used euphemisms, claiming that certain products would make people "more lovable" or "more popular." What is a recent development is the abandonment of any such polite double talk. Advertising today leaves no question about what is being sold along with the roasted

peanuts or artificial sweetener. "Tell us about your first time," coyly invites the innu-endo-filled magazine advertisement for Campari liquor. A billboard for Levi's shows two jeans-clad young men on the beach, hoisting a girl in the air. The boys' perfect, tan bodies are matched by hers, although we see a lot more of hers: bare midriff, short shorts, cleavage. She caresses their hair; they stroke her legs. A jolly gang-bang fantasy in the making. And a TV commercial promoting the Irish pop group The Cranberries blares nonstop the suggestive title of their latest album: "Everybody else is doing it, so why can't we?"

Indeed, just about everybody *is* doing it. Studies show that by the age of 20, 75 per- 9 cent of Americans have lost their virginity. In many high schools—and an increasing number of junior highs—virginity is regarded as an embarrassing vestige of childhood, to be disposed of as quickly as possible. Young people are immersed from their earliest days in a culture that parades sexuality at every turn and makes heroes of the advocates of sexual excess. Girls, from toddlerhood on up, shop in stores packed with clothing once thought suitable only for streetwalkers—lace leggings, crop tops, and wedge-heeled boots. Parents drop their children off at Madonna or Michael Jackson concerts, featuring simulated on-stage masturbation, or at Bobby Brown's show, where a fan drawn out of the audience is treated to a pretended act of copulation. Young boys idol-ize sports stars like Wilt Chamberlain, who claims to have bedded 20,000 women. And when the "Spur Posse," eight California high school athletes, were charged with systematically raping girls as young as 10 as part of a "scoring" ritual, the beefy young jocks were rewarded with a publicity tour of talk shows, while one father boasted to reporters about his son's "manhood."

In a late, lame attempt to counterbalance this sexual overload, most schools offer 10 sex education as part of their curriculums. (In 1995, forty-seven states recommended or required such courses.) But sex ed classes are heavy on the mechanics of fertiliza-tion and birth control—sperm, eggs, and condoms—and light on any discussion of sex-uality as only one part of a well-balanced life. There is passing reference to abstinence as a method of contraception, but little discussion of abstinence as an emotionally or spiritually satisfying option. Promiscuity is discussed for its role in spreading sexually transmitted diseases. But the concept of rejecting casual sex in favor of reserving sex for an emotionally intimate, exclusive, trusting relationship—much less any mention of waiting until marriage—is foreign to most public school settings. "Love and stuff like that really wasn't discussed" is the way one Spur Posse member remembers his high school sex education class.

Surely teenagers need the factual information provided by sex education courses. 11 But where is "love and stuff like that" talked about? Where can teens turn for a more balanced view of sexuality? Who is telling young people like Elaine, my former house-guest, that sex is not an adequate basis for a healthy, respectful relationship? Along with warnings to keep condoms on hand, is anyone teaching kids that they have a right to be valued for something other than their sexuality? Madison Avenue, Hollywood, and the TV, music, and fashion industries won't tell them that. Who will?

No one has told Elaine—at least, not in a way she comprehends. I haven't seen her 12 for a long time, but I hear of her occasionally. The baby boy she bore while living in my house is in a foster home, a few miles from his older half-sister, who is also in foster care. Elaine herself is working in a local convenience store—and she is pregnant again. This time, I understand, she is carrying twins.

Illustration   255

Questions for Close Reading

1. What is the selection's thesis? Locate the sentence(s) in which Garity states her main idea. If she doesn't state the thesis explicitly, express it in your own words.

2. Why would Elaine love the ads in the teen fashion magazines at Garity's beauty salon? Why doesn't Garity react to the ads as Elaine would? What, according to Garity, *don't* the ads tell us?

3. In Garity's opinion, how does our culture reinforce advertisements' sexually explicit messages?

4. Why, according to Garity, don't sex education courses refute our culture's distorted messages about sex and relationships? What does she believe schools *should* teach about sex?

5. Refer to your dictionary as needed to define the following words used in the selection: *waif* (paragraph 3), *croon* (4), *spontaneity* (6), *abandon* (6), *pedestrian* (6), *irony* (7), *euphemisms* (8), *innuendo* (8), *vestige* (9), *simulated* (9), *copulation* (9), *abstinence* (10), and *exclusive* (10).

Questions About the Writer's Craft

1. The pattern. The numerous examples that Garity provides in paragraphs 3–6 and 8–9 would have been sufficient to convey her central point. Why, then, do you think she decided to include the extended example about Elaine? What does this lengthy example add to the essay?

2. Other patterns. Garity reinforces her thesis by highlighting a number of contrasts. Identify three of these contrasts and explain how they underscore the author's central point.

3. Other patterns. Several cause-effect chains underlie Garity's essay. Identify some of these chains. How do they help Garity convey her thesis?

4. How would you characterize Garity's tone—and her attitude—toward her subject? How do Garity's sentence structure and word choices help to create this tone?

Writing Assignments Using Illustration as a Pattern of Development

1. Select a single aspect of American popular culture—for example, TV commercials, movies, magazine advertisements, or rock music—and write an essay supporting Garity's point that our society helps create irresponsible sexuality. Like Garity, provide a number of specific, highly detailed examples to illustrate your thesis. Before writing, read Ann McClintock's "Propaganda Techniques in Today's Advertising" (page 277), Pete Hamill's "Crack and the Box" (page 356), and Caryl Rivers's "What Should Be Done About Rock Lyrics?" (page 473); these essays will deepen your understanding of popular culture.

∞ **2.** Look closely at and reach some conclusions about the way advertisements and commercials depict a subject other than sex. You might, for example, examine media messages about any of the following: alcohol, academic success, the world of work, or parent-child relationships. Are the media images accurate, or are they distorted? Including persuasive examples of different ads and commercials, write an essay supporting your conclusion. To lend credibility to your analysis of advertising strategies, cite some points raised by Ann McClintock in "Propaganda Techniques in Today's Advertising" (page 277).

Writing Assignments Using Other Patterns of Development

3. Although she doesn't provide all the details, Garity indicates that Elaine and her children are on welfare. Recently, there has been strong sentiment nationwide to deny welfare payments to unmarried teenagers with more than one child. Read about this controversial issue in the library, and discuss it with friends, classmates, and family members. Then determine your position and support it in a persuasive essay. Try to refute as many of the opposing views as you can.

4. Brainstorm with others to discover ways our society might counteract the influence of what Garity calls our "sex-saturated" culture. Then write an essay showing the specific steps that parents or schools or communities or religious organizations could take to provide youngsters with a more balanced view of relationships and sex. Describe the steps in enough detail so that readers can fully understand the potentially positive effects these steps would have on children—and on society at large.

Illustration   257

ADDITIONAL
WRITING
TOPICS:
ILLUSTRATION

General Assignments

Use illustration to develop one of the following topics into a well-organized essay.

1. Many of today's drivers have dangerous habits.

2. Drug and alcohol abuse is (or is not) a serious problem among many young people.

3. One rule of restaurant dining is, "Management often seems oblivious to problems that are perfectly obvious to customers."

4. Children today are not encouraged to use their imaginations.

5. The best things in life are definitely not free.

6. A part-time job is an important experience that every college student should have.

7. Television commercials stereotype the elderly (or another minority group).

8. Today, salespeople act as if they're doing you a favor by taking your money.

9. Most people behave decently in their daily interactions with each other.

10. You can tell a lot about people by observing what they eat.

Assignments with a Specific Purpose, Audience, and Point of View

1. A friend of yours has taken a job in a big city or moved to a small town. To prepare your friend for this new environment, write a letter giving examples of what life in a big city or small town is like. You might focus on those benefits or dangers with which your friend is unlikely to be familiar.

2. Shopping for a new car, you become annoyed at how many safety features are available only as expensive options. Write a letter of complaint to the auto manufacturer, citing at least three examples of such options. Avoid sounding hostile.

3. Lately, many people at your college or workplace have been experiencing stress. As a member of the campus (or company) Committee on Morale, you've been asked to prepare a pamphlet illustrating different strategies for reducing stress. Decide what strategies you'll discuss and explain them with helpful examples.

4. Assume that you're an elementary school principal planning to give a speech in which you'll try to convince parents that television distorts children's perceptions of reality. Write the speech, illustrating your point with vivid examples.

5. A pet food company is having an annual contest to choose a new animal to feature in its advertising. To win the contest, you must convince the company that your pet is personable, playful, unique. Write an essay giving examples of your pet's special qualities.

6. For your college humor magazine, write an article on what you consider to be the "three best consumer products of the past twenty-five years." Support your opinion with lively, engaging specifics that are consistent with the magazine's offbeat and slightly ironic tone.

14
DIVISION-
CLASSIFICATION

WHAT IS DIVISION-CLASSIFICATION?

IMAGINE what life would be like if this were how an average day unfolded:

> You plan to stop at the supermarket for only a few items, but your marketing takes over an hour because all the items in the store are jumbled together. Clerks put new shipments anywhere they please; milk is with vegetables on Monday but with laundry detergent on Thursday. Next, you go to the drugstore to pick up some photos you left to be developed. You don't have time, though, to wait while the cashier roots through the large carton into which all the pick-up envelopes have been thrown. You return to your car and decide to stop at the town hall to pay a parking ticket. But the town hall baffles you. The offices are unmarked, and there isn't even a directory to tell you on which floor the Violations Bureau can be found. Annoyed, you get back into your car and, minutes later, end up colliding with another car that was driving toward you in your lane. When you wake up in the hospital, you find there are three other patients in your room: a middle-aged man with a heart problem, a young boy ready to have his tonsils removed, and a woman about to go into labor.

Such a muddled world, lacking the most basic forms of organization, would make daily life chaotic. All of us instinctively look for ways to order our environment. Without systems, categories, or sorting mechanisms, we would be overwhelmed by life's complexity. An organization like a college or university, for example, is made manageable by being divided into various schools (Liberal Arts, Performing Arts, Engineering, and so on). The schools are then separated into departments (English, History, Political Science), and each department's offerings are grouped into distinct categories—English, for instance, into Literature and Composition—before being further divided into specific courses.

The kind of ordering system we've been discussing is called **division-classification,** a way of thinking that allows us to make sense of a complex world.

Division and classification, though separate processes, often complement each other. **Division** involves taking a single unit or concept, breaking it down into parts, and then analyzing the connection among the parts and between the parts and the whole. For instance, if we wanted to organize the chaotic hospital described at the beginning of the chapter, we might think about how the single concept *hospital* could be broken down into its components. We might come up with the following breakdown: pediatric wing, cardiac wing, maternity wing, and so on.

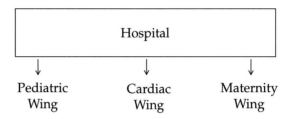

What we have just done involves division: We've taken a single entity (a hospital) and divided it into some of its component parts (wings), each with its own facilities and patients.

In contrast, **classification** brings two or more related items together and categorizes them according to type or kind. If the disorganized supermarket described earlier were to be restructured, the clerks would have to classify the separate items arriving at the store. Cartons of lettuce, tomatoes, cucumbers, butter, yogurt, milk, shampoo, conditioner, and setting lotion would be assigned to the appropriate categories:

HOW DIVISION-CLASSIFICATION FITS
YOUR PURPOSE AND AUDIENCE

The reorganized hospital and supermarket show the way division and classification work in everyday life. But division and classification also come into play during the writing process. Because division involves breaking a subject into parts, it can be a helpful strategy during prewriting, especially if you're analyzing a broad, complex subject: the structure of a film; the motivation of a character in a novel; the problem your community has with vandalism; the controversy surrounding school prayer. An editorial examining a recent hostage crisis, for example, might divide the crisis into three areas: how the hostages were treated by (1) their captors, (2) the governments negotiating their release, and (3) the media. The purpose of the editorial might be to show readers that the governments' treatment of the hostages was particularly exploitative.

Classification can be useful for imposing order on the hodgepodge of ideas generated during prewriting. You examine that material to see which of your rough ideas are alike and which are dissimilar, so that you can cluster related items in the same category. Classification would, then, be a helpful strategy when analyzing topics like these: techniques for impressing teachers; comic styles of talk-show hosts; views on abortion; reasons for the current rise in volunteerism. You might, for instance, use classification in a paper showing that Americans are undermining their health through their obsessive pursuit of various diets. Perhaps you begin by brainstorming all the diets that have gained popularity in recent years (Weight Watchers, Slim-Fast, Jenny Craig, whatever). Then you categorize the diets according to type: high fiber, low protein, high carbohydrate, and so on. Once the diets are grouped, you can discuss the problems within each category, demonstrating to readers that none of the diets is safe or effective.

Division-classification can be crucial when responding to college assignments like the following:

> Based on your observations, what kinds of appeals do television advertisers use when selling automobiles? In your view, are any of these appeals morally irresponsible?

> Analyze the components that go into being an effective parent. Indicate those you consider most vital for raising confident, well-adjusted children.

> Describe the hierarchy of the typical high school clique, identifying the various parts of the hierarchy. Use your analysis to support or refute the view that adolescence is a period of rigid conformity.

> Many social commentators have observed that discourtesy is on the rise. Indicate whether you think this is a valid observation by characterizing the types of everyday encounters you have with people.

These assignments suggest division-classification through the use of such words as *kinds, components, parts,* and *types.* Generally, though, you won't receive such clear signals to use division-classification. Instead, the broad purpose of the essay—and the point you want to make—will lead you to the analytical thinking characteristic of division-classification.

Sometimes division-classification will be the dominant technique for structuring an essay; other times it will be used as a supplemental pattern in an essay organized primarily according to another pattern of development. Let's look at some examples. Say you want to write a paper *explaining a process* (surviving divorce; creating a hit recording; shepherding a bill through Congress; using the Heimlich maneuver on people who are choking). You could *divide* the process into parts or stages, showing, for instance, that the Heimlich maneuver is an easily mastered skill that readers should acquire. Or imagine you plan to write a light-spirited essay analyzing the *effect* that increased awareness of sexual stereotypes has had on college students' social lives. In such a case, you might use *classification*. To show readers that shifting gender roles make young men and women comically self-conscious, you could categorize the places where students scout each other out: in class, at the library, at parties, in dorms. You could then show how students—not wishing to be macho or coyly feminine—approach each other with laughable tentativeness in these four environments.

Now imagine that you're writing an *argumentation-persuasion* essay urging that the federal government prohibit the use of growth-inducing antibiotics in livestock feed. The paper could begin by *dividing* the antibiotics cycle into stages: the effects of antibiotics on livestock; the short-term effects on humans who consume the animals; the possible long-term effects of consuming antibiotic-tainted meat. To increase readers' understanding of the problem, you might also discuss the antibiotics controversy in terms of an even larger issue: the dangerous ways food is treated before being consumed. In this case, you would consider the various procedures (use of additives, preservatives, artificial colors, and so on), *classifying* these treatments into several types—from least harmful (some additives or artificial colors, perhaps) to most harmful (you might slot the antibiotics here). Such an essay would be developed using both division *and* classification: first, the division of the antibiotics cycle and then the classification of the various food treatments. Frequently, this interdependence will be reversed, and classification will precede rather than follow division.

PREWRITING STRATEGIES

The following checklist shows how you can apply to division-classification some of the prewriting techniques discussed in Chapter 2.

☑ DIVISION-CLASSIFICATION: A PREWRITING CHECKLIST

Choose a Subject to Analyze

☐ What fairly complex subject (sibling rivalry, religious cults) can be made more understandable through division-classification?

☐ Will you divide a single entity or concept (domestic violence) into parts (toward spouse, parent, or child)? Will you classify a number of similar things (college courses) into categories (easy, of average difficulty, tough)? Or will you use both division and classification?

Determine Your Purpose, Audience, Tone, and Point of View

☐ What is the purpose of your analysis?

☐ Toward what audience will you direct your explanations?

☐ What tone and point of view will make readers receptive to your explanation?

> *Use Prewriting to Generate Material on Parts or Types*
>
> ☐ How can brainstorming, mapping, or any other prewriting technique help you divide your subject into parts? What differences or similarities among parts will you emphasize?
>
> ☐ How can brainstorming, mapping, or any other prewriting technique help you categorize your subjects? What differences or similarities among categories will you emphasize?
>
> ☐ How can the patterns of development help you generate material about your subjects' parts or categories? How can you describe the parts or categories? What can you narrate about them? What examples illustrate them? What process do they help explain? How can they be compared or contrasted? What causes them? What are their effects? How can they be defined? What arguments do they support?

STRATEGIES FOR USING DIVISION-CLASSIFICATION IN AN ESSAY

After prewriting, you're ready to draft your essay. The following suggestions will be helpful whether you use division-classification as a dominant or supportive pattern of development.

1. Select a principle of division-classification consistent with your purpose. Most subjects can be divided or classified according to *several different principles.* For example, when writing about an ideal vacation, you could divide your subject according to any of these principles: location, cost, recreation available. Similarly, when analyzing students at your college, you could base your classification on a variety of principles: students' majors, their racial or ethnic background, whether they belong to a fraternity or sorority. In all cases, though, the principle of division-classification you select must meet one stringent requirement: It must help you meet your overall purpose and reinforce your central point.

Sometimes a principle of division-classification seems so attractive that you latch on to it without examining whether it's consistent with your purpose. Suppose you want to write a paper asserting that several episodes of a new television comedy are destined to become classics. Here's how you might go wrong. You begin by doing some brainstorming about the episodes. Then, as you start to organize the prewriting material, you hit upon a possible principle of classification: grouping the characters in the show according to the frequency with which they appear (main characters appearing in every show, supporting characters appearing in most shows, and guest characters appearing once or twice). You name the characters and explain which characters fit where. But is this principle of classification significant? Has it anything to do with why the shows will become classics? No, it hasn't. Such an essay would be little more than a meaningless exercise.

In contrast, a significant principle of classification might involve categorizing a number of shows according to the easily recognized human types portrayed: the Pompous Know-It-All, the Boss Who's Out of Control, the Lovable Grouch, the Surprisingly Savvy Innocent. You might illustrate the way certain episodes offer delightful twists on these stock figures, making such shows models of comic plotting and humor.

When you write an essay that uses division-classification as its primary method of development, a *single principle* of division-classification provides the foundation for each major section of the paper. Imagine you're writing an essay showing that the success of contemporary music groups has less to do with musical talent than with the group's ability to market themselves to a distinct segment of the listening audience. To develop your point, you might categorize several performers according to the age ranges they appeal to (preteens, adolescents, people in their late twenties) and then analyze the marketing strategies the musicians use to gain their fans' support. The essay's logic would be undermined if you switched, in the middle of your analysis, to another principle of classification—say, the influence of earlier groups on today's music scene.

Don't, however, take this caution to mean that essays can never use more than one principle of division-classification as they unfold. They can—as long as the *shift from one principle to another* occurs in *different parts* of the paper. Imagine you want to write about widespread disillusionment with student government leaders at your college. You could develop this point by breaking down the dissatisfaction into the following: disappointment with the students' qualifications for office; disenchantment with their campaign tactics; frustration with their performance once elected. That section of the essay completed, you might move to a second principle of division—how students can get involved in campus government. Perhaps you break the proposed involvement into the following possibilities: serving on nominating committees; helping to run candidates' campaigns; attending open sessions of the student government.

2. Apply the principle of division-classification logically. In an essay using division-classification, you need to demonstrate to readers that your analysis is the result of careful thought. First of all, your division-classification should be as *complete* as possible. Your analysis should include—within reason—all the parts into which you can divide your subject, or all the types into which you can categorize your subjects. Let's say you're writing an essay showing that where college students live is an important factor in determining how satisfied they are with college life. Keeping your purpose in mind, you classify students according to where they live: with parents, in dorms, in fraternity and sorority houses. But what about all the students who live in rented apartments, houses, or rooms off campus? If these places of residence are ignored, your classification won't be complete; you will lose credibility with your readers because they'll probably realize that you have overlooked several important considerations.

Your division-classification should also be *consistent:* the parts into which you break your subject or the groups into which you place your subjects should be as mutually exclusive as possible. The parts or categories should not be mixed, nor should they overlap. Assume you're writing an essay describing the animals at the zoo in a nearby city. You decide to describe the zoo's mammals, reptiles, birds, and endangered species. But such a classification is inconsistent. You begin by cat-egorizing the animals according to scientific class (mammals, birds, reptiles), then switch to another principle when you classify some animals according to whether they are endangered. Because you drift over to a different principle of classifica-tion, your categories are no longer mutually exclusive: endangered species could overlap with any of the other categories. In which section of the paper, for instance, would you describe an exotic parrot that is obviously a bird but is also nearly extinct? And how would you categorize the zoo's rare mountain gorilla? This impressive creature is a mammal, but it is also an endangered species. Such overlapping categories undercut the logic that gives an essay its integrity.

3. Prepare an effective thesis. If your essay uses division-classification as its dom-inant method of development, it might be helpful to prepare a thesis that does more than signal the paper's subject and suggest your attitude toward that sub-ject. You might also want the thesis to state the principle of division-classification at the heart of the essay. Furthermore, you might want the thesis to reveal which part or category you regard as most important.

Consider the two thesis statements that follow:

Thesis 1

`As the observant beachcomber moves from the tidal area to the upper beach to the sandy dunes, rich variations in marine life become apparent.`

Thesis 2

`Although most people focus on the dangers associated with the dis-posal of toxic waste in the land and ocean, the incineration of toxic matter may pose an even more serious threat to human life.`

The first thesis statement makes clear that the writer will organize the paper by classifying forms of marine life according to location. Since the purpose of the essay is to inform as objectively as possible, the thesis doesn't suggest the writer's opinion about which category is most significant.

The second thesis signals that the essay will evolve by dividing the issue of toxic waste according to methods of disposal. Moreover, because the paper takes a stance on a controversial subject, the thesis is worded to reveal which aspect of the topic the writer considers most important. Such a clear statement of the writer's position is an effective strategy in an essay of this kind.

You may have noted that each thesis statement also signals the paper's plan of development. The first essay, for example, will use specific facts, examples, and details to describe the kinds of marine life found in the tidal area, upper beach, and dunes. However, thesis statements in papers developed primarily through division-classification don't have to be so structured. If a paper is well written, your principle of division-classification, your opinion about which part or category is most important, and the essay's plan of development will become apparent as the essay unfolds.

4. Organize the paper logically. Whether your paper is developed wholly or in part by division-classification, it should have a logical structure. As much as possible, you should try to discuss *comparable points* in each section of the paper. In the essay on seashore life, for example, you might describe life in the tidal area by discussing the mollusks, crustaceans, birds, and amphibians that live or feed there. You would then follow through, as much as possible, with this arrangement in the paper's other sections (upper beach and dunes). Forgetting to describe the birdlife thriving in the dunes, especially when you had discussed birdlife in the tidal and upper-beach areas, would compromise the paper's structure. Of course, perfect parallelism is not always possible—there are no mollusks in the dunes, for instance. You should also use *signal devices* to connect various parts of the paper: "*Another* characteristic of marine life battered by the tides"; "A *final* important trait of both tidal and upper-beach crustaceans"; "*Unlike* the creatures of the tidal area and the upper beach." Such signals clarify the connections among the essay's ideas.

5. State any conclusions or recommendations in the paper's final section. The analytic thinking that occurs during division-classification often leads to surprising insights. Such insights may be introduced early on, or they may be reserved for the end, where they are stated as conclusions or recommendations. A paper might categorize different kinds of coaches—from inspiring to incompetent—and make the point that athletes learn a great deal about human relations simply by having to get along with their coaches, regardless of the coaches' skills. Such a paper might conclude that participation in a team sport teaches more about human nature than several courses in psychology. Or the essay might end with a proposal: Rookies and seasoned team members should be paired, so that novice players can get advice on dealing with coaching eccentricities.

REVISION STRATEGIES

Once you have a draft of the essay, you're ready to revise. The following checklist will help you and those giving you feedback apply to division-classification some of the revision techniques discussed in Chapters 7 and 8.

 DIVISION-CLASSIFICATION: A REVISION CHECKLIST

Revise Overall Meaning and Structure

☐ What is the principle of division-classification at the heart of the essay? How does this principle contribute to the essay's overall purpose and thesis?

□ Does the thesis state the essay's principle of division-classification? Should it? Does the thesis signal which part or category is most important? Should it? Does the thesis reveal the essay's plan of development? Should it?

□ Is the essay organized primarily through division, classification, or a blend of both?

□ If the essay is organized mainly through division, is the subject sufficiently broad and complex to be broken down into parts? What are the parts?

□ If the essay is organized mainly through classification, what are the categories? How does this categorizing reveal similarities and/or differences that would otherwise not be apparent?

Revise Paragraph Development

□ Are comparable points discussed in each of the paper's sections? What are these points?

□ In which paragraphs does the division-classification seem illogical, incomplete, or inconsistent? In which paragraphs are parts or categories not clearly explained?

□ Are the subject's different parts or categories discussed in separate paragraphs? Should they be?

□ What conclusions or recommendations are stated or implied in the closing paragraph(s)?

Revise Sentences and Words

□ What signal devices ("Another characteristic"; "A third type"; "The most important trait") help integrate the paper? Are there enough signals? Too many?

□ Where should sentences and words be made more concrete and specific in order to clarify the parts and categories being discussed?

STUDENT ESSAY: FROM PREWRITING THROUGH REVISION

The student essay that follows was written by Gail Oremland in response to this assignment:

In "Propaganda Techniques in Today's Advertising," Ann McClintock describes the flaws in many of the persuasive strategies used by advertisers. Choose another group of people whose job is also to communicate—for example, parents, bosses, teachers. Then, in an essay of your own, divide the group into types according to the flaws they reveal when communicating.

Gail wanted to prepare a light-spirited paper about college professors' foibles. Right from the start, she decided to focus on three kinds of professors: the "Knowledgeable One," the "Leader of Intellectual Discussion," and the "Buddy." She used the *patterns of development* to generate prewriting material about each kind, typing whatever ideas came to mind as she focused on one pattern at a time. Reprinted here is Gail's prewriting for the Knowledgeable One. Note that not every pattern sparked ideas. When Gail later reviewed her prewriting, she added some details and deleted others. The handwritten marks on the prewriting indicate Gail's later efforts to refine her rough material.

After annotating her prewriting for all the categories, Gail prepared her first draft, without shaping her prewriting further or making an outline. As she wrote, though, she frequently referred to her warm-up material to retrieve specifics about each professorial type.

Prewriting Using the Patterns of Development

Knowledgeable One

Even in a blizzard or hurricane — **Narration**: Enters, walks to podium, puts notes on stand, begins lecture exactly on schedule. Talks on and on, stating facts. ~~Even when she had a cold, she kept on lecturing, although we could hardly hear her and her voice kept cracking.~~ Always ends lecture exactly on time. Packs her notes. Hurries away. *Shoots out the back door. Back to the privacy of her office, away from students.*

Description: Self-important air, yellowed notes, all weather, drones, students' glazed eyes, yawns

Doesn't stop, so students feel they can't interrupt — **Cause-Effect**: Thinks she's an expert and that students are ignorant, so students are intimidated. States one dry fact after another, so students get bored. Addresses students as "Mr." or "Miss," so she establishes distance.

Definition: A fact person

Illustration: History prof who knows death toll of every battle; biology prof who knows all the molecules; accounting prof who knows every clause of tax form

Comparison-Contrast: Interest in specialized academic area vs. no interest in students

Now read Gail's paper, "The Truth About College Teachers," noting the similarities and differences between her prewriting and final essay. As you may imagine, the patterns of development that yielded the most details during prewriting became especially prominent in the final essay. Note, too, that Gail's prewriting consisted of unconnected details within each pattern, whereas the essay flows easily. To achieve such coherence, Gail used commentary and transitional phrases to connect the prewriting details. As you read the essay, also consider how well it applies the principles of division-classification discussed in this chapter. (The commentary that follows the paper will help you look at the essay more closely and will give you some sense of how Gail went about revising her first draft.)

The Truth About College Teachers
by Gail Oremland

1   A recent TV news story told about a group of college professors from a nearby university who were hired by a local school system to help upgrade the teaching in the community's public schools. The professors were to visit classrooms, analyze teachers' skills, and then conduct workshops to help the teachers become more effective at their jobs. But after the first round of workshops, the superintendent of schools decided to cancel the whole project. He fired the learned professors and sent them back to their ivory tower. Why did the project fall apart? There was a simple reason. The college professors, who were supposedly going to show the public school teachers how to be more effective, were themselves poor teachers. Many college students could have predicted such a disastrous outcome. They know, firsthand, that college teachers are strange. They know that professors often exhibit bizarre behaviors, relating to students in ways that make it difficult for students to stay awake, or—if awake—to learn.

2   One type of professor assumes, legitimately enough, that her function is to pass on to students the vast store of knowledge she has acquired. But because the "Knowledgeable One" regards herself as an expert and her students as the ignorant masses, she adopts an elitist approach that sabotages learning. The Knowledgeable One enters a lecture hall with a self-important air, walks to the podium, places her yellowed-with-age notes on the stand, and begins her lecture at the exact second the class is officially scheduled to begin. There can be a blizzard or hurricane raging outside the lecture hall; students can be running through freezing sleet and howling winds

Introduction

Thesis

Topic sentence

The first of three paragraphs on the first category of teacher

The first paragraph in a three-part chronological sequence: What happens before *class*

to get to class on time. Will the Knowledgeable One wait for them to arrive before beginning her lecture? Probably not. The Knowledgeable One's time is precious. She's there, set to begin, and that's what matters.

Topic sentence ———————→ Once the monologue begins, the Knowledgeable One drones on   3
and on. The Knowledgeable One is a fact person. She may be the

The second para-
graph on the first
category of teacher
history prof who knows the death toll of every Civil War battle, the biology prof who can diagram all the common biological molecules, the accounting prof who enumerates every clause of the federal tax form. Oblivious to students' glazed eyes and stifled yawns, the Knowledgeable One delivers her monologue, dispensing one dry fact after another. The only advantage to being on the receiving end of this boring monologue is that students do not have to worry about being called on to question

The second
paragraph in the
chronological
sequence: What
happens *during*
class
a point or provide an opinion; the Knowledgeable One is not willing to relinquish one minute of her time by giving students a voice. Assume for one improbable moment that a student actually manages to stay awake during the monologue and is brave enough to ask a question. In such a case, the Knowledgeable One will address the questioning student as "Mr." or "Miss." This formality does not, as some students mistakenly suppose, indicate respect for the student as a fledgling member of the academic community. Not at all. This impersonality represents the Knowledgeable One's desire to keep as wide a distance as possible between her and her students.

Topic sentence ———————→ The Knowledgeable One's monologue always comes to a   4
close at the precise second the class is scheduled to end. No sooner has she delivered her last forgettable word than the

The third
paragraph on the
first category of
teacher

The final
paragraph in the
chronological
sequence: What
happens *after* class
Knowledgeable One packs up her notes and shoots out the door, heading back to the privacy of her office, where she can pursue her specialized academic interests--free of any possible interruption from students. The Knowledgeable One's hasty departure from the lecture hall makes it clear she has no desire to talk with students. In her eyes, she has met her obligations; she has taken time away from her research to transmit to students what she knows. Any closer contact might mean she would risk contagion from students, that great unwashed mass. Such a danger is to be avoided at all costs.

5   Unlike the Knowledgeable One, the "Leader of Intellectual
Discussion" seems to respect students. Emphasizing class
discussion, the Leader encourages students to confront ideas
("What is Twain's view of morality?" "Was our intervention in
Vietnam justified?" "Should big business be given tax breaks?")
and discover their own truths. Then, about three weeks into the   — Topic sentence
semester, it becomes clear that the Leader wants students to
discover his version of the truth. Behind the Leader's demo-   Paragraph on the
cratic guise lurks a dictator. When a student voices an opinion   second category of
that the Leader accepts, the student is rewarded by hearty nods   teacher
of approval and "Good point, good point." But if a student
is rash enough to advance a conflicting viewpoint, the Leader
responds with killing politeness: "Well, yes, that's an interesting perspective. But don't you think that . . .?" Grade-
conscious students soon learn not to chime in with their viewpoint. They know that when the Leader, with seeming honesty,
says, "I'd be interested in hearing what you think. Let's open
this up for discussion," they had better figure out what the
Leader wants to hear before advancing their own theories.
"Me-tooism" rather than independent thinking, they discover,
guarantees good grades in the Leader's class.

6   Then there is the professor who comes across as the stu-   Topic sentence
dents' "Buddy." This kind of professor does not see himself as
an imparter of knowledge or a leader of discussion but as a pal,   Paragraph on the
just one in a community of equals. The Buddy may start his   third category of
course this way: "All of us know that this college stuff--   teacher
grades, degrees, exams, required reading--is a game. So let's
not play it, okay?" Dressed in jeans, sweatshirt, and scuffed
sneakers, the Buddy projects a relaxed, casual attitude. He
arranges the class seats in a circle (he would never take a
position in front of the room) and insists that students call
him by his first name. He uses no syllabus and gives few tests,
believing that such constraints keep students from directing
their own learning. A free spirit, the Buddy often teaches
courses like "The Psychology of Interpersonal Relations" or
"The Social Dynamics of the Family." If students choose to use
class time to discuss the course material, that's fine. If they
want to discuss something else, that's fine, too. It's the
self-expression, the honest dialog, that counts. In fact, the

Buddy seems especially fond of digressions from academic
subjects. By talking about his political views, his marital
problems, his tendency to drink one too many beers, the Buddy
lets students see that he is a regular guy--just like them.
At first, students look forward to classes with the Buddy. They
enjoy the informality, the chitchat, the lack of pressure.
But after a while, they wonder why they are paying for a course
where they learn nothing. They might as well stay home and
watch the soaps.

Conclusion   Obviously, some college professors are excellent. They are   7
learned, hardworking, and imaginative; they enjoy their work
and like being with students. On the whole, though, college
Echoes opening   professors are a strange lot. Despite their advanced degrees
anecdote   and their own exposure to many different kinds of teachers,
they do not seem to understand how to relate to students.
Rather than being hired as consultants to help others upgrade
their teaching skills, college professors should themselves
hire consultants to tell them what they are doing wrong and how
they can improve. Who should these consultants be? That's easy:
the people who know them best--their students.

Commentary

Introduction and Thesis

After years of being graded by teachers, Gail took special pleasure in writing an
essay that gave her a chance to evaluate her teachers—in this case, her college professors. Even the essay's title, "The Truth About College Teachers," implies that
Gail is going to have fun knocking profs down from their ivory towers. To introduce her subject, she uses a timely news story. This brief anecdote leads directly to
the essay's *thesis:* "Professors often exhibit bizarre behaviors, relating to students
in ways that make it difficult for students to stay awake, or—if awake—to learn."
Note that Gail's thesis isn't highly structured; it doesn't, for example, name the
specific categories to be discussed. Still, her thesis suggests that the essay is going
to *categorize* a range of teaching behaviors, using as a *principle of classification* the
strange ways that college profs relate to students.

Purpose

As with all good papers developed through division-classification, Gail's essay
doesn't use classification as an end in itself. Gail uses classification because it

helps her achieve a broader *purpose*. She wants to *convince* readers—without moralizing or abandoning her humorous tone—that such teaching styles inhibit learning. In other words, there's a serious undertone to her essay. This additional layer of meaning is characteristic of satiric writing.

Categories and Topic Sentences

The essay's body, consisting of five paragraphs, presents the three categories that make up Gail's analysis. According to Gail, college teachers can be categorized as the Knowledgeable One (paragraphs 2–4), the Leader of Intellectual Discussion (5), or the Buddy (6). Obviously, there are other ways professors might be classified. But given Gail's purpose, audience, tone, and point of view, her categories are appropriate; they are reasonably *complete, consistent,* and *mutually exclusive*. Note, too, that Gail uses *topic sentences* near the beginning of each category to help readers see which professorial type she's discussing.

Overall Organization and Paragraph Structure

Gail is able to shift smoothly and easily from one category to the next. How does she achieve such graceful transitions? Take a moment to reread the sentences that introduce her second and third categories (paragraphs 5 and 6). Look at the way each sentence's beginning (in italics here) links back to the preceding category or categories: "*Unlike the Knowledgeable One,* the 'Leader of Intellectual Discussion' seems to respect students"; and the "Buddy...*does not see himself as an imparter of knowledge or a leader of discussion* but as a pal...."

Gail is equally careful about providing an easy-to-follow structure within each section. She uses a *chronological sequence* to organize her three-paragraph discussion of the Knowledgeable One. The first paragraph deals with the beginning of the Knowledgeable One's lecture; the second, with the lecture itself; the third, with the end of the lecture. And the paragraphs' *topic sentences* clearly indicate this passage of time. Similarly, *transitions* are used in the paragraphs on the Leader of Intellectual Discussion and the Buddy to ensure a logical progression of points: "*Then,* about three weeks into the semester, it becomes clear that the Leader wants students to discover *his* version of the truth" (5), and "*At first,* students look forward to classes with the Buddy.... But *after a while,* they wonder why they are paying for a course where they learn nothing" (6).

Tone

The essay's unity can also be traced to Gail's skill in sustaining her satiric tone. Throughout the essay, Gail selects details that fit her gently mocking attitude. She depicts the Knowledgeable One lecturing from "yellowed-with-age notes..., oblivious to students' glazed eyes and stifled yawns," unwilling to wait for students who "run...through freezing sleet and howling winds to get to class on time." Then she presents another tongue-in-cheek description, this one focusing on the way the Leader of Intellectual Discussion conducts class: "Good point, good point.... Well, yes, that's an interesting perspective. But don't you think that…?" Finally, with similar killing accuracy, Gail portrays the Buddy, democratically garbed in "jeans, sweatshirt, and scuffed sneakers."

Other Patterns of Development

Gail's satiric depiction of her three professorial types employs a number of techniques associated with *narrative* and *descriptive writing:* vigorous images, highly connotative language, and dialog. *Definition, illustration, causal analysis,* and *comparison-contrast* also come into play. Gail defines the characteristics of each type of professor; she provides numerous examples to support her categories; she explains the effects of the different teaching styles on students; and, in her description of the Leader of Intellectual Discussion, she contrasts the appearance of democracy with the dictatorial reality.

Unequal Development of Categories

Although Gail's essay is unified, organized, and well developed, you may have felt that the first category outweighs the other two. There is, of course, no need to balance the categories exactly. But Gail's extended treatment of the first category sets up an expectation that the others will be treated as fully. One way to remedy this problem would be to delete some material from the discussion of the Knowledgeable One. Gail might, for instance, omit the first five sentences in the third paragraph (about the professor's habit of addressing students as Mr. or Miss). Such a change could be made without taking the bite out of her portrayal. Even better, Gail could simply switch the order of her sections, putting the portrait of the Knowledgeable One at the essay's end. Here, the extended discussion wouldn't seem out of proportion. Instead, the sections would appear in *emphatic order,* with the most detailed category saved for last.

Revising the First Draft

It's apparent that an essay as engaging as Gail's must have undergone a good deal of revising. Along the way, Gail made many changes in her draft, but it's particularly interesting to see how she changed her original introduction (reprinted here). The annotation represents her general impressions of the paragraph's problems.

Original Version of the Introduction

Too serious.
Doesn't fit rest
of essay.

Despite their high IQs, advanced degrees, and published papers, some college professors just don't know how to teach. Found almost in any department, in tenured and untenured positions, they prompt student apathy. They fail to convey ideas effectively and to challenge or inspire students. Students thus finish their courses having learned very little. Contrary to popular opinion, these professors' ineptitude is not simply

```
a matter of delivering boring lectures or not caring about
students. Many of them care a great deal. Their
failure actually stems from their unrealistic perceptions
of what a teacher should be. Specifically, they adopt teaching
styles or roles that alienate students and undermine
learning. Three of the most common ones are "The Knowledgeable
One," "The Leader of Intellectual Discussion," and "The Buddy."
```

When Gail showed the first draft of the essay to her composition instructor, he laughed—and occasionally squirmed—as he read what she had prepared. He was enthusiastic about the paper but felt there was a problem with the introduction's tone; it was too serious when compared to the playful, lightly satiric mood of the rest of the essay. When Gail reread the paragraph, she agreed, but she was uncertain about the best way to remedy the problem. After revising other sections of the essay, she decided to let the paper sit for a while before going back to rewrite the introduction.

In the meantime, Gail switched on the TV. The timing couldn't have been better; she tuned into a news story about several supposedly learned professors who had been fired from a consulting job because they had turned out to know so little about teaching. This was exactly the kind of item Gail needed to start her essay. Now she was able to prepare a completely new introduction, making it consistent in spirit with the rest of the paper.

With this stronger introduction and the rest of the essay well in hand, Gail was ready to write a conclusion. Now, as she worked on the concluding paragraph, she deliberately shaped it to recall the story about the fired consultants. By echoing the opening anecdote in her conclusion, Gail was able to end the paper with another poke at professors—a perfect way to close her clever and insightful essay.

ACTIVITIES: DIVISION-CLASSIFICATION

Prewriting Activities

1. Imagine you're writing two essays: One is a humorous paper showing how to impress college instructors; the other is a serious essay explaining why volunteerism is on the rise. What about the topics might you divide and/or classify?

2. Use group brainstorming to identify at least three possible principles of division for *one* of the following topics. For each principle, determine what your thesis might be if you were writing an essay.

  a. Prejudice
  b. Rock music
  c. A shopping mall
  d. A good horror movie

3. Through group brainstorming, identify three different principles of classification that might provide the structure for an essay about the possible effects of a controversial decision to expand your college's enrollment. Focusing on one of the principles, decide what your thesis might be. How would you sequence the categories?

Revising Activities

4. Following is a scratch outline for an essay developed through division-classification. On what principle of division-classification is the essay based? What problem do you see in the way the principle is applied? How could the problem be remedied?

Thesis: The same experience often teaches opposite things to different people.

- What working as a fast-food cook teaches: Some learn responsibility; others learn to take a "quick and dirty" approach.

- What a negative experience teaches optimists: Some learn from their mistakes; others continue to maintain a positive outlook.

- What a difficult course teaches: Some learn to study hard; others learn to avoid demanding courses.

- What the breakup of a close relationship teaches: Some learn how to negotiate differences; others learn to avoid intimacy.

5. Following is a paragraph from the first draft of an essay urging that day-care centers adopt play programs tailored to children's developmental needs. What principle of division-classification focuses the paragraph? Is the principle applied consistently and logically? Are parts/categories developed sufficiently? Revise the paragraph, eliminating any problems you discover and adding specific details where needed.

Within a few years, preschool children move from self-absorbed to interactive play. Babies and toddlers engage in solitary play. Although they sometimes prefer being near other children, they focus

primarily on their own actions. This is very different from the
highly interactive play of the elementary school years. Sometime
in children's second year, solitary play is replaced by parallel
play, during which children engage in similar activities near one
another. However, they interact only occasionally. By age three,
most children show at least some cooperative play, a form that
involves interaction and cooperative role-taking. Such role-taking
can be found in the "pretend" games that children play to explore
adult relationships (games of "Mommy and Daddy") and anatomy (games
of "Doctor"). Additional signs of youngsters' growing awareness of
peers can be seen at about age four. At this age, many children
begin showing a special devotion to one other child and may want to
play only with that child. During this time, children also begin to
take special delight in physical activities such as running and
jumping, often going off by themselves to expend their abundant
physical energy.

PROFESSIONAL
SELECTIONS:
DIVISION-CLASSIFICATION

ANN McCLINTOCK

Formerly Director of Occupational Therapy at Ancora State Hospital in New Jersey,
Ann McClintock (1946–) has also worked as a free-lance writer and editor. She speaks
frequently to community groups about the effects of advertising on American life. The
following essay, revised for this collection, is part of a work-in-progress about the use of
propaganda techniques in the marketing of products and candidates.

PROPAGANDA TECHNIQUES
IN TODAY'S ADVERTISING

1   Americans, adults and children alike, are being seduced. They are being brainwashed. And few of us protest. Why? Because the seducers and the brainwashers are
the advertisers we willingly invite into our homes. We are victims, content—even

eager—to be victimized. We read advertisers' propaganda messages in newspapers and magazines; we watch their alluring images on television. We absorb their messages and images into our subconscious. We all do it—even those of us who claim to see through advertisers' tricks and therefore feel immune to advertising's charm. Advertisers lean heavily on propaganda to sell their products, whether the "products" are a brand of toothpaste, a candidate for office, or a particular political viewpoint.

Propaganda is a systematic effort to influence people's opinions, to win them over to a certain view or side. Propaganda is not necessarily concerned with what is true or false, good or bad. Propagandists simply want people to believe the messages being sent. Often propagandists will use outright lies or more subtle deceptions to sway people's opinions. In a propaganda war, any tactic is considered fair.

When we hear the word "propaganda," we usually think of a foreign menace: anti-American radio programs broadcast by a totalitarian regime or brainwashing tactics practiced on hostages. Although propaganda may seem relevant only in the political arena, the concept can be applied fruitfully to the way products and ideas are sold in advertising. Indeed, the vast majority of us are targets in advertisers' propaganda war. Every day, we are bombarded with slogans, print ads, commercials, packaging claims, billboards, trademarks, logos, and designer brands—all forms of propaganda. One study reports that each of us, during an average day, is exposed to over *five hundred* advertising claims of various types. This saturation may even increase in the future since current trends include ads on movie screens, shopping carts, video cassettes, even public television.

What kind of propaganda techniques do advertisers use? There are seven basic types:

1. *Name Calling*   Name calling is a propaganda tactic in which negatively charged names are hurled against the opposing side or competitor. By using such names, propagandists try to arouse feelings of mistrust, fear, and hate in their audiences. For example, a political advertisement may label an opposing candidate a "loser," "fence-sitter," or "warmonger." Depending on the advertiser's target market, labels such as "a friend of big business" or "a dues-paying member of the party in power" can be the epithets that damage an opponent. Ads for products may also use name calling. An American manufacturer may refer, for instance, to a "foreign car" in its commercial—not an "imported" one. The label of foreignness will have unpleasant connotations in many people's minds. A childhood rhyme claims that "names can never hurt me," but name calling is an effective way to damage the opposition, whether it is another car maker or a congressional candidate.

2. *Glittering Generalities*   Using glittering generalities is the opposite of name calling. In this case, advertisers surround their products with attractive—and slippery—words and phrases. They use vague terms that are difficult to define and that may have different meanings to different people: *freedom, democratic, all-American, progressive, Christian,* and *justice.* Many such words have strong, affirmative overtones. This kind of language stirs positive feelings in people, feelings that may spill over to the product or idea being pitched. As with name calling, the emotional response may overwhelm logic. Target audiences accept the product without thinking very much about what the glittering generalities mean—or whether they even apply to the product. After all, how can anyone oppose "truth, justice, and the American way"?

7   The ads for politicians and political causes often use glittering generalities because such "buzz words" can influence votes. Election slogans include high-sounding but basically empty phrases like the following:

"He cares about people." (That's nice, but is he a better candidate than his opponent?)

"Vote for progress." (Progress by *whose* standards?)

"They'll make this country great again." (What does "great" mean? Does "great" mean the same thing to others as it does to me?)

"Vote for the future." (What kind of future?)

"If you love America, vote for Phyllis Smith." (If I don't vote for Smith, does that mean I don't love America?)

8   Ads for consumer goods are also sprinkled with glittering generalities. Product names, for instance, are supposed to evoke good feelings: *Luvs* diapers, *New Freedom* feminine hygiene products, *Joy* liquid detergent, *Loving Care* hair color, *Almost Home* cookies, *Yankee Doodle* pastries. Product slogans lean heavily on vague but comforting phrases: Kinney is "The Great American Shoe Store," General Electric "brings good things to life," and Dow Chemical "lets you do great things." Chevrolet, we are told, is the "heartbeat of America," and Chrysler boasts cars that are "built by Americans for Americans."

9   3. *Transfer*   In transfer, advertisers try to improve the image of a product by associating it with a symbol most people respect, like the American flag or Uncle Sam. The advertisers hope that the prestige attached to the symbol will carry over to the product. Many companies use transfer devices to identify their products: Lincoln Insurance shows a profile of the President; Continental Insurance portrays a Revolutionary War minuteman; Amtrak's logo is red, white, and blue; Liberty Mutual's corporate symbol is the Statue of Liberty; Allstate's name is cradled by a pair of protective, fatherly hands.

10   Corporations also use the transfer technique when they sponsor prestigious shows on radio and television. These shows function as symbols of dignity and class. Kraft Corporation, for instance, sponsored a "Leonard Bernstein Conducts Beethoven" concert, while Gulf Oil is the sponsor of *National Geographic* specials and Mobil supports public television's *Masterpiece Theatre.* In this way, corporations can reach an educated, influential audience and, perhaps, improve their public image by associating themselves with quality programming.

11   Political ads, of course, practically wrap themselves in the flag. Ads for a political candidate often show either the Washington Monument, a Fourth of July parade, the Stars and Stripes, a bald eagle soaring over the mountains, or a white-steepled church on the village green. The national anthem or "America the Beautiful" may play softly in the background. Such appeals to Americans' love of country can surround the candidate with an aura of patriotism and integrity.

12   4. *Testimonial*   The testimonial is one of advertisers' most-loved and most-used propaganda techniques. Similar to the transfer device, the testimonial capitalizes on the admiration people have for a celebrity to make the product shine more brightly— even though the celebrity is not an expert on the product being sold.

Print and television ads offer a nonstop parade of testimonials: here's Cher for Holi- 13
day Spas; here's basketball star Michael Jordan eating Wheaties; Michael Jackson sings
about Pepsi; American Express features a slew of well-known people who assure us
that they never go anywhere without their American Express card. Testimonials can
sell movies too; newspaper ads for films often feature favorable comments by well-
known reviewers. And, in recent years, testimonials have played an important role in
pitching books; the backs of paperbacks frequently list complimentary blurbs by celebrities.

Political candidates, as well as their ad agencies, know the value of testimonials. 14
Barbara Streisand lent her star appeal to the presidential campaign of Bill Clinton,
while Arnold Schwarzenegger endorsed George Bush. Even controversial social issues
are debated by celebrities. The nuclear freeze, for instance, starred Paul Newman for
the pro side and Charlton Heston for the con.

As illogical as testimonials sometimes are (Pepsi's Michael Jackson, for instance, is a 15
health-food adherent who does not drink soft drinks), they are effective propaganda.
We like the *person* so much that we like the *product* too.

5. *Plain Folks*   The plain folks approach says, in effect, "Buy me or vote for me. I'm 16
just like you." Regular folks will surely like Bob Evans' Down on the Farm Country
Sausage or good old-fashioned Countrytime Lemonade. Some ads emphasize the idea
that "we're all in the same boat." We see people making long-distance calls for just the
reasons we do—to put the baby on the phone to Grandma or to tell Mom we love her.
And how do these folksy, warmhearted (usually saccharine) scenes affect us? They're
supposed to make us feel that AT&T—the multinational corporate giant—has the same
values we do. Similarly, we are introduced to the little people at Ford, the ordinary
folks who work on the assembly line, not to bigwigs in their executive offices. What's
the purpose of such an approach? To encourage us to buy a car built by these honest,
hardworking "everyday Joes" who care about quality as much as we do.

Political advertisements make almost as much use of the "plain folks" appeal as they 17
do of transfer devices. Candidates wear hard hats, farmers' caps, and assembly-line cov-
eralls. They jog around the block and carry their own luggage through the airport. The
idea is to convince voters that the candidates are average people, not the elite—not
wealthy lawyers or executives but the common citizen.

6. *Card Stacking*   When people say that "the cards were stacked against me," they 18
mean that they were never given a fair chance. Applied to propaganda, card stacking
means that one side may suppress or distort evidence, tell half-truths, oversimplify the
facts, or set up a "straw man"—a false target—to divert attention from the issue at
hand. Card stacking is a difficult form of propaganda both to detect and to combat.
When a candidate claims that an opponent has "changed his mind five times on this
important issue," we tend to accept the claim without investigating whether the candidate had good reasons for changing his mind. Many people are simply swayed by the
distorted claim that the candidate is "waffling" on the issue.

Advertisers often stack the cards in favor of the products they are pushing. They 19
may, for instance, use what are called "weasel words." These are small words that usually slip right past us, but that make the difference between reality and illusion. The
weasel words are underlined in the following claims:

"Helps <u>control</u> dandruff symptoms." (The audience usually interprets this as *stops* dandruff.)

"Most dentists <u>surveyed</u> recommend sugarless gum for their patients <u>who chew gum</u>." (We hear the "most dentists" and "for their patients," but we don't think about how many were surveyed or whether or not the dentists first recommended that the patients not chew gum at all.)

"Sticker price $1000 lower than <u>most comparable</u> cars." (How many is "most"? What car does the advertiser consider "comparable"?)

20   Advertisers also use a card stacking trick when they make an unfinished claim. For example, they will say that their product has "twice as much pain reliever." We are left with a favorable impression. We don't usually ask, "Twice as much pain reliever as what?" Or advertisers may make extremely vague claims that sound alluring but have no substance: Toyota's "Oh, what a feeling!"; Vantage cigarettes' "the taste of success"; "The spirit of Marlboro"; Coke's "the real thing." Another way to stack the cards in favor of a certain product is to use scientific-sounding claims that are not supported by sound research. When Ford claimed that its LTD model was "400% quieter," many people assumed that the LTD must be quieter than all other cars. When taken to court, however, Ford admitted that the phrase referred to the difference between the noise level inside and outside the LTD. Other scientific-sounding claims use mysterious ingredients that are never explained as selling points: "Retsyn," "special whitening agents," "the ingredient doctors recommend."

21   *7. Bandwagon*   In the bandwagon technique, advertisers pressure, "Everyone's doing it. Why don't you?" This kind of propaganda often succeeds because many people have a deep desire not to be different. Political ads tell us to vote for the "winning candidate." The advertisers know we tend to feel comfortable doing what others do; we want to be on the winning team. Or ads show a series of people proclaiming, "I'm voting for the Senator. I don't know why anyone wouldn't." Again, the audience feels under pressure to conform.

22   In the marketplace, the bandwagon approach lures buyers. Ads tell us that "nobody doesn't like Sara Lee" (the message is that you must be weird if you don't). They tell us that "most people prefer Brand X two to one over other leading brands" (to be like the majority, we should buy Brand X). If we don't drink Pepsi, we're left out of "the Pepsi generation." To take part in "America's favorite health kick," the National Dairy Council urges us to drink milk. And Honda motorcycle ads, praising the virtues of being a follower, tell us, "Follow the leader. He's on a Honda."

23   Why do these propaganda techniques work? Why do so many of us buy the products, viewpoints, and candidates urged on us by propaganda messages? They work because they appeal to our emotions, not to our minds. Often, in fact, they capitalize on our prejudices and biases. For example, if we are convinced that environmentalists are radicals who want to destroy America's record of industrial growth and progress, then we will applaud the candidate who refers to them as "treehuggers." Clear thinking requires hard work: analyzing a claim, researching the facts, examining both sides of an issue, using logic to see the flaws in an argument. Many of us would rather let the propagandists do our thinking for us.

Because propaganda is so effective, it is important to detect it and understand how 24
it is used. We may conclude, after close examination, that some propaganda sends a
truthful, worthwhile message. Some advertising, for instance, urges us not to drive
drunk, to become volunteers, to contribute to charity. Even so, we must be aware that
propaganda is being used. Otherwise, we will have consented to handing over to others our independence of thought and action.

Questions for Close Reading

1. What is the selection's thesis? Locate the sentence(s) in which McClintock states
her main idea. If she doesn't state the thesis explicitly, express it in your own
words.

2. What is *propaganda*? What mistaken associations do people often have with this
term?

3. What are "weasel words"? How do they trick listeners?

4. Why does McClintock believe we should be better informed about propaganda
techniques?

5. Refer to your dictionary as needed to define the following words used in the
selection: *seduced* (paragraph 1), *warmonger* (5), and *elite* (17).

Questions About the Writer's Craft

1. The pattern and other patterns. Before explaining the categories into which
propaganda techniques can be grouped, McClintock provides a definition of propaganda. Is the definition purely informative, or does it have a larger objective? If
you think the latter, what is the definition's broader purpose?

2. In her introduction, McClintock uses loaded words like *seduced* and *brainwashed*. What effect do these words have on the reader?

3. Locate places where McClintock uses questions. Which are rhetorical and
which are genuine queries?

4. What kind of conclusion does McClintock provide for the essay?

Writing Assignments Using Division-Classification as a Pattern of Development

∞ **1.** McClintock cautions us to be sensitive to propaganda in advertising. Young
children, however, aren't capable of this kind of awareness. With pen or pencil in
hand, watch some television commercials aimed at children, such as those for
toys, cereals, and fast food. Then analyze the use of propaganda techniques in
these commercials. Using division-classification, write an essay describing the

main propaganda techniques you observed. Support your analysis with examples drawn from the commercials. Remember to provide a thesis that indicates your opinion of the advertising techniques used on television. To gain insight into television's powerful influence, read Pete Hamill's "Crack and the Box" (page 356).

2. Like advertising techniques, television shows can be classified. Avoiding the obvious system of classifying according to game shows, detective shows, and situation comedies, come up with your own original division-classification principle. Possibilities include how family life is depicted, the way work is presented, how male-female relationships are portrayed. Using one such principle, write an essay in which you categorize popular TV shows into three types. Refer to specific shows to support your classification system. Your attitude toward the shows being discussed should be clear.

Writing Assignments Using Other Patterns of Development

3. McClintock says that card stacking "distort[s] evidence, tell[s] half-truths, over-simplif[ies] the facts" (18). Focusing on an editorial, a political campaign, a print ad, or a television commercial, analyze the extent to which card stacking is used as a persuasive strategy.

4. To increase further your sensitivity to the moral dimensions of propaganda, write a proposal outlining an ad campaign for a real or imaginary product or elected official. The introduction to your proposal should identify who or what is to be promoted, and the thesis or plan of development should indicate the specific propaganda techniques you suggest. In the paper's supporting paragraphs, explain how these techniques would be used to promote your product or candidate.

DEBORAH TANNEN

Deborah Tannen (1945–) is a linguistics professor at Georgetown University and has been a Distinguished McGraw Lecturer at Princeton University. She has shared her research with the general public through appearances on the *Today* show and CNN, through pieces in the *New York Times* and the *Washington Post,* and in books, including *That's Not What I Meant: How Conversational Style Makes or Breaks Relationships* (1987), and *You Just Don't Understand: Women and Men in Conversation* (1990). The following selection is from *Talking from 9 to 5: How Women's and Men's Conversational Styles Affect Who Gets Ahead, Who Gets Credit, and What Gets Done at Work* (1994).

BUT WHAT DO YOU MEAN?

1   Conversation is a ritual. We say things that seem obviously the thing to say, without thinking of the literal meaning of our words, any more than we expect the question "How are you?" to call forth a detailed account of aches and pains.

Unfortunately, women and men often have different ideas about what's appropriate, 2 different ways of speaking. Many of the conversational rituals common among women are designed to take the other person's feelings into account, while many of the conversational rituals common among men are designed to maintain the one-up position, or at least avoid appearing one-down. As a result, when men and women interact—especially at work—it's often women who are at the disadvantage. Because women are not trying to avoid the one-down position, that is unfortunately where they may end up.

Here, the biggest areas of miscommunication.   3

1. Apologies

Women are often told they apologize too much. The reason they're told to stop 4 doing it is that, to many men, apologizing seems synonymous with putting oneself down. But there are many times when "I'm sorry" isn't self-deprecating, or even an apology; it's an automatic way of keeping both speakers on an equal footing. For example, a well-known columnist once interviewed me and gave me her phone number in case I needed to call her back. I misplaced the number and had to go through the newspaper's main switchboard. When our conversation was winding down and we'd both made ending-type remarks, I added, "Oh, I almost forgot—I lost your direct number, can I get it again?" "Oh, I'm sorry," she came back instantly, even though she had done nothing wrong and *I* was the one who'd lost the number. But I understood she wasn't really apologizing; she was just automatically reassuring me she had no intention of denying me her number.

Even when "I'm sorry" *is* an apology, women often assume it will be the first step in 5 a two-step ritual: I say "I'm sorry" and take half the blame, then you take the other half. At work, it might go something like this:

A: When you typed this letter, you missed this phrase I inserted.
B: Oh, I'm sorry. I'll fix it.
A: Well, I wrote it so small it was easy to miss.

When both parties share blame, it's a mutual face-saving device. But if one person, 6 usually the woman, utters frequent apologies and the other doesn't, she ends up looking as if she's taking the blame for mishaps that aren't her fault. When she's only partially to blame, she looks entirely in the wrong.

I recently sat in on a meeting at an insurance company where the sole woman, 7 Helen, said "I'm sorry" or "I apologize" repeatedly. At one point she said, "I'm thinking out loud. I apologize." Yet the meeting was intended to be an informal brainstorming session, and *everyone* was thinking out loud.

The reason Helen's apologies stood out was that she was the only person in the 8 room making so many. And the reason I was concerned was that Helen felt the annual bonus she had received was unfair. When I interviewed her colleagues, they said that Helen was one of the best and most productive workers—yet she got one of the smallest bonuses. Although the problem might have been outright sexism, I suspect her speech style, which differs from that of her male colleagues, masks her competence.

9   Unfortunately, not apologizing can have its price too. Since so many women use ritual apologies, those who don't may be seen as hard-edged. What's important is to be
aware of how often you say you're sorry (and why), and to monitor your speech based
on the reaction you get.

2. Criticism

10   A woman who cowrote a report with a male colleague was hurt when she read a
rough draft to him and he leapt into a critical response—"Oh, that's too dry! You have
to make it snappier!" She herself would have been more likely to say, "That's a really
good start. Of course, you'll want to make it a little snappier when you revise."

11   Whether criticism is given straight or softened is often a matter of convention. In
general, women use more softeners. I noticed this difference when talking to an editor
about an essay I'd written. While going over changes she wanted to make, she said,
"There's one more thing. I know you may not agree with me. The reason I noticed the
problem is that your other points are so lucid and elegant." She went on hedging for
several more sentences until I put her out of her misery: "Do you want to cut that
part?" I asked—and of course she did. But I appreciated her tentativeness. In contrast,
another editor (a man) I once called summarily rejected my idea for an article by barking, "Call me when you have something new to say."

12   Those who are used to ways of talking that soften the impact of criticism may find it
hard to deal with the right-between-the-eyes style. It has its own logic, however, and
neither style is intrinsically better. People who prefer criticism given straight are operating on an assumption that feelings aren't involved: "Here's the dope. I know you're
good; you can take it."

3. Thank-Yous

13   A woman manager I know starts meetings by thanking everyone for coming, even
though it's clearly their job to do so. Her "thank-you" is simply a ritual.

14   A novelist received a fax from an assistant in her publisher's office; it contained suggested catalog copy for her book. She immediately faxed him her suggested changes
and said, "Thanks for running this by me," even though her contract gave her the right
to approve all copy. When she thanked the assistant, she fully expected him to reciprocate: "Thanks for giving me such a quick response." Instead, he said, "You're welcome." Suddenly, rather than an equal exchange of pleasantries, she found herself
positioned as the recipient of a favor. This made her feel like responding, "Thanks for
nothing!"

15   Many women use "thanks" as an automatic conversation starter and closer; there's
nothing literally to say thank you for. Like many rituals typical of women's conversation, it depends on the goodwill of the other to restore the balance. When the other
speaker doesn't reciprocate, a woman may feel like someone on a seesaw whose partner abandoned his end. Instead of balancing in the air, she has plopped to the ground,
wondering how she got there.

4. Fighting

Many men expect the discussion of ideas to be a ritual fight—explored through ver- 16
bal opposition. They state their ideas in the strongest possible terms, thinking that if
there are weaknesses someone will point them out, and by trying to argue against
those objections, they will see how well their ideas hold up.

Those who expect their own ideas to be challenged will respond to another's ideas 17
by trying to poke holes and find weak links—as a way of *helping.* The logic is that
when you are challenged you will rise to the occasion: Adrenaline makes your mind
sharper; you get ideas and insights you would not have thought of without the spur of
battle.

But many women take this approach as a personal attack. Worse, they find it impos- 18
sible to do their best work in such a contentious environment. If you're not used to ritual fighting, you begin to hear criticism of your ideas as soon as they are formed. Rather
than making you think more clearly, it makes you doubt what you know. When you
state your ideas, you hedge in order to fend off potential attacks. Ironically, this is more
likely to *invite* attack because it makes you look weak.

Although you may never enjoy verbal sparring, some women find it helpful to learn 19
how to do it. An engineer who was the only woman among four men in a small company
found that as soon as she learned to argue she was accepted and taken seriously. A doctor attending a hospital staff meeting made a similar discovery. She was becoming more
and more angry with a male colleague who'd loudly disagreed with a point she'd made.
Her better judgment told her to hold her tongue, to avoid making an enemy of this powerful senior colleague. But finally she couldn't hold it in any longer, and she rose to her
feet and delivered an impassioned attack on his position. She sat down in a panic, certain she had permanently damaged her relationship with him. To her amazement, he
came up to her afterward and said, "That was a great rebuttal. I'm really impressed. Let's
go out for a beer after work and hash out our approaches to this problem."

5. Praise

A manager I'll call Lester had been on his new job six months when he heard that 20
the women reporting to him were deeply dissatisfied. When he talked to them about it,
their feelings erupted; two said they were on the verge of quitting because he didn't
appreciate their work, and they didn't want to wait to be fired. Lester was dumbfounded: He believed they were doing a fine job. Surely, he thought, he had said nothing to give them the impression he didn't like their work. And indeed he hadn't. That
was the problem. He had said *nothing*—and the women assumed he was following the
adage "If you can't say something nice, don't say anything." He thought he was showing confidence in them by leaving them alone.

Men and women have different habits in regard to giving praise. For example, Deir- 21
dre and her colleague William both gave presentations at a conference. Afterward,
Deirdre told William, "That was a great talk!" He thanked her. Then she asked, "What
did you think of mine?" and he gave her a lengthy and detailed critique. She found it
uncomfortable to listen to his comments. But she assured herself that he meant well,

and that his honesty was a signal that she, too, should be honest when he asked for a critique of his performance. As a matter of fact, she had noticed quite a few ways in which he could have improved his presentation. But she never got a chance to tell him because he never asked—and she felt put down. The worst part was that it seemed she had only herself to blame, since she *had* asked what he thought of her talk.

22   But had she really asked for his critique? The truth is, when she asked for his opinion, she was expecting a compliment, which she felt was more or less required following anyone's talk. When he responded with criticism, she figured, "Oh, he's playing 'Let's critique each other' "—not a game she'd initiated, but one which she was willing to play. Had she realized he was going to criticize her and not ask her to reciprocate, she would never have asked in the first place.

23   It would be easy to assume that Deirdre was insecure, whether she was fishing for a compliment or soliciting a critique. But she was simply talking automatically, performing one of the many conversational rituals that allow us to get through the day. William may have sincerely misunderstood Deirdre's intention—or may have been unable to pass up a chance to one-up her when given the opportunity.

6. Complaints

24   "Troubles talk" can be a way to establish rapport with a colleague. You complain about a problem (which shows that you are just folks) and the other person responds with a similar problem (which puts you on equal footing). But while such commiserating is common among women, men are likely to hear it as a request to *solve* the problem.

25   One woman told me she would frequently initiate what she thought would be pleasant complaint-airing sessions at work. She'd talk about situations that bothered her just to talk about them, maybe to understand them better. But her male office mate would quickly tell her how she could improve the situation. This left her feeling condescended to and frustrated. She was delighted to see this very impasse in a section in my book *You Just Don't Understand,* and showed it to him. "Oh," he said, "I see the problem. How can we solve it?" Then they both laughed, because it had happened again: He short-circuited the detailed discussion she'd hoped for and cut to the chase of finding a solution.

26   Sometimes the consequences of complaining are more serious: A man might take a woman's lighthearted griping literally, and she can get a reputation as a chronic malcontent. Furthermore, she may be seen as not up to solving the problems that arise on the job.

7. Jokes

27   I heard a man call in to a talk show and say, "I've worked for two women and neither one had a sense of humor. You know, when you work with men, there's a lot of joking and teasing." The show's host and the guest (both women) took his comment at face value and assumed the women this man worked for were humorless. The guest said, "Isn't it sad that women don't feel comfortable enough with authority to see the

humor?" The host said, "Maybe when more women are in authority roles, they'll be more comfortable with power." But although the women this man worked for *may* have taken themselves too seriously, it's just as likely that they each had a terrific sense of humor, but maybe the humor wasn't the type he was used to. They may have been like the woman who wrote to me: "When I'm with men, my wit or cleverness seems inappropriate (or lost!) so I don't bother. When I'm with my women friends, however, there's no hold on puns or cracks and my humor is fully appreciated."

The types of humor women and men tend to prefer differ. Research has shown that 28 the most common form of humor among men is razzing, teasing, and mock-hostile attacks, while among women it's self-mocking. Women often mistake men's teasing as genuinely hostile. Men often mistake women's mock self-deprecation as truly putting themselves down.

Women have told me they were taken more seriously when they learned to joke the 29 way the guys did. For example, a teacher who went to a national conference with seven other teachers (mostly women) and a group of administrators (mostly men) was annoyed that the administrators always found reasons to leave boring seminars, while the teachers felt they had to stay and take notes. One evening, when the group met at a bar in the hotel, the principal asked her how one such seminar had turned out. She retorted, "As soon as you left, it got much better." He laughed out loud at her response. The playful insult appealed to the men—but there was a trade-off. The women seemed to back off from her after this. (Perhaps they were put off by her using joking to align herself with the bosses.)

There is no "right" way to talk. When problems arise, the culprit may be style differ- 30 ences—and *all* styles will at times fail with others who don't share or understand them, just as English won't do you much good if you try to speak to someone who knows only French. If you want to get your message across, it's not a question of being "right"; it's a question of using language that's shared—or at least understood.

Questions for Close Reading

1. What is the selection's thesis? Locate the sentence(s) in which Tannen states her main idea. If she doesn't state the thesis explicitly, express it in your own words.

2. Describe the differences in the way men and women perceive women's use of apologies. According to Tannen, how does this difference in perception create a problem?

3. What is the difference between "straight" and "softened" criticism (11)? Does Tannen like one style more than the other? Why or why not?

4. What is a "ritual fight" (16)? How, according to Tannen, do men and women differ in their responses to ritual fighting?

5. Refer to your dictionary as needed to define the following words used in the selection: *synonymous* (paragraph 4), *self-deprecating* (4), *reciprocate* (14), *contentious* (18), *dumbfounded* (20), *soliciting* (23), *commiserating* (24), *malcontent* (26).

Questions About the Writer's Craft

1. The pattern. Are Tannen's seven categories of male-female miscommunication mutually exclusive, or do they overlap? Cite specific examples to support your view. Why do you think she divided them as she did?

2. Other patterns. Besides identifying the differences in men's and women's conversation rituals, Tannen often analyzes the causes and effects of these differences. Trace the causal chain in Tannen's discussion of apologies (paragraphs 7–9). How does this causal chain help Tannen reinforce her thesis?

3. Social scientists like Tannen often write impersonally, relying on statistics and a third-person point of view. Why do you suppose Tannen writes from the first-person point of view? What advantage does this point of view offer?

4. How would you characterize Tannen's tone in this selection? How does Tannen's attitude toward her subject and readers reinforce the essay's purpose?

Writing Assignments Using Division-Classification as a Pattern of Development

1. Tannen's essay shows how typical male-female conversational patterns may put women at a disadvantage. Focus on two other closely related groups whose relationship is imbalanced because the communication behaviors of one are at odds with the group's best self-interest. You might examine the relationship between parents and children, teachers and students, or employers and employees. Like Tannen, categorize the areas in which the imbalance is apparent, and be sure to explain the consequences as well as the origins of the counterproductive communication behavior.

2. Tannen's essay focuses on conversational patterns in the workplace. Select another setting you know well—perhaps a dormitory, classroom, subway, party, or sporting event. Focus on a specific type of speech (for example, gossip, compliments, or complaints) that occurs in this setting, and write an essay investigating the component parts of that kind of speech. Reach some conclusion about the language behaviors you observe. Do you consider them funny, sad, frustrating, or something else? Be sure your tone is consistent with the conclusions you reach.

Writing Assignments Using Other Patterns of Development

∞ **3.** Tannen discusses differences in men's and women's communication rituals. Extending her work, examine another area where you perceive significant gender differences. Possibilities include the way men and women eat, socialize, shop for clothes, furnish their rooms, or watch television. Write an essay comparing and contrasting the sexes' attitudes and behaviors in this area. Brainstorm with others to gather anecdotes that convincingly exemplify the behaviors you describe. Your essay may be serious, light-hearted, or both. Before writing, read Susan Douglas's "Managing Mixed Messages" (page 247) and Nancy Gibbs's "When Is It Rape?" (page 423). You may also want to read relevant portions of Tannen's *You Just Don't Understand* or *Talking from 9 to 5.*

4. In this selection, Tannen shows that verbal behavior can be misunderstood. Write an essay showing that nonverbal behaviors can also be misinterpreted. Before you write, research nonverbal communication in the library or on the Internet. Armed with background information, spend time observing people's nonverbal communication in a variety of campus settings. When you write, do more than provide instances of misunderstanding; be sure to offer explanations of why such communication breakdowns occur.

MEG GREENFIELD

A graduate of Smith College, Meg Greenfield (1930–) began her journalism career as a researcher for *Reporter* magazine and joined the *Washington Post* in 1968. She won a Pulitzer Prize in 1978 for editorial writing and, since 1979, has served as the editor of the *Post*'s editorial page. The following essay first appeared in 1986 as one of her columns for *Newsweek.*

WHY NOTHING IS "WRONG" ANYMORE

There has been an awful lot of talk about sin, crime and plain old antisocial behavior   1
this summer—drugs and pornography at home, terror and brutality abroad. Maybe it's just the heat; or maybe these categories of conduct (sin, crime, etc.) are really on the rise. What strikes me is our curiously deficient, not to say defective, way of talking about them. We don't seem to have a word anymore for "wrong" in the moral sense, as in, for example, "theft is wrong."

Let me quickly qualify. There is surely no shortage of people condemning other peo-   2
ple on such grounds, especially their political opponents or characters they just don't care for. Name-calling is still very much in vogue. But where the concept of wrong is really important—as a guide to one's own behavior or that of one's own side in some dispute—it is missing; and this is as true of those on the religious right who are going around pronouncing great masses of us sinners as it is of their principal antagonists, those on the secular left who can forgive or "understand" just about anything so long as it has not been perpetrated by a right-winger.

There is a fairly awesome literature that attempts to explain how we have changed   3
as a people with the advent of psychiatry, the weakening of religious institutions and so forth, but you don't need to address these matters to take note of a simple fact. As a guide and a standard to live by, you don't hear so much about "right and wrong" these days. The very notion is considered politically, not to say personally, embarrassing,

since it has such a repressive, Neanderthal ring to it. So we have developed a broad range of alternatives to "right and wrong." I'll name a few.

4   **Right and stupid:** This is the one you use when your candidate gets caught stealing, or, for that matter, when anyone on your side does something reprehensible. "It was really so dumb of him"—head must shake here—"I just can't understand it." Bad is dumb, breathtakingly dumb and therefore unfathomable; so, conveniently enough, the effort to fathom it might just as well be called off. This one had a big ploy during Watergate and has had mini-revivals ever since whenever congressmen and senators investigating administration crimes turn out to be guilty of something similar themselves.

5   **Right and not necessarily unconstitutional:** I don't know at quite what point along the way we came to this one, the avoidance of admitting that something is wrong by pointing out that it is not specifically or even inferentially prohibited by the Constitution or, for that matter, mentioned by name in the criminal code or the Ten Commandments. The various parties that prevail in civil-liberty and civil-rights disputes before the Supreme Court have gotten quite good at making this spurious connection: it is legally permissible, therefore it is morally acceptable, possibly even good. But both as individuals and as a society we do things every day that we know to be wrong even though they may not fall within the class of legally punishable acts or tickets to eternal damnation.

6   **Right and sick:** Crime or lesser wrongdoing defined as physical and/or psychological disorder—this one has been around for ages now and as long ago as 1957 was made the butt of a great joke in the "Gee Officer Krupke!" song in *West Side Story.* Still, I think no one could have foreseen the degree to which an originally reasonable and humane assumption (that some of what once was regarded as wrongdoing is committed by people acting out of ailment rather than moral choice) would be seized upon and exploited to exonerate every kind of misfeasance. This route is a particular favorite of caught-out officeholders who, when there is at last no other recourse, hold a press conference, announce that they are "sick" in some way and throw themselves and their generally stunned families on our mercy. At which point it becomes gross to pick on them; instead we are exhorted to admire them for their "courage."

7   **Right and only to be expected:** You could call this the tit-for-tat school; it is related to the argument that holds moral wrongdoing to be evidence of sickness, but it is much more pervasive and insidious these days. In fact it is probably the most popular dodge, being used to justify, or at least avoid owning up to, every kind of lapse: the other guy, or sometimes just plain circumstance, "asked for it." For instance, I think most of us could agree that setting fire to live people, no matter what their political offense, is— dare I say it?—wrong. Yet if it is done by those for whom we have sympathy in a conflict, there is a tendency to extenuate or disbelieve it, receiving it less as evidence of wrongdoing on our side than as evidence of the severity of the provocation or as enemy-supplied disinformation. Thus the hesitation of many in the anti-apartheid movement to confront the brutality of so-called "necklacing," and thus the immediate leap of Sen. Jesse Helms to the defense of the Chilean government after the horrifying incineration of protesters there.

8   **Right and complex:** This one hardly takes a moment to describe; you know it well. "Complex" is the new "controversial," a word used as "controversial" was for so long to flag trouble of some unspecified, dismaying sort that the speaker doesn't want to have to step up to. "Well, you know, it's very complex...." I still can't get this one out of my own vocabulary.

In addition to these various sophistries, we also have created a rash of "ethics com-   9
mittees" in our government, of course, whose function seems to be to dither around
writing rules that allow people who have clearly done wrong—and should have known
it and probably did—to get away because the rules don't cover their offense (see **Right
and not necessarily unconstitutional**). But we don't need any more committees or
artful dodges for that matter. As I listen to the moral arguments swirling about us this
summer I become ever more persuaded that our real problem is this: the "still, small
voice" of conscience has become far too small—and utterly still.

Questions for Close Reading

1. What is the selection's thesis? Locate the sentence(s) in which Greenfield states
her main idea. If she doesn't state the thesis explicitly, express it in your own
words.

2. What is the "simple fact" that Greenfield refers to in paragraph 3?

3. How many excuses does Greenfield cite to illustrate her belief that wrongdoing
is widely condoned these days? What are the excuses?

4. In particular, whose ethics does Greenfield question? Locate places in the essay
where she indicates who her actual target is.

5. Refer to your dictionary as needed to define the following words used in the
selection: *antagonists* (paragraph 2), *perpetrated* (2), *repressive* (3), *Neanderthal* (3),
reprehensible (4), *unfathomable* (4), *inferentially* (5), *spurious* (5), *misfeasance* (6), *insidious* (7), *extenuate* (7), *anti-apartheid* (7), and *sophistries* (9).

Questions About the Writer's Craft

1. The pattern. Does Greenfield use division, classification, or both to organize
her essay? Does she apply her principle of division-classification consistently?

2. Greenfield repeats the phrase "right and" before each of her alternatives to
"wrong." Why do you suppose she uses this strategy? How is this repetition
related to her thesis?

3. Locate places in the essay where Greenfield employs the first person. What
effect does her use of "I" have on the essay's tone and persuasiveness?

4. How does Greenfield tie her opening and closing paragraphs together? What
issue in her introductory paragraph does she resolve in her conclusion?

Writing Assignments Using Division-Classification as a Pattern of Development

∞ **1.** Greenfield names various excuses that politicians and others use in uncomfortable situations. Choose a disquieting situation in which people sometimes find

themselves, and write an essay categorizing the excuses they typically devise. For example, you could write about the types of excuses that students use when they hand in late papers or that drivers use to justify speeding. Like Greenfield, reveal your attitude toward these people. John Leo's "Absolutophobia" (page 429) provides an interesting perspective on the tendency to justify wrongful behavior.

2. Using a personal, authoritative tone like Greenfield's, write an essay classifying the kinds of mistakes that people make in a specific situation. You might, for example, write about people's bumbling attempts to improve their social lives or their errors of judgment in selecting a college. Your essay might be light or serious.

Writing Assignments Using Other Patterns of Development

3. What does the concept *wrong* mean to you? Write an essay defining this word and clarifying your standards for determining if an action is "wrong."

4. In an essay, draw upon either several vivid illustrations or a single compelling example to show that people are capable of highly moral, even altruistic behavior. To demonstrate your appreciation of the complexities of human behavior, cite at some point in your essay the research of John Darley and Bibb Latané (see "Why People Don't Help in a Crisis," page 392).

ADDITIONAL WRITING TOPICS: DIVISION-CLASSIFICATION

General Assignments

Choose one of the following subjects and write an essay developed wholly or in part through division-classification.

Division

1. A shopping mall

2. A video or stereo system

3. A particular kind of team

4. A school library

5. A playground, gym, or other recreational area

6. A significant event

7. A college campus

8. A television show or movie

Classification

1. People in a waiting room

2. Parents

3. Holidays

4. Students in a class

5. Summer movies

6. College courses

7. Television watchers

8. Commercials

Assignments with a Specific Purpose, Audience, and Point of View

1. You are a dorm counselor. During orientation week, you'll be talking to students on your floor about the different kinds of problems they may have with roommates. Write your talk, describing each kind of problem and explaining how to cope.

2. As a driving instructor, you decide to prepare a lecture on the types of drivers that your students are likely to encounter on the road. In your lecture, categorize drivers according to a specific principle and show the behaviors of each type.

3. You have been asked to write a pamphlet for "new recruits"—new workers on your job, new students in your college class, new members of your sports team, or the like. In the pamphlet, identify at least three general qualities needed for the recruits' success.

4. A seasoned camp counselor, you've been asked to prepare, for new counselors, an informational sheet on children's emotional needs. Categorizing those needs into types, explain what counselors can do to nurture youngsters emotionally.

5. As your college newspaper's TV critic, you plan to write a review of the fall shows, most of which—in your opinion—lack originality. To show how stereotypical the programs are, select one type (for example, situation comedies or crime dramas). Then use a specific division-classification principle to illustrate that the same stale formulas are trotted out from show to show.

6. Asked to write an editorial for the campus paper, you decide to do a half-serious piece on taking "mental health" days off from classes. Structure your essay around three kinds of occasions when "playing hooky" is essential for maintaining sanity.

15
PROCESS
ANALYSIS

WHAT IS PROCESS ANALYSIS?

PERHAPS you've noticed the dogged determination of small children when they learn how to do something new. Whether trying to tie their shoelaces or tell time, little children struggle along, creating knotted tangles, confusing the hour with the minute hand. But they don't give up. Mastering such basic skills makes them feel less dependent on the adults of the world—all of whom seem to know how to do everything. Actually, none of us is born knowing how to do very much. We spend a good deal of our lives learning—everything from speaking our first word to balancing our first bank statement. Indeed, the milestones in our lives are often linked to the processes we have mastered: how to cross the street alone; how to drive a car; how to make a speech without being paralyzed by fear.

Process analysis, a technique that explains the steps or sequence involved in doing something, satisfies our need to learn as well as our curiosity about how the world works. All the self-help books flooding the market today (*Managing Stress, How to Make a Million in Real Estate, Ten Days to a Perfect Body*) are examples of process analysis. The instructions on the federal tax form and the recipes in a cookbook are also process analyses. Several television classics, now seen in reruns, capitalize on our desire to learn how things happen: *The Wild Kingdom* shows how animals survive in faraway lands, and *Mission: Impossible* has great fun detailing elaborate plans for preventing the triumph of evil. Process analysis can be more than merely interesting or entertaining, though; it can be of critical importance. Consider a waiter hurriedly skimming the "Choking Aid" instructions posted on a restaurant wall or an air-traffic controller following emergency procedures in an effort to prevent a midair collision. In these last examples, the consequences could be fatal if the process analyses are slipshod, inaccurate, or confusing.

Undoubtedly, all of us have experienced less dramatic effects of poorly written process analyses. Perhaps you've tried to assemble a bicycle and spent hours sorting through a stack of parts, only to end up with one or two extra pieces never mentioned in the instructions. Or maybe you were baffled when putting up a set of wall shelves because the instructions used unfamiliar terms like *mitered cleat, wing nut,* and *dowel pin.* No wonder many people stay clear of anything that actually admits "assembly required."

HOW PROCESS ANALYSIS FITS
YOUR PURPOSE AND AUDIENCE

You will use process analysis in two types of writing situations: (1) when you want to give step-by-step instructions to readers showing how they can do something, or (2) when you want readers to understand how something happens even though they won't actually follow the steps outlined. The first kind of process analysis is **directional;** the second is **informational.**

When you look at the cooking instructions on a package of frozen vegetables or follow guidelines for completing a job application, you're reading directional process analysis. A serious essay explaining how to select a college and a humorous essay telling readers how to get on the good side of a professor are also examples of directional process analysis. Using a variety of tones, informational process analyses can range over equally diverse subjects; they can describe mechanical, scientific, historical, sociological, artistic, or psychological processes: for example, how the core of a nuclear power plant melts down; how television became so important in political campaigns; how abstract painters use color; how to survive a blind date.

Process analysis, both directional and informational, is often appropriate in *problem-solving situations.* In such cases, you say, "Here's the problem and here's what should be done to solve the problem." Indeed, college assignments frequently take the form of problem-solving process analyses. Consider these examples:

> Because many colleges and universities have changed the eligibility requirements for financial aid, fewer students can depend on loans or scholarships. How can students cope with the increasing costs of obtaining a higher education?

> Over the years, there have been many reports citing the abuse of small children in day-care centers. What can parents do to guard against the mistreatment of their children?

> Community officials have been accused of mismanaging recent unrest over the public housing ordinance. Describe the steps the officials took, indicating why you think their strategy was unwise. Then explain how you think the situation should have been handled.

Note that the last assignment asks students to explain what's wrong with the current approach before they present their own step-by-step solution. Problem-solving process analyses are often organized in this way. You may also have noticed that none of the assignments explicitly requires an essay response using process analysis. However, the wording of the assignments—"*Describe* the *steps*," "*What* can parents *do*," "*How* can students *cope*"—indicates that process analysis would be an appropriate strategy for developing the responses.

Assignments don't always signal the use of process analysis so clearly. But during the prewriting stage, as you generate material to support your thesis, you'll often realize that you can best achieve your purpose by developing the essay—or part of it—using process analysis.

Sometimes process analysis will be the primary strategy for organizing an essay; other times it will be used to help make a point in an essay organized around another pattern of development. Let's take a look at process analysis as a supporting strategy.

Assume that you're writing a *causal analysis* examining the impact of television commercials on people's buying behavior. To help readers see that commercials create a need where none existed before, you might describe the various stages in an advertising campaign to pitch a new, completely frivolous product. In an essay *defining* a good boss, you could convey the point that effective managers must be skilled at settling disputes by explaining the steps your boss took to resolve a heated disagreement between two employees. If you write an *argumentation-persuasion* paper urging the funding of programs to ease the plight of the homeless, you would have to dramatize for readers the tragedy of these people's lives. To achieve your purpose, you could devote part of the paper to an explanation of how the typical street person goes about finding a place to sleep and getting food to eat.

PREWRITING STRATEGIES

The following checklist shows how you can apply to process analysis some of the prewriting strategies discussed in Chapter 2.

> ✔ PROCESS ANALYSIS: A PREWRITING CHECKLIST
>
> *Choose a Process to Analyze*
> ☐ What processes do you know well and feel you can explain clearly (for example, how to jog without injury, how lobbyists influence legislators)?
> ☐ What processes have you wondered about (how to meditate; how the greenhouse effect works)?
> ☐ What process needs changing if a current problem is to be solved?

Determine Your Purpose, Audience, Tone, and Point of View

☐ What is the central purpose of your process analysis? Do you want to inform readers so that they will acquire a new skill (how to buy a used car)? Do you want readers to gain a better understanding of a complex process (how young children develop a conscience)? Do you want to persuade readers to accept your point of view about a process, perhaps even urge them to adopt a particular course of action ("If you disagree with the proposed plan for reorganizing academic advisement, you should take the following steps to register your protest with college officials")?

☐ What audience are you writing for? What will they need to know to understand the process? What will they not need to know?

☐ What point of view will you adopt when addressing the audience?

☐ What tone do you want to project? Do you want to come across as serious, humorous, sarcastic, ironic, objective, impassioned?

Use Prewriting to Generate the Stages of the Process

☐ How could brainstorming or mapping help you identify primary and secondary steps in the process?

☐ How could brainstorming or mapping help you identify the ingredients or materials that the reader will need?

STRATEGIES FOR USING PROCESS ANALYSIS IN AN ESSAY

After prewriting, you're ready to draft your essay. The following suggestions will be helpful whether you use process analysis as a dominant or supportive pattern of development.

1. Formulate a thesis that clarifies your attitude toward the process. Like the thesis in any other paper, the thesis in a process analysis should do more than announce your subject ("Here's how the college's work-study program operates"). It should also state or imply your attitude toward the process: "Enrolling in the college's work-study program has become unnecessarily complicated. The procedure could be simplified if the college adopted the helpful guidelines prepared by the Student Senate."

2. Keep your audience in mind when deciding what to cover. Only after you gauge how much your readers already know (or don't know) about the process can you determine how much explanation to provide. Suppose you've been asked to write an article informing students of the best way to use the university computer center. The article will be published in a newsletter for computer science majors. You would seriously misjudge your audience—and probably put them to sleep— if you explained in detail how to transfer material from disk to disk or how to delete information from a file. However, an article on the same topic prepared for a general audience—your composition class, for instance—would probably require such detailed instructions. The audience's level of knowledge also determines whether you should define technical terms. The computer science majors wouldn't need terms such as "modem," "interface," and "byte" defined, whereas students in your composition class would likely require easy-to-understand explanations. Indeed, with any general audience, you should use as little specialized language as possible.

To determine how much explanation is needed, put yourself in your readers' shoes. Don't assume readers will know something just because you do. Ask questions like these about your audience: "Will my readers need some background about the process before I describe it in depth?" and "If my essay is directional, should I specify near the beginning the ingredients, materials, and equipment needed to perform the process?" (For more help in analyzing your audience, see the checklist on page 21.)

3. Focusing on your purpose, thesis, and audience, explain the process—one step at a time. After using prewriting techniques to identify primary and second-ary steps and needed equipment, you're ready to organize your raw material into an easy-to-follow sequence. At times your purpose will be to explain a process with a *fairly fixed chronological sequence:* how to make a pizza, how to pot a plant, how to change a tire. In such cases, you should include all necessary steps in the correct chronological order. However, if a strict chronological ordering of steps means that a particularly important part of the sequence gets buried in the mid-dle, the sequence probably should be juggled so that the crucial step receives the attention it deserves.

Other times your goal will be to describe a process having *no commonly accepted sequence.* For example, in an essay explaining how to discipline a child or how to pull yourself out of a blue mood, you will have to come up with your own defini-tion of the key steps and then arrange those steps in some logical order. You may also use process analysis to *reject* or *reformulate* a traditional sequence. In this case, you would propose a more logical series of steps: "Our system for electing con-gressional representatives is inefficient and undemocratic; it should be reformed in the following ways."

Whether the essay describes a generally agreed-on process or one that is not commonly accepted, you must provide all the details needed to explain the pro-cess. Your readers should be able to understand, even visualize, the process. There should be no fuzzy patches or confusing cuts from one step to another. Don't, however, go into obsessive detail about minor stages or steps. If you dwell for sev-eral hundred words on how to butter the pan, your readers will never stay with you long enough to learn how to make the omelet.

It's not unusual, especially in less defined sequences, for some steps in a pro-cess to occur simultaneously and to overlap. When this happens, you should present the steps in the most logical order, being sure to tell your readers that several steps are not perfectly distinct and may merge. For example, in an essay explaining how a species becomes extinct, you would have to indicate that overpopulation of hardy strains and destruction of endangered breeds are often simultaneous events. You would also need to clarify that the depletion of food sources both precedes and follows the demise of a species.

4. Sort out the directional and informational aspects of the process analysis. As you may have discovered when prewriting, directional and informational process analyses are not always distinct. In fact, they may be complementary: You may need to provide background information about a process before outlining its steps. For example, in a paper describing a step-by-step approach for losing weight, you might first need to explain how the body burns calories. Or, in a paper on gardening, you could provide some theory about the way organic fertilizers work before detailing a plan for growing vegetables. Although both approaches may be appropriate in a paper, one generally predominates.

The kind of process analysis chosen has implications for the way you will relate to your reader. When the process analysis is *directional,* the reader is addressed in the *second person:* "You should first rinse the residue from the radiator by..." or "Wrap the injured person in a blanket and then...." (In the second example, the pronoun *you* is implied.)

If the process analysis has an *informational* purpose, you won't address the reader directly but will choose from a number of other options. For example, you might use the *first person.* In a humorous essay explaining how not to prepare for finals, you could cite your own disastrous study habits: "Filled with good intentions, I sit on my bed, pick up a pencil, open my notebook, and promptly fall asleep." The *third-person singular or plural* can also be used in informational process essays: "The door-to-door salesperson walks up the front walk, heart pounding, more than a bit nervous, but also challenged by the prospect of striking a deal," or "The new recruits next underwent a series of important balance tests in what was called the 'horror chamber.'" Whether you use the first, second, or third person, avoid shifting point of view midstream.

You might have noticed that in the third-person examples, the present tense ("walks up") is used in one sentence, the past tense ("underwent") in the other. The past tense is appropriate for events already completed, whereas the present tense is used for habitual or ongoing actions. ("A dominant male goose usually flies at the head of the V-wedge during migration.") The present tense is also effective when you want to lend a sense of dramatic immediacy to a process, even if the steps were performed in the past. ("The surgeon gently separates the facial skin and muscle from the underlying bony skull.") As with point of view, be on guard against changing tenses in the middle of your explanation.

5. Provide readers with the help they need to follow the sequence. As you move through the steps of a process analysis, don't forget to *warn readers about difficulties* they might encounter. For example, in a paper on the artistry involved in butterflying a shrimp, you might write something like this:

Next, make a shallow cut with your sharpened knife along the
convex curve of the shrimp's intestinal tract. The tract, usually a
faint black line along the outside curve of the shrimp, is faintly
visible beneath the translucent flesh. But some shrimp have a thick
orange, blue, or gray line instead of a thin black one. In all
cases, be careful not to slice too deeply, or you will end up with
two shrimp halves instead of one butterflied shrimp.

You have told readers what to look for, citing the exceptions, and have warned
them against making too deep a cut. Anticipating spots where communication
might break down is a key part of writing an effective process analysis.

Transitional words and phrases are also critical in helping readers understand the
order of the steps being described. Time signals like *first, next, now, while, after,
before,* and *finally* provide readers with a clear sense of the sequence. Entire sentences can also be used to link parts of the process, reminding your audience of
what has already been discussed and indicating what will now be explained:
"Once the panel of experts finishes its evaluation of the exam questions, randomly
selected items are field-tested in schools throughout the country."

6. Select and maintain an appropriate tone. When writing a process analysis
essay, be sure your tone is consistent with your purpose, your attitude toward
your subject, and the effect you want to have on readers. When explaining how
fraternities and sororities recruit new members, do you want to use an objective,
nonjudgmental tone, or do you want to project an angry, even accusatory tone? To
decide, take into account readers' attitudes toward your subject. Does your audience have a financial or emotional investment in the process being described?
Does your own interest in the process coincide or conflict with that of your audience? Awareness of your readers' stance can be crucial. Consider another example: Assume you're writing a letter to the director of the student health center
proposing a new system to replace the currently chaotic one. You'd do well to be
tactful in your criticisms. Offend your reader, and your cause is lost. If, however,
the letter is slated for the college newspaper and directed primarily to other students, you could adopt a more pointed, even sarcastic tone. Readers, you would
assume, will probably share your view and favor change.

Once you settle on the essay's tone, maintain it throughout. If you're writing a
light piece on the way computers are taking over our lives, you wouldn't include
a grim step-by-step analysis of the way confidential computerized medical
records may become public.

7. Open and close the process analysis effectively. A paper developed primarily
through process analysis should have a strong beginning. The introduction
should state the process to be described and imply whether the essay has an informational or directional intent.

If you suspect readers are indifferent to your subject, use the introduction to
motivate them, telling them how important the subject is:

Do you enjoy the salad bars found in many restaurants? If you do, you probably have noticed that the vegetables are always crisp and fresh--no matter how many hours they have been exposed to the air. What are the restaurants doing to make the vegetables look so inviting? There's a simple answer. Many restaurants dip and spray the vegetables with potent chemicals to make them look appetizing.

If you think your audience may be intimidated by your subject (perhaps because it's complex or relatively obscure), the introduction is the perfect spot to reassure them that the process being described is not beyond their grasp:

Studies show that many people prefer to accept a defective product rather than deal with the uncomfortable process of making a complaint. But once a few easy-to-learn basics are mastered, anyone can register a complaint that gets results.

Most process analysis essays don't end as soon as the last step in the sequence is explained. Instead, they usually include some brief final comments that round out the piece and bring it to a satisfying close. This final section of the essay may summarize the main steps in the process—not by repeating the steps verbatim but by rephrasing and condensing them in several concise sentences. The conclusion can also be an effective spot to underscore the significance of the process, recalling what may have been said in the introduction about the subject's importance. Or the essay can end by echoing the note of reassurance that may have been included at the start.

REVISION STRATEGIES

Once you have a draft of the essay, you're ready to revise. The following checklist will help you and those giving you feedback apply to process analysis some of the revision techniques discussed in Chapters 7 and 8.

✔ PROCESS ANALYSIS: A REVISION CHECKLIST

Revise Overall Meaning and Structure

☐ What purpose does the process analysis serve? To inform, to persuade, or to do both?

☐ Where does the process seem confusing? Where have steps been left out? Which steps need simplifying?

□ What tone does the essay project? Is the tone appropriate for the essay's purpose and readers? Where are there distracting shifts in tone?

Revise Paragraph Development

□ Does the introduction specify the process to be described? Does it provide an overview? Should it? Does it mention ingredients or materials the reader needs to know about? Should it?

□ Which paragraphs are difficult to follow? Have any steps been explained in unnecessary detail? Have key steps been omitted? Which paragraphs should warn readers about potential trouble spots or overlapping steps?

□ Where do time signals (*after, before, next*) clarify the sequence within and between paragraphs? Where does overreliance on time signals make the sequence awkward and mechanical?

□ Which paragraph describes the most crucial step in the sequence? How has the step been highlighted?

□ What closing comments round out the piece? Would the conclusion be more effective if the main stages were summarized? Or would such a conclusion be too repetitive?

Revise Sentences and Words

□ What technical or specialized terms appear in the essay? Have they been sufficiently defined or explained? Where could simpler, less technical language be used?

□ Are there any places where the essay awkwardly switches from say, second person to third person? How could this problem be corrected?

□ Does the essay use correct verb tenses—the past tense for completed events, the present tense for habitual or ongoing actions?

□ Where does the essay use the passive voice ("The earth is hoed")? Would the active voice ("You hoe the earth") be more effective?

STUDENT ESSAY: FROM PREWRITING THROUGH REVISION

The student essay that follows was written by Robert Barry in response to this assignment:

In "Watching the Animals," Richard Rhodes describes how the meat that Americans love to eat is processed. Think of something else that Americans enjoy and show, step by step, how it has worked its way into Americans' everyday life. Your essay, either serious or light in tone, might focus on a form of entertainment, a pastime, an invention, or the like.

Before writing his essay, Robert used the prewriting strategy of *mapping* to generate material for the subject he decided to write on: VCR addiction. Then, with his map as a foundation, he prepared a topic outline that organized and developed his thoughts more fully. Both the map and the outline are reprinted here.

Mapping

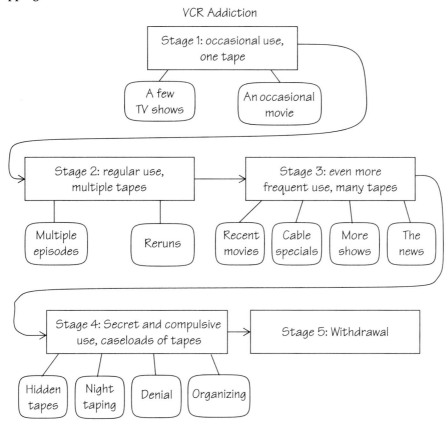

VCR Addiction

Outline

Thesis: Without realizing it, a person can turn into a compulsive videotaper. This movement from innocent hobby to full-blown addiction occurs in several stages.

    I. Stage One: Occasional use (only one tape)

        A. TV show reruns

           1. Star Trek

           2. Miami Vice

       B. An occasional movie

  II. Stage Two: More frequent use (more tapes)

       A. Many episodes of <u>Star Trek</u>

       B. Reruns of <u>The Honeymooners</u> and <u>Mission: Impossible</u>

 III. Stage Three: Much more frequent use (stockpile of tapes)

       A. Taping of news shows

       B. Taping of recent movies--add examples

       C. Not enough time to watch taped cable shows plus regularly taped shows

  IV. Stage Four: Secret and compulsive use (caseloads of tapes)

       A. Reaction to family's concern

         1. Denial

         2. Hiding tapes in suitcase

         3. Nighttime taping

       B. Obsessive organization of tapes

   V. Stage Five: Withdrawal

       A. Forced withdrawal at college

       B. Success at last

Now read Robert's paper, "Becoming a Videoholic," noting the similarities and differences among his map, outline, and final essay. You'll see that Robert dropped one idea (taping news shows), expanded other points (his obsessive organization of tapes into Westerns, comedies, and horror movies), and added some completely new details (his near backsliding during withdrawal). Note, too, that the analogy between VCR addiction and alcoholism doesn't appear in either the map or the outline. The analogy didn't occur to Robert until he began writing his first draft. Despite these differences, the map and outline depict essentially the same five stages in VCR addiction as the essay. Finally, as you read the essay, consider how well it applies the principles of process analysis discussed in this chapter. (The commentary that follows the paper will help you look at Robert's essay more closely and will give you some sense of how he went about revising.)

Becoming a Videoholic

by Robert Barry

Introduction   In the last several years, videocassette recorders (VCRs)   1
have become popular additions in many American homes. A recent
newspaper article notes that one in three households has a VCR,
with sales continuing to climb every day. VCRs seem to be the
most popular technological breakthrough since television

itself. No consumer warning labels are attached to these
rapidly multiplying VCRs, but they should be. VCRs can be
dangerous. Barely aware of what is happening, a person can turn Start of two-sentence thesis
into a compulsive videotaper. The descent from innocent hobby
to full-blown addiction takes place in several stages. Topic sentence

2   In the first innocent stage, the unsuspecting person buys
a VCR for occasional use. I was at this stage when I asked my
parents if they would buy me a VCR as a combined birthday and
high school graduation gift. With the VCR, I could tape reruns First stage in process (VCR addiction)
of Star Trek and Miami Vice, shows I would otherwise miss on
nights I was at work. The VCR was perfect. I hooked it up to the
old TV in my bedroom, recorded the intergalactic adventures of
Captain Kirk and the high-voltage escapades of Sonny Crockett,
then watched the tapes the next day. Occasionally, I taped a
movie that my friends and I watched over the weekend. I had just
one cassette, but that was all I needed since I watched every
show I recorded and simply taped over the preceding show when Beginning of analogy to alcoholism
I recorded another. In these early days, my VCR was the
equivalent of light social drinking. Topic sentence

3   In the second phase on the road to videoholism, an indi- Second stage in process
vidual uses the VCR more frequently and begins to stockpile
tapes rather than watch them. My troubles began in July when my
family went to the shore for a week's vacation. I programmed
the VCR to tape all five episodes of Star Trek while I was at
the beach perfecting my tan. Since I used the VCR's long-play
mode, I could get all five Star Treks on one cassette. But that
ended up creating a problem. Even I, an avid Trekkie, didn't
want to watch five shows in one sitting. I viewed two shows, but
the three unwatched shows tied up my tape, making it impossible
to record other shows. How did I resolve this dilemma? Very
easily. I went out and bought several more cassettes. Once I
had these additional tapes, I was free to record as many Star
Treks as I wanted, plus I could tape reruns of classics like The
Honeymooners and Mission: Impossible. Very quickly, I accumulated six Star Treks, four Honeymooners, and three Mission:
Impossibles. Then a friend--who shall go nameless--told me that
only eighty-two episodes of Star Trek were ever made. Excited
by the thought that I could acquire as impressive a collection
of tapes as a Hollywood executive, I continued recording Star

Continuation of — *Trek,* even taping shows while I watched them. Clearly, my once
analogy   innocent hobby was getting out of control. I was now using the
                 VCR on a regular basis--the equivalent of several stiff drinks
                 a day.

Topic sentence ——→ In the third stage of videoholism, the amount of taping   4
                 increases significantly, leading to an even more irrational
                 stockpiling of cassettes. The catalyst that propelled me into
Third stage in   this third stage was my parents' decision to get cable TV.
process   Selfless guy that I am, I volunteered to move my VCR and hook
                 it up to the TV in the living room, where the cable outlet was
Continuation of — located. Now I could tape all the most recent movies and cable
analogy   specials. With that delightful possibility in mind, I went out
                 and bought two six-packs of blank tapes. Then, in addition to
                 my regulars, I began to record a couple of other shows every
                 day. I taped Rocky III, Magnum Force, a James Bond movie, an HBO
                 comedy special with Eddie Murphy, and an MTV concert featuring
                 Mick Jagger. Where did I get time to watch all these tapes? I
                 didn't. Taping at this point was more satisfying than watching.
                 Reason and common sense were abandoned. Getting things on tape
                 had become an obsession, and I was taping all the time.

Topic sentence ——→ In the fourth stage, videoholism creeps into other parts   5
                 of the addict's life, influencing behavior in strange ways.
                 Secrecy becomes commonplace. One day, my mother came into my
Fourth stage in room and saw my bookcase filled with tapes--rather than with
process   the paperbacks that used to be there. "Robert," she exclaimed,
Continuation of — "isn't this getting a bit out of hand?" I assured her it was
analogy   just a hobby, but I started hiding my tapes, putting them in a
                 suitcase stored in my closet. I also taped at night, slipping
                 downstairs to turn on the VCR after my parents had gone to bed
                 and getting down first thing in the morning to turn off the VCR
                 and remove the cassette before my parents noticed. Also, denial
                 is not unusual during this stage of VCR addiction. At the din-
                 ner table, when my younger sister commented, "Robert tapes all
                 the time," I laughingly told everyone--including myself--that
                 the taping was no big deal. I was getting bored with it and was
                 going to stop any day, I assured my family. Obsessive behavior
                 also characterizes the fourth stage of videoholism. Each week,
                 I pulled out the TV magazine from the Sunday paper and went
                 through it carefully, circling in red all the shows I wanted to

tape. Another sign of addiction was my compulsive organization
of all the tapes I had stockpiled. Working more diligently than
I ever had for any term paper, I typed up labels and attached
them to each cassette. I also created an elaborate list that
showed my tapes broken down into categories such as Westerns,
horror movies, and comedies.

                                                 — Topic sentence

6   In the final stage of an addiction, the individual either
succumbs completely to the addiction or is able to break away   — Continuation of
from the habit. I broke my addiction, and I broke it cold tur-   analogy
key. This total withdrawal occurred when I went off to college.
There was no point in taking my VCR to school because TVs were
not allowed in the freshman dorms. Even though there were many
things to occupy my time during the school week, cold sweats
overcame me whenever I thought about everything on TV I was not
taping. I even considered calling home and asking members of my   Final stage in
family to tape things for me, but I knew they would think I was   process
crazy. At the beginning of the semester, I also had to resist
the overwhelming desire to travel the three hours home every
weekend so I could get my fix. But after a while, the urgent
need to tape subsided. Now, months later, as I write this, I
feel detached and sober.

7   I have no illusions, though. I know that once a videoholic,   Conclusion
always a videoholic. Soon I will return home for the holidays,
which, as everyone knows, can be a time for excess eating--and   — Final references to
taping. But I will cope with the pressure. I will take each day   analogy
one at a time. I will ask my little sister to hide my blank
tapes. And if I feel myself succumbing to the temptations of
taping, I will pick up the telephone and dial the videoholics'
hot line: (800) VCR-TAPE. I will win the battle.

Commentary

Purpose, Thesis, and Tone

    Robert's essay is an example of *informational process analysis;* his purpose is to
describe—rather than teach—the process of becoming a "videoholic." The title,
with its coined term *videoholic,* tips us off that the essay is going to be entertaining.
And the introductory paragraph clearly establishes the essay's playful, mock-
serious tone. The tone established, Robert briefly defines the term *videoholic* as a
"compulsive videotaper" and then moves to the essay's *thesis:* "Barely aware of

what is happening, a person can turn into a compulsive videotaper. The descent from innocent hobby to full-blown addiction takes place in several stages."

Throughout the essay, Robert sustains the introduction's humor by mocking his own motivations and poking fun at his quirks: "Selfless guy that I am, I volunteered to move my VCR" (paragraph 4), and "Working more diligently than I ever had for any term paper, I typed up labels" (5). Robert probably uses a bit of *dramatic license* when reporting some of his obsessive behavior, and we, as readers, understand that he's exaggerating for comic effect. Most likely he didn't break out in a cold sweat at the thought of the TV shows he was unable to tape, and he probably didn't hide his tapes in a suitcase. Nevertheless, this tinkering with the truth is legitimate because it allows Robert to create material that fits the essay's lightly satiric tone.

Organization and Topic Sentences

To meet the requirements of the assignment, Robert needed to provide a *step-by-step* explanation of a process. And because he invented the term *videoholism*, Robert also needed to invent the stages in the progression of his addiction. During his prewriting, Robert discovered five stages in his videoholism. Presented *chronologically*, these stages provide the organizing focus for his paper. Specifically, each supporting paragraph is devoted to one stage, with the *topic sentence* for each paragraph indicating the stage's distinctive characteristics.

Transitions

Although Robert's essay is playful, it is nonetheless a process analysis and so must have an easy-to-follow structure. Keeping this in mind, Robert wisely includes *transitions* to signal what happened at each stage of his videoholism: "*Once* I had these additional tapes, I was free to record" (paragraph 3); "*Then,* in addition to my regulars, I began to record" (4); "*One day,* my mother came into my room" (5); and "*But after a while,* the urgent need to tape subsided" (6). In addition to such transitions, Robert uses crisp questions to move from idea to idea within a paragraph: "How did I resolve this dilemma? Very easily. I . . . bought several more cassettes" (3), and "Where did I get time to watch all these tapes? I didn't" (4).

Other Patterns of Development

Even though Robert's essay is a process analysis, it contains elements of other patterns of development. For example, his paper is unified by an *analogy*—a sustained *comparison* between Robert's video addiction and the obviously more serious addiction to alcohol. Handled incorrectly, the analogy could have been offensive, but Robert makes the comparison work to his advantage. The analogy is stated specifically in several spots: "In these early days, my VCR was the equivalent of light social drinking" (2); "I was now using the VCR on a regular basis—the equivalent of several stiff drinks a day" (3). Another place where Robert touches wittily on the analogy occurs in the middle of the fourth paragraph: "I went out and bought two six-packs of blank tapes." To illustrate his progression toward videoholism, Robert depicts the *effects* of his addiction. Finally, he generates numerous lively details or *examples* to illustrate the different stages in his addiction.

Two Unnecessary Sentences

Perhaps you noticed that Robert runs into a minor problem at the end of the fourth paragraph. Starting with the sentence "Reason and common sense were abandoned," he begins to ramble and repeat himself. The paragraph's last two sentences fail to add anything substantial. Take a moment to read paragraph 4 aloud, omitting the last two sentences. Note how much sharper the new conclusion is: "Where did I get time to watch all these tapes? I didn't. Taping at this point was more satisfying than watching." This new ending says all that needs to be said.

Revising the First Draft

When it was time to revise, Robert—in spite of his apprehension—showed his paper to his roommate and asked him to read it out loud. Robert knew this strategy would provide a more objective point of view on his work. His roommate, at first an unwilling recruit, nonetheless laughed as he read the essay aloud. That was just the response Robert wanted. But when his roommate got to the conclusion, Robert heard that the closing paragraph was flat and anticlimactic. His roommate agreed, so the two of them brainstormed ways to make the conclusion livelier and more in spirit with the rest of the essay.

Reprinted here is Robert's original conclusion. The handwritten notes, numbered in order of importance, represent both Robert's ideas for revision and those of his roommate.

Original Version of the Conclusion

③ Shorten first sentence

    I have no illusions, though, that I am over my videoholism.

    Soon I will be returning home for the holidays, which can be a   ① Get back to analogy

    time for excess taping. All I can do is ask my little sister to

    hide my blank tapes. After that, I will hope for the best.   ② Boring. Add humor.

As you can see, Robert and his roommate decided that the best approach would be to reinforce the playful, mock-serious tone that characterized earlier parts of the essay. Robert thus made three major changes to his conclusion. First, he tightened the first sentence of the paragraph ("I have no illusions, though, that I am over my videoholism"), making it crisper and more dramatic: "I have no illusions, though." Second, he added a few sentences to sustain the light, self-deprecating tone he had used earlier: "I know that once a videoholic, always a videoholic"; "But I will cope with the pressure"; "I will win the battle." Third, and perhaps most important, he returned to the alcoholism analogy: "I will take each day one at a time.... And if I feel myself succumbing to the temptations of taping, I will pick up the telephone and dial the videoholics' hotline...."

These weren't the only changes Robert made while reworking his paper, but they help illustrate how sensitive he was to the effect he wanted to achieve. Certainly, the recasting of the conclusion was critical to the overall success of this amusing essay.

ACTIVITIES: PROCESS ANALYSIS

Prewriting Activities

1. Imagine you're writing two essays: One defines the term *comparison shopping;* the other contrasts two different teaching styles. Jot down ways you might use process analysis in each essay.

2. Look at the essay topics that follow. Assuming that your readers will be students in your composition class, which topics would lend themselves to directional process analysis, informational process analysis, or a blend of both? Explain your responses.

  a. Going on a job interview
  b. Using a computer in the college library
  c. Cleaning up oil spills
  d. Negotiating personal conflicts
  e. Curing a cold
  f. Growing vegetables organically

3. For *one* of the following essay topics, decide—given the audience indicated in parentheses—what your purpose, tone, and point of view might be. Then use brainstorming, questioning, mapping, or another prewriting technique to identify the steps you'd include in a process analysis for that audience. After reviewing the material generated, delete, add, and combine points as needed. Then organize the material in the most logical sequence.

  a. How to write effective essays (*college students*)
  b. How to get along with parents (*high school students*)
  c. How the college administration handled a controversial campus issue (*alumni*)
  d. How to deal with a bully (*elementary school children*)
  e. How a specific ceremony is performed in your religion (*an adult unfamiliar with the practice*)
  f. How malls encourage spending sprees (*general public*)

4. Select *one* of the essay topics that follow and determine what your purpose, tone, and point of view would be for each audience indicated in parentheses. Then use prewriting to identify the points you'd cover for each audience. Finally, organize the raw material, noting the differences in emphasis and sequence for each group of readers.

a. How to buy a car (*young people who have just gotten a driver's license; established professionals*)

b. How children acquire their values (*first-time parents; elementary school teachers*)

c. How to manage money (*grade-school children; college students*)

d. How loans or scholarships are awarded to incoming students on your campus (*high school graduates applying for financial aid; high school guidance counselors*)

e. How arguments can strengthen relationships (*preteen children; young adults*)

f. How to relax (*college students; parents with young children*)

5. For *one* of the following process topics, identify an appropriate audience, purpose, tone, and point of view. Then use prewriting to generate raw material showing that there's a problem with the way the process is performed. After organizing that material, use prewriting once again—this time to identify how the process *should* be performed. Sequence this new material in a logical order.

a. How students select a college or a major

b. How local television news covers national events

c. How a specific group of people mismanage their finances

d. How your campus or your community is handling a difficult situation

Revising Activities

6. The following paragraph is from an essay making the point that over-the-phone sales can be a challenging career. The paragraph, written as a process analysis, describes the steps involved in making a sales call. Revise the paragraph, deleting any material that undermines the paragraph's unity, organizing the steps in a logical sequence, and supplying transitions where needed. Also be sure to correct any inappropriate shifts in person. Finally, do some brainstorming—individually or in a group—to generate details to bolster underdeveloped steps in the sequence.

```
     Establishing rapport with potential customers is the most chal-
lenging part of phone sales. The longer you can keep customers on
the phone, the more you can get a sense of their needs. And the more
you know about customers, the more successful the salesperson is
bound to be. Your opening comments are critical. After setting the
right tone, you gently introduce your product. There are a number of
ways you can move gracefully from your opening remarks to the actual
selling phase of the call. Remember: Don't try to sell the customer
at the beginning. Instead, try in a friendly way to keep the pro-
spective customer on the phone. Maintaining such a connection is
easier than you think because many people have an almost desperate
```

need to talk. Their lives are isolated and lonely--a sad fact of
contemporary life. Once you shift to the distinctly selling phase of
the call, you should present the advantages of the product, especially the advantages of price and convenience. Mentioning install-
ment payments is often effective. If the customer says that he or
she isn't interested, the salesperson should try to determine--in a
genial way--why the person is reluctant to buy. Don't, however, push
aggressively for reasons or try to steamroll the person into thinking his or her reservations are invalid. Once the person agrees to
buy, try to encourage credit card payment, rather than check or
money order. The salesperson can explain that credit card payment
means the customer will receive the product sooner. End the call as
you began--in an easy, personable way.

7. Reprinted here is a paragraph from the first draft of a humorous essay advising
shy college students how to get through a typical day. Written as a process analysis,
the paragraph outlines techniques for surviving class. Revise the paragraph, deleting digressions that disrupt the paragraph's unity, eliminating unnecessary repetition, and sequencing the steps in the proper order. Also correct inappropriate shifts
in person and add transitions where needed. Feel free to add any telling details.

Simply attending class can be stressful for shy people. Several
strategies, though, can lessen the trauma. Shy students should time
their arrival to coincide with that of most other class members--
about two minutes before the class is scheduled to begin. If you
arrive too early, you may be seen sitting alone or, even worse, may
actually be forced to talk with another early arrival. If you arrive
late, all eyes will be upon you. Before heading to class, the shy
student should dress in the least conspicuous manner possible--say,
in the blue jeans, sweatshirt, and sneakers that 99.9 percent of
your classmates wear. That way you won't stand out from everyone
else. Take a seat near the back of the room. Don't, however, sit at
the very back since professors often take sadistic pleasure in calling on students back there, assuming they chose those seats because
they didn't want to be called on. A friend of mine who is far from
shy uses just the opposite ploy. In an attempt to get in good with
her professors, she sits in the front row and, incredibly enough,
volunteers to participate. However, since shy people don't want to
call attention to themselves, they should stifle any urge to sneeze
or cough. You run the risk of having people look at you or offer you
a tissue or cough drop. And of course, never, ever volunteer to

answer. Such a display of intelligence is sure to focus all eyes on you. In other words, make yourself as inconspicuous as possible. How, you might wonder, can you be inconspicuous if you're blessed (or cursed) with great looks? Well, ... have you ever considered earning your degree through the mail?

PROFESSIONAL
SELECTIONS:
PROCESS ANALYSIS

DIANE COLE

Diane Cole (1952–), a former contributing editor of *Psychology Today,* has written articles for numerous publications, including the *Wall Street Journal, Newsweek, Ms.,* and *Mademoiselle.* Cole has also written several books, among them *Hunting the Head Hunters: A Woman's Guide* (1988) and *After Great Pain: Coping with Loss and Change* (1996). The following selection, which first appeared in the *New York Times* in 1989, was underwritten by the Anti-Defamation League of B'nai B'rith as part of its ongoing campaign against prejudice.

DON'T JUST STAND THERE

1   It was my office farewell party, and colleagues at the job I was about to leave were wishing me well. My mood was one of ebullience tinged with regret, and it was in this spirit that I spoke to the office neighbor to whom I had waved hello every morning for the past two years. He smiled broadly as he launched into a long, rambling story, pausing only after he delivered the punch line. It was a very long pause because, although he laughed, I did not: This joke was unmistakably anti-Semitic.

2   I froze. Everyone in the office knew I was Jewish; what could he have possibly meant? Shaken and hurt, not knowing what else to do, I turned in stunned silence to the next well-wisher. Later, still angry, I wondered, what else should I—could I—have done?

3   Prejudice can make its presence felt in any setting, but hearing its nasty voice in this way can be particularly unnerving. We do not know what to do and often we feel another form of paralysis as well: We think, "Nothing I say or do will change this person's attitude, so why bother?"

4   But left unchecked, racial slurs and offensive ethnic jokes "can poison the atmosphere," says Michael McQuillan, adviser for racial/ethnic affairs for the Brooklyn

borough president's office. "Hearing these remarks conditions us to accept them; and if we accept these, we can become accepting of other acts."

Speaking up may not magically change a biased attitude, but it can change a person's 5 behavior by putting a strong message across. And the more messages there are, the more likely a person is to change that behavior, says Arnold Kahn, professor of psychology at James Madison University, Harrisonburg, Virginia, who makes this analogy: "You can't keep people from smoking in *their* house, but you can ask them not to smoke in *your* house."

At the same time, "Even if the other party ignores or discounts what you say, people 6 always reflect on how others perceive them. Speaking up always counts," says LeNorman Strong, director of campus life at George Washington University, Washington, D.C.

Finally, learning to respond effectively also helps people feel better about them- 7 selves, asserts Cherie Brown, executive director of the National Coalition Building Institute, a Boston-based training organization. "We've found that, when people felt they could at least in this small way make a difference, that made them more eager to take on other activities on a larger scale," she says. Although there is no "cookbook approach" to confronting such remarks—every situation is different, experts stress— these are some effective strategies.

> When the "joke" turns on who you are—as a member of an ethnic or religious group, a person of 8 color, a woman, a gay or lesbian, an elderly person, or someone with a physical handicap—shocked paralysis is often the first response. Then, wounded and vulnerable, on some level you want to strike back.

Lashing out or responding in kind is seldom the most effective response, however. 9 "That can give you momentary satisfaction, but you also feel as if you've lowered yourself to that other person's level," Mr. McQuillan explains. Such a response may further label you in the speaker's mind as thin-skinned, someone not to be taken seriously. Or it may up the ante, making the speaker, and then you, reach for new insults—or physical blows.

"If you don't laugh at the joke, or fight, or respond in kind to the slur," says Mr. 10 McQuillan, "that will take the person by surprise, and that can give you more control over the situation." Therefore, in situations like the one in which I found myself—a private conversation in which I knew the person making the remark—he suggests voicing your anger calmly but pointedly: "I don't know if you realize what that sounded like to me. If that's what you meant, it really hurt me."

State how *you* feel, rather than making an abstract statement like, "Not everyone 11 who hears that joke might find it funny." Counsels Mr. Strong: "Personalize the sense of 'this is how I feel when you say this.' That makes it very concrete"—and harder to dismiss.

Make sure you heard the words and their intent correctly by repeating or rephrasing 12 the statement: "This is what I heard you say. Is that what you meant?" It's important to give the other person the benefit of the doubt because, in fact, he may *not* have realized that the comment was offensive and, if you had not spoken up, would have had no idea of its impact on you.

13   For instance, Professor Kahn relates that he used to include in his exams multiple-choice questions that occasionally contained "incorrect funny answers." After one exam, a student came up to him in private and said, "I don't think you intended this, but I found a number of those jokes offensive to me as a woman." She explained why. "What she said made immediate sense to me," he says. "I apologized at the next class, and I never did it again."

14   But what if the speaker dismisses your objection, saying, "Oh, you're just being sensitive. Can't you take a joke?" In that case, you might say, "I'm not so sure about that, let's talk about that a little more." The key, Mr. Strong says, is to continue the dialogue, hear the other person's concerns, and point out your own. "There are times when you're just going to have to admit defeat and end it," he adds, "but I have to feel that I did the best I could."

15   When the offending remark is made in the presence of others—at a staff meeting, for example—it can be even more distressing than an insult made privately.

16   "You have two options," says William Newlin, director of field services for the Community Relations division of the New York City Commission on Human Rights. "You can respond immediately at the meeting, or you can delay your response until afterward in private. But a response has to come."

17   Some remarks or actions may be so outrageous that they cannot go unnoted at the moment, regardless of the speaker or the setting. But in general, psychologists say, shaming a person in public may have the opposite effect of the one you want: The speaker will deny his offense all the more strongly in order to save face. Further, few people enjoy being put on the spot, and if the remark really was not intended to be offensive, publicly embarrassing the person who made it may cause an unnecessary rift or further misunderstanding. Finally, most people just don't react as well or thoughtfully under a public spotlight as they would in private.

18   Keeping that in mind, an excellent alternative is to take the offender aside afterward: "Could we talk for a minute in private?" Then use the strategies suggested above for calmly stating how you feel, giving the speaker the benefit of the doubt, and proceeding from there.

19   At a large meeting or public talk, you might consider passing the speaker a note, says David Wertheimer, executive director of the New York City Gay and Lesbian Anti-Violence Project: You could write, "You may not realize it, but your remarks were offensive because...."

20   "Think of your role as that of an educator," suggests James M. Jones, Ph.D., executive director for public interest at the American Psychological Association. "You have to be controlled."

21   Regardless of the setting or situation, speaking up always raises the risk of rocking the boat. If the person who made the offending remark is your boss, there may be an even bigger risk to consider: How will this affect my job? Several things can help minimize the risk, however. First, know what other resources you may have at work, suggests Caryl Stern, director of the A World of Difference—New York City campaign: Does your personnel office handle discrimination complaints? Are other grievance procedures in place?

22   You won't necessarily need to use any of these procedures, Ms. Stern stresses. In fact, she advises, "It's usually better to try a one-on-one approach first." But simply

knowing a formal system exists can make you feel secure enough to set up that meeting.

You can also raise the issue with other colleagues who heard the remark: Did they 23 feel the same way you did? The more support you have, the less alone you will feel. Your point will also carry more validity and be more difficult to shrug off. Finally, give your boss credit—and the benefit of the doubt: "I know you've worked hard for the company's affirmative action programs, so I'm sure you didn't realize what those remarks sounded like to me as well as the others at the meeting last week...."

If, even after this discussion, the problem persists, go back for another meeting, Ms. 24 Stern advises. And if that, too, fails, you'll know what other options are available to you.

It's a spirited dinner party, and everyone's having a good time, until one guest starts reciting a rac- 25 ist joke. Everyone at the table is white, including you. The others are still laughing, as you wonder what to say or do.

No one likes being seen as a party-pooper, but before deciding that you'd prefer not 26 to take on this role, you might remember that the person who told the offensive joke has already ruined your good time.

If it's a group that you feel comfortable in—a family gathering, for instance—you 27 will feel freer to speak up. Still, shaming the person by shouting "You're wrong!" or "That's not funny!" probably won't get your point across as effectively as other strategies. "If you interrupt people to condemn them, it just makes it harder," says Cherie Brown. She suggests trying instead to get at the resentments that lie beneath the joke by asking open-ended questions: "Grandpa, I know you always treat everyone with such respect. Why do people in our family talk that way about black people?" The key, Ms. Brown says, "is to listen to them first, so they will be more likely to listen to you."

If you don't know your fellow guests well, before speaking up you could turn dis- 28 creetly to your neighbors (or excuse yourself to help the host or hostess in the kitchen) to get a reading on how they felt, and whether or not you'll find support for speaking up. The less alone you feel, the more comfortable you'll be speaking up: "I know you probably didn't mean anything by that joke, Jim, but it really offended me...." It's important to say that *you* were offended—not state how the group that is the butt of the joke would feel. "Otherwise," LeNorman Strong says, "you risk coming off as a goody two-shoes."

If you yourself are the host, you can exercise more control; you are, after all, the one 29 who sets the rules and the tone of behavior in your home. Once, when Professor Kahn's party guests began singing offensive, racist songs, for instance, he kicked them all out, saying, "You don't sing songs like that in my house!" And, he adds, "they never did again."

At school one day, a friend comes over and says, "Who do you think you are, hanging out with 30 Joe? If you can be friends with those people, I'm through with you!"

Peer pressure can weigh heavily on kids. They feel vulnerable and, because they are 31 kids, they aren't as able to control the urge to fight. "But if you learn to handle these situations as kids, you'll be better able to handle them as an adult," William Newlin points out.

32   Begin by redefining to yourself what a friend is and examining what friendship means, advises Amy Lee, a human relations specialist at Panel of Americans, an inter-group-relations training and educational organization. If that person from a different group fits your requirement for a friend, ask, "Why shouldn't I be friends with Joe? We have a lot in common." Try to get more information about whatever stereotypes or resentments lie beneath your friend's statement. Ms. Lee suggests: "What makes you think they're so different from us? Where did you get that information?" She explains: "People are learning these stereotypes from somewhere, and they cannot be blamed for that. So examine where these ideas came from." Then talk about how your own experience rebuts them.

33   Kids, like adults, should also be aware of other resources to back them up: Does the school offer special programs for fighting prejudice? How supportive will the principal, the teachers, or other students be? If the school atmosphere is volatile, experts warn, make sure that taking a stand at that moment won't put you in physical danger. If that is the case, it's better to look for other alternatives.

34   These can include programs or organizations that bring kids from different back-grounds together. "When kids work together across race lines, that is how you break down the barriers and see that the stereotypes are not true," says Laurie Meadoff, pres-ident of CityKids Foundation, a nonprofit group whose programs attempt to do just that. Such programs can also provide what Cherie Brown calls a "safe place" to express the anger and pain that slurs and other offenses cause, whether the bigotry is directed against you or others.

35   In learning to speak up, everyone will develop a different style and a slightly differ-ent message to get across, experts agree. But it would be hard to do better than these two messages suggested by teenagers at CityKids: "Everyone on the face of the earth has the same intestines," said one. Another added, "Cross over the bridge. There's a lot of love on the streets."

Questions for Close Reading

1. What is the selection's thesis? Locate the sentence(s) in which Cole states her main idea. If she doesn't state the thesis explicitly, express it in your own words.

2. Why does Cole believe it is better to speak up against prejudice rather than to keep silent or ignore it?

3. Although Cole acknowledges that there is no "cookbook approach" for dealing with offensive comments, she nevertheless presents some general steps that can be followed. What are these general steps? Cole also describes more specific steps that can be taken in particular situations. What are the situations and the steps to be taken?

4. According to Cole's sources, what types of comments and responses are *not* useful in dealing with prejudicial jokes and remarks?

5. Refer to your dictionary as needed to define the following words used in the selection: *ebullience* (paragraph 1), *anti-Semitic* (1), *slurs* (4), *discounts* (6), *lashing* (9), *ante* (9), *abstract* (11), *personalize* (11), *rift* (17), *grievance* (21), and *volatile* (33).

Questions About the Writer's Craft

1. The pattern. Does Cole's process analysis have a primarily informative or persuasive purpose? How do you know? Where does the author suggest her purpose? How does her use of the second person "you" reinforce that purpose?

2. Other patterns. What examples does Cole provide to illustrate the process she's explaining? Why do you think she provides so many examples?

3. Cole uses quotations extensively in the essay. Why do you suppose she quotes so many people? What effect do you think Cole hopes the quotations will have on her readers?

4. What purpose do the essay's three sections set off with smaller type serve? Why might Cole have chosen to set off these sections? Which one of the three sections seems to address a different audience than the other two? Taking into account why this essay was written and where it was published (see the biographical note), do you think Cole is justified in shifting her essay's focus in this way? Why or why not? Is the shift effective? Explain.

Writing Assignments Using Process Analysis as a Pattern of Development

1. Cole describes a process for handling offensive *comments*, but there are many times when we wonder whether to protest someone's objectionable *behavior*. Write an essay explaining a process for dealing with one such behavior. You might describe a process for confronting a friend who forgets to repay loans, a teacher who grades unfairly, or a boss who treats employees rudely. Like Cole, tell readers what they should do if a step in the process doesn't yield the hoped-for results.

2. In paragraph 27, Cole describes a family gathering during which a grandchild confronts a grandfather as one adult to another. However, dealing with older relatives in such a forthright manner can be difficult, especially when the older adults don't perceive the grown-up child as a mature individual. Write an essay describing the process by which a grown child can confront such relatives and request that they treat the "child" like an adult. Use examples from your own family and from friends' families when explaining how to deal—and not deal—with such relatives.

Writing Assignments Using Other Patterns of Development

3. Cole writes about one type of behavior that most of us find obnoxious. But, as we all know, there are many types of obnoxious or annoying people. Focusing on a specific setting (a library, a highway, a store, a classroom) write a light-spirited essay in which you categorize the kinds of obnoxious people you typically encounter there. Be sure to provide vivid descriptions of the behavior that makes these people so unpleasant.

4. When confronted by offensive language and behavior, people should—Cole argues—take a stand. Write an essay constructing your personal definition of *assertiveness.* Illustrate your definition by providing specific examples of what it is and what it isn't. To gain additional insight into assertiveness, read "Why People Don't Help in a Crisis" (page 392) by John Darley and Bibb Latané.

MALCOLM X

Malcolm X (1925–65) was born Malcolm Little but took the name Malcolm X when he become a Black Muslim. An impassioned speaker and influential civil rights leader, Malcolm X was assassinated by a follower of a rival political and religious group. The following selection is from *The Autobiography of Malcolm X* (1964), which was originally dictated to Alex Haley, later known as the author of *Roots.*

MY FIRST CONK

1   Shorty soon decided that my hair was finally long enough to be conked. He had promised to school me in how to beat the barbershops' three- and four-dollar price by making up congolene, and then conking ourselves.

2   I took the little list of ingredients he had printed out for me, and went to a grocery store, where I got a can of Red Devil lye, two eggs, and two medium-sized white potatoes. Then at a drugstore near the poolroom, I asked for a large jar of Vaseline, a large bar of soap, a large-toothed comb and a fine-toothed comb, one of those rubber hoses with a metal spray-head, a rubber apron and a pair of gloves.

3   "Going to lay on that first conk?" the drugstore man asked me. I proudly told him, grinning, "Right!"

4   Shorty paid six dollars a week for a room in his cousin's shabby apartment. His cousin wasn't at home. "It's like the pad's mine, he spends so much time with his woman," Shorty said. "Now, you watch me—"

5   He peeled the potatoes and thin-sliced them into a quart-sized Mason fruit jar, then started stirring them with a wooden spoon as he gradually poured in a little over half the can of lye. "Never use a metal spoon; the lye will turn it black," he told me.

6   A jelly-like, starchy-looking glop resulted from the lye and potatoes, and Shorty broke in the two eggs, stirring real fast—his own conk and dark face bent down close. The congolene turned pale-yellowish. "Feel the jar," Shorty said. I cupped my hand against the outside, and snatched it away. "Damn right, it's hot, that's the lye," he said. "So you know it's going to burn when I comb it in—it burns bad. But the longer you can stand it, the straighter the hair."

7   He made me sit down, and he tied the string of the new rubber apron tightly around my neck, and combed up my bush of hair. Then, from the big Vaseline jar, he took a handful and massaged it hard all through my hair and into the scalp. He also thickly Vaselined my neck, ears and forehead. "When I get to washing out your head, be sure to tell me anywhere you feel any little stinging," Shorty warned me, washing his

hands, then pulling on the rubber gloves, and tying on his own rubber apron. "You always got to remember that any congolene left in burns a sore into your head."

The congolene just felt warm when Shorty started combing it in. But then my head 8 caught fire.

I gritted my teeth and tried to pull the sides of the kitchen table together. The comb 9 felt as if it was raking my skin off.

My eyes watered, my nose was running. I couldn't stand it any longer; I bolted to 10 the washbasin. I was cursing Shorty with every name I could think of when he got the spray going and started soap-lathering my head.

He lathered and spray-rinsed, lathered and spray-rinsed, maybe ten or twelve times, 11 each time gradually closing the hot-water faucet, until the rinse was cold, and that helped some.

"You feel any stinging spots?"   12

"No," I managed to say. My knees were trembling.   13

"Sit back down, then. I think we got it all out okay."   14

The flame came back as Shorty, with a thick towel, started drying my head, rubbing 15 hard. *"Easy, man, easy!"* I kept shouting.

"The first time's always worst. You get used to it better before long. You took it real 16 good, homeboy. You got a good conk."

When Shorty let me stand up and see in the mirror, my hair hung down in limp, 17 damp strings. My scalp still flamed, but not as badly; I could bear it. He draped the towel around my shoulders, over my rubber apron, and began again Vaselining my hair.

I could feel him combing, straight back, first the big comb, then the fine-tooth one. 18

Then, he was using a razor, very delicately, on the back of my neck. Then finally, 19 shaping the sideburns.

My first view in the mirror blotted out the hurting. I'd seen some pretty conks, but 20 when it's the first time, on your *own* head, the transformation, after the lifetime of kinks, is staggering.

The mirror reflected Shorty behind me. We both were grinning and sweating. And 21 on top of my head was this thick, smooth sheen of shining red hair—real red—as straight as any white man's.

How ridiculous I was! Stupid enough to stand there simply lost in admiration of my 22 hair now looking "white," reflected in the mirror in Shorty's room. I vowed that I'd never again be without a conk, and I never was for many years.

This was my first really big step toward self-degradation: when I endured all of that 23 pain, literally burning my flesh to have it look like a white man's hair. I had joined that multitude of Negro men and women in America who are brainwashed into believing that the black people are "inferior"—and white people "superior"—that they will even violate and mutilate their God-created bodies to try to look "pretty" by white standards.

Look around today, in every small town and big city, from two-bit catfish and soda- 24 pop joints into the "integrated" lobby of the Waldorf-Astoria, and you'll see conks on black men. And you'll see black women wearing these green and pink and purple and red and platinum-blonde wigs. They're all more ridiculous than a slapstick comedy. It makes you wonder if the Negro has completely lost his sense of identity, lost touch with himself.

You'll see the conk worn by many, many so-called "upper class" Negroes, and, as 25 much as I hate to say it about them, on all too many Negro entertainers. One of the reasons that I've especially admired some of them, like Lionel Hampton and Sidney

Poitier, among others, is that they have kept their natural hair and fought to the top. I admire any Negro man who has never had himself conked, or who has had the sense to get rid of it—as I finally did.

26   I don't know which kind of self-defacing conk is the greater shame—the one you'll see on the heads of the black so-called "middle class" and "upper class," who ought to know better, or the one you'll see on the heads of the poorest, most downtrodden, ignorant black men. I mean the legal-minimum-wage ghetto-dwelling kind of Negro, as I was when I got my first one. It's generally among these poor fools that you'll see a black kerchief over the man's head, like Aunt Jemima; he's trying to make his conk last longer, between trips to the barbershop. Only for special occasions is this kerchief-protected conk exposed—to show off how "sharp" and "hip" its owner is. The ironic thing is that I have never heard any woman, white or black, express any admiration for a conk. Of course, any white woman with a black man isn't thinking about his hair. But I don't see how on earth a black woman with any race pride could walk down the street with any black man wearing a conk—the emblem of his shame that he is black.

27   To my own shame, when I say all of this I'm talking first of all about myself—because you can't show me any Negro who ever conked more faithfully than I did. I'm speaking from personal experience when I say of any black man who conks today, or any white-wigged black woman, that if they gave the brains in their heads just half as much attention as they do their hair, they would be a thousand times better off.

Questions for Close Reading

1. What is the selection's thesis? Locate the sentence(s) in which Malcolm X states his main idea. If he doesn't state the thesis explicitly, express it in your own words.

2. What are the ingredients of "congolene"? What is their effect? Why are the Vaseline, soap, spray hose, apron, and gloves needed?

3. Why does Malcolm X permit his friend Shorty to give him a "conk"? Why does he refer to it as "my first really big step toward self-degradation"?

4. What kind of black man does Malcolm X say he admires? What does he imply is more important than trying to change one's appearance?

5. Refer to your dictionary as needed to define the following words used in the selection: *self-degradation* (paragraph 23) and *self-defacing* (26).

Questions About the Writer's Craft

1. The pattern. After detailing the steps in the process of conking, Malcolm X places conking in the context of another, larger process. What is that process? How is it related to Malcolm X's purpose in writing this essay?

2. Other patterns. Rather than just presenting the process of conking, Malcolm X narrates his own experience with hair-straightening. What does his use of personal narrative add to the essay?

3. In paragraphs 22–26, Malcolm X places quotation marks around a number of words. How do these quotation marks reinforce the essay's thesis?

4. Do you think Malcolm X is writing primarily for a black audience or for a white one? How can you tell?

Writing Assignments Using Process Analysis as a Pattern of Development

∞ **1.** Malcolm X writes of the pressure to conform to majority opinions and practices. Relate the steps you took to resist pressures exerted by a specific group (your family, an employer, the educational system). Explain whether your resistance was or was not in your own best interests. George Orwell's "Shooting an Elephant" (page 203), Diane Cole's "Don't Just Stand There" (page 315), and Joseph H. Suina's "And Then I Went to School" (page 361) offer insights into the possible effects of the need to conform.

∞ **2.** Malcolm X describes an arduous process that had a demoralizing effect. In an essay, show how your mastery of a difficult process increased your self-esteem. Guide readers through the process step by step, revealing how your achievement enhanced your self-image. Maya Angelou's "Sister Flowers" (page 175) will spark some ideas worth exploring.

Writing Assignments Using Other Patterns of Development

3. In his youth, Malcolm X valued the straight hair of many whites. As he matured, however, he took pride in his natural appearance. Select some quality you possess or a custom you follow that you presently value more or less than you used to. Contrast your current attitude with your earlier one. Reveal what brought about the change.

∞ **4.** Narrate a time you initially misjudged someone because of his or her appearance. Convey the individual's genuine character, as well as your progressive discovery of the real person behind the appearance. To get a better idea of how prejudice can distort our perception of others, read Brent Staples's "Black Men and Public Space" (page 398).

RICHARD RHODES

Following his graduation with honors from Yale University, Richard Rhodes (1937–) worked for Hallmark Cards before becoming a contributing editor for *Playboy* and *Harper's*. Rhodes's fascination with the step-by-step unfolding of a process is evident in many of his books, including *The Making of the Atomic Bomb* (1987), *Dark Sun: The Making of the Hydrogen Bomb* (1995), and *How to Write: Advice and Reflections*

(1996). He is also the author of *Deadly Feasts: Tracking the Secrets of a Terrifying New Plague* (1997). The excerpted selection reprinted here was first published in *Harper's* in 1970.

WATCHING THE ANIMALS

The loves of flint and iron are naturally a little rougher than those of the nightingale and the rose.

—Ralph Waldo Emerson

1   I remembered today about this country lake in Kansas where I live: that it is artificial, built at the turn of the century, when Upton Sinclair was writing *The Jungle,** as an ice lake. The trains with their loads of meat from the Kansas City stockyards would stop by the Kaw River, across the road, and ice the cars. "You have just dined," Emerson once told what must have been a shocked Victorian audience, "and however scrupulously the slaughterhouse is concealed in the graceful distance of miles, there is complicity, expensive races—race living at the expense of race...."

2   The I-D Packing Company of Des Moines, Iowa: a small outfit which subcontracts from Armour the production of fresh pork. It can handle about 450 pigs an hour on its lines. No beef or mutton. No smoked hams or hot dogs. Plain fresh pork. A well-run outfit, with federal inspectors alert on all the lines.

3   The kind of slaughterhouse Upton Sinclair was talking about doesn't exist around here any more. The vast buildings still stand in Des Moines and Omaha and Kansas City, but the operations are gone. The big outfits used to operate on a profit margin of 1.5 per cent, which didn't give them much leeway, did it. Now they are defunct, and their buildings, which look like monolithic enlargements of concentration-camp barracks, sit empty, the hundreds of windows broken, dusty, jagged pieces of glass sticking out of the frames as if the animals heard the good news one day and leaped out the nearest exit....

4   There are no stockyards inside the I-D Packing Company. The pigs arrive by trailer truck from Sioux City and other places. Sometimes a farmer brings in two or three in the back of his pickup. He unloads them into the holding pens, where they are weighed and inspected, goes into the office and picks up his check....

5   Down goes the tail gate and out come the pigs, enthusiastic after their drive. Pigs are the most intelligent of all farm animals, by actual laboratory test. Learn the fastest, for example, to push a plunger with their foot to earn a reward of pelletized feed. And not as reliable in their instincts. You don't have to call cattle to dinner. They are waiting outside the fence at 4:30 sharp, having arrived as silently as the Vietcong.† But perhaps that is pig intelligence too: let you do the work, laze around until the last minute, and then charge over and knock you down before you can slop the garbage into the trough. Cattle will stroll one by one into a row of stalls and usually fill them in serial

---

*Upton Sinclair (1878–1968) was an American writer and social reformer. His novel *The Jungle* (1906) is an exposé of the inhumane conditions found in Chicago's stockyards in the early 1900s (editors' note).
†Vietnamese Communist rebels, noted for moving silently through the jungle (editors' note).

order. Not pigs. They squeal and nip and shove. Each one wants the entire meal for himself. They won't stick together in a herd, either. Shoot out all over the place, and you'd damned better have every gate closed or they'll be in your garden and on your lawn and even in your living room, nodding by the fire.

They talk a lot, to each other, to you if you care to listen. I am not romanticizing 6 pigs. They always scared me a little on the farm, which is probably why I watched them more closely than the other animals. They do talk: low grunts, quick squeals, a kind of hum sometimes, angry shrieks, high screams of fear.

I have great respect for the I-D Packing Company. They do a dirty job and do it as 7 cleanly and humanely as possible, and do it well. They were nice enough to let me in the door, which is more than I can say for the Wilson people in Omaha, where I first tried to arrange a tour. What are you hiding, Wilson people?

Once into the holding pen, the pigs mill around getting to know each other. The I-D 8 holding pens are among the most modern in the nation, my spokesman told me. Tubular steel painted tinner's red to keep it from rusting. Smooth concrete floors with drains so that the floors can be washed down hygienically after each lot of pigs is run through.

The pigs come out of the first holding pen through a gate that allows only one to 9 pass at a time. Just beside the gate is a wooden door, and behind the door is the first worker the pigs encounter. He has a wooden box beside him filled with metal numbers, the shape of each number picked out with sharp needles. For each lot of pigs he selects a new set of numbers—2473, say—and slots them into a device like a hammer and dips it in nontoxic purple dye. As a pig shoots out of the gate he hits the pig in the side with the numbers, making a tattoo.* The pig gives a grunt—it doesn't especially hurt, pigskin is thick, as you know—and moves on to one of several smaller pens where each lot is held until curtain time. The tattoo, my spokesman told me, will stay on the animal through all the killing and cleaning and cutting operations, to the very end. Its purpose is to identify any animal or lot of animals which might be diseased, so that the seller can be informed and the carcasses destroyed. Rather too proud of his tattooing process, I thought, but then, you know the tattoos I am thinking about.†

It would be more dramatic, make a better story, if the killing came last, but it comes 10 first. We crossed a driveway with more red steel fencing. Lined up behind it, pressing into it because they sensed by now that all was not well with them, were perhaps a hundred pigs. But still curious, watching us go by in our long white canvas coats. Everyone wore those, and hard plastic helmets, white helmets for the workers, yellow helmets for the foremen. I got to be a foreman.

Before they reach their end, the pigs get a shower,‡ a real one. Water sprays from 11 every angle to wash the farm off of them. Then they begin to feel crowded. The pen narrows like a funnel; the drivers behind urge the pigs forward, until one at a time they climb onto a moving ramp. The ramp's sides move as well as its floor. The floor is created to give the pigs footing. The sides are made of blocks of wood so that they will not bruise, and they slant inward to wedge the pigs along. Now they scream, never having been on such a ramp, smelling the smells they smell ahead. I do not want to overdra-

*, †, ‡ Rhodes's description of the pigs' slaughter echoes Germany's extermination of Jews and other minorities during World War II. Uprooted from their homes, the prisoners were sent to death camps, where they were tattooed with identification numbers. Then, having been told they were going to be allowed to shower, the unsuspecting prisoners were herded into gas chambers, where they were put to death (editors' note).

matize, because you have read all this before. But it was a frightening experience, seeing their fear, seeing so many of them go by. It had to remind me of things no one wants to be reminded of anymore, all mobs, all death marches, all mass murders and extinctions, the slaughter of the buffalo, the slaughter of the Indian, the Inferno, Judgment Day, complicity, expensive races, race living at the expense of race. That so gentle a religion as Christianity could end up in Judgment Day. That we are the most expensive of races, able in our affluence to hire others of our kind to do this terrible necessary work of killing another race of creatures so that we may feed our oxygen-rich brains. Feed our children, for that matter.

12   At the top of the ramp, one man. With rubber gloves on, holding two electrodes that looked like enlarged curling irons except that they sported more of those needles. As a pig reached the top, this man jabbed the electrodes into the pig's butt and shoulder, and that was it. No more pain, no more fear, no more mudholes, no more sun in the lazy afternoon. Knocked instantly unconscious, the pig shuddered in a long spasm and fell onto a stainless steel table a foot below the end of the ramp. Up came another pig, and the same result. And another, and another, 450 an hour, 3,600 a day, the belts returning below to coax another ride.

13   The pigs are not dead, merely unconscious. The electrodes are humane, my spokesman said, and relatively speaking, that is true. They used to gas the pigs—put them on a conveyor belt that ran through a room filled with anesthetic gas. That was humane too. The electrodes are more efficient. Anesthesia relaxes the body and loosens the bowels. The pigs must have been a mess. More efficient, then, to put their bodies in spasm.

14   They drop to the table, and here the endless chain begins. A worker takes the nearest dangling chain by its handle as it passes. The chain is attached at the top to a belt of links, like a large bicycle chain. At the bottom the dangling chain has a metal handle like the handle on a bike. The chain runs through the handle and then attaches to the end of the handle, so that by sliding the handle the worker forms a loop. Into the loop he hooks one of the pig's hind feet. Another worker does the same with the other foot. Each has his own special foot to grab, or the pig would go down the line backwards, which would not be convenient. Once hooked into the line, the pig will stay in place by the force of its own weight.

15   Now the line ascends, lifting the unconscious animal into the air. The pig proceeds a distance of ten feet, where a worker standing on a platform deftly inserts a butcher knife into its throat. They call it "sticking," which it is. Then all hell breaks loose, if blood merely is hell. It gushes out, at about a 45-degree angle downward, thick as a ship's hawser, pouring directly onto the floor. Nothing is so red as blood, an incandescent red and most beautiful. It is the brightest color we drab creatures possess. Down on the floor below, with a wide squeegee on a long handle, a worker spends his eight hours a day squeegeeing that blood, some of it clotted, jellied, now, into an open drain. It is cycled through a series of pipes into a dryer, later to be made into blood meal for animal feed.

16   The line swings around a corner, high above the man with the squeegee, around the drain floor, turns left at the next corner, and begins to ascend to the floor above. This interval—thirteen seconds, I think my spokesman said, or was it thirty?—so that the carcass may drain completely before further processing. Below the carcass on the ascent is a trough like those lowered from the rear of cement trucks, there to catch the last drainings of blood.

17   Pigs are not skinned, as cattle are, unless you are after the leather, and we are after the meat. But the hair must be taken off, and it must first be scalded loose. Courteously, the

line lowers the carcass into a long trough filled with water heated to 180 degrees. The carcass will float if given a chance, fat being lighter than water, so wooden pushers on crankshafts spaced equally along the scalding tank immerse and roll the carcasses. Near the end of the trough, my spokesman easily pulls out a tuft of hair. The line ascends again, up and away, and the carcass goes into a chamber where revolving brushes as tall as a man whisk away the hair. We pass to the other side of the chamber and find two workers with wide knives scraping off the few patches of hair that remain. The carcasses then pass through great hellish jets of yellowish-blue gas flame to singe the skin and harden it. The last step is polishing: more brushes. Our pig has turned pink and clean as a baby.

One of the small mercies of a slaughterhouse: what begins as a live animal loses all   18
similarity as the processing goes on, until you can actually face the packaged meat at the exit door and admire its obvious flavor.

The polished carcasses swing through a door closed with rubber flaps, and there,   19
dear friends, the action begins. Saws. Long knives. Butcher knives. Drawknives. Boning knives. Wails from the saws, large and small, that are driven by air like a dentist's drill. Shouts back and forth from the men, jokes, announcements, challenges. The temperature down to 50 degrees, everyone keen. Men start slicing off little pieces of the head right inside the door, each man his special slice, throwing them onto one of several lines that will depart for special bins. A carcass passes me and I see a bare eyeball staring, stripped of its lids. Deft knives drop the head from the neck, leaving it dangling by a two-inch strip of skin. Around a corner, up to a platform, and three men gut the carcasses, great tubs of guts, each man taking the third carcass as it goes by. One of them sees me with my tape recorder and begins shouting at us something like "I am the greatest!" A crazy man, grinning and roaring at us, turning around and slipping in the knife, and out comes everything in one great load flopped onto a stainless-steel trough. And here things divide, and so must our attention.

My spokesman is proud of his chitterling machine. "I call them chitlins, but they're   20
really chitterlings." It is the newest addition to his line. A worker separates the intestines from the other internal organs and shoves them down a slide, gray and shiny. Another worker finds one end and feeds it onto a steel tube flushed with water. Others trim off connective tissue, webbings, fat. The intestines shimmer along the tube into a washing vat, shinny up to the top of the machine where they are cooled, shinny back down where they are cooled further, and come out the other side ready for the supermarket. A worker drops them into wax buckets, pops on a lid, and packs them into shipping boxes. That is today's chitlin machine. They used to have to cool the chitlins overnight before they could be packaged. Now five men do the work of sixteen, in less time.

The remaining organs proceed down a waist-high conveyor; on the other side of the   21
same walkway, the emptied carcasses pass; on a line next to the organ line the heads pass. By now all the meat has been trimmed off each head. A worker sockets them one at a time into a support like a footrest in a shoeshine parlor and a wedge neatly splits them in half. Out come the tongues, out come the brains, and at the end of the line, out come the pituitaries, each tiny gland being passed to a government inspector in white pants, white shirt, and a yellow hard hat, who looks it over and drops it into a wax bucket. All these pieces, the brain, the tongue, the oddments of sidemeat off the head and carcass, will become "by-products": hot dogs, baloney, sausage. You are what you eat....

And that is a tour of a slaughterhouse, as cheerful as I could make it.   22

23   But the men there. Half of them blacks, some Mexicans, the rest whites. It gets
harder and harder to hire men for this work, even though the pay is good. The production line keeps them hopping; they take their breaks when there is a break in the line,
so that the killing floor breaks first, and their break leaves an empty space ten minutes
long in the endless chain, which, arriving at the gutting operation, allows the men there
to break, and so on. Monday morning absenteeism is a problem, I was told. Keeping the
men under control can be a problem, too, I sensed: when the line broke down briefly
during my tour, the men cheered as convicts might at a state license-plate factory when
the stamping machine breaks down. It cannot be heartening to kill animals all day....

24   The technology at the I-D Packing Company is humane by present standards, at least
so far as the animals are concerned. Where the workers are concerned, I'm not so sure.
They looked to be in need of lulling.

25   Beyond technology is the larger question of attitude. Butchering on the farm when I
was a boy had the quality of a ceremony. We would select, say, a steer, and pen it separately overnight. The next morning several of us boys—this was a boys' home as well
as a farm—would walk the steer to a large compound and leave it standing, trusting as
hell, near the concrete-floored area where we did the skinning and gutting. Then the
farm manager, a man of great kindness and reserve, would take aim with a .22 rifle at
the crosspoint of two imaginary lines drawn from the horns to the opposite eyes. And
hold his bead until the steer was entirely calm, looking at him, a certain shot, because
this man did not want to miss, did not want to hurt the animal he was about to kill.
And we would stand in a spread-out circle, at a respectful distance, tense with the
drama of it, because we didn't want him to miss either.

26   The shot cracked out, the bullet entered the brain, and the animal instantly collapsed.
Then the farm manager handed back the rifle, took a knife, ran forward, and cut into the
throat. Then we dragged the steer onto the concrete, hooked its back legs through the
Achilles tendons to a cross tree, and laboriously winched it into the air with a differential pulley. Four boys usually did the work, two older, two younger. The younger boys
were supposed to be learning this skill, and you held your stomach together as best you
could at first while the older boys played little tricks like, when they got there in the
skinning, cutting off the pizzle and whipping it around your neck, but even these crudi-
ties had their place: they accustomed you to contact with flesh and blood.

27   And while the older boys did their work of splitting the halves with a hacksaw, you
got to take the guts, which on the farm we did not save except for the liver, the heart,
and the sweetbreads, in a wheelbarrow down to the back lane where you built with
wood you had probably cut yourself, a most funereal pyre. Then we doused the guts
with gasoline, tossed in a match, and Whoosh! off they went. And back on the concrete, the sawing done, the older boys left the sides hanging overnight in the winter
cold to firm the meat for cutting.

28   By now it was noon, time for lunch, and you went in with a sort of pride that you
had done this important work, and there on the table was meat some other boys had
killed on some other ceremonial day. It was bloody work, of course, and sometimes I
have wondered how adults could ask children to do such work, but it was part of a
coherent way of life, as important as plowing or seeding or mowing or baling hay. It
had a context, and I was literary enough even then to understand that burning the guts
had a sacrificial significance. We could always have limed them and dumped them into
a ditch. Lord knows they didn't burn easily.

I never saw our farm manager more upset than the day we were getting ready to 29
butcher five pigs. He shot one through the nose rather than through the brain. It ran
screaming around the pen, and he almost cried. It took two more bullets to finish the
animal off, and this good man was shaking when he had finished. "I hate that," he said
to me. "I hate to have them in pain. Pigs are so damned hard to kill clean."

But we don't farm anymore. The coherence is gone. Our loves are no longer the 30
loves of flint and iron, but of the nightingale and the rose, and so we delegate our killing. Our farm manager used to sleep in the sheep barn for nights on end to be sure he
was there to help the ewes deliver their lambs, ewes being so absentminded they
sometimes stop labor with the lamb only halfway out. You saw the beginning and the
end on the farm, not merely the prepackaged middle. Flint and iron, friends, flint and
iron. And humility, and sorrow that this act of killing must be done, which is why in
those days good men bowed their heads before they picked up their forks.

Questions for Close Reading

1. What is the selection's thesis? Locate the sentence(s) in which Rhodes states his
main idea. If he doesn't state the thesis explicitly, express it in your own words.

2. How are pigs slaughtered at the I-D Packing Company? What steps are
involved? How do the plant workers react to the process?

3. According to Rhodes, what are pigs like? What is it about their personalities
and reactions that makes them so compelling?

4. What is the difference between the way farm animals were killed in the past
and the way they are killed at the I-D Packing House? How does Rhodes know
about the way farm animals used to be killed?

5. Refer to your dictionary as needed to define the following words used in the
selection: *defunct* (paragraph 3), *monolithic* (3), *hygienically* (8), *complicity* (11), *affluence* (11), *hawser* (15), *deft* (19), *chitterlings* (20), *lulling* (24), *winched* (26), *differential*
(26), *pizzle* (26), *coherent* (28), *sacrificial* (28).

Questions About the Writer's Craft

1. The pattern. Throughout this disturbing but riveting piece, Rhodes uses several techniques to help readers follow the sequence of steps in the butchering process. Identify some of these techniques and explain how each of them keeps
readers focused on the part of the process being explained.

2. Why do you think Rhodes chose to preface his essay with the quotation from
Ralph Waldo Emerson? How does this quotation and the subsequent references to
Emerson (in paragraphs 1, 11, and 30) reinforce Rhodes's central point?

3. Other patterns. Although Rhodes's description becomes especially graphic
from paragraph 11 on, the descriptive elements in earlier paragraphs play a critical

role in establishing Rhodes's thesis. How, for example, do the descriptive details in paragraphs 3–9 reinforce Rhodes's thesis?

4. Rhodes often uses a breezy colloquial style. Consider, for example, the fragment combined with a full sentence at the end of paragraph 5: "Shoot out all over the place, and you'd damned better have every gate closed...." Locate other examples of this informal style. Why might Rhodes have chosen to express himself so informally at various points in the essay?

Writing Assignments Using Process Analysis as a Pattern of Development

1. Like Rhodes, write an essay describing a process you think is wrong or flawed in some way. You might, for example, describe how your college determines competency in writing, how a particular business handles customer complaints, how a township approaches recycling. Describe the process so fully that readers will have no question about the need for reform.

2. Focus on a societal problem that concerns you. Perhaps you're upset that cheating is on the rise among elementary schoolchildren, that tensions between college students and townspeople have escalated in your community, that a local newspaper discourages debate by failing to publish views that differ from those of the editorial board. Write an essay explaining step by step what needs to be done to resolve the problem. To demonstrate the need for change, begin the paper with a brief yet dramatic description of the problem. Caryl Rivers's "What Should Be Done About Rock Lyrics?" (page 473), Edwin Koch's "Death and Justice" (page 477), and David Bruck's "The Death Penalty" (page 482) should provide some ideas for writing an essay that exposes a significant social problem.

Writing Assignments Using Other Patterns of Development

3. Rhodes implies that, at some level, we know about the suffering experienced by animals but choose to close our eyes to it. There are, of course, other kinds of suffering that people often push out of their minds. Write an essay narrating the story of a single representative of a group whose pain or difficulty tends to be ignored or disregarded. Possibilities include an adult who cannot read, a child with special learning needs, a family without medical insurance. Using vivid narrative details to dramatize what the person's life is like, make a strong case for treating the whole group more sympathetically. Before writing, read George Orwell's "Shooting an Elephant" (page 203) and Natalie Angier's "A Granddaughter's Fear" (page 388), for two powerful depictions of human insensitivity.

4. Besides criticizing the methods used to kill animals, many animal rights activists cite what they consider other kinds of animal abuse: hunting or fishing, the eating of meat, confining animals in zoos, the wearing of fur or leather, the use of animals in circuses, and so on. Select *one* such issue, read about it in the library, and discuss it with people holding diverse viewpoints. Review the material gathered to determine your own position. Then write an essay supporting your viewpoint with persuasive reasons and examples, remembering to refute opposing views whenever you can.

ADDITIONAL WRITING TOPICS: PROCESS ANALYSIS

General Assignments

Using process analysis, write an essay on one of the following topics.

Directional: How to Do Something

1. How to improve a course you have taken

2. How to drive defensively

3. How to get away with _____

4. How to improve the place where you work or study

5. How to relax

6. How to show appreciation to others

7. How to get through school despite personal problems

8. How to complain effectively

Informational: How Something Happens

1. How a student becomes burned out

2. How a library's card catalog or computerized catalog organizes books

3. How a dead thing decays (or some other natural process)

4. How the college registration process works

5. How *homo sapiens* chooses a mate

6. How a VCR (or some other machine) works

7. How a bad habit develops

8. How people fall into debt

Assignments with a Specific Purpose, Audience, and Point of View

1. An author of books for elementary school children, you want to show children how to do something—take care of a pet, get along with siblings, keep a room clean. Explain the process in terms a child would understand yet not find condescending.

2. To help a sixteen-year-old friend learn how to drive, explain a specific driving maneuver one step at a time. You might, for example, describe how to make a three-point turn, parallel park, or handle a skid. Remember, your friend lacks self-confidence and experience.

3. Write an article for *Consumer Reports* on how to shop for a certain product. Give specific steps explaining how to save money, buy a quality product, and the like.

4. Write a process analysis showing how to save a life by CPR, rescue breathing, the Heimlich maneuver, or some other method. Your audience will be people from your neighborhood who are taking a first-aid class.

5. Your best friend plans to move into his or her own apartment but doesn't know the first thing about how to choose one. Explain the process of selecting an apartment—where to look, what to investigate, what questions to ask before signing a lease.

6. You write an "advice to the lovelorn" column for the campus newspaper. A correspondent writes saying that he or she wants to break up with a steady boyfriend/girlfriend but doesn't know how to do it without hurting the person. Give the writer guidance on how to end a meaningful relationship with a minimal amount of pain.

16
COMPARISON-CONTRAST

WHAT IS COMPARISON-CONTRAST?

WE frequently try to make sense of the world by finding similarities and differences in our experiences. Seeing how things are alike (**comparing**) and seeing how they are different (**contrasting**) helps us impose meaning on experiences that otherwise might remain fragmented and disconnected. Barely aware of the fact that we're comparing and contrasting, we may think to ourselves, "I woke up in a great mood this morning, but now I feel uneasy and anxious. I wonder why I feel so different." This inner questioning, which often occurs in a flash, is just one example of the way we use comparison and contrast to understand ourselves and our world.

Comparing and contrasting also helps us make choices. We compare and contrast everything—from two brands of soap we might buy to two colleges we might attend. We listen to a favorite radio station, watch a preferred nightly news show, select a particular dessert from a menu—all because we have done some degree of comparing and contrasting. We often weigh these alternatives in an unstudied, casual manner, as when we flip from one radio station to another. But when we have to make important decisions, we tend to think rigorously about how things are alike or different: Should I live in a dorm or rent an apartment? Should I accept the higher-paying job or the lower-paying one that offers more challenges? Such a deliberate approach to comparison-contrast may also provide us with needed insight into complex contemporary issues: Is television's coverage of political candidates more or less objective than it used to be? What are the merits of the various positions on abortion?

HOW COMPARISON-CONTRAST FITS
YOUR PURPOSE AND AUDIENCE

When is it appropriate in writing to use the comparison-contrast pattern of development? Comparison-contrast works well if you want to demonstrate any of the following: (1) that one thing is better than another (the first example below); (2) that things which seem different are actually alike (the second example below); (3) that things which seem alike are actually different (the third example below).

> Compare and contrast the way male and female relationships are depicted in *Cosmopolitan, Ms., Playboy,* and *Esquire.* Which publication has the most limited view of men and women? Which has the broadest perspective?

> Football, basketball, and baseball differ in the ways they appeal to fans. Describe the unique drawing power of each sport, but also reach some conclusions about the appeals the three sports have in common.

> Studies show that both college students and their parents feel that post-secondary education should equip young people to succeed in the marketplace. Yet the same studies report that the two groups have a very different understanding of what it means to succeed. What differences do you think the studies identify?

Other assignments will, in less obvious ways, lend themselves to comparison-contrast. For instance, although words like *compare, contrast, differ,* and *have in common* don't appear in the following assignments, essay responses to the assignments could be organized around the comparison-contrast format:

> The emergence of the two-career family is one of the major phenomena of our culture. Discuss the advantages and disadvantages of having both parents work, showing how you feel about such two-career households.

> Some people believe that the 1950s, often called the golden age of television, produced several never-to-be equaled comedy classics. Do you agree that such shows as *I Love Lucy* and *The Honeymooners* are superior to the situation comedies aired on television today?

> There has been considerable criticism recently of the news coverage by the city's two leading newspapers, the *Herald* and the *Beacon.* Indicate whether you think the criticism is valid by discussing the similarities and differences in the two papers' news coverage.

Note: The last assignment shows that a comparison-contrast essay may cover similarities *and* differences, not just one or the other.

As you have seen, comparison-contrast can be the key strategy for achieving an essay's purpose. But comparison-contrast can also be a supplemental method used to help make a point in an essay organized chiefly around another pattern of development. A serious, informative essay intended for laypeople might *define* clinical depression by contrasting that state of mind with ordinary run-of-the-mill blues. Writing humorously about the exhausting *effects* of trying to get in shape, you might dramatize your plight for readers by contrasting the leisurely way you used to spend your day with your current rigidly compulsive exercise regimen. Or, in an urgent *argumentation-persuasion* essay on the need for stricter controls over drug abuse in the workplace, you might provide readers with background by comparing several companies' approaches to the problem.

PREWRITING STRATEGIES

The following checklist shows how you can apply to comparison-contrast some of the prewriting strategies discussed in Chapter 2.

✔ COMPARISON-CONTRAST: A PREWRITING CHECKLIST

Choose Subjects to Compare and Contrast

☐ What have you recently needed to compare and contrast (subjects to major in, events to attend, ways to resolve a disagreement) in order to make a choice? What would a comparison-contrast analysis disclose about the alternatives, your priorities, and the criteria by which you judge?

☐ Can you show a need for change by contrasting one way of doing something (say, the way your college awards athletic scholarships) with a better way (either imagined or actual)?

☐ Do any people you know show some striking similarities and differences? What would a comparison-contrast analysis reveal about their characters and the personal qualities you prize?

☐ How does your view on an issue (the legal drinking age, birth control, a new policy at your college) differ from that of other people (your parents, a friend, most students at your college)? What would a comparison-contrast analysis of these views indicate about your values?

Determine Your Purpose, Audience, Tone, and Point of View

☐ Is your purpose primarily to inform readers of similarities and differences? To evaluate your subjects' relative merits? To persuade readers to choose between alternative courses of action?

☐ What audience are you writing for? To what tone and point of view will they be most receptive?

Use Prewriting to Generate Points of Comparison-Contrast

☐ How could brainstorming, freewriting, mapping, or journal entries help you gather information about your subjects' most significant similarities and differences?

STRATEGIES FOR USING COMPARISON-CONTRAST IN AN ESSAY

After prewriting, you're ready to draft your essay. The following suggestions will be helpful whether you use comparison-contrast as a dominant or supportive pattern of development.

1. Be sure your subjects are at least somewhat alike. Unless you plan to develop an *analogy* (see the following numbered suggestion), the subjects you choose to compare or contrast should share some obvious characteristics or qualities. It makes sense to compare different parts of the country, two comedians, or several college teachers. But a reasonable paper wouldn't result from, let's say, a comparison of a television game show with a soap opera. Your subjects must belong to the same general group so that your comparison-contrast stays within logical bounds and doesn't veer off into pointlessness.

2. Stay focused on your purpose. When writing, remember that comparison-contrast isn't an end in itself. That is, your objective isn't to turn an essay into a mechanical list of "how *A* differs from *B*" or "how *A* is like *B*." As with the other patterns of development discussed in this book, comparison-contrast is a strategy for making a point or meeting a larger purpose.

Consider the assignment on page 335 about the two newspapers. Your purpose here might be simply to *inform*, to present information as objectively as possible: "This is what the *Herald*'s news coverage is like. This is what the *Beacon*'s news coverage is like."

More frequently, though, you'll use comparison-contrast to *evaluate* your subjects' pros and cons, your goal being to reach a conclusion or make a judgment: "Both the *Herald* and the *Beacon* spend too much time reporting local news," or "The *Herald*'s analysis of the recent hostage crisis was more insightful than the *Beacon*'s." Comparison-contrast can also be used to *persuade* readers to take action: "People interested in thorough coverage of international events should read the *Herald* rather than the *Beacon*." Persuasive essays may also propose a change, contrasting what now exists with a more ideal situation: "For the *Beacon* to compete with the *Herald*, it must assign more reporters to international stories."

Yet another purpose you might have in writing a comparison-contrast essay is to *clear up misconceptions* by revealing previously hidden similarities or differences. For example, perhaps your town's two newspapers are thought to be sharply different. However, a comparison-contrast analysis might reveal that—although one paper specializes in sensationalized stories while the other adopts a more muted approach—both resort to biased, emotionally charged analyses of local politics. Or the essay might illustrate that the tabloid's treatment of the local arts scene is surprisingly more comprehensive than that of its competitor.

Comparing and contrasting also make it possible to *draw an analogy* between two seemingly unrelated subjects. An analogy is an imaginative comparison that delves beneath the surface differences of subjects in order to expose their significant and often unsuspected similarities or differences. Your purpose may be to show that singles bars and zoos share a number of striking similarities. Or you may want to illustrate that wolves and humans raise their young in much the same way, but that wolves go about the process in a more civilized manner. The analogical approach can make a complex subject easier to understand—as, for example, when the national deficit is compared to a household budget gone awry. Analogies are often dramatic and instructive, challenging you and your audience to consider subjects in a new light. But analogies don't speak for themselves. You must make clear to the reader how the analogy demonstrates your purpose.

3. Formulate a strong thesis.   An essay that is developed primarily through comparison-contrast should be focused by a solid thesis. Besides revealing your attitude, the thesis will often do the following:

- Name the subjects being compared and contrasted
- Indicate whether the essay focuses on the subjects' similarities, differences, or both
- State the essay's main point of comparison or contrast

Not all comparison-contrast essays need thesis statements as structured as those that follow. Even so, these examples can serve as models of clarity. Note that the first thesis statement signals similarities, the second differences, and the last both similarities and differences:

Middle-aged parents are often in a good position to empathize with adolescent children because the emotional upheavals experienced by the two age groups are much the same.

The priorities of most retired people are more conducive to health and happiness than the priorities of most young professionals.

College students in their thirties and forties face many of the same pressures as younger students, but they are better equipped to withstand these pressures.

4. Select the points to be discussed.   Once you have identified the essay's subject, purpose, and thesis, you need to decide which of the many points generated during prewriting you will discuss: You have to identify which aspects of the subjects to compare or contrast. College professors, for instance, could be compared and contrasted on the basis of their testing methods, ability to motivate students, confidence in front of a classroom, personalities, level of enthusiasm, and so forth.

When selecting points to cover, be sure to consider your audience. Ask yourself: "Will my readers be familiar with this item? Will I need it to get my message across? Will my audience find this item interesting or convincing?" What your readers know, what they don't know, and what you can project about their reactions should influence your choices. And, of course, you need to select points that support your thesis. If your essay explains the differences between healthy, sensible diets and dangerous crash diets, it wouldn't be appropriate to talk about aerobic exercise. Similarly, imagine you want to write an essay making the point that, despite their differences, hard rock of the 1960s and punk rock of the 1970s both reflected young people's disillusionment with society. It wouldn't make much sense to contrast the long uncombed hairstyles of the 1960s with the short spiky cuts of the 1970s. But contrasting song lyrics (protest versus nihilistic messages) would help support your thesis and lead to interesting insights.

5. Organize the points to be discussed.   After deciding which points to include, you should use a systematic, logical plan for presenting those ideas. If the points aren't organized, your essay will be little more than a confusing jumble of ideas. There are two common ways to organize an essay developed wholly or in part by comparison-contrast: the one-side-at-a-time method and the point-by-point method. Although both strategies may be used in a paper, one method usually predominates.

In the **one-side-at-a-time method** of organization, you discuss everything relevant about one subject before moving to another subject. For example, responding to the earlier assignment that asked you to analyze the news coverage in two local papers, you might first talk about the *Herald*'s coverage of international, national, and local news; then you would discuss the *Beacon*'s coverage of the same categories. Note that the areas discussed should be the same for both newspapers. It wouldn't be logical to review the *Herald*'s coverage of international, national, and local news and then to detail the *Beacon*'s magazine supplements, modern living section, and comics page. Moreover, the areas compared and contrasted should be presented in the same order.

This is how you would organize the essay using the one-side-at-a-time method:

Everything about subject *A*   *Herald*'s news coverage:
- International
- National
- Local

Everything about subject *B*   *Beacon*'s news coverage:
- International
- National
- Local

In the **point-by-point method** of organization, you alternate from one aspect of the first subject to the same aspect of your other subject(s). For example, to use this method when comparing or contrasting the *Herald* and the *Beacon*, you would first discuss the *Herald*'s international coverage, then the *Beacon*'s international coverage; next, the *Herald*'s national coverage, then the *Beacon*'s; and finally, the *Herald*'s local coverage, then the *Beacon*'s.

An essay using the point-by-point method would be organized like this:

First aspect of subjects *A* and *B*	*Beacon:* International coverage
	Herald: International coverage
Second aspect of subjects *A* and *B*	*Beacon:* National coverage
	Herald: National coverage
Third aspect of subjects *A* and *B*	*Beacon:* Local coverage
	Herald: Local coverage

Deciding which of these two methods of organization to use is largely a personal choice, though there are several factors to consider. The one-side-at-a-time method tends to convey a more unified feeling because it highlights broad similarities and differences. It is, therefore, an effective approach for subjects that are fairly uncomplicated. This strategy also works well when essays are brief; the reader won't find it difficult to remember what has been said about subject *A* when reading about subject *B*.

Because the point-by-point method permits more extensive coverage of similarities and differences, it is often a wise choice when subjects are complex. This pattern is also useful for lengthy essays since readers would probably find it difficult to remember, let's say, ten pages of information about subject *A* while reading the next ten pages about subject *B*. The point-by-point approach, however, may cause readers to lose sight of the broader picture, so remember to keep them focused on your central point.

6. Supply the reader with clear transitions.   Although a well-organized comparison-contrast format is important, it doesn't guarantee that readers will be able to follow your line of thought easily. *Transitions*—especially those signaling similarities or differences—are needed to show readers where they have been and where they are going. Such cues are essential in all writing, but they're especially crucial in a paper using comparison-contrast. By indicating clearly when subjects are being compared or contrasted, the transitions help weave the discussion into a coherent whole.

The transitions (in boldface) in the following examples could be used to *signal similarities* in an essay discussing the news coverage in the *Herald* and the *Beacon:*

- The *Beacon* **also** allots only a small portion of the front page to global news.
- **In the same way,** the *Herald* tries to include at least three local stories on the first page.
- **Likewise,** the *Beacon* emphasizes the importance of up-to-date reporting of town meetings.
- The *Herald* is **similarly** committed to extensive coverage of high school and college sports.

The transitions (in boldface) in these examples could be used to *signal differences:*

- **By way of contrast,** the *Herald*'s editorial page deals with national matters on the average of three times a week.

- **On the other hand,** the *Beacon* does not share the *Herald*'s enthusiasm for interviews with national figures.
- The *Beacon*, **however,** does not encourage its reporters to tackle national stories the way the *Herald* does.
- **But** the *Herald*'s coverage of the Washington scene is much more comprehensive than its competitor's.

REVISION STRATEGIES

Once you have a draft of the essay, you're ready to revise. The following checklist will help you and those giving you feedback apply to comparison-contrast some of the revision techniques discussed in Chapters 7 and 8.

✔ COMPARISON-CONTRAST: A REVISION CHECKLIST

Revise Overall Meaning and Structure

☐ Are the subjects sufficiently alike for the comparison-contrast to be logical and meaningful?

☐ What purpose does the essay serve? Does it inform? Evaluate? Persuade readers to accept a viewpoint and perhaps take action? Eliminate misconceptions or draw a surprising analogy?

☐ What is the essay's thesis? How could the thesis be stated more effectively?

☐ Is the overall essay organized primarily by the one-side-at-a-time method or by the point-by-point method? What is the advantage of that strategy for this essay?

☐ Regardless of the method used to organize the essay, are the same features discussed for each subject? What are the features? Are they discussed in the same order?

☐ Which points of comparison and/or contrast might be unfamiliar to readers? Do these need further development? Which points should be deleted because they're unconvincing or irrelevant? Where do significant points seem to be missing? How has the most important point of similarity or difference been emphasized?

Revise Paragraph Development

☐ If the essay uses the one-side-at-a-time method, which paragraph marks the switch from one subject to another?

☐ If the essay uses the point-by-point method, do paragraphs consistently alternate between subjects (one aspect of one subject, then the same aspect for another subject, and so on)? If this alternation becomes too elaborate or predictable, what could be done to eliminate the problem?

☐ If the essay uses both the one-side-at-a-time and the point-by-point methods, which paragraph marks the switch from one method to the other? If the switch is confusing, how could it be made less so?

☐ Where would transitions signaling similarities (*also, likewise, in contrast*) make it easier to follow the line of thought within and between paragraphs?

Revise Sentences and Words

☐ Where do too many transitions make sentences awkward and mechanical?

☐ Which sentences and words fail to convey the intended tone?

STUDENT ESSAY: FROM PREWRITING THROUGH REVISION

The student essay that follows was written by Carol Siskin in response to this assignment:

In "And Then I Went to School," Joseph Suina contrasts his home and school environments, showing that one was much more favorable than the other. In an essay of your own, contrast two personality types, life-styles, or stages of life, demonstrating that one is superior to the other.

Having recently turned forty, Carol decided to write an essay taking issue with the idea that being young is better than being old. From time to time, Carol had used her *journal* to explore what it means to grow older. Rather than writing a new journal entry on the subject, she decided to look at earlier entries to see if they contained any helpful material for the assignment. One rather free-ranging entry, typewritten the evening of her birthday, proved especially valuable. The original entry starts below. The handwritten marks indicate Carol's later efforts to shape and develop this raw material. Note the way Carol added details, circled main ideas, and indicated a possible sequence. These annotations paved the way for her outline, which is presented after the journal entry.

Journal Entry

Forty years old today. At 20 I thought 40 would mean the end of everything, but that's not the case at all. I'm much happier now.

Possible conclusion

Mom and Dad made a dinner for the occasion. Talking of happy, they look great. Mom said this is the best part of their lives. They love retirement--and obviously each other. I hope

Mitch and I will be that happy when we're in our sixties. And Dave and Elaine seem as good as ever. They look right together. What a pleasure it is to be a couple. I remember how lonely I was before Mitch and how lonely Dave was after his divorce. I sure don't envy young singles.

Dave seems content now. He looks handsome and robust, partly because he feels good about his life, partly because he tries to run pretty regularly. I remember how desperately he used to work out with weights because he worried about his appearance. I'm glad I don't have to be obsessed with my appearance the way I used to be. Mitch loves me the way I am. And I'm not obsessed anymore with being super stylish. Or thin. In fact, tonight, with no qualms whatever, I ate two healthy slices of birthday cake.

Dave says that Nancy (I can't believe she's 22) is thinking of going to graduate school, but she's not sure what to study. I can remember all the confusion I felt about schools and majors. I don't miss those days at all. Dave thinks Nancy is just plain confused about who she is and what she wants. Her goals change from day to day, especially because she's trying to please everyone. One day she feels confident; the next she's frightened. And she blames her parents' unhappy marriage for her confusion. No wonder she can't decide whether to marry and have kids. What chaos!

Tonight, though, was anything but chaos and confusion. It was an evening of quiet contentment. All of us enjoyed each other and got along. Quite different from the way it used to be. How I used to fight with Mom and Dad. I remember slamming the door and yelling, "It's your fault I was born." What unhappy times those were.

I (Appearance)

My diets. Hated big waist and legs.

blazers vs. leather jackets

II (Decisions)

III (Sense of self)

II

Outline

Thesis: Being young is good, but being older is better.

    I. Appearance
        A. Dave and I when young
            1. Dave's weight lifting to build himself up
            2. My constant dieting to change my body
            3. Both begging for "right" clothes

B. Attitudes now

   1. My contentment with my rounded shape

   2. Dave's satisfaction with his thinness

   3. Our clothes fashionable but comfortable

II. Decisions

  A. My major decisions mostly in the past

   1. About education

   2. About marriage and children

  B. Nancy's major decisions mostly in the future

   1. About education

   2. About marriage and children

III. Sense of self

  A. Nancy's uncertainty

   1. Unclear values and goals

   2. Strong need to be liked

   3. Unresolved feelings about parents

  B. Older person's surer self-identity

   1. Have clearer values and goals

   2. Can stand being disliked

   3. Don't blame parents

Now read Carol's paper, "The Virtues of Growing Older," noting the similarities and differences among her journal entry, outline, and final essay. You'll see that the essay is more developed than either the journal entry or outline. In the essay, Carol added numerous specific details—like those about Dave gobbling vitamins and milk shakes when he was a teen. In contrast, she omitted from the essay some journal material because it would have required burdensome explanations. For instance, if she hadn't eliminated the reference to Nancy, it would have been necessary to explain that Nancy is the daughter of Dave's wife by her first marriage. Despite these differences, you'll note that the essay's basic plan is derived largely from the journal entry and outline. As you read the essay, also consider how well it applies the principles of comparison-contrast discussed in this chapter. (The commentary that follows the paper will help you look at Carol's essay more closely and will give you some sense of how she went about revising her first draft.)

The Virtues of Growing Older

by Carol Siskin

The first of a two-paragraph introduction

Our society worships youth. Advertisements convince us to 1 buy Grecian Formula and Oil of Olay so we can hide the gray in our hair and smooth the lines on our face. Television shows

feature attractive young stars with firm bodies, perfect complexions, and thick manes of hair. Middle-aged folks work out in
gyms and jog down the street, trying to delay the effects of age.

2   Wouldn't any person over thirty gladly sign with the devil
just to be young again? Isn't aging an experience to be
dreaded? Perhaps it is un-American to say so, but I believe the
answer is "No." Being young is often pleasant, but being older
has distinct advantages.

3   When young, you are apt to be obsessed with your
appearance. When my brother Dave and I were teens, we worked
feverishly to perfect the bodies we had. Dave lifted weights,
took megadoses of vitamins, and drank a half-dozen milk shakes
a day in order to turn his wiry adolescent frame into some
muscular ideal. And as a teenager, I dieted constantly. No
matter what I weighed, though, I was never satisfied with the
way I looked. My legs were too heavy, my shoulders too broad,
my waist too big. When Dave and I were young, we begged and
pleaded for the "right" clothes. If our parents didn't get them
for us, we felt our world would fall apart. How could we go to
school wearing loose-fitting blazers when everyone else would
be wearing smartly tailored leather jackets? We could be
considered freaks. I often wonder how my parents, and parents
in general, manage to tolerate their children during the
adolescent years. Now, however, Dave and I are beyond such
adolescent agonies. My rounded figure seems fine, and I don't
deny myself a slice of pecan pie if I feel in the mood. Dave
still works out, but he has actually become fond of his tall,
lanky frame. The two of us enjoy wearing fashionable clothes,
but we are no longer slaves to style. And women, I'm
embarrassed to admit, even more than men, have always seemed to
be at the mercy of fashion. Now my clothes--and my brother's--
are attractive yet easy to wear. We no longer feel anxious
about what others will think. As long as we feel good about how
we look, we are happy.

4   Being older is preferable to being younger in another way.
Obviously, I still have important choices to make about my
life, but I have already made many of the critical decisions
that confront those just starting out. I chose the man I wanted
to marry. I decided to have children. I elected to return to

The second
introductory
paragraph

Thesis

First half of topic
sentence for point
1: Appearance

Start of what it's
like being young

Second half of
topic sentence
for point 1

Start of what it's
like being older

First half of topic
sentence for point
2: Life choices

Start of what it's
like being older

Second half of
topic sentence
for point 2

Start of what
it's like being
younger

college to complete my education. But when you are young, major
decisions await you at every turn. "What college should I
attend? What career should I pursue? Should I get married?
Should I have children?" These are just a few of the issues
facing young people. It's no wonder that, despite their carefree facade, they are often confused, uncertain, and troubled
by all the unknowns in their future.

Topic sentence
for point 3:
Self-concept

Start of what
it's like being
younger

But the greatest benefit of being forty is knowing who I   5
am. The most unsettling aspect of youth is the uncertainty you
feel about your values, goals, and dreams. Being young means
wondering what is worth working for. Being young means feeling
happy with yourself one day and wishing you were never born the
next. It means trying on new selves by taking up with different
crowds. It means resenting your parents and their way of life

Start of what it's
like being older

one minute and then feeling you will never be as good or as
accomplished as they are. By way of contrast, forty is sanity.
I have a surer self-concept now. I don't laugh at jokes I don't
think are funny. I can make a speech in front of a town meeting
or complain in a store because I am no longer terrified that
people will laugh at me; I am no longer anxious that everyone
must like me. I no longer blame my parents for my every
personality quirk or keep a running score of everything they
did wrong raising me. Life has taught me that I, not they,
am responsible for who I am. We are all human beings--neither
saints nor devils.

Conclusion

Most Americans blindly accept the idea that newer is   6
automatically better. But a human life contradicts this
premise. There is a great deal of happiness to be found as we
grow older. My own parents, now in their sixties, recently told
me that they are happier now than they have ever been. They
would not want to be my age. Did this surprise me? At first,
yes. Then it gladdened me. Their contentment holds out great
promise for me as I move into the next--perhaps even better--
phase of my life.

Commentary

Purpose and Thesis

In her essay, Carol disproves the widespread belief that being young is preferable to being old. The *comparison-contrast* pattern allows her to analyze the drawbacks of one and the merits of the other, thus providing the essay with an

evaluative purpose. Using the title to indicate her point of view, Carol places the *thesis* at the end of her two-paragraph introduction: "Being young is often pleasant, but being older has distinct advantages." Note that the thesis accomplishes several things. It names the two subjects to be discussed and clarifies Carol's point of view about her subjects. The thesis also implies that the essay will focus on the contrasts between these two periods of life.

Points of Support and Overall Organization

To support her assertion that older is better, Carol supplies examples from her own life and organizes the examples around three main points: attitudes about appearance, decisions about life choices, and questions of self-concept. Using the *point-by-point method* to organize the overall essay, she explores each of these key ideas in a separate paragraph. Each paragraph is further focused by one or two sentences that serve as a topic sentence.

Sequence of Points, Organizational Cues, and Paragraph Development

Let's look more closely at the way Carol presents her three central points in the essay. She obviously considers appearance the least important of a person's worries, life choices more important, and self-concept the most critical. So she uses *emphatic order* to sequence the supporting paragraphs, with the phrase "But the greatest benefit" signaling the special significance of the last issue. Carol is also careful to use *transitions* to help readers follow her line of thinking: "*Now, however,* Dave and I are beyond such adolescent agonies" (3); "*But* when you are young, major decisions await you at every turn" (4); and "*By way of contrast,* forty is sanity" (5).

Although Carol has worked hard to write a well-organized paper—and has on the whole been successful—she doesn't feel compelled to make the paper fit a rigid format. As you've seen, the essay as a whole uses the point-by-point method, but each supporting paragraph uses the *one-side-at-a-time method*—that is, everything about one age group is discussed before there is a shift to the other age group. Notice too that the third and fifth paragraphs start with young people and then move to adults, whereas the fourth paragraph reverses the sequence by starting with older people.

Other Patterns of Development

Carol uses the comparison-contrast format to organize her ideas, but other patterns of development also come into play. To illustrate her points, she makes extensive use of *illustration,* and her discussion also contains elements typical of *causal analysis.* Throughout the essay, for instance, she traces the effect of being a certain age on her brother, herself, and her parents.

A Problem with Unity

As you read the third paragraph, you might have noted that Carol's essay runs into a problem. Two sentences in the paragraph disrupt the *unity* of Carol's discussion: "I often wonder how my parents, and parents in general, manage to tolerate their children during the adolescent years," and "women, I'm embarrassed to admit...have always seemed to be at the mercy of fashion." These sentences should be deleted because they don't develop the idea that adolescents are overly concerned with appearance.

Conclusion

Carol's final paragraph brings the essay to a pleasing and interesting close. The conclusion recalls the point made in the introduction: Americans overvalue youth. Carol also uses the conclusion to broaden the scope of her discussion. Rather than continuing to focus on herself, she briefly mentions her parents and the pleasure they take in life. By bringing her parents into the essay, Carol is able to make a gently philosophical observation about the promise that awaits her as she grows older. The implication is that a similarly positive future awaits us, too.

Revising the First Draft

To help guide her revision, Carol asked her husband to read her first draft aloud. As he did, Carol took notes on what she sensed were the paper's strengths and weaknesses. She then jotted down her observations, as well as her husband's, onto the draft. Because Carol wasn't certain which observations were most valid, she didn't rank them. Carol made a number of changes when revising the essay. You'll get a good sense of how she proceeded if you compare the annotated original introduction reprinted here with the final version in the full essay.

Original Version of the Introduction

Boring paragraph
First sentence dull

Cut?

        America is a land filled with people who worship youth. We admire dynamic young achievers; our middle-aged citizens work out in gyms; all of us wear tight tops and colorful sneakers-- clothes that look fine on the young but ridiculous on aging bodies. Television shows revolve around perfect-looking young

Make point about TV more specific

stars, while commercials entice us with products that will keep us young.

Make questions more vigorous

        Wouldn't every older person want to be young again? Isn't aging to be avoided? It may be slightly unpatriotic to say so, but I believe the answer is "No." Being young may be pleasant at times, but I would rather be my forty-year-old self. I no longer have to agonize about my physical appearance, I have

Maybe cut plan of development

already made many of my crucial life decisions, and I am much less confused about who I am.

After hearing her original two-paragraph introduction read aloud, Carol was dissatisfied with what she had written. Although she wasn't quite sure how to proceed, she knew that the paragraphs were flat and that they failed to open the essay on a strong note. She decided to start by whittling down the opening sentence, making it crisper and more powerful: "Our society worships youth." That done, she eliminated two bland statements ("We admire dynamic young achievers" and "all of us wear tight tops and colorful sneakers") and made several vague references more concrete and interesting. For example, "Commercials entice us with products that will keep us young" became "Grecian Formula and Oil of Olay...hide the gray in our hair and smooth the lines on our face"; "perfect-looking young stars" became "attractive young stars with firm bodies, perfect complexions, and thick manes of hair." With the addition of these specifics, the first paragraph became more vigorous and interesting.

Carol next made some subtle changes in the two questions that opened the second paragraph of the original introduction. She replaced "Wouldn't every older person want to be young again?" and "Isn't aging to be avoided?" with two more emphatic questions: "Wouldn't any person over thirty gladly sign with the devil just to be young again?" and "Isn't aging an experience to be dreaded?" Carol also made some changes at the end of the original second paragraph. Because the paper is relatively short and the subject matter easy to understand, she decided to omit her somewhat awkward *plan of development* ("I no longer have to agonize about my physical appearance, I have already made many of my crucial life decisions, and I am much less confused about who I am"). This deletion made it possible to end the introduction with a clear statement of the essay's thesis.

Once these revisions were made, Carol was confident that her essay got off to a stronger start. Feeling reassured, she moved ahead and made changes in other sections of her paper. Such work enabled her to prepare a solid piece of writing that offers food for thought.

ACTIVITIES:
COMPARISON-
CONTRAST

Prewriting Activities

1. Imagine you're writing two essays: One explores the effects of holding a job while in college; the other explains how to budget money wisely. Jot down ways you might use comparison-contrast in each essay.

2. Suppose you plan to write a series of articles for your college newspaper. What purpose might you have for comparing and/or contrasting each of the following subject pairs?

    a. Audio tapes and compact discs

    b. Paper or plastic bags at the supermarket

    c. Two courses—one taught by an inexperienced newcomer, the other by an old pro

    d. Cutting class and not showing up at work

3. Use the patterns of development or another prewriting technique to compare and/or contrast a current situation with the way you would like it to be. After reviewing your prewriting material, decide what your purpose, audience, tone, and point of view might be if you were to write an essay. Finally, write out your thesis and main supporting points.

4. Using your journal or freewriting, jot down the advantages and disadvantages of two ways of doing something (for example, watching movies in the theater versus watching them on a VCR at home; following trends versus ignoring them; dating one person versus playing the field; and so on). Reread your prewriting and determine what your thesis, purpose, audience, tone, and point of view might be if you were to write an essay. Make a scratch list of the main ideas you would cover. Would a point-by-point or a one-side-at-a-time method of organization work more effectively?

Revising Activities

5. Of the statements that follow, which would *not* make effective thesis statements for comparison-contrast essays? Identify the problem(s) in the faulty statements and revise them accordingly.

    a. Although their classroom duties often overlap, teacher aides are not as equipped as teachers to handle disciplinary problems.

    b. This college provides more assistance to its students than most schools.

    c. During the state's last congressional election, both candidates relied heavily on television to communicate their messages.

    d. There are many differences between American and foreign cars.

6. The following paragraph is from the draft of an essay detailing the qualities of a skillful manager. How effective is this comparison-contrast paragraph? What revisions would help focus the paragraph on the point made in the topic sentence? Where should details be added or deleted? Rewrite the paragraph, providing necessary transitions and details.

    A manager encourages creativity and treats employees courteously, while a boss discourages staff resourcefulness and views it as a threat. At the hardware store where I work, I got my boss's approval to develop a system for organizing excess stock in the storeroom. I shelved items in roughly the same order as they were

displayed in the store. The system was helpful to all the salespeople, not just to me, since everyone was stymied by the boss's
helter-skelter system. What he did was store overstocked items
according to each wholesaler, even though most of us weren't there
long enough to know which items came from which wholesaler. His
supposed system created chaos. When he saw what I had done, he was
furious and insisted that we continue to follow the old slap-dash
system. I had assumed he would welcome my ideas the way my manager
did last summer when I worked in a drugstore. But he didn't and
I had to scrap my work and go back to his eccentric system. He
certainly could learn something about employee relations from the
drugstore manager.

PROFESSIONAL
SELECTIONS:
COMPARISON-
CONTRAST

TONI MORRISON

One of the most honored contemporary American writers, Nobel Prize-winner Toni Morrison (1931–) also received the National Book Critics Circle Award for Fiction for her novel *Song of Solomon* (1977) and the Pulitzer Prize for her novels *Tar Baby* (1981) and *Beloved* (1986). Her other books include *Dancing Mind* (1967) and *Paradise* (1997). In her capacity as an editor for Random House, she worked on autobiographies of boxer Muhammed Ali and civil rights activist Angela Davis, as well as on *To Die for the People* (1995), an account of the Black Panther Party. The essay reprinted here first appeared in the *New York Times Magazine* on July 4, 1976, the date of the American bicentennial.

A SLOW WALK OF TREES

1   His name was John Solomon Willis, and when at age 5 he heard from the old folks that "the Emancipation Proclamation was coming," he crawled under the bed. It was his earliest recollection of what was to be his habitual response to the promise of white

people: horror and an instinctive yearning for safety. He was my grandfather, a musician who managed to hold on to his violin but not his land. He lost all 88 acres of his Indian mother's inheritance to legal predators who built their fortunes on the likes of him. He was an unreconstructed black pessimist who, in spite of or because of emancipation, was convinced for 85 years that there was no hope whatever for black people in this country. His rancor was legitimate, for he, John Solomon, was not only an artist but a first-rate carpenter and farmer, reduced to sending home to his family money he had made playing the violin because he was not able to find work. And this during the years when almost half the black male population were skilled craftsmen who lost their jobs to white ex-convicts and immigrant farmers.

His wife, however, was of a quite different frame of mind and believed that all things   2
could be improved by faith in Jesus and an effort of the will. So it was she, Ardelia Willis, who sneaked her seven children out of the back window into the darkness, rather than permit the patron of their sharecropper's existence to become their executioner as well, and headed north in 1912, when 99.2 percent of all black people in the U.S. were native-born and only 60 percent of white Americans were. And it was Ardelia who told her husband that they could not stay in the Kentucky town they ended up in because the teacher didn't know long division.

They have been dead now for 30 years and more and I still don't know which of   3
them came closer to the truth about the possibilities of life for black people in this country. One of their grandchildren is a tenured professor at Princeton. Another, who suffered from what the Peruvian poet called "anger that breaks a man into children," was picked up just as he entered his teens and emotionally lobotomized by the reformatories and mental institutions specifically designed to serve him. Neither John Solomon nor Ardelia lived long enough to despair over one or swell with pride over the other. But if they were alive today each would have selected and collected enough evidence to support the accuracy of the other's original point of view. And it would be difficult to convince either one that the other was right.

Some of the monstrous events that took place in John Solomon's America have been   4
duplicated in alarming detail in my own America. There was the public murder of a President in a theater in 1865 and the public murder of another President on television in 1963. The Civil War of 1861 had its encore as the civil-rights movement of 1960. The torture and mutilation of a black West Point Cadet (Cadet Johnson Whittaker) in 1880 had its rerun with the 1970's murders of students at Jackson State College, Texas Southern and Southern University in Baton Rouge. And in 1976 we watch for what must be the thousandth time a pitched battle between the children of slaves and the children of immigrants—only this time, it is not the New York draft riots of 1863, but the busing turmoil in Paul Revere's home town, Boston.

Hopeless, he'd said. Hopeless. For he was certain that white people of every politi-   5
cal, religious, geographical and economic background would band together against black people everywhere when they felt the threat of our progress. And a hundred years after he sought safety from the white man's "promise," somebody put a bullet in Martin Luther King's brain. And not long before that some excellent samples of the master race demonstrated their courage and virility by dynamiting some little black girls to death. If he were here now, my grandfather, he would shake his head, close his eyes and pull out his violin—too polite to say, "I told you so." And his wife would pay

attention to the music but not to the sadness in her husband's eyes, for she would see what she expected to see—not the occasional historical repetition, but, *like the slow walk of certain species of trees from the flatlands up into the mountains,* she would see the signs of irrevocable and permanent change. She, who pulled her girls out of an inadequate school in the Cumberland Mountains, knew all along that the gentlemen from Alabama who had killed the little girls would be rounded up. And it wouldn't surprise her in the least to know that the number of black college graduates jumped 12 percent in the last three years: 47 percent in 20 years. That there are 140 black mayors in this country; 14 black judges in the District Circuit, 4 in the Courts of Appeals and one on the Supreme Court. That there are 17 blacks in Congress, one in the Senate; 276 in state legislatures—223 in state houses, 53 in state senates. That there are 112 elected black police chiefs and sheriffs, 1 Pulitzer Prize winner; 1 winner of the Prix de Rome; a dozen or so winners of the Guggenheim; 4 deans of predominantly white colleges.... Oh, her list would go on and on. But so would John Solomon's sweet sad music.

6   While my grandparents held opposite views on whether the fortunes of black people were improving, my own parents struck similarly opposed postures, but from another slant. They differed about whether the moral fiber of white people would ever improve. Quite a different argument. The old folks argued about how and if black people could improve themselves, who could be counted on to help us, who would hinder us and so on. My parents took issue over the question of whether it was possible for white people to improve. They assumed that black people were the humans of the globe, but had serious doubts about the quality and existence of white humanity. Thus my father, distrusting every word and every gesture of every white man on earth, assumed that the white man who crept up the stairs one afternoon had come to molest his daughters and threw him down the stairs and then our tricycle after him. (I think my father was wrong, but considering what I have seen since, it may have been very healthy for me to have witnessed that as my first black-white encounter.) My mother, however, *believed* in them—their possibilities. So when the meal we got on relief was bug-ridden, she wrote a long letter to Franklin Delano Roosevelt. And when white bill collectors came to our door, it was she who received them civilly and explained in a sweet voice that we were people of honor and that the debt would be taken care of. Her message to Roosevelt got through—our meal improved. Her message to the bill collectors did not always get through and there was occasional violence when my father (self-exiled to the bedroom for fear he could not hold his temper) would hear that her reasonableness had failed. My mother was always wounded by these scenes, for she thought the bill collector knew that she loved good credit more than life and that being in arrears on a payment horrified her probably more than it did him. So she thought he was rude because he was white. For years she walked to utility companies and department stores to pay bills in person and even now she does not seem convinced that checks are legal tender. My father loved excellence, worked hard (he held three jobs at once for 17 years) and was so outraged by the suggestion of personal slackness that he could explain it to himself only in terms of racism. He was a fastidious worker who was frightened of one thing: unemployment. I can remember now the doomsday-*cum*-graveyard sound of "laid off" and how the minute school was out he asked us, "Where you workin'?" Both my parents believed that all succor and aid came

from themselves and their neighborhood, since "they"—white people in charge and those not in charge but in obstructionist positions—were in some way fundamentally, genetically corrupt.

So I grew up in a basically racist household with more than a child's share of con- 7 tempt for white people. And for each white friend I acquired who made a small crack in that contempt, there was another who repaired it. For each one who related to me as a person, there was one who in my presence at least, became actively "white." And like most black people of my generation, I suffer from racial vertigo that can be cured only by taking what one needs from one's ancestors. John Solomon's cynicism and his deployment of his art as both weapon and solace, Ardelia's faith in the magic that can be wrought by sheer effort of the will; my mother's open-mindedness in each new encounter and her habit of trying reasonableness first; my father's temper, his impatience and his efforts to keep "them" (throw them) out of his life. And it is out of these learned and selected attitudes that I look at the quality of life for my people in this country now. These widely disparate and sometimes conflicting views, I suspect, were held not only by me, but by most black people. Some I know are clearer in their positions, have not sullied their anger with optimism or dirtied their hope with despair. But most of us are plagued by a sense of being worn shell-thin by constant repression and hostility as well as the impression of being buoyed by visible testimony of tremendous strides. There *is* repetition of the grotesque in our history. And there *is* the miraculous walk of trees. The question is whether our walk is progress or merely movement. O.J. Simpson leaning on a Hertz car* *is* better than the Gold Dust Twins on the back of a soap box. But is *Good Times*† better than Stepin Fetchit? Has the first order of business been taken care of? Does the law of the land work for us?

Questions for Close Reading

1. What is the selection's thesis? Locate the sentence(s) in which Morrison states her main idea. If she doesn't state the thesis explicitly, express it in your own words.

2. How did Morrison's grandfather and grandmother feel about opportunities for blacks? Why did they disagree?

3. Why does Morrison say she grew up in a "racist household"? To what extent does Morrison consider herself a racist?

4. What evidence is there, according to Morrison, that life for blacks in the United States has improved? What evidence does she cite to the contrary?

---

*Prior to his arrest and trial for the murder of his ex-wife, O.J. Simpson, a former football superstar, was the spokesperson for Hertz Rent-a-Car (editors' note).
†A popular 1970s television show featuring an African American family. Many critics felt that the show perpetuated harmful stereotypes (editors' note).

5. Refer to your dictionary as needed to define the following words used in the selection: *unreconstructed* (paragraph 1), *rancor* (2), *sharecropper* (2), *lobotomized* (3), *virility* (5), *irrevocable* (5), *hinder* (6), *arrears* (6), *fastidious* (6), *succor* (6), *vertigo* (7), and *deployment* (7).

Questions About the Writer's Craft

1. The pattern. Morrison builds her essay around the comparison-contrast between first, her grandparents, and then her parents. However, numerous other comparisons and contrasts appear in the essay. Identify some of these and explain how Morrison uses them to reinforce her thesis.

2. Look closely at paragraph 5. How does Morrison's sentence structure there underscore her central point?

3. Examine the lengthy analysis of the differences between Morrison's parents (paragraph 6). How does Morrison shift the focus from her grandparents to her parents, then from one parent to the other?

4. Reread the final seven sentences in paragraph 7, starting with "There *is* repetition...." Why do you suppose Morrison italicized the word *is* in the first, second, and fourth sentences, but not in the third?

Writing Assignments Using Comparison-Contrast as a Pattern of Development

∞ 1. Morrison writes that when she was a child, occasionally "a white friend...made a small crack" in her distrust of whites. Who in your life has "made a crack" in your generalizations about an issue, about people, or about yourself? Perhaps an aging but energetic relative changed your opinion that the elderly are to be pitied, or a friend's passion for Bach and Chopin challenged your belief that those who like classical music are boringly highbrow, or a neighbor showed you that you had real athletic potential. Write an essay contrasting your "before" and "after" beliefs, remembering to provide vivid details to bring the contrast to life. You may want to read Maya Angelou's "Sister Flowers" (page 175) to gain insight into the way one person can alter another individual's entrenched views.

2. Write an essay contrasting the belief systems of two individuals whose views affected the way you think about a particular aspect of life—for example, academic success, tolerance for others, financial well-being. Like Morrison, begin by describing the differences in the individuals' beliefs.

Writing Assignments Using Other Patterns of Development

3. Morrison writes that her grandfather's "rancor [toward whites] was legitimate." Write an essay in which you offer your personal definition of the phrase "legitimate rancor." Develop your definition by narrating a single event that shows the circumstances under which you believe rancor would be a valid response. Let the power of your details rather than inflamed language show that anger would be a justified reaction.

4. Despite the racism they encountered, Morrison's grandparents and parents believed in themselves and lived lives of great dignity. Focus on a specific group of individuals who, because of prejudice, often struggle to maintain their self-esteem. Possibilities include immigrants, the elderly, the overweight, the learning-disabled, the physically challenged. Write an essay describing the specific steps that *one* group (for example, parents, schools, communities, or religious organizations) can take to encourage a healthy sense of optimism and possibility in these people.

PETE HAMILL

Pete Hamill (1935–) started his professional writing career at the *New York Post* in 1960. Since then, he has published the autobiographical *A Drinking Life* (1993); nonfiction, including *Why Sinatra Matters* (1998); novels, like *Snow in August* (1997); and several collections of essays that originally appeared in the *New York Post* and the *Village Voice.* "Crack and the Box" is from his 1996 collection of essays, *Piecework.*

CRACK AND THE BOX

One sad rainy morning last winter, I talked to a woman who was addicted to crack cocaine. She was twenty-two, stiletto-thin, with eyes as old as tombs. She was living in two rooms in a welfare hotel with her children, who were two, three, and five years of age. Her story was the usual tangle of human woe: early pregnancy, dropping out of school, vanished men, smack and then crack, tricks with johns in parked cars to pay for the dope. I asked her why she did drugs. She shrugged in an empty way and couldn't really answer beyond "makes me feel good." While we talked and she told her tale of squalor, the children ignored us. They were watching television.

Walking back to my office in the rain, I brooded about the woman, her zombielike children, and my own callous indifference. I'd heard so many versions of the same story that I almost never wrote them anymore; the sons of similar women, glimpsed a dozen years ago, are now in Dannemora or Soledad or Joliet;* in a hundred cities, their daughters are moving into the same loveless rooms. As I walked, a series of homeless

---

*Names of United States prisons (editors' note).

men approached me for change, most of them junkies. Others sat in doorways, staring at nothing. They were additional casualties of our time of plague, demoralized reminders that although this country holds only 2 percent of the world's population, it consumes 65 percent of the world's supply of hard drugs.

3   *Why,* for God's sake? Why do so many millions of Americans of all ages, races, and classes choose to spend all or part of their lives stupefied? I've talked to hundreds of addicts over the years; some were my friends. But none could give sensible answers. They stutter about the pain of the world, about despair or boredom, the urgent need for magic or pleasure in a society empty of both. But then they just shrug. Americans have the money to buy drugs; the supply is plentiful. But almost nobody in power asks, *Why?* Least of all, George Bush and his drug warriors....

4   And then, on that rainy morning in New York, I saw another one of those ragged men staring out at the rain from a doorway. I suddenly remembered the inert postures of the children in that welfare hotel, and I thought: *television.*

5   Ah, no, I muttered to myself: too simple. Something as complicated as drug addiction can't be blamed on television. Come on.... But I remembered all those desperate places I'd visited as a reporter, where there were no books and a TV set was always playing and the older kids had gone off somewhere to shoot smack, except for the kid who was at the mortuary in a coffin. I also remembered when I was a boy in the '40s and early '50s, and drugs were a minor sideshow, a kind of dark little rumor. And there was one major difference between that time and this: television.

6   We had unemployment then; illiteracy, poor living conditions, racism, governmental stupidity, a gap between rich and poor. We didn't have the all-consuming presence of television in our lives. Now two generations of Americans have grown up with television from their earliest moments of consciousness. Those same American generations are afflicted by the pox of drug addiction.

7   Only thirty-five years ago, drug addiction was not a major problem in this country. Yes: There were drug addicts. We had some at the end of the nineteenth century, too, hooked on the cocaine in patent medicines. During the placid '50s, Commissioner Harry Anslinger pumped up the budget of the old Bureau of Narcotics with fantasies of reefer madness. Heroin was sold and used in most major American cities, while the bebop generation of jazz musicians got jammed up with horse.

8   But until the early '60s, narcotics were still marginal to American life; they weren't the $129-billion market they make up today. If anything, those years have an eerie innocence. In 1955 there were 31,700,000 TV sets in use in the country (the number is now past 184 million). But the majority of the audience had grown up without the dazzling new medium. They embraced it, were diverted by it, perhaps even loved it, but they weren't *formed* by it. That year, the New York police made a mere 1,234 felony drug arrests; in 1988 it was 43,901. They confiscated ninety-seven *ounces* of cocaine for the entire year; last year it was hundreds of pounds. During each year of the '50s in New York, there were only about a hundred narcotics-related deaths. But by the end of the '60s, when the first generation of children *formed* by television had come to maturity (and thus to the marketplace), the number of such deaths had risen to 1,200. The same phenomenon was true in every major American city.

9   In the last Nielsen survey of American viewers, the average family was watching television seven hours a day. This has never happened before in history. No people has

ever been entertained for seven hours a *day*. The Elizabethans didn't go to the theater seven hours a day. The pre-TV generation did not go to the movies seven hours a day. Common sense tells us that this all-pervasive diet of instant imagery, sustained now for forty years, must have changed us in profound ways.

Television, like drugs, dominates the lives of its addicts. And though some lonely 10 Americans leave their sets on without watching them, using them as electronic companions, television usually absorbs its viewers the way drugs absorb their users. Viewers can't work or play while watching television; they can't read; they can't be out on the streets, failing in love with the wrong people, learning how to quarrel and compromise with other human beings. In short, they are asocial. So are drug addicts.

One Michigan State University study in the early '80s offered a group of four- and 11 five-year-olds the choice of giving up television or giving up their fathers. Fully one third said they would give up Daddy. Given a similar choice (between cocaine or heroin and father, mother, brother, sister, wife, husband, children, job), almost every stone junkie would do the same.

There are other disturbing similarities. Television itself is a consciousness-altering 12 instrument. With the touch of a button, it takes you out of the "real" world in which you reside and can place you at a basketball game, the back alleys of Miami, the streets of Bucharest, or the cartoony living rooms of Sitcom Land. Each move from channel to channel alters mood, usually with music or a laugh track. On any given evening, you can laugh, be frightened, feel tension, thump with excitement. You can even tune in *MacNeil/Lehrer* and feel sober.   13

But none of these abrupt shifts in mood is *earned*. They are attained as easily as popping a pill. Getting news from television, for example, is simply not the same experience as reading it in a newspaper. Reading is *active*. The reader must decode little symbols called words, then create images or ideas and make them connect; at its most basic level, reading is an act of the imagination. But the television viewer doesn't go through that process. The words are spoken to him by Dan Rather or Tom Brokaw or Peter Jennings. There isn't much decoding to do when watching television, no time to think or ponder before the next set of images and spoken words appears to displace the present one. The reader, being active, works at his or her own pace; the viewer, being passive, proceeds at a pace determined by the show. Except at the highest levels, television never demands that its audience take part in an act of imagination. Reading always does.

In short, television works on the same imaginative and intellectual level as psycho- 14 active drugs. If prolonged television viewing makes the young passive (dozens of studies indicate that it does), then moving to drugs has a certain coherence. Drugs provide an unearned high (in contrast to the earned rush that comes from a feat accomplished, a human breakthrough earned by sweat or thought or love).

And because the television addict and the drug addict are alienated from the hard 15 and scary world, they also feel they make no difference in its complicated events. For the junkie, the world is reduced to him and the needle, pipe, or vial; the self is absolutely isolated, with no desire for choice. The television addict lives the same way. Many Americans who fail to vote in presidential elections must believe they have no more control over such a choice than they do over the casting of *L.A. Law.*

The drug plague also coincides with the unspoken assumption of most television 16 shows: Life should be *easy*. The most complicated events are summarized on TV news in a minute or less. Cops confront murder, chase the criminals, and bring them to justice (usually violently) within an hour. In commercials, you drink the right beer and you get the girl. *Easy!* So why should real life be a grind? Why should any American have to spend years mastering a skill or a craft, or work eight hours a day at an unpleasant job, or endure the compromises and crises of marriage? Nobody *works* on television (except cops, doctors, and lawyers). Love stories on television are about falling in love or breaking up; the long, steady growth of a marriage—its essential *dailiness*—is seldom explored, except as comedy. Life on television is almost always simple: good guys and bad, nice girls and whores, smart guys and dumb. And if life in the real world isn't simple, well, hey, man, have some dope, man, be happy, feel good.

17   The doper always whines about how he *feels;* drugs are used to enhance his feelings or obliterate them, and in this the doper is very American. No other people on earth spend so much time talking about their feelings; hundreds of thousands go to shrinks, they buy self-help books by the millions, they pour out intimate confessions to virtual strangers in bars or discos. Our political campaigns are about emotional issues now, stated in the simplicities of adolescence. Even alleged statesmen can start a sentence, "I feel that the Sandinistas should..." when they once might have said, "I *think*...." I'm convinced that this exaltation of cheap emotions over logic and reason is one by-product of hundreds of thousands of hours of television.

18   Most Americans under the age of fifty have now spent their lives absorbing television; that is, they've had the structures of drama pounded into them. Drama is always about conflict. So news shows, politics, and advertising are now all shaped by those structures. Nobody will pay attention to anything as complicated as the part played by Third World debt in the expanding production of cocaine; it's much easier to focus on Manuel Noriega,* a character right out of *Miami Vice,* and believe that even in real life there's a Mister Big.

19   What is to be done? Television is certainly not going away, but its addictive qualities can be controlled. It's a lot easier to "just say no" to television than to heroin or crack. As a beginning, parents must take immediate control of the sets, teaching children to watch specific television *programs,* not "television," to get out of the house and play with other kids. Elementary and high schools must begin teaching television as a subject, the way literature is taught, showing children how shows are made, how to distinguish between the true and the false, how to recognize cheap emotional manipulation. All Americans should spend more time reading. And thinking.

20   For years, the defenders of television have argued that the networks are only giving the people what they want. That might be true. But so is the Medellin cartel.†

Questions for Close Reading

1. What is the selection's thesis? Locate the sentence(s) in which Hamill states his main idea. If he doesn't state the thesis explicitly, express it in your own words.

---

*Former President of Panama; tried and convicted of drug trafficking in the United States; currently serving a 40-year sentence in a Florida prison (editors' note).
†The largest group of drug suppliers in Colombia (editors' note).

2. What difference does Hamill perceive between the 1940s and 1950s of his youth and the present?

3. Referring to the points that Hamill makes in paragraphs 10–17, briefly cite what he considers the basic similarities between television and drug addiction.

4. After examining the television-drug connection, Hamill offers possible ways to remedy the situation. What measures does he propose as a means of reducing television's "addictive qualities" (19)?

5. Refer to your dictionary as needed to define the following words used in the selection: *squalor* (paragraph 1), *brooded* (2), *callous* (2), *stupefied* (3), *inert* (4), *diverted* (8), *confiscated* (8), *phenomenon* (8), *all-pervasive* (9), *coherence* (14), *alienated* (15), *enhance* (17), and *obliterate* (17).

Questions About the Writer's Craft

1. The pattern. In his essay, Hamill compares and contrasts different subjects. What is the selection's central comparison-contrast ? Identify some of the secondary comparisons and contrasts he explores. Overall, which does Hamill emphasize more in his essay, comparison or contrast? Why do you think he chooses this approach?

2. Other patterns. Hamill begins the essay with a brief first-hand account. How does this personal anecdote help Hamill reinforce his thesis?

3. Other patterns. In addition to using the comparison-contrast pattern, Hamill draws upon cause-effect analysis when developing his thesis. Identify the central causal chain that Hamill explores, beginning with paragraphs 5–6.

4. What purpose do you think Hamill had in mind when writing this essay? How would you characterize his tone? How does this tone support his purpose?

Writing Assignments Using Comparison-Contrast as a Pattern of Development

1. Hamill believes that TV changed forever many aspects of everyday life. Write an essay comparing and/or contrasting what life was before and after the advent of another new technology. Consider focusing on *one* of the following: VCR's, cable television, microwave ovens, credit cards, cash machines, and so on. Your essay may have a serious or lighthearted tone. In either case, use vivid examples, drawn from your own and other people's experience, to point out the similarities and differences in life before and after the introduction of the technology.

2. Many points that Hamill makes regarding television are now being made about computers, particularly the Internet. Write an essay comparing and/or contrasting television's effects to those of the Internet. In addition to gathering information by speaking to others, do some research in the library or on the Internet. Draw upon all these sources of information when writing your essay.

Writing Assignments Using Other Patterns of Development

3. Hamill points to the "all-consuming presence of television in our lives," with the objective of illustrating its negative legacy. But many would respond that television has significantly enhanced the quality of viewers' lives. Focus on a particular kind of television that is often criticized—for example, tabloid TV talk shows, situation comedies, game shows, local news broadcasts, children's Saturday morning cartoons, and so on. Write an essay in which you defend the genre *or* argue that the criticism is merited. Brainstorm with others to generate material to support your position. When you write, remember to acknowledge opposing viewpoints, dismantling as many of them as you can.

4. TV addiction is only one of many forms of addiction. People may, for example, be addicted to gambling, cars, sex, sports, alcohol, computer games, chocolate, shopping, and so forth. Write an essay on one such addiction, explaining step by step how the addiction takes hold and how it can be overcome. Depending on your subject, your essay may have a serious or playful tone. Robert Barry's "Becoming a Videoholic" (page 306) offers help on ways you might approach your essay.

JOSEPH H. SUINA

Still living on the Cochiti Pueblo Reservation in New Mexico where he grew up, Joseph H. Suina (1944–) teaches in the Multicultural Teacher Education Program at the University of New Mexico. Suina's work as an educator led to his coauthoring a book for teachers, *The Learning Environment: An Instructional Strategy* (1982). The following selection first appeared in *Linguistic and Cultural Influences on Learning Mathematics,* edited by Rodney Cocking and Jose Mestre (1988).

AND THEN I WENT TO SCHOOL

1   I lived with my grandmother from the ages of 5 through 9. It was the early 1950s when electricity had not yet invaded the homes of the Cochiti Indians. The village day school and health clinic were first to have it and to the unsuspecting Cochitis this was the approach of a new era in their uncomplicated lives.

2   Transportation was simple then. Two good horses and a sturdy wagon met most needs of a villager. Only five or six individuals possessed an automobile in the Pueblo of 300. A flatbed truck fixed with wooden rails and a canvas top made a regular Saturday trip to

Santa Fe. It was always loaded beyond capacity with Cochitis taking their wares to town for a few staples. With an escort of a dozen barking dogs, the straining truck made a noisy exit, northbound from the village.

During those years, Grandmother and I lived beside the plaza in a one-room house. 3
It consisted of a traditional fireplace, a makeshift cabinet for our few tin cups and dishes, and a wooden crate that held our two buckets of all-purpose water. At the far end of the room were two rolls of bedding we used as comfortable sitting "couches." Consisting of thick quilts, sheepskin, and assorted blankets, these bed rolls were undone each night. A wooden pole the length of one side of the room was suspended about 10 inches from the ceiling beams. A modest collection of colorful shawls, blankets, and sashes was draped over the pole making this part of the room most interesting. In one corner was a bulky metal trunk for our ceremonial wear and a few valuables. A dresser, which was traded for some of my grandmother's well-known pottery, held the few articles of clothing we owned and the "goody bag." Grandmother always had a flour sack filled with candy, store bought cookies, and Fig Newtons. These were saturated with a sharp odor of moth balls. Nevertheless, they made a fine snack with coffee before we turned in for the night. Tucked securely in my blankets, I listened to one of her stories or accounts of how it was when she was a little girl. These accounts seemed so old fashioned compared to the way we lived. Sometimes she softly sang a song from a ceremony. In this way I fell asleep each night.

Earlier in the evening we would make our way to a relative's house if someone had 4
not already come to visit us. I would play with the children while the adults caught up on all the latest. Ten-cent comic books were finding their way into the Pueblo homes. For us children, these were the first link to the world beyond the Pueblo. We enjoyed looking at them and role playing as one of the heroes rounding up the villains. Everyone preferred being a cowboy rather than an Indian because cowboys were always victorious. Sometimes, stories were related to both children and adults. These get-togethers were highlighted by refreshments of coffee and sweet bread or fruit pies baked in the outdoor oven. Winter months would most likely include roasted pinon nuts or dried deer meat for all to share. These evening gatherings and sense of closeness diminished as the radios and televisions increased over the following years. It was never to be the same again.

The winter months are among my fondest recollections. A warm fire crackled and 5
danced brightly in the fireplace and the aroma of delicious stew filled our one-room house. To me the house was just right. The thick adobe walls wrapped around the two of us protectingly during the long freezing nights. Grandmother's affection completed the warmth and security I will always remember.

Being the only child at Grandmother's, I had lots of attention and plenty of reasons 6
to feel good about myself. As a pre-schooler, I already had the chores of chopping firewood and hauling in fresh water each day. After "heavy work," I would run to her and flex what I was certain were my gigantic biceps. Grandmother would state that at the rate I was going I would soon attain the status of a man like the adult males in the village. Her shower of praises made me feel like the Indian Superman of all times. At age 5, I suppose I was as close to that concept of myself as anyone.

In spite of her many years, Grandmother was still active in the village ceremonial 7
setting. She was a member of an important women's society and attended all the functions, taking me along to many of them. I would wear one of my colorful shirts she

handmade for just such occasions. Grandmother taught me the appropriate behavior at these events. Through modeling she taught me to pray properly. Barefooted, I would greet the sun each morning with a handful of cornmeal. At night I would look to the stars in wonderment and let a prayer slip through my lips. I learned to appreciate cooperation in nature and my fellowmen early in life. About food and material things, Grandmother would say, "There is enough for everyone to share and it all comes from above, my child." I felt very much a part of the world and our way of life. I knew I had a place in it and I felt good about me.

8   At age 6, like the rest of the Cochiti 6-year-olds that year, I had to begin my schooling. It was a new and bewildering experience. One I will not forget. The strange surroundings, new concepts about time and expectations, and a foreign tongue were overwhelming to us beginners. It took some effort to return the second day and many times thereafter.

9   To begin with, unlike my grandmother, the teacher did not have pretty brown skin and a colorful dress. She was not plump and friendly. Her clothes were one color and drab. Her pale and skinny form made me worry that she was very ill. I thought that explained why she did not have time just for me and the disappointed looks and orders she seemed to always direct my way. I didn't think she was so smart because she couldn't understand my language. "Surely that was why we had to leave our 'Indian' at home." But then I did not feel so bright either. All I could say in her language was "yes teacher," "my name is Joseph Henry," and "when is lunch time." The teacher's odor took some getting used to also. In fact, many times it make me sick right before lunch. Later, I learned from the girls that this odor was something she wore called perfume.

10   The classroom too had its odd characteristics. It was terribly huge and smelled of medicine like the village clinic I feared so much. The walls and ceiling were artificial and uncaring. They were too far from me and I felt naked. The fluorescent light tubes were eerie and blinked suspiciously above me. This was quite a contrast to the fire and sunlight that my eyes were accustomed to. I thought maybe the lighting did not seem right because it was man-made, and it was not natural. Our confinement to rows of desks was another unnatural demand from our active little bodies. We had to sit at these hard things for what seemed like forever before relief (recess) came midway through the morning and afternoon. Running carefree in the village and fields was but a sweet memory of days gone by. We all went home for lunch because we lived within walking distance of the school. It took coaxing and sometimes bribing to get me to return and complete the remainder of the school day.

11   School was a painful experience during those early years. The English language and the new set of values caused me much anxiety and embarrassment. I could not comprehend everything that was happening but yet I could understand very well when I messed up or was not doing so well. The negative aspect was communicated too effectively and I became unsure of myself more and more. How I wished I could understand other things just as well in school.

12   The value conflict was not only in school performance but in other areas of my life as well. For example, many of us students had a problem with head lice due to "the lack of sanitary conditions in our homes." Consequently, we received a severe shampooing that was rough on both the scalp and the ego. Cleanliness was crucial and a washing of this type indicated to the class how filthy a home setting we came from. I recall that after one such treatment I was humiliated before my peers with a statement

that I had "She'na" (lice) so tough that I must have been born with them. Needless to say, my Super Indian self-image was no longer intact.

My language, too, was questionable from the beginning of my school career. "Leave 13 your Indian (language) at home" was like a trademark of school. Speaking it acciden-tally or otherwise was a sure reprimand in the form of a dirty look or a whack with a ruler. This punishment was for speaking the language of my people which meant so much to me. It was the language of my grandmother and I spoke it well. With it, I sang beautiful songs and prayed from my heart. At that young and tender age, comprehend-ing why I had to part with it was most difficult for me. And yet at home I was encour-aged to attend school so that I might have a better life in the future. I knew I had a good village life already but this was communicated less and less each day I was in school. . . .

I had to leave my beloved village of Cochiti for my education beyond Grade 6. I left to 14 attend a Bureau of Indian Affairs boarding school 30 miles from home. Shined shoes and pressed shirt and pants were the order of the day. I managed to adjust to this just as I had to most of the things the school shoved at me or took away from me. Adjusting to leaving home and the village was tough indeed. It seemed the older I got, the further away I became from the ways I was so much a part of. Because my parents did not own an auto-mobile, I saw them only once a month when they came up in the community truck. They never failed to come supplied with "eats" for me. I enjoyed the outdoor oven bread, dried meat, and tamales they usually brought. It took a while to get accustomed to the diet of the school. I longed for my grandmother and my younger brothers and sisters. I longed for my house. I longed to take part in a Buffalo Dance. I longed to be free.

I came home for the 4-day Thanksgiving break. At first, home did not feel right any- 15 more. It was much too small and stuffy. The lack of running water and bathroom facili-ties were too inconvenient. Everything got dusty so quickly and hardly anyone spoke English. I did not realize I was beginning to take on the white man's ways, the ways that belittled my own. However, it did not take long to "get back with it." Once I estab-lished my relationships with family, relatives, and friends I knew I was where I came from and where I belonged.

Leaving for the boarding school the following Sunday evening was one of the sad- 16 dest events in my entire life. Although I enjoyed myself immensely the last few days, I realized then that life would never be the same again. I could not turn back the time just as I could not do away with school and the ways of the white man. They were here to stay and would creep more and more into my life. The effort to make sense of both worlds together was painful and I had no choice but to do so. The schools, television, automobiles, and other white man's ways and values had chipped away at the simple cooperative life I grew up in. The people of Cochiti were changing. The winter evening gatherings, exchanging of stories, and even the performing of certain ceremonies were already only a memory that someone commented about now and then. Still the demands of both worlds were there. The white man's was flashy, less personal, but comfortable. The Indian was both attracted and pushed toward these new ways that he had little to say about. There was no choice left but to compete with the white man on his terms for survival. For that I knew I had to give up a part of my life.

Determined not to cry, I left for school that dreadfully lonely night. My right hand 17 clutched tightly the mound of cornmeal Grandmother placed there and my left hand brushed away a tear as I made my way back to school.

Questions for Close Reading

1. What is the selection's thesis? Locate the sentence(s) in which Suina states his main idea. If he doesn't state the thesis explicitly, express it in your own words.

2. How did the Cochiti instill their values and native culture in their children? How was the Cochiti approach different from the teaching methods used in the white school Suina attended?

3. What non-native influences appear in Suina's town and life before he starts attending school?

4. Why is Suina forced to attend a white school and learn about the whites' life-style and language? What does he find confusing about school? How does school change him?

5. Refer to your dictionary as needed to define the following words used in the selection: *adobe* (paragraph 5), *ego* (12), and *belittled* (15).

Questions About the Writer's Craft

1. The pattern. Comparison-contrast essays organize material according to the point-by-point or one-side-at-a-time method. Which method predominates in this essay? Why do you think Suina uses this method? Locate places where Suina uses the other method of organization.

2. Other patterns. Suina uses description to evoke the simple, emotional warmth of the Native American life-style as well as the sterile, stark coldness of the white school. Locate places in the essay where Suina provides sensory details to help readers understand the differences between the two cultures.

3. Consider Suina's word choice in the opening paragraph. How do the words *invade* and *unsuspecting* help establish the essay's overall tone? What do these terms reveal about Suina's attitude toward the transformation of Native American culture?

4. Where in paragraph 14 does Suina use repetition? What is the effect of the repetition?

Writing Assignments Using Comparison-Contrast as a Pattern of Development

1. As a Native American, Suina is made to feel like an outsider in the white school. But cultural differences aren't the only factors that cause children to feel uncomfortable in school. For example, they may have trouble fitting in because they have a learning disability, are shy, are extroverted, or need more (or less) structure than the school provides. Focusing on *one* such problem, write an essay comparing and contrasting present-day education with the way it should be.

2. After attending boarding school for a few months, Suina reappraises his home and earlier life-style. In a similar way, separation can cause the rest of us to view our home, our school, another institution, or an individual in a more positive or a more negative light. Write an essay comparing and contrasting the feelings you had for a person, place, or institution with your attitude after being separated for a while. Provide vigorous details to show why your attitude changed.

Writing Assignments Using Other Patterns of Development

∞ **3.** Suina reports that his grandmother showered him with praise and made him feel like a "Superman." However, once he entered school, the constant scoldings, dirty looks, and ruler slaps eroded his self-esteem. Write an essay illustrating how a person affected your view of yourself, either by praising or by criticizing your efforts. Provide several dramatic examples or a single, richly detailed example to show how this person affected you. Before writing, read Maya Angelou's "Sister Flowers" (page 175) and Russell Baker's "Selling the Post" (page 214), two essays that illustrate the influence of powerful individuals.

4. In school, Suina is pressured to abandon the language of his home and to speak only English. Conduct some library research on the subject of bilingualism in education. Then write an essay arguing that schools either should or should not teach non-English-speaking students in their native language until they become sufficiently proficient in English to join regular classes. At some point, you should acknowledge and perhaps refute opposing views.

ADDITIONAL WRITING TOPICS: COMPARISON-CONTRAST

General Assignments

Using comparison-contrast, write an essay on one of the following topics.

1. Two-career family versus one-career family

2. Two approaches for dealing with problems

3. Children's pastimes today and yesterday

4. Two attitudes toward money

5. Watching a movie on television versus viewing it in a theater

6. Two approaches to parenting

7. Two approaches to studying

8. Marriage versus living together

9. Two views on a controversial issue

10. The coverage of an event on television versus its coverage in a newspaper

Assignments with a Specific Purpose, Audience, and Point of View

1. You would like to change your campus living arrangements. Perhaps you want to move from a dormitory to an off-campus apartment or from home to a dorm. Before you do, though, you'll have to convince your parents (who are paying most of your college costs) that the move will be beneficial. Write out what you would say to your parents. Contrast your current situation with your proposed one, explaining why the new arrangement would be better.

2. As a store manager, you decide to write a memo to all sales personnel explaining how to keep customers happy. Compare and/or contrast the needs and shopping habits of several different consumer groups (by age, spending ability, or sex), and show how to make each group comfortable in your store.

3. Write a guide on "Passing Exams" for first-year college students, contrasting the right and wrong ways to prepare for and take exams. Although your purpose is basically serious, leave the section on how *not* to approach exams with some humor.

4. You work as a volunteer for a mental health hot line. Many people call simply because they feel "stressed out." Prepare a brochure for these people, recommending a "Type B" approach to stressful situations. Focus the brochure on the contrast between "Type A" and "Type B" personalities: the former is nervous, hard-driving, competitive; the latter is relaxed and noncompetitive. Give specific examples of how each "type" tends to act in stressful situations.

5. As president of your student senate, you're concerned about the way your school is dealing with a particular situation (for example, advisement, parking, financial assistance). Write a letter to your college president contrasting the way your school handles the situation with another school's approach. In your conclusion, point out the advantages of adopting the other college's strategy.

6. Your old high school has invited you back to make a speech before an audience of seniors. The topic will be "how to choose the college that is right for you." Write your speech in the form of a comparison-contrast analysis. Focus on the choices available (two-year versus four-year schools, large versus small, local versus faraway, and so on), showing the advantages and/or disadvantages of each.

17
CAUSE-EFFECT

WHAT IS CAUSE-EFFECT?

Superstition has it that curiosity killed the cat. Maybe so. Yet our science, technology, storytelling, and fascination with the past and future all spring from our determination to know "Why" and "What if." Seeking explanations, young children barrage adults with endless questions: "Why do trees grow tall?" "What would happen if the sun didn't shine?" But children aren't the only ones who wonder in this way. All of us think in terms of cause and effect, sometimes consciously, sometimes unconsciously: "Why did they give me such an odd look?" we wonder, or "How would I do at another college?" we speculate. This exploration of reasons and results is also at the heart of most professions: "What led to our involvement in Vietnam?" historians question; "What will happen if we administer this experimental drug?" scientists ask.

Cause-effect writing, often called **causal analysis,** is rooted in this elemental need to make connections. Because the drive to understand reasons and results is so fundamental, causal analysis is a common kind of writing. An article analyzing the unexpected outcome of an election, a report linking poor nutrition to low academic achievement, an editorial analyzing the impact of a proposed tax cut—all are examples of cause-effect writing.

Done well, cause-effect pieces uncover the subtle and often surprising connections between events or phenomena. By rooting out causes and projecting effects, causal analysis enables us to make sense of our experiences, revealing a world that is somewhat less arbitrary and chaotic.

HOW CAUSE-EFFECT FITS YOUR PURPOSE AND AUDIENCE

Many assignments and exam questions in college involve writing essays that analyze causes, effects, or both. Sometimes, as in the following examples, you'll be asked to write an essay developed primarily through the cause-effect pattern:

> Although divorces have leveled off in the last few years, the number of marriages ending in divorce is still greater than it was a generation ago. What do you think are the causes of this phenomenon?

> Political commentators were surprised that so few people voted in the last election. Discuss the probable causes of this weak voter turnout.

> Americans never seem to tire of gossip about the rich and famous. What effect has this fascination with celebrities had on American culture?

> The federal government is expected to pass legislation that will significantly reduce the funding of student loans. Analyze the possible effects of such a cutback.

Other assignments and exam questions may not explicitly ask you to address causes and effects, but they may use words that suggest causal analysis would be appropriate. Consider these examples, paying special attention to the italicized words:

Cause

> In contrast to the socially involved youth of the 1960s, many young people today tend to remove themselves from political issues. What do you think are the *sources* of the political apathy found among 18- to 25-year-olds?

Effect

> A number of experts forecast that drug abuse will be the most significant factor affecting American productivity in the coming decade. Evaluate the validity of this observation by discussing the *impact* of drugs on the workplace.

Cause and Effect

> According to school officials, a predictable percentage of entering students drop out of college at some point during their first year. What *motivates* students to drop out? What *happens* to them once they leave?

In addition to serving as the primary strategy for achieving an essay's purpose, causal analysis can also be a supplemental method used to help make a point in an essay developed chiefly through another pattern of development. Assume, for example, that you want to write an essay *defining* the term *the homeless*. To help readers see that unfavorable circumstances can result in nearly anyone becoming homeless, you might discuss some of the unavoidable, everyday factors causing people to live on streets and in subway stations. Similarly, in a *persuasive* proposal urging your college administration to institute an honors program, you would probably spend some time analyzing the positive effects of such a program on students and faculty.

PREWRITING STRATEGIES

The following checklist shows how you can apply to cause-effect some of the prewriting techniques discussed in Chapter 2.

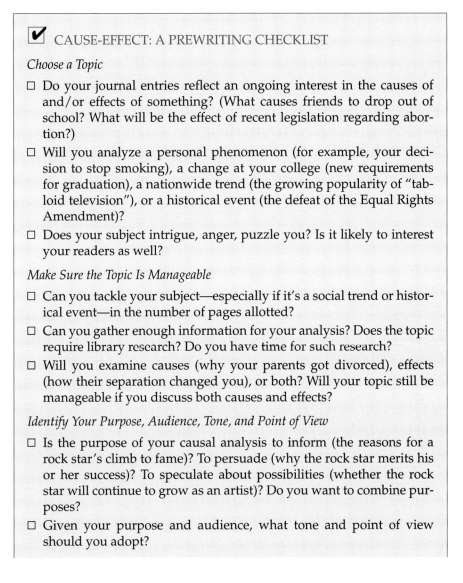

☑ CAUSE-EFFECT: A PREWRITING CHECKLIST

Choose a Topic

☐ Do your journal entries reflect an ongoing interest in the causes of and/or effects of something? (What causes friends to drop out of school? What will be the effect of recent legislation regarding abortion?)

☐ Will you analyze a personal phenomenon (for example, your decision to stop smoking), a change at your college (new requirements for graduation), a nationwide trend (the growing popularity of "tabloid television"), or a historical event (the defeat of the Equal Rights Amendment)?

☐ Does your subject intrigue, anger, puzzle you? Is it likely to interest your readers as well?

Make Sure the Topic Is Manageable

☐ Can you tackle your subject—especially if it's a social trend or historical event—in the number of pages allotted?

☐ Can you gather enough information for your analysis? Does the topic require library research? Do you have time for such research?

☐ Will you examine causes (why your parents got divorced), effects (how their separation changed you), or both? Will your topic still be manageable if you discuss both causes and effects?

Identify Your Purpose, Audience, Tone, and Point of View

☐ Is the purpose of your causal analysis to inform (the reasons for a rock star's climb to fame)? To persuade (why the rock star merits his or her success)? To speculate about possibilities (whether the rock star will continue to grow as an artist)? Do you want to combine purposes?

☐ Given your purpose and audience, what tone and point of view should you adopt?

> *Use Individual and Group Brainstorming, Mapping, and/or Freewriting to Explore Causes and Effects*
>
> ☐ *Causes:* What happened? What are the possible reasons? Which are most likely? Who was involved? Why?
> ☐ *Effects:* What happened? Who was involved? What were the observable results? What are some possible future consequences? Which consequences are negative? Which are positive?

STRATEGIES FOR USING CAUSE-EFFECT IN AN ESSAY

After prewriting, you're ready to draft your essay The following suggestions will be helpful whether you use causal analysis as a dominant or supportive pattern of development.

1. Stay focused on the purpose of your analysis.   When writing a causal analysis, don't lose sight of your overall purpose. Consider, for example, an essay on the causes of widespread child abuse. If you're concerned primarily with explaining the problem of child abuse to your readers, you might take a purely *informative* approach:

> Although parental stress is the immediate cause of child abuse, the more compelling reason for such behavior lies in the way parents were themselves mistreated as children.

Or you might want to *persuade* your audience about some point or idea concerning child abuse:

> The tragic consequences of child abuse provide strong support for more aggressive handling of such cases by social workers and judges.

Then again, you could choose a *speculative* approach, your main purpose being to suggest possibilities:

> Psychologists disagree about the potential effect on youngsters of all the media attention given to child abuse. Will children exposed to this media coverage grow up assertive, self-confident, and able to protect themselves? Or will they become fearful and distrustful?

These examples illustrate that an essay's causal analysis may have more than one purpose. For instance, although the last example points to a paper with a primarily speculative purpose, the essay would probably start by informing readers of experts' conflicting views. The paper would also have a persuasive slant if it ended by urging readers to complain to the media about their sensationalized treatment of the child-abuse issue.

2. Adapt content and tone to your purpose and readers. Your purpose and audience determine what supporting material and what tone will be most effective in a cause-effect essay. Assume you want to direct your essay on child abuse to general readers who know little about the subject. To *inform* readers, you might use facts, statistics, and expert opinion to provide an objective discussion of the causes of child abuse. Your analysis might show the following: (1) adults who were themselves mistreated as children tend to abuse their own offspring; (2) marital stress contributes to the mistreatment of children; and (3) certain personality disorders increase the likelihood of child abuse. Sensitive to what your readers would and wouldn't understand, you would stay away from a technical or formal tone. Rather than writing "Pathological pre-abuse symptomatology predicts adult transference of high aggressivity," you would say "Psychologists can often predict, on the basis of family histories, who will abuse children."

Now imagine that your purpose is to *convince* future social workers that the failure of social service agencies to act authoritatively in child-abuse cases often has tragic consequences. Hoping to encourage more responsible behavior in the prospective social workers, you would adopt a more emotional tone in the essay, perhaps citing wrenching case histories that dramatize what happens when child abuse isn't taken seriously.

3. Think rigorously about causes and effects. Cause-effect relationships are usually complex. To write a meaningful analysis, you should do some careful thinking about your subject. (The two sets of questions at the end of this chapter's Prewriting Checklist [page 372] will help you think creatively about causes and effects.)

If you look beyond the obvious, you'll discover that a cause may have many effects. Imagine you're writing a paper on the effects of cigarette smoking. A number of consequences might be discussed, some less obvious but perhaps more interesting than others: increased risk of lung cancer and heart disease, evidence of harm done by secondhand smoke, legal battles regarding the rights of smokers and nonsmokers, lower birth weights in babies of mothers who smoke, and developmental problems experienced by such underweight infants.

In the same way, an effect may have multiple causes. An essay analyzing the reasons for world hunger could discuss many causes, again some less evident but perhaps more thought-provoking than others: overpopulation, climatic changes, inefficient use of land, and poor management of international relief funds.

Your analysis may also uncover a **causal chain** in which one cause (or effect) brings about another, which, in turn, brings about another, and so on. Here's an example of a causal chain: Prohibition went into effect; bootleggers and organized crime stepped in to supply public demand for alcoholic beverages; ordinary citizens began breaking the law by buying illegal alcohol and patronizing speak-easies; disrespect for legal authority became widespread and acceptable. As you can see, a causal chain often leads to interesting points. In this case, the subject of Prohibition leads not just to the obvious (illegal consumption of alcohol) but also to the more complex issue of society's decreasing respect for legal authority.

Don't grapple with so complex a chain, however, that you become hopelessly entangled. If your subject involves multiple causes and effects, limit what you'll discuss. Identify which causes and effects are *primary* and which are *secondary*. How extensively you cover secondary factors will depend on your purpose and audience. In an essay intended to inform a general audience about the harmful effects of pesticides, you would most likely focus on everyday dangers—polluted drinking water, residues in food, and the like. You probably wouldn't include a discussion of more long-range consequences (evolution of resistant insects, disruption of the soil's acid-alkaline balance).

Similarly, decide whether to focus on *immediate,* more obvious causes and effects, or on less obvious, more *remote* ones. Or perhaps you need to focus on both. In an essay about a faculty strike at your college, should you attribute the strike simply to the faculty's failure to receive a salary increase? Or should you also examine other factors: the union's failure to accept a salary package that satisfied most professors; the administration's inability to coordinate its negotiating efforts? It may be more difficult to explore more remote causes and effects, but it can also lead to more original and revealing essays. Thoughtful analyses take these less obvious considerations into account.

When developing a causal analysis, be careful to avoid the **post hoc fallacy.** Named after the Latin phrase *post hoc, ergo propter hoc,* meaning "after this, therefore because of this," this kind of faulty thinking occurs when you assume that simply because one event *followed* another, the first event *caused* the second. For example, if the Republicans win a majority of seats in Congress and, several months later, the economy collapses, can you conclude that the Republicans caused the collapse? A quick assumption of "Yes" fails the test of logic, for the timing of events could be coincidental and not indicative of any cause-effect relationship. The collapse may have been triggered by uncontrolled inflation that began well before the congressional elections. (For more on *post hoc* thinking, see pages 453–454 in Chapter 19.)

Also, be careful not to mistake *correlation* for *causation.* Two events correlate when they occur at about the same time. Such co-occurrence, however, doesn't guarantee a cause-effect relationship. For instance, while the number of ice cream cones eaten and the instances of heat prostration both increase during the summer months, this doesn't mean that eating ice cream causes heat prostration! A third factor—in this case, summer heat—is the actual cause. When writing causal analyses, then, use with caution words that imply a causal link (such as *therefore* and *because*). Words that express simply time of occurrence (*following* and *previously*) are safer and more objective.

Finally, keep in mind that a rigorous causal analysis involves more than loose generalizations about causes and effects. Creating plausible connections may require library research, interviewing, or both. Often you'll need to provide facts, statistics, details, personal observations, or other corroborative material if readers are going to accept the reasoning behind your analysis.

4. Write a thesis that focuses the paper on causes, effects, or both. The thesis in an essay developed through causal analysis often indicates whether the essay will deal mostly with causes, effects, or both. Here, for example, are three thesis statements for causal analyses dealing with the public school system. You'll see that each thesis signals that essay's particular emphasis:

Causes

Our school system has been weakened by an overemphasis on trendy electives.

Effects

An ineffectual school system has led to crippling teachers' strikes and widespread disrespect for the teaching profession.

Causes and Effects

Bureaucratic inefficiency has created a school system unresponsive to children's emotional, physical, and intellectual needs.

Note that the thesis statement—in addition to signaling whether the paper will discuss causes or effects or both—may also point to the essay's plan of development. Consider the last thesis statement; it makes clear that the paper will discuss children's emotional needs first, their physical needs second, and their intellectual needs last.

The thesis statement in a causal analysis doesn't have to specify whether the essay will discuss causes, effects, or both. Nor does the thesis have to be worded in such a way that the essay's plan of development is apparent. But when first writing cause-effect essays, you may find that a highly focused thesis will help keep your analysis on track.

5. Choose an organizational pattern. There are two basic ways to organize the points in a cause-effect essay: you may use a chronological or an emphatic sequence. If you select *chronological order,* you discuss causes and effects in the order in which they occur or will occur. Suppose you're writing an essay on the causes for the popularity of imported cars. These causes might be discussed in chronological sequence: American plant workers became frustrated and dissatisfied on the job; some workers got careless while others deliberately sabotaged the production of sound cars; a growing number of defective cars hit the market; consumers grew dissatisfied with American cars and switched to imports.

Chronology might also be used to organize a discussion about effects. Imagine you want to write an essay about the need to guard against disrupting delicate balances in the country's wildlife. You might start the essay by discussing what happened when the starling, a non-native bird, was introduced into the American environment. Because the starling had few natural predators, the starling population soared out of control; the starlings took over food sources and habitats of native species; the bluebird, a native species, declined and is now threatened with extinction.

Although a chronological pattern can be an effective way to organize material, a strict time sequence can present a problem if your primary cause or effect ends up buried in the middle of the sequence. In such a case, you might use *emphatic order,* reserving the most significant cause or effect for the end. For example, time order could be used to present the reasons behind a candidate's unexpected victory: Less than a month after the candidate's earlier defeat, a full-scale fundraising campaign for the next election was started; the candidate spoke to many crucial power groups early in the campaign; the candidate did exceptionally well in the pre-election debates; good weather and large voter turnout on election day favored the candidate. However, if you believe that the candidate's appearance before influential groups was the key factor in the victory, it would be more effective to emphasize that point by saving it for the end. This is what is meant by emphatic order—saving the most important point for last.

Emphatic order is an especially effective way to sequence cause-effect points when readers hold what, in your opinion, are mistaken or narrow views about a subject. To encourage readers to look more closely at the issues, you present what you consider the erroneous or obvious views first, show why they are unsound or limited, then present what you feel to be the actual causes and effects. Such a sequence nudges the audience into giving further thought to the causes and effects you have discovered. Here are informal outlines for two causal analyses using this approach:

```
Subject: The causes of the riot at a rock concert

1. Some commentators blame the excessively hot weather.
2. Others cite drug use among the concertgoers.
3. Still others blame the liquor sold at the concessions.
4. But the real cause of the disaster was poor planning by the con-
   cert promoters.


Subject: The effects of campus crime

1. Immediate problems
   a. Students feel insecure and fearful.
   b. Many night-time campus activities have been curtailed.
2. More significant long-term problems
   a. Unfavorable publicity about campus crime will affect future
      student enrollment.
   b. Unfavorable publicity about campus crime will make it diffi-
      cult to recruit top-notch faculty.
```

When using emphatic order, you might want to word the thesis in such a way that it signals which point your essay will stress. Look at the following thesis statements:

Although many immigrants arrive in this country without marketable
skills, their most pressing problem is learning how to make their
way in a society whose language they don't know.

The space program has led to dramatic advances in computer technology
and medical science. Even more importantly, though, the program has
helped change many people's attitudes toward the planet we live on.

These thesis statements reflect an awareness of the complex nature of cause-effect relationships. While not dismissing secondary issues, the statements establish which points the writer considers most noteworthy. The second thesis, for instance, indicates that the paper will touch on the technological and medical advances made possible by the space program but will emphasize the way the program has changed people's attitudes toward the earth.

Whether you use a chronological or emphatic pattern to organize your essay, you'll need to provide clear *signals* to identify when you're discussing causes and when you're discussing effects. Expressions such as "Another reason" and "A final outcome" help readers follow your line of thought.

6. Use language that hints at the complexity of cause-effect relationships. Because it's difficult—if not impossible—to identify causes and effects with certainty, you should avoid such absolutes as "It must be obvious" and "There is no doubt." Instead, try phrases like "Most likely" or "It is probable." Such language isn't indecisive; it's reasonable and reflects your understanding of the often tangled nature of causes and effects. Don't, however, go to the other extreme and be reluctant to take a stand on the issues. If you have thought carefully about causes and effects, you have a right to state your analysis with conviction.

REVISION STRATEGIES

Once you have a draft of the essay, you're ready to revise. The following checklist will help you and those giving you feedback apply to cause-effect writing some of the revision techniques discussed in Chapters 7 and 8.

 CAUSE-EFFECT: A REVISION CHECKLIST

Revise Overall Meaning and Structure

☐ Is the essay's purpose informative, persuasive, speculative, or a combination of these?

☐ What is the essay's thesis? Is it stated specifically or implied? Where? Could it be made any clearer? How?

☐ Does the essay focus on causes, effects, or both? How do you know?

☐ Where has correlation been mistaken for causation? Where is the essay weakened by *post hoc* thinking?

☐ Where does the essay distinguish between primary and secondary causes and effects? How do the most critical causes and effects receive special attention?

☐ Where does the essay dwell on the obvious?

Revise Paragraph Development

☐ Which paragraphs fail to support the essay's thesis?

☐ Are the essay's paragraphs sequenced chronologically or emphatically? Was the decision to use that order a good one? Why or why not?

☐ Where would signal devices (such as *afterward, before, then,* and *next*) make it easier to follow the progression of thought within and between paragraphs?

☐ Which paragraphs would be strengthened by vivid examples, such as statistics, facts, anecdotes, or personal observations, that support the causal analysis?

Revise Sentences and Words

☐ Where do expressions like *as a result, because,* and *therefore* mislead the reader by implying a cause-effect relationship? Would words such as *following* and *previously* eliminate the problem?

☐ Do any words or phrases convey an arrogant or dogmatic tone (*there is no question, undoubtedly, always, never*)? What other expressions (*most likely, probably*) would improve credibility?

STUDENT ESSAY: FROM PREWRITING THROUGH REVISION

The student essay that follows was written by Carl Novack in response to this assignment:

> In "Black Men and Public Space," Brent Staples reminds us that, sadly, racist attitudes have not changed much over the years. There are, though, some areas in which people's attitudes *have* changed dramatically. Identify a significant shift in an activity, practice, or institution. Then write an essay in which you discuss the factors that you believe are responsible for the attitudinal change.

After deciding to write about Americans' changing food habits, Carl used the *mapping technique* to generate material on his subject. His map is shown on page 379. The marks in color indicate Carl's later efforts to organize and elaborate the original map. Note that he added some branches, eliminated others, drew arrows indicating that some topics should be moved, and changed the wording of some key ideas. These annotations paved the way for Carl's topic outline, which is presented after the map.

Mapping

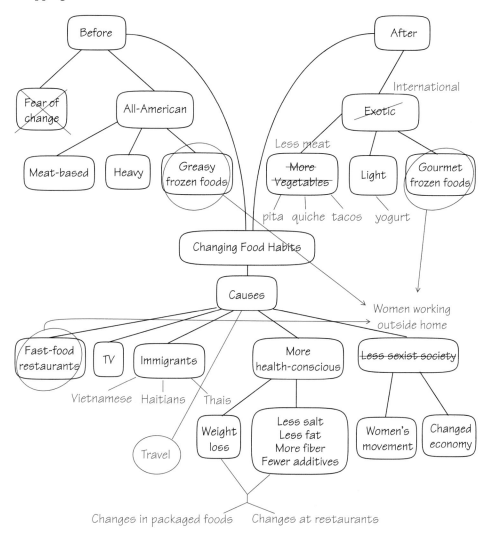

Outline

Thesis: America has changed and so has what we Americans eat and how we eat.

    I. We used to eat "All-American" meals.

        A. Heavy

        B. Meat-based

II. Now our tastes are more international.

   A. Lighter--yogurt

   B. Less meat--pita, quiche, tacos

III. There are several reasons for our tastes becoming more
      international.

   A. Television

   B. Travel abroad

   C. Immigrants in this country

IV. Two social trends have also changed how and what we eat.

   A. Health consciousness

     1. Concern about weight

     2. Concern about salt, fat, fiber, additives

       a. Changes in packaged foods (lunch meat, canned
          vegetables, soups)

       b. Changes in restaurants (salad bars)

   B. More women working outside the home because of the
      economy and the women's movement

     1. Increase in fast-food restaurants

     2. More frozen foods, some even gourmet

Now read Carl's paper, "Americans and Food," noting the similarities and differences among his map, outline, and final essay. See, for example, how the diagram suggests a "before" and "after" contrast—a contrast the essay develops. Also note Carl's decision to move "frozen foods" and "fast-food restaurants" to the "women working outside home" section of the diagram. This decision is reflected in the outline and in the final essay, where frozen foods and fast-food restaurants are discussed in the same paragraph. As you read the essay, also consider how well it applies the principles of causal analysis discussed in this chapter. (The commentary that follows the paper will help you look at Carl's essay more closely and will give you some sense of how he went about revising his first draft.)

Americans and Food

by Carl Novack

Introduction   An offbeat but timely cartoon recently appeared in the   1
local newspaper. The single panel showed a gravel-pit operation
with piles of raw earth and large cranes. Next to one of the
cranes stood the owner of the gravel pit--a grizzled, tough-
looking character, hammer in hand, pointing proudly to the new
sign he had just tacked up. The sign read, "Fred's Fill Dirt and
Croissants." The cartoon illustrates an interesting phenomenon:

the changing food habits of Americans. Our meals used to consist of something like home-cooked pot roast, mashed potatoes
laced with butter and salt, a thick slice of apple pie topped
with a healthy scoop of vanilla ice cream--plain, heavy meals,
cooked from scratch, and eaten leisurely at home. But America
has changed, and because it has, so have what we Americans eat   — Thesis
and how we eat it.

2   We used to have simple, unsophisticated tastes and looked
with suspicion at anything more exotic than hamburger. Admittedly, we did adopt some foods from the various immigrant
groups who flocked to our shores. We learned to eat Chinese
food, pizza, and bagels. But in the last few years, the inter-   — Topic sentence:
national character of our diet has grown tremendously. We can   Background
walk into any mall in Middle America and buy pita bread,   paragraph
quiche, and tacos. Such foods are often changed on their journey from exotic imports to ordinary "American" meals (no Paki-
stani, for example, eats frozen-on-a-stick boysenberry-flavored
yogurt), but the imports are still a long way from hamburger on   Topic sentence:
a bun.   Three causes
                                                                   answer the
3   Why have we become more worldly in our tastes? For one   question
thing, television blankets the country with information about
new food products and trends. Viewers in rural Montana know   — First cause
that the latest craving in Washington, D.C., is Cajun cooking
or that something called tofu is now available in the local
supermarket. Another reason for the growing international fla-   Second cause
vor of our food is that many young Americans have traveled
abroad and gotten hooked on new tastes and flavors. Backpacking
students and young professionals vacationing in Europe come
home with cravings for authentic French bread or German beer.
Finally, continuing waves of immigrants settle in the cities
where many of us live, causing significant changes in what we   Third cause
eat. Vietnamese, Haitians, and Thais, for instance, bring their
native foods and cooking styles with them and eventually open
small markets or restaurants. In time, the new food will become
Americanized enough to take its place in our national diet.   Topic sentence:
4   Our growing concern with health has also affected the way   Another cause
we eat. For the last few years, the media have warned us about
the dangers of our traditional diet, high in salt and fat, low
in fiber. The media also began to educate us about the dangers

Start of a — of processed foods pumped full of chemical additives. As a
causal chain   result, consumers began to demand healthier foods, and manufacturers started to change some of their products. Many foods,
such as lunch meat, canned vegetables, and soups, were made
available in low-fat, low-sodium versions. Whole-grain cereals
and high-fiber breads also began to appear on the grocery
shelves. Moreover, the food industry started to produce
all-natural products--everything from potato chips to ice
cream--without additives and preservatives. Not surprisingly,
the restaurant industry responded to this switch to healthier
foods, luring customers with salad bars, broiled fish, and
steamed vegetables.

Topic sentence: → Our food habits are being affected, too, by the rapid   5
Another cause   increase in the number of women working outside the home. Soci-
ologists and other experts believe that two important factors
triggered this phenomenon: the women's movement and a changing
economic climate. Women were assured that it was acceptable,
even rewarding, to work outside the home; many women also discovered that they had to work just to keep up with the cost
of living. As the traditional role of homemaker changed, so
did the way families ate. With Mom working, there wasn't time
for her to prepare the traditional three square meals a day.
Instead, families began looking for alternatives to provide
Start of a —   quick meals. What was the result? For one thing, there was a
causal chain   boom in fast-food restaurants. The suburban or downtown strip
that once contained a lone McDonald's now features Wendy's, Roy
Rogers, Taco Bell, Burger King, and Pizza Hut. Families also
began to depend on frozen foods as another time-saving alternative. Once again, though, demand changed the kind of frozen
food available. Frozen foods no longer consist of foil trays
divided into greasy fried chicken, watery corn niblets, and
lumpy mashed potatoes. Supermarkets now stock a range of supposedly gourmet frozen dinners--from fettucini in cream sauce
to braised beef en brochette.

Conclusion   It may not be possible to pick up a ton of fill dirt and a   6
half-dozen croissants at the same place, but America's food
habits are definitely changing. If it is true that "you are
what you eat," then America's identity is evolving along with
its diet.

Commentary

Title and Introduction

Asked to prepare a paper analyzing the reasons behind a change in our lives, Carl decided to write about a shift he had noticed in Americans' eating habits. The title of the essay, "Americans and Food," identifies Carl's subject but could be livelier and more interesting.

Despite his rather uninspired title, Carl starts his *causal analysis* in an engaging way—with the vivid description of a cartoon. He then connects the cartoon to his subject with the following sentence: "The cartoon illustrates an interesting phenomenon: the changing food habits of Americans." To back up his belief that there has been a revolution in our eating habits, Carl uses the first paragraph to summarize the kind of meal that people used to eat. He then moves to his *thesis:* "But America has changed, and because it has, so have what Americans eat and how we eat it." The thesis implies that Carl's paper will focus on both causes and effects.

Purpose

Carl's purpose was to write an *informative* causal analysis. But before he could present the causes of the change in eating habits, he needed to show that such a change had, in fact, taken place. He therefore uses the second paragraph to document one aspect of this change—the internationalization of our eating habits.

Topic Sentences

At the start of the third paragraph, Carl uses a question—"Why have we become more worldly in our tastes?"—to signal that his discussion of causes is about to begin. This question also serves as the paragraph's *topic sentence,* indicating that the paragraph will focus on reasons for the increasingly international flavor of our food. The next two paragraphs, also focused by topic sentences, identify two other major reasons for the change in eating habits: "Our growing concern with health has also affected the way we eat" (paragraph 4), and "Our food habits are being affected, too, by the rapid increase in the number of women working outside the home" (5).

Other Patterns of Development

Carl draws on two patterns of development—*comparison-contrast* and *illustration*—to develop his causal analysis. At the heart of the essay is a basic *contrast* between the way we used to eat and the way we eat now. And throughout his essay, Carl provides convincing *examples* to demonstrate the validity of his points. Consider for a moment the third paragraph. Here Carl asserts that one reason for our new eating habits is our growing exposure to international foods. He then presents concrete evidence to show that we have indeed become more familiar with international cuisine: Television exposes rural Montana to Cajun cooking; students traveling abroad take a liking to French bread; urban dwellers enjoy the exotic fare served by numerous immigrant groups. The fourth and fifth paragraphs use similarly specific evidence (for example, "low-fat, low-sodium versions" of "lunchmeat, canned vegetables, and soups") to illustrate the soundness of key ideas.

Causal Chains

Let's look more closely at the evidence in the essay. Not satisfied with obvious explanations, Carl thought through his ideas carefully and even brainstormed with friends to arrive at as comprehensive an analysis as possible. Not surprisingly, much of the evidence Carl uncovered took the form of *causal chains*. In the fourth paragraph, Carl writes, "The media also began to educate us about the dangers of processed foods pumped full of chemical additives. As a result, consumers began to demand healthier foods, and manufacturers started to change some of their products." And the next paragraph shows how the changing role of American women caused families to look for alternative ways of eating. This shift, in turn, caused the restaurant and food industries to respond with a wide range of food alternatives.

Making the Paper Easy to Follow

Although Carl's analysis digs beneath the surface and reveals complex cause-effect relationships, he wisely limits his pursuit of causal chains to *primary* causes and effects. He doesn't let the complexities distract him from his main purpose: to show why and how the American diet is changing. Carl is also careful to provide his essay with abundant *connecting devices,* making it easy for readers to see the links between points. Consider the use of *transitions* (signaled by italics) in the following sentences: "*Another* reason for the growing international flavor of our food is that many young Americans have traveled abroad" (paragraph 3); "*As a result,* consumers began to demand healthier foods" (4); and "*As* the traditional role of homemaker changed, so did the way families ate" (5).

A Problem with the Essay's Close

As you read the essay, you probably noticed that Carl's conclusion is a bit weak. Although his reference to the cartoon works well, the rest of the paragraph limps to a tired close. Ending an otherwise vigorous essay with such a slight conclusion undercuts the effectiveness of the whole paper. Carl spent so much energy developing the body of his essay that he ran out of the stamina needed to conclude the piece more forcefully. Careful budgeting of his time would have allowed him to prepare a stronger concluding paragraph.

Revising the First Draft

When Carl was ready to revise, he showed the first draft of his essay to several classmates who used the revision checklist on pages 377–378 to focus their feedback. Listening carefully, Carl jotted down their most helpful comments and eventually transferred them, numbered in order of importance, to his draft. Comparing Carl's original version of his fourth paragraph (shown on the next page) with his final version in the essay will show you how he went about revising.

Original Version of the Fourth Paragraph

(A growing concern with health has also affected the way we
eat, especially because the media has sent us warnings the last
few years about the dangers of salt, sugar, food additives, and
high-fat and low-fiber diets.) We have started to worry that our
traditional meals may have been shortening our lives. As a
result, consumers demanded healthier foods and manufacturers
started taking some of the salt and sugar out of canned foods.
"All-natural" became an effective selling point, leading to
many preservative-free products. Restaurants, too, adapted
their menus, luring customers with light meals. Because we now
know about the link between overweight and a variety of health
problems, including heart attacks, we are counting calories. In
turn, food companies made fortunes on diet beer and diet cola.
Sometimes, though, we seem a bit confused about the health
issue; we drink soda that is sugar-free but loaded with chemical sweeteners. Still, we believe we are lengthening our lives
through changing our diets.

② First sentence
cluttered, too
long

③ Add specifics

① Doesn't fit
point being
made

On the advice of his classmates, Carl decided to omit all references to the way
our concern with weight has affected our eating habits. It's true, of course, that
calorie-counting has changed how we eat. But as soon as Carl started to discuss
this point, he got involved in a causal chain that undercut the paragraph's unity.
He ended up describing the paradoxical situation in which we find ourselves: In
an attempt to eat healthy, we stay away from sugar and turn to possibly harmful
artificial sweeteners. This is an interesting issue, but it detracts from Carl's main
point—that our concern with health has affected our eating habits in a *positive*
way.

Carl's editing team also pointed out that the fourth paragraph's first sentence
contained too much material to be an effective topic sentence. Carl corrected the
problem by breaking the overlong sentence into two short ones: "Our growing
concern with health has also affected the way we eat. For the last few years, the
media have warned us about the dangers of our traditional diet, high in salt and
fat, low in fiber." The first of these sentences serves as a crisp topic sentence that
focuses the rest of the paragraph.

Finally, when Carl heard the essay read aloud, he realized the fourth paragraph
lacked convincing specifics. When revising, he changed "manufacturers started
taking some of the salt and sugar out of canned foods" to the more specific "Many
foods, such as lunch meats, canned vegetables, and soups, were made available in
low-fat, low-sodium versions." Similarly, generalizations about "light meals" and
"all-natural" products gained life through the addition of concrete examples: restaurants lured "customers with salad bars, broiled fish, and steamed vegetables,"

and the food industry produced "everything from potato chips to ice cream—without additives and preservatives."

Carl did an equally good job revising other sections of his paper. With the exception of the weak spots already discussed, he made the changes needed to craft a well-reasoned essay, one that demonstrates his ability to analyze a complex phenomenon.

ACTIVITIES: CAUSE-EFFECT

Prewriting Activities

1. Imagine you're writing two essays: One proposes the need for high school courses in personal finance (how to budget money, balance a checkbook, and the like); the other explains how to show appreciation. Jot down ways you might use cause-effect in each essay.

2. Use mapping, collaborative brainstorming, or another prewriting technique to generate possible causes and/or effects for *one* of the following topics. Then organize your raw material into a brief outline, with related causes and effects grouped in the same section.

    a. Pressure on students to do well

    b. Children's access to soft-core pornography on cable television

    c. Being physically fit

    d. Spiraling costs of a college education

3. For the topic you selected in activity 2, note the two potential audiences indicated below in parentheses. For each audience, devise a thesis and decide whether your essay's purpose would be informative, persuasive, speculative, or some combination of these. Then, with your thesis statements and purposes in mind, review the outline you prepared for the preceding activity. How would you change it to fit each audience? What points should be added? What points would be primary causes and effects for one audience but secondary for the other? Which organizational pattern—chronological, spatial, or emphatic—would be most effective for each audience?

    a. Pressure on students to do well (*college students, parents of elementary school children*)

    b. Children's access to soft-core pornography on cable television (*cable executives, parents of young children*)

c. Being physically fit (*those who show a reasonable degree of concern, those who are obsessed with being fit*)

d. Spiraling costs of a college education (*college officials, high school students planning to attend college*)

Revising Activities

4. Explain how the following statements demonstrate *post hoc* thinking and confuse correlation and cause-effect.

a. Our city now has many immigrants from Latin American countries. The crime rate in our city has increased. Latin American immigrants are the cause of the crime wave.

b. The divorce rate has skyrocketed. More women are working outside the home than ever before. Working outside the home destroys marriages.

c. A high percentage of people in Dixville have developed cancer. The landfill, used by XYZ Industries, has been located in Dixville for twenty years. The XYZ landfill has caused cancer in Dixville residents.

5. The following paragraph is from the first draft of an essay arguing that technological advances can diminish the quality of life. How solid is the paragraph's causal analysis? Which causes and/or effects should be eliminated? Where is the analysis simplistic? Where does the writer make absolute claims even though cause-effect relationships are no more than a possibility? Keeping these questions in mind, revise the paragraph.

How did the banking industry respond to inflation? It simply introduced a new technology--the automated teller machine (ATM). By making money more available to the average person, the ATM gives people the cash to buy inflated goods--whether or not they can afford them. Not surprisingly, automatic teller machines have had a number of negative consequences for the average individual. Since people know they can get cash at any time, they use their lunch hours for something other than going to the bank. How do they spend this new-found time? They go shopping, and machine-vended money means more impulse buying, even more than with a credit card. Also, because people don't need their checkbooks to withdraw money, they can't keep track of their accounts and therefore develop a casual attitude toward financial matters. It's no wonder children don't appreciate the value of money. Another problem is that people who would never dream of robbing a bank try to trick the machine into dispensing money "for free." There's no doubt that this kind of fraud contributes to the immoral climate in the country.

PROFESSIONAL
SELECTIONS:
CAUSE-EFFECT

NATALIE ANGIER

Natalie Angier (1958–), a Pulitzer-Prize-winning science writer for the *New York Times,* began her professional career as a staff writer for *Discover* magazine. She has published two books: *Natural Obsessions* (1988) and *The Beauty of the Beastly* (1995). "A Granddaughter's Fear" first appeared in the *New York Times* magazine in May 1989.

A GRANDDAUGHTER'S FEAR

1   I was talking business with a colleague late one afternoon when the first call came. The voice on the other end was loud and panicked; my colleague looked over at me, horrified.

2   "Natalie, is that you?" screamed my grandmother. "Natalie, I need you to do me a favor!"

3   I cupped the telephone mouthpiece. "What's wrong, Grandma?"

4   She started to cry, her voice heaving and gasping. She told me that she'd been alone since 12 o'clock—for five hours!—and that nobody was scheduled to visit her until 10 that night. She couldn't stand it; she was going crazy; they'd left her all alone, and she was so afraid. She'd been calling everybody, everybody—her son (my uncle), her stepson, her grandsons. And now me.

5   "So what do you want me to do?" I muttered, although I knew the answer.

6   "Please, darling, come over! Can't you come here? Please Natalie! I'm ALL ALONE!"

7   "O.K., O.K.," I said. "I'm coming over. I'll be up there as soon as I can."

8   I hung up and told my colleague that I'd have to leave in a few minutes. But I didn't think there was any immediate crisis. My grandmother lives in an apartment building on New York's Upper East Side where plenty of people know her and stop by to see how she is. She just wanted company—and, damn it, I was busy. I continued my business discussion for another 20 minutes. Until the second call came.

9   This time my grandmother was genuinely hysterical. "Natalie, WHERE ARE YOU?" she cried. "You said you were coming right over! Please darling!"

10   Now I really did hurry, racing out the door and grabbing a cab. But the moment I arrived at her apartment I wanted to run the other way again. She clutched my arm and pulled me inside. Her face was a gray blur of tears and her thin white hair stood up in wild peaks. Her bathrobe had half fallen off; I'd never seen my grandmother's naked body before. The apartment smelled stale. I threw open a window and sat down stiffly on the couch.

11 For the next few minutes I didn't say a word as my grandmother shuffled around the living room, ranting against the world. She complained about my uncle, who had deserted her earlier in the day (he had to go to work). She railed against my mother—her daughter—who was vacationing in Australia. She talked madly about how they were trying to steal her money, how they'd taken away her keys, how they never spent more than 10 minutes at a time with her—although I knew only too well that both her children structured their days and nights around her needs.

12 As she sputtered on, I felt more and more helpless and resentful. Finally, my rage overwhelmed my judgment. I stood up and started yelling at her. I told her that nobody and nothing could help her. The only person who could help you is *you!*" I said in righteous fury. "Do you understand me? You've got to stop being so damned dependent on everybody!"

13 At which point she let out a piercing shriek of agony and hurled herself on her bed. The only thing I'd accomplished with my idiotic lecture was to heighten both her hysteria and my sense of impotence.

14 My grandmother is 80, but she seems much older. Although she suffers from a host of physical ailments—mild diabetes, glaucoma, asthma, arthritis—her real problems are neurological and psychological. She may have Alzheimer's, she may have been stricken by a series of small, silent strokes. Her doctor isn't sure, and he says that, frankly, the precise diagnosis doesn't matter: her condition is irreversible. What is clear is that she hates being old, she can't stand being left alone for even minutes at a time, and she'll do anything to surround herself with people.

15 These days, much of the family conversation centers on her. What are we going to do about Grandma? Put her in a nursing home? (Too awful.) Hire a live-in companion? (Too expensive.) Put her on some new psychotherapeutic medication? (Nothing seems to work.) Not only does my grandmother demand companionship during the day; she also needs somebody around every night. So another question my family grapples with is: whose turn is it to sleep over on Grandmother's sofa bed?

16 By far the most debilitating consequence of the ordeal is the guilt. Because we can't seem to make my grandmother happy, we feel frustrated. That frustration leads us to either explode in anger or to drop out of sight—immature reactions that come prepackaged with shame. No matter how much she does, my mother worries she's not doing enough. At the same time, she bitterly resents her mother's nonstop demands. The result is that my mother visits and calls my grandmother constantly, but then ends up lashing out in senseless indignation. My uncle usually represses his emotions, but he's starting to gain weight and to look his 56 years.

17 I manage to combine the worst of all worlds. I neglect to call my grandmother for weeks at a stretch. When I do visit, I lapse into the role of boot-camp sergeant. As a fitness fanatic, I tell her it's never too late to take up exercise. I turn away from her tears. My mother accuses me of being heartless; she's right.

18 My grandmother is the first person I have watched grow old. I used to adore her: she still keeps loving poems and letters I wrote to her. She was always a vivid, energetic woman, selling bonds for Israel, working long hours in charity thrift shops. She told stories about her past with the narrative panache of Isaac Bashevis Singer.* Wherever

---

*A Polish-born American Yiddish writer (1904–1991), winner of the 1978 Nobel Prize for literature (editors' note).

she went, she made flocks of friends—a trait that I, a lonely and sullen girl, particularly admired.

But then hard times began to pile up around her like layers of choking silt. Although 19 she'd stoutly nursed three husbands through terminal illnesses, she became increasingly depressed when her siblings—all older than she—started to die. After she lost her last remaining sister, in 1982, my grandmother just about lost her mind. She still had many friends, but she clamored for ever more attention from her children and grandchildren. She became an emotional hair-trigger, she'd have temper tantrums at parties, seders,* my sister's wedding.

As my grandmother has worsened, so too has my response to her. My mother 20 implores me to be decent and stay in touch, and I launch into all the reasons why I don't. But my excuses sound shallow and glib, even to myself. The truth is that my grandmother terrifies me.

I have in my mind a pastel confection of the perfect old woman. She is wise and dig- 21 nified, at peace with herself and quietly proud of the life she has forged. She doesn't waste time seeking approval or cursing the galaxy. Instead, she works at her craft. She is Georgia O'Keeffe painting, Louise Nevelson sculpturing, Marianne Moore[†] writing. Or she is a less celebrated woman, who reads, listens to Bach,[‡] and threads together the scattered days into a private whole.

Of course, there are many things my fantasy doyenne is *not.* She's not strapped for 22 money. Her joints don't ache, her breath doesn't rattle. She isn't losing her memory, her reason, her eyesight. Above all, she is not the old woman I know best.

I love my grandmother. She still has her good hours, when her mind is quick and 23 clear. Inevitably, though, her mad despair bursts to the surface again. She discovers a new reason to weep, blame and backstab, and I discover a new excuse for staying away.

I want to age magnificently, as O'Keeffe and Moore did. I want to be better in half a 24 century than I am at 31, but I doubt that I will. When I look at my grandmother, fragile, frightened, unhappy, wanting to die but clinging desperately to life, I see myself—and I cannot stand the sight.

Questions for Close Reading

1. What is the selection's thesis? Locate the sentence(s) where Angier states her main idea. If she doesn't state the thesis explicitly, express it in your own words.

2. How does Angier react to her grandmother? Why does she respond as she does?

---

*Feasts commemorating the exodus of the Jews from Egypt, celebrated by Jewish people on the first two nights of Passover (editors' note).
[†]American painter (1887–1986), Russian-born American sculptor (1899–1988), American poet (1887–1972) (editors' note).
[‡]Johann Sebastian Bach (1685–1750), German composer and organist of the baroque period (editors' note).

3. How does Angier's reaction to the grandmother compare with her mother's and uncle's?

4. Describe Angier's fantasy of "the perfect old woman." How does Angier's grandmother differ from this ideal?

5. Refer to your dictionary as needed to define the following words used in the selection: *railed* (paragraph 11), *impotence* (13), *psychotherapeutic* (15), *debilitating* (16), *indignation* (16), *panache* (18), *stoutly* (19), *clamored* (19), *confection* (21), and *doyenne* (22).

Questions About the Writer's Craft

1. The pattern. In her essay, Angier explores two related causal chains: the effect of the grandmother's decline on the family and the reasons for the grandmother's decline. Which causal chain does Angier explore first? Why do you think that Angier made this decision?

2. Why do you think Angier chose the title "A Granddaughter's Fear" instead of, say, "My Fear"?

3. Other patterns. Angier's causal analysis includes a strong narrative component. As such, it focuses on a number of conflicts. What conflicts do you detect in this selection? Are they resolved? How do the conflicts help Angier convey her thesis?

4. Other patterns. In the narrative parts of her essay, Angier uses dialog fairly often, mixing actual dialog (paragraphs 2, 3, 5, 6, 7, 9, and 12) and dialog paraphrasing (4). Why might she have chosen first-hand dialog in some places and second-hand paraphrasing in others? What effect does each of these narrative techniques have on the way the story is told?

Writing Assignments Using Cause-Effect as a Pattern of Development

1. "A Granddaughter's Fear" presents an intimate portrait of Angier's conflicted feelings about her aging and increasingly infirm grandmother. Consider an elderly person you either know well or have encountered only briefly, and write a causal analysis showing how this person's aging affected you. You might explain, as Angier does, that the individual's old age had a wrenching effect on you. Or you might show that the person's energy and enthusiasm caused you to reinterpret what it means to grow older. In either case, be sure to provide plentiful examples to illustrate the person's impact on you.

∞ 2. Angier describes a profound change in her grandmother. Write a causal analysis exploring the reasons for and consequences of a fundamental change in someone you know well—perhaps a family member, a friend, even yourself. The changes you focus on may be positive or negative. State briefly what the person was once like; then examine in detail what caused the individual to change. End by showing how the shift affected everyone concerned. Before writing your paper, read Maya Angelou's "Sister Flowers" (page 175) to gain insight into the way seemingly minor experiences can bring about life-altering changes.

Writing Assignments Using Other Patterns of Development

∞ 3. Near the end of her essay, Angier contrasts the painful reality of her grandmother's aging with an idealized notion of the aging process. Brainstorm with friends, family, and classmates to gain insight into other situations that are less than ideal. Possibilities include a campus problem, an aspect of male-female interaction, or people's behavior at a specific event. Select *one* situation to write about and continue group brainstorming to gather material to develop a paper contrasting the way things are with the way they should be. Before writing the paper, read several of the following essays, all of which illustrate a clash between reality and an ideal: Audre Lorde's "The Fourth of July" (page 210), Joseph Suina's "And Then I Went to School" (page 361), Brent Staples's "Black Men and Public Space" (page 398), Nancy Gibbs's "When Is It Rape?" (page 423), Fern Kupfer's "Institution Is Not a Dirty Word" (page 470), and Caryl Rivers's "What Should Be Done About Rock Lyrics?" (page 473).

4. Write an essay in which you support or refute the following argument: "People in today's society neglect and mistreat the elderly." For whichever position you choose, brainstorm with others to assemble compelling, real-life examples to support your position. In the course of defending your argument, remember to acknowledge opposing viewpoints, refuting them when you can.

JOHN M. DARLEY
BIBB LATANÉ

John M. Darley (1938–), professor of psychology at Princeton University, studies the principles of moral judgment in children and adults. Bibb Latané (1937–), the former director of the Behavioral Sciences Laboratory at Ohio State University, is professor of psychology at the University of North Carolina, Chapel Hill. Darley and Latané are coauthors of *The Unresponsive Bystander: Why Doesn't He Help* (1970) and *Help in a Crisis: Bystander Response to an Emergency* (1976). Based on their research into the origins of noninvolvement, "Why People Don't Help in a Crisis" (1968) was awarded an essay prize from the American Association for the Advancement of Science.

WHY PEOPLE DON'T HELP IN A CRISIS

1   Kitty Genovese is set upon by a maniac as she returns home from work at 3 A.M. Thirty-eight of her neighbors in Kew Gardens, N.Y., come to their windows when she cries out in terror; not one comes to her assistance, even though her assailant takes half an hour to murder her. No one so much as calls the police. She dies.

2   Andrew Mormille is stabbed in the head and neck as he rides in a New York City subway train. Eleven other riders flee to another car as the 17-year-old boy bleeds to death; not one comes to his assistance, even though his attackers have left the car. He dies.

3   Eleanor Bradley trips and breaks her leg while shopping on New York City's Fifth Avenue. Dazed and in shock, she calls for help, but the hurrying stream of people simply parts and flows past. Finally, after 40 minutes, a taxi driver stops and helps her to a doctor.

4   How can so many people watch another human being in distress and do nothing? Why don't they help?

5   Since we started research on bystander responses to emergencies, we have heard many explanations for the lack of intervention in such cases. "The megalopolis in which we live makes closeness difficult and leads to the alienation of the individual from the group," says the psychoanalyst. "This sort of disaster," says the sociologist, "shakes the sense of safety and sureness of the individuals involved and causes psychological withdrawal." "Apathy," say others. "Indifference."

6   All of these analyses share one characteristic: they set the indifferent witness apart from the rest of us. Certainly not one of us who reads about these incidents in horror is apathetic, alienated or depersonalized. Certainly these terrifying cases have no personal implications for us. We needn't feel guilty, or re-examine ourselves, or anything like that. Or should we?

7   If we look closely at the behavior of witnesses to these incidents, the people involved begin to seem less inhuman and a lot more like the rest of us. They were not indifferent. The 38 witnesses of Kitty Genovese's murder, for example, did not merely look at the scene once and then ignore it. They continued to stare out of their windows, caught, fascinated, distressed, unwilling to act but unable to turn away.

8   Why, then, didn't they act?

9   There are three things the bystander must do if he is to intervene in an emergency: *notice* that something is happening; *interpret* that event as an emergency; and decide that he has *personal responsibility* for intervention. As we shall show, the presence of other bystanders may at each stage inhibit his action.

The Unseeing Eye

10   Suppose that a man has a heart attack. He clutches his chest, staggers to the nearest building and slumps sitting to the sidewalk. Will a passerby come to his assistance? First, the bystander has to notice that something is happening. He must tear himself away from his private thoughts and pay attention. But Americans consider it bad manners to look closely at other people in public. We are taught to respect the privacy of others, and when among strangers we close our ears and avoid staring. In a crowd, then, each person is less likely to notice a potential emergency than when alone.

Experimental evidence corroborates this. We asked college students to an interview 11
about their reactions to urban living. As the students waited to see the interviewer,
either by themselves or with two other students, they filled out a questionnaire. Solitary students often glanced idly about while filling out their questionnaires: those in
groups kept their eyes on their own papers.

As part of the study, we staged an emergency: smoke was released into the waiting 12
room through a vent. Two thirds of the subjects who were alone noticed the smoke
immediately, but only 25 percent of those waiting in groups saw it as quickly. Although
eventually all the subjects did become aware of the smoke—when the atmosphere
grew so smoky as to make them cough and rub their eyes—this study indicates that the
more people present, the slower an individual may be to perceive an emergency and
the more likely he is not to see it at all.

Seeing Is Not Necessarily Believing

Once an event is noticed, an onlooker must decide if it is truly an emergency. Emer- 13
gencies are not always clearly labeled as such; "smoke" pouring into a waiting room
may be caused by fire, or it may merely indicate a leak in a steam pipe. Screams in the
street may signal an assault or a family quarrel. A man lying in a doorway may be having a coronary—or he may simply be sleeping off a drunk.

A person trying to interpret a situation often looks at those around him to see how 14
he should react. If everyone else is calm and indifferent, he will tend to remain so; if
everyone else is reacting strongly, he is likely to become aroused. This tendency is not
merely slavish conformity; ordinarily we derive much valuable information about new
situations from how others around us behave. It's a rare traveler who, in picking a road-
side restaurant, chooses to stop at one where no other cars appear in the parking lot.

But occasionally the reactions of others provide false information. The studied non- 15
chalance of patients in a dentist's waiting room is a poor indication of their inner anxiety. It is considered embarrassing to "lose your cool" in public. In a potentially acute
situation, then, everyone present will appear more unconcerned than he is in fact. A
crowd can thus force inaction on its members by implying, through its passivity, that
an event is not an emergency. Any individual in such a crowd fears that he may appear
a fool if he behaves as though it were.

To determine how the presence of other people affects a person's interpretation of 16
an emergency, Latané and Judith Rodin set up another experiment. Subjects were paid
$2 to participate in a survey of game and puzzle preferences conducted at Columbia
University by the Consumer Testing Bureau. An attractive young market researcher
met them at the door and took them to the testing room, where they were given questionnaires to fill out. Before leaving, she told them that she would be working next
door in her office, which was separated from the room by a folding room-divider. She
then entered her office, where she shuffled papers, opened drawers and made enough
noise to remind the subjects of her presence. After four minutes she turned on a high-
fidelity tape recorder.

On it, the subjects heard the researcher climb up on a chair, perhaps to reach for a 17
stack of papers on the bookcase. They heard a loud crash and a scream as the chair collapsed and she fell, and they heard her moan, "Oh, my foot...I...I...can't move it. Oh,
I...can't get this...thing off me." Her cries gradually got more subdued and controlled.

18   Twenty-six people were alone in the waiting room when the "accident" occurred. Seventy percent of them offered to help the victim. Many pushed back the divider to offer their assistance; others called out to offer their help.

19   Among those waiting in pairs, only 20 percent—8 out of 40—offered to help. The other 32 remained unresponsive. In defining the situation as a nonemergency, they explained to themselves why the other member of the pair did not leave the room; they also removed any reason for action themselves. Whatever had happened, it was believed to be not serious. "A mild sprain," some said. "I didn't want to embarrass her." In a "real" emergency, they assured us, they would be among the first to help.

The Lonely Crowd

20   Even if a person defines an event as an emergency, the presence of other bystanders may still make him less likely to intervene. He feels that his responsibility is diffused and diluted. Thus, if your car breaks down on a busy highway, hundreds of drivers whiz by without anyone's stopping to help—but if you are stuck on a nearly deserted country road, whoever passes you first is likely to stop.

21   To test this diffusion-of-responsibility theory, we simulated an emergency in which people overheard a victim calling for help. Some thought they were the only person to hear the cries; the rest believed that others heard them, too. As with the witnesses to Kitty Genovese's murder, the subjects could not *see* one another or know what others were doing. The kind of direct group inhibition found in the other two studies could not operate.

22   For the simulation, we recruited 72 students at New York University to participate in what was referred to as a "group discussion" of personal problems in an urban university. Each student was put in an individual room equipped with a set of headphones and a microphone. It was explained that this precaution had been taken because participants might feel embarrassed about discussing their problems publicly. Also, the experimenter said that he would not listen to the initial discussion, but would only ask for reactions later. Each person was to talk in turn.

23   The first to talk reported that he found it difficult to adjust to New York and his studies. Then, hesitantly and with obvious embarrassment, he mentioned that he was prone to nervous seizures when he was under stress. Other students then talked about their own problems in turn. The number of people in the "discussion" varied. But whatever the apparent size of the group—two, three or six people—only the subject was actually present; the others, as well as the instructions and the speeches of the victim-to-be, were present only on a pre-recorded tape.

24   When it was the first person's turn to talk again, he launched into the following performance, becoming louder and having increasing speech difficulties: "I can see a lot of er of er how other people's problems are similar to mine because er I mean er they're not er e-easy to handle sometimes and er I er um I think I I need er if if could er er somebody er er er give me give me a little er give me a little help here because er I er *uh* I've got a a one of the er seiz-er er things coming *on* and and er uh uh (choking sounds)..."

25   Eighty-five percent of the people who believed themselves to be alone with the victim came out of their room to help. Sixty-two percent of the people who believed there was *one* other bystander did so. Of those who believed there were four other bystanders,

only 31 percent reported the fit. The responsibility-diluting effect of other people was so strong that single individuals were more than twice as likely to report the emergency as those who thought other people also knew about it.

The Lesson Learned

People who failed to report the emergency showed few signs of the apathy and indif- 26 ference thought to characterize "unresponsive bystanders." When the experimenter entered the room to end the situation, the subject often asked if the victim was "all right." Many of them showed physical signs of nervousness; they often had trembling hands and sweating palms. If anything, they seemed more emotionally aroused than did those who reported the emergency. Their emotional behavior was a sign of their continuing conflict concerning whether to respond or not.

Thus, the stereotype of the unconcerned, depersonalized *homo urbanus,* blandly 27 watching the misfortunes of others, proves inaccurate. Instead, we find that a bystander to an emergency is an anguished individual in genuine doubt, wanting to do the right thing but compelled to make complex decisions under pressure of stress and fear. His reactions are shaped by the actions of others—all too frequently by their inaction.

And we are that bystander. Caught up by the apparent indifference of others, we 28 may pass by an emergency without helping or even realizing that help is needed. Once we are aware of the influence of those around us, however, we can resist it. We can choose to see distress and step forward to relieve it.

Questions for Close Reading

1. What is the selection's thesis? Locate the sentence(s) in which Darley and Latané state their main idea. If they don't state the thesis explicitly, express it in your own words.

2. According to the authors, what three factors prevent people in a crowd from helping victims during an emergency?

3. Why did Darley and Latané isolate the subjects in separate rooms during the staged emergency described in paragraphs 21–26?

4. What kind of person, according to the authors, would tend to ignore or bypass a person experiencing a problem? What might encourage this person to act more responsibly?

5. Refer to your dictionary as needed to define the following words used in the selection: *megalopolis* (paragraph 5), *apathy* (5), *indifference* (5), *alienated* (6), *depersonalized* (6), *inhibit* (9), *corroborates* (11), *coronary* (13), *slavish* (14), *nonchalance* (15), *diffused* (20), and *blandly* (27).

Questions About the Writer's Craft

1. The pattern. What techniques do Darley and Latané use to help readers focus on the causes of people's inaction during an emergency?

2. Other patterns. The three brief narratives that open the essay depict events that happened well before Darley and Latané wrote their essay. Why might the authors have chosen to recount these events in the present tense rather than in the past tense?

3. Locate places where Darley and Latané describe the experiments investigating bystander behavior. How do the authors show readers the steps—and the implications—of each experiment?

4. What purpose do you think the authors had in mind when writing the selection? How do you know?

Writing Assignments Using Cause-Effect as a Pattern of Development

∞ **1.** Write an essay showing the "responsibility-diluting effect" that can occur when several people witness a critical event. Brainstorm with others to gather examples of this effect; then select two or three dramatic situations as the basis of your essay. Be sure to acknowledge other factors that may have played a role in inhibiting people's ability to act responsibly. To gain additional insight into the pressures that can compel group conformity, read George Orwell's "Shooting an Elephant" (page 203) and Diane Cole's "Don't Just Stand There" (page 315).

2. Although Darley and Latané focus on times when individuals fail to act responsibly, people often respond with moral heroism during difficult situations. Brainstorm with others to identify occasions in which people have taken the initiative to avert a crisis. Focusing on two or three compelling instances, write an essay in which you analyze the possible motives for people's responsible behavior. Also show how their actions affected the other individuals involved.

Writing Assignments Using Other Patterns of Development

3. How could families or schools or communities or religious organizations encourage children to act rather than withdraw when confronted by someone in difficulty? Focusing on *one* of these institutions, talk with friends, classmates, and family members to gather their experiences and recommendations. Select the most provocative ideas, and write an essay explaining the steps that this particular institution could take to help develop children's sense of responsibility to others. Develop your points with specific examples of what has been done and what could be done.

∞ **4.** Darley and Latané cite social critics who believe that the United States has become a nation of strangers, alienated and withdrawn from one another. Write an essay refuting this claim by presenting several vivid instances of small acts of everyday kindness—examples in which people demonstrate their sense of connectedness to those around them. Generate examples by drawing on your own and other people's experiences. Before writing, you might want to read Maya Angelou's "Sister Flowers" (page 175) for a portrait of an individual who shows—in small, quiet ways—that she cares for others.

BRENT STAPLES

After earning a Ph.D. in psychology from the University of Chicago, Brent Staples (1951–) soon became a nationally recognized essayist. He has worked on numerous newspapers and is now assistant metropolitan editor of the *New York Times.* Staples's autobiography, *Parallel Time: Growing Up in Black and White* was published in 1995. This selection first appeared in slightly different form in *Ms.* magazine (1986) and then in *Harper's* (1987).

BLACK MEN AND PUBLIC SPACE

My first victim was a woman—white, well dressed, probably in her early twenties.   1 I came upon her late one evening on a deserted street in Hyde Park, a relatively affluent neighborhood in an otherwise mean, impoverished section of Chicago. As I swung onto the avenue behind her, there seemed to be a discreet, uninflammatory distance between us. Not so. She cast back a worried glance. To her, the youngish black man—a broad six feet two inches with a beard and billowing hair, both hands shoved into the pockets of a bulky military jacket—seemed menacingly close. After a few more quick glimpses, she picked up her pace and was soon running in earnest. Within seconds she disappeared into a cross street.

That was more than a decade ago. I was twenty-two years old, a graduate student   2 newly arrived at the University of Chicago. It was in the echo of that terrified woman's footfalls that I first began to know the unwieldy inheritance I'd come into—the ability to alter public space in ugly ways. It was clear that she thought herself the quarry of a mugger, a rapist, or worse. Suffering a bout of insomnia, however, I was stalking sleep, not defenseless wayfarers. As a softy who is scarcely able to take a knife to a raw chicken—let alone hold one to a person's throat—I was surprised, embarrassed, and dismayed all at once. Her flight made me feel like an accomplice in tyranny. It also made it clear that I was indistinguishable from the muggers who occasionally seeped into the area from the surrounding ghetto. That first encounter, and those that followed, signified that a vast, unnerving gulf lay between nighttime pedestrians—particularly women—and me. And I soon gathered that being perceived as dangerous is a hazard in itself. I only needed to turn a corner into a dicey situation, or crowd some frightened, armed person in a foyer somewhere, or make an errant move after being pulled over by a policeman. Where fear and weapons meet—and they often do in urban America—there is always the possibility of death.

3   In that first year, my first away from my hometown, I was to become thoroughly familiar with the language of fear. At dark, shadowy intersections, I could cross in front of a car stopped at a traffic light and elicit the *thunk, thunk, thunk, thunk* of the driver—black, white, male, or female—hammering down the door locks. On less traveled streets after dark, I grew accustomed to but never comfortable with people crossing to the other side of the street rather than pass me. Then there were the standard unpleasantries with policemen, doormen, bouncers, cabdrivers, and others whose business it is to screen out troublesome individuals *before* there is any nastiness.

4   I moved to New York nearly two years ago and I have remained an avid night walker. In central Manhattan, the near-constant crowd cover minimizes tense one-on-one street encounters. Elsewhere—in SoHo, for example, where sidewalks are narrow and tightly spaced buildings shut out the sky—things can get very taut indeed.

5   After dark, on the warrenlike streets of Brooklyn where I live, I often see women who fear the worst from me. They seem to have set their faces on neutral, and with their purse straps strung across their chests bandolier-style, they forge ahead as though bracing themselves against being tackled. I understand, of course, that the danger they perceive is not a hallucination. Women are particularly vulnerable to street violence, and young black males are drastically overrepresented among the perpetrators of that violence. Yet these truths are no solace against the kind of alienation that comes of being ever the suspect, a fearsome entity with whom pedestrians avoid making eye contact.

6   It is not altogether clear to me how I reached the ripe old age of twenty-two without being conscious of the lethality nighttime pedestrians attributed to me. Perhaps it was because in Chester, Pennsylvania, the small, angry industrial town where I came of age in the 1960s, I was scarcely noticeable against a backdrop of gang warfare, street knifings, and murders. I grew up one of the good boys, had perhaps a half-dozen fistfights. In retrospect, my shyness of combat has clear sources.

7   As a boy, I saw countless tough guys locked away; I have since buried several, too. They were babies, really—a teenage cousin, a brother of twenty-two, a childhood friend in his mid-twenties—all gone down in episodes of bravado played out in the streets. I came to doubt the virtues of intimidation early on. I chose, perhaps unconsciously, to remain a shadow—timid, but a survivor.

8   The fearsomeness mistakenly attributed to me in public places often has a perilous flavor. The most frightening of these confusions occurred in the late 1970s and early 1980s, when I worked as a journalist in Chicago. One day, rushing into the office of a magazine I was writing for with a deadline story in hand, I was mistaken for a burglar. The office manager called security and, with an ad hoc posse, pursued me through the labyrinthine halls, nearly to my editor's door. I had no way of proving who I was. I could only move briskly toward the company of someone who knew me.

9   Another time I was on assignment for a local paper and killing time before an interview. I entered a jewelry store on the city's affluent Near North Side. The proprietor excused herself and returned with an enormous red Doberman pinscher straining at the end of a leash. She stood, the dog extended toward me, silent to my questions, her

eyes bulging nearly out of her head. I took a cursory look around, nodded, and bade her good night.

Relatively speaking, however, I never fared as badly as another black male journalist. 10 He went to nearby Waukegan, Illinois, a couple of summers ago to work on a story about a murderer who was born there. Mistaking the reporter for the killer, police officers hauled him from his car at gunpoint and but for his press credentials would probably have tried to book him. Such episodes are not uncommon. Black men trade tales like this all the time.

Over the years, I learned to smother the rage I felt at so often being taken for a crim- 11 inal. Not to do so would surely have led to madness. I now take precautions to make myself less threatening. I move about with care, particularly late in the evening. I give a wide berth to nervous people on subway platforms during the wee hours, particularly when I have exchanged business clothes for jeans. If I happen to be entering a building behind some people who appear skittish, I may walk by, letting them clear the lobby before I return, so as not to seem to be following them. I have been calm and extremely congenial on those rare occasions when I've been pulled over by the police.

And on late-evening constitutionals I employ what has proved to be an excellent 12 tension-reducing measure: I whistle melodies from Beethoven and Vivaldi and the more popular classical composers. Even steely New Yorkers hunching toward night-time destinations seem to relax, and occasionally they even join in the tune. Virtually everybody seems to sense that a mugger wouldn't be warbling bright, sunny selections from Vivaldi's *Four Seasons.* It is my equivalent of the cowbell that hikers wear when they know they are in bear country.

Questions for Close Reading

1. What is the selection's thesis? Locate the sentence(s) in which Staples states his main idea. If he doesn't state the thesis explicitly, express it in your own words.

2. How did Staples first learn that he was considered a threat by many people? How did this discovery make him feel?

3. What are some of the dangers that Staples has encountered because of his race? How has he handled each dangerous situation?

4. What "precautions" does Staples take to appear nonthreatening to others? Why do these precautions work?

5. Refer to your dictionary as needed to define the following words used in the selection: *uninflammatory* (paragraph 1), *dicey* (2), *bandolier* (5), *lethality* (6), *bravado* (7), *berth* (11), and *constitutionals* (12).

Questions About the Writer's Craft

1. The pattern. Brent Staples reveals both causes and effects of people's reacting with fear to a black male. Does the essay end with a discussion of causes or of effects? Why do you suppose Staples concludes the essay as he does?

2. **Other patterns.** Why do you think Staples opens the piece with such a dramatic, yet intentionally misleading narrative? What effect does he achieve?

3. Is Staples writing primarily for whites, blacks, or both? How do you know?

4. What is Staples's tone? Why do you think he chose this tone?

Writing Assignments Using Cause-Effect as a Pattern of Development

1. Write an essay showing how your or someone else's entry into a specific public space (for example, a bus, party, elevator, or table at the library) influenced other people's behavior. Identify the possible reasons that others reacted as they did, and explain how their reactions, in turn, affected the newcomer. Use your analysis to reach some conclusions about human nature.

2. Staples describes circumstances that often result in fear. Focusing on a more positive emotion, like admiration or contentment, illustrate the situations that tend to elicit that emotion in you. Discuss why these circumstances have the effect they do.

Writing Assignments Using Other Patterns of Development

∞ 3. Staples describes how others' expectations oblige him to alter his behavior. Narrate an event during which you felt forced to conform to what others expected. What did you learn from the experience? George Orwell's "Shooting an Elephant" (page 203), Diane Cole's "Don't Just Stand There" (page 315), Malcolm X's "My First Conk" (page 321), and Joseph H. Suina's "And Then I Went to School" (page 361) may prompt some interesting thoughts on the issue of conformity.

4. When he encounters a startled pedestrian, Staples feels some fear but manages to control it. Write an essay showing the steps you took one time when you felt afraid but, like Staples, remained in control and got through safely. Convey your initial fear, your later relief, and any self-discovery that resulted from the experience.

ADDITIONAL WRITING TOPICS: CAUSE-EFFECT

General Assignments

Write an essay that analyzes the causes and/or effects of one of the following topics.

1. Sleep deprivation

2. Having the parents you have

3. Lack of communication in a relationship

4. Overexercising or not exercising

5. A particular TV or rock star's popularity

6. Skill or ineptitude in sports

7. A major life decision

8. Changing attitudes toward the environment

9. Voter apathy

10. An act of violence or cruelty

Assignments with a Specific Purpose, Audience, and Point of View

1. A debate about the prominence of athletics at colleges and universities is going to be broadcast on the local cable station. For this debate, prepare a speech pointing out either the harmful or the beneficial effects of "big-time" college athletic programs.

2. Why do students "flunk out" of college? Write an article for the campus newspaper outlining the main causes of failure. Your goal is to steer students away from dangerous habits and situations that lead to poor grades or dropping out.

3. Write a letter to the editor of your favorite newspaper, analyzing the causes of the country's current "trash crisis." Be sure to mention the nationwide love affair with disposable items and the general disregard of the idea of thrift.

4. As part of a pamphlet for first-year college students, write an advice piece on the effects—both negative and positive—of combining a part-time job with college studies.

5. Why do you think teenage suicide is on the rise? Write a fact sheet for parents of teenagers and for high school guidance counselors, describing the factors that could make a young person desperate enough to attempt suicide. At the end, suggest what parents and counselors can do to help confused, unhappy young people.

6. Write a letter to the mayor of your town or city suggesting a "Turn Off the TV" public relations effort, convincing residents to stop watching television for a month. Cite the positive effects that "no TV" would have on parents, children, and the community in general.

18
DEFINITION

WHAT IS DEFINITION?

IN Lewis Carroll's wise and whimsical tale *Through the Looking Glass*, Humpty Dumpty proclaims, "When I use a word...it means just what I choose it to mean—neither more nor less." If the world were filled with characters like Humpty Dumpty, all of them bending the meanings of words to their own purposes and accepting no challenges to their personal definitions, communication would creak to a halt.

For language to communicate, words must have accepted definitions. Dictionaries, the sourcebooks for definitions, are compilations of current word meanings, enabling speakers of a language to understand one another. But as you might suspect, things are not as simple as they first appear. We all know that a word like *discipline* has a standard dictionary definition. We also know that parents argue every day over the meaning of *discipline*, as do teachers and school administrators. Moreover, many of the wrenching moral debates of our time are attempts to resolve questions of definition. Much of the controversy over abortion, for instance, centers on what is meant by "life" and when it "begins."

Words can, in short, be slippery. Each of us has unique experiences, attitudes, and values that influence the way we use words and the way we interpret the words of others. Lewis Carroll may have been exaggerating, but to some degree Humpty Dumpty's attitude exists in all of us.

In addition to the idiosyncratic interpretations we may attach to words, some words shift in meaning over time. The word *pedagogue*, for instance, originally meant "a teacher or leader of children." However, with the passage of time, *pedagogue* has come to mean "a dogmatic, pedantic teacher." And, of course, we invent new words as the need arises. For example, *modem* and *byte* are just two of many new words created in response to recent breakthroughs in computer technology.

Writing a **definition,** then, is no simple task. Primarily, the writer tries to answer basic questions: "What does _____ mean?" and "What is the special or true nature of _____?" The word to be defined may be an object, a concept, a type of person, a place, or a phenomenon. Potential subjects might be the "user-friendly" computer, animal rights, a model teacher, cabin fever. As you will see, there are various strategies for expanding definitions far beyond the single-word synonyms or brief phrases that dictionaries provide.

HOW DEFINITION FITS YOUR PURPOSE AND AUDIENCE

Many times, short-answer exam questions call for definitions. Consider the following examples:

Define the term _mob psychology._
What is the difference between a metaphor and a simile?
How would you explain what a religious cult is?

In such cases, a good response might involve a definition of several sentences or several paragraphs.

Other times, definition may be used in an essay organized mainly around another pattern of development. In this situation, all that's needed is a brief formal definition or a short definition given in your own words. For instance, a _process analysis_ showing readers how computers have revolutionized the typical business office might start with a textbook definition of the term _artificial intelligence._ In an _argumentation-persuasion_ paper urging students to support recent efforts to abolish fraternities and sororities, you could refer to the definitions of _blackballing_ and _hazing_ found in the university handbook. Or your personal definition of _hero_ could be the starting point for a _causal analysis_ that explains to readers why there are few real heroes in today's world.

But the most complex use of definition, and the one we focus on in this chapter, involves exploring a subject through an **extended definition.** Extended definition allows you to apply a personal interpretation to a word, to propose a revisionist view of a commonly accepted meaning, to analyze words representing complex or controversial issues. _Pornography, gun control, secular humanism,_ and _right to privacy_ would be good subjects for extended definition; each is multifaceted, often misunderstood, and fraught with emotion. _Junk food, anger, leadership,_ and _anxiety_ could also make interesting subjects, especially if the extended definition helped readers develop a new understanding of the word. You might, for example, define _anxiety_ not as a negative state but as a positive force that propels us to take action.

An extended definition may run several paragraphs or a few pages. Keep in mind, however, that some definitions require a chapter or even an entire book to develop. Theologians, philosophers, and pop psychologists have devoted entire texts to concepts like *evil* and *love*.

PREWRITING STRATEGIES

The following checklist shows how you can apply to definition some of the prewriting techniques discussed in Chapter 2.

✔ DEFINITION: A PREWRITING CHECKLIST

Choose Something to Define

☐ Is there something you're especially qualified to define? What about that thing do you hope to convey?

☐ Do any of your journal entries reflect an attempt to pinpoint something's essence: courage, pornography, a well-rounded education?

☐ Will you define a concept (energy), an object (the microchip), a type of person (the bigot), a place (the desert), a phenomenon (the rise in volunteerism), a complex or controversial issue (euthanasia)?

☐ Can your topic be meaningfully defined within the space and time allotted?

Identify Your Purpose, Audience, Tone, and Point of View

☐ Do you want simply to inform and explain—that is, to make meaning clear? Or do you want to persuade readers to accept your understanding of a term? Do you want to do both?

☐ Will you offer a personal interpretation? Propose a revised meaning? Explain an obscure or technical term? Discuss shifts in meaning over time? Distinguish one term from another, closely related term? Show conflicts in definition?

☐ Are your readers apt to be open to your interpretation of a term? What information will they need to understand your definition and to feel that it is correct and insightful?

☐ What tone and point of view will make your readers receptive to your definition?

Use Prewriting to Develop the Definition

☐ How might mapping, brainstorming, freewriting, and speaking with others generate material that develops your definition?

☐ Which of the prewriting questions on the next page would generate the most details and, therefore, suggest patterns for developing your definition?

Question	Pattern
How does X look, taste, smell, feel, and sound?	Description
What does X do? When? Where?	Narration
What are some typical instances of X?	Illustration
What are X's component parts? What different forms can X take?	Division-classification
How does X work?	Process analysis
What is X like or unlike?	Comparison-contrast
What leads to X? What are X's consequences?	Cause-effect

STRATEGIES FOR USING DEFINITION IN AN ESSAY

After prewriting, you're ready to draft your essay. The following suggestions will be helpful whether you use definition as a dominant or supportive pattern of development.

1. Stay focused on the essay's purpose, audience, and tone.   Since your purpose for writing an extended definition shapes the entire paper, you need to keep that objective in mind when developing your definition. Suppose you decide to write an essay defining *jazz*. The essay could be purely *informative* and discuss the origins of jazz, its characteristic tonal patterns, and some of the great jazz musicians of the past. Or the essay could move beyond pure information and take on a *persuasive* edge. It might, for example, argue that jazz is the only contemporary form of music worth considering seriously.

Just as your purpose in writing will vary, so will your tone. A strictly informative definition will generally assume a detached, objective tone ("Apathy is an emotional state characterized by listlessness and indifference"). By way of contrast, a definition essay with a persuasive slant might be urgent in tone ("To combat student apathy, we must design programs that engage students in campus life"), or it might take a satiric approach ("An apathetic stance is a wise choice for any thinking student").

As you write, keep thinking about your audience as well. Not only do your readers determine what terms need to be defined (and in how much detail), but they also keep you focused on the essay's purpose and tone. For instance, you probably wouldn't write a serious, informative piece for the college newspaper about the "mystery meat" served in the campus cafeteria. Instead, you would adopt a light tone as you defined the culinary horror and might even make a persuasive pitch about improving the food prepared on campus.

2. Formulate an effective definition.   A definition essay sometimes begins with a brief **formal definition**—the dictionary's, a textbook's, or the writer's—and then expands that initial definition with supporting details. Formal definitions are traditionally worded as three-part statements, including (1) the **term,** (2) the **class** to which the term belongs, and (3) the **characteristics** that distinguish the term from other members of its class. Consider these examples of formal definition:

Term	Class	Characteristics
The peregrine falcon,	an endangered bird,	is the world's fastest flyer.
A bodice-ripper	is a paperback book,	usually read by women, that deals with highly charged romance in exotic places and faraway times.
Back to basics	is a trend in education	that emphasizes skill mastery through rote learning.

A definition that meets these three guidelines—term, class, and characteristics—will clarify what your subject *is* and what it *is not.* These guidelines also establish the boundaries or scope of your definition. For example, defining *back to basics* as "a trend that emphasizes rote...learning" signals a certain boundary; it lets readers know that other educational trends (such as those that emphasize children's social or emotional development) won't be part of the essay's definition.

Because they are formulaic, formal definitions tend to be dull. For this reason, it's best to reserve them for clarifying potentially confusing words—perhaps words with multiple meanings. For example, the term *the West* can refer to the western section of the United States, to the United States and its non-Communist allies (as in the "Western world"), or to the entire Western Hemisphere. Before discussing the West, then, you would need to provide a formal definition that clarifies your use of the term. Highly specialized or technical terms may also require clarification. Few readers are likely to feel confident about their understanding of the term *cognitive dissonance* unless you supply them with a formal definition: "a conflict of thoughts arising when two or more ideas do not go together."

If you decide to include a formal definition in your essay, avoid tired openings like "the dictionary says" or "according to *Webster's.*" Such weak starts lack imagination. You should also keep in mind that a strict dictionary definition may actually confuse readers. Suppose you're writing a paper on the way people tend to absorb their ideas and values from the media. Likening this automatic response to the process of osmosis, you decide to open the paper with a dictionary definition. If you write "Osmosis is the tendency of a solvent to disperse through a semipermeable membrane into a more concentrated medium," readers are apt to be baffled. *Remember:* The purpose of a definition is to clarify meaning, not obscure it.

You should also stay clear of ungrammatical "is when" definitions: "Blind ambition is when you want to get ahead, no matter how much other people are hurt." Instead, write "Blind ambition is wanting to get ahead, no matter how much other people are hurt." A final pitfall to avoid in writing formal definitions is **circularity,** saying the same thing twice and therefore defining nothing: "A campus tribunal is a tribunal composed of various members of the university community." Circular definitions like this often repeat the term being defined (*tribunal*) or use words having the same meaning (*campus; university community*). In this case, we learn nothing about what a campus tribunal is; the writer says only that "*X* is *X*."

3. Develop the extended definition.   You can use the patterns of development when formulating an extended definition. Description, narration, process analysis, comparison-contrast, or any of the other patterns discussed in this book may be drawn upon—alone or in combination. Imagine you're planning to write an extended definition of *robotics*. You might develop the term by providing *examples* of the way robots are currently being used in scientific research; by *comparing* and *contrasting* human and robot capabilities; or by *classifying* robots, starting with the most basic and moving to the most advanced or futuristic models. (To deepen your understanding of which patterns to use when developing a particular extended definition, take a moment to review the last item in this chapter's Prewriting Checklist.)

4. Organize the material that develops the definition.   If you use a single pattern to develop the extended definition, apply the principles of organization suited to that pattern, as described in the appropriate chapter of this book. Assume that you're defining *fad* by means of *process analysis*. You might organize your paragraphs according to the steps in the process: a fad's slow start as something avant-garde or eccentric; its wildfire acceptance by the general public; the fad's demise as it becomes familiar or tiresome. If you want to define *character* by means of a single *narration,* you would probably organize paragraphs chronologically.

   In a definition essay using several methods of development, you should devote separate paragraphs to each pattern. A definition of *relaxation,* for instance, might start with a paragraph that *narrates* a particularly relaxing day; then it might move to a paragraph that presents several *examples* of people who find it difficult to unwind; finally, it might end with a paragraph that explains a *process* for relaxing the mind and body.

5. Write an effective introduction.   It can be helpful to provide—near the beginning of a definition essay—a brief formal definition of the term you're going to develop in the rest of the paper. Beyond this basic element, the introduction might include a number of other features. You may explain the *origin* of the term being defined: "*Acid rock* is a term first coined in the 1960s to describe music that was written or listened to under the influence of the drug LSD." Similarly, you could explain the *etymology,* or linguistic origin, of the key word that focuses the paper: "The term *vigilantism* is derived from a Latin word meaning 'to watch and be awake.'"

   You may also use the introduction to clarify what your subject is *not.* Such **definition by negation** can be an effective strategy at a paper's beginning, especially if readers don't share your view of the subject. In such a case, you might write something like this: "The gorilla, far from being the vicious killer of jungle movies and popular imagination, is a sedentary, gentle creature living in a closely knit family group." Such a statement provides the special focus for your essay and signals some of the misconceptions or fallacies soon to be discussed.

In addition, you may include in the introduction a **stipulative definition,** one that puts special restrictions on a term: "Strictly defined, a mall refers to a one- or two-story enclosed building containing a variety of retail shops and at least two large anchor stores. Highway-strip shopping centers or downtown centers cannot be considered true malls." When a term has multiple meanings, or when its meaning has become fuzzy through misuse, a stipulative definition sets the record straight right at the start, so that readers know exactly what is, and is not, being defined.

Finally, the introduction may end with a *plan of development* that indicates how the essay will unfold. A student who returned to school after having raised a family decided to write a paper defining the mid-life crisis that had led to her enrollment in college. After providing a brief formal definition of *mid-life crisis,* the student rounded off her introduction with this sentence: "Such a mid-life crisis often starts with vague misgivings, turns into depression, and ends with a significant change in life-style."

REVISION STRATEGIES

Once you have a draft of the essay, you're ready to revise. The following checklist will help you and those giving you feedback apply to definition some of the revision techniques discussed in Chapters 7 and 8.

✔ DEFINITION: A REVISION CHECKLIST

Revise Overall Meaning and Structure

☐ Is your essay's purpose informative, persuasive, or both?

☐ Is the term being defined clearly distinguished from similar terms?

☐ Where does a circular definition cloud meaning?

☐ Where would a word's historical or linguistic origin clarify meaning? Where would a formal definition, stipulative definition, or definition by negation help?

☐ Where are technical, nonstandard, or ambiguous terms a source of confusion?

☐ Which patterns of development are used to develop the definition? How do these help the essay achieve its purpose?

☐ If the essay uses only one pattern, is the essay's method of organization characteristic of that pattern (step by step for process analysis, chronological for narration, and so on)?

☐ Where could a dry formal definition be deleted without sacrificing overall clarity?

Revise Paragraph Development

☐ If the essay uses several patterns of development, where would separate paragraphs for different patterns be appropriate?

☐ Which paragraphs (or passages) are flat or unconvincing? How could they be made more compelling?

Revise Sentences and Words

☐ Which sentences and words are inconsistent with the essay's tone?

☐ Where should overused phrases like "the dictionary says" and "according to *Webster's*" be replaced by more original wording?

☐ Have "is when" definitions been avoided?

STUDENT ESSAY: FROM PREWRITING THROUGH REVISION

The student essay that follows was written by Laura Chen in response to this assignment:

In "Entropy," K. C. Cole takes a scientific term from physics and gives it a broader definition and a wider application. Choose another specialized term and define it in such a way that you reveal something significant about contemporary life.

Before writing her essay, Laura sat down at a computer and *brainstormed* material on the subject she decided to write about: inertia in everyday life. Later on, when she started shaping this material, she jotted down notes in the margin, starred important ideas, crossed out an item, added other ideas, drew connecting arrows, and used numbers and letters to sequence points. In the process, the essay's underlying structure began to emerge so clearly that an outline seemed unnecessary; Laura felt she could move directly from her brainstormed material to a first draft. Laura's original brainstormed list is reprinted on page 412. The handwritten marks indicate her later efforts to organize the preliminary material.

Now read Laura's paper, "Physics in Everyday Life," noting the similarities and differences between her prewriting and final essay. You'll see, for example, that Laura's decision to discuss national inertia *after* individual inertia makes the essay's sequence of points more emphatic. Similarly, by moving the mention of gravity to the essay's end, Laura creates a satisfying symmetry: The paper now opens and closes with principles of physics. As you read the essay, also consider how well it applies the principles of definition discussed in this chapter. (The commentary that follows the paper will help you look at Laura's essay more closely and will give you some sense of how she went about revising her first draft.)

Brainstorming

Entropy--an imp. term in physics. (Put in _conclusion_? Just like gravity.)

Formal definition
Boulder sitting or rolling

③National inertia (save broadest for last)

3b **We accept pollution**

3a **Accept shoddy products**

~~Accept growing homelessness~~
3c Go ahead with genetic engineering even though uncomfortable
3d **Keep producing nuclear arms**

3e **Watch too much TV, despite all the reports**

1c **Racial discrimination remains a problem**   Move to section
                                                  on the individual

①**Individual inertia, too**

We resist change

1a **Vote the same way all the time**

1b **Need jolts to change (a perfect teenage daughter becomes
   pregnant)** Add example here

②**But on TV--no inertia**

2a **Soap operas, commercials--everyone changes easily**   give
                                                            specifics

2b **In real life--wear same hairstyle, use same products,
   wars and national problems drag on**

Physics in Everyday Life

by Laura Chen

Introduction   A boulder sits on a mountainside for a thousand years. The   1
            boulder will remain there forever unless an outside force inter-
            venes. Suppose a force does affect the boulder--an earthquake,

for instance. Once the boulder begins to thunder down the mountain, it will remain in motion and head in one direction only--downhill--until another force interrupts its progress. If the boulder tumbles into a gorge, it will finally come to rest as gravity anchors it to the earth once more. In both cases, the boulder is exhibiting the physical principle — *Formal definition*
of inertia: the tendency of matter to remain at rest or, if moving, to keep moving in one direction unless affected by an — *Thesis*
outside force. Inertia, an important factor in the world of physics, also plays a crucial role in the human world. Inertia ← *Plan of development*
affects our individual lives as well as the direction taken by society as a whole. — *Topic sentence*

2   Inertia often influences our value systems and personal growth. Inertia is at work, for example, when people cling to certain behaviors and views. Like the boulder firmly fixed to the mountain, most people are set in their ways. Without thinking, they vote Republican or Democratic because they have always voted that way. They regard with suspicion a couple having no children, simply because everyone else in the neighbor- — *Start of a series of causes and effects*
hood has a large family. It is only when an outside force--a jolt of some sort--occurs that people change their views. A white American couple may think little about racial discrimination, for instance, until they adopt an Asian child and must comfort her when classmates tease her because she looks different. Parents may consider promiscuous any unmarried girl who has a baby until their 17-year-old honors student confesses that she is pregnant. Personal jolts like these force people to think, perhaps for the first time, about issues that now affect them directly. — *Topic sentence*

3   To illustrate how inertia governs our lives, it is helpful to compare the world of television with real life. On TV, iner- — *Start of a series of contrasts*
tia does not exist. Television shows and commercials show people making all kinds of drastic changes. They switch brands of coffee or try a new hair color with no hesitation. In one car commercial, an ambitious young accountant abandons her career with a flourish and is seen driving off into the sunset as she heads for a small cabin by the sea to write poetry. In a soap opera, a character may progress from homemaker to hooker to nun

in a single year. But in real life, inertia rules. People tend
to stay where they are, to keep their jobs, to be loyal
to products. A second major difference between television
and real life is that, on television, everyone takes prompt
and dramatic action to solve problems. The construction worker
with a thudding headache is pain-free at the end of the sixty-
second commercial; the police catch the murderer within
an hour; the family learns to cope with their son's life-
threatening drug addiction by the time the made-for-TV movie
ends at eleven. But in the real world, inertia persists,
so that few problems are solved neatly or quickly. Illnesses
drag on, few crimes are solved, and family conflicts last
for years.

Topic sentence ──────────→ Inertia is, most importantly, a force at work in the   4
life of our nation. Again, inertia is two-sided. It keeps
us from moving and, once we move, it keeps us pointed in
one direction. We find ourselves mired in a certain path,
accepting the inferior, even the dangerous. We settle for toys

Start of a series ──────────
of examples   that break, winter coats with no warmth, and rivers clogged
with pollution. Inertia also compels our nation to keep moving
in one direction--despite the uncomfortable suspicion that
it is the wrong direction. We are not sure if manipulating
genes is a good idea, yet we continue to fund scientific
projects in genetic engineering. More than fifty years ago,
we were shaken when we saw the devastation caused by an atomic
bomb. But we went on to develop weapons hundreds of times
more destructive. Although warned that excessive television
viewing may be harmful, we continue to watch hours of
television each day.

Conclusion   We have learned to defy gravity, one of the basic   5
laws of physics; we fly high above the earth, even float
in outer space. But most of us have not learned to defy
inertia. Those special individuals who are able to act
when everyone else seems paralyzed are rare. But the fact
that such people do exist means that inertia is not all-
powerful. If we use our reasoning ability and our
creativity, we can conquer inertia, just as we have
conquered gravity.

Commentary

Introduction

As the title of her essay suggests, Laura has taken a scientific term (inertia) from a specialized field and drawn on the term to help explain some everyday phenomena. Using the *simple-to-complex* approach to structure the introduction, she opens with a vivid *descriptive* example of inertia. This description is then followed by a *formal definition* of inertia: "the tendency of matter to remain at rest or, if moving, to keep moving in one direction unless affected by an outside force." Laura wisely begins the paper with the easy-to-understand description rather than with the more-difficult-to-grasp scientific definition. Had the order been reversed, the essay would not have gotten off to nearly as effective a start. She then ends her introductory paragraph with a *thesis,* "Inertia, an important factor in the world of physics, also plays a crucial role in the human world," and with a *plan of development,* "Inertia affects our individual lives as well as the direction taken by society as a whole."

Organization

To support her definition of inertia and her belief that it can rule our lives, Laura generates a number of compelling examples. She organizes these examples by grouping them into three major points, each point signaled by a *topic sentence* that opens each of the essay's three supporting paragraphs (2–4).

A definite organizational strategy determines the sequence of Laura's three central points. The essay moves from the way inertia affects the individual to the way it affects the nation. The phrase "most importantly" at the beginning of the fourth paragraph indicates that Laura has arranged her points emphatically, believing that inertia's impact on society is most critical.

A Problem with Organization and a Weak Example

When reading the fourth paragraph, you might have noticed that Laura's examples aren't sequenced as effectively as they could be. To show that we, as a nation, tend to keep moving in the same direction, Laura discusses our ongoing uneasiness about genetic engineering, nuclear arms, and excessive television viewing. The point about nuclear weapons is most significant, yet it gets lost in the middle. The paragraph would be stronger if it ended with the point about nuclear arms. Moreover, the example about excessive television viewing doesn't belong in this paragraph since, at best, it has limited bearing on the issue being discussed.

Other Patterns of Development

In addition to using numerous *examples* to illustrate her points, Laura draws on several other patterns of development to show that inertia can be a powerful force. In the second and fourth paragraphs, she uses *causal analysis* to explain how inertia can paralyze people and nations. The second paragraph indicates that only "an outside force—a jolt of some sort—" can motivate inert people to change. To support this view, Laura provides two examples of parents who experience such jolts. Similarly, in the fourth paragraph, she contends that inertia causes the persistence of specific national problems: shoddy consumer goods and environmental pollution.

Another pattern, *comparison-contrast*, is used in the third paragraph to highlight the differences between television and real life: on television, people zoom into action, but in everyday life, people tend to stay put and muddle through. The essay also contains a distinct element of *argumentation-persuasion* since Laura clearly wants readers to accept her definition of inertia and her view that it often governs human behavior.

Conclusion

Laura's *conclusion* rounds off the essay nicely and brings it to a satisfying close. Laura refers to another law of physics, one with which we are all familiar—gravity. By creating an *analogy* between gravity and inertia, she suggests that our ability to defy gravity should encourage us to defy inertia. The analogy enlarges the scope of the essay; it allows Laura to reach out to her readers by challenging them to action. Such a challenge is, of course, appropriate in a definition essay having a persuasive bent.

Revising the First Draft

When it was time to rework her essay, Laura began by reading her paper out loud. Then, referring to the revision checklist on pages 410–411, she noted in the margin of her draft the problems she detected, numbering them in order of importance. After reviewing her notes, she started to revise in earnest, paying special attention to her third paragraph. The first draft of that paragraph, together with her annotations, is reprinted here:

Original Version of the Third Paragraph

① Paragraph rambles
④ First two sentences awkward

⑦ Make more specific

③ Delete part about annoyed wives and hairstyles

The ordinary actions of daily life are, in part, determined by inertia. To understand this, it is helpful to compare the world of television with real life, for, in the TV-land of ads and entertainment, inertia does not exist. For example, on television, people are often shown making all kinds of drastic changes. They switch brands of coffee or try a new hair color with no hesitation. In one car commercial, a <u>young accountant leaves her career</u> and sets off for a cabin by the sea to write poetry. In a soap opera, a character may progress from homemaker to hooker to nun in a single year. In contrast, inertia rules in real life. People tend to stay where they are, to keep their jobs, to be loyal to products (wives get annoyed if a husband brings home the wrong brand or color of bathroom tissue

from the market). Middle-aged people wear the hairstyles
or makeup that suited them in high school. A second major
difference between television and real life is that, on TV,
everyone takes prompt and dramatic action to solve problems. (A
woman finds the solution to dull clothes) at the end of a
commercial; the police catch the murderer within an hour; the
family learns to cope with a son's disturbing life-style by
the time the movie is over. In contrast, the law of real-life
inertia means that few problems are solved neatly or quickly.
Things, once started, tend to stay as they are. Few crimes are
actually solved. Medical problems are not easily diagnosed.
Messy wars in foreign countries seem endless. National problems
are identified, but Congress does not pass legislation to solve
them.

⑤ Trite—replace

⑥ Point about life-style not clear

② Last two sentences don't belong

After rereading her draft, Laura realized that her third paragraph rambled. To give it more focus, she removed the last two sentences ("Messy wars in foreign countries seem endless" and "National problems are identified, but Congress does not pass legislation. . . .") because they referred to national affairs but were located in a section focusing on the individual. Further, she eliminated two flat, unconvincing examples: wives who get annoyed when their husbands bring home the wrong brand of bathroom tissue and middle-aged people whose hairstyles and makeup are outdated. Condensing the two disjointed sentences that originally opened the paragraph also helped tighten this section of the essay. Note how much crisper the revised sentences are: "To illustrate how inertia rules our lives, it is helpful to compare the world of television with real life. On TV, inertia does not exist."

Laura also worked to make the details and the language in the paragraph more specific and vigorous. The vague sentence "A woman finds the solution to dull clothes at the end of the commercial" is replaced by the more dramatic "The construction worker with a thudding headache is pain-free at the end of the sixty-second commercial." Similarly, Laura changed a "son's disturbing life-style" to a "son's life-threatening drug addiction"; "by the time the movie is over" became "by the time the made-for-TV movie ends at eleven"; and "a young accountant leaves her career and sets off for a cabin by the sea to write poetry" was changed to "an ambitious young accountant abandons her career with a flourish and is seen driving off into the sunset as she heads for a small cabin by the sea to write poetry."

After making these changes, Laura decided to round off the paragraph with a powerful summary statement highlighting how real life differs from television: "Illnesses drag on, few crimes are solved, and family conflicts last for years."

These third-paragraph revisions are similar to those that Laura made elsewhere in her first draft. Her astute changes enabled her to turn an already effective paper into an especially thoughtful analysis of human behavior.

ACTIVITIES: DEFINITION

Prewriting Activities

1. Imagine you're writing two essays: One explains an effective strategy for registering a complaint; the other contrasts the styles of two stand-up comics. Jot down ways you might use definition in each essay.

2. Use the prewriting questions for the patterns of development on pages 406–407 to generate material for an extended definition of *one* of the terms that follow. Then answer these questions about your prewriting material: What thesis does the prewriting suggest? Which pattern(s) yielded the most supporting material? In what order would you present this support when writing an essay?

   a. popularity
   b. cruelty
   c. a "dweeb"
   d. self-esteem
   e. a "wimp"
   f. loneliness

3. Select a term whose meaning varies from person to person or one for which you have a personal definition. Some possibilities include:

success	femininity	a liberal
patriotism	affirmative action	a housewife
individuality	pornography	intelligence

Brainstorm with others to identify variations in the term's meaning. Then examine your prewriting material. What thesis comes to mind? If you were writing an essay, would your purpose be informative, persuasive, or both? Finally, prepare a scratch list of the points you might cover.

Revising Activities

4. Explain why each of the following is an effective or ineffective definition. Rewrite those you consider ineffective.

   a. *Passive aggression* is when people show their aggression passively.
   b. A *terrorist* tries to terrorize people.
   c. *Being assertive* means knowing how to express your wishes and goals in a positive, noncombative way.

d. *Pop music* refers to music that is popular.

e. *Loyalty* is when someone stays by another person during difficult times.

5. The following introductory paragraph is from the first draft of an essay contrasting walking and running as techniques for reducing tension. Although intended to be a definition paragraph, it actually doesn't tell us anything we don't already know. It also relies on the old-hat *"Webster's* says." Rewrite the paragraph so it is more imaginative. You might use a series of anecdotes or one extended example to define "tension" and introduce the essay's thesis more gracefully.

According to <u>Webster's</u>, <u>tension</u> is "mental or nervous strain, often accompanied by muscular tightness or tautness." Everyone feels tense at one time or another. It may occur when there's a deadline to meet. Or it could be caused by the stress of trying to fulfill academic, athletic, or social goals. Sometimes it comes from criticism by family, bosses, or teachers. Such tension puts wear and tear on our bodies and on our emotional well-being. Although some people run to relieve tension, research has found that walking is a more effective tension reducer.

PROFESSIONAL
SELECTIONS:
DEFINITION

K. C. COLE

K. C. Cole (1946–) has contributed articles on science to numerous national publications and has written a regular column for *Discovery* magazine. Her essays are collected in *Sympathetic Vibrations: Reflections on Physics as a Way of Life* (1985). She has written several books, including *Facets of Light: Color Images and Things That Glow in the Dark* (1980), *Order in the Universe: The Shape of Relative Motion* (1986), and *Finding Your Way: Navigation Essays from the Exploratorium* (1992). The selection that follows first appeared as a "Hers" column in the *New York Times* (1982).

ENTROPY

1   It was about two months ago when I realized that entropy was getting the better of me. On the same day my car broke down (again), my refrigerator conked out and I learned that I needed root-canal work in my right rear tooth. The windows in the bedroom were still leaking every time it rained and my son's baby sitter was still failing to

show up every time I really needed her. My hair was turning gray and my typewriter was wearing out. The house needed paint and I needed glasses. My son's sneakers were developing holes and I was developing a deep sense of futility.

After all, what was the point of spending half of Saturday at the Laundromat if the   2
clothes were dirty all over again the following Friday?

Disorder, alas, is the natural order of things in the universe. There is even a precise   3
measure of the amount of disorder, called entropy. Unlike almost every other physical property (motion, gravity, energy), entropy does not work both ways. It can only increase. Once it's created it can never be destroyed. The road to disorder is a one-way street.

Because of its unnerving irreversibility, entropy has been called the arrow of time.   4
We all understand this instinctively. Children's rooms, left on their own, tend to get messy, not neat. Wood rots, metal rusts, people wrinkle and flowers wither. Even mountains wear down; even the nuclei of atoms decay. In the city we see entropy in the rundown subways and worn-out sidewalks and torn-down buildings, in the increasing disorder of our lives. We know, without asking, what is old. If we were suddenly to see the paint jump back on an old building, we would know that something was wrong. If we saw an egg unscramble itself and jump back into its shell, we would laugh in the same way we laugh at a movie run backward.

Entropy is no laughing matter, however, because with every increase in entropy   5
energy is wasted and opportunity is lost. Water flowing down a mountainside can be made to do some useful work on its way. But once all the water is at the same level it can work no more. That is entropy. When my refrigerator was working, it kept all the cold air ordered in one part of the kitchen and warmer air in another. Once it broke down the warm and cold mixed into a lukewarm mess that allowed my butter to melt, my milk to rot and my frozen vegetables to decay.

Of course the energy is not really lost, but it has defused and dissipated into a cha-   6
otic caldron of randomness that can do us no possible good. Entropy is chaos. It is loss of purpose.

People are often upset by the entropy they seem to see in the haphazardness of their   7
own lives. Buffeted about like so many molecules in my tepid kitchen, they feel that they have lost their sense of direction, that they are wasting youth and opportunity at every turn. It is easy to see entropy in marriages, when the partners are too preoccupied to patch small things up, almost guaranteeing that they will fall apart. There is much entropy in the state of our country, in the relationships between nations—lost opportunities to stop the avalanche of disorders that seems ready to swallow us all.

Entropy is not inevitable everywhere, however. Crystals and snowflakes and galax-   8
ies are islands of incredibly ordered beauty in the midst of random events. If it was not for exceptions to entropy, the sky would be black and we would be able to see where the stars spend their days; it is only because air molecules in the atmosphere cluster in ordered groups that the sky is blue.

The most profound exception to entropy is the creation of life. A seed soaks up some   9
soil and some carbon and some sunshine and some water and arranges it into a rose. A seed in the womb takes some oxygen and pizza and milk and transforms it into a baby.

The catch is that it takes a lot of energy to produce a baby. It also takes energy to   10
make a tree. The road to disorder is all downhill but the road to creation takes work. Though combating entropy is possible, it also has its price. That's why it seems so hard to get ourselves together, so easy to let ourselves fall apart.

11   Worse, creating order in one corner of the universe always creates more disorder somewhere else. We create ordered energy from oil and coal at the price of the entropy of smog.

12   I recently took up playing the flute again after an absence of several months. As the uneven vibrations screeched through the house, my son covered his ears and said, "Mom, what's wrong with your flute?" Nothing was wrong with my flute, of course. It was my ability to play it that had atrophied, or entropied, as the case may be. The only way to stop that process was to practice every day, and sure enough my tone improved, though only at the price of constant work. Like anything else, abilities deteriorate when we stop applying our energies to them.

13   That's why entropy is depressing. It seems as if just breaking even is an uphill fight. There's a good reason that this should be so. The mechanics of entropy are a matter of chance. Take any ice-cold air molecule milling around my kitchen. The chances that it will wander in the direction of my refrigerator at any point are exactly 50-50. The chances that it will wander away from my refrigerator are also 50-50. But take billions of warm and cold molecules mixed together, and the chances that all the cold ones will wander toward the refrigerator and all the warm ones will wander away from it are virtually nil.

14   Entropy wins not because order is impossible but because there are always so many more paths toward disorder than toward order. There are so many more different ways to do a sloppy job than a good one, so many more ways to make a mess than to clean it up. The obstacles and accidents in our lives almost guarantee that constant collisions will bounce us on to random paths, get us off the track. Disorder is the path of least resistance, the easy but not the inevitable road.

15   Like so many others, I am distressed by the entropy I see around me today. I am afraid of the randomness of international events, of the lack of common purpose in the world; I am terrified that it will lead into the ultimate entropy of nuclear war. I am upset that I could not in the city where I live send my child to a public school; that people are unemployed and inflation is out of control; that tensions between sexes and races seem to be increasing again; that relationships everywhere seem to be falling apart.

16   Social institutions—like atoms and stars—decay if energy is not added to keep them ordered. Friendships and families and economies all fall apart unless we constantly make an effort to keep them working and well oiled. And far too few people, it seems to me, are willing to contribute consistently to those efforts.

17   Of course, the more complex things are, the harder it is. If there were only a dozen or so air molecules in my kitchen, it would be likely—if I waited a year or so—that at some point the six coldest ones would congregate inside the freezer. But the more factors in the equation—the more players in the game—the less likely it is that their paths will coincide in an orderly way. The more pieces in the puzzle, the harder it is to put back together once order is disturbed. "Irreversibility," said a physicist, "is the price we pay for complexity."

Questions for Close Reading

1. What is the selection's thesis? Locate the sentence(s) in which Cole states her main idea. If she doesn't state the thesis explicitly, express it in your own words.

2. How does entropy differ from the other properties of the physical world? Is the image "the arrow of time" helpful in establishing this difference?

3. Why is the creation of life an exception to entropy? What is the relationship between entropy and energy?

4. Why does Cole say that entropy "is no laughing matter"? What is so depressing about the entropy she describes?

5. Refer to your dictionary as needed to define the following words used in the selection: *futility* (paragraph 1), *dissipated* (6), *buffeted* (7), *tepid* (7), and *atrophied* (12).

Questions About the Writer's Craft

1. The pattern. What is Cole's underlying purpose in defining the scientific term *entropy*? What gives the essay its persuasive edge?

2. What tone does Cole adopt to make reading about a scientific concept more interesting? Identify places in the essay where her tone is especially prominent.

3. Cole uses such words as *futility, loss,* and *depressing.* How do these words affect you? Why do you suppose she chose such terms? Find similar words in the essay.

4. Other patterns. Many of Cole's sentences follow a two-part pattern involving a contrast: "The road to disorder is all downhill but the road to creation takes work" (paragraph 10). Find other examples of this pattern in the essay. Why do you think Cole uses it so often?

Writing Assignments Using Definition as a Pattern of Development

1. Define *order* or *disorder* by applying the term to a system that you know well— for example, your school, dorm, family, or workplace. Develop your definition through any combination of writing patterns: by supplying examples, by showing contrasts, by analyzing the process underlying the system, and so on.

2. Choose, as Cole does, a technical term that you think will be unfamiliar to most readers. In a humorous or serious paper, define the term as it is used technically; then show how the term can shed light on some aspect of your life. For example, the concept in astronomy of a *supernova* could be used to explain your sudden emergence as a new star on the athletic field, in your schoolwork, or on the social scene. Here are a few suggested terms:

symbiosis	volatility	resonance
velocity	erosion	catalyst
neutralization	equilibrium	malleability

Writing Assignments Using Other Patterns of Development

3. Can one person make much difference in the amount of entropy—disorder and chaos—in the world? Share your view in an essay. Use examples of people who have tried to overcome the tendency of things to "fall apart." Make clear whether you think these people succeeded or failed in their attempts.

4. Cole claims that our lives contain a distressing amount of "haphazardness" (paragraph 7). Write an essay arguing that people either do or do not control their own fates. Support your point with a series of specific examples.

NANCY GIBBS

Employed by *Time* since 1985, Nancy Gibbs was named a senior editor in 1991. She has worked in a number of the magazine's departments, writing articles on a wide range of issues, including health care, child labor laws, and racism on campus. Gibbs's book *Children of Light,* a history of Quaker education in New York City, was published in 1985. *Mad Genius: The Odyssey, Pursuit, and Capture of the Unabomber,* a book she coauthored, was published in 1996. The selection reprinted here first appeared in *Time* (1991).

WHEN IS IT RAPE?

1   Be careful of strangers and hurry home, says a mother to her daughter, knowing that the world is a frightful place but not wishing to swaddle a child in fear. Girls grow up scarred by caution and enter adulthood eager to shake free of their parents' worst nightmares. They still know to be wary of strangers. What they don't know is whether they have more to fear from their friends.

2   Most women who get raped are raped by people they already know—like the boy in biology class, or the guy in the office down the hall, or their friend's brother. The familiarity is enough to make them let down their guard, sometimes even enough to make them wonder afterward whether they were "really raped." What people think of as "real rape"—the assault by a monstrous stranger lurking in the shadows—accounts for only one out of five attacks.

3   So the phrase "acquaintance rape" was coined to describe the rest, all the cases of forced sex between people who already knew each other, however casually. But that was too clinical for headline writers, and so the popular term is the narrower "date rape," which suggests an ugly ending to a raucous night on the town.

4   These are not idle distinctions. Behind the search for labels is the central mythology about rape: that rapists are always strangers, and victims are women who ask for it. The mythology is hard to dispel because the crime is so rarely exposed. The experts guess—that's all they can do under the circumstances—that while one in four women will be raped in her lifetime, less than 10 percent will report the assault, and less than 5 percent of the rapists will go to jail.

When a story of the crime lodges in the headlines, the myths have a way of cluttering the search for the truth. The tale of Good Friday in Palm Beach landed in the news because it involved a Kennedy,* but it may end up as a watershed case, because all the mysteries and passions surrounding date rape are here to be dissected. William Kennedy Smith met a woman at a bar, invited her back home late at night and apparently had sex with her on the lawn. She says it was rape, and the police believed her story enough to charge him with the crime. Perhaps it was the bruises on her leg; or the instincts of the investigators who found her, panicked and shaking, curled up in the fetal position on a couch; or the lie-detector tests she passed. 5

On the other side, Smith has adamantly protested that he is a man falsely accused. 6
His friends and family testify to his gentle nature and moral fiber and insist that he could not possibly have committed such a crime. Maybe the truth will come out in court—but regardless of its finale, the case has shoved the debate over date rape into the minds of average men and women. Plant the topic in a conversation, and chances are it will ripen into a bitter argument or a jittery sequence of pale jokes.

Women charge that date rape is the hidden crime; men complain it is hard to pre- 7
vent a crime they can't define. Women say it isn't taken seriously; men say it is a concept invented by women who like to tease but not take the consequences. Women say the date-rape debate is the first time the nation has talked frankly about sex; men say it is women's unconscious reaction to the excesses of the sexual revolution. Meanwhile, men and women argue among themselves about the "gray area" that surrounds the whole murky arena of sexual relations, and there is no consensus in sight.

In court, on campus, in conversation, the issue turns on the elasticity of the word 8
rape, one of the few words in the language with the power to summon a shared image of a horrible crime.

At one extreme are those who argue that for the word to retain its impact, it must 9
be strictly defined as forced sexual intercourse: a gang of thugs jumping a jogger in Central Park, a psychopath preying on old women in a housing complex, a man with an ice pick in a side street. To stretch the definition of the word risks stripping away its power. In this view, if it happened on a date, it wasn't rape. A romantic encounter is a context in which sex *could* occur, and so what omniscient judge will decide whether there was genuine mutual consent?

Others are willing to concede that date rape sometimes occurs, that sometimes a 10
man goes too far on a date without a woman's consent. But this infraction, they say, is not as ghastly a crime as street rape, and it should not be taken as seriously. The *New York Post,* alarmed by the Willy Smith case, wrote in a recent editorial, "If the sexual encounter, *forced or not,* has been preceded by a series of consensual activities—drinking, a trip to the man's home, a walk on a deserted beach at three in the morning—the charge that's leveled against the alleged offender should, it seems to us, be different than the one filed against, say, the youths who raped and beat the jogger."

---

*William Kennedy Smith, the nephew of John, Robert, and Edward Kennedy, was accused of raping a woman on Good Friday (1991) in Palm Beach, Florida. Kennedy was acquitted, but his trial, broadcast on television, generated heated debate on the issue of date rape.

11   This attitude sparks rage among women who carry scars received at the hands of men they knew. It makes no difference if the victim shared a drink or a moonlit walk or even a passionate kiss, they protest, if the encounter ended with her being thrown to the ground and forcibly violated. Date rape is not about a misunderstanding, they say. It is not a communications problem. It is not about a woman's having regrets in the morning for a decision she made the night before. It is not about a "decision" at all. Rape is rape, and any form of forced sex—even between neighbors, co-workers, classmates and casual friends—is a crime.

12   A more extreme form of that view comes from activists who see rape as a metaphor, its definition swelling to cover any kind of oppression of women. Rape, seen in this light, can occur not only on a date but also in a marriage, not only by violent assault but also by psychological pressure. A Swarthmore College training pamphlet once explained that acquaintance rape "spans a spectrum of incidents and behaviors, ranging from crimes legally defined as rape to verbal harassment and inappropriate innuendo."

13   No wonder, then, that the battles become so heated. When innuendo qualifies as rape, the definitions have become so slippery that the entire subject sinks into a political swamp. The only way to capture the hard reality is to tell the story.

14   A thirty-two-year-old woman was on business in Tampa last year for the Florida supreme court. Stranded at the courthouse, she accepted a lift from a lawyer involved in her project. As they chatted on the ride home, she recalls, "he was saying all the right things, so I started to trust him." She agreed to have dinner, and afterward, at her hotel door, he convinced her to let him come in to talk. "I went through the whole thing about being old-fashioned," she says. "I was a virgin until I was twenty-one. So I told him talk was all we were going to do."

15   But as they sat on the couch, she found herself falling asleep. "By now, I'm comfortable with him, and I put my head on his shoulder. He's not tried anything all evening, after all." Which is when the rape came. "I woke up to find him on top of me, forcing himself on me. I didn't scream or run. All I could think about was my business contacts and what if they saw me run out of my room screaming rape.

16   "I thought it was my fault. I felt so filthy, I washed myself over and over in hot water. Did he rape me? I kept asking myself. I didn't consent. But who's gonna believe me? I had a man in my hotel room after midnight." More than a year later, she still can't tell the story without a visible struggle to maintain her composure. Police referred the case to the state attorney's office in Tampa, but without more evidence it decided not to prosecute. Although her attacker has admitted that he heard her say no, maintains the woman, "he says he didn't know that I meant no. He didn't feel he'd raped me, and he even wanted to see me again."

17   Her story is typical in many ways. The victim herself may not be sure right away that she has been raped, that she had said no and been physically forced into having sex anyway. And the rapist commonly hears but does not heed the protest. "A date rapist will follow through no matter what the woman wants because his agenda is to get laid," says Claire Walsh, a Florida-based consultant on sexual assaults. "First comes the dinner, then a dance, then a drink, then the coercion begins." Gentle persuasion gives way to physical intimidation, with alcohol as the ubiquitous lubricant. "When that fails, force is used," she says. "Real men don't take no for an answer."...

So here, of course, is the heart of the debate. If rape is sex without consent, how 18
exactly should consent be defined and communicated, when and by whom? Those
who view rape through a political lens tend to place all responsibility on men to make
sure that their partners are consenting at every point of a sexual encounter. At the
extreme, sexual relations come to resemble major surgery, requiring a signed consent
form. Clinical psychologist Mary P. Koss of the University of Arizona in Tucson, who is
a leading scholar on the issue, puts it rather bluntly: "It's the man's penis that is doing
the raping, and ultimately he's responsible for where he puts it."

Historically, of course, this has never been the case, and there are some who argue 19
that it shouldn't be—that women too must take responsibility for their behavior, and
that the whole realm of intimate encounters defies regulation from on high. Anthropologist Lionel Tiger has little patience for trendy sexual politics that make no reference to
biology. Since the dawn of time, he argues, men and women have always gone to bed
with different goals. In the effort to keep one's genes in the gene pool, "it is to the male
advantage to fertilize as many females as possible, as quickly as possible and as efficiently as possible." For the female, however, who looks at the large investment she
will have to make in the offspring, the opposite is true. Her concern is to "select" who
"will provide the best set up for their offspring." So, in general, "the pressure is on the
male to be aggressive and on the female to be coy."

What is lost in the ideological debate over date rape is the fact that men and 20
women, especially when they are young, and drunk, and aroused, are not very good at
communicating. "In many cases," says [Susan] Estrich,* "the man thought it was sex,
and the woman thought it was rape, and they are both telling the truth." The man may
envision a celluloid seduction, in which he is being commanding, she is being coy. A
woman may experience the same event as a degrading violation of her will. That some
men do not believe a woman's protests is scarcely surprising in a society so drenched
with messages that women have rape fantasies and a desire to be overpowered.

By the time they reach college, men and women are loaded with cultural baggage, 21
drawn from movies, television, music videos and "bodice ripper" romance novels.
Over the years they have watched Rhett sweep Scarlett up the stairs in *Gone with the
Wind;* or Errol Flynn, who was charged twice with statutory rape, overpower a protest-
ing heroine who then melts in his arms; or Stanley rape his sister-in-law Blanche du
Bois while his wife is in the hospital giving birth to a child in *A Streetcar Named
Desire.* Higher up the cultural food chain, young people can read of date rape in Homer
or Jane Austen, watch it in *Don Giovanni* or *Rigoletto.*†

The messages come early and often, and nothing in the feminist revolution has been 22
able to counter them. A recent survey of sixth- to ninth-graders in Rhode Island found

*The victim of a rape in the 1970s, law professor Susan Estrich has written a book, *Real Rape,* about
her ordeal (editors' note).
†Traditionally, the Greek poet Homer is conjectured to be the author of the epics *The Iliad* and *The
Odyssey,* both dated around 850 BC. Jane Austen was an English novelist (1775–1817). *Don Giovanni,* an opera by Wolfgang Amadeus Mozart (1756–1791), tells the tale of a notorious libertine and
womanizer. *Rigoletto,* an opera by Giuseppe Verdi (1813–1901), recounts a story of abduction and
seduction.

that a fourth of the boys and a sixth of the girls said it was acceptable for a man to force a woman to kiss him or have sex if he has spent money on her. A third of the children said it would not be wrong for a man to rape a woman who had had previous sexual experiences.

23   Certainly cases like Palm Beach, movies like *The Accused* and novels like Avery Corman's *Prized Possessions** may force young people to re-examine assumptions they have inherited. The use of new terms, like acquaintance rape and date rape, while controversial, has given men and women the vocabulary they need to express their experiences with both force and precision. This dialogue would be useful if it helps strip away some of the dogmas, old and new, surrounding the issue. Those who hope to raise society's sensitivity to the problem of date rape would do well to concede that it is not precisely the same sort of crime as street rape, that there may be very murky issues of intent and degree involved.

24   On the other hand, those who downplay the problem should come to realize that date rape is a crime of uniquely intimate cruelty. While the body is violated, the spirit is maimed. How long will it take, once the wounds have healed, before it is possible to share a walk on a beach, a drive home from work or an evening's conversation without always listening for a quiet alarm to start ringing deep in the back of the memory of a terrible crime?

Questions for Close Reading

1. What is the selection's thesis? Locate the sentence(s) in which Gibbs states her main idea. If she doesn't state the thesis explicitly, express it in your own words.

2. What does Gibbs mean by the "elasticity of the word *rape*" (paragraph 8)? How does this "elasticity" lead to problems in definition?

3. What, in Gibbs's opinion, is the "typical" scenario in a case of date rape? According to the consultant that Gibbs quotes, what is it about men that causes them to enact this scenario?

4. An author cited by Gibbs states that in a case of rape both the man and the woman "are telling the truth" (20). What anthropological and cultural factors might contribute to this conflict in perception?

5. Refer to your dictionary as needed to define the following words used in the selection: *watershed* (paragraph 5), *fetal* (5), *psychopath* (9), *omniscient* (9), *infraction* (10), *innuendo* (12, 13), *coercion* (17), *intimidation* (17), *ubiquitous* (17), *ideological* (20), *celluloid* (20), *statutory* (21), and *dogmas* (23).

The Accused is a 1988 film about a woman who pursues retribution for a gang-rape she endured. *Prized Possessions* is a 1990 novel about the rape of a first-year college student.

Questions About the Writer's Craft

1. The pattern. Writers often use definition by negation in the beginning of a definition essay (see page 409). Where in the essay does Gibbs employ this strategy? How does it help her reinforce her thesis?

2. Other patterns. Definition essays frequently draw upon other patterns of development to explain the meaning of a term. Locate places in the selection where Gibbs uses comparison-contrast and narration. How do these patterns help clarify her definition of date rape?

3. What emotionally charged language does Gibbs use in her introduction and conclusion? What effect do you think she hoped these words would have on readers? How do these words help create an effective beginning and end for the piece?

4. Gibbs uses statistics (paragraphs 2 and 4), refers to several dramatic cases of rape (5–6, 9–10), often cites experts or writers in the field of sexual assault (17–20), and summarizes the results of recent opinion surveys (22). Why do you think she includes such factual material? What type of audience does she seem to assume will read her essay?

Writing Assignments Using Definition as a Pattern of Development

1. Interview some people, both male and female, to get their definitions of date rape. Then, in an essay, point out any differences between the two sexes' perspectives. That done, present your own definition of date rape, explaining both what it is and what it isn't.

∞ **2.** One of Gibbs's authorities on date rape comments sarcastically, "Real men don't take no for an answer" (paragraph 17). Brainstorm with several people to see how they define a "real man." After evaluating that material, write an essay constructing your own definition of a "real man." Susan Douglas's "Managing Mixed Messages" (page 247), Deborah Tannen's "But What Do You Mean?" (page 283), and Caryl Rivers's "What Should Be Done About Rock Lyrics?" (page 473) will prompt some ideas worth exploring.

Writing Assignments Using Other Patterns of Development

∞ **3.** Date rape seems to be on the rise. Brainstorm with others to identify what may be causing its increased incidence. Focusing on several related factors, write an essay showing how these factors contribute to the problem. Some possible factors include the following: the way males and females are depicted in the media (advertisements, movies, television, rock videos); young people's use of alcohol; the emergence of co-ed college dorms. At the end of the essay, offer some recommendations about what can be done to create a safer climate for dating. Susan Douglas's "Managing Mixed Messages" (page 247), Deborah Tannen's "But What Do You Mean?" (page 283), and Caryl Rivers's "What Should Be Done About Rock Lyrics?" (page 473) may provide insights to draw on in your paper.

4. Determine what your college is doing about date rape. Does it have a formal policy defining date rape, a hearing process, ongoing workshops, discussions for incoming students? Write a paper explaining how your college deals with date rape. Then argue either that more attention should be devoted to this issue or that your college has adopted measures sufficient to deal with the problem. If you feel the college should do more, indicate what steps should be taken.

JOHN LEO

Syndicated columnist John Leo (1935–) writes a controversial, widely read column in *U.S. News and World Report.* A former writer for the *New York Times* and *Time* magazine, Leo also began the "Press Clips" column of media criticism for the *Village Voice.* He is the author of *How the Russians Invented Baseball and Other Essays of Enlightenment* (1989) and a collection of columns, *Two Steps Ahead of the Thought Police* (1994). "Absolutophobia" first appeared in *U.S. News* in July 1997.

ABSOLUTOPHOBIA

1   In 20 years of college teaching, Prof. Robert Simon has never met a student who denied that the Holocaust happened. What he sees quite often, though, is worse: students who acknowledge the fact of the Holocaust but can't bring themselves to say that killing millions of people is wrong. Simon reports that 10 to 20 percent of his students think this way. Usually they deplore what the Nazis did, but their disapproval is expressed as a matter of taste or personal preference, not moral judgment. "Of course I dislike the Nazis," one student told Simon, "but who is to say they are morally wrong?"

2   Overdosing on nonjudgmentalism is a growing problem in the schools. Two disturbing articles in the *Chronicle of Higher Education* say that some students are unwilling to oppose large moral horrors, including human sacrifice, ethnic cleansing, and slavery, because they think that no one has the right to criticize the moral views of another group or culture.

3   One of the articles is by Simon, who teaches philosophy at Hamilton College in Clinton, N.Y. The other is by Kay Haugaard, a freelance writer who teaches creative writing at Pasadena City College in California. Haugaard writes that her current students have a lot of trouble expressing any moral reservations or objections about human sacrifice. The subject came up when she taught her class Shirley Jackson's *The Lottery,* a short story about a small American farm town where one person is killed each year to make the crops grow. In the tale, a woman is ritually stoned to death by her husband, her 12-year-old daughter, and her 4-year-old son.

Haugaard has been teaching since 1970. Until recently, she says, "Jackson's mes- 4 sage about blind conformity always spoke to my students' sense of right and wrong." No longer, apparently. A class discussion of human sacrifice yielded no moral comments, even under Haugaard's persistent questioning. One male said the ritual killing in *The Lottery* "almost seems a need." Asked if she believed in human sacrifice, a woman said, "I really don't know. If it was a religion of long standing...." Haugaard writes: "I was stunned. This was the woman who wrote so passionately of saving the whales, of concern for the rain forests, of her rescue and tender care of a stray dog."

The Aztecs did it. Both writers believe multiculturalism has played a role in 5 spreading the vapors of nonjudgmentalism. Haugaard quotes a woman in her class, a "50-something red-headed nurse," who says, "I teach a course for our hospital personnel in multicultural understanding, and if it is part of a person's culture, we are taught not to judge...." Simon says we should "welcome diversity rather than fear it" but says his students often think they are so locked into their own group perspectives of ethnicity, race, and gender that moral judgment is impossible, even in the face of great evils.

In the new multicultural canon, human sacrifice is hard to condemn, because the 6 Aztecs practiced it. In fact, however, this nonjudgmental stance is not held consistently. Japanese whaling and the genital cutting of girls in Africa are criticized all the time by white multiculturalists. Christina Hoff Sommers, author and professor of philosophy at Clark University in Massachusetts, says that students who can't bring themselves to condemn the Holocaust will often say flatly that treating humans as superior to dogs and rodents is immoral. Moral shrugging may be on the rise, but old-fashioned and rigorous moral criticism is alive and well on certain selected issues: smoking, environmentalism, women's rights, animal rights.

Sommers points beyond multiculturalism to a general problem of so many students 7 coming to college "dogmatically committed to a moral relativism that offers them no grounds to think" about cheating, stealing, and other moral issues. Simon calls this "absolutophobia"—the unwillingness to say that some behavior is just plain wrong. Many trends feed this fashionable phobia. Postmodern theory on campuses denies the existence of any objective truth: All we can have are clashing perspectives, not true moral knowledge. The pop-therapeutic culture has pushed nonjudgmentalism very hard. Intellectual laziness and the simple fear of unpleasantness are also factors. By saying that one opinion or moral stance is as good as another, we can draw attention to our own tolerance, avoid antagonizing others, and get on with our careers.

The "values clarification" programs in the schools surely should come in for some 8 lumps, too. Based on the principle that teachers should not indoctrinate other people's children, they leave the creation of values up to each student. Values emerge as personal preferences, equally as unsuited for criticism or argument as personal decisions on pop music or clothes.

But the wheel is turning now, and "values clarification" is giving way to "character 9 education," and the paralyzing fear of indoctrinating children is gradually fading. The search is on for a teachable consensus rooted in simple decency and respect. As a spur to shaping it, we might discuss a culture so morally confused that students are showing up at colleges reluctant to say anything negative about mass slaughter.

Questions for Close Reading

1. What is the selection's thesis? Locate the sentence(s) in which Leo states his main idea. If he doesn't state the thesis explicitly, express it in your own words.

2. Leo discusses Kay Haugaard's experience in teaching Shirley Jackson's "The Lottery." Why are both Leo and Haugaard troubled by students' responses to this short story?

3. According to Leo, how does multiculturalism spread "the vapors of nonjudgmentalism"(6)?

4. According to Leo, what current trends encourage "absolutophobia"?

5. Refer to your dictionary as needed to define the following words used in the selection: *conformity* (paragraph 4), *perspective* (5), *rigorous* (6), *dogmatically* (7), *relativism* (7), *phobia* (7), *antagonizing* (7), and *indoctrinate* (8).

Questions About the Writer's Craft

1. The pattern. Leo provides a definition of "absolutophobia" in paragraph 7. Why do you suppose he waits until nearly the end of the essay to offer his definition?

2. Other patterns. Where does Leo use the cause-effect pattern in his essay? How does this pattern contribute to Leo's overall purpose?

3. Other patterns. At the end of his essay, Leo contrasts "values clarification" and "character education." Why do you think Leo concludes his essay with this contrast?

4. How does Leo's language reveal his attitude toward "absolutophobia"?

Writing Assignments Using Definition as a Pattern of Development

1. Building upon Leo's comments in paragraph 9, formulate your own definition of "character education." Identify the basic premise(s) of such a philosophy, and brainstorm with others the possible advantages and disadvantages of such an approach. Then write an essay defining the term and assessing its validity as an educational philosophy. Focus on a specific level of schooling, and provide examples based on your own and other people's experience.

2. In his essay, Leo discusses a new term, "absolutophobia." In an essay of your own, focus on an already existing term or definition that you think is misused or misunderstood. Possibilities include "feminism," "new age," "senior citizen," "adolescence," "illiteracy," "homeless," "addiction," "liberal," "family," or "the disabled." Provide several examples showing how the word is commonly mis-used. Then offer your own definition, using clear examples to convey why your understanding of the word is more accurate.

Writing Assignments Using Other Patterns of Development

∞ **3.** Leo explains the phenomenon of "absolutophobia" in terms of students' unwillingness to make moral judgments in the classroom. Brainstorm with others to identify additional areas of life where there is evidence of this reluctance to make judgments. Focusing on *one* such area, write an essay in which you provide compelling examples of moral paralysis in that setting. The following essays will provide insight into the complexities of morality: George Orwell's "Shooting an Elephant" (page 203), Joyce Garity's "Is Sex All That Matters?" (page 252), Diane Cole's "Don't Just Stand There" (page 315), Meg Greenfield's "Why Nothing is 'Wrong' Anymore" (page 290), Nancy Gibbs's "When Is It Rape?" (page 423), and Caryl Rivers's "What Should Be Done About Rock Lyrics?" (page 473).

4. Leo suggests that the moral fiber of young people has deteriorated. Ask several people of varying ages to read Leo's essay. Do they think his view is valid? Why or why not? Encourage each person to provide one personal experience that explains why he or she agrees or disagrees with Leo. Review all the material you gather, and write an essay arguing your own position. Use convincing examples from the interviews and your own experience to support your viewpoint. Near the beginning of your essay, acknowledge and, when possible, refute opposing viewpoints.

ADDITIONAL WRITING TOPICS: DEFINITION

General Assignments

Using definition, write an essay on one of the following topics.

1. Fads

2. Helplessness

3. An epiphany

4. Empowerment

5. A Yiddish term such as *mensch, klutz, chutzpah,* or *dreck,* or a term from some other ethnic group

6. Idiomatic expressions

7. Hypocrisy

8. Inner peace

9. Exploitation

10. A double bind

Assignments with a Specific Purpose, Audience, and Point of View

1. *Newsweek* magazine runs a popular column called "My Turn," consisting of readers' opinions on subjects of general interest. Write a piece for this column defining *today's college students.* Use the piece to dispel some negative stereotypes (for example, that college students are apathetic, ill-informed, self-centered, and materialistic).

2. You're an attorney arguing a case of sexual harassment—a charge your client has leveled against an employer. To win the case, you must present to the jury a clear definition of exactly what *sexual harassment* is and isn't. Write such a definition for your opening remarks in court.

3. You have been asked to write part of a pamphlet for students who come to the college health clinic. For this pamphlet, define *one* of the following conditions and its symptoms: *depression, stress, burnout, test anxiety, addiction* (to alcohol, drugs, or TV), *workaholism.* Part of the pamphlet should describe ways to cope with the condition described.

4. A new position has opened in your company. Write a job description to be sent to employment agencies that will screen candidates. Your description should define the job's purpose, state the duties involved, and outline essential qualifications.

5. Part of your job as a peer counselor in the student counseling center involves helping students communicate more effectively. To assist students, write a definition of some term that you think represents an essential component of a strong interpersonal relationship. You might, for example, define *respect, sharing, equality,* or *trust*. Part of the definition should employ definition by negation, a discussion of what the term is *not*.

6. Having waited on tables for several years at a resort hotel, you've been asked by the hotel manager to give some pointers to this year's new dining hall staff. Prepare a talk in which you define *courtesy*, the quality you consider most essential to the job. Use specific examples to illustrate your definition.

19
ARGUMENTATION-PERSUASION

WHAT IS ARGUMENTATION-PERSUASION?

"You can't possibly believe what you're saying."

"Look, I know what I'm talking about, and that's that."

Does this heated exchange sound familiar? Probably. When we hear the word *argument*, most of us think of a verbal battle propelled by stubbornness and irrational thought, with one person pitted against the other.

Argumentation in writing, though, is a different matter. Using clear thinking and logic, the writer tries to convince readers of the soundness of a particular opinion on a controversial issue. If, while trying to convince, the writer uses emotional language and dramatic appeals to readers' concerns, beliefs, and values, then the piece is called **persuasion.** Besides encouraging acceptance of an opinion, persuasion often urges readers (or another group) to commit themselves to a course of action. Assume you're writing an essay protesting the federal government's policy of offering aid to those suffering from hunger in other countries while many Americans go hungry. If your purpose is to document, coolly and objectively, the presence of hunger in the United States, you would prepare an argumentation essay. Such an essay would be filled with statistics, report findings, and expert opinion to demonstrate how widespread hunger is nationwide. If, however, your purpose is to shake up readers, even motivate them to write letters to their Congressional representatives and push for a change in policy, you would write a persuasive essay. In this case, your essay might contain emotional accounts of undernourished children, ill-fed pregnant women, and nearly starving elderly people.

Because people respond rationally *and* emotionally to situations, argumentation and persuasion are usually *combined*. Suppose you decide to write an article for the campus newspaper advocating a pre-Labor Day start for the school year. Your audience includes the college administration, students, and faculty. The article might begin by *arguing* that several schools starting the academic year earlier were able to close for the month of January and thus reduce heating and other maintenance expenses. Such an argument, supported by documented facts and figures, would help convince the administration. Realizing that you also have to gain student and faculty support for your idea, you might argue further that the proposed change would mean that students and faculty could leave for winter break with the semester behind them—papers written, exams taken, grades calculated and recorded. To make this part of your argument especially compelling, you could adopt a *persuasive* strategy by using emotional appeals and positively charged language: "Think how pleasant it would be to sleep late, spend time with family and friends, toast the New Year—without having to worry about work awaiting you back on campus."

When argumentation and persuasion blend in this way, emotion *supports* rather than *replaces* logic and sound reasoning. Although some writers resort to emotional appeals to the exclusion of rational thought, when you prepare argumentation-persuasion essays, you should advance your position through a balanced appeal to reason and emotion.

HOW ARGUMENTATION-PERSUASION FITS YOUR PURPOSE AND AUDIENCE

You probably realize that argumentation, persuasion, or a combination of the two is everywhere: an editorial urging the overhaul of an ill-managed literacy program; a commercial for a new shampoo; a scientific report advocating increased funding for AIDS research. Your own writing involves argumentation-persuasion as well. When you prepare a *causal analysis, descriptive piece, narrative,* or *definition essay,* you advance a specific point of view: MTV has a negative influence on teens' view of sex; Cape Cod in winter is imbued with a special kind of magic; a disillusioning experience can teach people much about themselves; *character* can be defined as the willingness to take unpopular positions on difficult issues. Indeed, an essay organized around any of the patterns of development described in this book may have a persuasive intent. You might, for example, encourage readers to try out a *process* you've explained, or to see one of the two movies you've *compared.*

Argumentation-persuasion, however, involves more than presenting a point of view and providing evidence. Unlike other forms of writing, it assumes controversy and addresses opposing viewpoints. Consider the following assignments, all of which require the writer to take a position on a controversial issue:

In parts of the country, communities established for older citizens or childless couples have refused to rent to families with children. How do you feel about this situation? What do you think are the rights of the parties involved?

Citing the fact that the highest percentage of automobile accidents involve young men, insurance companies consistently charge their highest rates to young males. Is this practice fair? Why or why not?

Some colleges and universities have instituted a "no pass, no play" policy for athletes. Explain why this policy is or is not appropriate.

It's impossible to predict with absolute certainty what will make readers accept the view you advance or take the action you propose. But the ancient Greeks, who formulated our basic concepts of logic, isolated three factors crucial to the effectiveness of argumentation-persuasion: *logos, pathos,* and *ethos.*

Your main concern in an argumentation-persuasion essay should be with the *logos,* or **soundness,** of your argument: the facts, statistics, examples, and authoritative statements you gather to support your viewpoint. This supporting evidence must be unified, specific, sufficient, accurate, and representative (see pages 46–49 and 68–72). Imagine, for instance, you want to convince people that a popular charity misappropriates the money it receives from the public. Your readers, inclined to believe in the good works of the charity, will probably dismiss your argument unless you can substantiate your claim with valid, well-documented evidence that enhances the *logos* of your position.

Sensitivity to the *pathos,* or the **emotional power of language,** is another key consideration for writers of argumentation-persuasion essays. *Pathos* appeals to readers' needs, values, and attitudes, encouraging them to commit themselves to a viewpoint or course of action. The *pathos* of a piece derives partly from the writer's language. *Connotative* language—words with strong emotional overtones—can move readers to accept a point of view and may even spur them to act.

Advertising and propaganda generally rely on *pathos* to the exclusion of logic, using emotion to influence and manipulate. Consider the following pitches for a man's cologne and a woman's perfume. The language—and the attitudes to which it appeals—are different in each case:

Brawn: Experience the power. Bold. Yet subtle. Clean. Masculine. The scent for the man who's in charge.

Black Lace is for you—the woman who dresses for success but who dares to be provocative, slightly naughty. Black Lace. Perfect with pearls by day and with diamonds by night.

The appeal to men plays on the impact that the words *Brawn, bold, power,* and *in charge* may have for some males. Similarly, the charged words *Black Lace, provocative, naughty,* and *diamonds* are intended to appeal to business women who—in the advertiser's mind, at least—may be looking for ways to reconcile sensuality and professionalism. (For more on slanted language, read Ann McClintock's "Propaganda Techniques in Today's Advertising," page 277).

Like an advertising copywriter, you must select language that reinforces your message. In a paper supporting an expanded immigration policy, you might use evocative phrases like "land of liberty," "a nation of immigrants," and "America's open-door policy." However, if you were arguing for strict immigration quotas, you might use language like "save jobs for unemployed Americans," "flood of unskilled labor," and "illegal aliens." Remember, though: Such language should *support, not supplant,* clear thinking. (See page 443 for additional information on persuasive language.)

Finally, whenever you write an argumentation-persuasion essay, you should establish your *ethos,* or **credibility** and **reliability.** You cannot expect readers to accept or act on your viewpoint unless you convince them that you know what you're talking about and that you're worth listening to. You will come across as knowledgeable and trustworthy if you present a logical, reasoned argument that takes opposing views into account. Make sure, too, that your appeals to emotion aren't excessive. Overwrought emotionalism undercuts credibility.

Writing an effective argumentation-persuasion essay involves an interplay of *logos, pathos,* and *ethos.* The exact balance among these factors is determined by your audience and purpose (that is, whether you want the audience simply to agree with your view or whether you also want them to take action). More than any other kind of writing, argumentation-persuasion requires that you *analyze your readers* and tailor your approach to them. You need to determine how much they know about the issue, how they feel about you and your position, what their values and attitudes are, what motivates them.

In general, most readers will fall into one of three broad categories: supportive, wavering, or hostile. Each type of audience requires a different blend of *logos, pathos,* and *ethos* in an argumentation-persuasion essay.

1. A supportive audience. If your audience agrees with your position and trusts your credibility, you don't need a highly reasoned argument dense with facts, examples, and statistics. Although you may want to solidify support by providing additional information (*logos*), you can rely primarily on *pathos*—a strong emotional appeal—to reinforce readers' commitment to your shared viewpoint. Assume that you belong to a local fishing club and have volunteered to write an article encouraging members to support threatened fishing rights in state parks. You might begin by stating that fishing strengthens the fish population by thinning out overcrowded streams. Since your audience would certainly be familiar with this idea, you wouldn't need to devote much discussion to it. Instead, you would attempt to move them emotionally. You might evoke the camaraderie in the sport, the pleasure of a perfect cast, the beauty of the outdoors, and perhaps conclude with "If you want these enjoyments to continue, please make a generous contribution to our fund."

2. A wavering audience. At times, readers may be interested in what you have to say but may not be committed fully to your viewpoint. Or perhaps they're not as informed about the subject as they should be. In either case, because your readers need to be encouraged to give their complete support, you don't want to risk alienating them with a heavy-handed emotional appeal. Concentrate instead on *ethos* and *logos,* bolstering your image as a reliable source and providing the evidence needed to advance your position. If you want to convince an audience of high school seniors to take a year off to work between high school and college, you might establish your credibility by recounting the year you spent working and by showing the positive effects it had on your life (*ethos*). In addition, you could cite studies indicating that delayed entry into college is related to higher grade point averages. A year's savings, you would explain, allow students to study when they might otherwise need to hold down a job to earn money for tuition (*logos*).

3. A hostile audience. An apathetic, skeptical, or hostile audience is obviously most difficult to convince. With such an audience you should avoid emotional appeals because they might seem irrational, sentimental, or even comical. Instead, weigh the essay heavily in favor of logical reasoning and hard-to-dispute facts (*logos*). Assume your college administration is working to ban liquor from the student pub. You plan to submit to the campus newspaper an open letter supporting this generally unpopular effort. To sway other students, you cite the positive experiences of schools that have gone dry. Many colleges, you explain, have found their tavern revenues actually increase because all students—not just those of drinking age—can now support the pub. With the greater revenues, some schools have upgraded the food served in the pubs and have hired disc jockeys or musical groups to provide entertainment. Many schools have also seen a sharp reduction in alcohol-related vandalism. Readers may not be won over to your side, but your sound, logical argument may encourage them to be more tolerant of your viewpoint. Indeed, such increased receptivity may be all you can reasonably expect from a hostile audience. (*Note:* The checklists on pages 21 and 439–440 provide additional guidelines for analyzing your audience.)

PREWRITING STRATEGIES

The following checklist shows how you can apply to argumentation-persuasion some of the prewriting techniques discussed in Chapter 2.

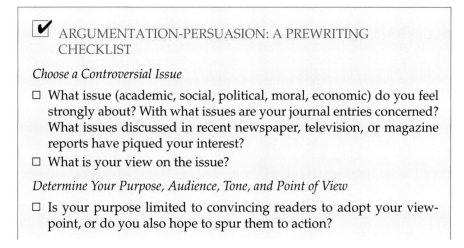

☑ ARGUMENTATION-PERSUASION: A PREWRITING
    CHECKLIST

Choose a Controversial Issue

☐ What issue (academic, social, political, moral, economic) do you feel
   strongly about? With what issues are your journal entries concerned?
   What issues discussed in recent newspaper, television, or magazine
   reports have piqued your interest?

☐ What is your view on the issue?

Determine Your Purpose, Audience, Tone, and Point of View

☐ Is your purpose limited to convincing readers to adopt your viewpoint, or do you also hope to spur them to action?

☐ Who is your audience? How much do your readers already know about the issue? Are they best characterized as supportive, wavering, or hostile? What values and needs may motivate readers to be responsive to your position?

☐ What tone is most likely to increase readers' commitment to your point of view? Should you convey strong emotion or cool objectivity?

☐ What point of view is most likely to enhance your credibility?

Use Prewriting to Generate Supporting Evidence

☐ How might brainstorming, journal entries, freewriting, or mapping help you identify personal experiences, observations, and examples to support your viewpoint?

☐ How might the various patterns of development help you generate supporting material? What about the issue can you describe? Narrate? Illustrate? Compare and contrast? Analyze in terms of process or cause-effect? Define or categorize in some especially revealing way?

☐ How might interviews or library research help you uncover relevant examples, facts, statistics, expert opinion?

STRATEGIES FOR USING ARGUMENTATION-PERSUASION IN AN ESSAY

After prewriting, you're ready to draft your essay. The following suggestions will help you prepare a convincing and logical argument.

1. At the beginning of the paper, identify the controversy surrounding the issue and state your position. Your introduction should clarify the controversy about the issue. In addition, it should provide as much background information as your readers are likely to need.

The thesis of an argumentation-persuasion paper is often called the **assertion** or **proposition**. Occasionally, the proposition appears at the paper's end, but it is usually stated at the beginning. If you state the thesis right away, your audience knows where you stand and is better able to evaluate the evidence presented.

Remember: Argumentation-persuasion assumes conflicting viewpoints. Be sure your proposition focuses on a controversial issue and indicates your view. Avoid a proposition that is merely factual; what is demonstrably true allows little room for debate. To see the difference between a factual statement and an effective thesis, examine the two statements that follow.

Fact

In the last few years, the nation's small farmers have suffered financial hardships.

Thesis

Inefficient management, rather than competition from agricultural conglomerates, is responsible for the financial plight of the nation's small farmers.

The first statement is certainly true. It would be difficult to find anyone who believes that these are easy times for small farmers. Because the statement invites little opposition, it can't serve as the focus of an argumentation-persuasion essay. The second statement, though, takes a controversial stance on a complex issue. Such a proposition is a valid starting point for a paper intended to argue and persuade. However, don't assume that this advice means that you should take a highly opinionated position in your thesis. A dogmatic, overstated proposition ("Campus security is staffed by overpaid, badge-flashing incompetents") is bound to alienate some readers.

Remember also to keep the proposition narrow and specific, so you can focus your thoughts in a purposeful way. Consider the following statements:

Broad Thesis

The welfare system has been abused over the years.

Narrowed Thesis

Welfare payments should be denied to unmarried mothers under the age of eighteen.

If you tried to write a paper based on the first statement, you would face an unmanageable task—showing all the ways that welfare has been abused. Your readers would also be confused about what to expect in the paper: Will it discuss unscrupulous bureaucrats, fraudulent bookkeeping, dishonest recipients? In contrast, the revised thesis is limited and specific. It signals that the paper will propose severe restrictions. Such a proposal will surely have opponents and is thus appropriate for argumentation-persuasion.

The thesis in an argumentation-persuasion essay can simply state your opinion about an issue, or it can go a step further and call for some action:

Opinion

The lack of affordable day-care centers discriminates against low-income families.

Call for Action

The federal government should support the creation of more day-care centers in low-income neighborhoods.

In either case, your stand on the issue must be clear to your readers.

2. Offer readers strong support for your thesis. Finding evidence that relates to your readers' needs, values, and experience (see pages 21 and 439–440) is a crucial part of writing an argumentation-persuasion essay. Readers will be responsive to evidence that is *unified, adequate, specific, accurate, dramatic,* and *representative* (see pages 46–49 and 68–72). The evidence might consist of personal experiences or observations. Or it could be gathered from outside sources—statistics; facts; examples; or expert opinion taken from books, articles, reports, interviews, and documentaries. A paper arguing that elderly Americans are better off than they used to be might incorporate the following kinds of evidence:

- *Personal observation or experience:* A description of the writer's grandparents who are living comfortably on Social Security and pensions.
- *Statistics from a report:* A statement that the per-capita after-tax income of older Americans is $335 greater than the national average.
- *Fact from a newspaper article:* The point that the majority of elderly Americans do not live in nursing homes or on the streets; rather, they have their own houses or apartments.
- *Examples from interviews:* Accounts of several elderly couples living comfortably in well-managed retirement villages in Florida.
- *Expert opinion cited in a documentary:* A statement by Dr. Marie Sanchez, a specialist in geriatrics: "An over-sixty-five American today is likely to be healthier, and have a longer life expectancy, than a fifty-year-old living only a decade ago."

You may wonder whether to use the *first-person* ("I") or *third-person* ("he," "she," "they") point of view when presenting evidence based on personal observation, experience, or interviews. The subjective immediacy typical of the first person often delivers a jolt of persuasive power; however, many writers arguing a point prefer to present personal evidence in an objective way, using the third person to keep the focus on the issue rather than on themselves. When you write an argumentation-persuasion essay, your purpose, audience, and tone will help you decide which point of view will be most effective. If you're not sure which point of view to use, check with your instructor. Some encourage a first-person approach; others expect a more objective stance.

As you seek outside evidence, you may—perhaps to your dismay—come across information that undercuts your argument. Resist the temptation to ignore such material; instead, use the evidence to arrive at a more balanced, perhaps somewhat qualified viewpoint. Conversely, don't blindly accept or disregard flaws in the arguments made by sources agreeing with you. Retain a healthy skepticism, analyzing the material as rigorously as if it were advanced by the opposing side.

Also, keep in mind that outside sources aren't infallible. They may have biases that cause them to skew evidence. So be sure to evaluate your sources. If you're writing an essay supporting a woman's right to abortion, the National Abortion Rights Action League (NARAL) can supply abundant statistics, case studies, and reports. But realize that NARAL won't give you the complete picture; it will probably present evidence that supports its "pro-choice" position only. To counteract such bias, you should review what those with differing opinions have to say. You should, for example, examine material published by such "pro-life" organizations as the National Right-to-Life Committee—keeping in mind, of course, that this material is also bound to present support for its viewpoint only. Remember, too, that there are more than two sides to a complex issue. To get as broad a perspective as possible, you should track down sources that have no axe to grind—that is, sources that make a deliberate effort to examine all sides of the issue. For example, published proceedings from a debate on abortion or an in-depth article that aims to synthesize various views on abortion would broaden your understanding of this controversial subject.

Whatever sources you use, be sure to *document* (give credit to) that material. Otherwise, readers may dismiss your evidence as nothing more than your subjective opinion, or they may conclude that you have *plagiarized*—tried to pass off someone else's ideas as your own. (Documentation isn't necessary when material is commonly known or is a matter of historical or scientific record.) In brief informal papers, documentation may consist of simple citations like "Psychologist Aaron Beck believes depression is the result of distorted thoughts" or "*Newsweek* (May 1, 1989) reports that most college-admissions procedures are chaotic." (For information about documenting sources in longer, more formal papers, see Chapters 20 and 21.)

3. Seek to create goodwill. Since your goal is to convince others of your position's soundness, you need to be careful about alienating readers—especially those who don't agree with you. Be careful, then, about using close-minded, morally superior language ("*Anyone* can see that..."). Exaggerated, overly emotional language can also antagonize readers. Consider an essay in which you argue that the speed limit shouldn't be raised from 55 m.p.h. to 65 m.p.h. Some readers may tune you out if you write "Truckers, the beer-bellied bullies of the highways, have no respect for other drivers or for the speed limit. They roar along the highway, tailgating and driving at least 20 m.p.h. over the speed limit. Now, with the new 65 m.p.h. speed limit, they're racing up on our bumpers at 80 m.p.h.—with disastrous consequences." Readers will probably be more receptive if you use less charged language: "The majority of truck drivers have more driving experience than anyone else on the road, and they handle their rigs responsibly. But when delivery deadlines encourage truckers to drive above the speed limit, an accident at 65 m.p.h. rather than at 55 m.p.h. will almost certainly be fatal." Last, guard against using confrontational language: "*My opponents* find the existing laws more effective than the proposed legislation" sounds adversarial, whereas "*Opponents* of the proposed legislation...," "*Those opposed* to the proposed legislation...," and "*Supporters* of the existing laws..." seems more even-handed and respectful. The last three statements also focus—as they should—on the issue, not on the people involved in the debate.

Goodwill can also be established by finding a *common ground*—some points on which all sides can agree, despite their differences. Assume a township council has voted to raise property taxes. The additional revenues will be used to preserve, as parkland, a wooded area that would otherwise be sold to developers. Before introducing its tax-hike proposal, the council would do well to remind homeowners of everyone's shared goals: maintaining the town's beauty and preventing the community's overdevelopment. This reminder of the common values shared by the town council and homeowners will probably make residents more receptive to the tax hike.

4. Organize the supporting evidence. The support for an argumentation-persuasion paper can be organized in a variety of ways. Any of the patterns of development described in this book (description, narration, definition, cause-effect, and so on) may be used—singly or in combination—to develop the essay's proposition. Imagine you're writing a paper arguing that car racing should be banned from television. Your essay might contain a *description* of a horrifying accident that was televised in graphic detail; you might devote part of the paper to a *causal analysis* showing that the broadcast of such races encourages teens to drive carelessly; you could include a *process analysis* to explain how young drivers "soup up" their cars in a dangerous attempt to imitate the racers seen on television. If your essay includes several patterns, you may need a separate paragraph for each.

When presenting evidence, arrange it so you create the strongest possible effect. In general, you should end with your most compelling point, leaving readers with dramatic evidence that underscores your proposition's validity.

5. Use Rogerian strategy to acknowledge differing viewpoints. If your essay has a clear thesis and strong logical support, you've taken important steps toward winning readers over. However, because argumentation-persuasion focuses on controversial issues, you should also take opposing views into account. As you think about and perhaps research your subject, seek out conflicting viewpoints. As journalist Walter Lippman argued more than sixty years ago in an essay aptly titled "The Indispensable Opposition," it is through the "confrontation of opinion in debate" that we test our views. A good argument seeks out contrary viewpoints, acknowledges them, perhaps even admits they have some merit. Such a strategy strengthens your argument in several ways. It helps you anticipate objections, alerts you to flaws in your own position, and makes you more aware of the other sides' weaknesses. Further, by acknowledging the dissenting views, you come across as reasonable and thorough—qualities that may disarm readers and leave them more receptive to your argument. You may not convince them to surrender their views, but you can enlarge their perspectives and encourage them to think about your position.

Psychologist Carl Rogers took the idea of acknowledging contrary viewpoints a step further. He believed that argumentation's goal should be to *reduce conflict*, rather than to produce a "winner" and a "loser." But he recognized that people identify so strongly with their opinions that they experience any challenge to those opinions as highly threatening. Such a challenge feels like an attack on their very identity. And what's the characteristic response to such a perceived attack? People become defensive; they dig in their heels and become more adamant than ever about their position. Indeed, when confronted with solid information that calls their opinion into question, they devalue that evidence rather than allow themselves to be persuaded. The old maxim about the power of first impressions demonstrates this point. Experiments show that after people form a first impression of another person, they are unlikely to let future conflicting information affect that impression. If, for example, they initially perceive someone to be unpleasant and disagreeable, they tend to reject subsequent evidence that casts the person in a more favorable light.

Taking into account this tendency to cling tenaciously to opinions in the face of a challenge, Rogerian strategy rejects the adversarial approach that often characterizes argumentation. It adopts, instead, a respectful, conciliatory posture—one that demonstrates a real understanding of opposing views, one that emphasizes shared interests and values. Such an approach makes it easier to negotiate differences and arrive at—ideally—a synthesis: a new position that both parties find at least as acceptable as their original positions.

How can you apply Rogerian strategy in your writing? Simply follow these steps:

- Begin by making a conscientious effort to *understand* the viewpoints of those with whom you disagree. As you listen to or read about their opinions, try to put yourself in their shoes; focus on *what they believe* and *why they believe it,* rather than on how you will challenge their beliefs.

- Open your essay with an unbiased, even-handed *restatement of opposing points of view.* Such an objective summary shows that you're fair and open-minded—and not so blinded by the righteousness of your own position that you can't consider any other. Typically, people respond to such a respectful approach by lowering their defenses. Because they appreciate your ability to understand what they have to say, they become more open to your point of view.

- When appropriate, *acknowledge the validity* of some of the arguments raised by those with differing views. What should you do if they make a well-founded point? You'll enhance your credibility if you concede that point while continuing to maintain that, overall, your position is stronger.

- Point out areas of *common ground* (see pages 443–444) by focusing on interests, values, and beliefs that you and those with opposing views share. When you say to them, "Look at the beliefs we share. Look at our common concerns," you communicate that you're not as unlike them as they first believed.

- Finally, *present evidence* for your position. Since those not agreeing with you have been "softened up" by your noncombative stance and disarmed by the realization that you and they share some values and beliefs, they're more ready to consider your point of view.

Let's consider, more specifically, how you might draw upon essentially Rogerian strategy when writing an argumentation-persuasion essay. In the following paragraphs, we discuss three basic strategies. As you read about each strategy, keep in mind this key point: The earlier you acknowledge alternate viewpoints, the more effective you will be. Establishing—right at the outset—your awareness of opposing positions shows you to be fair-minded and helps reduce resistance to what you have to say.

First, you may acknowledge the opposing viewpoint in a two-part proposition consisting of a subordinate clause followed by a main clause. The *first part of the proposition* (the subordinate clause) *acknowledges opposing opinions;* the *second part* (the main clause) *states your opinion* and implies that your view stands on more solid ground. (When using this kind of proposition, you may, but don't have to, discuss opposing opinions.) The following thesis illustrates this strategy (the opposing viewpoint is underlined once; the writer's position is underlined twice):

> <u>Although some instructors think that standardized finals restrict academic freedom,</u> <u><u>such exams are preferable to those prepared by individual professors.</u></u>

Second, *in the introduction,* you may provide—separate from the proposition—a *one- or two-sentence summary of the opposing viewpoint.* Suppose you're writing an essay advocating a ten-day waiting period before an individual can purchase a handgun. Before presenting your proposition at the end of the introductory paragraph, you might include sentences like these: "Opponents of the waiting period argue that the ten-day delay is worthless without a nation-wide computer network that can perform background checks. Those opposed also point out that only a percentage of states with a waiting period have seen a reduction in gun-related crime."

Third, you can take *one or two body paragraphs* near the beginning of the essay to *present in greater detail arguments raised by opposing viewpoints.* After that, you *grant* (when appropriate) the validity of some of those points ("It may be true that . . . ," "Granted, . . ."). Then you go on to *present evidence* for your position ("Even so . . . ," "Nevertheless . . ."). Imagine you're preparing an editorial for your student newspaper arguing that fraternities and sororities on your campus should be banned. Realizing that many students don't agree with you, you "research" the opposing viewpoint by seeking out supporters of Greek organizations and listening respectfully to the points they raise. When it comes time to write the editorial, you decide not to begin with arguments for your position; instead, you start by summarizing the points made by those supporting fraternities and sororities. You might, for example, mention their argument that Greek organizations build college spirit, contribute to worthy community causes, and provide valuable contacts for entry into the business world. Following this summary of the opposing viewpoint, you might concede that the point about the Greeks' contributions to community causes is especially valid; you could then reinforce this conciliatory stance by stressing some common ground you share—perhaps you acknowledge that you share your detractors' belief that enjoyable social activities with like-minded people are an important part of campus life. Having done all that, you would be in a good position to present arguments why you nevertheless think fraternities and sororities should be banned. Because you prepared readers to listen to your opinion, they would tend to be more open to your argument.

6. Refute differing viewpoints. There will be times, though, that acknowledging opposing viewpoints and presenting your own case won't be enough. Particularly when an issue is complex and when readers strongly disagree with your position, you may have to *refute* all or part of the *dissenting views.* Refutation means pointing out the problems with opposing viewpoints, thereby highlighting your own position's superiority. You may focus on the opposing sides' inaccurate or inadequate evidence; or you may point to their faulty logic. (Some common types of illogical thinking are discussed on pages 448–451 and 453–455.)

Let's consider how you could refute a competing position in an essay you're writing that supports sex education in public schools. Adapting the Rogerian approach to suit your purposes, you might start by acknowledging the opposing viewpoint's key argument: "Sex education should be the prerogative of parents." After granting the validity of this view in an ideal world, you might show that many parents don't provide such education. You could present statistics on the number of parents who avoid discussing sex with their children because the subject makes them uncomfortable; you could cite studies revealing that children in single-parent homes are apt to receive even less parental guidance about sex; and you could give examples of young people whose parents provided sketchy, even misleading information.

There are various ways to develop a paper's refutation section. The best method to use depends on the paper's length and the complexity of the issue. Two possible sequences are outlined here:

First Strategy

- State your proposition.
- Cite opposing viewpoints and the evidence for those views.
- Refute opposing viewpoints by presenting counterarguments.

Second Strategy

- State your proposition.
- Cite opposing viewpoints and the evidence for those views.
- Refute opposing viewpoints by presenting counterarguments.
- Present additional evidence for your proposition.

In the first strategy, you simply refute all or part of the opposing positions' arguments. The second strategy takes the first one a step further by presenting *additional evidence* to support your proposition. In such a case, the additional evidence *must be different* from the points made in the refutation. The additional evidence may appear at the essay's end (as in the preceding outline), or it may be given near the beginning (after the proposition); it may also be divided between the beginning and end.

No matter which strategy you select, you may refute opposing views *one side at a time* or *one point at a time.* When using the one-side-at-a-time approach, you cite all the points raised by the opposing side and then present your counter-argument to each point. When using the one-point-at-a-time strategy, you mention the first point made by the opposing side, refute that point, then move on to the second point and refute that, and so on. (For more on comparing and contrasting the sides of an issue, see pages 339–340.) No matter which strategy you use, be sure to provide clear signals so that readers can distinguish your arguments from the other sides': "Despite the claims of those opposed to the plan, many think that . . ." and "Those not in agreement think that. . . ."

7. Use induction or deduction to think logically about your argument. The line of reasoning used to develop an argument is the surest indicator of how rigorously you have thought through your position. There are two basic ways to think about a subject: inductively and deductively. Though the following discussion treats induction and deduction as separate processes, the two often overlap and complement each other.

Inductive reasoning involves examination of specific cases, facts, or examples. Based on these specifics, you then draw a conclusion or make a generalization. This is the kind of thinking scientists use when they examine evidence (the results of experiments, for example) and then draw a *conclusion:* "Smoking increases the risk of cancer." All of us use inductive reasoning in everyday life. We might think the following: "My head is aching" (evidence); "My nose is stuffy" (evidence); "I'm coming down with a cold" (conclusion). Based on the conclusion, we might go a step further and take some action: "I'll take an aspirin."

With inductive reasoning, the conclusion reached can serve as the proposition for an argumentation-persuasion essay. If the paper advances a course of action, the proposition often mentions the action, signaling an essay with a distinctly persuasive purpose.

Let's suppose that you're writing a paper about a crime wave in the small town where you live. You might use inductive thinking to structure the essay's argument:

Several people were mugged last month while shopping in the center of town. (*evidence*)

Several homes and apartments were burglarized in the past few weeks. (*evidence*)

Several cars were stolen from people's driveways over the weekend. (*evidence*)

The police force hasn't adequately protected town residents. (*conclusion, or proposition, for an argumentation essay with probable elements of persuasion*)

The police force should take steps to upgrade its protection of town residents. (*conclusion, or proposition, for an argumentation essay with a clearly persuasive intent*)

This inductive sequence highlights a possible structure for the essay. After providing a clear statement of your proposition, you might detail recent muggings, burglaries, and car thefts. Then you could move to the opposing viewpoint: a description of the steps the police say they have taken to protect town residents. At that point, you would refute the police's claim, citing additional evidence that shows the measures taken have not been sufficient. Finally, if you wanted your essay to have a decidedly persuasive purpose, you could end by recommending specific action the police should take to improve its protection of the community.

As in all essays, your evidence should be *unified, specific, accurate, dramatic, sufficient,* and *representative* (see pages 46–49 and 68–72). These last two characteristics are critical when you think inductively; they guarantee that your conclusion would be equally valid even if other evidence were presented. Insufficient or atypical evidence often leads to **hasty generalizations** that mar the essay's logic. For example, you might think the following: "Some elderly people are very wealthy and do not need Social Security checks" (evidence), and "Some Social Security recipients illegally collect several checks" (evidence). If you then conclude, "Social Security is a waste of taxpayers' money," your conclusion is invalid and hasty because it's based on only a few atypical examples. Millions of Social Security recipients aren't wealthy and don't abuse the system. If you've failed to consider the full range of evidence, any action you propose ("The Social Security system should be disbanded") will probably be considered suspect by thoughtful readers. It's possible, of course, that Social Security should be disbanded, but the evidence leading to such a conclusion must be sufficient and representative.

When reasoning inductively, you should also be careful that the evidence you collect is *recent* and *accurate.* No valid conclusion can result from dated or erroneous evidence. To ensure that your evidence is sound, you also need to evaluate the reliability of your sources. When a person who is legally drunk claims to have seen a flying saucer, the evidence is shaky, to say the least. But if two respected scientists, both with 20-20 vision, saw the saucer, their evidence is worth considering.

Finally, it's important to realize that there's always an element of uncertainty in inductive reasoning. The conclusion can never be more than an *inference,* involving what logicians call an **inductive leap.** There could be other explanations for the evidence cited and thus other positions to take and actions to advocate. For example, given a small town's crime wave, you might conclude not that the police force has been remiss but that residents are careless about protecting themselves and their property. In turn, you might call for a different kind of action—perhaps that the police conduct public workshops in self-defense and home security. In an inductive argument, your task is to weigh the evidence, consider alternative explanations, then choose the conclusion and course of action that seem most valid.

Unlike inductive reasoning, which starts with a specific case and moves toward a generalization or conclusion, **deductive reasoning** begins with a generalization that is then applied to a specific case. This movement from general to specific involves a three-step form of reasoning called a **syllogism.** The first part of a syllogism is called the **major premise,** a general statement about an entire group. The second part is the **minor premise,** a statement about an individual within that group. The syllogism ends with a **conclusion** about that individual.

Just as you use inductive thinking in everyday life, you use deductive thinking—often without being aware of it—to sort out your experiences. When trying to decide which car to buy, you might think as follows:

Major Premise   In an accident, large cars are safer than small cars.
Minor Premise   The Turbo Titan is a large car.
Conclusion   In an accident, the Turbo Titan will be safer than a small car.

Based on your conclusion, you might decide to take a specific action, buying the Turbo Titan rather than the smaller car you had first considered.

To create a valid syllogism and thus arrive at a sound conclusion, you need to avoid two major pitfalls of deductive reasoning. First, be sure not to start with a *sweeping* or *hasty generalization* (see page 228 in Chapter 13) as your *major premise.* Second, don't accept as truth a *faulty conclusion.* Let's look at each problem.

Sweeping major premise. Perhaps you're concerned about a trash-to-steam incinerator scheduled to open near your home. Your thinking about the situation might follow these lines:

Major Premise Trash-to-steam incinerators have had serious problems and pose significant threats to the well-being of people living near the plants.

Minor Premise The proposed incinerator in my neighborhood will be a trash-to-steam plant.

Conclusion The proposed trash-to-steam incinerator in my neighborhood will have serious problems and pose significant threats to the well-being of people living near the plant.

Having arrived at this conclusion, you might decide to join organized protests against the opening of the incinerator. But your thinking is somewhat illogical. Your *major premise* is a *sweeping* one because it indiscriminately groups all trash-to-steam plants into a single category. It's unlikely that you're familiar with all the trash-to-steam incinerators in this country and abroad; it's probably not true that *all* such plants have had serious difficulties that endangered the public. For your argument to reach a valid conclusion, the major premise must be based on repeated observations or verifiable facts. You would have a better argument, and thus reach a more valid conclusion, if you restricted or qualified the major premise, applying it to some, not all, of the group:

Major Premise A *number* of trash-to-steam incinerators have had serious problems and posed significant threats to the well-being of people living near the plants.

Minor Premise The proposed incinerator in my neighborhood will be a trash-to-steam plant.

Conclusion *It's possible* that the proposed trash-to-steam incinerator in my neighborhood will run into serious problems and pose significant threats to the well-being of people living near the plant.

This new conclusion, the result of more careful reasoning, would probably encourage you to learn more about trash-to-steam incinerators in general and about the proposed plant in particular. If further research still left you feeling uncomfortable about the plant, you would probably decide to join the protest. On the other hand, your research might convince you that the plant has incorporated into its design a number of safeguards that have been successful at other plants. This added information could reassure you that your original fears were unfounded. In either case, the revised deductive process would lead to a more informed conclusion and course of action.

Faulty conclusion. Your syllogism—and thus your reasoning—would also be invalid if your *conclusion reverses the "if...then" relationship implied in the major premise.* Assume you plan to write a letter to the college newspaper urging the resignation of the student government president. Perhaps you pursue a line of reasoning that goes like this:

Major Premise	Students who plagiarize papers must appear before the Faculty Committee on Academic Policies and Procedures.
Minor Premise	Yesterday Jennifer Kramer, president of the student government, appeared before the Faculty Committee on Academic Policies and Procedures.
Conclusion	Jennifer must have plagiarized a paper.
Action	Jennifer should resign her position as student government president.

Such a chain of reasoning is illogical and unfair. Here's why. *If* students plagiarize their term papers and are caught, *then* they must appear before the committee. However, the converse isn't necessarily true—that *if* students appear before the committee, *then* they must have plagiarized. In other words, not *all* students appearing before the Faculty Committee have been called up on plagiarism charges. For instance, Jennifer could have been speaking on behalf of another student; she could have been protesting some action taken by the committee; she could have been seeking the committee's help on an article she plans to write about academic honesty. The conclusion doesn't allow for these other possible explanations.

Now that you're aware of the problems associated with deductive reasoning, let's look at the way you can use a syllogism to structure an argumentation-persuasion essay. Suppose you decide to write a paper advocating support for a projected space mission. You know that controversy surrounds the space program, especially since seven astronauts died in a 1986 launch. Confident that the tragedy has led to more rigorous controls, you want to argue that the benefits of an upcoming mission outweigh its risks. A deductive pattern could be used to develop your argument. In fact, outlining your thinking as a syllogism might help you formulate a proposition, organize your evidence, deal with the opposing viewpoint, and—if appropriate—propose a course of action:

Major Premise	Space programs in the past have led to important developments in technology, especially in medical science.
Minor Premise	The *Cosmos* Mission is the newest space program.
Proposition (*essay might be persuasive*)	The *Cosmos* Mission will most likely lead to important developments in technology, especially in medical science.
Proposition (*essay is clearly persuasive*)	Congress should continue its funding of the *Cosmos* Mission.

Having outlined the deductive pattern of your thinking, you might begin by stating your proposition and then discuss some new procedures developed to protect the astronauts and the rocket system's structural integrity. With that background established, you could detail the opposing claim that little of value has been produced by the space program so far. You could then move to your refutation, citing significant medical advances derived from former space missions. Finally, the paper might conclude on a persuasive note, with a plea to Congress to continue funding the latest space mission.

8. Use Toulmin logic to establish a strong connection between your evidence and thesis. Whether you use an essentially inductive or deductive approach, your argument depends on strong evidence. In *The Uses of Argument,* Stephen Toulmin describes a useful approach for strengthening the connection between evidence and thesis. Toulmin divides a typical argument into three parts:

- **Claim**—the thesis, proposition, or conclusion
- **Data**—the evidence (facts, statistics, examples, observations, expert opinion) used to convince readers of the claim's validity
- **Warrant**—the underlying assumption that justifies moving from evidence to claim.

Here's a sample argument using Toulmin's terminology:

The train engineer was under the influence of drugs when the train crashed.

(Data)

Transportation employees entrusted with the public's safety should be tested for drug use.

(Claim)

Transportation employees entrusted with the public's safety should not be allowed on the job if they use drugs.

(Warrant)

As Toulmin explains in his book, readers are more apt to consider your argument valid if they know what your warrant is. Sometimes your warrant will be so obvious that you won't need to state it explicitly; an *implicit warrant* will be sufficient. Assume you want to argue that the use of live animals to test product toxicity should be outlawed. To support your claim, you cite the following evidence: first, current animal tests are painful and usually result in the animal's death; second, human cell cultures frequently offer more reliable information on how harmful a product may be to human tissue; and third, computer simulations often can more accurately rate a substance's toxicity. Your warrant, although not explicit, is nonetheless clear: "It is wrong to continue product testing on animals when more humane and valid test methods are available."

Other times, you'll do best to make your *warrant explicit.* Suppose you plan to argue that students should be involved in deciding which faculty members are granted tenure. To develop your claim, you present some evidence. You begin by noting that, currently, only faculty members and administrators review candidates for tenure. Next, you call attention to the controversy surrounding two professors, widely known by students to be poor teachers, who were nonetheless granted tenure. Finally, you cite a decision, made several years ago, to discontinue using student evaluations as part of the tenure process; you emphasize that since that time complaints about teachers' incompetence have risen dramatically. Some readers, though, still might wonder how you got from your evidence to your claim. In this case, your argument could be made stronger by stating your warrant explicitly: "Since students are as knowledgeable as the faculty and administrators about which professors are competent, they should be involved in the tenure process."

The more widely accepted your warrant, Toulmin explains, the more likely it is that readers will accept your argument. If there's no consensus about the warrant, you'll probably need to *back it up*. For the preceding example, you might mention several reports that found students evaluate faculty fairly (most students don't, for example, use the ratings to get back at professors against whom they have a personal grudge); further, students' ratings correlate strongly with those given by administrators and other faculty.

Toulmin describes another way to increase receptivity to an argument: *qualify the claim*—that is, explain under what circumstances it might be invalid or restricted. For instance, you might grant that most students know little about their instructors' research activities, scholarly publications, or participation in professional committees. You could, then, qualify your claim this way: "Because students don't have a comprehensive view of their instructors' professional activities, they should be involved in the tenure process but play a less prominent role than faculty and administrators."

As you can see, Toulmin's approach provides strategies for strengthening an argument. So, when prewriting or revising, take a few minutes to ask yourself the following questions:

- What data (*evidence*) should I provide to support my claim (*thesis*)?
- Is my warrant clear? Should I state it explicitly? What back-up can I provide to justify my warrant?
- Would qualifying my claim make my argument more convincing?

Your responses to these questions will help you structure a convincing and logical argument.

9. Recognize logical fallacies. When writing an argumentation-persuasion essay, you need to recognize **logical fallacies** both in your own argument and in points raised by the opposing side. Work to eliminate such gaps in logic from your own writing and, when they appear in the opposing argument, try to expose them in your refutation. Logicians have identified many logical fallacies—including the sweeping or hasty generalization and the faulty conclusion discussed earlier in this chapter. Other logical fallacies are described in Ann McClintock's "Propaganda Techniques in Today's Advertising" (page 277) and in the paragraphs that follow.

The *post hoc* **fallacy** (short for a Latin phrase meaning "after this, therefore because of this") occurs when you conclude that a cause-effect relationship exists simply because one event preceded another. Let's say you note the growing number of immigrants settling in a nearby city, observe the city's economic decline, and conclude that the immigrants' arrival caused the decline. Such a chain of thinking is faulty because it assumes a cause-effect relationship based purely on co-occurrence. Perhaps the immigrants' arrival was a factor in the economic slump, but there could also be other reasons: the lack of financial incentives to

attract business to the city, restrictions on the size of the city's manufacturing facilities, citywide labor disputes that make companies leery of settling in the area.
Your argument should also consider these possibilities. (For more on the *post hoc*
fallacy, see page 374 in Chapter 17.)

The *non sequitur* **fallacy** (Latin for "it does not follow") is an even more blatant
muddying of cause-effect relationships. In this case, a conclusion is drawn that has
no logical connection to the evidence cited: "Millions of Americans own cars, so
there is no need to fund public transportation." The faulty conclusion disregards
the millions of Americans who don't own cars; it also ignores pollution and road
congestion, both of which could be reduced if people had access to safe, reliable
public transportation.

An *ad hominem* **argument** (from the Latin meaning "to the man") occurs when
someone attacks a person rather than a point of view. Suppose your college plans
to sponsor a physicians' symposium on the abortion controversy. You decide to
write a letter to the school paper opposing the symposium. Taking swipes at two
of the invited doctors who disapprove of abortion, you mention that one was
recently involved in a messy divorce and that the other is alleged to have a drinking problem. By hurling personal invective, you avoid discussing the issue. Mud-
slinging is a poor substitute for reasoned argument. And as politician Adlai
Stevenson once said, "He who slings mud generally loses ground."

Appeals to questionable or faulty authority also weaken an argument. Most of
us have developed a healthy suspicion of phrases like *sources close to, an unidenti-
fied spokesperson states, experts claim,* and *studies show.* If these people and reports
are so reliable, they should be clearly identified.

Begging the question involves failure to establish proof for a debatable point.
The writer expects readers to accept as given a premise that's actually controversial. For instance, you would have trouble convincing readers that prayer should
be banned from public schools if you based your argument on the premise that
school prayer violates the U.S. Constitution. If the Constitution does, either explicitly or implicitly, prohibit prayer in public education, your essay must demonstrate that fact. You can't build a strong argument if you pretend there's no
controversy surrounding your premise.

A **false analogy** disregards significant dissimilarities and wrongly implies that
because two things share *some* characteristics, they are therefore *alike in all respects.*
You might, for example, compare nicotine and marijuana. Both, you could mention, involve health risks and have addictive properties. If, however, you go on to
conclude, "Driving while smoking a cigarette isn't illegal, so driving while smoking marijuana shouldn't be illegal either," you're employing a false analogy.
You've overlooked a major difference between tobacco and marijuana: Marijuana
impairs perception and coordination—important aspects of driving—while
there's no evidence that tobacco does the same.

The *either/or* **fallacy** occurs when you assume that a particular viewpoint or
course of action can have only one of two diametrically opposed outcomes—
either totally this or totally that. Say you argue as follows: "Unless colleges continue to offer scholarships based solely on financial need, no one who is underprivileged will be able to attend college." Such a statement ignores the fact that

bright, underprivileged students could receive scholarships based on their potential or their demonstrated academic excellence.

Finally, a **red herring** argument is an intentional digression from the issue—a ploy to deflect attention from the matter being discussed. Imagine you're arguing that condoms shouldn't be dispensed to high school students. You would introduce a red herring if you began to rail against parents who fail to provide their children with any information about sex. Most people would agree that parents *should* provide such information. However, the issue being discussed is not parents' irresponsibility but the pros and cons of schools' distributing condoms to students.

REVISION STRATEGIES

Once you have a draft of the essay, you're ready to revise. The following checklist will help you and those giving you feedback apply to argumentation-persuasion some of the revision techniques discussed in Chapters 7 and 8.

☑ ARGUMENTATION-PERSUASION: A REVISION CHECKLIST

Revise Overall Meaning and Structure

☐ What issue is being discussed? What is controversial about it?

☐ What is the essay's thesis? How does it differ from a generalization or mere statement of fact?

☐ What is the essay's purpose? To win readers over to a point of view? To spur readers to action? What action?

☐ For what audience is the essay written? What strategies are used to make readers receptive to the essay's thesis?

☐ What tone does the essay project? Is the tone likely to win readers over? Why or why not?

☐ If the essay's argument is essentially deductive, is the major premise sufficiently restricted? What repeated observations or verifiable facts is the premise based on? Are the minor premise and conclusion valid? If not, how could these problems be corrected?

☐ Where is the essay weakened by hasty generalizations, a failure to weigh evidence honestly, or a failure to draw the most valid conclusion?

☐ Where does the essay commit any of the following *logical* fallacies: Concluding that a cause-effect relationship exists simply because one event preceded another? Attacking a person rather than an issue? Drawing a conclusion that isn't logically related to the evidence? Failing to establish proof for a debatable point? Relying on questionable or vaguely specified authority? Drawing a false analogy? Resorting to *either/or* thinking?

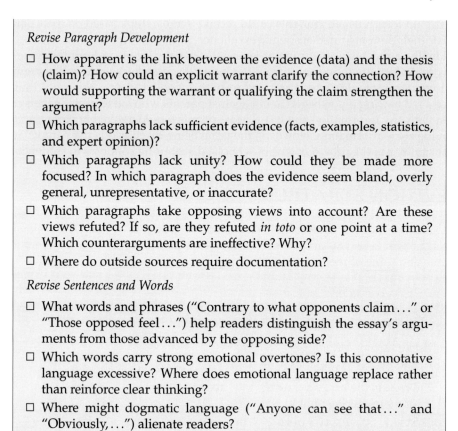

Revise Paragraph Development

☐ How apparent is the link between the evidence (data) and the thesis (claim)? How could an explicit warrant clarify the connection? How would supporting the warrant or qualifying the claim strengthen the argument?

☐ Which paragraphs lack sufficient evidence (facts, examples, statistics, and expert opinion)?

☐ Which paragraphs lack unity? How could they be made more focused? In which paragraph does the evidence seem bland, overly general, unrepresentative, or inaccurate?

☐ Which paragraphs take opposing views into account? Are these views refuted? If so, are they refuted *in toto* or one point at a time? Which counterarguments are ineffective? Why?

☐ Where do outside sources require documentation?

Revise Sentences and Words

☐ What words and phrases ("Contrary to what opponents claim . . ." or "Those opposed feel . . .") help readers distinguish the essay's arguments from those advanced by the opposing side?

☐ Which words carry strong emotional overtones? Is this connotative language excessive? Where does emotional language replace rather than reinforce clear thinking?

☐ Where might dogmatic language ("Anyone can see that . . ." and "Obviously, . . .") alienate readers?

STUDENT ESSAY: FROM PREWRITING THROUGH REVISION

The student essay that follows was written by Mark Simmons in response to this assignment:

> In "Institution Is Not a Dirty Word," Fern Kupfer invites controversy by disputing the notion that placing a severely mentally disabled child in an institution is cruel and irresponsible. Select another controversial issue, one that you feel strongly about. Using logic and solid evidence, convince readers that your viewpoint is valid.

Before writing his essay, Mark used the prewriting strategy of *group brainstorming* to generate material on the subject he decided to write about: compulsory national service. In a lively give-and-take with friends, Mark jotted down, as they occurred, ideas that seemed especially promising. Later on, he typed up his jottings so he could review them more easily. At that point, he began to organize the material.

Mark's typed version of the brainstormed list is on page 457. The handwritten marks indicate his later efforts to organize the material. As you can see, he started organizing the list by crossing out one item (the possibility of low morale) and adding several others (for example, that compulsory national service would be a relatively inexpensive way to repair bridges and roads). Then he labeled points raised by the opposing side and his counterarguments. In the process, the essay's underlying structure began to emerge so clearly that he had no trouble preparing an outline, which is presented on pages 458–459.

Brainstorming

```
Compulsory service--ages 17-25

Two years--military or public service              Definition
Serve after high school or college

Israel has it, and it works well                   Example. Where to
                                                   use?

Nazi Germany had it, too

Too authoritarian                    Opposing position: Point 3
                                     (potentially fascist)
Start of a dictatorship

Can choose what kind of service

No uniforms                          Refutation of point 3
                                     (not fascist)
U.S. not a fascist country

Americans very lucky--economic opportunity,
right to vote, etc.

Take without giving                                Introduction

Should have to give--program provides that chance

Program too expensive

Pay--at least minimum wage           Opposing position:
                                     Point 1 (too expensive)
Have to provide housing, too

Can live at home
Payments from participating towns, cities, states      Less costly way to
                                                       repair bridges and
                                     Refutation of point 1   roads and help
Could be like AmeriCorps's small budget  (not expensive)  elderly and disabled

Low morale because forced? (Unlike Volunteer Peace Corps)
```

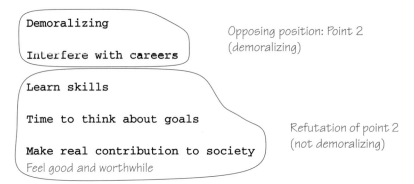

Demoralizing

Interfere with careers

*Opposing position: Point 2
(demoralizing)*

Learn skills

Time to think about goals

Make real contribution to society

Feel good and worthwhile

*Refutation of point 2
(not demoralizing)*

Outline

Thesis: Compulsory national service would be good for both young
people and the country.

   I. Definition of compulsory national service

  II. Cost of compulsory national service

     A. Would be expensive

       1. Would have high administrative costs

       2. Would have high salary and housing costs

     B. Wouldn't be expensive

       1. Could follow AmeriCorps model

       2. Would require the towns, cities, and states using the
corps to pay salary and housing costs

       3. Would cut costs by having young people live at home

       4. Would provide a cost-efficient way to repair deteriorat-
ing bridges, roads, and neighborhoods

       5. Would provide a cost-efficient way to help the elderly
and homeless

 III. Effect of compulsory national service on young people

     A. Would be demoralizing

       1. Would interrupt career plans

       2. Would waste young people's time by making them do work
that isn't personally meaningful

     B. Wouldn't be demoralizing

       1. Would give young people time to evaluate life and career
goals

       2. Would equip young people with marketable skills

       3. Would make young people from different backgrounds feel
good about coming together to contribute to society

  IV. Effect of compulsory national service on American democracy

A. Could encourage fascism, as it did in Germany

B. Wouldn't encourage fascism

   1. Wouldn't undermine our present system of checks and balances

   2. Would offer young people choices about when they would serve and in which branch they would serve

   3. Wouldn't require uniforms or confinement in a barracks

   4. Wouldn't be that different from a regular nine-to-five job

Now read Mark's paper, "Compulsory National Service," noting the similarities and differences between his prewriting, outline, and final essay. One difference is especially striking: During prewriting, Mark and his friends tended to identify an objection to compulsory service, brainstorm an appropriate counterargument, then move to the next objection and its counterargument. Mark used the same *point-by-point* format in his outline. When drafting his paper, though, Mark decided to use the *one-side-at-a-time* format. He summarized all reservations first, then devoted the rest of the essay to a detailed refutation. This change in organization strengthened Mark's argument because his rebuttals acquired greater force when gathered together, instead of remaining scattered throughout the paper. As you read the essay, also consider how well it applies the principles of argumentation-persuasion discussed in this chapter. (The commentary that follows the paper will help you look at Mark's essay more closely and will give you some sense of how he went about revising his first draft.)

Compulsory National Service

by Mark Simmons

1   Our high school history class spent several weeks studying the events of the 1960s. The most intriguing thing about that decade was the spirit of service and social commitment among young people. In the 60s, young people thought about issues beyond themselves; they joined the Peace Corps, worked in poverty-stricken Appalachian communities, and participated in freedom marches against segregation. Most young people today, despite their obvious concern with careers and getting ahead, would also like an opportunity to make a worthwhile contribution to society. Convinced that many young adults are indeed eager for such an opportunity, the Clinton administration implemented in 1994 a pilot program of voluntary national service. The following year, the program was formalized and given the name AmeriCorps. The program holds out so much promise that

Introduction

Common knowledge: No need to document

it seems only natural to go one step further and make participation for young people required. By instituting a program of
compulsory national service, our country could tap youth's idealistic desire to contribute. Such a system would yield
significant benefits.

Start of two-sentence thesis

Definition paragraph

Compulsory national service means that everyone between the   2
ages of 17 and 25 would serve the country for two years. Young
people could choose between two major options: military service
or a public-service corps. They could serve their time at any
point within the eight-year span. The unemployed or the uncertain could join immediately after high school; college-bound
students could complete their education before joining the
national service.

The idea of compulsory national service has been discussed   3
for many years, and some nations such as Israel have embraced
it wholeheartedly. The idea could also be workable in this
country. Unfortunately, detractors have prevented the idea from
taking hold. Opponents contend, first of all, that the program
would cost too much; they argue that a great deal of money would
have to be spent administering the program. In addition, young
people would have to receive at least a minimum wage for their
work, and some of them would need housing--both costly items.
Another argument against compulsory national service is that it
would demoralize young people; the plan would prevent the young
from getting on with their careers and would make them feel as
though they were engaged in work that had no personal reward. A
final argument is that compulsory service would lay the groundwork for a military state. The picture is painted of an army of
young robots totally at the mercy of the government, like the
Hitler Youth of the Second World War.

Topic sentence

Beginning of summary of three points raised by opposing viewpoint

Topic sentence: Refutation of first point

Despite opponents' claims that compulsory national service   4
would involve exorbitant costs, the program would not have
to be that expensive to run. AmeriCorps has already provided
an excellent model for achieving substantial benefits at reasonable cost. Also, the sums required for wages and housing
could be reduced considerably through payments made by the
towns, cities, and states using the corps' services. And
the economic benefits of the program could be significant.

The public-service corps could repair deteriorating bridges, highways, public buildings, and inner-city neighborhoods. The corps could organize recycling projects; it could staff public health clinics, day-care centers, legal aid centers, and homeless shelters. The corps could also monitor pollution, clean up litter, and help care for the country's growing elderly population. All of these projects would help solve many of the problems that plague our nation, and they would probably cost much less than if they were handled by traditional government bureaucracies or the private sector.

5   Also, rather than undermining the spirit of young people, as opponents contend, the program would probably boost their morale. Many young people feel enormous pressure and uncertainty. They are not sure what they want to do, or they have trouble finding a way to begin their careers. Compulsory national service could give young people a much-needed breathing space and could even equip them with the skills needed to start a career. Moreover, participating in compulsory national service could provide an emotional boost for the young; all of them would experience the pride that comes from working hard, reaching goals, acquiring skills, and handling responsibilities. A positive mind-set would also result from the sense of community that would be created by serving in the national service. All young people--rich or poor, educated or not, regardless of sex or social class--would come together during this time. Young people would grow to understand one another and learn that every person has an ability to aid the welfare of the whole group. Each young person would have the satisfaction of knowing that he or she has made a real contribution to the nation.

Topic sentence: Refutation of second point

6   Finally, contrary to what opponents claim, compulsory national service would not signal the start of a dictatorship. Although the service would be required, young people would have complete freedom to choose any two years between the ages of 17 and 25. They would also have complete freedom to choose the branch of the military or public-service corps that suits them best. And the corps would not need to be outfitted in military uniforms or to live in barracks-like camps. It could

Topic sentence: Refutation of third point

be set up like a regular job, with young people living at home
as much as possible, following a nine-to-five schedule, enjoying all the personal freedoms that would ordinarily be theirs.
Also, a dictatorship would no more likely emerge from a program
of compulsory national service than it has from our present
military system. We would still have a series of checks and
balances to prohibit the taking of power by one group or
individual. We should also keep in mind that our system is
different from that of fascist regimes; our long tradition of
personal liberty makes improbable the seizing of absolute power
by one person or faction. A related but even more important
point to remember is that freedom does not mean people are
guaranteed the right to pursue only their individual needs.
That is mistaking selfishness for freedom. And, as everyone
knows, selfishness leads only to misery. It cannot lead to a
happy life. The national service would not take away freedom.
On the contrary, it would help young people grasp this larger
concept of freedom, a concept that is badly needed to counteract the deadly "look out for number one" attitude that is
spreading like a poison across the nation.

Conclusion:
Echoes material in
introduction

Perhaps there will never be a time like the 1960s when so   7
many young people were concerned with remaking the world.
Still, a good many of today's young people want meaningful
work. They want to feel that what they do makes a difference. A
program of compulsory national service would tap this willingness in young people, helping them realize the best in themselves. Such a program would also allow us as a nation to make
substantial headway against the social problems that haunt the
country. AmeriCorps, an efficient and successful program of
voluntary service, has paved the way. Now seems the perfect
time to expand the concept and make compulsory national service
a reality.

Commentary

Blend of Argumentation and Persuasion

In his essay, Mark tackles a controversial issue: He takes the position that compulsory national service would benefit both the country as a whole and its young
people in particular. Mark's essay is a good example of the way argumentation

and persuasion often mix; although the paper presents Mark's position in a logical, well-reasoned manner (argumentation), it also appeals to readers' personal values and suggests a course of action (persuasion).

Audience Analysis

When planning the essay, Mark realized that his audience—his composition class—would consist largely of two kinds of readers. Some, not sure of their views, would be inclined to agree with him if he presented his case well. Others would probably be reluctant to accept his view. Because of this mixed audience, Mark knew he couldn't depend on *pathos* (an appeal to emotion) to convince readers. Rather, his argument had to rely mainly on *logos* (reason) and *ethos* (credibility). So Mark organized his essay around a series of logical arguments and evoked his own authority, drawing on his knowledge of history and his "inside" knowledge of young people.

Introduction and Thesis

Mark introduces his subject by discussing an earlier decade when large numbers of young people worked for social change. Mark's references to the Peace Corps, community work, and freedom marches reinforce his image as a knowledgeable source and establish a context for his position. These historical references, combined with the comments about President Clinton's program of voluntary national service, lead into the two-sentence thesis at the end of the introduction: "By instituting a system of compulsory national service, our country could tap youth's idealistic desire to contribute. Such a system would yield significant benefits."

Background Paragraph

The next paragraph is developed around a *definition* of compulsory national service. The definition guarantees that Mark's readers will share his understanding of the essay's central concept.

Acknowledging the Opposing Viewpoint

Mark is now in a good position to move into the body of his essay. Even though the assignment didn't call for research, Mark wisely decided to get together with some friends to brainstorm some issues that might be raised by the dissenting view. Using the *one-side-at-a-time* format, he acknowledges this position in the *topic sentence* of the essay's third paragraph: "Unfortunately, opponents have prevented the idea from taking hold." Next he summarizes the main points the dissenting opinion might advance: compulsory national service would be expensive, demoralizing to young people, and dangerously authoritarian. Mark uses the rest of the essay to counter these criticisms.

Refutation

The next three paragraphs (4–6) *refute* the opposing stance and present Mark's evidence for his position. Adapting material he brainstormed with friends, Mark structures the essay so that readers can follow his *counterargument* with ease. Each paragraph argues against one opposing point and begins with a *topic sentence* that serves as Mark's response to the dissenting view. Note the way the italicized portion of each topic sentence recalls a dissenting point cited earlier: "Despite opponents' claims that *compulsory national service would involve exorbitant costs,* the program would not have to be that expensive to run" (paragraph 4); "Also, rather than *undermining the spirit of young people,* as opponents contend, the program would probably boost their morale" (5); "Finally, contrary to what opponents claim, *compulsory national service would not signal the start of a dictatorship*" (6). Mark also guides the reader through the various points in the refutation by using *transitions* within paragraphs: "*And* the economic benefits...could be significant" (4); "*Moreover,* participating in compulsory national service could provide an emotional boost..." (5); "*Also,* a dictatorship would no more likely emerge..." (6).

Some Problems with the Refutation

Overall, Mark's three-paragraph refutation is strong, but it would have been even more effective if the paragraphs had been resequenced. As it now stands, the last paragraph (6) seems anticlimactic. The refutation would have been more persuasive if Mark had placed the final paragraph in the refutation in a less emphatic position. He could, for example, have put it first or second in the sequence, saving for last either of the other two more convincing paragraphs.

You may also have felt that there's another problem with the third paragraph in the refutation. Here, Mark seems to lose control of his counterargument. Beginning with "And, as everyone knows...," Mark falls into the *logical fallacy* called *begging the question.* He shouldn't assume that everyone agrees that a selfish life inevitably brings misery. He also indulges in charged emotionalism when he refers—somewhat melodramatically—to the "deadly 'look out for number one' attitude that is spreading like a poison across the nation."

Inductive Reasoning

Mark arrived at his position *inductively*—through an *inference* or *inductive leap.* He started with a number of specific observations about the nation and its young people. To support those observations, he added his friends' comments and insights. Combined, this material led him to the general *conclusion* that compulsory national service would be both workable and beneficial. In other words, Mark's evidence, as thoughtful and convincing as it may be, consists not of researched fact but of reasonable speculation.

Other Patterns of Development

To develop his argument, Mark draws on several patterns of development. The second paragraph relies on *definition* to clarify what is meant by compulsory national service. The introduction and conclusion *compare* and *contrast* young people of the 1960s with those of today. Finally, to support his position, Mark uses a kind of *causal analysis* that speculates on the likely consequences of compulsory national service.

Conclusion

Despite some minor problems along the way, Mark closes the essay effectively. He echoes the point made in the introduction about the 1960s and restates his thesis. The essay then ends with a crisp assertion that suggests a course of action.

Revising the First Draft

Mark revised his first draft with the help of two classmates, who used the checklist on pages 455–456 to focus their comments. After jotting his classmates' suggestions on a separate sheet, Mark transferred those he found most helpful to the margin of his paper. He then numbered the comments in order of importance. As Mark reviewed these notes, he realized that his introduction needed special attention.

A comparison of the introduction's original and final versions reveals the way Mark proceeded when revising. The annotations on the original (reprinted here) signal the problems that Mark and his partners saw in the first version.

Original Introduction

> "There's no free lunch." "You can't get something for nothing." "You have to earn your way." In America, these sayings are not really true. In America, we gladly take but give back little. In America, we receive economic opportunity, legal protection, the right to vote, and, most of all, a personal freedom unequaled throughout the world. How do we repay our country for such gifts? In most cases, we don't. This unfair relationship must be changed. The best way to make a start is to institute a system of national compulsory service for young people. This system would be of real benefit to the country and its citizens.

③ Choppy

① Focus right from start on young people—maybe mention youth of the 1960s

② Need stronger link between early part of paragraph and thesis

Following his classmates' suggestion, Mark deleted the introduction's references to Americans in general. He made this change because the paper focuses not on all Americans but on American youth. To reinforce this emphasis, he also added the point about the social commitment of young people who joined the Peace Corps in the 1960s and AmeriCorps in the 1990s. Besides providing a logical lead-in to the thesis, these references gave the discussion an important historical perspective and lent a note of authority to Mark's argument. Mark was also pleased to see that adding this new material helped unify and smooth out the paragraph.

These are just a few of the many changes Mark made while reworking his essay. Because he budgeted his time carefully, he was able to revise thoroughly. With the exception of some weak spots in the sixth paragraph, Mark's essay is well reasoned and convincing.

ACTIVITIES: ARGUMENTATION-PERSUASION

Prewriting Activities

1. Imagine you're writing two essays: One defines hypocrisy; the other contrasts license and freedom. Identify an audience for each essay (college students, professors, teenagers, parents, employers, employees, or some other group). Then jot down how each essay might argue the merits of certain ways of behaving.

2. Following are several thesis statements for argumentation-persuasion essays. For each thesis, determine whether the three audiences indicated in parentheses are apt to be supportive, wavering, or hostile. Then select *one* thesis and use group brainstorming to identify, for each audience, general concerns on which you might successfully base your persuasive appeal (for example, the concern for approval, for financial well-being, for self-respect, for the welfare of others).

   a. The minimum wage should be raised every two years (*low-income employees, employers, congressional representatives*).
   b. Students should not graduate from college until they have passed a comprehensive exam in their majors (*college students, their parents, college officials*).
   c. Abandoned homes owned by the city should be sold to low-income residents for a nominal fee (*city officials, low-income residents, general citizens*).
   d. The town should pass a law prohibiting residents near the reservoir from using pesticides on their lawns (*environmentalists, homeowners, members of the town council*).
   e. Faculty advisors to college newspapers should have the authority to prohibit the publication of articles that reflect negatively on the school (*alumni, college officials, student journalists*).

3. Using the thesis you selected in activity 2, focus—for each group indicated in parentheses—on one or two of the general concerns you identified. Then brainstorm with others to determine the specific points you'd make to persuade each group. How would Rogerian argument (pages 444–445) and other techniques (page 439) help you disarm the most hostile audience?

4. Clip an effective advertisement from a magazine or newspaper. Through brainstorming, determine to what extent the ad depends on *logos, ethos,* and *pathos.* Consider the persuasive approaches described in Ann McClintock's "Propaganda Techniques in Today's Advertising" (page 277) as well as the logical fallacies discussed in this chapter. After reviewing your brainstorming, devise a thesis that expresses your feelings about the ad's persuasive strategies. Are they responsible? Why or why not?

5. In a campus, local, or major newspaper, find an editorial with which you disagree. Using the patterns of development, freewriting, or another prewriting technique, generate points that refute the editorial. You may, for example, identify any logical fallacies in the editorial. Then, following one of the refutation strategies discussed in this chapter, organize your rebuttal, keeping in mind the power of Rogerian argument.

Revising Activities

6. Examine the following sets, each containing *data* (evidence) and a *claim* (thesis), For each set, identify the implied *warrant*. Which sets would benefit from an explicit warrant? Why? How might the warrant be expressed? In which sets would it be helpful to support the warrant or qualify the claim? Why? How might the warrant be supported or the claim qualified?

a. *Data:* An increasing number of Americans are buying Japanese cars. The reason, they report, is that Japanese cars tend to have superior fuel efficiency and longevity. Japanese cars are currently manufactured under stricter quality control than American models.
Claim: Implementing stricter quality controls is one way for the American auto industry to compete with Japanese imports.

b. *Data:* Although laws guarantee learning-impaired children an education suitable to their needs, no laws safeguard the special needs of intellectually gifted children. There are, proportionately, far more programs that assist the slow learner than there are those that challenge the fast learner.
Claim: Our educational system is unfair to gifted children.

c. *Data:* To date, no woman or nonwhite and only one non-Protestant (John F. Kennedy) has ever been elected president of the United States.
Claim: Until prejudicial attitudes change, American voters will not elect a president who is a female, a member of a racial minority, or a non-Protestant.

d. *Data:* Minors aren't permitted to vote, marry without parental consent, or sign contracts. Nevertheless, the Supreme Court has ruled that a minor can receive the full penalty of the law—in some cases, even be executed—for a crime.
Claim: Minors who engage in criminal acts should be treated with greater leniency than adults.

7. Examine the faulty chains of reasoning that follow. Which use essentially inductive logic? Which use essentially deductive logic? In each set, determine, in general terms, why the conclusion is invalid. (The next activity offers practice in identifying specific logical fallacies that render conclusions invalid.)

a. Whenever I work in the college's computer lab, something goes wrong. The program crashes, the cursor freezes, the margins unset themselves.
Conclusion: The college needs to allocate additional funds to repair and upgrade the computers in the lab.

b. Many cars in the student parking lot are dented and look as though they have been in accidents.
Conclusion: Students are careless drivers.

c. Many researchers believe that children in families where both parents work develop confidence and independence. In a nearby community, the number of two-career families increased 15 percent over a two-year period.
Conclusion: Children in the nearby community will develop confidence and independence.

d. The local Chamber of Commerce elected a woman as president. The all-male Metropolitan Business Club approved a woman for membership.
Conclusion: Traditionally conservative male groups are starting to accept women's role in business.

e. Anyone found guilty of sexual harassment will be fired by XYZ Corporation. Curt A. was fired by XYZ Corporation.
Conclusion: Curt A. is guilty of sexual harassment.

8. Each set of statements that follows contains at least one of the logical fallacies described earlier in the chapter and in Ann McClintock's essay "Propaganda Techniques in Today's Advertising" (page 277). Identify the fallacy or fallacies in each set and explain why the statements are invalid.

a. Grades are irrelevant to learning. Students are in college to get an education, not good grades. The university should eliminate grading altogether.

b. The best policy is to put juvenile offenders in jail so that they can get a taste of reality. Otherwise, they will repeat their crimes again and again.

c. Legal experts say that this bill will weaken consumers' rights. Based on their views, we should petition legislators not to sign the bill.

d. So-called sex education programs do nothing to decrease the rate of teenage pregnancy. Further expenditures on these programs should be curtailed.

e. This country should research environmentally sound ways to use coal as an energy source. If we don't, we will become enslaved to the oil-rich Middle East nations.

f. If we allow abortion, people will think it's acceptable to kill the homeless or pull the plug on sick people—two groups that are also weak and frail.

g. The curfews that some towns impose on teenagers are as repressive as the curfews in totalitarian countries.

h. Each day, Americans throw out ton after ton of edible food; it isn't true that some Americans suffer from hunger.

i. Two members of the state legislature have introduced gun-control legislation. Both have led sheltered, pampered lives that prevent them from seeing how ordinary people need guns to protect themselves.

j. Some say that auto insurance rates need to be more strictly regulated, but how strict are regulations on health insurance?

k. Last year, a few students managed to avoid paying for their parking decals. This year's increased student parking fees unfairly penalize everyone for the dishonesty of a few.

9. Following is the introduction from the first draft of an essay advocating the elimination of mandatory dress codes in public schools. Revise the paragraph, being sure to consider these questions: How effectively does the writer deal with the opposing viewpoint? Does the paragraph encourage those who might disagree with the writer to read on? Why or why not? Do you see any logical fallacies in the writer's thinking? Where? Does the writer introduce anything that veers away from the point being discussed? Where? Before revising, you may find it helpful to do some brainstorming—individually or in a group—to find ways to strengthen the paragraph.

After reworking the paragraph, take a few minutes to consider how the rest of the essay might unfold. What persuasive strategies could be used? How could Rogerian argument win over readers? What points could be made? What action could be urged in the effort to build a convincing argument?

```
In three nearby towns recently, high school administrators
joined forces to take an outrageously strong stand against stu-
dents' constitutional rights. Acting like Fascists, they issued an
edict in the form of a preposterous dress code that prohibits stu-
dents from wearing expensive jewelry, designer jeans, leather jack-
ets--anything that the administrators, in their supposed wisdom,
consider ostentatious. Perhaps the next thing they'll want to do
is forbid students to play rock music at school dances. What
prompted the administrators' dictatorial prohibition against cer-
tain kinds of clothing? Somehow or other, they got it into their
heads that having no restrictions on the way students dress cre-
ates an unhealthy environment, where students vie with each other
for the flashiest attire. Students and parents alike should pro-
test this and any other dress code. If such codes go into effect,
we might as well throw out the Constitution.
```

PROFESSIONAL
SELECTIONS:
ARGUMENTATION-
PERSUASION

FERN KUPFER

A teacher of writing at Iowa State University, Fern Kupfer (1946–) lectures nationally as an advocate for families with disabled children. Her works include three novels, *Surviving the Seasons* (1989), *No Regrets* (1990), *Love Lies* (1994), as well as *Before and After Zachariah* (1982), a book about the institutionalization of her severely disabled son. The following essay first appeared in *Newsweek* in 1982.

INSTITUTION IS NOT A DIRTY WORD

I watched Phil Donahue recently. He had on mothers of handicapped children who   1
talked about the pain and blessing of having a "special" child. As the mother of a
severely handicapped six-year-old boy who cannot sit, who cannot walk, who will be in
diapers all of his days, I understand the pain. The blessing part continues to elude
me—notwithstanding the kind and caring people we've met through this tragedy.

What really makes my jaws clench, though, is the use of the word "special." The   2
idea that our damaged children are "special," and that we as parents were somehow
picked for the role, is one of the myths that come with the territory. It's reinforced by
the popular media, which present us with heartwarming images of retarded people
who marry, of quadriplegics who fly airplanes, of those fortunate few who struggle out
of comas to teach us about the meaning of courage and love. I like these stories myself.
But, of course, inspirational tales are only one side of the story. The other side deals
with the daily care of a family member who might need more than many normal families can give. Parents who endure with silent stoicism or chin-up good humor are
greeted with kudos and applause. "I don't know how you do it," the well-wishers say,
not realizing, of course, that no one has a choice in this matter. No one would consciously choose to have a child anything less than healthy and normal. The other truth
is not spoken aloud: "Thank God, it's not me."

One mother on the Donahue show talked about how difficult it was to care for her   3
severely brain-damaged daughter, but in the end, she said serenely, "She gives much
more than she takes from our family." And no, she would never institutionalize her
child. She would never "put her away." For "she is my child," the woman firmly concluded as the audience clapped in approval. "I would never give her up."

Everyone always says how awful the institutions are. Don't they have bars on the   4
windows and children lying neglected in crowded wards? Aren't all the workers
sadists, taking direction from the legendary Big Nurse? Indeed, isn't institutionalizing a

child tantamount to locking him away? Signing him out of your life forever? Isn't it proof of your failure as a parent—one who couldn't quite measure up and love your child, no matter what?

5   No, to all of the above. And love is beside the point.

6   Our child Zachariah has not lived at home for almost four years. I knew when we placed him, sorry as I was, that this was the right decision, for his care precluded any semblance of normal family life for the rest of us. I do not think that we "gave him up," although he is cared for daily by nurses, caseworkers, teachers and therapists, rather than by his mother and father. When we come to visit him at his "residential facility," a place housing 50 severely physically and mentally handicapped youngsters, we usually see him being held and rocked by a foster grandma who has spent the better part of the afternoon singing him nursery rhymes. I do not feel that we have "put him away." Perhaps it is just a question of language. I told another mother who was going through the difficult decision regarding placement for her retarded child, "Think of it as going to boarding school rather than institutionalization." Maybe euphemisms help ease the pain a little bit. But I've also seen enough to know that institution need not be a dirty word.

7   The media still relish those institution horror stories: a page-one photo of a retarded girl who was repeatedly molested by the janitor on night duty. Oh, the newspapers have a field day with something like that. And that is how it should be, I suppose. To protect against institutional abuse we need critical reporters with sharpened pencils and a keen investigative eye. But there are other scenes from the institution as well. I've seen a young caseworker talk lovingly as she changed the diapers of a teen-age boy. I've watched as an aide put red ribbons into the ponytail of a cerebral-palsied woman, wiped away the drool and kissed her on the cheek. When we bring Zach back to his facility after a visit home, the workers welcome him with hugs and notice if we gave him a haircut or a new shirt.

8   The reporters don't make news out of that simple stuff. It doesn't mesh with the anti-institutional bias prevalent in the last few years, or the tendency to canonize the handicapped and their accomplishments. This anti-institutional trend has some very frightening ramifications. We force mental patients out into the real world of cheap welfare hotels and call it "community placement." We parole youthful offenders because "jails are such dangerous places to be," making our city streets dangerous places for the law-abiding. We heap enormous guilt on the families that need, for their own survival, to put their no-longer-competent elderly in that dreaded last stop: the nursing home.

9   Another danger is that in a time of economic distress for all of us, funds could be cut for human-service programs under the guise of anti-institutionalization. We must make sure, before we close the doors of those "awful" institutions, that we have alternative facilities to care for the clientele. The humanitarians who tell us how terrible institutions are should be wary lest they become unwilling bedfellows to conservative politicians who want to walk a tight fiscal line. It takes a lot of money to run institutions. No politician is going to say he's against the handicapped, but he can talk in sanctimonious terms about efforts to preserve the family unit, about families remaining independent and self-sufficient. Translated, this means, "You got your troubles, I got mine."

10   Most retarded people do not belong in institutions any more than most people over 65 belong in nursing homes. What we need are options and alternatives for a heterogeneous population. We need group homes and halfway houses and government subsidies

to families who choose to care for dependent members at home. We need accessible housing for independent handicapped people; we need to pay enough to foster-care families to show that a good home is worth paying for. We need institutions. And it shouldn't have to be a dirty word.

Questions for Close Reading

1. What is the selection's thesis? Locate the sentence(s) in which Kupfer states her main idea. If she doesn't state the thesis explicitly, express it in your own words.

2. What myths about disabled children does Kupfer identify?

3. According to Kupfer, what role do the media play in determining how we think about the disabled? What aspects of the problem do the media tend to ignore?

4. What are some of the negative effects of the "anti-institutional bias" that Kupfer points out?

5. Refer to your dictionary as needed to define the following words used in the selection: *quadriplegics* (paragraph 2), *stoicism* (2), *kudos* (2), *tantamount* (4), *fiscal* (9), *sanctimonious* (9), and *heterogeneous* (10).

Questions About the Writer's Craft

1. The pattern. The author of an argumentation-persuasion essay needs to establish his or her credibility. How does Kupfer do this?

2. Where does Kupfer refer to the opposing viewpoint? What strategy does she use to counter this view?

3. Other patterns. Locate places in the essay where Kupfer uses highly connotative, descriptive language. How do these descriptive passages affect her portrayal of the opposing view and help her develop her own position?

4. How would you describe Kupfer's tone? What roles do word choice, sentence structure, and punctuation (especially quotation marks) play in establishing this tone?

Writing Assignments Using Argumentation-Persuasion as a Pattern of Development

1. In paragraph 8, Kupfer mentions other institutions she believes our society is biased against: mental hospitals, jails for juvenile offenders, nursing homes for the elderly. In an essay, argue for or against one of these institutions as a way to handle a social problem. Devote at least one paragraph to refuting the opposing viewpoint.

2. As a lead-in to her argument, Kupfer describes a talk-show discussion. Watch or listen to a talk show dealing with a controversial life-style or community problem.

After evaluating the points of view expressed, write an argumentation-persuasion essay that advances your position on the issue. Part of the essay should acknowledge, perhaps rebut, the opposing viewpoint.

Writing Assignments Using Other Patterns of Development

∞ **3.** Kupfer's essay tells the "other side" of an experience. In an essay of your own, do the same. Contrast the way the media have portrayed some situation or event with the way it really is. For example, you might contrast your college newspaper's account of an unruly student senate meeting with what really happened. Or you might contrast television's glamorous depiction of two-career families with the grinding everyday reality. For insight into the media's often skewed portrayal of life, read Joyce Garity's "Is Sex All That Matters?" (page 252) and Pete Hamill's "Crack and the Box" (page 356).

4. Kupfer objects to the use of the word *special* for severely disabled children. In an essay, explain why you object to some other term (perhaps *senior citizen, yuppie,* or *tree hugger*) used to describe a particular group of people. Use examples to show why you feel the term is inaccurate or unfair.

CARYL RIVERS

A journalism professor at Boston University, Caryl Rivers (1937–) has authored numerous articles for newspapers and magazines. Her many books include three novels, *Virgins* (1984), *Intimate Enemies* (1987), and *Indecent Behavior* (1990), as well as works on contemporary culture: *More Joy Than Rage: Crossing Generations with the New Feminism* (1991); *Slick Spins and Fractured Facts: How Cultural Myths Distort the News* (1996); and *He Works/She Works: How the American Family Is Making It Work* (1996), which she coauthored. The following essay first appeared in the *Boston Globe* in 1985.

WHAT SHOULD BE DONE ABOUT ROCK LYRICS?

1   After a grisly series of murders in California, possibly inspired by the lyrics of a rock song, we are hearing a familiar chorus: don't blame rock and roll. Kids will be kids. They love to rebel, and the more shocking the stuff, the better they like it.

2   There's some truth in this, of course. I loved to watch Elvis shake his torso when I was a teenager, and it was even more fun when Ed Sullivan wouldn't let the cameras show him below the waist. I snickered at the forbidden "Rock With Me, Annie" lyrics by a black rhythm and blues group, which were deliciously naughty. But I am sorry, rock fans, that is not the same thing as hearing lyrics about how a man is going to force a woman to perform oral sex on him at gunpoint in a little number called "Eat Me Alive." It is not in the same league with a song about the delights of slipping into a

woman's room while she is sleeping and murdering her, the theme of an AC/DC ballad that allegedly inspired the California slayer.

Make no mistake, it is not sex we are talking about here, but violence. Violence 3 against women. Most rock songs are not violent—they are funky, sexy, rebellious, and sometimes witty. Please do not mistake me for a Mrs. Grundy. If Prince wants to leap about wearing only a purple jock strap, fine. Let Mick Jagger unzip his fly as he gyrates, if he wants to. But when either one of them starts garroting, beating, or sodomizing a woman in their number, that is another story.

I always find myself annoyed when "intellectual" men dismiss violence against 4 women with a yawn, as if it were beneath their dignity to notice. I wonder if the reaction would be the same if the violence were directed against someone other than women. How many people would yawn and say, "Oh, kids will be kids" if a rock group did a nifty little number called "Lynchin," in which stringing up and stomping on black people were set to music? Who would chuckle and say, "Oh, just a little adolescent rebellion" if a group of rockers went on MTV dressed as Nazis, desecrating synagogues and beating up Jews to the beat of twanging guitars?

I'll tell you what would happen. Prestigious dailies would thunder on editorial 5 pages; senators would fall over each other to get denunciations into the *Congressional Record.* The president would appoint a commission to clean up the music business.

But violence against women is greeted by silence. It shouldn't be.   6

This does not mean censorship, or book (or record) burning. In a society that pro- 7 tects free expression, we understand a lot of stuff will float up out of the sewer. Usually, we recognize the ugly stuff that advocates violence against any group as the garbage it is, and we consider its purveyors as moral lepers. We hold our nose and tolerate it, but we speak out against the values it proffers.

But images of violence against women are not staying on the fringes of society. No 8 longer are they found only in tattered, paper-covered books or in movie houses where winos snooze and the scent of urine fills the air. They are entering the mainstream at a rapid rate. This is happening at a time when the media, more and more, set the agenda for the public debate. It is a powerful legitimizing force—especially television. Many people regard what they see on TV as the truth; Walter Cronkite once topped a poll as the most trusted man in America.

Now, with the advent of rock videos and all-music channels, rock music has grabbed 9 a big chunk of legitimacy. American teenagers have instant access, in their living rooms, to the messages of rock, on the same vehicle that brought them *Sesame Street.* Who can blame them if they believe that the images they see are accurate reflections of adult reality, approved by adults? After all, Big Bird used to give them lessons on the same little box. Adults, by their silence, sanction the images. Do we really want our kids to think that rape and violence are what sexuality is all about?

This is not a trivial issue. Violence against women is a major social problem, one 10 that's more than a cerebral issue to me. I teach at Boston University, and one of my most promising young journalism students was raped and murdered. Two others told me of being raped. Recently, one female student was assaulted and beaten so badly she had $5,000 worth of medical bills and permanent damage to her back and eyes.

It's nearly impossible, of course, to make a cause-and-effect link between lyrics and 11 images and acts of violence. But images have a tremendous power to create an atmosphere in which violence against certain people is sanctioned. Nazi propagandists knew that full well when they portrayed Jews as ugly, greedy, and powerful.

12   The outcry over violence against women, particularly in a sexual context, is being legitimized in two ways: by the increasing movement of these images into the mainstream of the media in TV, films, magazines, albums, videos, and by the silence about it.

13   Violence, of course, is rampant in the media. But it is usually set in some kind of moral context. It's usually only the bad guys who commit violent acts against the innocent. When the good guys get violent, it's against those who deserve it. Dirty Harry blows away the scum; he doesn't walk up to a toddler and say, "Make my day." The A team does not shoot up suburban shopping malls.

14   But in some rock songs, it's the "heroes" who commit the acts. The people we are programmed to identify with are the ones being violent, with women on the receiving end. In a society where rape and assaults on women are endemic, this is no small problem, with millions of young boys watching on their TV screens and listening on their Walkmans.

15   I think something needs to be done. I'd like to see people in the industry respond to the problem. I'd love to see some women rock stars speak out against violence against women. I would like to see disc jockeys refuse air play to records and videos that contain such violence. At the very least, I want to see the end of the silence. I want journalists and parents and critics and performing artists to keep this issue alive in the public forum. I don't want people who are concerned about this issue labeled as bluenoses and bookburners and ignored.

16   And I wish it wasn't always just women who were speaking out. Men have as large a stake in the quality of our civilization as women do in the long run. Violence is a contagion that infects at random. Let's hear something, please, from the men.

Questions for Close Reading

1. What is the selection's thesis? Locate the sentence(s) in which Rivers states her main idea. If she doesn't state the thesis explicitly, express it in your own words.

2. What about rock music does Rivers find acceptable—even enjoyable? What does Rivers mean when she says in paragraph 3 that she doesn't want to be mistaken for a "Mrs. Grundy"?

3. How, according to Rivers, does television contribute to the problem of rock music's violence against women?

4. Why does Rivers think that the "outcry against violence" is legitimate, even necessary? What form does Rivers believe this outcry should take?

5. Refer to your dictionary as needed to define the following words used in the selection: *grisly* (paragraph 1), *garroting* (3), *purveyors* (7), *sanction* (9 and 11), *cerebral* (10), *propagandists* (11), *endemic* (14), and *contagion* (16).

Questions About the Writer's Craft

1. The pattern. When presenting her argument, Rivers often refers to opposing views. Which opposing views does she refute? Which does she concede? Why do you think she proceeds in this manner?

2. Other patterns. Rivers uses comparison-contrast in several places in the essay. Locate some of these comparisons and/or contrasts. How does Rivers's use of comparison-contrast help support her thesis?

3. Throughout much of her essay, Rivers writes in the first person and, in paragraph 2, she addresses the reader directly. What effect does her use of the first and second person have on her credibility and on her essay's tone?

4. Rivers sprinkles highly connotative language throughout the essay. Locate some of this language in the selection. What effect do you think Rivers hoped such language would have on the reader?

Writing Assignments Using Argumentation-Persuasion as a Pattern of Development

1. Spend some time watching rock videos on television, taking notes on those that support and those that refute Rivers's criticism. Weigh your observations carefully and decide whether you agree with Rivers that rock music's images and lyrics promote violence against women. Remembering to acknowledge opposing views, write an essay agreeing or disagreeing with Rivers. Use your observations to support your thesis.

∞ **2.** Asserting that we live in a time when "assaults on women are endemic," Rivers attributes this problem mainly to rock lyrics. But there are other factors in our society that contribute to the problem: substance abuse, advertising messages, cultural definitions of appropriate male and female behavior, and so on. Select *one* of these factors, or another that seems important, and write an essay arguing that this factor is *more* critical than rock music in inciting violence against women. Near the beginning of the essay, point out the limitations of Rivers's perspective. Susan Douglas's "Managing Mixed Messages" (page 247) and Deborah Tannen's "But What Do You Mean?" (page 283) will provide insights to draw on when you write.

Writing Assignments Using Other Patterns of Development

3. Rivers is outraged by the silence surrounding rock music's violence against women. In an essay, present the steps that *one* of the following—families, schools, or religious institutions—should take to end the silence. Before explaining what should be done, present several vivid examples to dramatize that there is indeed a problem that needs to be addressed.

∞ **4.** Critics accuse not only rock videos but also television in general of fostering harmful images of women, men, teenagers, ethnic and racial minorities, and the elderly. Write an essay illustrating television's distorted depiction of *one* of these groups. Brainstorm with others to gather compelling examples to support your thesis. Where appropriate, cite points made by Pete Hamill in "Crack and the Box" (page 356).

Debating the Issues: Capital Punishment

EDWARD I. KOCH

Following a stint in the U.S. House of Representatives, controversial and outspoken Edward I. Koch (1924–) served as mayor of New York City from 1977 to 1989. He was elected after campaigning on an anti-crime and anti-spending platform. Koch, who now presides over a popular TV courtroom show, has written two autobiographical books, *Mayor* (1984) and *Politics* (1985). He also coauthored the book *His Eminence and Hizzoner* (1989) with the equally controversial John Cardinal O'Connor. The following essay was published in the *New Republic* in 1985.

DEATH AND JUSTICE

1   Last December [1984] a man named Robert Lee Willie, who had been convicted of raping and murdering an 18-year-old woman, was executed in the Louisiana state prison. In a statement issued several minutes before his death, Mr. Willie said: "Killing people is wrong....It makes no difference whether it's citizens, countries, or governments. Killing is wrong." Two weeks later in South Carolina, an admitted killer named Joseph Carl Shaw was put to death for murdering two teenagers. In an appeal to the governor for clemency, Mr. Shaw wrote: "Killing is wrong when I did it. Killing is wrong when you do it. I hope you have the courage and moral strength to stop the killing."

2   It is a curiosity of modern life that we find ourselves being lectured on morality by cold-blooded killers. Mr. Willie previously had been convicted of aggravated rape, aggravated kidnapping, and the murders of a Louisiana deputy and a man from Missouri. Mr. Shaw committed another murder a week before the two for which he was executed, and admitted mutilating the body of the 14-year-old girl he killed. I can't help wondering what prompted these murderers to speak out against killing as they entered the death-house door. Did their newfound reverence for life stem from the realization that they were about to lose their own?

3   Life is indeed precious, and I believe the death penalty helps to affirm this fact. Had the death penalty been a real possibility in the minds of these murderers, they might well have stayed their hand. They might have shown moral awareness before their victims died, and not after. Consider the tragic death of Rosa Velez, who happened to be home when a man named Luis Vera burglarized her apartment in Brooklyn. "Yeah, I shot her," Vera admitted. "She knew me, and I knew I wouldn't go to the chair."

4   During my 22 years in public service, I have heard the pros and cons of capital punishment expressed with special intensity. As a district leader, councilman, congressman, and mayor, I have represented constituencies generally thought of as liberal. Because I support the death penalty for heinous crimes of murder, I have sometimes been the subject of emotional and outraged attacks by voters who find my position reprehensible or worse. I have listened to their ideas. I have weighed their objections carefully. I still support the death penalty. The reasons I maintained my position can be best understood by examining the arguments most frequently heard in opposition.

5   ***1. The death penalty is "barbaric."*** Sometimes opponents of capital punishment horrify us with tales of lingering death on the gallows, of faulty electric chairs, or of agony in the gas chamber. Partly in response to such protests, several states such as

North Carolina and Texas switched to execution by lethal injection. The condemned person is put to death painlessly, without ropes, voltage, bullets, or gas. Did this answer the objections of death penalty opponents? Of course not. On June 22, 1984, the *New York Times* published an editorial that sarcastically attacked the new "hygienic" method of death by injection, and stated that "execution can never be made humane through science." So it's not the method that really troubles opponents. It's the death itself they consider barbaric.

Admittedly, capital punishment is not a pleasant topic. However, one does not have   6
to like the death penalty in order to support it any more than one must like radical surgery, radiation, or chemotherapy in order to find necessary these attempts at curing cancer. Ultimately we may learn how to cure cancer with a simple pill. Unfortunately, that day has not yet arrived. Today we are faced with the choice of letting the cancer spread or trying to cure it with the methods available, methods that one day will almost certainly be considered barbaric. But to give up and do nothing would be far more barbaric and would certainly delay the discovery of an eventual cure. The analogy between cancer and murder is imperfect, because murder is not the "disease" we are trying to cure. The disease is injustice. We may not like the death penalty, but it must be available to punish crimes of cold-blooded murder, cases in which any other form of punishment would be inadequate and, therefore, unjust. If we create a society in which injustice is not tolerated, incidents of murder—the most flagrant form of injustice—will diminish.

2. No other major democracy uses the death penalty. No other major democ-   7
racy—in fact, few other countries of any description—are plagued by a murder rate such as that in the United States. Fewer and fewer Americans can remember the days when unlocked doors were the norm and murder was a rare and terrible offense. In America the murder rate climbed 122 percent between 1963 and 1980. During that same period, the murder rate in New York City increased by almost 400 percent, and the statistics are even worse in many other cities. A study at M.I.T. showed that based on 1970 homicide rates a person who lived in a large American city ran a greater risk of being murdered than an American soldier in World War II ran of being killed in combat. It is not surprising that the laws of each country differ according to differing conditions and traditions. If other countries had our murder problem, the cry for capital punishment would be just as loud as it is here. And I daresay that any other major democracy where 75 percent of the people supported the death penalty would soon enact it into law.

3. An innocent person might be executed by mistake. Consider the work of   8
Adam Bedau, one of the most implacable foes of capital punishment in this country. According to Mr. Bedau, it is "false sentimentality to argue that the death penalty should be abolished because of the abstract possibility that an innocent person might be executed." He cites a study of the 7,000 executions in this country from 1893 to 1971, and concludes that the record fails to show that such cases occur. The main point, however, is this. If government functioned only when the possibility of error didn't exist, government wouldn't function at all. Human life deserves special protection, and one of the best ways to guarantee that protection is to assure that convicted murderers do not kill again. Only the death penalty can accomplish this end. In a recent case in New Jersey, a man named Richard Biegenwald was freed from prison after serving 18 years for murder; since his release he has been convicted of committing four murders. A

prisoner named Lemuel Smith, while serving four life sentences for murder (plus two life sentences for kidnapping and robbery) in New York's Green Haven Prison, lured a woman corrections officer into the chaplain's office and strangled her. He then mutilated and dismembered her body. An additional life sentence for Smith is meaningless. Because New York has no death penalty statute, Smith has effectively been given a license to kill.

9   But the problem of multiple murder is not confined to the nation's penitentiaries. In 1981, 91 police officers were killed in the line of duty in this country. Seven percent of those arrested in the cases that have been solved had a previous arrest for murder. In New York City in 1976 and 1977, 85 persons arrested for homicide had a previous arrest for murder. Six of these individuals had two previous arrests for murder, and one had four previous murder arrests. During those two years the New York police were arresting for murder persons with a previous arrest for murder on the average of one every 8.5 days. This is not surprising when we learn that in 1975, for example, the median time served in Massachusetts for homicide was less than two and a half years. In 1976 a study sponsored by the Twentieth Century Fund found that the average time served in the United States for first degree murder is ten years. The median time served may be considerably lower.

10   **4. *Capital punishment cheapens the value of human life.*** On the contrary, it can be easily demonstrated that the death penalty strengthens the value of human life. If the penalty for rape were lowered, clearly it would signal a lessened regard for the victims' suffering, humiliation, and personal integrity. It would cheapen their horrific experience, and expose them to an increased danger of recurrence. When we lower the penalty for murder, it signals a lessened regard for the value of the victim's life. Some critics of capital punishment, such as columnist Jimmy Breslin, have suggested that a life sentence is actually a harsher penalty for murder than death. This is sophistic nonsense. A few killers may decide not to appeal a death sentence, but the overwhelming majority make every effort to stay alive. It is by exacting the highest penalty for the taking of human life that we affirm the highest value of human life.

11   **5. *The death penalty is applied in a discriminatory manner.*** This factor no longer seems to be the problem it once was. The appeals process for a condemned prisoner is lengthy and painstaking. Every effort is made to see that the verdict and sentence were fairly arrived at. However, assertions of discrimination are not an argument for ending the death penalty but for extending it. It is not justice to exclude everyone from the penalty of the law if a few are found to be so favored. Justice requires that the law be applied equally to all.

12   **6. *Thou shalt not kill.*** The Bible is our greatest source of moral inspiration. Opponents of the death penalty frequently cite the sixth of the Ten Commandments in an attempt to prove that capital punishment is divinely proscribed. In the original Hebrew, however, the Sixth Commandment reads, "Thou Shalt Not Commit Murder," and the Torah specifies capital punishment for a variety of offenses. The biblical viewpoint has been upheld by philosophers throughout history. The greatest thinkers of the nineteenth century—Kant, Locke, Hobbes, Rousseau, Montesquieu, and Mill—agreed that natural law properly authorizes the sovereign to take life in order to vindicate justice. Only Jeremy Bentham was ambivalent. Washington, Jefferson, and Franklin endorsed it. Abraham Lincoln authorized executions for deserters in wartime. Alexis de Tocqueville, who expressed profound respect for American institutions, believed that the death

penalty was indispensable to the support of social order. The United States Constitution, widely admired as one of the seminal achievements in the history of humanity, condemns cruel and inhuman punishment, but does not condemn capital punishment.

7. The death penalty is state-sanctioned murder. This is the defense with 13 which Messrs. Willie and Shaw hoped to soften the resolve of those who sentenced them to death. By saying in effect, "You're no better than I am," the murderer seeks to bring his accusers down to his own level. It is also a popular argument among opponents of capital punishment, but a transparently false one. Simply put, the state has rights that the private individual does not. In a democracy, those rights are given to the state by the electorate. The execution of a lawfully condemned killer is no more an act of murder than is legal imprisonment an act of kidnapping. If an individual forces a neighbor to pay him money under threat of punishment, it's called extortion. If the state does it, it's called taxation. Rights and responsibilities surrendered by the individual are what give the state its power to govern. This contract is the foundation of civilization itself.

Everyone wants his or her rights, and will defend them jealously. Not everyone, 14 however, wants responsibilities, especially the painful responsibilities that come with law enforcement. Twenty-one years ago a woman named Kitty Genovese was assaulted and murdered on a street in New York. Dozens of neighbors heard her cries for help but did nothing to assist her. They didn't even call the police. In such a climate the criminal understandably grows bolder. In the presence of moral cowardice, he lectures us on our supposed failings and tries to equate his crimes with our quest for justice.

The death of anyone—even a convicted killer—diminishes us all. But we are diminished even more by a justice system that falls to function. It is an illusion to let ourselves believe that doing away with capital punishment removes the murderer's deed from our conscience. The rights of society are paramount. When we protect guilty lives, we give up innocent lives in exchange. When opponents of capital punishment say to the state: "I will not let you kill in my name," they are also saying to murderers: "You can kill in your *own* name as long as I have an excuse for not getting involved."

It is hard to imagine anything worse than being murdered while neighbors do noth- 16 ing. But something worse exists. When those same neighbors shrink back from justly punishing the murderer, the victim dies twice.

Questions for Close Reading

1. What is the selection's thesis? Locate the sentence(s) in which Koch states his main idea. If he doesn't state the thesis explicitly, express it in your own words.

2. According to Koch, what is it about the death penalty that its opponents find objectionable? Are such objections, in Koch's opinion, justified? Why or why not?

3. What arguments does Koch use to try to convince readers that the death penalty doesn't run counter to traditional religious and philosophical thought?

4. In Koch's view, how does the death penalty affirm the fact that "life is...precious"? Why, according to Koch, would punishing murderers with anything less than the death penalty be unjust?

5. Refer to your dictionary as needed to define the following words used in the selection: *reverence* (paragraph 2), *constituencies* (4), *heinous* (4), *reprehensible* (4), *lethal* (5), *implacable* (8), and *sophistic* (10)

Questions About the Writer's Craft

1. The pattern. Where does Koch try to establish his *ethos*? What does this attempt to establish his credibility say about Koch's perception of his audience's point of view?

2. Where does Koch draw upon hard evidence to develop his argument? What is the effect of this evidence?

3. What instances do you find in Koch's essay of emotional appeals and connotative language? How do you think Koch intends readers to react to such appeals and emotionally charged language?

4. Why might Koch have decided to conclude his essay with the Kitty Genovese anecdote? How does this anecdote contribute to his arguments in support of capital punishment?

Writing Assignments Using Argumentation-Persuasion as a Pattern of Development

∞ **1.** Koch bases his refutation of the standard arguments against capital punishment on a number of principles to which he is strongly committed. Some of these are stated clearly in the text:

- "If we create a society in which injustice is not tolerated, the incidence of murder—the most flagrant form of injustice—will diminish" (paragraph 6).
- "It is 'false sentimentality to argue that the death penalty should be abolished because of the abstract possibility that an innocent person might be executed'" (8).
- "The death penalty strengthens the value of human life" (10).

Drawing upon what you've read in "Death and Justice" and on what you know about the issue of capital punishment, write an essay that supports or refutes one of these principles or any other that Koch cites in his essay. Part of your paper should acknowledge and, if possible, refute the opposing viewpoint. To become more familiar with that viewpoint, read David Bruck's "The Death Penalty" (page 482).

2. Using the same organizational strategy as Koch, write an essay that argues for or against a particular stand on another controversial issue. Begin by stating and defending your position. Then, identify and refute several of the standard opposing arguments. Possible topics include the banning of college fraternities and sororities, allowing prayer in public schools, and implementing new graduation requirements at a college.

Writing Assignments Using Other Patterns of Development

3. Read David Bruck's "The Death Penalty," below, an essay written in response to Koch's. Then write a strictly informative paper comparing and contrasting Koch's and Bruck's views. Don't ally yourself with either side, but do focus on those points you consider most important to an objective discussion of the capital punishment issue.

4. Have you or anyone you know well ever witnessed or been a victim of violence? If so, write a narrative about the incident. Use taut sentences, descriptive detail, and climactic time order to convey the fear, helplessness, and anger that you or the person you're writing about felt. End with a statement about the event's impact on your life or on the other person's.

DAVID BRUCK

A lecturer and consultant on the death penalty, attorney David Bruck (1949–) has represented numerous death row clients. He has published articles in the *Washington Post* and the *New York Times* and has discussed capital punishment on a variety of national television programs. Writing in response to Ed Koch's argument in favor of the death penalty (see page 477), Bruck prepared the following piece, which first appeared in the *New Republic* in 1985.

THE DEATH PENALTY

Mayor Ed Koch contends that the death penalty "affirms life." By failing to execute   1
murderers, he says, we "signal a lessened regard for the value of the victim's life." Koch suggests that people who oppose the death penalty are like Kitty Genovese's neighbors, who heard her cries for help but did nothing while an attacker stabbed her to death.

This is the standard "moral" defense of death as punishment: even if executions   2
don't deter violent crime any more effectively than imprisonment, they are still required as the only means we have of doing justice in response to the worst of crimes.

Until recently, this "moral" argument had to be considered in the abstract, since no   3
one was being executed in the United States. But the death penalty is back now, at least in the southern states, where every one of the more than 30 executions carried out over the last two years has taken place. Those of us who live in those states are

getting to see the difference between the death penalty in theory, and what happens when you actually try to use it.

4   South Carolina resumed executing prisoners in January with the electrocution of Joseph Carl Shaw. Shaw was condemned to death for helping to murder two teenagers while he was serving as a military policeman at Fort Jackson, South Carolina. His crime, propelled by mental illness and PCP, was one of terrible brutality. It is Shaw's last words ("Killing was wrong when I did it. It is wrong when you do it. . . .") that so outraged Mayor Koch: he finds it "a curiosity of modern life that we are being lectured on morality by cold-blooded killers." And so it is.

5   But it was not "modern life" that brought this curiosity into being. It was capital punishment. The electric chair was J. C. Shaw's platform. (The mayor mistakenly writes that Shaw's statement came in the form of a plea to the governor for clemency: actually Shaw made it only seconds before his death, as he waited, shaved and strapped into the chair, for the switch to be thrown.) It was the chair that provided Shaw with celebrity and an opportunity to lecture us on right and wrong. What made this weird moral reversal even worse is that J. C. Shaw faced his own death with undeniable dignity and courage. And while Shaw died, the TV crews recorded another "curiosity" of the death penalty— the crowd gathered outside the death-house to cheer on the executioner. Whoops of elation greeted the announcement of Shaw's death. Waiting at the penitentiary gates for the appearance of the hearse bearing Shaw's remains, one demonstrator started yelling, "Where's the beef?"

6   For those who had to see the execution of J. C. Shaw, it wasn't easy to keep in mind that the purpose of the whole spectacle was to affirm life. It will be harder still when Florida executes a cop-killer named Alvin Ford. Ford has lost his mind during his years of death-row confinement, and now spends his days trembling, rocking back and forth, and muttering unintelligible prayers. This has led to litigation over whether Ford meets a centuries-old legal standard for mental competency. Since the Middle Ages, the Anglo-American legal system has generally prohibited the execution of anyone who is too mentally ill to understand what is about to be done to him and why. If Florida wins its case, it will have earned the right to electrocute Ford in his present condition. If it loses, he will not be executed until the state has first nursed him back to some semblance of mental health.*

7   We can at least be thankful that this demoralizing spectacle involves a prisoner who is actually guilty of murder. But this may not always be so. The ordeal of Lenell Jeter— the young black engineer who recently served more than a year of a life sentence for a Texas armed robbery that he didn't commit—should remind us that the system is quite capable of making the very worst sort of mistake. That Jeter was eventually cleared is a fluke. If the robbery had occurred at 7 p.m. rather than 3 p.m., he'd have had no alibi, and would still be in prison today. And if someone had been killed in that robbery, Jeter probably would have been sentenced to death. We'd have seen the usual execution-day interviews with state officials and the victim's relatives, all complaining that Jeter's

---

*On June 26, 1986, the Supreme Court prohibited the execution of convicted murderers who are so insane they do not understand they will be executed. However, if Ford regains his sanity, Florida may execute him.

appeals took too long. And Jeter's last words from the gurney would have taken their place among the growing literature of death-house oration that so irritates the mayor.

Koch quotes Hugo Adam Bedau, a prominent abolitionist, to the effect that the record fails to establish that innocent defendants have been executed in the past. But this doesn't mean, as Koch implies, that it hasn't happened. All Bedau was saying was that doubts concerning executed prisoners' guilt are almost never resolved. Bedau is at work now on an effort to determine how many wrongful death sentences may have been imposed: his list of murder convictions since 1900 in which the state eventually *admitted* error is some 400 cases long. Of course, very few of these cases involved actual executions: the mistakes that Bedau documents were uncovered precisely because the prisoner was alive and able to fight for his vindication. The cases where someone is executed are the very cases in which we're least likely to learn that we got the wrong man.

I don't claim that executions of entirely innocent people will occur very often. But they will occur. And other sorts of mistakes already have. Roosevelt Green was executed in Georgia two days before J. C. Shaw. Green and an accomplice kidnapped a young woman. Green swore that his companion shot her to death after Green had left, and that he knew nothing about the murder. Green's claim was supported by a statement that his accomplice made to a witness after the crime. The jury never resolved whether Green was telling the truth, and when he tried to take a polygraph examination a few days before his scheduled execution, the state of Georgia refused to allow the examiner into the prison. As the pressure for symbolic retribution mounts, the courts, like the public, are losing patience with such details. Green was electrocuted on January 9, while members of the Ku Klux Klan rallied outside the prison.

Then there is another sort of arbitrariness that happens all the time. Last October, Louisiana executed a man named Ernest Knighton. Knighton had killed a gas station owner during a robbery. Like any murder, this was a terrible crime. But it was not premeditated, and is the sort of crime that very rarely results in a death sentence. Why was Knighton electrocuted when almost everyone else who committed the same offense was not? Was it because he was black? Was it because his victim and all 12 members of the jury that sentenced him were white? Was it because Knighton's court-appointed lawyer presented no evidence on his behalf at his sentencing hearing? Or maybe there's no reason except bad luck. One thing is clear: Ernest Knighton was picked out to die the way a fisherman takes a cricket out of a bait jar. No one cares which cricket gets impaled on the hook.

Not every prisoner executed recently was chosen that randomly. But many were. And having selected these men so casually, so blindly, the death penalty system asks us to accept that the purpose of killing each of them is to affirm the sanctity of human life.

The death penalty states are also learning that the death penalty is easier to advocate than it is to administer. In Florida, where executions have become almost routine, the governor reports that nearly a third of his time is spent reviewing the clemency requests of condemned prisoners. The Florida Supreme Court is hopelessly backlogged with death cases. Some have taken five years to decide, and the rest of the Court's work waits in line behind the death appeals. Florida's death row currently holds more than 230 prisoners. State officials are reportedly considering building a special "death prison" devoted entirely to the isolation and electrocution of the condemned. The state is also considering the creation of a special public defender unit that will do nothing else but handle death penalty appeals. The death penalty, in short, is spawning death agencies.

13   And what is Florida getting for all of this? The state went through almost all of 1983 without executing anyone: its rate of intentional homicide declined by 17 percent. Last year Florida executed eight people—the most of any state, and the sixth highest total for any year since Florida started electrocuting people back in 1924. Elsewhere in the U.S. last year, the homicide rate continued to decline. But in Florida, it actually rose by 5.1 percent.

14   But these are just the tiresome facts. The electric chair has been a centerpiece of each of Koch's recent political campaigns, and he knows better than anyone how little the facts have to do with the public's support for capital punishment. What really fuels the death penalty is the justifiable frustration and rage of people who see that the government is not coping with violent crime. So what if the death penalty doesn't work? At least it gives us the satisfaction of knowing that we got one or two of the sons of bitches.

15   Perhaps we want retribution on the flesh and bone of a handful of convicted murderers so badly that we're willing to close our eyes to all of the demoralization and danger that come with it. A lot of politicians think so, and they may be right. But if they are, then let's at least look honestly at what we're doing. This lottery of death both comes from and encourages an attitude toward human life that is not reverent, but reckless.

16   And that is why the mayor is dead wrong when he confuses such fury with justice. He suggests that we trivialize murder unless we kill murderers. By that logic, we also trivialize rape unless we sodomize rapists. The sin of Kitty Genovese's neighbors wasn't that they failed to stab her attacker to death. Justice does demand that murderers be punished. And common sense demands that society be protected from them. But neither justice nor self-preservation demands that we kill men whom we have already imprisoned.

17   The electric chair in which J. C. Shaw died earlier this year was built in 1912 at the suggestion of South Carolina's governor at the time, Cole Blease. Governor Blease's other criminal justice initiative was an impassioned crusade in favor of lynch law. Any lesser response, the governor insisted, trivialized the loathsome crimes of interracial rape and murder. In 1912 a lot of people agreed with Governor Blease that a proper regard for justice required both lynching and the electric chair. Eventually we are going to learn that justice requires neither.

Questions for Close Reading

1. What is the selection's thesis? Locate the sentence(s) in which Bruck states his main idea. If he doesn't state the thesis explicitly, express it your own words.

2. Bruck refers to Ed Koch's (see page 477) belief that being lectured on morality by convicted killers is a "curiosity of modern life." Bruck then goes on to mention things he finds even more curious about the death penalty. What are they?

3. What does Bruck's essay reveal about the J. C. Shaw case that Koch's essay does not? How do these new facts support Bruck's thesis?

4. In paragraph 12, Bruck writes that states now executing prisoners are "learning that the death penalty is easier to advocate than…to administer." What does he mean? What evidence does he give to support this point?

5. Refer to your dictionary as needed to define the following words used in the selection: *semblance* (paragraph 6), *retribution* (9), *impaled* (10), *clemency* (12), *spawning* (12), *tiresome* (14), and *trivialize* (16).

Questions About the Writer's Craft

1. The pattern. Where in the essay does Bruck use appeals to reason to support his argument? Where does he use appeals to emotion? Which does he emphasize? What does this emphasis say about the way Bruck perceives his readers?

2. Like many writers of argumentation-persuasion essays, Bruck spends time refuting opposing opinions, in this case those of former New York City Mayor Ed Koch. Which of Koch's points provide the organizational framework for Bruck's argument? Why might Bruck have selected these points and not others?

3. In paragraph 10, Bruck uses a series of *rhetorical questions*—questions he doesn't expect his readers to answer. What is the effect of these questions?

4. In the essay's conclusion, Bruck explains that the electric chair in which J. C. Shaw died had been built at the suggestion of Governor Cole Blease, a man who also fervently supported lynch law. Why do you think Bruck introduces this new fact at the very end of the essay? What purpose does it serve?

Writing Assignments Using Argumentation-Persuasion as a Pattern of Development

∞ **1.** Bruck bases his argument against the death penalty on several important key points, the following among them:

- The death penalty negates the sanctity of human life.
- The death penalty offers no more practical deterrent to violent crime than imprisonment.
- The death penalty is pronounced disproportionately against minorities.
- The death penalty may result in the execution of innocent people.

Write an essay either defending or challenging *one* of these points. No matter which position you take, one section of your paper should recognize and, if possible, rebut opposing viewpoints. If you haven't already done so, be sure to read Ed Koch's "Death and Justice" (page 477) before planning your paper.

2. Develop an argument in which you try to persuade readers that life imprisonment is a just way of punishing convicted murderers and that there is no need to impose the death penalty. Try to anticipate and refute objections others might have to your position.

Writing Assignments Using Other Patterns of Development

3. Bruck believes that many people support the death penalty out of frustration with the criminal justice system rather than out of commitment to a particular ideology. Write an essay analyzing the consequences of this disillusionment with the criminal justice system. What other effects does it have on our beliefs and on the way we lead our lives?

4. Think of a law, regulation, procedure, or policy that has, like the death penalty, run into difficultly being implemented. Possible subjects include banning alcohol from campus parties, legalizing gambling, and building low-income housing in middle-income neighborhoods. Write an essay explaining the steps that should be taken to make things run more efficiently. Before presenting your step-by-step discussion, describe problems with the current law or policy.

Debating the Issues: Multiculturalism

YUH JI-YEON

Yuh Ji-Yeon was born in Seoul, Korea, in 1965. Her family immigrated to the United States and settled in Chicago when Yuh was five years old. A 1987 graduate of Stanford University, she worked as a reporter for the *Omaha World-Herald* and *Long Island Newsday* and is currently pursuing a doctorate at the University of Pennsylvania. The essay reprinted here originally appeared in the *Philadelphia Inquirer* in 1991.

LET'S TELL THE STORY OF ALL AMERICA'S CULTURES

1   I grew up hearing, seeing and almost believing that America was white—albeit with a little black tinge here and there—and that white was best.

2   The white people were everywhere in my 1970s Chicago childhood: Founding Fathers, Lewis and Clark, Lincoln, Daniel Boone, Carnegie, presidents, explorers and industrialists galore. The only black people were slaves. The only Indians were scalpers.

3   I never heard one word about how Benjamin Franklin was so impressed by the Iroquois federation of nations that he adapted that model into our system of state and federal

government. Or that the Indian tribes were systematically betrayed and massacred by a greedy young nation that stole their land and called it the United States.

I never heard one word about how Asian immigrants were among the first to turn   4 California's desert into fields of plenty. Or about Chinese immigrant Ah Bing, who bred the cherry now on sale in groceries across the nation. Or that plantation owners in Hawaii imported labor from China, Japan, Korea and the Philippines to work the sugar cane fields. I never learned that Asian immigrants were the only immigrants denied U.S. citizenship, even though they served honorably in World War I. All the immigrants in my textbook were white.

I never learned about Frederick Douglass, the runaway slave who became a leading   5 abolitionist and statesman, or about black scholar W. E. B. Du Bois. I never learned that black people rose up in arms against slavery. Nat Turner wasn't one of the heroes in my childhood history class.

I never learned that the American Southwest and California were already settled by   6 Mexicans when they were annexed after the Mexican-American War. I never learned that Mexico once had a problem keeping land-hungry white men on the U.S. side of the border.

So when other children called me a slant-eyed chink and told me to go back where   7 I came from, I was ready to believe that I wasn't really an American because I wasn't white.

America's bittersweet legacy of struggling and failing and getting another step closer   8 to democratic ideals of liberty and equality and justice for all wasn't for the likes of me, an immigrant child from Korea. The history books said so.

Well, the history books were wrong.   9

Educators around the country are finally realizing what I realized as a teenager in 10 the library, looking up the history I wasn't getting in school. America is a multicultural nation, composed of many people with varying histories and varying traditions who have little in common except their humanity, a belief in democracy and a desire for freedom.

America changed them, but they changed America too.   11

A committee of scholars and teachers gathered by the New York State Department 12 of Education recognizes this in their recent report, "One Nation, Many Peoples: A Declaration of Cultural Interdependence."

They recommend that public schools provide a "multicultural education, anchored 13 to the shared principles of a liberal democracy."

What that means, according to the report, is recognizing that America was shaped 14 and continues to be shaped by people of diverse backgrounds. It calls for students to be taught that history is an ongoing process of discovery and interpretation of the past, and that there is more than one way of viewing the world.

Thus, the westward migration of white Americans is not just a heroic settling of an 15 untamed wild, but also the conquest of indigenous peoples. Immigrants were not just white, but Asian as well. Blacks were not merely passive slaves freed by northern whites, but active fighters for their own liberation.

In particular, according to the report, the curriculum should help children "to assess 16 critically the reasons for the inconsistencies between the ideals of the U.S. and social realities. It should provide information and intellectual tools that can permit them to contribute to bringing reality closer to the ideals."

17   In other words, show children the good with the bad, and give them the skills to help improve their country. What could be more patriotic?

18   Several dissenting members of the New York committee publicly worry that America will splinter into ethnic fragments if this multicultural curriculum is adopted. They argue that the committee's report puts the focus on ethnicity at the expense of national unity.

19   But downplaying ethnicity will not bolster national unity. The history of America is the story of how and why people from all over the world came to the United States, and how in struggling to make a better life for themselves, they changed each other, they changed the country, and they all came to call themselves Americans.

20   *E pluribus unum.* Out of many, one.

21   This is why I, with my Korean background, and my childhood tormentors, with their lost-in-the-mist-of-time European backgrounds, are all Americans.

22   It is the unique beauty of this country. It is high time we let all our children gaze upon it.

Questions for Close Reading

1. What is the selection's thesis? Locate the sentence(s) in which Yuh states her main idea. If she doesn't state the thesis explicitly, express it in your own words.

2. Yuh makes the rather shocking claim that "the history books were wrong" (paragraph 9). Why does she make this statement? What evidence does she offer to support it?

3. According to Yuh, what changes are needed in American history courses?

4. Why does Yuh feel it is critical that American students receive more than the traditional whites-only version of our nation's history? Who will be served by making history books more multicultural?

5. Refer to your dictionary as needed to define the following words used in the selection: *albeit* (paragraph 1), *tinged* (1), *galore* (2), *multicultural* (10, 13, 18), *interdependence* (12), *indigenous* (15), *dissenting* (18), *ethnicity* (18), and *bolster* (19).

Questions About the Writer's Craft

1. The pattern. Where in her argument does Yuh present the opposing viewpoint? Why do you suppose she waits so long to deal with the dissenting opinion? What effect does this delay have on her argument's effectiveness?

2. Other patterns. Why might Yuh have decided to use so many examples in paragraphs 2 through 6? How do these examples contribute to the persuasiveness of her position? Why might she have placed these examples before her thesis statement?

3. Yuh mixes the subjective and the objective in her argument. Where does she use specifics from her own life? How do these personal details help persuade readers to accept her viewpoint?

4. Yuh often uses parallelism and repetition of phrases, particularly in paragraphs 1 through 6 and paragraph 15. What effect do you think she intended these two stylistic devices to have on her readers?

Writing Assignments Using Argumentation-Persuasion as a Pattern of Development

∞ **1.** Read several articles about the ongoing debate over multiculturalism's role in contemporary education. Also discuss the issue with friends, family, and classmates. Review all the material gathered, and decide whether or not you support the idea of a multicultural curriculum. Then write an essay in which you argue your position, refuting as many of the opposing views as possible. To support your position, include your library research as well as your own and other people's experiences. If you haven't already done so, read Arthur Schlesinger's "The Cult of Ethnicity: Good and Bad" (page 491) before writing your paper.

2. Yuh cites a problem she encountered in her education. Brainstorm the problems or insufficiencies you found in your own education. Then select a single problem at one level of education, and meet with others to discuss their experiences with the problem. Drawing upon the most compelling examples, write a persuasive essay directed at those who think all is well in our educational system.

Writing Assignments Using Other Patterns of Development

3. Because the mainstream culture they lived in didn't recognize the presence of minorities, the author's classmates considered Yuh almost a nonbeing. To what extent, in your opinion, does television contribute to the dehumanization of minorities? For several days, watch a variety of television shows, noting how a particular ethnic or minority group (such as African Americans, Hispanic Americans, or the elderly) is portrayed. Then write an essay showing that television's depiction of this group is either accurate *or* distorted. Support your main idea with plentiful references to specific television shows, including newscasts, situation comedies, talk shows, and so forth.

4. The New York State Department of Education report (paragraphs 12–14) argues that curriculum should encourage young people to examine "the reasons for the inconsistencies between the ideals of the U.S. and social realities." Like most people, you probably detected such disparities when you were growing up. Perhaps you heard an admired neighbor brag about padding an expense account or learned that an esteemed high school coach took kickbacks from college recruiters. Focus on one such clash between the ethical ideal and the everyday reality, and write about the incident's effect on you. At the end of the essay, reach some conclusions about the way children can be helped to deal with such collisions between ideals and reality.

ARTHUR SCHLESINGER, JR.

Special advisor to the Kennedy administration from 1961–64, Arthur Schlesinger, Jr., won a Pulitzer Prize for *A Thousand Days* (1965), his book on John F. Kennedy. A professor at the graduate school of the City University of New York, Schlesinger is a widely regarded author of American history. His many publications include *The Politics of Upheaval* (1974), *The Imperial Presidency* (1973), *Robert Kennedy and His Times* (1980), *The Age of Jackson* (1988), and *The Disunity of America* (1992). "The Cult of Ethnicity, Good and Bad" was first published in *Time* in 1991.

THE CULT OF ETHNICITY: GOOD AND BAD

1   The history of the world has been in great part the history of the mixing of peoples. Modern communication and transport accelerate mass migrations from one continent to another. Ethnic and racial diversity is more than ever a salient fact of the age.

2   But what happens when people of different origins, speaking different languages and professing different religions, inhabit the same locality and live under the same political sovereignty? Ethnic and racial conflict—far more than ideological conflict—is the explosive problem of our times.

3   On every side today ethnicity is breaking up nations. The Soviet Union,* India, Yugoslavia,† Ethiopia, are all in crisis. Ethnic tensions disturb and divide Sri Lanka, Burma, Indonesia, Iraq, Cyprus, Nigeria, Angola, Lebanon, Guyana, Trinidad—you name it. Even nations as stable and civilized as Britain and France, Belgium and Spain, face growing ethnic troubles. Is there any large multiethnic state that can be made to work?

4   The answer to that question has been, until recently, the United States. "No other nation," Margaret Thatcher has said, "has so successfully combined people of different races and nations within a single culture." How have Americans succeeded in pulling off this almost unprecedented trick?

5   We have always been a multiethnic country. Hector St. John de Crèvecoeur, who came from France in the 18th century, marveled at the astonishing diversity of the settlers—"a mixture of English, Scotch, Irish, French, Dutch, Germans and Swedes... this promiscuous breed." He propounded a famous question: "What then is the Amer-

---

*In 1991, the Soviet Union was dissolved into fifteen separate nations, partly because of the very ethnic conflicts Schlesinger describes (editors' note).
†In 1991, Yugoslavia also split into six nations because of ethnic rivalries (editors' note).

ican, this new man?" And he gave a famous answer: "Here individuals of all nations are melted into a new race of men." *E pluribus unum.* *

The U.S. escaped the divisiveness of a multiethnic society by a brilliant solution: the 6 creation of a brand-new national identity. The point of America was not to preserve old cultures but to forge a new, *American* culture. "By an intermixture with our people," President George Washington told Vice President John Adams, immigrants will "get assimilated to our customs, measures and laws: in a word, soon become one people." This was the ideal that a century later Israel Zangwill crystallized in the title of his popular 1908 play *The Melting Pot.* And no institution was more potent in molding Crèvecoeur's "promiscuous breed" into Washington's "one people" than the American public school.

The new American nationality was inescapably English in language, ideas and insti- 7 tutions. The pot did not melt everybody, not even all the white immigrants; deeply bred racism put black Americans, yellow Americans, red Americans and brown Americans well outside the pale. Still, the infusion of other stocks, even of nonwhite stocks, and the experience of the New World reconfigured the British legacy and made the U.S., as we all know, a very different country from Britain.

In the 20th century, new immigration laws altered the composition of the American 8 people, and a cult of ethnicity erupted both among non-Anglo whites and among non-white minorities. This had many healthy consequences. The American culture at last began to give shamefully overdue recognition to the achievement of groups subordinated and spurned during the high noon of Anglo dominance, and it began to acknowledge the great swirling world beyond Europe. Americans acquired a more complex and invigorating sense of their world—and of themselves.

But, pressed too far, the cult of ethnicity has unhealthy consequences. It gives rise, 9 for example, to the conception of the U.S. as a nation composed not of individuals making their own choices but of inviolable ethnic and racial groups. It rejects the historic American goals of assimilation and integration. And, in an excess of zeal, well-intentioned people seek to transform our system of education from a means of creating "one people" into a means of promoting, celebrating and perpetuating separate ethnic origins and identities. The balance is shifting from *unum* to *pluribus.*

That is the issue that lies behind the hullabaloo over "multiculturalism" and "politi- 10 cal correctness," the attack on the "Eurocentric" curriculum and the rise of the notion that history and literature should be taught not as disciplines but as therapies whose function is to raise minority self-esteem. Group separatism crystallizes the differences, magnifies tensions, intensifies hostilities. Europe—the unique source of the liberating ideas of democracy, civil liberties and human rights—is portrayed as the root of all evil, and non-European cultures, their own many crimes deleted, are presented as the means of redemption.

I don't want to sound apocalyptic about these developments. Education is always in 11 ferment, and a good thing too. The situation in our universities, I am confident, will soon right itself. But the impact of separatist pressures on our public schools is more troubling. If a Kleagle of the Ku Klux Klan wanted to use the schools to disable and handicap black Americans, he could hardly come up with anything more effective than

*A reference to the official motto of the United States, *E pluribus unum,* a Latin phrase meaning "Out of many, one." Schlesinger suggests that the emphasis is shifting from one (*unum*) single American nationality to many (*pluribus*) separate ethnic groups.

the "Afrocentric" curriculum. And if separatist tendencies go unchecked, the result can only be the fragmentation, resegregation and tribalization of American life.

12   I remain optimistic. My impression is that the historic forces driving toward "one people" have not lost their power. The eruption of ethnicity is, I believe, a rather superficial enthusiasm stirred by romantic ideologues on the one hand and by unscrupulous con men on the other: self-appointed spokesmen whose claim to represent their minority groups is carelessly accepted by the media. Most American-born members of minority groups, white or nonwhite, see themselves primarily as Americans rather than primarily as members of one or another ethnic group. A notable indicator today is the rate of intermarriage across ethnic lines, across religious lines, even (increasingly) across racial lines. "We Americans," said Theodore Roosevelt, "are children of the crucible."

13   The growing diversity of the American population makes the quest for unifying ideals and a common culture all the more urgent. In a world savagely rent by ethnic and racial antagonisms, the U.S. must continue as an example of how a highly differentiated society holds itself together.

Questions for Close Reading

1. What is the selection's thesis? Locate the sentence(s) in which Schlesinger states his main idea. If he doesn't state the thesis explicitly, express it in your own words.

2. According to Schlesinger, how has the United States, despite its ethnic diversity, managed to forge a unified national identity?

3. What, in Schlesinger's opinion, are the possible benefits of a "cult of ethnicity"? What are its drawbacks?

4. Why is Schlesinger optimistic about America's future as a unified, undivided nation?

5. Refer to your dictionary as needed to define the following words used in the selection: *salient* (paragraph 1), *sovereignty* (2), *ideological* (2), *unprecedented* (4), *promiscuous* (5), *assimilated* (6), *crystallized* (6), *potent* (6), *infusion* (7), *reconfigured* (7), *spurned* (8), *Anglo* (8), *inviolable* (9), *zeal* (9), *apocalyptic* (11), *ferment* (11), *Kleagle* (11), *crucible* (12), and *rent* (13).

Questions About the Writer's Craft

1. The pattern. Where in the essay does Schlesinger cite the opposing viewpoint? How does his characterization of this viewpoint help him achieve his purpose?

2. Schlesinger poses a series of questions in paragraphs 2–4. How do these questions help him convey his ideas to an audience of mainstream readers?

3. Other patterns. Throughout his essay, Schlesinger uses terms that have become "buzzwords"—words with specialized, often emotional connotations. Two examples are *Anglo* (paragraph 8) and *Eurocentric* (10). Locate other instances. Why do you think Schlesinger decided not to define these terms? How do these undefined terms help Schlesinger reinforce his argument?

4. Schlesinger includes a number of quotations in his essay. Locate several of them. Why might he have decided to quote these particular sources?

Writing Assignments Using Argumentation-Persuasion as a Pattern of Development

∞ **1.** Write an essay defending *or* challenging Schlesinger's point that heightened ethnic awareness may have "unhealthy consequences." To gather material on both sides of the issue, speak to individuals with varying viewpoints, drawing on their experiences as well as your own to support your position. For additional insights on multicultural perspectives, read Joseph H. Suina's "And Then I Went to School" (page 361) and Yuh Ji-Yeon's "Let's Tell the Story of All America's Cultures" (page 487).

2. Schlesinger states that the twentieth century gave "shamefully overdue recognition" to several groups long overlooked. Write an essay arguing that a specific group of people typically fails to receive the recognition it deserves. You might focus on the accomplishments of a particular ethnic, racial, or religious group, or on the achievements of a group distinguished in some other way—for example, single parents or caregivers of the elderly. Assume that some of your readers are apathetic about the group you're writing about, so be sure to provide compelling examples that challenge their indifference.

Writing Assignments Using Other Patterns of Development

3. Schlesinger implies that Americans are more similar than they are different. Write an essay about a racial, ethnic, generational, gender, or other tension that you have observed—perhaps at your college, in your community, in your home, or on the job. Begin the paper with a vivid example that demonstrates the nature of the conflict. Then explain what steps *one* group—for example, students, administrators, townspeople, the clergy, parents, and so on—could take to improve the situation. How might they defuse hostilities by highlighting the similarities between the groups at odds?

∞ **4.** As Schlesinger points out, public education has functioned as a strong unifying national force. However, it has also tended, perhaps in the service of that unity, to ignore some of the less heroic, more shameful events in American history: for example, the massacre of Native Americans in the West and the internment of Japanese Americans during World War II. Write an essay in which you show how children are affected by the withholding of this information. Then discuss how they might be affected if they were taught some of these harsh truths. To deepen your understanding of the issue, be sure to read Yuh Ji-Yeon's "Let's Tell the Story of All America's Cultures" (page 487). Talking with others and conducting some library research will also help you sort out the issue's complexities.

ADDITIONAL WRITING TOPICS: ARGUMENTATION-PERSUASION

General Assignments

Using argumentation-persuasion, develop one of the following topics in an essay.

1. Hiring quotas

2. Giving birth-control devices to teenagers

3. Prayer in the schools

4. Spouses sharing housework equally

5. Big-time sports in college

6. Music videos

7. Drugs and alcohol on campus

8. Requiring college students to pass a comprehensive exam in their majors before graduating

9. Putting elderly parents in nursing homes

10. Financial aid to college students

Assignments with a Specific Purpose, Audience, and Point of View

1. A college has rejected your or your child's application on the basis of low SAT scores. Write to the college admissions director, arguing that SAT scores are not a fair indicator of your or your child's abilities and potential.

2. As a staff writer for the college opinion magazine, you've been asked to nominate the "Outstanding Man or Woman on Campus," to be featured on the magazine's cover. Write a letter to your supervising editor in support of your nominee.

3. You and your parents don't agree on some aspect of your romantic life (you want to live with your boyfriend/girlfriend and they don't approve; you want to get married and they want you to wait; they simply don't like your partner). Write your parents a letter explaining why your preference is reasonable. Try hard to win them over to your side.

4. As a high school teacher, you support some additional restriction on students. The restriction might be "no radios in school," "no T-shirts," "no food in class," "no smoking on school grounds." Write an article for the school newspaper, justifying this new rule to the student body.

5. Someone you know is convinced that the music you listen to is trashy or boring. Write a letter to the person arguing that your music has value. Support your contention with specific references to lyrics, musical structure, and performers' talent.

6. Assume you're a member of a racial, ethnic, religious, or social minority. You might, for example, be a Native American, an elderly person, a female executive. On a recent television show or in a TV commercial, you saw something that depicts your group in an offensive way. Write a letter (to the network or the advertiser) expressing your feelings and explaining why you feel the material should be taken off the air.

PART IV

THE
RESEARCH
PAPER

20
SELECTING A SUBJECT, USING THE LIBRARY AND THE INTERNET, AND TAKING NOTES

SOME GENERAL COMMENTS ABOUT THE RESEARCH PAPER

IF you're like many of the students we know, **research papers** probably make you nervous. Why, you may wonder, do instructors assign them? Such projects take time, and the payoff, you may feel, doesn't seem worth the effort. If this *is* how you feel, we hope to show you that conducting research and writing up your findings can be rewarding, even fun.

Think of library research as a treasure hunt. The deeper you dig, the more you unearth material that's new to you. Besides experiencing the pleasure of such discovery, you become an expert of sorts in your subject and grow more comfortable with research methods. Most important, writing a research paper enlarges your perspective. As you test your own views against existing evidence, evaluate conflicting opinions, and learn how to detect other people's biases, you acquire analytic skills that will benefit you throughout life. These skills enable you to move beyond casual, off-the-top-of-the-head opinions to those that are well reasoned and thoughtful. In everyday conversation, most of us feel free to voice all kinds of opinions, even if they're based on nothing more than emotion and secondhand information. Researched opinions, though, are sounder and more logical. They're based on authoritative evidence rather than on limited personal experience, on fact rather than on hearsay. Instead of being rooted in unexamined personal belief, researched opinions emerge from a careful consideration of the evidence.

All of this may sound intimidating, but keep in mind that writing a research paper expands what you already know about writing essays; many of the steps are the same. The two major differences are the greater length of the research paper—usually five or more pages—and the kind of support you offer for your thesis. Rather than relying on your own experience or that of friends or family, you use published information and expert opinion to support your thesis. Even so, writing a research paper *can* be a challenge. One way to make the project more manageable is to view it as a process consisting of two major phases: (1) the **research stage,** when you find out all you can about your subject and identify a working thesis, and (2) the **writing stage,** when you present in an accepted format what you've discovered. This chapter focuses on the first stage; the next, Chapter 21, examines the second stage. Although we discuss the research process as a series of steps, we encourage you to modify the sequence to suit your subject, your personal approach to writing, and the requirements of a particular assignment.

During the first stage of the research process, you do the following:

- Plan the research
- Find sources in the library
- Prepare a working bibliography
- Take notes to support the thesis with evidence

PLAN THE RESEARCH

Understand the Paper's Boundaries

Your first step in planning the research is to *clarify the project's requirements.* How long is the paper supposed to be? How extensively should you deal with opposing viewpoints? Are there any restrictions about the number and type of sources? Are popular magazines and books acceptable, or should you use only scholarly sources? Has the instructor limited your subject choices?

Also, be sure you *understand the paper's overall purpose.* Unless you've been assigned a purely informative report ("explain several psychologists' theories of hostility"), your research paper shouldn't simply display all the information you have gathered. Instead of merely patching together ideas from a variety of sources, you should develop your own position, using outside sources to arrive at a balanced but definitive conclusion.

One more point: You should be aware that most instructors expect students to use the third-person point of view in research papers. If you plan to include any personal experiences, observations, or interviews (see below and pages 564–565) along with your outside research, ask your instructor whether the use of the first-person point of view would be appropriate.

Understand Primary Versus Secondary Research

You should determine whether your instructor expects you to conduct any **primary research**—information gathered from firsthand observations, personal interviews, and the like. Most college research papers involve **library** or **secondary research**—information gathered secondhand from the Internet (see pages 520–532) or from published print sources. Such material includes information gathered from published accounts, including statistics, facts, case studies, expert opinion, critical interpretations, and experimental results. Occasionally, though, you may want or be asked to conduct primary research. You may, for example, run an experiment, visit an organization, observe a situation, schedule an interview, or conduct a survey. In such cases of primary research, you'll need to prepare carefully and establish a strict deadline schedule for yourself. (See pages 564–565 for hints on incorporating primary research into a paper.)

Conducting Interviews in Person, by Phone, and Through E-Mail

If you plan to go on an information-gathering interview, put some careful thought into how you will proceed. If you use a letter rather than a telephone call to request an interview, get feedback on the letter's overall effectiveness before mailing it. When you set up your appointment, request enough time (30–60 minutes) to discuss your topic in depth; keep in mind, however, that the person may not be able to set aside as much time as you'd like. If you hope to tape-record the interview, you must obtain permission to do so beforehand. (Some organizations don't permit employees to be recorded during interviews.) Also, when making the appointment, ask if you may quote the person directly; he or she is entitled to know that all comments will be "on the record."

Most important, plan the interview carefully. First, determine what you want to accomplish: Do you want to gather general background material or do you want to clear up confusion about a specific point? Then, well in advance of the interview, prepare a list of questions geared toward that goal. During the interview, though, remain flexible—follow up on interesting remarks even if they diverge somewhat from your original plan. (If you discover that your interviewee isn't as informed as you had hoped, graciously request the names of other people who might help you further.) Throughout the interview, take accurate and complete notes (unless, of course, you're taping). If certain remarks seem especially quotable, make sure you get the statements down correctly. Finally, soon after the interview ends, be sure to fill in any gaps in your notes.

If a face-to-face interview isn't feasible, a phone interview often will provide the information you need. Don't, however, call the person and expect a phone interview on the spot. Instead, call, explain the kind of help you would like, and see if the person is willing to schedule time to talk at a later date. If so, follow the guidelines above for conducting a focused interview.

Another way to conduct an interview is through the Internet. Perhaps you read an article and have questions about several of the author's points. Or maybe you want to see if the author can direct you to additional material on your topic. You note that the author's e-mail address is provided, so you decide to connect with the author electronically. Your e-mail correspondence should describe the topic you're researching, explain your reasons for establishing contact, and list clearly and concisely the information you would like the author to provide. It's also a good idea to give the date by which you hope the author can get back to you. If the author's e-mail address isn't provided, the following search directories can help you track down the address:

Inter Nic (International Network Informational Services Directory and Database provided by AT&T) at <http://ds.internic.net>

Netfind at <http://lut.ac.uk/dir/netfind.html>

(For additional information about the Internet and e-mail interviews, see pages 520–532).

Conducting Surveys

A survey helps you gather a good deal of information from many people (called "respondents")—and in a much shorter period of time than would be needed to interview each person individually. If you believe that citing the opinions of a group of people will strengthen your paper, you might want to conduct a survey. Bear in mind, though, that designing, administering, and interpreting a survey questionnaire are time-consuming tasks that demand considerable skill. Be sure, then, to have someone knowledgeable about surveys evaluate both your questionnaire and the responses it evokes.

When you write your survey questions, make them as clear and precise as possible. For example, if your goal is to determine the frequency with which something occurs, do not ask for vague responses such as "seldom," "often," and "occasionally." Instead, ask the respondents to identify more specific time periods: "weekly," "1–3 times a week," "4–6 times a week," and "daily." Also, steer away from questions that favor one side of an issue or that restrict the range of responses. Consider the following survey questions:

Should already overburdened college students be required to participate in a community-service activity before they can graduate?

Yes _____   No _____   Maybe _____

In your opinion, how knowledgeable are college students about jobs in their majors?

Knowledgeable _____   Not knowledgeable _____

Both of the preceding questions need to be revised but for different reasons. The first, by assuming that students are "already overburdened," biases respondents to reply negatively. To make the question more neutral, you would have to eliminate the prejudicial words. The second question asks respondents to answer in terms of a simple contrast: "Knowledgeable" or "Not knowledgeable." It ignores the likelihood that some respondents may wish to reply "Very knowledgeable," "Somewhat knowledgeable," and so on.

You should include in your survey only those items that will yield useful information. For example, if administering a survey to students on your campus, you would ask respondents some questions about their age, college year, major, and so forth—as long as you planned to break responses into subgroups. But these questions would be unnecessary if you didn't intend to analyze responses in such a manner. In any case, be sure to limit the number of questions you ask. If you don't, you'll regret it later on when you sort out the responses.

When you conduct a survey, it's unlikely that you'll be able to poll every member of the group whose opinions you seek. Instead, you must poll a *representative subgroup* of the whole. By *representative,* we mean "having characteristics similar to the group as a whole." Imagine you're writing a research paper on unfair employment practices. As part of your data collection, you decide to poll students on campus about their job experiences. If you, a first-year student, give the questionnaire only to students in your introductory courses, your sample won't be representative of the student body as a whole. Upper-level students might have significantly different work experiences and thus quite different opinions about employer fairness. So, to gauge students' attitudes at your college with accuracy, you'll have to hand out your survey in numerous places and on varied occasions on the campus. That way, your responses will be drawn from the whole spectrum of undergraduate backgrounds, majors, ages, and so forth.

This method of collecting student responses still wouldn't amount to what is called a *random sample.* To achieve a random sample, you must choose respondents by a scientific method—one that would, theoretically, give each person in the group to be studied the chance to respond. For example, to survey undergraduates on your campus, you would have to obtain a comprehensive list of all enrolled students. From this list, you would pick names at a regular interval, perhaps every tenth; to each tenth person, you would deliver (or mail) a survey, or you would telephone to ask the questions orally. With this method, every enrolled student has the potential of being chosen as a respondent.

Since there's so much cost and time involved in doing a random sample, you'll most likely use an informal method of collecting responses. Using the "street corner" approach, you might hand your survey to passersby or to people seated in classes, in student lounges, and so on. Or, if you're collecting information about the service provided at a particular facility, you might (with permission) place a short questionnaire where respondents can pick it up, quickly fill it out, and return it. Because of your informal methods, your results would be an *approximate* portrait of the group polled; however, the more people you survey, the more accurate your profile of the larger population is likely to be. (See pages 564–565 for hints on incorporating survey results into a research paper.)

Once you're sure of the paper's boundaries and understand your instructor's expectations regarding primary and secondary research, it's time for you to move on. At this point, you'll need to (1) choose a general subject, (2) limit that subject, (3) conduct preliminary research, (4) identify a working thesis, and (5) make a schedule.

Choose a General Subject

Your instructor may provide a list of acceptable topics for a research paper, or you may be free to select a topic on your own. In the latter case, your second step in planning the research is to *choose a general subject.* If you have an area of interest —say, Native American culture or animal rights—the subject might be suitable for a research paper. If you don't immediately know what you'd like to research, consider current events, journal entries, the courses you're taking, the reading you've done on your own, or some of the selections in this book. A sociology course may have piqued your interest in child abuse or the elderly. Current events might suggest research on water pollution or business ethics. Several of your journal entries may focus on an issue that concerns you—maybe, for example, use of drugs in college athletics. Perhaps you've come across a provocative article on nuclear power or the nation's health-care crisis. Maybe you find yourself disagreeing with what Caryl Rivers says about rock music in "What Should Be Done About Rock Lyrics" on pages 473–475 of this book. (In the activities at the end of this chapter, you'll find a list of suggested research topics derived from the readings in this text.)

If you're still not sure of what subject to research, go to the library and do some background reading on several possible general subjects. Also try using one or more prewriting techniques to identify areas that interest or puzzle you. Brainstorming, questioning, freewriting, and mapping (see pages 25–29) should help you generate ideas worth exploring. As soon as you have a list of possible topics, use the following checklist to help you determine which of these subjects would or would not be appropriate for a research paper.

☑ SELECTING AN APPROPRIATE SUBJECT TO RESEARCH:
   A CHECKLIST

☐ Will you enjoy learning about the subject for the substantial period of time you'll be working on the research paper? If you think you might get bored, select another subject.

☐ Can you obtain enough information on the subject? Recent developments (an ongoing government scandal or a controversial new program to help the homeless) can be investigated only through mass-circulation newspapers and magazines. Books as well as specialized or scholarly journal articles on recent events may not be available for some time.

☐ Has the topic been researched so often (the legalization of marijuana, violence in sports) that there's nothing new or interesting left to say about it?

☐ Is the topic surrounded by unreliable testimony (ESP, UFOs, the Bermuda Triangle), making it unsuitable for a research paper?

☐ Is the topic (a rock star's conflict with the recording industry, for example) too trivial for an academic project?

☐ Does the subject lend itself to or call for research? If it doesn't, think about selecting another topic. For example, the dangers of smoking are now almost universally acknowledged and so probably wouldn't make an appropriate topic for a research paper.

☐ Has the topic been written about by only one major source? If so, your research will be one-sided.

☐ Can you be objective about your topic? Researching both sides of an issue about which you feel strongly usually deepens your understanding of the issue's complexity. But if you feel so committed to a point of view that you'll have trouble considering opposing opinions, it's best to avoid that subject altogether.

Once you have a general topic in mind, you may want to clear it with your instructor. Or you can wait until the next stage to do so—after you've narrowed the topic further.

Prewrite to Limit the General Subject

The next step in planning your research is to *limit* or *narrow your topic.* "Pollution" is too broad a topic, but "The Effect of Acid Rain on Urban Structures" poses a realistic challenge. Similarly, "Cable Television" is way too general, but "Trends in Cable Comedy" is manageable. Remember, you aren't writing a book but a paper of probably five to fifteen pages.

Sometimes you'll know the particular aspect of a subject you want to explore. Usually, though, you'll have to do some work to restrict your subject. In such cases, try using the prewriting techniques of questioning, mapping, freewriting, and brainstorming described in Chapter 2. Discussing the topic with other people and doing some background reading on your subject can also help focus your thinking. (For more on limiting general subjects, see pages 25–27.)

Conduct Preliminary Research

Frequently, you won't be able to narrow your topic until you learn more about it. When that's the case, background reading, often called **preliminary research,** is necessary. Just as prewriting precedes a first draft, preliminary research precedes the in-depth research you conduct further along in the process.

At this point, you don't have to track down highly specialized material. Instead, you simply browse the Internet (see pages 520–532) and skim books and mass-market or newspaper articles on your topic to get an overview and to identify possible slants on your subject. If your broad subject is inspired by a class, you can check out the topic in your textbook. And, of course, you can consult library sources—the *computerized* or *card catalog*, the *reference section*, and *periodical indexes* such as the *Readers' Guide to Periodical Literature*. All of these sources break broad subjects into subtopics, thus helping you focus your research. These and other library resources, discussed in greater detail later in the chapter, are among the most valuable tools available to researchers.

After you locate several promising books or articles on your general subject, glance through the material rapidly to get a sense of issues and themes. Do the sources suggest a particular angle of inquiry? If you don't find much material on your subject, think about selecting another topic, one about which more has been written.

While conducting preliminary research, there's no need to take notes, unless you want to jot down possible limited topics. However, you should keep an informal record of the books and articles you skim. Using a sheet of paper or preferably an index card for each source, note the following information: For each book, record the author, title, and call number; for each article, record the date and the page numbers. Such basic information will help you relocate material later on, when you'll need to look at your sources more closely. Also, it's a good idea to jot down the authors and titles of other works mentioned in the sources you skim. You may decide to consult them at another point.

Once you arrive at your limited topic—or several possibilities—ask your instructor for feedback, listening carefully to any reservations he or she may have about your idea. Moreover, even though you've identified a limited subject, don't be surprised if it continues to shift and narrow further as you go along. Such reshaping is part of the research process.

Identify a Working Thesis

Once you have done some preliminary research on your limited topic and have determined there's sufficient material available, your next step is to form a **working thesis**—an idea of your own that is in some way original.

Having a tentative thesis guides your research and helps you determine which sources will be appropriate. However, general statements like "Congress should not make further cuts in social programs," "Prayer in public schools should not be allowed," and "Higher education is male-dominated" are so broad that they fail to restrict the scope of research. Whole books have been written on welfare, just one of many social programs. Be sure, then, that your working thesis focuses on a *limited subject*. The thesis should also take a stand by *expressing your point of view*, or *attitude, about the subject*. Note the difference between the broad statements above and the effective limited thesis statements that follow (the limited subjects are underlined once, the attitudes twice):

> The Congressional decision to reduce funding of school lunch programs has had unfortunate consequences for disadvantaged children.

> A moment of silence in public schools does not violate the constitutional separation of church and state.

> The funding of college athletics discriminates against women.

It's important for you to view your working thesis as tentative; you probably won't have a thesis until your research is almost complete and all the facts are in. Indeed, if your thesis *doesn't* shift as you investigate your topic, you may not be tapping a wide enough range of sources, or you may be resisting challenges to your original point of view. *Remember:* Gathering information with a closed mind undermines the purpose of a research project.

In its *final* form, your thesis should accomplish at least one of three things. First, it may offer your personal synthesis of multiple findings, your own interpretation of "what it all means." Second, it may refine or extend other people's theories or interpretations. Third, it may offer a perspective that differs from or opposes the one you find expressed in most of your sources. (For more on thesis statements, see pages 36–41.)

Make a Schedule

Having identified your working thesis, you're nearly ready to begin the research stage of your project. Before you begin, though, *make a schedule*. First, list what you need to do. Then, working back from your paper's due date, set rough time limits for the different phases of the project: locating and reading relevant periodicals and books; taking notes; interviewing an expert or sending away for information; drafting, revising, and editing the paper.

FIND SOURCES IN THE LIBRARY

Now is the time to start your research in earnest. Always keep in mind that you're looking for material to support your working thesis. What should you do if you come across material that contradicts your thesis? Resist the temptation to disregard such material. Instead, evaluate it as objectively as you can, and use it to arrive at a more valid statement of your thesis.

Even if your paper contains some primary research, most of your information-gathering will take place in your college library or its equivalent. If the college library is new to you, look for informative handouts near the main desk, and sign up for a library tour if one is offered. Most college libraries contain several floors of bookshelves (often called *stacks*), with fiction and nonfiction arranged according to the Dewey Decimal or Library of Congress system of classification (see pages 509–510). You'll also find sections for periodicals, microfilm and microfiche files, reference works, reserved books, government documents, rare books, and the like. Special collections may be housed in the main library or elsewhere; for example, an extensive music library may be located in the music department. In any case, the main library catalog lists all the material contained in such special collections.

The pages ahead provide detailed information about using library resources—the computerized or card catalog, the reference section, and periodicals.

The Computerized Catalog

Most college libraries now have **computerized catalogs** of their book holdings. If computer technology makes you nervous, you'll be pleased to learn that most computerized systems are equipped with on-screen prompts that make it easy to search for sources. Even so, don't wait until your paper is due to familiarize yourself with your college's on-line catalog system. It can be overwhelming to learn the system *and* conduct research at the same time. Instead, early in the academic year, spend an hour or so at the library. Take an orientation tour, read any handouts that are provided, speak to the librarian, experiment with the system. The confidence you gain will make all the difference when you begin researching in earnest.

In a typical on-line search, you'll be asked by the computer whether you want to search by *author, title,* or *subject.* If you're searching by author or title, you type into the terminal the author's first and last names or the title, respectively. If you're searching by subject, you type in a key word or phrase that summarizes your topic. You may have to try several key terms to discover under which term(s) the computer lists sources on your topic. Assume you're conducting research to identify classroom strategies that undermine student success. You might start by keying in the word *Education.* But that word would probably yield so many possibilities that you wouldn't know where to start. You might narrow your search by keying in "teaching techniques," "classroom practices," or "academic failure." For help in identifying appropriate key terms, speak with your college librarian. He or she will probably have you consult the *Library of Congress Subject Headings* or a bound or on-screen thesaurus of headings used in your library's data base.

One other point: When you search for a book by subject, the screen will usually indicate narrower subheadings under that topic. As soon as one of those subheads is clicked, the screen provides a list of books on that subject. To get complete bibliographic information about a specific book, follow the computer's instructions. The book's publisher, publication date, call number, and so on will then appear on the screen. Most computerized catalogs also indicate the status of a book—whether it is out on loan, overdue, lost, or available on loan. Here is one college's computerized card catalog display for a book on education in the inner city:

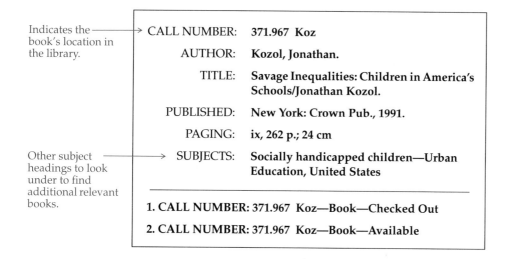

Indicates the book's location in the library.

CALL NUMBER: **371.967 Koz**

AUTHOR: **Kozol, Jonathan.**

TITLE: **Savage Inequalities: Children in America's Schools/Jonathan Kozol.**

PUBLISHED: **New York: Crown Pub., 1991.**

PAGING: **ix, 262 p.; 24 cm**

Other subject headings to look under to find additional relevant books.

SUBJECTS: **Socially handicapped children—Urban Education, United States**

1. CALL NUMBER: 371.967 Koz—Book—Checked Out

2. CALL NUMBER: 371.967 Koz—Book—Available

Once the computer identifies books on your subject, you can copy down the authors, titles, and call numbers (see pages 510–512) of promising books; or, in many libraries, you can direct the computer to print out a list. By mastering your library's computerized catalog, you'll find that it will take only minutes to identify sources that in the past might have taken you several hours to track down. One caution, however, about computerized catalogs: Few libraries have their entire collections on-line. Special collections and older books may not be included. If the data base isn't posted near the terminals, check with the librarian. You'll have to use the traditional card catalog to track down those sources not covered by the computerized catalog.

The Card Catalog

If your library isn't computerized, you'll need to use the traditional **card cata-log,** a file of cards listing all the books in the library. The catalog is arranged alphabetically by word rather than letter by letter: *music* would come before *musicians; social reformers* before *socialism.* If you're not sure with what word or term to start your search, consult a reference book that lists (alphabetically) the card catalog's subject headings. For libraries using the Dewey Decimal system, this book is the *Sears List of Subject Headings;* for libraries using the more common Library of Congress system, it is the *Library of Congress Subject Headings.*

Subject, Title, and Author Cards

To locate books on your topic, look under the appropriate subject headings; that is, use the catalog's **subject cards.** You'll find a card for each book the library owns on that subject. Again, suppose you're researching the classroom factors that inhibit student success. You could start by looking under the subject heading *Education*, jotting down the titles and call numbers (see below) of promising books. One might be the classic work *Why Children Fail* by John Holt. If you don't find appropriate books under the first subject heading (or if that heading yields a daunting number of prospects), try alternative headings. They are often listed on a separate card at the front of each catalog section devoted to a major subject heading. The *Education* card, for example, might list *Learning, styles of* and *Teaching strategies*. If you don't find such a cross-reference card, consult the *Library of Congress Subject Headings* or brainstorm words related to your topic. You could, for instance, look under *Instruction* or *Schools*.

The catalog also indexes books by *title* and by *author*. Imagine you already know about Holt's ground-breaking book and want to start your research by reading it. To see if your library has the book, you would look under the title (*How Children Fail*) or under the author (Holt). **Title cards** are arranged alphabetically according to the first word in the title, or according to the second word if the first is *A, An,* or *The.* **Author cards** are arranged alphabetically according to the author's last name. If a book has more than one author, there's a card for each.

Some libraries file author, title, and subject cards in a single catalog; others maintain one catalog for subject cards and a second for author and title cards.

Subject, title, and author cards contain the same information. The only difference is that subject cards have subject headings at the top, while title and author cards have, respectively, titles and authors' names at the top. Look carefully at the example below of a subject card, paying special attention to the information it provides.

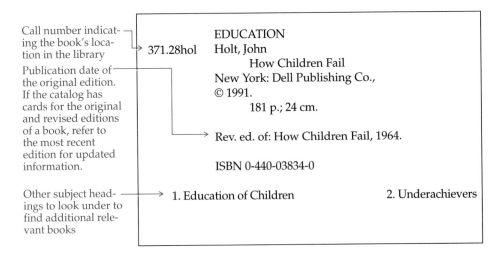

How to Find a Book

To locate a book on the shelves, use its **call number.** Besides appearing in the upper-left corner of the catalog card, the call number is printed on the spine of the book. There are two systems of call numbers in use in the United States—the **Dewey Decimal** and the **Library of Congress.** Most college libraries use the latter system, though some still reference older books by the Dewey Decimal system and more recent acquisitions by the Library of Congress. Check with the librarian to see which system(s) your library uses. Listed here are both systems' call numbers and the subjects they represent:

Dewey Decimal System

000–099 General Works
100–199 Philosophy and Psychology
200–299 Religion
300–399 Social Science
400–499 Language

500–599 Pure Science
600–699 Technology (Applied Sciences)
700–799 The Arts
800–899 Literature
900–999 History

Library of Congress System

A	General works—Polygraphy
B	Philosophy—Religion
C	History—Auxiliary Sciences
D	History and Topography (except America)
E–F	America
G	Geography—Anthropology
H	Social Sciences
J	Political Science
K	Law
L	Education
M	Music
N	Fine Arts
P	Language and Literature
Q	Science
R	Medicine
S	Agriculture—Plant and Animal Industry
T	Technology
U	Military Science
V	Naval Science
Z	Bibliography and Library Science

Once you have a book's call number, consult a map or list posted near the card catalog to determine the book's location in the stacks. If you don't see a list, ask the librarian. In libraries with closed stacks, make out a call slip so that a member of the staff can get the book for you.

If you can't find a book in the stacks, don't assume that it's been checked out. Perhaps it's tossed on a table close by, or it may have been replaced carelessly; take a look at books tucked at the ends of the shelves and placed sideways. If you still can't locate the book, consult the person at the circulation desk. If the book has been checked out, you can usually fill out a form to have the current borrower notified that you're waiting for the book, which will be held for you as soon as it is returned. You might also check with a librarian to see if the book has been put on reserve or moved to a special collection, or if it is available through an inter-library loan system. In libraries with computerized circulation systems, all you need to do is type in the book's call number, and the computer screen will tell you whether the book has been checked out, moved to a special location, or lost.

The Reference Section

As you already know, **reference works** can help you conduct preliminary research on a topic. Though they have limitations, reference volumes can also be useful at this point. Some reference works (*Encyclopaedia Britannica* and the *World Almanac and Book of Facts*) cover a wide range of subjects. Others (*Mathematics Dictionary* and *Dance Encyclopedia*) are more specialized and provide information about specific fields. Despite these differences, all reference volumes present significantly condensed information. They provide basic facts but not much interpretation. Explanations are brief. Most reference works are, then, unsuitable as sources for in-depth research. In fact, they're usually omitted from the list of Works Cited at the end of a paper.

How do you track down reference works that might be helpful? Start by looking up your subject in your library's card catalog or in its computerized catalog—or, if your library has one, in the separate card catalog for reference books. Record the call numbers and titles of those books marked "Ref" (Reference). The Library of Congress call number for reference is "Z," but a library may keep only some of its "Z" books in the reference section and the rest in the stacks. Most libraries arrange reference shelves alphabetically by subject ("Art," "Economics," "History"), making it easy to browse for other useful references once you've identified one on a subject. Keep in mind that reference materials don't circulate; that is, they cannot be checked out, so you must consult them while in the library.

Listed here are some of the common reference books found in most college libraries:

Biography

International Who's Who
Who's Who in America

Business/Economics

Dictionary of Banking and Finance
Encyclopedia of Economics

Ethnic/Feminist Studies

Encyclopedia of Feminism
Harvard Encyclopedia of American Ethnic Groups

Fine Arts

New Grove Dictionary of American Music
The New Harvard Dictionary of Music
The Oxford Companion to Art
The Thames and Hudson Dictionary of Art Terms

Literature/Film

The Oxford Companion to American Literature
The Oxford Companion to English Literature
World Encyclopedia of the Film

History/Political Science

Editorials on File
Encyclopedia of American Political History
Facts on File
A Political Handbook of the World

Philosophy/Religion

A Dictionary of Non-Christian Religions
The Encyclopedia of American Religions
An Encyclopedia of Philosophy

Science/Technology/Mathematics

A Dictionary of Mathematics
Encyclopedia of Medical History
McGraw-Hill Encyclopedia of Science and Technology
The Merck Index of Chemicals and Drugs

Psychology/Education

Encyclopedia of Education
Encyclopedia of Psychology
Encyclopedia of Special Education

Social Sciences

Dictionary of Anthropology
Encyclopedia of Crime and Justice
International Encyclopedia of the Social Sciences

Periodicals

Periodicals are publications issued at periodic (regular or intermittent) intervals throughout the year. There are three broad types of periodicals: general, scholarly, and serious.

General periodicals (daily newspapers and magazines such as *Time, Newsweek,* and *Psychology Today*) are designed for the average person. Such publications often adopt a personal or anecdotal writing style and offer easy-to-read overviews of subjects. Usually written by generalists rather than experts, the articles in such mass-market publications provide background information, but their lack of comprehensive coverage limits their usefulness for in-depth research. Moreover, since general circulation periodicals usually give only the briefest credit to the writers whose ideas they mention, readers have difficulty tracking down sources and being assured that information is reliable.

Intended for readers with specialized knowledge, **scholarly periodicals** (*Journal of Experimental Child Psychology, Renaissance Drama,* and *Veterinary Medicine*) provide objective, in-depth analyses written by authorities in the field. Such publications develop ideas with facts, studies, and well-reasoned commentary; they document fully the ideas they borrow.

Serious periodicals (*National Geographic, Scientific American,* and *Smithsonian*) are designed for well-educated laypeople rather than experts. These publications develop subjects with less depth than scholarly periodicals but provide a broader perspective. Like scholarly publications, they use a generally objective tone and back up their ideas with information and logic. Documentation is provided but often isn't as complete as it is in scholarly publications.

Periodical Indexes, Abstracts, and Bibliographies

Periodical indexes, issued anywhere from every two weeks to once a year, are cumulative directories that list articles published in certain journals, newspapers, and magazines. In addition, major newspapers, including the *New York Times,* publish annual subject directories. Most periodical indexes arrange listed articles under subject headings. Beneath the headings, individual articles are organized alphabetically by authors' last names.

To locate periodical indexes, you must learn how your library is organized. If there's a periodicals room, you'll probably find the periodical indexes located there, arranged alphabetically by title. In such a case, simply scan the shelves to find the index you want. Sometimes, periodical indexes are located in a separate alphabetically arranged section in the reference room, or, less helpfully, are shelved with reference volumes according to call number. Occasionally, you may find the periodical index to a highly specialized field shelved in the stacks near books in the same field of study. If you can't find the index you want in any of these locations, check with the librarian. You may have to use the computerized card catalog to find the index you want.

You're probably familiar with one index—the *Readers' Guide to Periodical Literature.* It lists general-interest articles published by popular newsstand magazines, such as *U.S. News & World Report* and *Sports Illustrated*. The *Readers' Guide* is issued twice a month in softcover volumes, which are compiled into quarterly, semiannual, and annual issues; once a year is ended, a library retains only the annual hardbound volume. When you were in high school, you probably used the *Readers' Guide* because it indexes accessible, nontechnical publications. To locate articles appropriate for college-level research, you'll need to consult indexes that list articles from more academic, professional, and specialized publications. The college equivalents of the *Readers' Guide* are the *Humanities Index* and the *Social Sciences Index* (below). You should become familiar with these indexes as well as with the major indexes for the field in which you plan to major (see pages 515–516).

Some specialized indexes provide brief descriptions of the articles they list. These indexes are usually called **abstracts.** Examples are *Abstracts of Folklore Studies, Criminal Justice Abstracts,* and *Psychological Abstracts.* Abstracts usually contain fewer listings than other types of indexes and are restricted to a limited field. In contrast to indexes that list only articles, **bibliographies** like the *Modern Language Association International Bibliography* list books as well as articles.

Listed here are representative indexes, abstracts, and bibliographies found in most college libraries. To save time, check with the librarian to see which of these sources can be accessed electronically at your library. (For information on indexes, abstracts, and bibliographies that are available in electronic form, see page 517.)

General

Biography Index
Humanities Index
New York Times Index
Readers' Guide to Periodical Literature
Social Sciences Index
Speech Index

Arts/Literature

Art Index
Book Review Index
Film Literature Index
Modern Language Association International Bibliography
Music Index
New York Times Book Review Index
Play Index

Business/Economics

Business Periodicals Index
International Bibliography of Economics
Wall Street Journal Index

Education

Education Abstracts
Education Index
ERIC (Education Resources Information Center)

History, Political Science, Government

Historical Abstracts
Monthly Index to United States Government Publications
Political Science Bibliographies
Public Affairs Information Service
Vertical File Index

Philosophy/Religion

Philosopher's Index
Religion Index

Psychology/Sociology

Psychological Abstracts
Sociological Abstracts

Sciences

Applied Science and Technology Index
Biological Abstracts
Botanical Bibliographies
Chemical Abstracts
Engineering Index Annual
Environment Index
International Computer Bibliography

Women's and Ethnic Studies

Bibliography on Women
Ethnic Newswatch
Hispanic American Periodicals Index
Index to Periodical Articles by and About Blacks
Women's Resources International

Computerized Indexes, Abstracts, and Bibliographies

A growing number of college libraries now offer computerized searches of many of the major indexes, abstracts, and bibliographies listed on page 517. In some libraries, a database that groups directories alphabetically by subject is maintained in the same system as the computerized catalog for books (see pages 508–509). In other libraries, there may be a separate bank of terminals for searching periodical directories. These terminals are usually hooked up to a **CD-ROM** (compact disc, read-only memory) player containing compact discs on which periodical indexes are stored. The CDs are usually updated monthly so that the information is more current than that found in the bound versions of the directories.

Here is a list of some of the most popular CD-ROM indexes. There are many others. Check to see which your library subscribes to.

- *Academic Search FullTEXT* (provides complete text of many articles, plus an index to the *New York Times*)
- *Art Index*
- *Business Periodicals Index*
- *Education Index*
- *Government Publications Index*
- *Health Index*
- *Humanities Index*
- *InfoTrac Academic Index* (includes the previous six months of the *New York Times*)
- *InfoTrac Magazine Index* (provides full text for many articles)
- *InfoTrac National Newspaper Index*
- *Magazine Index Plus*
- *Modern Language Association International Bibliography*
- *National Newspaper Index* (covers the *New York Times* and other important national newspapers like the *Atlanta Constitution* and the *Los Angeles Times*)
- *News Bank*
- *ProQuest General Periodicals Ondisc*
- *Readers' Guide to Periodical Literature*
- *Social Sciences Index*

More and more libraries offer telephone access to databases located off campus. Because access occurs through a telephone, there's usually a charge and possibly a time delay for retrieval of information. These telephone-access databases not only list the titles of specific journal articles but also print out the articles themselves— a feature that certainly justifies the small fee involved. Some major on-line databases are Dialog, Wilsonline, Nexis, and EBSCOhost.

As you no doubt realize, library technology is changing rapidly. Book catalogues, major reference works, as well as periodical indexes, abstracts, and bibliographies are available at some colleges not just on the library's computer terminals but also campus-wide through a complex computer network. At such technically sophisticated schools, students can conduct much of their research from their dorms at any time of the day or night. Other colleges have just begun to computerize their library operations. (For more information on accessing electronic information, see pages 520–532.)

Using Computerized and Printed Indexes

Besides saving time, computerized directories have the advantage of being current. Most are updated monthly (unlike print volumes, which are generally updated quarterly or annually). Plus, in many libraries the computer terminals at which you view database listings are hooked up to printers, enabling you to print out the listings rather than record them from the screen. Some on-line and CD-ROM databases offer access to the full text of selected articles or books. These texts may be read on screen and, if the computer terminal connects to a printer, printed out. Even when full text isn't available, you may have the option of printing out the *abstract* of a work that seems promising. Remember, though, an abstract is simply a summary. Although it can help you decide whether you should track down the original complete text, an abstract can't be cited as a source in your paper.

Being able to print out computerized text of work that originally appeared in print form is, of course, a real time-saver. However, computerized text has its drawbacks. Most on-line and CD-ROM databases don't indicate where page breaks occurred in the original. So, if you read computerized text of an article that originally appeared on, say, pages 22, 23, and 26 of a magazine, you'll have no way of knowing where one page ended and another began. Since you won't be able to provide exact page numbers, your readers may have difficulty locating, in the original, specific passages cited in your paper. The lack of page breaks underscores the fact that computerized text often works best for accessing texts that are unavailable or difficult to obtain in print; otherwise, it may be preferable to read and take notes on texts in their original print form.

Many computerized databases catalog only recent material, from the past few years or decades. When researching a topic with a historical component, you may find computerized indexes inadequate. For instance, to discover how J. D. Salinger's novel *The Catcher in the Rye* was received when it first appeared in 1951, you would need to identify articles and reviews written in that year. Bound volumes of the *Modern Language Association International Bibliography, Book Review Index,* and the *New York Times Book Review Index* would provide you with the needed information.

Whether a periodicals directory is in computerized or print form, you can search by subject (keywords) to uncover titles of relevant articles. If you don't find your subject listed in a printed index, or if a computerized database yields no titles when you type in keywords, try alternate terms for your topic. Suppose you're researching the subject of business ethics. In addition to using "Business ethics" as your subject heading or keywords, you might try "Bribery" or "Fraud" to find relevant articles. Both computerized and print indexes also show cross-references. By looking under "Business ethics," you might see suggested search terms such as "Advertising ethics," "Banking, ethical aspects," and "Commercial crime."

Periodicals directories in print form list articles alphabetically, both by subject and by author. Under each subject, articles are listed alphabetically by title. When using a computerized guide to articles in periodicals, type in either an author's name or your subject. The database will then list appropriate articles, usually in reverse chronological order (most recent first). The precise procedures for searching computerized databases vary; libraries usually post instructions for the particular databases they offer.

Printed indexes such as the *Readers' Guide to Periodical Literature* and computerized indexes supply basically the same information. Take a look at the sample *Readers' Guide* entry and the corresponding entry from a computerized database (EBSCOhost).

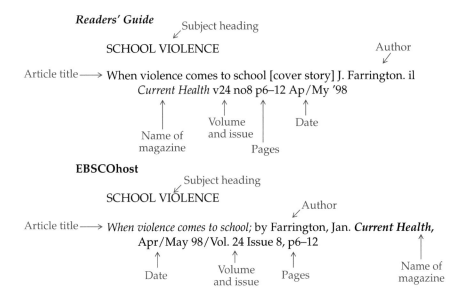

Both entries provide all the information you need to find an article. The front of the *Readers' Guide* volume that you're using lists abbreviations and their meanings. In the event of any puzzling abbreviations or symbols in computerized guides, ask your librarian either to explain their meaning or to direct you to a printed key for an explanation.

Be sure not to end your search for appropriate material until you've consulted the most pertinent indexes and bibliographies. For a paper on the psychology of child abuse, you might start with the *New York Times Index* and then move to more specialized volumes, such as *Psychological Abstracts, Child Development Abstracts,* and *Mental Health Book Review Index.* To ensure that you don't miss current developments in your subject area, always start with the most recent years and work your way back.

Locating Specific Issues of Periodicals

If you can't print out computerized text of relevant articles, you'll need to obtain the original text. To do so, you first have to determine whether your library owns the specific periodicals and the issues you want. If your library catalogs its periodicals on-line, search for a periodical by typing in its name. Does that particular name appear on screen? If it does, your library owns issues of that publication. With a few additional keystrokes, you can obtain more detailed information—such as the specific volumes held by your library and the periodical's call number and location in the library.

If your library doesn't catalog its periodicals on line, look for a card catalog of holdings. Some libraries list the periodicals they own in the general card catalog. Other libraries have a separate periodicals card catalog, usually located in the periodicals or reference room. Whether the card catalog you use is general or restricted to periodicals, look up periodicals by name. A periodical card will usually tell you the issues owned by the library, their call number, and their location. Issue numbers and dates given at the top of the card usually refer to the first issues published, not to the first issues owned by the library. Information about issues owned by the library generally appears at the bottom of the card.

If your library maintains neither an on-line catalog nor a card catalog that references periodicals, check with your librarian. He or she will direct you to a computer printout, a spiral-bound volume, or some other source that lists the library's periodicals.

Recent issues of magazines, newspapers, and journals are kept in the library's current periodicals section, where they are arranged alphabetically by name. Less current issues can be found in the periodicals room, in the stacks, or on microfilm. Bound volumes of periodicals don't circulate. Back issues of major newspapers are usually stored on microfilm filed in cabinets in a separate location.

USE THE INTERNET

Computer technology—in one form or another—is part of nearly everyone's life nowadays. Nothing demonstrates the staggering impact of the computer revolution more powerfully than the growth of the **Internet,** also called the **Net.** This global network of interlinked computer systems puts a massive storehouse of information within the reach of anyone with access to a personal computer and a **modem,** a device that transmits electronic data over a telephone line.

Such a wealth of material presents obvious research benefits to you as a student. However, when faced with the task of using the Internet, you may feel overwhelmed and unsure of how to proceed. The following pages will help; they'll introduce you to the Internet, show you how to access its resources, and offer pointers on evaluating the material you find there.

The Internet and the World Wide Web

The Internet is the catch-all term for the global network that links individual computer networks at tens of thousands of educational, scientific, state, federal and commercial agencies in over 63 countries. While the **World Wide Web** exists *on* the Internet, the two are not synonymous. The Internet is the nuts-and-bolts of the network: the cables and computers. The World Wide Web refers to a global information system existing *within* the Internet. The Web consists of uncounted millions of Web

sites. Some Web sites feature text only; others contain graphics; still others contain audio and video components. Although there's great variation in the content and design of Web sites, all contain a *home page* (modeled after the contents page of a book) that provides the site's title, introductory descriptive material about the site, and a menu consisting of **links** to the information that can accessed from the site. A link is a stepping stone to other pages on the site or to a related Web site. You can jump from the first location to the next just by clicking on the link. (For more on links, see page 526).

What the Web Offers

While often compared to a library, the Web is more accurately thought of as an enormous storage shed, piled to the ceiling with boxes and crates and items of every description. Because it's not subject to a central system of organization, and because anyone—from Nobel Prize winners to representatives of the most extreme fringe groups—can post material on it at any time, the Web is in a state of constant flux. The quality of information found on the Web ranges from authoritative to speculative to fraudulent. It's impossible to say with certainty even how large the Web is. Anywhere from 20 to 50 million pages of data may be represented by the millions of Web sites in operation.

What can be stated with confidence is that the World Wide Web offers a collection of data that surpasses anything the world has ever seen. With the click of a mouse, you can read electronic versions of the *Washington Post* or the *London Times;* you can search the holdings of the Library of Congress, check the temperature in Moscow, or get up-to-the-minute stock quotes; you can scan breaking news from Associated Press or learn the latest information on alternative treatments for arthritis.

The Advantages and Limitations of the Library and the Web

The availability of the Web makes doing research over the computer an attractive option. But that doesn't mean that libraries have become obsolete. Both the library and the Web have strengths and weaknesses. Depending upon your topic and its focus, one may be a better starting point than the other. Here are some issues to consider:

- The library is *consistently organized.* With some guidance from the catalog system and the reference librarian, you can quickly locate materials that are relevant to your topic.
- Because the Web *doesn't have a centralized organizational structure,* you are automatically—and somewhat haphazardly—exposed to a staggering array of material. If you're not sure how to focus your topic, browsing the Web may help you narrow your topic by identifying directions you wouldn't have thought of on your own. Conversely, the sheer volume of material on your subject may leave you stunned and glassy-eyed, the information overload making you feel all the more confused about how to proceed.

- Some sources in the library may be dated or even no longer accurate. By contrast, on-line material is almost always up-to-date because it can be posted on the Web as soon as it's created. (See pages 531–532 for hints on evaluating the currency of electronic data.)

- The instantaneous nature of Web postings can create problems, though. Library materials certainly aren't infallible, but most have gone through a process of editorial review before being published. This is often *not* the case with material on the Web. Most of us realize that the claim "I saw it in the newspaper!" doesn't ensure that information is accurate or valid. "I saw it on the Web!" is even less of a guarantee. Given this basic limitation, it's a good idea not to rely solely on the Web when you research your topic. Consider using it as a supplement to, rather than a substitute for, library research. (For more about evaluating the validity of material on the Web, see pages 531–532.)

Accessing the Web

Access to the Web ("going on-line") is provided through a software program called a **web browser.** Netscape, Internet Explorer, and Mosaic are several widely used browsers. If you're a student at one of the many colleges or universities providing Web access to students, you'll probably use one of these browsers. Commercial on-line services, such as America Online, Prodigy, and CompuServe, have their own browsers.

If you don't have access to a college-provided browser, you'll probably want to subscribe to a commercial on-line service and use its browser. (Most commercial services offer two options: You pay only for the time you're on-line—which is best if you use the service only occasionally and for brief periods—or you pay a flat monthly fee that allows you all the on-line time you want.) An on-line service, along with your modem and a printer, makes it possible for you to conduct a good deal of your research at home.

Using On-line Time Efficiently

Whether you access the Web through a university-provided service or a commercial provider, you need to learn how to make efficient use of your on-line time. The Internet is known as the "information superhighway," and the analogy is a good one. Like any superhighway, the Internet has its rush hours and even its periods of gridlock. Here are some suggestions to keep you cruising in the express lane:

- Experiment with logging on at different times of day and evening. Typically, evening hours (approximately 6 p.m. to 10 p.m.) are times of peak Internet traffic. If you have trouble getting through to particular sites, you may have more success earlier in the day or later at night.

- If it takes more than a couple of minutes to retrieve files from a Web site, hit the "Stop" or "Cancel" button and try again later.

- If you don't need to see the graphics (illustrations, photographs, charts, and so on) included in a Web site, check if your browser offers a "text only" option. If it does, activate that option. Waiting for graphics to download can increase your on-line time substantially.

• Just as you do when conducting library research, be sure to record sufficient information about your on-line source so you can provide full documentation when it comes time to write your paper. Specifically, when you print information from the Web, make sure your browser is set so that the material's title, date, page as well as the date of your retrieval appear on the printed copy. You also need to check that the **URL** (*uniform resource locator*), or Internet **address**, appears clearly on the copy. Having the address makes it possible for you to return to the site in the future.

Here is the address—broken down into elements—for the daily edition of the newspaper *The Hong Kong Standard:*

http://www.hkstandard.com/online/news/001/hksnews.htm

You'll note that *http*: ("hypertext transfer protocol") is the first element in the Web address. It tells the sending and receiving computers how to transfer the information. Next is *www.hkstandard.com,* with *www.* indicating that the site is located on the World Wide Web. After that comes the Internet address of the institution, agency, corporation, or organization (in this case the *Hong Kong Standard,* represented by *hkstandard*). The *.com* portion indicates that the site is a commercial one.* Following the slash, the *online/news/00l/hksnews.htm* tells where the site's files are stored, the path to those files, and the name of the particular file being retrieved. (The *.htm*—often written as *html*—stands for *hypertext mark-up language,* the language in which these particular Web pages are written.)

It's critical that you key in an address exactly as it appears on the Web site's home page. Don't capitalize something that originally was in lowercase letters, and don't leave extra space between elements in the address. Keying in even slight changes in the address usually makes it impossible to access the site.

• When you find a Web site that you like and may want to visit again, use your browser's **Bookmark** or **Favorite Places** option. (Typically, you will find the bookmark option on your browser's pull-down menu.) After you "bookmark" a site, its address is saved in your personal file, so you can click on its name and instantly return to the site, without having to remember (and key in) its address.

---

*The **domain name** is that portion of the address indicating the type of organization at a specific address. The domain name consists of the organization's name (in the case above, *hkstandard*), followed by a period (called a **dot**) and one of several domain abbreviations (in the example above, *.com* for the *Hong Kong Standard*). The primary domains are as follows:

.com—commercial   .mil—military
.net—Internet service providers   .org—non-profit organizations
.edu—educational institutions   .gov—government

For example, tusk.edu is the domain name for Tuskegee University.

Using the Net to Find Books on Your Topic

Assume that you've used your college's computerized catalog to track down several books on your subject. Now you'd like to go on-line to see if there are additional books you might find helpful. In such a case, you access one or both of the following national booksellers:

Barnes and Noble Books at http://www.barnesandnoble.com

Amazon Books at http://www.amazon.com

At either site, you would use the "Browse Subjects" box on the bookseller's home page to identify relevant books. Let's say you want to investigate the way the experience of childhood poverty affected the politics of specific American presidents. Using the "Browse Subjects" box, you note that one of the subject listings is "Biography." Clicking on "Biography," you see that one of the subcategories is "Presidents." Click on "Presidents," and a list of books on American presidents appears. By clicking on specific titles from the list, you obtain information about each book, including reviewer and reader comments. With this information, you can usually determine which books are appropriate for your purpose. At that point, you might purchase the relevant books on-line or, more likely, check the availability of the books at a library other than the one at your college.

On-line booksellers can also help you narrow your topic. Perhaps you want to research the topic of illiteracy. As soon as you type the word "illiteracy" in the "Key Words" box on the bookseller's home page, you receive a long list of books on the subject. Simply looking at the range of titles can help you narrow your research. You might, for example, decide to focus on illiteracy in the workplace, teenagers' declining reading scores, or programs that teach marginally literate parents how to read to their children.

Using the Net to Find Articles and Other Materials on Your Topic

What do you do if you want to go online to track down articles, speeches, legislation, TV transcripts, and so on about your subject? How, given the staggering array of online material, can you identify sources that will be pertinent? Search directories and search engines will help.

Search Directories

A **search directory,** a service that organizes Web sites by categories, will begin pointing you in the right direction. New search directories crop up regularly, but one of the most popular and user-friendly is Yahoo! The address of Yahoo! is http://www.yahoo.com.* Figure 20.1 (page 525) is an approximation of what you'll see when you go to Yahoo's home page. (Bear in mind that Web sites change

---

*Addresses are subject to change. Addresses given in the chapter are current as of April 1999.

Search advanced search

Yahoo! Mail - Get your **free** e-mail account today!

Shopping - Yellow Pages - People Search - Maps - Travel Agent - Classifieds - Personals - Games - Chat
Email - Calendar - Pager - My Yahoo! - Today's News - Sports - **Weather** - TV - Stock Quotes - more...

Arts & Humanities
Literature, Photography...

Business & Economy
Companies, Finance, Jobs...

Computers & Internet
Internet, WWW, Software, Games...

Education
Universities, K-12, College Entrance...

Entertainment
Cool Links, Movies, Humor, Music...

Government
Military, Politics, Law, Taxes...

Health
Medicine, Diseases, Drugs, Fitness...

News & Media
Full Coverage, Newspapers, TV...

Recreation & Sports
Sports, Travel, Autos, Outdoors...

Reference
Libraries, Dictionaries, Quotations...

Regional
Countries, Regions, US States...

Science
Biology, Astronomy, Engineering...

Social Science
Archaeology, Economics, Languages...

Society & Culture
People, Environment, Religion...

In the News
- U.S. jets hit targets in N Iraq
- Albright clashes with China over rights
- Weekend's top movies
  more...

Marketplace
- Y! Auctions - a shopping treasure hunt
- Looking for a car? job? house?
  more...

Inside Yahoo!
- Y! Clubs - create your own
- Free Fantasy Baseball - sign up today
- Y! Tax Center - organize, prepare and file
- Y! Entertainment
  more...

World Yahoo!s *Europe* : Denmark - France - Germany - Italy - Norway - Spain - Sweden - UK & Ireland
Pacific Rim : Australia & NZ - HK - Japan - Korea - Singapore - Taiwan -- Asia - Chinese
Americas : Canada - Spanish

Yahoo! Get Local LA - NYC - SF Bay - Chicago - more...   Enter Zip Code

Other Guides Autos - Computers - Employment - Local Events - Net Events - Message Boards - **Movies**
Music - Real Estate - Small Business - Ski & Snow - Y! Internet Life - Yahooligans!

How to Suggest a Site - Company Info - Privacy Policy - Contributors - Openings at Yahoo!

Figure 20.1   Yahoo! home page.

constantly. What appears on your computer screen may not be identical to what is presented here.)

Making Use of Links on the Web.   As you see, Yahoo! divides Web sites into 14 categories: Arts & Humanities, Business & Economy, and so on. Each category is presented as a **link** (see page 521). Typically, a link shows up as an underlined word or phrase that is a different color from the type elsewhere on the page. When you click on a link, you're automatically transported to a related site. There you are presented with a more detailed list of Web sites to choose from. As you move from link to link, you move from the general topic to more specific aspects of the topic. For example, say you are researching the legal rights of the disabled. You notice that there's a section titled "Law" under the category "Government." Click on "Law" and you're presented with a screen that lists several dozen law-related links, from "arbitration and mediation" to "trade." (There's even a link for "lawyer jokes.") When you see the link "disabilities," you know you're on the right track. You click on that link; Figure 20.2 (page 527) presents what would then appear on your screen. Clicking on any of the displayed links provides access to that web site as well as related ones.

Exploring Other Search Directories.   Yahoo! is only one of many search directories worth using as you explore the Internet. Here are addresses and brief descriptions of several additional directories:

- Excite (http://www.excite.com) claims to have more than 11.5 million Web pages indexed. This site receives high "relevancy rankings" (indications of how closely hits match a request) from users.
- Galaxy (http://www.einet.net) bills itself as "The Web's resources, compiled for professionals" rather than for those conducting scholarly research. It has a relatively small database, divided into nine categories.
- Infoseek (http://www.infoseek.com) has the reputation of doing a good job of maintaining its bank of Web sites, which saves the annoyance of trying to connect to a site and finding that it's no longer active. Information is returned in an especially easy-to-understand format.
- Internet Services List (http://sirius.we.lc.ehu.es/internet/inet.services.html) is more specialized than Yahoo! and lets you search over a hundred subject categories. For example, "botany," "biology," and "physics" each has its own category, rather than being lumped under "sciences"; similarly, there's a category for "ham radio," not just for "hobbies."
- LookSmart (http://www.looksmart.com/r?lmp&hl), rather than immediately offering links to other sites, displays more and more specialized menus on the screen while keeping visible the menus you've already moved through. Such an approach makes this an especially easy and enjoyable directory to use.
- Magellan (http://www.mckinley.com) offers useful reviews and ratings of the Web sites in its database. These rankings can save you a good deal of time by helping you focus on the sites that are most useful.

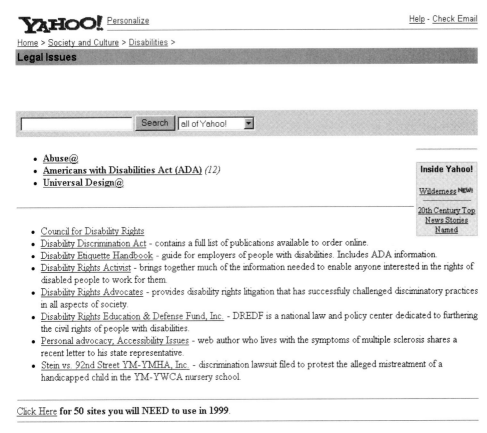

Figure 20.2   Disability legal issues page from Yahoo!

- My Virtual Reference Desk (http://www.refdesk.com) is an amazing collection that lets you access daily newspapers from around the world, on-line magazines, encyclopedias, almanacs, and links to several hundred search engines (see below). Don't pass this site up!

Search Engines

Search directories, like Yahoo!, are wonderful tools when you begin exploring your topic. But when you're refining your investigation, you'll want to use another kind of resource—the **search engine.** Search engines are tools that comb through the vast amount of information on the Web for sites or documents that match your research needs. You activate a search engine by typing in key words or phrases that tell the engine what to look for.

Here is a list of several popular search engines and their addresses. You'll notice that some overlap with the partial list of search directories on page 526. Why? The reason is that some search directories, such as LookSmart, have their own built-in search engines.

- AltaVista (http://www.altavista.digital.com) offers the largest data base of all the search engines. Because of the huge size of its Web site collection, you'll find it an excellent place to hunt for out-of-the-ordinary subjects. But, if you're researching a more common subject, you may become frustrated having to wade through the enormous number of hits you'll get.
- AOL Netfind (http://www.aol.com/netfind) is the search engine built into America Online. Other large commercial service providers (such as CompuServe and Prodigy) have similar built-in search engines. Users of such online providers are automatically routed to the service's search engine when they click on the "Search the Internet" option offered on the welcome menu.
- Electric Library (http://www.Elibrary.com) contains the full text of millions of newspaper and magazine articles as well as thousands of book chapters and television and radio transcripts.
- HotBot (http://www.hotbot.com) allows you to tailor your search by limiting the number of hits returned (from 10 to 100), the date the material was posted (from in the last week to anytime), and the geographical area from which the material originated.
- LookSmart (http://www.looksmart.com) prefaces each hit that comes back with a brief description as well as a note of where the hit is categorized in LookSmart's search directory.
- Lycos (http://www.lycos.com), one of the first and still one of the largest search engines, has some of the same pros and cons as AltaVista: a huge data base, but a sometimes overwhelming number of hits. Some hits may lead to outdated or no longer functioning sites.
- Yahoo! (http://www.yahoo.com) is a popular search engine as well as a search directory. When you click on the "options" button beside the search box, you'll receive especially helpful suggestions for tailoring your search. Once you're on the "options" page, clicking on "help" provides even more specific tips for tracking down material.
- WebCrawler (http://www.webcrawler.com) lets you see summaries of the Web sites you've hit before accessing the sites themselves. WebCrawler's "what's hot" feature indicates the fifty most accessed links from the previous week.

Tips for Using Search Engines.   When you reach the home page of a search engine, it's a good idea to click on the "help" or "tips" button. When you do, you'll receive specific guidelines for using that particular search engine efficiently. As you proceed, don't forget to "bookmark" (see page 523) the search engines you use so you can return to them easily at a later date.

Figure 20.3 (page 529) is an example of a search engine home page, this one from Lycos. Note that at the top of the Lycos home page, there's an empty box beside "Search for." That's where you type in the word or words describing your research topic. After you click on "Go Get It" (or whatever your search engine calls its "search" command), the engine scans the Web for your keyword(s). It then

Figure 20.3   Lycos home page.

provides you with a list of "hits," or links, to Web sites where your keyword is found. Most search engines also provide a brief description of each site.

How to Limit Your Search.   The success of your search depends on how carefully you follow your search engine's guidelines and on how specific and descriptive your search terms are. For example, say you're doing research on animal-rights activism. Depending upon your search engine, if you simply enter the words *animal rights activism* in the search box, the engine may provide a list of *every* document that contains the word "animal" or "rights" or "activism"—hundreds of thousands of hits. Again, the most efficient way to limit the number of hits you get is to follow with great care your search engine's specific guidelines. If no guidelines are provided or if the guidelines are confusing, try these suggestions:

- Put quotation marks around the phrase you are searching for—in this case, "animal rights activism." Many search engines interpret the quotation marks to mean you want only those documents that include the words *animal rights activism* next to each other. If you don't include the quotation marks, you may receive listings for each word.
- To focus your search further, use the plus (+) and minus (-) signs, leaving no space before or after the signs. Say you're interested in animal-rights activism as it applies to protests against the wearing of fur. Try typing this in the search box:

  +"animal rights activism"+fur

  The + signs before *animal rights activism* and before *fur* instruct the search to locate items that contain both sets of keywords. A minus (–) sign has the opposite effect. If you want information about animal-rights activism, *excluding* information about fur, you would type your search phrase like this:

  +"animal rights activism"–fur

- Use the Boolean* operative words AND, OR, and NOT to limit your search. When you investigate a topic via a search engine that recognizes Boolean logic (the search tips will indicate if it does, or you can experiment on your own as you type in search phrases), using these operatives between key terms broadens or narrows the range of your search. For example, assume you typed the following: reggae music AND Rastafarians AND Jamaica. Using the operative *AND* instructs the search engine to return only those documents containing all three search terms.

Using Discussion Groups and Newsgroups

Thousands of discussion groups and newsgroups operate on the Web, focusing on every topic imaginable. You can find addresses for these groups in various ways: in computer publications and special-interest magazines, or by conducting a search through a search engine.

An online **discussion group** consists of individuals who share a similar interest, with members of the group communicating with one another through e-mail. Each e-mail message is automatically distributed to everyone on the discussion

---

*Named for George Boole, a nineteenth-century mathematician, Boolean logic modifies search items through the use of the "operators" AND, OR, and NOT.

group's membership list. A **newsgroup** operates in a similar fashion, except that no membership is required. Instead of communicating through e-mail, people post messages on a central "bulletin board," where anyone can read and respond to a message. In a moderated newsgroup, contributions are reviewed by a group facilitator before being posted to the group at large. In unmoderated newsgroups, there is no such review. Not surprisingly, unmoderated newsgroups tend to have a high ratio of junk mail.

Keep in mind that anyone—scholar, fraud, con artist, or saint—can voice an opinion in a discussion group. Also, be careful not to assume that a talkative member of a group is necessarily an expert: any self-styled "authority" can access an on-line group. Despite these problems, newsgroups and discussion groups *can* be helpful sources of information and provide valuable leads as you do your research. They may also put you in e-mail touch with respected authorities in your field of research.

Evaluating Internet Materials

As noted in the preceding section and on page 522, you need to take special care to evaluate the worth of material you find on the Web. Electronic documents may appear seemingly out of nowhere and can disappear without a trace. And anyone with access to a computer and modem can create a Web page or state a position in a discussion group. How, then, do you know if a source found on the Net is credible? Here are some questions to ask when you work with on-line material:

- Who is the author of the material? Does the author offer his or her credentials in the form of a résumé or biographical information? Do these credentials qualify the author to provide information on the topic? Does the author provide an e-mail address so you can request more information? The less you know about an author, the more suspicious you should be about using the data.

- Can you verify the accuracy of the information presented? Does the author refer to studies or to other authors you can investigate? If the author doesn't cite other works or other points of view, that may suggest the document is opinionated and one-sided. In such a case, it's important to track down material addressing alternative points of view.

- Who is sponsoring the Web site? Many sites are published by organizations— businesses, agencies, lobby groups—as well as by individuals. If a sponsor pushes a single point of view, you should use the material with great caution. And once again, make an extra effort to locate material addressing other sides of the issue.

- Is the information cited recent and up-to-date? Being on the Internet doesn't guarantee that information is current. To assess the timeliness of Internet materials, check at the top or bottom of the document for copyright date, publication date, and/or revision date. Having those dates will help you determine whether the material is recent enough for your purposes.

Using Other Internet Tools

The World Wide Web is not the only portion of the Internet that you'll find interesting or useful. Other aspects of the Net include Telnet, a software networking tool that allows you to log onto another computer and access its files; FTPs (File Transfer Protocols), through which you download files from remote computers and upload files to computers to which you have access; and Gopher, a comprehensive menu-based program developed at the University of Minnesota. If you become interested in the workings of the Net beyond the World Wide Web and want to investigate further, your favorite search engine—and your college librarian—should provide the help you need. Finally, don't be shy about asking any Net-savvy folks you know for advice. Most computer buffs are more than willing to share their knowledge. With very little prodding from you, they'll be happy to explain the ins and outs of the Net and provide valuable assistance for accessing its wealth of information.

PREPARE A WORKING BIBLIOGRAPHY

As you gather promising books, reference volumes, print articles, and on-line material about your subject, prepare a **working bibliography**—a master list of potential sources. Having such a list means you won't have to waste time later tracking down a source whose title you remember only vaguely.

Since you want to read as much as you can about your subject, the working bibliography will contain more sources than your instructor requires for the final paper. In the long run, you probably won't use all the sources in your working bibliography. Some will turn out to be less helpful than you thought they would be; others may focus on an aspect of your topic you decide not to cover after all.

The working bibliography may be compiled on standard notebook paper or, preferably, on index cards, one card for each source. We recommend 4 × 6-inch cards rather than 3 × 5-inch ones or sheets of paper. Unlike sheets of paper, index cards can be arranged in alphabetical order quickly, making it easy to prepare your Works Cited list (see page 556). And the larger index cards give you room to comment on a source's value ("Good discussion of landfill regulations") or availability ("See if book is on reserve").

Whether you use notebook paper or index cards to prepare your working bibliography, take time to record the following information (to see sample bibliography cards, turn to pages 536–538):

- If the source is a book, write down its title, author, and call number.
- If the source is an article in a reference volume, note the titles of both the article and the reference work, the article's author, and the reference work's call number.

- If the source is an article in a periodical, note the titles of both the article and periodical, the article's author, and the article's date and pages.
- If you obtain an article title by using a CD-ROM or going on-line, write down the same information you would if you were using a print directory. If you don't expect to locate the article in print form (because a print version is either nonexistent or difficult to obtain), then also note any information essential for accessing the article electronically. For example, if you want later on to locate the article's text on the same CD-ROM you are using as an index, write down "CD-ROM" and the data base (for example, *ERIC*). For an on-line source, note the data base (for example, *Magazine Database Plus*); the computer network or service through which you access the data base (for example, CompuServe), and any keyboard commands you need to access the material, especially the on-line address).

Recording this basic information helps you locate these potentially useful sources later on. In the next stage, as you start taking notes, you'll refine the information in your working bibliography.

TAKE NOTES TO SUPPORT THE THESIS WITH EVIDENCE

Why Take Notes?

Now that you've formed a working thesis, identified promising sources, and compiled a working bibliography, it's almost time to take notes. Your goal at this point is to find support for your preliminary thesis—*and* to pay close attention to material suggesting alternative viewpoints. Sifting through this conflicting information will enable you to refine your working thesis with more precision. (For more about evaluating contrasting positions, see pages 534–535). At this point you may be wondering why you should take notes at all. Why not simply read the sources and then draft the research paper, referring to the sources when you need to check a fact or quote something?

Such an approach is bound to create problems. For one thing, you may have to return a source to the library before you're ready to start writing. Taking the time to go back to the library to retrieve the source later on can slow you down considerably—and, in fact, someone else could have checked out the only copy of the source. With note cards, though, you'll have all the necessary information at hand without having to return to the original source.

Moreover, if you have your sources in front of you as you write, you'll be tempted to move large chunks of material directly from your sources to your paper, without first evaluating and distilling the material. Writing directly from your sources also aggravates any tendency you may have to string together one quotation after another, without providing many ideas of your own. Worst of all, such an approach often leads to *plagiarism:* passing off someone else's work as your own. (For more on plagiarism, see pages 542, 547–548, and 565–573.)

Note-taking can eliminate such problems. When done well, it encourages you to assess, synthesize, and react to your sources. Keeping your working thesis firmly in mind, you examine what others have to say about your subject. Some authors will support your working thesis; others will serve as "devil's advocates," prodding you to consider opposing viewpoints. In either case, note-taking helps you refine your position and develop a sound basis for your conclusions.

Before Note-Taking: Evaluate Sources

You shouldn't take notes on a source until after you've evaluated its *relevance, timeliness, seriousness of approach,* and *objectivity.* Titles can be misleading. If a source turns out to be irrelevant, skip note-taking; just indicate on your working bibliography that you consulted the source and found it didn't relate to your topic. Next, consider the source's age. To some extent, the topic and kind of research you're doing determine whether a work is outdated. If you're researching a historical topic such as the internment of Japanese Americans during World War II, you would most likely consult sources published in the 1940s and 1950s, as well as more up-to-date sources. In contrast, if you're investigating a recent scientific development—*in vitro* fertilization, for example—it would make sense to restrict your search to current material. For most college research, a source older than ten years is considered outdated unless it was the first to present key concepts in a field.

You should also ask yourself if each source is serious and scholarly enough for your purpose and your instructor's requirements. Finally, examine your sources for possible bias, keeping in mind that a strong conclusion or opinion is *not in itself* a sign of bias. As long as a writer doesn't ignore opposing positions or distort evidence, a source can't be considered biased. A biased source presents only those facts that fit the writer's predetermined conclusions. Such a source is often marked by emotionally charged language (see pages 22–23). Publications sponsored by special interest groups—a particular industry, religious association, or political party—are usually biased. Reading such materials *does* familiarize you with a specific point of view, but remember that contrary evidence has probably been ignored or skewed.

A special problem occurs when you find a source that takes a position contrary to the one that you had previously considered credible. When you come across such conflicting material, you can be sure you've identified a pivotal issue within your topic. To decide which position is more valid, you need to take good notes from both sources (see pages 539–549) or carefully annotate your photocopies (see pages 541–542). Then evaluate each source for bias. On this basis alone, you might discover serious flaws in one or both sources. Also compare the key points and supporting evidence in the two sources. Where do they agree? Where do they disagree? Does one source argue against the other's position, perhaps even discrediting some of the opposing view's evidence? The answers to these questions may very well cause you to question the quality, completeness, or fairness of one or both sources. To resolve such a conflict of sources, you can also research your subject more fully. For example, if your conflicting sources are at the general or serious level (see page 514), you should probably turn to more scholarly sources. By referring to more authoritative material, you may be able to determine which of the conflicting sources is more valid.

When you try to resolve discrepancies between sources, be sure not to let your own bias come into play. Try not to favor one position over the other simply because it supports your working thesis. Remember, your goal is to arrive at the most well-founded position you can. In fact, researching a topic may lead you to change your original viewpoint. In this case, you shouldn't hesitate to revise your working thesis to accord with the evidence you gather.

Before Note-Taking: Refine Your Working Bibliography

After determining the sources from which you will take notes, spend some time refining the relevant entries in your working bibliography. With the sources in front of you, use the following guidelines to fill in any missing information. (At times, the guidelines include a bit more information than MLA requires. This precision will often be helpful if you use a format other than MLA.)

- Take down the *authors' names* exactly as they appear on the title pages of the original works and in the order shown there. The author listed first is considered the primary author, so don't rearrange the names alphabetically. Occasionally, a work will be attributed to an organization, university, or institute rather than to a person. If so, consider that organization the author.
- For a *book*, record from the title page the full title (including any subtitle) and the publisher's name, noting only key words (Townsend, *not* Townsend Press). Also, record the publisher's location. If the publisher is international, use the publishing location in your country, if there is one. If several locations within your country are listed, use as the city of publication the one that's listed first on the title page. Also record the copyright year, the most recent year in which the text was registered, as well as the volume number for multivolume books. If you have doubts whether your edition is the most recent, check the computerized on-line or card catalog to see if the library has a later one. Remember, the number of editions in which a book has appeared is not the same as the number of printings the book has gone through. A book may say "ninth printing," yet be only the second edition. Finally, don't forget to note the book's call number.
- For a *mass-publication magazine*, note the author's name (if any), the article title, the magazine title, the date (usually month and year), and the pages on which the article appears.
- For a *newspaper article*, take down the author's name (if any), the article title, the newspaper title, the date (month, day, and year), the edition, and the section and pages where the article appears.

- For an *article in a book-length collection*, record the authors of the article, the article title, the book title, the book's editor, the publisher and its location, the copyright date, and the specific book pages on which the article appears.
- For an *article in a scholarly or serious journal*, note the article's author(s), the article title, the journal title, the date (including month and year), the volume and issue (if any), and the pages on which the article appears. Also indicate whether the journal is paginated continuously from issue to issue throughout a given year or whether each issue is paginated separately. Take down the publisher's location only if two periodicals have the same name. In such a case, indicate the city of publication by placing it in parentheses after the periodical's name.
- For all periodicals, note the library location of relevant issues.
- For *text obtained on CD-ROM or on-line*, note the identical information you would for a printed source in the same category (for example, a magazine article), with the possible exception of page numbers. If the data base doesn't specify an article's precise page numbers (see pages 562–563), write down the page number (if available) on which the article began in the original, plus the number of pages or number of paragraphs in the article. In addition, for CD-ROM text, note the data base (for instance, *New York Times Ondisc*), CD-ROM publisher (for example, UMI-ProQuest), and CD-ROM publication date. For text accessed on-line, note the data base (for instance, *New York Times Online*), the computer service or network (for example, Nexis), your date of access, and any other information someone would need to retrieve the text (such as the on-line address).

We suggest that you display bibliographic information as it appears in the sample cards below and on the next two pages. Be sure to include any information you might need for your paper's Works Cited or References page. If your working bibliography is accurate and complete, you won't need to refer to your sources later on when preparing your paper's final reference list.

QL785.27
.M37
1995

Masson, Jeffrey Moussaieff, and Susan
      McCarthy. When Elephants Weep:
      The Emotional Lives of Animals.
      New York: Delacorte, 1995.

Bibliography Card: Book

Current Periodicals

Toch, Thomas. "Will Teachers Save Public
Schools?" U.S. News & World
Report 20 July 1998: 16–19.

Bibliography Card: Article in a General-Interest Magazine

Microfilm

Roth, Cliff. "Commercials Need to Be
Rated Too." Washington Post 30
Dec 1998, final ed.: C3.

Bibliography Card: Newspaper Article

Bound Periodicals

Gulong, Wu; Peter Kuhn. "A Theory of
Holdouts in Wage Bargaining."
American Economic Review 388.3
(June 1998): 428–449.

**Bibliography Card: Article in a Scholarly Journal That Is
Paginated Continuously**

Bound Periodicals

Weiner, Sandra. "Lying and Truth-Telling
Among Preschool Children." The
Young Child 2:3 (1995): 12–14.

Bibliography Card: Article in a Scholarly Journal That Paginates Each Issue Separately

---

CD-ROM

Berman, Marlene, and Marilyn Maxwell.
"To Ban or Not to Ban: Confronting
the Issue of Censorship in the
English Class." Journal of
Adolescent & Adult Literacy. Oct.
1997. 41: 92–96 (10 pars.). ERIC
Database. CD-ROM. U.S.
Department of Education, 1998.

Bibliography Card: Magazine Article on CD-ROM

On-line

"Out of Order in the World Court."
Progressive Jan. 1998: 62
(8 pars.). Proquest Direct.
On-line. 19 Dec. 1998.
[http://proquest.umi.com]

Bibliography Card: Magazine Article Obtained On-line

Before Note-Taking: Read Your Sources

At this point, you should spend some time analyzing each source for its *central ideas*, *main supporting points*, and *key details.* As you read, keep asking yourself how the source's content meshes with your working thesis and with what you know about your subject. Does the source repeat what you already know? If so, you may not need any notes. But if a source provides detailed support for important ideas, plan to take full notes.

When Note-Taking: What to Select

What, specifically, should you take notes on? Your notes might include any of the following: facts, statistics, anecdotal accounts, expert opinion, case studies, surveys, reports, results of experiments. If a source suggests a new angle on your subject, thoughtful and extensive notes are in order. As you begin taking notes, you may not be able to judge how helpful a source will be. In that case, you probably should take fairly detailed notes. After a while, you'll become more selective.

As you go along, you may come across material that challenges your working thesis and forces you to think differently about your subject. Indeed, the more you learn, the more difficult it may be to state anything conclusively. This is a sign that you're synthesizing and weighing all the evidence. In time, the confusion will lessen, and you'll emerge with a clearer understanding of your subject.

When Note-Taking: How to Record Statistics

As you read your sources, you'll probably come across statistics that reinforce points you want to make. Follow these guidelines when taking notes on statistics:

• Check that you record the figures accurately. Also note how and by whom the statistics were gathered as well as where and when they were first reported.

• Take down your source's interpretation of the statistics, but be sure to scrutinize the interpretation. Although the source's figures may be correct, they could have been given a "spin" that distorts them. For example, if 80 percent of Americans think violent crime *is* our number one national problem, that doesn't mean that violent crime is our main problem; it simply means that 80 percent of the people polled *think* it is. And if a "majority" of people think that homelessness should be among our top national priorities, it may be that a mere 51 percent—a bare majority—feels that way. In short, make sure the statistics mean what your sources say they mean.

• Examine each source for possible bias. If a source takes a highly impassioned stance, you should regard its statistics with healthy skepticism. Indeed, it's a good idea to corroborate such figures elsewhere; tracking down the original source of a statistic is the best way to ensure that numbers are being reported fairly.

- Be suspicious of statistics that fail to indicate the number of respondents or that are based on a small nonrepresentative sample (see pages 502-503). For instance, assume the claim is made that 90 percent of the people sampled wouldn't vote for a candidate who had an extramarital affair. However, if only ten people were polled one Sunday as they left church, then the 90 percent statistic is meaningless. (For hints on using statistics in a paper, see page 573.)

When Note-Taking: Use Index Cards

With your sources and bibliography cards close at hand, you're ready to begin taking notes on a second set of index cards. Your instructor will probably ask you to take notes on 4 × 6-inch (or larger) cards. On each card, record notes from only *one source* and on only *one subtopic* of your subject.

Note cards have several advantages over sheets of paper. First, cards help you break information into small, easy-to-manage chunks. Second, they allow you to rearrange information since they can be piled and sorted, unlike information on pages, which must be cut and taped. You can also delete information easily by simply removing a card. Last, note cards save time once you begin writing; you can, for example, staple a quotation on a card right onto your first draft.

For every note card, do the following:

- *Key* each card *to the appropriate source* in your working bibliography by writing the author's last name on each note card. If you have more than one source by the same author, also record the source's title.
- Record the *page* or *pages* in the source that the note refers to. If the note card material is drawn from several pages, indicate clearly where the page breaks occur in the source. That way, if you use only a portion of the material later, you will know its exact page number.
- Write a key word or phrase at the top of each note card, indicating the gist of the note and the aspect of your topic the card focuses on. Often your key terms will themselves develop subtopics. For example, a paper on erosion may have two major stacks of cards: "Beach erosion" and "Mountain erosion," with beach erosion being divided into "Dune" and "Shoreline" erosion.
- Finally, write down the actual note. Pages 542–549 describe specific kinds of notes to take. In the meantime, here's some general advice. Some cards will have only a line or two; others will be quite full. If you run out of space on a card, don't use the other side; this makes it hard to see at a glance what the noteis about. Instead, use a second card, being sure to record the source, page, and so on. Also label successive cards carefully (1 of 2, 2 of 2) and clip them to the first card in the series.

It's up to you where on the note card you place identifying information. The sample card shown here illustrates one way. Whichever way you set up your note cards, be consistent. When you scan your cards before finishing with a source, you'll be more inclined to notice any missing information if you've prepared them in some consistent style. You'll also find it easier to retrieve information later on from well-organized note cards.

Unethical business behavior: causes   Etzioni, p. 22
    Economists suggest that people's desire
for profit causes them to cheat—cheat to
stay ahead.
    But recent studies by social scientists
show otherwise—"social ties" and other non-
economic factors cause ethical or noneth.
behav.
    Most important "social ties"—family mores
and the culture of one's business peers.

Note cards may also include your comments about a source. Enclosing your observations in square brackets ["helpful summary," "controversial interpretation"] keeps these interpretive remarks separate from your notes on a source. If taking notes sparks new ways of looking at your subject, get down such thoughts, carefully separating them from your source material. Write "Me" or "My idea" on the card, or enclose your observations in a box. If your own comments become extensive, use separate note cards, clearly labeling them as your own ideas.

Two Other Note-Taking Approaches

Although index cards are the most efficient way to take notes, there are other methods available. If you can't get the hang of the note-card system, try using **sheets of paper.** To minimize the problems you may encounter later when you start organizing the paper, head each sheet with a key to the source. Then enter all notes from that source, along with page numbers, on the same sheet. If you run out of space, don't take notes on the other side. Instead, start a new sheet, entering on each a key to the source, and continue to keep track of the pages in the source from which you're taking notes. Mark each sheet in the sequence clearly (1 of 3, 2 of 3, and so on). Using key phrases to signal subtopics will also make it easier to organize your notes later.

Duplicating material is another way to gather information. You have the right to copy published work as long as you use it for your own research and give credit for borrowed material. Photocopying *does* have advantages. It allows unhurried analysis and reconsideration of research material at home. It can also be a way of ensuring accuracy since sources can be checked so easily. Duplicating can be especially useful if you need to retrieve a detail that initially seemed unimportant.

However, photocopying is not without dangers, especially if you're an inexperienced researcher. You may get a false sense of security if you convince yourself that once you've photocopied material, you've done most of the work. *Remember:* You still have to evaluate and synthesize your source material, figuring out what evidence supports your working thesis. That means you should dig into the photocopied material, underlining or boxing sections you might use, jotting subtopics in the margins, recording your reaction to the material.

There's one more pitfall to consider: Working with duplicated material can encourage *plagiarism*. Instead of recasting material in your own words, you may be tempted to copy others' language and ideas. If that is the case, you'd be better off steering clear of duplicating altogether. (For more on plagiarism, see pages 533–534, 547–548, and 565–573.)

If you do photocopy, don't forget to include the duplicated sources in your working bibliography and to write complete source information on the photocopy itself.

Kinds of Notes

There are four broad kinds of notes: direct quotations, summaries, paraphrases, and combined notes. Knowing how and when to use each type is an important part of the research process.

Direct Quotations

A **quotation note** reproduces, word for word, that which is stated in a source. Although quoting can demonstrate the thoroughness with which you reviewed relevant sources, don't take one direct quote note card after another; such a string of quotations means you haven't evaluated and synthesized your sources sufficiently. When should you quote? If a source's ideas are unusual or controversial, record a representative quotation in your notes so you can include it in your paper to show you have accurately conveyed the source's viewpoint. Also record a quotation if a source's wording is so eloquent or convincing that it would lose its power if you restated the material in your own words. And, of course, you should take down a quotation if a source's ideas reinforce your own conclusions. If the source is a respected authority, such a quotation will lend authority to your own ideas. When taking notes, you might aim for one to three quotations from each major source. More than that can create a problem when you write the paper.

A card containing a direct quotation from a source should be clearly indicated by quotation marks, perhaps even a handwritten note like "Direct Quotation" or "DQ." Whenever your source quotes someone else (a secondary source) and you want to take notes on what that other person said, put the statement in quotes and indicate its original source. (See pages 572–573 for more on quoting secondary sources.

When copying a quotation, you must record the author's statement *exactly* as it appears in the original work, right down to the punctuation. As long as you don't change the meaning of the original, you may delete a phrase or sentence from a quotation if it's not pertinent to the point you're making. In such cases, insert three periods, called an **ellipsis** (. . .), in place of the deleted words. Leave a space before the second and the third period but not before the first or after the third. To make it clear that the ellipsis stands for material that you rather than your source deleted, place brackets around the ellipsis points.*

Original Passage

The plot, with one exciting event after another, was representative of the usual historical novel. But *Gone With the Wind* placed its emphasis as much on the private individual as on the panorama.

Ellipsis Used to Show Material Omitted

When omitting material *in or near the middle* of the original sentence, proceed as follows: Leave a space before the first bracket, provide the ellipsis, and leave a space after the final bracket before continuing with the quoted matter:

"The plot [. . .] was representative of the usual historical novel. But <u>Gone With the Wind</u> placed its emphasis as much on the private individual as on the panorama."

If you drop material from the end of a sentence, the period that ends the sentence appears in its usual place, followed by the three spaced periods that signal the omission:

Ellipsis at the End

When deleting material *at the end* of the original sentence, proceed as above, but follow the last bracket with the period that ends the sentence; then provide the closing quotation mark:

"The plot, with one exciting event after another, was representative of the usual historical novel [. . .]."

You don't need an ellipsis if you omit material at the start of a quotation. Simply place the quotation marks where you begin quoting directly. Also, don't capitalize the first word in the quotation unless it ordinarily requires capitalization:

---

*The 1999 edition of the *MLA Handbook for Writers of Research Papers* was the first edition calling for the use of brackets with ellipsis points. Earlier editions required only the ellipses. To be consistent with the most recent guidelines, the examples here and on page 561 use brackets with the ellipses. Check with your instructors to see which guidelines they want you to follow.

No Ellipsis Needed

```
Gone With the Wind's piling up of "one exciting event after another"
was typical of the historical potboiler.
```

This last example also illustrates that you can omit the ellipsis if all you quote is a key term or short phrase. In such cases, just enclose the borrowed material in quotation marks. (For more examples of the ellipsis, see pages 566–567.)

If, for clarity's sake, you need to add a word or short phrase to a quotation (for example, by changing a verb tense or replacing a vague pronoun with a noun), enclose your insertion in **brackets:**

```
"Not only did it [Gone With the Wind] for a short time become Amer-
ica's speediest-selling novel, but over the long haul, it became the
nation's largest-selling novel."
```

When a source you're quoting quotes another source, place single quotation marks around the words of the secondary source:

```
"Despite its massive scope, Gone With the Wind sustained, according
to one reviewer, 'remarkable continuity in its plot and character
development.'"
```

Summaries

By **summaries,** we mean *condensing* someone else's ideas and restating them *in your own words.* Skim the source; then, using your own language, condense the material to its central idea, main supporting points, and key details. Summary note cards may be written as lists, brief paragraphs, or both. You may use abbreviations and phrases as well as complete sentences. *A caution:* When summarizing, don't use the ellipsis and brackets to signal that you have omitted some ideas. The ellipsis and brackets are used only when quoting.

The length of the summary depends on your topic and purpose. Read the following excerpt from page 8 of Julian Stamp's book, *The Homeless and History.* Then look at the subsequent summary note cards.

> The key to any successful homeless policy requires a clear understanding of just who are the homeless. Since fifty percent of shelter residents have drug and alcohol addictions, programs need to provide not only a place to sleep but also comprehensive treatment for addicts and their families. Since roughly one-third of the homeless population is mentally ill, programs need to offer psychiatric care, perhaps even institutionalization, and not just housing subsidies. Since the typical head of a homeless family (a young woman with fewer than six months' working experience) usually lacks the know-how needed to maintain a job and a home, programs need to supply

employment and life skills training; low-cost housing alone will not ensure the family's stability.

However, if we switch our focus from the single person to the larger *economic* issues, we begin to see that homelessness cannot be resolved solely at the level of individual treatment. Since the 1980s, the gap between the rich and the poor has widened, buying power has stagnated, industrial jobs have fled overseas, and federal funding for low-cost housing has been almost eliminated. Given these developments, homelessness begins to look like a product of history, our recent history, and only by addressing shifts in the American economy can we begin to find effective solutions for people lacking homes. Moreover, these solutions—ranging from renewed federal spending to tax laws favoring job-creating companies—will require a sustained national commitment that transcends partisan politics.

The summary notes on page 546 were taken by two students writing on related but different topics. Although both students eventually used more scholarly and detailed sources in their papers, they found—in the early stages of their research—that Stamp's book provided helpful background and perspective. The first student, planning to write on the causes of homelessness, prepared an in-depth summary card labeled "Personal and Economic Causes of Homelessness." The second student, planning to write on the day-to-day experience of homeless families, took a much shorter note under the heading "Profile: Heads of Homeless Families."

Summarizing problems.   The sample note cards on page 546 were prepared by students who were careful about translating ideas into their own language. The note cards on page 547, however, were prepared by students who had difficulty recasting ideas from the Stamp passage. In the first example, the student was so determined to put things her way that she added her own ideas and ended up *distorting* Stamp's meaning. For instance, note the way she emphasizes personal problems over economic issues, making the former the cause of the latter. Stamp does just the opposite and highlights economic solutions rather than individual treatment. In the second example, the student worked so hard to compress material that he prepared an *overly condensed* note card. His excessively terse statement, lacking detail and explanation, renders the summary almost meaningless.

Paraphrases

You may have heard of another kind of note prepared in your own words: **paraphrase notes.** Unlike a summary, which condenses the original, a paraphrase recasts material by using roughly the same number of words, retaining the same level of detail, and adopting the same style as the original. Since the research process requires you to distill information, you'll probably find summary note cards much more helpful than paraphrases.

Personal and Economic Causes   Stamp, p. 8
of Homelessness

Point: As individuals, homeless have personal problems.

    50% in shelters are substance abusers.

    33% of all homeless suffer mental illnesses.

    Head of homeless family usually has little or no job
    experience.

    Treatment program needed to solve these problems.

                                Stamp, p. 8 cont.

Point: As a nation, homelessness is an economic
problem. Since 1980:

    Growing gulf between rich and poor.
    Decline in industrial jobs.
    Loss of federal money for housing.

    Only economic treatment—from government
    spending to new tax laws—can permanently
    solve the homeless problem.

First Student's Summary Cards

Profile: Heads of Homeless Families   Stamp, p. 8

Most homeless families are led by young women who
haven't held a job for longer than six months. Without
training in work skills and household management,
these women can't maintain their families or any
housing that might be available.

Second Student's Summary Card

Who Are the Homeless?   Stamp, p. 8

The homeless are people with big problems like
addiction, mental illness, and poor job skills. Because
they haven't been provided with proper treatment
and training, the homeless haven't been able to
adapt to a changing economy. So their numbers have
soared since the 1980s.

Summary: Distorting the Original

Effective Homeless Programs   Stamp, p. 8

Homeless need economic—not psychiatric—
treatment and solutions.

Summary: Overly Condensed

Plagiarism

One problem with paraphrases is that they can lead to **plagiarism**—which occurs when a writer borrows someone else's ideas, facts, or language but doesn't properly credit that source. Look, for example, at the first note card on page 548. When preparing his paraphrase, the student stayed too close to the source and borrowed much of Stamp's language *word for word*. Note, for example, the underlined words, which are taken directly from Stamp. If the student transferred this phrasing to his paper without supplying quotation marks, he'd be guilty of plagiarism. Indeed, even if this student acknowledged Stamp in the paper, he'd still be plagiarizing—the lack of quotation marks implies that the language is the student's when, in fact, it is Stamp's.

As the second sample card on page 548 shows, another student believed, erroneously, that if she changed a word here and omitted a word there, she'd be preparing an effective paraphrase. Note that the language is all Stamp's except for the underlined words, which signal the student's slight rephrasings of Stamp. Notice, too, that the student occasionally deleted a word from Stamp, thinking that such

---

Homelessness: An Economic Problem   Stamp, p. 8

Only by addressing changes in the American
economy—from the gap between the wealthy and the
poor to the loss of industrial jobs to overseas
markets—can we begin to find solutions for the
homeless. And these solutions, ranging from renewed
federal spending to tax laws favoring job-creating
companies, will not be easy to find or implement.

Plagiarized Paraphrase: Word-for-Word

Homelessness: An Economic Problem   Stamp, p. 8

Only by addressing shifts in the economy can we find
solutions for the homeless. These solutions will
require a sustained federal commitment that avoids
partisan politics.

Plagiarized Paraphrase: Near-Quotes

changes would constitute a legitimate paraphrase. For instance, Stamp's "only by
addressing shifts in the American economy can we begin to find effective solutions" became "only by addressing shifts in the economy can we find solutions."
The student couldn't place quotation marks around these *near-quotes* because her
wording wasn't identical to that of the source. Yet to place the near-quotes in a
paper without quotation marks would be deceptive; the lack of quotation marks
would suggest that the language was the student's when actually it's substantially
(but not exactly) Stamp's. Such near-quotes are also considered plagiarism, even
if, when writing the paper, the student supplied a note citing the source. (For hints
on steering clear of plagiarism when you actually write a research paper, see the
discussion of documentation on pages 565–573).

Combined Notes

When taking notes, you may summarize someone else's ideas in your own words but also include some of the source's exact wording. The result, a **combined note,** is legitimate as long as you put quotation marks around the source's language. The combined note cards shown below are based on the same passage from Stamp's book.

Combination note cards are effective. They allow you to retain key phrases as well as eloquent or controversial statements from your source; you don't have to spend time recasting material that resists translation into your own words. At the same time, combined notes indicate that you're actively involved with your research material, that you're continually asking yourself, "What should I state in my own words? What is so informative, so interesting, so provocative that I want to use it exactly as it is, word for word?" Such questions prompt discipline and careful thought, two qualities that will serve you well as you move ahead to the next phase of your research—organizing and writing the paper, our focus in Chapter 21.

> Homelessness: An Economic Problem   Stamp, p. 8
>
> Beyond the individual problems of homeless people, homelessness is a matter of "larger _economic_ issues." Since 1980:
>
> > Growing gulf between rich and poor
> > Flat growth in "buying power"
> > Decline in industrial jobs and federal money
> > > for housing

> Stamp, p. 8 cont.
>
> Only "by addressing shifts in the American economy"—through government spending and new tax laws—can we permanently solve the homeless problem.

One Student's Combined Note Cards

ACTIVITIES: SELECTING A SUBJECT, USING THE LIBRARY AND THE INTERNET, AND TAKING NOTES

1. Use the card or computer catalog to answer the following questions:

   a. What are three books dealing with the subject of adoption? Of television? Of urban violence? Of genetic research?
   b. What is the title of a book by Betty Friedan? By John Kenneth Galbraith?
   c. Who is the author of *The Invisible Man?* Of *A Country Year?*

2. Examine this entry from a computerized catalog and then use it to answer the questions that follow.

CALL NUMBER:	**PE1128.A2 S63**
AUTHOR:	**Spagenberg-Urbschat, Karen; Robert Pritchard.**
TITLE:	**Kids Come in All Languages: Reading Instruction for ESL Students**
PUBLISHED:	**Newark, Del.: International Reading Association, 1994.**
PAGING:	**vii, 231p.; 22 cm.**
SUBJECTS:	**English (ESL) Education, United States–Bilingual Education, United States**

1. **CALL NUMBER: PE1128.A2 S63—Book—Checked Out**

2. **CALL NUMBER: PE1128.A2 S63—Book—Available**

---

   a. Which catalog system does this library use?
   b. What is the title of the book?
   c. How many authors does the book have? What are their names?
   d. Under what subjects is this book listed in the catalog?
   e. When was the book published?
   f. Assume you're writing a paper about the way children not born in this country learn English. Considering the information on the card, would you try to locate this book? Why or why not?

3. Prepare a bibliography card for each of the following books. Gather all the information necessary at the library so that you can write accurate and complete bibliography cards:

    a. Barbara Tuchman, *Practicing History*

    b. L. Jacobs, *The Documentary Tradition*

    c. Margaret Mead, *Coming of Age in Samoa*

    d. Stephen Bank, *The Sibling Bond*

    e. Ronald Gross, *The New Old*

    f. Matthew Arnold, *Culture and Anarchy*

4. Using reference works available in your library, find the answers to the following questions:

    a. When was the Persian Gulf War fought?

    b. Who invented Kodachrome film, and when?

    c. What is the medical condition *rosacea*?

    d. What television show won the Emmy in 1973–74 for Outstanding Comedy Series?

    e. What was artist John Sartain known for?

    f. When was an African American first elected to Congress?

    g. In economics, what is Pareto's Law?

    h. In art, what is *écorché*?

    i. Give two other names for a *mbira*, a musical instrument.

    j. In the religion of the Hopi Native Americans, what are *kachinas*?

5. Select *one* of the following limited topics. Then, using the appropriate periodical indexes and bibliographies (see pages 514-520), locate three periodicals that would be helpful in researching the topic. Examine each periodical to determine whether it is aimed at a general, serious, or scholarly audience.

    a. Drug abuse among health-care professionals

    b. Ethical considerations in organ-transplant surgery

    c. Women in prison

    d. Deforestation of the Amazon rain forest

    e. The difference between *Sense and Sensibility* as a novel and as a film

6. Select *one* of the following limited topics. Then, using the Internet, locate at least three relevant articles on the topic: one from a general-interest magazine, one from a newspaper, one from a serious or scholarly journal. Make a bibliography card for each article.

    a. Ordaining women in American churches

    b. Attempts to regulate pornography

    c. The popularity of novelist and essayist Isak Dinesen

    d. The growing interest in painter David Hockney

    e. AIDS education programs

    f. The global economy

7. Listed here are some of this book's professional essays, along with broad research topics that they suggest. Choose *one* of these general subjects and, using the Internet and/or the library's resources, do some background reading. (You should find helpful some of the sources listed on pages 512–513 and 514–520.) On either index cards or notebook paper, keep an informal record of the works you consult. As you read, jot down potential limited topics. After doing some further reading on *one* of the limited topics, devise a working thesis. (Don't, by the way, feel constrained by the point of view expressed in the essay[s] that initially prompted your research.)

    a. "Sister Flowers" (page 175); "The Fourth of July" (page 210); "My First Conk" (page 321); "A Slow Walk of Trees" (page 351); "And Then I Went to School" (page 361); "Black Men and Public Space" (page 398); "Let's Tell the Story of All America's Cultures" (page 482); "The Cult of Ethnicity" (page 491)

    Preservation of cultural differences

    Teaching about diversity

    Relations between different racial or ethnic groups

    b. "Shooting an Elephant" (page 203); "The Fourth of July" (page 210); "Is Sex All That Matters?" (page 252); "Why Nothing Is 'Wrong' Anymore" (page 290); "Don't Just Stand There" (page 315); "When Is It Rape?" (page 423); "Absolutophobia" (page 429)

    Teaching morality to children

    Morality in the mass media

    Morality in the workplace

    Sexual morality

    c. "Managing Mixed Messages" (page 247); "Is Sex All That Matters?" (page 252); "But What Do You Mean?" (page 283); "When Is It Rape?" (page 423); "What Should Be Done About Rock Lyrics?" (page 473);

    Raising non-sexist children

    The mass-media depiction of gender roles

    Sexism on the college campus

8. Referring to paragraphs 1–5 in Ann McClintock's "Propaganda Techniques in Today's Advertising" (page 277), prepare three note cards: a direct quotation, a summary, and a combined note. Assume you're using the McClintock essay to research advertisers' use of emotional appeals to sell products.

21
WRITING
THE
RESEARCH
PAPER

AFTER you complete your note-taking, you're ready to begin the writing phase of the research project. When writing the paper, you'll probably find it helpful to follow these steps:

- Refine your working thesis.
- Sort the note cards.
- Organize the evidence by outlining.
- Prepare the Works Cited list.
- Write the first draft.
- Document borrowed material.
- Revise, edit, and proofread.

REFINE YOUR WORKING THESIS

This is a good time to *reexamine your working thesis*; it's undoubtedly evolved since you first started your research. Indeed, now that you're more informed about the topic, you may feel that your original thesis oversimplifies the issue. To clarify your position, begin by sifting through your note cards; your goal is to formulate a position that makes the most sense in light of the research you've done and the information you've gathered. Then, revise your working thesis, keeping in mind the evidence on your note cards. This refined version of your thesis will serve as the starting point for your first draft. Remember, though—as you write the paper, new thoughts may emerge that will cause you to modify your thesis even further. (For more on thesis statements, see Chapter 3.)

SORT THE NOTE CARDS

Keeping your refined thesis in mind, *sort your note cards* into piles *by topic.* If, for example, your thesis is "Lotteries are an inefficient means of raising money for state programs," you might form one pile of note cards on administrative costs, another on types of state programs, a third on the way money is allocated, and so on. Although you can sort by the key terms or headings you previously placed at the tops of cards, it's a good idea to reread the cards. You may find, for example, that a heading needs to be changed because its information better suits some other category. If some cards don't fit into any pile—and this is likely—put them aside. You don't need to use every note card. At this point, though, you should consider which organizational approach (see pages 54–56) will help you sequence your material. Arrange your topic piles to reflect this order.

Once you've arranged your note cards according to the topic headings at the top, sort each topic pile by *subtopic.* For example, the pile of cards about types of state programs might be divided into these three subtopic piles: programs for the elderly, programs for preschool children, programs for the physically disabled. Next, using the patterns of development and organizational approaches discussed, respectively, on pages 45–46 and 54–56, order each set of subtopic cards to match the sequence in which you think you'll discuss those subtopics in your paper. This sorting will make your next step—preparing an outline—much easier.

ORGANIZE THE EVIDENCE BY OUTLINING

Whether or not your instructor requires an *outline,* it's a good idea to prepare one before you begin writing the paper. Because an outline groups and sequences points, it provides a blueprint you can follow when writing. Outlining clarifies what your main ideas are, what your supporting evidence is, and how everything fits together. It reveals where your argument is well supported and where it is weak.

To design your outline, focus first on the paper's body. How can you best explain and support your thesis? For now, don't worry about your introduction or conclusion. General guidelines on outlining are discussed in Chapter 5 (pages 56–58). To apply those guidelines to a research paper, keep the following points in mind:

- Base your outline on your organized piles of note cards.
- Label your *main topic* headings (those on your main pile of cards) with Roman numerals (I, II, III, and so on) to indicate the order in which you plan to discuss each topic in the paper.

- Label the *subtopics* grouped under each main topic heading with capital letters (A, B, C). Indent the subtopic entries under their respective main topics, listing them in the order you plan to discuss them.
- Label *supporting points* (ideas noted on your cards) with arabic numerals (1, 2, 3) and indent them under the appropriate subtopics.
- Label *specific details* (facts, quotations, statistics, examples, expert opinion) with lowercase letters (a, b, c) and indent them under the appropriate supporting points. Use shorthand for details. For example, write "Bitner quote here" instead of copying the entire quotation into your outline.
- Where appropriate, map out sections of the paper that will provide background information or define key terms.

Here's how the various outline elements look when they're properly labeled and indented:

```
 I. Main topic
    A. Subtopic
       1. Supporting point
       2. Supporting point
          a. Specific detail
          b. Specific detail
    B. Subtopic
       1. Supporting point
       2. Supporting point
II. Main topic
    A. Subtopic
       1. Supporting point
       2. Supporting point
          a. Specific detail
          b. Specific detail
    B. Subtopic
```

Your first outline probably won't be a formal full-sentence one; rather, it's more likely to be a *topic* (or phrase) *outline,* like those on pages 305–306, 343–344, and 458–459. A topic outline helps you clarify a paper's overall structure. A *full-sentence outline* (see pages 232–233 and 584–586) or a *combined topic and sentence outline* (see pages 379–380) is better suited to mapping out in detail the development of a paper's ideas. If you're preparing an outline that will be submitted with the paper, find out in advance which kind your instructor prefers.

Before you go any further, it's a good idea to get some feedback on your outline—from an instructor or a critical friend—to make sure others agree that your meaning and organization are logical and clear. Then, based on your readers' reactions, make whatever changes seem necessary.

Finally, key your note cards to your outline. Label each card according to the section of the paper in which the card will be used: "IA," "IIB2," and so on. Using a different color ink for each main-topic section makes it easier to locate appropriate card stacks when you write the paper later on.

PREPARE THE WORKS CITED LIST: MLA FORMAT

At this point, you should draft a tentative **Works Cited list** (or bibliography) before you write the paper. That way, each time you include borrowed material in your paper, you can easily key that material to the appropriate item on the Works Cited list.

The following discussion focuses on the MLA—Modern Language Association— format for preparing the Works Cited list. The **MLA format** is used widely in the liberal arts. (The system used in the social sciences—that of the American Psychological Association [APA]—is described on pages 576–580. On page 580, you'll also find a description of the format used in the hard sciences and in technical fields.)

As a first step in preparing your Works Cited list, pull out the bibliography cards (or working bibliography) for the sources you think you'll actually refer to in your paper. Alphabetize them by the authors' last names. For now, put any anonymous works at the end.

The Works Cited list, which will appear at the end of your final paper, should include only those works you actually quote, summarize, or otherwise directly refer to in your paper. Don't list other sources, no matter how many you may have read. Placed on its own page, the Works Cited list provides readers with full bibliographic information about the sources you cite in the paper.

Double-space the entries on the Works Cited list, and *don't* add extra space between entries. The first line of each new entry should start at the left margin; if an entry extends beyond one line of type, all subsequent lines should be indented five spaces. The major items in a bibliographic entry (the author's full name, the title, all the information on publication) are separated with periods. (See the sample Works Cited list on pages 595–596.)

The following sample entries will help you prepare an accurate Works Cited list.

Book Sources

Here is the basic format for listing a book in Works Cited:

- Start with the author's name, last name first, then first name and any initial, with a comma between the first and last names. Put a period after the first name or initial. Leave one space between the period and the next item.
- Give the complete book title. If the book has a subtitle, separate it from the title with a colon. Leave a space after the colon. Underline the full title and follow it with a period. Leave one space between the period and the next item.

- Next, give the city of publication, followed by a colon. Leave a space between the colon and the next item. If the publisher has more than one location, use the city listed first on the book's title page. If the book is published in the United States, give only the city. If it is published in another country, give the city as well as the country, separating them with a comma.
- Supply the publisher's name, giving only key words and omitting the words *Company, Press, Publishers, Inc.,* and the like. (For example, write *Rodale* for Rodale Press, *Allyn* for Allyn and Bacon, and *Wiley* for John Wiley.) In addition, use *UP* to abbreviate the names of university presses (as in *Columbia UP* and *U of California P*). Place a comma and a space after the publisher's name.
- End with the publication date and a period. Supply the most recent year of copyright. Don't use the year of the most recent printing.

Here is a sample entry for a book in the MLA format:

Book with One Author

Nyberg, David. <u>The Varnished Truth: Truth Telling and Deceiving in</u>
    <u>Ordinary Life</u>. Chicago: U of Chicago P, 1993.

For books varying from this basic entry, consult the examples that follow. If you don't spot a sample entry for the type of source you need to document, consult the latest edition of the *MLA Handbook for Writers of Research Papers* for more comprehensive examples.

Two or More Works by the Same Author

Knapp, Caroline. <u>Drinking: A Love Story</u>. New York: Dell, 1996.

---. <u>Pack of Two: The Intricate Bond Between People and Dogs</u>. New
    York: Dial, 1998.

If you use more than one work by the same author, list each book separately. Give the author's name in the first entry only; begin the entries for other books by that author with three hyphens followed by a period. Arrange the works alphabetically by title. The words *A, An,* and *The* are ignored when alphabetizing by title.

Book with Two or Three Authors

Canfield, Jack, and Mark Victor Hansen. <u>A Fifth Portion of Chicken</u>
    <u>Soup for the Soul</u>. Deerfield Beach: Health Communications,
    1998.

For a book with two or three authors, give all the authors' names but reverse only the first name. List the names in the order shown on the title page.

Book with Four or More Authors

Dansker, Isadora, et al. <u>Geological Formations Along the Eastern
    Seaboard</u>. Boston: Newtown, 1995.

For a work with four or more authors, give only the first author's name followed by a comma and *et al.* (Latin for "and others").

Revised Edition of a Book

Graydon, Don, and Kurt Hanson, eds. <u>Mountaineering: The Freedom of
    the Hills</u>. 6th ed. Seattle: Mountaineers, 1997.

Follow the title with the edition, identified either by number (for example, 2nd) or by the abbreviation *Rev.* (for *Revised*), depending on how the book itself indicates edition.

Book with an Editor or Translator

Kafka, Franz. <u>The Metamorphosis and Other Stories</u>. Trans. Donna
    Freed. New York: Barnes, 1996.

Place the editor's or translator's name after the title, with the identifying abbreviation *Ed.* or *Trans.* before the person's name. Don't reverse the first and last name of the editor or translator.

Anthology or Compilation of Works by Different Authors

O'Hearn, Claudine Chiawei, ed. <u>Half and Half: Writers on Growing Up
    Biracial and Bicultural</u>. New York: Pantheon, 1998.

If you refer in general to an edited book—rather than to the individual authors whose work it contains—give the editor's name in the author position, followed by a comma and the abbreviation *ed.*

Section of an Anthology or Compilation by Different Authors

Macdonald, Cynthia. "The Lady Pitcher." <u>A Whole Other Ball Game:
    Women's Literature on Women's Sports</u>. Ed. Joli Sandoz. New
    York: Noonday, 1997. 85-86.

If you use only a section from an anthology, list first the author of that particular selection or chapter. The remaining information should be presented in this order: selection title (in quotation marks), book title (underlined), editor's name (preceded by the abbreviation *Ed.*), publication data, and the selection's page numbers. Don't use *p.* or *page.*

Section or Chapter in a Book by One Author

```
Hegelsen, Sally. "Why Women Are Leading the Way." Everyday Revolu-
     tionaries: Working Women and the Transformation of American
     Life. New York: Doubleday, 1998. 41-69.
```

If you use only one named section or chapter of a book, give the section's title in quotation marks before the title of the book. At the end, give the section's page numbers. Don't use *p.* or *page.* If you use several sections, don't name each of them; just put the page numbers for all the sections at the end of the entry.

Book by an Institution or Corporation

```
American Medical Women's Association. The American Medical Women's
     Association Guide to Fertility and Reproductive Health. New
     York: Dell, 1996.
```

Give the name of the institution or corporation in the author position, even if the same institution is the publisher.

Articles in Periodicals

Here is the basic format for listing periodical articles in Works Cited:

- Start with the author's last name, following the guidelines for a book author. If the article is unsigned, begin with its title.
- Give the article's complete title, enclosed in quotation marks, and follow it with a period. Leave one space between the period and the next item in the entry.
- Supply the periodical's name, underlining it. Don't place any punctuation after it.
- Give the date of publication. For newspapers and weekly magazines, include the day, month, and year—in that order. Abbreviate the month (using the first three letters) if it is five letters or longer. For scholarly journals, give the volume number, issue number (if appropriate), and year. In both cases, follow the date with a colon. Leave a space between the colon and the next item.
- Provide page number(s) without using *p., pp., page,* or *pages* before the numbers. If the pages in an article are continuous, give the page range (for example, 67–72). If the pages in an article aren't continuous (for example, 67–68, 70, 72), write the first page number and a plus sign (67+). Place a period after the page-number information.

The following sample entries for articles in periodicals are formatted in the MLA style. If you don't spot an entry for the type of source you need to document, consult the *MLA Handbook* for more comprehensive examples.

Authored or Anonymous Article from a Weekly or Biweekly Magazine

Garrett, Major. "Congress Snuffs Out the Tobacco Bill." <u>U.S. News</u> 29
    June 1998: 30-33.

Article from a Monthly or Bimonthly Magazine

Davis, Kristin. "The Bonnie and Clyde of Credit Card Fraud."
    <u>Kiplinger's Personal Finance Magazine</u> July 1998: 65-71.

Article from a Daily Newspaper

Schellhardt, Timothy D. "Relocating Mom: A Primer of New Perks."
    <u>Wall Street Journal</u> 23 June 1998, eastern ed.: B1+.

Greenhouse, Linda. "Blowing the Dust off the Constitution That Was."
    <u>New York Times</u> 28 May 1995, natl. ed., sec. 4: 1+.

Use the newspaper's name as it appears on the masthead, but delete any initial
The. If the title doesn't specify the paper's location and the paper lacks nationwide
recognition, put the town or city and (if necessary) the state in brackets after the
title: *Today's Sunbeam* [Salem, NJ]. If the paper is a large daily, indicate the particular edition (late, early, national, and so on) after the date, abbreviating longer
words such as national (*natl.*) and edition (*ed.*). For a newspaper with sections, if
the section letter is part of each page number (see the first example above), provide the page and section designation exactly as they appear (for example, A15 or
10C). However, if the section designation isn't part of the page number (see the
second example above), use the abbreviation *sec.* followed by the section number
or letter, a colon, and then the page number (for example, sec. 3: 5 or sec. C: 2+).
For a newspaper without sections, simply provide the page number.

Editorial, Letter to the Editor, or Reply to a Letter

Isaacson, Walter. "The Nerve Gas Story." Editorial. <u>Time</u> 29 June
    1998: 4.

List as you would any signed or unsigned article, but indicate the nature of the
piece by adding *Editorial, Letter,* or *Reply to letter of [letter writer's name]* after the
article's title.

Article from a Scholarly Journal

Milspaw, Yvonne J. "Regional Style in Quilt Design." <u>Journal of
    American Folklore</u> 110 (1997): 363-90.

```
Linder, Regina. "Exploring Diversity in an Undergraduate Science
     Program." Transformations 6.1 (1995): 76-84.
```

Some journals are paged continuously (the first example); the first issue of each year starts with page one, and each subsequent issue picks up where the previous one left off. For such journals, use numerals to indicate the volume number after the title, and then indicate the year in parentheses. Note that neither *volume* nor *vol.* is used. The article's page or pages appear at the end, separated from the year by a colon. For a journal that pages each issue separately (the second example), use numerals to indicate the volume *and issue* numbers; separate the two with a period, but leave no space after the period.

Nonprint Sources (Other Than Computerized)

Television or Radio Program

```
"D-Day." The American Experience. World War II. PBS. WHYY-TV,
     Philadelphia. 6 Feb. 1998.
```

List, at a minimum, the program's title (underlined), the network that carried the program, the local station on which the program was seen or heard, and the city and date of the broadcast. If, as in the example above, the program is an episode in a continuing series, give the episode title first (in quotation marks), then the program title (underlined), then the series title, if any (neither underlined nor in quotation marks). You might also include additional information such as the director or narrator before the series title.

Movie, Recording, Videotape, Filmstrip, or Slide Program

```
Secrets of the Titanic. Dir. Nicolas Noxon. Videotape. Warner Home
     Video, 1997.

Winfrey, Oprah, perf. Oprah: Make the Connection. Videotape. Harper
     Video, 1997.
```

List the title (underlined), director, distribution company, and year. The writer, main performers, or producers may be listed after the director and before the company. If the work is a videotape, filmstrip, or slide program, indicate the original release date (if applicable) and the medium (for example, videotape, filmstrip, etc.). If you use the source to discuss the work of a particular individual, begin with that person's name followed by his or her position (as in the second example above).

Personal and Phone Interview

Harrow, Morgan. Personal interview. 5 Aug. 1998.

Susskin, Carrie. Phone interview. 13 Sept. 1998.

Lecture

Akers, Sharon. "Managing Pension Funds." Workshop. Association of
    Retirement Communities. Plaza Conference Hall, Miami. 14 Dec.
    1998.

Kahn, Linda. "Resolving Family Conflicts." Lecture. Sociology 202,
    William Patterson College. Wayne, New Jersey. 10 Oct. 1995.

Start with the speaker's name, followed by the lecture's title (in quotation marks) if there is one. If not, identify the lecture with an appropriate label such as *Keynote address* or *Lecture*. Then provide the sponsoring organization's name, the site of the lecture, and the date.

Computerized Sources

Computer Software

Lynch, Peter. The Stock Shop. CD-ROM. Windows 3.1 and 95. Houghton-
    Mifflin Interactive, 1997.

List the program's author, if known, then the title (underlined), the software medium (CD-ROM, Diskette, Magnetic tape), the edition or version (if relevant), the distributor, and the year.

Article on CD-ROM

Krauss, Clifford. "Crime Statistics in the Big Apple." New York
    Times 12 Mar. 1998, late ed.: B1 (6 pars.). New York Times
    Ondisc. CD-ROM. UMI-ProQuest. Oct. 1998.

For text on CD-ROM, give the same information you would for printed text of the same kind (for example, a newspaper article), with the possible exception of page numbers. If the CD-ROM doesn't indicate an article's page numbers, give the page number (if available) on which the article begins and the article's length in pages or paragraphs (for example, *4 pp.* or *14 pars.*). Then give the data-base title (underlined), publication medium (CD-ROM), CD-ROM publisher, and CD-ROM publication date. (*Note:* When citing an article stored on CD-ROM, don't provide the date you accessed the material. Unlike on-line material which can be revised or updated at any time, material stored on CD-ROM is unchangeable and will stay the same no matter when it is accessed.)

Article Obtained from an On-line Data Base

```
Fumento, Michael. "'Road Rage' Versus Reality." Atlantic Monthly
     282:2 (Aug. 1998): 6 pp. 2 Sept. 1998
     <http://www.theatlantic.com/issues/98aug/roadrage.htm>.
```

For text obtained on-line, supply the same information you would for printed text of the same kind, with the possible exception of the page numbers. If the data base doesn't indicate an article's page numbers, give the page number (if available) on which the article starts, along with the article's length in pages or paragraphs in parentheses (for example, *4 pp.* or *14 pars.*). Complete your listing with the date on which you accessed the material, followed by the address of the Web site in angle brackets. (*Note:* Unlike material stored on CD-ROM, on-line material can be revised or updated at any time. Providing the date on which you accessed the material is critical since that date is the only way to identify the version you retrieved.)

E-Mail Messages

```
Bernard, Lynn. "Adult Literacy Seminar." E-mail to Ronnie Hotis. 30
     Aug. 1998.
```

To cite e-mail, provide the name of the writer; the title of the message (if any), taken from the subject line of the posting and enclosed in quotation marks; a description of the message that includes the recipient (for example, "E-mail to the author"); and the date of the message.

WRITE THE FIRST DRAFT

Once you've refined your working thesis, sorted your note cards, constructed an outline, and prepared a preliminary Works Cited page, you're ready to write your first draft. As with the early versions of an essay, don't worry at this stage about grammar, spelling, or style. Just try to get down as much of the paper's basic content and structure as you can.

Chapter 6 offers general guidelines for writing a first draft (pages 64–65). When applying those guidelines to a research paper, keep the following points in mind:

• As you write, refer to your note cards and outline. Don't rely on your memory for the information you've gathered.
• Feel free to deviate from your outline if, as you write, you discover a more effective sequence, realize some material doesn't fit, or see new merit in previously discarded information.

- Include any quotations and summaries in the draft. Rather than recopy, you may tape or staple the appropriate note cards to the page.
- Provide rough documentation (see pages 565–573) for all material borrowed from your sources.
- Use the present tense when quoting or summarizing a source ("Stamp *reports* that..." rather than "Stamp *reported* that...").
- Use the third-person point of view throughout, unless your instructor has indicated that you may use the first person when presenting primary research (see pages 500–501).

There are two contrasting strategies for generating a first draft. One is to *overwrite*, explaining each point as fully as possible, even including alternative explanations and wordings. The other strategy is to *underwrite*. In this approach, you jot down your ideas quickly, leaving gaps where points need to be expanded, making notations like "Insert a quote here." The disadvantage of this strategy is that it simply defers filling in the gaps until a later time, when it might be difficult to recapture your original train of thought. The advantage is that generating material quickly can make a long piece of writing more manageable and less forbidding. Some writers combine the two strategies—writing out parts of the paper fully but only sketching out those sections where getting all the details down would interrupt the flow of thought.

Whichever strategy you use, keep in mind that your draft shouldn't merely string together other people's words and ideas. Rather than simply presenting fact after fact or quotation after quotation, you must *analyze* and *comment on* your research, clearly showing how it supports your thesis. Similarly, when drafting the paper, be sure your language doesn't stay too close to that of your sources. To avoid overreliance on your sources' language, refer to your note cards as you write, not to the sources themselves. Remember, too, that taking source material and merely changing a word here and there still constitutes *plagiarism*—passing off someone else's thoughts or language as your own. Such a charge is valid even if you acknowledge your source. (For more pointers on steering clear of plagiarism, see pages 533–534, 542, 547–548, and 565–573.)

Presenting the Results of Primary Research

If your instructor requires you to conduct primary research (see pages 501–502), you might be tempted to include in the draft every bit of information you gathered through any surveys, experiments, or interviews you conducted. Remember, though, your primary purpose is to provide evidence for your thesis, so include only that material which furthers your goal. To preserve the draft's overall unity, you should also avoid the temptation to mass, without commentary, all your primary research in one section of the paper. Instead, insert the material at those places where it supports the points you want to make. Sometimes instructors will ask you to devote one part of the paper to a detailed discussion of the process you used to conduct primary research—everything from your methodology to a detailed interpretation of your results. In such a case, before writing your draft, ask your instructor where you should cover that information. Perhaps it should be placed in a separate introductory section or in an appendix.

HOW TO AVOID PLAGIARISM: DOCUMENT BORROWED MATERIAL USING MLA FORMAT

Copyright law and the ethics of research require that you give credit to those whose words and ideas you borrow; that is, you must provide full and accurate **documentation.** A lack of such documentation results in *plagiarism*—borrowing someone's ideas, facts, and words without properly crediting your source. Faulty documentation undermines your credibility. For one thing, readers may suspect that you're hiding something if you fail to identify your sources clearly. Further, readers planning follow-up research of their own will be perturbed if they have trouble locating your sources. Finally, weak documentation makes it difficult for readers to distinguish your ideas from those of your sources.

To avoid plagiarizing, you must provide documentation in the following situations:

- When you include a *word-for-word quotation* from a source.

- When you *summarize or restate in your own words* ideas or information from a source, *unless* that material is *commonly known* and *accepted* (whether or not you yourself were previously aware of it) *or* is a *matter of* historical or scientific *record.*

- When you *combine* a *summary* and a *quotation.*

One exception to formal documentation occurs in writing for the general public. For example, you may have noticed that the authors of this book's essays don't use full documentation when they borrow ideas. *Academic writers,* though, *must provide full documentation* for all borrowed information. The next section explains how to do this.

Indicate Author and Page

Both the MLA documentation system described here and the APA system described later in the chapter use the **parenthetic reference,** a brief note in parentheses inserted into the text after borrowed material. The parenthetic reference doesn't provide full bibliographic information, but it provides enough so that readers can turn to the Works Cited list for complete information. If the method of documentation you learned in high school involved footnotes or endnotes, you'll be happy to know that parenthetic documentation, which is currently preferred, is much easier to use and is accepted by most professors. To be on the safe side, though, check with your professors to determine their documentation preferences.

Whenever you use borrowed material, you must, within your paper's text, do two things. First, you must *identify the author.* (Since the Works Cited page is arranged according to authors' last names, readers can refer to that listing for title, publisher, and so on.) Second, you must *specify the page(s)* in your source on which the material appears.

Using Only Parentheses

The simplest way to provide documentation involves the use of *parentheses* for both *author* and *page* references. The examples that follow, based on references to Julian Stamp's *The Homeless and History,* illustrate this method. (If you like, turn to pages 544–545 for the extract from Stamp's book and compare the original there with the documentation here. And turn to page 543 if you would like to review the use of ellipses and brackets when deleting material from a source.)

Counseling and other support services are not enough to solve the problem of homelessness; proposed solutions must address the complex economic issues at the heart of homelessness (Stamp 8).

It is no coincidence that as "the gap between the rich and the poor has widened[...]" (Stamp 8), homelessness has emerged as a social ill.

If we look beyond the problems of homeless people "to larger economic issues, we[...]see that homelessness cannot be resolved solely at the level of individual treatment (Stamp 8).

Because half of those taking refuge in shelters have substance-abuse problems, "programs need to provide not only a place to sleep but also comprehensive treatment for addicts [...]" (Stamp 8).

Take a moment to look again at the preceding examples. Note the following:

What to Provide Within the Parentheses

- Give the author's last name only, even when the author is cited for the first time.
- Write the page number immediately after the author's last name, with no punctuation between. (If the source is only one page, only the author's name is needed.) Provide a full page range of the summary or quotation if it spans more than one page. Don't use the designation *p.* or *page.*

Where to Place the Parentheses

- Immediately *after* the borrowed material, at a natural pause in the sentence, or at the end of the sentence

- Before any internal punctuation (comma, semicolon) or terminal punctuation (period, question mark)
- After an ellipsis and bracket at the end of a quotation but before the final period

Using Parentheses and Attributions

Skilled writers indicate clearly where their ideas stop and those of their sources begin. So, besides providing careful parenthetic documentation, writers often provide **attributions**—nonparenthetical source identifiers like those (underlined) in the following two *summary* statements:

<u>Julian Stamp argues that</u> homelessness must be addressed in terms of economics--and not simply in terms of individual counseling, addiction therapy, or job training (8).

<u>According to statistics</u>, one-half of the homeless individuals in shelters are substance abusers (Stamp 8).

A *quotation* should also be inserted smoothly with an attribution. Don't just drop a quotation into your text, as in this example:

Incorrect

"The key to any successful homeless policy requires a clear understanding of just who are the homeless" (Stamp 8).

Instead, provide an attribution for the quoted statement:

Correct

<u>As Stamp states</u>, "The key to any successful homeless policy requires a clear understanding of just who are the homeless" (8).

<u>One social scientist points out that</u> "the key to any successful homeless policy requires a clear understanding of just who are the homeless" (Stamp 8).

Glance back at the examples on this page and note the following:

- An attribution may specify the author's name (*Julian Stamp argues that; As Stamp states*), or it may refer to a source more generally (*According to statistics; One social scientist points out*). If you want to call attention to a specific author, use an attribution indicating the author's name. Otherwise, use a more general attribution—or a parenthetic citation that includes the name along with the page.

- The first time an author is referred to in the text, the author's full name is provided; afterwards, only the last name is given.
- When the author's name is provided in the text, the name is *not* repeated in the parentheses. (Later nonparenthetic references to the same author give only the last name.)

Sometimes, to inform readers of an author's area of expertise, you may identify that person by profession (*Social scientist Julian Stamp*). Don't, however, use such personal titles as *Mr.* or *Ms.* Finally, as part of an attribution, you may mention your source's title (In *The Homeless and History,* Stamp maintains that...). No matter what information you include, try to vary your attributions. In addition to those already mentioned, you might try the following lead-ins, placing them wherever they fit best—at the beginning, middle, or end of the sentence:

As _____ states, . . .

The information compiled by _____ shows . . .

In _____'s opinion, . . .

_____ contends that . . .

_____'s study reveals that . . .

Also, aim for smooth, graceful attributions, avoiding such awkward constructions as these: "According to Julian Stamp, he says that..." and "In the book by Julian Stamp, he argues that...."

Special Cases of Authorship

In some situations, providing authorship in the attribution or in the parenthetic citation becomes slightly more complicated. The guidelines that follow will help you deal with special types of authorship.

More Than One Source by the Same Author. When your paper includes references to more than one work by the same author, you must specify the particular work being cited. You do this by providing the *title,* as well as the author's name and the page(s). As with the author's name, the title may be given in *either* the attribution *or* the parenthetic citation. Here are some examples:

In <u>The Language and Thought of the Child</u>, Jean Piaget states that "discussion forms the basis for a logical point of view" (240).

Piaget considers dialog essential to the development of logical thinking (<u>Language and Thought</u> 240).

<u>The Child's Conception of the World</u> shows that young children think that the name of something can never change (Piaget 81).

Young children assume that everything has only one name and that no others are possible (Piaget, <u>Child's Conception</u> 81).

Notice that when a work is named in the attribution, the full title appears; when a title is given in the parenthetic citation, only the first few significant words appear. (However, don't use the ellipsis to indicate that some words have been omitted from a title; the ellipsis is used only when quoting a source.) In the preceding examples, the work is a book, so its title is underlined. If the source is an article or a selection from a compilation, the title is placed in quotation marks.

Two or Three Authors.   Supply all the authors' last names in either the attribution or parentheses.

More Than Three Authors.   In either the attribution or parentheses, give the last name of the first author followed by *et al.* (which means "and others").

Two or More Authors with the Same Last Names.   When you use two or more sources written by authors with the same last names, you must include (in either the attribution or parentheses) each author's first name or initial(s).

A Source with No Author.   For a source without a named author, use, in your attribution or parenthetic reference, the title of the work *or* the name of the issuing organization—whichever you used to alphabetize the source on the Works Cited list.

Information Found in Two or More Sources.   During your research, you may come across several sources who cite the same *general* information or who share the same *widely accepted* opinion. Such material is considered *common knowledge* and *doesn't* need to be documented. However, when you come across several sources who cite the same *highly specialized* information or who share the same *controversial* opinion, that material *does* need to be documented. In such a case, state the material in your own words. Then present in the parenthetic citation each source, listed in the order in which it appears on the Works Cited list. Here's an example:

A number of educators agree that an overall feeling of competence-- rather than innate intelligence--is a key factor in determining which students do well the first year in college (Smith 465; Jones 72; Greene 208).

If you use a quotation to express an idea that occurs in several sources, provide an attribution for the quoted source and, in the parentheses, give the source's page number followed by a note that other sources make the same point:

Educator Henry Schneider argues that "students with low self-esteem tend to disregard the academic success they achieve" (23; also pointed out in Rabb 401).

Special Cases of Pagination

Occasionally, a source will have unusual pagination. Here's how to deal with such situations.

A Source with No Page Numbers.   The parenthetic citation simply lacks a page number and the Works Cited list indicates "unpaged" with the abbreviation *N. pag.*

Each Volume of a Multivolume Source Paged Separately.   Indicate the volume number, then the page number, with a colon between the two (Kahn 3:246). Do not use *vol.* or *v.*

A Nonprint Source (Television Show, Lecture, Interview).   In a parenthetic citation, give only the item (title, speaker, person interviewed) you used to alphabetize the source on your Works Cited list. Or provide the identifying information in the attribution, thus eliminating the need for parenthetic information:

```
In the documentary Financing a College Education, Cheryl Snyder

states that...
```

Blending Quotations into Your Text

On the whole, you should try to state borrowed material in your own words. A string of quotations signals that you haven't sufficiently evaluated and distilled your sources. Use quotations sparingly; draw upon them only when they dramatically illustrate key points you want to make or when they lend authority to your own conclusions. Also, keep in mind that supplying the appropriate citation may not be enough to blend the quotation smoothly into your own writing; additional wording may be needed to achieve a smooth transition. Finally, don't forget that a quotation, by itself, won't always make your case for you; it may be necessary to interpret the quotation, showing why it's significant and explaining how it supports your central points. Indeed, such commentary is often precisely what's needed to blend quoted material gracefully into your discussion.

Consider the following examples, noting how the first quotation is dropped awkwardly into the text, without any transition or commentary. In contrast, brief interpretive remarks in the second example provide a transition that allows the quotation to merge easily with the surrounding material:

Original

Recent studies of parenting styles are designed to control researcher bias. "Recent studies screen out researchers whose strongly held attitudes make objectivity difficult" (Layden 10).

Revised

Recent studies of parenting styles are designed to control researcher bias. Psychologist Marsha Layden, a harsh critic of earlier studies, acknowledges that nowadays most investigations "screen out researchers whose strongly held beliefs make objectivity difficult" (10).

Besides following the guidelines on page 543 for using ellipses and brackets, you should be familiar with the following capitalization and punctuation conventions when quoting.

Capitalization and Punctuation of Short Quotations

The way a short quotation is used in a sentence determines whether it begins or doesn't begin with a capital letter and whether it is or isn't preceded by a comma.

1. When an attribution introduces a short quotation that can stand alone as a sentence, *do capitalize* the quotation's *first word*. Also, *precede the quotation with a comma*:

According to Stamp, "Since the explosion of homelessness as a social problem in the 1980s, the gap between the rich and the poor has widened, buying power has stagnated, industrial jobs have fled overseas, and federal funding for low-cost housing has been almost eliminated" (8).

Stamp observes, "Since the explosion of homelessness as a social problem in the 1980s, the gap between the rich and the poor has widenened, buying power has stagnated, industrial jobs have fled overseas, and federal funding for low-cost housing has been almost eliminated" (8).

2. When blending a short quotation into the structure of your own sentence, *don't capitalize* the quotation's *first word* and *don't procede it with a comma*:

Stamp observes that "since the explosion of homelessness as a social problem in the 1980s, the gap between the rich and the poor has widened, buying power has stagnated, industrial jobs have fled overseas, and federal funding for low-cost housing has been almost eliminated" (8).

Even if—as in this case—the material being quoted originally started with a capital letter, you still use lowercase when incorporating the quotation into your own sentence. Quotations often merge with your own words in this way when they are introduced, as in the preceding example, by a pronoun (*that, which, who*)—either stated or implied.

3. If, for variety, you *interrupt a full-sentence quotation* with an attribution, *place commas on both sides of the attribution,* and *resume* the quotation with a *lowercase* letter:

```
"The key to any successful homeless policy," Stamp comments,
"requires a clear understanding of just who are the homeless" (8).
```

Long Quotations

A quotation longer than four lines starts on a new line and is indented, throughout, ten spaces from the left margin. Since this **block format** indicates a quotation, quotation marks are unnecessary. Double-space the block quotation, as you do the rest of your paper. Don't leave extra space above or below the quotation. Long quotations, always used sparingly, require a lead-in. A lead-in that *isn't* a full sentence is followed by a comma; a lead-in that *is* a full sentence (see below) is followed by a colon:

```
Stamp cites changing economic conditions as the key to a national
homeless policy:
```

```
        Since the 1980's, the gap between the rich and the poor
        has widened, buying power has stagnated, industrial jobs
        have fled overseas, and federal funding for low-cost hous-
        ing has been almost eliminated. Given these developments,
        homelessness begins to look like a product of history, our
        recent history, and only by addressing shifts in the Amer-
        ican economy can we begin to find effective solutions for
        people lacking homes. Moreover, these solutions--ranging
        from renewed federal spending to tax laws favoring job-
        creating companies--will require a sustained national com-
        mitment that transcends partisan politics. (8)
```

Notice that the page number in parentheses appears *after* the period, not before as it would with a short quotation.

Quoting or Summarizing a Source Within a Source

If you quote or summarize a *secondary source* (someone whose ideas come to you only through another source), you need to make this clear. The parenthetic documentation should indicate "as quoted in" with the abbreviation *qtd. in:*

```
According to Sherman, "Recycling has, in several communities, cre-
ated unanticipated expenses" (qtd. in Pratt 3).
```

```
Sherman explains that recycling can be surprisingly costly (qtd. in
Pratt 3).
```

If the material you're quoting includes a quotation, place single quotation marks around the secondary quotation:

```
Pratt believes that "recycling efforts will be successful if, as
Sherman argues, 'communities launch effective public-education
campaigns'" (2).
```

Note: Your Works Cited list should include the source you actually read (Pratt), rather than the source you refer to secondhand (Sherman).

Presenting Statistics

Citing statistics can—if done well—be an effective strategy for supporting your ideas. In your enthusiasm to make your points, though, be careful not to misinterpret the data or twist its significance. When presenting statistics in your paper, remember to provide an attribution indicating their source. Also, be sure not to overwhelm readers with too many statistics; include only those that support your central points in compelling ways. Keep in mind, too, that statistics won't speak for themselves. You need to interpret them for readers, showing how the figures cited reinforce your key ideas. Suppose you're writing a paper showing that Medicare reform is needed to control increasing costs. It wouldn't be effective if you simply provided an attribution, then presented one statistic after the other, without explanatory commentary:

Incorrect

The Health Care Financing Administration reports that 1992 revenues ($185 billion) exceeded spending ($120 billion). But in 1997, revenues ($204 billion) and spending ($208 billion) were almost the same. It is projected that by the year 2010, revenues will be $310 billion and spending $410 billion (Mohr 14).

Instead, after providing an attribution, present only the most telling statistics, being sure to explain their significance:

Correct

The Health Care Financing Administration reports that in 1992, Medicare revenues actually exceeded spending by about $65 billion. But five years later, costs had increased so much that they exceeded revenues by about $4 billion. This trend toward escalated costs is expected to continue. It's projected that by the year 2010, revenues will be only $310 billion, whereas spending—if not controlled—will climb to at least $410 billion (Mohr 14).

(For more on statistics, see pages 539–540)

REVISE, EDIT, AND PROOFREAD
THE FIRST DRAFT

After completing your first draft, reward yourself with a break. Set the paper aside for a while, as least for a few hours. When you pick up the draft later, you'll have a fresh, more objective point of view on it. Then, referring to the checklist on pages 98–99 and the first section of the revision checklist that follows, reread your entire draft to get a general sense of how well the paper works. Outlining the draft (see page 98)—*without* referring to the outline that guided the draft's preparation—is a good way to evaluate the paper's overall meaning and structure.

Despite all the work you've done, you may find when you reread the paper that a main point in support of your thesis seems weak. Sometimes a review of your note cards—including those you didn't use for your draft—will uncover appropriate material that you can add to the paper. Other times, though, you may need another trip to the library to gather additional information. Once you're confident that the paper's overall meaning and structure are strong, go ahead and write your introduction and conclusion—if you haven't already done so.

That done, move ahead and evaluate your paper's paragraph development. To focus your revision, use the checklist on pages 100–101, as well as the second section of the revision checklist that follows. As you work, it's a good idea to pay special attention to the way you present evidence in the paragraphs. Does your evidence consist of one quotation after another, or do you express borrowed ideas in your own words? Do you simply insert borrowed material without commentary, or do you interpret the material and show its relevance to the points you want to make?

Before moving to the next stage in the revision process, look closely at the way you introduce borrowed material. If you prepared the draft without providing many attributions, now is the time to supply them. Then, consulting the checklists on pages 118 and 128, as well as the third section of the revision checklist that follows, go ahead and refine your draft's words and sentences.

Finally, when you start editing and proofreading, allow enough time to verify the accuracy of quoted and summarized material. Check such material against your note cards, and check your documentation against both your bibliography cards and Works Cited list, making sure everything matches. When preparing the final copy of your paper, follow the format guidelines on pages 134–136, using the sample research paper (pages 582–596) as a model. Note that the research paper, when accompanied by an outline, has a separate title page. For a research paper without an outline, the title and other identifying information are usually placed at the top of the paper's first page.

Chapters 7, 8, and 9 discuss techniques for revising and editing an essay draft. The following checklist will help you and those giving you feedback apply those techniques to the research paper.

✔ REVISING THE RESEARCH PAPER: A CHECKLIST

Revise Overall Meaning and Structure

- ☐ What is the thesis of the research paper? Where is it stated? How could the thesis be expressed more clearly?
- ☐ Where would background material or a definition of terms clarify overall meaning?
- ☐ Where does research evidence (facts, statistics, expert opinion, surveys, and experimental results) seem irrelevant or contradict the thesis? What can be done to correct these problems?
- ☐ What principle of organization (chronological, spatial, emphatic, simple-to-complex) does the paper use? How does this organizing principle reinforce the paper's thesis and make it easy for readers to follow the paper's line of reasoning?

Revise Paragraph Development

- ☐ In which paragraphs is evidence solid and compelling? Where is it confusing, insufficient, irrelevant, too abstract, inaccurate, nonrepresentative, or predictable? How can these problems be remedied?
- ☐ Which paragraphs merely present research, without analyzing and relating it to the thesis? How can the research material be better incorporated into the paper's point of view?
- ☐ Which paragraphs simply string together quotations, without interpretive commentary? Where is commentary needed? Which quotations could be eliminated?

Revise Sentences and Words

- ☐ Where is more documentation needed to avoid plagiarism? Where do another author's words appear but without quotation marks? Where is a source's language only slightly modified? Which borrowed ideas are summarized but not credited?
- ☐ Where would attributions help signal more clearly where a source's ideas begin and stop?
- ☐ How could attributions be made more graceful and varied?

Edit and Proofread

- ☐ Where is parenthetic documentation lacking required information? Where must an author's name, a title, publication data, or page numbers be added?
- ☐ Which parenthetic citations contain punctuation errors? Where should a title be underlined or placed in quotation marks? Where should a comma be added or deleted?

☐ Where are quotations punctuated incorrectly? Which should start with a capital letter? Which should begin in lowercase? Which should be preceded by a comma? Which should not? Where should a capital letter be deleted? Where is a comma needed to connect the quotation to the text? Where should a comma be deleted?

☐ Where is the format for long quotations incorrect? How can it be corrected?

☐ Where is the format for the Works Cited list incorrect? Which entries are out of alphabetical order? Which titles should be underlined or placed in quotation marks? Where should commas or periods be added or deleted? Where should page numbers be added?

APA DOCUMENTATION FORMAT

MLA documentation style is appropriate for research papers written for courses in the humanities, such as your composition course. Researchers in the social sciences and in education use a different citation format, one developed by the American Psychological Association (APA). If you're writing a paper for a course in sociology, psychology, anthropology, economics, or political science, your professor will probably expect **APA-style documentation.** History, philosophy, and religion are sometimes considered humanities, sometimes social sciences, depending on your approach to the topic.

Parenthetic Citations

As in the MLA format, APA citations are enclosed in parentheses within the text and provide the author's last name. The main difference between the two formats is that the APA parenthetic note *always includes the year* of publication but *may not include the page number.* Specifically, the page number is *required* when a source is *quoted* or when *specific parts* of a source are *paraphrased* or *summarized.* (A paraphrased or summarized citation without a page number refers to the source as a whole.) Also, APA citations are punctuated with commas between the author's name and the year and between the year and the page. Finally, *p.* or *pp.* appears before the page number(s).

Here are some examples of APA parenthetic citations:

APA Format

```
Reports indicate that "intelligence is not nearly as important as
schooling, background, personality, and chance in determining how a
person's life turns out" (Summers, 1998, p. 35).
```

```
The degree of success in a person's life depends less on intelli-
gence than on other factors, including education, socioeconomic
status, temperament, and good luck (Summers, 1998, p. 35).
```

Here are the same citations in MLA style:

MLA Format

```
Reports indicate that "intelligence is not nearly as important as
schooling, background, personality, and chance in determining how a
person's life turns out" (Summers 35).
```

```
The degree of success in a person's life depends less on intelli-
gence than on other factors, including education, socioeconomic
status, temperament, and good luck (Summers 35).
```

In APA format, if you lead into a quotation, paraphrase, or summary with an attribution that gives the author's name, the publication year follows the author's name in parentheses, and the page number appears at the end:

```
Carol Simons (1998) notes that Channel One has "an MTV format that
undercuts the significance of important issues" (p. 54).
```

```
Carol Simons (1998) believes that Channel One's scattershot style
trivializes serious issues (p. 54).
```

If a work has two authors, cite both. Join their names by *and* within the attribution and by an ampersand (&) within a parenthetic reference:

```
Martin A. Lee and Norman Solomon (1998) find much television cover-
age of international news to be "superficial, incomplete, or mis-
leading" (p. 257).
```

```
Much television coverage of international news is "superficial,
incomplete, or misleading" (Lee & Solomon, 1998, p. 257).
```

If a work has three to five authors, name all authors in the first citation. In subsequent citations, name only the first author followed by *et al.* If there are six or more authors, cite the first author followed by *et al.*

References List

As in the MLA style, a double-spaced alphabetical list of sources appears at the end of a research paper using APA documentation style. However, whereas the MLA titles this list "Works Cited," the APA gives it the heading **References.**

The MLA and APA formats for listing sources include the same basic information, but they present it in different ways. Here are some of the distinguishing features of APA-style entries:

- The first line of each entry should start at the left margin; subsequent lines are indented on the same margin as your paper's paragraphs.*
- The publication date is placed in parentheses directly after the author's name and is followed by a period.
- Two or more works by the same author are arranged according to publication date, with the earliest appearing first.
- Two or more works written by the same author and published in the same year are differentiated by lowercase letters—(1996a), (1996b)—and are alphabetized by title.
- All authors' names, no matter how many, are given in the reference. When there are two or more authors, use the ampersand instead of *and.*
- All authors' names are inverted. In addition, an author's first and middle names are represented by initials only.
- Only the first letter of a book or article title (and subtitle) and any proper names contained within it are capitalized.
- All titles appear *with* any initial *A, An,* or *The.*

Here's a sample APA-style reference for a *book with a single author:*

Coren, S. (1997). <u>Sleep Thieves: An eyeopening exploration into the science and mysteries of sleep.</u> New York: Free Press.

What about articles listed on the References page? Unlike the MLA, the APA uses no quotation marks around article titles. And, as noted, only the first word of an article's title and subtitle is capitalized. However, as in MLA style, a periodical's name is underlined and all major words within it are capitalized. Include any initial *A* or *An* in a periodical's name but drop any initial *The.* A

---

*For papers being published in a book or journal that follows APA style, the first line of each entry should be indented five spaces from the left; subsequent lines are flush left. The typesetting system used by the book or journal will convert the entries to the format you see above and on the following pages.

journal title is immediately followed by a comma, a space, and the volume number (also underlined). Finally, precise and inclusive page numbers are required for all types of articles, even when the pages are not consecutive. In citations for a newspaper source, encyclopedia entry, or article or chapter in an edited book, *p.* or *pp.* precedes the page number(s). Otherwise, only the numbers themselves are given.

Here are sample APA listings for articles in print sources:

Magazine Article

Neimark, J. (1998, July-August). Night life. <u>Psychology Today,</u>
     <u>18,</u> 30–33, 66.

Journal Article (Paginated by Issue)

Kokeev, M. (1998). Global climate and politics. <u>International</u>
     <u>Affairs, 44,</u> 38–44.

Article in an Anthology

Edelman, P. B. (1995). Responsibility for reducing poverty. In R.
     Lavelle (Ed.), <u>America's new war on poverty</u> (pp. 223–226).
     San Francisco: Blackside.

Computerized Sources

APA recommendations regarding the format for listing computerized sources are complicated—and in flux. Indeed, the 1995 edition of the Publication Manual of the American Psychological Association acknowledges that "at the time of writing this edition, a standard has not yet emerged" for citing computerized sources. Because APA style for documenting computerized sources has not been determined fully, it's a good idea to ask your instructor for guidance if you need to cite a computerized source using APA format. In the meantime, the following sample listings will provide some initial guidance.

Article on CD-ROM

Cassell, A. (1997, December 24). Unease and prosperity. <u>Philadel-</u>
     <u>phia Inquirer</u> [CD-ROM], D01 (14 pars.). Dialog.

In general, to list an article on CD-ROM, put *CD-ROM* in brackets after the periodical's title. Follow the article's page numbers (or other available information on pagination and article length) with the name of the publisher of the computerized database.

Article Obtained from an On-line Data Base

```
Stevens, William K. (1998, June 23). Debating nature of nature in
    Yellowstone. New York Times (67 pars.) Science Section.
    <http://archives.nytimes.com/archive/bin/
    checksub?docid=161665>. (1998, August 7).
```

For an article accessed on-line, include author, date and title information, followed by the article's page numbers (or other available information on pagination and article length) in parentheses, and then the title of the Web site. The Web site address should appear in angle brackets at the end of the citation, followed by the date on which the site was accessed (in parentheses).

More information about APA documentation format can be found in the latest edition of the *Publication Manual of the American Psychological Association.*

E-Mail Messages

According to the APA style, personal correspondence, including e-mail, doesn't need to be documented in your reference list. Instead, cite the person's name in your essay and in parentheses write *personal communication* and the date.

A NOTE ABOUT OTHER DOCUMENTATION SYSTEMS

Generally, professionals in the hard sciences (biology, chemistry, medicine, physics) and technical fields (computer science and electrical engineering) use neither the MLA nor the APA system of documentation. Rather, using bracketed or superscripted (raised) reference numbers, they key each item of borrowed material to an entry on the References page. The References list, therefore, isn't alphabetized; instead, the numbered sources simply appear in the order in which they are mentioned in the paper.

When you write a paper for a science course, ask your professor whether you should use the MLA, APA, or the system found in most science and technical journals. If your instructor prefers the last, find out which publication can serve as your model. That way, you won't be unpleasantly surprised by any criticism that you've used an inappropriate system of documentation.

STUDENT RESEARCH PAPER: MLA-STYLE DOCUMENTATION

The sample outline and research paper that follow were written by Brian Courtney for a composition class. In his paper, Brian uses the MLA documentation system. To help you spot various types of sources, quotations, and attributions, we've annotated the paper. Our marginal comments also flag key elements, such as the paper's thesis statement, plan of development, and concluding summary.

Note that the main headings in Brian's outline parallel, to a large degree, the topic sentences of the paper's paragraphs; subheadings generally represent the points that develop those paragraphs. The outline contains no sections corresponding to Brian's introduction and conclusion because he wrote those only after completing the body of his paper. As you read the paper, pay special attention to the way Brian incorporates source material and uses it to support his own ideas.

As you'll see, Brian provided a title page because his paper was preceded by an outline. For a paper submitted without an outline, use a top heading rather than a title page. Here is the format for a first page with a top heading:

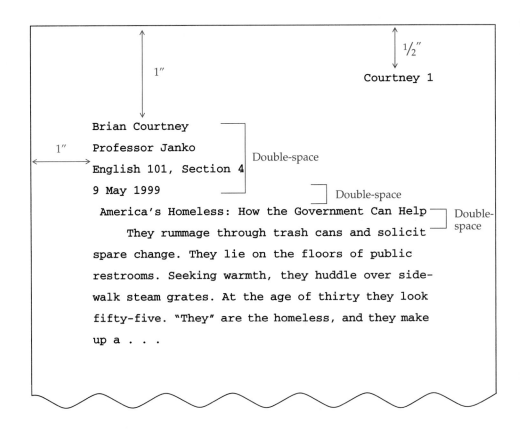

America's Homeless:

How the Government Can Help

by

Brian Courtney

English 101, Section 19

Professor Janko

9 May 1999

Although a title page isn't necessary, you may be asked to provide one.

A paper *with* an outline often has a separate title page.

Title begins about one-third of the way down the page.

Center the title. Double-space between lines of the title and your name.

Course and section, instructor's name, and date, on separate lines, are double-spaced and centered.

After the title page, number all pages in upper-right corner— a half-inch from the top. Place your name before the page number. Use small Roman numerals on outline pages. Use arabic numbers on pages following the outline.

The word *Outline* (without underlining or quotation marks) is centered one inch from the top. Double-space to first line of outline.

Double-space both outline and text. Leave one-inch margins at top, bottom, and sides.

1″

1″

Courtney i

Outline

Thesis: The federal government should do more to help the homeless toward independence.

  I. Homelessness is a major problem in the United States.

   A. Experts disagree about the number of Americans who are homeless.

   B. Experts agree that the number of homeless, particularly homeless families, is growing.

 II. Finding ways to help the homeless is difficult.

   A. Even if the homeless find shelter, they still often wander the street.

    1. Some homeless people are addicted to alcohol or drugs.

    2. Some have serious psychiatric problems.

    3. Others lack basic survival skills.

   B. Comprehensive programs are needed to address the complex problems that many homeless people have.

III. Some programs offer exactly this kind of broad assistance to the homeless.

   A. Project Renewal and Pine Street Inn offer substance-abuse programs.

   B. Lenox Hill Neighborhood House and CANP also offer psychological-support programs for the homeless.

    1. Counseling sessions are attended by those with substance-abuse problems.

    2. Counseling sessions are attended by runaway teens.

1″

1″

Courtney ii

3. Counseling sessions are attended by
those overwhelmed by personal difficulties.

IV. Some broad-assistance programs provide
training in everyday survival skills.

A. Homes for the Homeless offers workshops on
everything from nutrition to interview
techniques.

B. Project Hope shows clients how to apply for
food stamps and other benefits to which
they are entitled.

C. House of Hope provides instruction in
household budgeting and home maintenance.

V. Some broad-assistance programs help the homeless get a job.

A. Many of the homeless have no jobs or have
never worked more than six months.

B. CANP provides training in résumé writing
and interviewing.

C. CANP's job training has a high success
rate.

VI. The federal government should help such broad-
assistance programs.

A. CANP's funding has slipped.

B. Project Hope doesn't have the resources
needed to meet the growing demands on its
services.

VII. The government should also raise the minimum
wage.

A. Some of the homeless have jobs, but their
low incomes put most housing out of their
reach.

B. The last two decades have seen a dramatic
   drop in minimum-wage buying power.
VIII. A lack of affordable housing is at the center
   of the homeless problem.
   A. One magazine argues that people's deep dis-
      turbances--not the unavailability of inex-
      pensive housing--are at the heart of the
      homeless problem.
   B. Numerous studies and many experts refute
      this viewpoint and show that recent trends
      in housing are the real culprit.
IX. The federal government should finance more
   low-cost housing.
   A. Affordable private housing is almost non-
      existent.
      1. Gentrification increases the price of
         previously low-cost housing units, put-
         ting them beyond the reach of poor peo-
         ple.
      2. Even rundown SRO hotels charge more than
         the poor can afford.
   B. Public housing can accommodate only a small
      percentage of those seeking relief from
      high costs in the private housing market.
      1. The federal government has cut funding
         of public housing and housing subsidies.
      2. Cities have slashed funding for the
         construction of public housing and
         shelters.

Courtney 1

America's Homeless: How the Government Can Help

1   They rummage through trash cans and solicit
spare change. They lie on the floors of public
restrooms. Seeking warmth, they huddle over sidewalk
steam grates. At the age of thirty, they look fifty-
five. "They" are the homeless, and they make up a
growing percentage of America's population. Indeed,
homelessness has reached such proportions that the
private sector and local governments can't possibly
cope. To help homeless people toward independence,
the federal government must support rehabilitation
and job training programs, raise the minimum wage,
and fund more low-cost housing.

2   Not everyone agrees on the number of Americans
who are homeless. Estimates range anywhere from
650,000 to 5 million at any given time (Link et al.
353; "Prevalence"). Although the figures may vary,
analysts agree on another matter: that the number of
homeless, particularly of homeless families, is
increasing (Nunez 3). A U.S. Conference of Mayors'
survey found that in the past several years requests
for shelter access increased in three quarters of
the country's top twenty-nine cities, while 90% of
those cities reported increases in families requesting such aid ("Meaner"; Nunez 3).

3   Finding ways to assist this growing and changing homeless population has become increasingly difficult. Even when homeless individuals or families
manage to find a shelter that will give them three
meals a day and a place to sleep at night, a good
number have trouble moving beyond the shelter system
and securing a more stable lifestyle. Part of the
problem, explains sociologist Christopher Jenks in
his now classic study, is that many homeless adults

For a paper with an
outline, you may
repeat the paper's
title, centered, on the
first page of the text.
Double space
between the title and
text.

Introduction

Thesis, with plan of
development

Parenthetic citation
for information that
appears in two
sources. Sources
given in order they
appear on Works
Cited list. First cita-
tion indicates a
work with more
than three authors;
page number *and*
first author's name
given since author is
not cited earlier in
the sentence. No
author or page
number given for
the second source
since it is an anony-
mous one-page
article.

Parenthetic
citation for a single-
author source. Page
number *and* author
are given since
author is not cited
earlier in the
sentence.

Common
knowledge is not
documented.

Attribution gives
author's name and
area of expertise.
Parenthetical refer-
ence at end of sen-
tence gives just the
page number since
the author is cited
in the attribution.

Courtney 2

are addicted to alcohol and drugs (41-42). And psy-
chiatrist E. Fuller Torrey adds that nearly one-
third of the homeless have serious psychiatric disorders (17). While not addicted or mentally ill,
many others simply lack the everyday survival skills
needed to turn their lives around. Reporter Lynette
Holloway notes that New York City officials believe
the situation will improve only when shelters provide comprehensive programs that address the many
needs of the homeless (B1). As Catherine Howard,
Director of the Bronx-based Paradise Transitional
Housing Program, wrote in a letter to the New York
Times, "Identifying the needs of the homeless and
linking them with services in the community is as
important as finding suitable housing. Many homeless
people return to the [...] shelter system and eventually to the street because of the lack of such
support services" (A26).

Luckily, a number of agencies are beginning to   4
act on the belief that the homeless need "more than
a key and a lease" if they are to acquire the attitudes, skills, and behaviors needed to stay off the
street (Howard A26). Besides providing shelter, non-
profit agencies such as New York City's Project
Renewal and Boston's Pine Street Inn offer substance-abuse programs and intensive follow-ups to
ensure that clients remain sober and drug-free (Holloway B1; United States 29). To help the homeless
cope with psychological programs, New York City's
Lenox Hill Neighborhood House and Boston's Community
Action Now Program (CANP) provide in-house social
workers and psychiatric care (Holloway B1; Van
Meder). Joan Van Meder, CANP's cofounder and director, explained in an e-mail interview that her orga-

Parenthetic reference gives page but not author since author is cited in the paper.

Full-sentence quotation is preceded by a comma and begins with a capital letter.

Ellipses enclosed in brackets indicate that some material has been deleted from the middle of the original sentence.

Quotation blends into rest of the sentence (no comma; quotation's first word is not capitalized).

Second source is a government publication.

No page number given for second source in parenthetic citation because source is an e-mail interview.

E-mail interview source is identified.

Courtney 3

nization offers one-on-one and group sessions helping not only recovering substance abusers but also
runaway teenagers (some of whom are pregnant) as
well as individuals overwhelmed by personal traumas
like divorce, death of a family member, or loss of a
job. Staff counselors refer individuals with more
severe psychological disturbances to community
health agencies.

5   In addition to providing psychological support,
many organizations instruct the homeless in basic
survival skills. Adapting the principles of "Continuum of Care," a project sponsored by the Department
of Housing and Urban Development, such agencies provide training in the everyday skills that clients
need to live independently (Halper and McCrummen ← —— Parenthetic citation
26). New York City's Homes for the Homeless has   for a work with two
                                                             authors
established facilities called "American Family
Inns." Functioning as "residential, literacy,
employment, and training centers for entire
families," these centers emphasize good nutrition,
effective parenting, education, household-
management skills, and job-search and interview
techniques (Nunez 72). Boston's Project Hope also
works to guide the homeless toward self-sufficiency,
showing them how to apply for jobs and how to obtain
disability compensation and veterans' benefits
(Leonard 12-13). At St. Martin de Porres House of
Hope, a Chicago shelter, homeless women and their
children are assigned household jobs upon their
arrival and learn the basics of domestic budgeting
and home maintenance (Driscoll 46). Such increased
responsibility teaches the homeless how to cope with
life's everyday challenges--and prepares them for
the demands of working life.

Courtney 4

Since many of the homeless have little work   6
experience, it is not surprising that vocational
training is a key service provided by broad-based
agencies. According to Jenks's often-cited survey,
94% of the homeless lack steady work (50). The same
survey shows that most heads of homeless families
have never worked longer than six months (Nunez 28).
Through challenging instruction that includes practice in writing a resume and interviewing for a
position, CANP and other agencies coach the homeless
in getting and keeping a job. As a result of such
intensive training, CANP has an outstanding job
placement rate, with 75% of those completing its
job-training program moving on to self-sufficiency
(Van Meder).

E-mail interview
source provided in
parentheses since
no attribution giv-
en in the sentence

Unfortunately, organizations like CANP are   7
struggling to survive on dwindling allocations. Boston's Project Hope, for example, served as a short-
term way-station for homeless families through the
late 1980s, until the recession of the early 90s.
Then new welfare and public-assistance policies
reduced the program's operating budget. Fewer families now meet the tighter eligibility requirements
to stay at the shelter, and those who do are forced
to stay longer because so few housing subsidies are
available (Leonard 11-12). It's apparent that government aid is necessary if suppliers of comprehensive assistance--like CANP and Project Hope--are to
meet the needs of a growing population.

Besides funding local programs for the home-   8
less, the government also needs to raise the minimum wage. Some homeless people are employed, but
their limited education locks them into minimum-
wage positions that make it nearly impossible for

Courtney 5

them to afford available housing. Dennis Culhane,
Professor of Social Welfare Policy at the University
of Pennsylvania, explains that employed homeless
individuals--who typically receive the minimum-
wage--pay such a high percentage of their salary on
housing that "their income doesn't cover their housing costs" (qtd. in United States 12). Patrick Markee also points to this disastrous decline in
minimum-wage buying power:

> Indeed, the causes of modern mass home-
> lessness are a matter of little debate,
> and reside in what many academics and
> advocates call the affordability gap:
> the distance between the affordability
> (and availability) of secure, stable
> housing and the income levels of poor
> Americans[...]. The other side of the
> affordability gap has two elements, one
> of which is by now familiar to most Amer-
> icans: the steep decline in real wages
> since the mid-seventies; the steady ero-
> sion of the minimum wage; the widening
> gulf between rich and poor during the
> past two decades; and the growing sever-
> ity of poverty. (27)

9   The Economist concedes that this escalating
affordability gap makes it difficult for poor people
to find suitable housing. Even so, the magazine
argues, eroding incomes and a lack of affordable
housing aren't at the center of the homeless problem. For the Economist, at the heart of homelessness
is an essentially dysfunctional population with "a
range of social problems. No matter what changes

Where a secondary source is quoted—in a government publication

Attribution leading to a long quotation. Attribution is followed by a colon since the lead-in is a full sentence. If the lead-in isn't a full sentence, use a comma after the attribution.

Long quotation indented ten spaces. Double-space the quotation, as you do the rest of the paper. Don't leave extra space above or below the quotation.

The word *Americans* is followed by ellipses enclosed in brackets plus a period, indicating that some material has been deleted from the end of the original sentence.

Attribution naming periodical source for the article cited in parentheses later in the paragraph

Courtney 6

Quotation with brackets indicating that the student writer added words for clarity

economically, many [of the homeless] will still live on the margin" ("Economics Focus"). Numerous studies dispute such an interpretation; they conclude, as does one urban researcher, that a lack of affordable housing--not "an enduring internal state" like addiction or mental illness--plays the critical role in putting people on the street (Schinn). In Making Room: The Economics of Homelessness, Brendan O'Fla-herty points out that large-scale deinstitutional-ization for the mentally ill occurred between 1960 and 1975; however, it wasn't until the 1980s--a period marked by sharp cuts in subsidized housing--that large numbers of the mentally ill wound up liv-ing on the streets (235). Shinn cites a study that supports the view that a lack of affordable housing is at the center of the homelessness problem. She conducted a longitudinal study of homeless families who received subsidized housing in New York City and found that "whatever other problems families may have had, an average of 5 years after entering shel-ter, 61% were stably housed in their own apartments for at least a year and an average of 3 years. Only 4% were in shelter." Shinn concludes, "Receipt of subsidized housing was both a necessity and a suffi-cient condition for achieving stability." Even Jenks, whose views are similar to those of the Economist, believes that more affordable "housing is still the first step in dealing with the homeless problem. Regardless of why people are on the streets, giving them a place to live[...]is usually the most important thing we can do to improve their lives" (qtd. in United States 7).

Clearly, the federal government must increase   10
its funding of low-cost housing. Such a commitment

No author or page number is given since source is an anonymous one-page article.

Parenthetic citation for article obtained on-line; author pro-vided but no page given since elec-tronic text does not follow the pagina-tion of the original

Attribution naming book and its author

Quotation preceded by *that* blends into the rest of the sentence (no com-ma; quotation's first word is not capitalized).

No parenthetic citation needed because author's name appears in text and because electronic text does not follow pagina-tion of the original

Courtney 7

is essential given recent developments in both the
private and public housing markets. As Markee
explains, affordable private housing has become
increasingly scarce in the last several decades
(27). The major problem affecting the private market
is gentrification, a process by which low-cost units
are transformed into high-cost housing for affluent
professionals. As neighborhoods gentrify, housing
that formerly trickled down to the poor is taken off
the low-cost market, increasing homelessness
(O'Flaherty 117). Also, in gentrified areas, many of
the tenements and SRO (single room occupancy) hotels
in which the desperately poor used to live have been
gutted and replaced by high-priced condominiums. And
the tenements and SRO's that remain generally demand
more rent than the poor can pay (Halper and McCrummen 29).

11   Where can people turn to seek relief from these
inflated costs in the private housing market? What
remains of public housing can hardly answer the
problem. As Markee notes, the 1980s saw the federal
government cut spending on public housing and housing subsidies by 75%. In 1980, for example, federal
agencies helped build 183,000 housing units. By the
mid 1980s, that number had fallen to 20,000 (27). To
counteract these reductions, many cities invested
heavily in new housing in the late 1980s. In the
1990s, though, city budgets slashed such investments
in half (Halper and McCrummen 28). Municipal money
now goes to constructing temporary shelters that can
house only 2% of the cities' homeless population
(Halper and McCrummen 27).

12   In light of all these problems, one conclusion
seems inevitable: the federal government must take a

Conclusion pro-
vides a summary
and restates the
thesis.

Courtney 8

more active role in helping America's homeless.
While debate may continue about the extent and the
causes of homelessness, we know which approaches
work and which do not. The government must increase
its support of programs that make a demonstrable
difference. Such programs do more than provide food
and shelter; they also offer substance-abuse counseling, psychological support, instruction in basic
survival skills, and job training. Finally, unless
the government guarantees a decent minimum wage and
affordable housing, even skilled, well-adjusted
individuals may be forced to live on the street. The
government can't continue to walk past the homeless,
face averted. In doing so, it walks past millions in
need.

Courtney 9

Works Cited

Driscoll, Connie. "Responsibility 101: A Chat with
    Sister Connie Driscoll." Interview with Bruce
    Upbin. <u>Forbes</u> 19 May 1997: 46–47.

"Economics Focus: Down and Out." <u>Economist</u> 8 Feb.
    1997: 86. <u>Academic Universe</u>. On-line. Lexis-
    Nexis. 30 Oct. 1998.

Halper, Evan, and Stephanie McCrummen. "Out of Sight,
    Out of Mind: New York City's New Homeless
    Policy." <u>Washington Monthly</u> April 1998: 26–29.

Holloway, Lynette. "Shelters Improve Under Private
    Groups, Raising a New Worry." <u>New York Times</u> 12
    Nov. 1997, late ed.: B1+.

Howard, Catherine. Letter. <u>New York Times</u>. 18 Nov.
    1997, late ed.: A26. <u>New York Times</u> Ondisc.
    CD-ROM. UMI-ProQuest. Oct. 1998.

Jenks, Christopher. <u>The Homeless</u>. Cambridge:
    Harvard UP, 1994.

Leonard, Margaret A. "Project Hope: An Interview
    with Margaret A. Leonard." Interview with
    George Anderson. <u>America</u> 2 Nov. 1996: 10–14.

Link, Bruce, et al. "Lifetime and Five-Year Preva-
    lence of Homelessness in the United States: New
    Evidence on an Old Debate." <u>American Journal of</u>
    <u>Orthopsychiatry</u> 65.3 (1995): 347–54.

Markee, Patrick. "The New Poverty: Homeless Families
    in America." Review of <u>The New Poverty</u>, by
    Ralph Nunez, <u>The Nation</u> 14 Oct. 1996: 27–28.

"Meaner Streets for the Homeless." Editorial.
    <u>America</u> 1 Feb. 1997: 3.

Interview published in a weekly magazine—interview's pages are consecutive

Anonymous magazine article obtained through an on-line data base. Electronic text indicates that the article is a single page in the original.

Article by two authors, in a monthly magazine; pages are consecutive

Article in a daily newspaper—section indicated along with pages; pages are not consecutive

Letter to a daily newspaper, obtained from a CD-ROM

Book by one author—publisher's name is abbreviated

Article, by more than three authors, in a scholarly journal with continuous pagination

Book review in a monthly magazine

Anonymous editorial in a weekly magazine

Courtney 10

Nunez, Ralph da Costa. <u>The New Poverty: Homeless</u>
        <u>Families in America</u>. New York: Insight, 1996.

O'Flaherty, Brendan. <u>Making Room: The Economics of</u>
        <u>Homelessness</u>. Cambridge: Harvard UP, 1998.

"The Prevalence of Homelessness." <u>Harvard Mental</u>
        <u>Health Letter</u> Apr. 1996: 6.

"Room at the Top: Housing for the Poor." <u>Economist</u> 1
        June 1996: 24.

Shinn, Marybeth. "Family Homelessness: State
        or Trait?" <u>American Journal of Community</u>
        <u>Psychology</u> 25.6 (1997): 755-70 (27 pars.).
        <u>Expanded Academic Index ASAP</u>. On-line. Infotrac
        Search Bank. 30 Oct. 1998.

Torrey, E. Fuller. <u>Out of the Shadows: Confronting</u>
        <u>America's Mental Illness Crisis</u>. New York:
        Wiley, 1997.

United States. Cong. House. Subcommittee on Housing
        and Community Opportunity of the Committee on
        Banking and Financial Services. <u>Hearing on</u>
        <u>Homeless Housing Programs Consolidation and</u>
        <u>Flexibility Act</u>. 105th Cong., 1st sess. Wash-
        ington: GPO, 1997.

Van Meder, Joan. E-mail interview. 28 Oct. 1998.

Article in a scholarly journal obtained through an on-line data base. Electronic text does not duplicate original pagination; text is 27 paragraphs long.

Government publication

E-mail interview

Commentary

Brian begins his introduction with an evocative description of a typical street person's struggle to survive. These descriptive passages prepare readers for a general statement of the problem of homelessness. This two-sentence statement, starting with "'They' are the homeless" and ending with "the private sector and local governments can't possibly cope," leads the way to Brian's *thesis:* "To help homeless people toward independence, the federal government must support rehabilitation and job training programs, raise the minimum wage, and fund more low-cost housing."

By researching his subject thoroughly, Brian was able to marshal many compelling facts and opinions. He sorted through this complex web of material and arrived at a logical structure that reinforced his thesis. He describes the extent of the problem (paragraph 2), analyzes some of the causes of the problem (3, 4, 8–11), and points to solutions (4–6, 8, 10–11). He draws upon *statistics* to establish the severity of the problem and quotes *expert opinion* to demonstrate the need for particular types of programs. Note, too, that Brian writes in the *present tense* and uses the *third-person point of view.*

Beyond being clearly organized and maintaining a consistent point of view, the paper is *unified* and *coherent.* For one thing, Brian makes it easy for readers to follow his line of thought. He often uses *transitions:* "And" (3), "In addition" (5), "Besides" (8), and so forth. In other places, he asks a *question* (for example, at the beginning of the eleventh paragraph), or he uses a *bridging sentence* (for instance, at the beginning of the fifth, sixth, and eighth paragraphs). Moreover, he always provides clear attributions and parenthetic references so that readers know at every point along the way whose idea is being presented. Brian has, in short, prepared a well-written, carefully documented paper.

ACTIVITIES:
WRITING THE
RESEARCH
PAPER

1. Imagine that you've just written a research paper exploring how parents can ease their children's passage through adolescence. Prepare a *Works Cited* list for the following sources, putting all information in the correct MLA format.

   a. "A Circle of Friends: It's Not Peer Pressure, It's the Adolescent Way of Life," a chapter in Patricia Hersch's book titled *A Tribe Apart: Journey into the Heart of American Adolescence.* The chapter runs from page 125 to 148. The book was published by the Ballantine Publishing Group (New York) in 1998.

b. One radio broadcast within a series called *Family Matters,* hosted by Dr. Daniel Gottlieb and produced by Laura Jackson. The broadcast, titled "Getting Along with Adolescents," was aired on 10 September 1998, on WHYY-FM of Philadelphia, PA.

c. An article titled "The Relationship Between Early Maltreatment and Teenage Parenthood," by Ellen C. Herrenkohl and three coauthors. The article appeared in volume 21, issue 3 (1998) of the *Journal of Adolescence* and ran from page 291 to 303. The article, which has 20 paragraphs, was found on the *ProQuest* data base on December 19, 1998. The URL of *ProQuest* is http://proquest.umi.com.

d. A book and an article by Laurence Steinberg. The book, *You and Your Adolescent: A Parent's Guide for Ages 10–20,* was published in 1997 by HarperCollins Publishing (PA). The article, "Ethnicity and Adolescent Achievement," appeared on pages 28 to 35 and 44 to 48 in the Summer 1996 issue of *American Educator.*

e. An eight-page guidebook issued in 1998 by the U.S. Department of Education. The guidebook is titled *How Can We Support Girls in Early Adolescence?*

f. An article from pages 3 and 5, section C of the September 6, 1998, issue of the *New York Times.* Written by Donna Greene, the article is titled "Charting a Safe Course for Adolescence" and has 11 paragraphs. The article was found on the ERIC Database CD-ROM, published by the U.S. Department of Education in 1998.

2. Assume you're writing a research paper on date rape. You decide to incorporate into your paper points made by Nancy Gibbs in "When Is It Rape?" (page 423). To practice using attributions, parenthetic citations, and correct punctuation with quoted material, do the following:

a. Choose a statement from the essay to quote. Then write one sentence or more that includes the quotation, a specific attribution, and the appropriate parenthetic citation.

b. Choose an idea to summarize from the essay. Then write one sentence or more that includes the summary and the appropriate parenthetic documentation.

c. Find a place in the essay where the author quotes an expert. Use this quotation to write one or more sentences in which you:

- first, quote the expert quoted by Gibbs
- second, summarize the ideas of the expert quoted by Gibbs

Each of the above should include the appropriate attribution and parenthetic citation.

PART V

THE LITERARY PAPER AND EXAM ESSAY

22
WRITING
ABOUT
LITERATURE

DOES the idea of writing a **literary analysis** make you anxious? If it does, we'd like to reassure you that in some ways writing a literary analysis is easier than writing other kinds of essays. For one thing, you don't have to root around, trying to figure out what you want to accomplish: Your purpose in any literary analysis is simply to share with readers some insights about an aspect of a poem, play, story, or novel.* Second, in a literary analysis, your thesis and supporting evidence grow directly out of your reading of the text. All you have to do is select the textual evidence that supports your thesis.

By examining both *what* the author says and *how* he or she expresses it, you increase your readers' understanding and appreciation of the work. And, of course, literary analysis rewards you as well. Close textual analysis develops your ability to think critically and independently. Studying literature also strengthens your own writing. As you examine literary works, you become familiar with the strategies that skilled writers use to convey meaning with eloquence and power. Finally, since literature deals with the largest, most timeless issues, literary analysis is one way to learn more about yourself, others, and life in general.

---

*For the sake of simplifying a complex subject, we discuss literary analysis as though it focuses on a single work. In practice, though, a literary analysis often examines two or more works.

ELEMENTS OF LITERARY WORKS

Before you can analyze a literary text, you need to become familiar with literature's key elements. The following list of literary terms will help you understand what to look for when reading and writing about literature.

List of Literary Terms

Theme: a work's controlling idea, the main issue the work addresses (for example, loyalty to an individual versus loyalty to a cause; the destructive power of a lie). Most literary analyses deal with theme, even if the analysis focuses on the methods by which that theme is conveyed.

Plot: the series of events that occurs within the work. Typically, plays and stories hinge on plot much more heavily than poetry, which is often constructed around images and ideas rather than actions.

Structure: a work's form, as determined by plot construction, act and scene divisions, stanza and line breaks, repeated images, patterns of meter and rhyme, and other elements that create discernible patterns. (See also *image, meter, rhyme,* and *stanza.*)

Setting: the time and place in which events unfold (the present, on a hot New York City subway car; a nineteenth-century sailing vessel in the South Pacific).

Character: an individual within a poem, play, story, or novel (Tom Sawyer, Ophelia, Oliver Twist, Bigger Thomas).

Characterization: the way in which the author develops an individual within the work.

Conflict: a struggle between individuals, between an individual and some social or environmental force, or within an individual.

Climax: the most dramatic point in the action, usually near the end of a work and usually involving the resolution of conflict.

Foreshadowing: hints, within the work, of events to come.

Narrator or **speaker:** the individual in the work who relates the story. It's important to remember that the narrator is not the same as the author. The opening of Mark Twain's *Huckleberry Finn* makes this distinction especially clear: "You don't know me, without you have read a book by the name of *The Adventures of Tom Sawyer,* but that ain't no matter. That book was made by Mr. Mark Twain, and he told the truth, mainly." A poorly educated boy named Huck Finn is the narrator; it is *his* captivating but ungrammatical voice that we hear. In contrast, Twain, the author, was a sophisticated middle-aged man whose command of the language was impeccable.

Point of view: the perspective from which a story is told. In the **first-person** ("I") point of view, the narrator tells the story as he or she experienced it ("*I* saw the bird flap its wings"). The first-person narrator either participates in or observes the action. In the **third-person** point of view, the narrator tells the story the way someone else experienced it ("*Dave* saw the bird flap its wings").

The third-person narrator is not involved in the action. He or she may simply report outwardly observable behavior or events, enter the mind of only one character, or enter the minds of several characters. Such a third-person narrator may be *omniscient* (all-knowing) or have only *limited knowledge* of characters and events.

Irony: a discrepancy or incongruity of some kind. *Verbal irony,* which is often tongue-in-cheek, involves a discrepancy between the literal words and what is actually meant ("Here's some news that will make you sad. You received the highest grade in the course"). If the ironic comment is designed to be hurtful or insulting, it qualifies as *sarcasm* ("Congratulations! You failed the final exam"). In *dramatic irony,* the discrepancy is between what the speaker says and what the author means or what the audience knows. The wider the gap between the speaker's words and what can be inferred about the author's attitudes and values, the more ironic the point of view.

Satire: ridicule (either harsh or gentle) of vice or folly, with the purpose of developing awareness—even bringing about reform. Besides using wit, satire often employs irony to attack absurdity, injustice, and evil.

Figure of speech: a non-literal comparison of dissimilar things. The most common figures of speech are **similes,** which use the word *like* or *as* ("*Like* a lightning bolt, the hawk streaked across the sky"); **metaphors,** which state or imply that one thing *is* another ("All the world's a stage"); and **personification,** which gives human attributes to something nonhuman ("The angry clouds unleashed their fury").

Image: a short, vivid description that creates a strong sensory impression ("A black flag writhed in the wind").

Imagery: a combination of images.

Symbol: an object, place, characteristic, or phenomenon that suggests one or more things (usually abstract) in addition to itself (rain as mourning; a lost wedding ring as betrayal). Usually, though, symbols don't convey meaning in pat, unambiguous ways. Rain, for example, may suggest purification as well as mourning; a lost wedding ring may suggest a life-affirming break from a destructive marriage as well as betrayal.

Motif: a recurring word, phrase, image, figure of speech, or symbol that has particular significance.

Meter: a basic, fixed rhythm of accented and unaccented syllables that the lines of a particular poem follow.

Rhyme: a match between two or more words' final sounds (*Cupid, stupid; mark, park*).

Stanza: two or more lines of a poem that are grouped together. A stanza is preceded and followed by some blank space.

Alliteration: repetition of initial consonant sounds (such as the "b" sounds in "A *b*utterfly *b*looms on a *b*uttercup").

Assonance: repetition of vowel sounds (like the "a" sounds in "m*a*d *a*s *a* h*a*tter").

Sonnet: a fourteen-line, single-stanza poem following a strict pattern of meter and rhyme. The Italian, or *Petrarchan*, sonnet consists of two main parts: eight lines in the rhyme pattern *a b b a, a b b a,* followed by six lines in the pattern *c d c, c d c* or *c d e, c d e*. The English, or *Shakespearean,* sonnet consists of twelve lines in the rhyme scheme *a b a b, c d c d, e f e f,* followed by two rhymed lines *g g* (called a *couplet*). Traditionally, sonnets are love poems that involve some change in tone or outlook near the end.

HOW TO READ A LITERARY WORK

Read to Form a General Impression

The first step in analyzing a literary work is to read it through for an overall impression. Do you like the work? What does the writer seem to be saying? Do you have a strong reaction to the work? Why or why not?

Ask Questions About the Work

One way to focus your initial impressions is to ask yourself questions about the literary work. You could, for example, select from the following checklist those items that interest you the most or those that seem most relevant to the work you're analyzing.

☑ ANALYZING A LITERARY WORK: A CHECKLIST

☐ What *themes* appear in the work? How do *structure, plot, characterization, imagery,* and other literary strategies reinforce theme?

☐ What gives the work its *structure* or shape? Why might the author have chosen this form? If the work is a poem, how do *meter, rhyme, alliteration, assonance,* and *line breaks* emphasize key ideas? Where does the work divide into parts? What words and images are repeated? What patterns do they form?

☐ How is the *plot* developed? Where is there any *foreshadowing*? What are the points of greatest suspense? Which *conflicts* add tension? How are they resolved? Where does the *climax* occur? What does the *resolution* accomplish?

☐ What do the various *characters* represent? What motivates them? How is character revealed through dialog, action, commentary, and physical description? In what ways do major characters change? What events and interactions bring about the changes?

☐ What is the relationship between *setting* and *action*? To what extent does setting mirror the characters' psychological states?

☐ Who is the *narrator*? Is the story told in the *first* or the *third person*? Is the narrator omniscient or limited in his or her knowledge of characters and events? Is the narrator recalling the past or reporting events as they happen?

☐ What is the author's own *point of view*? What are the author's implied *values* and *attitudes*? Does the author show any religious, racial, sexual, or other biases? Is there any discrepancy between the author's values and attitudes and those of the narrator? To whom in the work does the author grant the most status and consideration? Who is presented as less worthy of consideration?

☐ What about the work is *ironic* or surprising? Where is there a discrepancy between what is said and what is meant?

☐ What role do *figures of speech* play? What *metaphors*, if any, are sustained and developed? Why might the author have used these metaphors?

☐ What functions as a *symbol*? How can you tell?

☐ What *flaws* do you find in the work? Which elements fail to contribute to thematic development? Where does the work lose impact because ideas are stated directly rather than implied? Do any of the characters seem lifeless or inconsistent? Are any of them unnecessary to the work's key events and themes?

Reread and Annotate

Focusing on what you consider the most critical questions from the preceding checklist, begin a second, closer reading of the literary work. With pen or pencil in hand, look for answers to your questions, being sure to note telling details and patterns. Underline striking words, images, and ideas. Draw connecting lines between related items. Jot down questions, answers, and comments in the margins. Of course, if you don't own the work, then you can't write in it. In this case, make notes on a sheet of paper or on index cards.

We've marked the accompanying poem to give you an idea of just what annotation involves. The poem is Shakespeare's Sonnet 29, first published in 1609. Notice that the annotations reveal patterns crucial to an interpretation. For example, jotting down the *rhyme scheme* (*a b a b, c d c d,* and so on) leads to the discovery that one change in rhyme corresponds to a turning point in the narrator's thoughts (see line 9). Similarly, the circling or underlining of repeated or contrasting words highlights ideas developed throughout the poem. The words, *I, my,* and *state,* for instance, are emphasized by repetition. The marginal comments also capture possible *themes,* such as love's healing, redemptive power and the futility of self-absorption and envy.

Contrast between unhappy self-absorption ("beweep") and joyous love ("haply"), between "outcast state" and "scorn to change my state."

When, in disgrace with Fortune and men's eyes,   *a*

I all alone beweep my outcast state,   *b*

And trouble deaf heaven with my bootless cries,   *useless*   *a*

And look upon myself and curse my fate,   *b*

Envy {

Wishing me like to one more rich in hope,   *good looks*   *c*

Featur'd like him, like him with friends possess'd,   *d*

Desiring this man's art, and that man's scope,   *talent knowledge*   *c*

With what I most enjoy contented least;   *d*

}

Changes to increasing → joy. Turns away from self-absorption.

Yet in these thoughts myself almost despising   *e*

Haply I think on thee, and then my state,   *(First time lover is mentioned.)*   *b*

Joyous images. New beginning. Healing power of love.

Like to the lark at break of day arising   *e*

From sullen earth, sings hymns at heaven's gate;   *b*

For thy sweet love rememb'red such wealth brings   *f*

That then I scorn to change my state with kings.   *don't want to trade places*   *f*

Modify Your Annotations

Your annotations will help you begin to clarify your thoughts about the work. With these ideas in mind, try to read the work again; make further annotations on anything that seems relevant and modify earlier annotations in light of your greater understanding of the work. At this point, you're ready to move into the actual analysis.

WRITE THE LITERARY ANALYSIS

When you prepare a literary analysis, the steps you follow are the same as those for writing an essay. You start with prewriting; next, you identify your thesis, gather evidence, write the draft, and revise; finally, you edit and proofread your paper.

Prewrite

Early in the prewriting stage, you should take a moment to think about your purpose, audience, point of view, and tone. Your **purpose** in writing a literary analysis is to share your insights about the work. Even if your paper criticizes some aspect of the work (perhaps it finds fault with the author's insensitive depiction of the poor), your primary purpose is still to convey your interpretation of the work's meaning and methods. When writing literary analysis, you customarily assume that your **audience** is composed of readers already familiar with the work. This makes your task easier. In the case of a play or story, for example, there's no need to rehash the plot.

As you write, you should adopt an objective, **third-person point of view.** Even though you're expressing your own interpretation of the work, guard against veering off into first-person statements like "In my opinion" and "I feel that." The **tone** of a literary analysis is generally serious and straightforward. However, if your aim is to point out that an author's perspective is narrow or biased or that a work is artistically unworthy of high regard, your tone may also have a critical edge. Be careful, though, to concentrate on the textual evidence in support of your view; don't simply state your objections.

   Prewriting actually begins when you annotate the work in light of several key questions you pose about it (see pages 604–605). After refining your initial annotations (see page 606), try to impose a tentative order on your annotations. Ask yourself, "What points do my annotations suggest?" List the most promising of these points on a separate sheet; then link these points to your annotations. There are a number of ways to proceed. You could, for instance, simply list the annotations under the points they support. Or you can number each point and give relevant annotations the same number as that point. Another possibility is to color-code your annotations: Give each point a color; then underline or circle in the same color any annotation related to that point. Finally, prepare a scratch outline of the main points you plan to cover, inserting your annotations in the appropriate spots. (For more on scratch outlines, see pages 31–33 in Chapter 2.)

   If you have trouble generating and focusing ideas in this way, experiment with other prewriting strategies. You might, for example, *freewrite* a page or two on what you have highlighted in the literary text, *brainstorm* a list of ideas, or *map out* the work's overall structure (see pages 27–30 in Chapter 2). Mapping is especially helpful when analyzing a poem.

   If the work still puzzles you, it may be helpful to consult outside sources. Encyclopedias, biographies of the author, and history books can clarify the context in which the work was written. Such reference books as *The Oxford Companion to American Literature* and *The Oxford Companion to English Literature* offer brief biographies of authors and summaries of their major works. In addition, *Twentieth-Century Short Story Explication: Interpretations, 1900–1975, of Short Fiction* lists books and articles on particular stories; and *Poetry Explication: A Checklist of Interpretation Since 1925 of British and American Poems Past and Present* does the same for individual poems.

Identify Your Thesis

   Looking over your scratch list and any supplementary prewriting material or research notes you've collected, try to formulate a **working thesis.** As in other kinds of writing, your thesis statement for a literary analysis should include both your *limited subject* (the literary work you'll analyze and what aspect of the work you'll focus on), as well as your *attitude* toward that subject (the claim you'll make about the work's themes, the author's methods, the author's attitudes, and so on).

   Here are some effective thesis statements for literary analysis:

```
In the poem "The Garden of Love," William Blake uses sound and imag-
ery to depict what he considers the deadening effect of organized
religion.
```

`The characters in the novel `<u>`Judgment Day`</u>` illustrate James Farrell's`
`belief that psychology, not sociology, determines fate.`

`The figurative language in Marge Piercy's poem "The Longings of`
`Women" reveals much about women's feelings and their struggle for`
`power.`

If your instructor asks you to include commentary from professional critics, or if you explore such sources at your own initiative, proceed with caution. To avoid merely adopting others' ideas, try to formulate your thesis about the work *before* you read anyone else's interpretation. Then use others' opinions as added evidence in support of your thesis or as opposing viewpoints that you can counter. (For more on thesis statements, see pages 37–41 in Chapter 3.)

Thesis Statements to Avoid

Guard against a *simplistic* thesis. A statement like "The author shows that people are often hypocritical" doesn't say anything surprising and fails to get at a work's complexity. More likely, the author shares insights about the *nature* of hypocrisy, the *reasons* underlying it, the *forms* it can take, or its immediate and long-term *effects.*

An *overly narrow* thesis is equally misguided. Don't limit your thesis to the time and place in which the work is set. You shouldn't, for example, sum up the theme of Hawthorne's *The Scarlet Letter* with the thesis "Hawthorne examines the intolerance of seventeenth-century Puritan New England." Hawthorne's novel probes the general, or universal, nature of communal intolerance. Puritan New England is simply the setting in which the work's themes are dramatized.

Also, make sure your thesis is *about the work.* Discussion of a particular *social* or *political issue* is relevant only if it sheds light on the work. If you feel a work has a strong feminist theme, it's fine to say so. It's a mistake, however, to stray to a nonliterary thesis such as "Feminism liberates both men and women."

A *biographical thesis* is just as inappropriate as a sociopolitical one. By all means, point out the way a particular work embodies an author's prejudices or beliefs ("Through a series of striking symbols, Yeats pays tribute in 'Easter, 1916' to the valiant struggle for Irish independence"). Don't, however, devise a thesis that passes judgment on the author's personal or psychological shortcomings ("Poe's neurotic attraction to inappropriate women is reflected in the poem 'To Helen'"). It's usually impossible to infer such personal flaws from the text alone. Perhaps the author had a mother fixation, but that determination belongs in the domain of psychoanalysis, not literary analysis.

Support the Thesis with Evidence

Once you've identified a working thesis, return to the text to make sure that nothing in the text contradicts your theory. Also, keeping your thesis in mind, search for previously overlooked **evidence** (*quotations* and *examples*) that develops your thesis. Consider, too, how *summaries* of portions of the work might support your interpretation.

   If you don't find solid textual evidence for your thesis, either drop or modify it. Don't—in an effort to support your thesis—cook up possible relationships among characters, twist metaphors out of shape, or concoct elaborate patterns of symbolism. As Sigmund Freud once remarked, "Sometimes a cigar is just a cigar." Be sure there's plentiful evidence in the work to support your interpretation. The text of Shakespeare's *Romeo and Juliet,* for instance, doesn't support the view that the feud between the lovers' two families represents a power struggle between right-wing and left-wing politics.

Organize the Evidence

   When it comes time to **organize your evidence,** look over your scratch list and evaluate the main points, textual evidence, and outside research it contains. Focusing on your thesis, decide which points should be deleted and which new ones should be added. Then identify an effective sequence for your points. That done, check to see if you've placed textual evidence and outside research under the appropriate points. If you plan to refute what others have said about the work, the discussion on pages 446–447 will help you block out the outline's refutation section. What you're aiming for is a solid, well-developed outline that will guide your writing of the first draft. (For more on outlining, see pages 56–59 in Chapter 5.)

   When preparing your outline, remember that the patterns of development can help you sequence material. If you're writing in response to an assignment, the assignment itself may suggest certain patterns. Consider these examples:

Comparison-Contrast

   In Mark Twain's *Huckleberry Finn,* what traits do the Duke and the Dauphin have in common? In what ways do the two characters differ?

Definition

   How does Ralph Waldo Emerson define "forbearance" in his poem of that name?

Process Analysis

   Discuss the stages by which Morgan Evans is transformed into a scholar in Emlyn Williams's play *The Corn Is Green.*

   Notice that, in these assignments, certain words and phrases (*have in common; in what ways . . . differ; define;* and *discuss the stages*) signal which pattern would be particularly appropriate. Often, though, you'll write on a topic of your own choice. For help in deciding which pattern(s) of development you might use in such circumstances, turn to pages 67–68 in Chapter 6.

Write the First Draft

At this point, you're all set to write. As you rough out your first draft, try to include textual evidence (quotations, examples, summaries), as well as any outside commentary you may have gathered. However, if you get bogged down either incorporating all the evidence or making it blend smoothly with your own points, move on. You can go back and smooth out any rough spots later. In general, proceed as you would in a research paper when blending quotations and summaries with your own words (see pages 570–573 in Chapter 21).

When preparing the draft, you should also take into account the following four conventions of literary analysis.

Use the Present Tense

Literary analysis is written in the **present,** not the past, tense:

```
In "Arrangement in Black and White," Dorothy Parker depicts the
self-deception of a racist who is not conscious of her own racism.
```

The present tense is used because the literary work continues to exist after its completion. Use of the past tense is appropriate only when you refer to a time earlier than that in which the narrator speaks.

Identify Your Text

Even if your only source is the literary work itself, some instructors may want you to identify it by author, title, and publication data in a formal bibliographic note. In such a case, the first time you refer to the work in the paper, place an asterisk after its title. Then, at the bottom of the page, type an asterisk, and, after it, provide full bibliographic information. Here's an example of such a bibliographic footnote:

```
*Marianne Moore, "To a Steam Roller," The Voice That Is Great Within
Us: American Poetry of the Twentieth Century, ed. Hayden Carruth
(New York: Bantam, 1985) 126.
```

(For more about bibliographic footnotes, consult the most recent edition of the *MLA Handbook for Writers of Research Papers*.)

Use Parenthetic References

If you're writing about a very short literary work, your instructor may not require documentation. Usually, however, documentation is expected.

Fiction quotations are followed by the page number(s) in parentheses (89); poetry quotations, by the line number(s) (12–14); and drama quotations, by act, scene, and line numbers (2.1.34–37). The parenthetic reference goes right after the quotation, even if your own sentence continues. When your sentence concludes with the quotation, the final period belongs *after* the parenthetic reference. If you use sources other than the literary text itself, document these as you would quotations or borrowed ideas in a research paper, and provide a Works Cited page. In this case, the literary work you're writing about should also be listed on the Works Cited page, rather than in a bibliographic footnote. (For more on parenthetic documentation and Works Cited listings, see Chapter 21.)

Quote Poetry Appropriately

If you're writing about a short poem, it's a good idea to include the poem's entire text in your paper. When you need to quote fewer than four lines from a poem, you can enclose them in quotation marks and indicate each line break with a slash (/): "But at my back I always hear / Time's winged chariot hurrying near." (Notice that space appears before and after the slash.) Verse quotations of four or more lines should be indented ten spaces from the left margin of your paper and should appear line for line, as in the original source—without slashes to indicate line breaks.

Revise Overall Meaning, Structure, and Paragraph Development

After completing your first draft, you'll gain helpful advice by showing it to others. The checklist that follows will help you and your readers apply to literary analysis some of the revision techniques discussed in Chapters 7 and 8.

 REVISING A LITERARY ANALYSIS: A CHECKLIST

Revise Overall Meaning and Structure

☐ What is the thesis of the analysis? According to the thesis, which elements of the work (such as theme and structure) will be discussed? In what ways, if any, is the thesis simplistic or too narrow? In what ways, if any, does it introduce extraneous social, political, or biographical issues?

☐ What main points support the thesis? If any points stray from or contradict the thesis, what changes should be made?

☐ How well supported by textual evidence is the essay's thesis? What evidence, crucial to the thesis, needs more attention? What other interpretation, if any, seems better supported by the evidence?

☐ Which patterns of development (comparison-contrast, process analysis, and so on) help shape the analysis? How do these patterns support the thesis?

☐ What purpose does the analysis fulfill? Does it simply present a straightforward interpretation of some aspect of the work? Does it point out some flaw in the work? Does it try to convince readers to accept an unconventional interpretation?

□ How well does the analysis suit an audience already familiar with the work? How well does it suit an audience that may or may not share the interpretation expressed?

□ What tone does the analysis project? Is it too critical or too admiring? Where does the tone come across as insufficiently serious?

Revise Paragraph Development

□ What method of organization underlies the sequence of paragraphs? How effective is the sequence?

□ Which paragraphs lack sufficient or sufficiently developed textual evidence? Where does textual evidence fail to develop a paragraph's central point? What important evidence, if any, has been overlooked?

□ Which paragraphs contain too much textual evidence? Which quotations are longer than necessary?

□ Where could textual evidence in a paragraph be more smoothly incorporated into the analysis?

□ If any of the paragraphs include outside research (expert commentary, biographical data, historical information), how does this material strengthen the analysis? If any of the paragraphs consider alternative interpretations, are these opposing views refuted? Should they be?

Revise Sentences and Words

□ Which words and phrases wrongly suggest that there is only one correct interpretation of the work ("Everyone must agree...," "Obviously...")?

□ What words give the false impression that it is possible to read an author's mind ("Clearly, Dickinson intends us to see the flowers as ...," "With Willy Loman's suicide, Miller wants to show that...").

□ Where does the analysis fail to maintain the present tense? Which uses of past tense aren't justified—that is, which don't refer to something that occurred earlier that the narrator's present?

□ Where is there inadequate or incorrect documentation?

□ Where does language lapse into needless literary jargon?

□ If poetry is quoted, where should slash marks indicate line breaks? Where should lines be indented?

Edit and Proofread

When editing and proofreading your literary analysis, you should proceed as you would with any other type of essay (see pages 133–136 in Chapter 9). Be sure, though, to check textual quotations with special care. Make sure you quote correctly, use ellipses appropriately, and follow punctuation and capitalization conventions.

PULLING IT ALL TOGETHER

Read to Form a General Impression

By this time, you're familiar with the steps involved in writing a literary analysis, so you're probably ready to apply what you've learned. The following short story was written by Langston Hughes (1902–67), a poet and fiction writer who emerged as a major literary figure during the Harlem Renaissance of the 1920s. Published in 1963, the story first appeared in *Something in Common,* a collection of Hughes's work. Read the story and gather your first impressions. Then follow the suggestions after the story.

LANGSTON HUGHES
EARLY AUTUMN

1   When Bill was very young, they had been in love. Many nights they had spent walking, talking together. Then something not very important had come between them, and they didn't speak. Impulsively, she had married a man she thought she loved. Bill went away, bitter about women.

Yesterday, walking across Washington Square, she saw him for the first time in years.

"Bill Walker," she said.

He stopped. At first he did not recognize her, to him she looked so old.

5   "Mary! Where did you come from?"

Unconsciously, she lifted her face as though wanting a kiss, but he held out his hand. She took it.

"I live in New York now," she said.

"Oh"—smiling politely. Then a little frown came quickly between his eyes.

"Always wondered what happened to you, Bill."

10   "I'm a lawyer. Nice firm, way downtown."

"Married yet?"

"Sure. Two kids."

"Oh," she said.

A great many people went past them through the park. People they didn't know. It was late afternoon. Nearly sunset. Cold.

15   "And your husband?" he asked her.

"We have three children. I work in the bursar's office at Columbia."

"You're looking very..." (he wanted to say *old*) "...well," he said.

She understood. Under the trees in Washington Square, she found herself desperately reaching back into the past. She had been older than he then in Ohio. Now she was not young at all. Bill was still young.

"We live on Central Park West," she said. "Come and see us sometime."

20   "Sure," he replied. "You and your husband must have dinner with my family some night. Any night. Lucille and I'd love to have you."

The leaves fell slowly from the trees in the Square. Fell without wind. Autumn dusk. She felt a little sick.

"We'd love it," she answered.

"You ought to see my kids." He grinned.

Suddenly the lights came on up the whole length of Fifth Avenue, chains of misty brilliance in the blue air.

"There's my bus," she said.

He held out his hand, "Good-by."

25

"When..." she wanted to say, but the bus was ready to pull off. The lights on the avenue blurred, twinkled, blurred. And she was afraid to open her mouth as she entered the bus. Afraid it would be impossible to utter a word.

Suddenly she shrieked very loudly, "Good-by!" But the bus door had closed.

The bus started. People came between them outside, people crossing the street, people they didn't know. Space and people. She lost sight of Bill. Then she remembered she had forgotten to give him her address—or to ask him for his—or tell him that her youngest boy was named Bill, too.

Ask Questions About the Work

Now that you've read Hughes's story, consult the questions on pages 604–605 so you can devise your own set of questions to solidify your first impressions. Here are some questions you might consider:

1. How does *setting* help bring out the theme?
   Answer: Both the time of year, "early autumn," and the time of day, "nearly sunset" suggest that time is running out. The place, a crowded walkway in a big city, highlights the idea of all the people with whom we never make contact—that is, of life's missed connections.

2. From what *point of view* is the story told? How does this relate to the story's meaning?
   Answer: The point of view is the third-person omniscient. This enables the author to show the discrepancy between what characters are thinking and what they are willing or able to communicate.

3. What *words* and *images* are repeated in the course of the story? How do these *motifs* reflect the story's theme?
   Answer: The words *young* and *old* appear a number of times. This repetition helps bring out the theme of aging, of time running out. *Walking* is another repeated word that gives the reader the sense of people's uninterrupted movement through life. The repeated phrase *people they don't know* emphasizes how hard it is for people to genuinely communicate and connect with one another. *Love,* another repeated word, underscores the tragedy of love lost or unfulfilled.

Reread and Annotate

In light of the questions you develop, reread and annotate Hughes's story. Then consider the writing assignments that follow.

1. Analyze how Hughes develops the theme that it is urgently important for people to "take time out" to communicate with one another.

2. Discuss some strategies that Hughes uses to achieve universality. You might, for example, call attention to the story's impersonal point of view, the lack of descriptive detail about the characters' appearances, and the generality of the information about the characters' lives.

3. Explain how Hughes uses setting to reveal the characters' psychological states and to convey their sense of loss.

STUDENT ESSAY

Which of the preceding assignments appeals to you most? Student Karen Vais decided to write in response to the first assignment. After using questions to focus her initial impressions and guide her annotations, Karen organized her prewriting and began to draft her literary analysis. The final version of her analysis follows. As you read the essay, consider how well Karen addresses both *what* Hughes expresses and *how* he expresses it. What literary devices does Karen discuss? How are these related to the story's theme? Also note that Karen doesn't identify "Early Autumn" with a bibliographic footnote. Because the story was assigned in class and everyone used the same text, she didn't need to provide such a footnote. Similarly, her instructor didn't require parenthetic documentation of quoted material because the story is so brief.

Stopping to Talk

by Karen Vais

1   In his short story "Early Autumn," Langston Hughes dramatizes the idea that hurried movement through life prevents people from forming or maintaining meaningful relationships. Hughes develops his theme of "walking" versus "talking" through such devices as setting, plot construction, and dialog.

Introduction

Thesis with plan of development

2   The story's setting continually reminds the reader that time is running out; it is urgent for people to stop and communicate before it is too late. The meeting between the two characters takes place on a busy walkway, where strangers hurry past one another. The season is autumn, the time is "late afternoon," the temperature is "cold." The end of the renewed connection between Mary and Bill coincides with the blurring of the streetlights. The chilly, dark setting suggests the coming of winter, of night, even of death.

First supporting paragraph: focus on setting

3   In keeping with the setting, the plot is a series of lost chances for intimacy. When they were young and in love, Bill and Mary used to "walk...[and] talk...together," but that was years ago. Then "something not very important...[came] between

Second supporting paragraph: focus on plot

them, and they didn't speak." When she says Bill's name, Mary halts Bill's movement through the park, and, for a short time, Bill "Walker" stops walking. But when Mary hurries onto the bus, the renewed connection snaps. Moreover, even their brief meeting in the park is already a thing of the past, having taken place "yesterday."

Third supporting paragraph: focus on dialog

Like their actions, the characters' words illustrate a   4
reluctance to communicate openly. The dialog consists of little more than platitudes: "I live in New York now. . . . We have three kids. . . . You and your husband must have dinner with my family some night." The narrator's telling comments about what remains <u>unspoken</u> ("he <u>wanted</u> to say . . .," "she <u>wanted</u> to say . . .") underscore Bill and Mary's separateness. Indeed, Mary fails to share the one piece of information that would have revealed her feelings for Bill Walker--that her youngest son is also named Bill.

Conclusion

The theme of walking vs. talking runs throughout "Early   5
Autumn." "Space and people," Hughes writes, once again come between Bill and Mary, and, as in the past, they go their separate ways. Through the two characters, Hughes seems to be urging each of us to speak--to slow our steps long enough to make emotional contact.

Commentary

Note that Karen states her *thesis* in the opening paragraph; this first sentence addresses the *what* of the story: "the idea that hurried movement through life prevents...meaningful relationships." The next sentence addresses the *how*: "Hughes develops his theme...through such devices as setting, plot construction, and dialog." This second sentence also announces the essay's *plan of development*. Karen will discuss setting, then plot, then dialog, with one paragraph devoted to each of these literary elements. In the body of the analysis, Karen backs up her thesis with *textual evidence* in the form of summaries and quotations. The quotations are no longer than is necessary to support her points. In the concluding paragraph, Karen repeats her thesis, reinforcing it with Hughes's own words. She ends by pointing out the relevance of the story's theme to the reader's own life.

Writing Assignment on "Early Autumn"

Having seen what one student did with "Early Autumn," look back at the second and third writing assignments on page 615 and select one for your own analysis of Hughes's story. Then, in light of the assignment you select, read the story again, making any adjustments in your annotations. Next, organize your prewriting annotations into a scratch list, identify a working thesis, and organize your ideas into an outline. That done, write your first draft. Before submitting your analysis, take time to revise, edit, and proofread it carefully.

ADDITIONAL SELECTIONS AND WRITING ASSIGNMENTS

The two selections that follow—a poem by Elizabeth Bishop and a short story by Kate Chopin—will give you further practice in analyzing literary texts. No matter which selection you decide to write on, the following guidelines should help you approach the literary analysis with confidence.

Start by reading the text once to gain an overall impression. Then, draw on any of the questions on pages 604–605 to help you focus your first impressions and guide your annotations. When deciding what to write about, you may select a topic of your own, a subject proposed by your instructor, or one of the assignments suggested after the readings. With your topic in mind, reread the selection and evaluate the appropriateness of your earlier annotations. Make whatever changes are needed before moving your annotations into an informal scratch list. Next, review the scratch list so you can formulate a working thesis and prepare an outline of your ideas. Then go ahead and write your first draft, making sure you revise, edit, and proofread thoroughly before handing in your analysis.

ELIZABETH BISHOP

The recipient of a Pulitzer Prize, Elizabeth Bishop (1911–79) is considered one of the country's leading twentieth-century poets. Her sensitivity to life in all its forms, expressed in simple yet powerful images, is reflected in the poem reprinted here. The poem first appeared in 1946 in *North and South*, a collection of Bishop's work.

THE FISH

1   I caught a tremendous fish
    and held him beside the boat
    half out of water, with my hook
    fast in a corner of his mouth.
5   He didn't fight.
    He hadn't fought at all.

He hung a grunting weight,
battered and venerable
and homely. Here and there
his brown skin hung in strips   10
like ancient wallpaper,
and its pattern of darker brown
was like wallpaper:
shapes like full-blown roses
stained and lost through age.   15
He was speckled with barnacles,
fine rosettes of lime,
and infested
with tiny white sea lice,
and underneath two or three   20
rags of green weed hung down.
While his gills were breathing in
the terrible oxygen
—the frightening gills,
fresh and crisp with blood,   25
that can cut so badly—
I thought of the coarse white flesh
packed in like feathers,
the big bones and the little bones,
the dramatic reds and blacks   30
of his shiny entrails,
and the pink swim bladder
like a big peony.
I looked into his eyes
which were far larger than mine   35
but shallower, and yellowed,
the irises backed and packed
with tarnished tinfoil
seen through the lenses
of old scratched isinglass.*   40
They shifted a little, but not
to return my stare.
—It was more like the tipping
of an object toward the light.
I admired his sullen face,   45
the mechanism of his jaw,
and then I saw
that from his lower lip
—if you could call it a lip—
grim, wet, and weaponlike,   50

---

isinglass: mica, a thin, nearly transparent mineral.

            hung five old pieces of fish line,
            or four and a wire leader
            with the swivel still attached,
            with all their five big hooks
    55   grown firmly in his mouth.
            A green line, frayed at the end
            where he broke it, two heavier lines,
            and a fine black thread
            still crimped from the strain and snap
    60   when it broke and got away.
            Like medals with their ribbons
            frayed and wavering,
            a five-haired beard of wisdom
            trailing from his aching jaw.
    65   I stared and stared
            and victory filled up
            the little rented boat,
            from the pool of bilge
            where oil had spread a rainbow
    70   around the rusted engine
            to the bailer rusted orange,
            the sun-cracked thwarts,*
            the oarlocks on the strings,
            the gunnels†—until everything
    75   was rainbow, rainbow, rainbow!
            And I let the fish go.

Writing Assignments on "The Fish"

1. The language that Bishop uses to describe the fish is striking. Analyze Bishop's images and figures of speech in the poem, showing what they reveal about the fish and its history. Explain how this history relates to the poet's vision of the sanctity of life.

2. Discuss the way the narrator's attitude toward the fish changes as the poem unfolds. Consider the foreshadowing that Bishop provides to prepare readers for the change.

3. In the biblical story of Noah and the flood, a rainbow is a sign of God's promise never again to threaten the world with destruction. Discuss the symbolism of the rainbow in Bishop's poem. Explain why you think the poem's climax follows the appearance of the rainbow.

---

thwarts: the seats of a boat.
†*gunnels:* the upper sides of a boat.

KATE CHOPIN

Fiction-writer Kate Chopin (1851–1904) is best known for her novel *The Awakening* (1899). When first published, the novel shocked readers with its frank sensuality and the independent spirit of its female protagonist. The story that follows, first published in *Vogue* in 1894, shows a similar defiance of socially prescribed expectations and norms.

THE STORY OF AN HOUR

Knowing that Mrs. Mallard was afflicted with heart trouble, great care was taken to break to her as gently as possible the news of her husband's death. 1

It was her sister Josephine who told her, in broken sentences, veiled hints that revealed in half concealing. Her husband's friend Richards was there, too, near her. It was he who had been in the newspaper office when intelligence of the railroad disaster was received, with Brently Mallard's name leading the list of "killed." He had only taken the time to assure himself of its truth by a second telegram, and had hastened to forestall any less careful, less tender friend in bearing the sad message. 2

She did not hear the story as many women have heard the same, with a paralyzed inability to accept its significance. She wept at once, with sudden, wild abandonment, in her sister's arms. When the storm of grief had spent itself she went away to her room alone. She would have no one follow her. 3

There stood, facing the open window, a comfortable, roomy armchair. Into this she sank, pressed down by a physical exhaustion that haunted her body and seemed to reach into her soul. 4

She could see in the open square before her house the tops of trees that were all aquiver with the new spring life. The delicious breath of rain was in the air. In the street below a peddler was crying his wares. The notes of a distant song which someone was singing reached her faintly, and countless sparrows were twittering in the eaves. 5

There were patches of blue sky showing here and there through the clouds that had met and piled one above the other in the west facing her window. 6

She sat with her head thrown back upon the cushion of the chair, quite motionless, except when a sob came up into her throat and shook her, as a child who has cried itself to sleep continues to sob in its dreams. 7

She was young, with a fair, calm face, whose lines bespoke repression and even a certain strength. But now there was a dull stare in her eyes, whose gaze was fixed away off yonder on one of those patches of blue sky. It was not a glance of reflection, but rather indicated a suspension of intelligent thought. 8

There was something coming to her and she was waiting for it, fearfully. What was it? She did not know, it was too subtle and elusive to name. But she felt it, creeping out of the sky, reaching toward her through the sounds, the scents, the color that filled the air. 9

Now her bosom rose and fell tumultuously. She was beginning to recognize this thing that was approaching to possess her, and she was striving to beat it back with her will—as powerless as her two white slender hands would have been. 10

When she abandoned herself a little whispered word escaped her slightly parted lips. She said it over and over under her breath: "Free, free, free!" The vacant stare and the look of terror that had followed it went from her eyes. They stayed keen and bright. Her pulses beat fast, and the coursing blood warmed and relaxed every inch of her body. 11

12   She did not stop to ask if it were not a monstrous joy that held her. A clear and exalted perception enabled her to dismiss the suggestion as trivial.

13   She knew that she would weep again when she saw the kind, tender hands folded in death; the face that had never looked save with love upon her, fixed and gray and dead. But she saw beyond that bitter moment a long procession of years to come that would belong to her absolutely. And she opened and spread her arms out to them in welcome.

14   There would be no one to live for during those coming years; she would live for herself. There would be no powerful will bending her in that blind persistence with which men and women believe they have a right to impose a private will upon a fellow creature. A kind intention or a cruel intention made the act seem no less a crime as she looked upon it in that brief moment of illumination.

15   And yet she had loved him—sometimes. Often she had not. What did it matter! What could love, the unsolved mystery, count for in face of this possession of self-assertion which she suddenly recognized as the strongest impulse of her being.

16   "Free! Body and soul free!" she kept whispering.

17   Josephine was kneeling before the closed door with her lips to the keyhole, imploring for admission. "Louise, open the door! I beg; open the door—you will make yourself ill. What are you doing, Louise? For heaven's sake open the door."

18   "Go away. I am not making myself ill." No; she was drinking in a very elixir of life through that open window.

19   Her fancy was running riot along those days ahead of her. Spring days, and summer days, and all sorts of days that would be her own. She breathed a quick prayer that life might be long. It was only yesterday she had thought with a shudder that life might be long.

20   She arose at length and opened the door to her sister's importunities. There was a feverish triumph in her eyes, and she carried herself unwittingly like a goddess of Victory. She clasped her sister's waist, and together they descended the stairs. Richards stood waiting for them at the bottom.

21   Some one was opening the front door with a latchkey. It was Brently Mallard who entered, a little travel-stained, composedly carrying his gripsack and umbrella. He had been far from the scene of accident, and did not even know there had been one. He stood amazed at Josephine's piercing cry; at Richards' quick motion to screen him from the view of his wife.

22   But Richards was too late.

23   When the doctors came they said she had died of heart disease—of joy that kills.

Writing Assignments on "The Story of an Hour"

1. Show how Chopin uses imagery and descriptive detail to contrast the rich possibilities for which Mrs. Mallard yearns with the drab reality of her everyday life.

2. Argue that "The Story of an Hour" dramatizes the theme that domesticity saps a woman's spirit and physical strength.

3. Does Chopin's characterization of Mrs. Mallard justify the story's unexpected and ironic climax? Explain your response.

23
WRITING
EXAM
ESSAYS

YOU may never consider **exam essays** fun, but once you develop the knack, writing an essay as part of an exam can be as much of a learning experience as writing an essay or report out of class. There are differences, of course. At home, you can "hatch" your essay over several hours, days, or even weeks; you can write and rewrite; you can produce an impressively typed final copy.

Exam essays, though, are different. Time pressure is the name of the game. If you have trouble writing essays at home, the idea of preparing one in a test situation may throw you into a kind of panic. How, you may wonder, can you show what you know in such a short time? Indeed, you may feel that such tests are designed to show you at your worst.

Befuddling students and causing anxiety are not, however, the goals that instructors have in mind when they prepare essay exams. Instructors intend such exams to reveal your understanding of the subject—and to stimulate you to interpret course material in perceptive, new ways. They realize that the writing done under time pressure won't result in a masterpiece; such writing may include misspellings and awkward sentences. However, they *do* expect reasonably complete essay answers: no brief outlines, no rambling lists of unconnected points. Focused, developed, coherent responses are what instructors are looking for. Such expectations are not as unrealistic as they may first seem when you realize that all the writing techniques discussed in this book are applicable to taking essay tests.

THREE FORMS OF WRITTEN ANSWERS

There are three general types of questions that require written answers—some as short as one or two sentences, others as long as a full, several-paragraph essay.

Short Answers

One kind of question calls for a **short answer** of only a few sentences. Always read the instructions carefully to determine exactly what's expected. Such questions often ask you to identify (or define) a term *and* explain its importance. An instructor may give full credit only if you answer *both* parts of the question. Also, unless the directions indicate that fragmentary responses are acceptable, be prepared to write one to three full sentences.

Here are several examples of short answers for an exam in modern art history.

Directions: Identify and explain the significance of the following:

1. *Composition with Red, Yellow, and Blue,* 1921: Like most of Piet Mondrian's "compositions," this painting consists of horizontal and vertical lines and the primary colors, red, yellow, and blue. The painting also shows Matisse's influence on Mondrian since Matisse believed that art should express a person's spirit through pure form and color rather than depict real objects or scenes.
2. "Concerning the Spiritual in Art": This is an essay written by Wassily Kandinsky in 1912 to justify the abstract painting style he used. Showing Matisse's influence, the essay maintains that pure forms and basic colors convey reality more accurately than true-to-life depictions.
3. The Eiffel Tower Series: Done around 1910 by Robert Delaunay, this is a series of paintings having the Eiffel Tower as subject. Delaunay used a cubist approach, analyzing surface, space, and interesting planes.

Paragraph-Length Answers

Questions requiring a **paragraph-length answer** may signal—directly or indirectly—the length of response expected. For example, such questions may indicate "answer in a few sentences," or they may be followed by a paragraph-sized space on the answer sheet. In any case, a successful answer should address the question as completely yet as concisely as possible. Beginning with a strong topic sentence will help you focus your response.

Following is a paragraph-length answer to a question on a political science exam:

Directions: Discuss the meaning of the term *interest group* and comment briefly on the role such groups play in the governing of democratic societies.

An interest group is an "informal" type of political organization; its goal is to influence government policy and see legislation enacted that favors its members. An interest group differs from a political party; the interest group doesn't want to control the government or have an actual share in governing (the whole purpose of a political party). Interest groups are considered "informal" because they are not officially part of the governing process. Still, they exert tremendous power. Democratic governments constantly respond to interest groups by passing new laws and policies. Some examples of interest groups are institutions (the military, the Catholic Church), associations (the American Medical Association, Mothers Against Drunk Driving), and nonassociational groups (car owners, television viewers).

Essay-Length Answers

You will frequently be asked to write an **essay-length answer** as part of a longer examination. Occasionally, an exam may consist of a single essay, as in a "test-out" exam at the end of a writing course.

Here is a typical essay question from an exam in an introductory course in linguistics. A response to this question can be found on pages 630–631.

Account for the differences in American and British English by describing at least *three* major influences that affected the way this country's settlers spoke English. Give as many examples as you can of words derived from these influences.

The rest of this chapter discusses the features of a strong essay response and shows how the writing process can be adapted to a test-taking situation.

HOW TO PREPARE FOR EXAM ESSAYS

Being able to write a good exam essay is the result of a certain type of studying. There are times when cramming is probably unavoidable, but you should try to avoid this last-minute crunch whenever possible. It prevents you from gaining a clear overview of a course and a real understanding of a course's main issues. In contrast, spaced study throughout the semester gives you a sense of the *whys* of the subject, not just the *who, what, where,* and *when.*

As you prepare for an exam essay, you should try to follow these steps:

• In light of the main concepts covered in the course, identify key issues that the exam might logically address.
• With these issues in mind, design several exam essay questions.

- Draft an answer for each anticipated question.
- Commit to memory any facts, quotations, data, lists of reasons, and so forth that you would include in your answers.

Although you may not anticipate the exam's actual questions, preparing some questions and answers can give you practice analyzing and working with the course material. In the process, you'll probably allay some pre-exam jitters as well.

AT THE EXAMINATION

Survey the Entire Test

Look over the entire written-answer section of a test before working on any part of it. Note which sections are worth the highest point value and plan to spend the longest time on those sections. Follow any guidelines that the directions may provide about the length of the response. When "a brief paragraph" is all that is required, don't launch into a full-scale essay.

If you're given a choice about which exam questions to answer, read them all before choosing. Of course, select those you feel best equipped to answer. If it's a toss-up between two, you might quickly sketch out answers to both (see page 627) before deciding which to do. To avoid mistakes, circle questions you plan to answer and cross out those you'll skip. Then give yourself a time limit for writing each response and, within reason, stick with your plan.

Understand the Essay Question

Once you've selected the question on which you're going to write, you need to make sure you know what the question is looking for. Examine the question carefully to determine its slant or emphasis. Most essay questions ask you to focus on a specific issue or to bring together material from different parts of a course.

Many questions use **key directional words** that suggest an answer developed according to a particular pattern of development. Here are some key directional words and the patterns they suggest:

Key Directional Words	Pattern of Development
Provide details about . . .	Description
Give the history of . . . Trace the development of . . .	Narration
Explain . . . List . . . Provide examples of . . .	Illustration
Analyze the parts of . . . Discuss the types of . . .	Division-classification

Key Directional Words	Pattern of Development
Analyze... Explain how... Show how...	Process analysis
Discuss advantages and disadvantages of... Show similarities and differences between...	Comparison-contrast
Account for... Analyze... Discuss the consequences of... Explain the reasons for... Explain why... Show the influence of...	Cause-effect
Clarify... Explain the meaning of... Identify...	Definition
Argue... Defend... Evaluate... Justify... Show the failings or merits of... Support...	Argumentation-persuasion

The following sample questions show the way key directional words imply the approach to take. In each example, the key words are italicized. Note that some essay questions call for two or more patterns of development. The key terms could, for example, indicate that you should *contrast* two things before *arguing* the merits of one.

1. Galileo, now recognized as having made valuable contributions to our under-standing of the universe, was twice tried by the Vatican. *Explain the factors* that *caused* the church and the astronomer to fall into what one historian has termed a "fatal collision of opposite philosophies." [Cause-effect]
2. *Define* the superego and *explain how,* according to Freud, the superego develops. [Definition; process analysis]
3. *Explain the difference* between "educational objectives" and "instructional objectives." *Provide specific examples* of each, focusing on the distinction between students' immediate and long-term needs. [Comparison-contrast; illustration]

WRITE THE ESSAY

The steps in the writing process are the same, whether you compose an essay at home or prepare an essay response in a classroom test situation. The main difference is that during a test the process is streamlined. Following are some helpful guidelines for handling each writing stage when you prepare an essay as part of an exam.

Prewrite

Prewriting begins when you analyze the essay question and determine your essay's basic approach (see pages 625–626). We suggest that you do your analysis of the question on the exam sheet: Underline key directional terms, circle other crucial words, and put numbers next to points that the question indicates you should cover.

Then, still using your exam page or a piece of scratch paper, make notes for an answer. (Writing on the exam sheet means you won't have several pieces of paper to keep track of.) Jot down main points as well as facts and examples. If you feel blocked, try brainstorming, freewriting, mapping, or another prewriting technique (see pages 25–30) to get yourself going.

What to Avoid. Don't get overinvolved in the prewriting stage; you won't have time to generate pages of notes. Try using words and phrases, not full sentences or paragraphs. Also, don't spend time analyzing your audience (you know it's your instructor) or choosing a tone (exams obviously require a serious, analytic approach).

Identify Your Thesis

Like essays written at home, exam essays should have a **thesis.** Often, the thesis is a statement answering the exam question. For example, in response to a question asking you to "Discuss the origins of apartheid," your thesis might begin, "The South African law of 'separateness,' or apartheid, originated in 1948, a result of a series of factors that...." Similarly, the essay answer to a question asking you to "Discuss the process by which nations are admitted to the European Community..." might start, "Nations are admitted to the European Community through the process of...." Note that these thesis statements are somewhat informal. They state the *subject* of the essay but *not* the writer's *attitude* toward the subject. In a test-taking situation, these less-structured thesis statements are perfectly acceptable. (For more on thesis statements, see Chapter 3.)

Support the Thesis with Evidence

In the prewriting stage, you jotted down material needed to answer the question. At this point, you should review the **evidence** quickly to make sure it's *adequate*. Does it provide sufficient support for your thesis? If not, make some additional quick notes. Also, check that support for your thesis is *unified, specific, accurate,* and *representative* (see pages 46–49 and 68–72).

Organize the Evidence

Before you start writing, devise some kind of **outline.** You may simply sequence your prewriting jottings by placing numbers or letters beside them. Or you can quickly translate the jottings into a brief, informal outline.

However you proceed, go back and review the essay question one more time. If the question has two or three parts, your outline should tackle each one in turn.

Suppose a question asks you to "Consider the effects of oil spills on wildlife, ocean ecology, and oil reserves." Your answer should address each of these three areas, with separate paragraphs for each area.

Also, focus again on the question's *key directional words*. If the question asks you to discuss similarities and differences, your outline should draw on one of the two basic *comparison-contrast* formats (see pages 338–339). Since many exam questions call for more than one task (for example, you may be asked both to *define* a theory and to *argue* its merits), you should make sure your outline reflects the appropriate patterns of development.

Many outlines use an *emphatic* approach to organize material ("Discuss which factors are most critical in determining whether a wildlife species will become extinct"). However, when discussing historical or developmental issues (for example, in psychology), you often structure material *chronologically*. In some fields (art history is one) you may choose a *spatial* approach—for instance, if you describe a work of art. Quickly assess the situation to determine which approach would work best, and keep it in mind as you sequence the points in your outline. (Turn to pages 56–59 and 54–56 for more on, respectively, outlining and emphatic, chronological, spatial, and simple-to-complex plans.)

What to Avoid. Don't prepare a formal or many-leveled outline; you'll waste valuable time. A phrase outline with two levels of support should be sufficient in most cases.

Write the Draft

Generally, you won't have time to write a formal introduction, so it's fine to begin the essay with your thesis, perhaps followed by a plan of development (see pages 38–39). Write as many paragraphs as you need to show you have command of the concepts and facts taught in the course. Refer to your outline as you write, but, if inspiration strikes, feel free to add material or deal with a point in a different order.

As you draft your response, you may want to write on every other line or leave several blank spaces at the bottom of the page. That way, you can easily slot in any changes you need to make along the way. Indeed, you shouldn't feet hesitant about crossing out material—a quotation you didn't get quite right, a sentence that reads awkwardly, a fact that should be placed elsewhere. *Do* make these changes, but make them neatly.

When preparing the draft, remember that you'll be graded in part on how *specific, accurate*, and *representative* your evidence is (see pages 47–49 and 69–72). Provide concrete, correct, true-to-type evidence. Make sure, too, that your response is *unified* (see pages 46–47 and 68–69). Don't include interesting but basically irrelevant information. Stay focused on the question. Using topic sentences to structure your paragraphs will help you stay on track.

Your instructor will need transitions and other markers to understand fully how your points connect to one another. Try to show how your ideas relate by using *signal devices*, such as *first, second, however, for instance*, and *most important* (see pages 74–75).

As you near the end of the essay, check the original question. Have you covered everything? Does the question call for a final judgment or evaluative comment? If so, provide it. Also, if you have time, you may want to close with a brief, one- or two-sentence summary.

What to Avoid. Don't write your essay on scrap paper and plan to recopy. You probably won't have enough time. Even if you do, you may, in your haste, leave out words, phrases, or whole sentences. Your first and only draft should be the one written on the exam booklet or paper. Also, unless your instructor specifically requests it, don't waste time recopying the question in your exam booklet.

Instructors find it easier to evaluate what you know if you've used paragraphs. Don't, then, cast your answer as one long paragraph spanning three pages. If you've outlined your ideas, you'll have a clear idea where paragraph breaks should occur. Finally, don't cram your response with everything you know about the subject. Most instructors can detect padded answers in a second. Give focused, intelligent responses, not one rambling paragraph after another.

Revise, Edit, and Proofread

If you've budgeted your time, you should have a few minutes left to review your essay answer. (Don't skip rereading it just so you can leave the room a few minutes early.) Above all, read your response to be sure it answers the question fully. Make any changes that will improve the answer—perhaps add a fact, correct a quotation, tighten a sentence. If you want to add a whole sentence or more, write the material in some nearby blank space and use an arrow to show where it goes. If something is in the wrong place, use an arrow and a brief note to indicate where it should go.

Instructors will accept insertions and deletions—as long as such changes are made with consideration for their sanity. Use a few bold strokes, not wild spidery scribbles, to cross out text. Use the standard editing marks such as the caret (see page 136) to indicate additions and other changes.

As you reread, check grammar and spelling. Obvious grammatical errors and spelling mistakes—especially if they involve the subject's key terms—may affect your grade. If spelling is a problem for you, request permission to have your dictionary at hand.

SAMPLE ESSAY ANSWER

The essay that follows was written by Andrew Kahan in response to this exam question:

Account for the <u>differences</u> in <u>American</u> and <u>British English</u> by describing at least <u>three major influences</u> that affected the way this country's settlers spoke English. Give as many <u>examples</u> as you can of <u>words derived</u> from these <u>influences</u>.

① Maritime pidgin (Portug. influ.)
② African pidgin (Slaves comm. with each other and with owners)
③ Native-American pidgin (words for native plants and animals)

Andrew started by underlining the question's key words. Then he listed in the margin the main points and some of the supporting evidence he planned to include in his answer. That done, he formulated a thesis and began writing his essay. The handwritten annotations reflect the changes Andrew made when he refined his answer before handing in his exam.

American English diverged from British English because those who settled the New World had contact with people that those back in England generally did not. As a result of this contact, several pidgin languages developed. A pidgin language, which has its own grammar and vocabulary, comes about when the speakers of two or more unrelated languages communicate ~~for a while~~ over a period of time. Maritime pidgin, African pidgin, and Indian pidgin were three influences that helped shape American English.

By the time the New World began to be settled, sailors and sea merchants of all the European nations had traveled widely. A maritime pidgin thus ~~immerged~~ emerged that enabled diverse groups to communicate.* Since Portugal controlled the seas around the time the colonies were settled, maritime pidgin was largely influenced by the Portuguese. Such Portuguese-derived words as "cavort," "palaver," and "savvy" first entered American English in this way.

The New World's trade with Africa also ~~effec~~ affected American English. The slave trade, in particular, took American sailors and merchants all over the African continent. Since the traders mixed up slaves of many tribes to prevent them from becoming unified, the Africans had to rely on their own pidgin to communicate with each other. Moreover, slave owners relied on this African-based pidgin to communicate with their slaves.** Since slaves tended to be settled in the heavily populated American coastal areas, elements of the African pidgin readily worked their way into the language of the New World. Words and phrases derived from African pidgins include "caboodle" and "kick the bucket." Other African-based words include "buckaroo" and "goobers," plus words known only in the Deep South, like "cooter" for turtle. African-based slang terms and constructions ("uptight," "put-on," and "hip," meaning "cool" or "in") continue to enter mainstream English from black English even today.

Another important influence on American English, in the nation's early days, was contact with Native American culture. As settlers moved inland from coastal areas, they confronted Native Americans, and new pidgins grew up, melding English and Native-American terms. Native-

*and trade with each other   **until they mastered English.

American words like "squaw," "tomahawk," and "papoose" entered English. Also, many words for Native American plants and animals have Native-American roots: "squash," "raccoon," and "skunk" are just a few. Another possible effect of Native American languages on American English may be the tendency to form noun-noun compounds ("apple butter" and "shade tree"). While such constructions do occur in British English, they are more frequent in American English.

    British and American English differ because the latter has been shaped by contact with European languages like Portuguese, as well as by contact with non-European languages--especially those spoken by Africans and Native Americans.

Commentary

    Alert to such phrases as *account for* and *influences that affected* in the question, Andrew wrote an essay that describes three *causes* for the divergence of American from British English. The three causes are organized roughly chronologically, beginning with the influence of maritime exploration, moving to the effect of contact with African culture, and concluding with the influence of Native Americans.

    Although the essay is developed mainly through a decision of causes, other patterns of development come into play. The first paragraph *defines* the term *pidgin*, while the second, third, and fourth paragraphs draw on *process analysis;* they describe how pidgins developed, as well as how they affected the language spoken by early settlers. Finally, the essay includes numerous *examples,* as the exam question requested. Andrew's response shows a solid knowledge of the material taught in the course and demonstrates his ability to organize the material into a clear, coherent statement.

ACTIVITY:
WRITING
EXAM ESSAYS

    In preparation for an exam with essay questions, devise four possible essay questions on the material in one of your courses. For each, do some quick prewriting, determine a thesis, and jot down an outline. Then, for one of the questions, write a full essay answer, giving yourself a time limit of fifteen to twenty-five minutes, whatever is appropriate for the question. Don't forget to edit and proofread your answer.

PART VI

A
CONCISE
HANDBOOK

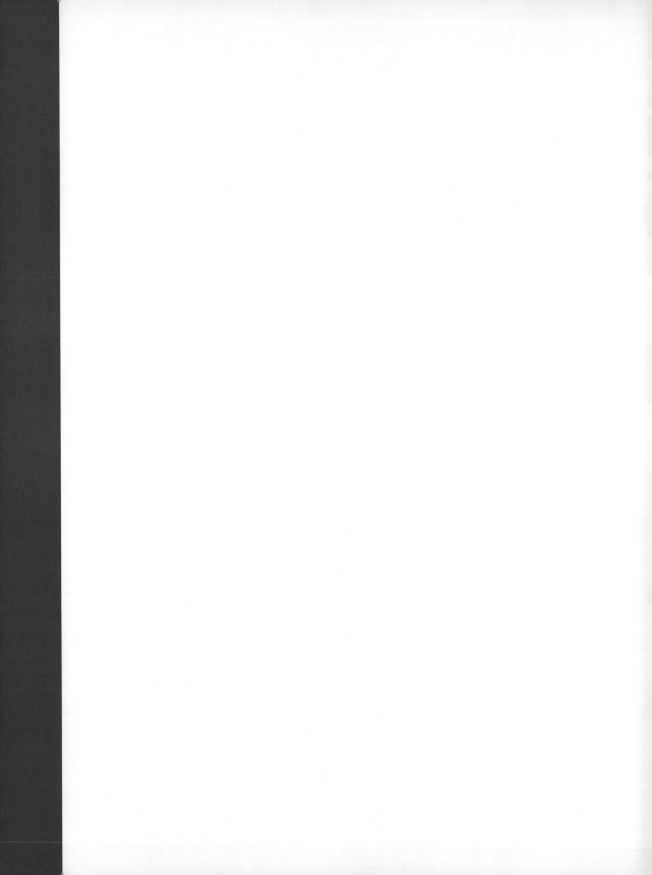

OPENING COMMENTS

MANY students consider grammar a nuisance. Hoping for an easy way out, they cross their fingers and trust they haven't made too many mistakes. They assume that their meaning will come across, even if their writing contains some errors—perhaps a misplaced comma here or a dangling modifier there. Not so. Surface errors annoy readers and may confuse meaning. Such errors also weaken a writer's credibility because they defy language conventions—customs that readers expect writers to honor. By mastering grammar, punctuation, and spelling conventions, you increase your power and versatility as a writer. When you know the rules, you have the option of breaking them, occasionally, for *stylistic* effect. Sentence fragments serve as a good example. Used well, fragments can add dramatic emphasis. (Consider "Not so" a few sentences back.) If, however, fragments appear frequently in your writing because you can't distinguish them from full sentences, they'll only detract from your message.

This concise Handbook will help you brush up on the rules and conventions of writing. It's organized according to the broad skill areas that give writers the most trouble. (The areas are identified in the list on the next page.) Throughout the Handbook, grammatical terminology is kept to a minimum. Although we assume you know the major parts of speech (noun, verb, pronoun, and so on), we *do*, when appropriate, provide on-the-spot definitions of more technical grammatical terms.

Consult the Handbook whenever your instructor points out that you're on shaky ground about some aspect of grammar or punctuation. Certainly, use it also whenever you feel unsure about the correctness of what you've written. Most instructors won't devote much class time to grammar and punctuation, so it's your responsibility to take the steps needed to sharpen your skills.

Here's how the Handbook is arranged:

There are a few other things you should know about the Handbook:

- Each problem area is treated separately. This means that you don't have to study earlier skills before reviewing one that comes later.
- In the margin beside each problem area is a symbol or abbreviation that your instructor may use in marking your papers. A list of these symbols and the

page locations where the corresponding skills are discussed in the Handbook can be found on the inside front cover of this book.

- On the whole, we've adopted a "do this—don't do this" approach. However, because things aren't always so simple, we also explain when you may break grammatical convention to achieve a specific effect.

Once you get used to looking up items in the Handbook, you'll find it's like any other tool—the more you use it, the more proficient you become. If you refer to the Handbook often, you can uncross your fingers and feel confident that your work is polished and correct.

SENTENCE FAULTS

frag | FRAGMENTS

A full **sentence** satisfies two conditions: (1) it has a subject and a verb, and (2) it can stand alone as a complete thought. Although a **fragment** is punctuated like a full sentence—with a capital letter at the beginning and a period at the end—it doesn't satisfy these two requirements.* There are two kinds of fragments: phrase fragments and dependent clause fragments.

Phrase Fragments

A group of words missing either a subject or a verb is only a phrase, not a complete sentence. If you punctuate a phrase as if it is a sentence, the result is a **phrase fragment.** We illustrate here five kinds of phrase fragments (identified by italics in the examples). Then we present ways to correct such fragments.

Noun Phrase Fragment

I was afraid of my wrestling coach. *A harsh and sarcastic man.* He was never satisfied with my performance.

Added-Detail Phrase Fragment

Many people have difficulty getting up in the morning. *Especially on Mondays after a hectic weekend.* They wish they had one more day to relax.

---

*For information on the way an occasional fragment may be used for emphasis, see pages 116–117 in Chapter 8.

Prepositional Phrase Fragment

After a long day at work. I drove to the bank that opened last week. *On the corner of Holly Avenue and Red Oak Lane. Next to the discount supermarket.*

Every summer millions of Americans burn themselves to a crisp. *Despite warnings about the sun's dangers.* They spend hours at the beach, often without applying any protective lotion.

Present Participle, Past Participle, or Infinitive Phrase Fragment

Waiting [present participle] *to buy tickets for the concert.* The crowd stood quietly in line. No one cared that the box office would be closed until the morning.

The children presented the social worker with a present. *Wrapped* [past participle] *in gold aluminum foil.*

After years of negotiating, several nations signed a treaty. *To ban* [infinitive] *the sale of ivory in their countries.*

Missing-Subject Phrase Fragment

Every weekend, the fraternities sponsored a joint open-house party. *And blared music all night long.* Not surprisingly, neighbors became furious.

How to Correct Phrase Fragments

There are four strategies for eliminating phrase fragments from your writing. When using these strategies, you may need to reword sentences slightly to maintain smoothness.

1. Attach the fragment to the preceding or following sentence, changing punctuation and capitalization as needed. When attaching a phrase fragment to the *beginning of a preceding sentence,* place a comma between the fragment and the start of the original sentence:

Fragment	Environmentalists predict a drought this summer. *In spite of heavy spring rains.* Everyone hopes the predictions are wrong.
Correct	In spite of heavy spring rains, environmentalists predict a drought this summer. Everyone hopes the predictions are wrong.

To attach a phrase fragment to the *end of a preceding sentence,* change the period at the end of the preceding sentence to a comma and change the first letter of the fragment to lowercase:

Fragment	I spent several hours in the college's Career Services Office. *Trying to find an interesting summer job.* Nothing looked promising.
Correct	I spent several hours in the college's Career Services Office, trying to find an interesting summer job. Nothing looked promising.

To attach a phrase fragment to the *beginning of a full sentence that follows it,* change the period at the end of the fragment to a comma and make the capital letter at the start of the full sentence lowercase:

Fragment	*Overwhelmed by school pressures and family demands.* She decided to postpone her education. That was a mistake.
Correct	Overwhelmed by school pressures and family demands, she decided to postpone her education. That was a mistake.

2. Insert the fragment into the preceding or following sentence, adding commas as needed:

Fragment	The tests were easy. *Especially the essay questions.* We felt confident that we had done well.
Correct	The test, especially the essay questions, were easy. We felt confident that we had done well. [fragment inserted into preceding sentence]

Fragment	*A robust girl who loved physical activity from the time she was a baby.* My sister qualified for the Olympics when she was seventeen.
Correct	My sister, a robust girl who loved physical activity from the time she was a baby, qualified for the Olympics when she was seventeen. [fragment inserted into following sentence]

3. Attach the fragment to a newly created sentence:

Fragment	Although I proudly call it mine, my apartment does have some problems. *For example, very little heat in the winter.*
Correct	Although I proudly call it mine, my apartment does have some problems. For example, *it has* very little heat in the winter.

4. Supply the missing subject:

Fragment	Although they argued frequently, my grandparents doted on each other. *And held hands wherever they went.*
Correct	Although they argued frequently, my grandparents doted on each other. *They* held hands wherever they went.
or	
Correct	Although they argued frequently, my grandparents doted on each other *and* held hands wherever they went.

Dependent Clause Fragments

Unlike phrases, which lack either a subject or a full verb, **clauses** contain both a subject and a full verb. Clauses may be **independent** (expressing a complete thought and able to stand alone as a sentence) or **dependent** (not expressing a complete thought and, therefore, not able to stand alone). A dependent clause (often called a **subordinate clause**) begins with a word that signals the clause's reliance on something more for completion. Such introductory words may take the form of **subordinating conjunctions** or **relative pronouns:**[*]

---

[*]Dependent clauses introduced by relative pronouns are often referred to as *relative clauses.*

Subordinating Conjunctions		Relative Pronouns
after	once	that
although	since	what
as	so that	which
because	unless	who
even though	until	whoever
if	when	whom
in order that	while	whose

If you punctuate a dependent clause as though it is a complete sentence, the result is a **dependent clause fragment** (identified by italics in the examples):

Fragment   *Because my parents wanted to be with their children at bedtime.* They arranged to leave their late-shift jobs a few minutes early.

Fragment   The mayor, after months of deliberation, proposed a housing ordinance. *Which antagonized almost everyone in town.*

How to Correct Dependent Clause Fragments

There are two main ways to correct dependent clause fragments. When using the strategies, you may need to reword sentences slightly to maintain smoothness.

1. Connect the fragment to the preceding or following full sentence, adding a comma if needed:

Fragment   I thought both my car and I would be demolished. *When the motorcycle hit me from behind.*

Correct   When the motorcycle hit me from behind, I thought both my car and I would be demolished. [fragment attached, with a comma, to beginning of preceding sentence]

or

Correct   I thought both my car and I would be demolished when the motorcycle hit me from behind. [fragment attached, without a comma, to end of preceding sentence]

Fragment   *Although the clean-up crew tried to scrub the oil-coated rocks thoroughly.* Many birds nesting on the rocky shore are bound to die.

Correct   Although the clean-up crews tried to scrub the oil-coated rocks thoroughly, many birds nesting on the rocky shore are bound to die. [fragment attached, with a comma, to beginning of following sentence]

or

Correct   Many birds nesting on the rocky shore are bound to die, although the clean-up crews tried to scrub the oil-coated rocks thoroughly. [fragment attached, with a comma, to end of following sentence]

When you connect a dependent clause to a full sentence, you need to decide whether to insert a comma. Consider the following:

Guidelines for Using Commas with Dependent Clauses

- If a dependent clause with a subordinating conjunction (like *when* or *although*) precedes the full sentence, the dependent clause is followed by a comma (as in the first and third corrected sentences on page 641).
- If a dependent clause follows the full sentence, it isn't preceded by a comma (as in the second corrected sentence on page 641).
- The exception is dependent clauses beginning with such words as *although* and *though*—words that show contrast. When such clauses follow a full sentence, they are preceded by a comma (as in the last corrected sentence on page 641).

When connecting a relative clause to a full sentence, you *set off* the *relative clause* with a comma if the clause is **nonrestrictive** (that is, if it is *not essential* to the sentence's meaning):

Fragment As a child, I went to the mountains with my parents. *Who never relaxed long enough to enjoy the lazy times there.*
Correct As a child, I went to the mountains with my parents, who never relaxed long enough to enjoy the lazy times there.

Note that in the corrected version there's a comma between the independent and relative clauses because the relative clause (*who never relaxed long enough to enjoy the lazy times there*) is nonrestrictive. In other words, it isn't needed to identify the writer's parents.

Take a look, though, at the following:

Fragment As a child, I went to the mountains with the family. *Who lived next door.*
Correct As a child, I went to the mountains with the family who lived next door.

In this case, the relative clause (*who lived next door*) is needed to identify which family is being referred to; that is, the clause is **restrictive** (*essential*) and, therefore, is *not* set off with a comma. (For information on punctuating restrictive and nonrestrictive phrases, see pages 670–671.)

When a relative clause beginning with *that* is attached to a nearby sentence, no comma is used between the relative and independent clauses:

Fragment My uncle got down on his hands and knees to rake away the dry leaves. *That he felt spoiled the beauty of his flower beds.*
Correct My uncle got down on his hands and knees to rake away the dry leaves that he felt spoiled the beauty of his flower beds.

2. Remove or replace the dependent clause's first word:

Fragment   The typical family-run farm is up for sale these days. *Because few small farmers can compete with agricultural conglomerates.*

Correct   The typical family-run farm is up for sale these days. Few small farmers can compete with agricultural conglomerates.

PRACTICE: CORRECTING SENTENCE FRAGMENTS

Correct any phrase and dependent clause fragments that you find in the following sentences. Be careful, though; some of the sentences may not contain fragments, and others may contain more than one.

1. Even though there must be millions of pigeons in the city. You never see a baby pigeon. It makes you wonder where they're hiding.

2. Children between the ages of eight and twelve often follow teenagers' trends. And look up to teens as role models. Mimicking their behavior in frequently disconcerting ways.

3. The least expensive remote-control toy car costs over fifty dollars. Which is more than many budget-conscious parents want to pay. Such high costs are typical in the toy industry.

4. The student's dorm room looked like a disaster area. Heaps of dirty clothes, crumpled papers, and half-eaten snacks were strewn everywhere. Keeping the room neat was obviously not a priority.

5. Because they feel urban schools are second-rate. Many parents hope to move their families to the suburbs. Even though they plan to continue working in the city.

6. Pulling the too-short hospital gown around his wasted body, the patient wandered down the hospital corridor. Unaware of the stares of the healthy people streaming by.

7. Last year, the student government overhauled its charter and created chaos. A confusing set of guidelines that muddled already contradictory policies. This year's senate has to find a way to remedy the situation.

8. Out of all the listed apartments we looked at that dreary week. Only one was affordable. And suitable for human habitation.

9. My grandfather likes to send off-beat greeting cards. Like the one with a picture of a lion holding on to a parachute. The card reads, "Just wanted to drop you a lion."

10. About a year ago, my mother was unexpectedly laid off by the restaurant. Where she had been hired five years earlier as head chef. The experience made her realize that she wanted to go into business for herself.

11. Occasionally looking up to see if anyone interesting had entered the room, the students sat hunched over their desks in the study carrels. Cramming for final exams. Scheduled to start the next day.

12. As prices have come down, compact-disc players have gained great popularity. With the development of these sophisticated sound systems, listening to concert music is more enjoyable than ever. Indeed, nearly as pleasurable as being at the concert itself.

13. Through the local adult education program, my parents took a course in electrical wiring last spring. They plan to enroll in a plumbing course this winter. Their goal is to save money on household repairs. Which cost them hundreds of dollars last year.

14. For breakfast, my health-conscious roommate drinks a strange concoction. That consists of soybean extract, wheat germ, and sunflower meal. It doesn't look very appealing.

15. Last night, I went to the hospital to visit my uncle. Who had been hospitalized four days earlier with a heart attack. I was relieved to see how healthy he looked.

16. The BB gun has changed dramatically. Over the last few years. Today's top-of-the-line gun can fire BBs or pellets 800 feet per second. Almost as fast as some handguns.

17. The hyacinths and daffodils in the garden were blooming beautifully. Until a freakish spring storm blasted their growth. Within hours, they shriveled up. And lay flat on the ground.

18. During last week's heated town meeting, several municipal officials urged the town council to adopt a controversial zoning ordinance. A proposal that had already been rejected by the town residents.

19. Strategically placed pine trees concealed the junkyard from nearby residents. Who otherwise would have protested its presence in the neighborhood. Well known for its lush lawns and colorful gardens.

20. In an effort to cover his bald spot. Al combs long strands of hair over the top of his head. Unfortunately, no one is fooled by his strategy. Especially not his wife. Who wishes her husband would accept the fact that he's getting older.

COMMA SPLICES AND RUN-ON SENTENCES

cs r-o

Consider the following faulty sentences:

Almost everyone in the office smokes, cigarette breaks are more important than coffee breaks.

My grades are good too bad my social life isn't.

The first example is a **comma splice:** A comma is used to join, or splice together, two complete thoughts, even though a comma alone is not strong enough to connect the two independent clauses. The second example is a **run-on,** or **fused, sentence:** Two sentences are connected, or run together, without any punctuation at all to indicate where the first sentence ends and the second begins.

Three Common Pitfalls

Here we describe three situations that often lead to comma splices or run-on sentences. Then we present ways to correct these sentence errors.

1. When the second sentence starts with a personal or demonstrative pronoun
The following are **personal pronouns:** *I, you, he, she, it, we,* and *they. This, that, these,* and *those* are **demonstrative pronouns.**

Comma Splice	The college's computerized billing system needs to be overhauled, *it billed more than a dozen students twice for tuition.*
Run-on	Lobsters are cannibalistic and will feed on each other *this is one reason they are difficult to raise in captivity.*

2. When the second sentence starts with a transition   Some common **transitions** include the words *finally, next, second,* and *then.*

Comma Splice	You start by buttering the baking dish, *next you pour in milk and mix it well with the butter.*
Run-on	The dentist studied my X-rays *then she let out an ominous sigh.*

3. When two sentences are connected by a transitional adverb   Here are some of the most common **transitional adverbs:**

Transitional Adverbs

accordingly	furthermore	meanwhile	still
also	however	moreover	therefore
anyway	indeed	nevertheless	thus
besides	instead	nonetheless	
consequently	likewise	otherwise	

Comma Splice	We figured the movie tickets would cost about five dollars, *however, we forgot to calculate the cost of all the junk food we would eat.*
Run-on	Fish in a backyard pond will thrive simply by eating the bugs, larvae, and algae in the pond *nevertheless, many people enjoy feeding fish by hand.*

How to Correct Comma Splices and Run-on Sentences

There are four strategies for eliminating comma splices and run-on sentences from your writing.

1. Place a period, question mark, or exclamation point at the end of the first sentence and capitalize the first letter of the second sentence:

Comma Splice	Our team played badly, *we deserved to lose by the wide margin we did.*
Correct	Our team played badly. We deserved to lose by the wide margin we did.

| Run-on | Which computer do experts recommend for the average college student *which system do experts consider most all-purpose?* They seldom agree. |
| Correct | Which computer do experts recommend for the average college student? Which system do experts consider most all-purpose? They seldom agree. |

2. Use a semicolon (;) to mark where the first sentence ends and the second begins:

| Comma Splice | In the eighteenth century, beauty marks were considered fashionable, *people even glued black paper dots to their faces.* |
| Correct | In the eighteenth century, beauty marks were considered fashionable; people even glued black paper dots to their faces. |

| Run-on | Many men use hairstyling products, facial scrubs, and cologne *however, most draw the line at powder and eye makeup.* |
| Correct | Many men use hairstyling products, facial scrubs, and cologne; however, most draw the line at powder and eye makeup. |

Note that when the second sentence starts with a transitional adverb (such as *however* in the last corrected sentence above), a *comma* is placed *after* the transition.[*]

3. Turn one of the sentences into a dependent clause:[**]

| Comma Splice | The camping grounds have no electricity, *however, people flock there anyway.* |
| Correct | *Although* the camping grounds have no electricity, people flock there anyway. |

| Run-on | The highway was impassable *it had snowed all night and most of the morning.* |
| Correct | The highway was impassable *because* it had snowed all night and most of the morning. |

When using this strategy, refer to the list of guidelines on page 651 to help you decide whether you should (as in the first corrected example) or shouldn't (as in the second corrected example) use a comma between the independent and dependent clauses.

4. Keep or add a comma at the end of the first sentence, but follow the comma with a coordinating conjunction. The following words are **coordinating conjunctions:** *and, but, for, nor, or, so, yet.*

---

[*]For information on punctuating transitional adverbs when they appear midsentence, see page 671.
[**]See page 641 for a list of words that introduce dependent clauses.

Comma Splice	Well-prepared and confident, I expected the exam to be easy, *it turned out to be a harrowing experience.*
Correct	Well-prepared and confident, I expected the exam to be easy, but it turned out to be a harrowing experience.
Run-on	Last election we campaigned enthusiastically *this year we expect to be equally involved.*
Correct	Last election we campaigned enthusiastically, *and* this year we expect to be equally involved.

PRACTICE: CORRECTING COMMA SPLICES AND RUN-ON SENTENCES

Correct any comma splices and run-ons that you find in the following sentences. Be careful, though; some commas belong just where they are.

1. Since the town appeared to be nearby, they left the car on the side of the road and started walking toward the village, they soon regretted their decision.

2. As we rounded the bend, we saw hundreds of crushed cars piled in neat stacks, the rusted hulks resembled flattened tin cans.

3. With unexpected intensity, the rain hit the pavement, plumes of heat rose from the blacktop, making it difficult to drive safely.

4. According to all reports, the day after Thanksgiving is the worst day of the year to shop, the stores are jammed with people, all looking for bargains.

5. Plants should be treated regularly with an organic insecticide, otherwise, spider mites and mealy bugs can destroy new growth.

6. Have you ever looked closely at a penny, do you know whether Lincoln faces right or left?

7. As we set up the tent, flies swarmed around our heads, we felt like day-old garbage.

8. If the phone rings when my parents are eating dinner, they don't answer it, they assume that, if the person wants to reach them, he or she will call back.

9. The library's security system needs improving, it allows too many people to sneak away, with books and magazines hidden in their pockets, purses, or briefcases.

10. Ocean air is always bracing, it makes everyone feel relaxed and carefree, as though the world of work is far away.

11. In the last few years, many prestigious art museums have developed plans to add on to buildings designed by such legendary architects as Frank Lloyd Wright and Louis Kahn, however, many irate museum-goers want the buildings to stay just as they are.

12. The salesperson stapled my bag in six places I must have looked like a shoplifter.

13. Throughout the last decade, publishing companies doled out huge advances to lure big-time authors, now many publishers, struggling with massive losses, regret the strategy.

14. Several communities in the country sponsor odd food festivals, in fact, one of the strangest takes place in Vineland, New Jersey, this small rural community celebrates spring with a dandelion-eating contest.

15. Only the female mosquito drinks blood the males live on plant juices.

16. Every Friday evening, my parents go out to eat, by themselves, at the local diner, then they do their marketing for the week.

17. Television commercials are valuable they give everyone a chance to stretch, visit the bathroom, and get a snack.

18. I start by wetting my feet in the lake's cold water then I wade up to my knees before plunging in, shivering all the while.

19. In this country, roughly three hundred new pizza parlors open every week, this shows that pizza has become a staple in the American diet, exceeding even hamburgers and hot dogs in popularity.

20. The first wave of crack babies is approaching school age, and health and social workers are discovering a whole new set of drug-related problems.

FAULTY PARALLELISM

Words in a pair or in a series should be placed in parallel (matching) grammatical structures. If they're not, the result is **faulty parallelism:**

Faulty Parallelism   After the exam, we were *exhausted, hungry,* and *experienced depression.*

In the preceding sentence, three items make up the series. However, the first two items are adjectives (*exhausted* and *hungry*), while the last one is a verb plus a noun (*experienced depression*).

Words that follow correlative conjunctions (*either...or, neither...nor, both... and, not only...but also*) should also be parallel:

Faulty Parallelism   Every road into the city is either *jammed* or *is closed* for repairs.

Here, *either* is followed by an adjective (*jammed*), but *or* is followed by a verb (*is*).

How to Correct Faulty Parallelism

To correct faulty parallelism, *place words in a pair or in a series in the same grammatical structure*:

Faulty Parallelism   After the car baked in the sun for hours, the steering wheel was hot, the seats were sticky, and there was stuffiness in the air.

Correct   After the car baked in the sun for hours, the steering wheel was hot, the seats were sticky, and the air was stuffy.

or

Correct   After the car baked in the sun for hours, the steering wheel was hot, the seats sticky, and the air stuffy.

Faulty Parallelism   Parents are either too permissive or they are too strict.
Correct   Parents are either too permissive or too strict.

or

Correct   Parents either are too permissive or are too strict.

or

Correct   Either parents are too permissive, or they are too strict.

(For more on parallelism, see pages 115–116 in Chapter 8.)

PRACTICE: CORRECTING FAULTY PARALLELISM

Correct any faulty parallelism that you find in the following sentences. Be careful, though; not every sentence contains an error.

1. The professor's tests were long, difficult, and produced anxiety.

2. Medical tests showed that neither being allergic to dust nor seasonal hay fever caused the child's coughing fits.

3. One option that employees had was to accept a pay cut; the other was working longer hours.

4. The hairstylist warned her customers, "I'm a beautician, not a magician. This is a comb; it's not a wand."

5. The renovated concert hall is both beautiful and it is spacious.

6. My roommates and I are not only learning Japanese but also Russian.

7. The game-show contestants were told they had to be quick-witted, friendly, and demonstrate enthusiasm.

8. Having good rapport, being open to ideas, and believing strongly in a common goal can help group members complete a project.

9. While waiting in line at the supermarket, people often flip through the tabloids to read about celebrities, the latest scandals, and how to lose weight.

10. Smoking either will be eventually made illegal or people will give it up on their own.

VERBS

s-v agr

PROBLEMS WITH SUBJECT-VERB AGREEMENT

A **verb** should *match its subject in number.* If the subject is singular (one person, place, or thing), the verb should have a singular form. If the subject is plural (two or more persons, places, or things), the verb should have a plural form.

How to Correct Faulty Subject-Verb Agreement

The six situations described here often lead to problems with subject-verb agreement. To deal with each of these problems, you must determine the *verb's subject* and make sure the *verb agrees with it,* rather than with some other word in the sentence.

1. When there are two or more subjects   When the word *and* joins two or more subjects in a sentence, use a plural verb:

Correct   A beautiful maple *and* a straggly oak *flank* [not *flanks*] the building.

However, when the word *or* joins the subjects, use a singular verb:

Correct   A maple *or* an oak *offers* [not *offer*] good shade in the summer.

2. When the subject and verb are separated by a prepositional phrase   Be sure to match the verb to its subject—not to a word in a prepositional phrase that comes between the subject and the verb:

Correct

One of the desserts *was* [not *were*] too sweet even for me.

To pass inspection, the *plumbing* in all the apartments *needs* [not *need*] to be repaired.

650

3. When the words *either...or* or *neither...nor* connect subjects   When *either ...or* or *neither...nor* link two subjects, use the verb form (singular or plural) that agrees with the subject *closer* to the verb:

Correct

   Neither the students *nor* the *professor likes* [not *like*] the textbook.

   Neither the professor *nor* the *students like* [not *likes*] the textbook.

4. When the subject is an indefinite pronoun   Some **indefinite pronouns** (such as *anyone, anything, each, either, every, everyone, everybody, everything, neither,* and *nobody*) take a *singular verb*—whether they act as a pronoun subject (as in the first sentence that follows) or as an adjective in front of a noun subject (as in the second sentence):

Correct

   Neither of the libraries *was* [not *were*] open.

   Neither library was [not *were*] open.

Other indefinite pronouns (such as *all, any, most,* and *some*) take a *singular or a plural verb,* depending on whether they refer to one thing or to a number of things. In the following sentence, *some* refers to a single tutoring session, so the verb is singular:

Correct   The student reported that only *some* of her tutoring *session was* helpful.

In this next sentence, however, *some* refers to multiple sessions, so the verb is plural:

Correct   The student reported that only *some* of her tutoring *sessions were* helpful.

5. When there is a group subject   When the subject of a sentence refers to a group acting in unison, or as a unit, use a singular verb:

Correct   The debate *club is* [not *are*] on a winning streak.

However, when the subject is a group whose members are acting individually, rather than as a unit, use a plural verb:

Correct   *The debate club argue* [not *argues*] among themselves constantly.

If, in this case, the plural verb sounds awkward, reword the sentence so that the group's individual members are referred to directly:

Correct   The debate club *members argue* among themselves constantly.

6. When the verb comes before the subject   Words such as *here, there, how, what, when, where, which, who,* and *why,* as well as *prepositional phrases,* are apt to invert normal sentence order, causing the verb to precede the subject. In such cases, look ahead for the subject and make sure it and the verb agree in number:

Correct

There *is* [not *are*] always a long *line* of students at the library's duplicating machine.

What *are* [not *is*] the *reasons* for consumers' complaints about the car?

Near the lifeguard station, looking for us everywhere, *were* [not *was*] our *parents.*

PRACTICE: CORRECTING PROBLEMS WITH SUBJECT-VERB AGREEMENT

Correct any errors in subject-verb agreement that you find in the following sentences. Be careful, though; some sentences may not contain any errors.

1. There is many secretaries who do their bosses' jobs, as well as their own.
2. At the back of the closet, behind all the clothes, are some old records.
3. Each of the children wear a name tag when the play group takes a field trip.
4. Next week, the faculty committee on academic standards plans to pass a controversial resolution, one that the student body have rejected in the past.
5. In the garage, leaning against the back wall, are a rusty sled and a broken tricycle.
6. Neither the sales representative nor the customers were happy with the price increase, which is scheduled to go into effect next month.
7. The human spinal column, with its circular discs, resemble a stack of wobbly poker chips.
8. Both the students and the instructor dislikes experimental music.
9. In most schools, either the college president or the provost is responsible for presenting the budget to the board of trustees. The board of trustees, in turn, are responsible for cutting costs whenever possible.
10. Nobody in the two classes think that the exam, which lasted three hours, was fair.
11. Chipped ceramic pots and half-empty bags of fertilizer lines the shelves of my grandparents' storage shed.
12. In the middle of the campus, near the two new dorms, are a row of spindly elms. The trees, especially the one at the end, were badly damaged in last week's storm.
13. A strong, secure bond between parent and child are formed when parents responds quickly and consistently to their babies' needs.
14. The crowd, consisting of irate teachers and parents, were quiet, but the police were alerted anyway.
15. The guidelines issued by the supervisor states that personal calls made during the business day violate company policy.

PROBLEMS WITH VERB TENSE

vt

A **verb's tense** indicates the time—*past, present,* or *future*—of an event. Here we show how to correct two common problems with verb tense: (1) inappropriate shifts in tense, and (2) faulty use of past tense.

How to Correct Inappropriate Shifts in Verb Tense

The first sentence that follows switches from the past tense (*bought*) to the present (*breaks*), even though both events took place in the same (past) period of time. The second sentence switches from the present tense (*is*) to the past (*was*). To avoid such inappropriate shifts, *use the same verb tense to relate all events occurring in the same time period:*

Inappropriate Tense Shift	The township *bought* a powerful new lawn mower, which *breaks* down after two weeks.
Correct	The township *bought* a powerful new lawn mower, which *broke* down after two weeks.

Inappropriate Tense Shift	The restaurant's homemade bread *is* thick and crunchy. It *was* a meal in itself.
Correct	The restaurant's homemade bread *was* thick and crunchy. It *was* a meal in itself.

When writing, decide which verb tense will be most effective; then use that tense throughout—unless you need to change tenses to indicate a different time period.

Much of the writing you do in college will use the past tense:

Changes in the tax law *created* chaos for accounting firms.

However, when writing about literature, you generally use the present tense:

Twain *examines* the conflict between humane impulses and society's prejudices.

How to Correct Faulty Use of Past Tense

The following sentence uses the **simple past tense** (*finished, burst*) for both verbs, even though one event ("the plane finished rolling down the runway") *preceded* the other (the plane "burst into flames"). To distinguish one past event from an earlier one, use the **past perfect tense** ("*had* washed," "*had* gone," "*had* finished") for the earlier event:

Faulty Past Tense	The plane already *finished* rolling down the runway when it *burst* into flames.
Correct	The plane *had* already *finished* [past perfect] rolling down the runway when it *burst* [simple past] into flames.

Correct any errors in verb tense that you find in the following sentences. Be careful, though; some tenses shouldn't be changed.

1. I parked illegally, so my car is towed and gets dented in the process.

2. We had already ordered a truckload of lumber when we decided not to build a deck after all.

3. Although the union leaders called a strike, the union members voted not to stop working.

4. Dr. Alice Chase wrote a number of books on healthy eating. In 1974, she dies of malnutrition.

5. By the time we hiked back to the campsite, the rest of the group collected their gear to go home.

6. In her poetry, Marge Piercy often pays tribute to women's strength and resilience.

7. As a boy, Thomas Edison was told he will never succeed at anything.

8. The Museum of Modern Art once hung a painting upside down. The mistake goes unnoticed for more than a month.

9. When doctors in Los Angeles went on strike in 1976, the death rate drops 18 percent.

10. John Steinbeck's *The Grapes of Wrath* conveyed the horrors of poverty

11. The championship players slapped each other's backs, hooted and hollered, and poured champagne all over the coach.

12. The aspiring comic walked to the front of the small stage. As he looked out at the audience, a wave of nausea sweeps over him.

PRONOUNS

PROBLEMS WITH PRONOUN USE

Pronouns are words that take the place of nouns (persons, places, things, and concepts). Indeed, the word *pronoun* means "for a noun." As the following sentences show, pronouns keep you from repeating words unnecessarily:

After I fertilized the plant, *it* began to flourish. [*it* takes the place of *plant*]

When the students went to register *their* complaint, *they* were told to come back later. [*their* and *they* replace *students*]

When using pronouns, you need to be careful not to run into problems with case, agreement, and reference.

Pronoun Case

case

A pronoun's correct form, or **case,** depends on the way the pronoun is used in the sentence. A pronoun acting as a *subject* requires the **nominative case.** One acting as a *direct object* (receiving a verb's action), an *indirect object* (indicating to or for whom the action is performed), or an *object of a preposition* (following a preposition such as *at, near,* or *to*) requires the **objective case.** And a pronoun indicating *possession* takes the **possessive case**. The list that starts here and continues on the next page classifies pronouns by case:

Nominative Case	Objective Case	Possessive Case	
I	me	my	mine
we	us	our	ours
you	you	your	yours
he	him	his	his
she	her	her	hers

655

Nominative Case	Objective Case	Possessive Case	
it	it	its	its
they	them	their	theirs
who	whom	whose	

How to Correct Faulty Pronoun Case

The five situations described here often lead to errors in pronoun case. To correct any of these problems, *determine whether the pronoun is used as object or subject; then put the pronoun in the appropriate case.*

1. Pronoun pairs or a pronoun and a noun   Use the nominative case when two pronouns act as subjects:

Correct   *He* and *I* [not *Him* and *me*] are different ages, but we have several traits in common.

Also use the nominative case when a pronoun and noun serve as subjects:

Correct   *She* [not *Her*] and *several transfer students* enrolled in the new course.

Conversely, use the objective case when a pronoun pair acts as direct object, indirect object, or object of a preposition:

Correct (Direct Objects)   My parents sent *her* [not *she*] and *me* [not *I*] to the store to buy decorations for the holiday.
Correct (Indirect Objects)   The committee presented *him* [not *he*] and *me* [not *I*] with the award.

Similarly, use the objective case when a pronoun and noun function as direct object, indirect object, or object of a preposition:

Correct (Object of Preposition)   The doctor gave the pills to the three other patients and *me* [not *I*].

A hint: When a pronoun is paired with another pronoun or with a noun, and you're not sure which case to use, imagine the sentence with only one pronoun. For example, perhaps you wonder whether it's correct to write "The student senate commended my roommates and *I* for our actions." "The student senate commended *I*" doesn't sound right, so you know *me* is the correct form.

2. A pronoun-noun pair acting together as subject or object   If a pronoun-noun pair acts as the subject, use the nominative case:

Correct   *We* [not *Us*] *dorm residents* plan to protest the ruling.

If the pronoun-noun pair serves as an object, use the objective case:

Correct   The dropout rate among *us* [not *we*] *commuting students* is high.

3. Pronouns following forms of the verb *to be*   In formal English, use the nominative case in constructions like the following:

Correct

It is *I* [not *me*].

This is *she* [not *her*].

In such constructions, the objective case (*me* and *her*, for example) is so common that the formally correct nominative case may sound strange. However, before using the more colloquial objective case, check with your instructor to make sure such informality will be acceptable.

4. Pronouns following the comparative *than*   Comparisons using the word *than* tend to imply, rather than state directly, the sentence's final word (placed in brackets in the following sentence):

The other employees are more willing to negotiate *than we* [are].

To determine the appropriate case for the pronoun in a sentence with a *than* comparison, simply add the implied word. For example, maybe you're not sure whether *we* or *us* is correct in the preceding sentence. As soon as you supply the implied word (*are*), it becomes clear that *we*, not *us*, is correct.

5. *Who* and *whom*   When, as in the first example that follows, a pronoun acts as the subject of a sentence or clause, use *who* (the nominative case). When, as in the second example, the pronoun acts as the object of a verb or preposition, use *whom* (the objective case). You can test whether *who* or *whom* is correct by answering the question stated or implied in the *who/whom* portion of the sentence. The pronoun that answers *who/whom* will reveal which case to use:

"*Who/Whom* did you meet at the jazz festival"? → "I met *him* at the festival." → Since *him* is the objective case, use *whom*.

"The employees want to know *who/whom* will supervise the project." → "*She* will supervise the project." → Since *she* is the nominative case, use *who*.

PRACTICE: CORRECTING PROBLEMS WITH PRONOUN CASE

Correct any problems with pronoun case that you find in the following sentences. Be careful, though; some pronouns are used correctly.

   1. At this college, neither the president nor the dean automatically assumes that, on every issue, the faculty is better informed than us students.

   2. Between you and I, each of the dorms should have their security systems replaced.

   3. The theater critic, whom slipped into her seat right before the curtain went up, gave him and the other actors favorable reviews.

4. Neither of the boys impressed she or me with their musical ability.

5. The salesperson explained to my husband and I that each of the video-cassette recorders had its drawbacks.

6. My grandfather, who found knitting relaxing, made me and my brother beautiful scarves and sweaters.

7. After enjoying prosperity through most of the 1980s, she and him were unprepared for the rigors of the next decade.

8. To whom did the theater manager give the free passes?

9. Many of us baby boomers came of age in an era of social activism.

10. The people who lived next door, me and my roommates concluded, had no intention of being neighborly.

11. The director of housing, whom we had contacted two months ago, finally asked us dorm residents to itemize our complaints.

12. The plot twisted and turned so much it was difficult for my sister and I to keep track of who cheated on who.

pro agr

Pronoun Agreement

A pronoun must **agree in number** with its **antecedent**—the noun or pronoun it replaces or refers to. If the antecedent is singular, the pronoun must be singular. If the antecedent is plural, the pronoun must be plural.

How to Correct Faulty Pronoun Agreement

The four situations described here often lead to problems with pronoun agreement. To deal with these problems, either *change the pronoun so it agrees in number and person with its antecedent* or *change the noun to agree with the pronoun you have used.*

1. Compound nouns   Compound (two or more) nouns joined by *and* are plural and require plural pronouns:

Correct   Both the oak *tree* and the rose *bushes* had trouble regaining *their* strength after the storm.

However, when compound nouns are joined by *or* or *nor,* whichever noun is closer to the verb determines whether the pronoun should be singular or plural:

Faulty Pronoun Agreement   Neither the oak tree nor the rose *bushes* regained *its* strength after the storm.

Correct   Neither the oak tree nor the rose *bushes* regained *their* strength after the storm.

Correct   Neither the rose bushes nor the oak *tree* regained *its* strength after the storm.

2. Collective nouns   Collective nouns represent a collection of people or things. Some examples are *company, university, team,* and *committee.* If the collective noun refers to a group or entity that acts as one unit, use the singular pronoun:

Faulty Pronoun Agreement   The *band* showed *their* appreciation by playing several encores.
Correct   The *band* showed *its* appreciation by playing several encores.

If, in this case, the singular pronoun form sounds awkward, simply make the antecedent plural. Then use the plural pronoun:

Correct   The band *members* showed *their* appreciation by playing several encores.

When the collective noun refers to members of a group who act individually, use a plural pronoun:

Correct   *The band* disagreed among *themselves* about the songs to be played.

3. Indefinite pronouns   Here is a list of indefinite pronouns:

Indefinite Pronoun	Possessive Form		Reflexive Form
anybody	his, her	his, hers	himself, herself
everybody	his, her	his, hers	himself, herself
nobody	his, her	his, hers	himself, herself
somebody	his, her	his, hers	himself, herself
anyone	his, her	his, hers	himself, herself
everyone	his, her	his, hers	himself, herself
no one	his, her	his, hers	himself, herself
someone	his, her	his, hers	himself, herself
either	his, her	his, hers	himself, herself
neither	his, her	his, hers	himself, herself
each	his, her	his, hers	himself, herself
one	one's		oneself

In everyday speech, we often use plural pronouns (*their* and *themselves*) because such pronouns cause us to picture more than one person. For example, we may say *"Everyone* should bring *their* own computer disks." In formal writing, though, indefinite pronouns are considered singular and thus take singular pronouns:

Correct

Each of the buildings had *its* [not *their*] lobby redecorated.

Neither of the ballerinas was pleased with *her* [not *their*] performance.

Using the singular form with indefinite pronouns may mean that you find yourself in the awkward situation of having to choose between *his* or *her* or between *himself* and *herself.* As a result, you may end up writing sentences that exclude either males or females: "Everybody in the mall seemed lost in *his* own thoughts." (Surely some of the shoppers were female.) To avoid this problem, you may make the antecedent plural and use the plural pronoun:

The *shoppers* in the mall seemed lost in *their* own thoughts.

(See pages 126–128 in Chapter 8 for other ways to avoid language that excludes one sex or the other.)

4. A shift in person   Within a sentence, pronouns shouldn't—as in the following sentences—disrupt pronoun-antecedent agreement by shifting person (point of view):

Faulty Pronoun Agreement

To drop a course, *students* [third person] should go to the registrar's office, where *you* [second person] obtain a course-change card.

Most of *us* [first person] enjoy eating out, but *you* [second person] can never be sure that a favorite restaurant won't lower its standards.

Such shifts are most often from the third or first person to the second person (*you*). In the first example, *you* should be *they;* in the second example, *you* should be *we.*

PRACTICE: CORRECTING PROBLEMS WITH PRONOUN AGREEMENT

Correct any problems with pronoun agreement that you find in the following sentences. Be careful, though; some pronouns are used correctly.

1. We proponents of the recycling plan challenged everyone on the town council to express their objections.

2. Officials have asked every man competing in the weight-lifting event to sign a statement saying that he has never used steroids.

3. All job applicants must call for an appointment, so that the personnel office can interview you.

4. The committee passed their resolution that each of the apartments was to be free of asbestos before occupancy.

5. Typically, one of the girls loses their schedule of upcoming games, so the coach always reminds the team of its next event at the start of each competition.

6. I like living in a small town because there's always someone who remembers you as a child.

7. The instructor reminded everyone in class to pick up their term papers before they left for the semester break.

8. Neither the bank manager nor the bank officers admitted to their error in approving the risky loan.

9. Despite poor attendance last year, the library staff decided once again to hold their annual party at the Elmhurst Inn.

10. Many amateur photographers like to use one-step cameras that you don't have to focus.

pro ref

Pronoun Reference

Besides agreeing with its antecedent in number and person, a pronoun must have a *clear antecedent.* A sentence that lacks clear **pronoun reference** is vague and ambiguous.

How to Correct Unclear Pronoun Reference

To make sure that each pronoun has an unmistakable antecedent, use the four strategies described here.

1. Leave no ambiguity about the noun to which a pronoun refers:

Unclear Antecedent	The newcomer battled the longtime champion for the tennis prize. In the end, she won. [Who won? The newcomer or the longtime champion?]
Correct	The newcomer battled the longtime champion for the tennis prize. In the end, *the newcomer* won.

2. Replace a pronoun that lacks an antecedent with the appropriate noun:

Omitted Antecedent	In his talk on child abuse, the caseworker pointed out the number of *them* mistreated by day-care employees. [*Them* is meant to refer to *children,* but this word doesn't appear in the sentence.]
Correct	In his talk on child abuse, the caseworker pointed out the number of *children* mistreated by day-care employees.

3. Make sure a pronoun doesn't refer to the possessive form of a noun or to an adjective:

Omitted Antecedent	In *journalists' articles, they* often quote unidentified sources. [*They* refers to *journalists,* which is in the possessive case.]
Correct	*Journalists* often quote unidentified sources in *their* articles.

4. Place pronouns near their antecedents:

Unclear Antecedent	The *dancers,* performing almost daily, traveled by bus and train. The trip spanned several states. *They* returned exhausted and out of debt.
Correct	Performing almost daily, traveling by bus and train on a trip that spanned several states, the *dancers* returned exhausted. *They* were also out of debt.

PRACTICE: CORRECTING PROBLEMS WITH PRONOUN REFERENCE

Correct any problems with pronoun reference that you find in the following sentences. Be careful, though; some pronouns are used correctly.

1. In Anne Tyler's novels, she gives us a picture of family life—at its best and at its worst.

2. To keep children away from dangerous chemicals, lock them in a storage closet.

3. The student sat down glumly as soon as the professor began to criticize his research paper. After a few moments, though, he turned away in frustration, trying to collect his thoughts.

4. Many patients' lawsuits against doctors end when they receive an out-of-court settlement.

5. All too often, arguments between a big and a little sister are ended by the younger one, when she threatens to blackmail her sister with some violation of household rules.

6. In Ibsen's *A Doll's House,* he dramatizes the story of a woman treated as a plaything.

7. The swirling of the magician's cape distracted the audience as he opened the trap door slowly.

8. Since the old man's morning was planned around reading the newspaper, he became upset when it was delivered late.

9. The supervisor explained to the employee that he would be transferred soon.

10. Although the school board members talked far into the night, they couldn't reach an agreement. Opinions on the principal's performance were mixed, with some highly positive and others sharply critical. They decided to continue the discussion the following week.

MODIFIERS

PROBLEMS WITH MODIFICATION

Misplaced and Ambiguous Modifiers

A **modifier** is a word or group of words that describes something else. Sometimes sentences are written in such a way that modifiers are **misplaced** or **ambiguous.** Here are examples of misplaced and ambiguous modifiers:

Misplaced Modifier	Television stations carried the story of the disastrous fire *in every part of the nation.* [The fire was in every part of the nation?]
Ambiguous Modifier	Singers who don't warm up *gradually* lose their voices. [What does the sentence mean: that singers who don't warm up will lose their voices gradually or that singers who don't gradually warm up will lose their voices?]

How to Correct Misplaced or Ambiguous Modifiers

We describe here two strategies for correcting misplaced or ambiguous modifiers.

1. Place the modifier next to the word(s) it describes:

Misplaced Modifier	We scanned the menu *with hungry eyes.* [The menu had hungry eyes?]
Correct	With hungry eyes, we scanned the menu.
Misplaced Modifier	The paramedics covered the boy's forehead with a cold compress, *which was bruised and swollen.* [The cold compress was bruised and swollen?]
Correct	The paramedics covered the boy's forehead, which was bruised and swollen, with a cold compress.
Misplaced Modifier	They *only* studied a few minutes for the exam. [Doesn't the word *only* describe *a few minutes,* not *studied*?]
Correct	They studied *only* a few minutes for the exam.

663

2. Rewrite the sentence to eliminate ambiguity:

Ambiguous Modifier   Giving money *frequently* relieves people's guilt about living well.

Writing the sentence this way could mean *either* that the frequent giving of gifts relieves guilt or that giving gifts relieves guilt frequently. Moving the modifier to the front of the sentence conveys the first meaning.

Frequently, giving money relieves people's guilt about living well.

The second meaning, however, can be conveyed only by rewriting the sentence:

Giving money *on a frequent basis* relieves people's guilt about living well.

---

dgl

Dangling Modifiers

An introductory modifier must modify the subject of the sentence. If it doesn't, the result is a **dangling modifier.** Here's an example of a dangling modifier:

Dangling Modifier   *Driving along the highway,* the blinding sun obscured our view of the oncoming car. [The sentence says that the sun was driving along the highway.]

How to Correct Dangling Modifiers

To eliminate a dangling modifier, you may *rewrite the sentence by adding to the modifying phrase the word being described* (as in the first corrected example that follows). Or you may *rewrite the sentence so that the word being modified becomes the sentence's subject* (as in the second corrected example):

Dangling Modifier   *While relaxing in my backyard hammock,* a neighbor's basketball hit me on the head. [The basketball was relaxing in the backyard?]
Correct   While *I* was relaxing in my backyard hammock, a neighbor's basketball hit me on the head.

or

Correct   While relaxing in my backyard hammock, *I* was hit on the head by my neighbor's basketball.

PRACTICE: CORRECTING PROBLEMS WITH MODIFICATION

Correct any misplaced, ambiguous, or dangling modifiers that you find in the following sentences. Be careful, though; not every sentence is incorrect.

   1. While cooking dinner, the baby began to howl.

   2. Swaying from the boughs of a tall tree, the children were intrigued by the ape's agility and grace.

3. When pondering her problems, it finally struck Laura that her life was filled with many pleasures.

4. At the end of the semester, I realized that I only needed tutoring in one course.

5. While waiting for the plumber, the hot-water tank began to leak all over the basement floor.

6. After swimming the entire length of the lake, the coach, much to his embarrassment, passed out.

7. Dogs and cats can scare small children wandering loose.

8. Faded and brittle with age, we read the old newspaper clipping with difficulty.

9. The reporters indicated that they only wanted a few minutes of the candidate's time.

10. With disgust, I threw the greasy hamburger into the trash can that had been dripping all over me.

11. Investigating the crime scene, the detectives made a surprising discovery.

12. An outfit that can only be worn once or twice a year isn't a practical investment.

13. Spinning wildly on the barn roof, the boys noticed an old copper weathervane.

14. We bought our dining room table at a discount store which cost less than one hundred dollars.

15. Pushing a shopping cart and muttering to herself, the homeless woman approached me warily.

PUNCTUATION

p

Correct **punctuation** is no trivial matter. Notice how a single comma alters the meaning of this sentence.

Their uncle would be the only visitor they feared.

Their uncle would be the only visitor, they feared.

The first sentence suggests that the uncle's visit is a source of anxiety; the second sentence suggests that the uncle is, unfortunately, the only person to pay a visit. So choose your punctuation carefully. Skillful punctuation helps you get your message across; careless punctuation can undermine your credibility and spoil an otherwise effective piece of writing.

In the pages ahead, we discuss, first, end punctuation (the period, question mark, and exclamation point) and then other punctuation marks (such as the comma, semicolon, and colon).

PERIOD (.)

The most frequent misuse of the **period** is at the end of a *fragment*—a word or group of words that doesn't constitute a full sentence, only part of one. (For more on sentence fragments, see pages 638–643 of the Handbook.) The correct uses of the period are outlined here.

1. At the end of full statements A period correctly completes any full sentence not worded as a question or exclamation:

The dognappers were caught with three pets that they planned to sell to a medical laboratory.

The campus senators asked when the college administrators would approve the new plan.

Although the second sentence reports that a question was asked, the sentence itself is a statement. For this reason, it ends with a period, not with a question mark.

2. With some abbreviations   A period is also used to indicate a shortened form of a word; that is, an abbreviation:

Prof. (Professor)   Dec. (December)
Rev. (Reverend)   p.m. (*post meridiem,* Latin phrase meaning "after noon")

When an abbreviation ends a sentence, only one period is needed at the sentence's close:

They didn't place the order until 3 a.m.

Some abbreviations, though, have no period at all. These include the abbreviated titles of organizations and government agencies, as well as the official U.S. Postal Service abbreviations for state names:

NFL (National Football League)
FDA (Food and Drug Administration)
ME (Maine)

In addition, it is becoming increasingly acceptable to omit the periods in frequently used abbreviations—for example, *MTV* (Music Television) and *mph* (miles per hour). If you're in doubt whether to include a period in an abbreviation, consult a recent dictionary. Many dictionaries have a separate section near the beginning that lists abbreviations.

3. In decimal numbers   A period precedes the fractional portion of a decimal number:

5.38 (five and thirty-eight hundredths)

Since money is counted according to the decimal system, a period occurs between dollars and cents:

$10.35

(For more information on writing numerals, see pages 690–692 of the Handbook.)

?

QUESTION MARK (?)

1. At the end of direct questions   Just as a period concludes a statement, a **question mark** concludes a question:

Where can a dorm resident find peace and solitude?

The panelists debated the question, "Should drugs be legalized?"

Did the consultants name their report "The Recycling Crisis"?

Notice that in the second example above, the actual question occurs only within the quotation marks. Therefore, the question mark is placed *before* the final quotation marks. In the third example, though, the whole sentence is a question, so the question mark goes *after* the final quotation marks.

2. In parentheses, following an item of questionable accuracy   Whenever you're unable to confirm the accuracy of a name, date, or other item, indicate your uncertainty by following the item with a question mark enclosed in parentheses:

The fraud, begun in 1977 **(?)**, was discovered only this year.

!

EXCLAMATION POINT (!)

At the end of emphatic sentences   An **exclamation point** is placed at the end of a sentence to indicate strong emotion:

That's the worst meal I've ever eaten!

Use exclamation points sparingly; otherwise, they lose their effectiveness.

,

COMMA (,)

The **comma** is so frequent in writing that mastering its use is essential. By dividing a sentence into its parts, commas clarify meaning. Compare the following:

As soon as we had won the contest was declared illegal.

As soon as we had won**,** the contest was declared illegal.

The comma shows the reader where to pause in order to make sense of the sentence. The following pages discuss the correct use of the comma.

1. Between sentences joined by a coordinating conjunction   When joining two complete sentences with a coordinating conjunction (*and, but, for, nor, or, so, yet*), place a comma *before* the coordinating conjunction:

My father loves dining out, *but* he is fussy about food.

It's permissible to omit the comma, though, if the two complete sentences are very short:

They lied *yet* they won the case.

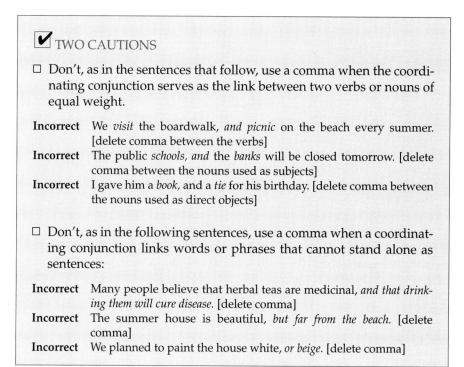

☑ TWO CAUTIONS

□ Don't, as in the sentences that follow, use a comma when the coordinating conjunction serves as the link between two verbs or nouns of equal weight.

Incorrect   We *visit* the boardwalk, *and picnic* on the beach every summer. [delete comma between the verbs]
Incorrect   The public *schools, and* the *banks* will be closed tomorrow. [delete comma between the nouns used as subjects]
Incorrect   I gave him a *book,* and a *tie* for his birthday. [delete comma between the nouns used as direct objects]

□ Don't, as in the following sentences, use a comma when a coordinating conjunction links words or phrases that cannot stand alone as sentences:

Incorrect   Many people believe that herbal teas are medicinal, *and that drinking them will cure disease.* [delete comma]
Incorrect   The summer house is beautiful, *but far from the beach.* [delete comma]
Incorrect   We planned to paint the house white, *or beige.* [delete comma]

2. Between items in a series   As the examples in the preceding box show, you do *not* use a comma between *two* items in a series. However, you *do* use a comma to separate *three or more* items in a series:

Bicycle racing requires practice, stamina, and determination.

It was a long, lonely, frightening drive to the cabin.

Notice that in both examples a comma appears before the last item in the series, whether or not this last item is preceded by *and* or *or.* (Although journalists and popular writers often omit the last comma in a series, its inclusion is expected in most other writing.)

However, if each item in the series is joined by *and* or *or,* do not place commas between them:

We didn't applaud *or* support *or* encourage the protesters.

3. Between adjectives of equal weight   A comma can substitute for the word *and* between adjectives of *equal weight* that describe the same noun:

Collecting exotic, colorful plants is one of my grandparents' hobbies.

In this sentence, the adjectives *exotic* and *colorful* contribute equally to the description of the noun *plants*. To test whether two adjectives have equal weight, reverse them or imagine the word *and* between them. If the sentence sounds fine, the adjectives have equal weight; thus, there should be a comma between them.

> ☑ CAUTION
>
> Don't, as in the sentence that follows, use a comma between adjectives of *unequal weight*:
>
> **Incorrect:**   We bought a new, American-made stereo.
>
> The fact that the stereo is *American-made* has more weight than the fact that it is *new*. Moreover, the sentence would sound strange if the adjectives were reversed or if *and* appeared between them. For these reasons, there should be no comma between *new* and *American-made*.

4. Setting off nonrestrictive word groups   When a word, phrase, or clause describes a noun but isn't crucial for identifying that noun, it is *set off* from the rest of the sentence *with a comma*. Such a word or group of words is considered **nonrestrictive,** or **nonessential.**

Here's an example:

The professor asked the class to read Twain's *Pudd'nhead Wilson*, a novel both droll and dark.

Because *Pudd'nhead Wilson* identifies the novel sufficiently, the phrase *a novel both droll and dark* is nonrestrictive and, thus, set off with a comma. If the nonrestrictive phrase appears midsentence, it is preceded and followed by commas:

The professor asked the class to read Twain's *Pudd'nhead Wilson*, a novel both droll and dark, by the end of the week.

In the next sentence, however, the book's title is *not set off by a comma* because the word group making up the title is **restrictive,** or **essential;** that is, it is needed for identification (Twain wrote more than one novel):

The professor asked the class to read Twain's droll and dark novel *Pudd'nhead Wilson*.

(For a discussion of restrictive and nonrestrictive clauses, turn to page 642 in the Handbook.)

5. Setting off words that precede the main body of the sentence   When introductory material precedes the sentence's main subject and verb, such material is usually followed by a comma:

Yes, I'll be happy to read the report.

Like most children, my little sister loves animals.

Because English Composition is a required course, sections are always filled.

If, however, the introductory material is very brief, you may often omit the comma:

Surely everyone has an urge to see exotic places.

6. Setting off words that follow the main body of the sentence   Material attached to the end of a sentence—after the main subject and verb—is preceded by a comma:

Many people think a walk is a waste of time, *like napping or daydreaming.*

You should start any new exercise program slowly, *making sure not to push yourself.*

7. Setting off interrupting words and phrases   Some words and phrases inserted into the body of a sentence can be removed without significant loss of meaning. Such *interrupting* elements are preceded and followed by commas when they occur midsentence:

Dr. Helen Rafton, *standing by the door and chatting with reporters*, is a celebrated botanist.

I told him, *when he mentioned the accident*, my version of what had happened.

The snowfall was heavy; classes, *however*, were held as usual.

 CAUTION

Note that a *pair of commas* must be used to set off interrupting words or phrases that occur midsentence. A single comma, as in the following sentences, is *not* enough to set off interrupting elements:

Incorrect   The high school reunion, scheduled for Memorial Day weekend should be well-attended. [comma needed after *weekend*]

Incorrect   They reported with considerable anxiety, the results of the test. [comma needed before *with*]

Incorrect   The autumn day was surprisingly warm; we therefore, decided to go on a picnic. [comma needed before *therefore*]

In the last sentence, the transitional adverb *therefore* should be flanked by commas because it occurs *within* an independent clause. But when a transitional adverb comes *between* two independent clauses, it is preceded by a semicolon and followed by a comma (see page 646 in the Handbook).

8. Setting off words in direct address   Use a comma before and/or after the name of a person or group being addressed directly:

> Ladies and gentlemen, the meeting is about to begin.

> "Remember, Janet, to turn the thermostat down," my father always warned.

9. Between a short quotation and the phrase that indicates the quotation's source   Use a comma between a short quotation and a reference to its source or speaker:

> My roommate remarked, "You remind me of a hungry bulldog."

> "You can't block access to the building," the police informed the striking employees.

(For more on punctuating quotations, see pages 676–678 of the Handbook.)

10. Between the elements of a date or place   Use a comma to separate the non-numerical portions of a mailing address, as well as the numbers in a date:

> The witness testified that the package was delivered to 102 Glendale Road, Kirkwood, New Jersey 08043 on January 23, 1999.

Also, place a comma after the year if the date appears before the end of the sentence:

> They were married on June 28, 1974, in New York City.

When you reverse the day and month in a date or give only the month and year or the month and day, do not use commas. Also, don't put a comma between a state and a ZIP code:

> February 14, 1999
> 14 February 1999
> February 1999
> February 14
> New York, NY 10022

PRACTICE: CORRECTING COMMA ERRORS

Where appropriate, provide or eliminate commas in the following sentences. Be careful, though; some of the commas belong just where they are.

1. The local movie theater, despite efforts to attract customers finally closed its doors, and was purchased by a supermarket chain.

2. As a little boy, I dreamed about wearing a plaid flannel shirt and, like Paul Bunyan, camping out underneath towering trees.

3. Their parents, always risk takers divorced in August and remarried in February just six months later.

4. Shaken by the threat of a hostile takeover, the board of directors, and the stockholders voted to sell the retail division which had been losing money for years.

5. Despite my parents' objections I read Stephen King's novels *The Shining,* and *Carrie* when I was in junior high. The books terrified me; nevertheless, I couldn't put them down.

6. We skimmed the chapter, looked quickly at the tables, and charts, realized we didn't know enough to pass the exam, and began to panic.

7. After years of saving his money my brother bought a used car and then his problems started.

8. I discovered last week, that my neighbors, whose friendship I had always treasured, intend to sue me.

9. Late yesterday afternoon, I realized that Dan was lying, and had driven my car without permission.

10. Although it can be annoying, and frustrating, forgetting things usually isn't an early sign of Alzheimer's disease, as many people think.

11. "Going to New York" Maria said, "was like walking onto a movie set."

12. The long, pretentious report issued on May 11, 1992 neither analyzed the problem adequately, nor proposed reasonable solutions.

13. By going to a party alone a single person stands a better chance of meeting someone, and of having a good time.

14. Janet and Sandy her younger sister run three miles each day even in the winter.

15. Al pleaded "Let me borrow your notes and I'll never ask for anything again. I promise."

16. Mumbling under his breath, the man picked over the tomatoes, and cucumbers in the market's produce department.

17. All too often these days people assume that a bank statement is correct, and that there's no need to open the envelope, and examine the statement closely.

18. In the last two seconds of the game the quarterback seized the ball, and plunged across the goal line, scoring the game's winning point.

19. After the uprising was quelled, numerous dissidents were imprisoned but an unknown number remained at large, waiting for the right moment to stage a revolution.

20. Our psychology professor, who has an active, clinical practice, talked about the pressures, and rewards of being in a helping profession.

;

SEMICOLON (;)

1. Between independent clauses closely related in meaning   You may connect two independent clauses with a **semicolon,** rather than writing them as separate sentences. When you do, though, the clauses should be closely related in meaning. They might, for example, *reinforce* each other:

> Making spaghetti sauce is easy; most people can do it after only a few tries.

Or the clauses might *contrast* with each other:

> Many homebuyers harbor suspicious feelings about the real estate industry; most realtors, however, are honest and law-abiding.

Use of the semicolon is especially common when the *clauses* are *short:*

> Smile when you are introduced; nod or bow slightly to acknowledge applause; wait for silence; pause a second; then begin your speech.

You may also use a semicolon (instead of a period) between independent clauses linked by *transitions* (like *then* and *next*) or by *transitional adverbs* (such as *moreover* and *however*):

> We continually lost track of our sales; *finally,* a friend showed us a good accounting system.

> Customers kept requesting food items other than produce; *therefore,* the owners expanded their fruit and vegetable market into a general convenience store.

Note that when the second independent clause starts with a transitional expression, a comma is placed *after* the transition. However, if a comma is placed *before* the transition, a *comma splice* results (see pages 644–647 of the Handbook on ways to avoid comma splices).

2. Between items in a series, when any of the items contains a comma   When individual items in a series have internal commas, another form of punctuation is needed to signal clearly where one item ends and another begins. For this purpose, use the semicolon:

> After dinner, we had to choose between seeing a movie classic, like *Casablanca, Rear Window,* or *It's a Wonderful Life*; playing Clue, Scrabble, or Monopoly; or working out at the gym.

3. Before coordinating conjunctions used to join independent clauses, when any of the clauses contains a comma   Ordinarily, independent clauses joined by a coordinating conjunction (*and, but, for, nor, or, so, yet*) have a comma, not a semicolon, between them. However, when any such clause has internal commas, a semicolon is needed between the clauses:

> The mist settled in the valley, hiding the fields, the foliage, and the farms; and the pleasant road became a menace.

COLON (:)

1. To introduce an illustrative statement or list of examples   Use a **colon** to introduce lengthy illustrative material—either a full statement or a number of examples—whenever that material is preceded by a full sentence:

> In the spring, the city has a special magic: Street musicians, jugglers, and ethnic festivals enthrall tourist and resident alike.

> Having nine brothers and sisters determined a number of my character traits: my love of solitude, my craving for attention, my resentment of anything secondhand.

As the first example shows, when the material following the colon can stand alone as a complete sentence, it begins with a capital letter (*Street*). Otherwise, as in the second example, the material after the colon starts with a lowercase letter (*my*).

2. To introduce a long quotation   Use a colon when a complete sentence introduces a long quotation (five or more lines) that is set off in block (indented) form without quotation marks:

```
The witness to the accident told the police:
            I was walking to my car in the parking lot when I
            glanced over at the other side of the street. I saw
            the traffic light turn yellow, and a silver convert-
            ible started to slow down. Just then, a red station
            wagon came racing down the street. When the convert-
            ible stopped for the light, the station wagon kept
            going--right into the convertible's rear fender.
```

(See pages 570–573 in Chapter 21 for more information on the format for long and short quotations.)

3. After the opening of a business letter   Follow the opening of a business letter with a colon:

> Dear Ms. Goldwin:

Use a comma, however, in the salutation of a personal letter.

4. Between parts of certain conventional notations   A number of standard notations include colons. One example is time notation, with hours and minutes separated by a colon:

> 4:52 p.m.

In a ratio, a colon substitutes for the word *to*:

> By a ratio of 3:2, Americans prefer Glocko cleanser.

In a reference to the Bible, the colon separates chapter and verse numbers:

> Genesis 2:14

Titles and subtitles (of books, journal articles, short stories, works of art, films, and so on) are also separated by a colon:

> *Election Handbook: A Participant's Guide*

QUOTATION MARKS (" ")

1. Direct quotations   A *direct quotation* reproduces exactly the wording, punctuation, and spelling of the source. It is also enclosed in *double* **quotation marks:**

> "Youngsters in elementary school should learn the importance of budgeting money," the psychologist said.

A quotation within a quotation is enclosed in *single* (' ') quotation marks.

> The psychologist said, "It was gratifying when my children told me, 'We're glad you taught us how to spend money sensibly.'"

✔ CAUTION

Indirect Quotations

> *Indirect quotations*—those referred to or paraphrased rather than reproduced word for word—*don't* get quotation marks:

Correct   The psychologist said that even young children should be taught how to manage money wisely.

As in the preceding sentence, the word *that* is often used to introduce an indirect quotation. There is *no comma* before or after *that* in this case.

Use a comma between a short quotation and an identifying phrase like *they commented* or *he said*. Such phrases may be placed before, after, or within the quotation:

> *She argued*, "They won't reject the plan."
>
> "They won't reject the plan," *she argued.*
>
> "They won't reject the plan," *she argued*, "if they understand its purpose."

When, as in the last example, the identifier interrupts the quotation midsentence, commas flank both sides of the identifier. But if the identifier comes between two quoted sentences, it is followed by a period:

"They won't reject the plan," *she argued*. "They understand its purpose."

✔ CAUTION

More on Punctuating Direct Quotations:

☐ Always place a period or comma *inside* the closing quotation marks:

Correct   "You know what you meant to say," the instructor remarked, "but the reader doesn't."

☐ Always place a colon or semicolon *outside* the closing quotation marks:

Correct   The article stated, "Rice is the major foodstuff of all Asian peoples"; in particular, the Japanese eat ten times more rice than Americans.

☐ Place question marks and exclamation points according to their context. If a quotation is itself a question or exclamation, the question mark or exclamation point goes *inside* the closing quotation marks. No other end punctuation is used:

Correct   "Who's responsible for this decision?" the chief executive demanded. Each department head responded, "Not me!"

As the first sentence here shows, no comma is used when an identifying phrase follows a quoted question or exclamation.

If the entire sentence, not just the quotation, is a question or an exclamation, the question or exclamation mark goes *outside* the quotation marks, at the end of the entire sentence:

Correct

Who taught you to ask for things by saying "Gimme"?

I eagerly await the day when people will again say "Please" and "Thank you"!

☐ Use no punctuation other than quotation marks when a quotation is blended (with or without the word *that*) into the rest of a sentence:

Correct

People who believe that **"rules are made to be broken"** only substitute their own rules.

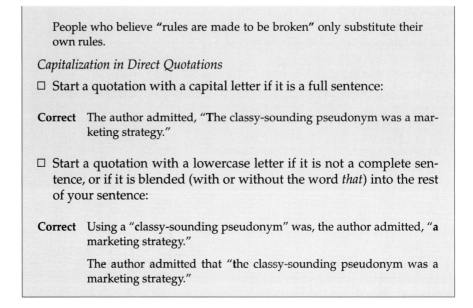

People who believe "rules are made to be broken" only substitute their own rules.

Capitalization in Direct Quotations

☐ Start a quotation with a capital letter if it is a full sentence:

Correct   The author admitted, "The classy-sounding pseudonym was a marketing strategy."

☐ Start a quotation with a lowercase letter if it is not a complete sentence, or if it is blended (with or without the word *that*) into the rest of your sentence:

Correct   Using a "classy-sounding pseudonym" was, the author admitted, "a marketing strategy."

The author admitted that "the classy-sounding pseudonym was a marketing strategy."

(For information on adding to or deleting from quotations, see pages 542–544 in Chapter 20.)

2. Titles of short works   Put quotation marks around the titles of short works—book chapters, poems, stories, articles, editorials, essays, individual episodes of a television or radio program—that are part of a larger work or series:

The business professor spent almost two weeks discussing the chapter "Ethics in the Workplace."

Kenneth Koch's poem "Mending Sump" parodies Robert Frost's "Mending Wall."

Titles of longer works are underlined or italicized (see pages 689–690 of the Handbook).

3. Calling attention to a word's use   To focus attention on a particular word or term, you may enclose it in quotation marks:

The report started with a discussion of just what "sex education" signifies.

People frequently say "between" when they should say "among."

Quotation marks also enclose words being used humorously or ironically:

To celebrate their victory, the team members indulged in such "adult" behavior as pouring champagne over each other's heads.

(See page 690 of the Handbook on highlighting words with italics.)

ELLIPSIS (. . .)

An **ellipsis,** consisting of three spaced periods (. . .), indicates that *words* have been *omitted from quoted material.* To use the ellipsis correctly, follow the guidelines presented here.

1. When to use the ellipsis   You may use an ellipsis to shorten a quotation, as long as you don't distort its meaning:

Original

The judge commented, "It won't surprise you to learn that this has been the most disturbing and the most draining case I have tried in all my years on the bench."

With Ellipsis

The judge commented, "It won't surprise you to learn that this has been the most disturbing . . . case I have tried in all my years on the bench."

When you drop words from the end of a sentence or omit an entire sentence, the period that ends the sentence appears in its usual place, followed by the three spaced periods that signal the omission:

The judge commented, "It won't surprise you to learn that this has been the most disturbing and the most draining case I have tried. . . ."

Notice that in this case, there is no space between the last word in the sentence and the sentence's period.

2. When *not* to use the ellipsis   When you omit words from the beginning of a quotation, do not use an ellipsis; just begin your quotation at the point you've selected:

The judge commented, "This has been the most disturbing and the most draining case I have tried in all my years on the bench."

(For more on using the ellipsis, see pages 543–544 and 565–566.)

APOSTROPHE (')

1. In place of omitted letters   In standard contractions, an **apostrophe** replaces any omitted letters:

can't, don't, I'm, it's, she's, we've

Apostrophes also replace any letters dropped for the purpose of reproducing casual speech or slang:

"Keep singin' an' marchin'!" he shouted.

2. To indicate possession   To show the possessive form of most *singular nouns,* add *'s*:

The singer**'s** debut was a disaster.

Several of Salinger**'s** books have been banned from high school libraries.

The boss**'s** office was small and poorly lit.

Plural nouns ending in *s* add only an apostrophe to show possession:

Students**'** grades improved after computer-assisted instruction.

Plural nouns that do *not* end in *s* need both an apostrophe and an *s* to show possession:

The children**'s** school was set on fire.

To show *joint possession* (two or more owners of the same thing), make only the last noun possessive:

Lubin and Wachinsky**'s** firm handled the defense.

To show *individual possession* of more than one thing, make each noun possessive:

The girl**'s** and the boy**'s** parents urged them to date other people.

✔ CAUTION

☐ The possessive forms of personal pronouns do *not* include an apostrophe. Here are the correct forms:

mine, yours, his, hers, its, ours, theirs

☐ Note that *its* (*without* an apostrophe) is the *possessive* form of *it*:

Correct   The theater closed *its* [not *it's*] doors last week.

☐ The word *it's* means "it is" or "it has" (the apostrophe takes the place of the omitted letters):

> **Correct**
>
> *It's* [meaning "it is"] cold today.
>
> *It's* [meaning "it has"] been a difficult time for us.
>
> ☐ Similarly, *whose* (*without* an apostrophe) is the possessive form of *who:*
>
> **Correct**   *Whose* [not *who's*] coat is on the table?
>
> ☐ The word *who's* means "who is" or "who has" (the apostrophe takes the place of the omitted letters):
>
> **Correct**
>
> We wonder *who's* [meaning "who is"] going to take her place.
>
> They want to know *who's* [meaning "who has"] been tabulating the results.

Amounts (of time, money, weight, and so on) should also be written in possessive form when appropriate:

Employees can accumulate a maximum of a month**'s** sick leave.

We could buy only five dollars**'** worth of gas.

3. To indicate some plurals   When a letter, symbol, or word treated as a word is made plural, an apostrophe often precedes the final *s:*

I got mostly C**'s** my first semester of college.

Her letters seem to shout; they contain so many !**'s**.

He uses too many *and***'s** to connect one thought to another.

However, common abbreviations such as *VCR, ESP,* and *SAT* don't take the apostrophe in the plural:

The local television station reported that residents sighted three *UFO***s** last summer.

When you refer to a decade, you may omit the apostrophe:

The 1960**s** were turbulent and exciting.

An apostrophe is required only to replace omitted numerals that indicate the century:

The '60s were turbulent and exciting.

☑ CAUTION

☐ Don't, as in the following sentences, use an apostrophe when forming the simple plural of a noun:

Incorrect   The *plant's* (or *plants'*) need to be watered. [delete apostrophe]
Incorrect   The young people played three *radio's* (or *radios'*) at the same time.
              [delete apostrophe]

This kind of error is most likely to occur with a noun that is short
(*plant*) or that ends in a vowel (*radio*). The preceding sentences should
read:

Correct   The *plants* need to be watered.
Correct   The young people played three *radios* at the same time.

☐ Don't, as in the following sentence, use an apostrophe when forming the third-person singular form of the verb:

Incorrect   The television *blare's* all day in many homes.
Correct   The television *blares* all day in many homes.

( )

PARENTHESES ( )

Parentheses enclose subordinate but related ideas, facts, or comments—items
that would unnecessarily interrupt the sentence if set off by commas. A parenthetic remark may be located anywhere in a sentence except at the beginning, but
it should immediately follow the item to which it refers. The presence of parentheses does not otherwise affect a sentence's punctuation. Here are some guidelines
to follow when using parentheses.

**1. A parenthetic sentence between two other sentences or at the end of a para-
graph**   If you place a parenthetic sentence between two other sentences or at the
end of a paragraph, simply write the parenthetic sentence as you normally would;
then enclose it in parentheses. The sentence in parentheses should begin with a
capital letter and end with a period or other end punctuation:

Writing home from summer camp is a chore most youngsters avoid. **(S**ome camps
have children write home once a week.**)** Most parents, though, eagerly await letters
from their kids.

2. At the end of a sentence   Material that extends or illustrates a sentence should be inserted in parentheses at the end of the sentence *before* the closing period. Such parenthetic material shouldn't start with a capital letter. Also, the parenthetic material doesn't have its own period.

> It is a cruel irony that everything I am allergic to is wonderful (like chocolate, roses, and dogs).

> It is a cruel irony that everything I am allergic to is wonderful (for example, I can't get enough of chocolate, roses, and dogs).

3. A parenthetic sentence inside another sentence   When parenthetic material that can stand alone as a full statement occurs within another sentence, the parenthetic material should *not* begin with a capital letter or end with a period:

> Watering a garden the right way (yes, there's a wrong way) is important.

If, however, the parenthetic material is a question, do end it with a question mark:

> Watering a garden the right way (you didn't think there was a wrong way?) is important.

4. After a word that would be followed by a comma   When you insert a parenthetic comment after a word that would otherwise be followed by a comma, move the comma to the end of the parenthetic element:

Original   Without sufficient water, the trees started to lose their leaves in July.
Parenthetic Without sufficient water (only half an inch the whole month), the trees started to lose their leaves in July.

5. Enclosing numbers or letters assigned to items in a series   Use parentheses to enclose the numbers or letters assigned to items in a series. The items in a series are followed by commas:

> Before making a drastic change in your life, you should (1) discuss it with friends, (2) seek the advice of people who have had a similar change, and (3) determine whether a less dramatic change would be sufficient.

> Research indicates that (a) 58% of hospitalized patients improve, (b) 20% stay the same, and (c) 22% get worse.

6. Enclosing inserted dates and organizations' abbreviations   When you add information such as dates and abbreviations to an otherwise complete sentence, enclose this information in parentheses:

> Frank Lloyd Wright (1869–1959) was one of America's foremost architects.

> Angry commuters founded Students for the Abolition of Privileged Parking (SAPP) and vowed to eliminate faculty-only lots.

BRACKETS [ ]

1. To clarify a quotation   When, for the purpose of clarification or correction, you insert your own words into a quotation, enclose them within **brackets:**

> "In its entire history, the mining company [founded 1858] has never experienced a strike," the owner said.

> "Research done at that laboratory [Sci-Tech] is suspect," the physician testified.

Use parentheses, not brackets, to insert a comment within your *own* sentence or paragraph.

2. To signal a linguistic irregularity within a quotation   Quotations sometimes contain linguistic irregularities—such as colloquialisms or errors in spelling, grammar, or usage. In such cases, you may want to follow the irregularity with the Latin term *sic* in brackets, thus indicating that the questionable word or expression appears exactly as used by the quoted writer or speaker:

> "None of the tenents [sic] complained about the building," the landlord wrote in a letter to the housing authority.

(For information about the use of brackets when quoting material in a research paper, see page 543. For more on quotations, see pages 542–544, 565–573, and 676–678.)

HYPHEN (-)

A **hyphen** consists of one short line about the width of a lowercase *n*.

1. To break a word   A word that is too long to fit at the end of a typed line may be divided between two syllables, with a hyphen indicating the break. (Check the dictionary if you're uncertain where the syllables begin and end.)

> Once a clear contest between good and evil, between right and wrong, tele-
> vision wrestling now features stereotype-defying and ambiguous protag-
> onists.

Most word-processing programs automatically either break long words at the end of lines or move them to the next line (called "word wrapping").

2. To combine words into an adjective or noun   When you combine two or more words to form a new adjective or noun, use hyphens between the original words:

> The question is whether this country should maintain first-strike capability.

The only exception is a compound adjective that contains an adverb ending in *ly*. In this case, don't place a hyphen after the *ly:*

> The poorly constructed VCR jammed within the week.

In a series of hyphenated compound adjectives or nouns all having the same final word, write that word only at the end of the series:

> First-, second-, and third-year students must take one semester of gym.

3. Between a combined number and word   Hyphenate a numeral combined with a word:

> The new car has a 2.6-liter engine.

4. After certain prefixes   Compound words beginning in *self* or *ex* take a hyphen after the prefix:

> My ex-roommate is self-employed as a computer consultant.

So do words that, without the hyphen, would be misread as other words.

> A growing number of young professionals live in co-ops.

5. To write certain numbers   Use a hyphen when writing most numbers composed of two words:

> The zoning ordinance outlines twenty-one restrictions.

Note, however, that two-word numbers like *one hundred* and *two thousand* don't take a hyphen.

A hyphen is required when a fraction is used as a compound modifier:

> The class was almost one-half empty.

(For more on writing numbers, see pages 690–692 of the Handbook.)

DASH (--)

A **dash** (—) is composed of two typed hyphens (--). Don't leave a space between the hyphens or between the words that precede or follow the dash.

To highlight a thought or idea   A dash *signals* an *added* or *interrupting thought* and, unlike parentheses, highlights that thought. When the added thought occurs at the sentence's end, it is preceded by a single dash:

The package finally arrived--badly damaged.

When the added thought occurs midsentence, it receives two dashes, one before the added thought and another after:

The ambassador--after serving for more than two decades--suddenly resigned her post.

PRACTICE: CORRECTING PROBLEMS WITH PUNCTUATION

Correct any punctuation problems that you find in the following sentences. Be careful, though; some of the punctuation marks belong just where they are.

1. The New Madrid fault, which lies in the central part of the country will be the site of a major earthquake within the next thirty years.

2. In the children's story, the hero carries a fresh, yellow rose rather than a sword.

3. I asked "Wasn't Uncle Pete drafted into the army in 1943?"

4. "Branch offices, and drive-in windows," the bank president announced, "will be closed January 4, the day of the governors funeral".

5. Some people avoid physical work; others seek out, and enjoy it. But, probably no one likes it all the time.

6. The scientists said that "they wondered how anyone could believe stories of outer-space visitors."

7. On one of the office's paneled wall's the executive had a framed copy of the poem, *If.*

8. Many children collect stamps according to a theme, like wildlife, aeronautics, or sports, but adults usually prefer to collect on the basis of stamps' rarity.

9. Shoplifters often believe they are doing no harm; nevertheless shoplifting is stealing and therefore, illegal.

10. The young people fell in love with the house, that stood next to a clear cold stream.

11. The kennel owner sent birthday cards' and small gifts to all the dog's she had boarded during the year.

12. The polished floor in the hallway, and dining room lost it's sheen after only a week.

13. According to the lawyer, the property is clearly ours' and not the other family's.

14. The celebration was loud, and unruly; finally police arrived at the scene around 11:00 p.m..

15. The parents know it's too early to tell whose children will need tutoring.

16. Did the visiting journalist make her speech, "Preserving a Source's Confidentiality?"

17. In the student handbook, the Dean wrote, "A student may be suspended for any of the following; using drugs, plagiarizing papers, cheating on exams, vandalizing college property..."

18. They asked us what courses we planned to take during the summer?

19. In the closet, (which hadn't been opened for years) we found three baseball bats, and half a dozen badminton sets.

20. Who's notes will you borrow to study for tomorrows exam.

MECHANICS

cap

CAPITALIZATION

Always capitalize the pronoun *I* and the first word of a sentence. Following are other **capitalization** guidelines.

1. Proper names   Whether they appear in noun, adjective, or possessive form, proper names are always capitalized. **Proper names** include the following: names of individuals; countries, states, regions, and cities; political, racial, and religious groups; languages; institutions and organizations; days, months, and holidays; historical periods; product brand names; fully specified academic degrees (Master's of Science in Chemistry); and particular academic courses. Here are some examples:

> *Representative O'Dwyer,* a *Democrat* from the *Midwest,* introduced several bills in *Congress* last *March.*

> According to my *Marketing 101* professor, *Cuddles Cat Chow* set new sales records in the *Southwest.*

> All *Buddhists* are vegetarians.

> *Latin* and *Greek* regained widespread popularity during the *Renaissance.*

Do not capitalize the names of ideologies and philosophies, such as *communism* and *idealism* (unless the name is derived from that of an individual—for example, *Marxism*). Similarly, avoid capitalizing compass directions, unless the direction serves as the name of a region (the *West,* the *Northeast*) or is attached to the name of a continent, country, or city (*North America, South Angola, West Philadelphia*).

Finally, don't capitalize the following: seasons; animal breeds (unless part of the name is derived from that of a place—such as *French poodle* and *Labrador retriever*); types of academic degrees (*bachelor's, master's, doctorate*); or academic subjects and areas (*sociology, mathematics*), unless they're part of a course title or department name (*Sociology I, Mathematics Department*). Here are some more examples:

On one side of the Continental Divide, rivers flow *east;* on the other, they flow *west.*

In San Francisco, there is little temperature variation between *spring* and *summer.*

Only one professor in the Psychology Department doesn't have a *doctorate.*

2. Titles of literary and other artistic works   When writing a title, capitalize the first word and all other words, except articles (*a, an, the*), conjunctions (*and, but*), and prepositions (*on, to*) of fewer than five letters.

In *The Structure of Scientific Revolutions,* Thomas Kuhn discusses the way the scientific establishment resists innovation. However, Anna Stahl disputes Kuhn's argument in *The Controversy Over Scientific Conservatism.*

3. Official and personal titles   Capitalize official and personal titles when they precede a name or are used in place of the name of a specific person:

Only *Reverend* Zager could stretch a sermon to an hour and a half.

President Clinton met with the Japanese delegation.

Weeks before Father's Day, the stores start featuring gifts for *Dad.*

Do not capitalize such titles otherwise:

The *reverend* encouraged the congregation to donate food and clothing to the poor.

We elect the *president* of the United States every four years.

His *dad* writes for the local paper.

UNDERLINING AND ITALICS

ital

In machine-printed text, ***italicizing*** (*slanted type*) serves the same purposes as **underlining.**

1. Titles of individual works   Underline or italicize the titles of works that are published individually—not as part of a magazine, anthology, or other collection. Such works are often lengthy—entire books, magazines, journals, newspapers, movies, television programs, musical recordings, plays, and so on. They may, however, also be works of visual art, such as paintings and sculptures. Here are some examples:

When I was a child, my favorite book was <u>At the Back of the North Wind</u>.

The movie critic panned <u>Friday the 13th</u>, <u>Part 83</u>.

Titled <u>The Lost</u>, the sculpture looks like a giant staple.

However, titles of certain historical documents and major religious writings, such as the books of the Bible, are neither italicized nor enclosed in quotation marks, but important words begin with a capital letter:

the Bible	Declaration of Independence
Song of Solomon	Bill of Rights
Old Testament	U.S. Constitution
the Koran	Monroe Doctrine

(See page 678 of the Handbook for ways to designate the titles of short works like poems and short stories.)

2. Foreign terms   Foreign words not fully incorporated into mainstream English should be underlined or italicized:

Before protesters knew what was happening the legislation was a <u>fait accompli</u>.

3. For emphasis   Underline or italicize words you wish to stress, but do so sparingly because too many italicized words actually weaken emphasis:

The campaign staff will <u>never</u> allow the candidate to appear in an open forum.

4. Letters and numbers referred to as words   Underline or italicize letters or numbers when they function as words:

In the local high school, teachers give <u>A</u>'s and <u>B</u>'s only to outstanding students.

5. Calling attention to a word's use   To call attention to the way a word is being used, you may underline or italicize it:

Why use <u>conflagration</u> when a simple word like <u>fire</u> will do?

The most common prepositions are <u>at</u>, <u>for</u> and <u>to</u>.

(See page 678 of the Handbook for another way to highlight words.)

6. Vehicles of transportation   Underline or italicize the names of ships, planes, trains, and spacecraft:

A design flaw led to the explosion of the space-shuttle <u>Challenger</u>.

num

NUMBERS

1. When to use words   Generally, *words* instead of numerals are used for **numbers** that can be written out in *one* or *two words*. When written out, numbers between 21 and 99 (except round numbers) are hyphenated (*twenty-one; ninety-nine*). If the number requires *three or more words*, use *numerals;* a hyphenated number counts as one word. Also use words for any number that occurs at the start of a sentence:

The store manager came up with *three* fresh ideas for attracting more customers.

They retired when they were only *forty-five.*

The paper reported that more than *six hundred* birds died in the forest fire.

Two hundred forty-eight people were on the hijacked plane.

You may prefer to rephrase a sentence that begins with a long number, so that you can use numerals instead of words:

The hijacked plane had *248* people on board.

2. When to use numerals   Numerals are generally used to indicate measurements:

The office was approximately *10 feet, 8 inches* wide.

Dates, times, addresses, page numbers, decimals, and percentages are also usually given as numerals. When a date includes the day as well as the month and year, give only the numeral to identify the day (for example, write *March 4,* not *March 4th; May 2,* not *May 2nd*):

The builder claims that the wood delivered on *August 3, 1989,* was defective.

Use numerals when a time reference contains *a.m.* or *p.m.* or specifies the minutes as well as the hour:

We set the alarm for *5 a.m.* and left the house by *5:45.*

However, use words with *o'clock:*

My roommate has trouble getting up before *eleven o'clock* in the morning.

In addresses, the house or building number is always given in numerals:

Last weekend, I visited my childhood home at *80 Manemet Road.*

For a numbered street, use numerals unless the number is less than ten or the building and street numbers would be written next to each other—a potential source of confusion:

The shelter moved from 890 East 47th Street to *56 Second Avenue.*

Always give page numbers as numerals. It's also standard to give percentages and decimal amounts in numerals:

Sales increased *5%* last year.

More than *2.5 million* boxes of oat bran were sold last year.

He lost *0.007 pounds* on the supposedly miraculous new diet.

---

ab

ABBREVIATIONS

1. Personal and professional titles   The **abbreviations** for some personal titles appear *before* the person's name:

Dr. Tony Michelin   *Ms.* Carla Schim

Others come *after*:

Houston J. Marshall, *Esq.*   Nora Rubin, *MD*

Professional titles such as *Professor, Senator,* and *Governor* may be abbreviated only before a full name:

Prof. Eleanor Cross   Rep. George M. Dolby
Professor Cross   Representative Dolby

2. Common terms and organizations   Use the standard initials for common terms and widely known organizations:

VCR	MTV	AIDS
CIA	UFO	ESP
FBI	NATO	AT&T

Notice that these abbreviations do not include periods.

The first time you refer to a less familiar organization, give its full name, followed by the abbreviation in parentheses. Thereafter, you may refer to the organization with only the abbreviation. If the organization uses an ampersand (&) for *and* or abbreviations for terms such as *Incorporated* (Inc.) and *Company* (Co.), you may use them as well.

3. Time   Use the Latin abbreviations *a.m.* (*ante meridiem*) and *p.m.* (*post meridiem*) for time of day:

They started work at *4 a.m.* and got home at *6:15 p.m.*

Use numerals with the abbreviations *AD* (*anno Domini*—"in the year of the Lord"), *BC* ("before Christ"), *CE* (the common era), and *BCE* (before the common era), unless you refer to centuries rather than specific years. In that case, write out the century before the abbreviation:

The pottery was made around *AD 56,* but the tools date back to the *third century BC.*

Note that the year precedes BC (*684 BC*) but follows AD (*AD 1991*).

4. Latin terms   If you use the Latin abbreviations *i.e.* (for "that is") and *e.g.* (for "for example"), remember that they should be followed by a comma and used parenthetically:

Employees are enthusiastic about recent trends in the business world (*e.g.,* the establishment of on-site day-care programs and fitness centers).

Whenever possible, however, replace these abbreviations with their English equivalents.

In addition, try to avoid *etc.* ("and so on") by citing all examples you have in mind, instead of leaving them up to the reader's imagination.

5. Names of regions   Except in addresses, don't abbreviate geographic regions:

With a student rail pass, you can tour *Great Britain* [not *G.B.*] at discount rates.

Exceptions to this rule include *Washington, D.C.,* and *U.S.* when it is used as a modifier (*U.S. policy,* for example).

In addresses, states' names are abbreviated according to the postal designations—with two capital letters and no periods:

NY   RI   NJ

6. Units of measure   Don't abbreviate common units of measure:

The bedroom was *15 feet, 9-1/2 inches* wide.

Among other extravagances, the couple offered guests *ten pounds* of imported caviar.

However, do abbreviate such technical units of measure as millimeters (*mm.*) and revolutions per minute (*rpm*).

(Turn to page 697 for a practice exercise on mechanics.)

SPELLING

SPELLING

Spelling need not be a mystery. For reference, always have on hand a recent standard dictionary or a spelling dictionary. If you use a word processor, an automatic "spell check" program may be valuable. Another strategy is to keep a personal inventory of the words you misspell or need to look up repeatedly (see page 134 for instructions). Finally, knowing about basic spelling rules and commonly misspelled words can help you minimize spelling errors. Here are some guidelines you should find helpful.

1. When *i* and *e* are adjacent Do you remember the familiar rhyme for spelling a word with an adjacent *i* and *e*?

i before *e*	except after *c*	or when pronounced like *a* as in *neighbor* and *weigh*
achieve	ceiling	beige
piece	conceited	freight
thief	deceive	reign
yield	receive	their

The rule does *not* apply if the *i* and *e* are in separate syllables: *science, society*. It also does not apply to the following exceptions:

caffeine	inveigle	seize
either	leisure	sleight
financier	neither	species
foreign	protein	weird

2. Doubling the final consonant   This rule applies to words that satisfy the following conditions:

- The word's last three letters must be consonant, vowel, consonant *and*
- The word must be either one syllable (*plan*) or accented on the final syllable (*control*).

In such cases, double the final consonant before adding an ending that begins with a vowel (such as *-ed, -er, -al,* and *-ing*):

plan/plan**ned**   control/controll**er**
refer/refer**ral**   begin/begin**ning**

However, do *not* double the final consonant in the following cases:

- Words that end in a silent *e* (*pave/paved, mope/moping*)*
- Words ending in two vowels and a consonant or in two consonants (*appear/appearance, talk/talking*)
- Words whose accent is not on the final syllable (*develop/developing*)
- Words that no longer are accented on the final syllable when the ending is added (*refer/reference, prefer/preferable*). An exception is the word *questionnaire*, which does contain a double *n*.

3. Dropping the final silent *e*

For a word that ends in a silent (not pronounced separately) *e*, drop the *e* before adding an ending that begins with a vowel:

cope/cop**ing**   receive/receiv**able**
cute/cut**est**   guide/guid**ance**

But keep the *e* before an ending beginning with a consonant:

sincere/sincer**ely**   base/bas**ement**
definite/definit**ely**   nine/nin**ety**

Exceptions include the following: *truly, awful, argument; dyeing* and *singeing* (to avoid confusion with *dying* and *singing*); *changeable, courageous, manageable, noticeable,* and similar words where the final *e* is needed to keep the sound of the *g* or *c* soft.

4. Adding to words that end in *y*   For most words ending in *y*, change the *y* to *ie* before adding an *s*:

city/cit**ies**   study/stud**ies**   story/stor**ies**

---

*An exception is *write/written*. Note, however, that the *-ing* form of *write* is *writing*, not *writting*.

Change the *y* to *i* before all other endings, except *-ing:*

copy/cop**ies**   cry/cr**ies**   study/stud**ies**

The *y* remains when the ending is *-ing:*

cop**ying**   cr**ying**   stud**ying**

The *y* also stays when it is preceded by a vowel:

delay/dela**ys**/dela**yed**/dela**ying**

5. Words ending in *-f* and *-fe*   Words ending in *-f* and *-fe* normally change to *-ves* in the plural:

leaf/lea**ves**   life/li**ves**
knife/kni**ves**   wife/wi**ves**

An exception is ***roof,*** whose plural simply adds an *-s.*

6. Common spelling errors   **Homonyms** are words that sound alike but have different spellings and meanings. (A spelling dictionary will provide a complete list of homonyms and other commonly confused words.) If you're not sure of the differences in meaning between any of the homonym pairs listed, check your dictionary. Here are a few of the most troublesome:

accept/except	knew/new	their/there/they're
affect/effect	lose/loose	to/too/two
complement/compliment	principal/principle	whose/who's
its/it's	than/then	your/you're

Cognates are words with the same root. However, they may not always have the same spelling:

curious/curiosity   disaster/disastrous
generous/generosity   four/forty

Some words contain *silent* (or nearly silent) *letters* that are often erroneously omitted when the word is spelled:

environment   sophomore
February   supposed to
government   used to
library

Finally, avoid *nonexistent forms* of words. For example, there is no such word as *its'; a lot* is two words, not one; and few instructors consider *alright* an acceptable variant of *all right.*

PRACTICE: CORRECTING PROBLEMS WITH MECHANICS AND SPELLING

Correct any mechanics or spelling problems that you find in the following sentences. Be careful, though; not every sentence contains an error, and some sentences may contain more than one.

1. "Emerging Nations in today's World," one of the supplementary texts in Modern History I, is on reserve at the libary.

2. Last year, while visiting my parents in central Florida, I took a disastrous coarse in Sociology.

3. The analysts of the election-eve pole concluded, "Its a toss-up."

4. For some reason, Spring tends to have a depressing affect on me.

5. Rev. Astor's teeth chattered at my brother's outdoor wedding, held in March in Northern Massachusetts.

6. Weighing in at 122 lbs. was Tim Fox, a sophmore from a community college in Ala.

7. In the fall, when the foliage is at it's peek, many people pack their hiking gear and head for the country.

8. 300 students signed up for the experimental seminar that Prof. Julia Cruz plans to offer through the Business Department. The class is scheduled to meet at eight a.m. on Monday.

9. Senator Miller, who was suppose to end the press conference once the subject of the enviroment came up, got embroiled in an arguement with several reporters.

10. Listen to nutritionists; many of them contend that their are advantages to limiting the amount of protein in you're diet.

11. My roommate, who's native language is French, recieved an award for writting a provocative series of articles on student pressures.

12. The President of the company distributed to key management 30 copies of the book How To win in Business. Many employees, though, are offended by the books emphasis on what it calls economic opportunism.

13. My parents always reminded me to watch my p's and q's. Not surprisingly, they were frequently complemented on my good behavior.

14. In the South during the summer months, it is light well after nine o'clock in the evening.

15. Prof. Mohr excepts no if's, and's, or but's when a student tries to hand in a paper past it's due date.

ACKNOWLEDGMENTS

Angelou, Maya. "Sister Flowers." From *I Know Why the Caged Bird Sings* by Maya Angelou. Copyright © 1969 and renewed 1997 by Maya Angelou. Reprinted by permission of Random House, Inc.

Angier, Natalie. "A Granddaughter's Fear." From *The New York Times*, May 7, 1989. Copyright © 1989 by The New York Times. Reprinted by permission.

Baker, Russell. "Selling the Post." Reprinted from *Growing Up* by Russell Baker, © 1982. Used with permission of Congdon and Weed, Inc., and NTC/Contemporary Publishing Group, Inc.

Bishop, Elizabeth. "The Fish." From *The Complete Poems 1927–1979* by Elizabeth Bishop. Copyright © 1979, 1983 by Alice Helen Methfessel. Reprinted by permission of Farrar, Straus & Giroux, Inc.

Bruck, David. "The Death Penalty." Reprinted by permission of *The New Republic*, © 1985, The New Republic, Inc.

Ciardi, John. "Dawn Watch." From *Manner of Speaking* by John Ciardi. Reprinted by permission of the Ciardi Family.

Cole, Diane. "Don't Just Stand There." From *The New York Times*, 1982. Reprinted by permission of the author.

Cole, K. C. "Entropy." From *The New York Times*, March 18, 1982. Copyright © 1982 by The New York Times. Reprinted by permission.

Darley, John M., and Bibb Latané. "Why People Don't Help in a Crisis." From *Psychology Today*, December 1968. Reprinted with permission from Psychology Today Magazine, Copyright © 1968 (Sussex Publishers, Inc.).

Douglas, Susan. "Managing Mixed Messages." From *Where the Girls Are* by Susan Douglas. Copyright © 1994 by Susan J. Douglas. Reprinted by permission of Times Books, a division of Random House, Inc.

Garity, Joyce. "Is Sex All That Matters?" Reprinted by permission of Joyce Garity.

Gibbs, Nancy. "When Is It Rape?" From *Time*, June 3, 1991. © 1991 Time Inc. Reprinted by permission.

Goodman, Ellen. "Family Counterculture." From *Value Judgements* by Ellen Goodman. © 1993, The Boston Globe Newspaper Co./Washington Post Writers Group. Reprinted with permission.

Greenfield, Meg. "Why Nothing Is 'Wrong' Anymore." From *Newsweek*, July 28, 1986. Copyright © 1986 Newsweek, Inc. Reprinted by permission, all rights reserved.

Hamill, Peter. "Crack and the Box." From *Piecework* by Peter Hamill. Copyright © 1996 by Deidre Enterprises Inc. By permission of Little, Brown and Company.

Hughes, Langston. "Early Autumn." From *Short Stories* by Langston Hughes. Copyright © 1996 by Ramona Bass and Arnold Rampersad. Reprinted by permission of Hill and Wang, a division of Farrar, Straus & Giroux, Inc.

Koch, Ed. "Death and Justice." Reprinted by permission of *The New Republic*, © 1985, The New Republic, Inc.

Kupfer, Fern. "Institution Is Not a Dirty Word." From "My Turn" column of *Newsweek*, December 13, 1982. Reprinted by permission of Fern Kupfer.

Leo, John. "Absolutophobia." From *U.S. News & World Report,* July 21, 1997. Copyright, July 21, 1997, *U.S. News & World Report.*

Lindbergh, Anne Morrow. "The Channeled Whelk." From *Gift from the Sea* by Anne Morrow Lindbergh. Copyright © 1955, 1975 by Anne Morrow Lindbergh. Reprinted by permission of Pantheon Books, a division of Random House, Inc.

Lorde, Audre. "The Fourth of July." Reprinted with permission from "The Fourth of July" in *Zami: A New Spelling of My Name* by Audre Lorde. © 1982. Published by The Crossing Press: Freedom, CA.

Lycos home page. © 1998 Lycos, Inc. Lycos® is a registered trademark of Carnegie Mellon University. All rights reserved.

Malcolm X. "My First Conk." From *The Autobiography of Malcolm X* by Malcolm X with the assistance of Alex Haley. Copyright © 1964 by Malcolm X and Alex Haley. Copyright © 1965 by Alex Haley and Betty Shabazz. Reprinted by permission of Random House, Inc.

McClintock, Ann. "Propaganda Techniques in Today's Advertising." Reprinted by permission of Ann McClintock.

Morrison, Toni. "A Slow Walk of Trees." From *The New York Times,* July 4, 1976. Reprinted by permission of International Creative Management, Inc. Copyright © 1976 by Toni Morrison.

Orwell, George. "Shooting an Elephant." From *Shooting an Elephant and Other Essays* by George Orwell, copyright 1950 by Sonia Brownell Orwell and renewed 1978 by Sonia Pitt-Rivers, reprinted by permission of Harcourt Brace & Company.

Rhodes, Richard. "Watching the Animals." Copyright © 1971 by Richard Rhodes. Originally published in *Harper's.* Reprinted by permission of the author.

Rivers, Caryl. "What Should Be Done about Rock Lyrics?" Reprinted by permission of Caryl Rivers.

Schlesinger, Arthur, Jr. "The Cult of Ethnicity: Good and Bad." From *Time,* July 8, 1991. © 1991 Time Inc. Reprinted by permission.

Staples, Brent. "Black Men and Public Space." Reprinted by permission of Brent Staples.

Suina, Joseph. "And Then I Went to School." From *Linguistic and Cultural Influences on Learning Mathematics* by Cocking and Mestre. Reprinted by permission of Joseph Suina and Lawrence Erlbaum Associates, Inc.

Tannen, Deborah. "But What Do You Mean?" From *Talking from 9 to 5* by Deborah Tannen. Copyright © 1994 by Deborah Tannen. Reprinted by permission of William Morrow & Company, Inc.

White, E. B. "Once More to the Lake." From *One Man's Meat,* text copyright © 1941 by E. B. White. Reprinted by permission of Tilbury House, Publishers, Gardiner, Maine.

Woolf, Virginia. "The Death of the Moth." From *The Death of the Moth and Other Essays* by Virginia Woolf, copyright 1942 by Harcourt Brace & Company and renewed 1970 by Marjorie T. Parsons, Executrix, reprinted by permission of the publisher.

Yahoo! home page and Disability Legal Issues page. Courtesy of Yahoo! Inc.

Yuh, Ji-Yeon. "Let's Tell the Story of All America's Cultures." From the *Philadelphia Inquirer,* June 30, 1991. Reprinted with permission from the *Philadelphia Inquirer.*

INDEX

Quotations *(continued)*
conclusions using, 81
direct, 193–194, 197, 199, 200, 274, 676–678
ellipses with, 543–544, 679
humorous or ironic use, 678
indirect, 676
interrupted, 572, 676–678
introductions using, 78
in literary analysis, 610–611
MLA documentation of, 565–572
near-quotes, 548–549
in note-taking, 542–544, 546–548
in other quotations, 572–573
plagiarism, 546–548
punctuation in, 570–572, 677–678
in research paper, 542–549, 565–572
sample note cards of, 541, 546–548
single, 572–573
source within a source, 572–573
statistics, 573

Random sample, in surveying, 502–503
Raw material, generating, 19, 27–31, 45–46, 305, 379
Readers' Guide to Periodical Literature, 514–515, 517, 519
Reading process, 3–11
model selection, 6–9
questions for evaluating essays, 5–6
steps in effective reading, 4–6
Reasoning. *See* Logic
Redundancy, 106–107
Reference books, list of common, 512–513
Reference, pronoun, 660–662

Reference section in library, 505, 512–513
"References" list, in APA format, 578–579
Refutation, 446–447, 460–464
Relative clauses, 109–110, 111, 640–641
Relative pronouns, 640–641
Remote causes, 373–374
Repeated words, 75
Repetition, for emphasis, 106–107
Research, conducting
activities for, 550–552
and bibliography, working, 532–533, 535–538
card catalog and, 509–510
evaluating sources, 534–535
Humanities Index and, 515
interviews and, 501–502
in library, 507–532
note-taking and, 533–549
plagiarism and, 534, 542, 546–548
preliminary, 505–506
primary, 501–504
Readers' Guide to Periodical Literature and, 514–515, 517, 519
schedule for, 507
secondary, 501
Social Sciences Index and, 515
survey, 501–502
Research paper
activities for, 597–598
APA format for, 565, 576–580
attributions in, 567–568
checklist for subject selection, 504–505
checklist, revising, 575–576
documentation of, 553, 556–563, 565–570
APA, 565, 576–580
authorship, 556–559, 568–569
MLA, 556–563, 565–569
draft of, writing, 563–564

limiting subject of, 505
note-taking for, 533–549
outline for, 553, 554–556, 584–586
plagiarism and, 534, 542, 546–548, 565–573
planning, 500–507
purpose of, 499–500
quotations in, 542–549, 565–572
research stages for, 500, 553
revising, editing, and proofreading, 553, 574–576
sample, 581–597
schedule for, 507
statistics in, 539–540, 573
subject of, choosing, 504–505
supporting points in, 554–556
thesis of, 506
Works Cited list in, 553, 556–563
Restrictive clauses, 112, 670
Revising. *See also* Revising activities; Revising checklists
argumentation-persuasion, 455–456, 465
of body paragraphs, 166–167, 201, 237–238, 384–386, 416–417
cause-effect, 377–378, 384–386
comparison contrast, 341–342, 348–349
conclusions, 274–275, 311
definition, 410–411, 416–417
description, 160–161, 166–167
division-classification, 266–267, 274–275
of exam essays, 629
illustration, 230–231, 237–238
introductions, 101, 128–129, 274–275, 348–349, 465
in literary analysis, 611–612
narration, 195–196, 201

THE MACMILLAN WRITER

Instructor's Manual

FOURTH EDITION

JUDITH NADELL

LINDA McMENIMAN
Rowan University

JOHN LANGAN
Atlantic Community College

ALLYN AND BACON

Boston   London   Toronto   Sydney   Tokyo   Singapore

Printed in the United States of America

10 9 8 7 6 5 4 3 2 1   04 03 02 01 00 99

CONTENTS

SETS OF THEMATICALLY RELATED ESSAYS

Throughout *The Macmillan Writer*, a number of assignments relate two or more essays by theme. In the book, all such assignments are marked with a special symbol (   ). These assignments encourage students to make connections between essays, giving them a richer background of material to draw on in their writing. Instructors wishing to stress themes and recurrent ideas will find these assignments especially helpful. All essays thematically related in this way are shown below as sets, under appropriate theme headings.

Communication and Language

Managing Mixed Messages (247) / Sister Flowers (175) / But What Do You Mean? (283) / When Is It Rape? (423)

Is Sex All That Matters? (252) / Propaganda Techniques in Today's Advertising (277) / Crack and the Box (356) / What Should We Do About Rock Lyrics? (473)

Is Sex All That Matters? (252) / Propaganda Techniques in Today's Advertising (277)

Propaganda Techniques in Today's Advertising (277) / Don't Just Stand There (315) / Crack and the Box (356) / Why People Don't Help in a Crisis (392)

When Is It Rape? (423) / What Should We Do About Rock Lyrics? (473)

Ethics and Morality

Once More to the Lake (169) / A Granddaughter's Fear (388)

Shooting an Elephant (203) / My First Conk (321)

Shooting an Elephant (203) / Selling the Post (214) / A Granddaughter's Fear (388)

The Fourth of July (210) /Shooting an Elephant (203) / A Granddaughter's Fear (388)

The Fourth of July (210) / Managing Mixed Messages (247) / Black Men and Public Space (398) / When Is It Rape? (423)

Why Nothing Is "Wrong" Anymore (290) / Institution Is Not a Dirty Word (470)

Why Nothing Is "Wrong" Anymore (290) / Absolutophobia (429)

Why Nothing Is "Wrong" Anymore (290) / Why People Don't Help in a Crisis (392)

Don't Just Stand There (315) / Why People Don't Help in a Crisis (392)

Watching the Animals (324) / Shooting an Elephant (203)

Family and Children

Government and Law

Human Groups and Societies

Meaning in Life

Memories and Autobiography

THEMATIC CONTENTS

Family and Children

Government and Law

Health and Medicine

Human Groups and Societies

Humor and Satire

Meaning in Life

COLLABORATIVE AND/OR PROBLEM-SOLVING ACTIVITIES

Exercises and activities on the following pages encourage students to work together to tackle a variety of rhetorical tasks. In addition, many writing assignments for the professional selections lend themselves to group work.

TEACHING COMPOSITION WITH
THE MACMILLAN WRITER

Teaching offers many pleasures. Among the foremost, for us, is the chance to get together with colleagues for some shoptalk. Trading ideas, airing classroom problems, sharing light moments, speculating about why some assignments set off fireworks and others fizzle—all of this helps us in our day-to-day teaching.

In this Instructor's Manual, we would like to share with you some thoughts about teaching freshman composition and about using *The Macmillan Writer*. We'll explain our approach for introducing each pattern of development and indicate what we emphasize when discussing the professional essays in each section. We'll provide suggested answers to the activities that conclude each of the writing process chapters and to the prewriting and revising activities that follow the introductions to the patterns of development. We'll also offer suggested answers to the "Questions for Close Reading" and "Questions About the Writer's Craft" found after each professional essay. These responses aren't meant to be definitive. Although we purposely avoided open-ended, anything-goes questions, we intend the responses to represent *our* views only. You may not agree with all our interpretations. That's fine. If nothing else, our answers may suggest another way of viewing an essay.

At the Start of the Course

Frankly, many students dread freshman composition—a bitter pill to swallow for those of us who have made the teaching of writing our life's work. But it's important to understand that many students' past experiences with writing have not been positive. Rather than trying to pretend that all our students are pleased about being in a writing class, we work to get out in the open any unhappiness they may have about writing and writing teachers.

Here's how we go about airing any negative feelings that may exist. On the first day of class, we acknowledge students' feelings by saying something like this: "I guess some of you wish that you didn't have to take this course. In fact, you may feel that the only thing worse would be having to take a course in public speaking." Our remark elicits smiles of self-recognition from many students, and the whole class seems to relax a bit. Then, we ask students to talk about why they have such uneasy feelings about taking a writing course. Many have sad tales to tell about previous writing classes and writing teachers. Here are summaries of some of the comments we've heard over the years.

— In the past, my papers were returned so covered with red ink that I could barely make out my own writing. I felt discouraged to see how much I had done wrong and angry to see my work covered over with comments.

— I could never figure out what my teachers wanted. Different teachers seemed to look for different things. Since there were no clear standards, I've never understood the qualities that make up good writing.

— Writing papers always took me too much time and felt like an endless chore. Getting a first draft done was hard enough, but revising was even worse. And the payoff for writing several drafts didn't seem worth the effort.

— I knew in my head what I wanted to say but didn't know how to get my thoughts down on paper. My ideas never came out quite right.

— I had writer's block whenever I sat down to put pen to paper. I started at the desk, daydreamed, fidgeted, and had real trouble getting started. Finally, just before an assignment was due, I dashed off something to hand in, just to get it over with.

As such sentiments are aired, students discover that their experience has not been unique; they learn that others in class have had similar frustrating experiences. In addition, we tell the class that each semester many of our students recount comparable sagas of woe. We reassure the class that we understand the obstacles, both inner and outer, that they have to face when writing. And, we tell them that we will work to make the freshman writing course as positive an experience as possible. But we also say that we'd be dishonest if we told them that writing is easy. It isn't. And, unfortunately, we have no magic formula for turning them into A-plus writers. On the other hand, because we are writers and because we work with writers, we know that the composing processes can be satisfying and rewarding. We tell the class that we hope they'll come to share our feelings as the semester progresses.

From here, we move to an activity that continues the ice breaking while also familiarizing the class with the workshop format we use frequently during the semester. Students form groups of two and then four, chatting with each other for about five minutes each time. To get them moving, we put some questions on the board: what are their names, where are they from, where are they living while attending college, what other courses are they taking, what is their intended major, and so on. After a few seconds of nervous silence, the class begins to buzz with friendly energy.

When ten minutes or so have passed, we stop the activity and explain why we have devoted some precious class time to socializing. During the semester, we explain, the class will often meet in small groups and respond to each other's work, learning a good deal from each other about writing as they do so. So it makes sense for them to get to know each other a bit right at the outset. Also, we explain our hope that they will find sharing their writing as interesting and enjoyable as chatting together. Then, as a final step in building a spirit of community, we create a class phone directory by circulating a piece of paper on which all the students write their names and phone numbers. Before the next class, we have the sheet typed and reproduced so that everyone can have a copy.

Assigning the First Chapters in the Book

During the first or second class, we emphasize to students that the course should help them become sharper readers as well as stronger writers. With that in mind, we assign the chapter on "The Reading Process" before moving on to work on the writing process.

When students come to class having read the reading chapter, we answer any questions they may have and go over the "Questions for Close Reading" and "Questions About the Writer's Craft" that follow the selection from Ellen Goodman (see page 19 of this manual).

After this discussion of reading, we begin introducing the writing process, explaining how helpful it is for a writer to break down the task of writing into stages. We've found that many students have never viewed writing as a process, and our explanation of the steps is a great revelation to them. We are careful to emphasize that not everyone writes the same way; we explain that, after trying out our recommendations about each stage of the process, students will most likely vary the process in a way that works best for them. We then assign the first part of Chapter 2, "Getting Started Through Prewriting" (up to "Discovering Your Essay's Limited Subject"). In the next class, we discuss and practice prewriting. We tell the class that prewriting loosens a writer up. Exploratory and tentative, prewriting helps reduce the anxiety many people feel when facing the blank page. With prewriting, a writer doesn't have to worry, "This better be good." After all, no one except the writer is going to read the prewritten material. We work briefly with activities, such as Activities 1 and 3 at the end of Chapter 2, but we tell our students that the best way for them to discover what prewriting is like is for them to try it for themselves. So, we say, "Let's suppose you had to write an essay on why students dislike English classes or what teachers could do to make English courses more interesting." Then, we ask them to select one prewriting technique discussed in the book (questioning the subject, brainstorming, freewriting, or mapping) to generate the raw material for such an essay. Often, we distribute scrap paper or yellow lined paper for them to use, reinforcing the message that prewriting is tentative and vastly different from finished work. Instructors who ask students to keep a journal might instead have them write a first journal entry in class.

At the end of the class, we ask students to save the prewriting just prepared in class for possible use as the basis for an essay later in the term. And we assign the rest of the prewriting chapter and an additional end-of-chapter activity; we also ask them to begin keeping a journal.

In the next class, we finish the discussion of prewriting and work again in class on getting familiar with the various prewriting techniques. After this, we introduce the patterns of development as invaluable aids to the writing process, from prompting ideas to organizing them coherently to easing the flow during the writing of a draft. For the next class, we assign either Chapter 11, "Description," or Chapter 12, "Narration," as the first in-depth study of a pattern of development. We have found both patterns invaluable in helping beginning writers attend to detail, discover appropriate sequencing, and become aware of the reader's needs. Throughout the course, we alternate in-depth study of the stages of the writing process with work on the patterns of development. And we frequently have students reach back to material generated in the early prewriting sessions and, after feedback from other students, use it as the basis for more polished work.

Ways to Use the Book

The Macmillan Writer is arranged in six sections; most writing courses will emphasize Part Two, the nine chapters on the writing process, and Part Three, covering the nine patterns of development: description, narration, illustration, division-classification, process, comparison-contrast, cause-effect, definition, and argumentation-persuasion. The study of the writing process can be handled in at least two ways. You might wish to spread in-depth work on each of the writing process steps through the semester, while also assigning professional selections and discussing some of the patterns of development. Or you may wish to devote the first unit of the course to work on the writing process before moving into the selections and the patterns of development. In Part Three, the introduction to each pattern shows how the writing process applies to the pattern; the more accessible experiential patterns are presented first, before moving on to the more demanding analytic patterns.

If you organize your course according to the patterns of development, you need not feel confined by the order of patterns in the book; each chapter is self-contained, making it possible for you to sequence the modes however you wish. And, of course, there's no need to cover all the essays in a chapter or even all the patterns. You may wish to concentrate on one or two of the selections demonstrating a pattern rather than attempt to cover them all in depth. A word of warning: If you tell the class which of several assigned selections will be emphasized, some students will read only those. You'll probably want to explain to students that there are many ways to use a pattern and that reading *all* the assigned essays will give them an understanding of the options available.

For courses organized according to the patterns, we suggest that you emphasize early in the semester that professional writers don't set out to write an essay organized a particular way. Rather, the patterns emerge as writers prewrite and organize their ideas; writers come to see that their points can best be made by using a particular pattern of development or combination of patterns.

It's helpful, we've learned, to assign selections before *and after* students write an essay. For example, if students are going to write a causal analysis, you might have them read "A Granddaughter's Fear" and "Black Men and Public Space." Then, after reviewing their drafts and seeing the problems they have had, for example, with a chain of causes and effects, you might have them examine the way Darley and Latané handle the interplay of causes and effects in "Why People Don't Help in a Crisis."

Some instructors using the patterns of development approach in their courses place a special emphasis on exposition. If this is your orientation, you might want to focus early on the illustration chapter. That chapter stresses the importance of establishing a point. Then, you might move to the description and narration chapters; these underscore the importance of, respectively, a dominant impression and a narrative point, both developed through specific supporting details.

If you prefer to design the course around themes rather than development patterns, the thematic table of contents (at the front of the textbook) and the sets of thematically related essays (at the front of this manual) will help you select essays on timely issues. For such a course, we recommend that you have students read a number of essays on a given theme. The fact that several essays on the same theme use different patterns of development helps students see that the patterns are not ends in themselves, but techniques that writers use to make their points.

Creating a Process-Oriented Class Environment

We've found that creating a workshop atmosphere in the classroom helps students view writing as a process. When a new paper is assigned, we try to give students several minutes to start their prewriting in class. In other classes, time may be set aside for students to rework parts of their first draft. We may, for instance, ask them to sharpen their introductions, conclusions, sentence structure, or transitions.

In our experience, it's been especially productive to use class time for peer evaluations of first drafts. For these feedback sessions, students may be paired with one other classmate, or they may meet with three or four other classmates. (We've found groups of more than five unwieldy.) Feedback from someone other than the course instructor motivates students to put in more time on a draft. Otherwise, some of them will skip the revision stage altogether; as soon as they've got a draft down on paper, they'll want to hand it in. Hearing from other classmates that a point is not clear or that a paragraph is weakly developed encourages students to see that revision involves more than mechanical tinkering. They start to understand that revision often requires wholesale rethinking and reworking of parts of the essay. And, after a few feedback sessions, students begin to identify for themselves the problem areas in their writing.

You'll find that many students squirm at the thought of reacting to their classmates' work. So it's not surprising that they tend to respond to each other's papers with either indiscriminate praise or unhelpful neutrality. To guide students, we prepare a brief checklist of points to consider when responding to each other's work. You might, for example, adapt the checklists on pages 98, 100, 128, and 134 to fit a particular assignment. With such a checklist in front of them, students are able to focus their impressions and provide constructive feedback.

There are a number of ways to set up peer feedback sessions. Here are a few you may want to use:

— After pairing students or placing them in small groups, have each essay read aloud by someone other than the author. Students tell us that hearing another person read what they've written is invaluable. Awkward or unclear passages in a paper become more obvious when someone who has never before seen the essay reads it aloud.

4

— Place students in small groups and ask them to circulate their papers so that everyone has a chance to read all the essays. Then, have each group select one especially effective paper to read aloud to the rest of the class. Everyone discusses each paper's strengths and what might be done to sharpen the sections that miss the mark.

— Ask one or two students to photocopy their drafts of an assignment, making enough copies so that everyone can look at the papers. In class, the other students—either as a whole or in groups—react to the papers up for scrutiny that day.

A quick aside: At the start of the course, students are reluctant to "offer their papers up for sacrifice"—as one student put it. But, once they're accustomed to the process, they are not at all skittish and even volunteer to be "put on the chopping block"—another student's words. They know that the feedback received will be invaluable when the time comes to revise.

As you can no doubt tell, we have a special liking for group work. Since it gives students the chance to see how others approach the same assignment, they come to appreciate the personal dimension of writing and develop an awareness of rhetorical options. The group process also multiplies the feedback students get for their work, letting them see that their instructor is just one among many readers. Group activities thus help students gain a clearer sense of purpose and audience. Finally, we have found that peer review encourages students to be more active in the classroom. When students assume some of the tasks traditionally associated with the instructor, the whole class becomes more animated.

Some Cautions About Group Work

If you are new to group work, you may have the uneasy feeling that the group process can deteriorate into enjoyable but unproductive rap sessions. That *can* happen if the instructor does not guide the process carefully.

Here are several suggestions to steer you clear of some traps that can ensnare group activities. First, we recommend you give very clear instructions about how students are to proceed. Providing a checklist, for example, directs students to specific issues you want them to address. Second, we believe in establishing a clear time schedule for each group activity. We might say, "Take five minutes to read to yourself the paper written by the person on your left," or "Now that all the papers in your group have been read, you should vote to determine which is the strongest paper. Then, take five minutes to identify one section of the essay that needs additional attention." Third, although we try to be as inconspicuous as possible during group work, we let students know that we are available for help when needed. Sometimes we circulate among the groups, listening to comments, asking a question or two. But, more often, we stay at the desk and encourage students to consult with us when they think our reaction would be helpful.

Responding to Student Work

Beyond the informal, in-class consultations just described, we also meet during the course with each student for several one-on-one conferences of about fifteen to thirty minutes. Depending on our purpose, student needs, class size, and availability of time, a number of things may occur during the individual conferences. We may review a paper that has already been graded and commented on, highlighting the paper's strengths and underscoring what needs to be done to sharpen the essay. Or we may use the conference to return and discuss a recent essay that has or has not been graded. In the last few years, we have tended not to grade or write comments on papers we're going to review in conference. Instead, we take informal notes about the papers and refer to them when meeting with students. We've found that this approach encourages students to interact with us more freely since their attention isn't riveted to the comments and grade already recorded on the paper. Finally, we end each conference by jotting down a brief list of what the student needs to concentrate on when revising or writing the next assignment. Students tell us this individualized checklist lets them know exactly what they should pay attention to in their work.

When students hand in the final draft of a paper, we ask them to include their individualized checklists. Having a checklist for each student enables us to focus on the elements that typically give the student trouble. And, candidly, having the checklist in front of us tames our not-so-noble impulse to pounce on every problem in an essay.

In our oral and written comments, we try to emphasize what's strong in the essay and limit discussion of problems to the most critical points. Like everyone else, students are apt to overlook what they've done well and latch on to things that haven't been so successful. If every error a student makes is singled out for criticism, the student—again like everyone else—often feels overwhelmed and defeated. So unless a student is obviously lackadaisical and would profit from some hard-hitting teacherly rebukes, we try to make our comments as positive and encouraging as possible. And, rather than filling the paper with reworked versions of, let's say, specific sentences and paragraphs, we make liberal use of such remarks as these: "Read these last three sentences aloud. Do you hear the awkwardness? How could you streamline these sentences?" or "Doesn't this paragraph contradict what you say at the beginning of the preceding paragraph? What could you do to eliminate the confusion?"

When responding to a paper, we often suggest that the student review or reread a professional essay, the introduction to a rhetorical pattern, or a specific chapter on the writing process. And, we always end our comments with a brief list of points to be added to the student's personalized checklist.

Using Portfolios to Assess Student Progress

You may wish to have your students present a portfolio of their work for grading at the conclusion of the course, instead of giving grades for each paper in succession. Using such a portfolio system alters somewhat the way you respond to individual student papers as they are submitted, because you assign no grades to them. The written and oral feedback on a paper is geared solely to making the essay a more effective piece of communication rather than to justifying a particular low or high grade. This forces all concerned—instructors and students—to stay focused on how to improve writing rather than on what might pull a paper down or on what score a paper should get. If students balk at "floating free" of grades for the whole course, you might occasionally supply a tentative grade or give students grades on one or two essays so they get a feel for the standards. As the course progresses, however, the issue of what a strong paper is like should be resolved. The students will be reading the successful papers in the text, examining and commenting on the essays of other students, and hearing a plenitude of helpful comments about writing.

You should indicate clearly at the start of the course that students must complete each essay as well as all other practices, journal entries, and so forth that you assign, but that the writing component of their final grade will be based upon a portfolio of polished work. Clearly establish the minimum number of essays to be included in a completed portfolio. Typically, a course might be represented by four final-draft essays, plus some late-in-the-term in-class writing. In addition, you may wish to examine the successive drafts for one of the revised papers. To receive a grade, each student meets with the instructor for a conference about the writing progress demonstrated in the portfolio. After a dialogue about the writing's strengths and areas needing improvement, the instructor and student agree on a grade.

Such a portfolio system has several advantages. It stresses to students that writing well is an ongoing process and encourages them to make subsequent revisions of their essays as they acquire new insights into writing. It forces them to take responsibility for their progress beyond the achievement they reach in the first submitted version of an essay. It instills the notion of a writing community, for once they have gotten beyond the initial series of structured feedback sessions that you have built into the course, students must initiate feedback from their peers and from the instructor on any revisions they do. Finally, such a system dramatizes the reality that writers write for other people, and that reaching the audience, not jumping hurdles to get a grade, is the goal of writing.

At the End of the Course

Since our students keep all their papers in a folder, they have no trouble retrieving essays written weeks or even months earlier. So, near the end of the semester, we ask students to select—for one more round of revision—three or four essays, with each paper illustrating a different rhetorical pattern. We use these reworked versions of the essays to assign a final grade to each student. If you structure your course around themes and issues, you'll probably want to require that each paper deal with a different theme.

As the semester draws to a close, we also ask students to complete the questionnaire at the back of the book. Their responses let us know which selections worked well and which did not, helping us make adjustments in what we assign in future semesters. So that you too can find out how the class reacted to the assigned selections, you might ask students to give the completed forms to you rather than having students mail their questionnaire to the publisher. If you do collect the forms, we hope that you'll forward them on to us at Allyn & Bacon after you've had a chance to look them over. This kind of student feedback will be crucial when we revise the book.

An especially rewarding way to end the semester is to have the class publish a booklet of the best writing. Students revise and then submit two of their strongest papers to a class-elected editorial board. This board selects one essay from each student in the class, making an effort to choose essays that represent a mix of styles and rhetorical approaches. After a table of contents and a cover have been prepared, the essays are retyped, duplicated, and stapled into booklet form. Depending on the equipment and funds available, the booklet may be photocopied or designed on a computer.

Students respond enthusiastically to this project. After all, who can resist the prospect of being published? And knowing that their writing is going public encourages students to revise in earnest. The booklets yield significant benefits for us, too. They help build a bank of student writing to use as examples in subsequent semesters. As a bonus, the booklets allow us to reconnect with the experiences, thoughts, and feelings of the students passing through our classes year after year. Such booklets have been an ongoing source of pleasure.

A SUGGESTED SYLLABUS

On the following pages we present a syllabus that will give you some further ideas on how to use *The Macmillan Writer*. Note that the syllabus assumes the course meets twice a week for an hour and a half per session over the course of fifteen weeks. The syllabus can, of course, be adjusted to fit a variety of course formats.

WEEK 1

Class 1

- Provide an introduction to the course and handle necessary business matters.

- Direct a "getting to know each other" activity (see page 2 of this manual).

- Have students prepare an in-class writing sample to get an initial sense of their writing needs.

- Assignment—Ask students to read Chapter 1, "Becoming a Strong Reader."

Class 2

- Discuss Chapter 1, "Becoming a Strong Reader," including the reading and craft questions following "Family Counterculture."

- Return the in-class papers. Review common sentence skills and mechanical problems.

- Introduce the writing process, with emphasis on prewriting.

- Assignment—Have students read up to "Discover Your Essay's Limited Subject" (p. 24) in Chapter 2, "Getting Started Through Prewriting."

WEEK 2

Class 3

- Discuss and answer questions about the first part of Chapter 2, "Getting Started Through Prewriting."

- Have students do some practice prewriting or a practice journal entry; ask for a few volunteers to submit their writing to be read aloud anonymously.

- Have students, in groups or as a class, do Activities 1 and 3 at the end of Chapter 2. Discuss answers as a class.

8

- Assignments—Have students:

  a. Finish Chapter 2, "Getting Started Through Prewriting." Do Activity 1 at the end of Chapter 2.

  b. Begin keeping a journal, number and length of entries to be specified by the instructor.

Class 4

- Discuss and answer questions about the second part of Chapter 2, "Getting Started Through Prewriting." Go over Activity 1 at the end of Chapter 2.

- Have students do in class Activity 5 at the end of the chapter. Discuss results as a class; have volunteers read their prewriting aloud or submit for anonymous reading. Or have students share their prewriting with each other in groups.

- Introduce the first pattern of development, "Description" (or "Narration," as you choose).

- Assignment—Have students read Chapter 11, "Description," up to "Revision Strategies" (p. 160), or alternatively, Chapter 12, "Narration," up to "Revision Strategies" (p. 195).

WEEK 3

Class 5

- Discuss descriptive or narrative writing and answer student questions.

- Have students do in class Activities 1 and 6 at the end of Chapter 11, "Description." Alternatively, have them do Activities 1 and 3 at the end of Chapter 12, "Narration." Discuss the results as a class, or have student groups share the results of Activity 6 if done individually.

- Assignments—Have students:

  a. Finish Chapter 11, "Description," or Chapter 12, "Narration." Complete Activity 2 or 3 at the end of Chapter 11 or Activity 2 or 5 at the end of Chapter 12.

  b. Read "Once More to the Lake" by E. B. White or another selection in Chapter 11. Alternatively, read "Shooting an Elephant" by George Orwell or another selection in Chapter 12. Prepare to discuss the reading and craft questions following the assigned selection.

Class 6

- Discuss the assigned selection.

- Finish discussion of Chapter 11, "Description," or Chapter 12, "Narration." Have students do Activities 5 and 6 at the end of Chapter 11 or Activities 4 or 6 at the end of Chapter 12. Arrange groups so students may share their revisions of Activity 6 in Chapter 12 or Activity 6 in Chapter 12.

- Have students do prewriting for one of the writing assignments at the end of the assigned description or narration selection or at the end of Chapter 11 or 12. Using groups, have students share their prewriting and get feedback.

- Assignments—Have students:

  a. Read a second assigned selection from Chapter 11 or 12 and prepare to discuss the reading and craft questions following it.

  b. Prepare a draft of the description or narration essay.

WEEK 4

Class 7

- Discuss the assigned selection.

- Initiate group feedback on students' description or narrative essays (see pages 4–5 of this manual). Give students the option of handing in their papers now or revising them by the next class.

- Assignments—Have students

  a. Revise the description or narrative essay (optional).

  b. Read Chapter 3, "Identifying Your Thesis."

Class 8

- Pass back and discuss students' description or narrative essays; collect essays from students who chose to revise.

- Discuss and answer questions about Chapter 3, "Identifying Your Thesis."

- Have students do Activities 1, 3, and 4 at the end of Chapter 3. Discuss the results.

- Assignments—Have students:

  a. Do Activities 2 or 5 and 6 at the end of Chapter 3, "Identifying Your Thesis."

  b. Read Chapter 13, "Illustration," up to "Revision Strategies" (p. 230).

WEEK 5

Class 9

- Discuss assigned Activities 2 or 5 and 6 at the end of Chapter 3, "Identifying Your Thesis."

- Discuss and answer questions on Chapter 13, "Illustration."

- Have students do in class Activities 1 and 2 at the end of Chapter 13. Use groups or pairs to share responses to both activities. Read aloud responses to Activity 2.

- Assignments—Have students:

  a. Do Activity 4 at the end of Chapter 13, "Illustration."

  b. Read "Channelled Whelk" by Anne Morrow Lindbergh or another selection in Chapter 13 and prepare to discuss the reading and craft questions following it.

  c. Read Chapter 4, "Supporting the Thesis With Evidence." Complete Activity 1 at the end of Chapter 4.

Class 10

- Have students share results of Activity 4 at the end of Chapter 13, "Illustration," either in groups or by reading aloud to the class. If there is not enough time for group work, collect student responses and review quickly at home, without marking.

- Discuss the assigned reading selection.

- Discuss and answer questions on Chapter 4, "Supporting the Thesis With Evidence," and on Activity 1.

- Have students do in class Activity 2 at the end of Chapter 4. Also arrange groups and have them do Activity 3 or 4. Discuss the results.

- Assignment—Have students finish Chapter 13, "Illustration," and do Activity 5 at the end of the chapter. Also do Activity 5 at the end of Chapter 4.

WEEK 6

Class 11

- Go over Activity 5 at the end of Chapter 4.

- Discuss and answer questions on the rest of Chapter 13, "Illustration." Discuss the results of Activity 5 in Chapter 13.

- Have students do Activity 6 or 7 at the end of Chapter 13; arrange groups so students may share their revisions.

- Have students do prewriting for one of the writing assignments at the end of the assigned selection or at the end of Chapter 13. Using groups, have students share their prewriting and get feedback.

- Assignments—Have students:

a. Prepare a draft of the illustration essay.

b. Read a second assigned selection from Chapter 13, "Illustration," and prepare to discuss the reading and craft questions at the end of the selection.

Class 12

- Initiate group feedback on students' illustration essays (see pages 4–5 of this manual). Give students the option of handing in their papers now or revising them by the next class.

- Discuss the assigned reading selection.

- Introduce Chapter 5, "Organizing the Evidence."

- Assignments—Have students:

    a. Revise the illustration essay (optional).

    b. Read Chapter 5, "Organizing the Evidence."

WEEK 7

Class 13

- Pass back and discuss students' illustration essays; collect essays from students who chose to revise.

- Discuss and answer questions on Chapter 5, "Organizing the Evidence." Have students do Activities 1, 2, and 4 at end of Chapter 5.

- Assignments—Have students:

    a. Do Activity 5 at end of Chapter 5, "Organizing the Evidence."

    b. Read Chapter 14, "Division-Classification," up to "Revision Strategies" (p. 266) and do Activities 1 and 2 at end of Chapter 14. Alternatively, read Chapter 15, "Process Analysis," up to "Revision Strategies" (p. 303) and do Activities 1 and 2 at the end of Chapter 15.

    c. Read "Propaganda Techniques in Today's Advertising" by Ann McClintock or another selection in Chapter 14. Alternatively, read "My First Conk" by Malcolm X or another selection in Chapter 15. Prepare to discuss the reading and craft questions at the end of the selection.

Class 14

- Discuss Activity 3 at the end of Chapter 5, "Organizing the Evidence."

- Discuss and answer questions about Chapter 14, "Division-Classification." Go over Activities 1 and 2 at the end of Chapter 14. Have students do in class Activities 3 and 4 at end of Chapter 14. Alternatively, discuss and answer questions about Chapter 15, "Process Analysis," and go over Activities 1 and 2 at the end of Chapter 15. Have students do in class Activities 3, 4 or 5 at the end of Chapter 15.

- Discuss the assigned reading selection.

- Assignments—Have students:

  a. Finish Chapter 14, "Division-Classification," or Chapter 15, "Process Analysis."

  b. Read "Why Nothing Is 'Wrong' Anymore" by Meg Greenfield or another reading selection in Chapter 14. Alternatively, read "Don't Just Stand There" by Diane Cole in Chapter 15. Prepare to discuss the reading and craft questions at the end of the selection.

WEEK 8

Class 15

- Discuss the rest of Chapter 14, "Division-Classification," and have students do Activity 5 at the end of the chapter. Alternatively, discuss the rest of Chapter 15, "Process Analysis," and have students do Activity 6 at the end of Chapter 15. Use groups to share results.

- Discuss the assigned reading selection.

- Have students do prewriting for one of the writing assignments at the end of the assigned division-classification or process analysis selection or at the end of Chapter 14 or 15. Using groups, have students share their prewriting and get feedback.

- Assignments—Have students:

  a. Prepare a draft of the division-classification or process analysis essay.

  b. Read Chapter 6, "Writing the Paragraphs in the First Draft," up to "Write Other Paragraphs in the Essay's Body" (p. 76) and do Activity 1 at the end of Chapter 6.

Class 16

- Initiate group feedback on students' division-classification or process analysis essays (see pages 4–5 of this manual). Give students the option of handing in their papers now or revising them by the next class.

- Discuss and answer questions on Chapter 6, "Writing the Paragraphs in the First Draft." Go over Activity 1. Have students do in class Activity 2 or 3 at the end of the chapter.
- Assignments—Have students:

  a. Revise the division-classification or process analysis essay (optional).

  b. Finish Chapter 6, "Writing the Paragraphs in the First Draft," and do Activity 2 or 3 at the end of the chapter if not assigned in class.

  c. Read Chapter 10, "An Overview of the Patterns of Development."

Class 17

- Pass back and discuss students' division-classification or process analysis essays; collect essays from students who chose to revise.

- Continue discussing Chapter 6, "Writing the Paragraphs in the First Draft," and Activities 2 and 3 at the end of the chapter. Have students do Activities 4 and 5 or 6 at the end of the chapter.

- Discuss Chapter 10, "An Overview of the Patterns of Development."

- Introduce "Comparison-Contrast."

- Assignment—Have students:

  a. Read Chapter 16, "Comparison-Contrast," up to "Revision Strategies (p. 341). Do Activity 2 at the end of the chapter.

  b. In Chapter 6, "Writing the Paragraphs in the First Draft," do Activity 9 at the end of the chapter.

Class 18

- Discuss and answer questions on Chapter 16, "Comparison-Contrast," and go over Activity 2 at the end of the chapter. Have students do in class Activity 1 and either 3 or 4 at the end of the chapter. Use groups to share responses to Activity 3 or 4.

- Go over Activity 9 at the end of Chapter 6, "Writing the Paragraphs in the First Draft."

- In class, read "A Slow Walk of Trees" by Toni Morrison in Chapter 16. Discuss the selection as an example of "one-side-at-a-time" format.

- Assignments—Have students:

  a. Read an additional selection in Chapter 16, "Comparison-Contrast," and prepare to discuss the selection's use of the "point-by-point" format. Also prepare to discuss the reading and craft questions following the selection.

  b. Finish Chapter 16, "Comparison-Contrast," and do Activity 6 at the end of the chapter.

WEEK 10

Class 19

- Discuss the assigned selection.

- Discuss the rest of Chapter 16, "Comparison-Contrast," and go over Activity 6 at the end of the chapter, perhaps using groups to share revisions. Have students do in class Activity 5 at the end of the chapter.

- Have students do prewriting for one of the writing assignments at the end of the assigned comparison-contrast selections or at the end of Chapter 16. Using groups, have students share their prewriting and get feedback.

- Assignments—Have students:

  a. Prepare a draft of the comparison-contrast essay.

  b. Read Chapter 7, "Revising Overall Meaning, Structure, and Paragraph Development."

Class 20

- Initiate group feedback on students' comparison-contrast essays (see pages 4–5 of this manual). Ask students to use the guidelines and checklists on pages 98 and 100 in Chapter 7 during the feedback process. Require students to revise their essays by the next class.

- Discuss and answer questions on Chapter 7, "Revising Overall Meaning, Structure, and Paragraph Development." Have students do in class Activities 1 and 3 at the end of the chapter.

- Assignments—Have students:

  a. Revise the comparison-contrast essay, using the revision checklists on pages 98 and 100.

  b. Bring in journal entries, previously written essays, or material generated for Activity 6 at the end of Chapter 6 for revision practice in class.

WEEK 11

Class 21

- Collect the comparison-contrast essays.

- Go over Activity 3 at the end of chapter 7, "Revising for Overall Meaning, Structure, and Paragraph Development," or use groups to share revisions of journal entries or previous papers.

- Assignment—Have students read Chapter 8, "Revising Sentences and Words," up to "Make Sentences Emphatic" (p. 114).

Class 22

- Pass back and discuss the students' comparison-contrast essays.

- Discuss the first part of Chapter 8, "Revising Sentences and Words." Have students do Activities 1 and 2 at the end of the chapter.

- Introduce "Cause-Effect."

- Assignments—Have students:

  a. Finish Chapter 8, "Revising Sentences and Words." Do Activity 13 at the end of the chapter.

  b. Read Chapter 17, "Cause-Effect," up to "Revision Strategies" (p. 377).

WEEK 12

Class 23

- Discuss and answer questions on the rest of Chapter 8, "Revising Sentences and Words." Go over Activity 13 at the end of the chapter. In class, have students do Activities 3 and 4 at the end of the chapter.

- Discuss and answer questions on Chapter 17, "Cause-Effect." In class, have students do Activities 1 and 2 at the end of the chapter.

- Assignments—Have students:

  a. Do Activity 5 at the end of Chapter 8.

  b. Finish Chapter 17, "Cause-Effect," and do Activities 3 and 5 at the end of the chapter.

Class 24

- Go over Activity 5 at the end of Chapter 8, "Revising Sentences and Words." Have students do in class Activity 6 at the end of the chapter and discuss results. Using groups, have students work on Activity 8 at the end of the chapter.

- Discuss and answer questions on the rest of Chapter 17, "Cause-Effect." Go over Activities 3 and 5 at the end of the chapter. Have students do in class Activity 4 at the end of the chapter.

- Assignments—Have students:

  a. Do Activity 11 at the end of Chapter 8, "Revising Sentences and Words."

  b. Read two selections in Chapter 17, one emphasizing causes, "Why People Don't Help in a Crisis," by John Darley and Bibb Latané, and one emphasizing effects, "Black Men and Public Space," by Brent Staples. Prepare to discuss the reading and craft questions following the selections.

WEEK 13

Class 25

- Go over Activity 11 of Chapter 8, "Revising Sentences and Words." Have students do in class Activity 9 or 10 at the end of the chapter.

- Discuss the assigned selections in Chapter 17, "Cause-Effect."

- Have students do prewriting for one of the writing assignments at the end of the assigned cause-effect selections or at the end of Chapter 17. Using groups, have students share their prewriting and get feedback.

- Assignment—Have students prepare a draft of the cause-effect essay.

Class 26

- Initiate group feedback on students' cause-effect essays (see pages 4–5 of this manual). Ask students to use the checklists on pp. 98, 100, 128, and 134 during the feedback session.

- Introduce "Definition" or "Argumentation-Persuasion," as you choose.

- Assignments—Have students:

  a. Revise the cause-effect essay using the checklists on pp. 98, 100, 128, and 134.

  b. Read Chapter 18, "Definition," up to "Revision Strategies" (p. 410). Alternatively, read Chapter 19, "Argumentation-Persuasion," up to "Revision Strategies" (p.455).

WEEK 14

Class 27

- Collect the cause-effect essays.

- Discuss and answer questions about Chapter 18, "Definition," and have students work in class on Activity 2 at the end of the chapter and share responses in groups. Also, do Activity 1 at the end of the chapter. Alternatively, discuss Chapter 19, "Argumentation-Persuasion," and have students work in class on Activity 2 at the end of the chapter and share responses in groups. Also, do Activities 1 and 3 at the end of Chapter 19.

- Ask students to read "Entropy" by K. C. Cole or another selection in Chapter 18. Alternatively, assign "Institution is Not a Dirty Word" by Fern Kupfer or another selection at the end of Chapter 19. Discuss the reading and craft questions following the selection.

  Assignments—Have students:

  a. Finish Chapter 18, "Definition," and do Activity 3 at the end of the chapter. Alternatively, finish Chapter 19, "Argumentation-Persuasion." Do Activity 4 at the end of the chapter.

  b. Read "Absolutophobia" by John Leo or another selection at the end of Chapter 18. Alternatively, read "Death and Justice" by Edward I. Koch or "The Death Penalty" by David Bruck at the end of Chapter 19. Prepare to discuss the reading and craft questions for the assigned selection(s).

  c. Read Chapter 9, "Editing and Proofreading."

Class 28

- Pass back and discuss students' cause-effect essays.

- Discuss and answer questions about the rest of Chapter 18, "Definition." Go over Activity 3 at the end of the chapter. Have students do in class Activity 4 at the end of the chapter. Alternatively, discuss the rest of Chapter 19, "Argumentation-Persuasion." Go over Activity 4 at the end of Chapter 19. Have students do in class Activities 6 and 7 at the end of the chapter.

- Discuss the assigned reading selections.

- Have students do prewriting for one of the writing assignments at the end of the assigned definition or argumentation-persuasion selections or at the end of Chapter 18 or 19. Using groups, have students share their prewriting and use the checklists on pages 98, 100, 128, and 134 when providing feedback.

- Assignments—Have students:

  a. Prepare a draft of the definition or argumentation-persuasion essay.

  b. Do Activity 1 at the end of Chapter 9, "Editing and Proofreading."

WEEK 15

Class 29

- Go over Activity 1 at the end of Chapter 9, "Editing and Proofreading."

- Initiate group feedback on students' definition or argumentation-persuasion essays.

- Have students work in class on Activity 5 at the end of Chapter 18, "Definition." Alternatively, have students work in class on Activities 8 and 9 at the end of Chapter 19, "Argumentation-Persuasion."

- Assignment—Have students revise the definition or argumentation-persuasion essay.

Class 30

- Pass back and discuss students' definition or argumentation-persuasion essays.

- Have students submit their folders of revised work.

- Conclude the course.

ANSWER KEY

FAMILY COUNTERCULTURE

Ellen Goodman

Questions for Close Reading (p. 11)

1. According to Goodman, parenting today entails a constant struggle against what the popular marketplace presents as attractive to children. She asserts, "What the media delivers to children by the masses, you are expected to rebut one at a time" (paragraph 14). In the past, she tells us, parents raised their children "in accordance with the dominant cultural message" (2). But today, they must "raise their children in opposition" (14) to it. Responsible parenting, Goodman feels, is now a matter of resistance, making child raising an increasingly difficult task.

2. Both the grocers' association and PR people "assembled under the umbrella marked 'parental responsibility'" (5) protested the ban. Goodman takes the PR people more seriously because she considers them a symptom of a dangerous phenomenon: the tendency to call for more parental responsibility precisely at the time the marketplace becomes more irresponsible. To Goodman, this demand for an unrealistic degree of parental accountability absolves the marketplace of its responsibility.

Questions About the Writer's Craft (p. 11)

1. In the first two paragraphs, Goodman uses the second-person point of view to establish the fact that she is aiming her essay at parents: "All *you* [italics added] need to join is a child" and "At some point between LaMaze and the PTA, it becomes clear that one of *your* [italics added] main jobs as a parent is to counter the culture." The specific parents Goodman addresses are those struggling to raise their children in opposition to mainstream culture. Goodman's use of "we" and "our" (16) makes it clear that she allies herself with these beleaguered adults. She argues that it's unfair to think that parents should be considered successful only if they can counter the culture. Such a standard, she asserts, is impossible to attain, given the pervasive power of media messages.

2. In paragraph 16, Goodman repeats the word "it's" four times. Goodman may repeat this word to illustrate just how familiar readers are with the problem: It is no longer necessary to identify the problem by name; it is so much a part of their daily lives that they already know, perhaps too well, to what she is referring. This repetition also reflects the ongoing nature of the struggle, the short, clipped assertions summing up the problem succinctly.

ANSWERS FOR CHAPTER 2
"GETTING STARTED THROUGH PREWRITING" (p. 15)

Below we provide suggested responses to selected activities at the end of Chapter 2 (p. 33). In some cases, other responses are possible.

1. **Set A**

   3 Abortion
   2 Controversial social issue
   5 Cutting state abortion funds
   4 Federal funding of abortions
   1 Social issues

   Set B

   4 Business majors
   3 Students' majors
   1 College students
   2 Kinds of students on campus
   5 Why students major in business

2. "Day care," "male and female relationships," and "international terrorism" are clearly too broad to be used as topics for a 2- to 5-page essay.

3. Here are some descriptions of possible purposes, tones, and points of view for the various topics and audiences.

   Overcoming shyness

   — for ten-year-olds
   　　Purpose: to reassure them, help them feel safer
   　　Tone: lively, optimistic
   　　Point of view: ex-shy adult
   — for teachers of ten-year-olds
   　　Purpose: to help teachers encourage shy children
   　　Tone: explanatory
   　　Point of view: psychologist
   — for young singles
   　　Purpose: to show how easy talking to others can be
   　　Tone: pep-talk
   　　Point of view: an extroverted young single

Telephone solicitations

— for people training for a job
        Purpose: to motivate
        Tone: up-beat
        Point of view: high-powered successful phone salesperson
— for homeowners
        Purpose: to advise how to handle
        Tone: angry
        Point of view: experienced homeowner
— for readers of a humor magazine
        Purpose: to make fun of telephone sales pitches
        Tone: mocking
        Point of view: call recipient

Smoking

— for people who have quit
        Purpose: to reinforce their decision with benefits
        Tone: supportive and informative
        Point of view: medically informed quitter
— for smokers
        Purpose: to demolish their reasons for smoking
        Tone: sarcastic
        Point of view: a smoke-hater
— for elementary school children
        Purpose: to warn them of dangers
        Tone: serious
        Point of view: a concerned parent

5. Here are some possible patterns that might work with these topics and purposes:

   a. Topic: the failure of recycling efforts on campus
      Pattern: cause-effect

   b. Topic: the worst personality trait that someone can have
      Pattern: description or illustration

   c. Topic: the importance of being knowledgeable about national affairs
      Pattern: argumentation-persuasion

ANSWERS FOR CHAPTER 3
"IDENTIFYING A THESIS" (p. 36)

Below we provide suggested responses to selected activities at the end of Chapter 3 (p. 41). In many cases, other responses are possible.

1. a. **Limited Subject**: The ethics of treating severely handicapped infants

   FS   Some babies born with severe handicaps have been allowed to die.

   TB   There are many serious issues involved in the treatment of handicapped newborns.

   OK   The government should pass legislation requiring medical treatment for handicapped newborns.

   A   This essay will analyze the controversy surrounding the treatment of severely handicapped babies who would die without medical care.

   b. **Limited Subject:** Privacy and computerized records

   TB   Computers raise significant questions for all of us.

   FS   Computerized records keep track of consumer spending habits, credit records, travel patterns, and other personal information.

   OK   Computerized records have turned our private lives into public property.

   A   In this paper, the relationship between computerized records and the right to privacy will be discussed.

2. Here are some possible thesis statements for the topics:

   a. Topic: the failure of recycling efforts on campus
      Thesis: Campus apathy about recycling results from poor planning by the campus housing department.

   b. Topic: the worst personality trait that someone can have
      Thesis: Bossiness is an intolerable trait in a friend.

   c. Topic: the importance of being knowledgeable about national affairs
      Thesis: Gaining awareness of current events is a significant part of becoming a responsible adult.

3. Below are possible thesis statements for each pair of general and limited subjects.

General Subject	Limited Subject	Possible Thesis
Psychology	The power struggles in a classroom	The classroom is often a battlefield, with destructive struggles for power going on among students and teacher.
Health	Doctors' attitudes towards patients	In hospitals, doctors often treat patients like robots rather than human beings.
The elderly	Television's depiction of the elderly	Television sitcoms either ignore or trivialize the elderly
Work	Minimum-wage jobs for young people	The minimum wage is too low to inspire young people to work hard and advance themselves.

4. Below are possible thesis statements for each set of points.

Set A

Possible thesis: Students in college today are showing signs of increasing conservatism.

Set B

Possible thesis: If not closely monitored, experiments in genetic engineering could yield disastrous results.

ANSWERS FOR CHAPTER 4
"SUPPORTING THE THESIS WITH EVIDENCE" (p. 44)

Below we provide suggested responses to selected activities at the end of Chapter 4 (p. 50). In many cases, other responses are possible.

1. **Thesis**:   Colleges should put less emphasis on sports.

    OK   High-powered athletic programs encourage grade-fixing.

    TG   Too much value is attached to college sports.

    IA   Athletics have no educational value.

    OK   Competitive athletics can lead to extensive and expensive injuries.

    OK   Athletes can spend too much time on the field and not enough on their studies.

    IA   Good athletic programs create a strong following among former undergraduates.

2. Below are possible supporting points for each of the thesis statements.

    Thesis: Rude behavior in movie theaters seems to be on the rise.

    — People feel free to chat loudly with their companions during films.

    — Some shout out humorous or vulgar comments about the characters and events on the screen.

    — Others smoke and visit the popcorn stand without any concern for those they disturb.

    Thesis: Recent television commercials portray men as incompetent creatures.

    — College male washing colors and whites together, to horror of older woman in laundromat.

    — Father caring for child but unable to cope with emergency.

    — Men concerned only with taste of product, while wives are knowledgeable about healthfulness.

Thesis: The local library fails to meet the public's needs.

— The hours are limited and inconvenient.

— The part-time, inexperienced staff provide insufficient assistance.

— The collection is outdated and incomplete.

Thesis: People often abuse public parks.

— Litter spoils picnic and other recreation areas.

— Off-road vehicles and dirt bikes destroy fields, seashores, and woodlands.

— Illegal camping, hunting, and fire-making can cause long-term damage.

ANSWERS FOR CHAPTER 5
"ORGANIZING THE EVIDENCE" (p. 53)

Below we provide suggested response to selected activities at the end of Chapter 5 (p. 60). In many cases, other responses are possible.

1. **Thesis**: Our schools, now in crisis, could be improved in several ways.

      I. Schedules
         A. Longer school days
         B. Longer school year
      II. Teachers
         A. Certificate requirements for teachers
         B. Merit pay for outstanding teachers
      III. Curriculum
         A. Better textbooks for classroom use
         B. More challenging course content

2. **Set A**

   Thesis: Traveling in a large city can be an unexpected education.

   Purpose 1:   To explain, in a humorous way, the stages in learning to cope with the city's cab system.

   This purpose would clearly require a *chronological* approach to depict "the stages in learning to cope. . . ."

   Purpose 2:   To describe, in a serious manner, the vastly different sections of the city as viewed from a cab.

   This purpose would require a *spatial* approach, moving from section to section.

   Set B

   Thesis: The student government seems determined to improve its relations with the college administration.

   Purpose 1:   To inform readers by describing efforts that student leaders took, month by month, to win administrative support.

   This purpose would require a *chronological* approach.

   Purpose 2:   To convince readers by explaining straightforward as well as intricate pro-administration resolutions that student leaders passed.

   This purpose would require a *simple-to-complex* approach.

Set C

Thesis: Supermarkets use sophisticated marketing techniques to prod consumers into buying more than they need.

Purpose 1: To convince readers that positioning products in certain locations encourages impulse buying.
This purpose would require a *spatial* approach, covering the locations in order.

Purpose 2: To persuade readers not to patronize those chains using especially objectionable sales strategies.

This purpose would require an *emphatic* approach.

4. **Set A**

Thesis: Friends of the opposite sex fall into one of several categories: the pal, the confidante, and the pest.

Overall pattern of development: *Division-classification*

— Frequently, an opposite-sex friend is simply a "pal."

Pattern of development: *Definition*

— Sometimes, though, a pal turns, step by step, into a confidante.

Pattern of development: *Process analysis*

— If a confidante begins to have romantic thoughts, he or she may become a pest, thus disrupting the friendship.

Pattern of development: *Cause-effect*

Set B

Thesis: What happens when a child gets sick in a two-income family? Numerous problems occur.

Overall pattern of development: *Cause-effect*

— Parents often encounter difficulties as they take steps to locate a baby sitter or make other child care arrangements.

Pattern of development: *Process analysis*

— If no child care helper can be found, a couple must decide which parent will stay at home—a decision that may create conflict between husband and wife.

Pattern of development: *Cause-effect*

— No matter what they do, parents inevitably will incur at least one of several kinds of expenses.

Pattern of development: *Division-classification* or *illustration*

ANSWERS FOR CHAPTER 6
"WRITING THE FIRST DRAFT" (p. 63)

Below we provide suggested responses to selected activities at the end of Chapter 6 (p. 85). In many cases, other responses are possible.

1. a. The topic is the final sentence of the paragraph: "Clearly, being an expert doesn't guarantee a clear vision of the future."

   b. There is no explicit topic sentence in this paragraph. The point of the paragraph could be expressed this way: "Several cities have resorted to drastic measures to limit automobile traffic."

   c. The first sentence of this paragraph is the topic sentence: "A small town in Massachusetts that badly needed extra space for grade school classes found it in an unlikely spot." The final sentence identifies this "unlikely spot" as a saloon.

   d. The topic sentence of this paragraph appears in the middle: "New research, though, shows that neurotics are indeed likely to have physical problems."

   e. The topic sentence is the first sentence: "Many American companies have learned the hard way that they need to know the language of their foreign customers."

2. Below are possible revised versions of the paragraphs.

   a. Other students can make studying in the college library difficult. For one thing, some students spread out their books, coats, backpacks, and other paraphernalia so that they take up a whole library table, leaving no room for anyone else. Whispering and giggling with friends, chomping gum, even eating sandwiches, others indulge in thoughtless behavior that makes concentration impossible. Still others, tapping their feet, clicking their pens, shifting noisily every two minutes, disrupt the quiet. Worst of all, some students remove books and magazines from their assigned locations and don't return them. Some even tear out pages, making it impossible for another person to find needed material.

   b. Some people have dangerous driving habits. Acting as though no one else is on the road, they blithely drop into a lane without giving other motorists any warning. Others seem unsure of where they're going; they move around the road without signaling, hustling into the turn lane and then veering back to their original position. The truly confused, of which there seem to be many, conscientiously blink for a right turn and then turn left. Finally, some motorists drive ten or even twenty mph over the speed limit, while others mosey along at 25 in a 55 mph zone. Both speedballs and slowpokes cause accidents.

c. Things people used to think were safe are now considered dangerous. Foods once thought healthy, such as eggs and even milk, are now under suspicion of causing heart disease. Similarly, some habits people thought were harmless are not considered risky, like smoking or having a few drinks. Even things in the home, in the work place, and in the air have been found to be harmful. Recent reports show that asbestos, radon gas, and perhaps even electromagnetic waves cause lung disease and a variety of life-threatening cancers. So much has been discovered in recent years about what is harmful that it makes you wonder: What additional dangers lurk in the environment?

d. Society encourages young people to drink. For one thing, youngsters learn early that their parents and other relatives find alcohol consumption a necessity on birthdays, anniversaries, and graduations. They see their parents buying scotch to give as presents to clients and ordering liquor by the case for business functions. Memorial Day, Independence Day, and other national holidays also cause adults to break out the Budweiser, the Johnny Walker, and even the champagne. But, the place where youngsters see alcohol depicted most enticingly is on television. Prime-time shows, like major sports events and popular sitcoms, are typically sponsored by beer and wine commercials and show healthy, jubilant people drinking liquor and having the time of their lives.

3. The major flaws in each paragraph are indicated below.

a. This paragraph lacks unity (U). Sentences five and nine ("Of course, participants' observations. . ."; "Such findings underscore. . .") are digressions from the main point.

b. This paragraph lacks unity (U); it moves from the children's cheating to children growing up with "distorted values" to adult cheating. It also lacks specific support (S) throughout.

c. The support consists of the same point about brain size repeated over and over (R). The paragraph needs tightening.

d. A problem in coherence (C) is caused by the lack of a transition between the first and second sentences as well as by insufficient transitions to signal the second and third steps that adults can take to reduce their cholesterol level. Unity (U) is spoiled by the digression of the fifth sentence ("Physicians warn . . ."). The placement of the sixth sentence ("for those unwilling . . .") leads to another problem in coherence (C). Since this sentence develops the point about vegetarianism, it should go after the third sentence ("Since only foods . . ."), the sentence that first discusses vegetarianism.

4. Here is one way to revise the paragraph. (Transitional signals are italicized.)

As a camp counselor this past summer, I learned that leading young children is different from leading people your own age. I was president of my high school Ecology Club, *and* I ran it democratically. *When* we wanted to bring a speaker to the school, we decided to do a fund raiser. I solicited ideas from everybody, *and then* we got together to figure out which was best. It became obvious that a raffle with prizes donated by local merchants was the most profitable. *So,* everybody got behind the effort.

This summer, on the other hand, I learned that little kids operate differently. *With them,* I had to be more of a boss than a democratic leader. *Once,* I took suggestions from the group on the main activity of the day. Everyone *then* voted for the best suggestion. Some kids got especially upset, *especially* those whose ideas were voted down. *As a result,* I learned to make the suggestions myself *and* allow the children to vote on them. *That way,* no one was overly attached to any of the suggestions. *Usually,* they felt the outcome of the voting was fair, *and* I basically got to be in charge.

5. Below are the patterns of development implied by each topic sentence.

Thesis: The college should make community service a requirement for graduation.

Definition	"Mandatory community service" is a fairly new and often misunderstood concept.
Description	Certainly the conditions in many communities signal serious need.
Narration	Here's the story of one student's community involvement.
Division-Classification	There are, though, many other kinds of programs in which students can become involved.
Illustration	Indeed, a single program offers students numerous opportunities.
Cause-Effect	Such involvement can have a real impact on student's lives.
Process Analysis	This is the way mandatory community service might work on this campus.
Comparison-Contrast	However, the college could adopt two very approaches—one developed by a university, the other by a community college.
Argumentation-Persuasion	In any case, the college should begin exploring the possibility of making community service a graduation requirement.

30

9. It's a good idea to have students share their analysis of Harriet's first draft with each other in small groups. Such group discussion can help students understand all the ways in which Harriet's draft is working well.

Here are the strengths of Harriet's draft:

— An explicit statement of the thesis appears at the end of the introductory paragraph: "But being a parent today is much more difficult because nowadays parents have to shield/protect kids from lots of things, like distractions from schoolwork, from sexual material, and from dangerous situations."

— Numerous details and examples are provided to support the development of the three points.

— The essay follows the emphatic organizational pattern established in the thesis: "distractions from schoolwork, from sexual material, and from dangerous situations."

The essay does have some problems, however, besides those Harriet noted as she wrote. For example:

— The first body paragraph lacks unity because it contains a digression: the sentence beginning, "Unfortunately, though. . . ."

— The second paragraph contains a digression at the end: "The situation has gotten so out of hand that maybe the government should establish guidelines. . . ."

— The third paragraph organization could be improved by using chronological order, beginning with little children, moving to slightly older children, and ending with teenagers.

— The conclusion contains a vague reference to a fictional character; this unexpected allusion dilutes the impact of the ending.

ANSWERS FOR CHAPTER 7
"REVISING OVERALL MEANING, STRUCTURE, AND PARAGRAPH DEVELOPMENT" (p. 92)

Below we provide suggested responses to selected activities at the end of Chapter 7 (p. 102). In many cases, other responses are possible.

1. Students profit from working in a group on this activity; if you have students work alone, then set aside some time for them to share their evaluations of the draft. If students worked on Harriet's draft for activity #9 on page 90, they may wish to refer to their notes.

    Here are the problems, in addition to the ones she noted as she wrote, that Harriet will have to correct as she revises her essay.

    — The first body paragraph lacks unity because it contains a digression: The sentence beginning "Unfortunately, though . . ." has nothing to do with her thesis.

    — The second paragraph contains a digression at the end: "The situation has gotten so out of hand that maybe the government should establish guidelines. . . ."

    — The third paragraph's organization could be improved by using chronological order, beginning with little children, moving to slightly older children, and ending with teenagers.

    — The conclusion contains a vague reference to a fictional character; this unexplained allusion dilutes the impact of the ending.

3. The annotations below describe some of the essay's problems in meaning, structure and development.

The Extended School Day

Vague phrases.	Imagine a seven-year-old whose parents work until five each night. When she arrives home after school, she is on her own. She's a good girl, but still *a lot of things could happen.* She could *get into trouble* just by *being* curious. Or, *something could happen through no fault of her own.* All over the country, there are many "latch-key" children like this little girl. Some way must be found to deal with the problem. One suggestion
Thesis should be more specific.	is to keep elementary schools open longer than they now are. *There are many advantages to this idea.*
Support is weak, repetitive. 2nd	Parents wouldn't have to be in a state of uneasiness about whether their child is safe and happy at home. *They wouldn't get uptight about whether their children's needs are being met. They also wouldn't have to feel guilty because they are not able to help a child with homework.*

32

point belongs in next paragraph.
Support too personal, inadequate.

The longer day would make it possible for the teacher to provide such help. Extended school hours would also relieve families of the financial burden of hiring a home sitter. *As my family learned, having a sitter can wipe out the budget.* And, having a sitter doesn't necessarily eliminate all problems. Parents still have the hassle of worrying whether the person will show up and be reliable.

Digression.

Support repeats ideas already discussed.

Support too personal; inadequate.

Here support is specific.

Irrelevant support.

It's a fact of life that many children dislike school, which is a sad commentary on the state of education in this country. Even so, the longer school day would benefit children as well. *Obviously, the dangers of their being home alone after school would disappear because by the time the bus dropped them off after the longer school day, at least one parent would be home. The unnameable horrors feared by parents would not have a chance to happen.* Instead, the children would be in school, under trained supervision. There, they would have a chance to work on subjects that give them trouble. *In contrast, when my younger brother had difficulty with subtraction in second grade, he had to struggle along because there wasn't enough time to give him the help he needed.* The longer day would also give children a chance to participate in extracurricular activities. They could join a science club, play on a softball team, sing in a school chorus, take an art class. *Because school districts are trying to save money, they often cut back on such extracurricular activities. They don't realize how important such experiences are.*

Vague.
Give specifics.

Digression.

Finally, the longer school day would *also benefit teachers.* Having more hours in each day would relieve them of *a lot of pressure. This longer work day would obviously require schools to increase teachers' pay. The added salary would be an incentive for teachers to stay in the profession.*

Digression.

Good summary.

Strong concluding image.

Implementing an extended school day would be expensive, but I feel that many communities would willingly finance its costs because *it provides benefits to parents, children, and even teachers.* Young children, home alone, wondering whether to watch another TV show or wander outside to see what's happening, need this longer school day now.

ANSWERS FOR CHAPTER 8
"REVISING SENTENCES AND WORDS" (p. 105)

Below are suggested responses to selected activities at the end of Chapter 8 (p. 129). In many cases, other responses are possible.

1. Below are possible revisions of the sentences. Other versions are possible.

   a. Before subletting an apartment, a person should have a formal sublet contract.

   b. High school students often deny liking poetry because they fear mockery of others.

   c. Since college students are rare in my neighborhood, going to college gave me instant status.

   d. Many people observed that the new wing of the library resembles several nearby historical buildings.

   e. The professor aptly noted that students who complain about heavy course requirements tend to hold jobs.

3. The revisions below show one way the sentences could be made more emphatic.

   a. The old stallion's mane was tangled, his hooves chipped, his coat scraggly. (Parallelism)

   b. Most of us find it difficult to deal with rude salespeople. (Important item last)

   c. "I'll solve all your problems," promises the politician. (Inverted order)

   d. In the movies, we meet the gold digger, the dangerous vixen, and the "girl next door." Female stereotypes all. (Fragment)

   e. Wise teachers encourage discussion of controversial issues in the classroom. (Important item first)

4. Here is a version of the paragraph that eliminates murkiness and gets straight to the point. Other versions might work equally well.

   Since its founding, our student senate has had one main goal: to improve its student services. Two years ago, consultants from the National Council of Student Governing Boards agreed with the senate that its services were basically strong but also felt that additional funding from the administration would further improve student services. This has turned out to be true; services have significantly improved in the last fifteen months since the administration began contributing more money.

5. Here are some ways to use each word in a sentence that reinforces its connotations. Other versions are possible.

   a. On her chubby legs, the toddler stiffly lurched across the room.

      Proud of her voluptuous figure, the bride-to-be asked the dressmaker to lower the neckline and tighten the bodice of her gown.

      The portly lawyer eased himself into his desk chair and slowly went over the will with his client.

   b. The engaged couple strolled on the riverbank, breathing in the fragrance of the spring blooms.

      Dripping wet under their uniforms, the mail carriers trudged determinedly through the summer heat.

      Loitering near the liquor store, the vacant-eyed man beseeched passers-by for money to buy a sandwich and soup.

   c. The students were in turmoil over the suspension of the class president for cheating on an exam.

      The demonstration turned into anarchy as bands of youths began throwing rocks, robbing vendors, and smashing car windows.

      When the "Sold Out" sign was posted, the movie fans created a hubbub by jeering the manager and jostling each other.

8. The examples below show some ways to enliven the sentences.

   a. With a fever of 101 degrees, I shivered and coughed my way through the tour of the California wineries.

   b. In his new silver convertible, the balding middle-aged man glided to a halt at the crowded intersection.

   c. A yellow finch, feathers damp with rain, alighted on the wooden fence rail.

   d. Shifting in their seats, the math students doodled on their notebooks and restlessly tapped their pencils.

   e. Natasha Miles, the seasoned network reporter, put on a shocked face and assumed a hushed tone as she announced the crash of the international flight.

9. Below is a possible revision of the paragraph.

   The situation at Paul Godfrey's farm illustrates the problem of rural vandalism. Godfrey estimates that motorcyclists speeding over his land the past few weekends have destroyed over three acres of his crops. Such vandalism results from the suburbs encroaching on rural areas.

10. Here are non-sexist versions of the sentences.

   a. The manager of a convenience store has to guard *the* cash register carefully.

   b. When I broke my arm in a car accident, a *nurse*, aided by a physician's assistant, treated my injury.

   c. All of us should contact our *congressional representatives* if we're not happy with their performance.

   d. The chemistry professors agree that students shouldn't have to buy their own Bunsen burners.

ACTIVITIES FOR CHAPTER 9
"EDITING AND PROOFREADING" (p. 133)

Below we provide a suggested response to a selected activity at the end of Chapter 9 (p. 142). Other versions are possible.

1. Here is a corrected version of the letter.

Dear Mr. Eno:

As a sophomore at Harper College, I will be returning home to Brooktown this June, hoping to find a job for the summer. I would prefer a position that would give me further experience in the retail field. I have heard from my friend, Sarah Snyder, that you are hiring college students as assistant managers. I would be greatly interested in such a position.

I have quite a bit of experience in retail sales, having worked after school in a "Dress Place" shop at Mason Mall, Pennsylvania. I started there as a sales clerk; by my second year, I was serving as assistant manager.

I am re liable and responsible and truly enjoy sales work. Mary Carver, the owner of the "Dress Place," can verify my qualifications. She has been my supervisor for two years.

I will be visiting Brooktown from April 25 to 30. I hope to have an opportunity to speak to you about possible summer jobs at that time, and will be available for an interview at your convenience. Thank you for your consideration.

Sincerely,

Joan Ackerman

ANSWERS FOR CHAPTER 11
"DESCRIPTION" (p. 153)

Opening Comments

Some colleagues tell us they prefer to omit description when they teach freshman writing. Emphasizing the analytic side of exposition, they consider descriptive writing a digression, a luxury in an already crowded syllabus. To them, descriptive writing belongs in a creative writing course, not in freshman composition. On the other hand, some instructors *do* include description, but they discuss it after narration.

We feel that descriptive writing should be included in freshman composition. And we've found that description can be covered before narration with excellent results. In other words, we recommend that description be the first pattern studied in the course.

Why do we feel this way? For one thing, when students begin by writing descriptive essays, they learn the importance of specific details, and they start to develop the habit of observation. (The sensory chart illustrated on pages 161-62 is one way to encourage such attention to detail.) Also, since descriptive writing depends on creating a dominant impression, description helps students understand the concept of focus early in the semester.

Descriptive writing also teaches students to select details that enhance an essay's central point. Finally—and most importantly—students can discover real pleasure in writing descriptive pieces. They are challenged by the possibility that they can make readers feel as they do about a subject. They enjoy using words to share a place, person, or object that has personal significance to them. Every semester, we have students who admit that descriptive writing changed their attitude toward composition. For the first time, they see that writing, though difficult, can be rewarding and fun.

The selections in this chapter represent a wide range of techniques found in descriptive writing. You may wish to start with White's essay, "Once More to the Lake," celebrated for its clear rendering of natural details and poetic evocation of remembered events and scenes. Angelou's essay ("Sister Flowers") demonstrates the power of sensory details, while Ciardi's ("Dawn Watch") shows how carefully described details accumulate to create a dominant impression.

ACTIVITIES: DESCRIPTION

Below we provide suggested responses to selected activities at the end of Chapter 11. Of course, other approaches are possible.

Prewriting Activities (p. 167)

1. There are many ways to use description in these two essays; below we've listed some of the possibilities. In classroom use of this activity, we suggest you have students share their responses. They'll be surprised and often delighted to discover their neighbors have devised quite different uses for description in the essays. Sharing and comparing such prewriting conveys the invaluable point that writers are individual and their writing is unique.

   Topic: **How students get burned out**
   > Describe ineffective studying methods: cramming, skimming
   > Describe student with 6 courses struggling with homework
   > Draw portrait of aloof professor assigning too-difficult work
   > Describe student working and carrying full load

   Topic: **Being a spendthrift is better than being frugal**
   > Describe allure of some purchase: dress, sneakers, etc.
   > Describe appeal of shopping center or mall
   > Describe gourmet meal at expensive restaurant

   Topic: **Being a spendthrift is worse than being frugal**
   > Describe shocked clerk ringing up your large purchase
   > Describe empty pockets and meager lunches after a spree
   > Describe sleepless night after charging a lot

Revising Activities (p. 168)

4. Here are some possible ways to revise the sentences to create distinct, contrasting moods. Other versions are, of course, possible.

   a. Around the filthy, lopsided table slouched four grubby, droopy-eyed old men.

      Alert and eagle-eyed, the four natty old poker players sat tensely around the felt-topped table.

   b. Enticed by media attention to the movie's special effects, hordes of boisterous teenagers thronged the street outside the theatre showing *Race to Doom.*

      Snaking down the alley beside the theatre, a line of silent, slouch-hatted customers waited to see the notorious film.

   c. The skinny twelve-year-old girl teetered, wobbled, and finally tripped as she walked into church in her first pair of high heels.

With head held high, hips swaying, and eyes roving to see if anyone noticed, Mary Beth strolled down Main Street in her first pair of high heels.

5. Here are some ways to revise the sentences. Other versions are possible, of course. Encourage students to avoid other, similar cliches ("dull as dust," "jealous as sin," and so on).

   a. The workers were as quiet as children waiting for recess.

   The cafe cooks were suddenly quiet as water waiting to boil.

   b. My brother used to become as envious as a four-year-old at someone else's birthday party if I had a date and he didn't.

   My brother would look as if he just drank sour milk if I had a date and he didn't.

   c. Andrea is as proud as an Olympic champion of her new Girl Scout uniform.

   The little girl dressed in her new Girl Scout uniform twirled like a music box ballerina.

   d. The professor is as dull as a dead snail.

   Professor Tomari is as dull as an iceberg lettuce sandwich on white bread.

6. We suggest that you offer your students the chance to read each other's revisions of this paragraph. Such exposure to the versions of others helps them see a variety of possibilities in improving a piece of writing.

   Here are the main problems in the paragraph:

   — Details about driving on Route 334 are irrelevant and should be eliminated.

   — Statement that car has been "washed and waxed" detracts attention from arrival at farm.

   — Short, choppy sentences could be combined with others nearby: "Its paint must have worn off decades ago"; "They were dented and windowless." For example, such combined sentences might read: "Then I headed for the dirt-colored barn, its roof full of huge, rotted holes"; "As I rounded the bushes, I saw the dirt-colored house, its paint worn off decades ago"; "A couple of dented, windowless, dead-looking old cars were sprawled in front of the barn."

   — Spatial order is broken by placing description of house in between details about what is near the barn.

ONCE MORE TO THE LAKE

E. B. White

Questions for Close Reading (pp. 173-74)

1. White's thesis is implied. One way of stating it is as follows: "In taking his son to revisit the lake where he experienced so many significant childhood events, White learns that he can only partly recapture the feelings and the atmosphere of days long past. Instead, he gets in touch with a premonition of his own death."

2. White suggests that his return to the lake was rather casual and impulsive (1). While he normally preferred the ocean, he says, sometimes the turbulence of the sea made him long for the calm of a placid lake in the woods. In addition, he could take his son along and introduce him to fresh water fishing. On a deeper level, he seems to have longed to revisit a place of significance from his own youth and to share its pleasures with a son.

3. In paragraph 4, the author lies in his bed, hearing his son sneak out in the dawn light to take a motorboat out on the lake, just as White had himself done as a boy. His son's behavior is so similar to his own as a youth that he suddenly feels as if "he was I, and therefore . . . that I was my own father." Another significant transposition occurs when they are fishing (5). A dragonfly, an unchanging element of nature, alights on his rod and gives him the dizzying feeling that he has moved back in time, until he "didn't know which rod [he] was at the end of." Finally, in paragraph 10, he identifies deeply with his son's attempts to gain mastery over the motorboat; he feels again all the same feelings he had in his youth as he grew to have a "spiritual" relationship with the motor.

4. The visit shows that much has remained the same through the years. Nature has not changed much, nor has the town or the accommodations. In fact, White feels that the visit reveals the "pattern of life indelible" (8). In keeping with the times, however, some details have changed. The road has only two tracks, from the tires of automobiles, not three from horse-drawn carriages (7); also, the boat is a modern outboard, not the one- and two-cylinder inboard motors of his youth. The waitresses are still country girls, but, impressed by actresses in the movies, they keep their hair cleaner than the girls of the past (7). Finally, the store serves Coke rather than old-fashioned sodas like Moxie and sarsaparilla (11).

5. *incessant* (1): continuous, not stopping
   placidity (1): peacefulness, calmness
   primeval (3): primitive
   transportation (4): a reversal or switching of place
   undulating (6): rippling, moving in wave-like fashion
   indelible (8): permanent, unerasable
   petulant (10): irritable, grouchy
   languidly (13): lifelessly, spiritlessly, without energy

Questions About the Writer's Craft (p. 174)

1. White describes the present-day life objectively. For example, he writes: "There was a choice of pie for dessert, and one was blueberry and one was apple, and the waitresses were

the same country girls . . . the waitresses were still fifteen; their hair had been washed, that was the only difference—they had been to the movies and seen the pretty girls with clean hair." But White's descriptions of the past are sensuous and evocative, and full of imagery suggesting his memories are more powerful than the scenes of the present.

2. In paragraph 2, White calls the lake a "holy spot" and recalls a memory of the lake at dawn, when the woods along the shore seems to form a "cathedral." Later, in paragraph 10, he describes the experience of learning to operate a motorboat as getting "really close to it spiritually." He uses prayer-like language to evoke the summer at the lake in paragraph 8: "pattern of life indelible," "summer without end." These images convey White's almost religious reverence for nature: its beauty, peace, and permanence.

3. This passage uses the metaphor of a melodrama for the storm, a comparison that points out that the storm is full of noise and turbulence but, in reality, is not dangerous. The storm's "audience," the children, in particular, get all excited about it, but to White, an old hand at the lake, the storm's "drama of electrical disturbance" is familiar. The "gods grinning" suggests a pagan image of nature gods playing with the elements just to tease and scare humans, putting on a show for them, in a sense. The campers run about and swim in the rain, enjoying the harmless imitation of danger. Nevertheless, the violent storm sets the stage for White's premonition of death in the next paragraph.

4. The feeling grows out of a complex of events. The mock-danger of the storm has intensified everyone's reactions. White has enjoyed the storm as a piece of theater; he remains on the sidelines wittily analyzing the scene. But, the storm arouses the vitality of his son, who joins the frolicking campers. This action is the final example of how the son is growing up and away from his parent. (The boy takes the boat out by himself, for example.) When White feels a "sympathetic" iciness in his groin as his son dons a cold wet swimsuit, White is identifying sensuously (again) with the boy's experience. In "biblical" terms, a child is the fruit of its father's "groin," and so the iciness also represents White's sudden awareness that his vitality is decreasing; to use the image of the melodrama, his scene is ending, while his son is center-stage. The many transpositions of identity between father and son have hinted at this final thought; White feels more and more like his own father, who, we can assume, has died.

SISTER FLOWERS

Maya Angelou

Questions for Close Reading (p. 179)

1. The dominant impression is implied and can be stated as, "The care and attention of a loving mentor is crucial to a child's healthy development, particularly in times of crisis." In addition, Angelou seeks to draw a portrait of beloved Mrs. Flowers, the essence of whom Angelou expresses when she writes, "[Mrs. Flowers] was one of the few gentlewomen I have ever known, and has remained throughout my life the measure of what a human being can be" (paragraph 5).

2. Mrs. Flowers represents for Angelou the gentility and sophistication as well as the benevolence that she has read about in novels and seen in films, but has never encountered first-hand, especially not among her fellow townspeople. She says, "She appealed to me because she was like people I had never met personally" (11) and calls her "the aristocrat of Black Stamps" (2). Flowers's stunning beauty and impeccable grooming (2-4) powerfully impress Angelou, who lives in a community of relatively poor and minimally-educated people. Still more fascinating is Flowers's refined grace (12), dazzling intellect, and stirring eloquence (22), all of which inspire Angelou to strive for a standard she previously thought accessible only to privileged whites. Angelou reflects, "She made me proud to be Negro, just by being herself" (11). Most of all, Angelou is profoundly honored and grateful that Flowers would not only spend time with her but also impart to her the "lessons for living" that would form the foundation of Angelou's subsequent existence.

3. Angelou humorously describes her frustration and embarrassment when witnessing her unrefined Momma speaking to the highly-educated and proper Mrs. Flowers. In particular, Angelou is ashamed of Momma's calling Mrs. Flowers "*Sister* Flowers." To the young Angelou, such an informal appellation is inconsistent with what she considers the obvious superiority of her elegant neighbor. In Angelou's opinion, "Mrs. Flowers deserved better than to be called Sister" (7). Worse still is Momma's flawed grammar as she speaks to Flowers; Angelou agonizes over Momma's incorrect and missing verbs and says that she "hated [Momma] for showing her ignorance to Mrs. Flowers" (7). Despite Angelou's intense embarrassment over Momma, Momma and Flowers share an amicable and mutually respectful friendship—a fact which perplexes Angelou, who calls their relationship "strange" (6). Flowers does not object to Momma's calling her "Sister" and in fact might be pleased to be included in the community of women; similarly, Momma feels enough kinship with Flowers to call her "Sister." The two women often engage in "intimate conversation" with each other (10), and it is implied that Momma has asked Flowers's assistance in mentoring the withdrawn young Angelou. Years later, Angelou finally realizes that Momma and Flowers were indeed "as alike as sisters, separated only by formal education" (7), a notion reinforced by Flowers's insistence that Angelou appreciate the wisdom of "mother wit," such as that of Momma (35).

4. The first significant lesson Mrs. Flowers teaches Angelou is about the beauty and power of language. In the process of convincing young Angelou that she needs to participate verbally in class, Flowers explains that "it is language alone which separates [man] from the lower animals," a notion that was "a totally new idea" to Angelou (23). Soon after, in a statement that Angelou remembers as "valid and poetic," Flowers says, "It takes the human voice to infuse [words] with the shades of deeper meaning" (24). Flowers's melodic, invigorating reading of *A Tale of Two Cities* convincingly illustrates to Angelou the vast power of words. (Clearly, this lesson had a tremendous impact on Angelou, presently a renowned writer not only of novels but also of poetry.) The next important lesson concerns the nature of wisdom and intelligence. Probably perceiving Angelou's embarrassment at Momma's lack of refinement, Flowers informs her that many unschooled people are more knowledgeable and intelligent than some highly educated scholars. "Mother wit," she asserts, is every bit as valuable (if not more so) as book knowledge, for it contains "the collective wisdom of generations" (35). Flowers's lesson on knowledge is summed up when she advises Angelou to "always be intolerant of ignorance but understanding of illiteracy" (35). Following this advice, it seems likely that young Angelou would think twice before judging Momma harshly again. Beyond these explicitly-stated lessons, Angelou also receives the invaluable understanding that she is a unique and likable individual worthy of the attention of an exemplary woman, a realization that will help rebuild her wounded self-confidence.

5. *taut* (2): tightly pulled or strained
   voile (2): a light, sheer fabric
   benign (4): kind and gentle
   unceremonious (8): informal
   gait (8): particular way of walking
   moors (11): broad area of open land, often containing patches of wetness
   incessantly (11): continuing without interruption
   scones (11): small biscuit-like pastries
   crumpets (11): small, round, cake-like breads
   heath (11): large area of land containing low-growing shrubs
   chifforobe (17): tall piece of furniture containing drawers and space for hanging clothes
   sacrilegious (17): disrespectful of something held sacred
   infuse (24): to introduce into as if by pouring
   couched (35): expressed
   aura (42): an invisible atmosphere seeming to surround something or someone

Questions About the Writer's Craft (pp. 179-80)

1. Angelou relies primarily on visual and occasionally on both tactile and auditory impressions to convey Flowers's "aristocratic" appearance. In paragraph 2, Angelou describes her graceful bearing that never evidences extremes of weather and her thin frame which lacks the "taut look of wiry people." Flowers's attire is the next object of Angelou's attention as she observes the elegant woman's airy "printed voile dresses," "flowered hats," and gloves (2). Angelou then describes Flowers's "rich black" complexion, comparing it to the visual and tactile image of an easily peeled plum (3). Angelou also details Flowers's "slow dragging" smile (15), thin black lips, "even, small white teeth" (4) and "soft yet carrying voice" (6). Later, she mentions Flowers's "easy gait" (8). In general, Angelou organizes these details of Flowers' appearance spatially, moving first from her physical carriage and attire up to her face and zeroing in on her smile (although she returns to Flowers's "easy gait" later in the essay.)

   To describe her reaction when she first arrived at Flowers's home, Angelou invokes the sense of smell when, for example, she cites the "sweet scent of vanilla" (29). She then draws upon the visual sense to describe what she observes: "browned photographs" and "white, freshly done curtains" (32). The next part of the visit calls upon the visual as well as the taste faculty as Angelou describes eating Flowers's delectable cookies ("flat round wafers, slightly browned on the edges and butter-yellow in the center") and drinking the refreshing, cold lemonade (34). The tactile sense is appealed to when she mentions the "rough crumbs" of the cookies scratching against her jaw (34). And the sense of sound is evoked as Angelou remembers Flowers's reading voice, "cascading" and "nearly singing" (37). Overall, Angelou organizes this last set of richly-textured sensory impressions spatially as well as chronologically; that is, she presents the details as she moves through the house and as the afternoon progresses.

2. The first figure of speech is the simile Angelou uses in comparing herself to an old biscuit (1). This image establishes young Angelou's shame and withdrawal following the rape; indeed, her depression is what prompts Flowers to find time to talk with the child. Angelou then employs a series of striking figures of speech to describe Flowers's character and demeanor. The most powerful appear in paragraph 11. There Angelou provides a series of similes using "like" to compare Flowers with the gentle, elegant "women in English novels who walked the moors . . . with their loyal dogs racing at a respectful distance" and "the women who sat in front of

roaring fireplaces, drinking tea incessantly from silver trays full of scones and crumpets." The final simile of the paragraph is an implied one; although it lacks "like," it deliberately mirrors the structure of the previous two similes: "Women who walked over the 'heath' and read morocco-bound books and had two last names divided by a hyphen." The function of these similes comparing Flowers to female British gentility is to reinforce the notion of Flowers as "the aristocrat of Black Stamps" (2). The basis of Flowers's allure for Angelou is her otherworldly elegance and sophistication, particularly when juxtaposed with the ordinary citizens of Black Stamps. That this elegant and gracious woman actually seeks out the young Angelou is enough to transform the child from an "old biscuit" into one who excitedly runs down the road, flush with the pleasure of being liked.

3. The technique of imagined conversation injects humor into Angelou's portrait of herself as a child, while also allowing readers greater insight into her character by giving them access to her mental processes. The young Angelou's imagined scoldings of Momma resoundingly illustrate her embarrassment with "uncouth" Momma. Here, Angelou seems caught between two worlds: that of "backwards" Momma and Black Stamps and that of education and opportunity seemingly offered by the outside world. As Mrs. Flowers instructs, however, much wisdom resides in "mother wit" like Momma's, and given this lesson, young Angelou would probably be led to re-evaluate her embarrassed attitude toward Momma.

4. From Angelou's very first statement about Mrs. Flowers, it is apparent that race is a significant facet of life in Angelou's town. Flowers is said to be "the aristocrat of Black Stamps," a statement that draws its power from the notion that aristocrats have traditionally been white. This depiction of Flowers as being uniquely regal is heightened by Angelou's comparing her to British female gentry (11) and by her observation that Flowers behaves differently from the average "Negro woman" (14) in town. Most significantly, Angelou states that Flowers made her "proud to be a Negro, just by being herself" (11), a difficult feat given the racist climate of the day. The town's appellation "Black Stamps" (12) implies the existence of a "White Stamps," a fact later confirmed when Angelou mentions "powhitefolks" (13). Angelou indicates that no Negro, not even the elegant Flowers, is immune to the disrespect of the town's self-aggrandizing poor whites. Indeed, even Angelou's reverence for Flowers "would have been shattered like the unmendable Humpty-Dumpty" (13) if the "powhitefolks" had called this revered idol by her first name, Bertha. Angelou lives in a world that would sanction such racially-inspired disrespect and insult. In paragraph 42, Angelou refers to "Southern bitter wormwood," a subtle reference to racism. In such a world, it is difficult for a black child—especially one so traumatized and wounded—to develop a strong sense of self. But that is just what the encounter with Mrs. Flowers achieves; it makes young Angelou "feel proud" to be a Negro, and with that comes the loosening of trauma's hold on her.

DAWN WATCH

John Ciardi

Questions for Close Reading (p. 183)

1. Ciardi expresses the thesis very directly and clearly in the first line of the piece: "Unless a man is up for the dawn and for the half hour or so of first light, he has missed the best of the day."

The sensory details that he supplies in the rest of the essay help us understand what he might mean by "the best" and thus provide evidence for the thesis.

2. Ciardi never actually tells us directly what is best about the dawn. Rather, he describes the time of day for us as he experiences it, letting us infer what qualities make up this "best" time. These qualities include the special atmosphere provided by the "ghost of a mist," an "exhalation that will be gone three minutes after the sun comes over the treetops" (3) and the dewy brightness of the grass, which "shows a depth of green it will not show again all day" (4). The tones of cardinals, the appearance of the cat and the rabbit, and the dawn-only blossoming of certain weeds and flowers, the morning glory (8), dayflower (9), and "another blue morning weed whose name I do not know" (10), also contribute to his preference for this time of day. In addition to the freshness and opening-up of nature, the solitude also contributes to the specialness of this time.

3. Ciardi's immersion in the scene is clear right from the start when he speaks about the mist or "exhalation" that he knows "will be gone three minutes after the sun comes over the treetops" (3). He knows the deep green of the grass "will not show again all day" (4). He is acquainted with the tomcat, and gives us a sketch of his personality, "too can-fed and too lazy to hunt" (6). He further describes what it is like to weed out the dayflower and other blue-flowering weeds that he admires at dawn (9, 10), and he actually gets down and pulls out clumps of crabgrass (12). He predicts the dumped weeds will be covered by grass clippings from his next lawn mowing session. He recognizes a sound that might be mysterious to others—the brake squeak of the car delivering the paper (14). Finally, near the end, he remarks upon his family's disparagement of his love of the dawn, indicating that he frequently stays up to see it.

4. He has read the newspaper, leaving it in a "mess" (16), and found the news the same as every other day, "another disaster count. . . . bringing us tragedies faster than we can pity" (14). He suspects everyone will become "inured" and "emotionless." The hummingbird drinking from his favorite lily is a life-affirming image, one that offsets the negativity of the daily news. His saying that he will take the hummingbird for news indicates he prefers what the delicate, evanescent processes of nature convey about life as opposed to what the papers indicate about human existence. From this contrast can be inferred that Ciardi finds the everyday world depressing and numbing.

5. *exhalation* (3): that which is breathed out, such as air or vapor
   grackles (5, 13): large, crowlike blackbird with raucous call
   aspen (11): a type of poplar tree noted for its fluttery leaves
   spectrum (11): the band of colors produced when light passes through a prism
   germinating (12): taking root; beginning to grow
   inured (14): toughened by repeated exposure or experiences

Questions about the Writer's Craft (pp. 183-84)

1. Sights, sounds, smells, and touch all play a role in Ciardi's dawn watch. He sees the "exhalation" that seems to transform the air (3) and the lawns shining (4). He notices the tomcat, the rabbit, and his dog (6-7), and notices the morning glory (8), two blue flowered weeds (9-10), the seeming transparency of the Japanese red maple (11) and crabgrass in his zinnia garden (12). He watches the various birds swoop down to the birdseed and his dog break up the party. Finally, he sees a humming bird "the color of green crushed velvet" drink from one of his lilies. Sounds include the beginning of traffic (2), the calls of cardinals and

grackles in his trees (5), and the brake-squeak of the newspaper deliverer. He smells the heavy odor of the lily. Seeing the crabgrass "wrestling with the zinnias" causes him to pause and pull out the clumps of weeds (12), giving him the sensations of getting his thumb and forefinger dirty (touch). Finally, he smokes a cigarette, giving him another sensation of touch and of taste (though this has nothing to do with the dawn).

These numerous details are subtly structured in chronological order, according to the path of his walk, which he refers to as his "stroll-around first hour" (16). There are also several small narratives that he witnesses during the hour. The first detail is the traffic beginning to flow (2). Then, he notices the "exhalation" (3) and the shining of the grass (4) as a rabbit hops around.He then mentions the birds (5) and says he scatters birdseed for them. The first small narrative is the scene between the cat, the rabbit, and the dog (6-7). After this, Ciardi sees the morning glories and the flowering weeds (8, 9, 10), and the slant of the sun through the red maple (11). He portrays the weedy zinnia garden as a drama: the crabgrass "wrestling" with the flowers; he gets involved by pulling out the weeds (12). Then, he moves on to the thicket, where he dumps the crabgrass, and then returns, seeing the birds swoop down for the birdseed he scattered, and the dog scares the birds (13). He hears the brakes squeak as the paper is delivered; it is implied he goes and picks it up, takes it back and reads it on the patio. He notices the birds have stopped singing. The hummingbird arrives, he watches it and then recognizes that the dawn has ended.

2. The metaphors include the sound of a car being "almost like the sound of a brook a half mile down in the crease of a mountain I know—a sound that carries not because it is loud but because everything else is still" (2), the mist being "nearly the ghost of a mist" and "a phenomenon like side vision" (3), and the grackles sounding "like a convention of broken universal joints grating uphill" (5). Ciardi also likens the tomcat to "one of those poolroom braggarts" (6). Ciardi metaphorically calls the excess of dayflower that he has weeded "bales" (9), and he likens the red maple leaves' transparency to the aspen (11). In paragraph 12, he compares the crabgrass and zinnias to wrestlers and later compares the flowers of the lily to horns (15). The metaphors help us to feel, see, and hear the beauty of nature at dawn with something like the intensity and sensitivity of an acute observer such as Ciardi. Thus, the metaphors support the dominant impression in that they powerfully convey the specialness of dawn.

3. There are numerous processes described in the essay. In paragraph 3, for example, Ciardi describes the process by which one can view the "ghost of a mist" that transforms the air: "glance without focusing and something registers," "like side vision," he says (3). In the following paragraph, he explains the process by which he understands the shining of the grass is not caused by dew. In 8, he describes how the morning glory has come to grow in his mountain laurel, and in 9-10 and 12, he explains the process involved in weeding dayflower, the unnamed morning weed, and crabgrass. In 11, he explains the process by which aspen leaves become transparent in the fall, similar to the transparency of the red maple at dawn. Each of these processes shows Ciardi deeply engrossed in the scenes of the dawn, remembering and considering the meaning of each element he notices. The sharpness of his attention as he describes these processes supports the idea that for Ciardi, dawn is the best part of the day.

4. At the end of the essay, Ciardi suddenly talks to his dog ("Come on, boy") instead of the reader. This reminds us that Ciardi want us to feel as if as if the essay was composed as he took his dawn stroll. At the end of the dawn hour, he ends both his description and his walk, since there is nothing more to appreciate. He points out that the animals have shifted gears— the rabbits "won't come back until tomorrow"—and the birds will get on with their "work,"

and implies that so should he. The effectiveness of the last sentence is partly due to the pun it makes. Colloquially, "call it a day," means to end one's work day, to have put in enough hours at work to "call it a day." In the context of Ciardi's descriptive essay, however, the best part of day and of living is over, so one might just as well "call it a day" and end the work of awareness. Finally, in a literal sense, the moment has passed when one could "call it dawn," and so, Ciardi says, to "call it a day," that is, shift into the regular day full of light and activity. The colloquial expression is thus bestowed a fresh new meaning by its juxtaposition with Ciardi's poetic awareness of dawn.

ANSWERS FOR CHAPTER 12
"NARRATION" (p. 187)

Opening Comments

In our classes, we introduce narrative writing *after* description because we have found that descriptive writing helps students acquire many of the skills needed to write engaging narratives. For example, through descriptive writing, students discover the need to generate evocative details, use varied sentence structure, and establish a clear point of view.

At the start of the course, however, we often find students reluctant to write a narrative. Schooled to believe that lightning will strike them if they use "I" in an essay, they are more comfortable starting with description because it lends itself easily to the objective third-person point of view. (Obviously, both narration and description can use either the first or third person, but beginning writers tend to associate narration with the first and description with the third person.)

Even if it is not the first pattern covered, we suggest that narration be introduced near the beginning of the course. Everyone, after all, likes a good story. Also, most students have written narratives in high school and so feel comfortable tackling them in college. Despite some students' familiarity and seeming ease with the narrative pattern, it helps to keep in mind that narration requires a sophisticated repertoire of skills. Pacing, choice of details, telescoping of time, point of view—all offer a real challenge.

Students seem to have particular trouble understanding point of view. Because they tend to be more familiar with the first rather than the third person, we've found it useful to ask them to write two versions of the same narrative—one in the first and one in the third person. Such an assignment shows students how point of view changes a story and makes them aware of the advantages and limitation of each perspective.

Although each narrative in this chapter is filled with drama and tension, students find special power in the conflicts underlying Orwell's "Shooting an Elephant." In "The Fourth of July," Lorde uses narration to explore the anger and confusion created by her parents' silence in regard to prejudice. Baker's essay ("Selling the Post") mixes delightful humor with skillful manipulation of details and demonstrates the telescoping of events that occurred over years of time.

ACTIVITIES: NARRATION

Below we provide possible responses to selected activities at the end of Chapter 12. Of course, your students are bound to come up with their own inventive approaches.

Prewriting Activities (p. 202)

1. There are numerous ways to use narration to open these two essays. Below we've listed some of the possibilities. In going over this activity in class, we suggest you have students trade responses or read them aloud to each other, so that they are all aware of the diversity of responses to the assignment.

   Topic: The effect of insensitive teachers on young children

   > Teacher being sarcastic to student making a mistake
   > Teacher joking about student's clothes choices
   > Child's reading mistakes increasing as teacher corrects
   > Child crying after a teacher's cruel remark
   > Teacher punishing harshly for small transgression
   > Name-calling or labeling of a child for being different

   Topic: The importance of family traditions

   > Family seated at Sunday dinner
   > Sugary donuts for all at breakfast for a family birthday
   > Generations gathered at a holiday for a yearly reunion
   > Fourth of July kite-flying with all the cousins
   > Gathering at year's end to view selected family videos

3. Here are some possible conflicts for each situation:

   a. Friend criticizes your food choices as unhealthy
      Friend embarrasses you by snacking on food throughout store

   b. College choice is on the other side of the country
      College choice does not offer the major your parents wish you to take

   c. Counter-demonstrators accost your group
      Some protestors break the law by trespassing and are arrested

   d. Fighting the desire to go to the gym instead of studying
      Telling friends to be quiet or go away

Revising Activities (pp. 202-03)

5. Here are some ways to revise the sentence sets to create first a negative connotation and then a positive connotation. Other versions are possible, of course.

   a. The raucous clanging of the bell signaled that the last day of lectures and homework was finally over.

With a gentle dinging sound from the school bell, the last day of high school quietly ended.

b. We strode over to admonish our neighbors for polluting the air with burning leaves.

We had a neighborly chat with the Joneses, while the autumn leaves burned fragrantly in their yard.

c. The sun slicing through my window jolted me upright in bed, and I was forced to admit that daylight had come.

The lemony-yellow sunshine poured across my bed, and I sat up, grateful the new day was finally here.

6. It's a good idea to set aside some time for students to exchange their versions of the paragraph with others. Seeing how others handled the assignment can open their eyes to techniques they haven't thought of.

Students should keep in mind as they revise that this is an introductory anecdote. It needs to be brief and pointed. Here are the main problems in the paragraph:

— The reference to the type of car the writer was driving is irrelevant and should be deleted.

— The speeding car should be described.

— The description, "The car didn't slow down . . ." is slow-paced and indirect; rewrite to state that the car "sped. . . ."

— Description of car coming, light changing, couple crossing, is too slow; condense and make more dramatic.

— "Dressed like models" is irrelevant, unless other details are added later in the paragraph to indicate how rumpled and bloody their clothes now are.

— The sentence about the man "jump[ing] to the shoulder" is short and choppy.

— Describe man's and woman's locations and injuries more visually, instead of saying he "wasn't hurt" but "it was clear she was."

— Narrator's calling police is a digression; condense events to get to the point: she died.

— Give more visual details of speeding car stopping, driver getting out, instead of saying he "looked terrible"; give us a picture of him drunk.

— Use his repeated offenses as a lead-in or stronger transition to the final sentence, the thesis.

SHOOTING AN ELEPHANT

George Orwell

Questions for Close Reading (p. 208)

1. Orwell's thesis is implied. One possible way of stating it is: "Imperialistic rulers must behave so as not to lose face or power over the populace, even if it means doing something against their better judgment."

2. Orwell felt pressured by the people, almost overwhelmed by their power over him through their mere presence. In theory, he explains at the start of the selection, he "was all for the Burmese and all against their oppressors, the British" (2). But, in reality, Orwell says, he felt the common people of the country were "evil-spirited little beasts who tried to make my job impossible" (2). During the shooting incident the people were "happy and excited," and they watched him "as they would a conjurer about to perform a trick." He resentfully saw himself as having to spend his life "trying to impress the 'natives'" (7). He reports later that, as he fired a shot, the crowd emitted a "devilish roar of glee" (11). His choice of words shows that he resented and disliked the Burmese.

3. Orwell shoots the elephant because the two thousand native people standing behind him expect him to. They want vengeance for the man it killed, the meat the carcass will provide, and the entertainment of watching the shooting. "The people expected it of me and I had got to do it" (7), he writes. There is an implication that if he decided not to shoot the elephant, both he and the empire would suffer a loss of prestige, but the main concern in Orwell's mind is the "long struggle not to be laughed at" (7). He is even afraid to "test" the animal's mood by going closer for fear it might attack and kill him before he could shoot, thus giving the crowd a sight it would enjoy as much as the slaughter of the beast.

4. Despotic governments result from the need to maintain power over subtly resistant people. Such a government can rule only by fulfilling the people's expectations and responding to every crisis with the expected force. Orwell points to the irony that he stood armed in front of an unarmed crowd, yet he was powerless to do as he wished or as his judgment told him. Instead, he felt himself "an absurd puppet pushed to and fro by the will of those yellow faces behind" (7).

5. *imperialism* (2): a country's policy of gaining power by acquiring and ruling territories
   prostrate (2): lying face down, as in submission or adoration
   despotic (3): tyrannical, all-powerful
   mahout (3): the keeper and driver of an elephant
   miry (5): swampy, muddy
   conjurer (7): magician
   futility (7): uselessness, ineffectiveness
   sahib (7): "Master"; Indian title of respect when addressing Europeans

Questions About the Writer's Craft (pp. 208-209)

1. What Orwell calls a "tiny incident" lasted only a short time, perhaps only an hour. Orwell uses clear transitions of time to keep us oriented as to what is happening, but he provides no

specific clock time. "Early one morning," the narrative begins (3); after the death of the coolie, the action steps up and the transitions indicate things are happening at a rapid pace: "he could not have been dead many minutes" (4): "As soon as I saw the dead man" (4); "The orderly came back in a few minutes" (5); "meanwhile some Burmans had arrived" (5); "As soon as I saw" (6); "I thought then" (6); "But at that moment" (7); "And suddenly I realized" (7); "And it was at this moment" (7); "I perceived in this moment" (7); "But I had got to act quickly" (8); "For at that moment" (9); "When I pulled the trigger" (11); "In that instant, in too short a time" (11); "He looked suddenly stricken" (11); "At last, after what seemed a long time—it might have been five seconds" (11); "And then down he came" (11). Orwell then describes the refusal of the animal to die: "I waited a long time"; "Finally I fired"; "but still he did not die" (12). The incident ends with Orwell leaving the scene but learning later that the animal took half an hour to die.

2. The first two paragraphs introduce us to the alien, far-off world where the narrative took place. In addition to setting the scene, Orwell explains what he was doing in Burma and, more importantly, gives us an emotional perspective from which to view the event. We learn in a general way about the bitterness between the colonialists and the native inhabitants and about the psychological effect his job as a policeman had on him. His confession that he was "young and ill-educated" and not even aware the British Empire was collapsing helps us feel empathy for him in the incident that follows. Without this information, we might not be willing to forgive him for shooting the elephant or for its horrible death or be able to comprehend the sense of victimization he felt despite his position as an "authority."

3. Orwell uses analogies in three important places. Two of the analogies are from the theatre and relate to the sense of falseness that Orwell feels about his role in the colony. With the crowd watching him, he compares himself to "a conjurer about to perform a trick" with "the magic rifle." Then, he helps us to understand his own psychological state at that moment by using another theater image: "Here was I . . . seemingly the lead actor of the piece; but in reality I was only an absurd puppet pushed to and fro by the will of those yellow faces . . ."; in the East, he says, the white man "becomes a sort of hollow, posing dummy. . . . He wears a mask, and his face grows to fit it" (7). Paragraph 10 continues this analogy, as Orwell describes the crowd breathing "a deep, low, happy sigh, as of people who see the theatre curtain go up at last." The third analogy compares the elephant to an elderly person; as he watches the beast in the rice paddy, he feels it has a "preoccupied grandmotherly air."

4. After he fires the first shot, he says the elephant "looked suddenly stricken, shrunken, immensely old. . . . His mouth slobbered. An enormous senility seemed to have settled upon him. One could have imagined him thousands of years old" (11). Orwell vividly evokes the suffering of the elephant by carefully observing the animal's movements after the shot. He notices the subtle but "terrible change" that came over it, in which "every line of his body had altered." The analogy with an old man helps structure his observations that the elephant seemed paralyzed, then sagged to his knees and slobbered. Other trenchant details include the image of the animal standing "weakly upright" again and the image of him toppling "like a huge rock," "his trunk reaching skywards like a tree and trumpeting once" (11). In paragraph 12, Orwell provides a graphic description of the beast's death agony. He reports firing over and over; into a picture that has so far been in black-and-white, he interjects colors. He remembers that the elephant's "mouth was wide open" so that "he could see far down into caverns of pale pink throat," and that "the thick blood welled out of him like red velvet." In this paragraph, too, we hear sounds: the "dreadful noise" and the "tortured gasps" that continued "steadily as the ticking of a clock."

THE FOURTH OF JULY

Audre Lord

Questions for Close Reading (p. 212)

1. Here is one possible way of stating the essay's implied thesis: "Lorde's eighth grade graduation was supposed to mark the end of her childhood. But it was her Fourth of July graduation-present trip to Washington, D.C. that truly marked the end of her innocence, because there she encountered the harsh reality of racism."

2. This picnic is Lorde's mother's idea of what it means to take care of her family, even to the extent that she provides different pickles (one type for the father, another type for the kids), wraps peaches separately so they won't bruise, and puts in a tin of rosewater for messy hands. Being a good mother also means packing the things your family enjoys, like "'marigolds' . . . from Cushman's Bakery . . . and rock-cakes from Newton's" (paragraph 4). All these domestic details of a caring mother underscore the injustice, the horrific irony of the way the family is treated at the ice cream counter. Although Lorde's mother probably believed in her heart that packing the picnic was a way to keep her family safe from food touched by the hands of strangers, more importantly, it was also a way to keep her children away from the racist situation they would most likely encounter in the railroad dining car. In short, these elaborate picnic preparations were evidence of the mother's avoidance of unpleasantness at all cost.

3. There are two reasons Lorde gives us for her inability to comprehend her parents' admonitions against white people. First of all, Lorde's parents never gave her any reasons; they just expected her "to know without being told" (7) the logic behind their warnings and the source of their feelings regarding white people. In addition, she has difficulty accepting such a dictate when her mother, as she tells us, "looked so much like one of those people we were never supposed to trust" (7) The fuzziness of the dictate leaves Lorde doubly vulnerable to the experience she encounters at the ice cream counter.

4. In paragraphs 5 and 6, Lorde illustrates her mother's attempt to sidestep racism and her father's attempt to make up for it. By packing an elaborate picnic for the trip, Lorde's mother successfully avoids subjecting her family to the racism they would surely have encountered had they attempted to eat in the dining car. And when Lorde's sister is denied access to her own senior class trip because, truth be told, they would be staying in a hotel that "did not rent rooms to Negroes," Lorde's father tries to offset Phyllis's disappointment by planning a family trip instead. In paragraph 7, Lorde explains her parents' behavior more fully. She writes: "They handled it as a private woe. My mother and father believed that they could best protect their children from the realities of race in america and the fact of american racism by never giving them name, much less discussing their nature."

   In the picture Lorde draws for us in paragraph 18, her family does not so much deal with the situation as ignore it. After the waitress delivered her message, Lorde tells us, "Straight-backed and indignant, one by one, my family got down from the counter stools and turned around and marched out of the store, quiet and outraged, as if we had never been Black before." But when she questions her parents about this obvious injustice, they don't answer her. In fact, they never address the incident, "not because they had contributed to it, but because they felt they should have anticipated it and avoided it" (19). Lorde gets increasingly angry not only because her parents do not share her heated emotions, but also because they seem to accept responsibility for what happened. Also, her sisters mimic her parents' pretense of denial, and this invalidation of her response from all members of the family just heightens

Lorde's fury and anger. Moreover, while she is given the freedom to articulate her fury in a letter to the President of the United States, because her father insists upon reviewing the letter before she sends it off, we wonder whether she will be permitted to fully express her righteous rage.

5. *fabled* (1): famous; legendary
   injunction (7): order or demand
   progressive (8): favoring progress or reform
   dilated (9): enlarged
   vulnerable (9): unprotected
   travesty (10): a ridiculous representation of something
   decreed (13): ordered
   pretense (19): false appearance

Questions About the Writer's Craft (pp. 212-13)

1. Lorde uses transitions of time and place to let us know when and where events occur. In the first sentence of the essay, Lorde establishes a general time frame when she writes that events occurred "on the edge of . . . summer." The final sentence of paragraph 1 narrows that time frame down to the Fourth of July. In paragraph 2, we learn that Lorde's family took the trip "during the day" and that it was made by train. We know that the train leaves New York City and passes through Philadelphia; Lorde writes, "I remember it was Philadelphia because I was disappointed not to have passed by the Liberty Bell" (3). In paragraphs 8 and 12, she signals the family's arrival at their destination ("In Washington, D.C., we had one large room with two double beds and an extra cot for me") as well as the family's movement out of the hotel to see the sites ("I spent the whole next day after Mass squinting up at the Lincoln Memorial"). Paragraph 13 reveals the passage of time ("Later that Washington afternoon my family and I walked back down Pennsylvania Avenue"), while paragraphs 15 and 16 set the scene at the ice cream parlor ("Two blocks away from our hotel, the family . . . stopped . . . at a . . . soda fountain . . . . Corded and crisped and pinafored, the five of us seated ourselves one by one at the counter") and indicate Lorde's place in the scene ("There was I between my mother and father"). Paragraph 18 reveals the family's response to the waitress's refusal to serve them (". . . one by one, my family . . . got down from the counter . . . and marched out of the store"). That day ends with Lorde's writing a letter to the President of the United States, which her father promises she can type out on the "office typewriter next week" (19). The "whole rest of that trip," Lorde writes, she felt sick to her stomach (20).

2. In paragraphs 5-7, 9-11 and 19-20, Lorde moves from the events of the day to other discussions. Nevertheless, the information she provides in these instances is critical. The last sentence of paragraph 5 and the whole of paragraphs 6 and 7 are used to convey the way her parents handle racism and how their behavior affects her. Although the information in these paragraphs does not advance the narrative itself, what she reveals here has much to do with the experience she is describing. Her parents' failure to explain "the realities of race in america and the fact of american racism" leaves her open to the confusion and pain she feels while in Washington.
   In paragraphs 9-11, we learn that Lorde has trouble seeing clearly every summer; her eyes are unable to adjust to the "dazzling whiteness" of July. At first, this little aside about squinting seems arbitrary and unnecessary, but later we find that it is actually a metaphor for being blinded to racism: Just as her parents "did not approve of sunglasses, nor of their expense" (thus forcing her to squint her way through each summer, never seeing clearly), they

also did not approve of racism discussions, nor of the cost of exposing their children to the reality of racism (thus forcing Lorde into a sort of blindness that made the day of clarity all the more painful).

In paragraph 19, Lorde tells us that her sisters, like her parents, behaved as though nothing was wrong with what happened in the ice cream parlor. In fact, her whole family seemed to have a tacit agreement that denial was the best way to handle—or not handle—racism. Lorde feels alone in her inability to accept injustice. As a result, Washington, D.C. becomes a solid block of whiteness that makes her sick to her stomach, and the trip itself proves to be "[not] much of a graduation present after all" (20).

3. Lorde's use of the lower case is appropriate. Given the soul-searing incident she experiences in Washington, D.C., the nation's capital, on the holiday commemorating that nation's declaration of independence and its promise of freedom and justice for all, the use of lower-case letters conveys her lack of respect for a country and a leader that fail to uphold those promises implied in the celebration of the Fourth of July.

4. In paragraph 20, Lorde repeats the word "white" over and over again: "The waitress was white, and the counter was white, and the ice cream I never ate in Washington, D.C., that summer I left childhood was white, and the white heat and the white pavement and the white stone monuments of my first Washington summer made me sick to my stomach for the whole rest of that trip and it wasn't much of a graduation present after all." Like Lorde, who feels overcome by the prevalence of racism, we too are overcome by the word "white" and can understand Lorde's experience: Racism is constant and exists everywhere.

SELLING THE POST

Russell Baker

Questions for Close Reading (p. 219)

1. Baker's narrative point is that his mother gave him his early start, at eight years of age, in journalism (1). We quickly gather that Baker means this jokingly, for his early push into the world of work came, he says, as a result of his mother's belief that he needed to develop "gumption" in order to "make something" of himself in life (1-2). In addition, her intention was to push him into the business end of publishing, not into journalism, where he himself later chose to work. Throughout the essay, Baker humorously cites one situation after another in which his lack of gumption was exposed and his unsuitability for business transparent.

2. Young Russell Baker possessed some typical juvenile characteristics. He gets excited easily; he is cowed by adults; he is passive as a salesman, and he is obedient to his mother's campaign to make him a success. When his mother tells him someone is coming to visit them, he "burst in" from school to meet the unknown visitor—"an executive of the Curtis Publishing Company" (11). In the conversation that follows, Baker is quiet and perhaps benumbed, for his mother jumps in and answers the man's questions, while he follows up each time with the same two-word response: "That's right." And in the actual selling, Baker shows himself to be oblivious of the ways of the commercial world: he stands around on a corner with the bag of magazines slung around his neck, awaiting buyers (32).

Doris, although two years younger than Russell, possesses all the gumption that he lacks. She has energy and verve and determination. Baker provides a telling example of her personality: "When she was only seven she could carry a piece of short-weighted cheese back to the A & P, threaten the manager with legal action, and come back triumphantly with the full quarter-pound we'd paid for and a few ounces extra thrown in for forgiveness" (3).

The sister operates as a foil, or revealing opposite, to Baker. When he sells the *Saturday Evening Post* at a trickling pace, Doris is instructed to take him out to learn how it is done. She succeeds in a few minutes what he cannot accomplish in a week (52-55). Doris is a miniature adult at the young age of seven, a "midget" as Baker puts it in paragraph 53, and she scolds and rats on her older brother (56-59). Her maturity and spunk provide a shaming contrast to Baker, a boy who prefers reading to doing anything practical (2).

3. Mrs. Baker shows her self to be a conventionally-minded woman, always spouting maxims, and she clearly believed that success was achieved by "gumption" and work. Baker tells us she heartily believed that "The Lord helps those who help themselves" (4), and "If at first you don't succeed, try, try again." (61). Beyond this, however, she has experienced what life could be like when one's career choices were limited. Her husband, Baker's father, had been a "plain workman" and lived a hard life with little reward; he "died with a few sticks of mail-order furniture as [his] legacy" (46). After his death, she had to move her children and herself in with her brother, a successful salesman who could afford to take in "threadbare relatives" (31). Mrs. Baker wanted a better life for her children—better being a chance at a white-collar job and the luxuries of a big house, a Buick, and a vacation at the beach (46). Hence she felt it was crucial to instill the spirit of competition into her son, and perhaps, with her brother Allen as a model, believed sales was a solid career choice.

4. After three years of struggle as a magazine vendor, Russell still apparently demonstrated no greater aptitude for commerce, and his mother began to contemplate preparing him for "careers that demanded less competitive zeal" (62). One evening, after her seventh-grader son showed her a school composition that had gained an A, she suddenly realized that he might make a writer. Baker reports that he "clasped the idea to . . . heart" because he loved reading but also because he saw instantly that possessing "gumption" would not be a requirement for this career. In fact, he says, "so far as I could make out, what writers did couldn't even be classified as work" (65).

5. *gumption* (2): initiative or resourcefulness
   repose (2): dignified calmness
   interrogations (7): formal questions
   grit (14): courage
   spunk (26): dogged courage
   chasuble (30): sleeveless outer vestment worn by priests
   extracted (30): pulled out, drawn out
   intervened (42): came between
   aptitude (45): natural talent or ability
   wean (46): to free from a habit or attitude
   canvassed (47): solicited
   zeal (62): enthusiasm
   prose (63): ordinary language without meter or rhyme

Questions About the Writer's Craft (p. 219)

1. Baker's use of dialog is an important source of humor, and the dialog also helps to dramatize the differences between Baker and his mother. Early in the essay, we learn that Mrs. Baker, rather single-minded and determined, tends to communicate in maxims and to speak bluntly against traits she doesn't care for, such as lack of "gumption." The bluntness of her remarks may make the reader chuckle. "You've got no more gumption than a bump on a log, . . . Get out in the kitchen and help Doris do those dirty dishes," Baker reports her saying (2). And when he innocently says that, as a career, he would choose "garbage man," she immediately replies, "Have a little gumption, Russell" (9).

   Baker reports a long, three-way conversation between his mother, a *Saturday Evening Post* sales rep, and himself which displays Mrs. Baker's own determination and gumption—and his youthful lack of these traits. When the sales executive inquires pompously about Russell's desire and aptitude for selling the *Post*, Mrs. Baker matches the questions with her own exaggerated, enthusiastic responses, while her overwhelmed son can only add weakly, "That's right" (11-29). In a later conversation, his mother interrogates him bluntly about his first on-the-street sales stint, requesting all the details of his strategy, uncovering his failure to have any strategy: "How many did you sell, Buddy? . . . Where did you go? . . . What did you do? . . . You just stood there? . . . For God's sake, Russell!" (33-41). His uncle, rather than his mother, has some mercy on him, and subscribes to the *Post* then and there (42). Baker also presents other snippets of conversation with his mother that show her relentlessness and determination; she says things like, "If you think I'm going to raise a good-for-nothing, you've got another thing coming" (45), and "Better get out there and sell the rest of those magazines tonight" (48).

2. Baker's little sister Doris displays a personality opposite to his, and, in fact, is clearly the inheritor of his mother's assertive, competitive, resourceful traits. Doris displays her own gumption throughout the essay; in paragraph 3, where she is introduced, we learn she "had enough gumption for a dozen people," ripped through housework with great energy, and could in a snap get justice at the supermarket for a piece of short-weighted cheese. In the matter of selling the *Post*, we soon surmise that she, not Russell, is possessed of the "grit, the character, the never-say-quit spirit it takes to succeed in business," the personality prescribed by the *Post* sales rep (14). Sent out to help him, Doris gets the magazines sold in a few minutes with a characteristic aggressiveness, and when he springs for an apple to reward her, she parentally scolds him for wasting money and eating before supper.

   In addition to humorously delineating the characters of his mother and himself, the inclusion of assertive little Doris turns our expectations upside down. In this family, it is the women who have the spirit of competition and who seem not to care whose feelings might be trampled when they assert themselves. A final character who offers contrast is Uncle Allen, who, while a successful businessman, shows himself to be more considerate and nurturing than Baker's own mother. While she deplores his failure to sell any magazines on his first try, Uncle Allen feels sorry for him and buys a subscription as a way of encouragement.

3. The narrative of Baker's career in "journalism" (really, in sales) begins in paragraph 10, and is signalled the subordinating conjunction, "when." The scene then quickly shifts to the conversation with the Curtis Publishing Company representative, and this is also signalled by a clause starting with "when": "When I burst in that afternoon she was in conference in the parlor . . ." (11). This lengthy conversation (11-30) is followed in the next paragraph by a shift to the next week: "The following Tuesday . . ." (31), when Baker goes out to sell the magazines for the first time. The slow passage of time at his job is indicated by the transition, "For the next several hours . . ." (33) and his return home is marked by yet another "when"

clause: "When the angle of the light indicated it was suppertime, I walked back to the house" (33).

Some time passes, and Baker reports on a later attempt at selling. He eases our transition to this scene with the phrase, "One rainy night . . ." (52). After this incident in which Doris shows Russell how to really sell those magazines, Baker moves us along two years, using the phrase, "By the time I was ten . . ." (61). We reach the conclusion of his career in sales in paragraph 63, which Baker introduces with a transition of time: "One evening when I was eleven. . . ."

4. Numerous details establish that the narrative is occurring a couple of generations ago. Little details, such as the title of the book he read as a boy, *Dick Tracy Meets Stooge Viller*, the fact that the dishes are being washed by hand (2), and the problem of cheese cut and "short-weighted" at the grocery (3) tip readers off early in the essay that we are being taken back quite a few decades. Likewise, the comment that in those days the best career a spunky girl could have was as a nurse or teacher sets the story in the past (3). In paragraph 6, Baker comes right out and refers to "fifty years ago" as a time when people might seriously inquire of a young boy whether he wanted to be president someday; it was a time when grandfathers "could remember Lincoln's time." In paragraph 31, we learn explicitly that the story is occurring in a suburb of northern New Jersey, outside of the city of Newark, and that "it was 1932, the bleakest year of the Depression." Other details establish that life was hard, and that the Bakers, having suffered the loss of Mr. Baker, were living with Mrs. Baker's younger brother, a successful business man. These details set the scene for the drama of a mother and son, the mother determined—both from personality and from terror at the economic destitution everywhere at that time—to set her son on a path to success, and the son dumbfounded by the very concept of "gumption." Documenting how this conflict failed to produce a competent salesmen but instead, ironically and by default, set Baker on the road to national fame as a columnist is the heart of Baker's purpose.

ANSWERS FOR CHAPTER 13
"ILLUSTRATION" (p. 223)

Opening Comments

When we first started teaching, we were caught off guard by students' seeming inability to provide detailed, specific examples in their papers. But we soon uncovered the reason for the vagueness of their writing. Many of them arrived in college with the notion that good writing is abstract and full of highfalutin language. Warned over and over not to pad their papers, many students had come to regard specific details and "for instances" as fluff.

We've found an almost sure-fire way to help students appreciate how powerfully examples can affect a reader. We have them react (see page 229) to two versions of some student writing, one enlivened with specifics, the other flat, lifeless, and sorely in need of supporting details. When we question students about their reactions ("Which version is more interesting? Which gives you more of a sense of the writer?"), we actually see them coming to grasp the full importance of vigorous supporting details.

Next, we spend some class time on prewriting activities. This helps students learn how to generate examples for their essays.

That skill mastered, some of our eager-to-please students then give us too much of a good thing. They force readers to wade through a mass of specifics that don't add focus or drama to the essay's idea. When this happens, we emphasize that writers need to be selective and choose only the most striking, telling examples to support a point.

Varied in subject and mood, the professional selections in this chapter illustrate the power writing derives from rich supporting detail. In her gentle, reflective essay, "Channelled Whelk," Lindbergh sometimes uses a string of specifics (as in the eighth paragraph) to suggest the clutter of everyday life. Douglas tackles the barrage of conflicting messages the media creates, citing numerous examples to illustrate her struggle ("Managing Mixed Messages"). Finally, Garity ("Is Sex All That Matters?") provides an extended example as well as numerous small details to identify and explore a societal problem.

ACTIVITIES: ILLUSTRATION

Below we provide possible responses to selected activities at the end of Chapter 13. Of course, your students are bound to come up with their own approaches.

Prewriting Activities (p. 239)

1. There are many ways to use illustration in these two essays; the lists below only begin to name the possibilities. We suggest that you have students share their ideas for examples, perhaps with a partner or in small groups. Seeing what others have come up with makes the point clearly that writing involves invention and individuality.

   ### Topic: Why public school teachers quit

      Teacher who has to work a second job to support family
      Ex-teacher now a mail carrier, better paid
      Science teacher recruited by industry
      Teacher resenting blame and criticism of education today
      Teacher toiling late at night over tests and lesson plans

   ### Topic: Defining a preppie

      Female wearing pearls with baggy shorts on a chilly day
      Male wearing rugby striped shirt with a crest and loafers
      Preppies' conversation centering on grades and careers
      Preppie male going out for crew or tennis
      Preppie female playing intramural lacrosse or field hockey

Revising Activities (pp. 239-40)

We suggest you offer students the chance to read each other's revised versions of the paragraphs in activities 5, 6, and 7. Such exposure to others' work helps them to see new ways of handling the revision and can encourage them to be more creative.

5. Here are the main problems with the paragraph:

   — Needs examples of how stores might be modernized: new signs, more professional window display, interior renovation.

   — Nature of the improvements to streets should be shown by examples: potted plants, outdoor sculptures, decorative benches, outdoor cafes.

   — Examples needed of how town could be made more "fun to walk."

   — Examples of the "attention-getting events" should be provided.

6. Here are some notes about the problems in the paragraph:

   — "When we act foolishly or wildly" is general and self-evident.

   — The "qualms" felt later are vague.

   — The situation behind someone's wanting "revenge" is obscure, making this detail unconvincing.

   — What it is like to "feel bad" because of the superego's influence needs to be shown by illustration.

   Here's the way an extended example might work in this paragraph:

   The superego is the part of us that makes us feel guilty when we do something that we know is wrong. A young person might feel guilt after an evening of carrying on. For example, suppose a group of bored young men get "a fun idea" driving into town late one Saturday night. They buy cartons of eggs and bombard semi-conscious homeless men and haggard-looking prostitutes with raw eggs and unprintable names. Feeling superior, they laugh themselves silly. The next day, however, they might wake up depressed at the thought of their treatment of unfortunate human beings. Their superego is finally at work, making them recognize their own evil side. I can affirm the power of the superego, because in my senior year of high school I was involved in just such a caper.

7. It's a good idea to provide time in class for students to read over each other's revisions of this paragraph. Seeing how others handled the revision can give students a stronger sense of their revision options.

   Here are the main problems with the paragraph:

   — Vague descriptions ("trendy," "fine") need replacement by vigorous images. A strong example or two is needed here.

   — Point about trendy clothes should be tied in to the idea of the costliness.

   — Singling out women is sexist; at the very least such a charge needs supporting examples. Indeed, more thought may well show that men are similarly vulnerable.

   — Shampoo example should occur at the end of the paragraph, because the movement of the paragraph is from things that don't wear out to things that do wear out. Change the opening words of the sentence to fit it into its new location.

   — "Slight changes" is vague; an example is necessary.

   — Statement that men are "naive" and are "hoodwinked" is sexist and irrelevant; this point also needs to be more clearly tied in to the point that the desire for the new is costly to the consumer.

CHANNELLED WHELK

Anne Morrow Lindbergh

Questions for Close Reading (p. 245)

1. Lindbergh's thesis is implied. One way to express it is as follows: "A life with a simple shape, like that of the shell, is best; it leads to a feeling of being 'in grace,' to being 'at peace with oneself'" (5). Or: "Women's lives would be improved if they could minimize the complications and distractions that go along with being wives, mothers, and career women; they might then find inner harmony."

2. The shell, first of all, reminds Lindbergh of the creatures it housed, a sea snail and a hermit crab. Then, she admires its simple beauty, its color, texture, and shape. It is a simple, useful, and beautiful object.

3. Women perform several roles in life, as mothers, wives, and homemakers; in the modern world, they can also choose to be involved in community affairs and the professions (8). The problem of multiplicity does not affect men so much, because their lives have been more restricted to professional and community affairs; they have had far fewer responsibilities in the home. "Distraction is, always has been, and probably always will be, inherent in women's lives."

4. Although Lindbergh says she "could live in it always" (19), she must leave the beach house to return to her everyday responsibilities, her chosen life of wife and mother. She takes the shell of the channelled whelk with her to remind her of its message of simplicity. She also hopes it will encourage her to aspire to inner harmony and grace (21).

5. *apex* (2): pointed end, tip
   conductive (6): apt to produce or bring about
   myriad (12): a great number, various
   periphery (12): outskirts or surrounding area
   sedentary (17): marked by much sitting

Questions About the Writer's Craft (pp. 245-46)

1. The major use of extended example occurs in paragraphs 14 to 17; here, Lindbergh moves away from discussion and analysis to provide the specifics of what she has shed at the beach. Earlier, in paragraph 7, she has included an extended example of "the caravan of complications" that characterizes the life of a modern woman.

2. By beginning with an evocative description of the shell, Lindbergh conveys a powerful image of a natural, simple kind of life. These images provide an inviting introduction to the essay and also contrast with her description of her own busy, "blurred" and barnacled woman's life (3). In paragraph 13, she returns to the image of the shell, stating specifically that it gives her a clue about how to achieve balance. In paragraphs 19-21, she meditates upon it one last time, hoping the shell will continue to inspire her to seek "grace" in life once she takes it back to Connecticut with her.

3. "Tying a shoestring" stands for all the trivial but absolutely necessary duties people must perform to survive. At first, Lindbergh uses the phrase off-handedly—"one can hardly tie a shoestring"—to refer to how frustrating and difficult ordinary tasks can be when one is feeling "out of grace." By repeating the image in the next sentence, she lets us know she is using the phrase as a metaphor for life's drudgery.

4. In speaking directly to the shell, Lindbergh treats it as if it were a being or a presence in itself. In the previous paragraph, she discusses how the shell's message of simplification pertains to the "outside" of her life. In addressing the shell, she indicates it has become part of her inner life and that it has set her thoughts on an inward journey of awareness and change.

MANAGING MIXED MESSAGES

Susan Douglas

Questions for Close Reading (p. 250)

1. Douglas states her thesis in the second paragraph: "Having grown up with the mass media myself, and considering what that has done for me and to me, I bring all that to bear as I raise my own little girl, who will, in her own way, and with her own generation, have her hopes and fears shaped by the mass media too." She restates it in the final paragraph, where she expresses her outrage as well: "Like us, they will have to work hard to fend off what cripples them and amplify what empowers them. But why, after all these years, should they still have to work so hard and to resist so much?"

2. As Douglas sees it, *The Little Mermaid* and *Beauty and the Beast* make only small steps in the right direction. She tells us that although *The Little Mermaid's* main character, Ariel, "is indeed brave, curious, feisty and defiant" (3), the movie still propagates images of women that are either unrealistic or derogatory. For instance, Ariel has a waist "the diameter of a chive, and her salvation comes through her marriage—at the age of sixteen, no less—to Eric. And the sadistic, consummately evil demon in the movie is, you guessed it, an older, overweight woman with too much purple eyeshadow and eyeliner, a female octopus who craves too much power and whose nether regions evoke the dreaded vagina dentate" (3). Likewise, *Beauty and the Beast* serves to maintain the notion that a woman's "dreams of a more interesting, exciting life" can be "fulfilled through marriage alone" (6)

   According to Douglas, nonanimated movies like *Home Alone* and *Free Willy* do not do much better in providing girls with positive role models. Movies such as these, she asserts, all have "little boy leads, little boy adventures, and little boy heroism," which means ". . . gutsy, smart, enterprising, and sassy little girls remain, after all this time, absent, invisible, denied." According to Douglas, these movies reflect the fact that "Hollywood simply takes it for granted that little heroes, like big ones, are always boys" (4). Girls, like Douglas's own daughter, can only imagine themselves in the hero role. The ultimate effect is that while boys come to accept as a given their "hero" status, girls continue to yearn for movies in which they take center stage.

3. Unlike the other movies Douglas mentions, *The Wizard of Oz* presents a positive female image, one in which the girl does not have to compromise her femaleness in order to be strong or assertive, nor does the movie have love and romance as the heroine's ultimate goal and final reward. As Douglas proclaims in paragraph 5, ". . . here's a *girl* who has an adventure and doesn't get married at the end. She runs away from home, flies to Oz in a cyclone, kills one wicked witch and then another—although never on purpose—and helps Scarecrow get a brain, Tin Man get a heart, and Lion get some courage, all of which Dorothy already has in spades. Throughout the movie, Dorothy is caring, thoughtful, nurturing, and empathetic, but she's also adventuresome, determined, and courageous."

   The only problem Douglas finds with this movie has nothing to do with the story line itself, but with what went on in the background in order for the movie to be made. According to Douglas, "Judy Garland had to have her breasts strapped down for the part and was fed bucketfuls of amphetamines so she'd remain as slim as the studio wanted."

4. On a number of occasions, Douglas refers to her daughter's reactions to the media's presentation of gender roles. We witness her daughter either accepting, rejecting, or questioning what the media present. In each case, Douglas's references to her daughter's reactions reinforce her thesis: that her daughter's hopes and fears are being "shaped by the mass media too" (2).

   In the first paragraph, Douglas's point is that the media dictate what toys are appropriate for girls and boys; she uses her daughter's Saturday-morning requests as evidence of the media's success in dictating gender-appropriate toy preferences. Paragraphs 2-4 illustrate the ways in which television programs and movies support either the age-old notion of female success through beauty and marriage or the idea that only boys can be adventuresome and heroic. To help make the point that the presentation of such concepts makes girls feel invisible, at the close of paragraph 4, Douglas refers us to her daughter's comment: "Mommy, there should be more movies with girls." The information she provides in paragraph 6—her daughter's insistence upon dressing like a girl, her love of games like "wedding" and "family," and her abandonment of blocks and trucks for Barbie—anticipates the focus of paragraph 7: the nature-nurture debate. Finally, in paragraph 9, Douglas focuses for the last time on her daughter's struggle to manage "the mixed messages around her." At times, she resists the messages and asserts her desire to be in control ("she dictates the precise direction of her pretend games with the authority of a field marshal"); other times she succumbs because "it is also important to her that she be pretty, desired." For Douglas, her daughter's struggle is evidence of the truth that media imagery "holds out promises of female achievement with one hand and slaps her down with the other."

5. *implores* (1): begs
   semiotics (1): the analysis of the nature and relationship of signs in language
   consummately (3): totally
   nether (3): lower
   arbitrary (4): based on one's preference, notion, or whim
   flourishes (4): displays
   resurgence (5): rising again
   retrograde (7): a throwback to or reminder of the past
   succumbs (9): gives in
   demurs (10): objects
   impart (10): convey
   unharried (11): not bothered
   exhortations (11): appeals

Questions About the Writer's Craft (p. 251)

1. Although Douglas switches back and forth from one genre to the other, she signals her moves clearly. The first paragraph focuses on television commercials, but we know that the following paragraph will cover the gamut of media genres because she states in paragraph 2, "Ever since she was old enough to understand books, kids' movies, and *Sesame Street*, I have looked, in vain, for strong and appealing female characters for her to identify with." In paragraph 2, she indicates movement from TV shows to books with "Children's books are not much better" and then returns to television shows ("Television cartoons . . . still treat females . . . as nonexistent or . . . ancillary afterthoughts"). To indicate her switch to a discussion of movies, she begins paragraph 3 with the words "And then there are the movies." To make sure readers stay focused on films, she begins paragraph 5 with "The one movie that I was happy to have . . . ." And in paragraph 8, she once again aims her sights at kids' Saturday morning television: "In fact, kids' TV is worse than ever . . . ."

2. Douglas seems both exasperated by and disgusted with the media's depiction of girls. In the first paragraph, these emotions are conveyed in the words and phrases she uses to describe both the situation with her daughter and the items advertised on television. She wakes on a Saturday morning as her daughter "implores" her to come see the thing she wants on television. She has to "drag" her "hungover and inadequately caffeinated butt over to the TV set." Her daughter's eyes "shine like moonstones" as she gazes at the screen. What Douglas sees before her is "some hideous plastic doll, or pony, or troll," "pitched" to her daughter by "elated little girls, flashing lights, and rap music." And the colors seem to be the same for "everything," from "a troll doll in a wedding dress" to "Kitty Surprise or Cheerleader Skipper." Her daughter doesn't want that "Pentagon-inspired stuff" for boys; she wants "nothing more in the whole wide world" than "Rollerblade Barbie." Douglas's choice of words and phrases establishes her disdain for what the media present to young girls. We understand how she feels about the situation before she actually articulates her position.

3. In paragraph 1, we hear Douglas's daughter talk. Her words ("Mommy, Mommy, hurry, come quickly, *now*!" and "Can I get that, Mommy, can I, puleeze? Please, Mommy") convey how caught up she is. Her urgency illustrates that she accepts the media messages totally and underscores how infuriating it is that parents have to counter these forces. We hear Douglas speak in paragraph 4. As she tells us, when the media at long last actually present a worthy depiction of a female, parents are reduced to didactic commentary ("See how *strong* she is, honey?") in an effort to counterbalance the media's insidious influence.

4. The question posed at the end of the piece reinforces the exasperation and frustration Douglas establishes in the opening paragraph. The question also forces readers—presumed to be parents ("Like us, our daughters . . . ")—to confront the responsibility they have for countering the corrosive effects of the gender conditioning promoted by the media. In short, the question encourages readers to come up with a solution, which is probably what Douglas wanted, for certainly the essay as a whole encourages us to action.

IS SEX ALL THAT MATTERS?

Joyce Garity

Questions for Close Reading (p. 255)

1. Garity's thesis is implied. It might be stated, "Overly sexualized imagery in ads and popular culture gives teenagers a false message: that sexual activity is to be sought and practiced with abandon." The essay provides numerous examples of ads that use sex to sell products and, in addition, sell a sexy lifestyle as well.

2. Elaine is filled with envy at the lifestyle depicted in ads, a lifestyle where beautiful, scantily clad young people dally in luxurious surroundings (4). Garity says that while Elaine lived with her, she saw how much the young woman "yearn[ed] after magazine images, soap-opera heroines and rock goddesses" (6). To Elaine, the ads showed "the way life—her life—is supposed to be. . . . a world characterized by sexual spontaneity, playfulness, and abandon" (6). Garity sees through the ads, however, because she is older and more experienced, and therefore knows that the photos are not real. They are "a marketing invention." She writes, "I know that the moment the photo shoot was over, the beautiful room was dismantled, the models moved on the next job, and the technicians took over the task of doctoring the photograph until it reached full-blown fantasy proportions" (5). The ads and soap operas omit the "unsexy" realities of relationships: birth control, unwanted pregnancy, AIDS, and "shattered lives." They ignore the issues of "commitment or whether [people] should act on their sexual impulses" (6), and despite the extreme titillation that often goes on in the ads, the issue of rape is ignored (6).

3. Garity complains that our culture "parades sexuality at every turn and makes heroes of the advocates of sexual excess." Clothing stores sell "hooker-style" clothing for girls of all ages, and children are taken to see concerts of pop stars who are famous for their sexy style or where pretend sex occurs on stage. Sports heroes, the idols of young boys, boast of obsessive sexual conquest. The accused boys in a criminal case involving the systematic rape of girls were rewarded with talk-show appearances and excused by their parents as exhibiting their manhood (9).

4. Garity points out that most sex education focuses on the biology and excludes discussion of values, of "sexuality as only one part of a well balanced life." The biological dangers of pregnancy and sexually transmitted diseases are discussed, but the emotional components of sexuality— "love and stuff like that," in the words of a Spur Posse member— are ignored. Garity indicates that she feels the schools should teach specific ideas about sex: that abstinence can be "an emotionally or spiritually satisfying option," that sex should be saved for "an emotionally intimate, exclusive, trusting relationship" (10).

5. *waif* (3): a lost child
   croon (4): sing
   spontaneity (6): quality of acting on impulse
   abandon (6): freedom from constraint
   pedestrian (6): ordinary
   irony (7): an outcome opposite to what might have been
   euphemisms (8): mild indirect terms for vulgar or ordinary things
   innuendo (8): shade of meaning
   vestige (9): remnant

simulated (9): imitation
copulation (9): sexual intercourse
abstinence (10): avoidance of sexual activity
exclusive (10): shutting out all others from participation

Questions About the Writer's Craft (p. 255)

1. The case of Elaine, a girl so childlike and romantic, and so very irresponsible and pregnant, dramatizes the problems created in a culture where sex is portrayed as necessary, wonderful, and glamorous. The author's personal experience with this girl adds immediacy, even a sense of emergency, to the point that young people's lives are shattered when they innocently try to live like the kids in the ads. Elaine's situation, described in depth, provides a springboard for all the issues that Garity raises: the naive response of youth to media images, the cruel reality that can result from irresponsible sex, the failure of sex education to stem the sexual tide. Finally, the use of Elaine as an example helps the reader to understand that Garity's message is rooted in her humane and even maternal concern for the real suffering of young people; it lends her credibility, in a sense, for it implies that Garity is not just another anti-sex media critic.

2. Garity makes clear that she and Elaine would not see eye-to-eye on the subject of the way ads portray relationships. Elaine, in her unsophisticated way, would find the ads romantic and beautiful (4). Garity, while acknowledging the strong impact of the ads, would see through them to the false message they convey about the role of sex in relationships; she would also be aware of the craft that has created the illusion of perfect bodies, luxurious surroundings, and spontaneity (5). Garity also contrasts the way ads used to be and the way they currently are. Although it is a constant that ads have always used sex to lure unsuspecting consumers, older ads were more veiled and discrete, putting the focus on "popularity" or "lovableness." But today's ads explicitly suggest that happy sex results from consuming certain products (8). A third contrast occurs in the biological focus of sex education and Garity's preference for sex ed to highlight values, especially traditional values about sexual abstinence and committed relationships (10).

3. Garity suggests a cause-effect relationship between the excessively sexualized advertisements that inundate young people in our culture and Elaine's irresponsible sexual behavior and pregnancy. She writes, "Years of exposure to this media-invented, sex-saturated universe have done their work on Elaine" (7). In paragraph 8, Garity points out that the lure of lovableness or popularity has always caused "the masses" of ordinary people to be "susceptible to the notion that a particular product will make them more sexually attractive" and that this fact has resulted in advertisers' use of sex in ads. In addition to pointing out a cause-effect relationship between ads and sexual behavior, Garity suggests that other cultural factors have caused young people to be more sexual at an earlier age: sexy children's clothes, children's attendance at sexy rock concerts, sports heroes' boasts about their sexual appetites, and the rewards of publicity for those who commit sexual crimes (9). In addition, Garity implies that sex education that is limited to the hows of sexual biology can cause young people to ignore or be ignorant of the emotional or spiritual sides of intimacy (10).

4. Garity's essay bristles with concern and indignation about the forces that have victimized Elaine and other young people. The essay begins with her neutral description of Elaine's situation, but as the essay moves on, Garity's tone becomes more heightened. As she focuses on the media causes of her anger, she invokes her memories of Elaine using a repeated phrase: "I think about her often . . . I think of her as I page through . . . I think of Elaine . . ." anger

blares through. As she describe the ads she sees in a fashion magazine, she uses strong, even harsh, images: the magazines "trumpet sexuality page after leering page"; models wear "snug" dresses cut to "just below the crotch"; a "naked," "waif-thin" girl wears a look of "startled helplessness" (3). Her tone become sarcastic as she uses short, curt sentences to elaborate on the beauty that Elaine would perceive in the ads: "The faces and bodies they show are lovely. The lighting is superb. The hair and makeup are faultless" (4). Elaine "could only want to be the girl in the ads," Garity writes, adding, again sarcastically, "Heck, *I* want to be her" (4).

The sarcasm crops up again when Garity describes the factors omitted from this "marketing invention" of a world: "Nor, apparently," she complains, "do [these people] spend much time thinking about such pedestrian topics as commitment. . . ." She uses heightened language to contrast their "clean sunlit rooms" with the ignored realities of "AIDS, of unwanted pregnancy, of shattered lives" (6). In paragraphs 7-8, Garity continues her strong condemnatory imagery: "this media-invented, sex-saturated universe"; Elaine "melts over images from a sexual Shangri-la" (7) and is "not the first to be suckered by the cynical practice of using sex to sell underwear . . ." (8). As she describes more sexualized ads, she again grows sarcastic: an ad "coyly invites" a magazine's readers; a jeans ad shows "a jolly gang-bang fantasy in the making." (8).

Her tone becomes blunt in paragraph 9's description of the sexual mores of today's youth: "virginity is regarded as an embarrassing vestige of childhood, to be disposed of as quickly as possible." Again she relies upon strong imagery and straight-forward assertion of the facts to convey her anger: our culture "parades" sexuality and rock concerts feature "simulated on-stage masturbation" or a "pretended act of copulation"; boys "charged with systematically raping girls as young as 10 . . . were rewarded with a publicity tour." She accuses sex education of being a "late, lame attempt to counterbalance" the "sexual overload" (10). Her pounding series of questions in paragraph 11 is indignant and capped by her complaint: "No one has told Elaine" (12).

ANSWERS FOR CHAPTER 14
"DIVISION-CLASSIFICATION" (p. 259)

Opening Comments

We sometimes feel slightly uneasy about teaching division-classification as a distinct pattern of development. After all, the logic at its core comes into play often during the writing process. For example, when students generate and group ideas during the prewriting stage and when they outline their material, they necessarily draw on the ordering principles of division-classification. Even though many students can instinctively use it, we still teach division-classification as a discrete pattern of development. Understanding it helps students appreciate the demands of logical analysis.

We recommend covering division-classification early in the semester, although work on this pattern can be deferred. Students weak in analysis profit from an explicit discussion of the way to break down ideas and establish categories. And, all students gain from analyzing essays to determine whether division and/or classification forms the main organizational principle.

Working with division-classification can cause two problems for students. First, they sometimes become confused about the difference between division and classification. They think they're classifying when they're dividing and dividing when they're classifying. On page 260, we state as succinctly as we can the difference between these two related but separate processes: Division involves taking a *single unit* or a *concept, breaking the unit down* into its *parts*, and *analyzing the connection* among the parts and between the parts and the whole. Classification *brings two or more related items together* and *categorizes* them according to type or kind.

Second, some students view division-classification as a pointless exercise designed by overly particular composition teachers. When they learn that they've been using division-classification all along (when brainstorming, when outlining, and so on), they begin to understand that division-classification is a valuable tool for logical analysis. In this regard, the student essay, "The Truth About College Professors" (pages 269-72), will provide the class with a good laugh (perhaps even at your expense) and help students see how to use classification to make a point.

This chapter's professional essays show how division-classification can help writers shed light upon a subject. In "Propaganda Techniques in Today's Advertising," McClintock uses classification to sort the types of Madison Avenue tactics. Tannen ("But What Do You Mean?") classifies our most common forms of verbal interaction to explore the different ways men and women communicate. And Greenfield's "Why Nothing Is 'Wrong' Anymore" divides and categorizes the justifications by which wrong becomes acceptable in today's America.

ACTIVITIES: DIVISION-CLASSIFICATION

Below we provide possible responses to selected activities at the end of Chapter 14. Of course, other approaches are possible.

Prewriting Activities (pp. 275-76)

1. Division-classification can be used in a variety of ways in these two essays. Below are a few suggestions. It's a good idea to have students share their ideas on the use of division-classification with each other; this will provide a concrete demonstration of the possibilities.

    Topic: How to impress college instructors

    > Divide brown-nosing techniques into types
    > Classify students according to their favorite technique
    > Classify instructors according to what impresses them

    Topic: Why volunteerism is on the rise

    > Divide to obtain motivations for volunteerism
    > Classify people needing help
    > Classify kinds of people who are apt to volunteer

2. Here are some possible principles of division for each of the topics. Other principles of division and theses are possible.

    a. **Prejudice**

    Principle of division: According to how prejudice develops
    Thesis: A prejudice against a group may be learned from one's parents, absorbed from society, or based on a bad experience of one's own.

    Principle of division: According to whether the prejudice is dangerous
    Thesis: Most of us have prejudices; some are trivial, such as a bias against broccoli; others are harmless, such as an intolerance for whiners; still others are hurtful, such as a mistrust of a racial, ethnic, or religious group.

    Principle of division: According to the motivation for the prejudice
    Thesis: Prejudice against another group of people can be motivated by fear, jealousy, or ignorance.

    b. **Rock Music**

    Principle of division: According to era
    Thesis: Rock music styles fall into distinct eras: music of fifties, sixties, seventies, and eighties.

    Principle of division: According to audience
    Thesis: Rock music appeals to many audiences: the middle-aged, the yuppie, the college-aged, and the teenaged.

Principle of division: According to its origin
Thesis: Rock music has diverse influences: country music, rhythm and blues, and jazz.

c. **A Shopping Mall**

Principle of division: According to time of day at mall
Thesis: At different times of the day, different groups of people inhabit the mall: senior "mall-walkers" in the early morning, business people grabbing lunch at midday, mothers and babies in the early afternoon, and teenagers in the early evening.

Principle of division: According to what is sold
Thesis: The types of stores that prosper at Garvey Mall tell much about today's consumer; the majority of shops sell apparel, quite a few sell audio and video tapes, but only one sells books.

Principle of division: According to places people congregate
Thesis: The fountain, the fast-food arcade, and the movie theater patio at Garvey Mall are all social spots, but for different types of people.

d. **A Good Horror Movie**

Principle of division: According to person being victimized
Thesis: In *Kennel Horror II*, the victim is either an unsuspecting innocent, a helpless poor person, or a law-enforcement officer.

Principle of division: According to attack location
Thesis: The victims in *Kennel Horror II* are attacked in their own homes, in pleasant public places, or in isolated rural areas.

Principle of division: According to film shots
Thesis: Director Logan Bettari uses extreme close-ups, rapid pans, and jarring cuts to increase the tension in *Kennel Horror II*.

3. Here are some possible principles of classification and thesis statements for this topic. Your students, of course, may come up with different ones.

Topic: The effects of expanding the college enrollment

Principle of classification: According to which groups expansion would affect
Thesis: Expanding the college enrollment would severely affect the student body, the faculty, and the local townspeople.

Principle of classification: According to effects on various aspects of college life
Thesis: Expanding the college enrollment would have serious economic, social, and academic effects.

Principle of classification: According to consequences for various academic departments

> *Thesis:* Expanding the college's enrollment will minimally affect most departments, somewhat affect departments with popular majors, and seriously affect departments offering many required courses.

Revising Activities (pp. 276-77)

4. The essay is based on a principle of division; "experience" is divided according to areas: employment, academic, social.

   The principle of division is applied incorrectly in the second point. Instead of being about an area of experience, this point focuses on "negative" experiences, a broad division that doesn't fit with the other areas. Second of all, the point refers only to "optimists," while all the other points refer to everyone.

   The problem can be remedied by eliminating the second point, since there are already three other solid points to be made in the essay.

5. Make time for your students to share their revisions with each other. Seeing the work of others helps students see all the possibilities in revising.

   This paragraph divides the concept of "play" using as a principle of division how much the child's peers are involved in the play. The paragraph's organization is based on the chronological appearance of the stages in the child's growth. The principle is applied consistently, but there are some problems in organization and in the support offered.

   Here are the specific problems with the paragraph:

   — The discussion of the first stage ("babies and toddlers") needs a specific example or two of "their own actions."

   — The fourth sentence, about elementary children's play, is incorrectly located in the paragraph, which discusses the play of preschool children. Delete this sentence.

   — The discussion of the second stage ("parallel play") could use an example of the "similar activities" the children engage in and how the children might "occasionally" interact. Note the specific examples provided for the third stage.

   — The last sentence is irrelevant and contradictory because no connection is made between the "special delight in physical activities" and the social aspect of children's play. In addition, the second part of the sentence contradicts the topic (first) sentence. This point must be more thought out and more details should be added.

PROPAGANDA TECHNIQUES IN TODAY'S ADVERTISING

Ann McClintock

Questions for Close Reading (p. 282)

1. McClintock's thesis is located at the end of the first paragraph: "Advertisers lean heavily on propaganda to sell their products, whether the 'products' are a brand of toothpaste, a candidate for office, or a particular political viewpoint."

2. Propaganda is the "systematic effort to influence people's opinions, to win them over to a certain view or side" (2) in terms of product choices, political candidates, or social concerns. Many people associate propaganda solely with the subversive campaigns of foreign powers or with the spreading of outrageous lies to an unwitting, innocent populace. But actually, propaganda is all around us; it is used by all the special interests that vie for our attention, our dollars, and our votes. American advertising is pervaded with propaganda in its attempt to sell us commercial products, and our political climate suffers from blizzard after blizzard of propaganda before each election.

3. Advertisers use "weasel words" to "stack the cards" and distort facts so that their products appear superior. Weasel words are words that say more than they mean and suggest more value than they actually denote. For example, an ad might say a shampoo "helps control dandruff," but we might understand this to mean that it cures dandruff (19).

4. Consumers should be aware of propaganda techniques so they can resist the appeal of ads that distort the truth or pull at our emotions. Only when we can separate the actual message and evaluate it for ourselves are we doing the hard work of clear thinking: "analyzing a claim, researching the facts, examining both sides of an issue, using logic to see the flaws in an argument" (23).

5. *seduced* (1): enticed
   warmonger (5): person who attempts to start wars
   elitist (17): an exclusive or privileged group

Questions About the Writer's Craft (p. 282)

1. The definition of propaganda informs us about the term's true meaning and also clears up misunderstandings about the extent to which average Americans are subjected to propaganda. The broader purpose of providing us with this definition is to persuade us that advertising is indeed propaganda. McClintock hopes to motivate us to learn more about the various techniques of propaganda, so we can protect ourselves from its daily onslaughts.

2. "Seduced" and "brainwashed" are both words with strong negative connotations; we are likely to be shocked or disbelieving when we read that "Americans, adults and children alike, are being seduced. They are being brainwashed" (1). By using these terms, McClintock challenges our belief in our independence and free will. Through the use of these and other terms ("victims"), she provokes us to continue reading the essay. Ironically, this use of loaded words manipulates the readers' reactions in a manner similar to that of propaganda.

3. Questions appear in the discussions of glittering generalities and card stacking and in the conclusion to the essay. In both sections on propaganda techniques, the questions are rhetorical, in that they need no answers. They are questions used to make a point. For example, McClintock asks, "After all, how can anyone oppose 'truth, justice, and the American way'?" (6). The implied answer is, "No one can." In her discussion of specific empty phrases, the author asks questions to point out the meaningless of such statements as "He cares" and "Vote for Progress" (7). These questions are meant not to be answered, but to show the vagueness of glittering generalities. In the section on card stacking (18-20), the author suggests that readers ask questions to test the validity of a political accusation such as "My opponent has changed his mind five times." The questions in the essay's conclusion (23), however, are real questions to which McClintock provides answers.

4. Tied to McClintock's explanation of why propaganda works is a warning: that to remain blind to the power of propaganda is to consent "to handing over to others our independence of thought and action" (24). To prevent this fate, McClintock advises us to do the work that clear thinking requires. This ending is an example of a call-for-action conclusion.

BUT WHAT DO YOU MEAN?

Deborah Tannen

Questions for Close Reading (p. 288)

1. Tannen's thesis appears in paragraph 2. She explains there that "conversational rituals common among women are designed to take the other person's feelings into account" while the "rituals common among men are designed to maintain the one-up position, or at least avoid appearing one-down." These conversational differences, Tannen affirms, often place women at a disadvantage, particularly in professional situations. She writes: "Because women are not trying to avoid the one-down position, that is unfortunately where they may end up" (2).

2. Tannen finds that "women are often told they apologize too much" because, in men's speech, "apologizing seems synonymous with putting oneself down" (4). But women, Tannen explains, do not perceive apology as self-negating. They see it as a means "of keeping both speakers on an equal footing" (4). To illustrate this point, Tannen recounts in paragraph 4 a personal anecdote involving an apology ("Oh, I'm sorry") that isn't an admission of wrongdoing, but an attempt to provide reassurance of equality. This drive to foster equality often carries over into apologies that *are* intended to acknowledge wrongdoing. Frequently, Tannen states, a woman claims fault in expectation that the other speaker will also share the blame (5). In this way, both speakers apologize for some component of a mishap, and neither party loses status (6). To men unschooled in sharing blame, a woman's frequent apologies unfairly place her—again and again—in the one-down position (8).

3. As Tannen reports, in "straight" criticism an evaluator delivers commentary directly—"Oh, that's too dry! You have to make it snappier!" (10), while in "softened" criticism the evaluator offers reassuring markers—"That's a really good start" (10). Tannen believes that "women use more softeners" (11) in delivering criticism, but she states that "neither style is

intrinsically better" (12). To those familiar with softened critiques, a straight approach can be too blunt. However, to the straight talker, softened criticism is evasive and overly concerned with providing reassurance and protecting feelings (12). As Tannen sees it, the straight talker imagines that the subject of criticism does not need reassurance and "can take it" (12). Recipients of either approach, Tannen suggests, should recognize straight or softened criticism as first and foremost an *approach*—a style with a specific logic and goal (12). Such a view is consistent with Tannen's aims and conclusions. As she writes in the end of her essay, "There is no 'right' way to talk" (30). Problems in communication are better seen as problems in style, "and *all* styles will at times fail with others who don't share or understand them," just as English won't help one communicate with a speaker of French (30). One must learn to recognize the different speaking styles (just as English speakers traveling in France will find it advantageous to learn some French).

4. Tannen believes that men discuss ideas through a "ritual fight" or "verbal opposition": Men "state their ideas in the strongest possible terms, thinking that if there are weaknesses, someone will point them out, and by trying to argue against those objections, they will see how well their ideas hold up" (16). In short, for men, this battle-like scenario of proposal and interrogation is seen as a means of helping speakers sharpen and clarify their views. Women, however, may view such "verbal sparring" as a personal attack and consequently "find it impossible to do their best work" (18). As Tannen points out, "If you're not used to ritual fighting, you begin to hear criticism of your ideas as soon as they are formed" (18). As a result, a woman may doubt and not sharpen her ideas. She may also equivocate or "hedge in order to fend off potential attacks" (18), thereby making herself and her proposals look weak. This perceived weakness may, in turn, invite actual criticism and attack.

5. *synonymous* (4): having the same meaning
   self-deprecating (4): self-critique (often negative)
   reciprocate (14): to give and receive mutually
   contentious (18): prone to argument
   dumbfounded (20): speechless with surprise
   soliciting (23): asked repeatedly
   commiserating (23): sympathizing
   malcontent (26): a discontented person

Questions About the Writer's Craft (p. 289)

1. Although Tannen divides her essay into the seven "biggest areas of miscommunication" (3) between men and women—apologies, criticism, thank-yous, fighting, praise, complaints, and jokes—her categories actually describe *two* gendered tendencies. As Tannen explains, "conversation rituals common among women are designed to take the other person's feelings into account," while those "common among men are designed to maintain the one-up position" (2). As a result, Tannen's seven areas are not mutually exclusive, but demonstrate different instances of the same behaviors. Within each category, women's speech involves reciprocity, placing speakers "on an equal footing" (4)—one speaker apologizes, thanks, or complains, and the second speaker responds in kind—while men's verbal fighting, problem-solving, and teasing, conversely, function to determine a speaker's status. For example, when Tannen asks a female columnist for a forgotten telephone number, the columnist responds, "Oh, I'm sorry," even though *she* had not forgotten anything (4). However, when men fail to thank in turn, like the male assistant who did not return the novelist's pleasantry (14), they are following their status-seeking goals. Demonstrating the difference between women's exchanges and men's

positioning across her categories, Tannen reveals repeatedly that women, who "are not trying to avoid the one-down position" (2) in conversation, often end up there anyway.

2. In paragraphs 7-9, Tannen explores several branching effects that she considers damaging to women. Earlier, in paragraphs 4-5, she demonstrates how women use apology not to acknowledge mistakes but to preserve parity. Having established that point, she introduces the anecdote about Helen. When Helen frequently apologized at a company meeting, her attempts to foster parity set in motion a series of effects. Her apologies fell on completely male ears, "mask[ed] her competence" (8), placed her in a one-down position, decreased her status in the company (the prime concern of men's conversations), and ultimately compromised her compensation. This causal chain supports Tannen's concern that in male-dominated contexts, women's conversational rituals effectively relegate professional women to subordinate positions.

3. Tannen's essay focuses on conversational rituals—"things that seem obviously the thing to say, without thinking of the literal meaning" (1). In detailing how these obvious but empty words are used differently by men and women, Tannen tries to evoke the everyday world where such language happens. Her aim is not to explain scientific or sociological data; instead, she uses the first-person point of view to comment directly on those social interactions we all share. Refusing to be a distant observer, the essay's "I" becomes an active participant in the described behaviors. Tannen places herself in rituals like apology (4) and criticism (11), demonstrating what the behaviors signify to each speaker. Through her example and that of the world she knows, Tannen wants readers to recognize their own conversational approaches and understand those of others. Seen in this light, Tannen's use of the first person is not unlike a woman's conversational ritual: her aim is to establish parity between herself and readers and not to assert or secure her status. She does not, as a man might, propose her categories "in the strongest possible terms" (16), bracing the prose for interlocutors to examine holes or flaws in her theory. Instead, the first-person point of view builds rapport and supports Tannen's thesis: that speech is not "a question of being 'right'; it's a question of using language that's shared" (30).

4. Tannen's purpose is to explain how conversational rituals often place women at a professional disadvantage, yet she never adopts a strident tone to make her point. Rather than employing language rich in invective or anger at women's linguistic bind, Tannen remains non-abrasive and impartial throughout. When she writes, she always keeps clarity and common ground in mind. She begins the essay with a simple definition of conversation itself (1), and then moves on to observe that "unfortunately, women and men often have different ideas about what's appropriate, different ways of speaking" (2). While she emphasizes each sex's "different ideas"—that women seek rapport in conversation while men seek status—Tannen is at pains to distinguish these differences from notions of right and wrong. As she emphasizes in her conclusion, "there is no 'right' way to talk" (30), only various styles of talking. Since she suggests that conversation is "not a question of being 'right'; it's a question of using language that's shared—or at least understood" (30), Tannen does the same. Speaking in the first person and drawing on informal anecdotes, Tannen tries to explain how conversational rituals can cause "miscommunication" (3) between men and women. In explaining each of the seven categories, she sometimes addresses women directly; for example, in discussing ritual fighting in paragraph 19, she writes: "Although you may never enjoy verbal sparring, some women find it helpful to learn how to do it." Other times, she addresses men by implication, pointing out why Lester's employees might be dissatisfied with his lack of praise (20). In this way, Tannen works to explain to each sex, in a deliberately objective and fair fashion, the gendered speech of the other. Tannen's tone—personal, informal, engaging—suits her purpose; because she threatens neither men nor women, readers remain open to her analysis and leave with a clear understanding of gendered miscommunication.

WHY NOTHING IS "WRONG" ANYMORE

Meg Greenfield

Questions for Close Reading (p. 292)

1. Greenfield indicates her broad thesis at the end of the third paragraph: "So we have developed a broad range of alternatives to 'right and wrong.'" The rest of the essay explains these alternatives.

2. The "simple fact," something she says is readily apparent, is that there is little talk about "right and wrong" in today's world. The concept of "right and wrong," she says, is considered "embarrassing," because it "has such a repressive, Neanderthal ring to it." It just seems too old-fashioned.

3. Greenfield names five different excuses people give for wrongdoing. Sometimes wrongdoing is considered "stupid" rather than wrong (4); other times it is labeled "not unconstitutional" (5). Other instances of wrongdoing are ascribed to mental illness—they arc "sick" acts rather than wrong (6). Sometimes the circumstances are such that the wrong behavior is excused as "only to be expected" because provoked (7). Finally, some wrongdoing is described as "complex," as if the situation is too intricate and mysterious for any suspected of it to be labeled with the simplistic term "wrong" (8).

4. Politicians, government officials, and other public figures seem to be Greenfield's main subject. While she doesn't say explicitly that she is referring mainly to their excuses for wrongdoing, her examples suggest so. Early in the essay, she discusses name-calling in the public arena (2). She also mentions Watergate (4), Supreme Court disputes (5), "caught-out officeholders" (6), and violence in South Africa and Chile (7) as illustrations of faulty ethics in political life. Also, her second excuse, "right and not necessarily unconstitutional" could only be used by a government official.

5. *antagonists* (2): hostile opponents
   perpetrated (2): carried out, committed
   repressive (3): overly controlled, Puritanical
   Neanderthal (3): pertaining to primitive humans, old-fashioned
   reprehensible (4): blameworthy
   unfathomable (4): incomprehensible, not able to be understood
   inferentially (5): through a guess or supposition
   spurious (5): not genuine; false
   misfeasance (6): wrongful performance of a normally lawful act; wrongdoing
   insidious (7): stealthily deceitful or treacherous
   extenuate (7): lessen the seriousness of
   antiapartheid (7): opposed to the system of racial separation in the Republic of South Africa
   sophistries (9): plausible but false arguments

78

Questions About the Writer's Craft (p. 292)

1. Greenfield's essay *divides* the concept of "right and wrong" (1) into *categories* of excuses. Her principle of division-classification is applied consistently, so that each alternative is a type of excuse that could be offered for some act of wrongdoing.

2. "Right and stupid," "right and sick" are terms modeled on the phrase "right and wrong," but each introduces a different alternative to the idea of "wrong." Repeating the "right and. . ." formula drums in Greenfield's central point, that some things are right and others are the opposite, despite the excuses.

3. The first person appears occasionally throughout the essay. Early on, Greenfield writes, "What strikes me is" (1); "Let me quickly qualify" (2); "I'll name a few [excuses]" (3). Through the use of "me" and "I," we catch the tone of indignation at this new way of speaking about wrongdoing. In other places, the first person shows the mind of a reasonable person at work: "I don't know at quite what point along the way we came to this one." (5); "Still, I think no one could have foreseen . . ." (6); "For instance, I think most of us could agree that setting fire to live people . . . is—dare I say it?—wrong" (7); "I still can't get this one [complex] out of my vocabulary." (8); "As I listen to the moral arguments swirling about us this summer I become ever more persuaded that . . ." (9).

4. The introduction states that "there has been an awful lot of talk about sin, crime and plain old antisocial behavior this summer"; the conclusion returns to the topic of current "moral arguments swirling about us this summer." At start of the essay, however, Greenfield simply observes that "we don't seem to have a word anymore for 'wrong' in the moral sense. . ." By the conclusion, Greenfield takes a stronger stand about this absence of the word 'wrong' in our discussions of sin and crime. She writes, "our real problem is this: the 'still, small voice' of conscience has become far too small—and utterly still."

ANSWERS FOR CHAPTER 15
"PROCESS ANALYSIS" (p. 296)

Opening Comments

Like many of our colleagues, we cover process analysis early in the semester. This pattern of development teaches students a great deal about selectivity ("Which steps should I cover?" "How many examples should I provide?"), organization, and transition signals. Process analysis also highlights the importance of audience analysis. To explain the steps in a process clearly, the writer must identify what readers need to know and understand.

Students often expect process analysis to write itself; they expect it to unfold naturally and automatically. But, once they get feedback on their first draft, they realize that the sequence of steps was self-evident only to them and that they need to work harder to make the process accessible to their readers.

This chapter includes process analysis that vary widely in subject. You may want to start with Cole's "Don't Just Stand There,"a directional process analysis essay that provides readers with a number of methods to address prejudicial comments made in casual conversation. Malcolm X's essay, "My First Conk," illustrates that informational process analysis may take the form of a narrative. Rhodes's ("Watching the Animals") frank and detailed portrayal of the slaughter process creates a powerful impression of the casual cruelty inherent in our meat-eating culture.

ACTIVITIES: PROCESS ANALYSIS

Below we provide possible responses to selected activities at the end of Chapter 15. Of course, your students are bound to come up with their own approaches.

Prewriting Activities (pp. 312-13)

1. Process analysis lends itself to these essay topics in several ways. Below are some possibilities. In class, we suggest you have students share their responses. They will be delighted to discover that their neighbors have devised different uses for process analysis in these essays.

   ### Topic: *Defining comparison shopping*

   How a person might use a consumer magazine to compare VCRs' quality
   How a person might compare sneakers at a mall
   How someone might call up car dealers to get the best price

   ### Topic: *Contrasting two teaching styles*

   How two teachers respond to student questions
   How two teachers deal with students who don't understand
   How two teachers convey complex information

2. Many students will find a way to treat each topic both directionally and informationally, and you'll need to sort out in class what the most likely approaches would be in terms of a particular audience.

   a. Going on a job interview: Primarily directional, possible informational, or both

   b. Using a computer in the college library: Directional

   c. Cleaning up oil spills: Informational

   d. Negotiating personal conflicts: Primarily directional, possible informational, or both

   e. Curing a cold: Directional, informational, or both

   f. Growing vegetables organically: Primarily informational, possible directional, or both.

Revising Activities (pp. 313-15)

6. Encourage students to work together on this activity or have them share their revisions. Other students' responses will help them discover weaknesses in the paragraph they otherwise might overlook.

   Here are the main problems with the paragraph:

   — The chronology is disorganized. The second and third sentences, about keeping customers on the phone, should come later in the paragraph, after the opening of the phone call is discussed.

— How one performs the steps in the process of making such a call is left vague. More details are needed to explain such aspects of the process as "setting the right tone," "in a friendly way . . . keep[ing] the prospective customer on the phone," "determin[ing]—in a genial way—why the person is reluctant to buy," "encourag[ing] credit card payment," and "end[ing] . . . in an easy, personable way."

— The sentences discussing the loneliness of the typical person are a digression. The two sentences from "Maintaining such a connection . . ." through "a sad fact of contemporary life" should be deleted.

— Throughout the paragraph, the caller is variously referred to as "you" and as "the salesperson." This shift in person should be corrected by choosing one or the other and sticking to it. The third person ("salesperson") may be more appropriate since few readers will be telephone solicitors.

7. We suggest you offer your students the chance to read each other's revisions of this paragraph. Exposure to other versions helps them see many more possibilities in revising.

Here are the main problems in the paragraph:

— To preserve the paragraph's chronology, the sixth sentence (beginning "Before heading to class . . .") and the seventh should come earlier in the paragraph. These two sentences should be placed after "lessen the trauma."

— Throughout the paragraph, there's a shift in person; for instance, "they" is used in the second sentence, but the third sentence shifts to "you"; it goes back and forth from there. The writer should choose one or the other and stick to it.

— The tenth and eleventh sentences, running from "A friend of mine . . ." to "volunteers to participate" are irrelevant and should be deleted.

— The point that you should "never, ever volunteer to answer" should be moved up to occur immediately after the advice about where to sit in sentences 8 and 9.

— The transition, "however" (sentence 12), doesn't work when the paragraph is reorganized as described above. A transition such as "also" would work well.

— The last two sentences, though in keeping with the paragraph's light tone, nevertheless seem a bit jarring. Furthermore, since they don't develop the essay's overall point, they probably should be eliminated.

DON'T JUST STAND THERE

Diane Cole

Questions for Close Reading (p. 319)

1. Cole expresses her thesis in paragraph 5: "Speaking up may not magically change a biased attitude, but it can change a person's behavior by putting a strong message across." The rest of the essay supports this idea by providing "strategies" for how to state opposition to biased remarks and jokes.

2. According to Michael McQuillan, a source quoted by Cole, one major reason to speak up is that jokes based on ethnic stereotypes can cause listeners to accept the prejudicial attitudes on which the jokes are based. Keeping our society free of such attitudes and even of offensive acts means striking out against the offensive "jokes" that we hear (4). In addition, speaking up can have the positive result of changing people's behavior, even if it does not affect their underlying attitudes; such change can result when a person receives multiple messages opposing prejudiced remarks (5). In the main, people wish to make a positive impression; learning that others find their comments offensive may cause a toning-down of the problematic behavior (6). For example, later in the essay Cole describes a man who threw out some guests who began singing offensive songs; they never again attempted to repeat this action (29). Finally, responding to offensive behavior by others in an effective change-promoting manner can increase a person's sense of competence and self-esteem (7).

3. Cole recommends that if you find yourself offended by such remarks, you state your feelings in a concrete way (11). It is crucial that you express yourself concretely, by describing what *you feel,* rather than elaborate upon abstract ethical principles or rules of politeness. You should also give the person the benefit of a doubt—restate the meaning of what you think you have heard, so that the person may correct or alter the impression you received. Sometimes, people just don't realize the effect of what they have said (12). Cole then provides strategies for dealing with people who dismiss your reaction. She quotes LeNorman Strong, a George Washington University official in charge of campus life, who recommends creating a dialogue. He suggests listening first and then reiterating your position (14). For comments made in a public situation, Cole provides additional steps; speak to the person privately, not in public, or pass the speaker at a large gathering a note expressing your feelings (16-18, 19).

4. "Striking back" is not a useful strategy when you have been the target of prejudiced comments, although an outburst can make you feel better at the time. Later, however, you might regret having "lowered yourself to that other person's level," according to Michael McQuillan (9). Also, responding with anger or prejudice of your own might further convince the person that you and the group you are a member of "are not to be taken seriously." Finally, responding with anger might escalate the situation and lead to further insults or even violence (9).

5. *ebullience* (1): exuberance
   anti-Semitic (1): hostile to Jews
   slurs (4): disparaging remarks; put-downs
   discounts (6): disregards; minimizes
   lashing (9): attacking harshly with words
   ante (9): the stake added by each poker player in turn; price of something (slang)

abstract (11): general, unspecific
personalize (11): to make personal
rift (17): split or break
grievance (21): complaint
volatile (33): tending toward violence; explosive

Questions About the Writer's Craft (p. 320)

1. Cole's purpose is primarily persuasive. Early in the essay (paragraphs 4-6), she confronts the reader with the reasons one should speak up and refutes the reasons people have for ignoring offensive remarks. Throughout the essay, the information Cole provides about the process focuses on effectively refuting offensive points of view. She conveys that people themselves should be persuasive in their approach to racism and other hurtful remarks. She coaches the reader in how to refute others; if one is countered or "dismissed," one should "continue the dialogue," listen, and restate one's own view (14). Likewise, with bosses, one should use persistence and politeness (23). Cole's consistent use of "you" throughout the essay also adds to the persuasive effect. By hypothetically proposing the reader's appropriate behavior, she makes the process of responding to prejudice seem already a part of the reader's life: "Make sure you heard the words and their intent correctly . . ." (12) she writes, and later says, "You can also raise the issue with other colleagues . . ." (23).

2. Throughout the essay, Cole provides numerous examples of what to say in order to speak up effectively. The first instance of this occurs in paragraph 10: "I don't know if you realize what that sounded like to me. If that's what you meant, it really hurt me." Then, she provides an alternative through a quotation from LeNorman Strong: "Personalize the sense of 'this is how I feel when you say this'" (11). Then in paragraph 12, she describes what you might say to make sure you heard the remark correctly: "This is what I heard you say. Is that what you meant?" She also gives examples that clarify the many possible situations you might find yourself in: at a public meeting, at a private dinner, with a prejudiced boss (23), close relative (27), acquaintance (28), or prejudiced friend who comments about your other associations (32). She also provides examples showing the contingencies that might occur once you begin to state your side and demonstrating additional modes for responding. The many uses of "if" or "even if" in the essay set up hypothetical situations for which Cole provides a suggested resolution. In paragraph 14, she gives an example of how a person might reply defensively if you spoke up. "Oh, you're just being sensitive. Can't you take a joke?" such a person might say. Then Cole provides an example of your best response to such a person: "I'm not sure about that, let's talk about that a little more."

3. Cole quotes from numerous experts in psychology and human relations to convince us that speaking up, while difficult, is beneficial and effective. The experts also provide support for the various strategies that she recommends. Clearly, the process she suggests is to some extent based on interviews with these people. The quotations are effective in that they show that concern about offensive jokes is not just a private obsession of Cole's but an issue that numerous prestigious people in the field of human interaction are seriously concerned about. It changes the issue from just "personal offense" to a societal problem. The weight of all the experts might also truly persuade a reader to try the process the next time a situation occurs.

4. The three sections separate and introduce three different occasions or situations in which one might have to deal with offensive remarks. Using a different typeface calls attention to these hypothetical offensive situations and to their role as themes of major sections of the

essay. In addition, using such examples works well to plunge the reader into the conflict; the examples make the offending situations concrete in a way that just using headings as separators would not do. In the first example, remarks are made which are personally offensive to a group of which one is a member: "*When the 'joke' turns on who you are . . .*" (8). The second section introduces a discussion of how to handle remarks that offend but that are not directed at a group personally present or represented: "*. . . one guest starts reciting a racist joke. Everyone at the table is white, including you. The others are still laughing, as you wonder what to say or do*" (25). The last section poses a situation among children's friends into which racism intrudes (30). This final section seems jarring and less well connected to her theme than the other two. Cole might have included this material on how to help children counter racism because the essay was written for a supplement to the *New York Times* as part of a nationwide campaign against bigotry.

MY FIRST CONK

Malcolm X

Questions for Close Reading (p. 323)

1. The thesis of this selection is implied. One way of stating it might be: "Getting a 'conk' was a painful, shameful process that showed how desperate blacks were at that time to be rid of their racial characteristics." Malcolm X does explicitly call getting a conk a kind of "self-degradation" in paragraph 23 and discuss other implications of hair-straightening (24-26), but these analyses come too late to be thesis statements.

2. "Congolene" is made from lye, eggs, and potatoes, or starch. Mixed together, they become a searing hot jelly that straightens hair but also burns the scalp. The vaseline is applied first to the scalp and skin around the hairline to protect these areas from burning. The apron and gloves are also to protect the skin and clothes of the two people doing the conking. The soap and spray hose are used to wash out the congolene.

3. Malcolm X was unhappy with his kinky red hair and desired to have hair like a white man (21-22). He later realized that this desire to look white was a "self-degradation," because it was based on the belief that blacks and their typical racial characteristics, such as kinky hair, were inferior (23).

4. He admires people who have kept their hair natural but who have achieved success anyway. He names Sidney Poitier (an actor) and Lionel Hampton (a jazz musician) as two such men (25). He also admires men who have given up the conk (25). He implies that education, hard work, and determination are preferable to painful cosmetic treatments to acquire straight hair; he writes, if blacks would give "the brains in their heads just half as much attention as they do their hair, they would be a thousand times better off" (27).

5. *self-degradation* (23): a reduction in one's self-worth
   self-defacing (26): disfiguring the self

Questions About the Writer's Craft (pp. 323-24)

1. Malcolm X calls getting a conk "my first really big step toward self-degradation" (23), a process by which blacks reject their own identity and try to look or act white. His purpose in explaining the nature of a conk is to convince blacks to give up this pursuit of whiteness and instead have pride in themselves.

2. Rather than tell the story of someone else getting a conk, Malcolm X narrates his own experience; by this choice he lends authority and poignancy to the piece. In addition, by exposing himself as a man who conked "faithfully," Malcolm avoids the appearance of looking down on other blacks or of smug superiority. He shows that he knows about the process of self-degradation from the inside. That he himself got "rid of it" lends force to his recommendation that other blacks do the same.

3. Malcolm X uses quotation marks to suggest he does not agree with a particular label for a person, characteristic, or situation, that is, that he is using the term ironically. He speaks of hair "looking 'white'" (22), for example, of brainwashing that leads to black people being thought "inferior," white people "superior," and to the attempt to look "pretty" by white standards (23). He mentions the "'integrated' lobby of the Waldorf-Astoria," implying that it is not integrated at all (24). He writes of "'upper-class' Negroes" (25), and the "so-called 'middle class' and 'upper class,' who ought to know better" (26) and the poor men who try to look "sharp" and "hip" by showing off a conk (26).

4. Malcolm X is writing primarily for a black audience. He writes, first of all, about conking and congolene without defining them, assuming his audience will know what they are. By recounting his own embarrassing and painful experience with "self-degradation," he is appealing to other blacks to have pride in their identity, not shame. This appeal is stated powerfully in the last sentence; Malcolm X wants blacks to use their energy to focus on what is really important, not on their looks.

WATCHING THE ANIMALS

Richard Rhodes

Questions for Close Reading (p. 330)

1. Rhodes implies his thesis. It might be stated as, "Today's modern process for butchering pigs is humane but still shocking, and keeps us ignorant of the bloody realities involved in eating meat." The essay presents a detailed description of how hogs are butchered today. Furthermore, Rhodes indicates that he views the butchery of animals as emblematic of other savagery in our modern world: "It had to remind me of things no one wants to be reminded of anymore, all mobs, all death marches, all mass murders and extinctions, the slaughter of the buffalo, the slaughter of the Indian, the Inferno, Judgment Day, complicity, expensive races, race living at the expense of race" (11).

2. First, the pigs are kept briefly in a holding pen, which at I-D is state of the art—the steel fencing is painted "tinner's red to keep it from rusting" and the floor is of smooth cement with drains so water can be flushed through after each set of pigs (8). Then, the pigs are shunted

through a gate one at a time, to be tattooed with identifying lot numbers by a man holding a hammer-like tool (8). Held once again in a red-fenced pen, the pigs are showered from every angle with water. The pen funnels the pigs into a moving ramp where both the sides and the floor move so as to prevent bruising (8). The ramp takes them upward, where, at the top, a man electrocutes each pig by stabbing it with electrodes on tools "that looked like enlarged curling irons." The unconscious pig then drops a foot down onto a steel table (12). The pigs are then chained to hang by their rear legs on a line which lifts them into the air (14). Ten feet along, a man slices open the pig's throat so the blood can run out onto the floor below, where another worker sweeps it down a drain (15). Then each pig's carcass is dipped and rolled in a vat of hot water, so that the hair can then be whisked off by revolving brushes. Workers at the end of this line complete the hair removal with knives. Then the carcasses are flamed to harden the skin and polished by more brushes (17). At this point, the actual butchering begins (19).

The workers act impersonally, each performing his assembly-line style job with great efficiency. In the actual butchery areas, however, the workers seem more agitated. As Rhodes notes, "It cannot be heartening to kill animals all day " (23). In the butchery, he hears "shouts back and forth from the men, jokes, announcements, challenges. . . . everyone keen" (19). One of the men gutting the carcasses sees Rhodes taping and "begins shouting at us something like 'I am the greatest!' A crazy man, grinning and roaring at us, turning around and slipping in the knife . . ." (19). Rhodes points out that "it gets harder and harder to hire men for this work, even though the pay is good" (23). Many workers are minorities. The men get breaks of ten minutes, but they obviously work hard, so hard that a break down in the line brought on cheers, reminding Rhodes of how "convicts might [cheer] at a state license-plate factory when the stamping machine breaks down" (23). He comments that while he could see that the animals are treated humanely at I-D, "where the workers are concerned, I'm not so sure. They looked to be in need of lulling" (24).

3. They are quite intelligent, "the most intelligent of all farm animals, by actual laboratory test," he writes. They learn quickly and are not as docile as other farm animals, such as cows. They don't have the herd instinct, but instead "squeal and nip and shove," each wanting "the entire meal for himself." They "shoot out all over the place" when let out of a pen, and are likely to explore and wander (5). They "talk a lot," he writes, and express emotions: "low grunts, quick squeals, a kind of hum sometimes, angry shrieks, high screams of fear" (6). They are curious, watching the humans even while lined up in the holding pen (10). And they do express fear; "they scream, never having been on such a ramp, smelling the smells they smell ahead" (11). They have, in other words, many characteristics similar to humans.

4. Rhodes points out that when he was a child, he assisted butchering on the farm where he lived, and that the event "had the quality of a ceremony" (25). The boys felt pride at performing "this important work," Rhodes says. "It was part of a coherent way of life, . . . It had a context . . ." It was part of producing food, every bit as much as "plowing or seeding or baling hay" (28). And it was part of the whole process of life and death which everyone on the farm experienced. "You saw the beginning and the end on the farm, not merely the prepackaged middle" (30). People then felt "humility, and sorrow that this act of killing must be done, which is why in those days good men bowed their heads before they picked up their forks" (30).

In contrast, the slaughter of pigs at the I-D plant is impersonal and technological; it is broken up into numerous small tasks, with the result that no one person or people are "responsible" for the deaths. The actual butchering is accompanied by agitation: "shouts, . . . jokes, announcements, challenges" 19). There is an irreverence, even a craziness, about the men performing the bloodier tasks (19).

5. *defunct* (3): no longer functioning or existing
   monolithic (3): uniform, massive, rigid
   hygienically (8): in a heathy and clean manner
   complicity (11): partnership or involvement in wrongdoing
   affluence (11): wealth
   hawser (15): a heavy rope used to moor or tow ships
   deft (19): quick and skillful
   chitterlings (20): small intestines of pigs, eaten fried or in a sauce
   lulling (24): causing quietness or sleep
   winched (26): hoisted by a rope and pulley system
   differential (26): a type of gear
   pizzle (26): penis of an animal
   coherent (28): consistent or logical
   sacrificial (28): offered up to a higher force or power

Questions About the Writer's Craft (pp. 330-31)

1. Rhodes mostly avoids using the most obvious kind of transition device for explaining process, that is, using enumeration or "first, second, then, next," to indicate the steps. But he does use transitions of time and narrative to hold the process together; often, pointing out the physical movement of the pigs or of his own movement serves to cue the reader that one part of the process is finished and another one beginning. In addition, he also anticipates stages of the process ahead of time to let the reader know what is coming up.

   The first step is the delivery of the animals, indicated in paragraph 4 and the first sentence of paragraph 5: "Down goes the tail gate and out come the pigs. . . ." Paragraph 8 begins with the word "once," which signals to the reader that Rhodes is picking up the process after several paragraphs of digression in which he has expounded upon the personality of pigs. The next step, tattooing, is introduced by beginning a new paragraph: "The pigs come out of the first holding pen through a gate that allows only one to pass at a time"(9). The use of the word "first" here also helps the reader to get on track with the process at this point and indicates that there will be other holding pens. In fact, as soon as this tattooing is over, the pigs' movement "to one of several smaller pens" signals the next stage; the rest of this sentence—"where each lot is held until curtain time"—prepares the reader for the upcoming killing (9). The transition to the next stage of the process is indicated by the author's physical movement: "We crossed a driveway with more red steel fencing" (10). In paragraph 11, Rhodes uses a narrative transition, "Before they reach their end . . ." to move into the shower stage. Again, the reference to "their end" sets the reader up to hear about the slaughter. paragraph 11 contains other transitions of time: "*Then* they begin to feel crowded. . . . Now they scream. . . ."

   Paragraph 12 again uses movement or spatial location to indicate a new stage: "*At the top* of the ramp. . . . *As* a pig reached the top. . . . *Up came another* pig. . . . *And another, and another, . . .* " In paragraph 14, Rhodes describes another physical motion, "*They drop* to the table," and through a spatial transition and a direct announcement indicates that a major transition in the process occurs at this point: "and *here* the endless chain begins." The steps involved in attaching the pig to the "endless chain," what might be called the "disassembly line," are provided using spatial indicators of what motions the workers perform. At the start of the next paragraph, we encounter the narrative transition, "Now the line ascends . . . " (15). Then spatial indicators mix with narrative ones: "The pig proceeds a distance of ten feet, *where* a worker. . . . *Then* all hell breaks loose. . . . *Down* on the floor below, . . . "(15).

   Paragraph 16 begins without official transition, indicating a change in the process by motion: "The line swings *around* a corner . . . *around* the drain floor, *turns left,* . . . and *begins to ascend* . . ." The next step comes along as changes in movement: "the line *lowers* the carcass. . . . The line *ascends again, up and away*, and the carcass *goes into* . . ."(17). Rhodes and his guide then move "to the other side of the chamber" to observe another stage. Finally, Rhodes uses the narrative transition "then" and the phrase, "the last step" to conclude this phase of the process: "The carcasses *then* pass through great hellish jets. . . . The *last step* is polishing . . . " (17).

Rhodes indicates the change to the butchering stage by pointing out movement and directly announcing the event: "The polished carcasses *swing through* a door . . . and *there* . . . the *action begins*" (19). Narrative and spatial indicators help the reader follow this action: "Men *start* slicing. . . . A carcass *passes* me. . . . *Around a corner, up to a platform,* . . ." After this point, Rhodes points out, many things happen at once as the animal's carcass is cut up: "And here things divide, and so must our attention . . ." (19).

In paragraphs 20 and 21, Rhodes again uses a mixture of narrative actions and spatial indicators: "a worker *separates* . . . and *shoves* . . . . *Another* worker finds one end . . . *Others* trim off. . . . The *intestines shimmer* along . . . and *come out the other side* . . . A *worker drops* them . . ." (20). "The remaining organs *proceed down* a . . . conveyor; *on the other side* of the same walkway, the emptied carcasses pass; *on a line next to the organ line* the heads pass. *By now,* all the meat. . . . A worker *sockets them* one at a time. . . . and *at the end of the line* . . ." (21).

2. The prefatory quotation from Emerson is cryptic, because there is no indicator of who loves these items and because "flint" and "iron" seem unusual objects of love. In effect, what this quotation means in relation to the essay's subject is not revealed until the last paragraph (30). But the quotation from Emerson in paragraph one is clear and pointed. In this quotation, Emerson accuses his Victorian audience of being an "expensive race," a "race living at the expense of race" even though "the slaughterhouse is concealed in the graceful distance of miles." Rhodes wishes to use this revered American essayist to support his own challenge to our complacency and ignorance about eating animals. By revealing what occurs in the slaughterhouse these days, Rhodes can inform his audience of the bloody truth about their diet, which is "expensive" in that it costs other animals their lives.

In paragraph 11, at the point where he describes the pigs wedged onto a ramp taking them up to be electrocuted, Rhodes echoes this quotation about expense. He says the sight of the pigs going to slaughter reminded him of "things no one wants to be reminded of anymore . . . all mass murders and extinctions, . . . the Inferno, Judgment Day, complicity, expensive races, race living at the expense of race. . . . That we are the most expensive of races, able in our affluence to hire others of our kind to do this terrible necessary work of killing another race of creatures so that we may feed our oxygen-rich brains" (11). Here Rhodes adds another dimension to the idea of "expensive race" by extending it to refer to our affluence which allows us to afford the expense of paying other people to kill our food.

At the end of the essay, after Rhodes has described the way farm animals used to be killed, with a shotgun, he repeats the imagery of the first Emerson quotation: "Our loves are no longer the loves of flint and iron, but of the nightingale and the rose, and so we delegate our killing. . . . Flint and iron, friends, flint and iron" (30). Here the "flint and iron" imagery obviously refers to the personal killing of one's meat with a gun, the way people obtained food in a time past when there was "coherence" and "context"—the unity of growing and eating food (29), of knowing "the beginning and the end on the farm" (30). "Flint and iron" thus represent a hard reality, one that people were in touch with in the past, so that they "bowed their heads before they picked up their forks." But these days, we are more in touch with "the nightingale and the rose," two romantic and soft images representing our avoidance of the realities of killing to eat. Incorporating this imagistic material from Emerson reinforces Rhodes's point that we have dulled ourselves to an important aspect of our true nature and dwell in a "graceful" evasive ignorance.

3. These early descriptions in the essay focus less on the process of slaughter and more on background and context so that the killing of pigs has more meaning. Paragraph 3 details the ruins of the old packing houses that were criticized in Upton Sinclair's novel; the author's

comparison of the defunct buildings to "monolithic enlargements of concentration-camp barracks" introduces a sinister element to the meat-packing industry, one which the essay suggests endures, even though many elements of the industry have changed. One of those changes is explained in paragraph 4, where we learn that stockyards are a thing of the past; the animals are butchered quickly after they are delivered by truck. Paragraph 5-8 provide information about what pigs are like. We learn they have personality and intelligence. They are "enthusiastic after their drive," Rhodes writes. He explains that their superior intelligence has been established by "actual laboratory test," but then provides numerous descriptive details about how they act with intelligence on the farm. They run less on instinct than on responsiveness to the moment. They don't herd, they fight to get more for themselves, they wander and explore if let loose. Rhodes attributes some human characteristics to them also: "They talk a lot, to each other, to you if you care to listen," he writes, and lists some of the emotions they express through different sounds (6). He points out that in the holding pen, they "mill around getting to know each other," an irony since they will soon be killed (8). These descriptions force the reader to recognize that pigs are living beings who enjoy life and for whom slaughter is terrible; this is one of the hidden realities that Rhodes wishes to bring forth in the essay.

In paragraph 9, Rhodes describes the first event in the process, the tattooing of the pigs so that contaminated or diseased lots can be traced. This detail creates an allusion to Nazi Germany's treatment of Jews, who were tattooed with serial numbers in the concentration camps. This allusion is reinforced in paragraph 11, where the pigs receive a shower, "a real one"; in the death camps, the prisoners were lured into the gas chambers by the fiction that they were going to "the showers."

Throughout paragraph 9, the details reveal the crudeness of the process—the pigs are thunked with a big hammer holding an inked set of numbers on the end. Yet it is considered humane, because the animals have such thick hides. This combination of crudeness and consideration foreshadows all the other processes and presents the reader with the double-edged complexity of the slaughter as a whole—that it is horrible and shocking but not unnecessarily cruel. In addition, the very technology that permits this balance of death and humaneness also plays off human health with impersonal control: the tattooed numbers. Through this imagery, Rhodes connects animal slaughter with mass murder of humans, again forcing recognition that meat-eating comes at a terrible expense.

4. Other examples of colloquial language include: paragraph 7, "they [I-D Packing] do a dirty job . . .What are you hiding, Wilson people?"; "where each lot is held until curtain time'" (9); "this man jabbed the electrodes in to the pig's butt and shoulder" (12); "pink and clean as a baby" (17); "keeps them hopping" (23). Some of Rhodes's colloquial language creates drama or heightens the effect: the pigs "shooting out all over" and the company doing a "dirty job" well are examples of ordinary language that enlivens. But other examples of slangy language are actually euphemistic: the colloquialisms seem at first to soften or lighten the seriousness of what he is describing. But, when considered, this glibness heightens the horror all the more: "Curtain time," jabbing the pigs' "butts," the pigs looking pink as babies, and the workers being kept hopping are examples of this kind of language.

Other expressions are just downright smart-alecky: "didn't give them much leeway, did it?" (3); "What are you hiding, Wilson people?" (7); "It would be more dramatic, make a better story, if the killing came last, but it comes first" (10); "I got to be a foreman" (10); "a shower, a real one" (11); "Feed our children, for that matter" (11); "You are what you eat" (21); "And that is a tour of a slaughterhouse, as cheerful as I could make it" (22). These comments, blunt and sometimes comical, introduce a kind of double awareness; on the surface, Rhodes seems to be trying to be cheerful, even chipper, in the face of an atrocity. But it is a hollow cheer, one which mocks those in the public who would rather ignore than confront the horror of a process that is a commonplace in our society.

ANSWERS FOR CHAPTER 16
"COMPARISON-CONTRAST" (p. 334)

Opening Comments

Students learn early that comparison-contrast questions are one of the mainstays of essay exams: "Compare and/or contrast the organization of the Senate and the House of Representatives"; "Discuss the similarities and/or differences between psychotic and neurotic behavior."

We've found that students' familiarity with comparison-contrast doesn't necessarily mean they know how to structure their answers. On the contrary, many students tend to prepare helter-skelter papers that ramble every which way and back. Yet, once they are introduced to some basic strategies for organizing a comparison-contrast discussion, their overall ability to write clearly and logically often takes a quantum leap.

When first learning to use comparison-contrast, students may be overly concerned about making their ideas fit into a neat symmetrical pattern; they may try to squeeze their points into an artificial and awkward format. We find it helpful to remind students that comparison-contrast is not an end in itself but a strategy for meeting a broader rhetorical purpose. Our reminder loosens them up a bit and encourages them to be more flexible when organizing their papers. The student essay, "The Virtues of Growing Older" (pages 344-46), helps students appreciate that a well-organized comparison-contrast paper does not have to follow a rigid formula.

We selected the readings in this chapter because, in addition to being just plain interesting, all of them illustrate key points about the comparison-contrast format. In "A Slow Walk of Trees," Morrison uses the one-side-at-a-time structure to explore the divergent opinions within her own family about the prospects for blacks in America. The point-by-point approach enables Hamill ("Crack and the Box") to bring together two seemingly unrelated problems in the world today: excessive television viewing and drug addiction. Suina ("And Then I Went to School") employs both comparison-contrast strategies to evoke a confusing and painful time of adaptation in his childhood.

ACTIVITIES: COMPARISON-CONTRAST

Below we provide possible responses to selected activities at the end of Chapter 16. Of course, other approaches are possible.

Prewriting Activities (pp. 349-50)

1. There are numerous ways to use comparison-contrast in these two essays. Below are some possibilities. In going over this activity in class, we suggest you have students trade responses so that they can see how diverse the responses are.

   ### Topic: *The effects of holding a job in college*

   Comparing/contrasting job-holders' and non-job-holders' grades
   Comparing/contrasting on-campus and off-campus jobs
   Comparing/contrasting part-time and full-time jobs
   Comparing/contrasting job-holders' and non-job-holders' involvement in campus activities

   ### Topic: *How to budget money wisely*

   Comparing/contrasting formal and informal budgets
   Comparing/contrasting following a budget to buying on impulse
   Comparing/contrasting those who budget and those who don't
   Comparing/contrasting reasonable and unreasonable budgets

2. Here are some possible purposes for the topics.

   a. Audio tapes and compact disks
      To guide student purchases
      To explain the technologies

   b. Paper or plastic bags at the supermarket
      To contrast the environmental impact of each
      To help students decide which to use

   c. Two courses taught by inexperienced and "pro" instructors
      To argue a novice may convey more enthusiasm for a subject
      To give students information for choosing courses

   d. Cutting class and not showing up at work
      To illustrate the consequences of irresponsibility
      To show the similarities and differences between college and the "real world"

Revising Activities (pp. 350-51)

5. a. This statement works well as a thesis.

   b. This statement is unworkable as a thesis; it is too vague and broad since "assistance" could refer to academic, financial, or other kind of aid. A possible revision: "This college provides much more comprehensive job placement services to students than other colleges in the area."

c. This statement would be effective as a thesis if revised to state an attitude toward the candidates' use of television, for example, if one made legitimate use of the medium and the other none. A possible revision: "Joe Cooper's overwrought campaign tactics gained extensive media coverage, while Cooper's opponent, Nancy Ashbury, conducted a more subdued campaign that emphasized issues and failed to attract much attention."

d. This statement would not work as a thesis. First of all, it points out the obvious and sets up the writer for a pedantic recital of known information. Secondly, the statement is far too inclusive; in attempting to cover the topic, the writer would have to use a ream of paper. A possible revision: "Applying their technological know-how, Japanese car manufacturers learned how to make small engines more powerful, while American companies, showing very little foresight, simply added power to their cars by reintroducing larger engines."

6. Have students read each others' versions of this paragraph so that they get a stronger sense of what changes needed to be made and the revision strategies possible.

Here are the main problems with the paragraph:

— Since the paragraph discusses a boss and then a manager, the topic sentence should be reversed to read, "A boss discourages staff resourcefulness and views it as a threat, while a manager encourages creativity and treats employees courteously."

— The second sentence ("At the hardware store . . .") begins abruptly; a transition, such as "for example," would be helpful here.

— The boss's helter-skelter system is introduced awkwardly: "What he did was. . . ." Something like this might be more effective: "He organized overstocked items. . . ."

— The phrase "created chaos" is vague, possibly a bit extreme, and also somewhat slangy. Briefly describing the actual problems his system created would be helpful, as long as the paragraph doesn't veer off track and focus entirely on the chaos.

— Some language is possibly too judgmental: "helter-skelter" (4), "slapdash" (7), and "eccentric" (9). Students may want to describe the system with enough telling details so the readers can see for themselves the system's inefficiency.

— No reason is given for the boss's anger at the new system—or perhaps there was no reason other than that his ego was deflated. In either case, the source of his objections should be clarified.

— Some ideas are repeated at the end; sentences 8 and 9 ("I had assumed he would welcome my ideas. . .") repeat material conveyed at the beginning of the paragraph.

— The phrase "to scrap" is perhaps a bit slangy in tone.

A SLOW WALK OF TREES

Toni Morrison

Questions for Close Reading (pp. 354-55)

1. Morrison's thesis concerns whether despair or optimism is the more accurate attitude for African Americans to hold regarding the "possibilities of life for black people in this country" (3). She implies that she herself takes a middle ground or complex view, when she sums up the differences between her grandparent's attitudes by saying, "each would have selected and collected enough evidence to support the accuracy of the other's original point of view. And it would be difficult to convince either one that the other was right" (3). The rest of the essay explores the evidence for both points of view.

2. Morrison's grandmother and grandfather were very different in personality and had had quite different experiences relating to their race, leading to a divergence of opinion about the future for blacks. Her grandfather had owned inherited land, but had had it confiscated by whites through some legal connivings. Throughout his life, he couldn't find decent or significant work, despite his accomplishments as a craftsman, because of his race. As a result of these experiences, Morrison says, "he was an unreconstructed black pessimist who . . . was convinced for 85 years that there was no hope whatever for black people in this country." To get by, he worked as a travelling violinist, sending money back to his family (1). He believed that whites were out to get blacks and would prevent any real progress (5). Morrison's grandmother, on the other hand, "was of a quite different frame of mind," and she had, through her own efforts, experienced the improvement of her situation. She rescued her children from apparent threat of murder by sneaking them out a window in the middle of the night, and moved her family out of a town in which "the teacher didn't know long division" (2). Her temperament was as optimistic as his was pessimistic, and she "would see what she expected to see . . . the signs of irrevocable and permanent change." It was she who provided the image that gives the piece its title: "like the slow walk of certain species of trees from the flatlands up into the mountains," progress would occur (5).

3. Morrison confesses, "I grew up in a basically racist household with more than a child's share of contempt for white people." Her parents felt that blacks had to take care of themselves, because whites were "in some way fundamentally, genetically corrupt" (6). Morrison's parents disputed whether white people could be decent, even whether they were fully human, and this atmosphere of distrust and antipathy taught her to dislike whites. As Morrison puts it, her parents "assumed that black people were the humans of the globe, but had serious doubts about the quality and existence of white humanity." Here, as in the grandparents' generation, the man is more pessimistic; Morrison's father was completely suspicious of every white person and white behavior in relation to blacks. Morrison's mother, on the other hand, "*believed* in them—their possibilities."

    When she began to have her own experiences, she found that "for each white friend I acquired who made a small crack in that contempt, there was another who repaired it." She admits to a "racial vertigo" a disorientation, caused by the disparate and contradictory behavior of whites. She notes that "for each [white person] who related to me as a person, there was one who in my presence at least, became actively "'white.'" Making sense of these conflicting experiences was difficult to impossible, and so Morrison says she pulls from her ancestors "what [she] needs": the grandfather's "cynicism and deployment of his art as both weapon and solace," her grandmother's "faith in the magic that can be wrought by sheer effort of the will"; her mother's open-mindedness . . . and . . . reasonableness"; her father's "temper, . . . impatience," and avoidance of whites. She admits, thus, to being filled with "widely disparate and sometimes conflicting views," and suggests most blacks are likewise, because, in fact, history and present day life contains evidence for all these views. "There is repetition of the grotesque in our history. And there is the miraculous walk of trees" (7). So, while she does not claim to have overcome her antipathy for whites, whatever racist tendencies she has are complicated and balanced by a recognition that there are good people and positive events out there.

4. Morrison cites much evidence on both sides. On the negative side, she points to the horrific parallels in our history: Lincoln's and Kennedy's assassinations, the Civil War matched by the battle for civil rights a hundred years later, the murder of pioneering black college students a hundred years apart, and riots over racial progress in the streets of NY in 1865 and in Boston a century later (4).

But she also list much positive evidence; "the number of black college graduates jumped 12 percent in the last three years, 47 percent in 20 years." Major gains have come in government, with the numbers of black mayors, judges, congress-persons, senators, and police chiefs all rising. Likewise, blacks have won numerous and significant awards, including the Pulitzer Prize, the Prix de Rome, the Guggenheim (5). And the image of blacks in the media has improved; she cites O.J. Simpson advertising Hertz rental cars, but wonders if today's television shows, "Good Times" being an example, are better than the Stepin Fetchit stereotype. Her final attitude is one of questioning: "Has the first order of business been taken care of? Does the law of the land work for us?" (7).

5. *unreconstructed* (1): stubbornly maintaining earlier positions
rancor (1): bitter resentment or ill will
sharecropper's (2): a tenant farmer's
lobotomized (3): having had a cut made across a brain lobe to control severe mental illness
virility (5): masculinity
irrevocable (5): not able to be revoked or recalled
hinder (6): cause delay or difficulty
arrears (6): being late with a payment
fastidious (6): characterized by excessive care or delicacy
succor (6): timely aid in distress
vertigo (7): a feeling of whirling
deployment (7): a stationing systematically

Questions About the Writer's Craft (p. 355)

1. The numerous contrasts include: the contrast between the 99.2 percent of blacks who were native born in 1912 and the 60 percent of whites who were (2); the contrast between the two grandchildren, one a tenured Princeton professor (Morrison herself), and the other a man shattered by his time in reformatories and mental hospitals (3); her white friends and acquaintances, some of whom rectify her image of white people and some who justify it (7); the contrast between the "repetition of the grotesque in our history" and "the miraculous walk of trees" (7); the contrasts of O.J. Simpson and the Gold Dust Twins, of "Good Times" with Stepin Fetchit (7).

All of these contrasts highlight the issue that is for Morrison the main concern and that prompts her central question. This issue is the potential contrast between "then"—the way it was for blacks— and now, and the question is whether the contrast is real, or whether life for blacks today is just a small variation on the past. Morrison sets up these contrasts and then interrogates them. The questions in paragraphs 7: "Has the first order of business been taken care of? Does the law of the land work for us?" she wonders (7). Each seeming contrast between then and now could be, underneath, just more of the same. The contrasts thus weave a texture of mind-boggling complexity around the issue of whether life for blacks has improved or not.

The essay does also contain some comparisons. In paragraph 4, Morrison points out that "Some of the monstrous events that took place in John Solomon's America have been duplicated in alarming detail in my own America." Also the title of the essay results from the comparison of progress in racial justice to the "slow walk of trees" (5).

2. At the start of the paragraph, Morrison repeats the word, "hopeless," as a sentence fragment, doubling its effect and creating a flatness of tone. Then Morrison moves into a series of long sentences beginning with a coordinating conjunction, either "for," as in the second sentence, or "and." The tone becomes more flowing, as if the negative events of black history are overtaking, flooding the paragraph: "For he was certain . . . And a hundred years after . . . And not long before that. . . ." The second sentence also contains a series that conveys a sense of overwhelming odds: "white people of every political, religious, geographical and economic background would bank together. . . ." Morrison puts the word "promise" in quotation marks, adding irony to the image of "the white man's 'promise.'" She concludes the section of the paragraph with a sentence that stresses the image of the grandfather by repeating the sentence subject and of his despair by depicting a series of actions: "If he were here now, my grandfather, he would shake his head, close his eyes, and pull out his violin . . ."

As Morrison moves to discuss her grandmother in this same paragraph, some sentences again begin with "and," creating a flowing effect. One sentence, the first about Ardelia, uses a complex sentence with an appended description that breaks the mold of sentence structure to produce a unique statement. This introduces us to the unusual and poignant image that represents the grandmother's view of racial progress: *the slow walk of certain trees from the flatland up into the mountains.* The paragraph concludes with a series of sentence fragments, all flowing from the statement that "it wouldn't surprise her in the least to know that. . . ." These fragments provide statistics about recent black successes in America, successes strung together and pounded home: "That there are 17 blacks in Congress, one in the Senate; 276 in state legislatures—223 in state houses, 53 in state senates. That there are 112 elected black police chiefs and sheriffs, 1 Pulitzer prize winner; 1 winner of the Prix de Rome . . ." Here the sentences create a tone that is assertive and celebratory. "Oh, her list would go on and on," Morrison concludes. "But so would John Solomon's sweet sad music." These two final short sentences cap the paragraph and balance the two forces of despair and optimism that have flowed through it—neither side wins out, the complexity of our racial situation is underscored.

3. Morrison begins paragraph 6 with a linking sentence that summarizes the conflict between her grandparents and then flows into a succinct preview of her parents' differences: "While my grandparents held opposite views on whether the fortunes of black people were improving, my own parents struck similarly opposed postures, but from another slant." In handling the earlier contrast between the grandparents, Morrison began by using separate paragraphs for each person, but here she instead provides an analysis of the differences before she moves to the specifics of each parent's position. "Quite a different argument," she comments, and then repeats the theme of the grandparents' conflict and follows it with another summary of her parents' main point of contention: "whether it was possible for white people to improve."

She then moves to her father's ideas with the transitional word, "*Thus,*" and provides a specific example of his views in action. She switches to her mother, appropriately using a transition of change: "My mother, *however,* . . ." and then brings in examples, using transitions of addition, "*So* when the meal we got on relief was bug-ridden . . ."; "*And* when white bill collectors came. . . ." Later in the paragraph, she moves back to her father abruptly: "My father loved excellence. . . ." and then uses a transition to return to a discussion of their common values: "*Both* my parents believed. . . ."

4. Morrison uses the italicized "is" to convey her certainty of a few things, in an essay that is itself focused on the uncertainty and ambiguity of racial progress. So, she acknowledges and asserts that John Solomon was right: "There *is* repetition of the grotesque in our history"; and, Ardelia Willis was right, "there *is* the miraculous walk of trees." And, she is sure that the image of blacks in today's advertising is a gain over the past: "O.J. Simpson leaning on a Hertz car *is* better than the Gold Dust Twins on the back of a soap box." But there are still numerous racial issues that are not resolved, that one cannot be certain about. Her statement of this does not italicize the word "is": "The question is whether our walk is progress or merely movement." She thus follows with the example of the Hertz ads, where she feels a judgment is possible, and then with questions about some of the "movement" that may or may not be actual progress. "But is 'Good Times' better than Stepin Fetchit? Has the first order of business been taken care of? Does the law of the land work for us?"

CRACK AND THE BOX

Pete Hamill

Questions for Close Reading (pp. 359-60)

1. From the very outset, Hamill implies his thesis, selecting a title ("Crack and the Box"—a playful twist on the familiar "Jack in the Box") that suggests a connection between drugs and TV. Though he doesn't go on to state his thesis explicitly, one way of expressing it might be, "Drug abuse and excessive television viewing have similar origins and effects: Both reflect the tendency to seek easy solutions and instant gratification, and both can lead to stupefaction and alienation."

2. Unlike today, when drug abuse is rampant in many parts of the country, Hamill says that in the 1940s and 1950s, "drugs were a minor sideshow, a kind of dark little rumor" (5). Drugs, including "reefer," heroin, and "horse," were in circulation then, but only within small subcultures, such as that of jazz musicians. And while the unemployment, poverty, racism, and governmental ineptness of Hamill's youth are still with us today, an entirely new factor changes the equation completely: Since those earlier decades, television has assumed an "all-consuming presence" in our lives, with "two generations of Americans . . . [growing] up with television from their earliest moments of consciousness" (6). Though people during Hamill's youth may have marveled at the "dazzling new medium" of TV, "they weren't *formed* by it" the way we are today (8). In Hamill's estimation, this centrality of television in modern life carries detrimental consequences, ones that he believes parallel the effects of drug abuse.

3. In Hamill's estimation, the similarities between television viewing and drug use are numerous and complex. In general, his arguments are as follows: both television and drugs dominate and absorb the lives of addicts, particularly since these habits impede healthy socialization (10); both are "consciousness-altering instrument[s]" (12), allowing one to escape reality with little effort; both encourage "imaginative and intellectual" passivity (13-14); both foster in the addict a feeling of alienation, insignificance, and impotence (15); both champion Americans' destructive demand for instant gratification as well as the unrealistic notions that "Life should be *easy*" and that the world is simple (16); finally, both reinforce Americans' self-indulgent preoccupation with feelings rather than reason (17).

97

4. Hamill's suggestions revolve around parental guidance and control. He advises parents to "take immediate control of the [television] sets," permitting children to watch only specific television programs and sending them outside to play with other children (19). Next, he urges an educational solution: Elementary and high schools should teach television as an academic subject, training children how to evaluate television criticaliy and perceptively. Finally, Hamill declares, "All Americans should spend more time reading. And thinking" (19).

5. *squalor* (1): filthy or wretched condition
   brooded (2): meditated or was in deep thought
   callous (2): emotionally hardened; unfeeling
   stupefied (3): having dulled senses and/or faculties
   inert (4): not moving or acting
   diverted (8): entertained by being distracted
   confiscated (8): seized by authority
   phenomenon (8): circumstance perceptible by the senses
   all-pervasive (9): present throughout
   coherence (14): logical, orderly relationship of parts
   alienated (15): isolated emotionally
   enhance (17): to intensify
   obliterate (17): to do away with completely

Questions About the Writer's Craft (p. 360)

1. Hamill's objective in this essay is to highlight the similarities between two unlikely subjects of comparison: television and drug abuse. For this reason, comparison serves as the central, structuring frame of his essay. At specific points in the essay, though, Hamill uses contrast to develop his point. For example, in paragraph 6, he contrasts "then" (the 1940s and 1950s of his youth) with "now," first listing the various conditions (unemployment, illiteracy, etc.) shared by both eras, then discussing the crucial difference that television has made between yesteryear and the present. The contrast between the past and the present is further elaborated in paragraph 8, in which Hamill uses statistics to demonstrate the dramatic increase of both television and drug use over the past few decades. Later in the essay, Hamill contrasts the dynamic activity of reading with the static habit of television watching (13).

2. The opening anecdote establishes the central subject of the essay: the ravages of drug use and the similarly paralyzing effect of excessive television viewing. The wretched circumstances of Hamill's interviewee—a gaunt 22-year-old mother of three addicted to crack and willing to engage in dangerous behavior to support her habit—illustrates the seriousness of the drug problem. This initial image of children oblivious to all except the television while their mother admits how good drugs make her feel echoes throughout Hamill's subsequent points about the similarities between excessive television-watching and drug abuse. More specifically, this image of children "inert" before the TV set recurs in paragraph 4, when Hamill first articulates the possible connection between television and drug use.

   Hamill employs this initial anecdote to deliver a striking opening statement about the horrors of the drug problem and to illustrate the presence of television in the midst of it. Though he never actually refers to this anecdote later on, its image pervades the rest of the essay as he examines the connection between drugs and television. In addition, Hamill's first-person narration and his claim to extensive experience with drug addicts give him greater authority to discuss the issues of drugs and television as well as validate the impassioned tone he uses in the piece.

3. While Hamill's central purpose is to establish similarities between excessive television viewing and drug abuse, he also asserts that television is the *cause* of increased drug use and a variety of other negative social phenomena. In paragraphs 5 and 6, he claims that television provoked the pivotal change between past decades and the present; while other conditions have remained the same (for example, unemployment and governmental ineptness), television is the factor that fundamentally changed American society—according to Hamill, for the worse. Television has fostered viewers' physical and intellectual inertness (10, 13), feelings of alienation and powerlessness (10, 15), and an unrealistic, unhealthy demand for simple answers and instant gratification (12-14, 16). All these conditions, Hamill believes, have set the stage for increased drug use.

4. Hamill's purpose is to inform readers of the drug-television connection and to enlighten them about the magnitude of the problem. Aware that he is making a comparison between two unlikely subjects of comparison, Hamill seeks to convince readers of the validity of his analysis. To win readers over, he uses emotional appeals (for example, the sordid portrait presented in the opening anecdote and his impassioned questions in paragraphs 3 and 16) as well as logical arguments (for example, the abundant supporting points and statistical evidence in paragraphs 2 and 8-18).

   Given the appeals Hamill makes to achieve his purpose, it's not surprising that his tone fluctuates between objective rationality and impassioned emotion. In paragraphs 8, 11, 12 and elsewhere, Hamill remains—on the whole—objective in his presentation of supporting evidence. Yet overall, Hamill's emotional appeals prevail. In paragraph 3, Hamill's voice takes on a distressed and desperate tone when he queries people's reasons for drug abuse, "*Why*, for God's sake?" In paragraph 16, Hamill bristles with sarcasm as he ironically asks, "So why should real life be a grind? Why should any American have to spend years mastering a skill or a craft, or work eight hours a day at an unpleasant job, or endure the compromises and crises of marriage? . . . And if life in the real world isn't that simple, well, hey, man, have some dope, man, be happy, feel good." These shifts in tone are perfectly consistent with—indeed, even reinforce—Hamill's ultimate goal: to make readers aware of a problem that he considers critical.

AND THEN I WENT TO SCHOOL

Joseph H. Suina

Questions for Close Reading (p. 365)

1. Suina's thesis is implied by the comparison of his preschool lifestyle with his life after school begins. It could be stated as, "Attending school began the destruction of Suina's strong Indian self-image and of his attachment to Indian customs and values." Paragraph 16 also provides a thesis-like statement: "life would never be the same again. . . . the ways of the white man. . . . would creep more and more into my life."

2. Values were instilled through story-telling, praise, and direct instruction. Suina mentions several typical story-telling sessions; for example, his grandmother would tell him about "how it was when she was a little girl" (3). When the relatives gathered, a nightly occurrence, they too would tell stories to "both children and adults" (4). Praise was showered upon him by his grandmother so that he would be proud of his accomplishments; "her shower of praises," he

writes, "made me feel like the Indian Superman of all times" (6). Finally, his grandmother teaches him about his culture by taking him along with her to various ceremonies and teaching him "appropriate behavior" for these occasions. She also models how to pray, so that he learns both the words and the proper attitude (7). When Suina goes to school, he is shocked by the very different methods of teaching. Instead of praise, he receives "a dirty look or a whack with a ruler" when he speaks his native language (13). Personal hygiene is impressed upon him through a cruelly administered shampoo and caustic, embarrassing comments about his background (12). The language barrier meant that he couldn't comprehend all the lessons, but "yet [he] could understand very well when [he] messed up . . . The negative aspect was communicated too effectively. . ." (11).

3. The village begins to take in some non-Indian influences. There are automobiles, albeit very few of them. Suina's grandmother possesses a dresser in which she keeps some of her possessions; the dresser, a European type of furniture, was acquired by trading some of her famous hand-made pottery. And, in the dresser, she keeps goodies, which include "store bought cookies and Fig Newtons." (3). Even the tradition of going nightly to visit relatives to chat and tell stories is on the decline as radios and televisions cause people to stay home instead of going out (4). And, the children have access to some 10-cent comic books, which they read and use as the basis for fantasy games when their families get together at night. They imitate the cowboys-and-Indians plots in the comics, with, ironically, all the children wanting to be cowboys because they always won the conflicts. Suina sums up the encroachment of white culture in paragraph 16: "The schools, television, automobiles and other white man's ways and values had chipped away at the simple cooperative life I grew up in. The people of Cochiti were changing."

4. In paragraph 13, Suina indicates that the adults around him wanted him to attend school so that he "might have a better life in the future" (13). This idea is in itself confusing to him, because he felt he "had a good village life already" (13). Near the end of the essay, he recognizes that "there was no choice but to compete with the white man on his terms for survival" (16).

   Many elements of the school lifestyle are confusing to him. The teaching style, with whacks of a ruler, dirty looks, scoldings and embarrassing comments, is very alien to him. "The strange surroundings, new concepts about time and expectations, and a foreign tongue" were other elements that bewildered him (8). The teacher is so different in appearance from his grandmother that he thinks she is ill; she is also unfriendly and, he thinks, not very smart, because she couldn't speak his language. The classroom is so large it seems cold and ominous; the artificial building style and the fluorescent lighting also seem forbidding and alien. Instead of running freely, he must sit all day long. The most confusing thing to him, however, is that he must give up his language and speak English.

   Going to the boarding school clinches his separation from his native village culture. He lives in a white-style building and learns the comforts of indoor plumbing, spacious rooms, and ventilation. By the time he returns for a four-day break at Thanksgiving, the village lifestyle does "not feel right anymore" (15). Now living with whites 24-hours a day, he finds himself unaccustomed to the culture he was raised in. He soon "gets back with it" (15), he says, and then finds returning to school extremely difficult. His life has been transformed, and he "could not turn back the time just as [he] could not do away with school and the ways of the white man" (16).

5. *adobe* (5): sun-dried clay, usually in bricks
   ego (12): sense of self-importance
   belittled (15): to criticize something as unimportant or trivial

Questions About the Writer's Craft (p. 365)

1. The essay is predominantly organized according to the *one-side-at-a-time* pattern. First, Suina discusses his life as a preschooler residing in his grandmother's house (1-7). Then, he discusses what life was like for him after he was required to attend school (8-16). This pattern works well because the essay compares "before" and "after" stages of Suina's childhood, stages that occurred one after the other. The *one-side-at-a-time* strategy allows Suina to maintain the chronological order of events.

    There are some places within the description of his school life where he returns to talk about Indian ways; in these places he uses the *point-by-point* strategy. For example, at the start of paragraph 9, he describes his teacher, comparing her with his grandmother. In paragraph 10, he compares the fluorescent lighting to "the fire and sunlight that my eyes were accustomed to" and sitting at a desk all day with his previous life of "running carefree in the village and fields, . . ." In paragraph 13, he compares the attitude of the school towards his native language and his own childhood view of it: "This punishment was for speaking the language of my people that meant so much to me. It was the language of my grandmother and I spoke it well. With it, I sang beautiful songs and prayed from my heart" (13). Later, Suina compares the beloved home cooking that his family brings to him once a month with the school food: "I enjoyed the outdoor oven bread, dried meat, and tamales they usually brought. It took a while to get accustomed to the diet of the school." Finally, the last paragraphs of the essay use *point-by-point* organization to express the conflicts he felt when he returned home from boarding school for four days. In 16, he describes how disappointed he felt with his old home: "Home did not feel right anymore. It was much too small and stuffy. The lack of running water and bathroom facilities were too inconvenient. Everything got dusty so quickly and hardly anyone spoke English. I did not realize I was beginning to take on the white man's ways, the ways that belittled my own."

2. The numerous places where Suina evokes the Pueblo lifestyle and values include paragraph 3, where he describes the inside of his grandmother's one-room house in great detail. Most of the details here are visual, although Suina does mention the "sharp odor of mothballs" in the dresser and the flour sack containing the " goodies," which made a "fine snack" at night. We also learn that he frequently hears stories or a softly sung song from a ceremony in the house. There are further references to the foods they shared with relatives in paragraph 4, and in the next paragraph he notes the sound and glow of the fire and the smell of stew cooking. He contrasts these sensory descriptions with details about the school he attends. There, he notices the teacher's appearance is very different from his grandmother's; he smells her odor, which makes him sick (9). He provides details of the classroom: its "huge" size and medicine-like smell, its artificial walls and ceiling, its "eerie" and blinking fluorescent lights. He feels the hardness of the desk to which he is confined. Towards the end of the essay, he returns to some beloved details about his Indian culture, things that he savors when his parents visit him at boarding school: "outdoor oven bread, dried meat, and tamales" (14). Yet, once home for a four-day break, he discovers he longs for some of the conveniences of the school, for his home "was much too small and stuffy. The lack of running water and bathroom facilities were too inconvenient. Everything got dusty so quickly . . ." (15).

3. Into the simple factual information of the first two sentences, Suina inserts a word with strong negative connotations: "invade." This word is used metaphorically to suggest that the coming of electricity to the pueblo began a conquest of the Indian culture by that of the whites. Portraying the Indians as "unsuspecting" suggests their innocence in not being aware that they were being transformed. These images establish an ominous tone and convey Suina's ambivalence about the material goods and other elements of white lifestyle that altered his native culture. However, while suggesting negative forces are at work in the pueblo, Suina 's

tone remains calm, almost matter-of-fact. There is no sense of blaming or rage; because of this tone, the changes seem inevitable changes.

4. The last four sentences of paragraph 14 all begin with the phrase, "I longed for. . . ." This repetition drums into the reader the grief and yearning Suina felt at being parted from his home culture. The sentences seem to cry out with pain. In addition, the shortness and simplicity of the sentences effectively convey the depth and sense of unallayed need. The final sentence moves away from specific needs for his grandmother and siblings, his home, and the familiar ceremonies to asserting that he needs to be free to be himself, instead of being confined in the alien world of the boarding school.

ANSWERS FOR CHAPTER 17
"CAUSE-EFFECT" (p. 369)

Opening Comments

Along with comparison-contrast, cause-effect writing (often called "causal analysis") is frequently required of college students—especially in exam situations ("Analyze the causes of the country's spiraling divorce rate"; "Discuss the impact of the revised tax laws on middle-income families"). Since students can't deny that an ability to write sound causal analyses will serve them well, they're generally eager to tackle this pattern of development.

Not surprisingly, though, many students run into problems with their analyses. Although they enjoy the intellectual challenge of tracing causes and effects, they sometimes stop at the obvious—overly concerned as they are about getting closure on an issue.

We've found a classroom activity that helps counteract this urge to oversimplify. Here's what we do. We put on the board a broad, noncontroversial statement. (For example, "In the United States, many people work hard to keep physically fit.") Then, we ask students to take five minutes (we time them and announce when the time is up) to brainstorm the reasons *why* (causes) people are so involved in physical fitness. Then, we ask students to spend another five minutes brainstorming the *consequences* (effects) of this concern with physical fitness. Next, we put students in pairs and then in groups of four; each time, they exchange, first, their causes and then their effects. As you'd expect, this activity generates a good deal of energy. We hear a number of comments, such as, "That's interesting. I never thought of that." Such a reaction is precisely what we hope for. The activity sensitizes students to the complexity of cause-effect relationships and encourages them to dig deeply and not settle for the obvious.

For this chapter, we chose professional selections that dramatize the power of causal analysis to make the reader think. Using a personal narrative, Angier ("A Granddaughter's Fear") traces two related causal chains to explore the various effects of her grandmother's physical and emotional decline. Darley and Latané's "Why People Don't Help in a Crisis" provides a well-researched analysis of the causal factors behind bystanders' typical inaction. And Staples ("Black Men and Public Space") describes the corrosive effects of racism on his life.

ACTIVITIES: CAUSE-EFFECT

Below we provide possible responses to selected activities at the end of Chapter 17. Of course, other approaches are possible.

Prewriting Activities (pp. 386-87)

1. There are many ways to use cause-effect in these two essays; the lists below suggest only a few of the possibilities. We suggest that you have students share their ideas on ways to use cause-effect in these essays. Seeing others' ideas makes the point dramatically that writing involves invention and individuality.

Topic: The need for a high school course in personal finance

    Causes of many young people's casual attitude to money
    Causes of parents' reluctance to teach about finance
    Effects of a young person bouncing checks
    Effects of overspending

Topic: How to show appreciation

    Causes of people's callous disregard for each other
    Causes of an appreciative approach to good manners
    Effects of appreciation in everyday life
    Effects of not showing appreciation

2. Here are some possible causes and/or effects for the various topics. Others are possible. In the second part of the activity, outlining will depend upon the points generated.

  a. **Pressure on a student to do well**

    Causes:
        High career ambitions
        Parental demands
        Inner pressure; self-esteem

    Effects:
        Restricted social, campus, and physical activities
        Emotional instability, anger
        Less effective academic performance

  b. **Children's access to soft-core pornography on cable TV**

    Causes:
        Lenient parents
        Failure to purchase a TV lock
        Children visiting friends' homes

    Effects:
        Children grow up too soon
        Children get unrealistic view of adult relationships
        Children dating at too early an age

c. *Being physically fit*

Causes:
>Media attention to health concerns
>Trend to engage in sports
>Desire to look attractive

Effects:
>Better health
>Growing enrollments in health clubs
>Preoccupation with fitness

d. *Spiraling costs of college education*

Causes:
>Growing costs of faculty and staff
>Modernization going on: computers, for example
>Inflation
>Cutbacks in state and federal funds

Effects:
>Students burdened with more loans
>Concern about paying back loans influences career choices
>More students work during college
>Some students drop out

Revising Activities (p. 387)

4. a. The growing Latin American immigrant population and the crime rate may be correlated, that is, there may be some connection between the two. That both figures are increasing, however, does not mean that the rise in immigration has *caused* the rise in crime. To say so is *post hoc* thinking.

   b. This statement shows *post hoc* thinking because it assumes that one of two parallel events is causing the other; that is, that more women working is causing the divorce rate to rise. However, there are other possible reasons for the increase in the divorce rate: a change in American values regarding the family, for instance, or the "sexual revolution." Moreover, one could cite the same two facts—more women working and the divorce rate rising—and argue the opposite, that the divorce rate is causing more women to work outside the home. In any case, disregarding these other possible points of view and arguing that a clear-cut relationship necessarily exists is an example of *post hoc* thinking.

   c. These two parallel situations do not have a proven causal relationship. To say that one has caused the other is *post hoc* reasoning, unless other proof exists. Such proof might consist of information about what chemicals exist in the landfill, whether they are cancer-causing, whether the chemicals have leached into the soil, water, or air of the town, and whether other causes for the cancer might exist.

5. It's a good idea to provide time in class for students to read over each other's revisions of this paragraph. Seeing how others handled the activity can give students a stronger sense of their revision options.

Here are the main problems with the paragraph:

— Overall, the paragraph asserts that the bank machines have *caused* certain behaviors and attempts to support such a claim with broad generalizations stated in absolute terms. For example, the fourth sentence asserts that automatic tellers have negatively influenced the "average individual." Similarly, the next three sentences state—almost categorically—that people, once they have cash readily in hand, invariably spend their lunch hours shopping. Equivalent absolutes can be found throughout. The paragraph could be rescued if the writer toned down the absolute tone and provided qualifications that suggest that "for *some* people" or "for *many* people" these machines present problems.

— The writer assumes causation explains the circumstances (use of ATM cards and people shopping during lunch hour) when these may simply be correlated, that is, they may happen at the same time because they are a two results of some other earlier event. Or, the simultaneous appearance of increased spending and ATM card use may be a coincidence, meaning that the writer has committed the *post hoc* fallacy.

— Another problem with the paragraph is its lack of supporting examples. Although it isn't necessary for the writer to provide hard evidence in the form of research, he or she should have supported the paragraph with specific references to friends, family, etc., for whom automatic tellers have created problems.

— The point that children don't appreciate the value of money is an unfounded generalization; it also digresses from the paragraph's point and so should be eliminated.

— The last sentence categorically asserts ("There's no doubt. . .") that banking machine fraud is a *cause* of the "immoral climate in the country." This is an unsupported causal statement and would need evidence to be considered valid. It should be deleted.

A GRANDDAUGHTER'S FEAR

Natalie Angier

Questions for Close Reading (pp. 390-91)

1. The thesis is implied. One possible way of stating it is: "The physical and mental decline that accompanies old age can pose severe difficulties not only for the aging person, but also for his or her loved ones." In the final sentence of the selection, Angier acknowledges that her grandmother's deterioration evokes her own paralyzing fear of decline and mortality: "When I look at my grandmother, fragile, frightened, unhappy, wanting to die but clinging desperately to life, I see myself—and I cannot stand the sight" (24). Angier's admission of her fear explains why she behaves in the often questionable, even reprehensible way she does.

2. As demonstrated by the essay's opening telephone-call episode, Angier reacts to her grandmother with apprehension, impatience, and even embarrassment (3-8). She has difficulty understanding how her grandmother could be so demanding and overly dependent on family (8, 11), and the family's inability to comfort and satisfy the grandmother results in overwhelming frustration and guilt for everyone concerned (16). Angier's negative emotions are heightened when she encounters her grandmother in person. The latter's irrational behavior and unwarranted rantings initially render Angier "helpless and resentful" (12), then inspire "rage," "righteous fury" (12), and a "sense of impotence" (13). Increasingly, Angier avoids interaction with her grandmother, neglecting to call or visit "for weeks at a stretch" (17) because she is terrified (20) by what her grandmother has become.

     Underlying and complicating these troubling emotions, however, are Angier's love and caring for her grandmother. Angier demonstrates her concern by (eventually) rushing to see her grandmother and by being distressed by the old woman's disheveled appearance (10). Later, she says, "I love my grandmother" (23) and describes her admiration of and pride in her grandmother's former exuberance and achievements (18).

     This conflicted mixture of fearful disgust and loving concern, as well as a personal fear of the ruthless aging process, are at the root of Angier's "heartless" behavior (17). Her grandmother's rapid and painful deterioration after a vibrant, courageous, and independent life reminds Angier of her own mortality; she expresses an anxiety that this pattern of awful decline may run in the family, so that no matter what she does, Angier may be on the road to a similar fate. In the concluding sentence, she says that she sees in her grandmother a portrait of what she may become, and she "cannot stand the sight" (24).

3. Angier contrasts her own behavior with the way her mother and uncle deal with the grandmother. She describes the unflagging devotion and self-sacrifice exhibited by her mother and uncle, who have "structured their days and nights around her [the grandmother's] needs" (11, 15, 16). The stress of this responsibility causes her mother to lash out occasionally at the grandmother and then feel guilty, while the uncle's repressed emotions have become manifest in his weight gain and aging appearance (16).

     Unlike her mother and uncle, whose care of their mother has become a daily concern, Angier avoids her grandmother at all costs. She says she "combine[s] the worst of all worlds," for she neglects visiting or calling and then speaks harshly to her grandmother (like a "boot-camp sergeant") when she does contact her (17). Angier resists her mother's pleas that she be gentler and more attentive to her grandmother, preferring avoidance and emotional withdrawal as her means of coping with her grandmother's deterioration.

4. Angier describes what she imagines as "the perfect old woman" in paragraph 21: "wise and dignified, at peace with herself and quietly proud of the life she has forged." She is neither insecure nor angry, but always actively improving and enjoying herself and her life, "thread[ing] together the scattered days into a private whole." The narrator provides examples of famous women who embody these characteristics, such as Georgia O'Keeffe, Louise Nevelson, and Marianne Moore, renowned artists who continued creating through their later years.

    In the paragraph that follows (22), Angier lists the characteristics her "fantasy doyenne" would lack, all of which are evident, sadly enough, in her own grandmother. These include physical ailments, mental and emotional instability, and financial problems. When she was young, Angier looked up to and "adore[d]" (18) her grandmother, but now she regards her grandmother as the antithesis of what she would ever want to become.

5. *railed* (11): criticized with abusive language
    impotence (13): powerlessness
    psychotherapeutic (15): healing mental and emotional disorders
    debilitating (16): sapping the energy or strength of
    indignation (16): anger aroused by something unjust
    panache (18): vitality and flair
    stoutly (19): resolutely and uncompromisingly
    clamored (19): demanded loudly
    confection (21): wonderful combination of various elements
    doyenne (22): woman who is the eldest member of a group

Questions About the Writer's Craft (p. 391)

1. Angier illustrates the impact of her grandmother's situation on the family *before* she explains why her grandmother is in such a declining state. Since Angier's objective is to demonstrate the stressful and troubling effects of an elder's infirmities on his or her loved ones, it is logical that she would place greater emphasis on her family's response to her grandmother than on the circumstances of her grandmother's infirmity. Though the pre- and post-illness portrait of her grandmother helps explain Angier's feelings of guilt and frustration, this information is secondary to the essay's central purpose: demonstrating the profoundly painful conflicts a family may experience following a loved one's decline.

2. The title "A Granddaughter's Fear" enlarges the essay and supports Angier's implied point that the decline of an elderly person is difficult for everyone who cares for that person. Angier seeks to convey that although not everyone will share her family's precise circumstances or responses, the difficulty and pain of watching a loved one degenerate is universal—for granddaughters and other family members alike. This use of the more general "a granddaughter's" instead of "my" reinforces this notion of universality.

3. As evidenced by the opening episode, the central conflict in the essay is between Angier and her grandmother. Angier resists and resents her grandmother's irrational demands and discusses at length the shortcomings that render her grandmother a burdensome source of discord and suffering for the entire family. Yet as the essay progresses, another conflict increasingly assumes prominence: Angier's internal struggle between her selfish neglect of her grandmother and her guilt over violating her familial duties to this once beloved elder. This conflict is particularly evident when Angier acknowledges that she is being "heartless" (17) and that her excuses for avoiding her grandmother are "shallow and glib" (20). By the end of the essay, another facet of Angier's internal conflict surfaces: her own consuming fear of

mortality and decline, which restricts her ability to connect with her grandmother. She sees herself in her deteriorating grandmother, is terrified (20), and "cannot stand the sight" (24). Because Angier does not resolve these tensions neatly and tidily by the end of the piece, readers will most likely finish the essay feeling somewhat distressed and out of sorts—an appropriate reaction given the complex issues Angier tackles.

4. Angier uses dialog to give readers direct access to the characters and to give the scene narrative immediacy. In paragraphs 2 and 6-9, the grandmother's desperation becomes evident both in what the elderly woman says to her granddaughter ("I'm ALL ALONE!" and "Natalie, WHERE ARE YOU?") and in how she says it (she "screamed" and hysterically cried). Likewise, in paragraphs 5 and 7, Angier's discomfort and irritation are evident both in her curt responses ("So what do you want me to do?" and "O.K., O.K.") and in the way she delivers her responses (she "muttered"). Having given readers a first-hand taste of her grandmother's irrational, frantic dialog early on, Angier wisely compresses subsequent dialog into a paraphrased description of what her grandmother said. A precise recapping of the entire dialog would probably be lengthy as well as tedious, especially given the grandmother's meandering conversational tendencies. In short, Angier's condensed reportage of what her grandmother said conveys the old woman's anxiety more efficiently than a repetition of the entire exchange would. Moreover, the technique of dialog paraphrasing calls attention to Angier's role as narrator and reminds readers that they are getting the story solely from her point of view.

WHY PEOPLE DON'T HELP IN A CRISIS

John M. Darley and Bibb Latané

Questions for Close Reading (p. 396)

1. Darley and Latané state their thesis at the end of their introduction, as an answer to the question, "Why, then, didn't they [witnesses to an emergency] act?" (8). They write, "There are three things the bystander must do if he is to intervene in an emergency: *notice* that something is happening; *interpret* that event as an emergency; and decide that he has *personal responsibility* for intervention" (9). They then indicate that the rest of the essay will explains the research that has led the authors to this conclusion: "As we shall show, the presence of other bystanders may at each stage inhibit his action" (9).

2. People need to notice that a problem is occurring before they can help, which means they must be disturbed out of their mental distractions. In addition, Americans are taught to keep their eyes to themselves, to "close our ears and avoid staring," the authors write (10). This principle of polite behavior can cause people to ignore or not really see a critical situation happening near them (10).

   Then, after an event has attracted their attention, people must realize that someone needs help. But the presence of others can delay the realization that a problem is going on. Darley and Latané explain that people take their cues from those around them—"if everyone else is calm and indifferent, [a person] will tend to remain so" (14). People simply get the message that there's no problem because, in our culture, people usually try to remain cool and calm in public; "it is considered embarrassing to 'lose your cool'" (15). The collective nonchalance of a crowd can suppress anyone's urge to help, that is, to go against the prevailing passivity and rush to aid.

Finally, even when a person has determined that aid is required, he or she will not feel the personal requirement to perform the assistance if there are many others nearby. Darley and Latané call this the "diffusion of responsibility theory" (21). Such people are not hard-hearted but just confused about what to do when others around them are doing nothing (27). People's "reactions are shaped by the actions of others," be it response or passivity.

3. The researchers wanted to eliminate the possibility that the presence of others would prevent awareness of the emergency, so they designed an experiment in which an obvious crisis occurred and in which the subjects' awareness would not be blunted by others being in the room with them. The subjects were told to discuss with each other over headsets, used with the rationale of protecting everyone's privacy. In this way, the researchers could determine whether, even when one of the students reported a medical crisis, the knowledge that several people knew it was happening and could take responsibility would blunt the individuals' willingness to act. The experiment showed that, indeed, the response of subjects to the emergency deteriorated rapidly when the number of people linked by microphones increased. "The responsibility diluting effect of other people was so strong that single individuals were more than twice as likely to report the emergency as those who thought other people also knew about it" (25).

4. The authors indicate that any one of us could be that unresponsive bystander, because being unresponsive is not a defect of character or a sign of the decay of civility in urban life (5). Rather, the failure to respond occurs in particular situations which could befall any of us. When people are surrounded by others, they notice less (10), they conform to norms of public behavior (14), and they take less responsibility for events around them (20). As Darley and Latané write, "If we look closely at the behavior of witnesses to [emergencies], the people involved begin to seem a little less inhuman and a lot more like the rest of us" (7). Any person could be influenced by the "apparent indifference of others" to "pass by an emergency" (28). "We are that bystander," they conclude (28) and suggest that being aware that groups or crowds might encourage our passivity could help us to "see distress and step forward to relieve it" (28).

5. *megalopolis* (5): an urban region consisting of several adjoining cities
   apathy (5): lacking involvement or interest
   indifference (5): without interest or concern
   alienated (6): to cause to become indifferent or hostile
   depersonalized (6): to make impersonal
   inhibit (9): to block or hold back
   corroborates (11): supports with additional proof
   coronary (13): of the human heart
   slavish (14): deliberately dependent or slave-like
   nonchalance (15): coolly unconcerned or indifferent
   diffused (20): spread widely or thinly
   blandly (27): unemotionally or indifferently

Questions About the Writer's Craft (p. 397)

1. From the way the thesis is introduced to the way the essay is organized, the authors make it easy for the reader to determine the causes of inaction. Darley and Latané introduce their thesis in a dramatic way, as the answer to a one-paragraph question (paragraph 8). Setting off the question in one paragraph creates surprise in the reader. They then follow this with a clear and direct answer. In this sentence, the three causal factors are italicized to call attention to them (9).

They follow up this listing with a direct announcement of their intentions in the essay: "As we shall show, the presence of other bystanders may at each stage inhibit his action" (9). The rest of the essay is divided into sections, the next three of which reflect the three causes: "The Unseeing Eye," "Seeing Is Not Necessarily Believing," and "The Lonely Crowd." Each one of these sections begins with an anecdote about a hypothetical situation in which help is needed. Then after presenting the ambiguities in this situation, the authors present a hypothesis suggesting why people avoid or delay acting and then cite psychological research that has shown the hypothesis to be valid. In addition, the authors use bridging sentences, the beginnings of which link back to previous material. For example, paragraph 13 begins, "Once an event is noticed . . ." which repeats the idea of the previous section. And paragraph 20 uses the beginning clause, "Even if a person defines an event as an emergency . . ." to remind the reader of the previous point.

2. Using the present tense creates a dramatic introduction to draw readers in—or at least, not scare readers away—from a serious and analytic essay. Narratives of crime and danger are intrinsically interesting, but the style used here heightens the shock-effect of the situations. Each narrative begins bluntly, with no lead-in, using a direct statement of the victim's situation: "Kitty Genovese is set upon by a maniac"; "Andrew Mormille is stabbed in the head"; "Eleanor Bradley trips and breaks her leg." The present tense adds a sense of urgency, while the direct style seems almost like a narrative voice-over, telling us events as they happen. In addition, the present tense circumvents the need to provide background data, such as the year of occurrence and so on, data that would slow the reader down and introduce the analytic style too early in the essay. Finally, the present tense conveys the timelessness of the events, in the sense that given human nature, these past responses would hold true at any point in time.

3. The experiments are described in paragraphs 11-12, 16-19, and 22-25. Each experiment is introduced by a clear announcement, and throughout the description of the experiment and the results, numerous transitions make each stage of action crystal clear. In paragraph 11, Darley and Latané write, "Experimental evidence corroborates this. We asked college students to an interview. . . ." Paragraph 16 begins, "To determine how the presence of other people affects a person's interpretation of an emergency, Latané and Judith Rodin set up another experiment." And the third experiment is introduced in paragraph 21: "To test this diffusion-of-responsibility theory, we simulated an emergency . . ." and picked up again in paragraph 22: "For the simulation. . . ."

   Within each description of an experiment, the authors use numerous clear signals to indicate the stages of the process. In paragraphs 11-12, they use signals of time, as well as the colon, effectively: "as the students waited. . . . As part of the study, we staged an emergency: smoke was released. . . . Although eventually all . . .—when the atmosphere grew so smoky. . . . "

   In the injured-researcher experiment (16-19), narrative and spatial signals help the reader along: "An attractive young market researcher met them . . . and took them to . . . where they . . . Before leaving, she told them she would be working next door in her office, which was separated from. . . . She then entered . . . where she. . . . After four minutes. . . . "

   In the group-discussion experiment (21-25), narrative transitions predominate, along with spatial indicators and enumeration: "Each student was put in an individual room . . . Each person was to talk in turn. The first to talk . . . Then . . . Other students then talked . . .in turn. When it was the first person's turn . . ." (22-23). The authors interrupt the process to explain the hidden reality of the experiment, using transitions of contrast: "But whatever the apparent size . . . only the subject; the others, as well as the instructions . . . were present only on . . . tape" (23). Returning to the process of the experiment again in paragraph 24, the authors use a narrative transition plus an enumeration and a signal of repetition: "When it was the first person's turn to talk again. . . ."

The authors also often use balanced sentence structure to compare the reactions of subjects who were alone with those who were in groups of various sizes. In the leaking-vent emergency (11-12), they write, "Solitary students often glanced idly about while filling out their questionnaires; those in groups kept their eyes on their own papers" (11); "two thirds of the subjects who were alone noticed the smoke immediately, but only 25 percent of those waiting in groups saw it as quickly" (12). In the injured researcher experiment, the results are presented in two separate paragraphs, one for those who were alone (18), and one for those who were in groups of various sizes (19). Short direct sentences which put in the foreground the percentages of how many subjects responded in what way make the data easy to follow, and signals of contrast help the reader sort out the details: "Seventy percent . . . offered to help. . . .Many pushed back the divider . . . ; others called out to offer their help" (18). "Among those waiting in pairs, only 20 percent . . ." (19).

In reporting the results of the group-discussion simulation, Darley and Latané again rely upon direct statements that list the percentages explaining who responded how: "Eighty-five percent of the people who believed themselves to be alone. . . . Sixty-two percent of the people who believed there was one other bystander. . . . Of those who believed there were four other bystanders, only 31 percent reported. . . ."

4. At the start of the essay, the reader is likely to think of witnesses who do not help a victim as monsters, as aberrant and mean-spirited human beings. Darley and Latané wish to show that inaction is in fact a natural result of ordinary human psychology; as they write in paragraph 7, "If we look closely at the behavior of witnesses to these incidents, the people involved begin to seem a little less inhuman and a lot more like the rest of us." One of their goals is to show that the failure to take action is typical in certain situations, situations, in fact, in which there are multiple bystanders. "As we shall show, the presence of other bystanders may at each stage inhibit his action" (9).

At the end of the essay, they indicate that their ultimate purpose is to create the awareness that inaction is the norm when people are in a group. With this awareness, people might be able to counteract the paralyzing effect of other people and get involved in helping in a critical situation. "Caught up by the apparent indifference of others, we may pass by an emergency without helping or even realizing that help is needed. Once we are aware of the influence of those around us, however, we can resist it. We can choose to see distress and step forward to relieve it" (28).

BLACK MEN AND PUBLIC SPACE

Brent Staples

Questions for Close Reading (p. 400)

1. The closest thing to a direct statement of the thesis occurs in the second paragraph, in the second sentence: "I first began to know the unwieldy inheritance I'd come into—the ability to alter public space in ugly ways."

2. Staples first discovered that other people considered him a threat during his first year away from his hometown, when he was a graduate student in Chicago. There, he found that "nighttime pedestrians—particularly women" would run away (2) or cross to the other side of the street (3); people in cars would lock their doors as he crossed the street in front of

them (3); doormen, policemen, cabdrivers, and other such workers were unpleasant to him (3). He says he felt "surprised, embarrassed, and dismayed all at once" and "like an accomplice in tyranny" (2). Over time, he gained an awareness that he himself is in danger when he is perceived as dangerous (2). Later in the essay he remarks that there is a "kind of alienation that comes of being ever the suspect" (5).

3. In general, Staples says he has become aware of situations that can be hazardous to him: turning "a corner into a dicey situation" or crowding "some frightened, armed person in a foyer somewhere," or making "an errant move after being pulled over by a policeman" (2). Specifically, Staples recounts the most frightening incident when he was mistaken for a burglar; rushing into a magazine office to deliver an article on deadline, he was pursued through the halls by "an *ad hoc* posse" of employees. In another case, he stopped in a jewelry store to kill time and was confronted by a silent store owner with a huge Doberman pinscher. He handled these nonconfrontationally; in the first case, he dashed to the office of the editor who knew him and could vouch for his honesty. In the second, he simply nodded goodnight and left the store. He is clearly a nonviolent person.

4. At night and when he is dressed casually, Staples takes care to move slowly and keep a distance from people who look nervous. He avoids giving the appearance of following people when entering buildings. And, if he is pulled over by police, he acts extremely friendly and nonthreatening. His final tactic when taking late-night walks is to whistle classical music, communicating that he is educated and has a love of beauty, and thus is not a mugger (11-12). These precautions telegraph his real identity: a law-abiding nonpredatory, nonviolent, educated and cultured person.

5. *uninflammatory* (1): not arousing strong emotion
   dicey (2): risky or uncertain (*informal*)
   bandolier (5): belt with loops for carrying bullets worn over shoulder and across chest
   lethality (6): ability to cause death
   bravado (7): swaggering show of courage; false bravery
   berth (11): (as in "give a wide berth to") avoid
   constitutionals (12): a walk taken for health reasons

Questions About the Writer's Craft (pp. 400-01)

1. The essay concludes with discussions of effects; in paragraph 11, Staples focuses on the effects on him of the perception that he is a mugger. In the last paragraph, he describes the effects on other nighttime pedestrians of his whistling classical melodies. By discussing these effects, Staples shows the inconvenience and foresight necessary for him, and other black men, to go about their daily lives. By mentioning his "excellent tension-reducing measure"—whistling Vivaldi and "the more popular classical composers"—Staples returns to the issue that he began with in the first paragraph and also shows that he has handled a potentially humiliating problem with grace and style.

2. The phrase, "my first victim was a woman," is certainly an attention getter, and it may suggest to the reader that the essay narrates a criminal's confession That Staples goes on to relate a story of misperception shows how quickly people are to assume the worst, both on the street and in reading the essay.

3. Staples' audience would seem to be primarily white. Most blacks would know first-hand the problem he writes of; it is the whites who, in encountering him anonymously on the

street, need to be told that he, like most black men, is harmless. He signals that his audience is white when he reveals, "Black men trade tales like this all the time" (10). In addition, the essay relies on many references to European tradition: "bandolier" (5); "bravado" (7); "posse" (8); Beethoven, Vivaldi, "cowbells" and "bear country" (12). There are no similar references to black culture.

4. Staples' tone is sad and conciliatory but also tinged with irony. He uses many terms that indicate his unhappiness with his perpetual role as "would-be mugger": "surprised, embarrassed, and dismayed" (2); "feel like an accomplice in tyranny" (2); "a vast, unnerving gulf" (2); "alienation" (5). He is conciliatory in that he has smothered his rage (11); he attempts to see the other side (5) and the wider perspective (2). That a self-confessed "softy" like him (2) should be taken for a criminal prompts several ironic notes; certainly, his last image, in which he likens himself to an innocent hiker wearing a cowbell to protect himself from "the bears," is strongly ironic.

ACTIVITIES FOR CHAPTER 18
"DEFINITION" (p. 404)

Opening Comments

In high school and certainly in college, students are frequently asked to answer questions that call for definitions: "Define 'mitosis'"; "Explain what 'divestiture' means." Even so, we hold off discussing definition as a method of development until the last quarter of the course.

Our rationale for delaying definition is based on the need for other patterns of development in fleshing out an extended definition. At the very least, students need to know how to incorporate well-chosen *examples* so that their definitions can be grounded in specifics. Similarly, the *comparison-contrast* format can show students how to go about organizing a definition by negation. And *process analysis,* explaining how something works, can be essential when developing a definition. Once students feel comfortable with these and other strategies, they can approach definition essays with confidence, knowing that they have a repertoire of techniques to draw on.

For this chapter, we selected readings that illustrate a variety of approaches for writing definition essays. Touching on a wide range of topics, the pieces show how definition can explain difficult-to-understand scientific concepts, expand the meaning we attach to everyday words, and help us view our society in a new light. We often start with Cole since she mixes a number of strategies (examples, facts, personal anecdotes) to develop her definition of "Entropy." In "When Is It Rape?" Gibbs makes use of definition by negation to discuss the confusions surrounding relationships between the sexes. Finally, Leo provides compelling examples, as well as a causal analysis, to clarify what is meant by the term "Absolutophobia."

115

ACTIVITIES: DEFINITION

Below we provide possible responses to selected activities at the end of Chapter 18. In many cases, other responses are possible.

Prewriting Activities (p. 418)

1. There are many ways to use definition in these two essays. Below we've listed some of the possibilities. In classroom use of this activity; we suggest you have students share their responses. They will be surprised and often delighted to discover that their neighbors have quite different answers.

    Topic: How to register a complaint
    Define "effective" complaining
    Define a "no-win situation"
    Define "conflict resolution"
    Define "diplomacy"

    Topic: Contrasting two stand-up comics
    Define "black humor"
    Define "improvisational humor"
    Define "political humor"
    Define "put-down" humor

2. For this activity, as for #3, students will, of course, each have individual responses. When introducing the activity and discussing students' material, make students aware that their goal is to frame a definition that goes beyond "dictionary meanings" or the commonly understood sense of the term. An essay-worthy personal definition is one that discovers or affirms some less-understood dimension of a word.

Revising Activities (pp. 418-19)

4. Here's our appraisal of the effectiveness of the definitions:

    a. This definition is circular because it repeats the words of the term itself. In addition, the "is when" format is awkward if not ungrammatical. Here's one way to revise the definition: "Passive aggression is a personality disorder in which a person chronically performs poorly as a way of unconsciously showing resentment of the demands of an employer, teacher, or other person."

    b. This definition is also ineffective because of its circularity. One way to rewrite it might be: "A terrorist uses violence against innocent people to intimidate those in power."

    c. This definition is effective and clear.

    d. This is a circular definition that tells us nothing about the term being defined. A better version would be: "Pop music typically contains simple lyrics, a strong beat, and appealing harmonies."

    e. This definition needs rephrasing to eliminate the awkward "is when"; otherwise, it is a workable definition. "Standing by another person during difficult times is the essence of loyalty."

116

5. It is a good idea to have your students read each other's revisions of this material. Doing so gives them helpful exposure to alternative ways of rewriting a problem paragraph.

Here are our recommendations for rewriting the paragraph:

— The opening sentence is weak; relying on the dictionary only tells us (boringly) what we already know. The sentence should be rewritten to catch the reader's interest.

— Since the second sentence states the obvious, it should be deleted.

— The listing of times people feel tense (sentences 3, 4, and 5) consists of obvious, general situations. Dramatic examples would be appropriate here.

— Similarly, "Wear and tear on our bodies and on our emotional well-being" is overly general. "Wear and tear" is a cliche as well. Specifying some actual damage that can result from tension would be an effective revision strategy.

— The thesis (how to relieve tension with walking) seems tacked on. A transitional phrase or lead-in is needed to build more naturally to the thesis.

ENTROPY

K. C. Cole

Questions for Close Reading (pp. 421-22)

1. Cole's thesis is located at the start of paragraph 3, after her two-paragraph introduction: "Disorder, alas, is the natural order of things in the universe."

2. Entropy is unique in being irreversible; most physical processes "work both ways" (3). In nature, things fall apart and decay, and they do not naturally reverse and come together. The "arrow of time" image helps us understand that entropy occurs in relation to time; as time passes, disorder naturally accompanies it. Entropy is the "arrow" also in the sense that it is the weapon time uses to destroy things.

3. The creation of life is the ordering of the particles of matter into a living thing, be it a plant or a person, and so represents the major contradiction to entropy. Such creation, however, requires energy in the form of nutrients such as, for a plant, soil, sun, carbon dioxide, and water, and for a person, "oxygen and pizza and milk" (9). Cole's other examples show that countering entropy does generally require energy in the form of physical work, the work of cleaning up children's rooms, painting old buildings (4), or maintaining skill at flute-playing (12). Cole points out that creating order and countering entropy require energy whose expenditure causes an increase in entropy in another part of the system; she uses as an example our society's creation of electricity by burning oil and coal, only to produce smog.

4. Entropy is "no laughing matter" because it is inevitable, and it operates not only in nature, but in society as well. There are "always so many more paths toward disorder than toward order," Cole writes (14), and unless we are diligent, entropy will get the better of us individually and societally. This ever-present threat of disorder is especially distressing in the area of social institutions and international events. Cole believes that the ultimate randomness of entropy endangers us—the "lack of common purpose in the world" (15) threatens to create more and more disorder.

5. *futility* (1): sense of uselessness
    dissipated (6): scattered, spread out
    buffeted (7): hit, slapped, pushed
    tepid (7): lukewarm
    atrophied (12): deteriorated

Questions About the Writer's Craft (p. 422)

1. Entropy is a phenomenon we surely have noted—rooms getting messy, wood rotting, metal rusting—but it is not likely we have understood it to have a name or be a "principle" of the universe. So Cole's definition is informative about this scientific law. In explaining the need for energy to counteract entropy (10-12) and in relating entropy to societal and world events, however, Cole adopts a persuasive tone. In paragraph 16, she cautions, "Friendships and families and economies all fall apart unless we constantly make an effort to keep them working and well oiled." Clearly, she is making a pitch for us all to work harder at keeping order in our world.

2. Speaking like a common person with average concerns, such as her refrigerator breaking and her tooth needing root canal work, Cole encourages a reader to follow her into a discussion of entropy as an explanation for these ordinary problems. She achieves a friendly, almost breezy tone by using the first person, contractions, short sentences, and colloquialisms such as "lukewarm mess" (5), "to get ourselves together" (10), and "the catch is" (10). The question in the second paragraph is another example of her personable, casual tone.

3. These terms are blunt and jarring and carry an intense impact. Throughout the essay, Cole uses these emotional words to keep us aware of the personal dimensions of entropy. While entropy is a scientific concept, she wants us to understand that it also pertains to our personal lives and has effects we can respond to emotionally. Some other similar terms are "unnerving" (4), "lost and buffeted" (7), "distressed," "afraid," "terrified," and "upset" (15).

4. This sentence pattern emphasizes contrasts—it contains an inherent opposition between the elements of the first and second half. Cole may find this pattern useful because she is trying to dramatize the effects of entropy and convince us to counteract its power as best we can. The first example compares the two "roads" to disorder and creation, finding one downhill, the other uphill. The second example compares ways to do "a sloppy job" and a "good one." Other examples occur throughout the essay: "Once it's created, it can never be destroyed" (3); "When my refrigerator was working, it kept all the cold air ordered in one part of the kitchen. . . . Once it broke down, the warm and cold mixed into a lukewarm mess that allowed my butter to melt . . ." (5); "Though combating entropy is possible, it also has its price"; "That's why it seems so hard to get ourselves together, so easy to let ourselves fall apart" (10); "creating order in one corner of the universe always creates more disorder somewhere else"; "We create ordered energy from oil and coal at the price of the entropy of smog" (11); "The chances that it will wander in the direction of my refrigerator at any point are exactly 50-50. The chances that it will wander away from my refrigerator are also 50-50" (13); "There are always so many more paths toward disorder than toward order. There are so many more different ways to do a sloppy job than a good one, so many more ways to make a mess than to clean it up" (14); "The more pieces in the puzzle, the harder it is to put back together once order is disturbed" (17).

WHEN IS IT RAPE?

Nancy Gibbs

Questions for Close Reading (p. 427)

1. Gibbs's thesis is implied. She sets up the expectation that the essay will provide an answer to the question, "When is it rape?" and the bulk of the essay is an exploration into the various attitudes and assertions made on this subject by men and women, victims and perpetrators, as well as experts and consultants. Early on, she admits that there is a "'gray area' that surrounds the whole murky arena of sexual relations" (7). Her sustained discussion of the conditions and causes of acquaintance rape imply that she does consider it a crime that should be taken seriously by the courts. The example she provides in 14-16 clearly suggests that to dismiss claims of date rape as an exaggeration or a misunderstanding is to do a grave injustice to the

violated. One way of stating the thesis might be, "Our society needs to debate the issues surrounding acquaintance rape, to outline more clearly what is and is not acceptable behavior between the sexes, and to define rape in a way that takes 'date rape' into account."

2. Rape is defined in different ways by different people, Gibbs points out. At the start of the essay, she mentions that some people think there is a thing called "real rape," that is, rape by "a monstrous stranger lurking in the shadows" (2), a concept that implies that rape by an acquaintance or date is not "rape" or not "real" (2). In fact, the coining of the terms, "acquaintance rape" and "date rape," suggests that these events are some how different or lesser than "real rape" (3). In paragraphs 9-12, she explains some of the different perspectives on rape. She cites "one extreme" view that holds that rape should only refer to the crime committed when a stranger attacks a woman, and that sex on a date can never be construed as rape (9). Another view holds that, while date rape can occur, it is not as serious as "stranger rape," because the people have been socializing, and perhaps drinking and kissing (10). Many people, especially women who have been raped by a date or acquaintance, insist that the crime of date rape is just as much a violation as rape committed by a stranger, and that it should not be considered just a "misunderstanding" (11). And, finally, another extreme view holds that rape is best understood as a metaphor for all the injustices done to women and that it includes everything from the legally defined crime of rape to "verbal harassment and inappropriate innuendo" (12).

3. Typically, Gibbs says, victims of date rape are themselves unsure whether they were raped, or whether, as the Florida businesswoman thought, "it was [their] fault" (16). They feel confused that their adamant refusals were not heeded by men they had trusted. Usually, the rapist acknowledges that he heard the woman refuse, but continued anyway. In the opinion of a consultant on sexual assaults, men who commit date rape start out to seduce, but if their dates are not compliant, move on to threats and finally to force to accomplish their goal, "to get laid" (17). She implies that such men put their masculinity on the line, and believe that "real men don't take no for an answer" (17).

4. While both parties in a date rape are often poor communicators because they are "young, and drunk, and aroused" (20), larger cultural and even biological factors may come into play as well. One anthropologist cited by Gibbs thinks that men may have a predisposition to "fertilize as many females as possible, as quickly as possible and as efficiently as possible"; he seems to attribute women's resistance to a biological need to select one mate who will help her protect her offspring. The upshot is that men wind up "aggressive" and women act "coy" (19). In a date rape situation, the man may think the women is spinning out a mock resistance befitting her role as a demure, even pure woman, while he feels the impetus to be "commanding" (20).

   In addition, Gibbs cites the enormous "cultural baggage" that young people carry as a factor in the attempted seductions and forced intimacies of date rape. Movies, television, rock videos, and romance novels all portray women as seductive and ultimately desirous of sex while seeming to refuse (21). "The messages come early and often," she says; our culture is "drenched with messages that women have rape fantasies and a desire to be overpowered" (20). Gibbs describes the results of a survey taken among young teenagers of both sexes showing that many believe force is acceptable if the male has spent money on the female or if the female is already sexually experienced (22). Both young men and women are susceptible to the media messages, leading men to assume the overpowering role and women to play the role of seducer and to send mixed signals, even when sexual intimacy is not desired.

5. *watershed* (5): a major turning point
   fetal (5): curled up like an unborn child
   psychopath (9): a mentally ill person who exhibits antisocial behavior

omniscient (9): infinitely knowledgeable or aware

infraction (10): breach or violation of law or custom

innuendo (12, 13): a hint or suggestion of a derogatory nature

coercion (17): compelling or forcing by fear or psychological pressure

intimidation (17): to force by inducing fear

ubiquitous (17): being everywhere at the same time

ideological (20): referring to set beliefs or doctrines

celluloid (20): the colorless material used for photographic film

statutory (21): legally punishable

dogmas (23): doctrines firmly held or authoritatively put forth

Questions About the Writer's Craft (p. 428)

1. Gibbs uses definition by negation, that is, defining by telling what the subject is *not*, in the first four paragraphs of the essay to negate the common misbelief that rape is usually performed by a stranger. Through this negation, she introduces her point that "acquaintance rape" is "real rape." In the first two paragraphs, she asserts that "most women who get raped are raped by people they already know" (2). Only one out of five rapes is the result of "a monstrous stranger lurking in the shadows." In paragraph 4, she returns to this point, calling the belief that most rapists are strangers "the central mythology about rape," a mythology that continues because so few women—as few as 10%— report rape to the police. The distinction between "acquaintance" or "date rape" and what people think of as "real rape," a crime between strangers, results from people's adherence to that "central mythology." Elsewhere in the essay, definition by negation crops up again. Those who adhere to the myth of "real rape" define "date rape" by negation: At one extreme, some believe that "rape" can <u>not</u> be defined as something that happened on a date (9). Others more moderate still believe that date rape is <u>not</u> the same, and such not be punishable in the same way, as "street rape." (10). Women who have been raped by acquaintances also define such rape by negation: "Date rape is not about a misunderstanding. . . . It is not a communications problem. It is not about a woman's having regrets in the morning. . . . It is not about a 'decision' at all" (11). These definitions by negations support the author's belief that confusion abounds on the the subject of rape, but that at least today men and women can enter a "dialogue," to remove "some of the dogmas, old and new, surrounding the issue" (23).

2. Gibbs says that the only way to get at the "hard reality" of date rape is to look at an individual story. She then provides the *narrative* of one case of date rape, in which a business woman on a business trip is raped by a lawyer for her project. (14-15). After the narrative, Gibbs cites an expert's view of the typical *process* of a date rape: "First comes dinner, then a dance, then a drink, then the coercion begins," her expert explains. The process includes "gentle persuasion," moving on to "physical intimidation," and "when that fails, force is used" (17). By analyzing a particular narrative of a date rape case to show the process behind it, Gibbs is able to demonstrate that date rape is a particular phenomenon with unique characteristics, not just a "misunderstanding" or morning after "regret."

    Gibbs also uses *comparison-contrast* frequently to show the diversity of opinions that exist on the subject of what rape is and to guide us toward a view of rape that she thinks is fair. Comparison-contrast first emerges in paragraphs 5-6, where Gibbs first presents the victim's perspective in the William Kennedy Smith rape case, and then presents the alleged perpetrator's side. The comparison serves to show how divergent opinions can be in just one situation. Then, in paragraph 7, Gibbs strings together a point-by-point array of men's and women's views about date rape, only to conclude at the end that "there is no consensus in sight." A few paragraphs later, in 9-12, Gibbs compares four different views of date rape, two extreme and two more middle-ground. Again, she concludes, "the definitions have become so slippery that the entire subject sinks into a political swamp" (13). In paragraph 19, she presents the analysis of Lionel Tiger, who also proposes that men and women have different, contrasting biological needs in the sexual arena, needs that can't be reconciled. In 20, she quotes a writer who posits the typical contrast between the male's and female's view in a case of date rape. The essay concludes, however, by moving somewhat beyond the stalemate of the perpetual contrast of the male and female motives and opinions. In paragraphs 21 through 23, Gibbs describes the "cultural baggage" that may predispose young people to fall into the pattern of date rape. Then, she contrasts this "baggage" with what she deems is a newer and better cultural climate happening today in which date rape is taken seriously as a crime and in which people learn that communication and discussion are necessary.

3. In the introduction, Gibbs uses a number of words and phrases with intense negative connotations: "frightful," "swaddle a child in fear," "scarred by caution," and "worst nightmares." These terms establish the constrained climate in which young girls grow up, and which they internalize so that, as adults, they "know to be wary of strangers." Such emotionally charged words are likely to cause the reader to feel grieved that daughters must be trained in fear. The wording in which Gibbs introduces the essay's subject—"whether [girls] have more to fear from their friends"—shocks the reader by juxtaposing the alliterative "fear" with "friends." These highly connotative sentences create intense interest in the subject and rivet attention on the question of "date rape." In the conclusion, Gibbs uses highly connotative words to evoke the damage done in a case of date or acquaintance rape: "uniquely intimate cruelty," "the body is violated," "spirit is maimed," "wounds," "a quiet alarm," and "a terrible crime." By inducing in the reader a likely reaction of sympathy with the victim and anger about the crime, Gibbs helps ensure that the reader will see finish the essay agreeing that the definition of rape must include date rape.

4. Into her analysis of the various definitions and opinions people have about date rape, Gibbs inserts references to known examples and cites statistical evidence to give her analysis a solid basis in fact. She clearly wishes to move away from people's assumptions about date rape and toward the realities of the crime. As she says, "the myths have a way of cluttering the search for the truth" (5). In addition, she refers to numerous commentators on the subject (17, 18, 19, 20). She also gains credibility by demonstrating that she is knowledgeable and lends weight to her own analysis of the issue by grounding it in such evidence and examples. That she should need to marshall her credibility suggests that she expects an audience of mixed or even hostile readers. Her analysis of views on date rape (9-13) shows that there are numerous possible opinions about it, and so she cannot count on an audience of people who agree with her. There are other signs that she expects a mixed or hostile audience; she refers to a multitude of places where people might discuss date rape, "in court, on campus, in conversation . . ." (8). Also, she acknowledges the other side or sides in the debate over whether date rape is a "real rape" or not; for example, she cites the ideas of anthropologist Lionel Tiger regarding the naturalness of male aggression and female coyness (19), two elements in the typical date rape scenario. Also, the variety of examples in paragraph 21 suggests she expects to have readers of all ages and education levels.

ABSOLUTOPHOBIA

John Leo

Questions for Close Reading (p. 431)

1. In an opening paragraph, Leo presents the dilemma of Professor Robert Simon: While Simon's students do not deny the existence of the Holocaust, they are unwilling to condemn genocide as morally wrong. This example leads to Leo's thesis statement that "nonjudgmentalism is a growing problem in the schools" (2), with students thinking "that no one has the right to criticize the moral views of another group or culture" (2). Several phrases found later in the essay echo this initial statement of Leo's thesis—for example, when he refers to multiculturalism as "spreading the vapors of nonjudgmentalism" (5); when he indicates that "moral shrugging" (6) is increasing on campus; and when, borrowing Simon's term, he cites students' lamentable "'absolutophobia'—the unwillingness to say that some behavior is just plain wrong" (7).

2. Jackson's story depicts an ancient fertility ritual inexplicably practiced in an American small town: Each June, a townsperson is chosen to be sacrificed so that crops will grow. What concerns Haugaard and Leo is the students' nonjudgmentalism—their inability to object to the story's central action. While a woman is stoned to death by her husband and children, Haugaard's students refuse to condemn the ceremony. Questioned by Haugaard, one student would not oppose the practice, explaining that it might be "a religion of long standing" (4). The student's attempt at multicultural understanding worries both Haugaard and Leo, who see in it a troubling moral relativism. Haugaard likens it to another student's diversity training, wherein hospital staff "are taught not to judge" an action "if it is part of a person's culture" (5). Leo worries that such "moral shrugging" creates a generation "unwilling to oppose large moral horrors, including human sacrifice" (2). At the same time, both Leo and Haugaard note that students are not too reluctant to express "old-fashioned and rigorous moral criticism" on certain issues like smoking, environmentalism, and animal rights (4, 6). In Haugaard's and Leo's view, the student readers of "The Lottery" swing between cultural relativism and strident belief: As Leo explains, students hesitate to condemn egregious evils if such acts reflect cultural mores (2), but they don't hesitate to "say flatly that treating humans as superior to dogs and rodents is immoral" (6). To Leo, students' inability to experience moral outrage about historical evils is evidence that they have lost their moral compass.

3. According to Leo, multiculturalism plays a key role in developing student reluctance to denounce clearly immoral acts. While Leo mentions Simon's plea to "welcome diversity rather than fear it" (5), he uses both Simon and Haugaard to demonstrate the dangers of multicultural thinking. From Haugaard, Leo highlights the example of a nurse who teaches "multicultural understanding" to her staff, instructing them "not to judge" actions if they are "part of a person's culture" (5). From Simon, Leo cites students "so locked into their own group perspectives of ethnicity, race, and gender" that judgment outside the group view "is impossible" (5). As Leo describes it, multiculturalism replaces moral judgment with cultural relativism: Although another culture's practices (for example, the Aztec practice of human sacrifice) may seem cruel or barbaric to our view, we cannot impose our view on that culture. Moreover, Leo also finds multicultural thinking to be inconsistent. While the Aztecs might not be condemned, contemporary practices like whaling or female circumcision are routinely attacked by "white multiculturalists" (6). In short, Leo sees multiculturalism as both flawed and dangerous. As his opening example illustrates, without the ability to condemn another

culture, students might find themselves "unwilling to oppose large moral horrors" like the Holocaust, slavery, or ethnic cleansing (1, 2).

4. According to Leo, what "trends feed" (7) "absolutophobia"? According to Leo, several distinct developments in our culture contribute to "the unwillingness to say that some behavior is just plain wrong" (7). In colleges, postmodern theory instructs students to question any claim to objective truth (like a definite evil) in favor of "clashing perspectives" (7). Outside the campus, the general "pop-therapeutic culture" ("I'm OK, you're OK") fosters acceptance rather than disapproval of offensive attitudes and behavior (7). Additionally, Leo finds other factors in "intellectual laziness and the simple fear of unpleasantness" (7): Assuming that one moral view "is as good as another" lets us appear tolerant and avoid antagonism; such a relaxed stance perfectly suits a people whose only goal is to "get on with our careers" (7). Finally, Leo points to "values clarification" education as a dangerous trend in schooling. Under these programs, teachers "leave the creation of values up to each student" (8) so that they will not "indoctrinate other people's children" (8) with their own views. Ultimately, Leo believes that these trends make "values emerge as personal preferences, equally as unsuited for criticism or argument as personal decisions on pop music or clothes" (8). As a result, students never learn that some actions are unequivocally wrong.

5. *conformity* (4): compliance, agreement, acquiescence
   perspective (5): point of view
   rigorous (6): extremely strict, rigidly observed, or disciplined
   dogmatically (7): unthinkingly held or observed
   relativism (7): the comparative or relational (as opposed to objective) quality of knowledge
      or truth
   phobia (7): irrational fear
   antagonizing (7): causing opposition to
   indoctrinate (8): to teach or instruct (*often negative:* to teach without analysis, reflection,
      or room for dissent)

Questions About the Writer's Craft (p. 431)

1. Leo opens his essay dramatically. As opposed to the neutral language of a dictionary entry, the first paragraph presents a disturbing moral problem: Professor Robert Simon's students "acknowledge" the historical existence of the Holocaust, but they cannot condemn the genocide (1). As one student explains, "Of course I dislike the Nazis . . . but who is to say they are morally wrong?" (1) This opening example—of students unwilling or unable to condemn horrible acts—is echoed throughout the essay. In an extended discussion of Shirley Jackson's "The Lottery," a story about ritual sacrifice, Leo tells us that "a class discussion of human sacrifice yielded no moral comments" (4). Leo's purpose seems clear: He is outraged by the students' lack of moral outrage and wants to readers to share his shock and disbelief. Formal definitions would blunt the essay's impact, switching attention from the students' disconcerting moral relativism to the more cut and dry issue of definition. Leo wisely introduces definition only after the major work of his essay—establishing protest, shock, and disbelief at students' being "taught not to judge" (5)—has been accomplished.

2. Cause and effect are crucial to Leo's essay, as he strives first to demonstrate the shocking results of absolutophobia and then to unravel the genesis of the absolutophobia phenomenon. The first part of the essay (1-4) can be seen then as an inventory of effects, with Leo presenting examples (drawn from Simon and Haugaard) of students "unwilling to oppose large moral horrors" (2). After describing students who can neither judge the Nazis nor condemn human sacrifice, Leo moves to the sources of this growing moral quagmire. He offers a list of linked

causes, beginning with "multicultural understanding" and its injunction "not to judge" the practices of another culture (5). Postmodern theory and therapy closely follow, as each replaces objective judgments with divergent perspectives and points of view. Before citing the role that "values clarification" programs have had in eroding a strong moral sense (8), Leo suggests that "laziness" and "fear" (7) also feed absolutophobia. In short, all these factors create a culture where "values emerge as personal preferences" (8), with the failure to judge leading to moral paralysis. At the end, Leo suggests that the series of linked causes feeding absolutophobia have—ironically—paved the way for a counter-development: "character education." Noting that "the wheel is turning" (9), Leo implies that character education's emphasis on objective standards of morality has the potential to produce students who don't exhibit absolutophobia.

3. In paragraph 8, Leo focuses on "values clarification" instruction in schools: a pedagogy that "leave[s] the creation of values up to each student" (8). At one level, these programs are simply one more addition to Leo's litany of forces feeding absolutophobia. At another level, values clarification constitutes a final word on or summation of the essay's thesis: Absolutophobia is not only a manifestation of multicultural tolerance but also a "paralyzing fear" of moral commitment (9). In his final paragraph, Leo contrasts what he considers the insidious nature of values clarification programs with a better model: "character education." According to Leo, this second approach is rooted in the belief that there are agreed-upon standards by which the morality of actions can be judged. By focusing on the contrast between values clarification and character education, Leo is able to end his essay on a hopeful note. He says that "the wheel is turning" and "the search is on for a teachable consensus rooted in simple decency and respect" (9). The emergence of this counter-movement indicates that "the paralyzing fear of indoctrinating children" is ending (9).

4. Leo pulls no punches in his discussion of absolutophobia. His aim is clear: to describe and condemn the "growing problem" of nonjudgmentalism (2). In so doing, Leo does not hide his disdain. He uses figurative language to cast the absolutophobia phenomenon in a most unfavorable light. In paragraph 2, he describes students as "overdosing on nonjudgmentalism," evoking the unsavory world of drugs and addiction. He also describes multiculturalism as "spreading the vapors of nonjudgmentalism" (5), calling to mind strong odors, pollution, and disease. As he discusses Kay Haugaard's experience in teaching "The Lottery," he includes sarcastic asides and caustic descriptions. When Haugaard states that the story's "message about blind conformity always spoke to my students' sense of right and wrong" (4), Leo responds: "No longer, apparently" (4). He also makes sure to include Haugaard's dismissive description of one of her students as a "50-something red-headed nurse" (5). Finally, Leo uses language emphasizing his own judgments and moral beliefs. He calls absolutophobia both "moral shrugging" (6) and a "fashionable phobia" (7). All these examples of loaded, highly charged language clearly underscore Leo's belief that absolutophobia does not merit respect.

ANSWERS FOR CHAPTER 19
"ARGUMENTATION-PERSUASION" (p. 435)

Opening Comments

First-year composition courses often end with argumentation-persuasion. There are good reasons for this. Since an argumentation-persuasion essay can use a number of patterns of development, it makes sense to introduce this mode after students have had experience working with a variety of patterns. Also, argumentation-persuasion demands logical reasoning and sensitivity to the nuances of language. We've found that earlier papers—causal analysis and comparison-contrast, for example—help students develop the reasoning and linguistic skills needed to tackle this final assignment.

When teaching argumentation-persuasion, we stress that the pattern makes special demands. Not only do writers have to generate convincing support for their positions, but they also must acknowledge and deal with opposing points of view. Having to contend with a contrary viewpoint challenges students to dig into their subjects so that they can defend their position with conviction. Students should find the material on page 447 helpful; it illustrates different ways to acknowledge and refute the opposition.

Despite their initial moans and groans, students enjoy the challenge of argumentation-persuasion. To help them become more aware of the characteristics of this pattern of development, we often ask them to look through current newspapers and magazines and clip editorials and advertisements they find effective. In class, these items provide the basis for a lively discussion about the strategies unique to argumentation-persuasion. For example, the endorsement of a health club by a curvaceous television celebrity raises the issue of credibility, or *ethos*. An editorial filled with highly charged language ("We must unite to prevent this boa constrictor of a highway from strangling our neighborhood") focuses attention on the connotative power of words.

We often conclude our composition courses with an assignment based on a controversial issue. Depending on the time available and the skill of our students, the assignment may or may not require outside research. If it does call for research, we begin by having the class as a whole brainstorm as many controversial social issues as they can. Then, for each issue, the class generates a pair of propositions representing opposing viewpoints. Here are a few examples of what one of our classes came up with:

Controversial Subject	*Propositions*
School Prayer	Prayer in public schools *should/should not* be allowed.
Drug abuse in professional sports	Professional sports *should/should not* implement a program of mandatory drug-testing.
Adoption	Adopted children *should/should not* be given the means to contact their biological parents.

If the statement doesn't include research, we focus attention on more immediate local problems. Using the sequence just described, we start the activity by asking the class as a whole to

126

brainstorm as many controversial campus problems as they can. Here are some argumentation-persuasion topics that have resulted.

Controversial Subject	*Propositions*
Cheating	A student found guilty of cheating *should/should not* be suspended.
Fraternities and sororities	Fraternities and sororities *should/should not* be banned from campus.
Drinking	The college pub *should/should not* be licensed to serve liquor.

Once the propositions have been generated, the activity can go in one of two directions. We might ask students to pair up by issue, with the students in each pair taking opposing positions. Or, we might have the students in each pair select the same position. Although students often end up qualifying their propositions, starting with a definitive thesis helps focus students' work in the early stages of the activity.

We try to schedule the assignment so that there is enough time for students to write their essays and deliver their arguments orally. The presentations take about one class; we call this class either "Forum on Contemporary Social Issues" or "Forum on Critical Campus Issues." Students tell us that they enjoy and learn a good deal form these brief oral presentations. (By the way, we grade only the papers, not the talks.)

We have been pleased by the way this final activity energizes students, pulling them out of the inevitable end-of-semester slump. The forum creates a kind of learning fellowship—not a bad way to end the course.

This chapter's professional readings illustrate the mix of logical support and emotional appeal characteristic of argumentation-persuasion. To develop her proposition that "Institution is not a Dirty Word," Kupfer relates her own experiences as a mother of a handicapped child and thus establishes her *ethos*. In "What Should Be Done About Rock Lyrics?" Rivers protests against those who shrug off rock's pro-violence and anti-women lyrics to build her case for public opposition. Addressing the popular arguments posed by those against the death penalty, Koch ("Death and Justice") and Bruck ("The Death Penalty") advance sharply contrasting views about one of our most controversial issues. Arguing from personal experience as well as detailed knowledge of Asian contributions to our culture, Yuh ("Let's Tell the Story of All America's Cultures") gently argues for multicultural education, while Schlesinger's "The Cult of Ethnicity: Good and Bad" analyzes the factors creating our multi-ethnic nation and the effects of multiculturalism and warns against excessive emphasis of ethnic origins.

ACTIVITIES: ARGUMENTATION-PERSUASION

Below we provide possible responses to selected activities at the end of Chapter 19. Of course, your students will devise their own inventive approaches.

Prewriting Activities (pp. 466-67)

1. Listed below are some possible approaches to each of the topics. We recommend that you have students share their responses to this activity in groups or pairs. Seeing how others handled the assignments can provide inspiration for their own work.

   ### Topic: Defining hypocrisy

   Possible Audience: Employers
   Essay might argue the merit of these ways of behaving:

   Some employees react negatively to the hypocrisy of bosses not practicing what they preach. Employers should be careful to dispense advice that they themselves are willing to follow. For example, they shouldn't reprimand staff for taking office supplies if they also "borrow" such supplies; they shouldn't write memos outlawing personal phone calls if they themselves make such calls.

   ### Topic: The difference between license and freedom

   Possible Audience: College students
   Essay might argue the merit of these ways of behaving:

   While license involves nothing more than indulging one's every whim, freedom means acting with thoughtful regard for consequences. Students, then, should think before going out to party before an exam, should reconsider substituting an easy course for a difficult one, and so on.

2. Here are the audience analyses for each thesis:

   a. Low-income employees: Supportive
      Employers: Hostile
      Congressional representatives: Wavering

   b. College students: Hostile
      Parents: Wavering or hostile
      College officials: Wavering or supportive

   c. City officials: Hostile
      Low-income residents: Supportive
      General citizens: Wavering

   d. Environmentalists: Supportive
      Homeowners: Hostile
      Town council members: Wavering

   e. Alumni: Wavering or supportive
      College Officials: Supportive
      Student journalists: Hostile

Revising Activities (pp. 467-69)

6. a. ***Implied warrant***: Strict quality control is necessary to produce cars that have superior fuel efficiency and longevity.

   This warrant is clearly implied and probably does not need to be stated explicitly. The warrant does not need additional support, nor does the claim need qualification. The writer might, however, add more specific data to the argument.

   b. ***Implied warrant***: Gifted children require special educational programs, just as do the learning impaired.

   This warrant should be made explicit, and it should be backed up with additional data that proves that gifted children need special programs. The claim might also be qualified to state that "sometimes" or "often" the educational system is unfair to the gifted.

   c. ***Implied warrant***: Prejudice plays a major role in determining how citizens vote for president.

   This warrant should be made explicit; additional data should be provided to show that prejudice has actually influenced voters' behavior in specific contests.

   d. ***Implied warrant***: Minors should be treated consistently under the law. If they are thought to be too young to vote, marry, or sign contracts, then they should be considered too young to be punished to the same extent as adults.

   This warrant needs to be made explicit so it can be examined for its validity. The claim should probably be qualified to refer to "some minors," "minors who are first offenders," or "minors who commit crimes against property" (as opposed to minors who murder, rape, or otherwise harm people).

7. a. ***Inductive reasoning***, moving from the events in the computer lab to a general conclusion. The conclusion is invalid because there may be other causes of the problems in the lab; for example, perhaps the support staff need better training or perhaps the writer needs further instruction in the use of the programs.

   b. ***Inductive reasoning***, moving from the evidence of the dented cars to a general conclusion. The conclusion is invalid because there may be many reasons for the dents in the cars. For example, perhaps many students cannot afford new cars and thus drive used cars that were dented by previous owners.

   c. ***Deductive reasoning***, applying a general, true statement about the qualities shown by children of two-career families to a particular situation—specifically, that of the increase of such families in a nearby town. This conclusion is invalid because the conclusion is much broader than the evidence supports. It would be more valid to say that "Some children" or

129

"More children than ever" in the nearby town are likely to develop confidence and independence.

d. *Inductive reasoning*, using the evidence of changes in two organizations to support a general statement about the larger class of organizations. The conclusion is invalid because only two organizations are cited as evidence; the sample is too small. It would be more valid to state that "Some traditionally conservative male groups are starting to accept women's role in business."

e. *Deductive reasoning*, applying a general rule about how sexual harassment is handled at XYZ Corporation to a particular case—that of Curt A. The conclusion is invalid because it fails to consider that there are other possible reasons why Curt A. could have been fired. Perhaps he frequently arrived late, did sloppy work, or was hostile to his boss or co-workers. Since these alternative explanations are not taken into account, the conclusion is rash.

8. a. *Begging the Question*. The statement that "Grades are irrelevant to learning" requires proof, but this argument skips over this debatable premise. The second statement is also debatable; some students, those wishing to attend graduate school, for example, are in college to "get good grades."

b. *Over-generalization; Either/or; Begging the Question*.
Both statements are debatable; for example, that jail provides a "taste of reality" is questionable, and that juvenile offenders will repeat crimes "over and over" unless jailed needs to be proven. Moreover, the argument presents only two alternatives: "either" a juvenile offender is jailed, "or" the offender will repeat crimes. It is possible to imagine other outcomes from not jailing juvenile offenders: with therapy, community service, job training, or suspended sentences, some may "go straight"; others may commit different crimes instead of "repeating" their initial crimes.

c. *Questionable Authority*. This argument relies on the appeal to the authority of "legal experts." These "experts" are unnamed and thus cannot be given much credibility. A much stronger argument could be made by citing the experts by name and pointing out specifically how the provisions of the bill would curtail rights that consumers now have.

d. *Over-generalization; Begging the Question; Card-Stacking*.
The first statement in this argument is an overly general description of the programs: they "do nothing to decrease the rate of teenage pregnancy." In addition, the argument begs the question of whether the programs truly fail to curtail teen pregnancies. The argument also fails to address whether there are other valuable accomplishments of the programs that might make them worth keeping. (For example, such programs most likely help reduce instances of sexually transmitted diseases.) Finally, the phrase "so-called sex education programs" is also a way of card-stacking; this term denigrates the programs without saying what's wrong with them.

e. ***Either/Or; Card-Stacking***. This argument admits of only two possibilities; "either" our country should use coal "or" become "enslaved" to the countries that sell oil. In reality, there are many more options, including developing other fuel sources such as solar, wind, or water power and increasing our ability to find, recover, and process oil in our own country. In addition, the use of the highly connotative word "enslaved" stacks the cards by predisposing people towards unthinking agreement with the argument.

f. ***False Analogy; Non-Sequitur***. By likening abortion to killing the homeless and pulling the plug on sick people, this argument commits a false analogy. In reality, these are all quite different situations with differing moral issues, motivations, and outcomes. Secondly, it is a non-sequitur to assume that if abortion is permitted that people "will think it's acceptable" to commit the other actions mentioned. There's actually no demonstrated causal connection between society's permitting abortion and its accepting the murder of unfortunate people.

g. ***False Analogy***. This argument compares two unlike things: locally imposed curfews on teenagers (often parentally supported) and curfews imposed by totalitarian governments on some or all of their population.

h. ***Non-Sequitur***. Even though Americans throw away tons of food each day, it does not follow that there are no starving people in America. The only conclusion that can be drawn is that many Americans have more food than they can eat. This argument is a non-sequitur, that is, the conclusion has no logical connection to the evidence.

i. ***Ad Hominem***. This argument attacks the background of those who support gun control instead of dismantling the arguments for their position; it attempts to destroy the credibility of those who hold the anti-gun point of view. In fact, even if the credibility of the anti-gun legislators were negligible, there still may be valid reasons for supporting their point of view.

j. ***Red Herring***. This argument distracts from the issues at hand by inviting debate about how well health insurance is regulated instead of presenting evidence that car insurance should *not* be regulated.

k. ***Post Hoc***. This argument assumes a causal relationship between a few students cheating on their parking fees (cause) and the rise in parking fees the next year (effect). However, the parking fees might have been increased for any number of other reasons: to provide higher salaries for campus guards, to improve parking facilities, or to discourage students from bringing a car on campus.

9. It's a good idea to set aside some time for students to see how others went about revising this paragraph. They may discover options they hadn't considered.

Here are some of the problems with the introduction:

— Throughout the paragraph there's a hostile, confrontational tone that undercuts the impact of the position being advanced. Sarcastic descriptions of the administrators amount to an *ad hominem* attack: "acting like fascists" and "in their supposed wisdom" (both in sentence 2) and "somehow or another they got it into their heads" (sentence 5). These accusatory descriptions of the way the administration came to impose the dress code should be replaced with a more realistic explanation of why they made the decision they did. A more objective tone is called for.

— Inflammatory language used in the first two sentences *stacks the cards* in favor of the writer's point of view: "outrageously strong," "issued an edict," "preposterous dress code." Similar card-stacking occurs in the fourth sentence when the writer refers to the administrators' "dictatorial prohibition." Such phrases need to be replaced by more neutral language.

— The writer's point that students will lose their "constitutional rights" (sentence 2) is not substantiated in any way. A brief explanation of this point would be appropriate.

— The statement (sentence 3) that "Perhaps the next thing they'll want to do is forbid students to play rock music at school dances," is a *non-sequitur* ; instituting a dress code has no causal relationship to restricting music at school dances. This statement might also be considered a *red herring* because it brings in an unrelated issue about which the reader might have strong feelings. In any case, this unfounded prediction should be eliminated.

— There is no sound basis for the recommendation (sentence 6) that students and parents should protest all dress codes. Any such recommendation should be reserved for the end of the essay, after a logical, well-reasoned argument has been advanced. At that point, it would be appropriate to name specific actions parents could take, such as calling the principal or speaking out at a PTA meeting.

— The final statement that if dress codes are implemented, "we might as well throw out the Constitution" embodies at least two fallacies. It is an *either/or* statement, admitting of no lesser or even other consequences. It also is a *non-sequitur*, because no cause-effect relationship has been shown to exist between dress codes and the end of constitutional rights. This closing statement should be eliminated.

— Finally, the paragraph uses the cause-effect pattern but presents no evidence for the causal relationship it claims. The writer discounts the *causes* of the administrators' decision (the current dress habits of the student body) and predicts extreme and unsubstantiated *effects* of the dress code. In revising, students might choose some of the following options: dispute the administration's claims that the lack of a dress code creates problems; discuss other possible ways of handling these problems, or analyze possible negative effects of a dress code. Of course, not all of these options could be pursued in the introductory paragraph, but they point the way to possible strategies for developing the rest of the essay in a thoughtful, logical manner.

INSTITUTION IS NOT A DIRTY WORD

Fern Kupfer

Questions for Close Reading (p. 472)

1. Kupfer's thesis is implied. One way of stating it might be: "An institution may be the best recourse for certain types of handicapped children, best for the children and for the family."

2. The myths are that damaged children are "special" and that their parents are "somehow picked for the role" (2); that handicapped people can do normal or superior things (2); and, finally, that institutions are cruel and parents who avail themselves of them unloving (4).

3. The media distort the reality of the handicapped by its "tendency to canonize the handicapped and their accomplishments" (8)—they typically show heartwarming images of success and competence among the handicapped (2). They also present horror stories of institutions that treat children badly (7), thus creating an anti-institution bias among the public (8). Omitting the agony of caring for the severely handicapped at home and the cost, both financial and emotional, to the relatives who must provide it, the media show only a very slanted image of this problem.

4. The anti-institutional bias affects others besides the severely handicapped. Kupfer points to this bias as the reason that mental patients have been forced "out into the real world of cheap welfare hotels" and that youthful offenders are paroled even though they are dangerous to the public. In addition, families who place incompetent elderly in nursing homes are made to feel guilty (8).

5. *quadriplegics* (2): persons paralyzed from the neck down
   stoicism (2): indifference to pain; an attitude of endurance and bravery
   kudos (2): praise and glory for an accomplishment
   tantamount (4): equivalent in effect or value
   fiscal (9): pertaining to finances
   sanctimonious (9): pretending to be righteous
   heterogeneous (10): mixed; composed of parts of different kinds

Questions About the Writer's Craft (p. 472)

1. Kupfer lets us know right away that she is the parent of a severely handicapped child (1), a role that gives her great credibility in speaking about this issue. In addition, she relates some of her experienced to lend authority to her view that an institution may be a positive solution to the tragedy of a handicapped child ("I've seen enough to know. . . .") (6, 7). Also, she subtly let us know that she has been responsible and caring, in that she has not signed her child "out of her life forever" (4); she mentions visits, home visits for the boy, and gifts her family gives him (7).

2. There are numerous places where Kupfer refers to two types of opposing viewpoints, those that claim "specialness" and normalcy for the handicapped, first of all, and those that oppose institutionalization. Her opening paragraph describes a television talk show on which mothers of handicapped children discuss the "blessings" as well as the pain of having a handicapped child (1). In paragraph 2, she discusses the media tendency to

represent the handicapped through images of those who become competent and succeed in living a somewhat normal life. She specifically cites a mother who claimed her brain-damaged daughter gives back more than she takes and who insisted she would never institutionalize the child (3). Other opposing viewpoints, in paragraphs 7 and 8, are those that portray institutions as corrupt and harmful. Kupfer refutes these viewpoints (showing that they "are only one side of the story" (2)) by citing her own experience, first of all, in caring for a severely handicapped son (1,6), and second, of visiting her child in his institution and seeing him lovingly cared for (7).

3. Much highly connotative, often descriptive language can be found in the essay, both to portray the opposing position as extreme and to create positive images of institutionalization. In paragraphs 4 and 8, Kupfer uses strongly imagistic language to represent the opposite view, which believes that there are "bars on the windows and children lying neglected in crowded wards. . ." and workers who are "sadists." To these people, institutionalizing a child is "locking him away" or "signing him out of your life forever," a proof of "failure as a parent" (4). Later, she uses highly connotative language to condemn the "anti-institutional trend" for having "some very frightening ramifications": we "force" mental patients to live in "cheap welfare hotels," we "heap guilt" on families who place the elderly in homes (8). When she describes her own viewpoint, her language is still connotative, but more gentle; she portrays the realities of institutionalization as she has witnessed it. She speaks of her son's being "held and rocked by a foster grandma" (not a "foster grandmother") (6); she paints pictures of "a young caseworker" who talks "lovingly" while caring for the basic needs of a teenager and an aide who put "red ribbons into the ponytail of a cerebral-palsied woman." She does not, however, go overboard or become sentimental as she describes her experiences; in fact, she reports quite neutrally that "the workers welcome him [Zach] with hugs and notice if we gave him a haircut or a new shirt" (7).

4. Kupfer seems angry and sometimes a bit sarcastic in tone. Her own self-description is of a person whose "jaws clench" at "the use of the word 'special'" to describe handicapped children (2). Her anger comes across through a brisk, sometimes clipped style: "I like these stories myself. But, of course, inspirational tales are only one side of the story"; "The other truth is not spoken aloud . . ." (2). Another example is paragraph 5: "No, to all of the above. And love is beside the point." Her word choice also shows her anger; she writes unsympathetically about "the blessing part" (1) and notes that Zach's presence in her home "precluded any semblance of a normal family life" (6). The connotative words discussed previously also contribute to the tone. Finally, Kupfer uses quotation marks to show her skepticism about how the handicapped are described and treated. The word "special" is the primary example of this (1, 2), but she also encloses the phrases "put her away" (3), "gave him up," "residential facility," and "put him away" (6) in quotation marks. Later on in the essay, she uses quotation marks to show her lack of sympathy with what is termed "community placement" for the mentally ill. Finally, in paragraph 9, she speaks of "those 'awful' institutions," using quotation marks to show her disagreement with this assessment.

WHAT SHOULD BE DONE ABOUT ROCK LYRICS?

Caryl Rivers

Questions for Close Reading (p. 475)

1. At the end of paragraph 3, Rivers implies her thesis. She writes, "But when either one of them [Prince or Mick Jagger] starts garroting, beating, or sodomizing a woman in their number [that is, song performed on stage], that is another story." She states it directly in paragraph 6: "But violence against women [in rock music lyrics] is greeted by silence. It shouldn't be." The rest of the essay explains the reasons why rock music needs to be discussed and evaluated for what it is: a pop-culture force proclaiming the acceptability of violence against women.

2. Rivers appreciates that rock celebrates rebellion and that it is often sexy; she loved Elvis when young and enjoyed the sexual undercurrents in rhythm and blues hits. She says rock is often "funky, sexy, rebellious and sometimes witty" (3). And by saying she's not a "Mrs. Grundy," she's indicating that she's no prude. She doesn't mind rock stars undressing or cavorting sexily on stage. It's not sex in the lyrics or staging that offends her, but violence against women.

3. Through rock videos and MTV, young people are exposed to rock's images of violence and degradation of women as well as to the lyrics. But more than being just a vehicle for access, TV lends legitimacy to whatever is aired, and so the anti-female imagery of rock can seem acceptable and "mainstream" to young viewers. Rivers points out that Walter Cronkite, at one time television's most popular newscaster, was found to be the most trusted man in America (8). "Many people regard what they see on TV as the truth" (8), she writes. She reminds us that today's teens have been schooled by TV, particularly by Sesame Street. They are likely to believe the images on TV are "accurate reflections of adult reality" and are "approved by adults" (9).

4. She believes the time is ripe for an outcry because the violent imagery of rock is now widely accessible to most Americans as their children through TV and films. Such violent imagery was once, but is no longer, confined to the seamy fringes of our society. And, she believes that silence about the ugliness and dangerousness of such imagery adds to its seeming legitimization (12). Speaking out against the lyrics is Rivers's preferred form of outcry. While she isn't pro-censorship (7), she nevertheless pleads that the "silence" that condones the violence in rock lyrics should be broken. In paragraph 9, she says that adults sanction the violent lyrics of rock by their silence about it. Her thesis itself (6) opposes such silence, and the next paragraph urges people to speak out. Paragraph 15 proposes some concrete actions against violence, all of which involve breaking the silence: she believes female rock stars should go public with their opposition; DJs should refuse to spin the records and air the videos; journals, parents and others in authority should speak out so there is a public forum about the subject, and finally, men should also join the outcry (16).

5. *grisly* (1): ghastly or gruesome
   garroting (3): strangling
   purveyors (7): those in the business of selling
   sanction (9 and 11): approve
   cerebral (10): mental or intellectual
   propagandists (11): deliberate spreaders of an ideology
   endemic (14): particular to a group or region, as a disease
   contagion (16): communicable disease

Questions About the Writer's Craft (pp. 475-76)

1. In paragraphs 4-6, Rivers protests vehemently against "intellectual men" who refuse to see images of violence against women as a problem and argues that to shrug off such imagery is unjustifiable. In general, however, Rivers proceeds by conceding points to the opposition and then using this agreement as grounds for arguing a related point of her own. For instance, she admits that rock embodies rebellion (1-2), but then she adds that this doesn't mean that rock is innocent of inspiring or approving of violence against women. (2-3). She grants that censorship is bad and usually unnecessary in our society (7-8), but then refutes the idea that rock and its video images are similar to pornography or adult "x-rated" movies. Rather, she points out that rock is much more accessible and accepted than either of these media. Then, she grants that the causal relationship between rock music and violence is not certain or verifiable, but refutes the idea that such violent images don't affect society (11). In paragraph 13, she agrees with her opponents that violence is widespread in the media, but then she refutes the idea that rock violence is of the same tenor; she argues that mainstream media violence is directed at the guilty, but rock violence is aimed at the innocent, that is, at women (13-14).

2. Rivers begins the essay by contrasting today's rock with that of the past; she shows that while rock lyrics have always been sexy and rebellious, they were not always violent (2-3). In paragraph 4, she explores how people would react to violence that targeted other segments of our population; anti-black or anti-Jewish lyrics would be condemned quickly and loudly, she attests. But, she points out, violent lyrics against women are not condemned. In paragraphs 7-8, she contrasts the marginalization of most pornography with the legitimization of rock and its violent images through television and videos. In paragraph 13, she contrasts typical media violence, which is usually directed at the guilty of society, with rock violence, which is directed against women. In paragraph 11, she uses comparison to show how violent images have, in the past, caused widespread violence in society. She implies that violence against women is comparable to violence against any other group—and that unless checked, the violence advocated in rock lyrics could claim more victims, similar to the violence that has killed blacks or Jews. Rivers's use of comparison and contrast helps her support the idea that rock music's anti-female imagery is dangerous—as dangerous as other imagery that society has marginalized or that has led to real violence.

3. The use of the first person adds a sense of conviction to the essay. In paragraphs 2 and 3, using the first person allows Rivers to make a pitch for her own credibility; she indicates that as a young person, she was a fan of rock, and that her enjoyment of it had much to do with its rebellion and sexiness. She attempts to convince the reader that she is a balanced and fair critic of rock who will give credit where it is due. She makes a direct appeal to the readers, addressing them as "rock fans": "But I am sorry, rock fans," she writes, current rock images of such things as forced kinky sex go beyond the enticing naughtiness of old rhythm and blues lyrics. She uses the second person in paragraph 3 as well: "Please do not mistake me for a Mrs. Grundy" is her plea for the reader to accept her as a supporter of rock and not just a prude who doesn't understand it. In other places, such as paragraphs 4 and 5, her use of "I" gives the essay a tone of impassioned conviction. In paragraph 10, she writes of her personal awareness of violence against women, again adding credibility to her thesis and to her as a critic of rock. Again in paragraph 15, she uses a strong declarative tone and the first person to address what she sees as the solution to the silence around rock's violence. Her repetition of the word "I" adds rhetorical power to this paragraph.

4. Most readers will feel that Rivers's highly connotative language makes the essay lively and the thesis both understandable and believable. Rivers first uses such language to describe the enjoyments of rock and roll: she "snickered at . . . deliciously naughtily [lyrics]" (2); "Prince

wants to leap about" in a "purple jock strap" (3); "Jagger [can] unzip his fly as he gyrates" (3). These jolting descriptions make for enjoyable reading and may also predispose us to accept the author's thesis. Rivers also uses highly connotative language to indicate her complaints against rock today: "the delights of slipping into a women's room . . . and murdering her" (2); "garroting, beating, or sodomizing a woman . . ." (3). Her analogy in paragraph 4 is enlivened with images: "stringing up and stomping on black people," "desecrating synagogues and beating up Jews to the beat of twanging guitars" (4), dailies "would thunder on editorial pages," senators would fall over each other" (5). In paragraphs 7-9, she again uses such lively language to indicate society's strong condemnation of porn and our failure to react appropriately to rock: "stuff will float up out of the sewer"; "moral lepers"; "hold our nose" (7); "tattered, paper-covered books"; "where winos snooze and the scent of urine fills the air" (8); "grabbed a big chunk of legitimacy" (9). Startling imagery is used again in paragraph 13, where Rivers comments that "Dirty Harry blows away the scum; he doesn't walk up to a toddler and say, 'Make my day.'" In paragraph 15, she indicates the intensity of her feelings with a series of pronouncements about the solutions she wishes, and uses highly connotative language to reaffirm that people concerned about this issue shouldn't be considered "bluenoses and bookburners and ignored." Finally, in the last paragraph, she refers to violence as a "contagion."

DEATH AND JUSTICE

Edward I. Koch

Questions for Close Reading (pp. 480-81)

1. Koch states his thesis in paragraph 4: "I . . . support the death penalty."

2. Opponents of the death penalty find killing itself objectionable, regardless of the reason or method. Koch considers this view unjustifiable because he believes the death penalty would reduce the number of killings overall, by acting as a deterrent to murder.

3. Koch notes that the Sixth Commandment, in the original Hebrew, prohibits murder, rather than all killing, and that the Torah allows the death penalty for certain crimes. Koch also cites a number of philosophers and statesmen who supported capital punishment (12).

4. Koch believes that the possibility of being executed will make potential murderers think twice (4). He also argues that "any other form of punishment would be inadequate and, therefore, unjust" (6).

5. *reverence* (2): respect
    constituencies (4): groups of supporters
    heinous (4): abominable
    reprehensible (4): deserving censure
    lethal (5): deadly
    implacable (8): relentless
    sophistic (10): unsound

Questions About the Writer's Craft (p. 481)

1. Koch reminds his readers of his 22 years of public service. He adds that he has maintained his support of capital punishment despite the fact that he has been elected by "liberal" constituencies. Because his readers are likely to be liberal, Koch is prepared to address readers who object to the death penalty.

2. Koch relies on facts throughout the essay. He uses statistics and refers to sociological studies in paragraphs 7,8, and 9. He also uses examples in his three introductory paragraphs and in paragraphs 8, 12, and 14. The effect of all this evidence is to lend strength and credibility to his argument.

3. Koch's emotionally charged language includes "cold-blooded killers" (2), "mutilating" (2), "tragic" (3), "plagued" (7), "nonsense" (10), and "transparently false" (13). The author intends such language to arouse the reader's horror and indignation, and to convince readers that he is speaking plainly, not as some do who would mislead with subtle and unsound arguments.

4. The Kitty Genovese anecdote is especially shocking and, therefore, powerful. It also points to the fact that our society—currently *without* capital punishment—is so morally weak that neighbors will not even phone the police to save a woman from being murdered. By focusing on one victim, the anecdote also makes the reader feel emotionally involved, so that Koch's final phrase ("the victim dies twice") inflicts real pain.

THE DEATH PENALTY

David Bruck

Questions for Close Reading (pp. 485-86)

1. Bruck's thesis, stated piecemeal throughout the essay, is that the death penalty "doesn't work" (14) and that it "encourages an attitude toward human life that is not reverent, but reckless" (15).

2. Bruck finds it "curious" that "a crowd gathered outside the death-house to cheer on the executioner" while Shaw faced his death with dignity (5). He also points out that when Green was executed, KKK members "rallied outside the prison" (9). In addition, Bruck states that Florida has experienced a rise in the murder rate since capital punishment was reinstated.

3. According to Bruck, Shaw was mentally ill and under the influence of PCP when he committed the murders. Bruck also claims that Shaw's statement that all killing is wrong occurred only moments before he was executed (5). Bruck is citing evidence that Shaw may not have deserved the death penalty.

4. Bruck points out that administrative difficulties surround the death penalty. For example, the governor of Florida spends much of his time reviewing clemency requests, and the state's Supreme Court is "backlogged with death cases" (12).

5. *semblance* (6): appearance
   retribution (9): deserved punishment
   impaled (10): pierced through
   clemency (12): mercy
   spawning (12): giving birth to in great quantity
   tiresome (14): boring, annoying
   trivialize (16): reduce the importance of

Questions About the Writer's Craft (p. 486)

1. Bruck appeals to reason when he objectively cites statistics and facts, for example, the number of death convictions about which the state has since admitted error (8) and the fact that the Florida homicide rate has increased since the death penalty was reinstated. Most of the time, however, he appeals to emotion, perhaps because he perceives his readers as being highly emotional *about* the issue of capital punishment. He might also feel that it is safe to appeal to the emotions if he thinks his readers are likely to take the "liberal" position on the issue—that is, his position. Instances of emotional appeals include Bruck's reference to Ford as "trembling" and saying "prayers" (6), his mention of the Ku Klux Klan, his use of the word "death house" (5), his comparison of Ernest Knighton with an "impaled" cricket (10), and his equation of the electric chair to lynching.

2. Bruck argues the points that Koch numbers 1, 3, 4, and 5: that "the death penalty is barbaric" (Koch, paragraph 5), that "an innocent person might be executed by mistake" (Koch, paragraph 8), that "capital punishment cheapens the value of human life" (Koch, 10), and that "the death penalty is applied in a discriminatory manner" (Koch, 11). He also refers to some of the same individual murder cases, for example, Shaw's acts of murder and his execution and the stabbing of Kitty Genovese. Bruck seems to have omitted the arguments that could not be supported as colorfully, that is, with as vivid examples: state vs. individual rights, precedence for one's view in scripture and philosophy, the fact that other major democracies do not use the death penalty.

3. The rhetorical questions increase the chance that the reader will view Bruck's interpretation as the obvious, common-sense one, since rhetorical questions are those couched as if the answer didn't need stating.

4. By bringing in Blease, Bruck implies that being in favor of capital punishment indicates the same intolerance as racism. Bruck refers to lynching and the electric chair as similarly barbaric. He probably saves this comparison for the end because he hopes it will leave the reader with as strong a distaste for capital punishment as the reader is likely to feel for lynching. The reader may instead react with a feeling of indignation at Bruck's putting capital punishment in the same category as lynching.

LET'S TELL THE STORY OF ALL AMERICA'S CULTURES

Yuh Ji-Yeon

Questions for Close Reading (p. 489)

1. Yuh states her thesis in paragraph 10, after a long and tantalizing introduction. She writes, "Educators around the country are finally realizing what I realized as teenager in the library. . . . America is a multicultural nation, composed of many people with varying histories and varying traditions who have little in common except their humanity, a belief in democracy and a desire for freedom." She restates it in paragraph 19: "The history of America is the story of how and why people from all over the world came to the United States, and how in struggling to make a better life for themselves, they changed each other, they changed the country, and they all came to call themselves Americans." The essay as a whole argues that students should receive information about the many streams of ethnicities that compose our country so that they can appreciate the contributions and struggles of all types of Americans.

2. The history books she was assigned in school portrayed America as formed by and developed through the efforts of white people such as "Lewis and Clark, Lincoln, Daniel Boone, Carnegie, presidents, explorers, and industrialists" (2). These portrayals are limited and place white European-descended people as the central players in our history. Her own research as a teenager determined that many other nonwhite groups had made contributions, but these were left out of the history. In the field of agriculture, she discovered that immigrants from Asia had cultivated California's deserts and worked the sugar cane fields in Hawaii; an Asian had developed the popular breed of cherry that now carries his name, Bing. Asians had also served in the U.S. armed forces in the first world war, but were denied citizenship nevertheless (4). In looking into history texts, she discovered that the only references to nonwhites were over-simplified and one-dimensional. African Americans were discussed only as slaves. Native Americans were portrayed as "scalpers" (2), as wild and violent. Her investigations thus led her to the conclusion that "the history books were wrong" (9). She has a special interest in righting the wrong because she herself is a nonwhite immigrant from Asia. Her evidence includes numerous examples of Native American (3, 15), Asian (4), African American (5, 15), and Hispanic (6) contributions to American life.

3. Yuh believes that history courses should teach about the various cultural groups that helped shape the nation (10, 14). More than this, however, students should "be taught that history is an ongoing process of discovery and interpretation of the past, and that there is more than one way of viewing the world" (14). What might look like a "heroic" achievement from one point of view, for example, could be considered barbarism from another, she notes, referring to the American domination of the Native American lands of the west (15). She believes all the various points of view about events in the American past should be presented.

4. Yuh believes that the truth about American history is multiple and that "there is more than one way of viewing the world" (14). But the most important reason for rewriting American history is that given by a New York State Department of Education report: students should learn how to "assess critically the reasons for the inconsistencies between the ideals of the US and social realities." In addition, they should gain the knowledge and skills that can help them participate in "bringing reality closer to the ideals" (16).

5. *albeit* (1): even if or although
   tinged (1): with a slight trace of coloration
   galore (2): in plentiful amounts
   multicultural (10, 13, 18): drawing from many ethnic and cultural groups
   interdependence (12): reliance on connected groups
   indigenous (15): native or original
   dissenting (18): disagreeing with the majority
   ethnicity (18): membership in a cultural group based on ancestry
   bolster (19): prop up or support

Questions About the Writer's Craft (pp. 489–490)

1. Yuh waits until paragraph 18 to mention that some people have concerns about multicultural education being divisive. By this time in the essay, she has expansively rendered her own position in concrete and convincing terms. Delaying the mention of opposing views allows her to develop her rather complex reasons for advocating multicultural curricula: that exposing the ethnic forces and achievements in our history is more accurate (10), that it presents history as interpretations rather than dogma (14), that it will help students understand the discrepancies between our great American ideals and our current social realities (16), and give students the skills to help them improve our nation (16). Coming so late in the essay, the dissenting view of multiculturalism seems simplistic in comparison to Yuh's argued position, and so it is easier for Yuh to dispose of it as off the mark.

2. Yuh's examples demonstrate her point that schoolbook American history has restricted students' knowledge about what really happened in our past. She offers some specifics of traditional American history in paragraph 2: "Founding Fathers, Lewis and Clark, Lincoln, Daniel Boone, Carnegie, presidents . . ." and then contrasts this list with numerous more detailed examples of ethnic contributions to and viewpoints about America's past. Invoking images of Iroquois government, Asian agricultural talents, and black initiatives toward freedom from slavery, the author shows concretely that there is more to the building of America than the heroic efforts of white men. Recalling the massacre of the indigenous tribes, the denial of citizenship to Asians despite their honorable World War I service, and the American overtaking of Mexican populations in California and New Mexico, Yuh dramatically pictures how our history plowed under nonwhite peoples. These specifics indicate that there are additional facts and alternative viewpoints to those traditionally taught as our history. These specifics also fill in knowledge gaps that readers may harbor and that may leave them poorly equipped to understand and appreciate her position. Placing them before the thesis renders the reader more aware of the complexity of our history and thus more open to her position. Hence, supplying these details is crucial to the success of her argument.

3. Much of the introduction consists of the author's personal recounting of what education she received (1-2) or failed to receive (3-6) regarding ethnic forces in our history. In paragraph 7, Yuh shocks us by revealing the degrading but inevitable taunts of her childhood peers ("So when other children called me a slant-eyed chink and told me to go back where I came from . . ."). This personal approach tells us what the educational and emotional consequences are of ignoring the diversity of people who have helped build America, and so sets the groundwork for Yuh's argument in favor of multicultural curricula in history. She returns to the personal at the end of the essay. Here she affirms that focusing on ethnicity in our country's past is a way of demonstrating that "out of many" comes the "one" (20). She then underscores the link between her, a Korean immigrant, and her white-bread childhood "tormentors": the Americanness they have in common.

4. Yuh's stylistic repetitions begin immediately in the first paragraph, where she parallels two relative clauses: "I grew up . . . almost believing that America was white . . . and that white was best." The second paragraph uses this same device, paralleling the two last sentences and repeating the phrase, "the only": "The only black people were slaves. The only Indians were scalpers." These short parallel clauses and sentences are emphatic and create a sense that "that was that," a sense of finality about the impressions she gained.

   The following four paragraphs open with the same repeated phrase: "I never learned one word about. . . ." And the sentences that follow within each paragraph begin, "Or that . . ." or repeat the words, "I never learned that. . . ." By using these repetitions, Yuh creates a catalog of her enforced ignorance. Each repeated opening signals the reader that more historical omissions are coming, and more, and even more. Through the repetitions, the reader understands that what has been left out of American history is not just one or two details, but whole vistas and vantage points from which our past looks very different.

   In paragraph 15, Yuh resumes the cataloging of omissions, again using repetitions. The first sentence sets the pattern: "the westward migration . . . *is not just* an heroic settling of an untamed wild, *but also* the conquest of indigenous peoples." The following two sentences use this "not just . . . but" structure, with small variations in wording, to convey the multiplicity inherent in our history.

THE CULT OF ETHNICITY, GOOD AND BAD

Arthur Schlesinger, Jr.

Questions for Close Reading (p. 493)

1. Schlesinger's thesis is conveyed in a number of places. In paragraph 4, he quotes Margaret Thatcher approvingly: "No other nation has so successfully combined people of different races and nations within a single culture." Then he cites the observations of Hector St. John de Crevecoeur on America's long-standing multiethnicism, "a mixture of English, Scotch, Irish, French, Dutch, Germans and Swedes . . . this promiscuous breed" (5). And at the start of paragraph 6, Schlesinger himself states his main idea: "The U.S. escaped the divisiveness of a multiethnic society by a brilliant solution: the creation of a brand-new national identity." The rest of the essay argues the benefits of such mixing and cautions against the "cult of ethnicity," which works against the sense of national unity.

2. Schlesinger quotes the Latin motto, *E pluribus unum* (5), and explains through the words of George Washington that our country forged "a brand-new national identity" because immigrants "get assimilated to our customs, measures and laws, in a word, soon become one people . . . through "intermixture with our people." That this theme of joining a new culture has been important throughout our history is reinforced by the fact that an early twentieth-century playwright, Israel Zangwill, titled one of his plays, "The Melting Pot" (6), creating a phrase we have all heard from childhood. He sees our educational system as "a means of creating 'one people'" (9). The American school, Schlesinger believes, is the most important force in molding the diverse immigrant population into one culture (6). This culture has always been overwhelmingly English in "language, ideas and institutions," but still very different from Great Britain (7). Finally, Schlesinger notes that "most American-born members of minority groups . . . see themselves primarily as Americans rather than primarily as members

of one or another ethnic group." He continues, "A notable indicator today is the rate of intermarriage across ethnic lines, across religious lines, even (increasingly) across racial lines" (12).

3. Schlesinger sees that some positive results can come from emphasizing the ethnic background of people. In our century, we have finally begun to acknowledge that "the pot did not melt everybody" and that we have treated racial minorities very poorly. We have to some extent begun to cast off the deep racism that excluded some groups from full membership in our culture. We have begun "to give shamefully overdue recognition" to these groups. And, as a result, our culture has been invigorated with a new sense of its own complexity and richness (8).

   On the other hand, however, ethnicity breaks up nations, as we currently see happening around the globe. Schlesinger cites a long list of countries from every corner of the globe which are undergoing ethnic strife and collapse (3). In our own country, Schlesinger sees that too much focus on ethnicity "gives rise . . . to the conception of the U.S. as a nation composed not of individuals making their own choices but of inviolable ethnic and racial groups" (9). It also deflects emphasis from "historic American goals of assimilation and integration." Boosters of ethnicity also have tried to educate children to have ethnic pride, but this effort causes a perpetuation of ethnic identities. As Schlesinger writes, "The balance is shifting from *unum* to *pluribus*" (9). Overall, he sees that "group separatism crystallizes the differences, magnifies tensions, intensifies hostilities" (10). He explicitly warns that "unchecked," separatism will cause the "fragmentation, resegregation, and tribalization of American life" (11).

4. He believes that most minority group members still feel more American than ethnic, despite the increasing claims that ethnic background make on people today. As a sign of this solidarity, he cites and celebrates the increase in intergroup marriage, across ethnic, religious, and racial lines. He quotes Theodore Roosevelt on this score, "We Americans are children of the crucible" (12).

5. *salient* (1): conspicuously noticeable
   sovereignty (2): national authority
   ideological (2): pertaining to a strict body of political or social doctrines
   unprecedented (4): without previous similar cases or instances
   promiscuous (5): characterized by frequent indiscriminate sexual activity
   assimilated (6): mixed in without distinctions
   crystallized (6): to cause to assume a definite form; articulated
   potent (6): powerful
   infusion (7): introduction
   reconfigured (7): changed, rearranged
   spurned (8): repudiated
   Anglo (8): of English, or more broadly, European derivation
   inviolable (9): incapable of being violated or desecrated
   zeal (9): enthusiasm
   apocalyptic (11): pertaining to or predicting the end of the world
   ferment (11): agitation or unrest
   Kleagle (11): leader in the Ku Klux Klan
   crucible (12): a severe test
   rent (13): torn

Questions About the Writer's Craft (pp. 493-494)

1. In paragraphs 7 and 8, Schlesinger acknowledges some of the complaints the opposition holds about the melting-pot theory of America and grants that our country has been far from perfect in its handing of diversity. He notes sympathetically that the melting "pot did not melt everybody," and states outright that some minority groups were severely shortchanged. But in paragraph 9, Schlesinger begins to discuss those who take ethnic pride too far, here mounting a strong but polite attack on those who over-emphasize ethnicity. He cites the "unhealthy consequences" that result: viewing the U.S. as a nation of groups rather than a nation of individuals, rejecting assimilation as our national goal. He refers to his opponents in a polite way, acknowledging their positive goals; he describes them as "well-intentioned people," who have an "excess of zeal," implying they are not malicious or evil but mistaken. Throughout the next two paragraphs he avoids giving too much power to the opposition by using terms that downplay the problem. In 10, he refers to the "hullabaloo" over multiculturalism, using a term that suggests "fuss" and "turmoil" but not "crisis." Likewise, in paragraph 11, he comments "I don't want to sound apocalyptic" about the new stress on ethnicity in our culture. He puts quotation marks around "multiculturalism," "political correctness," "Eurocentric" (10) and "Afrocentric" (11), setting them apart from our regular vocabulary and treating them as a specialized and perhaps temporary terminology of the current debate. In 12, he somewhat dismisses the ethnicity problem as in part a "superficial enthusiasm stirred by romantic ideologues" and by "unscrupulous con men," "self-appointed spokesmen" for particular groups. Schlesinger handles his opposition by both treating them with respect—thus maintaining our respect for him as a rational and civil person— and by suggesting their claims are less weighty than they at first seem. Since Schlesinger's goal is to reinforce the theme of inclusion and assimilation in American history, his dubious tone when discussing the ethnic helps him achieve his purpose.

2. Schlesinger uses questions to help render his abstract topic, "the cult of ethnicity," accessible to his mainstream readers. If he had been writing for an academic audience of historians, used to abstract discussions, he would not have had to use this technique. The questions focus the reader's attention upon the central issue of his essay, whether diversity and unity can coexist. In paragraph 2, Schlesinger asks, "What happens when people of different origins . . . inhabit the same locality and live under the same political sovereignty?" His answer, that all too often, bloody conflict results, sets the stage for his argument that emphasis upon ethnicity is divisive and creates more problems than it solves.

   Paragraph 3 bursts with the names of countries troubled by ethnic division, and ends in the question that might lie unformulated in a reader's mind: "Is there any large multiethnic state that can be made to work?" Here, Schlesinger uses the question to focus more specifically on whether any exception to ethnic breakup can be found, thus leading the reader along to the next point, for "the U.S." is the answer. The question at the end of paragraph 4, "How have Americans succeeded in pulling off this . . . trick?" opens the doors for Schlesinger to argue that creating a common culture, rather than fostering ethnic groupings, is America's strength. In addition to pointing the reader toward the author's main ideas, this second question is phrased colloquially, almost jovially, using the slangy idiom, "pulling off this . . . trick." This tone invites the reader to continue on, to find out the solution to the "trick."

3. Other examples of such connotative words are "multiculturalism" (10), "political correctness" (10), and "Afrocentric" (11). Schlesinger doesn't define these terms because, most likely, he believes his audience is aware of the issues and already understands the terms. Furthermore, used without definition, the terms have greater emotional impact. In fact, each of these terms ignites the exact divisive passions which Schlesinger deplores.

4. Schlesinger quotes a variety of people—Margaret Thatcher, Hector St. John de Crevecoeur, Israel Zangwill, George Washington, and Theodore Roosevelt—but all the quotations are about the successful multiethnic amalgam that America has become. The female British Prime Minister (4), the eighteenth-century French visitor to America (5, 6), a Jewish-American twentieth-century playwright (6), the first U.S. president (6), and an important twentieth-century president (12) all agree that our nation's significance lies in its forging of a new national culture from many strands. Providing statements from a diverse group effectively broadens Schlesinger's viewpoint, for through them we can realize that many thinkers, across the centuries and across the ocean, have perceived just what Schlesinger is pointing out.

Below we provide possible responses to selected activities at the end of Chapter 20 (pp. 550-52). We hope these suggested responses convey the range of answers possible.

Using the card or computer catalogue (pp. 507-12)

1. Here are possible answers to A1 and A2 and the correct answers for A3:

   a. These are the titles and authors of some books on the four subjects. Many other answers are possible.

   Adoption:

   United States. *Families for Black Children: The Search for Adoptive Parents.*

       Washington: GPO, 1971-2.

   Sorosky, Arthur, Annette Baran, and Reuben Pannor. *The Adoption*

       Triangle. Garden City, NY: Anchor, 1984.

   Feigelman, William and Arnold P. Silverman. *Chosen Children: New*

       Patterns of Adoptive Relationships. New York: Praeger, 1983.

   Television:

   Council on Children, Media, and Merchandising. *Edible Television: Your*

       Child and Food Commercials. Washington: GPO, 1977.

   Dorr, Aimee. *Television and Children: A Special Medium for a Special*

       Audience. Beverly Hills: Sage, 1986.

   Stewart, David W., and David H. Furse. *Effective Television Advertising:*

       A Study of 1000 Commercials. Lexington, MA: Lexington Books, 1986.

   Urban Violence

   Anderson, Elijah. *Code of the Street: Decency, Violence, and the Moral Life of*

       Inner City. Norton, 1999.

   Decker, Scott H. et al. *Life in the Gang: Family, Friends, and Violence.*

       Cambridge: Cambridge UP, 1996.

Pinderhughes, Howard. *Race in the Hood: Conflict and Violence Among Urban Youth.*

  Minnesota: U of Minnesota P, 1997.

Genetic Research

Cherfas, Jeremy. *Man-Made Life: An Overview of the Science, Technology,*

  and Commerce of Genetic Engineering. New York: Pantheon, 1982.

Kant, P. W., ed. *New Approaches to Genetics: Developments in Molecular*

  Genetics. Stocksfield, UK.: Oriel, 1978.

Lipkin, Mack, Jr., and Peter T. Rowley, eds. *Genetic Responsibility: On*

  Choosing Our Children's Genes. New York: Plenum, 1974.

  b. Betty Friedan is the author of *The Feminine Mystique* and *The Second Stage.*

  c. *Invisible Man* was written by Ralph Ellison. (There is another book with a similar title, *The Invisible Man*, by H. G. Wells.) *A Country Year* was written by Sue Hubbell.

2. a. This library uses the *Library of Congress* catalog system.

  b. The book's title is *Kids Come in All Languages: Reading Instruction for ESL Students.*

  c. This book has two *authors.*

  d. The book is listed under three headings: "English (ESL) Education," "United States —Bilingual Education," and "United States."

  e. The book was published in 1994.

  f. Given the book's title and the subjects under which it is listed in the catalogue, the book *does* look useful for a paper.
The student should try to locate the book.

3. Here is the information necessary to write a bibliography card for each title:

  a. Tuchman, Barbara. *Practicing History.* New York: Knopf, 1981.

  b. Jacobs, Lewis, ed. *The Documentary Tradition.* 2nd ed. New York: Norton, 1979.

  c. Mead, Margaret. *Coming of Age in Samoa: A Psychological Study of Primitive*

   Youth for Western Civilization. NY: Blue Ribbon Books, 1928.

  d. Bank, Stephen and Michael D. Kahn. *The Sibling Bond.* New York: Basic, 1982.

e. Gross, Ronald, Beatrice Gross, and Sylvia Seidman, eds. *The New Old: Struggling for Decent Aging.* Garden City, NY: Anchor, 1978.

f. Arnold, Matthew. *Culture and Anarchy.* Cambridge, U.K.: Cambridge UP, 1960.

Using Reference Books (pp. 512-513)

4. The goal of this assignment is to induce students to explore various reference books; the answers to the questions must be sought in specialized reference works, not general encyclopedias. The answers that follow include some hints as to where the answers may be found.

   a. The Persian Gulf War began on January 17, 1991, and lasted until February 28, 1992. (Possible source: *Facts on File*).

   b. Kodachrome film was invented by L. D. Mannes and L. Godowsky in 1935. (Possible source: *Focal Encyclopedia of Photography*)

   c. *Rosacea* is a chronic disease of the skin of the face. Its symptoms include redness and pimples; it was once called acne rosacea. (Possible sources: *Oxford Companion to Medicine; Dorland's Illustrated Medical Dictionary*)

   d. *M*A*S*H* was the winner of the 1973-74 Outstanding Comedy Series Emmy. (Possible source: *The World Almanac*)

   e. John Sartain was an engraver and oil painter. (Possible sources: *Dictionary of American Biography; National Cylopedia of American Biography*)

   f. The first black was elected to Congress in 1868 during Reconstruction. (Possible source: *The American Negro Reference Book*)

   g. Pareto's Law is a law of economics that states that no matter what a nation's institutionalized economic structure, the distribution of income among citizens will be the same. (Possible source: *The Dictionary of Banking and Finance; The Dictionary of Business and Economics; The McGraw-Hill Dictionary of Modern Economics*)

   h. An *écorché* figure is a drawing of the human body without skin, displaying all the musculature. The word comes from the French for "flayed." Such drawings were once standard studies for art students. (Possible sources: *The Oxford Companion to Art: The Thames and Hudson Dictionary of Art Terms*)

   i. The mbira is an African instrument played with the fingers; it is also called a thumb piano, kalimba, marimba, sansa or sanza, and lamellaphone. (Source: *The New Harvard Dictionary of Music*)

   j. *Kachinas* are supernatural beings and also their masked impersonations at rituals and ceremonies. (Possible source: *The Encyclopedia of Religion*)

Using Periodicals (pp. 514-520)

5. Below are some indexes, in addition to the *Reader's Guide, Social Sciences Index*, and *New York Times Index,* that might be helpful in locating periodical articles on the various topics.

   a. Drug abuse in health-care professions
      Health Index
      Government Publications Index
      Nursing Abstracts

   b. Ethical considerations in organ transplant surgery
      Philosopher's Index
      Abridged Index Medicus

   c. Women in prison
      Criminal Justice Abstracts
      Sociological Abstracts

   d. Deforestation of the Amazon rain forest
      Environment Index
      International Political Science Abstracts

   e. The difference between *Sense and Sensibility* as a novel and as a film
      MLA International Index, vol. 4, under *"Motion Picture Criticism" and
         "Motion Picture Review"*
      Film Literature Index

Note-taking (pp. 542-549)

8. Here are examples of possible note cards taken from the paragraphs in McClintock's article:

Direct Quotation

A broad view of propaganda	McClintock, p. 278

> McClintock points out that the word propaganda is typically associated with a "totalitarian regime or brainwashing tactics practiced on hostages." But, she argues, "the concept can be applied fruitfully to the way products and ideas are sold in advertising."

Summary

Specific Propaganda Techniques   McClintock, p. 279

   The transfer technique bolsters the credibility of a product in consumers'
eyes by linking it with a traditionally respected symbol. One example:
naming an insurance company <u>Lincoln Insurance</u> and having a corporate logo
that features a profile of the celebrated president.

Combined note card

The consumer's challenge   McClintock, p. 282

   The corporate advertiser knows that pitches based on essentially
propaganda techniques get the job done. They work by bypassing rational
thought and appealing to "our emotions [. . .], our prejudices and biases." As
consumers, we must educate ourselves about advertising techniques so we can
rigorously examine the logic of an advertisement's claims. If we fail to do so,
we end up "handing over to others our independence of thought and action."

ANSWERS FOR CHAPTER 21
"WRITING THE RESEARCH PAPER" (p. 553)

1. Here is the correct *Works Cited* list for this paper:

"Getting Along with Adolescents." Host, Dr. Daniel Gottlieb. Prod. Laura Jackson.

Family Matters. WHYY-FM, Philadelphia. 10 Sept. 1998.

Greene, Donna. "Charting a Safe Course for Adolescence." New York Times 6 Sept.

1998: sec. C: 3-5 (11 pars). ERIC. CD-ROM. U.S. Department of Education, 1998.

Herrenkohl, Ellen, C., et al. "The Relationship Between Early Maltreatment and Teenage

Parenthood." Journal of Adolescence 21.3 (1998): 291-303. 19 Dec. 1998.

<http://proquest.umi.com.>

Hersch, Patricia. "A Circle of Friends: It's Not Peer Pressure, It's the Adolescent Way of

Life." *A Tribe Apart: Journey into the Heart of American Adolescence*. New York:

Ballantine, 1998. 125-148.

Steinberg, Laurence. "Ethnicity and Adolescent Achievement." American Educator

Summer 1996: 28-35, 44-48.

- - -. You and Your Adolescent: A Parent's Guide for Ages 10-20. Pennsylvania:

HarperCollins, 1997.

United States. Department of Education. "How Can We Support Girls in Early Adolescence?"

Washington: GPO, 1998.

2. The attribution may occur at the beginning, the middle, or the end of the sentence, but the citation should be placed at the end. The examples below show some possible responses; your students will undoubtedly have different ones.

   a. Journalist Nancy Gibbs argues that "the use of new terms, like acquaintance rape and date rape, has given men and women the vocabulary [. . .] to express their experiences [. . .] with precision" (427).

   "New terms, like acquaintance rape and date rape," journalist Nancy Gibbs argues, have "given men and women the vocabulary [. . .] to express their experiences [. . .] with precision" (427).

"The use of new terms, like acquaintance rape and date rape, has given men and women the vocabulary [. . .] to express their experiences [. . .] with precision." This point is made by journalist Nancy Gibbs (427).

b. One journalist argues that "the use of new terms, like acquaintance rape and date rape, has given men and women the vocabulary [. . .] to express their experiences [. . .] with precision" (427).

"The use of new terms, like acquaintance rape and date rape, has given men and women," one journalist argues, "the vocabulary [. . .] to express their experiences [. . .] with precision" (427).

"The use of new terms, like acquaintance rape and date rape, has given men and women the vocabulary [. . .] to express their experiences [. . .] with precision." This is the point made by one journalist (427).

c. Here are typical sentences quoting and summarizing one of the experts that Gibbs cites:

Direct Quotation

Anthropologist Lionel Tiger argues that any discussion of date rape must take into account the different biological imperatives driving sexual intercourse between men and women. Males, Tiger claims, seek to "fertilize as many females as possible, while females look for males who "will provide the best set up [. . .] for offspring" (qtd. in Gibbs 426).

Summary

Anthropologist Lionel Tiger argues that any discussion of date rape must take into account the different biological imperatives driving sexual intercourse between men and women. For Tiger, men are impelled by the biological need to impregnate as many women as they can, while women are impelled by the desire to find mates who will provide security for themselves and their children (qtd. in Gibbs 426).

ANSWERS FOR PART 6: "A CONCISE HANDBOOK"

Correcting Sentence Fragments (pp. 643-644)

Below are examples of how to rewrite the sentences that contain errors. Other answers, in some cases, are possible.

1. Even though there must be millions of pigeons in the city, you never see a baby pigeon. It makes you wonder where they're hiding.

2. Children between the ages of eight and twelve often follow teenagers' trends and look up to teens as role models, mimicking their behavior in frequently disconcerting ways.

3. The least expensive remote-controlled toy car costs over fifty dollars, which is more than many budget-conscious parents want to pay. Such high costs are typical in the toy industry.

4. Correct

5. Because they feel urban schools are second-rate, many parents hope to move their families to the suburbs, even though they plan to continue working in the city.

6. Pulling the too-short hospital gown around his wasted body, the patient wandered down the hospital corridor. He was unaware of the stares of the healthy people streaming by.

7. Last year, the student government overhauled its charter and created chaos. It produced a confusing set of guidelines that muddled already contradictory policies. This year's senate has to find a way to remedy the situation.

8. Out of all the listed apartments we looked at that dreary week, only one was affordable and suitable for human habitation.

9. My grandfather likes to send off-beat greeting cards, like the one with a picture of a lion holding on to a parachute. The card reads, "Just wanted to drop you a lion."

10. About a year ago, my mother was unexpectedly laid off by the restaurant where she had been hired five years earlier as head chef. The experience made her realize that she wanted to go into business for herself.

11. Occasionally looking up to see if anyone interesting had entered the room, the students sat hunched over their desks in the study carrels. They were cramming for final exams, scheduled to start the next day.

12. As prices have come down, compact disc players have gained great popularity. With the development of these sophisticated sound systems, listening to concert music is more enjoyable than ever. Indeed, it is nearly as pleasurable as being at the concert itself.

13. Through the local adult education program, my parents took a course in electrical wiring last spring. They plan to enroll in a plumbing course this winter. Their goal is to save money on household repairs, which cost them hundreds of dollars last year.

14. For breakfast, my health-conscious roommate drinks a strange concoction that consists of soybean extract, wheat germ, and sunflower meal. It doesn't look very appealing.

15. Last night, I went to the hospital to visit my uncle, who had been hospitalized four days earlier with a heart attack. I was relieved to see how healthy he looked.

16. The B-B gun has changed dramatically over the last few years. Today's top-of-the-line gun can fire B-Bs or pellets 800 feet per second, almost as fast as some handguns.

17. The hyacinths and daffodils in the garden were blooming beautifully until a freakish spring storm blasted their growth. Within hours, they shrivelled up and lay flat on the ground.

18. During last week's heated town meeting, several municipal officials urged the town council to adopt a controversial zoning ordinance that had already been rejected by the town residents.

19. Strategically placed pine trees concealed the junk yard from nearby residents, who otherwise would have protested its presence in the neighborhood, well-known for its lush lawns and colorful gardens.

20. In an effort to cover his bald spot, Al combs long strands of hair over the top of his head. Unfortunately, no one is fooled by his strategy, especially not his wife, who wishes her husband would accept the fact that he's getting older.

Correcting Comma Splices and Run-Ons (pp. 647-48)

Below are examples of how to rewrite the sentences that contain errors. Other answers, in some cases, are possible.

1. Since the town appeared to be nearby, they left the car on the side of the road and started walking toward the village. They soon regretted their decision.

2. As we rounded the bend, we saw hundreds of crushed cars piled in neat stacks. The rusted hulks resembled flattened tin cans.

3. With unexpected intensity, the rain hit the pavement. Plumes of heat rose from the blacktop, making it difficult to drive safely.

4. According to all reports, the day after Thanksgiving is the worst day of the year to shop. The stores are jammed with people, all looking for bargains.

5. Plants should be treated regularly with an organic insecticide; otherwise, spider mites and mealy bugs can destroy new growth.

6. Have you ever looked closely at a penny? Do you know whether Lincoln faces right or left?

7. As we set up the tent, flies swarmed around our heads. We felt like day-old garbage.

8. If the phone rings when my parents are eating diner, they don't answer it. They assume that, if the person wants to reach them, he or she will call back.

9. The library's security system needs improving. It allows too many people to sneak away with books and magazines hidden in their pockets, purses, or briefcases.

10. Ocean air is always bracing. It makes everyone feel relaxed and carefree, as though the world of work is far away.

11. In the last few years, many prestigious art museums have developed plans to add on to buildings designed by such legendary architects as Frank Lloyd Wright and Louis Kahn. However, many irate museum-goers want the buildings to stay just as they are.

12. The salesperson stapled my bag in six places. I must have looked like a shoplifter.

13. Throughout the last decade, publishing companies doled out huge advances to lure big-time authors. Now many publishers, struggling with massive losses, regret the strategy.

14. Several communities in the country sponsor odd food festivals. In fact, one of the strangest takes place in Vineland, New Jersey. This small rural community celebrates spring with a dandelion-eating contest.

15. Only the female mosquito drinks blood; the males live on plant juices.

16. Every Friday evening, my parents go out to eat by themselves at the local diner, and then they do their marketing for the week.

17. TV commercials are valuable because they give everyone a chance to stretch, visit the bathroom, and get a snack.

18. I start by wetting my feet in the lake's cold water, and then I wade up to my knees before plunging in, shivering all the while.

19. In this country, roughly three hundred new pizza parlors open every week. This shows that pizza has become a staple in the American diet, exceeding even hamburgers and hot dogs in popularity.

20. Correct

Correcting Faulty Parallelism (p. 649)

1. The professor's tests were long, difficult, and anxiety-producing.

2. Medical tests showed that neither a dust allergy nor seasonal hayfever caused the child's coughing fits.

3. One option that employees had was to accept a pay cut; the other was to work longer hours.

4. The hairstylist warned her customers, "I'm a beautician, not a magician. This is a comb, not a wand."

5. The renovated concert hall is both beautiful and spacious.

6. My roommates and I are learning not only Japanese but also Russian.

7. The game-show contestants were told they had to be quick-witted, friendly, and enthusiastic.

8. Correct

9. While waiting in line at the supermarket, people often flip through the tabloids to read about celebrities, the latest scandals, and weight-loss tricks.

10. Eventually, either society will make smoking illegal or people will give it up on their own.

Correcting Problems With Subject-Verb Agreement (p. 652)

1. There are many secretaries who do their bosses' jobs, as well as their own.

2. Correct

3. Each of the children wears a name tag when the play-group takes a field trip.

4. Next week, the faculty committee on academic standards plans to pass a controversial resolution, one that the student body has rejected in the past.

5. Correct

6. Correct

7. The human spinal column, with its circular disks, resembles a stack of wobbly poker chips.

8. Both the students and the instructor dislike experimental music.

9. In most schools, either the college president or the provost is responsible for presenting the budget to the board of trustees. The board of trustees, in turn, is responsible for cutting costs whenever possible.

10. Nobody in the two classes thinks that the exam, which lasted three hours, was fair.

11. Chipped ceramic pots and half-empty bags of fertilizer line the shelves of my grandparents' storage shed.

12. In the middle of the campus, near the two new dorms, is a row of spindly elms. The trees, especially the one at the end, were badly damaged in last week's storm.

13. A strong, secure bond between parent and child is formed when the parent responds quickly and consistently to the baby's needs.

14. The crowd, consisting of irate teachers and parents, was quiet, but the police were alerted anyway.

15. The guidelines issued by the supervisor state that personal calls made during the business day violate company policy.

Correcting Problems With Verb Tense (p. 654)

1. I parked illegally, so my car was towed and got dented in the process.

2. Correct

3. Although the union leaders had called a strike, the union members voted not to stop working.

4. Dr. Alice Chase wrote a number of books on healthy eating. In 1974 she died of malnutrition.

5. By the time we hiked back to the campsite, the rest of the group had collected their gear to go home.

6. Correct

7. As a boy, Thomas Edison was told he would never succeed at anything.

8. The Museum of Modern Art once hung a painting upside down. The mistake went unnoticed for more than a month.

9. When doctors in Los Angeles went on strike in 1976, the death rate dropped 18 percent.

10. John Steinbeck's *The Grapes of Wrath* conveys the horrors of poverty.

11. Correct

12. The aspiring comic walked to the front of the small stage. As he looked out at the audience, a wave of nausea swept over him.

Correcting Problems With Pronoun Case (pp. 657-58)

1. At this college, neither the President nor the Dean automatically assumes that, on every issue, the faculty is automatically better informed than we students.

2. Between you and me, each of the dorms should have its security system replaced.

3. The theatre critic, who slipped into her seat right before the curtain went up, gave him and the other actors favorable reviews.

4. Neither of the boys impressed her or me with his musical ability.

5. The salesperson explained to my husband and me that each of the videocassette recorders had its drawbacks.

6. Correct

7. After enjoying prosperity through most of the 1980s, she and he were unprepared for the rigors of the next decade.

8. Correct

9. Correct

10. The people who lived next door, my roommates and I concluded, had no intention of being neighborly.

11. Correct

12. The plot twisted and turned so much it was difficult for my sister and me to keep track of who cheated on whom.

Correcting Problems With Pronoun Agreement (p. 660)

1. We proponents of the recycling plan challenged everyone on the town council to express his or her objections. Or: We proponents of the recycling plan challenged the town council members to express their objections.

2. Correct

3. All job applicants must call for an appointment, so that the personnel office can interview them.

4. The committee passed its resolution that each of the apartments was to be free of asbestos before occupancy.

5. The committee passed its resolution that each of the apartments was to be free of asbestos before occupancy.

6. I like living in the same small town where I was raised because there's always someone who remembers me as a child.

7. The instructor reminded the class to pick up their term papers before leaving for semester break.

8. Correct

9. Despite poor attendance last year, the library staff decided once again to hold its annual part at the Elmhurst Inn.

10. Many amateur photographers like to use one-step cameras that they don't have to focus. Or, Many amateur photographers like to use one-step cameras that don't require focusing.

Correcting Problems With Pronoun Reference (pp. 661-62)

1. In her novels, Ann Tyler gives us a picture of family life—at its best and at its worst.

2. Lock dangerous chemicals in a storage closet to keep children away from them.

3. The student sat down glumly as soon as the professor began to criticize the student's research paper. After a few moments, though, the student turned away in frustration.

158

4. Many patients' lawsuits against doctors end when the patients receive out-of court settlements.

5. All too often, arguments between a big and little sister are ended by the younger one, who threatens to blackmail her older sister with some violation of household rules.

6. In *A Doll's House*, Ibsen dramatizes the story of a woman treated as a plaything.

7. The swirling cape of the magician distracted the audience as he opened the trap door slowly.

8. Since the old man planned his morning around reading the newspaper, he became upset when it was delivered late.

9. The supervisor explained to the employee that the employee would be transferred soon.

10. . . . The members decided to continue the discussion the following week.

Correcting Problems With Modification (pp. 664-65)

1. While I was cooking dinner, the baby began to howl.

2. Swaying from the boughs of a tall tree, the ape displayed an agility and grace that intrigued the children.

3. When pondering her problems, Laura finally realized that her life was filled with many pleasures.

4. At the end of the semester, I realized that I needed tutoring in only one course.

5. While we were waiting for the plumber, the hot water tank began to leak all over the basement floor.

6. Correct

7. Wandering loose, dogs and cats can scare small children.

8. With difficulty, we read the old newspaper clipping, which was faded and brittle with age.

9. The reporters indicated that they wanted only a few minutes of the candidate's time.

10. With disgust, I threw the greasy hamburger that had been dripping all over me into the trash.

11. Correct

12. An outfit that can be worn only once or twice a year isn't a practical investment.

13. The boys noticed an old copper weathervane spinning wildly on the barn roof.

14. We bought our dining room table, which cost less than one hundred dollars, at a discount store.

15. Correct

Correcting Comma Errors (pp. 672-73)

1. The local movie theatre, despite efforts to attract customers, finally closed its doors and was purchased by a supermarket chain.

2. Correct

3. Their parents, always risk-takers, divorced in August and remarried in February, just five months later.

4. Shaken by the threat of a hostile takeover, the board of directors and the stockholders voted to sell the retail division, which had been losing money for years.

5. Despite my parents' objections, I read Stephen King's novels *The Shining* and *Carrie* when I was in junior high. The books terrified me. Nevertheless, I couldn't put them down.

6. We skimmed the chapter, looked quickly at the tables and charts, realized we didn't know enough to pass the exam, and began to panic.

7. After years of saving his money, my brother bought a used car, and then his problems started.

8. I discovered last week that my neighbors, whose friendship I had always treasured, intend to sue me.

9. Late yesterday afternoon, I realized that Dan was lying and had driven my car without permission.

10. Although it can be annoying and frustrating, forgetting things usually isn't an early sign of Alzheimer's disease, as many people think.

11. "Going to New York," Maria said, "was like walking onto a movie set."

12. The long, pretentious report, issued at the end of May, neither analyzed the problem adequately nor proposed reasonable solutions.

13. By going to a party alone, a single person stands a better chance of meeting someone and of having a good time.

14. Janet and Sandy, her younger sister, run three miles each day, even in the winter.

15. Al pleaded, "Let me borrow your notes, and I'll never ask for anything again. I promise."

16. Mumbling under his breath, the man picked over the tomatoes and cucumbers in the market's produce department.

17. All too often these days, people assume that a bank statement is correct and that there's no need to open the envelope and examine the statement closely.

18. In the last two seconds of the game, the quarterback seized the ball and plunged across the goal line for a touchdown, scoring the game's wining point.

19. After the uprising was quelled, numerous dissidents were imprisoned, but an unknown number remained at large, waiting for the right moment to stage a revolution. Or: After the uprising was quelled, numerous dissidents were imprisoned. An unknown number remained at large, however, waiting for the right moment to stage a revolution.

20. Our psychology professor, who has an active clinical practice, talked about the pressures and rewards of being in a helping profession.

Correcting Problems With Punctuation (pp. 686-87)

1. The New Madrid fault, which lies in the central part of the country, will be the site of a major earthquake within the next thirty years.

2. In the children's story, the hero carries a fresh yellow rose rather than a sword.

3. I asked, "Wasn't Uncle Pete drafted into the army in 1943?"

4. "Branch offices and drive-in windows," the bank president announced, "will be closed January 4, the day of the governor's funeral."

5. Some people avoid physical work. Others seek out and enjoy it, but probably no one likes it all the time.

6. The scientists said that they wondered how anyone could believe stories of outer-space visitors.

7. On the office's paneled walls, the executive had a framed copy of the poem "If."

8. Correct

9. Shoplifters often believe they are doing no harm; nevertheless, shoplifting is stealing and, therefore, illegal.

10. The young people fell in love with the house that stood next to a clear, cold stream.

11. The kennel owner sent birthday cards and small gifts to all the dogs she had boarded during the year.

12. The polished floor in the hallway and dining room lost its sheen after only a week.

13. According to the lawyer, the property is clearly ours and not the other family's.

14. The celebration was loud and unruly; finally, police arrived at the scene around 11 pm.

15. Correct

16. Did the visiting journalist make her speech, "Preserving a Source's Confidentiality"?

17. In the student handbook, the Dean wrote, "A student may be suspended for any of the following: using drugs, plagiarizing papers, cheating on exams, vandalizing college property. . . ."

18. They asked us what courses we planned to take during the summer.

19. In the closet (which hadn't been opened for years), we found three baseball bats and half a dozen badminton sets.

20. Whose notes will you borrow to study for tomorrow's exam?

Correcting Problems With Mechanics and Spelling (p. 697)

1. *Emerging Nations in Today's World*, one of the supplementary texts in Modern History I, is on reserve at the library.

2. Last year, while visiting my parents in central Florida, I took a disastrous course in sociology.

3. The analysts of the election-eve poll concluded, "It's a toss-up."

4. For some reason, spring tends to have a depressing effect on me.

5. Reverend Astor's teeth chattered at my brother's outdoor wedding, held in March in northern Massachusetts.

6. Weighing in at 122 pounds was Tim Fox, a sophomore from a community college in Alabama.

7. In the fall, when the foliage is at its peak, many people pack their hiking gear and head for the country.

8. Three hundred students signed up for the experimental seminar that Prof. Julia Cruz plans to offer through the Business Department. The class is scheduled to meet at 8 a.m. on Monday.

9. Senator Miller, who was supposed to end the press conference once the subject of the environment came up, got embroiled in an argument with several reporters.

10. Listen to nutritionists; many of them contend that there are advantages to limiting the amount of protein in your diet.

11. My roommate, whose native language is French, received an award for writing a provocative series of articles on student pressures.

12. The president of the company distributed to key management thirty copies of the book *How to Win in Business*. Many employees, though, are offended by the book's emphasis on what it calls "economic opportunism." [or *economic opportunism*]

13. My parents always reminded me to watch my p's and q's. Not surprisingly, they were frequently complimented on my good behavior.

14. Correct

15. Professor Mohr accepts no if's, and's, or but's when a student tries to hand in a paper past its due date.